Marshal Stalin, President Truman and Mr. Winston Churchill at the Conference at Potsdam on 17 July 1945. To the left of Marshal Stalin is Major Birse (British interpreter). Between Marshal Stalin and Mr. Truman are M. Pavlov (Soviet interpreter) and Fleet Admiral Leahy. Between Mr. Truman and Mr. Churchill is Mr. Attlee.

DOCUMENTS ON
BRITISH POLICY OVERSEAS

EDITED BY

ROHAN BUTLER, C.M.G., M.A., D.Litt.

Fellow of All Souls College, Oxford

AND

M. E. PELLY, M.A.

ASSISTED BY

H. J. YASAMEE, M.A.

SERIES I

Volume I

LONDON

HER MAJESTY'S STATIONERY OFFICE

Printed in the United Kingdom
for Her Majesty's Stationery Office
Dd. 716912 C10 2/84

ISBN 0 11 591682 2*

DOCUMENTS ON BRITISH POLICY OVERSEAS

Series I   Volume I

The Conference at Potsdam
July — August 1945

PREFACE

I

The decision to publish a collection of Documents on British Policy Overseas was announced in the House of Commons by the then Secretary of State for Foreign and Commonwealth Affairs, Sir Alec Douglas-Home, in the following introductory terms:

'Her Majesty's Government have decided to extend into the post-war period the practice adopted for 1919–1939 of publishing documents on British foreign policy. The new collection of the most important documents in the archives of the Foreign and Commonwealth Office relating to British policy overseas will initially comprise two series to cover foreign policy in the periods 1945–1950 and 1950–1955 respectively. The preparation of both series will be undertaken simultaneously. So as to keep the work within manageable proportions, at the start the new series will normally include only Foreign Office documents, but, where appropriate, documents from the archives of the Colonial and Commonwealth Relations Offices will also be included' (*Parl. Debs., 5th ser., H. of C.*, 1973, vol. 859, col. 45).

Mr. Rohan Butler, Fellow of All Souls College, Oxford, was entrusted by the Secretary of State with the general planning and production of the publication, as Senior Editor. Mr. Butler, the Editor of the present volume, was joined at the outset by Mrs. M. E. Pelly as Joint Editor of the series.

The Secretary of State had further announced: 'The title of the new series will be "Documents on British Policy Overseas". It will in general follow the lines of "Documents on British Foreign Policy 1919–1939" and the editors will have the customary freedom in the selection and arrangement of documents. For the post-war period, however, the great increase in the bulk of the archives presents a special problem. To meet this, it is intended that in some cases the documents printed in the collection shall be followed by printed calendars briefly summarizing related documents. Microcopies of these calendared documents will be available for purchase, except in exceptional cases where it is necessary on security grounds to restrict the availability of a particular document, as will be indicated in the text of the calendars. The provision of calendars and microcopies should make it easier to deal with the problem inherent in the greater volume of post-war records while, at the same time, making available to scholars more, and hitherto unpublished, documents.'

In 1939 the number of documents received in the Foreign Office was 270,968. By 1945 this figure had all but doubled to 541,076. It has thus been necessary to apply with increased rigour, while generally continuing to follow, the established criteria for the selection of documents, as also for their arrangement and annotation: criteria set out in the preface to the collection of *Documents on British Foreign Policy 1919–1939*, printed in volumes I of the First and of the Second Series. The intention is to concentrate so far as possible upon diplomatic issues of leading political significance, and to print only such of the more technical material, notably in the fields of economics and defence, as is particularly important for an understanding of the development of British foreign policy.

In the present publication, as in its predecessor, the highest priority has been claimed by instructions sent to His Majesty's Missions abroad in execution of policy, by their reports of business transacted with foreign governments, and by records of negotiations and discussions at home and abroad. While such formal records must have pride of place, account has been taken of the extent to which the increased pressure of diplomatic business during and since the Second World War has tended towards a corresponding increase in semi-official correspondence. Also important can be informative reporting by Missions abroad and briefs for the Secretary of State and submissions at high level in recommendation of policy.

The Editors of *Documents on British Policy Overseas*, as of *Documents on British Foreign Policy*, have had to recognize that owing to the frequent practice in the Foreign Office of minuting incoming documents by a succession of officials, quite often at length by juniors upwards, to have attempted to include all minutes on documents printed would greatly have swollen the size of the collection without a proportionate increase in the presentation of fresh and authoritative material. Minutes have, however, been printed in a number of cases in which they provide significant or new information, as of an otherwise unrecorded decision or procedure. Here again, the frequency may be increased under increased pressure in the aftermath of war.

Similarly, for reasons of space, the general aim has been not to reprint documents already available to the public in print, apart from cases of special importance. Where appropriate, references in footnotes have been supplied to documents already printed or cited. Also footnoted to documents printed in this volume are any occasional omissions from their text, because of uncertainty in the filed copy or for whatever other reason indicated in the notes. Any omissions are marked by the insertion of dots in the texts of documents, which are otherwise all printed in full.

In accordance with the parliamentary announcement some of the documents here printed, while self-contained in themselves, are supplemented by microcopies of further related documents. Their contents are briefly indicated in calendars printed directly after the substantive document to which they are appended under subsidiary Roman numerals, e.g. Nos. 3.i–iv, 7.i. A reference in a main document to a document calendared under it is editorially indicated in the text by the insertion in square brackets of the relevant Roman numeral, as on page 136.

Calendars are employed flexibly, in some cases to summarize a document or to cover salient considerations, in others to give brief indications of a run of supplementary documents. This incidentally permits some coverage of subsidiary issues and of material not in strictly diplomatic form, as in the proiferation of interdepartmental correspondence. These calendared documents are reproduced in full, unedited, on microfiches available with each volume. This two-tier method is designed to meet the needs of both the general and the more specialized reader.

The arrangement of the documents printed on British policy overseas will in general follow previous practice in publishing volumes of British diplomatic documents in broadly chronological series. Volumes will cover varying periods and subjects. Each volume will be divided into chapters wherein the documents will usually be arranged chronologically under the subject-heading of each chapter. This arrangement will, however, be applied flexibly, as indicated below in regard to the present volume.

II

The decision to publish a postwar collection of British diplomatic documents, beginning in 1945, was in accordance with previous practice in not seeking to cover by documentary publication the conduct of foreign policy under the special conditions of war. In the First and Second World Wars military and strategic considerations were usually predominant. British diplomacy during the latter period is already extensively covered in the five volumes of the official history by Sir Llewellyn Woodward: *British Foreign Policy in the Second World War* (London, 1970 f.).

The further decision as to where in 1945 to begin *Documents on British Policy Overseas* called for careful consideration. One possibility would have been to begin with the three-power Crimea Conference held at Yalta on 4–11 February 1945. It is frequently held now that particular significance attaches to the preparatory decisions of this conference, ranging from the treatment of Germany, reconstitution of Poland and Declaration on Liberated Europe to the convocation of a Conference on the World Organization of the United Nations to meet at San Francisco on 25 April 1945. The Conference at Yalta was, however, in sequence with previous wartime conferences such as those held at Casablanca, Cairo, Tehran and Moscow before the final defeat of Germany.

When the succeeding three-power Conference of Berlin opened at Potsdam on 17 July 1945 the war against Japan continued but the venue of the conference marked the unconditional surrender of Germany two months earlier. It might have appeared strictly logical to begin the postwar documentation of British policy overseas immediately after the conclusion in Tokyo Bay of the Japanese surrender on 2 September 1945, or possibly after the preceding suspension of hostilities from 15 August. Even the earlier of these dates would, however, have left an unduly long interval in regard to Europe and elsewhere since the termination of hostilities against Germany. It therefore seemed best to start in that overlap between war and peace which characterized the Conference at Potsdam. This last of the great tripartite conferences from the Second World War was directly formative for international relations in the postwar period. Executive decisions at Potsdam wound up the wartime European Advisory Commission and established a Council of Foreign Ministers to prepare peace settlements.

To have begun the present documentation with the first meeting of the Potsdam Conference would have left its proceedings without the clarification of a considerable number of important British preparatory papers and reports explaining the context of the conference. Some introductory material appeared necessary. Here again an editorial concern was the best place at which to begin in that European aftermath wherein the military priorities of reverting from a great war were gradually being reduced in relation to political concentration upon securing future peace.

A possible starting-place would have been from the conclusion on 26 June 1945 of the Conference at San Francisco. That date was not, however, of specially close significance for the immediate preliminaries of the Potsdam Conference. The most satisfactory date on balance appeared to be 6 July, the day after polling in the first British general election for nearly ten years: an election whose results were postponed by voting procedure for armed forces abroad but were, when announced on 26 July, to affect directly the conduct of that Potsdam Conference which had convened during this British interim. Also, diplomatically, 6 July 1945 was the day upon which His Majesty's Government, in concert with the United States Government, recognized the Polish Provisional Government of National Unity: a broadening, following the Yalta Declaration on Poland, of the previous Provisional Government at Lublin to include other leaders of resistance from the Polish homeland and from the former Polish Government in London. It was hoped that recognition of this coalition would contribute towards resolving that question of Polish representative and democratic government which was described by Sir Archibald Clark Kerr (later Lord Inverchapel), then H.M. Ambassador in Moscow, as 'the greatest single source of friction between the Soviet Union and her western allies' (document No. 78) in the immediate aftermath of the defeat of Germany.

'The victorious British Army, after the battle, now finds itself charged with a task of reconstruction' wrote Sir William Strang (No. 103) as Political Adviser to Field-Marshal Sir Bernard Montgomery, Commander-in-Chief of the British Forces of Occupation in the British zone of a Germany divided and reduced. The Second World War had cost the lives of not less than thirtyfive million persons, had displaced at least forty millions from their homes, had largely destroyed Stalingrad, Warsaw, Berlin and other cities, had devastated western Russia, improverished continental Europe and also the United Kingdom in her long defence of liberty under the leadership of Mr. Winston Churchill, and under exacting pressures.

In this legacy of sacrifice and distress a brief for the United Kingdom Delegation to the Potsdam Conference (No. 114) pointed to the economic crux for Europe: 'The control of Germany will be difficult, if not impossible, in the absence of a minimum of food and fuel. There is a world shortage of both. To the extent Germany's needs are met, our Allies, and perhaps ourselves, will go short. The fact is that by her action Germany has placed all the liberated countries in a condition of serious fear and want.'

This economic dilemma had a close bearing upon political aspects of Allied control of Germany and of Austria. British and Allied planning then looked towards the early establishment under Allied control of certain German central departments, as distinct from a government, as agreed in the final protocol of the conference (cf. No. 74, annex 1; No. 603). The constitution of Allied military administration in Berlin promptly raised economic questions (cf. No. 70), related in turn to complicated issues of German reparation. In application of one of the warnings from the peace settlement of Versailles in 1919, reparation was levied this time in kind rather than in cash.

Such issues were initially considered by the Allied Reparation Commission in Moscow upon the basis of a statement of principles agreed there at that level on 6 July 1945. These principles (cf. No. 116) notably included the treatment of Germany as a single economic unit, especially important for the British zone, needing to balance the output of coal from the Ruhr with that from Silesia and to draw upon the traditional granaries of eastern Germany under Soviet occupation. This was affected by the unilateral Russian ascription to Poland of the administration of the Soviet zone of Germany east of the line of the Oder and Western Neisse rivers (cf. No. 219, minute 8; No. 436). At the last meeting of the conference attended by Mr. Churchill he emphasized the importance of reaching broad agreement 'on this network of problems lying at the very heart of their work' (No. 271, minute 3). Questions of interzonal deliveries in Germany and of reparations were subsequently taken up in an American initiative towards recognising the Oder-Neisse line as the provisional western frontier of Poland (cf. Nos. 437, 494–5).

The economic proposals advanced in this connection aroused concern in the United Kingdom Delegation in regard to the future treatment of Germany. On 30 July Sir David Waley from the Treasury 'pointed out that if a line is drawn across the middle of Europe, so that there is a frontier with Russia on one side and the Western Powers on the other side, this has an importance far transcending reparations' (No. 485; cf. No. 492). In the political dimension His Majesty's Government had recognized the Polish Provisional Government of National Unity under specific reservation that the British Government was not satisfied with previous assurances regarding the free participation of political parties in forthcoming elections in Poland (cf. Nos. 6, 100). It was only after intensive questioning of the Polish deputation to the Potsdam Conference by Mr. Churchill, Mr. Eden, Mr. Attlee and Mr. Bevin, and the receipt of Polish assurances, that the United Kingdom Delegation withdrew its previous opposition to the proposal that the provisional frontier of Poland in the west should follow the line of the Oder and Western Neisse rivers.

At the end of the conference Mr. Attlee wrote to Mr. Churchill: 'I think that the results achieved are not unsatisfactory having regard to the way the course of the war had dealt the cards' (No. 522). In reply Mr.

Churchill expressed regret concerning the line of the Western Neisse and likely repercussions upon Germany, but added: 'This was certainly not the fault of the British Delegation' (No. 604.i).

The issue of free political activity and elections in Poland was matched in varying degrees in Roumania, Bulgaria, Yugoslavia, Hungary and Czechoslovakia. These nations were among those covered by the Yalta Declaration on Liberated Europe. As Mr. Churchill put it to Mr. Truman: 'Were all these States which had passed into Russian control to be free and independent, or not?' (No. 181). Immediate questions here further included freedom of press-reporting, protection of British economic interests, notably in Roumania, and 'the catalogue of incidents to our missions in Bucharest and Sofia': the context in which (No. 258, minute 3) Mr. Churchill expressed to Marshal Stalin his dissatisfaction that 'an iron curtain had been rung down. *Premier Stalin* said that these were fairy tales.'

In this area, as often, British and American policies largely coincided in objectives while differing to some extent in approach and application. This was also broadly true in regard to Italy, which British policy hoped to build up to be 'a "bastion of democracy" in the Mediterranean' (No. 63), and to Greece where British initiative and military support to the same end had given a lead towards containing internal and external communist pressures. In the case of Iran the Potsdam Conference agreed to begin the withdrawal of the Allied forces of occupation.

British intervention in Syria and the Lebanon in the light of military requirements and of local interests had unhappily distressed French opinion and General de Gaulle in particular. At the same time His Majesty's Government gave leading support to French participation in the occupation of Germany. Neither ally, furthermore, lost sight of the importance of the early conclusion of a postwar treaty of Anglo-French alliance, for which the Foreign Office had already prepared a draft (No. 119, annex 1H). This draft was annexed to a brief of 12 July 1945 for the United Kingdom Delegation wherein such a treaty was regarded as the precondition for progress 'towards the constitution of a "Western Group"' in Europe. In this connection it was recognized that 'there would undoubtedly be very great advantages in close economic association between the countries of Western Europe, but the difficulties are formidable, as to make a successful job, it would be necessary to have a customs union' (No. 119, annex 1; cf. No. 398).

The importance of cooperation in Western Europe for British policy in relation to the United States and the Soviet Union as the greatest world-powers was recognized in a comprehensive memorandum, 'Stocktaking after VE-Day' (No. 102), by Sir Orme Sargent, who was to be active in deputizing as Permanent Under Secretary of State for Foreign Affairs during the absence at Potsdam of Sir Alexander Cadogan. This memorandum of 11 July also advocated a firm policy in Eastern Europe, a region which was, however, to focus criticism of the policies of the great powers. Mr. Eden minuted to Mr. Churchill before the Potsdam Conference: 'I find world outlook gloomy and signs of Russian penetration everywhere' (No. 111). Whereas, as Mr. Churchill observed at the Potsdam Conference, Great Britain 'came out of this war as the greatest debtor in the world' (No. 226, minute 8). British reaction to the abrupt curtailment by President Truman of previous arrangements for lend-lease reflected the degree of immediate indebtedness in Great Britain, as elsewhere in Europe, to generous economic assistance from the United States.

The provision of American supplies to Allied governments under lend-lease was initially limited by Mr. Truman in July 1945 to uses in the continuing war against Japan. In that war the role of the United States was preponderant. At the same time Great Britain needed to care for important imperial and Commonwealth interests in the Far East, as in relations with the governments of Australia and New Zealand. The war against Japan dominates the records printed here of meetings at Potsdam of the British Chiefs of Staff Committee, as also of the Anglo-American Combined Chiefs of Staff Committee and of the single tripartite military meeting with Soviet representatives (No. 256) concerning the forthcoming entry into that war of the Soviet Union.

The Soviet Government was at that time in negotiation with the Chinese Government in pursuance of agreements concluded at the Yalta Conference (cf. Nos. 133, 180) and was also in receipt of Japanese peace-feelers towards the Western Allies, as reported by Marshal Stalin to the Conference at Potsdam (cf. No. 173, No. 447, minute 3). On 24 July 1945, however, the Combined Chiefs of Staff at Potsdam recommended 'that for the purpose of planning production and the allocation of manpower, the planning date for the end of organized resistance by Japan be the 15th November, 1946, and that this date be adjusted periodically to conform to the course of the war' (cf. Nos. 249, 255). At Potsdam Mr. Truman briefly informed Marshal Stalin of possession of a new and unusually destructive weapon following the successful testing at Alamogordo on 16 July 1945 of the atomic bomb. The active part played by Great Britain in its development was explained in a statement by Mr. Churchill issued by Mr. Attlee on 6 August when the bomb was first employed, against Hiroshima, four days after the conclusion of the Potsdam Conference and nine days before the consequent termination of active hostilities against Japan.

This extraordinary sequence of events in curtailing a grim war was one illustration of particular difficulties in assessing the yield of the Potsdam Conference. The usual measure of indirection of developments in foreign affairs, as in others, was liable to be accentuated by such variables as uncertainties in regard to true Soviet intentions, the absence after all of an ensuing and comprehensive peace-settlement for Germany, and the technological revolution of atomic energy. In this perspective the Potsdam Conference at the conclusion of the Second World War was held upon the eve of a new era in world history.

III

The first chapter of this volume I presents the preliminaries of the Potsdam Conference. In this explanatory material only the more directly relevant records are printed. Chapters II, IV and VI supply the British records of the conference before and after the interruption of its main proceedings to allow for the announcement of the results of the British general election and the replacement of Mr. Churchill by Mr. Attlee as Prime Minister and head of the United Kingdom Delegation at Potsdam; the documents incidentally illustrate both the large measure of continuity maintained in British foreign policy and distinctive views of Mr. Attlee in foreign affairs. Now printed for the first time are the full British records of the thirteen plenary meetings of heads of governments and the eleven meetings of foreign ministers held in the Cecilienhof Palace at Potsdam from 17 July to 1 August 1945. The three chapters coincide in time with chapters III and V containing diplomatic correspondence and papers concerning relevant developments during the conference.

The present volume is thus exceptionally concentrated in time-span and extensive in range of issues. It has therefore been necessary to give exceptional emphasis within chapters to chronology over arrangement by subject. This may help to illustrate the kind of synoptic view which statesmen at the Potsdam Conference needed to take of problems across the world claiming their urgent consideration day by day. For the British delegation the issues noticed above, and many others were elucidated in briefs of which over sixty are printed or calendared in this volume. Such briefs and memoranda present, to an extent unusual in the daily records of British foreign policy, a conspectus of its salient concerns as evaluated in 'stock-taking' in preparation for postwar challenges to the British Commonwealth.

Such a broad presentation of material in each chapter has called for the consultation of a particularly large range of files across the greatly expanded bulk of modern diplomatic archives. Such factors and some other initial difficulties inherent in this volume have slowed its preparation but, it is hoped, facilitated that of its successors. In the present instance, in order to assist reference to main subjects, each entry in the chapter-summaries in the front of the volume is preceded by an indicative key-letter.

No agreed tripartite records of the plenary meetings or meetings of foreign ministers were kept at the Potsdam Conference. The present British records of these meetings, together with memoranda in the P. (Terminal) series of the United Kingdom Delegation and the agreed protocol of the proceedings of the conference, are printed from the filed copy of the final texts preserved in confidential print on F.O. 371/50867: U 6197/3628/70. On occasion these texts have been collated with typewritten texts and drafts in F.O. 934 and F.O. 93/1/238 (cf. No. 226, note 1; No. 602, note 3).

In particular cases where British records of meetings of the conference can be significantly elucidated they have been cross-referenced to the independent American records printed in *Foreign Relations of the United*

States: The Conference of Berlin 1945 (Washington, 1960) or the Soviet record printed in *The Tehran, Yalta & Potsdam Conferences: Documents* (Moscow, 1969). Further documents are printed in *Sovetskiy Soyuz na mezhdunarodnykh konferentsiyakh perioda Velikoy Otechestvennoy voyny, 1941–1945 gg*: tom vi, *Berlinskaya (Potsdamskaya) konferentsiya rukovoditeley trekh soyuznykh derzhav— SSSR, SShA i Velikobritanii (17 iyulya—2 avgusta 1945 g): sbornik dokumentov* (Moscow, 1980)—'The Soviet Union at international conferences at the time of the Great Patriotic War, 1941–1945; volume vi, The Conference of Berlin (Potsdam) between the leaders of the three Allied powers— U.S.S.R., U.S.A. and Great Britain (17 July–2 August 1945): collection of documents'. Where appropriate in the present volume footnote-references have been supplied to documents printed or cited in these sources, in Sir Winston Churchill's *The Second World War* and in a range of other publications.

For this volume the main sources, now open in the Public Record Office, have been the political files in classes indicated above: F.O. 371 for Foreign Office main records, and F.O. 934 for records of the United Kingdom Delegation to the Potsdam Conference. Where a document is entered on more than one file preference is generally given to that on which action is taken and relevant correspondence preserved. For papers from class F.O. 371 of the Public Record Office only the Foreign Office file reference is given (e.g. No. 3). For all other classes the file reference is preceded by the P.R.O. class and piece number (e.g. No. 1).

Further sources used in the records of the Foreign and Commonwealth Office have included archives from His Majesty's Embassy in Moscow (F.O. 181) and collections of the papers of Private Secretaries (F.O. 800/ 416–7) and of the private papers of Mr. Eden (Earl of Avon: F.O. 954), Sir Archibald Clark Kerr (Lord Inverchapel: F.O. 800/303) and Sir Ronald Campbell (Campbell Papers). Where appropriate the archives of the Foreign Office have been supplemented from those of the Dominions Office (e.g. No. 7).

In accordance with the Parliamentary announcement the Editors have had the customary freedom in the selection and arrangement of documents. This access to the archives of the Foreign and Commonwealth Office has included material which, as in the case of some of the private papers, may not yet be fully listed but will be included in the archives. The Editors also enjoy reference to special categories of material, such as records retained in the Department under Section 3(4) of the Public Records Act of 1958. They have followed the customary practice whereby editors do not consult personal files on individual members of the Diplomatic Service or specifically intelligence material. As explained in the Parliamentary announcement, in exceptional cases where it is still necessary on security grounds to restrict the availability of a particular document editorially selected in accordance with regular practice, this will be indicated by square brackets round the text of the relevant calendar. No such exceptional case has arisen in the present volume.

In appropriate cases the publication of the records of the Foreign and Commonwealth Office has been supported from those of other Departments. Some records of conclusions of Cabinet Meetings (e.g. No. 118) are included. Among documents printed from the archives of the Cabinet Office are records (Cab 99/39) of meetings of the British Chiefs of Staff, now extensively printed for the first time, and of the Combined Chiefs of Staff, the only agreed Anglo-American minutes of meetings prepared at Potsdam. Also used where necessary have been files of the Prime Minister from No. 10 Downing Street (Prem: e.g. No. 2) and of the Treasury (T. 236: e.g. No. 485).

Despatches and telegrams received in the Foreign Office from His Majesty's Missions abroad are regularly addressed to the Secretary of State for Foreign Affairs, and outward correspondence to the Head or Acting Head of Mission. This practice is observed in the headings to documents, which have been editorially standardized in accordance with previous conventions and in the light of any special considerations. Such considerations for this volume have been the absence abroad of the Secretary of State for the greater part of the time covered, and the interval between Mr. Attlee's assumption of office and the appointment of Mr. Bevin to succeed Mr. Eden (cf. No. 422, note 4). Omitted from the headings and formulations at end are some classifications regarding administration and circulation but the main security classifications (Top Secret, etc.) are included where present in such form on the filed copy.

In accordance with regular practice the time of despatch for incoming telegrams is given according to standard time in the place of despatch, unless otherwise indicated. Thus in some cases the recorded time of receipt may be earlier than that of despatch. Outward telegrams are printed under the time of despatch from the cypher-room of the Foreign Office. In the absence of a time of despatch, the time of origin, that is, of receipt in the cypher-room is given, where known.

Standard abbreviations are explained in the lists on pp. xxii–xxiii, or in footnotes to the text. In the text any matter in square brackets is editorial unless otherwise indicated. In the conditions for the publication of this initial volume it has not proved practicable for the Editor to provide an index of requisite standard. It is, however, proposed to provide indexes to volumes in addition to the summaries of contents in the chapter-summaries.

I am grateful to the Earl of Avon, O.B.E., T.D., D.L., for permission to use the letter from Mr. Eden to Mr. Attlee printed, from the Attlee papers, in note 1 to No. 527. I am also grateful to the Imperial War Museum for permission to reproduce the photograph in the frontispiece.

I should like to thank successive Permanent Under Secretaries of State for Foreign and Commonwealth Affairs, and also Lord Bridges, K.C.M.G., for their support in planning and launching the present publication. I would also thank the Head of the Library and Records Department of the Foreign and Commonwealth Office and her staff for their indispensable assistance. Kind help has been further received from the Records Branch of the Cabinet Office, the Army Historical Branch of the Ministry of Defence, and the staffs of the Public Record Office and of Her Majesty's Stationery Office. Within the Foreign and Commonwealth Office I am indebted for valuable assistance to Miss K. E. Crowe, B.A., Miss M. P. Flanagan, Mrs. I. Ennis and, especially, Mrs. H. J. Yasamee, M.A. This volume owes much to all her work.

ROHAN BUTLER

24 August 1983

CONTENTS

CONTENTS

ABBREVIATIONS FOR PRINTED SOURCES

Berlinskaya
konferentsiya

Sovetskiy Soyuz na mezhdunarodnykh konferentsiyakh perioda Velikoy Otechestvennoy voyny, 1941–1945 gg (Moscow, 1978–80), tom vi, *Berlinskaya (Potsdamskaya) konferentsiya rukovoditeley trekh soyuznykh derzhav—SSSR, SShA i Velikobritanii (17 iyulya—2 avgusta 1945 g): sbornik dokumentov—* The Soviet Union at international conferences at the time of the Great Patriotic War 1941–1945, volume vi, The Conference of Berlin (Potsdam) between the leaders of the three Allied powers—U.S.S.R., U.S.A. and Great Britain (17 July–2 August 1945): collection of documents.

B.F.S.P.

British and Foreign State Papers (London, 1841–1977).

Cmd./Cmnd.

Command Paper (to 1956)/(from 1956).

Conferences:
Soviet
Documents

The Tehran, Yalta & Potsdam Conferences: Documents (Moscow, 1969).

D.B.F.P.

Documents on British Foreign Policy 1919–1939 (H.M.S.O., London, 1946f.).

F.R.U.S.

Foreign Relations of the United States: Diplomatic Papers (Washington, 1861f.).

F.R.U.S.
Berlin

Foreign Relations of the United States: The Conference of Berlin (The Potsdam Conference), 1945 (Washington, 1960).

Parl. Debs.
5th ser.,
H. of C.

Parliamentary Debates (Hansard), Fifth Series, House of Commons, Official Report (London, 1909f.).

Stalin
Correspondence

Correspondence between the Chairman of the Council of Ministers of the U.S.S.R. and the Presidents of the U.S.A. and the Prime Ministers of Great Britain during the Great Patriotic War of 1941–1945 (Moscow, 1957).

ABBREVIATED DESIGNATIONS

A.C.A.	Ministerial Committee on Armistice Terms and Civil Administration: to which worked a committee of officials (A.C.A.O.).
A.C.C.	Allied Control Commission.
A.F.H.Q.	Allied Force Headquarters
A.M.G.	Allied Military Government.
A.M.S.S.O.	Air Ministry, Special Signals Office.
A.P.W.	Armistice and Post-War Committee.
Arfar	Ministry of Economic Warfare telegram series.
A.V.N.O.J.	Yugoslav Anti-Fascist Council of National Liberation.
B.M.M.	British Military Mission.
C.C.A.C.	Anglo-American Combined Civil Affairs Committee.
C.C.S.	Anglo-American Combined Chiefs of Staff.
C.F.B.	Anglo-American Combined Food Board.
C.I.G.S.	Chief of Imperial General Staff.
C.M.A.B.	Anglo-American Combined Munitions Assignments Board.
Coronet	Codename for American plan to invade Honshu.
C.O.S.	British Chiefs of Staff.
C.P.R.B.	Anglo-American Combined Production and Resources Board.
C.R.A.B.	Anglo-American Combined Resources and Allocations Board.
Don	Telegram series on civil affairs from British Joint Staff Mission (Washington) to Cabinet Office.
E.A.C.	European Advisory Commission.

E.A.M.	Greek National Liberation Front.
E.C.C.	European Control Committee of the Cabinet.
E.C.I.T.O.	European Central Inland Transport Organisation.
E.C.O.	European Coal Organisation.
E.D.E.S.	Greek National Republican League.
E.E.C.E.	Emergency Economic Committee for Europe.
E.I.P.S.	British Economic and Industrial Planning Staff.
Elfu	Ministry of Fuel and Power telegram series.
F.A.O.	Food and Agricultural Organisation.
F.E.A.	American Foreign Economic Administration.
G.M.T.	Greenwich Mean Time.
G.O.C.	General Officer Commanding.
Grub	Ministry of Food telegram series.
I.R.C.C.	International Red Cross Committee.
J.A.P.	British Joint Administrative Planning Staff.
J.A.S.	British Joint American Secretariat.
J.S.M.	British Joint Staff Mission (Washington).
Mailfist	Codename for projected British operation for recapture of Singapore.
M.I.R.A.	Relief organisation for wheat in the Levant, in succession to Office des Céréales Panifiables (O.C.P.).
Nod	Telegram series on civil affairs from Cabinet Office to J.S.M. (Washington).

N.K.V.D.	Narodny Kommissariat Vnutrennikh Del: Soviet People's Commissariat of Internal Affairs.	S.D.	Sicherheitsdienst, security service of the Nazi Schutzstaffeln (S.S.).
Onward	Telegram series to U.K. Delegation (Berlin).	S.E.A.C.	South-East Asia Command.
		Sever	Telegram series from R.A.F. Delegation (Washington) to Air Ministry for J.A.S.
O.R.C.	Overseas Reconstruction Committee.		
O.W.I.	American Office of War Information.	Sextant	Codename for the Allied Conferences at Cairo in 1943.
P.A.I.C.	Persia and Iraq Command of British forces (Paiforce) in the Middle East.		
		S.H.A.E.F.	Supreme Headquarters, Allied Expeditionary Force.
P.(Terminal)	Numbered series of conference papers circulated by U.K. Delegation (Berlin).	S.L.A.	Ministerial Committee on supply questions in liberated and conquered areas: to which worked a committee of officials (S.L.A.O.).
P.H.P.	Post Hostilities Planning Committee.		
P.I.D.	Political Intelligence Department, Foreign Office.	T.A.	Tube Alloys: codename for research and development of atomic energy.
P.W.E.	Political Warfare Executive.	Target	Telegram series from U.K. Delegation (Berlin).
Resmed	British Resident Minister, Mediterranean.	Terminal	Codename for the Conference at Potsdam.
S.A.	Sturmabteilungen, Nazi storm troops.	Torch	Codename for Allied landings in French-North Africa in 1942.
S.A.C.M.E.D.	Supreme Allied Commander, Mediterranean.	U.M.A.	United Maritime Authority.
S.A.C.S.E.A.	Supreme Allied Commander, South-East Asia.	U.N.R.R.A.	United Nations Relief and Rehabilitation Administration.
		Uslon	Telegram series from R.A.F. Delegation (Washington) to Air Ministry for J.A.S.
Safehaven	Codename for programme to forestall German concealment of assets abroad.		
		Victim	Telegram series concerning Allied Reparations Commission in Moscow.
S.C.A.E.F.	Supreme Commander, Allied Expeditionary Force.	Zipper	Codename for projected landings in Malaya.

CHAPTER SUMMARIES

KEY-LETTERS TO SUBJECTS

A   Austria.

C   Conference at Potsdam: procedure and administration.

E   General European questions or surveys.

F   Far East: Japan, China, etc.

G   Germany.

I   Italy.

M   Middle East and Mediterranean: the Levant, Palestine, Iran, North Africa, Tangier.

N   Northern Europe. Scandinavia: Denmark, Norway, Sweden, Finland.

P   Poland.

R   Soviet Union and Russian questions.

S   South-Eastern and Central Europe: Czechoslovakia, Hungary, Roumania, Bulgaria.

T   Turkey.

U   United States and South America.

W   Western Europe: France, Netherlands, Belgium, Luxembourg, Spain.

X   Special questions of worldwide or scientific application. Postwar planning. The United Nations. The atomic bomb.

Y   Greece and Yugoslavia.

Z   British internal administration and arrangements.

CHAPTER SUMMARIES

CHAPTER I

Preliminaries of the Conference at Potsdam
6—16 July 1945

	NAME	DATE	MAIN SUBJECT	PAGE
1 U	EARL OF HALIFAX Washington Tel. No. 4672	6 July	Personal message for Mr. Churchill. President Truman hopes to stay with King George VI at Buckingham Palace after the Conference at Potsdam. Mr. Truman's approach to forthcoming conference.	1
2 Z	To EARL OF HALIFAX Washington Tel. No. T. 1227/5	6 July	Reply to No. 1. Explains to Mr. Truman arrangements proposed for U.K. Delegation in relation to declaration of poll on 26 July in British general election.	2
3 E	To EARL OF HALIFAX Washington Tel. No. 7169 *Calendars:* **i** 6–10 July. To and from Moscow tels. Nos. 30–1, 41, 43, 46–7 Victim & to Washington tel. No. 35 Victim: German reparation and treatment of Germany as an economic unit. **ii** 6 July. Letter from Sir A. Cadogan to F.M. Sir A. Brooke: Polish armed forces. **iii** 6 July. Budapest tel. No. 223: Communist ascendancy in Hungary. **iv** 6 July f. Belgrade tel. No. 1074, letter from King Peter II to Regents; U.K. Delegation brief No. 17: Tito-Subasic agreement.	6 July	Instructions for early discussion with Mr. Byrnes of situation in Europe. Has impression that Americans take 'rosier view of European prospects than we do': economic situation and political problems.	3
4 U	To EARL OF HALIFAX Washington Tel. No. 7212	6 July	Desirability of preliminary exchange of views with Americans while respecting their fear of 'ganging up'.	8

CHAPTER II

Earlier proceedings of the Conference at Potsdam
17—26 July 1945

1

CHAPTER III

Developments during the first part of the Conference at Potsdam 17–26 July 1945

Proceedings of the Conference at Potsdam after assumption of office by Mr. Attlee

27 July—1 August 1945

CHAPTER V

Developments during the second part of the Conference at Potsdam
27 July–2 August 1945

CHAPTER VI

The conclusion of the Conference at Potsdam
2 August 1945

CHAPTER I

Preliminaries of the Conference at Potsdam
6 — 16 July 1945

No. 1

Earl of Halifax (Washington) to Mr. Eden[1] *(Received 6 July, 8.30 a.m.)*
No. 4672 Telegraphic [F.O. 954/30:US/45/145]

Immediate   WASHINGTON, *6 July 1945, 12.28 a.m.*

Personal and secret for the Prime Minister.

I saw the President today[2] and gave him letter from the King inviting him to stay at Buckingham Palace.[3] President is sending reply to say that he certainly hopes to do this unless anything unforeseen occurs to summon him back here which he does not anticipate.

2. He is looking forward keenly to meeting you and working very closely with you. He is quite prepared to be friends with U. J.[4] where the ground is good.

3. He hoped, and I think thought, that Senate would ratify charter[5] by about July 21st. He said he could not put his fingers on more than three senators who would vote against it. If he is right in this, as he may well be, it is an amazing transformation.

4. I am sure you will like him and will find him direct and anxious to come to clear decisions without any waste of time. He visualises your talks lasting two or three weeks.

---

[1] Lord Halifax and Mr. Anthony Eden were respectively H.M. Ambassador at Washington and Secretary of State for Foreign Affairs. During the absence of Mr. Eden owing to illness, until 9 July 1945, the Foreign Office was in the charge of the Prime Minister, Mr. Winston Churchill, who went on holiday to Biarritz after 6 July.

[2] This telegram was drafted on 5 July 1945.

[3] On President Truman's return from the forthcoming Conference at Potsdam (code-named Terminal). For the letter of 28 June 1945 from H.M. King George VI to President Truman, cf. John W. Wheeler-Bennett, *King George VI: His Life and Reign* (London, 1958), p. 642.

[4] i.e. Uncle Joe, Marshal of the Soviet Union, Generalissimo J. V. Stalin.

[5] Of the United Nations, adopted by the United Nations Conference on International Organisation at San Francisco on 26 June 1945: printed (Cmd. 7015 of 1946) in *British and Foreign State Papers* (London, 1841 f: hereafter cited as *B.F.S.P.*), vol. 145, pp. 805–32.

5. I hope you are none the worse for all your election labours[6] and that you have got a good feeling about it.

[6] Polls in a British general election had been held on 5 July 1945. The results, postponed by voting arrangements for the armed forces abroad, were due to be announced on 26 July.

No. 2

Mr. Churchill to Earl of Halifax (Washington)
Serial No. T. 1227/5 Telegraphic [PREM 3/430/14]

FOREIGN OFFICE, 6 July 1945, 10.35 p.m.[1]

Personal and Top secret and Private

Your No. 4672:[2]

1 Thank you very much.[3] Naturally I am looking forward very much to meeting the President. The political members of the British delegation will quit the Conference on July 25 in order to await the poll in England. This will avoid embarrassment when the results are made known. I am led to believe that the present Government will obtain a majority but, as the President knows, electioneering is full of surprises. It is most unlikely in any event that I should resign on an adverse declaration of the poll unless it amounted to a very extreme expression of national displeasure. I should await the result of a confidence vote in the House of Commons on the King's Speech,[4] and take my dismissal from the House. This would enable the various parties and individuals to define their position by a vote.

2. The British delegation could therefore return to Berlin on the 27th, and I should personally be able to stay there if necessary till about the 5th or 6th August. Parliament meets on the 1st to elect a Speaker and to swear in Members. But it is not till Wednesday, 8th, that the King opens Parliament, and the decisive division would not take place before Friday, 10th. I thought all these details, some of which are extremely private, would be of interest to the President.

3. I am delighted to hear that the President contemplates two or even three weeks, as I think it of the utmost importance that whatever happens in England the Conference should not be hurried. It was somewhat abruptly

[1] Time supplied from another copy of this telegram, there numbered No. 7230.
[2] No. 1.
[3] The rest of this message is printed in W. S. Churchill, *The Second World War* (London, 1948 f.), vol. vi, pp. 529–30: cf. *Foreign Relations of the United States: The Conference of Berlin (The Potsdam Conference) 1945* (Washington, 1960: henceforth cited as *F.R.U.S. Berlin*), vol. i, pp. 149–50.
[4] The Speech from the Throne, made at each opening of Parliament, outlining the Government's legislative programme for the session.

curtailed in the Crimea.[5] We have here to try to reach settlements on a great number of questions of the greatest consequence, and to prepare the way for a Peace Conference which presumably will be held later in the year or in the early Spring.

4. Pray give my warmest personal regards to the President.

[5] At the Conference at Yalta held on 4–11 February 1945 between President Roosevelt, Mr. Churchill and Marshal Stalin.

No. 3

Mr. Churchill to Earl of Halifax (Washington)
No. 7169 Telegraphic [Z 8083/39/72][1]

Immediate   FOREIGN OFFICE, *6 July 1945, 12.5 a.m.*
Repeated to Moscow No. 3785.

Please take an early opportunity of discussing the situation in Europe with the new Secretary of State.[2]

2. I have the impression that the Americans take a rosier view of European prospects than we do. They seem to think that, given the settlement of a few outstanding problems, and the enunciation of general political principles and desiderata Europe can safely be left to look after itself and that it will soon settle down to peaceful and orderly development. Our view, on the contrary, is that unless we all work very hard the situation in Europe will deteriorate rapidly and dangerously. In view of the approaching meeting, I think it very important to impress our point of view on the United States Government. The following paragraphs give our estimate of the economic situation and of the position in the more important countries. You should make the fullest use of this in your conversation with Mr. Byrnes.

Economic Situation

3. Food is short and levels of consumption are dangerously low. Normal surplus areas in Eastern and South Eastern Europe will barely be self-sufficient this year and the already serious situation of the deficit areas will thereby be aggravated. Substantial food imports will be required involving heavy financial burdens. Even if shipping could be made available, internal transport is disrupted; there is acute shortage of rolling stock, inland water transport and trucks. Raw materials are short, production is at a very low

[1] The present text of this telegram is an amended copy including additions made to the original version by Foreign Office telegram No. 7204 to Washington of 6.20 p.m. on 6 July 1945.

[2] Mr. James F. Byrnes had succeeded Mr. E. R. Stettinius as U.S. Secretary of State on 3 July 1945. On 28 June Mr. Stettinius had been appointed American representative on the Security Council of the United Nations.

ebb and masses of labour are not gainfully employed. Above all a critical coal shortage this winter is certain and it will affect the whole economic fabric of Europe. Even if raw materials could be supplied and transport were available, absence of coal will hamstring production and distribution and prolong unemployment. These conditions apply generally throughout Europe, and in the liberated areas endanger stable government. In Germany and Austria the situation will be still further aggravated by the widespread disruption inevitable from the imposition of the necessary measures of economic disarmament and the levies of reparation labour. There will also be the problem of the support and disposal of a large body of non-repatriable displaced persons. In these circumstances the control of Germany on a quadripatrite [*sic*] basis will in itself present a formidable task.

Germany

4. Here our problems have hardly begun. The Control Commission is not yet established and no one can safely predict how it will work. We will do our best to make it work and to avoid the disastrous alternative under which each Commander-in-Chief would be administering his own zone regardless of the policy followed in the others. But we cannot be sure of succeeding. There is little agreement so far on policy towards Germany. Though the British and United States Delegations have tabled a long list of policy directives with the European Advisory Commission,[3] not one had yet been agreed. We have still no common view on what we desire the new Germany to be. There is no agreement on German frontiers or on the future of German populations outside the frontiers, or on the constitution of a German Government. Only when these and suchlike matters have been decided in principle can we begin to think constructively. The negative aspects of our policy on which we hitherto concentrated—disarmament, demilitarisation, de-Nazification, etc.—are clearly not enough.

Western Europe

5. We hope that after the French elections in November a reasonably strong and moderate Government will emerge which will be easier to deal with than the present government. We must support this government and help it rebuild France. But its future will depend largely on its success in dealing with economic problems. Meat, coal and means of transport are all going to be desperately short during the winter, and the resulting hardships might bring about serious internal disturbances. To guard against this

[3] The European Advisory Commission (E.A.C.) of British, American and Soviet representatives had been constituted by the Moscow Conference of Foreign Ministers in November 1943 to study and make recommendations to their governments upon European questions connected with the termination of hostilities. On 11 November 1944 the Governments of the United Kingdom, the United States of America and the Union of Soviet Socialist Republics had invited the Provisional Government of the French Republic to join the commission. M. R. Massigli, French Ambassador in London, took his seat in the commission, as the French representative, at a meeting on 27 November 1944.

it is important for the United States and the United Kingdom to do all in their power to help the French get supplies from abroad—especially coal and meat. Failure to do so may not only entail collapse of new French Government but lasting ill feeling between France and the United States and United Kingdom. Material help is what France will need, not kind words.

6. The position in Holland and Belgium resembles that in France. The governments need outside economic help if they are to survive and to retain the confidence of their people.

Italy

7. A new and promising government has just been formed,[4] which must be given every help. It should be encouraged to hold early elections and to reform and decentralise Italian Government machinery. But much more important, the Italian Government must be given sufficient economic assistance to get through the critical winter without too much unemployment and distress. Otherwise Italy will swing violently to the Left. Coal is the crying need, but Italy must also be helped with food and raw materials (U[nited] N[ations] R[elief and] R[ehabilitation] A[dministration] should help here). The Italian Government must be enabled to maintain and equip an army sufficient to ensure internal order and resist local aggression. This is equally a United States and a United Kingdom interest. The two countries have jointly liberated Italy. They have a joint obligation and interest to see Italy re-established as a going democratic concern. But this can only be achieved if much material assistance is made available to Italy. Fine speeches will not suffice.

Poland

8. The formation of the Polish Provisional Government of National Unity[5] is but the first step towards the restoration of normal conditions in Poland. Although the government will enjoy the recognition of the principal Allied Powers, it is by no means fully representative of all currents of Polish political life. The most influential figures in the government are Communists and fellow travellers, who count on Russian support in imposing their policies. The bourgeois parties are in eclipse. When the Soviet forces will withdraw

[4] For the formation of this government under Signor F. Parri, cf. Sir Llewellyn Woodward, *British Foreign Policy during the Second World War* (H.M.S.O., 1970 f.), vol. iii, p. 484.

[5] This government, formed on 28 June 1945, was recognized by His Majesty's Government at 1 a.m. on 6 July in synchronization with the United States Government (5 July, 7 p.m. Eastern War Time). The official statement of recognition is printed in *The Times* of 6 July 1945, p. 4: cf. also No. 6 below. Members of the new Polish government included M. E. Osobka-Morawski as Prime Minister, MM. W. Gomulka and S. Mikolajczk as Deputy Prime Ministers and M. W. Rzymowski as Minister for Foreign Affairs. M. Mikolajczk had been Prime Minister of the Polish Government in London until succeeded in November 1944 by M. T. Arciszewski. From 6 July 1945 His Majesty's Government ceased to recognise M. Arciszewski's government, which had been diplomatically represented by Count Raczynski: cf. Count Edward Raczynski, *In Allied London* (London, 1962), pp. 364–6, for his note of protest addressed on 6 July to Mr. Eden.

cannot yet be foreseen; while they remain, most Poles will regard the present settlement with reserve. The resultant insecurity may breed disorder and civil strife unless the Western Powers are prepared to use all their influence in favour of moderation and to lend their assistance both political and economic in the restoration of stable conditions.

Czechoslovakia

9. The situation is dominated as in Poland by the presence of the Red Army. Even when it goes, Russian influence will continue to make itself felt in various ways, and the contrary pull of the bourgeois elements towards the West will set up strains in a country where the government's control is still tenuous. Only the constant influence of the Western Powers can diminish these strains and prevent overhasty solutions which would create grave problems for the Allied [*sic*] outside the borders of Czechoslovakia itself.

South-Eastern Europe

10. The ex-satellite countries,[6] Hungary, Roumania and Bulgaria, all have unrepresentative Communist-controlled government. There is no prospect of free elections. The American and British representatives on the Allied Control Commission are powerless, and in this respect, there has been no improvement since the end of hostilities.

11. In Yugoslavia, the provisions of the Tito-Subasic Agreement[7] are not being fulfilled by Marshal Tito. Here again, there is little chance of free elections or of democratic government in the Anglo-Saxon sense of the word. Meanwhile, as we have seen in Venezia Giulia[8], Tito is adopting an anti-

---

[6] Allies of Germany in the Second World War.

[7] This agreement of 1 November 1944 (cf. No. 3.iv.c) between Marshal J. B. Tito, President of the Yugoslav National Committee of Liberation, the executive organ of the Anti-Fascist Council of National Liberation (A.V.N.O.J.), and Dr. I. Subasic, Prime Minister in the Royal Yugoslav Government, had provided for the appointment by King Peter II of a Regency Council and for the formation of an interim government. A further agreement dated 7 December 1944 provided that elections for a Yugoslav Constituent Assembly would be decided upon within three months of the liberation of the whole country. The new Government of Yugoslavia was formed on 7 March 1945 with Marshal Tito as Prime Minister and Minister for National Defence, and Dr. Subasic as Minister for Foreign Affairs.

[8] For negotiations leading to the Anglo-American-Yugoslav Agreement at Belgrade on 9 June 1945, providing for the establishment of Allied Military Government west of a demarcation-line (the Morgan Line) between Allied and Yugoslav troops in occupation of Trieste and adjacent areas of Venezia Giulia (summarized in undated U.K. Delegation brief No. 11 on Venezia Giulia, not printed), see Sir L. Woodward, *op. cit.*, vol. iii, pp. 367–80, and C. R. S. Harris, *Allied Military Administration of Italy 1943–1945* (H.M.S.O., 1957), pp. 330–45. In his telegram No. 2163 of 6 July 1945 to Mr. P. Broad, in charge of the Office of the British Resident Minister at Caserta (Resmed), Mr. Churchill commented on a suggestion made by General Sir W. Morgan, Chief of Staff to Field-Marshal Alexander, Supreme Allied Commander in the Mediterranean, that discussion of a final settlement be brought forward to the meeting at Potsdam in order to forestall Yugoslav pressure. Mr. Churchill stated: 'I should have no objection of principle to a settlement of the Italian-Yugoslav frontier in advance of a general European settlement. There are however grave

British and anti-American attitude and is currying favour with Bulgaria while making demands on all his other neighbours.

In Greece we can claim that the situation is distinctly better, though it still calls for careful handling and there will never be a return to public confidence and stability so long as the Greek people have reason to fear a concerted aggression by Yugoslavia and Bulgaria against their northern territories.

Turkey

12. The Soviet Government has made serious demands on the Turks[9] without previous warning to their Allies. The resulting crisis, if not soon resolved, may become hardly less serious than the Polish issue which has so poisoned international relations in recent years.

CALENDARS TO No. 3

i *6–10 July 1945* (*a*) *To Sir A. Clark Kerr* (*H.M. Ambassador, Moscow*) *Tels. Nos. 30–1 & 46–7 Victim, and to Lord Halifax* (*Washington*) *Tel. No. 35 Victim:* concern at unilateral action by Mr. E. W. Pauley, U.S. representative on Allied Reparations Commission in Moscow, in sending instructions to U.S. zone for interim delivery of German goods to liberated territories and for restitution of works of art (cf. *F.R.U.S. Berlin*, vol. i, pp. 514–5); British policy, and treatment of Germany as an economic unit. Instructions for representations to U.S. Govt. and discussion with Mr. Pauley (cf. *ibid.* pp. 532–5) [UE 2780, 2723/624/77]. (*b*) *Sir A. Clark Kerr* (*Moscow*) *Tel. No. 41 Victim:* M. I. M. Maisky, Assistant Commissar for Foreign Affairs and Chairman of Allied Reparations Commission, suggested a committee in Berlin on interim deliveries; question of French participation in Moscow Commission [UE 2862/624/77]. (*c*) *Sir A. Clark Kerr* (*Moscow*) *Tel. No. 43 Victim.* British plan for fixing reparation shares of other powers; continued emphasis upon early French participation [UE 2857/624/77].

ii *6 July 1945 Letter from Sir A. Cadogan* (*Permanent Under Secretary of State for Foreign Affairs*) *to F.M. Sir A. Brooke* (*C.I.G.S.*) *with enclosure:* treatment of

practical difficulties in the way of this course, particularly from the point of view of the procedure to be adopted. General question of procedure for settling disputed frontiers is on the agenda for the forthcoming meeting; but it is doubtful whether much progress will be able to be made there on the particular case of Venezia Giulia' (R 11098/6/92).

[9] On 19 March 1945 the Soviet Government had denounced the Soviet-Turkish treaty of 17 December 1925 (printed in *B.F.S.P.*, vol. 125, pp. 1001–2). In reply to a Turkish proposal for the negotiation of a new treaty the Soviet Commissar for Foreign Affairs, M. V. M. Molotov, was reported to have made on 7 June 1945 the following prior stipulations: (i) the provisions of the Treaty of Kars of 13 October 1921 between Turkey and Armenia, Azerbaijan and Georgia, with the participation of the Russian Socialist Federal Soviet Republic (*op. cit.*, vol. 120, pp. 906–13), whereby Turkey received Kars, Artvin and Ardahan, should be revised; (ii) Turkey should cede bases in the Straits to the U.S.S.R.; (iii) a Soviet-Turkish agreement should be made for the revision of the International Montreux Convention of 20 July 1936 regarding the fortification of the Straits and the passage through them of warships (*op. cit.*, vol. 140, pp. 288–300; cf. generally Sir L. Woodward, *op. cit.*, vol. iv, pp. 206–9). See further No. 207.

Polish armed forces in 'rather long period' anticipated between recognition of new Polish Govt. and elections in Poland [N 8285/123/55].

iii *6 July 1945 Mr. A. D. F. Gascoigne (H.M. Political Representative, Budapest) Tel. No. 223.* Reasons of President of Hungarian National Assembly for delaying elections; communist ascendancy, and lack of freedom [R 11518/26/21].

iv *6 July 1945 f. (a) Mr. R. C. Skrine Stevenson (H.M. Ambassador, Belgrade) Tel. No. 1074:* conversation with Dr. Subasic on 4 July; non-implementation of Tito-Subasic agreement [R 11570/130/92]. *(b) Letter from Mr. D. F. Howard (Head of F.O. Southern Dept.) to Mr. Skrine Stevenson.* Transmits letter from King Peter II to the Regents criticising their inactivity and policy of Yugoslav Government [R 10996/19/92]. *(c) Brief No. 17 for U.K. Delegation (without annexes): Situation in Yugoslavia and the implementation of the Tito-Subasic Agreement:* Allied responsibility towards fulfilment of obligations undertaken by Yugoslav Govt. by virtue of Allied declaration on Yugoslavia issued on 11 Feb. 1945 as art. VII of Yalta Conference Report (see No. 30, note 2) and accepted by Marshal Tito on 9 Mar. 1945 [F.O. 934/6].

No. 4

Mr. Churchill to Earl of Halifax (Washington)
No. 7212 Telegraphic [F.O.800/416/63]

Immediate. Top secret　　　　　　　　FOREIGN OFFICE, *6 July 1945, 7.55 p.m.*
Repeated to Moscow No. 3802.

Your telegram No. 4641[1] (of July 4th) (not repeated to Moscow).

We have been considering whether there is any possibility of a preliminary meeting with the Americans before Terminal. We imagine that a high level meeting on the analogy of that at Malta[2] is unlikely; we do not suppose that the Americans would agree, in view of their fear of 'ganging-up', and circumstances are likely to make it impossible in any case. But a meeting at some level would be extremely useful and we very much hope that a member or members of the State Department might arrange to pass through London for an exchange of views with us before the meeting. This could be done

---

[1] Not printed. This telegram had reported that Mr. Joseph Davies, Special Adviser to President Truman, expected to spend 24 hours in London on his way to the conference at Potsdam. Lord Halifax had added: 'In the course of a talk I had yesterday with Admiral King, he told me that he had gathered from Harry Hopkins that Stalin was likely to raise a question of some further interpretation being provided for Japanese of the meaning of unconditional surrender. I understood from him that on the American side they would [be] disposed to favour this, while appreciating the necessity of great caution, both as regards the substance of what might be said and the timing.'

[2] Before the Yalta Conference discussions had been held at Malta from 30 January to 2 February 1945 between British and American representatives: cf. W. S. Churchill, *op. cit.*, vol. vi, pp. 296–301, and the Earl of Avon, *The Eden Memoirs* (London, 1960 f.), *The Reckoning*, pp. 510–2.

quite unobstrusively [*sic*] and there should be no danger of an accusation of ganging-up.

2. Report that Mr. Joseph Davies is coming here might give you an occasion to make the above suggestion. Appropriate representatives of the State Department might accompany Mr. Davies on this mission, in regard to which we have as yet no information other than that in your telegram.

No. 5

Mr. Churchill to Sir A. Clark Kerr (Moscow)
No. 3803 Telegraphic [F.O. 954/2 : Con/45/147]

FOREIGN OFFICE, *6 July 1945, 7.35 p.m.*

Most Immediate. Personal and Secret

Repeated to Washington No. 7213 (Immediate).

My telegram No. 3748[1] (of July 4th: publicity at Terminal).

Please convey following message from the Prime Minister to Premier Stalin dated July 6th.

I have heard from the President that in conformity with our understanding he is announcing to-day that the press will not be allowed at Terminal and that all that will be issued from Terminal will be such official communiques as may be decided upon from time to time. The President tells me that he is sending a similar message to you.

2. In anticipation of your concurrence, we are making a similar announcement in London to-day.

---

[1] Not printed. This telegram conveyed Mr. Churchill's message of 4 July 1945 to Marshal Stalin, printed together with the present message in *Correspondence between the Chairman of the Council of Ministers of the U.S.S.R. and the Presidents of the U.S.A. and the Prime Ministers of Great Britain during the Great Patriotic War of 1941–1945* (Moscow, 1957: hereafter cited as *Stalin Correspondence*), vol. i, pp. 371–2; cf. also *F.R.U.S. Berlin*, vol. i, p. 145.

No. 6

Letter from Sir A. Clark Kerr (Moscow) to M. Modzelewski[1]
[N 9716/6/55]

MOSCOW, *6 July 1945*

(Dear Mr Modzelewski),

In confirmation of the oral message which Mr Roberts gave you last

---

[1] A copy of this letter to the Polish Ambassador in Moscow was transmitted to the Foreign Office under cover of Moscow despatch No. 505 of 23 July 1945 (received on 3 August).

night,[2] I write to say that I have been instructed by my government to inform the Soviet Government, as one of the three parties to the Crimea decisions, that they are not satisfied with the assurances contained in your letter to me of July 4th regarding the participation of Polish political parties in the eventual elections. Mr Churchill has therefore reserved the right to raise this matter at his next meeting with Generalissimo Stalin and President Truman as affecting the implementation of the Crimea decisions.

2. A similar communication is also being addressed to the United States Government.[3]

(Yours sincerely),
ARCHIBALD CLARK KERR

[2] This oral message, untraced in Foreign Office archives, from Mr. F. K. Roberts, H.M. Minister in Moscow, was evidently in pursuance of instructions from Mr. Churchill in Foreign Office telegram to Moscow No. 3779 of 5 July: 'I am not satisfied with assurances from Polish Ambassador' on 4 July (see No. 45, sixth paragraph). 'Nevertheless, I do not desire to hold up recognition on this account' (cf. No. 3, note 5).

[3] Cf. F.R.U.S. Berlin, vol. i, pp. 737–8.

No. 7

Viscount Cranborne to Mr. Mackenzie King (Ottawa)[1]
D. No. 1172 Telegraphic [D.O. 35/1610: WF 321/15]

Top secret   DOMINIONS OFFICE, *6 July 1945, 2.50 p.m.*

My telegram D. No. 1133[2] of 29th June. Turco-Soviet relations.

We have decided to enter an immediate caveat with Soviet Government. Turkish Government are expecting us to act even without United States support. Moreover, we think it better to warn Soviet Government of our views in advance of forthcoming Three Power Conference even at risk of rendering atmosphere at the Conference on this question more difficult, rather than give them impression that we do not intend to take any action or to spring it on them for first time at the Conference.

2. United Kingdom Ambassador in Moscow has accordingly been instructed to express to Soviet Government our surprise at Soviet territorial claims and demands for bases in the Straits. Former should be considered in the light of general world organisation and latter affects the multilateral Montreux Convention. Moreover it was agreed at Yalta that Soviet Government should consult United Kingdom and United States Governments before approaching Turkish Government on matters affecting Montreux Convention. Marshal Stalin also agreed to take no action

[1] Lord Cranborne was Secretary of State for Dominion Affairs. Mr. Mackenzie King was Canadian Prime Minister and Secretary of State for External Affairs. This telegram was also sent to the governments of Australia, New Zealand and South Africa.

[2] Not printed.

affecting independence and integrity of Turkey and to adopt a reassuring attitude to Turkish Government.[3] Thus we have naturally been very much surprised at recent radio and Press campaign against Turkey. We wish the Soviet Government to be aware of our views as we consider the whole question will have to be discussed at forthcoming Three Power Conference.

3. We are informing United States Government of our proposed action, pointing out that we cannot agree that conversation between Molotov and Turkish Ambassador in Moscow can be regarded as 'exploratory' and 'a preliminary exchange of views'.[4] Turkish Government are also being informed.[5]

CALENDAR TO No. 7

i *6 July 1945* Sir M. Peterson (*H.M. Ambassador, Angora*) *Tel. No. 707*. Has informed Acting Turkish Minister for Foreign Affairs of British policy explained in No. 7. Minister expressed great satisfaction. Soviet Ambassador to Turkey, M. Vinogradov, alleged to have been surprised by his government's action at that time [R 11507/4476/44].

[3] Cf. Sir L. Woodward, *op. cit.*, vol. iv, pp. 204–5.
[4] For this British communication of 7 July 1945 to the United States Government see *F.R.U.S. Berlin*, vol. i, pp. 1047–8. This communication referred to the American memorandum of 23 June here quoted: printed *ibid.*, pp. 1027–8.
[5] The main substance of this telegram was transmitted to principal H.M. Missions abroad in circular telegram No. 55 Intel of 12.50 a.m. on 6 July.

No. 8

Viscount Cranborne to Mr. Mackenzie King (Ottawa)[1]
D. No. 83 Saving Telegraphic [C 3699/1/18]

Secret   DOMINIONS OFFICE, *6 July 1945*

Germany.
Directive has been issued to Field Marshal Montgomery[2] in following sense.
(1) He will be United Kingdom Member of Control Council for Germany.
(2) When Control Council has been established, he will, in conjunction with United States, Soviet and French colleagues on Council, exercise control over Germany in accordance with agreement on Control machinery (despatches 25th November, 1944, D. No. 161 and 12th May, 1945, D. No. 80)[3] read in conjunction with report of

[1] This telegram was also sent to the governments of Australia, New Zealand and South Africa.
[2] Commander-in-Chief of the British Forces of Occupation in Germany.
[3] These despatches, not preserved in Dominions Office archives, are untraced. The Tripartite Agreement of 14 November 1944 on Control Machinery in Germany and the Four-Power amendment thereto of 1 May 1945 are printed in Cmnd. 1552 of 1961, *Selected Documents on Germany and the Question of Berlin 1944–1961*, pp. 31–3 and 35–6 respectively.

E.A.C. of 14th November, 1944,[4] particularly paragraphs 3-6 thereof.

(3) First task will be to ensure that provisions of Declaration on Unconditional Surrender of Germany (despatch 7th June G. No. 32)[5] are strictly carried out.

(4) In concerting policy with his colleagues on Control Council he is to be guided by post-surrender directives (despatch D. No. 143 of 13th October, 1944, and subsequent despatches)[6] for Germany, bearing in mind that these have not yet been agreed with United States, Soviet and French Governments and represent policy of His Majesty's Government in United Kingdom only.

[4] Printed in *F.R.U.S. 1944*, vol. i, pp. 404–6.

[5] This despatch, not preserved in Dominions Office archives, is untraced. The Declaration regarding the defeat of Germany and the assumption of Supreme Authority with respect to Germany by the Governments of the United Kingdom, the United States of America, and the Union of Soviet Socialist Republics, and by the Provisional Government of the French Republic, signed in Berlin on 5 June 1945, is printed (Cmd. 6648 of 1945) in *B.F.S.P.*, vol. 145, pp. 796–802.

[6] These despatches, not preserved in Dominions Office archives, are untraced.

No. 9

Joint Staff Mission[1] *(Washington) to the Cabinet Office*
(Received 7 July, 5.40 a.m. G.M.T.)
No. Don 878 Telegraphic [UE 2949/139/71]

Secret. Immediate   WASHINGTON, *6 July 1945, 11.51 p.m. G.M.T.*[2]

Reference Don 863.[3]

As the result of further discussions with McCloy and Hilldring[4] it appears that the War Dept agrees with us on the following points:

(A) Objective is earliest efficient functioning on quadripartite base;

(B) That aim should be to establish so far as practicable common ration scales and comparable standards of life in Western Germany meanwhile;

(C) Maximum production of German coal;

[1] This representative body in Washington of the British Chiefs of Staff was headed by Field Marshal Sir H. Maitland Wilson; also serving on it were Admiral of the Fleet Sir J. F. Somerville, Lt. General Sir G. N. Macready and Air Marshal D. Colyer. Telegrams from Joint Staff Mission were received through the Special Signals Office of the Air Ministry (A.M.S.S.O.) in the Offices of the Cabinet and Minister of Defence.

[2] Time of origin.

[3] Not printed. This telegram of 30 June 1945 in this series for the Civil Affairs Directorate of the War Office referred to the continuation of combined supply machinery for Germany.

[4] Mr. J. McCloy, American Assistant Secretary of War, and Major-General J. Hilldring, Director of the Civil Affairs Division in the American War Department Special Staff, were members of the Combined Civil Affairs Committee (C.C.A.C.) in Washington on planning and administration of civil affairs in occupied areas.

(D) Imports to be first charge on German capacity to pay;

(E) Surpluses in one zone to be set off against deficiencies in other zones so as to minimize imports;

(F) Net import programmes for 3 zones to be established after consultation and after allowing for maximum use of total indigenous resources of Western Germany.

2. Mel 891[5] has produced negative first reaction both in War Dept and in State Dept. Objections stem primarily from political considerations, but also from procedure considerations discussed later in this telegram.

On political point, Americans feel that what is in effect continuation of SHAEF G–5[6] German Section under new title of CRAB might well give the Russians the impression that the 3 Western Allies were seeking to set up new organization for the Western Area of Germany prior to making any arrangements with them. However, McCloy has stated definitely that in his view there should not be any gap between end of combined arrangements and beginning of quadripartite functioning, and he indicated that if continuation of combined arrangements until quadripartite machinery could take over were treated as a liquidating function and carried out by a body whose title referred to such liquidation in his view the political objection was much weakened and should be outweighed by practical advantages of avoiding any hiatus.

3. On the financial side McCloy said that if the liquidation process were not complete by the time the existing War Debt [Dept.] appropriation had been exhausted (i.e. after some six months) then the War Dept would have no money left available for procuring supplies on a combined basis. However, if at that juncture the British were able to undertake the immediate financing of supplies for their own zone, this financial difficulty should be capable of being resolved. Whether War Dept would maintain this if Treasury took contrary view is uncertain particularly since McCloy has left Washington.

4. Embassy have pursued political aspects of question with State Dept on basis of discussion in para 1 above. State Dept are now considering these representations.

5. If State Dept can be brought into line, the problem will be to agree with the Americans the machinery and procedures required to put the combined supply policy into effect.

6. We should have liked to be able to persuade the Americans to agree to machinery inside Germany on the lines suggested in Mel 891[5], and the

---

[5] This telegram of 30 June (UE 3227/139/71: not printed) from the Supreme Headquarters of the Allied Expeditionary Force (S.H.A.E.F.) to the Combined Chiefs of Staff, for C.C.A.C., had reported the appointment of the Anglo-American Combined Resources and Allocations Board (C.R.A.B.) and the suggested machinery for the distribution of supplies in Germany: cf. F. S. V. Donnison, *Civil Affairs and Military Government North-West Europe 1944–6* (H.M.S.O., 1961), p. 413.

[6] The Civil Affairs Division of the General Staff of S.H.A.E.F.

simultaneous submission of the 3 programmes to the combined boards,[7] to their being given an equal priority by the boards and to the right of the Zone Commander by agreement to divert supplies from one zone to another in emergencies. It is however pretty clear that the Americans will not agree to the Mel 891[5] proposals as they stand because:

(A) They would regard the introduction of the French as full partners as inconsistent with the emphasis which they feel essential to place upon the liquidation aspect of the operations and

(B) The proposals create difficulties for them in so far as the CRAB would be responsible to Zone Commanders and not CCS. See particularly para 8 below.

7. We therefore think that the best we are likely to be able to persuade the Americans to accept is on the following lines. There should be in Germany a combined Anglo-American body responsible to the CCS with a title indicating its liquidating function which would exercise the functions set out in para 1 of MEL 891, and would have the right to divert supplies allocated for use in Germany from one zone to another in emergencies. The programmes of requirements agreed by this body for the 3 zones should be submitted to the CCS and screened and approved by the CCAC before being transmitted to the combined boards. The boards should treat the 3 programmes as having equal priority. In the event of availabilities falling short of requirements the shortfall should be allocated between the zones not on a percentage basis but on a basis consistent with the maintenance of equivalent standards of living in the 3 zones.

8. This arrangement might be regarded as derogating from the sovereign authority of the zone commander in his zone but in so far as this is the case it is the price which will have to be paid for American agreement to the continuation of combined supply arrangements. The programme for the U.S. zone will have War Dept. backing and we cannot hope to get the programmes for the other two zones treated with equal priority (i.e. with War Dept backing) unless we are prepared to give the War Dept the opportunity to screen the requirements of British and French zones in the same way as they have hitherto in CCAC screened the requirements for areas of combined supply responsibility under SHAEF including areas such as Holland where the local responsibility was British. War Dept will certainly not back the programmes for British and French zones unless satisfied that it can justify them if called upon to do so by Congress and they would not regard agreement by American Commander in the field as sufficient. We do not however feel that much difficulty would be likely to arise in practice provided that there is agreement on the principles set out in para 1. above.

---

[7] Combined Boards on Food (C.F.B.), Productions and Resources (C.P.R.B.), Shipping Adjustment (C.S.A.B.), Raw Materials (C.R.M.B.), Munitions Assignments (C.M.A.B.), and Communications (C.C.B.): cf. H. Duncan Hall, *North American Supply* (H.M.S.O., 1955), pp. 346f., and H. Duncan Hall and C. Wrigley, *Studies of Overseas Supply* (H.M.S.O., 1956), pp. 206–236.

9. It would be possible for the programme for each zone, after agreement by the co-ordinating body to be submitted by the zone commander to his government and by his government to Washington. This would however be a clumsy procedure. If machinery in para 7 is agreed simplest channel of communication would seem to be direct between CCS and combined organisation in the field with copies to War Office, War Dept and Zone Commanders. This is the channel which War Dept would prefer if Americans agree to this plan.

10. As far as the French are concerned we think that for the reason given in para 6 (A) above the Americans would accept informal participation in the field but no formal participation as part of a three party organisation and no participation in the Washington machinery.

11. Please telegraph urgently whether assuming political difficulties can be overcome you are prepared to accept as basis for negotiation the arrangements proposed in paras 7 to 10 above.[8]

CALENDARS TO No. 9

i *14 July 1945   J.S.M. (Washington) to Cabinet Office Tels. Nos. Don 897–8:* discussions and Anglo-French proposals on financial arrangements for coal production for export from British and French zones in Germany in the light of U.S. War Dept. only being prepared to finance supplies and equipment for coal production for consumption within Germany [UE 3009/139/71].

ii *14 July 1945   Cabinet Office to J.S.M. (Washington) Tel. No. Nod 885.* Welcomes progress reported in No. 9 and agrees procedure in para. 9 there. Suggests form of local supply-arrangements to be made by Zone Commanders [UE 3010/139/71].

iii *7 July 1945   Mr. A. Holman (H.M. Minister, Paris) Tel. No. 350 Saving.* French relationship to Anglo-American Oil Allocating Committee [W 9339/12/76].

iv *7–10 July 1945   (a) Emergency Economic Committee for Europe (E.E.C.E.), Sub-Committee on Food and Agriculture:* proposals for modification of methods for coordinated purchasing and allocation;   (b) *Foreign Office minutes* on relationships between E.E.C.E. and Combined Boards [UR 2377/1600/53; UR 2210/1791/851].

v *30 June–9 July 1945 Foreign Office minutes and correspondence* on relations of Anglo-American Combined Boards with other Allies: anxieties of Mr. F. R. Hoyer Millar and Mr. W. J. Hasler, respectively Heads of F.O. Western and Relief Depts. [Z8943/8254/72].

[8] J.S.M. Washington telegram DON 880 of 7 July requested the addition here of: 'If not, please instruct us what line we should take'. A copy of the present document was received in the Foreign Office on 13 July and was minuted as follows by Mr. A. H. Lincoln of Economic Relations Department: 'A generally favourable reply has been sent to DON 878 in the shape of NOD 885 [ii] of the 14th July.   2. Copies of these telegrams have been sent to our delegation at Terminal in view of the discussion there of the treatment of Germany as an economic unit and the presence of Mr. Macloy [*sic*]. A.H.L. 15/7.'

No. 10

Brief for the United Kingdom Delegation to the Conference at Potsdam
No. 39 [U 5397/5397/70]

FOREIGN OFFICE, *6 July 1945*

Disposal of the German Fleet

In anticipation of the German collapse the Admiralty agreed with the Soviet naval command (through the liaison machinery at Moscow) the terms of orders to be issued to the German Navy after the surrender, including orders to ships at sea to put into the nearest Allied port and should remain there pending further orders from 'the Allied representatives'. The Admiralty acted upon these orders, but, in the event, the Russians failed to do so and no German ships at sea surrendered to the Russians. Nor did the Russians capture any seaworthy vessels in German ports.

2. When Germany surrendered we took the view that German shipping falling into our hands in the Dutch, Danish and North-West German ports came under the tactical surrender by Admiral Friedeburg to Field Marshal Montgomery as G.O.C. 21st Army Group, and were to be regarded as 'captured in the course of operations' and assignable by the Combined Chiefs of Staff. German shipping in Norwegian waters, however, including a high proportion (some 90) of the total unsunk U-boats, came under the general surrender of the German armed forces signed successively at Rheims and Berlin[1] in which the Russians participated. In Russian eyes it would be the final surrender by Field Marshal Keitel in Berlin that counted, and this document (text at Annex A)[2] required all German forces to remain where they were and to carry out further orders 'issued by SCAEF[3] and by the Supreme High Command of the Red Army'.

3. With the agreement of the Americans and on the authority of the Prime Minister, the Admiralty, however, took unilateral action to move the sea-worthy U-boats from the Norwegian harbours to the United Kingdom. The Russians have not so far asserted that they should have been first consulted, but if they had done so, it was the Admiralty's intention to argue that it was necessary for practical reasons (e.g. difficulty in guarding) to move the U-boats from Norway, and that the Russians had anyhow forfeited their interest by failing to carry out the agreement reached at Moscow whereby they as well as ourselves would have broadcast orders for the control of German ships.

---

[1] The Act of Military Surrender by Germany to the Allied and Associated Powers, signed at Rheims at 2.41 a.m. on 7 May 1945 (printed in *B.F.S.P.*, vol. 154, p. 365), whereby all hostilities ceased at one minute after 11 p.m. on 8 May, was ratified in Berlin between 11.15 and 11.45 p.m. on 8 May: cf. Cmnd. 1552 of 1961, p. 37.

[2] Not printed: see note 1 above.

[3] Supreme Commander, Allied Expeditionary Force, General of the Army Dwight D. Eisenhower, also Commander-in-Chief of the American Forces of Occupation in Germany.

4. On 23rd May, Marshal Stalin, in messages[4] to the Prime Minister and President Truman, claimed a minimum of one-third of the Navy and merchant marine of Germany. The Prime Minister replied that the question should be discussed at Terminal.

5. The present position in regard to the German fleet; considerations bearing upon policy; and suggestions for the solution of the problem are contained in the Cabinet Paper by the Admiralty at Annex B;[5] the draft of which was concerted and agreed with the Foreign Office on the official level.

6. A separate brief is being written by the Ministry of War Transport, in concert with the Admiralty and Foreign Office, on the question of *German merchant shipping*. In our opinion this should be settled as a matter of 'Reparations,' but we agree with the Admiralty that it would be wise to allow the Russians meanwhile the *use* of a proportion of the many German ships in our hands.

7. It would clearly be in the interest of this country, and in the interest of the World as a whole, to scrap the entire German fleet. Only the action of the Germans in scuttling their ships in 1918 put an end to unpleasant controversies which were already beginning between the Allies. While there is unfortunately little chance of the Russians agreeing to scrap as a general policy it is suggested that we ought, if only for technical reasons, to support strongly any American initiative proposing the scrapping of the entire fleet. We should, however, first reach an understanding with the Americans that they would not suddenly go back upon this, leaving us in a minority of one; that is to say, our eventual abandonment of scrapping in favour of a policy of division should be concerted with the United States.

8. There is every indication that the Russians wish very strongly to obtain a substantial slice of the German fleet, both for prestige reasons and because they think that these ships would be useful to them. As we in fact hold all the undamaged ships, we are in a very strong position, and in fact this is about the best card we hold in our hand for Terminal.

9. It is therefore submitted that we should not hesitate to make the fullest use of this card, and that we should only consent to abandon our preference for scrapping and to give the Russians part of the fleet in return for some comparable concession by the Russians in another matter where they are in the strongest position. Experience in past negotiations suggests that the Russians would give us no real credit for spontaneously meeting their demand for the German ships at an early stage of the Conference, and that they would understand, and indeed respect us for it, if we drove a bargain.

10. The French claim to a share in the German fleet, which has already been put forward semi-officially to the Admiralty, is weak in equity. But

---

[4] Printed in *Stalin Correspondence*, vol. i, pp. 359–60; vol. ii, p. 238. Mr. Churchill's reply of 26 May is printed *op. cit.*, vol. i, p. 360.

[5] Not attached to filed copy: see No. 10. i.

the French are an equal partner in the Allied supreme authority and control over Germany, and it is in our interest to preserve the good relations between the Royal Navy and the French Navy and to encourage the latter to work with us in the future. Accordingly, it is submitted that we should allow the French a few ships, on the ground that the destruction of their ship-building and dockyards during the war will preclude France from replacing losses by her own construction for some time.

11. The Foreign Office agree with the Admiralty's policy in not allotting enemy ships to the Dutch, Norwegians and Greeks, as we have undertaken to look after these Navies in the future and it is in our interest, and also in the interest of the small Allies, that they should have British-built ships and equipment. The Admiralty agree, however, that this policy carries the corollary that we should inform the Allies why we are not giving them German ships, and tell [them] that we intend to continue to meet the needs of their Navies with British ships and to be reasonable over financial terms.

12. Another reason for not proposing to give any ships to the Minor Allies is that this would certainly provoke a demand by the Russians for an allotment to the Polish Navy. This would complicate the question of the disposal of the 'London' Polish Navy in our hands.

13. A separate brief[6] is being prepared on the dispersal [disposal] of the Italian fleet.

CALENDAR TO No. 10

i *7 July 1945 Memorandum C.P.(45)67 by Mr. Brendan Bracken, First Lord of the Admiralty, on disposal of German Fleet.* Outlines existing position and British reservations concerning American proposals of 1944 for almost wholesale scrapping of fleet. Russian contribution at sea does not justify claim to one third of fleet, and French claim to German warships has few merits; British requirements; proposals for division of fleet and tactics at Potsdam. As German warships are in Anglo-American hands the bargaining position is 'extremely strong' [U 5473/5397/70].

[6] Not printed. This undated brief No. 47 (ZM 3885/1/22) summarized considerations advanced in Nos. 99 and 118.

No. 11

Mr. Nichols[1] (Prague) to Mr. Eden (Received 6 July, 11 p.m.)
No. 188 Telegraphic [N 8193/207/12]

Important. Confidential   PRAGUE, *6 July 1945, 7.32 p.m. G.M.T.*
Repeated to Washington.

My telegram No 185.[2]
American withdrawal prior to the final Russian withdrawal would be a very great mistake. The following considerations are relevant.

[1] Mr. P. B. B. Nichols was H.M. Ambassador at Prague.
[2] Of 6 July 1945, not printed. This telegram summarized a Czechoslovak note of 3 July to the United States Government, printed in *F.R.U.S. 1945*, vol. iv, pp. 468–9.

(a) It is pretty clear that only Communists in the Government together with Prime Minister Fierlinger are anxious for early American evacuation. The Minister of Justice is most anxious that the Americans should remain and, so I learn from my United States colleague, are a number of other Ministers. If the Americans withdraw, this will certainly strengthen the position of the Communists and those who look to the East and not to the West.

(b) 10 higher officials of the Ministry of Foreign Affairs approached my United States colleague confidentially through his Military Attaché urging that the Americans should stay.

(c) Unilateral withdrawal by the Americans would be inconsistent with the general policy of joint action by the Big Three.

(d) If the Americans withdraw, this will be widely regarded here as indication that the Russians have put pressure on the Czechoslovak Government, who in their turn have persuaded the Americans to leave. Western, and not only Americans [sic], prestige will suffer and conversely Russian prestige will be enhanced.

(e) Finally, if the Americans go, the view will be held perhaps illogically, but none the less naturally, that no date will ever be put to final withdrawal of the Russians.

2. In my opinion there is no doubt whatever that the withdrawal of the Americans now would constitute serious blow to Western prestige. The present situation and its past history demand that final Russian American withdrawal should be simultaneous. It is not fair to this country nor to ours to allow nine divisions of Russian troops i.e. approximately 100,000 men to remain here without any counterbalance from the West.

3. My United States colleague is I understand telegraphing in similar vein to State Department.[3]

Please pass to Washington as my telegram No 10.

CALENDARS TO No. 11

i *6–22 July 1945* Tels. *from Mr. Nichols (Prague) Nos. 186, 240—and to, No. 199; Air Ministry Tel. No. AX 66 to H.Q. Frankfurt:* transfer of Czechoslovak Air Force squadrons from Britain to Czechoslovakia: assurance from Czechoslovak Prime Minister and President that Russian consent was unnecessary: their country was an independent one [N 8123, 8655, 8884/1904/12].

ii *13 & 28 July 1945* Mr. Nichols *(Prague) No. 47; Mr. Warner to Sir F. Bovenschen (Joint Permanent Under-Secretary of State for War).* Support for Czechoslovak wish to extend agreement on British supply to Czechoslovak 1st Armoured Corps, and for Czechoslovak efforts to maintain some connexion with the West [N 8913/365/12].

iii *21 July 1945* Mr. Nichols *(Prague) No. 64.* Formation of Association of Czechoslovak-British Soldiers [N 9511/365/12].

[3] Cf. *ibid.*, pp. 473–4.

No. 12

Earl of Halifax (Washington) to Mr. Eden (Received 7 July, 7.35 a.m.)
No. 4706 Telegraphic [ZM 3711/1/22]

Important WASHINGTON, *6 July, 1945, 11.26 p.m. G.M.T.*

Repeated to Rome, Caserta (Resmed's Office).

Your telegram No. 6962 apparently crossed my telegram No. 4531 in paragraph 4 of which I suggested that points made in your despatch No. 1020 should be taken up orally with State Department at a later date.[1]

2. I am still of the opinion that it would serve no useful purpose at this moment to pursue discussions with State Department about policy towards Italy. Moreover I have no doubt that the United States Government are in favour:

(*a*) of the establishment of a truly democratic government in Italy rather than a totalitarian one whether Communist or otherwise and,

(*b*) of rendering all possible economic aid to Italy to help her rehabilitation. The combined chiefs of staff have pointed out in FAN 515[2] that there are difficulties in the provision of equipment for an Italian army. But in this instance too there is no doubt that the United States Government would not wish to see Italy left completely disarmed and helpless in post war Europe.

3. Our aims towards Italy are therefore substantially the same. The Americans and ourselves are both agreed that early steps should be taken (1) to ensure holding of election in Italy and (2) to proceed with negotiation of a peace treaty with that country. There is however a good deal of public uncertainty on both these points and the indeterminate status of 'co-belligerent'[3] and the present standstill arrangement on the 'institutional' question[4] are naturally irritating to such commentators as Welles and Lippmann. There is nothing State Department can do to prevent criticism on these subjects which naturally tends to be anti-British, as British 'imperialism' will always be a convenient whipping boy. Our difficulties however will largely be resolved once we have decided on the next *positive* steps to be taken as regards both the election and the peace treaty and I

---

[1] These telegrams of 1 July and 29 June 1945 (ZM 3140/1/22 and ZM 3560/3/22) respectively are not printed. For Mr. Churchill's despatch No. 1020 of 13 June, not printed, see Sir L. Woodward, *op. cit.*, vol. iii, pp. 482–4.

[2] Of 30 March (ZM 1915/8/22), not printed.

[3] On 13 October 1943 the British, American and Soviet Governments had declared Italy, still juridically in a state of war with them, a co-belligerent. On the same day Italy declared war on Germany.

[4] The question as to the future constitutional form of government in Italy.

would therefore urge everything possible be done to expedite action on these two questions.[5]

[5] On 9 July Foreign Office telegram No. 7293 replied: 'This has crossed our telegrams Nos. 7215 and 7216 [i]. 2. We are most anxious that views expressed in our telegram No. 7215 and our despatch No. 1020 should be put on record with State Department without delay so that United States authorities may be aware of them before Terminal. We hope therefore that paragraph 2 of your telegram No. 4706 does not mean that you intend to take no (repeat no) action on these telegrams. On contrary we should be glad if you would act on these telegrams as soon as possible.'

No. 13

Mr. Kirkpatrick[1] *(Frankfurt am Main) to Mr. Eden (Received 12 July)*
No. 14 [C 3821/688/18]

FRANKFURT AM MAIN, *6 July 1945*

Sir,

I have the honour to report that thanks to Air Chief Marshal Tedder, who lent me his aircraft for the purpose, I was able to pay a short visit to 'Ashcan'[2] on July 5th. It can be said that with the exception of a few technicians such as Speer[3], who are housed in 'Dustbin', and of some secondary outliers, the surviving ministers of the Reich Government, together with the leaders of the party and bureaucratic hierarchy, are now all assembled in 'Ashcan'.

2. There is a melancholy interest attached to wrecks and ruins. You may, therefore, care to have a brief account of the prisoners and the conditions in which they are housed. 'Ashcan' is situated in a pleasant little watering-place, consisting principally of hotels and pensions. In one of these is housed the directing staff, Colonel Andrus of the U.S. Army and some forty U.S. Army officers. Colonel Andrus, who is responsible for administration and discipline, is an excellent choice. He combines resolution in his dealings with the prisoners with great courtesy towards the many visitors inflicted on him.

[1] Mr. I. A. Kirkpatrick was British Political Adviser to General Eisenhower at S.H.A.E.F.
[2] Code-name for the detention-centre maintained by S.H.A.E.F. at Bad Mondorf in Luxembourg for high-ranking German service and political personnel. The code-name for the detention-centre for German scientific and technological personnel was Dustbin.
[3] Professor A. Speer, former German Minister for Armaments and War Production.

His officers are partly combat officers in charge of the buildings and the guards and partly political officers concerned with interrogations and interpreting. I may say in passing that the interpreters could not have been more capable or obliging.

3. 'Ashcan' itself is a large hotel with a small garden surrounded by a high wire stockade, guarded at each corner by a sentry on a raised platform. Camouflage netting protects it from prying eyes and entry can only be made on foot through a double fence. In the centre of the garden is a fountain, which has been turned into a sundial for the benefit of the prisoners, who have been deprived on security grounds of their watches.

4. On arrival at the stockade accompanied by Colonel Andrus, our names were logged by the guard and we were then admitted into the compound. An extraordinary sight met our eyes. The Reich Government, with their satellite officials, were sunning themselves in wicker chairs along the whole length of the terrace, dressed in the oddest assortment of disreputable garments. The circumstance that ties and shoelaces are not allowed adds to the eccentricity of the inmates' appearance. The latter viewed our approach with pleasurable curiosity; it was evidently an event which broke the insufferable monotony of their existence. As we reached the terrace itself, the prisoners rose and stood to attention facing us. A few, in the remoter corners, including Admiral Dönitz,[4] failed by accident or design to notice our arrival. Colonel Andrus at once sent a soldier to order them to rise, and we waited until this had been done, During this brief period I managed, despite their bedraggled appearance, to recognise a number of old friends, among them Herr Meissner, Secretary of State to Hitler; Reichsminister Frick, Reichsminister von Ribbentrop, Gauleiter Bohle, Reichsminister Frank and Dr. Lammers.[5]

5. Upstairs I was shown the prisoners' quarters. Most of them have a bedroom to themselves. All the hotel furniture has been removed, as also looking-glasses, window glass and lamps. The only articles provided are a small chair and a camp bed with a mattress, a pillow and two army blankets. Sheets and pillow-slips are not allowed. I saw lunch being prepared. It seemed to consist partly of a repugnant looking soup, cooked out of doors in an army kitchen by two filthy German prisoners of war.

6. As we moved through the hotel on this little tour of inspection, we passed from time to time an obsequious notability of Hitler's regime slinking furtively along the passage. As we came down to the interrogation

---

[4] Grand Admiral Karl von Dönitz, former Commander-in-Chief of the German Navy, had become Head of the German State and Supreme Commander of the German armed forces following the death of Herr Hitler on 30 April 1945.

[5] Dr. W. Frick had been German Minister for the Interior (1933–43) and Reich Protector of Bohemia and Moravia (1943–5). Herr Joachim von Ribbentrop had been Minister for Foreign Affairs (1938–45). Gauleiter (i.e. regional leader) E. Bohle, Secretary of State in the German Foreign Ministry, had been head of the organisation of the Nazi party abroad. Herr Hans Frank had been Governor-General in the General Government (Poland), 1939–45. Dr. H. Lammers had been head of the Reich Chancery (1933–45).

room Herr von Ribbentrop, at attention, was awaiting us at the door with a guard in attendance. We subsequently interrogated Marshal Göring[6] and Gauleiter Bohle. Records of these interviews[7] will be sent to you in due course.

7. I had intended seeing Reichsminister Frank, but the officer in charge told me that he was suicidally inclined and asked that I should say nothing calculated to upset him. I felt that in the circumstances it would be waste of time to summon him. Moreover I was glad of any excuse to leave 'Ashcan'. The hotel with its Spartan regime was not in itself displeasing; in congenial company I should not have found a prisoner's lot intolerable. But it is difficult to describe the odour of corruption and decay emanating from these living corpses of the Third Reich. I noticed that my companions seemed just as pleased as I was to escape.

8. As we came out on to the terrace, the sentry, evidently determined to have no further trouble with Admiral Dönitz, loudly called the sunbathers to attention. On reaching the bottom of the steps I heard him stand them at ease. Out of the corner of my eye I saw that our departure was being watched and discussed with the same eager speculation as had greeted our arrival.[8]

I have, &c.,

IVONE KIRKPATRICK

[6] Reich Marshal Hermann Goering, President of the Reichstag (1932–45) and Commander in Chief of the German Air Force (1935–45).

[7] Not printed, from C 3859, 4129/44/18 respectively: cf. also No. 57, note 2.

[8] Mr. Harvey and Sir Orme Sargent, respectively Acting Assistant Under-Secretary of State (superintending German and Western Departments) and a Duputy Under-Secretary of State in the Foreign Office, minuted as follows on this despatch: 'How are the mighty fallen! O. C. Harvey 15/vii.' 'And the weapons of war perished! O. G. Sargent July 15.'

No. 14

Minute from Sir A. Cadogan to Mr. Churchill
No. P.M./45/320 [*F.O. 954/31 : War C/45/5*]

FOREIGN OFFICE, *6 July 1945*

The conversations[1] with the United States, French and Soviet representatives on the proposals to try the principal Nazi criminals and organisations have on the whole gone smoothly.

2. There is general agreement that if possible one inter-Allied tribunal should be set up probably in Germany with power to sit elsewhere to try the leading Nazis and Nazi organisations. The four Powers would each appoint

[1] Held in London on 26 June–8 August 1945. American records of the meetings are printed in *Report of Robert H. Jackson, United States Representative to the International Conference on Military Trials, London 1945* (Washington, 1949: hereafter cited as *Report of Robert H. Jackson*), *passim*.

a judge to the court and also a chief prosecuting counsel who with their experience would join together in preparing the charges and conducting the prosecution. The Attorney-General has already been appointed for the United Kingdom Government and Justice Jackson for the United States Government.

3. There are differences in procedure and approach which still remain unresolved, but apart from the question of where the court should sit for the trial or trials the existing differences appear to offer no serious difficulty. A most important point would be the selection of a place for the trials. In our view they should be held in Germany and the Russians have suggested Berlin, but apparently they would also consider Nuremberg. Another suggestion is Munich. The Americans and we do not want to have a major trial in a place which is solely controlled by the Soviet forces, and even if the trial were held in the inter-Allied zone [sic] in Berlin it seems likely that it would be difficult to prevent the Soviet authorities obtaining control of it. Munich has the advantage that it is one of the few German towns believed to be in a condition to offer suitable facilities and in addition it would seem to be a good choice:

(a) as having been the cradle of the Nazi Movement,

(b) as being a compliment to the Americans who have done so much work on all this matter,

(c) because it would relieve the British military authorities of the very heavy burden of making the physical arrangements for the trial.

The above considerations would almost equally apply to Nuremberg.

4. The other major point which still remains for discussion is the list of Nazis to be tried.

5. As suitable representatives of the Nazi Party and its criminal organisation and of the Reichswehr[2] the following preliminary list of ten has been suggested by us for the first trial. We are in no way precluded from adding to or subtracting from this list:

Goering.

Ribbentrop.

Hess[3] (if in a condition to be tried—a question which should perhaps be determined by the Inter-Allied Court itself).

Ley (The Labour Controller).

Frick (The Minister of the Interior).

Keitel (as representing the Reichswehr).

Rosenberg (who was in charge of the Baltic provinces and largely responsible for the Party's ideology).

Kaltenbrunner (Himmler's right-hand man).

Streicher (the Jew baiter).

Hans Frank (who was in charge of German occupied Poland).

[2] German Armed Forces.

[3] Herr Rudolf Hess had been a Reich Minister and deputy leader of the Nazi party, 1933–41.

6. It is hoped to have the major trial or trials in the Autumn and we are aiming at September, though this may prove to be too optimistic.

ALEXANDER CADOGAN

CALENDARS TO No. 14

i *12–13 July 1945 Minutes by Mr. Harvey, Mr. R. D. J. Scott Fox (F.O. War Crimes Section) and Sir A. Cadogan. Question of Swiss extradition of Signor Bastianini, former Italian Under-Secretary of State for Foreign Affairs* [U 5538/55/73].

ii *13 July 1945 Communication from Mr. P. H. Dean (Assistant Legal Adviser, Foreign Office) to Lord Wright (Chairman of the United Nations War Crimes Commission). General Eisenhower and F.-M. Alexander have been authorized to proceed with trials and execution of sentences against lesser war-criminals* [U 5415/29/73].

No. 15

Minute from Mr Churchill to Colonel Stanley[1]
No. M. 679/5 [E 4939/15/31]

Copy   [10, DOWNING STREET,] *6 July 1945*

The whole question of Palestine must be settled at the Peace table, though it may be touched upon at Terminal. I do not think we should take the responsibility upon ourselves of managing this very difficult place while the Americans sit back and criticize. Have you ever addressed yourself to the idea that we should ask them to take it over? I believe we should be the stronger the more they are drawn into the Mediterranean. At any rate the fact that we show no desire to keep the mandate will be a great help. I am not aware of the slightest advantage which has ever accrued to Great Britain from this painful and thankless task. Somebody else should have their turn now.[2] However, the Chiefs of Staff should examine the matter from the strategic point of view.[3]

W. S. C.

CALENDAR TO No. 15

i *10–11 July 1945 Minutes by Mr. H. Beeley, Mr. C. W. Baxter (F.O. Eastern Dept.), Sir R. Campbell (Assistant Under-Secretary of State, F.O.) Arguments advanced against offering mandate for Palestine to the United States* [E 4939/15/31].

[1] This minute to the Secretary of State for the Colonies was also addressed to the Chiefs of Staff Committee.

[2] This sentence and other extracts from the foregoing are cited by N. Bethell, *The Palestine Triangle* (London, 1979), p. 201.

[3] Mr. J. N. Henderson, Assistant Private Secretary to Mr. Eden, minuted on this: 'Colonel Stanley saw the S. of S. this afternoon about the P.M.'s minute. Col Stanley's view is that it is a mistake for us to raise this matter at the present juncture; he is addressing a minute to the P.M. discouraging him from raising it.   The S. of S. said that he entirely agreed with Colonel Stanley's line of action. J. N. Henderson 13.vii.'

No. 16

Sir R. Bullard (*Tehran*) to Mr. Skrine[1] (*Meshed*)
No. 79 Telegraphic [E 4924/31/34]

TEHRAN, *6 July 1945*[2]

Repeated to Government of India, Zahidan, Foreign Office No. 673.

I understand long range Squadron[3] is still operating in Eastern Persia. Does it serve any useful purpose? It seems difficult to argue that it contributes to the prosecution of the war with Japan.

Foreign Office please pass to Government of India as my telegram No. 176.[4]

[1] H.M. Ambassador at Tehran and H.M. Consul-General at Meshed respectively.

[2] A copy of this untimed telegram was received in the Foreign Office at 3 p.m. on 7 July 1945.

[3] The Indian Long Range Squadron had been sent from India to East Persia in order to provide security from bandits on the Zahidan–Meshed supply-route to Russia.

[4] Indian External Affairs Department telegram No. 6349 of 18 July (copy received in Foreign Office on 19 July) to Mr. L. S. Amery, Secretary of State for India and Burma, observed: 'We consider it would be undesirable to withdraw long range squadron unless withdrawal is part of agreed plan for withdrawal of all British and Indian troops in Persia.'

No. 17

Dominions Office Memorandum
[F 4114/364/23]

Secret   DOMINIONS OFFICE, *6 July 1945*

The Dominions and Armistice and Control Arrangements for Japan

At the second Australia–New Zealand Conference in Wellington, New Zealand, in November, 1944,[1] the following secret resolutions were adopted.

Armistice Arrangements

(1) The Conference has noted the communications which have been exchanged on the subject of armistice arrangements in Europe. It considers that the Dominions and other nations which have been actively engaged from the beginning in the war against the Axis Powers, and have contributed and are contributing materially to their defeat, both on the European Fronts and in other theatres of war, are entitled to an effective voice in the conclusion of the European armistice and the preparations for the peace settlements and participation in their own right in the control of armistice machinery.

[1] Cf. P. Hasluck, *The Government and the People 1942–1945*, (Canberra, 1970), pp. 495–9, in Series 4 (Civil), vol. ii of *Australia in the War of 1939–1945*.

(2) In the interests of solidarity of the United Nations, both Australia and New Zealand have felt obliged to acquiesce in their exclusion from those arrangements in Europe even though settlements of vital concern have been involved, but they cannot acquiesce in a similar situation in the Pacific and the Far East.

(3) Australia and New Zealand are agreed that they should take the strongest possible action to ensure that their Governments are consulted in regard to the drafting of armistices with Japan and Thailand, that they are represented directly at the conclusion of the armistice and that they have the right of participating in the armistice control arrangements.

2. At the fourth session of the British Commonwealth Meeting in London on 6th April, 1945, Dr. Evatt, the Australian Minister for External Affairs, raised the question of participation by powers other than the United Kingdom, the United States and Soviet Union in the preparation of armistice plans. He pressed strongly that, in the case of Japan, Australia and New Zealand, who were so directly concerned, should participate directly as principals. He was supported by Mr. Fraser, Prime Minister of New Zealand. Mr. Churchill said that he fully sympathised and did not think that the United States President (then Mr. Roosevelt) would tolerate the exclusion of Australia and New Zealand from the conclusion of armistices in the Far East. He (Mr. Churchill) would support the claims of Australia and New Zealand with all the influence he could use.

3. On 12th June, 1945, Mr. Bruce, High Commissioner for Australia in London, reminded the Dominions Office of this pledge and expressed the view that there is a need for early formulation of British Commonwealth policies in the matter of surrender terms, military government and control commission policy for Japan. He again alluded to the wish of the Australian Government to participate in the early formulation of Commonwealth policy for Japan and to follow with close attention any subsequent discussions with the United States.

4. It is clear that Australia will wish to know of any proposals in the mind of the United Kingdom Government before these are put to the United States Government and may have views to express on them. The Australian Government probably realise that secret discussion on these matters between the United Kingdom and United States Governments without Australian participation is inevitable but they will expect to be kept in close touch. New Zealand may be expected to take the same line.

5. Australia is likely to object to Pacific affairs being settled by any committee consisting solely of Great Powers. Australia will also expect a seat on any international body for the Pacific or Far East which comprises countries other than Great Powers. She might not object to a smaller committee of Great Powers provided that there is also a larger body comprising countries directly interested in the Pacific, such as Australia and the Netherlands. Australia is likely to support the claim of France to a voice in the Pacific settlement, but it would be very galling to Australia if Russia, France and China had a say, whilst Australia had not. The views of New

Zealand may be expected to follow closely those of Australia, though perhaps to be expressed less forcibly.

6. It would be desirable to give not only Australia and New Zealand, but also Canada and possibly South Africa, the opportunity of representation on any international body for the Pacific comprising other than Great Powers. It is not certain whether they would both accept places. Canada, Australia and New Zealand were all represented on the Pacific War Council in Washington which sat in 1942 and 1943. South Africa was not invited and did not complain. Canada, Australia, New Zealand and South Africa were represented on the similar Council in London.[2]

[2] A copy of this memorandum was received in the Far Eastern Department of the Foreign Office on 9 July 1945. On 12 July the Head of the Department, Mr. J. C. Sterndale Bennett, noted: 'A copy of this memo is being taken to Terminal by Mr. Foulds', of that department.

No. 18

Sir E. Grigg[1] (Cairo) to Mr. Eden (Received 7 July, 2.30 p.m.)
No. 667 Telegraphic [R 11559/4476/44]

Important. Secret   CAIRO, *7 July 1945, 11.54 a.m. G.M.T.*
Repeated to Istanbul (Constantinople), Beirut.

Turkish Minister came to see me at his request,

As soon as he arrived he started on Russo-Turkish relations. Though so far as he knew no written note had been handed to the Turkish Government by the Russians they had made it sufficiently clear that they wanted not only to claim a base of some sort on the Straits but also the return of Turkish eastern province of Kars Artevin. What would the British attitude be towards such a request? Turkish friendship was essential to the maintenance of British position in the Middle East. If Turkey was driven into the arms of Russia it would bring Russian influence down to the Red Sea and Persian Gulf as Arab League,[2] even if we were successful in bringing it off, would offer no useful defence against Russian influence and penetration. He scoffed at the Arab League and said that the Arabs would never be worth anything. Nevertheless he said our policy ought to be to eliminate the French from the Middle East, to strengthen the Arab League and most important of all to give Turkey full support.

As regards the report put out by observer[3] [*sic*] that Turkey and Russia had come to an agreement by which the latter would support Turkey's

[1] H.M. Minister Resident in the Middle East.
[2] Established under the pact signed on 22 March 1945 by Egypt, Syria, Lebanon, Iraq, Transjordan, Saudi Arabia, and subsequently by the Yemen: cf. *B.F.S.P.*, vol. 155, pp. 365–72.
[3] *The Observer* of 1 July 1945 had printed an article entitled 'Middle East frontiers may be modified.'

claim to Aleppo and to a rectification of Syro-Turkish frontier he attributed it to French propaganda put out to create trouble for us in Syria. I refrained from much comment on the above and said that Turkey lay outside my field of responsibility. But I said that I was nevertheless ready on my personal responsibility to say two things

(a) That we attached great importance to Turkish independence and Anglo-Turkish alliance and

(b) That we would not allow the question of the Straits to be treated as a bilateral Russo-Turkish affair.

He seemed reassured, but added that he had every reason to believe that Bulgaria and Yugoslavia would act against Turkey as Russia might direct. He afterwards stayed to lunch and kept on harping on Turkey's need of strong support from us.

No. 19

Sir A. Clark Kerr (Moscow) to Mr. Eden (Received 20 July)[1]
No. 460 [R 11617/4476/44]

MOSCOW, *7 July 1945*

His Majesty's Ambassador at Moscow presents his compliments to His Majesty's Principal Secretary of State for Foreign Affairs and has the honour to transmit to him the under-mentioned documents.

Reference to previous correspondence:

Foreign Office telegram No. 3766[2] of July 5th, 1945.

Description of Enclosure

Name and Date	*Subject*
To: Mr Molotov, People's Commissar for Foreign Affairs, dated 7th July, 1945.	Conversations between representatives of Soviet and Turkish Governments.

ENCLOSURE IN No. 19

(227/53/45)

BRITISH EMBASSY, MOSCOW

7th July, 1945

Secret

(Dear Mr. Molotov),

I write under instructions from my government to inform you that they have been consulted by the Turkish Government about the conversations which have

[1] Date on which this despatch was initialed in the Foreign Office by Mr. G. L. McDermott of Southern Department.

[2] Not printed. This telegram conveyed the instructions summarised in No. 7.

recently taken place between representatives of the Soviet and Turkish Governments.

2. According to the Turkish Government the Soviet Government put forward in the course of these conversations certain territorial claims and also discussed the question of bases in the Straits. My government were very much surprised to learn this, since these two matters cannot be regarded as concerning exclusively the Soviet and Turkish Governments. In my government's view the former falls to be considered in the light of the general world organisation, and the latter affects the multi-lateral Montreux Convention. I have been instructed moreover to point out that at Yalta it was agreed that the Soviet Government should consult my government and the American Government before approaching the Turkish Government on matters affecting the Montreux Convention. Premier Stalin also agreed to take no action affecting the independence and integrity of Turkey and to adopt a reassuring attitude towards the Turkish Government. In the light of this my government have also been very much surprised at the recent campaign against Turkey in the Soviet press and over the Soviet wireless.

3. My government wish the Soviet Government to be aware of their views on these recent developments since they consider that the whole question will have to be discussed at the forthcoming meeting of the heads of governments.

(Yours sincerely),
ARCHIBALD CLARK KERR

CALENDAR TO No. 19

i   *10 July 1945   Brief No. 10 for U.K. Delegation on Turco-Soviet relations* [R 11696/4476/44].

No. 20

Mr. Holman (Paris) to Mr. Eden (Received 9 July, 2.20 p.m.)
No. 349 Saving Telegraphic, by bag [E 4941/8/89]

PARIS, 7 July 1945

My immediately preceding Savingram.[1]

M. Teitgen then spoke of the Levant controversy.[2] He realised that France had behaved stupidly and he deprecated the recent pinprick policy of General de Gaulle. He was now thinking, however, of the future

---

[1] Not printed. This telegram (on Z 8205/255/17) of even date reported that at dinner with Mr. Holman the previous evening M. Teitgen, Minister of Justice in the French Provisional Government, had said that the trial of Marshal Pétain 'would start shortly . . . If he were judge, he would not have a moment's hesitation in condemning Pétain to death. (Sentence would no doubt have to be commuted to something less drastic). Pétain's Counsel . . . might try to make the most of the so called Anglo-French negotiations of 1940 [cf. No. 565.i] . . . After November 1942 Pétain had no defence for his policy. He should have left [Vichy] immediately for North Africa. Not having done so, he was guilty of treason.'

[2] For the despatch of French reinforcements to Syria in May 1945, ensuing clashes there leading to British intervention, and proposed negotiations in London, cf. Sir L. Woodward, *op. cit.*, vol. iv, pp. 329–41, also No. 64 below.

and not the past. He was a fervent supporter of an Anglo-French alliance and it was unthinkable to him that local difficulties in the Levant should overshadow the main issue, namely Anglo-French friendship, establishment of which was just as much in British as French interests. With the world as it was, in which there existed an Eastern and an American bloc, England could not stand by herself and must unite with France and the other Western Powers, but of course on a basis of friendship with the other two blocs. Whole future of Anglo-French friendship was, however, being wrecked by our differences in the Levant. All that France wanted to know now was what our policy was in the Middle East. What was France to expect to retain of her present position there? Did we intend to eliminate France completely and then to turn our attention to Algeria and Tunis and do the same there? France was entitled to know. If His Majesty's Government gave the word, the Levant States would give immediate satisfaction to French desiderata. Great Britain must realise that in dealing with Arab countries the disappearance of France meant that Great Britain would be the next to suffer. Reverting to the question of an alliance, Teitgen admitted that it might be British practice to begin with the signature of a general Anglo-French Pact as a jumping off point for more detailed negotiations, but French psychology was different. France preferred to postpone signing any document, until all questions at issue had been settled. In replying to M. Teitgen I used all the familiar arguments, but I particularly emphasised that French colonial policy seemed to be sadly out of place in the Levant of today. French officials employed there to implement French policy were certainly not of the highest quality. They had been there too long and could not shake off their old prejudices. He himself was well aware that many of them had served under Vichy and might be secretly pleased that policy of General de Gaulle had reached present unfortunate impasse. What was required was new blood and new ideas. M. Teitgen did not dissent.

Above record may be of interest as showing views of a Minister, who is not only educated and intelligent, but is also a firm friend of Great Britain and realises the value of an Anglo-French alliance.

No. 21

Earl of Halifax (Washington) to Mr. Eden (Received 7 July, 9.35 a.m.)
No. 4711 Telegraphic [UR 2311/2109/851]

    Immediate. Secret   WASHINGTON, *7 July 1945, 2.27 a.m. G.M.T.*
Repeated to Moscow.

Your telegram No. 7169.[1]

I had enquired this morning[2] whether Byrnes would receive me to-day

[1] No. 3.
[2] This telegram was drafted on 6 July 1945. President Truman and the American delegation to the Conference at Potsdam left Washington that evening and sailed for Europe on 7 July.

but learned that he and the majority of the party have already left. Your telegram which reached me this afternoon therefore arrived too late for discussion of it.

2. But I do not (repeat not) think you need feel any anxiety that the Administration are taking a rosy view of European prospects or are under any illusion that, given settlement of a few outstanding problems, Europe can safely be left to look after itself. I reported in my telegram No. 4311[3] Matthews'[4] expression of State Department's grave preoccupation over the probable political effect in Europe of economic want and of special importance they attach to the problem of coal. This was followed by the President's unnumbered telegram to the Prime Minister repeated to Washington as No. 6802[5] proposing specific action to increase production of coal in Germany and to make it available to other European countries.[6] Lew Douglas[7] has just been back on a visit from Germany preaching the importance of coal to all and sundry. McCloy who is going on to Terminal dined with me last night. He had spent the afternoon at a meeting of State Department and War Department representatives who discussed the economic and other problems of Europe. Stimson[8] shares McCloy's disquiet. I know from what he said to me yesterday that the President has his mind fully on all this and I have no doubt that Byrnes has also.

3. You will have learnt from United States Ambassador in London that United States Government are proposing constituting a Commission of the

[3] Of 21 June (on UE 2614/2610/53), not printed.

[4] Mr. H. Freeman Matthews was Director of European Affairs in the State Department.

[5] Of 26 June (on UR 2502/2109/851), not printed. Mr. Truman's message of 24 June to Mr. Churchill, with text of draft U.S. directive to General Eisenhower and proposal that a similar directive be sent to Field-Marshal Montgomery, is printed in *F.R.U.S. Berlin*, vol. i, pp. 612–14.

[6] Mr. Eden minuted against this sentence: 'What are we doing about this?' On 10 July Mr. J. E. Coulson, Acting Head of the Economic Relations Department of the Foreign Office, minuted to explain that the Prime Minister had replied that he was in general agreement with the draft directive but that the Foreign Office would communicate with the State Department on certain points (*v. op. cit.*, vol. i, p. 622). Mr. Coulson summarised these points communicated to State Department on 3 July (*v. ibid.*, pp. 624–5) as '(*a*) we must carry the Russians along with us, otherwise they will argue we are not living up to our proposal to treat Germany as an economic whole; (*b*) the American draft directive fettered the discretion of the Commander-in-Chief too much, and we proposed some amendments'. Mr. Eden noted against (*a*) 'I would not worry about this' and minuted below, 'I don't think anything of the two points. I hope action is not being held up for them—is it? A. E. July 11'. Washington telegram No. 4826 of 11 July (received 12 July) transmitted the reply from the State Department, printed *ibid.*, pp. 636–8. On 12 July Mr. Coulson minuted that the State Department 'have gone some distance to meeting our points but they do not go with us the whole way . . . I imagine that the Secretary of State will, in view of his minute above, agree that we can accept the American directive.' Mr. Eden minuted 'I agree. We must get this settled, more especially if it is affecting output. If my help is needed, please call for it. A. E. July 13.'

[7] Mr. Lewis Douglas was special adviser to Lieutenant-General Lucius Clay, Deputy Military Governor of the American Zone in Germany.

[8] Mr. Henry L. Stimson was American Secretary of War and Chairman of the Combined Policy Committee on atomic energy.

Foreign Secretaries of the five major powers which whilst dealing in the first instance with preparation of Peace Treaties, could also give its attention to other European problems of a state character. My telegrams Nos. 4708 and 4709[9] will also show that their list of topics includes as a separate item, the problem of co-operation in solving European economic problems.

4. I believe therefore that you will find at Terminal that the American Delegation from the President downwards fully share your preoccupations and are prepared to tackle the difficulties ahead of us with vigour. At the same time I judge that they attach great importance to securing the full co-operation of the Soviet Union in attempting to solve these difficulties and are reasonably hopeful of securing this co-operation provided the Russians are not made to feel that the Americans or we ourselves start with a fundamental hostility towards them. This does not (repeat not) mean that the President and Byrnes will be reluctant to stand up to the Russians with us when necessary but that their point of departure will be one of showing that they seek to establish a common ground with the Russians.

CALENDAR TO No. 21

i 9 *July 1945* Lord Halifax (*Washington*) *Tel. No. 4759.* Conversation on 8 July with Mr. J. C. Dunn, Assistant Sec. of State: American preoccupation over status of France and hope for H.M.G.'s support in obtaining Soviet approval for proposed Council of Foreign Ministers, which might perhaps consider question of ultimate dismemberment of Germany; U.S. Govt. were disquieted by Soviet behaviour over Polish western frontier and wished to discuss this with H.M.G. Mr. Dunn personally favoured detachment of Ruhr from Germany but was uncertain about a permanent solution. After European economic problems, Central European states were next priority: U.S. and U.K. should seek to have more say on Control Commissions and try for a broadening of local governments. He favoured speaking with complete frankness to the Russians. U.S. Govt. thought H.M.G. had acted soundly in regard to U.S.S.R. and Turkey [U 5559/5559/70].

[9] Not printed. These telegrams of 7 July are summarized by Sir L. Woodward, *op. cit.*, vol. v, pp. 346–7. The list of topics transmitted in Washington telegram No. 4708 was also sent that day to Mr. Eden by Mr. J. G. Winant, U.S. Ambassador in London: cf. *F.R.U.S. Berlin*, vol. i, pp. 226–7 and 233–4. Lord Halifax further reported in Washington telegram No. 4712 of 7 July (received that day): 'State Department have already given to the Russians a list of their topics for discussion at Terminal. They welcome suggestion that we should give the Russians our list also. But they are opposed to giving the Russians the idea:– (*a*) That there is a joint Anglo-American list or (*b*) That we or the Americans desire to agree with the Russians beforehand on a formal tripartite agenda.'

No. 22

Mr. Churchill to Sir A. Clark Kerr (*Moscow*)
No. 3808 Telegraphic [UE 2875/2875/77]

Immediate. Secret   FOREIGN OFFICE, 7 *July*, 1945 1.55 *p.m.*
Following for Mr. Mark Turner of Reparation Delegation.

We intend to raise at forthcoming Conference of Heads of Governments the question of the treatment of Germany as a economic unit. We have it in mind to do this on the basis of the formula in paragraph 2 below. You will recollect earlier correspondence on this subject and we would be grateful for your comments on the revised formula.

2. In the exercise of control over German economy for the purpose of carrying out the objectives of the occupation, Germany will be treated as far as possible as a single economic unit. This policy will apply in particular to the production, collection and distribution of foodstuffs and other goods essential to the economic existence of the German people, and to the maintenance and use of services necessary for this purpose. The freest possible interchange of goods and services between the zones will be permitted. Germany's standard of living will be based on her minimum essential needs, which shall not however result in Germany enjoying basic living standards on a higher level than those generally current for comparable categories of the population in liberated territories. These minimum needs shall be taken into account in determining what exports of material from Germany can be made, whether by way of reparation or otherwise. For this purpose a surplus of foodstuffs shall only be deemed to exist where the supplies available until the next harvest are clearly in excess of minimum essential needs for the same period.

Austria also shall, as far as possible, be treated as a single economic unit for the purpose of carrying out the objectives of the occupation.

CALENDARS TO No. 22

i *6 & 10 July 1945 Briefs by Mr. Hasler and Mr. N. B. Ronald (Assistant Under Sec. of State, F.O.) on European surpluses.* Questions raised in memo. C.P. (45) 44 of 20 June by President of Board of Trade and Minister of Production, Mr. Oliver Lyttelton, had included whether to inform Russians that Eastern Europe cannot look to the West for food supplies additional to U.N.R.R.A. Mr. Hasler held that Russians should not be asked for anything since 'we know fairly well that there is no surplus for them to give'. Mr. Eden noted against this: 'How do we know? We have no people to report. A. E.' (cf. ii below). Mr. Hasler's reasons for not favouring raising with the Russians at Potsdam this question or that of supplying Silesian coal to the West. Mr. Eden minuted on 9 July 'I don't find these arguments impressive'. Mr. Ronald next day considered that subject of European surpluses was unsuitable for unilateral British representations to U.S.S.R. but that detailed discussion at Potsdam of economic collaboration 'would merely raise all sorts of difficult questions with which the meeting will not have time to deal' [UR 2023/282/851].

ii *12 July 1945 Brief No. 41 for the U.K. Delegation at Potsdam on Eastern European Surpluses.* Summarizes Cabinet conclusions of 10 July re memo. CP (45) 44. Information on surpluses in Soviet zone of Germany and the Danube Basin [UR 2479/282/851].

34

No. 23

Mr. Churchill to Earl of Halifax (Washington)
No. 7240 Telegraphic [C 3456/205/3]

Important   FOREIGN OFFICE, 7 *July 1945, 3.45 p.m.*

Repeated to Paris No. 1596 Saving, Moscow No. 3810, Resmed's Office Caserta No. 201 Saving, Rome (for Mack)[1] No. 261 Saving.

My immediately following telegram[2] contains extract from political directive sent to General McCreery in his dual capacity as British Commander-in-Chief and representative on prospective Allied Council for Austria.

2. (Washington and Paris only).

Please inform United States/French Government in strictest confidence of general tenour of instructions that have been issued to General McCreery, adding that a similar communication has been made to the French/United States Government, but not (repeat not) to Soviet Government.

3. (Moscow only).

United States and French Governments are being informed, in strict confidence, of these instructions, but are not being specifically invited to concur in them. You should not (repeat not) make any communication to Soviet Government.

[1] Mr. W. H. B. Mack was Political Adviser to General Sir R. McCreery: see below.
[2] No. 24.

No. 24

Mr. Churchill to Earl of Halifax (Washington)
No. 7241 Telegraphic [C 3456/205/3]

FOREIGN OFFICE, 7 *July 1945, 6.45 p.m.*

Repeated to Paris No. 1597 Saving, Moscow No. 3811, Resmed's Office Caserta No. 202 Saving, Rome (for Mack) No. 262 Saving.

Following is text referred to in my immediately preceding telegram.[1]

The views of His Majesty's Government on the question of the establishment of self-government in Austria were set out in a memorandum (a copy of which you will have seen) which was circulated to the E.A.C. on 14th December, 1944, as E.A.C.(44)45.[2]

Developments in Austria since her liberation, in particular the constitution of a Provisional Government in Vienna under Dr. Renner, the delay in establishing quadripartite control and the formation of local governments or committees in the provinces under the occupation of the various powers, make it desirable that you should receive fresh guidance in dealing with this situation.

[1] No. 23.
[2] Printed in *F.R.U.S. 1944*, vol. i, pp. 478–83.

Central Government

It remains the policy of His Majesty's Government to secure the restoration of a free and independent Austrian State. In furtherance of this aim and with a view to lightening the burden of military government, it is considered essential that responsibility for the administration of Austria should be placed at as early a date as possible on the shoulders of the Austrians themselves, under Allied control and guidance. In order to attain this objective the early establishment of a Provisional Austrian Government which would be genuinely representative of Austria, both politically and territorially, and which could receive the recognition of the four occupying Powers, is of the first importance.

The existence of the Renner Government creates a situation which will require careful handling. This Government was constituted prematurely and unilaterally when only Vienna and a small part of Austria had been liberated. The Soviet Government claim that it was constituted on Austrian initiative. They have not hindered its operation in territory under their control. While they appear to have made use of it in certain respects, they have not, so far as is known, undertaken any long-term commitment towards it, nor have they accorded it *de jure* recognition. Provided it is not made a prestige matter, there is no reason to suppose that they will make difficulty about the substitution of a more representative body. The government's writ does not run in the provinces occupied by British, United States and French forces, and His Majesty's Government, the United States Government and the Provisional French Government have refused to recognise it.

One of your first tasks will be to secure, in agreement with your Soviet, United States and French colleagues, an early transition from the Renner Government to a fully representative Austrian Government which it will be possible for the four controlling Powers to recognise.

With a view to bringing this about, you should take the following line in discussion with your colleagues. While admitting that the Renner Government may have fulfilled a useful purpose at a time when only a limited part of Austria had been liberated, you should assume that there can be no question of that government, recruited on so narrow a territorial basis, continuing to survive once Austria is placed as a whole under Allied control. Allied forces have now moved into their allotted zones and provincial governments or committees have been formed in all or most of these. It is essential that the provinces should have a substantial say in the formation of any government which claims to call itself Austria. You should accordingly propose that delegates of the various provincial administrations should assemble in Vienna at an early date and submit to the Allied Council recommendations for the composition of a Provisional Austrian Government. The numbers of delegates from the provinces might be as follows: three men from Vienna; two each from Styria, Carinthia, Lower Austria, Upper Austria, Tyrol and Salzburg; and one each from Vorarlberg and Burgenland. A body so constituted should be capable of nominating a representative Austrian Government which would be recognised as such by the four

Powers and would hold office until free elections could be held.

The above plan represents the general lines on which His Majesty's Government consider that an Austrian Provisional Government might most satisfactorily be formed in the absence of elections.[3] They do not consider that a modification or reconstruction of the Renner Government as such would provide an agreeable solution except as a last resort. They do not however wish to fetter unduly your judgment and freedom of action. You accordingly have discretion, in consultation with your Political Adviser, to deviate from the plan set out in the foregoing paragraph in the light of circumstances and of the attitude adopted by your Soviet, United States and French colleagues, bearing in mind the importance attached by His Majesty's Government to the early establishment of an Austrian Provisional Government which could be recognised by the four Powers and would be sufficiently representative not merely of the political parties but also of the various provinces to establish its authority throughout Austria.

CALENDARS TO No. 24

i *16 July 1945 Record by Mr. C. D. W. O'Neill (F.O. German Dept.) of conversation with M. L. Roché (French Embassy).* Rumour of an early Anglo-American recognition of Renner Govt. is unfounded [C 4009/205/3].

ii *25 July 1945 Letter from Mr. G. W. Harrison (U.K. Del. Berlin) to Mr. J. M. Troutbeck (Head of F.O. German Dept.).* Transmits copy of U.S. brief on Austria (not here reproduced: see *F.R.U.S. Berlin*, vol. i, pp. 334–5) suggesting likely U.S. readiness to recognise reconstructed Renner Govt. Has explained British reservations to Mr. Riddleberger of U.S. Delegation [C 5213/317/3].

iii *27 July 1945 To Sir N. Charles (Rome) Tel. No. 1921*, for Mr. Mack. Draws attention to clauses of E.A.C. Agreement on Control Machinery in Austria from which U.K. Representative on the Allied Council may be able to draw support in advancing British view on the Renner Govt. [C 4220/205/3].

iv *27 July 1945 General McCreery (8th Army) Tel. No. AC/317.* Developments in Styria [C 4310/317/3].

[3] The main substance of the preceding text was incorporated in a memorandum of 10 July 1945 from the British Embassy in Washington to the State Department, printed in *F.R.U.S. Berlin*, vol. i, pp. 341–2. A corresponding communication was addressed by the British Embassy in Paris to the French Ministry for Foreign Affairs on 12 July.

No. 25

Mr. Kirkpatrick (Frankfurt am Main) to Mr. Eden
(Received 10 July, 10.38 a.m.)
No. 146 Telegraphic [N 8238/3936/38]

FRANKFURT AM MAIN, 7 *July* 1945[1]

My United States colleague and I have been asked for our views on

[1] This telegram was drafted on 7 July. The time and date of despatch are not recorded.

disposal of members of Vlassov army[2] who are under house arrest in the Tyrol together with members of General Schilenkow's Free Russian Committee. Whereabouts of Vlassov and Schilenkow themselves are unknown.[3] Presence of these people in the Tyrol is known to Soviet Liaison Officer attached to 7th United States Army.

2. May I have your instructions?

3. Foreign Office please repeat to Moscow and Washington and also to Mr. Steel[4] (Saving).[5]

CALENDARS TO No. 25

i *7 July 1945 Letters from (a) Sir A. Cadogan to Sir J. Grigg (Secretary of State for War), (b) Mr. Brimelow to Brigadier Firebrace (War Office), (c) Sir O. Sargent to M. Gousev (Soviet Ambassador in London), (d) Mr. I. L. Henderson (F.O. Refugee Dept.) to Mr. Kirkpatrick (S.H.A.E.F.).* Respective treatment of liberated prisoners and refugees by Soviet, by British and by French authorities [N 8217/1951/38; N 8109/409/38; N 8367/2977/59].

ii *12 July 1945 Letter from Mr. Brimelow to Mr. I. T. M. Pink (Political Division, Control Commission for Germany, British Element).* Refers to report by General Galloway, in reply to protest by Soviet General Golikov, on conditions of

[2] The Soviet Lieutenant-General A. A. Vlasov had been captured by German forces near Leningrad in July 1942 and had subsequently, under German authority, assumed command of the anti-Soviet Russian Liberation Army (R.O.A.) of the Committee for the Liberation of the Peoples of Russia (K.O.N.R.).

[3] This sentence is quoted by N. Tolstoy, *Victims of Yalta* (Revised ed. London, 1979), p. 378. In May 1945 General Vlasov had passed from American into Soviet custody.

[4] Mr. C. E. Steel was Political Liaison Officer with General Eisenhower.

[5] This telegram was minuted as follows in the Northern Department of the Foreign Office: 'I suggest that our reply to the telegram within should be that the members of these organisations should be considered as coming within the scope of the Crimea Agreement on P.O.W. i.e. Soviet citizens to be handed over to the Soviet Authorities for disposal. Personnel in these forces who were not Soviet citizens in 1939 should be retained as P.O.W., care being taken to sift out from this residue any persons wanted by the Russians as war criminals. The latter should be specifically segregated pending institution of the inter-allied war crimes procedure. ? reply on these lines. John E. Galsworthy, 9/7.' 'T. Brimelow 9/7.' 'P. D[ean] 13/vii/45.' 'J. M. T[routbeck] 13/7.' 'In view of the imminent dissolution of Shaef I asked Lt. Col. Hammer who would be dealing with the disposal of the people referred to in Mr. Kirkpatrick's telegram. He said that in view of the Americans' refusal to accept our interpretation of the Yalta Agreement, the Civil Affairs people at the War Office had, under pressure from Field Marshal Alexander, asked the Combined Civil Affairs Committee at Washington for a ruling to cover Italy, Austria & Germany. A reply can not be expected in less than a fortnight and it would be premature on our part to issue any instructions in reply to Mr. Kirkpatrick's telegram. T. Brimelow 13/7/45.' 'I subsequently learnt that this ruling was not asked for. The whole question is under consideration at the War Office. B[ring] U[p] in a fortnight. T. B. 6/8/45.' 'The S[ecretary of] S[tate] has just ruled, on other papers, that Cossacks (& *all* Soviet citizens in our sense of the term) must be repatriated to the U.S.S.R. regardless of their own wishes in the matter. This decision will be communicated by the W.O. to the military auth[orit]ies concerned, and we can therefore safely let this go by, I think. J. E. Galsworthy 21/8.' 'Yes. T. B. 21/8.'

Soviet displaced persons and ex-prisoners of war in British zone of Germany. Would be disastrous if, in view of impending dissolution of S.H.A.E.F., Soviet accusations passed unchallenged [N 7882/409/38].

iii *8 July 1945   Field-Marshal Sir H. Alexander (Caserta) to Sir J. Grigg. Tel. No. F/19321.* Requests instructions as to disposal of 500 Cossacks, rounded up in Austria, who are unwilling to be returned to Soviet authorities, now pressing for their return; this would probably involve British use of force (cited N. Tolstoy, *op. cit.*, p. 416) [N 9357/409/38].

iv *11 & 14 July 1945   Correspondence between Brigadier R. F. K. Belchem (21st Army Group) and Mr. Pink.* Requests guidance concerning (*a*) Russians formerly in the Wehrmacht, who do not wish to be repatriated, 'presumably largely . . . White Russians, although I have not yet confirmed this'; (*b*) Yugoslavs. Mr. Pink replies, on (*a*) in particular, 'Anyone who was living in the Soviet Union on or before 3 September 1939 must be regarded as a Soviet citizen and should be repatriated. Anyone who was living outside the Soviet Union on 3 September 1939 should not be repatriated if he says he does not wish to go to Russia' [N 10073/409/38].

No. 26

Joint Staff Mission (Washington) to the Cabinet Office
(Received 8 July, 1.35 a.m. G.M.T.)
No. J.S.M. 951 Telegraphic [UE 2942/32/71]

Immediate. Top secret   WASHINGTON, *7 July 1945, 10.33 p.m. G.M.T.*

We must seek your[1] urgent assistance over one of the many difficulties we are experiencing in regard to lend-lease.[2]

2. In accordance with COS(W) 992[3] we have put in a memorandum (CCS 887)[3] setting out all our military commitments now that the German War is over.

3. The idea that we should put in this paper came originally from the U.S. side, it being argued that if we can only persuade U.S. Chiefs of Staff to recognise all these commitments as being inescapable on military grounds, we should have far less difficulty in getting under lend-lease the military stores and equipment that are required to support them.

4. On present form however it seems to us very unlikely that the U.S. Chiefs of Staff will be prepared to recognise all these commitments. For some time now there has been a tendency on the U.S. side to suggest that no military supplies can be made available under lend-lease unless it can be shown that they are required for 'direct use in the war against Japan'.

[1] This telegram was evidently intended for the British Chiefs of Staff: see note 7 below.
[2] The lend-lease system of pooled resources and mutual aid derived from the U.S. Lend-Lease Act of March 1941 and the Anglo-American Agreement of 23 February 1942 on Principles applying to Mutual Aid in the prosecution of the War against Aggression: printed respectively in H. Duncan Hall, *op. cit.*, pp. 505–7, and Cmd. 6391 of 1942).
[3] These documents of 25 June and 2 July 1945 respectively are not printed.

This tendency is now hardening in to a definite policy which we suspect is being dictated by the U.S. Government,[4] it would appear too that a very rigid interpretation will be placed on 'direct use in the war against Japan'. For instance we are now being asked to withdraw unit equipment from areas which the Americans do not think have any relation to the Japanese War, rather than to submit fresh requirements.

5. We feel that we must force this matter into the open and find out just exactly what the scope of military lend-lease is going to be in the future. The ideal will be to secure agreement that all our military commitments should be eligible, but if this is to be achieved it is quite evident that the instructions under which the War Department is operating at the moment will have to be revised.

6. As the whole allocation and assignment machinery is virtually at a standstill and has been for some time, and as the prospects of getting our future requirements accepted look very bad, we feel justified in asking you to raise this at Terminal. The procedure we propose is that you should authorise us at once to table the following memorandum, and explain that you would like to get the answer to it at the Conference.

Memorandum by the British Chiefs of Staff—
Begins.

We have for some time been experiencing considerable difficulty in obtaining military supplies under the Lend-Lease Act. We understand that the machinery of assignment is virtually at a standstill. In the circumstances we should be glad if the United States Chiefs of Staff would confirm, at Terminal, that the military commitments with which we are faced now that the German war is over, as set out in CCS 887[3], are in fact eligible for Lend-Lease under normal procedures.
Memorandum ends.

7. A short memorandum on these lines would, we think succeed in forcing things into the open. If the answer is satisfactory no further action will be required at the Conference. If it is not, then the matter would be lifted to the higher level where we would hope that the Prime Minister would be able to persuade the President to take the broader view.

8. We hope very much that you will agree to raise this matter at the Conference. We have been in very deep water for some time now[5] and have been making great efforts to overcome the difficulties, in conjunction with the Supply Council.[6] But we see no prospect of making progress unless you are prepared to help at Terminal.[7]

[4] Cf. President Truman's directive of 5 July 1945: *F.R.U.S. Berlin*, vol. i, p. 818.

[5] The preceding words in this sentence are cited by H. Duncan Hall, *op. cit.*, p. 456.

[6] The British Supply Council had been established in Washington in January 1941 for the coordination of supply to the military services.

[7] This telegram, circulated to the Foreign Secretary, the First Sea Lord, the Chief of the Imperial General Staff, the Chief of the Air Staff and the Defence Office, was discussed by the Chiefs of Staff Committee on 9 July 1945. The Committee expressed doubt as to the desirability of tabling the memorandum proposed in this telegram and decided that the

i *6–16 July 1945   R.A.F. Delegation (Washington) to Air Ministry for Joint American Secretariat, Tels. Uslon 98–104 and Sever 1106.* Friendly conversation (Uslon No. 100 of 10 July) between Mr. R. H. Brand and Sir H. Self, respectively Chairman and Deputy Chairman of the British Supply Council, and Judge F. M. Vinson, American Director of War Mobilisation and Reconversion, who was categorical that he had given 'green light' to U.S. Service Departments on Stage II lend-lease agreements. Conversation and correspondence between Mr. Brand and Mr. Leo Crowley, Administrator of U.S. Foreign Economic Administration (F.E.A.) concerning sixth lend-lease appropriation in non-munitions programme [UE 2904, 2939, 3047/32/71].

ii *11 July 1945   British Joint Staff Mission (Washington) to Cabinet Office Tel. No. J.S.M. 959.* Official confirmation from U.S. War Dept. of situation foreshadowed in para. 4 of No. 26. No help from U.S. civil dept.s on British lend-lease requirements other than for direct use against Japan. Advantage of bringing, if necessary, this most serious situation in military lend-lease on to highest plane for settlement at Potsdam [UE 2956/32/71].

iii *12 July 1945   Sir H. Self (Washington) for Sir R. Sinclair (Chief Executive, Ministry of Production) Tel. No. MIN 270.* Analysis of possible origins of present U.S. policy on lend-lease. War Dept.'s appropriation has been cut from $60 to 40 billion: possible difficulty in meeting all their own requirements [UE 2939/32/71].

iv *13 July 1945   Minute from General Sir Hastings Ismay (Chief of Staff to Minister of Defence) to Mr. Churchill.* Attaches report from Chiefs of Staff, setting out grave difficulties over lend-lease military supplies, and draft memo. for remission to President Truman at Potsdam [PREM 4/17/15/1487–90].

Joint Staff Mission 'should be told to hold hard'. Later that day it was agreed at a meeting of the British members of the London Munitions Assignment Board with representatives of the Foreign Office and Treasury that 'the right course is for the Prime Minister to take the matter up with the President, basing himself upon the Agreements governing Lend-Lease supplies in Stage II [i.e. between the defeat of Germany and the defeat of Japan] which were reached in Washington last autumn' (UE 2899/32/71), pursuant to the agreement reached in discussion on 14 September 1944 between President Roosevelt and Mr. Churchill at the Second Conference at Quebec: cf. *F.R.U.S. The Conference at Quebec 1944*, pp.344–6, 468, *F.R.U.S. 1944*, vol. iii, pp. 58–83, and W. K. Hancock and M. M. Gowing, *British War Economy* (H.M.S.O., 1949), pp. 527–33.

No. 27

Earl of Halifax (Washington) to Mr. Eden (Received 8 July, 7.35 a.m.)
No. 4747 Telegraphic [FO 954/30: US/45/146]

WASHINGTON, *7 July 1945, 10.37 p.m.*

Immediate. Top secret. Personal and Private

Following for Prime Minister from Halifax.
Your telegram No. 7230.[1]

---

[1] No. 2. The remainder of the present telegram is printed in W. S. Churchill, *op. cit.*, vol. vi, p. 530.

The President had already left for Terminal when your telegram reached me. Grey [Grew][2] has arranged personally for your message to be relayed to him on board ship.

2. I am sure you will find Truman most anxious to work with us and fully alive to the long range implications as well as short term difficulties of the decisions we have to make. I judge that American tactics with the Russians will be to display at the outset confidence in Russian willingness to co-operate. I should also expect the Americans in dealing with us, to be more responsive to arguments based upon the danger of economic chaos in European countries than to the balder pleas about the risks of extreme Left governments or of the spread of Communism. They showed some signs of nervousness in my portrayal of Europe (whatever the facts) as the scene of a clash of ideas in which the Soviet and Western influence are likely to be hostile and conflicting. At the back of their minds there are still lingering suspicions that we want to back Right Wing governments or monuments [monarchies] for their own sake. This does not in the least mean that they will be unwilling to stand up with us against the Russians when necessary. But they are likely to pick their occasions with care and are half expecting to play or at any rate, to represent themselves as playing, a moderating role between ourselves and the Russians.

[2] Mr. J. C. Grew was Under Secretary of State and Acting Secretary of State during the absence of Mr. Byrnes at Potsdam.

No. 28

Minute by Mr. Churchill[1]
No. M. 681/5 [R 11515/4/19]

10 DOWNING STREET, *7 July 1945*

I do not agree with the idea that a constituent assembly should be elected pending a plebiscite on the regime. It is contrary to all my correspondence with President Roosevelt, which always considered that there should be a plebiscite on the King's return as soon as normal conditions were restored. Obviously the object of this State Department paper is to deny the Greek people a chance to say whether they will have the monarchy back or not. I must ask that no approving telegram should be sent which I have not had an opportunity of seeing.

W. S. C.

[1] This minute to the Foreign Office had reference to Washington telegram No. 4669 of 6 July 1945 (not printed) transmitting the main text of a memorandum of 5 July from the State Department concerning the holding of elections in Greece: printed in *F.R.U.S. Berlin*, vol. i, pp. 657–8.

i *6 & 7 July 1945 Lord Halifax (Washington) Tels. Nos. 4668 and 4694; Mr. H. Caccia (H.M. Minister, Athens) Tel. No. 1501.* Comments on proposals in U.S. memo. of 5 July for Greek elections to precede plebiscite. Mr. Caccia represents that proposals would breach Varkiza Agreement of 12 February 1945 between Greek Govt. and E.A.M. (text in C. M. Woodhouse, *Apple of Discord*—London, 1948, pp. 308–10) [R 11480, 11516, 11561/4/19].

ii *9–13 July 1945 To and from Lord Halifax (Washington) Tels. Nos. 7313, 7418, 4841; to and from Mr. Caccia (Athens) Tels. Nos. 1496, 1531–2.* Strong British opposition to suggestion for Anglo-American advice that Greek elections should precede plebiscite (cf. *F.R.U.S. Berlin*, vol. i, pp. 660–1). U.S. Govt. are not pressing this suggestion. Arrangements for concerted Anglo-American approach to Greek Govt. concerning Allied supervision of elections [R 11561, 11798, 11881/4/19].

iii *14 & 15 July 1945 From and to Lord Halifax (Washington) Tels. Nos. 4917 and 7487.* Timing and wording of invitation to be issued to Soviet and French Govt.s concerning Allied supervision of Greek elections [R 11918, 11955/4/19].

iv *9 July 1945 Sir C. Woolley (Governor and Commander-in-Chief, Cyprus) to Col. O. Stanley Tel. No. 362.* Strong local protest against statement attributed to M. Zakynthinos, Greek Under-Secretary for Information, concerning question of Cyprus as a case for arrangements between two Allies [R 12134/708/19].

No. 29

Minute by Viscount Hood[1]

[U 5596/20/70]

FOREIGN OFFICE, *7 July 1945*

O.R.C. (45) 3[2]

This paper will be taken by the Overseas Reconstruction Committee[3] on Wednesday.[4]

This draft agreement[5] prepared by the European Advisory Commission

---

[1] A member of the Reconstruction Department of the Foreign Office.

[2] Annex below, supplied from U 5360/20/70.

[3] The Overseas Reconstruction Committee (O.R.C.) of the Cabinet had been constituted on 5 July 1945, under the chairmanship of Mr. Eden, in replacement of the Armistice and Post-War Committee (A.P.W.) to consider, in particular, questions of policy in connexion with liberated and former enemy countries. For this and other committees mentioned below, cf. F. S. V. Donnison, *Civil Affairs and Military Government Central Organization and Planning* (H.M.S.O., 1966), pp. 38–43.

[4] 11 July 1945: see ii below.

[5] The draft agreement, or general order, attached as annex A (not here printed) to the Annex below was identic, down to the end of section XIII, with the agreement *ad referendum* of 25 July 1945 between the British, American, Soviet and French Governments, for the imposition of certain additional requirements on Germany, printed in *F.R.U.S. Berlin*, vol. ii, pp. 1011–23.   In annex A to the Annex the concluding formula of the draft read: 'Dated this   day of   194 . Signed by the Allied Representatives', with blanks for names and titles of signatories: cf. further No. 406.

is intended to supplement the Declaration signed in Berlin on June 5th. The latter announced our military terms; this agreement deals mainly with political and economic subjects.

The existence and indeed most of the text of this agreement is due to British initiative and it is to be hoped that the Committee will authorise the U.K. Representative to sign the agreement in its present form. Certain doubts have arisen recently (see paragraphs 3 and 4 of the covering paper), but they do not appear to be points of real substance and it would be very difficult to secure amendments at this late stage. The other three Delegations at the E.A.C. are ready to sign and now that the Allied Council in Germany is on the point of starting its work it is very desirable that these additional requirements should be agreed and announced without delay.

Hood

ANNEX TO No. 29

Memorandum by the Minister of Education[6]
O.R.C. (45) 3

Secret   *5 July 1945*

Additional Requirements to be imposed on Germany

Early in 1944 the United Kingdom Representative on the European Advisory Commission tabled the British draft Armistice for Germany (A.C.A. (44) 1).[7] In the discussions at the Commission it became clear that both the United States and Soviet Governments favoured a shorter document of a primarily military character and the Instrument of Surrender finally agreed by the Commission took this form. Sir William Strang[8] made his acceptance of this short Instrument conditional on the preparation by the Commission of a further document to cover those subjects which were dealt with in the British draft Armistice but not in the Instrument of Surrender. This further document has recently been under discussion at the Commission and a Draft Agreement between the four Governments has now been prepared in a form suitable for publication.[5] The texts of this Agreement and of the Commission's covering report[9] are attached (Annexes A and B).

2. This Agreement will supplement the Declaration signed at Berlin on the 5th June and sets out the requirements of the Allies in the fields not mentioned in the Declaration. The subjects dealt with are:—

> I. Abolition of the German armed forces and prohibition of military training.
> II. Evacuation of German officials and civilians.
> III. Control of Germany's external relations.

---

[6] Mr. R. K. Law, formerly Minister of State for Foreign Affairs (1943–5), had been appointed Minister of Education in May 1945.

[7] The British draft Armistice for Germany is printed in *F.R.U.S. 1944*, vol. i, pp. 121–39.

[8] Sir W. Strang had been the U.K. representative on the European Advisory Commission prior to his appointment on 5 June 1945 to be Political Adviser to Field-Marshal Montgomery.

[9] The unsigned text of this report at annex B, not printed, was the same as the signed text in the annex to No. 406.

IV. Control of inter-communications, broadcasting, press, &c.
V. Control of German economy and assets.
VI. Restitution, reparation, costs of occupation.
VII. Control of shipping.
VIII. Control of transport.
IX. Movement control.
X. War Criminals.
XI. Abolition of the Nazi Party, reform of German law and the legal, administrative, police and educational systems.
XII. Supply of information and rights of access.
XIII. Interpretation.

The provisions of the Agreement, like those of the Declaration, are general and will require to be supplemented by specific orders issued by the Commanders-in-Chief.

3. The powers assumed in this Agreement are conferred on the Allied Representatives, that is to say, the four Commanders-in-Chief, and the intention is that they will exercise those powers jointly as the result of quadripartite agreement. This is liable to cause us some embarrassment if the British Commander-in-Chief were criticised for action which he may already have taken unilaterally in the fields covered by this Agreement, for instance, in the matter of German merchant shipping, or which he may decide to take unilaterally in his own zone. Such difficulties are, however, inherent in the whole conception of Four-Power control of Germany, which, on general grounds, it is our aim and in our interests to establish. On balance, therefore, I consider that we should accept the principle that the powers conferred in this Agreement, which deals with matters affecting Germany as a whole, should be exercised by the Allied Representatives jointly. Whilst the broad policy to be pursued in the fields covered by the Agreement will thus be a matter for Four-Power Agreement, it will still be open to each Commander-in-Chief to give effect to that policy on his own authority in his own zone by virtue of the supreme authority which he exercises in his zone.

4. There is one particular point which calls for comment: research work relating to war or the production of war material (para. 13 (b) of the Agreement and para. 3 (a) of the Covering Report). The United Kingdom Representative, as a result of recent discussion at the A.C.A.O. Committee,[10] attempted to secure:—

(i) the addition of a further sub-paragraph in the Agreement prohibiting such research work apart from any exceptions permitted by the Allied Representatives.

(ii) the amendment of para. 3 (a) in the Covering Report so as to set a definite time limit of six months to the continuation of such research and so as to provide for the destruction or removal of research equipment.

These proposals were resisted by the Soviet Representative: the first, on the grounds that it would lead to destruction or concealment by the Germans of their research work; the second, on the grounds that such matters should be left to the Commanders-in-Chief. The United States Delegation, whilst generally sympathetic

---

[10] The official Committee on Armistice Terms and Civil Administration (A.C.A.O.) worked to the ministerial Armistice Terms and Civil Administration Committee (A.C.A.). The latter committee had been relieved of responsibility for the supply sector of civil affairs by the constitution of the ministerial Committee on Supply Questions in Liberated and Conquered Areas (S.L.A.), to which worked a corresponding official committee (S.L.A.O.).

considered that the existing paragraphs were adequate for present purposes. In these circumstances I would not propose to press our amendments.

5. In general, I consider that this Agreement serves a useful purpose as demonstrating agreed Allied policy towards Germany and indicating to the Germans the obligations they must fulfil. I propose to authorise the United Kingdom Representative to join in recommending it for approval of the Four Governments.

R. K. L.

Ministry of Education, S.W.1, 5th July, 1945

CALENDARS TO NO. 29

i *7 July 1945 Minutes from Sir R. Campbell and Lord Hood to Sir A. Cadogan (E.A.C. Summary No. 99):* An informal E.A.C. Meeting of 6 July discussed arrangements for (*a*) the occupation of Austria: M. Gousev refused to include mention in the Covering Report of free transit in Austria and common use of facilities in Vienna, but accepted an unsatisfactory American formula; (*b*) draft agreement on French zone in Germany: accepted, except that Soviet Govt. consider that French sector in Berlin should be found from British and American sectors. Further action on (*a*)—see No. 35—and (*b*) agreed [U 5364/473/70; U 5354/11/70].

ii *11 July 1945 O.R.C. (45) 1st Meeting.* Additional requirements to be imposed on Germany (draft agreement approved subject to a reservation regarding para. 3 d of Commission's covering report, concerning return to owners of vessels of the United Nations surrendered to Allied representatives). Occupation of Austria. Extension of work of Economic and Industrial Planning Staff to Far Eastern questions. Control and ownership by United Nations of German industrial concerns [U 5425/5342/70].

No. 30

Memorandum by Mr. Troutbeck

[*C 3816/24/18*]

FOREIGN OFFICE, *7 July 1945*

The attached leader in to-day's *Times*[1] follows what the *Manchester Guardian* has been saying for some time.

It is of course true that the Allies have not yet got very far in working out 'Policies for Germany'. The only two documents yet published are the Yalta statement[2] and the Declaration of Defeat. In addition the European Advisory Commission have agreed the 'additional requirements', which are broadly those parts of our original long terms which were omitted from the Declaration of Defeat. All this does not amount to very much in the way of policy.

---

[1] Not here printed. The article was entitled 'A Common Policy'.

[2] The report, or 'statement' or 'communique', of the Conference at Yalta, issued on 11 February 1945 (Cmd. 6598 of 1945), is printed in *B.F.S.P.*, vol. 151, pp. 221–9. The protocol of the proceedings of the conference was subsequently published (Cmd. 7088 of 1947): *op. cit.*, vol. 148, pp. 80–8.

The Times attributes this to drift and inertia, which is no doubt a very proper line for an editor to take. There are, however, other reasons:

(1) A proper reluctance to take decisions on matters of high policy in Germany until we knew what situation we should have to meet. President Roosevelt expressed this view strongly at one period;

(2) The need to await the natural death of a lot of half baked ideas like the Morgenthau plan.[3] To have had a head-on collision on such matters would have been bad tactics;

(3) The difficulty of making any plans until it was known whether our policy was to have a single Germany or to divide the country into a number of separate States;

(4) The fact that up to a short time ago our highest authorities were still bending all their energies to fighting the war;

(5) The impossibility, on account of the Russian attitude, of making progress in the E.A.C., where a whole series of British and American policy directives have long lain on the table unconsidered;

(6) The refusal of the Russians to agree to the Control Council meeting until agreement had been reached on the withdrawal of the British and American forces into their own zones. Even now there is, according to a telegram[4] from Sir W. Strang, little prospect of the Council meeting before Terminal. We do not know precisely why, nor do the War Office. Sir W. Strang will be in London on July 11.

But even if the Council were to meet immediately, it would probably not get very far with the major problems without a lead from a higher source. We are therefore hoping to get agreement at Terminal on certain broad matters of principle, viz:

(i) the establishment of a central German administration for certain specified purposes;[5]

(ii) the establishment of political parties;

(iii) the establishment of trade unions;

(iv) co-ordination of propaganda and information services to Germany;

(v) treatment of Germany as an economic whole.

Once broad agreement has been reached on such matters of principle, it may be hoped that there will be less divergence on such matters as political and trade union activities and that the Control Council will be able to start working on a satisfactory basis. So far as H.M.G. are concerned, they have provided for it 'officials qualified by training and experience' to deal with political and economic matters.

But on the economic side the going is bound to be slow. Communications are disrupted, the towns are destroyed, the populations dispersed, the

---

[3] For this plan advanced in 1944 by Mr. H. Morgenthau, U.S. Secretary of the Treasury, for the 'pastoralisation' of Germany, and for British views thereon see Sir L. Woodward, *op. cit.*, vol. v, pp. 222–9. Mr. Morgenthau had resigned on 5 July 1945.

[4] Telegram No. 26 (on C 3641/47/18) of 4 July 1945, from the Headquarters of the 21st Army Group at Bad Oeynhausen, not printed.

[5] Mr. Eden noted in the margin against this clause: 'Bevin against. A. E.'

country still has some three million foreigners on its hands, and may soon have to find room for millions of immigrants from Poland and Czechoslovakia. Moreover some time is bound to elapse before agreement is reached on reparation and the amount of destruction to be carried out in German industry in the interests of economic security. *The Times* talks of reconstruction. It should not be forgotten that the word was taboo while the Morgenthau ideas were ruling the day.[6]

On fraternisation the Cabinet took a decision yesterday.[7]

J. M. TROUTBECK

[6] Mr. Hall-Patch, an Assistant Under Secretary of State in the Foreign Office, minuted as follows on this memorandum: 'I agree that no rapid progress on the economic side is possible. Food, transport and coal are all critically short. To the inevitable disruption arising from a long drawn out war, of which these shortages are only the more apparent indications, will be added further dislocation from a declared policy of "draconian" measures of economic disarmament & heavy reparation deliveries. Economic revival in these circumstances can only be a lengthy and painful process. Unless we are prepared to abandon both economic disarmament and reparation the measures advocated by *The Times* would only hasten *economic* revival to a very limited extent. And these measures predicate active co-operation by our Allies, as our own efforts can only touch the fringes of the problem. This co-operation has not yet become apparent. With this background *The Times* shows a strange levity in talking of reconstruction. Reparation, linked with economic security, will be the major economic factor in Germany for some years. We have already agreed in Moscow a statement of principles on this subject [see No. 116, annex] which is suitable for publication. This statement gives a clear indication in general terms of our intended policy. How far these principles will be respected in practice does not rest with us alone. E. L. Hall-Patch, 8/7/45.'

[7] War Office telegram No. 58607 of 10 July communicated to Field-Marshal Montgomery this Cabinet decision for further gradual relaxation of non-fraternisation, subject to it 'being so timed that the attitude of British occupying troops is less severe in Austria than in Germany. . . . You should consult with General Eisenhower so that, if possible, similar policies may be followed in both the British and American zones.' Field-Marshal Alexander was correspondingly instructed in War Office telegram No. 58608 of even date.

No. 31

Minute by Viscount Hood
[*ZM 3840/1/22*]

FOREIGN OFFICE, 7 *July 1945*

Peace Treaty with Italy

This paper[1] will be taken by the Cabinet on Thursday[2].

It was drafted six weeks ago when we were in the midst of our row with

[1] Annexed was a memorandum (not here printed) of 5 July 1945 by Mr. Eden on a 'Peace Treaty with Italy', circulated to the Cabinet as C.P.(45)64. This memorandum, covering a skeleton draft of the political clauses of the proposed treaty, was as summarized by Sir L. Woodward, *op. cit.*, vol. iii, pp. 478–80.

[2] 12 July 1945.

Tito over Trieste.[3] The territorial provisions were thus deliberately left vague, in the sense that the future of the territories to be ceded by Italy is left to later decision by the Four Powers. There is much to be said for settling these territorial questions quickly. Some are easy: the Dodecanese could go outright to Greece, and Zara and the Adriatic Islands to Yugoslavia; others are more difficult: the Italo-Yugoslav frontier, Trieste and the Italian colonies. Notwithstanding these difficulties, it should be possible and might be desirable to make the territorial clauses in the Treaty more definite, but it will probably be wiser to defer a decision about this until after the Potsdam Conference where the procedure for peace-making will be discussed.[4]

The discussions at Potsdam may also affect the procedure for agreeing the Peace Terms with the other interested Allied Governments, but we still want Cabinet approval of the recommendation made in paragraph 13 of the paper that our present draft Heads of Treaty should be communicated at once to the Dominion Governments and then to the U.S. Government.

The Trusteeship chapter of the San Francisco Charter is relevant to the future of Pantellaria, the Pelagian Islands and the Italian colonies. The Mediterranean Islands and parts of the Italian colonies might well become 'strategic areas', and the suggestion made in our paper that Italy might retain administrative rights in these islands and in Tripolitania will not now be feasible until Italy has been elected to the World Organisation.[5]

Hood

CALENDARS TO No. 31

i *7 July 1945 Minutes by Mr. Hoyer Millar.* Records of a conversation with Signor Migone, Counsellor in Italian Embassy: prospective discussion regarding Italy at Potsdam. Mr. Hoyer Millar explained that conclusion of a comprehensive peace treaty would take time. Signor Migone did not think Italy would be unduly shocked to be deprived of her overseas territories; his views on withdrawal of Allied forces from Italy [U 5356/50/70; ZM 3925/58/22].

[3] See No. 3, note 8.

[4] Sir A. Cadogan here noted in the margin 'Yes. A.C.'.

[5] Mr. Hoyer Millar commented in a minute of 8 July on this paper: 'As regards the actual proposals, Sir N. Charles considers them fair and just, though rather tough. He particularly welcomes leaving Bolzano to Italy and the idea of giving the latter a chance of administering Tripolitania under the International Trusteeship plan. Field Marshal Alexander thinks that our terms are too severe and would favour letting Italy keep Tripolitania in full sovereignty and having the right to administer Eritrea. Both the Ambassador and the Field Marshal seem particularly concerned that we should not be too severe on the Italians in the matter of the Italian fleet. The P[ost] H[ostilities] P[lanning Committee] idea is to leave the Italians with something rather less than half of their present fleet. For political reasons we should be glad to be rather less hard-hearted since the Italians attach great psychological importance to the fleet, and the Italian Navy has played a useful part on our side in the war. But we must, I think, be guided by the Admiralty in this as there are obvious practical objections to letting the Italians have too big a fleet. And the Russians have already claimed a third of it.'

49

17 July 1945 To Mr. Duff Cooper (H.M. Ambassador, Paris) No. 1309. Indication of H.M.G.'s attitude towards Italy was given to M. Paris, Counsellor in French Embassy, on 5 July. The Foreign Office favour a final rather than a piecemeal settlement. Italy would require all possible military and economic assistance if she was to become a useful member of Western society. She might be afforded some colonial facilities, possibly in Tripoli, under trusteeship [ZM 3739/1/22].

No. 32

Brief for the United Kingdom Delegation to the Conference at Potsdam
No. 21 [N 8339/9/15]

Secret   FOREIGN OFFICE, *7 July 1945*[1]

Bornholm

1. The Soviet General Korotkov in a press interview on 1st June stated that the Soviet forces in Bornholm would stay there as long as Stalin, Truman and Churchill found it necessary. They alone would decide. Asked whether they would decide together he replied in the affirmative. General Korotkov has since let it be known that he was severely reprimanded in Moscow for these remarks. It therefore appears unlikely that the Russians will raise this question at the forthcoming meeting. If however they do so, it would probably involve a discussion of the position of British forces in Denmark.

2. Soviet forces began to land on Bornholm on 9th May, in order to dispose of some 25,000 German troops there. There are still reported to be some 6,000 Soviet troops there, but it is reported that there are no signs of Soviet preparations for a prolonged stay. Relations between the Russians and the Danes continue to be cordial. Though the Danes do not appear to be particularly anxious, it may be assumed that they would like to see the Russians leave.

3. Shortly after their arrival the Russians informe[d] the local authorities that they had only come to take the surrender of the German forces and would leave as soon as their task was completed. Later the Soviet Commander said to the Danish Minister for Foreign Affairs during his visit to the island: 'The Russian forces have come to the island exclusively to cleanse it of everything German and when this task is completed Denmark will remain a free and independent country'. On 23rd May, the Soviet Commanding Officer gave the Danish Governor of Bornholm a written communication including the words: 'Bornholm is a part of Denmark and is only occupied by our troops because it lies behind our German occupation zone. The island is occupied by Red Army troops provisionally until questions on Germany relating to the war are solved.'

---

[1] Date on which the draft of this brief was initialed by Mr. C. F. A. Warner, Head of Northern Department.

4. The Chiefs of Staff's view is that in present circumstances, Bornholm is of small strategic importance and control of it would not in itself give the Russians control of the entrance to the Baltic. The fact that the Russians are in the island does not necessitate on strategic grounds the retention of British forces in Denmark.

5. On present plans the complete withdrawal of British forces from Denmark is unlikely to take place before mid-October by which time it is hoped that they will have completed the evacuation of German military personnel and civilian refugees, and have disposed of German shipping and swept all mines. If however political considerations require, it should be possible for alternative arrangements to be made which would not call for the employment of fighting units, but only of administrative units. Operational air forces will not be required after the withdrawal of the land forces, though an Royal Air Force Staging Post will be required for some time. A proposal to establish local short term leave camps in Denmark is still under consideration.

6. The Danes have been reticent on the subject of Bornholm and His Majesty's Minister at Copenhagen concludes that they hope that by maintaining good relations, dealing exclusively with the Russians and refraining from arousing their suspicions of third party interference, they will be able sooner or later to obtain a complete Russian withdrawal.

7. Should the Danish Government ask us to withdraw before the military task is completed as a lever to get the Russians out of Bornholm, there would be no objection to our seeking to concert plans with the Danish Government whereby they would take over part of the military task thus enabling an earlier withdrawal of British fighting units to be effected.

8. Alternatively, it is possible (but seems unlikely) that the Danish Government may ask us not to withdraw until they have obtained some assurance from the Russians about simultaneous withdrawal from Bornholm.

9. The natural course would be to withdraw as soon as the military task has been completed, and to leave the withdrawal of Russian troops from Bornholm as a purely Danish-Russian issue.

10. It therefore appears that for us to raise the question of Bornholm with the Russians might be contrary to Danish wishes and of no assistance to them. If however the Russians should raise the question of the withdrawal of Allied forces from Denmark, it may be said that we are withdrawing them and propose to continue to do so as and when their tasks are completed and that we assume the Russians will do likewise.

CALENDAR TO No. 32

i *7 July 1945   Brief No. 20 for U.K. Delegation on Soviet Forces in North Norway.*
No apparent reason to raise with Russians question of withdrawal of Soviet occupying forces in Kirkenes and Finnmark. Norwegian Govt. has not expressed anxiety for their withdrawal. Anglo-American forces in Norway may not be withdrawn before end of year owing to difficulties of evacuating disarmed German forces there [F.O. 934/6].

No. 33

Sir A. Clark Kerr (Moscow) to Mr. Eden (Received 8 July 1.20 p.m.)
No. 2998 Telegraphic [Z 8319/1535/43]

Important   MOSCOW, *8 July 1945, 12.31 a.m. G.M.T.*

Your telegram No. 3720,[1] paragraph 5.

I think it would be valuable if we were to take up with the Soviet Government at Terminal their hostility to Swiss Government and also to governments of other small European countries with whom His Majesty's Government have specially close relations, such as Greece, Turkey and Portugal. We could perhaps then find out what particular grudges the Soviet Government nourish against these Governments and what steps could be taken to improve relations. It would I think be a tactical mistake to mention Franco-Spain in this context, since apart from other considerations memories of Blue Division[2] etc. are still very alive there.[3]

[1] Of 3 July 1945, not printed: paragraph 5 had reported that on 26 June the Swiss Minister in London had told Sir A. Cadogan 'that he hoped an opportunity might be taken at the forthcoming Three Power meeting to ascertain what in fact were the real Soviet grievances against Switzerland and to do something in order to remedy the present situation'. The telegram added: 'The desirability of raising the question of Soviet-Swiss relations at the Three Power Conference had already occurred to us.'

[2] In 1941 the Spanish Government under General Franco had sanctioned the passage of the Blue Division of Spanish volunteers to fight in support of the German forces upon the eastern front against the Soviet Union.

[3] This telegram was discussed at a meeting (no record traced) held in Sir A. Cadogan's room on 9 July 1945. In Moscow telegram No. 3229A of 21 July (received that day) Mr. F. K. Roberts recalled that on 26 June the Soviet Government had 'agreed to Swiss proposal that Soviet representatives should investigate conditions of Soviet refugees in Switzerland. . . . Since 3rd July I have seen no [Soviet press] references to Switzerland in any context. She is no longer even included among the countries regularly listed in editorials as affording sanctuary to German refugees and funds.'

No. 34

Mr. Broad (Caserta) to Mr. Eden (Received 8 July, 8.15 a.m.)
No. 1309 Telegraphic [R 11592/40/19]

CASERTA, *8 July 1945, 7.20 a.m.*

Repeated to Moscow, Athens.

My telegram No. 341[1] not repeated to Moscow.

Allied Force Headquarters have instructed the Allied Commission[2] to inform the head of the Russian Military Mission accredited to the Displaced

[1] Of 20 February 1945 (R 3529/3133/67), not printed.
[2] For Italy.

Persons Sub Commission, Allied Commission, that the Supreme Allied Commander has decided that in view of the fact that all Soviet citizens have now been repatriated from Greece and the Adriatic, the Russian Mission in Greece has completed its work and should be returned to Russia as soon as possible.

Foreign Office repeat to Moscow as my telegram No. 156.

No. 35

Mr. Churchill to Sir A. Clark Kerr (Moscow)
No. 3831 Telegraphic [U 5354/11/70]

Important   FOREIGN OFFICE, *8 July 1945, 3 p.m.*

My telegram No. 3421 (of the 18th June: text of Marshal Stalin's message of June 17th).[1]

As you will have learnt from telegrams exchanged with British and United States Military Missions in Moscow the Russian troops have refused to withdraw from Styria. Please inform Soviet Government that we are at a loss to understand this refusal which is contrary to undertaking given by Marshal Stalin in his message to the Prime Minister of June 17th that he would take all necessary measures in Germany and Austria for the simultaneous movements of troops in accordance with agreed plan. We have carried out our side of the bargain and we expect Soviet Government at once to carry out theirs. Whilst formal agreement has not yet been signed at the E.A.C. the limits of the respective zones of occupation in Austria were agreed in principle some time ago. We can thus see no reason why these zones should not be established forthwith. Movement of French troops into the French zones both in Germany and Austria has not (repeat not) been delayed pending the conclusion of formal agreements at the E.A.C.

2. As regards the Agreement on Zones of Occupation, which is at present under discussion at the E.A.C., you should state that final agreement has been held up owing to the inability of the Soviet Representative to accept the principle of free transit of goods throughout Austria and the common use of transport and other facilities and public utility services within the city of Vienna. We agree with Soviet representative's contention that the application and regulation of these principles are matters for the Allied Council, but we consider that it would be useful and necessary for the Allied Council to be informed that these principles are accepted by the Four Governments;[2] otherwise members of Council might not know that they must act on this basis and delays and difficulties might well ensue locally. Discussions at the E.A.C. have always proceeded on the assumption that these principles

[1] Not here printed: see W. S. Churchill, *op. cit.*, vol. vi, p. 527.
[2] The occupying powers: the United Kingdom, United States, Soviet Union and France.

would be observed and we cannot thus understand Soviet representatives' inability to accept a written statement that these principles are accepted by the Four Governments. We should be grateful if Soviet Government would instruct their representative to accept a written statement on these lines.[3]

[3] Foreign Office telegram No. 3846 of 11.20 a.m. on 9 July 1945 to Moscow instructed with reference to the present telegram: 'Please suspend action'. In a minute of 9 July Lord Hood explained that he had taken this action 'on hearing that M. Gousev was now prepared to include in the Commission's Covering Report a paragraph about transit and common use of facilities in Vienna.   At the E.A.C. this morning M. Gousev tabled a formula which though it speaks of "transit" rather than "free transit" seemed to me acceptable. The paragraph about airfields was also agreed on the basis of the Soviet offer of two; and the whole Agreement and Covering Report are to be signed tonight. I have telegraphed the texts to Mr. Mack and am arranging for them to be circulated for the O.R. Committee's meeting on Wednesday [see No. 29.ii] so that H.M.G.'s approval can be obtained.   I understand from the War Office that General Macleary [McCreery] is anxious to have a meeting of the four Commanders without delay and on hearing from me that the Agreement was to be signed tonight the War Office will now telegraph him approving his plan.'

No. 36

Mr. Churchill to Sir A. Clark Kerr (Moscow)
No. 3835 Victim Telegraphic [C 3465/317/3]

FOREIGN OFFICE, 8 July 1945, 7.5 p.m.

Repeated to Washington No. 7275, Paris No. 1606 Saving, Caserta No. 204 Saving, Rome No. 263 Saving (For Mr. Mack).

Following for Sir Walter Monckton.[1]

Reports from Military Mission recently in Vienna confirm systematic and large-scale removal by Russians, both there and in Styria, of industrial equipment and stocks of all kinds. This is of course over and above the extensive looting of private property by Red Army soldiers.

2. Further details are being sought from the British Element of the Austrian Commission, and we are not in the meantime proposing to make any representations to the Russians through either the diplomatic channel or the Reparation Commission. It seems however desirable that you should have this information, which must inevitably have an important bearing on the reparation question as well as on the whole economic prospects of the country.

3. In this latter connexion, the Soviet Government is of course in no doubt as to our views—see my telegram No. 1979[2] (of 21st April).

[1] Solicitor-General and Head of the British Delegation to the Allied Reparations Commission in Moscow.

[2] Not printed: cf. F.R.U.S. 1945, vol. iii, p. 70.

i   *12 July 1945   Minute from Mr. Eden to Mr. Churchill No. PM/45/323.* Comments on extract from letter of 29 June from Deputy Commissioner for Civilian Relief, Central Mediterranean Force, on conditions in Soviet-occupied Austria [C 3945/141/3].

No. 37

Mr. Churchill to Earl of Halifax (Washington)
No. 7277 Telegraphic [N 8193/207/12]

Immediate   FOREIGN OFFICE, *8 July 1945, 3.36 p.m.*

Repeated to Prague No. 123.

Prague telegram No. 188[1] (of 6th July: withdrawal of Soviet forces from Czechoslovakia).

Please inform the State Department urgently of Mr. Nichols' views and of my wholehearted endorsement of them. I very much hope that the United States forces will not be entirely withdrawn until the Russian forces are.

[1] No. 11.

No. 38

Mr. Hopkinson[1] (Rome) to Mr. Eden (Received 8 July, 3.55 p.m.)
No. 1113 Telegraphic [R 11583/24/92]

ROME, *8 July 1945, 12.18 p.m. G.M.T.*

Repeated to Caserta, Belgrade, Moscow, Washington.

I asked Minister for Foreign Affairs this morning[2] whether in putting forward the proposal in their programme[3] that Trieste question should be settled by direct negotiations with Yugoslav Government, they had any reason to believe such negotiations would be successful. He replied that he personally had no hopes at all since Yugoslavia had so far shown no willingness to discuss the matter. It appears probable that this proposal which has always been advocated by the Communist party was included at the suggestion of Senor [*sic*] Togliatti. The latter may well have some reason to believe that it would meet with the support of the Soviet Government.

[1] British Deputy High Commissioner in Italy with local rank of Minister, acting in the absence of Sir Noel Charles, British representative in Rome with the personal rank of Ambassador.

[2] This telegram was drafted on 7 July 1945.

[3] The programme of Signor Parri's government, wherein Signor A. de Gasperi was Foreign Minister and Signor P. Togliatti Minister of Justice, had been issued on 26 June 1945: cf. *The Times* of 27 June 1945, p. 3.

Doctor Subasic's statement to His Majesty's Ambassador Belgrade reported in Belgrade telegram number 1067[4] tends to confirm this.

Please repeat to Belgrade and Moscow as my telegrams 52 and 27 respectively.

CALENDARS TO No. 38

i *8 July 1945   Mr. Hopkinson (Rome) Tel. No. 1112.* Signor de Gasperi regretted that it had not been possible to draw the Morgan Line (see No. 3, note 8) so as to protect more Italians in Istria from Yugoslav acts of aggression: recent representations also from Signor Parri. Allied Forces Headquarters have been asked to investigate urgently [R 11579/24/92].

ii *6 July 1945   Col. J. R. S. Clarke (Military Attaché, Belgrade) to War Office. Tel. No. 334.* Reports Yugoslav arrests and measures taken against repatriated personnel of former Yugoslav Royal Army [R 12839/1728/92].

---

[4] Of 6 July (R 11512/24/92), not printed. Concerning the Italian proposal Dr. Subasic had told Mr. Stevenson on 5 July: 'He personally was in favour of a direct agreement with Italy if it could be reached. It was obviously the most sensible way of settling a very difficult question. He thought however that an agreement would be impossible without the assistance of the Great Powers. He had not yet made up his mind on the matter.'

No. 39

Mr. Churchill to Sir. A. Clark Kerr (Moscow)
No. 3819 Telegraphic [N 7794/28/12]

FOREIGN OFFICE, *8 July 1945, 1.50 p.m.*

Repeated to Washington No. 7267, Prague No. 122.

Your telegram No. 2832[1] (of 30th June: Soviet-Czechoslovak treaty on transfer of Serb [Sub]-Carpathian Ruthenia to Soviet Ukraine).

I feel that we are entitled to complain of failure of Soviet Government to consult or inform us before concluding this treaty. We need not labour the point or make a serious grievance of the conclusion of an agreement which apparently was freely entered into on both sides. The fact that we have recognised without protest the cession to the Soviet Union of Bessarabia and parts of Finland—not to mention the *de facto* annexation of Eastern Poland—makes it difficult on the occasion of this fresh annexation to argue that it constitutes a violation of Article 5 of the Anglo-Soviet Treaty.[2]

You should however express to the Soviet Government the surprise of His Majesty's Government that, as the Allies of the Soviet Government, the

---

[1] Not printed. The Soviet-Czechoslovak Agreement of 29 June 1945 is printed in *B.F.S.P.*, vol. 145, pp. 1096–7.
[2] The Anglo-Soviet treaty of alliance of 26 May 1942 is printed *op. cit.*, vol. 144, pp. 1038–41.

latter did not feel able to take them into their confidence about their intentions before concluding with another friendly state an agreement providing for such an important accession of territory to the Soviet Union at the expense of one of its neighbours. His Majesty's Government feel the more entitled to express this view since they have repeatedly made it plain that in their opinion all territorial changes in Europe should await the final peace settlement.[3]

CALENDAR TO No. 39

i *9 July 1945* Mr. *Nichols (Prague) Tel. No. 40 Saving.* Political activity in Czechoslovakia; reactions to the cession of Sub-Carpathian Ruthenia; question of Teschen [N 8412/207/12].

[3] The representation here instructed was made in a letter of 11 July 1945 from Sir A. Clark Kerr to M. Molotov.

No. 40

Mr. Churchill to Mr. Shepherd[1] *(Helsingfors)*
No. 235 Telegraphic [N 8050/2490/56]

Top Secret   FOREIGN OFFICE, *8 July 1945*, *5.30 a.m.*
Repeated to Moscow No. 3826.

Your telegram No. 257[2] (of 4th July: future relations with Finland).

Stalin replied to Prime Minister's message referred to in paragraph 4 of my telegram No. 13 Saving (of 16th June)[3] noting that proposals on this question would be sent to him in the near future and adding that he saw no reason to defer the restoration of diplomatic relations with Finland, which was fulfilling the armistice conditions.

[1] Mr. F. M. Shepherd was British Political Representative in Finland.
[2] Not printed.
[3] Not printed. This telegram, repeated to Moscow as No. 122 Saving, had informed Mr. Shepherd of Marshal Stalin's message to Mr. Churchill of 27 May 1945 proposing the resumption of diplomatic relations with Roumania, Bulgaria, Finland and, in due course, Hungary. Paragraph 4 of this telegram had stated that in reply Mr. Churchill had informed Marshal Stalin 'that we ourselves have been considering our future relations with Roumania, Bulgaria, Hungary and Finland, and that we hope shortly to put comprehensive proposals before him and the United States Government. The Prime Minister added that he hoped these proposals might then be discussed with Stalin when they next met.' Telegram No. 13 Saving to Helsingfors had further informed Mr. Shepherd in confidence of the British 'tentative conclusion . . . that the time had come to conclude peace' with Roumania, Bulgaria and Hungary 'and that it would be appropriate to negotiate a peace treaty with Finland at the same time. . . . It is not possible to restore formal diplomatic relations without first concluding peace, and no advantage is seen in entry into informal diplomatic relations on the Italian model.' Marshal Stalin's messages to Mr. Churchill of 27 May and 14 June 1945 and Mr. Churchill's message to Marshal Stalin of 10 June 1945 are printed in *Stalin Correspondence*, vol. i, pp. 361, 363–4.

2. No further message has been sent in reply by the Prime Minister. It is proposed however that matter should be discussed at forthcoming 'Big Three' meeting, and Finland can most conveniently be dealt with separately from the Balkan ex-enemies. Our position is that owing to the necessity of settling important matters of principle under discussion in connexion with the peace treaty with Italy draft of peace treaty with Finland is unlikely to be ready much before the end of the year. If however the Russians and Americans wish to enter into diplomatic relations with Finland without delay, we would be prepared to establish informal diplomatic relations on the Italian model in advance of conclusion of peace treaty.

3. Words 'had fulfilled' in second sentence of paragraph 2 of my telegram under reference should have read 'were fulfilling'.

No. 41

Mr. Churchill to Sir A. Clark Kerr (Moscow)
No. 3843 Telegraphic [N 8210/6/55]

Immediate   FOREIGN OFFICE, *8 July 1945, 11.12 p.m.*

Repeated to Washington No. 7289.

Your telegram No. 2966[1] (of the 6th July; visit of proposed Polish Commission).

It has been decided that it is necessary to establish a clear understanding with Warsaw Government as regards terms of reference for discussions with Commission before such discussions can start.

2. Please request your Polish colleague to inform his Government as follows:-
(Begins).

The situation as regards liquidation of affairs of London Polish Government is highly complicated, since as a refugee Government it was almost entirely financed and maintained out of credits advanced by His Majesty's Government in accordance with the terms of certain formal agreements with former Polish Governments commencing with loan agreement of 7th September 1939.[2] As a consequence there is, broadly speaking, little or no property of the Polish Government, properly so called, in this country, and His Majesty's Government have an overriding financial interest in all the affairs of the late Polish Government conducted from here. On this account His Majesty's Government have appointed 'The Interim Treasury Committee for Polish Questions' to administer the affairs and liquidate machinery

---

[1] Not printed. A message from the Polish Provisional Government, transmitted in Moscow telegram No. 2902 of 4 July 1945 (not printed), had informed H.M. Government of their appointment of a Commission to take over all Polish assets in Great Britain. Proposed members of the Commission, under the chairmanship of M. E. Drozniak, were MM. H. Lukasiak, L. Grosfeld, J. Drohojowski and H. Kolodziejski.

[2] This Anglo-Franco-Polish agreement is printed in Cmd. 6610 of 1939.

of the old Polish Government in this country and to ensure that Polish civilians in this country and abroad who have hitherto been dependent administratively and financially upon Polish Government in London should not suffer from a complete financial and administrative breakdown consequent upon the disappearance of the old Polish Government. His Majesty's Government have also taken measures of conservation with regard to such property as has hitherto been under the control of the London Polish Government.

Polish Provisional Government will realise from what precedes that it is with His Majesty's Government therefore and not with representatives or ex-officials of late Polish Government that these matters must be discussed and His Majesty's Government are glad to learn that representatives of the Polish Provisional Government will be available for such discussions. His Majesty's Government consider it necessary, however, to reach agreement with the Polish Provisional Government as to the scope of these discussions before making contact officially with the Polish representatives named in your telegram No. 2902[1] (of the 4th July). The following points will require to be covered in such discussions:-

1. The acknowledgement by the Polish Provisional Government of the liability for the credits heretofore advanced to the late Government in London and other outstanding debts.

2. The relation of any such advances to any assets of the Polish State which may be available in this country.

3. Questions arising out of the present anomalous situation, in which large numbers of Polish refugees and other Polish nationals have hitherto been and are at the present moment dependent for their care and maintenance upon funds provided by His Majesty's Government. It is to be remarked in connexion with this point that His Majesty's Government and the British people will regard it as a matter of the first importance that these Allied nationals should not be subjected to unnecessary suffering through any fault of His Majesty's Government as the result of the latter's transference of recognition from the old Polish Government to the Provisional Government of National Unity.

The Polish Provisional Government will understand therefore that His Majesty's Government must ensure that the liquidation of the affairs of the London Government and the provisional maintenance of essential services hitherto performed by its machinery should be conducted in an orderly manner and must also ensure that the financial interests of His Majesty's Government are fully safeguarded.

His Majesty's Government will be glad to learn that the Polish Provisional Government accept the above premises as the basis for discussions and that they will issue instructions to their Commission to take [sic] contact with the Interim Treasury Committee for Polish Questions for conversations on the above basis. So soon as His Majesty's Government have received such assurances they will be ready to start discussions with the Polish Commission.

(Ends).

3. Unfortunately two members and Secretary of Polish Provisional Government's Commission arrived here from Warsaw on July 6th with Mr. Winch[3] in spite of efforts to stop them in Berlin. Mr. Winch tells us that he gathers:–

(*a*) that the original purpose of the appointment of the members of the Commission was to explain the new Government's policy to Poles here and contact them with a view to securing their allegiance to the new Government and that task of the Commission was only changed at the last moment to its present purpose;

(*b*) That his fellow travellers expected to take direct contact with the London Poles as regards taking over Polish property.

4. Mr. Winch has conveyed to Mr. Drozniak that His Majesty's Government have not yet consented to receive the Commission and are in discussion with the Polish Provisional Government in order to arrange a proper basis for its work, and that until this is done there can be no official contact with the Commission, it has been arranged, however, that M. Drozniak and M. Kolodjewski should visit the Foreign Office unofficially on 9th July in order to have the situation explained to them on the above lines.

5. It must of course be made clear to the Commission that His Majesty's Government have temporarily taken over from the London Poles and that members of the Commission must not try to deal direct with the London Poles or to assert their claims to Polish property etc. here in a disorderly manner.

6. It may be well that you should emphasise to your Polish colleague that this is the case and that the chances of the new Government making a good impression upon both His Majesty's Government and Poles here would be largely determined by the manner in which the 'Commission' conduct themselves.

CALENDARS TO No. 41

i *8 July 1945 Circular Tel. No 407 to Sir F. Stonehewer-Bird (H.M. Ambassador, Bagdad), etc.* Appointment of Interim Treasury Committee for Polish Questions. Essential that administration of Polish welfare services should continue abroad also. H.M.G. will continue financial support for Polish refugees. Prescribes local relations with Polish representatives [N 8324/1938/55].

ii *26 July 1945 Mr. R. M. A. Hankey (H.M. Chargé d'Affaires at Warsaw) No. 6.* Transmits Polish reply to British note of 10 July remitted in pursuance of para. 2 of No. 41. Polish Provisional Govt. is inclined to recognize liabilities, considered appropriate, of former Polish govts. but cannot be burdened with 'care about the fascist and anti-democratic elements'. Polish Govt., however, is ready to accept all liabilities connected with care and repatriation of returning Poles [N 9869/6/55].

[3] Mr. M. B. Winch had been appointed First Secretary to H.M. Embassy at Warsaw.

No. 42

Earl of Halifax (Washington) to Mr. Eden (Received 9 July, 1.25 a.m.)
No. 4754 Telegraphic [AN 2108/4/45]

Important   WASHINGTON, *8 July 1945, 6.1 p.m.*

Weekly Political Summary.[1]

The general public mood is exceptionally benevolent and hopeful; indeed, wherever the average American looks he perceives favourable omens: President Truman's popularity is immense; the latest Gallup poll estimates that 87 per cent of the entire population approve of him, with Republicans scarcely less enthusiastic than Democrats. Indeed, a member of my staff was told by a typical Republican that, after twelve years of happy indignation 'against that man in the White House, it was no fun being a Republican today'.

2. With only Ickes, Wallace,[2] Stimson and Forrestal[3] remaining of the former administration the new Cabinet equally appears to satisfy everyone: the Charter is universally approved. In the foreign field the usual undercurrent of ultimate distrust of the Soviet Union has been muffled. Other problems seem on the way to solution. *Time* magazine even wonders what the Big Three will find to discuss. Shortages of civilian goods, and labour strikes are so many flies in the ointment (Ickes delivered a severe public warning on the 5th July about the critical coal situation). They are not however felt to be as acute as they might have been and, to the general public, the restoration of peace-time economy seems almost round the corner. The problem of feeding Europe this winter is fully appreciated by the Administration, but is not sufficiently realised elsewhere to disturb the prevailing buoyantly optimistic mood. The only serious exception is the casualty list of the Pacific war—hence an increase of sentiment in favour of modifying, or at any rate clarifying, the concept of unconditional surrender of Japan (see paragraph 16 below).

The San Francisco Charter

3. The way to rapid and complete passage of the Charter seems to have been paved by the apparent crumbling of the opposition (more than two-thirds of the Senate have already in effect pledged themselves to support the Charter) and the press estimates that no more than five Senators are still unyielding opponents of it. Connally,[4] whose eloquence on the subject was largely taken for granted, said that he was aiming at ratification by the

---

[1] The first two paragraphs down to 'Japan' and other extracts from this summary are printed in *Washington Despatches 1941–1945*, ed. H. G. Nicholas (London, 1981), pp. 588–90.

[2] Mr. H. L. Ickes was U.S. Secretary of the Interior; Mr. H. A. Wallace, formerly Vice-President, was Secretary of Commerce.

[3] U.S. Secretary of the Navy.

[4] Senator T. T. Connally was the chairman, and Senator A. H. Vandenberg the senior Republican member, of the Senate Foreign Relations Committee.

1st August, but thought it might not take place until the 16th. The President hopes it may be earlier. Vandenberg[4] offered the Senate a meticulous commentary on the Charter, and pointed out that the issue about which he and his friends had felt the strongest doubts—the veto power of the Big Five[5]—was indispensable if only to protect the sovereign rights of the United States itself. Equally enthusiastic support of the Charter has been given by Stassen,[6] whose reputation was greatly enhanced at San Francisco. He declared that the Charter should ensure peace for at least half a century and mentioned that he had accepted Mr. Roosevelt's invitation to participate in the American delegation at some political risk to himself. The assembled Governors[7] have now unanimously declared approval of the Charter.

4. In the circumstances just mentioned, the passage of the Charter may be regarded as virtually assured. The debate may however last a fortnight largely to enable Senators to make speeches for home consumption—what Connally has contemptuously termed 'honey-swoggling'. Gromyko[8] has said that it would be impressive if the United States of America and the U.S.S.R. ratified the Charter at about the same time. British ratification is taken for granted. All this does not mean that we are necessarily altogether out of the wood since, however unlikely on present showing, the real debate may yet be staged on the question of the degree of military assistance due from this country to the organisation, and on the powers of the United States delegate, with particular reference to his authority to use American armed forces without a specific vote by the Senate. The motion to confer such powers (in this case on Stettinius) will be debated in both Houses as it is likely to be made the object of a Senate-House resolution i.e., subject to a simple majority vote of the entire Congress. In any case, these questions are unlikely to come up before the autumn.

5. The press and public are comparing the vast difference in mood between the troubled and divided Senate to which Wilson[9] addressed himself in 1919, and the warm-hearted reception of Truman's short speech endorsing the Charter. I am told that such disgruntled isolationists as still exist up and down the country are reluctant to risk the sharp unpopularity which an open protest would to-day bring down upon them, and consequently feel frustrated and relatively impotent. Unless the next few months see a serious deterioration of the situation in Europe, there is no reason for apprehending that the opponents of international collaboration will succeed in raising their heads in time to do serious damage to the United Nations organisation.

[5] The governments of the United Kingdom, United States, Soviet Union, France and China as permanent members of the Security Council of the United Nations (cf. Sir L. Woodward, *op. cit.*, vol. v, pp. 309–12).

[6] Commander H. E. Stassen had been a member of the American delegation at the San Francisco Conference.

[7] Governors of the states of the United States of America and of Hawaii and the Virgin Islands had met in annual conference on 2–4 July 1945 at Mackinac Island, Michigan.

[8] Soviet Ambassador to the United States and delegate to the San Francisco Conference.

[9] President Woodrow Wilson.

Cabinet Changes

6. According to a completely reliable source, Morgenthau's resignation from the Treasury was primarily due to his feeling of personal incompatibility with Byrnes. He is said to have demanded a showdown on his authority from the President, who thought it easier to let him go. His resignation was nowhere welcomed so much as in the State Department, which had for long resented his incursions into what it deemed its exclusive province. Indeed the news was said to have been greeted with dancing in the corridors, particularly outside Mr. Riddleberger's German Division. The press has given him a courteous but not enthusiastic series of obituaries. Morgenthau's departure may possibly mean the retirement or diminution in influence of Dr. Harry White, the principal American architect of the Bretton Woods scheme[10] which is itself sufficiently far advanced not to suffer excessively from whatever is in store for that none too easy official. The White House announced to-day that on his return from the Big Three meeting the President will nominate as Morgenthau's successor Judge Vinson, of whose personality a short appreciation was sent in paragraph 9 of my economic summary No. 139 Saving[11] at the time of his appointment to the post of War Mobiliser. (Further comments will follow.)

7. As might be expected there is now much talk of other Cabinet changes. Of the original New Deal Cabinet[12] only Wallace and Ickes remain, and the fate of the latter is thought to be very precarious, although it may depend in some degree on his success in the oil negotiations, to conduct which he is about to proceed to London. It is rumoured that Ickes may be succeeded by Pauley or by Krug of the War Production Board. The general trend in Cabinet changes has been to reward loyal party members, particularly Congressional leaders, and not to cast about too much for outside talent. The eyes of the public are incident[al]ly now fixed on Truman to see whether he appoints a liberal or a conservative to succeed the Republican Justice Roberts (the investigator of Teapot Dome and Pearl Harbour incidents),[13] who at the age of 70 is retiring in the ordinary way of routine from the Supreme Court.

Foreign Affairs. General

8. As reported in my Despatch No. 749,[14] the prevailing outlook can be summarised somewhat as follows: In Big Three relations American influence

[10] The agreements made at the United Nations Monetary and Financial Conference, held at Bretton Woods on 1–22 July 1944, providing for the establishment of an International Monetary Fund and International Bank for Reconstruction and Development, are annexed to the Final Act printed in Cmd. 6546 of 1944.

[11] Of 11 March 1945 (on UE 1162/42/53), not printed.

[12] The cabinet of President Roosevelt's first administration of 1933, which had promoted the reforming programme of the New Deal.

[13] Investigations into, respectively, the leasing of oil reserves at Teapot Dome in Wyoming in 1922, and the circumstances of the Japanese attack on Pearl Harbour in Hawaii on 7 December 1941.

[14] Of 3 July 1945 (on AN 2136/245/45), not printed.

will be exerted to prevent collisions between Great Britain and the Soviet Union i.e., the notion of the United States as mediator; in bilateral dealings with Britain a tough businesslike and 100% American line will be kept to the fore. Energy will be displayed in dealings with other Great Powers and a sharp eye kept on the supposed efforts of the wily foreigner to outmanoeuvre the United States. The acceptance speech of Byrnes with its stress on the need to live in peace with nations of a widely dissimilar outlook (written I am told by Ben Cohen[15]) sets the general tone of a policy designed to promote toleration and to avoid major crises.

9. In a written reply to Congressmen who had questioned the State Department on the 31st May about American foreign policy, Mr. Grew has declared that 'it can be stated unequivocally that *the* United States Government has no tacit understanding or day-to-day working arrangement through which it has become *de facto* or otherwise a part of an Anglo-American or any other front against the Soviet Union'. He added that 'conversely there is no truth in the assertions made by some that we are playing into the hands of the Soviet Union to the detriment of the British Empire or any other nation.' This communication also referred to the former foreign policy of President Roosevelt 'whereby the United States participated as an active force in all foreign questions involving American interests or policy'. Mr. Grew assured the Congressmen that President Truman is continuing the policy of the late President who 'used his influence and that of the United States as mediator in those questions which, although not directly affecting our interests, might disturb international harmony if allowed to remain unsolved'.[16]

Big Three meeting

10. Much is naturally expected from the meeting of the Big Three, in particular as regards European rehabilitation and the part of the Soviet

---

[15] Personal Assistant to Mr. Byrnes.

[16] Mr. N. M. Butler, an Assistant Under Secretary of State in the Foreign Office, who had recently visited Washington when returning from the San Francisco Conference, stated in a minute of 12 July 1945 on this telegram: 'Mr. Lippmann is an exponent of the need for his country to "mediate" between us and the Russians, and I took him to task over it last week, saying that we required no outside mediation between ourselves and our Ally, and that all the questions on which we had disputes with the Soviet Government were questions of principle in which the United States Government were as concerned as ourselves. Mr. Lippmann's retort was that as a matter of history there were a number of subjects affecting a territory roughly between Gibraltar and India in which we had traditionally quarrelled with Russia, and that it was in questions of this kind that it would be for his country to play the part of reconciler, and not to take sides. Lord Halifax said to President Truman, also last week, that he had noticed at San Francisco that if the Americans and we said the same thing to the Russians we generally ended by getting the right answer from Moscow. It is a hopeful sign that President Truman replied that he had noticed the same thing too. But in view of American ideas such as Mr. Lippmann's and fears of entanglement, it is important that if we have a dispute with Russia on which we need the support of the United States we should try to make it some question of principle, rather than over some individual, as in the case of Count Sforza and Italy'. This minute was initialed by Sir A. Cadogan on 13 July.

Union in the Far Eastern war. There is little speculation in the press so far as to the likelihood of Soviet belligerency, hopes that it may take place are to some degree inhibited by nervousness as to how this might affect United States relations with the Soviet Union in the Far East. Soong's visit to Moscow[17] has aroused keen speculation about the prospects of a Sino-Soviet Treaty and the possibility of bridging the dangerous rift between Chungking and Yenan. A 'Chinese Yalta' is demanded to prevent serious obstacles to Allied unity in the Far East, with deep perplexity in higher official circles as to what policy it is best to pursue, e.g. with regard to the degree of help to the various Chinese parties.

Germany

11. The problem of governing Germany engages much attention. The evidence of Mr. Crowley and Mr. Baruch[18] before the Military Affairs (Kilgore) Sub Committee of the Senate (see paragraph 9 of my telegram No. 4575)[19] has brought it home to the public that it would be wrong to assume that German industry has been destroyed beyond repair and does not need intensive and continuous control in the future. There is a continuing feeling that (. . . ?U.S.S.R.)[20] is managing its part of Germany more efficiently than the Anglo-Americans display in their portions of Germany. In this connexion Drew Pearson[21] and in particular the columnist Marquis Childs have drawn attention to an unpublished directive issued to General Eisenhower by the President with the agreement of the State, War and Treasury Departments, and declare that it is so masterly and clear as to warrant immediate publication in order to allay American criticisms of the alleged dilly-dallying of American civil occupation authorities in Germany.

12. Lippmann plumps for an enforced decentralisation of Germany into its traditional i.e. pre-Bismarckian component states. He thinks that Germany will have to be dismembered in any case to meet the requirement of her Western neighbours and Poland and that the grievances of German nationalists will not be materially increased by a partition of the Reich itself, which would have the advantage of at once destroying the evil influence of Berlin and of putting an end to the dangerous doctrine that people of the same language have a claim to be integrated into a single political state.

Interest of the U.S.S.R. in European Problems

13. No particular suspicion has greeted Soviet interest in the Straits and Tangier, and singularly little attention has been paid to the transfer of

[17] On 30 June 1945 Dr. T. V. Soong, Chinese Foreign Minister and Acting President of the Executive Yuan, had arrived in Moscow for negotiations with the Soviet Government for a treaty of friendship on behalf of Generalissimo Chiang Kai-shek's Nationalist (Kuomintang) Government at Chungking (cf. No. 383). A rival Chinese administration had been set up by the Chinese communist party at Yenan.

[18] Mr. B. M. Baruch had been official adviser to Mr. Byrnes when Director of War Mobilisation, 1943–1944.

[19] Not printed.

[20] The text is here uncertain.

[21] A political columnist in Washington.

Ruthenia and the dispute over Teschen. There is a general tendency, to some extent encouraged by the highest quarters, to believe that whatever they portend in the long run Russian claims to be heard on problems of the Western Mediterranean are to be welcomed at the present time if only because they appear to justify an analogous United States interest in Eastern European questions. The Hearst and McCormick newspapers[22] continue their anti-Russian campaign and basic nervousness about the U.S.S.R. has not decreased. In a recent article in the 'Saturday Evening Post' Demaree Bess[23] preaches the thesis that the Russians respond best to toughness and that a firm line is probably the healthiest method of ensuring peaceful relations with them. This is not however a view which appears at present to be at all widespread in Administration circles. The liberal Chicago publisher Marshall Field recently told a British official that he had been horrified to discover that his normally Anglophile east coast friends were bitterly complaining that Britain intended to manoeuvre the United States of America into war with the Soviet Union and that they would die rather than permit this to happen. Although somewhat gullible, Marshall Field probably accurately voices the views of others like himself.

Poland

14. The recognition of the Warsaw Government seems to have been greeted with considerable relief and few tears—most[ly] crocodile ones at that—are being shed for the London Poles. The late Polish Ambassador is about to address a farewell press conference in which he will doubtless pour out his heart. A last minute attempt to sell or transfer the Polish Embassy in Washington to an American-Polish Society to prevent it from falling into the hands of the Warsaw Government was foiled by a war-time statute forbidding such transfers without United States Treasury permission. Jests are circulating that the Polish Ambassador may take it into his head to sell all objects labelled 'Polish' to his friends—e.g. the 'Polish Desk' in the State Department and the like.

Far East

15. Senator Capehart, a political tubthumper from Indiana, has stirred up discussion about peace terms for Japan by asserting that he had heard from an unimpeachable administration source that about a month ago Japan had made a definite offer of conditional surrender which the State Department had kept from Congress and the public. After a denial by Grew, Capehart asserted that it was nevertheless the truth. His general thesis was that unconditional surrender was not necessarily the best weapon for compassing Japan's downfall, and that conditions existed and could be formulated on which the United States could and should be prepared to end the Japanese war. His views, echoed by Senator White of Maine, the Republican

[22] Mr. Randolph Hearst was editor and proprietor of the Hearst press whose publications included the *Chicago Herald-American*, *New York Journal* and *San Francisco Examiner*. Mr. Robert McCormick was editor and publisher of *The Chicago Tribune*.

[23] War correspondent and associate editor of the *Saturday Evening Post*.

minority leader and by two Republican representatives, clearly represent those of at any rate a section of the Republicans in Congress as well as of United States soldiers back from the Pacific, including men of proven mettle and high rank.

16. A fairly strong trend against the purely unqualified 'unconditional surrender' formula is thus now under way, assisted by demands for clarification by such commentators as Swing. Senator Barkley, majority leader, enquired whether Senator White favoured a declaration of United States terms without prior consultation with at any rate Britain, a partner in the Pacific war. White gave him no clear reply, merely observing that he left a final decision to the good judgment of the President. Of the Left-Wing press Drew Pearson and others continue to assert that Grew and his friends in fact favour a 'soft' peace with Japan, preservation of the Mikado and so forth, and that only unwavering watchfulness by the American people can prevent a 'sell-out'. There has so far been no public pronouncement from any official source to guide uncertain but on the whole anti-Mikado public opinion. On the 5th July Krock[24] analysed the arguments for and against preserving the Mikado and spoke of the necessity for an authoritative decision which the public can do nothing to promote. Other sources also testify to a deep division of opinion between the two contending schools of thought, and there is said to be a good deal of rumbling on this topic among American soldiers. Even Lippmann warns against suicidal slaughter. Curiously enough Britain has so far not been used as an Aunt Sally in this connexion.

France

17. Widely divergent attitudes prevail about France. The Administration i.e. the White House and State Department, seem clearly anxious to be as friendly as possible to the French Government. Welles has complained of American apathy towards France and of the false impression conveyed by giving Britain a *carte blanche* in the Levant. He criticises de Gaulle and looks on Herriot[25] as a true representative of that French democracy which the United States should attempt to understand more sympathetically. Warmth for France is not displayed in the Senate where there is a mood of scorn for the French largely due to the contemptuous accounts of their defeatism and cynicism brought back by visiting Congressmen. The Senate War Investigating Committee has furthermore reported 'a tendency on the part of the army to lose interest in France, in French industry, in French transportation and in French rehabilitation', with the result that Germany is being restored more rapidly and effectively than France. The general public takes little interest in France, or indeed in her difficulties in the Levant and elsewhere. The 'New Republic' has published an article severely critical of British policy in Syria and Lebanon.

[24] Mr. Arthur Krock, an American journalist.
[25] M. Edouard Herriot, a former French Prime Minister, was President of the Radical Socialist party.

Latin America

18. The press continues to expose the excesses of the Argentine Government, principally in stories by Mr. Newman of the *New York Herald Tribune* and Mr. Cortesi of the *New York Times*. Now that the Rockefeller policy seems to the public in effect disavowed, the press and liberal opinion generally feels at liberty to shake a fist at Argentine Fascism, fulminations against which had to some extent been restrained by previous turns of United States policy and the prestige of Chapultepec.[26] A back to Hull movement now appears to be under way.[27] Addressing delegates attending the New York State Institute of Community Service, Franklin Johnson, editor of the American Exporter, declared that Latin America and not the Soviet Union or China would prove to be America's greatest post-war export market.

Savingram subjects

19. This week's supplementary savingram[28] contains

    (1) Appointment of Mr. Byrnes as Secretary of State and changes in the United States foreign service,

    (2) Un-American activities,

    (3) British elections,

    (4) Fair treatment of negroes,

    (5) India,

    (6) Presidential succession.

20. Foreign Office please repeat saving to His Majesty's Ambassadors Moscow and Cairo and High Commissioner Rome.

---

[26] The succession of Mr. Stettinius to Mr. Cordell Hull as U.S. Secretary of State in December 1944 and the appointment of Mr. Nelson Rockefeller as Under-Secretary of State in charge of Latin American affairs had been equated with some prospective modification of policy in regard to the then unrecognised Argentine Government under President E. J. Farrell. On 27 March 1945 Argentina had declared war on Germany and Japan, and on 4 April adhered to the Act of Chapultepec, a declaration on reciprocal assistance and American solidarity approved on 6 March 1945 at the Inter-American Conference held at Mexico City: cf. *Final Act of the Inter-American Conference on problems of war and peace* (Washington, 1945), pp. 40–4. On 9 April the United Kingdom and the United States had resumed diplomatic relations with Argentina.

[27] Mr. N. Butler further stated in his minute of 12 July 1945: 'Lord Halifax was not at all happy about the Argentine situation, fearing some incident any day that might set off the strong anti-Argentine feeling in the United States. I do not, however, think that the trend is quite correctly described as a "back to Hull movement". I found fairly widespread feeling that though the Stettinius/Rockefeller policy was all wrong, Mr. Hull also had made a considerable mess of things, and roused great unpopularity for the United States in Latin America without achieving any positive results.'

[28] This Washington telegram No. 355 Saving of even date is not here printed; for (1) below see *Washington Despatches 1941–45, ed. cit.,* pp. 586–8.

No. 43

Letter from Field-Marshal Sir B. Montgomery (Bad Oeynhausen)
to Mr. Eden (Received 11 July)[1]
[C 3787/24/18]

HEADQUARTERS, 21 ARMY GROUP, 8 July 1942 [1945]

My dear Eden

    Will you please read this paper: after which you can, if you wish, destroy it!

But please read it first.

Yrs. sincerely,
B. L. MONTGOMERY

ENCLOSURE IN No. 43

British Zone: Notes on the Present Situation by Field-Marshal Montgomery

Top Secret   *6 July 1945*

1. Two months have now passed since Germany surrendered and the country passed to the control of the Allied Nations.

During these two months the full extent of the debacle has become apparent; we now know the magnitude of the problem that confronts us in the rebuilding of Germany.

2. The coming winter will be a critical time. In the British Zone there will be a shortage of food, a very definite shortage of coal, inadequate services of transportation and distribution, and insufficient accommodation. Northwest Europe is very cold in the winter; the average temperature is freezing and heavy falls of snow are frequent; under such conditions people want food and warmth, and they are likely to lack both.

3. There are some 20 million German civilians in the British Zone, besides many thousands of displaced persons of other nations. There are some 2 million men of the German armed forces awaiting discharge to civil life; amongst these are many thousand ardent Nazis, who cannot possibly be discharged.

The influence of the discharged soldier when he gets back to his home is an unknown factor; there are grounds for thinking it may be anti-British.

There is much looting and sabotage being carried out by the displaced persons.

There is communist propaganda going on.

4. It is clear from paras 2 and 3 that there is much fertile soil for the seeds of trouble.

The great mass of 20 million people in the British Zone are in for a hard time this

---

[1] This manuscript letter was transmitted by Sir W. Strang under cover of the following minute of 9 July 1945 to Mr. Eden: 'Field-Marshal Montgomery gave me the annexed paper for you when I saw him yesterday afternoon. He has also sent a copy to the Secretary of State for War. I have given copies to the Department. From what I saw and heard during my tour of the British Zone last week, I can confirm the general lines of the Field-Marshal's paper. I have come to London with General Weeks to get instructions on the questions of food and fuel for Berlin, about which there will be another meeting with the Russians and Americans in Berlin tomorrow.'

winter; they are apprehensive about food, about housing, and about the general unsettled conditions.

The best way to counteract this fear is to give them 'hope'.

5. It is clear that we must tackle the 'battle of the winter' energetically, and we must win it; if we lost it, we would compromise the future.

We require a good short term plan to take us through the winter: this must be closely linked to the long term plan for the complete restoration of the economic life of Germany.

6. There are certain factors which are going to have a great bearing on the issue. These are outlined below (paras 8 to 18).

In my opinion they are basic and fundamental; they deal with the human factor and to neglect that factor will be to risk failure.

They are not points on which we can compromise; nor must there be any delay.

7. I think some of our troubles are due to a tendency to adhere rigidly to SHAEF instructions issued previously; many of these instructions are now out of date.

The only sure way to success is to take each case on its merits, to consider carefully the factors involved, and to decide on a method suitable to the occasion.

We require a broad general directive; the problem is too complex for rigid instructions.

In cases where we have not authority to act ourselves at once, we must get the necessary authority quickly.

Compromise and delay are dangerous.

Propaganda and Information

8. The German people have had National Socialism, and Nazi doctrines, pumped into them for many years; they have become receptive to propaganda.

Suddenly it all ceased; now they have nothing; their minds are blank, and something must fill the void.

They are hungry for information; we must give it to them, mixed with good and officially inspired propaganda.

By means of Hamburg radio and other stations, by newspapers, and by the cinemas, we must get propaganda and information across to the people.

9. In particular they must be told our policy, and what is going to happen to their country.

A good start could be made by taking my Personal Message of 30 May[2] and explaining, subject by subject, the detail of how it is being done and what progress has been made.

We could explain the various problems of Military Government, and the steps we are taking to solve them.

10. The vital point is that we must get this started at once; very energetic action is required, and must be forthcoming.

Meetings and Trade Unions

11. I consider the people should be allowed to hold meetings in towns and villages to discuss their problems, and generally to set on foot measures to help themselves.

At present meetings are forbidden unless permission is first obtained.

[2] Printed in *The Times* of 31 May 1945, p. 4.

The result of this policy will be that meetings will be held in secret, and once that starts great harm may follow.

I see no harm in letting the people discuss political matters.

I would let the people meet and discuss what they like; all Nazi matter being forbidden; we can keep in touch by sending agents to attend meetings occasionally.

12. I consider we should allow Trades Unions to be formed; they may be useful to us, and will give us some authority with which to deal in case of necessity. Our general attitude towards Trades Unions should be one of benevolent neutrality.

13. In general I consider we should let the people get down to their own life, and talk things over amongst themselves. We can keep in touch with what is going on, and can quickly stamp on anything dangerous.

Non-Fraternisation

14. We cannot resuscitate Germany without the help of the people themselves; we cannot re-educate 20 million people if we are never to speak to them.

15. We crossed the Rhine on 23 March and for nearly four months we have not spoken to the German population, except when duty has so demanded. The Germans have been told why we have acted thus; it has been a shock to them and they have learnt their lesson.

16. To continue this policy is merely to make our own task very difficult, if not impossible.

17. I consider that the ban on fraternisation should be lifted at once.

Fraternisation should be discouraged, but not forbidden.

Commanders-in-Chief should be given a free hand to decide the best methods of applying this general directive.[3]

18. At present the policy of the various Allies is not even the same.

In the Russian Zone an officer or man is allowed to speak to and mix with civilians; in the British Zone he is tried by court-martial for so doing.

The Allies must all adopt the same policy.

General

19. The nett result of paras 8 to 18 is that we get to work quickly on the human material involved in this problem; it is my opinion that until we do this we shall gain no success: indeed we may well fail.

20. There are two other matters.

I give them separately below, as they are not concerned with the human factor. But we want some guidance about them.

One Germany, or Two

21. At present there is free circulation in that part of Germany occupied by the western Allies, with freedom of movement by land and air, and free interchange of information.

22. The western Allies cannot enter the Russian Zone except by previous agreement; there is no freedom of movement by land or air for us in that zone; there is no free interchange of information.

There is in fact a complete 'wall' between the Russian Zone and the Zones of the western Allies.

---

[3] Cf. No. 30, note 7.

23. The Russians have altered the guage of the railways as far west as Berlin, and will presumably do so right up to the Elbe: in due course.

24. All this makes it difficult to see how Germany is ever going to become one economic whole under a supreme organ of control. In fact it cannot ever become so as long as the present conditions obtain.

Central German Ministries

25. I consider it is essential to set up a number of essential German ministries in Berlin; we can do this without in any way committing ourselves to what extent we shall use them when they are formed. We must begin to re-establish civil control from the top, and for this we shall need the German ministries; at present we are re-establishing civil control only from below: by military government.[4]

B. L. MONTGOMERY
Field-Marshal
C-in-C, British Zone.

Germany, 6-7-45

CALENDARS TO NO. 43

i *10 July 1945 Letter from Sir R. Bruce Lockhart (Deputy Under-Sec. of State and Director-General of Political Warfare Executive) to Mr. Harvey enclosing minute of 9 July* on difficulties over British information services in Germany, with reference to No. 43 above. Minutes by Mr. Harvey and Mr. Eden on proposed action [C 4048/23/18].

ii *14 July 1945 Field-Marshal Montgomery: Notes on the present situation* in the British Zone in Germany. Refers to No. 43 and outlines plans for rehabilitating the mentality of the German people; desirability of accord with the Americans [C 4673/24/18].

iii *6 & 20 July 1945 Tels. Nos. 7195 & 7664 to Lord Halifax (Washington).* Political Warfare Directives (European Theatre). Information and publicity to Germany and Austria [C 49/47/18].

---

[4] Mr. Pierson Dixon, Private Secretary to Mr. Eden, minuted on this paper on 10 July: 'Seen by the S[ecretary] of S[tate], who is in general agreement with F. M. Montgomery's views & proposals, though he feels some doubt about para. 11 (meetings).'

No. 44

Brief for the United Kingdom Delegation to the Conference at Potsdam
No. 34 [F.O. 934/6]

FOREIGN OFFICE, 8 July 1945[1]

Displaced Persons in Germany

A. *Preamble*

1. In any top level discussion between the three Great Powers about inter-Allied policy and machinery as regards Germany, the question of displaced persons is pretty sure to crop up.

---

[1] Date of agreement of the text of this undated brief.

2. By far the larger number of displaced persons in Germany belonging to Western European countries (France, Belgium and Holland) either have already been or very shortly will be repatriated direct through the agency of the Allied military authorities. They present no problem.

3. The major continuing problem is that of displaced persons in Germany coming from Eastern and South Eastern Europe (Russia, Poland, the former Baltic States and Yugoslavia).

B. The Soviet Attitude

4. The Soviet Government may be expected to press (under the Yalta Agreement of February 11th)[2] for the return from Germany of all Soviet citizens displaced in Germany and to include in their claim
    (*a*) inhabitants of the former Baltic States and Bessarabia.
    (*b*) inhabitants of former Polish territory east of the Curzon Line.

5. The bulk of both categories (*a*) and (*b*) above are unlikely to wish to be handed over to the Soviet authorities.

6. The Warsaw Government are understood to wish for the return of displaced Poles from Germany. Their claim is likely to be put forward by the Soviet Government. Large numbers of these Poles will be unwilling to return in present circumstances.

7. A similar situation may very likely arise in respect of displaced Yugoslavs in Germany.

C. Role of UNRRA

8. In theory, all those displaced persons from Allied countries (and also displaced persons of ex-enemy origin who have been victimised on grounds of race, religion or pro-United Nations activities) come within the ambit of UNRRA whose task is to repatriate them or return them to their homes as soon as practicable and to give them relief meanwhile.

9. UNRRA is not authorised to undertake these tasks except (*a*) at the invitation of the Government of the country of origin and (*b*) with the consent of the authorities of the territory where the displaced persons actually are. It cannot repatriate until it is satisfied that the country of origin is ready and able to receive the displaced persons concerned. Nor can it repatriate displaced persons against their will.

10. UNRRA's operations in Germany should in theory be subject to overriding control by the Allied Control Commission.

11. The Soviet Government have informed the European Advisory Commission that they will not admit UNRRA into the Soviet zone in

[2] This Anglo-Soviet Agreement relating to prisoners of war and civilians liberated by British and by Soviet forces is printed in *The Daily Telegraph* of 13 February 1945, p. 3, and in *B.F.S.P.*, vol. 147, pp. 1047–51. Also on 11 February were signed an identic American-Soviet Agreement, *mutatis mutandis* (printed *op. cit.*, vol. 149, pp. 934–7), and a secret Anglo-Soviet Agreement relating to the position of liberated Soviet citizens in the United Kingdom (text on U 1206/2/74 of 1945): cf. *The Times* of 13 February 1945, p. 3, also Order in Council No. 166: the Allied Forces (Union of Soviet Socialist Republics) of 22 February 1945.

Germany nor agree to UNRRA handling displaced Soviet citizens in the other Allied zones.

12. It has been accepted that UNRRA should handle displaced persons (other than Soviet citizens) in the United Kingdom, the United States and French zones: in each zone UNRRA's operations will be subject to overriding control by the Commander-in-Chief.

13. It should be added that it may be impossible for UNRRA to undertake this work at all unless it can be given the experienced and high-ranking Officers for whom it has asked to direct its operations. In that event the burden of displaced persons will fall back on the authorities of each zone.

D. Existing Policy

14. No difficulty of principle exists in handing over to the Soviet authorities persons coming under (a) and (b) of paragraph 4 who make no objection.

15. Persons coming under those categories who object to being handed over have been segregated from those who do not object and retained under the control of SCAEF.

16. Similarly, Poles who object to returning to Poland in present conditions are at present being retained east of the Rhine under the control of SCAEF.

17. Where Poles or Balts have been found in territory liberated by forces under the command of SCAEF but falling within the Soviet occupation zone, they are being discreetly withdrawn before SCAEF's forces evacuate. This course was agreed with the United States Government on the latter's initiative and had in fact been already initiated by SCAEF on his own responsibility.

18. In general, it is our policy to regard all persons displaced owing to the war as ultimately repatriable (pending the taking of final decisions on this point at some later date when all relevant factors can be assessed). While such persons should be safeguarded from forcible repatriation prematurely, they should not be encouraged to take up an attitude now which might prejudice their chances of being able to return in more hopeful circumstances later. This view has been impressed on our military authorities and on UNRRA.

E. Recommendations

19. It is not in our interest to raise the problem of displaced persons in Germany, but we must be prepared to discuss it since the Soviet Government will almost certainly raise it.

20. Broadly speaking, the sooner displaced persons can be repatriated in an orderly manner, the better.

21. We should maintain the principle that all displaced persons should be encouraged to return to their homes and we should take such steps as possible to see that meanwhile they are not exposed to propaganda in the contrary sense. It is however an essential preliminary of their reapatriation [sic] that conditions should be such that they can return safely and without prejudice to their future existence.

22. The Yalta Agreement of February 11th ought not to be construed as compelling the return of displaced persons (other than those who were undoubtedly Soviet citizens before the outbreak of the war) forthwith to territories now occupied by or conceded as justifiably claimed by the Soviet Union which were not Soviet territory prior to the war. Decision on this point might reasonably be postponed till after the final territorial settlement.

23. In the meantime we should not admit any Soviet contention that their objection to UNRRA caring for Soviet displaced persons in Germany extends to such persons: otherwise a heavy burden would be placed on the occupying authorities.

24. It should on general grounds be our policy to ensure that UNRRA (within the limits set by the Soviet attitude as recorded in paragraphs 11 and 12 above) should be enabled to relieve the occupying authorities of the task of caring for and executing the repatriation of displaced persons within its mandate: and that for this purpose we should help it to enlist the right people to carry out the job effectively.

CALENDARS TO NO. 44

i *8 July 1945 General Eisenhower (S.H.A.E.F.) to Field-Marshal Montgomery (21st Army Group), General O. Bradley (12th Army Group, Wiesbaden), General J. L. Devers (6th Army Group, Heidelberg), Commanding General Communications Zone (Paris) Tel. No. S.96030.* Civilians displaced through war who were uncovered by Allied Expeditionary Forces (A.E.F.) since 11 Feb. 1945 and who are held to be Soviet citizens will not be permitted option as to whether or not they desire to be repatriated [N 8459/409/38].

ii *14 July 1945 Combined Chiefs of Staff to Field-Marshal Sir H. Alexander (Caserta) Tel. No. FAN 595.* Should inform Soviet representative that disposal of Soviet citizens will continue to be in accordance with Yalta agreements; but should not inform him that Latvians, Estonians, Lithuanians and Poles from east of 1939 demarcation-line or of Curzon line will not be repatriated to Soviet Union unless they claim Soviet citizenship [N 8459/409/38].

iii *9 July 1945 Memo. by Mr. Galsworthy on the Andronov case, and minutes thereon.* Mr. P. Dean and Mr. T. Brimelow propose (10 July) to allow this family to remain in U.K.: approved by Mr. Eden: 'All right. Keep the family. But delay our answer as long as we can so that we can get as many of our people out as we can. I have some fear of reprisals. A. E. July 13' (cited, N. Bethell, *The Last Secret*—revised ed. 1976—p. 77) [N 8811/409/38].

No. 45

Brief for the United Kingdom Delegation to the Conference at Potsdam No. 15 [F.O. 934/6]

FOREIGN OFFICE, *8 July 1945*[1]

Poland (Outstanding Questions)

The only Polish question under this heading which we may wish to take

[1] Date on which the draft (on N 8388/6/55) of this undated brief was initialed by Mr. Warner.

the initiative in raising is that of the right of Polish Political Parties to take part in elections in Poland. At the time of our recognition of the Polish Provisional Government of National Unity in Warsaw we informed the Soviet and United States Governments that we were not satisfied with the assurances which we had so far received from the Poles on this question and reserved the right to raise it at Terminal as affecting the implementation of the Crimea decisions. The Polish Provisional Government were informed that we had made this communication to the Soviet and United States Governments.[2]

The Polish Government in London and the underground movement owing allegiance to it in Poland have throughout the war been based upon four main Parties:– National Democrat Party, Christian Labour Party, Peasant Party, Socialist Party.

The Lublin Committee (later 'Provisional Government') was based nominally upon a similar coalition consisting of: Democratic Party, Peasant Party, Socialist Party, Polish Workers Party (Communist). The present Provisional Government of National Unity is still based upon these same four Parties, although the representation of the Peasant and Socialist Parties has been considerably strengthened and made more genuinely representative of the Parties as a whole. The National Democrat and Christian Labour Parties are not at present represented in the Provisional Government of National Unity.

At the time of the Crimea Conference and since we have always hoped that it might be possible for all the main political parties to be brought into the new Provisional Government of National Unity, though realising that in the case of the National Democratic Party at least this might be difficult. In the House of Commons on the 28th February 1945 the Secretary of State declared 'It (the new Government) must be, [or] as far as it can be made, representative of all the Polish parties as they are known and include representative national Polish figures'.[3] M. Mikolajczyk in his original list of candidates proposed after the Crimea Conference for the consultations in Moscow (but not necessarily for inclusion in the new Government) five National Democrats as well as five representatives of each of the other three Parties in the London Government coalition. He has always expressed the view that certain National Democrat leaders such as Trampczynski were respectable democratic leaders untainted by any suggestion of collaboration,[4] or anti-Russianism. But neither he nor anyone else has any doubt that the right wing of the party is violently anti-Russian (it left the Sikorski Govern-

---

[2] See No. 6.

[3] See *Parl. Debs.*, *5th ser.*, *H. of C.*, vol. 408, col. 1505, which did not include the word 'all' above.

[4] The rest of this paragraph, and the last three paragraphs of this brief, were marked on the draft by Mr. Warner for omission if a copy were given to the American Delegation at Potsdam.

ment over the Stalin-Sikorski Agreement[5]) and reactionary, and has been involved in anti-Russian and anti-Yalta propaganda and activities here and in Poland.

As we have now recognised the new Government in which two of the main Parties are not represented, it becomes all the more important to ensure that those Parties shall at least enjoy 'the right to take part and to put forward candidates' in the elections as 'democratic and anti-Nazi Parties' in accordance with the Crimea decision.[6] There may be criticism in this country if the elections turn out to be merely a coupon election organised by the existing Government block with no effective opposition.

Shortly before our recognition of the new Government, Sir Archibald Clark Kerr obtained from the Polish Ambassador in Moscow assurances in writing that the Government coalition 'leaves freedom of choice to the former elements of the democratic Christian Labour Parties which are democratic and anti-Nazi to take part in the elections or in any other way'. The Ambassador's communication[7] stated, however, that the National Democratic Party no longer existed in its pre-war form. In an oral communication to Sir Archibald Clark Kerr the Polish Ambassador stated that the Democratic and Christian Labour Parties would 'have complete freedom of action in regard to the elections and in all other respects'. The Polish Ambassador also indicated that political leaders who wished to start or revive other Democratic Parties would be free to do so and that such Parties would participate in the election either independently or in blocks as they saw fit.

M. Popiel, the leader of the Christian Labour Party, has recently left for Warsaw to discuss co-operation with the new Government at their invitation; but they have made, so far as we know no move toward any National Democrats. It looks from the statements quoted in the immediately preceding paragraph as if the intention of the new Government were to dissolve the National Democrats, but to allow the formation of new parties.

There appears to be no prospect of elections in the near future and the situation may have much changed before any are held.

The United States Government have given no signs of concerning themselves with this matter.

We have of course a right to take it up with the United States and Soviet Governments as covering the fulfilment of the Crimea Decisions; but the Russians are likely to take the line that it is a matter which we should discuss with the new Polish Government. It might be well, if Mr. Hankey reaches

---

[5] M. A. Zaleski, Foreign Minister, and other Ministers resigned from the Polish Government in exile under General W. Sikorski within a month of the signature on 30 July 1941 by General Sikorski and M. Maisky, then Soviet Ambassador in London, of a Soviet-Polish Agreement for mutual aid: printed in *B.F.S.P.*, vol. 144, p. 869. On 4 December 1941 General Sikorski and Marshal Stalin signed in Moscow a declaration of friendship and mutual assistance (*op. cit.*, p. 873).

[6] In the declaration on Poland issued as article VII of the protocol of the proceedings of the Conference at Yalta: see No. 30, note 2.

[7] Of 4 July 1945, not printed: cf. No. 6, note 2.

Warsaw in time, to learn through him M. Mikolajczyk's views on the subject before doing so.

No. 46

Mr. Houstoun-Boswall[1] *(Sofia) to Mr. Eden (Received 9 July, 7.20 p.m.)*
No. 791 Telegraphic [R 11691/3168/67]

SOFIA, *9 July 1945, 4.10 p.m. G.M.T.*

Repeated to Bucharest, Belgrade, Budapest, Resmed's Office (Caserta) No. 85, Istanbul (Constantinople) No. 89.

I have read with amazement in the first leading article (agreement on Poland) in the '*Times*' of June 25th the following sentences:

'The suspicion entertained in some quarters that Russia will be concerned with the political complexion of the new government is not borne out by what has happened in other countries of Eastern Europe;'.

If this was written in good faith, (and the '*Times*' had no correspondent here) it would, I suggest, be a good thing to enlighten or regard the facts of the situation.

2. Such a gross mis-statement in a journal which is apt to be regarded by foreigners as an official organ of His Majesty's Government, can surely only serve

(*a*) to encourage the Russians smugly to pursue their present policy of raining [*sic*] from behind the scenes a sort of 'holy war' against the principles of western democracy;

(*b*) to render even more difficult than it will be anyway, the direct negotiations of His Majesty's Government at the forthcoming meeting of the Big Three in dealing with the internal situation of ex-satellite countries (Intel No. 53[A])[2];

(*c*) to mislead British public opinion, with the result that His Majesty's Government may be deprived of that support to which they are entitled in conducting foreign affairs;

(*d*) to make things no easier for British representatives in the Balkan countries.[3]

---

[1] Mr. W. E. Houstoun-Boswall was British Political Representative in Bulgaria.

[2] Not printed.

[3] In a minute of 11 July 1945 on this telegram Mr. D. L. Stewart of the Southern Department of the Foreign Office expressed his understanding that Mr. Eden was proposing to speak that afternoon to the Editor of *The Times* on the lines of the telegram; it was also being suggested that Mr. Eden should show the Editor a copy of No. 47 below: 'It is to be hoped, therefore, that after this *The Times* will overcome their reluctance to face facts'.

No. 47

Sir A. Clark Kerr (Moscow) to Mr. Eden (Received 9 July, 9.45 p.m.)

No. 3031 Telegraphic [R 11702/3/19]

Important   MOSCOW, 9 July 1945, 7.5 p.m. G.M.T.

Your telegram No. 3752[1] paragraph 3 and paragraph 4.

I welcome this news because it is dangerous for public opinion to be left uninformed of what is going on in South East Europe, and because experience seems to show that the Soviet Government are not wholly insensitive to sustained pressure from governments and public opinion abroad, and more particularly to informed and objective criticism in newspapers normally well disposed to Soviet Union.

2. It seems to me desirable that publicity should not confine itself to the position in individual countries, but should also bring out under-lying pattern of developments throughout the area under Soviet influence, which though flexible is nevertheless clearly recognisable.

3. Among these are tendency for police to be under control of a Communist Minister of the Interior or Public Security as the case may be; control of publicity; organisation of youth movements on totalitarian lines; conception of trades unions as instruments for rallying workers behind the government...[2] specific....[2] Government nomination of executive committees of trades union confederations; attempt to undermine independent peasant parties; and news blackout. These and several other points of similarity are all false-hoods of scene with which the outside world is unfamiliar and on which the Soviet Government is likely to prove sensitive.

4. Technique used with considerable effect by Soviet press is to quote telling extracts from foreign press. The Soviet press and press in the countries

---

[1] This telegram of 4 July 1945 (not printed) had instructed Sir A. Clark Kerr to 'speak strongly to Soviet Government in the following sense: we have been increasingly concerned at the criticism which has been allowed to appear in the Soviet press not only in respect of the Greek Government and of British policy, but also in respect of the conduct of General Scobie and of British troops in Greece, which we particularly resent and emphatically reject, as we do also the allegation that His Majesty's Government have infringed the Crimea decisions . . . . Tass correspondent in Athens . . . has to our knowledge sent reports which are totally incorrect as to facts.   3. For your own information it is probable that articles will appear shortly in the British press which will contain fairly strong criticism of Russian policy in Bulgaria and Roumania. It is important that our protest about Soviet press should be made before these articles appear, since the Soviet Government might otherwise claim that we are launching a press campaign against them at the very moment when we are asking them to moderate the tone of their own press . . . .   4. If opportunity arise matter might subsequently be raised at Big Three Meeting in the hope of reaching agreement for cessation of press criticism on both sides.' On 6 July Sir A. Clark Kerr wrote to M. Molotov and took the matter up orally with him on 11 July.

[2] The text is here uncertain.

concerned contain much material bearing on the points in my immediately preceding paragraph and I suggest the same technique might with advantage be used by British press. I shall continue to draw your attention to suitable items in Soviet press.

5. I assume that critical articles foreshadowed in paragraph 3 of your telegram under reference will be based on material normally available to the press, and that they will not appear in such a form as to give the Soviet Government a reply to the accusation of His Majesty's Government of inspiring a hostile press campaign.

6. While I have every sympathy with the objective in your paragraph 4 I cannot help feeling that any such proposal would take us into very deep waters. The Soviet Government would naturally interpret it as implying admission that His Majesty's Government can effectively control the press, which we have hitherto always denied. Even if we could, we should then be committed to participating in news blackout in Eastern Europe, against which we have protested so strongly, and which there is now some hope of lifting. Finally, we should lay ourselves open to charges of bad faith if individual British newspapers refused to come into line as seems only too likely. I hope therefore that we shall continue to concentrate our efforts upon

(a) Getting correspondents into Eastern Europe with full facilities to report and,

(b) Protesting against inaccurate and unfair comment in the Soviet press.[3]

CALENDARS TO No. 47

i *7 July 1945 Mr. H. Caccia (Athens) Tel. No. 127 Saving:* marked increase in Russian propaganda; founding of a Greek-Soviet League; British Council should receive all support [R 11703/3/19].

ii *15–24 July 1945 Sir A. Clark Kerr (Moscow) Tel. No. 3137. To Mr. Eden (Berlin) Tel. No. 177 Onward.* Soviet Govt. rejects grounds for British representations of 6 July (see No. 47, note 1), and draws attention to recent anti-Soviet speeches in Greece. Mr. Churchill minuted on 19 July 'F.O. What is the truth?' Reply of 23 July from Athens [R 11932/3/19; F.O. 934/1/1 (7 & 17)].

iii *17 July 1945 Mr. Gascoigne (Budapest) No. 182* (without enclosure). British publicity in Hungary. Strong desire of Hungarian officials for early renewal of cultural relations with Britain [LC 3155/1766/452].

[3] In reply Foreign Office telegram No. 3911 of 13 July 1945 to Moscow stated that the articles mentioned in paragraph 5 above should fulfil the requirements specified in paragraphs 2, 3 and 5 above. Telegram No. 3911 to Moscow added: 'On reflection, I agree that we should not proceed upon the lines of paragraph 4 of my telegram No. 3752 . . . . The question of entry of correspondents into Russian-controlled territories and of securing facilities for free reporting when they get there is on the agenda for Terminal.'

No. 48

Mr. Le Rougetel[1] *(Bucharest) to Mr. Eden (Received 10 July, 1.55 a.m.)*
No. 698 Telegraphic [R 12473/4698/67]

Important   BUCHAREST, *9 July 1945, 10.45 p.m. G.M.T.*

Following from Air Vice-Marshal Stevenson for Permanent Under Secretary War Office.[2]

My RAC 1,811/1254, Elfu 134[3] and Le Rougetel's telegram No. 689.[4]

It will have been clear from general trend of events as reported in our telegrams and conclusion of economic agreement between Russia and Roumania[5] under which formation Russo-Roumanian combines on a 50–50 basis in most leading industries in the country particularly in oil—are planned, that unless we are prepared to take a definite initiative in the very near future either by negotiating a treaty of peace or otherwise, British interests will certainly be destroyed in this country and with them will go all effectiv[e] British influence. So far as we here are able to judge there is no reason why by careful planning and determined action we should not even now succeed in averting such an act of surrender.

2. Broadly speaking our interests in Roumania may be divided into

(*a*) maintenance of existing investments and such expansion as can be undertaken without importing new capital,

(*b*) development of British trade with Roumania.

3. In view of British proposals for Roumania,[6] and our high prestige here, I firmly believe that failing deliberate discrimination we are on a good wicket.

4. I believe our aims can be achieved without preferential treatment, which would in any case be unobtainable with Russia next door and in a highly suspicious mood.

5. For many years to come, there should not be a real conflict of economic interests between ourselves and Russia in this market. Russian exports will

---

[1] Mr. J. H. Le Rougetel was British Political Representative in Roumania.

[2] Air Vice-Marshal D. F. Stevenson was British Commissioner on the Allied Control Commission in Roumania. Sir F. Bovenschen and Sir E. Speed, who had special responsibility for finance, were Joint Permanent Under Secretaries of State for War.

[3] Of 5 July 1945, not printed.

[4] This telegram of 17 June is missing from Foreign Office archives.

[5] This agreement for economic collaboration, concluded in Moscow on 8 May 1945, is printed in B.F.S.P., vol. 149, pp. 876–84.

[6] British proposals for re-opening Anglo-Roumanian trade and limited banking relations had been transmitted to General I. Z. Susaikov, Soviet Deputy Chairman of A.C.C., Roumania, on 26 April 1945, as reported in Air Vice-Marshal Stevenson's telegram to the War Office of even date, RAC 1143/1252 STAC 7 (R 7546/382/37), not printed. For British policy in regard to the protection of British oil-interests in Roumania see i below, also Mr. J. C. Grew's telegram of 29 June to Mr. Harriman in Moscow, printed in F.R.U.S. *Berlin*, vol. i, pp. 423–6; the text of this telegram was relayed to the Foreign Office by Lord Halifax in Washington telegram No. 377 Saving of 20 July by bag (received, 25 July: not printed).

presumably be limited to raw materials and semi-fabricated goods whereas we shall be seeking to export finished products such as chemicals and pharmaceuticals, plant, machinery, tools and instruments, motor vehicles, agricultural tractors and the like. It is extremely difficult to estimate total potential value of Roumania's foreign trade (exclusive of Soviet Union) but at a rough estimate she should be able to export about £3,000,000 worth of goods in 1946 and this may well grow to exceed 15,000,000 after reparations have been paid off in 1950. A market of this size is not one to be ignored in the coming drive for foreign trade.

6. It is my firm belief that unless they are vigorously opposed the Russians will continue to encroach on our interests (. . .? in)[7] every possible way, until finally we are driven out. But I am equally sure that if we insist on equal *economic* rights in this country they will see that we are determined to hold what we have and will call a halt. Moreover, I respectfully submit that the only effective way to Anglo-Russian understanding lies in resisting the Russians obvious intention to isolate this part of Europe.

7. It will be remembered that it was vigorous action of this kind which prevented seizure of the 100 octane plant from Astra Romana[8] last January and called a halt to Russian seizure of our napthenic acid supplies (RAC 1811/1254,[3] paragraph 2).

8. No detailed examination of our interests is needed. It will suffice to establish once and for all the following points:

(*a*) British companies, whether they are engaged in production and industry or only trading with Roumania, should be guaranteed absolute parity of treatment, as regards concessions, taxation, facilities etc, etc, with purely Roumanian companies and Russian companies.

(*b*) (. . .? Russians)[7] to agree immediately to proposals made on April 26th (RAC 1143/1252) for Lever [*sic*] banking and trading between United Kingdom and Roumania.[6]

(*c*) Russians to agree immediately to re-entry and exit of representatives of British firms and interests, having in mind that the Russian representatives already have this facility.

(*d*) A clear understanding with Russia on important question of war liability, custody of enemy property (Article 8 of the armistice) and application of inter-allied declaration against acts of dispossession.[9] I am most appreciative of the fact that the first of these is on agenda reported in paragraph 5(*d*) of Foreign Office telegram Intel No. 54 [53A].[10] As to the second I am not clear whether the Russians are entitled to seize for their own benefit unlimited goods, shareholdings etc. from Roumanian custodian

---

[7] The text is here uncertain.

[8] A Roumanian oil company with 77% British capital investment: cf. i below.

[9] The Inter-Allied Declaration of 5 January 1943 against acts of dispossession committed in territories under enemy occupation or control is printed (Cmd. 6418 of 1943) in *B.F.S.P.* vol. 151, pp. 217–21: *op. cit.*, vol. 145, pp. 506–12 for the Armistice Agreement of 12 September 1944 between the United Nations and Roumania.

[10] Not printed.

or direct from existing managements. The Russians stated last week that this right was agreed at Yalta Conference. Can this be confirmed?[11] As to the third point, I consider that Russia should be induced to hold all cases in suspense until the matter can be discussed and agreed between the Allies.

9. Since on the face of it Russian interest in this country is primarily strategic there is no apparent reason why we should not maintain normal commercial relations. If Russians intend to squeeze us out they can always do so but from the haste with which they are now moving, it is fairly clear that they wish to confront us with a *fait accompli* when impending negotiations begin. This haste suggests to me that they are not sure of themselves and I believe that if we join issue with them at once on points I have mentioned, we have the best possible chance of compelling them to give way.

CALENDARS TO NO. 48

i *7 & 11 July 1945* (a) *Brief No. 32 for U.K. Delegation:* Soviet removal of oil-equipment of British part-owned companies in Roumania; (b) *Sir A. Clark Kerr (Moscow) No. 473.* Representations to Soviet Govt. concerning injury to British interests from continued Soviet requisitioning and removal of oil equipment from Roumania [F.O. 934/6; R 12012/80/37].

ii *12 July 1945 Letters from Mr. Turner (Moscow) to Mr. Hall-Patch with F.O. minutes.* Suggestions for obtaining satisfaction over Soviet removal of British-owned oil equipment from Roumania [R 15624/335/37].

iii *13 July 1945 British Military Mission (Roumania) to the War Office Tel. No. RAC 1887/940.* Conversation of 11 July between Mr. Le Rougetel and Roumanian M.F.A.: Roumanian Government's concern not to discourage British enterprise in Roumania [R 11910/335/37].

iv *11–20 July 1945 Minutes by Lord Dunglass, Parliamentary Under-Secretary of State, and others.* British trade interests in the Balkans [R 12473/4698/67].

[11] This matter had not been discussed at the Conference at Yalta, but a relevant British note was circulated to the conference on 10 February 1945: see *F.R.U.S. The Conferences at Malta and Yalta 1945*, pp. 893 and 965.

No. 49

Earl of Halifax (Washington) to Mr. Eden (Received 10 July, 6.10 a.m.)
No. 4774 Telegraphic [N 8336/207/12]

Immediate. Top secret   WASHINGTON, *9 July 1945, 10.54 p.m.*

Repeated to Prague, Moscow.

Your telegram No. 7277.[1]

State Department have shown member of my staff the text of reply which United States Chargé d'Affaires is to make to Czechoslovakia's note of

[1] No. 37.

83

June 22nd regarding withdrawal of United States forces. United States reply states that orders have been sent to the Commanding General, United States Forces in European theatre of operations, 'to begin immediately a reduction of forces under his command'. It goes on, however, to say that United States Government 'look forward to day when assistance of Allied armies will no longer be necessary and both armies can be withdrawn'.[2]

2. State Department have explained confidentially that it is not (repeat not) their intention that there should be a unilateral withdrawal of United States troops from Czechoslovakia. United States forces will be reduced in proportion to reduction of Soviet forces now proceeding at a rate which, according to information furnished by United States Military Attaché in Prague, should bring Soviet total from 150,000 down to 40,000. (N.B. this estimate differs from that given in Prague telegram No. 188)[3]. State Department estimate that on this basis approximately 10,000 United States troops would be retained in Bohemia pending arrangements for final simultaneous withdrawal of all United States and Soviet troops. War Department have apparently been persuaded to accept State Department's point of view and have agreed not (repeat not) to proceed with complete withdrawal of United States forces until State Department have given the green light.

3. Although State Department thus favour complete and simultaneous withdrawal of both Soviet and United States armies at an early date, they are most anxious not to make it appear that Czechoslovakia is a bone of contention between U.S.S.R. and the two major Western Allies. They are therefore not (repeat not) in favour of raising this question themselves with the Russians on their own initiative. They have therefore instructed United States Chargé d'Affaires in Prague to indicate informally to Czechoslovak Government that, if latter wish to suggest to United States Government that there should be a simultaneous withdrawal of Russian and United States troops, the United States Government would be willing to put proposal to Soviet Government. State Department have also told United States Chargé d'Affaires that they do not (repeat not) contemplate unilateral withdrawal and Officer in Charge of Czechoslovak (. . .? desk)[4] said he felt sure that Mr. Klieforth would let President Benes[5] know this.

4. Foreign Office please pass immediately to Prague as my telegram No. 10.

---

[2] Cf. *F.R.U.S. 1945*, vol. iv, p. 474. On 10 July 1945 Mr. Nichols, in reporting in Prague telegram No. 197 the remission of this American note on 9 July and its summary contents, commented, 'This is satisfactory'; Mr. Churchill minuted on 12 July to the Foreign Office 'Why?'. Mr. V. G. Lawford, Assistant Private Secretary to Mr. Eden, explained in a letter of 24 July to Mr. J. R. Colville, Assistant Private Secretary to Mr. Churchill: 'This is "satisfactory", as Mr. Nichols says, in the sense that we shall not be confronted with a situation in which Soviet troops are the only foreign troops on Czech soil. Moreover, as is shown by Prague telegram No. 227 [No. 156], the Russians are in fact fulfilling their promise to withdraw their troops.'

[3] No. 11.

[4] The text is here uncertain.

[5] Mr. A. W. Klieforth was United States Chargé d'Affaires in Prague. Dr. Eduard Benes was President of Czechoslovakia.

Mr. Churchill to Sir A. Clark Kerr (Moscow)
No. 43 Victim Telegraphic [UE 2730/624/77]

Immediate FOREIGN OFFICE, *9 July 1945*, *11.5 p.m.*

Repeated to Washington No. 47 Victim. Paris No. 56 Victim Saving.

My telegram No. 22[1] (Victim of 2nd July: Soviet and American shares of reparation).

Following from Chancellor of the Exchequer for Solicitor General.

I have now discussed with my colleagues the question of the American share of reparation. We are prepared to accept Pauley's contention that the American share should be equal to ours, provided that you make it clear that our agreement is based on broad and general considerations of Anglo-American relations, and not on any precise calculation of effort and loss such as appeared to be contemplated in the Yalta agreement.

CALENDAR TO NO. 50

i *9 July 1945 Minutes of 3rd meeting of Ministerial Committee on Reparations—R.M. (45) 3rd Meeting.* Discussion of statement of principles on reparation (No. 116, annex), and of Allied shares. Approval of general policy in No. 50 above and telegram No. 44 Victim (not printed) of 10 July instructing Sir W. Monckton that he should, at his discretion, support a narrow definition of booty [UE 2906/624/77].

[1] This message from Sir John Anderson, Chancellor of the Exchequer, to Sir Walter Monckton read: 'I agree that it would be difficult for you to obtain any reduction of the Russian share in the light of the American attitude, and you may therefore agree to their having 50% excluding labour. This is subject to the general reservation contained in paragraph 14 of your instructions. 2. As regards the American share, the personal grounds on which Pauley has supported his claim for an equal share to ours has created a painful impression. I must, of course, consult my colleagues on the wider question raised by Mr. Harriman of the possible effect of this issue on our relations with the United States, but meanwhile you should know that my view is that we should not (repeat not) give way. 3. We must, in my view, maintain the principles laid down in paragraph 1 of the Yalta Protocol. No one here wishes to belittle the contribution made by the United States towards the organisation of victory, but our burden and our losses are at least equally real.'

No. 51

Earl of Halifax (Washington) to Mr. Eden (Received 9 July, 11 p.m.)
No. 4758 Telegraphic [F.O. 800/416/63]

Immediate WASHINGTON, *9 July 1945, 3.6 p.m.*

Repeated to Moscow.

Your telegram No. 7,212.[1]

Dunn said last night that he is leaving for Terminal by air July 11th. He

[1] No. 4.

will stop overnight only in Paris and expects to reach Berlin on July 13th. He much regrets that it will hardly be possible for him to break his journey in London. Had the suggestion been made 10 days ago he would most gladly have made arrangements accordingly. All the other senior American delegates have left except Clayton[2] who will travel with Dunn. Dunn is expecting the talks at Terminal to begin on July 15th. This would leave Saturday July 14th comparatively free. He would be delighted to have discussions with any of our delegates on that day if you wish. You may (. . . ? Americans)[3] separately.[4]

[2] Mr. W. L. Clayton was U.S. Assistant Secretary of State supervising economic affairs.
[3] The text is here uncertain.
[4] Mr. Eden minuted to Mr. Dixon on this telegram 'P.D. Someone should talk with him. A.E.' Mr. Dixon minuted 'Sir A. Cadogan is leaving 24 hours early in order to meet Mr. Dunn at Terminal. P.D. 10/7.'

No. 52

Joint Staff Mission (Washington) to the Cabinet Office
(Received 9 July, 3.30 p.m. G.M.T.)
No. J.S.M. 954 Telegraphic [N 8507/2/38]

Top secret. Important   WASHINGTON, *9 July 1945, 2.25 p.m. G.M.T.*[1]

Reference COS (W) 982.[2]

U.S. Chiefs of Staff have replied as follows (CCS 884/1).[3]

Begins

The United States Chiefs of Staff have considered the proposals of the British Chiefs of Staff in CCS 884[2] concerning the information which should be given to the Russians on Intelligence, Dispositions and plans in the war against Japan.

2. The United States Chiefs of Staff consider this matter is not an appropriate one for Combined Agreement. However, they will not, without prior agreement of the appropriate British authorities, pass to the Russians any information on dispositions or operational plans of Allied forces in areas of British strategic responsibility or any information that has been obtained from a British source.

Ends.[4]

[1] Time of origin.
[2] In this telegram of 21 June 1945 (not printed) the British Chiefs of Staff had instructed their Joint Staff Mission in Washington to present the proposals in memorandum CCS 884 of 22 June, printed in *F.R.U.S. Berlin*, vol. i, p. 931.
[3] This memorandum of 8 July is printed *ibid.*, p. 932.
[4] This telegram, circulated to the Foreign Secretary, the First Sea Lord, the Chief of the Imperial General Staff, the Chief of the Air Staff and the Defence Office, was discussed by the Chiefs of Staff Committee on 10 and 11 July 1945. On 11 July the Committee agreed 'that this matter should be discussed with the United States Chiefs of Staff at "Terminal" '.

No. 53

Sir D. Osborne[1] (The Vatican) to Mr. Eden (Received 16 July, 5.30 p.m.)
No. 24 Saving Telegraphic, by bag [ZM 3853/38/57]

THE VATICAN, *9 July 1945*

My despatch No. 129.[2]

My United States colleague informs me that, in the course of this audience, the Pope expressed his earnest hope that Allied troops might remain in Italy in sufficient force to maintain order until such time as conditions became normal again. He felt that the mere presence of these troops would symbolise law and order and serve as an effective deterrent; large numbers would therefore not be necessary.

2. His Holiness has on more than one occasion spoken to me in the same sense and it is a theme that is constantly repeated in responsible Italian circles, both lay and ecclesiastical. Recent sporadic disorders in various parts of Italy have strengthened the argument and its expression.

CALENDARS TO No. 53

i *11 July 1945   Sir A. Clark Kerr (Moscow) Tel. No. 3036.* 'The Soviet press campaign against the Vatican has recently been gaining momentum and no opportunity is lost to connect Vatican policy with reactionary and anti-Soviet tendencies throughout the world' [ZM 3772/36/57].

ii *14 July 1945   Sir D. Osborne (The Vatican) No. 143.* Comments on Vatican report 'that the Pope will not leave Rome before the end of the Potsdam Conference, since it is his intention not to revert to peacetime customs "until the problems arising out of the world conflict and its aftermath are well on their way to a fair solution". (In this case one may wonder whether Castel Gandolfo will ever see His Holiness again.) . . . He appears to be one of those unfortunates who are unable to relax and who cannot enjoy leisure or natural surroundings' [ZM 4063/38/57].

---

[1] H.M. Minister to the Holy See.

[2] This despatch of 29 June 1945 (received 11 July: not printed) reported that on 26 June Pope Pius XII had received in private audience Mr. J. A. Brunner, head of the American ex-servicemen's organization 'Veterans of Foreign Wars', and Colonel F. Heard, Deputy Director of the U.S. War Department Bureau of Public Relations.

No. 54

Sir D. Osborne (The Vatican) to Mr. Eden (Received 20 July)
No. 136 [N 8889/409/38]

THE VATICAN, *9 July 1945*

His Majesty's Minister at Holy See presents his compliments to H.M. Secretary of State and has the honour to transmit to him the under-mentioned documents.

Note from the Secretariat of State,   Transmits appeal by Russian
Vatican to H.M. Legation of   Colony in Rome not to be sent
July 4th/45.   back to Russia against their will.

ENCLOSURE IN No. 54

Copy

Secretariat of State   4th July, 1945
    of His Holiness
N. 97737/SA

The Secretariat of State of His Holiness has been asked by Prince Serge Romanovsky, Duke of Leuchtenberg and President of the Committee for the Russian Colony in Rome residing in Via Panama 79, Rome, to request the good offices of His Britannic Majesty's Minister to the Holy See with the competent Allied Authorities that Russians in Allied territory be not compelled to return to Russia against their will and that, in conformity with the principles of the Atlantic Charter[1] these expatriates be accorded the opportunity of enjoying that juridical status formerly provided for such persons by the Statute of the League of Nations.[2]

[1] This Anglo-American declaration of 14 August 1941 is printed in Cmd. 6321 of 1941.

[2] The League of Nations Arrangement with respect to the issue of Certificates of Identity to Russian Refugees, signed at Geneva on 5 July 1922 (printed in *League of Nations Treaty Series*, vol. 13, No. 355), initiated a series of League of Nations agreements on refugees. These included the Arrangement of 30 June 1928 relating to the Legal Status of Russian and Armenian Refugees (*op. cit.*, vol. 89, No. 2005), and the Convention relating to the International Status of Refugees of 28 October 1933 (*op. cit.*, vol. 159, No. 3663). In a minute of 23 July 1945 on the present document Mr. J. E. Galsworthy wrote: 'By the Yalta Agreement we are bound to repatriate all Soviet citizens liberated by the Allied Armies, regardless of individual wishes in the matter. We do not wish to attract attention to this aspect of the Agreement which is, of course, in opposition to our traditional attitude towards political refugees, and I submit that it wd. be preferable to return no reply to the communication within which, in any case, seems not to require an answer.' This minute was initialed by Mr. T. Brimelow on 24 July. On 28 July Mr. A. D. M. Ross of Western Department minuted 'I agree'. Mr. J. L. Pumphrey of Northern Department initialed on 1 August.

No. 55

Sir A. Clark Kerr (Moscow) to Mr. Eden (Received 10 July, 8.20 a.m.)
No. 54 Victim Telegraphic [UE 2900/624/77]

Immediate   MOSCOW, *9 July 1945*[1]

Repeated to Paris, Washington.

From United Kingdom Delegation Moscow.

My immediately following telegram[2] gives text of Note on interim deliveries presented by Mr. Pauley to Steering Committee this evening. On

[1] Date of drafting. This telegram, drafted as from Sir W. Monckton, was despatched at 1.40 a.m. on 10 July 1945.

[2] Not printed. The American note is printed in *F.R.U.S. Berlin*, vol. i, pp. 544–6.

seeing first draft of his paper yesterday, I pointed out to him Russian desire to obtain capital goods from the western zones is the only card which we have to play and that it is unwise to play this card until we have secured agreement with Russia on reparation plan as a whole. Mr. Pauley professed agreement with this and said he would do his best to revise the draft with this in mind, but in discussion this evening he gave us no support.

2. I explained that I had of course not been able to consult you on the document, but that I had had some indication of your views through a telegram referring to interim deliveries at an earlier stage before the Control Council had been set up (see telegrams 30 and 31).[3] I thought you would feel that the right way to expedite removal of war potential and the delivery of capital equipment which Russia so much needs would be to complete the reparation plan quickly and that you would not normally favour delivery of capital goods under a system of interim deliveries.

3. I also said that I felt you might not agree with the proposal that a sub-commission in Berlin of the Moscow Commission should exercise the executive functions proposed which you might feel to be within the scope of the Control Council.

4. I also tentatively suggested that as it had been agreed that payment for imports should be a first charge on current deliveries, you might feel that we should add at the end of paragraph 4 'pending such final accounting the recipient country shall pay in acceptable currencies for all interim deliveries subject to any refund required when the final accounting takes place'. If so I suggested that payment should be based on Reichsmark prices in 1938 plus 10 per cent converted into United States dollars at the official rate.

5. Mr. Maisky said that the exclusion of capital goods would make the system of interim deliveries useless to Russia. They needed capital goods most of all. His idea was that the Moscow Commission would, within the next few days, agree that certain German industries should be eliminated 100 per cent and others, say 75 per cent and that this proposal would be approved by the Berlin Conference and thereafter interim deliveries might be made up to 75 per cent in the case of industries which were to be eliminated 100 per cent and so on. He asked whether I thought that His Majesty's Government would be opposed to interim deliveries of capital goods until all the smaller nations had accepted the reparations plan, to which I replied that I thought the system of interim deliveries for capital goods might well start after the reparations plan had been approved by the Big Three and obviously it would be difficult to operate without the approval of France also.

6. As regards the sub-commission in Berlin, Mr. Maisky said that until the reparation plan comes into effect and some agency is appointed to execute it, the interim delivery plan should be executed by the Moscow commission through the sub-commission in Berlin. As regards paragraph 3 (*d*) of Mr.

[3] No. 3.i(*a*).

Pauley's paper, I said that I found it rather obscure on the first reading and must reserve my comments.

7. As regards payment, Mr. Maisky asked if this meant that the French have to pay United States dollars for reparation coal and shrugged his shoulders expressively. Waley said that when he had discussed the matter informally with Alphand,[4] Alphand's comments had been a forcibly verbal expression of Mr. Maisky's shrug and we realised that there was a lot to be said on both sides.

8. Mr. Maisky asked for words to be added to say that transport priority would be given for interim deliveries to which Mr. Pauley agreed. I asked him for assurances that a[5] consistent and co-ordinated policy would be followed in all zones

(b) priorities to be granted for deliveries required in the direct war effort against Japan. Mr. Pauley said he would include both points in a revised draft and Mr. Maisky raised no objection.

9. Mr. Maisky said that he had no objection to raise to anything in Mr. Pauley's draft but he would like to reflect and give his final view at the next meeting.

10. I promised to consult His Majesty's Government immediately, but I realise that it is impossible for me to receive a reply before Wednesday[6] and presumably the matter will have to be settled either at or after the Berlin Conference.

Foreign Office please repeat to Washington and Paris as my telegram Victim 40.

[4] Sir David Waley, an Under-Secretary in H.M. Treasury, was a member of the British delegation to the Allied Commission on Reparations. M. Hervé Alphand was Director of Economic Affairs in the French Foreign Ministry.
[5] It was suggested on the filed copy that this should read: (a).
[6] 11 July.

No. 56

*Minutes of a Meeting of the European Advisory Commission
held at Lancaster House, London, S.W.1. on Monday, 9 July 1945
at 9 p.m.*

E.A.C. (45) 5th Meeting [C 4714/317/3]

Secret

Present:

MR. F. T. GOUSEV (*in the Chair*), Mr. G. F. Saksin, Mr. N. V. Ivanov.
SIR R. I. CAMPBELL, Viscount Hood, Brigadier F. G. French.
MR. J. G. WINANT, Brigadier-General V. Meyer, Mr. P. E. Mosely.
MONSIEUR R. MASSIGLI, Monsieur de Leusse, Professor A. Gros.

Secretariat: Mr. E. P. Donaldson, Mr. T. A. Marchenko, Lieutenant M. W. Boggs, U.S.N., Mr. E. A. Paton-Smith, Mr. B. V. Ivanoff.

Agenda

1. Approval of the text of the Agreement between the Governments of the United Kingdom, the United States of America and the Union of Soviet Socialist Republics and the Provisional Government of the French Republic on Zones of Occupation in Austria and the Administration of the City of Vienna.[1]

2. Approval of the Report by the European Advisory Commission to the Governments of the United Kingdom, the United States of America and the Union of Soviet Socialist Republics and the Provisional Government of the French Republic.[2]

THE COMMISSION—

1. Approval of text of the Agreement between the Governments of the United Kingdom, the United States of America and the Union of Soviet Socialist Republics and the Provisional Government of the French Republic on Zones of Occupation in Austria and the Administration of the City of Vienna.

(*a*) approved the text of the Agreement between the Governments of the United Kingdom, the United States of America and the Union of Soviet Socialist Republics and the Provisional Government of the French Republic on the Zones of Occupation in Austria and the Administration of the City of Vienna, the boundaries of the zones of occupation in Austria being as marked on the annexed map 'A' and the boundaries of the areas of occupation in the City of Vienna being as marked on the annexed map 'B' (the text of the Agreement on the Zones of Occupation in Austria and the Administration of the City of Vienna, in English, Russian and French, and map 'A' and map 'B' are annexed);[3]

(*b*) decided to submit the Agreement between the Governments of the United Kingdom, the United States of America and the Union of Soviet Socialist Republics and the Provisional Government of the French Republic on the Zones of Occupation in Austria and the Administration of the City of Vienna, with the annexed map

---

[1] This agreement, not here printed, is printed in Cmd. 6958 of 1946, pp. 15–20. Under this agreement the British zone comprised 'the province of Carinthia, including Ost Tirol, and the province of Styria, except the area of the Burgenland as it existed before the Decree of the 1st October 1938'. This agreement followed upon that on Control Machinery in Austria approved by the European Advisory Commission on 4 July 1945: *ibid.*, pp. 3–6. On 9 July Lord Hood minuted that the latter agreement 'is substantially the same as the draft tabled by the U.K. Delegation. The Allied Commission for Austria is organised on much the same principles as the Allied Control Machinery in Germany. It consists of an Allied Council composed of four Commanders-in-Chief, an Executive Committee composed of four deputies and a number of divisions (see Article 4 (a)). After a long fight the Russians agreed to separate naval and air divisions, to which our Service Ministries attach importance. In deference to Russian wishes we agreed to include a reparation, deliveries and restitution division' (U 5393/11/70).

[2] This report, not here printed, is printed in *F.R.U.S. 1945*, vol. iii, pp. 158–9.

[3] See note 1 above. Neither the Russian nor the French text, nor the maps are annexed to the filed copy.

'A' and map 'B', to the Governments of the United Kingdom, the United States of America and the Union of Soviet Socialist Republics and the Provisional Government of the French Republic for consideration and approval.

THE COMMISSION—

2. *Report by the European Advisory Commission to the Governments of the United Kingdom, the United States of America and the Union of Soviet Socialist Republics and the Provisional Government of the French Republic.*

approved the text of the Report by the European Advisory Commission and decided to transmit it, signed by the four Representatives on the European Advisory Commission, as a covering document to the text of the Agreement on the Zones of Occupation in Austria and the Administration of the City of Vienna to the Governments of the United Kingdom, the United States of America and the Union of Soviet Socialist Republics and the Provisional Government of the French Republic. (The text of the Report in English, Russian and French is annexed.)[4]

Representative of the Government of the United Kingdom on the European Advisory Commission:	Representative of the Government of the United States of America on the European Advisory Commission:	Representative of the Government of the Union of Soviet Socialist Republics on the European Advisory Commission:	Representative of the Provisional Government of the French Republic on the European Advisory Commission:
(Signed)	*(Signed)*	*(Signed)*	*(Signed)*
RONALD I. CAMPBELL	JOHN G. WINANT	F. GOUSEV	R. MASSIGLI

Lancaster House, London, S.W.1, 9th July, 1945

CALENDAR TO No. 56

i *10 July 1945   Record of Informal Meetings of the E.A.C. on 9 July* [U 5395/473/70].

[4] See note 2 above. Neither the Russian nor the French text are annexed to the filed copy.

No. 57

Political Intelligence Report

J.I.C. S.H.A.E.F.(45)26 [C 4319/24/18]

SUPREME HEADQUARTERS, ALLIED EXPEDITIONARY FORCE, *9 July 1945*[1]

Secret

This is the last Political Intelligence Report which will be issued by Supreme Headquarters AEF. Like its predecessors it is not designed to give a comprehensive review of the political state of the countries in this theatre.

[1] A copy of this report was sent through the Chiefs of Staff Committee to the Foreign Office (received by 17 July as J.I.C.(45)222 of 16 July 1945).

Its purpose is to outline some aspects of the political situation with particular emphasis on those which affect the security of the Allied armed forces.

In this report we have attempted to outline what appears on the little evidence so far available to be Russia's policy with regard to her zone in Germany. An account of an interview with Von Ribbentrop[2] is also included. At Annex A[3] a report of a visit to a Russian Guards Division and at Annex B[4] the story of General Ritter von Epp's experiences during the last days of the war.

K. W. D. STRONG
T. J. BETTS[5]
I. KIRKPATRICK
G. F. REINHARDT

ENCLOSURE IN NO. 57

I.   Russia's policy in her zone

1. We have very little precise evidence from which to assess Russian policy towards the part of Germany which they occupy. Now that our troops are occupying Berlin, it is important that the maximum amount of intelligence be obtained about conditions in the Russian zone, so that a clearer picture can be obtained of how efficiently and towards what goal the Russians are leading their zone. As yet only the most tentative conclusions, which are given below, can be reached from the evidence so far available, and it is to be hoped that during the next two months a far more authoritative picture will be able to be drawn.

Russian Propaganda

2. The Russian propaganda line is clear. While ours is to bring home to the Germans the state to which their crimes have brought them, theirs is to try to persuade the Germans that they are not such ogres as Goebbels painted them. Moscow and Berlin broadcasts and local German newspapers under Russian control are at pains to emphasise how quickly the work of reconstruction is being carried out and how their zone is returning to normality. Every new train service is at once reported; much space is given to showing how essential services such as electric light, gas and water mains are being repaired; factories are beginning to produce; cinemas, theatres and variety halls are said to have reopened; and schools are said to be restarting. Moreover, reports stress that the Russians are beginning to establish some form of educational and cultural relations with the Germans. The good fellowship which exists between the Red Army and German workers is played up. A youth committee has been formed in Berlin to help reeducate German youth. This organisation is composed of two representatives each from Socialist, Communist, Democratic parties and from the Protestant, Catholic and Jewish religions. Radio Berlin notes that by permitting the formation

---

[2] This undated report of a recent S.H.A.E.F. interrogation of Herr von Ribbentrop was included as paragraph 15 of the enclosure, omitted from the filed copy and filed separately on C 4299/44/18, not printed.

[3] Not printed.

[4] Not annexed to filed copy. An undated record of this nature is filed on C 3836/44/18.

[5] Major General K. W. D. Strong and Brigadier T. J. Betts (U.S. Army) were respectively Chief and Deputy Chief of the Intelligence Division of S.H.A.E.F.

of 'controlled German voluntary organisations' the Soviets had followed a procedure 'quite different from that of the Allies'.

3. While this propaganda may partly be aimed at Germans living in the Russian zone in order to convince them that their lot, if they work, is not hopeless and that the future will be brighter, it is more likely to be directed primarily at the outside world. The Russians have always been sensitive to the reproach that their standard of living and efficiency in organisation is lower than that of the Western Powers and they are out to show that the reverse is in fact the case. They do not hesitate to point out that they are getting on with the job, leaving it to their hearers to infer that the Allies are not. This propaganda has achieved a certain success in that it has been widely quoted in European newspapers. It is indeed quoted by Germans who live in areas safe from Russian occupation, possibly in an attempt to prise more concessions out of the Allied military government. But it does not seem to have a great effect in such towns as Magdeburg, where the population was reported to have been extremely depressed at seeing the American troops depart.

Reality and Propaganda

4. As always what the Russians do and what they say for public consumption are two different matters. The main Russian policy is to rebuild Russia itself and the reconstruction of Germany except in so far as it will help the task of the occupying Red Army will certainly not take a high priority. Russian broadcasts within the USSR practically ignore the occupational problems. The Russians appear to be completely indifferent to the plight of the Germans. Contrary to their propaganda, food is very short in Berlin and they are now refusing to provide food or coal for the 1,700,000 Germans in the U.S./British zones [? sectors]. Meanwhile German machinery is being moved to Russia. The German male population in various areas is often reported as having been rounded up for reconstruction or agricultural labour in Germany. How far the Russians have moved large numbers of German workers to Russia is not known, but specialists and skilled engineers have undoubtedly been sent there to rebuild Russian industry. In any case practically no young and robust males are to be seen in Berlin and labour is requisitioned by tens of thousands to perform any taks the Russians desire regardless of their qualifications.

Political Policy

5. So far as can be seen the Russians appear to have no intention at this stage of building up a strong German state in the East. Nor at the moment particularly since Berlin is now under tripartite control is there any sign of a rump German government being set up after the manner of the Renner Government in Vienna. Marshal Stalin has already denied that he intends installing the Von Seydlitz Committee[6] and indeed it would seem that this is unlikely to be done since it would cause such international repercussions and would entail an acknowledgment that the Russians were prepared to use the very militarists whom they have been most prompt to denounce. They have been ruthless in their round-up of all leading Nazis in their zone but from all accounts they have probably been willing to accept the small-fry, who can claim that they were

[6] The German General Walther von Seydlitz-Kurzbach, after capture by Soviet forces, had become chairman in Moscow of the Union of German Officers in association with the National Committee for Free Germany.

party members only in order that they could hold their jobs, to fill minor administrative posts. This is not unlikely since the Russians do not possess any large number of competent administrators whom they could spare for governing Germany and they will rely principally on the Germans governing themselves with a minimum of administrative supervision from the Red Army. In the present unsettled conditions of Poland, they are probably anxious to avoid stirring up undue hostility in Germany and now that the preliminary purges have been carried out their political policy is probably one of live and let live.

6. Nor are there any signs as yet of the Russians sponsoring a strong Communist Party in their zone. Undoubtedly they draw support from the Workers' districts who are ready enough to accept communism again as their political creed; but the Russians claim that they are being wary of newly converted comrades and despite their radio propaganda there is no close accord between them and their former enemies. On the other hand, in contrast to our policy, they encourage political activity and are permitting trades unions to reorganise. They are also appointing numbers of anti-Nazis from concentration camps to local administration. A combined reconstruction committee has been formed including members of the Communist and Socialist parties.

Economic Policy

7. At present Russian economic policy towards their zone might be described as one of overt spoilation. Plant, prototypes and experts are all liable to be moved to Russia, and such factories as are producing will probably see their products disappear Eastwards as well. With regard to food the Russians should be eventually in a happy position for they have occupied Germany's principal grain producing areas and they may also expect large surplus potato crops. This does not mean that the Germans benefit from the surplus which probably is spent in feeding the Red Army who live off the land and the millions of homeless Russians and Poles. In Berlin itself everything transportable has been stripped from the U.S./British zones. Out of the 36 telephone exchanges in the area only eight remained when we arrived and furniture and fittings have been treated in the same way.

To Sum Up

8. There is therefore nothing peculiarly sinister about Russia's policy in her zone. It appears in fact to be a perfectly simple policy of using German industry as a means of rebuilding Russia and of eliminating all possible political opposition in their own territory. It remains to be seen how far the Russians will continue the economic policy which they have instituted in Eastern Europe of eliminating all large landowners and collectivising farms.[7] For the rest they will probably have to rely largely on Germans for administering their own districts. The degree to which they win over the Germans to wholehearted cooperation will depend to a great extent on the efficiency of their administration. There seems to be little doubt that, in direct contradiction to their propaganda, they are completely indifferent to whether the Germans have a bare subsistence to live upon this winter and they seem to regard them as a useful source of cheap labour whose future is unimportant. Since this ruthless policy is clear-cut, they do not worry overduly about such moral policies as non-fraternisation. Much the most important question from the Allied point of view is how far the Soviet Government will go

[7] Marginal note in the Foreign Office, 'Where?'.

in developing a four power policy for Germany and treating the country as an economic unit with one policy as regards communications, education, etc.

Germany

General Situation

9. It is now just over two months ago that Germany capitulated at Rheims. At that time the Allies were faced with the problem of a country which had completely disintegrated. Not only were its armies hopelessly beaten and being herded into captivity. It had no central government worthy of the name, its leading administrators had either been made prisoner, fled or died and, most profound effect of all, Germany had ceased to exist as an economic unit. It was cut up into three zones; its transport system had been throughly wrecked; its pits, its factories, its steel works, all the heavy industry needed to repair the enormous damage were stilled. The miseries which the Germans had inflicted on other European countries were now visited fifty fold upon themselves.

10. By far the most critical problems in Germany are food transport and fuel. Firstly there is insufficient labour to produce enough food for the needs of the American and British zones. Moreover, the most productive agricultural areas containing the rye and food stuff growing districts are now in Russian hands. Secondly the breakdown in transportation has made distribution most difficult. The sugar beet crop may well rot in the fields this year owing to lack of coal stocks. With regard to the railways a vicious circle exists. Until the railways are repaired and working, little coal can be exported from the Ruhr; and until coal is exported and distributed to fuel locomotives the railways cannot run. Through traffic is greatly hampered by the number of bridges which have been blown and many of these cannot be repaired until steel and concrete is available from factories which are now idle owing to lack of raw materials which should be brought by railway. Inland waterways are also badly blocked by blown bridges and bomb damage.

11. The breakdown of transport has made reconstruction almost impossible. To clear the damage inflicted on cities like Cologne, Munich, Frankfurt and Mainz would take months even if fleets of bulldozers, cranes and hundreds of lorries were available which they are not. A beginning has, however, been made and the less hopelessly damaged houses are being cleared and made to some extent habitable. Given the necessary equipment the Germans might clear up war damage quicker than might be expected, as there is no doubt that they would organise such an enterprise with their usual efficiency. At the present rate of clearance, however, it will be many years before damage is cleared and large scale rebuilding undertaken.

Political Activity

12. In the field of political activity, there is little to report. The freedom granted to trade union activity has resulted in some union meetings which have served, thus far, to illustrate the effects of Nazi success in suppressing political liberty. Nine meetings were reported by the Fifteenth Army.[8] At the four attended by American representatives, the large audiences appeared generally apathetic and reluctant to respond to invitations from the leaders for general discussion. Once

---

[8] The U.S. Fifteenth Army, of General Omar Bradley's Twelfth Army Group, had headquarters at Bad Neuenahr under the command of Lieut.-General L. T. Gerow.

freedom of speech is forgotten, it is not easily recovered and it seems doubtful whether the Germans will recover the ability to discuss affairs freely and advocate political action, particularly since on all major issues they are bound by Allied decisions.

Security

13. The confused waters are gradually subsiding. Allied troops are being redeployed into their final positions, the numbers of itinerant Displaced Persons have been vastly reduced, Germans are gradually returning to their homes and prisoners are being demobilised. As a result static controls such as road blocks are becoming more effective and more numerous arrests of Germans travelling without permits or with forged identity papers and orders are reported. One woman was able to travel two hundred miles from Italy with invalid travel orders before finally being stopped. A photostatic copy of a pass was also successfully used. A NCO[9] in a Military Government office endorsed this pass when the civilian claimed that the original had been destroyed, the NCO evidently failing to realise that a photostatic copy could not have been made after the original was destroyed.

14. No acts of overt resistance traceable to an organised resistance movement have been reported. The rapid collapse of Germany and the thoroughness of counter-intelligence methods have broken up all efforts by the Sicherheits Dienst to form resistance groups and encourage Werewolf activity:[10] subversive activity now only amounts to scattered and unconnected incidents of sabotage. If in fact active resistance develops in the future it will arise more from disaffection during the prolonged occupation than from the original Werewolf planning.

Belgium

16.[2] The constitutional crisis is creaking to its close. The procession[11] of dignitaries from the Belgian Prime Minister M. Van Acker to an anonymous hairdresser has continued throughout the past week. It has become clear even to King Leopold that he cannot form a government, but he has not yet been able to bring himself to the point of signing his abdication. Nevertheless it seems likely that his hand will be forced. Van Acker's latest visit is designed to put a finish to the whole affair once and for all. Either the King abdicates or Van Acker threatens to stop acting as the leader of a caretaker government and to publish the evidence of the King's relations with the Nazis. This has been obtained from two independent testimonies of Schmidt, Hitler's interpreter and Meissner, his Chief of Protocol. Even if such evidence were not legally admissible, it is most powerful political dynamite which will probably make the King accept the Government's demands.

17. Both the Allied governments have throughout been at pains to emphasize their neutrality in this political debate, and elaborate instructions have been

---

[9] Non-commissioned officer.

[10] The Sicherheitsdienst (S.D.) was the Security Service of the Schutzstaffeln (S.S.), a defence echelon originally constituted as Herr Hitler's bodyguard in distinction from the general body of the Sturmabteilungen (S.A.), National-Socialist Storm Troops. Werewolf was the code name for an embryonic Nazi association for organised resistance to Allied occupation.

[11] To Salzburg where King Leopold III of the Belgians was then residing during the constitutional crisis concerning his return.

issued to the Army Groups concerned in order to prevent any action suggesting that we favour one side or the other.

No. 58

Memorandum by Sir W. Strang
[*UE 3021/607/53*]

FOREIGN OFFICE, *9 July 1945*

The annexed telegram from Field-Marshal Montgomery to the War Office about food and coal for Berlin will, I understand, be before the Cabinet at its special meeting tomorrow morning.

The broad position is that the Russians have asked that we and the Americans should contribute food for the feeding of the German population in our own sectors and our quota of fuel for maintaining the public utilities of the City.

The figures mentioned at the meeting with Marshal Zhukov in Berlin on July 7th[1] were 20,000 tons of food per month for each[2] of the British and American sectors, and a joint Anglo-American contribution of 5,000[2] tons of coal per day.

These figures are probably rather inflated. If, as we maintain, the food and fuel supply of Berlin should be on the same scale as in other centres of population in Germany, e.g. Hamburg, the reduction might be considerable. I have consulted Economic Relations Department, who say that they have not of course complete data, but they share our view that the Russian figure for coal is probably much too high.

General Weeks'[3] suggestion is that we and the Americans should agree, as an emergency measure, to supply some food and some coal for Berlin to cover the period of a month starting from about the end of July. He understands from a technical study made by the British and American military authorities in Germany that it would be possible to find and to transport an amount of food and fuel which would probably serve to bridge the gap for this period.

It would be made clear to the Russians that this would be without prejudice to the final settlement of the question of the supply of Berlin, which could be thrashed out by the Commanders concerned in the immediate future.

We understand from General Weeks that if food and fuel were found for Berlin for the proposed period of a month, the food would be found at the expense of other Germans, though the fuel might to some extent be at the

---

[1] See the annex and i below. Marshal G. K. Zhukov was Chief of the Soviet Military Administration and Commander-in-Chief of the Soviet Forces of Occupation in Germany.

[2] Underlined by Mr. Eden, to whom this memorandum was addressed.

[3] Lieut.-General Sir R. Weeks was Chief of Staff to Field-Marshal Montgomery for control matters.

expense of exports.[4] I annex a minute [ii] by Mr. Coulson on this aspect of the question.

If we declined to find food and fuel even on an emergency basis, we might well risk throwing the whole 4-Power occupation of Berlin into the melting-pot, with adverse effect also upon the whole idea of 4-Power responsibility for Germany. In any event, it would not be a reasonable proposition for us to maintain that we should make no contribution of food and fuel to Berlin. The question rather is, what should our quota be? Thus, in 1936–1937, between 40% and 50% of the hard coal consumed in Greater Berlin came from the Ruhr.[4]

I understand from General Weeks that the question of the feeding of Berlin was on the agenda proposed for the meeting of Marshal Zhukov, General Weeks and General Clay held at the end of June to make a plan for the withdrawal to the British and American zones and for the entry of the British and American contingent into Berlin;[5] but that it was only at their meeting on July 7th that the question was discussed.

ANNEX TO No. 58

Field-Marshal Sir B. Montgomery to the War Office
Unnumbered Telegraphic

Secret
Copy

[BAD OEYNHAUSEN,] *8 July 1945, 3.30 p.m.*

From C in C Brit. Zone

First. At a meeting in Berlin on Saturday 7th July Marshal Zhukov General Weeks General Clay discussed problem of administration of Berlin. The general arrangements for setting up the Berlin Council of three (subsequently four) Komendatura[6] and their terms of reference were settled satisfactorily and a document embodying these arrangements is being prepared and will be signed on Tuesday next 10th July at a further meeting with Marshal Zhukov.

Second. 2 points have been raised as regards food and coal on which no decision was reached and the questions were put back for discussion 10th July. As regards food the Russians claim that the responsibility for feeding the Germans in the sectors of the Berlin zone falls to the Powers occupying each sector. In brief we are asked as Mil Government in our Berlin sector as from date which is not yet stated to supply and distribute food to 909,000 Germans involving on the Russian estimate (which may not be unreasonable) a supply from our main zone in Germany approx 20,000 tons per month of varying categories of foodstuffs.

Third. The stock position of various commodities in Berlin as a whole varies at the moment according to Russian figures from 5 days in important items to 20 days in less important items. Figures of a similar nature apply to the Americans who have a somewhat smaller German population. We and the Americans have taken the line that the whole question is a matter for Governments as regards

[4] The preceding clause was underlined by Mr. Eden.
[5] For this meeting of 29 June 1945, cf. *F.R.U.S. Berlin*, vol. i, pp. 136–7; F. S. V. Donnison, *Civil Affairs and Military Government North West Europe*, pp. 267–8.
[6] i.e. the Inter-Allied Governing Authority for Berlin.

long term but the short term solution requires an immediate decision on Tuesday. Although it is inconvenient and will cause all manner of disturbances as regards our own main zone (details of which are being gone into at the moment) it may be possible as from 3 or more weeks time to put into Berlin the equivalent of 1 month's food for the Germans in the British sector. The actual breakdown of the commodities to be supplied would be a matter of detail but wheat would figure largely.

Fourth. Coal presents the same sort of problem. The total requirements in Berlin for public utilities etc. (not including any domestic requirements) is estimated by the Russians as 7,500 tons per day of which 1000 tons is brown coal. The Russians are likely to bid on us for 5000 tons per day. Stocks are stated to be 4 to 5 days but are believed to be a bit higher. Here again supply to Berlin will conflict with all our present arrangements in the British zone and with coal exports.[4] The question of rail transport to Berlin is also involved. The Bridge at Magdeburg will not be ready until 25 July.[2] The coal question is also to be considered on 10th July.

Fifth. General Weeks will be in London tomorrow Monday 9th and will discuss above problems. In the meantime studies are being made here of the possibility of implementing some short term supply without prejudice to long term Government or Control Council decisions.

CALENDARS TO NO. 58

i *7 June [July] 1945   Notes of a meeting held at Marshal Zhukov's Headquarters* [C 3849/24/18].

ii *9 July 1945   Minute by Mr. Coulson:* Effect on Hyndley-Potter Report (of 7 June: cf. F. S. V. Donnison, *op. cit.*, pp. 404–5 and *F.R.U.S. Berlin*, vol. i, pp. 619—21) of supplying coal from the Ruhr to Berlin: would reduce coal available for Western Europe and seriously prejudice the report's recommendations. Annotations by Mr. Eden [UE 3021/607/53].

No. 59

Minute by Mr. Harrison[1]
[C 3675/95/18]

FOREIGN OFFICE, *9 July 1945*

Transfer of German populations

I attach a copy of the brief [i] on this subject which has been prepared for Terminal.

In a covering brief[2] it is suggested that if the U.S. Delegation do not raise the question, 'it will probably be desirable that we should do so, though of the three Powers we are the least directly interested, our zone being furthest removed from the Polish and Czechoslovak frontiers'. Since the

---

[1] Mr. G. W. Harrison was a member of the German Department of the Foreign Office.
[2] See Annex below.

above was drafted the Americans have definitely said[3] that they do not themselves propose to take the initiative in raising the question.

There is no doubt of the pressing nature of this question of transfer of German populations from Czechoslovakia and to a lesser extent from Poland and Polish occupied Germany. We cannot ourselves avoid some general responsibility for what is done. There have indeed already been a few P[arliamentary] Q[uestion]s in the House of Commons.[4] Moreover, if there is a large influx of Germans into Germany it is bound to have some effect on our zone even though it is furthest removed from Poland and Czechoslovakia.[5]

On the other hand any unorganised influx of Germans is going in the first instance to affect the Russians and the Americans, and to this extent it is arguable that they have a greater interest than ourselves in securing an orderly and organised transfer. Moreover, the principle itself of these large scale transfers is quite likely to be attacked from various quarters, not least in powerful organs of the British press such as the *Times*, *Manchester Guardian* etc. Do we in these circumstances wish to incur the 'odium' of having taken the initiative in raising this question? Would it be better simply to have concurred?

This is a very important question of tactics which can only be settled at the highest level.[6]

A secondary question is how we should handle this question vis-a-vis the Czechoslovak Government. In our telegrams Nos. 6651 and 6652 of June 22nd to Washington,[7] we instructed H.M. Embassy to inform the U.S. Government of the lines on which we proposed Mr. Nicholls [*sic*] should reply to a demarche from the Czechoslovak Government regarding the transfer to Germany both of Reich German evacuees and the Sudeten minority. Since then Mr. Nicholls has reported[8] the receipt of a further note from the Czechoslovak Government which concludes by requesting that the point of view of President Benes and his Government on this subject of transfers should be conveyed to H.M.G. 'in order that Prime Minister Churchill may be informed and with a view to ensuring that this question may be a subject of discussion and decision at the forthcoming Conference

[3] As reported in Washington telegram No. 4709: cf. No. 21, note 9.

[4] Cf. *Parl. Debs.*, 5th ser., *H. of C.*, vol. 411, cols. 1632–3 and 1686–7.

[5] Mr. Troutbeck here noted in the margin: 'A very considerable effect. We cannot refuse to accept our share in any arrangement agreed on. J.M.T.'

[6] Mr. Harrison here added a marginal reference to a further undated minute, evidently written on 9 July 1945, which read: 'It has since been agreed at a meeting in Sir A. Cadogan's room that we had better raise the question, but that we might do so in the form of an enquiry to the U.S. and Soviet Representatives as to how they propose to handle the large number of transferees from Czechoslovakia & Poland. G.W.H.'

[7] Not printed. For a paraphrase of Foreign Office telegram No. 6651 see *F.R.U.S. Berlin*, vol. i, pp. 644–5. The gist of the two telegrams is indicated in No. 59.i below in connexion with the attitude of His Majesty's Government towards Czechoslovakia.

[8] This Prague telegram No. 180 of 5 July is not printed. The Czechoslovak note (copy received in the Foreign Office on 14 July) is printed in *Die Deutschen in der Tschechoslowakei 1933–1947: Dokumentensammlung*, ed. V. Král (Prague, 1964), pp. 550–1.

of the Three'. A similar note has been addressed to the U.S. and Soviet Governments.

I see little likelihood of getting any comments out of the State Department before the Berlin meeting, since the State Secretary is reported already to have left Washington. I think there would be advantage in instructing Mr. Nicholls to put in at once a note to the Czechoslovak Government on the lines of our telegram No. 6652 to Washington.[7] In doing so Mr. Nicholls should add that he has not failed to communicate to H.M.G. the Czechoslovak note of July 3rd summarised in his telegram No. 180.[8]

I do not believe that this independent action would do us any harm vis-a-vis the Americans and I think might do us good vis-a-vis the Czechs.

To save time I submit a draft telegram[9] to Mr. Nicholls in case action on the above lines is approved.[10]

G. W. HARRISON

ANNEX TO No. 59

Transfer of German populations from Poland,
Czechoslovakia and Hungary

We have proposed to the Americans that they should take the initiative in raising this question at the Conference. While agreeing that it should be raised, Mr. Mat[t]hews of the State Department said he was not sure that the United States Delegation would necessarily wish to take the initiative. The question is becoming so acute that, if they do not, it will probably be desirable that we should do so, though of the 3 Powers, we are the least directly interested, our zone being furthest removed from the Polish and Czechoslovak frontiers.

The present position

The position is that the Polish, Czechoslovak and Hungarian Governments wish to get rid of the overwhelming majority of the Germans in the territory which they control. So far as the Germans in territory controlled by Poland and Czechoslovakia are concerned, we, like the United States Government, are more or less committed to the principle of their transfer to Germany, though we have never tied ourselves down to details such as numbers, timetable etc. The Russians, too, are understood to be in favour of organised transfers.

It is impossible to give any serious estimate of the numbers involved, particularly as we have little knowledge of the numbers who have fled already, especially from Poland. Dr. Benes will probably wish to get rid of something in the neighbourhood of 2½ millions in addition to the Reich Germans who have been imported into Czechoslovakia since 1938; those from Poland and Polish occupied Germany may be anything between 5¼ and 9 millions and still more if the Western Neisse is accepted as the frontier; those in Hungary, which clearly has lower priority, perhaps ¼ million.

[9] Not printed. The resultant Foreign Office telegram No. 149 to Prague of 13 July conveyed to Mr. Nichols instructions for the reply to the Czechoslovak Government made in his note of 14 July, printed *ibid.*, pp. 551-2.

[10] Sir A. Cadogan and Mr. Eden minuted on this memorandum: 'This problem ought to be discussed at Terminal and a solution found, if possible. Otherwise the thing might get out of hand, with possibly disastrous results. A.C. July 10, 1945.' 'I agree. A.E. July 12.'

Mr. Nichols has reported that hatred of the Germans pervades the whole atmosphere in Czechoslovakia. At present Dr. Benes accepts the view that the expulsion of the German minority shall be dealt with in agreement with the Soviet, United States and British Governments. But there is the danger that, unless a decision satisfactory to the Czechs is reached at the forthcoming Three Power meeting, Dr. Benes may be obliged by domestic pressure to take matters into his own hands.

The position in Poland and Polish occupied territory is obscure. But there is every reason to suppose that the Poles are as anxious as the Czechs to get rid of what is left of the Germans under their control.

The Hungarian Government raised with His Majesty's Minister last May the question of the transfer of a large number of Schwaben[11] to Germany.

Argument

After the last war an attempt was made to safeguard the rights of minority populations by treaty. It is generally admitted that the attempt failed. Not only did it in practice prove impossible to safeguard the rights of minority populations, but in addition experience showed that such minorities could be a mortal danger to the countries harbouring them. It is not surprising therefore that the Polish, Czechoslovak and Hungarian Governments are anxious to expel the German populations from their territories.

There is a very strong case for the repatriation to Germany of German populations in neighbouring countries. None the less account must be taken of the fact that transfers on the scale involved will create immense short and long term economic problems both in Germany and in the expelling countries, but more severe by far in Germany. Nor can certain political aspects be ignored. For instance, the human suffering involved will inevitably be great, and the resettlement of the expelled Germans in Germany will create serious political and practical problems in that country which will greatly increase the burden of the occupying Powers. Indeed an unregulated flow of migrants in large numbers might well lead to a complete breakdown of administration in Germany. The displacement of the German population in Germany, as a result of evacuation and other causes, has been on so colossal a scale during the closing stages of the war that the effect on the repatriated populations may be less severe than would have been the case in more normal circumstances. None the less the migrants are likely to be penniless, homeless, workless, and embittered and will for a long time represent a distinct and undigested element in the population of Germany as a whole.

If therefore the principle of the transfer of the bulk of the German populations in Poland, Czechoslovakia and possibly Hungary is accepted, it will be essential that it should be carried out in as orderly and humane a manner as possible.

Recommendation

In the circumstances it is suggested that at the forthcoming conference we should formally accept the principle of the transfer to Germany of the German minorities in territory controlled by Poland, Czechoslovakia and possibly Hungary. We should, however, seek to establish that such transfers which, on the scale contemplated, will present many complex problems, should be regarded

[11] Swabians, as a designation of a German minority in Hungary.

as a matter of general international concern and should be subject to careful supervision and regulation.

We might aim therefore to secure general agreement to a formula somewhat on the following lines:

'The Three Powers, having considered the question in all its aspects, have agreed that the transfer to Germany of German populations from Central and South Eastern Europe is in principle desirable. They have further agreed that any transfers that take place should be carefully supervised and controlled, in order that they may be effected in as orderly and humane a manner as possible. They consider that the actual procedure for the transfer of these persons to Germany should be worked out by the Allied Control Council in Germany in consultation with the Governments concerned, due regard being paid to the capacity of Germany to absorb them.'

CALENDARS TO No. 59

i *Undated Brief No. 3 for U.K. Delegation:* transfer of German populations from Czechoslovakia, Poland and Hungary. Attitude of H.M.G. in regard to (i) Poland, (ii) Czechoslovakia in light of H.M.G.'s approval in 1942 of general principle of a postwar transfer to Germany of German minorities in Central and South East Europe in appropriate cases. H.M.G. would like to confirm this view to Czechoslovak Government, adding, however, that it must be for the Allied Control Council in Germany to decide the method and timing of the transfer of the expelled German populations to Germany. Generally similar attitudes of U.S. and Soviet Govt.s [C 3794/95/18].

ii *11 July 1945 Brief No. 35 for U.K. Delegation:* protection of minorities in Europe and the Middle East [U 5398/1578/70].

iii *16 July 1945 Tel. No. 35 Onward to Berlin transmitting Prague Tel. No. 222:* execution of instructions noted in note 9 above: expression of Czechoslovak concern 'lest once again it would be said here that Western Powers had let Czechoslovakia down' [F.O. 934/3/13(1)].

iv *23 July 1945 Letter from Mr. Nichols (Prague) to Mr. C. F. A. Warner:* reports generally satisfactory interview given on 11 July by President Benes to Reuters on transfer of Germans; considers reasons, however, for his reducing to 3–500,000 the figure of those expected to be allowed to remain [C 4799/95/18].

No. 60

Mr. Nichols (Prague) to Mr. Eden (Received 18 July
No. 40 [U 5834/16/73]

PRAGUE, *9 July 1945*

Sir,

With reference to my telegram No. 6 Saving[1] of June 12th, I have the

[1] Not preserved in Foreign Office archives.

honour to transmit to you herewith an interesting report[2] by Mr. Murray, First Secretary at this Embassy, who visited the camp at Terezin (Theresienstadt) on July 2nd, accompanied by an official of the Ministry of Foreign Affairs, in order to interview a number of persons claiming to be of British or Palestinian nationality. I have reported the results of Mr. Murray's investigation on this subject in my telegrams Nos. 177, 178 and 179[3] of July 4th.

2. The enclosed report[2] shows that conditions at Terezin were on a par with those with which we are already familiar from accounts of Belsen and Buchenwald. Terezin was, however, largely used as a staging camp for Jews who were subsequently sent to Poland for extermination. To one who has some former knowledge of Central European conditions, one of the most striking differences between today and yesterday is the almost complete absence of Jews. I remember well the very large number of Jews to be seen in Vienna after the last war. I have scarcely seen a Jew in Prague to-day. Comment is unnecessary.

I have, &c.,

PHILIP NICHOLS

[2] The enclosed report of 6 July 1945 by Mr. J. D. Murray on his visit to the former German concentration camp and ghetto at Terezin is not printed. Mr. Murray included in his report that he had there been 'introduced to Dr. Georg Vogel, the chief of the Czechoslovak camp administration, himself a former prisoner, who told me that he was the only surviving member of the first Jewish Council which the Germans set up to act as a buffer between them and the prisoners . . . . He told me that he came to Terezin with the first working party sent there by the Germans after they decided to use the place as a concentration camp. The first task of the first working party was to build a crematorium with a capacity for 200 bodies a day.'

[3] Untraced in Foreign Office archives.

No. 61

Record by Mr. Warner of a conversation with members of a Commission of the Polish Provisional Government

[N 8401/6/55]

FOREIGN OFFICE, 9 July 1945

As agreed with the Treasury and Sir A. Cadogan, I saw this morning the two members of the Polish Provisional Government's Commission who arrived here prematurely on the 6th July. They brought with them with my agreement, M. Drohojowski, an ex-member of the Polish Diplomatic Service and ex-Secretary General of the Polish Ministry of Information here, who has been acting as one of M. Mikolajczyk's representatives here since M. Mikolajczyk left for Moscow. He is one of those appointed by the Warsaw Government to the Commission. Mr. Allen[1] and Mr. Winch were also present, the latter to check M. Drohojowski's interpretation.

[1] Mr. W. D. Allen was a member of the Northern Department of the Foreign Office.

2. M. Drozniak, the Chairman of the Commission made quite a good impression upon me. He seemed able and business-like. He is 'president' of the new bank which the Lublin Government set up as the State Bank and Bank of Issue, and I should think that he was at least a competent bank official and probably of higher calibre than the average bank official. M. Kolodziejski, the other member of the Commission to come from Warsaw, used to be Librarian of the Sejm.[2] He is an oldish man and looked very worn and rather down-at-heel. He had been described to me by Count Raczynski as one who had always been active behind the scenes of the political world, and although known to be a man of the left, he had succeeded before the war in keeping on good terms with men of all political colours, including Pilsudskists.[3] He had a reputation as a conciliator and one who, although a string-puller, exercised his art rather in bringing people together and pouring oil on troubled waters than in making mischief. According to Count Raczynski he is a Jew by race. Although he was described by M. Drozniak as an economist, the impression M. Kolodziejski made bore out Count Raczynski's account of him, and I should suspect that he had been sent here to win over Poles and to advise the Commission on tactics rather than on finance and the business side of the Commission's work.

M. Drohojowski, who is normally a tiresome individual, confined himself to the role of interpreter, which according to Mr. Winch he performed quite well and accurately.

I started by welcoming M. Drozniak and M. Kolodziejski as the first official representatives of the new Government to arrive in this country from Warsaw, and M. Drozniak immediately responded by saying how glad they were to be here and how anxious they were to make contact with H.M.G.

I then explained the situation to them fully, informing them that they had arrived prematurely, and telling them laughingly that it was lucky for them that we had foreseen the possibility of their getting through without any British documents and had therefore taken precautions to see that they were spared the inconveniences which normally befell those who arrived here without permission. I then explained that we could not make official contact with the Commission until we had reached agreement with the Warsaw Government as to the basis of discussions, and proceeded to explain our attitude, the complications of the situation with which we were faced and the steps we had taken to meet it.

After I had outlined at M. Drozniak's request, the basis of discussions which we had proposed to Warsaw, on the lines of points 1, 2 and 3 of the communication to the Warsaw Government embodied in our telegram No. 3843[4] of the 8th July, Mr. Drozniak said that the Commission had come over to discuss these matters, and he believed that Poland in her short

[2] The Polish parliament.

[3] Followers of Marshal Jozef Pilsudski, former Polish Chief of State (1918–22), Prime Minister (1926–8, 1930), Minister of War (1926–35).

[4] No. 41.

recent period of independence had a good reputation for fulfilling her obligations; he did not, however, see how the Provisional Government could acknowledge these financial obligations referred to in point 1 of our telegram without knowing precisely what they were. I replied that this was perfectly understood, and that of course the Treasury Committee would be prepared to explain the obligations in detail so soon as it was agreed with the Warsaw Government that discussions should start with the Treasury Committee on the basis that I had outlined. Although M. Drozniak implied that the question of financial obligations was just what his Commission expected to discuss, I had the impression that, in fact, this point was a surprise to them; and Mr. Winch, as stated in our telegram No. 3843[4] of the 8th July to Moscow, paragraph 3, received the impression during the trip from Warsaw that the Commission was originally appointed to deal direct with the London Poles and that its principal task would be to win as many as possible over to Warsaw.

M. Drozniak then went on to say that he felt uncertain whether the Warsaw Government would understand the communication we had sent them. In the first place, he thought they might think they were being asked to acknowledge the financial obligations of the previous Government before discussions started, and therefore without knowing precisely what they were; secondly, he was afraid that they would not understand, and would be suspicious of, our arrangements for dealing with the machinery of the ex-London Government.

I replied that it was precisely in order to make our intentions clear, to explain the extremely anomalous and difficult situation which we had to deal with, to convince him of the necessity of making the provisional arrangements we had made, and to convince him of the excellence of our intentions in doing so, that I had been instructed to have this unofficial conversation with him. I felt sure that we should be ready to facilitate the conveyance to his Government of any explanations he wished to give them as a result of this conversation. We then had some discussion on this and it was decided that the Poles should think the matter over and let us know whether they would like us to send messages to their Government for them through Moscow; whether they should send a report to their Government by the hand of Mr. Hankey; or whether, as I suggested, one or more of them should return to Warsaw urgently. They have since asked us to lay on facilities for two of them to return to Warsaw. I suggested that, as it was most important for them to understand thoroughly our attitude and outlook before returning to their Government, they should check with us, before they sent a report or an emissary to Warsaw, the explanations which they proposed to give their Government.

M. Drozniak then said that Poland had suffered from internal dissensions and was still suffering from the activities of those Poles who would not accept or were uncertain about the new regime and ignorant of the present state of affairs in Poland. He felt unhappy about our employing officials connected with this critical group in the interim period. I made it clear that our plan was designed, so far as possible, to put control in the hands of the Treasury Committee for the triple purpose of liquidating the ex-London Ministries carrying on the necessary activities provisionally, and safeguarding our own financial interest; I made it clear that the status of the Polish ex-officials was that of servants of the Committee. The Poles then broached the question of the personalities we were employing, and I replied that we had heard the criticisms made by Professor Kot[5], that we had taken them into consideration, and that all I could say at the moment was that we understood M. Drozniak's point of view and were continuing to consider and watch the matter. He suggested that we should substitute officials who were known to be favourable to Warsaw, but I did not respond to that suggestion.

M. Drozniak then raised the question of the displaced persons in Germany, and said that on his way over here he had been told by Poles that he had met in Osnabruck that emissaries of the London Government were in touch with the displaced persons and disuading [sic] them from going back. I told M. Drozniak that our policy in the interim period had been, so far as possible, to keep the Polish displaced persons in cold storage for obvious reasons, but that the situation had at the beginning necessarily been chaotic, and it was a matter for SHAEF. I was not, therefore, in a position to say how far it had been possible to carry out our intention completely in practice.

The Poles then asked whether they could go and work in the Embassy or in one of the buildings leased by the London Polish Government. I explained that their Government had asked us to hand over the Embassy to M. Lukasiak, but that we had been compelled to reply that we could only do so if he was formally notified to us as Chargé d'Affaires and could therefore take full responsibility on behalf of his Government. We had heard no more and we were therefore unable to hand over the Embassy, although in point of fact I knew that Count Raczynski would be ready to move out to-morrow. The Poles then asked whether they could be provided with two or three rooms elsewhere to work in. After consulting Sir Orme Sargent, I have since informed them that it is unfortunately impossible to find rooms for them anywhere, and that various other foreign missions who have been coming over here have all had to work in their hotel bedrooms because there was no room elsewhere.

M. Drozniak said that he hoped we would understand the difficulties of the new Government. The intelligentsia in Poland had been largely exterminated and they were hard put to it to find personnel. We must excuse their ignorance in matters of protocol, and we must remember that they were not in control of their own communications. (This was the only reference, but a significant one, to Russian influence in Poland. Mr. Winch had already told me that he got a definite impression in Warsaw that the bulk of the population and the majority of the Ministers, including even the Prime Minister, were anxious to establish contacts with the West as a

---

[5] Formerly Polish Ambassador in Moscow (1941–2), and Minister of Information in the Polish Government in London (1942–4).

set-off to Russian influence, and hoped that the establishment of the new Government would help them to rid themselves of the Russian Army, whose looting and general attitude of conquerors made them in the highest degree unpopular with almost every Pole.)

M. Drozniak then asked whether the B.B.C. would broadcast a non-political message in Polish, expressing his pleasure at being here as the first representative of the new Government to come from Poland. I said we would consider this. I am having enquiries made as to whether the B.B.C. have yet said anything about his arrival.

I terminated a very long meeting by repeating that it seemed to me of the greatest importance that M. Drozniak should fully understand our proposed basis of discussions, and our reasons for the action we had taken, and should ensure that they were understood by his Government. It was of the greatest interest to both Governments that this very difficult matter should be successfully handled in an orderly way and with full comprehension on both sides. The success with which this could be done would no doubt have a great effect on the initial relations between the two Governments. M. Drozniak entirely agreed.

The whole interview appeared to me to go quite well; the atmosphere was friendly and M. Drozniak appeared extremely quick in taking our points.[6]

C. F. A. WARNER

CALENDAR TO No. 61

i   *10 July 1945   To Lord Halifax (Washington) Tel. No. 7321.* Explains administrative measures taken for Polish armed forces pending discussions as to their future; establishment of Interim Treasury Committee for Polish Questions [N 8209/6/55].

[6] Sir A. Cadogan minuted on this record: 'This seems to have passed off satisfactorily. Any inclination on the part of Warsaw to establish reasonable contacts with the West is to be encouraged if possible.   A. C. July 10, 1945.'

No. 62

Brief for the United Kingdom Delegation to the Conference at Potsdam No. 30 [U 5365/764/70]

FOREIGN OFFICE, 9 *July 1945*

Declaration on Liberated Europe[1]

This figures on both our own and the American agendas for Terminal[2] in the following terms:–

(i) *United Kingdom item:* 'Application of Yalta Declaration on liberated Europe'

[1] Issued as article V of the report of the Yalta Conference: cf. No. 30, note 2.
[2] Cf. No. 21, note 9, and No. 111, note 2.

(ii) *United States item:* 'Implementation of Yalta Declaration as [on] liberated Europe'.

2. The text of the Declaration, as agreed at the Crimea Conference and published in the Report on the Conference on 11th February 1945, is at *Annex A*.[3] Although the United Kingdom Delegation tried un-successfully at the Moscow Conference in October 1943 to obtain a Three Power Declaration of principles regarding liberated territory, the Crimea Declaration was in fact an American initiative and draft. There was no time at the Conference to consider its wording carefully, and although the United Kingdom Delegation were alive to its vagueness and drafting imperfections, it was thought best to accept it since it would at least have the great advantage of associating the United States more closely with European affairs.

3. The Soviet Delegation at the Crimea Conference were at first suspicious of the Declaration, which Monsieur Molotov described as an interference in the affairs of liberated Europe, They did not, however, make any serious difficulty before approving it.

4. On Monsieur Molotov's suggestion, which was supported by Mr. Eden, the hope was inserted in the Declaration that the Provisional French Government would associate itself with the Declaration. The approach to the French was made by the American Embassy in Paris. The French reaction was to ask the Americans and ourselves separately a series of questions, differing in certain respects. These questions, which related to the machinery for giving effect to the Declaration and the answers returned are shown in *Annexes B and C*.[4]

5. The French attitude was made clear by Monsieur Bidault when he visited the Secretary of State at Binderton on 25th February. His line was unless an organisation were set up to enforce clear principles France could not share in the responsibility. The Secretary of State agreed that if the French Government proposed the establishment of permanent machinery to deal with questions arising under the Declaration His Majesty's Government would support them. (Extract from the record of conversation in *Annex D*).[5]

6. The Franch [sic] have not pursued the matter and never seemed to have formally associated themselves with the Declaration. There have been indications that the French would prefer to keep out of the wrangles which they expect to result from its application.

7. The Americans however lost little [time] in invoking the Declaration in

---

[3] Not here printed.

[4] Not printed. Annex B, dated 23 February 1945, set out the French questions to H.M. Government with the British replies. Annex C comprised a telegram of 21 February from the State Department to the American Embassy in London setting out the corresponding French questions to the American Government with the American replies: cf. *F.R.U.S. 1945*, vol. iv, pp. 670–2.

[5] Not printed. For this visit to England by M. Georges Bidault, Minister for Foreign Affairs in the French Provisional Government, see Sir L. Woodward, *op. cit.*, vol. iii, pp. 97–9.

respect of the situation in Roumania, where they and we were opposing the Russian action forcing upon the country the minority Groza Government. The Soviet Government rejected the American appro[a]ch, on the ground that the informformation [*sic*] on which it was based was incorrect, and declined by implication to discuss the question under the Declaration. The American representations were repeated and again rejected.

8. We had supported the American demarche, about Roumania, but before the Russian reply had been received we took up with the Americans our doubts about the exact interpretation of the Declaration, particularly whether it meant that:–

(*a*) All three Governments must jointly agree before action could be taken under the Declaration, or:

(*b*) Whether the Declaration meant that no single one of the signatory Governments might take unilateral action in any liberated State (including the former Axis satellites) upon broad matters dealt with in the Declaration.

A copy of our telegram No. 2212 of 8th March to Washington is at *Annex E*.[6]

9. The considered reply of the State Department in Washington telegram No. 1640 of 14th March is at *Annex F*.[7] The American interpretation, as we expected it must be, was that alternative (*a*) in paragraph 4[8] above was correct. The effect of this appeared to the Foreign Office to be broadly that:–

(i) When a specific case arose in a 'liberated' country, it was open to a signatory Government to try to get the other Governments to agree to joint discussions, but that;

(ii) If any one Government refused (as the Soviet Government did over Roumania) there was nothing more which could be done under the Declaration.

10. The passage of time, the dubious attitude of the French and the fact that one Government has the power to block action must all be regarded as gravely weakening the practical utility of the declaration. Moreover, we must take into account the direct conflict of interpretation which exists between the Russians on the one hand and the Americans and ourselves on the other upon what constitute 'democratic elements' and 'free elections'. Our experience over Roumania appears to show that the Russians will take all advantage of their power to block action and will resolutely prevent any attempt to apply the declaration as we and the Americans interpret it to the Balkan countries under their control. While, therefore, the United States Government, without specifically invoking the declaration, are still pressing for the application of its principles, it appears that there is no prospect of any effective action under it, and that the more probable result of any attempt to revive the declaration would be merely to draw further attention

[6] Not printed. For a summary of the memorandum sent by H.M. Embassy at Washington to the State Department in accordance with this telegram see *F.R.U.S. 1945*, vol. v, pp. 515–6.

[7] Not printed. The American reply is printed *ibid.*, p. 516.

to the fact that we have undertaken obligations which it is impossible for us to fulfil.

No. 63

Record of a meeting in Sir O. Sargent's room in the Foreign Office on 9 July 1945

[*ZM 3777/1/22*]

FOREIGN OFFICE, *9 July 1945*

A meeting was held in Sir Orme Sargent's room at the Foreign Office on the morning of Monday, July 9th, to consider the situation in Italy. In addition to Sir Orme Sargent, who was in the Chair, the following were present:–

Sir F. Bovenschen	
Major-General Anderson }	War Office
Senior Commander Stones	
Sir Noel Charles	H.M. Ambassador, Rome.
Brigadier Lush	Allied Commission, Italy.
Mr. Harvey	
Mr. Hoyer Millar.	

The meeting considered the situation in Italy in the light of the report from Admiral Stone to SACMED dated June 23rd[1] and of other recent communications from H.M. Ambassador in Rome. The meeting assumed that H.M.G.'s policy towards Italy should be one of helping Italy to re-establish herself as a useful member of the European comity, of encouraging Italy to look to the West rather than to the East, and of building Italy up to a 'bastion of democracy' in the Mediterranean. The meeting also assumed that it was agreed that this objective was as much an American as a British

---

[1] This report from Rear Admiral Ellery Stone U.S.N.R., Chief Commissioner on the Allied Commission for Italy, is untraced in Foreign Office archives.

interest and that the United States authorities should be encouraged to take their full share in the undertaking. It was appreciated that this policy might mean the acceptance by ourselves of additional obligations. On these assumptions the meeting came to the following conclusions:–

1. *Elections*. It was very desirable that the Italian elections to the Constituent Assembly should be held before the end of the year, while Allied troops were still in Italy in considerable numbers and before the hardships of the winter had had time to exercise a disturbing influence on the voters. Although the Italian authorities were at present believed only to be contemplating holding elections in the Spring, enquiries of the Allied Commission had shown that given efficiency and energy on the part of the Italians it might be possible to hold elections before the end of the year. The Foreign Office were therefore telegraphing to Washington suggesting that the State Department should instruct the United States Ambassador in Rome to join with his British colleague in pressing the Italian Government to do everything possible to hold elections before the end of November.[2] It was, however, problematical to say the least whether the elections would in fact be held before next Spring.

2. *Allied Forces in Italy*. This question was now under consideration by the Chiefs of Staff and would no doubt come under discussion at Terminal. From the purely political point of view the Foreign Office representatives felt that there would be great advantage if Anglo-American troops could remain on in Italy (other than Venezia Giulia) until the Italian elections had been held. (The retention of the troops might of course also be desirable from the 'bastion' point of view). The presence of the troops would exercise a stabilising influence and encourage the Italians to exercise their votes freely and without fear. Both the War Office and the Foreign Office representatives agreed, however, that if such arrangements were made it was most important that the troops should be Anglo-American and not British alone. It would be essential to lay down that the troops would in no way supervise the holding of the elections or attempt to influence the voting.

3. *The Italian Army*. It was important that the Italian Government should be enabled to build up their armed forces quickly to a level sufficiently strong to enable them to maintain internal security and resist local aggression. An Italian army was, too, necessary if Italy was to prove an effective 'bastion'. For the Italian Government to be able to maintain such armed forces they would require appreciable assistance from the Allied Governments as regards equipment and training. The question of how this assistance should be provided and the extent to which the United States authorities should share in the undertaking is now under consideration by the Chiefs of Staff. From the political point of view, however, it seems highly desirable that if possible arrangements should be made for the Americans to undertake a part of the task.

4. *The Military Mission*. As part of the assistance to be given in this way

[2] See No. 12.i.

to the Italian army, a military mission would have to be set up on the dissolution of the Allied Commission. Whether this mission was an Anglo-American mission or purely British would depend to some extent on the decisions reached as to whether or not the United States took a part in the equipping of the Italian forces. It was, however, felt important that the mission should in any case be only advisory and not executive.

5. *Police Mission.* Admiral Stone has pressed for the appointment of a police mission and a telegram received during the last few days from H.M. Embassy in Rome supported this proposal, which was warmly endorsed by Sir Noel Charles and Brigadier Lush. It was felt, however, that if a British mission were to be appointed considerable difficulties would be experienced in the way of finding suitable personnel, more especially as the War Office would be in the market for similar personnel for work in Germany and such suitable persons as were available have already been selected for the Greek mission.[3] In these circumstances it might be better to press for the mission to be either American or provided by one of the Dominions. There were considerable political advantages in the mission being American or at all events in it not being British. It will be necessary to give the matter further thought before reaching any conclusion.

6. *Future of the Allied Commission.* The Allied Commission would inevitably disappear on the conclusion of the Peace Treaty. This might not, however, happen for several months to come, and in the meantime it seemed desirable that the Allied Commission, after the handing back to the Italian Government of the rest of Italy (other than Venezia Giulia and Bolzano), should gradually shed as many of its functions as possible without waiting for the conclusion of the Peace Treaty. The Allied Commission would of necessity have to retain its responsibility for the implementation of the military clauses of the armistice until the latter was replaced by the Peace Treaty. It would seem desirable, however, that the Allied Commission's present responsibilities in the economic sphere—i.e. in respect of the import of supplies and of the general control of the economy of Italy—should be got rid of as soon as practicable. It was hoped that U.N.R.R.A. would take over the responsibility for the import of supplies in a few months' time and plans were already under consideration for the early establishment of some kind of Anglo-American economic advisory machinery to take over from the Allied Commission the latter's work regarding the control of the Italian economy. The form which this new machinery should take was about to be discussed by the A.C.A.O.–S.L.A.O. Committee.[4] It was felt, however, that the hand-over from the Allied Commission should take place as soon as practicable.

7. *Publicity.* Admiral Stone had suggested that a useful part could be played in the political education of the Italian public during the period before the elections by the maintenance throughout the country of a certain number of liaison officers from the Allied Commission. It was agreed that it

---

[3] Cf. No. 84.i below.   [4] See No. 29, note 10.

would be desirable for both the British and American authorities to do what they could in the publicity and propaganda direction to spread an appreciation among the Italians of 'the democratic way of life', but it was thought that on the face of it this was more properly a job for the British and United States Embassies. Since, however, the Allied Commission was not likely to be brought to an end all of a sudden and since some of its duties would continue until the conclusion of the Peace Treaty, no doubt some of their officers would have in any case to remain in various parts of Italy and would be able by their presence to exert a useful influence from the publicity point of view.

8. *The Peace Treaty.* It was agreed that it was very desirable to press on with the early conclusion of a peace treaty. Both Sir Noel Charles and Brigadier Lush emphasised the importance which the Italian people attached from the psychological point of view to the Italian fleet. To have to surrender a very large part of the fleet in the Peace Treaty would therefore be very unwelcome to the Italian people. Brigadier Lush also suggested the desirability of including in the Treaty some definite statement promising Italy Allied support in the matter of supplies and more particularly of coal. It was felt, however, that to include any commitment on so definite lines would be both inappropriate and inadvisable.

9. *Coal.* The necessity of helping Italy to obtain as large supplies of coal as possible during the coming winter was emphasised by Sir Noel Charles and Brigadier Lush. They were assured that the authorities in London were fully alive to the point and that the question of how best to provide for the presentation of Italian claims before the European Coal Organisation was now under consideration.

F. R. HOYER MILLAR

CALENDARS TO NO. 63

i 7 *July 1945   Memo. by Chairman of the S.L.A.O. Committee, with F.O. minutes,* on economic arrangements in Italy and withdrawal of combined military control [ZM 3731/18/22].

ii *10 July 1945   Letter from Mr. J. Leckie (Board of Trade) to Mr. A. D. M. Ross.* Considers question of American commercial penetration in Italy and suggestion that British economic policy there is perhaps too passive [ZM 3809/2854/22].

No. 64

Brief for the United Kingdom Delegation to the Conference at Potsdam
No. 1 [E 4987/8/89]

FOREIGN OFFICE, 9 July 1945[1]

The Levant States

It is not proposed that the British Delegation should raise the question of the Levant States at Terminal. The Americans, who have agreed with us in

---

[1] Date of submission of this undated brief by Mr. C. W. Baxter, and of its initialing by Sir R. Campbell.

wishing to confine any immediate discussion of this question to the Powers directly concerned, are also presumably unlikely to raise it. If it is raised at all, it will therefore be by the Russians.

2. The only communication received from the Soviet Government about the Levant dispute is their note of the 1st June (copy attached),[2] to which we replied on the 9th June that developments in the Levant had necessitated the temporary intervention of British troops to restore order.

3. The present position is as follows:– The French Government proposed that a conference of French, British, American, Chinese and Soviet representatives should be called to consider current questions in the Near and Middle East. The United States Government replied that they did not think that an international conference on Near Eastern questions as a whole would be appropriate at the present time. His Majesty's Government informed the French Government that they agreed with the United States Government's view that discussion of the Levant problem should be confined to those directly interested. They therefore proposed that Anglo-American-French conversations should be held in London, with which the Syrian and Lebanese Governments would be associated.

4. The French Government have not replied to His Majesty's Government's proposal, though M. Massigli apparently believes that M. Bidault would not be prepared to come to London for a conference. Meanwhile Count Ostrorog[3] has returned to the Levant with certain proposals, the full nature of which is not yet known, but which have already resulted in the agreement to transfer the Troupes Speciales[4] to the Levant Governments.

[2] Not printed. This note was the same, subject to verbal variation, as that of even date from the Soviet Government to the American Government, printed in *F.R.U.S. 1945*, vol. viii, pp. 1128–9. The Soviet note to His Majesty's Government stated in particular: 'According to information received, fighting is at present taking place on the territory of Syria and the Lebanon, and the French troops have come into conflict with the Syrians and Lebanese, firing with artillery and mortars on Damascus, the capital of Syria. Damascus is being bombed from the air . . . . The Soviet Government considers that the events in Syria and the Lebanon are not in accordance with the spirit of the decisions taken at Dumbarton Oaks or with the aims of the Conference of the United Nations now in session at San Francisco . . . . The Soviet Government therefore considers that urgent measures should be taken to bring the fighting in Syria and the Lebanon to a conclusion and to settle by peaceful means the conflict which has arisen.' In his reply Mr. Churchill further stated: 'I note that the Soviet Government share the view taken by His Majesty's Government of the disturbing developments in the Levant States in recent weeks.' The British reply enclosed for information texts of the statements made in the House of Commons by Mr. Eden on 31 May 1945 and by Mr. Churchill on 5 June: see *Parl. Debs., 5th ser., H. of C.*, vol. 411, cols. 378–9 and 689–94.

[3] Count Stanislas Ostrorog, a member of the French Delegation General in the Levant, had recently visited Paris.

[4] The Troupes Spéciales were locally recruited military units under French command in the Levant: see Sir L. Woodward, *op. cit.*, vol. iv. p. 239, note 3; also p. 342 for the French announcement on 8 July 1945 of their transfer, under arrangements to be announced within fortyfive days, to the Syrian and Lebanese Governments. Next day Sir A. Cadogan recorded a conversation with the French Ambassador that afternoon on this subject: 'M. Massigli rather deplored the attitude of the British press which was inclined to insinuate that this

5. If the Soviet representatives raise the question of the Levant their purpose will presumably be to urge that the Soviet Government should not be excluded from any conference on this question. It is suggested that our own reply, if the United States Delegation agree, should be to the following effect. Failing any direct settlement between the French and the Levant Governments, the question of the future of the Levant States will in due course have to be referred to the World Organisation. At that stage, the Soviet Government would naturally participate in any discussions. Meanwhile, our main concern is the settlement of immediate practical questions in the Levant, whose solution has an obvious bearing on the conduct of the Far Eastern war. We adhere to our view that these questions can best be settled by direct discussion between the parties directly concerned and that they should not be combined with any general discussion of the Middle East as a whole.

CALENDARS TO No. 64

i *9 July 1945   To Mr. Duff Cooper (Paris) Tel. No. 1618 Saving.* 'Reason for our unwillingness to produce real figures of British troops in the Levant has been not that there were so many, but that there were so few. Under the Lyttelton-de Gaulle Agreement [of 25 July 1941, printed, with letters exchanged, by Sir L. Woodward, *op. cit.*, vol. i, pp. 589–93: cf. also *ibid.*, pp. 569–70.], French are entitled to claim operational as well as territorial command in any "zone of action" in which their troops are more numerous.' But considered that in view of attitude of French military this would render impossible the position of British forces there [E 4130/14/89].

ii *9 July 1945   Mr. J. E. M. Carvell (H.M. Consul-General, Algiers) No. 116.* Reports conversation on 3 July with two members of Parti Populaire Algérien. They expressed Arab gratification at British intervention in Syria, and evidently sought some assurance or encouragement to think that H.M.G. would intervene in Algeria in the event of disturbances. Mr. Carvell 'was most careful not to give the slightest encouragement to this wild wishful thinking'. Impression that nationalist elements in Algeria were fanatically determined [Z 8618/900/69].

was a matter in which the French could not help themselves and to belittle this action on the part of the French Government. I said that I had noticed this tendency and had thought that perhaps a little more credit could have been given to the French Government. On the other hand ... there was probably a long road to travel yet. M. Massigli did not dissent but he asked whether we could help to induce a little more generosity on the part of our press and assist locally by good advice to the Levant Governments. I said we would certainly consider both these points.   A. C. 9th July, 1945' (E 5033/14/89).

No. 65

Earl of Halifax (Washington) to Mr. Eden (Received 21 July)
No. 776 [U 5589/12/70]

Confidential   WASHINGTON, *9 July 1945*
Sir,
   I have the honour to transmit herewith a memorandum by Mr. Hadow[1]

[1] This memorandum of 5 July 1945 by Mr. R. H. Hadow, a Counsellor in H.M. Embassy at Washington, is not printed.

on the trends which he observed among the Latin American delegations during the course of the United Nations Conference on International Organisation at San Francisco.

2. As reported from San Francisco, the Latin American delegations were at times somewhat of a problem; by reason principally of their voting strength, their limited horizons and their nervous fear of Soviet Russia. These difficulties were, however, surmounted largely through the close contact which Mr. Nelson Rockefeller maintained with their delegations; and also thanks to the more broad-minded views and persuasive powers of Señor Parra Perez, of Venezuela, perhaps the outstanding Latin American delegate at this conference.

3. Señor Fernandez y Fernandez, of Chile, unfortunately entered at an early stage into a private understanding with Mr. Evatt, of Australia, the principal effect of which was to tie the Chilean vote over the veto question.[2] Useful and co-operative wheel horses—especially in the United States—were Señor Andrade, of Bolivia, Señor Galo Plaza Lasso, of Ecuador, and, once he had recovered from a slight bout of nationalism, Señor Lleras Camergo [Camargo], of Colombia. Señor Belaunde, of Peru—who professes unbounded admiration for Great Britain—treated the Assembly to two examples of fervent Latin American oratory over the admission of Argentina and the Mexican Declaration[3] against admission of Franco Spain respectively. The Brazilian delegation on the whole eschewed polemics and kept out of the limelight; their main grievance—wisely kept within bounds—being the repression of their ambition to reach the seats of the mighty. This disappointment was also shared by Mexico; which may account for the unexpected eclipse of Señor Padilla in comparison with his performances at Rio and Mexico.[4] His appointment as *rapporteur* to the Steering Committee acted as somewhat heady wine to Señor Belt Ramirez,[5] of Cuba.

4. On the whole their first contact for some years with world forces of which they had had but little practical experience probably sent the majority of the Latin American delegations back to their several countries in a wiser and more sober frame of mind than had prevailed among them at the outset.

5. Their contacts with the United Kingdom delegation were friendly throughout the conference; and it was perhaps inevitable that the mantle of

[2] Cf. No. 42, note 5.

[3] For this resolution and the discussion preceding its adoption on 19 June 1945 by Commission I of the San Francisco Conference see *Documents of the United Nations Conference on International Organisation, San Francisco 1945* (London, 1945), vol. vi, pp. 127–36.

[4] Dr. Ezequiel Padilla, Mexican Foreign Minister and delegate to the Conference of San Francisco, had been President of the Conference in Mexico City (cf. No. 42, note 26) and delegate at the Pan-American conference at Rio de Janeiro in January 1942: cf. Sir. L. Woodward, *op. cit.*, vol. iv, pp. 72–3.

[5] Dr. Guillermo Belt was Cuban Ambassador in Washington and head of the Cuban Delegation at San Francisco.

leadership should have seemed to them to have fallen, so far as this hemisphere is concerned, upon American shoulders.

I have, &c.,

HALIFAX

No. 66

Mr. Eden to Earl of Halifax (Washington)
No. 7304 Telegraphic [E 4206/420/89]

Important   FOREIGN OFFICE, *10 July 1945, 12.25 a.m.*

Repeated to Beirut No. 513, M.E. Min[ister] No. 1202, Paris Saving No. 1616.

My telegram No. 6763[1] (25th June: American assistance in Levant States).

Have you yet received any further indication of United States Government's views?

2. We are strongly in favour of suggestion in paragraph 3 of Sir E. Grigg's telegram No. 652[2] (30th June) that Americans should take over equipment and training of Syrian and Lebanese gendarmeries. Inability of States Governments to maintain order with their present resources will become an increasingly serious danger, particularly if to general insecurity there is added trouble between Moslems and Christians. Material interests such as oil pipe line may also be threatened. It would be particularly invidious for His Majesty's Government to undertake this task, since our known desire to improve the efficiency of the gendarmeries was a constant source of suspicion on the part of the French. We very much hope therefore that United States Government, whom the French have never accused of attempts to supplant them, will be prepared to supply a small mission as they have done in Persia and Saudi Arabia, as well as any further equipment which may be necessary.

3. If United States Government agree in principle, we suggest that United States Minister should be instructed to discuss detailed implications of this proposal with His Majesty's Minister and General Officer Commanding 9th Army.

---

[1] Not printed. This telegram had conveyed approval that the British Embassy in Washington had explored with Mr. Loy Henderson, Director of Near Eastern and African Affairs in the State Department, questions concerning possible American assistance in the Levant States, including the possible despatch of an American warship to the Levant. The telegram added: 'I appreciate difficulties in obtaining participation of American token force. We should however be very glad if the Americans were able to help the Levant States by sending advisers and technical help generally in any form acceptable to the Levant States', such as participation of some American officers in M.I.R.A., a temporary wheat organisation, set up by British military authorities in consultation with the Syrian and Lebanese governments, for the collection and distribution of the harvest in the Levant following the suspension of the Anglo-French Office des Céréales Panifiables (O.C.P.) in June 1945. In regard to the financing of M.I.R.A. Foreign Office telegram No. 522 of 12 July to Beirut explained that Mr. Eden was 'most anxious not to give French the impression that we are excluding their cooperation if that is obtainable in any form.'
[2] Not printed.

4. Our own military authorities are already seriously concerned at the growing danger of internal insecurity in the Levant, and you should impress on State Department that the question is one of real urgency. The agreement over the transfer of the Troupes Speciales does not of itself suffice to remove this danger.

No. 67

Mr. Duff Cooper (Paris) to Mr. Eden (Received 10 July, 7.40 p.m.)
No. 979 Telegraphic [Z 8234/103/17]

Immediate   PARIS, *10 July 1945, 6.58 p.m.*

Following for Hasler from Wyndham White.[1]

At weekly meeting with M. Pineau[2] and Ministry of Food officials on July 5th the French made urgent appeal for stop gap assistance on sugar and fats. We immediately telephoned details to Ministry of Food confirming by letter. We have so far had no firm reply. It would be very embarrassing to us to go to the next meeting on July 12th without being able to give an answer and we should be grateful therefore if you could expedite reply.

2. I realise that Broadley and Harrison[3] are doing their best and some extra weight may help them.

CALENDARS TO No. 67

i *10 July 1945 Ministry of Food to Mr. Pinnock (British Food Mission, Copenhagen) Tel. No. 39 Grub X.* Refers to S.H.A.E.F. decision on Danish surpluses (cf. No. 98, para. 3.i). Suggests agreement be sought to limit French purchases; otherwise French appear able to take whatever quantities they wish prior to declaration of an exportable surplus available for distribution. [UR 2620/1590/851].

ii *13 July 1945 Mr. Hutton (British Food Mission, Washington) to Ministry of Food Tel. No. Amaze 5311.* Mr. Parisius of F.E.A. has warned M. Pineau of dangers of independent action to secure meat for France [UR 2393/1857/851].

iii *13 July 1945 Mr. Duff Cooper (Paris) No. 758.* Transmits report by Mr. Wyndham White of a conversation with M. Pleven, Minister of Finance and National Economy. Supplies and difficulties of coal situation discussed. Generally, M. Pleven considered only comparatively modest Allied help required to pull France through. He complained of French exclusion from Commodity Committees of the Combined Board responsible for planning allocation of supplies [Z 8572/103/17].

---

[1] Economic Adviser to H.M. Embassy, Paris.

[2] M. Pineau, French Minister of Food, was shortly to visit Washington. In Foreign Office telegram No. 7669 of 20 July 1945 to Washington, concerning the desirability of British assistance in the success of M. Pineau's mission, Mr. O. C. Harvey informed Mr. R. M. Makins, H.M. Minister there: 'Pineau is an excellent man who deserves encouragement, and any help you can give him would be much valued.'

[3] Mr. H. Broadley, Deputy Secretary at the Ministry of Food, was Chairman of a Sub-committee on Food and Agriculture of the Emergency Economic Committee for Europe (E.E.C.E.). Mr. A. R. W. Harrison was Deputy Director of Public Relations in the Ministry of Food.

No. 68

Mr. Eden to Mr. Churchill (Biarritz)
No. 2 Victor Telegraphic [F.O. 954/1:AU/45/61]

FOREIGN OFFICE, 10 July 1945, 7 p.m.

Most Immediate. Personal and Top secret

Following for Colville from Rowan.[1]

1. Assheton[2] states he is generally satisfied with reports from constituencies about polling.

2. E.A.C. have settled zones of occupation in Austria. Text of agreement[3] by tomorrow's bag.

3. Committees and Cabinet working hard. Housing squad and Reparations[4] met yesterday. Manpower and European Control today plus two meetings of Cabinet.

---

[1] Mr. T. L. Rowan was Principal Private Secretary to Mr. Churchill.

[2] The Rt. Hon. Ralph Assheton, M.P., was Chairman of the Conservative Party Organization.

[3] See No. 56, note 1.

[4] i.e. the Housing and the Reparations Ministerial Committees of the Cabinet.

No. 69

Mr. Eden to Mr. Churchill (Biarritz)
No. 6 Victor Telegraghic [F.O. 954/2:Con/45/151]

Immediate   FOREIGN OFFICE, 10 July 1945, 9.50 p.m.

Personal for Prime Minister from Secretary of State for Foreign Affairs.

Arrived back this morning. Feeling very good though a little shaky on my legs. Nothing of outstanding note at to-day's Cabinet, where we missed you very much. Have to cope with Joe Davies for my sins tomorrow.[1]

I hope you are really making holiday and that the rest is doing you good. If opportunity offers don't forget to back No. 17.[2]

I look forward to our meeting at Terminal on Sunday.[3] From what I can see of things we shall not lack problems for discussion when we get there.

---

[1] Cf. No. 4, note 1. On 12 July 1945 *The Times* reported that Mr. Eden 'had a long talk' (record untraced) with Mr. Davies at luncheon on 11 July.

[2] The reference may have been to roulette.

[3] 15 July.

No. 70

Sir W. Strang (Lübbecke) to Sir J. Grigg (Received 12 July, 2 p.m.)[1]
No. M. 1194 Telegraphic [C 3853/24/18]

Immediate. Top secret   LÜBBECKE, *10 July 1945, 8.40 p.m.*

Repeated to Berlin District.

From General Weeks.

First. At meeting in Berlin today with Marshal Zhukov and General Clay, attended by Sir William Strang and Mr. Robert Murphy,[2] agreement was signed setting up inter-Allied Military Commandature for administration of greater Berlin[3]. Agreement follows closely the provisions previously agreed at EAC. First meeting of Commandature called for 11th July with Major General Lyne controlling British sector of Berlin. Text of agreement will reach you shortly.

Second. Provision of food and coal was then considered on clear understanding that this was on a[n] *ad hoc* basis and without prejudice to questions of principle which would be discussed at Terminal. Clay and I agreed jointly to provide food for one month up to approximate total figure of 40,000 tons per month, made up of wheat, potatoes, sugar and salt, last three items being supplied from indigenous resources. Russian estimates to be reviewed jointly by experts on 11th July to ensure approximate conformity with ration scales elsewhere in Germany. Delivery to begin at exchange points on border of Russian zone 15th July. Russians responsible for supplying to Commandature food equivalent to that received at exchange points. Russian Military Government Staffs will be withdrawn from non-Russian sectors within one or two days.

Third. Coal. Marshal Zhukov reiterated his statement made at previous meeting that territory east of Oder-Neisse line was not within his jurisdiction and therefore that Silesian coal could not be taken into consideration. Sir William Strang made it clear that British Government reserved their position on this question. Marshal Zhukov confirmed previous Russian estimate of Berlin's total requirements as 7500 tons per day which would have to be met by the four powers, but agreed that this figure should be examined jointly by experts on 11th July with view to effecting all possible economy.

I emphasised that figure appeared unreasonably high by comparison with all our previous experience and indicated serious repercussions on quantities for export movement of Russian displaced persons and other matters. After prolonged discussion it was agreed to start on basis of supplying an initial figure of 3 trains per day, say 2400 tons, to commence from a date to be

---

[1] Date and time of receipt in Foreign Office.

[2] Political Adviser on German affairs to General Eisenhower.

[3] This Allied agreement on the quadripartite administration of Berlin is printed under date of 7 July 1945 (cf. No. 58, annex) in Cmd. 1552 of 1961, p. 45.

determined by expert examination of transportation facilities available. Meanwhile requirements to be closely scrutinised with a view to more accurate estimates and the general question of future supply to be referred to Governments as in the case of food.

Fourth. Meeting then considered proposal tabled by Clay for early establishment of control council, co-ordinating committee, inter-allied secretariat and control staff. British and United States representatives both stressed importance attached by Governments to early action. Proposal to establish certain German central administrative agencies covering whole of Germany was explained by Clay in detail to Marshal Zhukov to whom conception seemed to be somewhat unfamiliar but he agreed to refer question to his Government and was obviously sympathetic. Agreement was reached that action to find suitable accommodation for central control should be initiated forthwith by Allied representatives now in Berlin.

Fifth. Agreement reached that French should be invited to participate with equal status in all future meetings of Allied co-ordinating committee and Commandature.

Sixth. General atmosphere of meeting was good. Joint communique summarising results was drafted by political advisers and has been issued.[4] Similar steps will be taken at subsequent meetings.

CALENDARS TO NO. 70

i *11 July 1945   Sir W. Strang (Lübbecke) (a) Tel. No. 36; (b) Letter to Mr. Harvey*, without enclosure: further accounts of meeting reported in No. 70. Owing to oversight no French liaison representative attended but account of proceedings is being communicated to French authorities and French member will be invited to first meeting of the Commandature on 11 July. General Lyne has established good relations with Russian Generals and will make every effort to collaborate with them. There is complete freedom of movement throughout sectors of Berlin. Impression of bad economic situation in Soviet zone. Only in Berlin are results of Soviet occupation likely to be visible to other Allies [C 3807/24/18; C 3905/1/18].

ii *10 July 1945   Memorandum by Viscount Hood:* delimitation of French sector in Berlin. In view of difficulties about supplies in Berlin it might be desirable to reduce British sector. Assumes, however, that British policy remains that U.S.S.R. should contribute, and submits that question should be raised at Berlin. Minuting in the Foreign Office in general agreement [U 6116/20/70].

---

[4] Cf. *The Times* of 11 July 1945, p. 4, for a summary of this communique.

No. 71

Mr. Eden to Earl of Halifax (Washington)
No. 7338 Telegraphic [N 8342/5074/55]

Secret   FOREIGN OFFICE, *10 July 1945, midnight*

My immediately preceding telegram.[1]

Following is text.

Joint OWI/PID Directive on Polish Provisional Government of National Unity, issued on 7th July.

A. Point out that His Majesty's Government and United States Government are satisfied that the formation of the Polish Provisional Government of National Unity constitutes a substantial step in the fulfilment of the Yalta agreement on Poland.

B. Refrain from giving undue prominence to any published news of charges or hostile criticism against the former Polish Government in London or of the London ex-Government's criticism of the new Polish Provisional Government of National Unity.

C. Give prominence to all news which would tend to cause Poles in in Germany to turn to Warsaw for a positive solution of their problems.

D. In comment do not give the impression that His Majesty's Government and United States Government are eager to force the Polish people to return home. Emphasise the fact that the Polish people themselves can do more to shape their own future if they go back to their native land than if they remain in Germany as exiles.

E. Point out that the structure of the new Provisional Government of National Unity, formed by the main Polish parties, allows for all Poles to have a share in the shaping of their country's destinies.

F. Make use of any reliable material showing how the new Provisional Government is fulfilling its pledges concerning the elections and is taking steps to provide employment and security to returning Poles.

G. Official appeals from the Provisional Government to Polish displaced persons in Germany prompting them to return should be used whenever available.

[1] Not printed. This telegram No. 7336, despatched at 11.33 p.m. on 10 July 1945, stated that the directive printed below had been agreed in London between the Political Intelligence Department of the Foreign Office and the American Office of War Information. This had been approved by the Foreign Office and issued as an internal directive for the guidance of the British Broadcasting Corporation and Allied Press Service output.

No. 72

Mr. Stevenson (Belgrade) to Mr. Eden (Received 16 July, 11.50 a.m.)
No. 78 Saving Telegraphic, by bag [R 13005/11/67]

BELGRADE, *10 July 1945*

Repeated to Resmed Caserta No. 49 Saving, Moscow No. 7 Saving, Washington No. 11 Saving.

M. Anto [Ante] Radojevic, Vice-President of the Radical Party and a former Minister of Communications, called on me this morning. He was in a highly nervous state. After inveighing for some time against the iniquities of the present régime, he told me that he was convinced that the leaders of the Communist Party were taking steps to remove any possible opposition leaders, among whom he figured. In support of this accusation he showed me a summons to appear before the Court of Serbian National Honour at Cacak. The Summons was a printed form which required his attendance at the Court on the grounds that he was 'suspected'. The space in the form provided for the insertion of a description of the activities of which he was suspected was left blank.

2. M. Radojevic said that if he went to Cacak in answer to this Summons he would probably be 'killed while trying to escape' or at best would be sentenced to some years of hard labour. The Court in question consisted of a Communist lawyer as President, and two workmen. He stated that this Court had been responsible for the liquidation of 2,000 people. He intended to write to the Court explaining that he was ill, and demand trial in Belgrade. He asked for my protection, adding that his wife was of Scottish birth and that he had two young children.

3. I pointed out to M. Radojevic that as he knew very well, I was not in a position to protect him in any way. All that I could do would be to speak on his behalf to Dr. Subasic and that I promised to do. He said that he understood the position perfectly well but would be grateful for anything I could do in the matter.

4. This evening I mentioned the case to Dr. Subasic and the latter took note of it. He said that the state of tension and nervousness in Belgrade was particularly bad at the moment but he did not think that there was any likelihood of the life of an ex-Minister such as M. Radojevic being in danger, though it might well be that a decision had been taken to bring him to trial. I pointed out that he had been imprisoned by the Germans for some time and that he had declined to have anything to do with the Cetnik movement.[1] It seemed odd, therefore, that he should be suspected of anything except perhaps of being out of sympathy with the present régime. Dr. Subasic promised to make some enquiries.

5. As an illustration of the wild rumours that were going about Belgrade in the present atmosphere of nervous tension, Dr. Subasic said that two days ago M. Trifunovic, another of the leaders of the Radical Party, had had occasion to call at the Ministry of Foreign Affairs on some routine business and had asked to see him. He had received M. Trifunovic, who expressed the greatest possible surprise at finding him there, having heard that very morning, on what he considered to be the highest authority, that Dr. Subasic had been arrested!

6. Speaking of the general political situation, Dr. Subasic said that he was disheartened and discouraged by the amount of attention that was

[1] Guerilla organisation in Serbia led by General Draza Mihailovic, Yugoslav Minister of War and Commander-in-Chief, 1942–4.

being given to politics, not only by the people in general but by the leaders of the régime. What was wanted was that everyone should be set to work to restore their ravaged country. Communications *must* be re-established at the earliest possible moment. Winter was approaching and he feared that the country would be faced with the impossibility of distributing even the relief which was now arriving from abroad. In many parts of Yugoslavia communications were non-existent and he shuddered to think of next winter unless something was done, and that quickly. 'It is not politics we should be discussing now but how to save the lives of the people'.[2]

7. I asked him why in these circumstances the army was not being demobilised. It seemed to me absurd now that the war with Germany was over to have so many men idle. He replied that Marshal Tito probably had a number of reasons for keeping the army on a war footing, not reasons of foreign politics, he hastened to add, but of internal affairs. The country was still in a disturbed state; many people had arms hidden away; and there were still bands of Cetniks in the mountains. He evidently thought that the retention of men in the army was probably justified but he added that it did not help to solve the labour problem.

CALENDAR TO NO. 72

i *10 July 1945 Letter from Mr. L. S. Amery to Mr. Eden.* Encloses tel. from Dr. M. Krek, former Yugoslav Deputy Prime Minister, asking that Slovenia should be placed under Allied Military Government at Trieste. Mr. Amery refers to fear expressed earlier by Dr. Krek that large proportion of 11,000 repatriated Slovenes have been put to death: seemingly strong argument for H.M.G. retaining present military administration as long as possible [R 11815/6/92].

[2] Mr. Stevenson further reported in Belgrade telegram No. 1102 of 12 July 1945 proposals for a Yugoslav congress to form a single national front, and Dr. Subasic's terms for his participation in the light of his fear of a national front becoming 'a thinly disguised one-party régime': Dr. Subasic was anxious (para. 7) for a reminder from Potsdam about the Tito-Subasic agreement. This telegram (printed in *F.R.U.S. Berlin*, vol. ii, pp. 1207–8), was transmitted by the Foreign Office to the British Delegation at Potsdam and was minuted as follows by Mr. Hayter, a member of Southern Department and Secretary-General of the British Delegation at Potsdam, by Sir A. Cadogan and Mr. Eden: 'Para. 7 of this is interesting. We hope to get some kind of reminder on the lines suggested, & the Americans seemed to agree yesterday [see No. 142]. As the Russians sponsored the Tito-Subasic Agreement at Yalta they can hardly refuse. W. G. Hayter 15/7.' 'Yes. S. of S.'s attention sh[oul]d be called to §7. A. C. July 16, 1945.' 'Americans should be told of this. It is important to enlist their help over Yugoslavia. A. E. July 17.'

No. 73

*Record of a meeting in Sir O. Sargent's room
in the Foreign Office at 5 p.m. on 10 July 1945*
[*N 7652/211/55*]

Minutes of meeting in Sir Orme Sargent's room at 5 p.m. on 10th July to discuss the attitude and policy to be adopted by His Majesty's Chargé d'Affaires at Warsaw.

Present:

Sir Orme Sargent, Mr. Warner, Mr. Hankey, Mr. Winch, Mr. Storrs.[1]

Mr. HANKEY asked to what extent His Majesty's Embassy at Warsaw should be prepared to let the Russians take the lead diplomatically and in general to admit that they had any authority on Polish territory.

SIR ORME SARGENT expressed the hope that our representative in Warsaw would have greater influence than his counterparts in Sofia and Bucharest, but that this depended on the extent to which he and his Mission would be dependent on the Russians, particularly as regards currency.

MR WINCH said that he had questioned the French Ambassador, Monsieur Garreau, regarding his liberty of movement during the time he had been in Poland. Monsieur Garreau had told him that at first he had had complete freedom and that he had been able without any difficulty to take a ticket for flights to Cracow, Danzig and other places. He had had to ask for a guard to be put on his house to protect it from robbery by the Russian soldiery. The guard encountered by Mr. Winch appeared to be an ordinary Polish peasant in uniform and not an N.K.V.D.[2] man, Russian or Polish.

MR. HANKEY considered that we should assume from the start that members of our Mission would have complete freedom, and that we should not put any ideas about restrictions into the Russians heads by applying for any sort of permission to travel about Poland.

To Sir Orme Sargent's question about the number of Russians now in Warsaw, MR. WINCH replied that he had seen extremely few in the centre of the City and not very many in Praga. He was told by individual Poles that there were many more Russians in small towns round about and that all traffic was controlled by the Russians. SIR ORME SARGENT asked about the Warsaw airport.

MR. WINCH said that this was guarded by a few sentries. He was not sure whether they were Russian or Polish, but that all the airfield staff were Russian as well as the pilots of the LOT air services now operating all over Poland as a nominally Polish service. He thought that we should always approach the Poles direct, on the assumption that they were independent, to a fair degree, of Russian control. He had, however, heard that an N.K.V.D. officer had attempted to turn the Voivode[3] of Lublin out of the car in which he was travelling and was only prevented from doing so by the intervention of the French Ambassador who happened to be a passenger in the car.

MR. HANKEY asked whether we should admit the right of the N.K.V.D. to arrest and deport Polish citizens or whether we should give some degree of support to the Poles in resisting such action. As a means of solving this problem, should we encourage the Poles to negotiate an agreement with the

---

[1] Mr. M. B. Storrs had been designated a Secretary in H.M. Embassy at Warsaw.

[2] Narodny Kommissariat Vnutrennikh Del: People's Commissariat of Internal Affairs (Soviet Union).

[3] Provincial Governor.

Russians, laying down the precise areas in which the Soviet military authorities should have control for purposes of communications with the Soviet zone in Germany and those in which Polish authorities should be paramount?

Mr. Warner remarked that the Russians had made with the Norwegians an agreement on this subject on exactly the same model as we had made with Norway and with countries in North-West Europe through which we had lines of communication. He thought the Poles would be very careful in their approach to us for any sort of backing against the Russians.

Sir Orme Sargent thought that Mikolajczyk might invite some on the quiet, as President Benes had done in Czechoslovakia and it was agreed that Mr. Hankey should consult with Mikolajczyk on such points, so far as he could without compromising him. But that we should not be drawn into the position of championing the Poles openly *vis à vis* of the Russians since we were unlikely to be able to exert much influence in practice in face of Russian opposition.

Mr. Winch said that those Poles who owed their present position to the Russians were very quick to resent any sign of ridicule or dislike of the Russians from other quarters. They would, however, welcome any concrete benefit which the Western Powers could bestow upon Poland.

Mr. Warner thought that we should certainly not mediate in any way between the Russians and the Poles.

Sir Orme Sargent raised the question of relations with the United States Mission in Warsaw. He thought they would probably be unwilling to 'gang up' with us in any way which might prejudice their relations with the Russians. They would probably be confident that the Poles would come to them rather than to the British for help. There was a tendency at the present time for the United States of America to regard themselves and the Union of Soviet Socialist Republics as the two first-rank powers in the world and to wish to keep clear of what they regarded as intra-European squabbles.

Mr. Warner remarked that the tendency was bound to be for the United States Mission to want to take the lead and to get as much credit as possible. They would claim greater impartiality and might well belittle us to the Poles. He thought that British big business would be chary of involving themselves in business in the new Poland—as indeed they were with the old.

Mr. Hankey said he had heard that the Prudential Assurance Company and various textile firms who had had an interest in Polish mills before the war were now anxious to renew their contacts. He asked whether we should given them active assistance.

Mr. Warner said that the protection of British interests was certainly one of Mr. Hankey's first duties.

Sir Orme Sargent said that a more important point—and one in which the Secretary of State was much interested was in getting British journalists to Poland in the immediate future.

Mr. Hankey said that the *Times* and the *Exchange Telegraph* had already appointed correspondents to proceed as soon as possible and that several other papers would follow suit. SIR ORME SARGENT felt that this depended largely on the conditions prevailing as regards censorship and transmission of reports.

MR. WINCH said that there was now no Russian censorship in Warsaw, and that the Warsaw radio station, which should be working by the end of July, would broadcast messages from foreign correspondents. The objection to this would be that such messages would not be exclusive to any one paper, and that reception of them might prove difficult in London. He believed that the French Ambassador was at present negotiating an agreement for the inauguration of telegraphic communication between Poland and France. We should do likewise as soon as possible.

MR. WARNER said that the General Post Office were, he believed, already concerning themselves with this.

SIR ORME SARGENT asked whether we should permit journalists to send their despatches in the diplomatic bag until other arrangements are possible. It was agreed that this facility should be given and that when possible individual journalists should be given seats in our courier plane.

MR. HANKEY thought it was important that we should not appear to be establishing a commercial air service by too frequently carrying passengers other than staff and an occasional journalist or important official or business man.

MR. WARNER said that our Transport Command service to Prague carried many Czechoslovaks and that the Czechoslovak authorities were anxious that we should start a commercial service as soon as possible.

MR. HANKEY asked what attitude we should adopt over the extensive removal by the Russians of factory and industrial equipment.

SIR ORME SARGENT said he thought that the Russians would claim that much of this counted as booty, particularly such machinery as was removed from the part of German Silesia now under Polish control. He suggested that the matter should be discussed with the Southern Department who would say what the position was in Roumania, from which country a great deal of equipment had been removed.

Frontiers

MR. HANKEY said he believed that few Poles were resigned to the loss of Lwow.[4]

MR. WINCH added that even the Ministers of the Lublin Administration and Modzelewski, the Polish Ambassador in Moscow, were distressed at this particular amputation.

MR. HANKEY asked about Teschen and Glatz.

SIR ORME SARGENT said emphatically that these disputed areas were not our concern, and that we should not allow ourselves to be drawn into discussion about them. The Soviet Government would maintain that the dispute was one to be settled between the Czechoslovaks and Poles without even

---

[4] The chief city in the Polish territory of Galicia annexed by the Soviet Union in November 1939.

Russian intervention. We should concentrate on the far more important question of the Polish German frontier. The Berlin Conference may or may not prove helpful in the settlement of this problem, but even if we do not bring it up the Americans almost certainly will.

Mr. WARNER thought that our attitude should be that the Four Powers should arrange among themselves for an orderly transference of Germans from the surrendered territories. We should discourage Russian backing to extravagant Polish claims.

Sir ORME SARGENT said that the Prime Minister had agreed at Tehran to the Oder Line as the Western frontier of Poland.[5] The Russians had pushed this claim and the Poles had fallen into the trap by attempting to seize the territory before the peace settlement. This issue might well be the cause of another war.

Mr. WARNER said that both we and the Americans considered that the frontier should be further East, but that we may not be able to obtain Russian agreement to this.

Elections

Mr. HANKEY asked whether His Majesty's Government thought that Polish elections should be held before or after the return of Polish soldiers from abroad.

Sir ORME SARGENT said that His Majesty's Government had no views on this subject. They would watch events. The dissolution of the National Democratic Party[6] was not agreeable to us.

Mr. WARNER said that we had reserved the right to bring up the question of which parties were to be accepted as 'anti-Nazi and Democratic'[7] at the 'Big Three' Meeting.

Mr. WINCH considered that the right wing of the National Democratic Party was definitely Fascist. He said that Monsieur Mikolajczyk was telling members of the National Democratic Party to join other parties. At present Poles applying for identity cards were being asked about their political affiliations. Most local officials appeared to be members of the P.P.R.,[8] but in fact the Communist Party was losing support to the Socialists.

Sir ORME SARGENT thought that they might well try to regain it by the use of force.

Mr. HANKEY asked whether it was desirable that previous supporters of General Sikorski should be disfranchised by the dissolution of the party.

Sir ORME SARGENT said that the party had two wings and that if the bad were suppressed the good would also be lost. It ought to be for the electorate, and not the government, to decide whether the party should be suppressed.

---

[5] For preliminary discussion of Polish questions at the Conference of Tehran, attended by Mr. Churchill, President Roosevelt and Marshal Stalin, 28 November–1 December 1943, cf. W. S. Churchill, *op. cit.*, vol. v, pp. 319–20, 350–1, 356–7 *passim*.

[6] Cf. No. 45, seventh paragraph.

[7] See No. 45, note 6.

[8] Polska Partia Robotnicza, the Polish Workers Party.

MR. HANKEY asked whether His Majesty's Government favoured the supervision of the elections by an international commission, such as was being proposed in Greece.

SIR ORME SARGENT considered that any such arrangement would be deplorable and that we should do everything to discourage it, although the United States might support the idea.

MR. WARNER said that the Polish Government should strive to be quite independent and not remain in leading strings, international or otherwise.

SIR ORME SARGENT added that whatever the result of the elections under international supervision we should be held responsible. MR. WINCH thought that there might be no elections, but MR. HANKEY thought the Poles abroad would want them before the internal system inspired real confidence. SIR ORME SARGENT thought this was not certain, and that they would watch the system now in operation.

Return of Poles abroad

MR. WARNER reported that Mr. Savery[9] had talked to a young Polish officer who thought that the bulk of the soldiers would return. Mr. Warner did not think there would be a bulk return at once as the service authorities appeared anxious to keep soldiers and to allow the 'London' Polish military authorities to preserve their hold over the troops.

MR. HANKEY said that if a large proportion did not return it would not look good for us.

MR. WARNER said that a minute submitted to the Prime Minister suggested that the maximum number should return. The Prime Minister's views were not yet known.

MR. HANKEY said he presumed we should not give sanctuary to compromised Poles. He noticed that our missions in the Balkans had been made use of as places of refuge by prominent men who were in trouble with the Soviet authorities.

MR. WARNER said we should not. Our contribution to the Polish resistance had not been as great as it was sometimes thought. What we had supplied to the Poles had been used by them to help Poland and not ourselves, and we should not feel ourselves to be under an obligation to Poles who might ask for protection.

Reparations

MR. HANKEY asked whether we should support the claim of the Poles to join the Reparations Commission.

MR. WARNER replied that if we continued to sponsor the inclusion of the French we should probably have to agree to the Russian condition that the Poles and Yugoslavs must be represented on the Commission.

[9] Mr. F. Savery had been Counsellor in H.M. Embassy to the former Polish Government in London.

United Nations Relief and Rehabilitation Administration

Mr. WINCH said that at present U.N.R.R.A. was not being properly administered in Poland. He had noticed that an U.N.R.R.A. car was being used by the Foreign Office and relief goods were not being fairly distributed. They were mostly going to State employees who were already better provided for than other members of the community. Mr. WARNER said that U.N.R.R.A. were faced with the choice of doing nothing for Poland or doing it on the only conditions the Russians would allow viz such that U.N.R.R.A. could not properly supervise the distribution of their supplies in Poland. They had chosen the latter alternative.

Mr. WARNER told Mr. Hankey that His Majesty's Government would presumably welcome the new Polish Government in the international coal and transport organisations, but Mr. Hankey should speak to Mr. Ronald on this point.

Mr. HANKEY said he understood the Anglo-Polish Treaty[10] was not considered to have lapsed.

Mr. WARNER replied that it had not, and that we considered that the new Government in Warsaw inherited all the international obligations of the old Government but the Treaty was limited to the case of aggression by Germany.

Mr. HANKEY said that, in the absence of any other instructions, he would consider the decisions reached at this meeting as representing the line that he should follow as Chargé d'Affaires in Warsaw.

[10] The Anglo-Polish Agreement of Mutual Assistance and Protocol of 25 August 1939 are respectively printed in *B.F.S.P.*, vol. 143, pp. 301–3, and vol. 158, pp. 393–4.

No. 74

Memorandum by Mr. Troutbeck
[*C 3786/267/18*]

FOREIGN OFFICE, *10 July 1945*

A brief for Terminal on political questions relating to Germany is attached.[1] In general it coincides with the political proposals suggested in Field Marshal Montgomery's notes of the 6th July.[2] It may be thought desirable to get Cabinet approval on the general line suggested in this brief before the meeting in Germany.

The first item, entitled 'General' needs little comment. Field Marshal Montgomery has drawn attention to the danger of Germany being divided

[1] The brief, filed as an annex under date of 9 July 1945 (Annex 1 below), was in fact a revision (cf. the reference below to the 'General' item) made by Mr. Harrison in the light of a meeting in Mr. Eden's room at 5.15 p.m. on 11 July: cf. *The Diaries of Sir Alexander Cadogan O.M., 1938–1945*, ed. D. Dilks (London, 1971), p. 760.

[2] Enclosure in No. 43.

into two watertight areas, and the best hope of preventing this happening must lie in co-ordination of Allied policy through the Control Council.

The question of building up a *central German administration* for certain specified purposes was discussed in London a week or so ago, and Field Marshal Montgomery's proposal[s] were approved by the Prime Minister after consideration by the A.C.A.O. Committee.

No consideration by Ministers has ever been given to the question of establishing a *central German government*. A paper on the subject was prepared about a year ago, but not submitted to Ministers.

The question of dismemberment has been discussed in the past by the A.P.W. Committee without, however, any firm conclusion having been recorded.

Our general attitude to *political and trade union activities* was laid down in the General Directive on Policy towards Germany[3] which was approved by the A.P.W. Committee. Subsequently the A.P.W. Committee approved more detailed proposals about trade unions. They have never given further consideration to our policy towards political parties. The present proposal that the formation of democratic political parties should be actually encouraged is a new departure which seems to be in harmony with Field Marshal Montgonery's [*sic*] ideas. If, as he suggests, the German people should be allowed to discuss political matters, it is only a small step towards their forming political parties, which has already been done in the Soviet zone.

The question of *co-ordinating propaganda and information services to Germany* has never been specifically considered by any Ministerial committee, its desirability having been considered too obvious.

If it is thought desirable to get Cabinet approval to the general line suggested in this brief, it might perhaps be worth while adding a paragraph in which attention would be drawn to the fact that these political aspects of the German problem are, for all their importance, probably to-day of less importance than the economic problems. The fact is that neither propaganda nor any of the suggestions which Field Marshal Montgomery includes under what he describes as 'the human factor' will fill empty stomachs or give warmth to a population without coal. Field Marshal Montgomery states that we must tackle the battle of the winter energetically, and we must win it. He therefore calls for a good short term plan. In certain respects this is proceeding. Plans are in hand for providing some imports of food, though on a minimum scale, and encouragement is being given to the greatest possible use of the soil. But in other respects our plans will inevitably make the Field Marshal's task more difficult. The Hyndley-Potter Report, which has been endorsed by President Truman and with some reservations by the Cabinet, is based on the idea of removing from Germany all the

[3] This draft general directive for Germany in the post-surrender period, circulated to the European Advisory Commission by Sir W. Strang on 30 May 1944, is printed in *F.R.U.S. 1944*, vol. i, pp. 226–7.

coal we can extract. Secondly, our policy is to enforce 'draconian' measures of economic disarmament and heavy reparation deliveries, to an extent which will leave the standard of living of the German population not 'exceeding the average of the standard of living of Middle European countries'. (Statement of principles agreed at Moscow).[4] It is clear from telegrams received from our Delegation at Moscow that the Russians intend by this means to de-industrialise Germany. Again, we agree in principle to the forcible transfer of Germans from Czechoslovakia and Poland and, once the principle is formally agreed, it will be difficulty [sic] to hold up *all* action on it, nor shall we be able to avoid our quota of immigrants, with the result that there will be more hungry mouths to feed.

In these circumstances, it seems idle to imagine that the German population is going to be kept content by any psychological action, and it would be a mistake to put too much trust in the 'human factor'. The fact is that by her action Germany has placed all the liberated countries in a condition of serious want and fear, and her population could now only be saved from the most dire consequences at the expense of the political and economic needs of our Allies. One must hope that the British public will be made and kept aware that the responsibility for all this lies at the door not merely of the Nazi leaders but of the whole German population.

If it is decided to submit a paper to the Cabinet it would seem desirable that it should be a joint one by the Secretary of State and the Secretary of State for War seeing that the latter is formally responsible for the control of Germany. It might be suggested to him that he should at the same time circulate Field Marshal Montgomery's notes.

J. M. Troutbeck

Annex 1 to No. 74

Germany: Political Questions

There are a number of questions connected with Germany on which it would be very useful to secure broad agreement between the Prime Minister, President Truman and Marshal Stalin at the forthcoming meeting.

1. *Establishment of Allied Control Council in Berlin*

It is our earnest hope that the Allied Control Council in Berlin will be successful in co-ordinating Allied policy in regard to the control and administration of Germany. We should try to ensure that it meets soon and continues to meet regularly as laid down in the Four Power Agreement on 'Control Machinery in Germany'.

2. *European Advisory Commission*

The British and U.S. Commanders-in-Chief in Germany have received from their Governments a large number of general and specific directives to guide them. These have been circulated in the E.A.C. and the Soviet and French Governments are familiar with them even though they have not approved them or tabled any of their own.

---

[4] Annex to No. 116.

It is very desirable that there should be Four Power Agreement on Germany over as wide a field as possible. It is understood that the U.S. and Soviet Governments both consider that the E.A.C. has served its purpose and should close down.

We should therefore recommend that agreement on all outstanding questions relating to Germany and Austria with which the E.A.C. has been unable to deal should henceforward be sought in the Allied Control Council in Berlin and the Allied Commission in Vienna respectively, possibly through the Political Advisers. (There is a separate brief on the future of the E.A.C.[5])

Meanwhile, there are a number of important German political questions on which the Big Three could usefully give general guidance to the A.C.C. for Germany.

(a) German administration

First, there is the question of building up a central German administration, in order to give effect to our policy that the burden of administering Germany should rest on German shoulders, subject to overall Allied control. Field Marshal Montgomery has submitted proposals aiming at 'the re-formation of the essential German ministries for the whole country, located in Berlin and controlled by the quadripartite Commission . . . this[6] central administration to include only those ministries which are essential to the proper running of the country, and to allow the greatest possible measure of decentralisation which in the light of experience proves possible and advisable'.

This proposal has been approved by the Prime Minister and it might be useful to try and secure the agreement of President Truman and Marshal Stalin.

(b) German Government

It would be inadvisable for us to raise the question at what point we should aim to establish the first Central German Government. Our view is that there are strong arguments against establishing one yet.

(c) Dismemberment

The intention of the Allied Governments in regard to the dismemberment of Germany is obviously relevant to the question of establishing a Central German Government. In his Proclamation to the Soviet people on the 9th May, Marshal Stalin said that the Soviet Union did not intend 'either to dismember or destroy Germany'. Nor was the word 'dismember' included, as proposed at Yalta, in the German surrender document, though it was covered by a vaguer phrase. None of the representatives on the London Dismemberment Committee, which was set up at Yalta, has submitted proposals.

The question arises whether it would be better to take the initiative in raising the matter at the forthcoming meeting or simply to let things continue to drift as at present. As the Foreign Secretary is Chairman of the London Dismemberment Committee and therefore accountable for its work, the best course might be to enquire of the Russians and Americans whether it is their intention to encourage separatist tendencies in their zones, a policy which H.M.G. have always favoured; and whether it is desired that the London Dismemberment Committee should become active.

[5] No. 76.i.
[6] Punctuation as in original citation of a version of No. 74.i.

135

(d) Political and Trade Union Activity

An unfortunate impression has been created both in Germany and elsewhere that, whereas the formation of trade unions and political parties is being encouraged in the Soviet zone, it is being restricted in the Western zones. There has for instance, been no statement on our side of the same authority as Marshal Zhukov's proclamation of the 10th June permitting the formation of trade unions and political parties in the Soviet zone.[7] This proclamation was followed by the formation in Berlin of Communist, Social Democrat, Christian Democrat, Cultural, etc. groups, who have issued manifestos which have received considerable publicity.

Both the British and the United States Commanders-in-Chief have authority, under their respective directives, to allow political and trade union activity. We have been rather more liberal than the Americans in encouraging the formation of trade unions in our zone, but the competent members of the British, American and French Elements of the Control Commission have now reached agreement regarding the procedure to be followed in the three zones. This procedure aims to give immediate effect to Allied policy, which is stated in the following terms:

'It is Allied policy to create conditions in which trade unions and employers federations can develop on democratic lines and ultimately enjoy their full powers and privileges, so long as the pursuit of this policy does not interfere with the maintenance of law and order or become a threat to the security of the occupying forces'.

It is understood that the formation of political parties is still banned in all three Western zones.

The trade union question is a very delicate one politically for the reasons given in the attached note by Sir Frederick Leggett [iii.*b*]. We and the Russians will never agree on a definition of what constitutes legitimate trade union activity and it is clearly of the highest importance to avoid any discussion of this thorny subject. None the less there would be obvious advantage, in order to show Germany and the world that the three Powers are broadly in agreement, if acceptance of the following principle could be publicly announced in the course of the forthcoming meeting:

'It is Allied policy, subject to the necessity for maintaining military security and smooth administration, to encourage the formation of free trade unions in Germany'.

It would also seem desirable that the ban on the formation of political parties should now be raised in the British and American zones, subject to the same limitation. The principle might be enunciated somewhat on the following lines:

'It is also Allied policy to encourage the formation in Germany of democratic political parties, which may form the basis of an ordered and peaceful German society in the future'.

Co-ordination of propaganda and information services to Germany (Brief D) [iv].

This question was first taken up over a year ago by Mr. Winant with the United Kingdom and Soviet Delegations to the European Advisory Commission. It has been impossible to extract any reaction from the Soviet Government.

---

[7] Cf. B. R. von Oppen, *Documents on Germany under occupation 1945–54* (London, 1955), pp. 37–8.

The experiences of the past two months since the collapse of Germany have clearly demonstrated the need for some degree of co-ordination between the four occupying Powers. Whether it will be practicable to attain the degree of co-ordination originally proposed by Mr. Winant is more than doubtful. But the effect of propaganda from one zone on the population in neighbouring zones has been very apparent and has hitherto worked to our disadvantage and to the Russian advantage. The rosy picture painted by both the Soviet and Soviet controlled broadcasts to Germany, together with the fact that Germans are apparently running the Berlin broadcasting station have created the impression that the Russians are adopting a more liberal policy towards the German population in their zone than we and the Americans are in ours. While the arrival of the Allied contingents in Berlin may make it possible to get things in better perspective, continued lack of co-ordination can only be of advantage to the Germans.

It is unlikely that we shall be able to get any detailed agreement with the Russians on the subject. Nevertheless we should try to get general agreement on the desirability of a regular exchange of views between the competent members of the Allied Control Council, with a view to maintaining in all four zones a common and consistent propaganda and information policy towards Germany. This would constitute powerful evidence to the Germans of Allied unity of purpose. The Allied Control Council might be directed to set up the necessary machinery.

(A separate set of briefs on German economy is being prepared).[8]

Foreign Office, S.W.1., 9 July 1945

Calendars to No. 74

i   *2 July 1945   Annex 2 to No. 74: F.O. memorandum on the build-up of the German administration* with enclosures. Attaches proposals of June 1945 by Field-Marshal Montgomery (Annex 3 to No. 74) for the build-up of German administration from below and the establishment in Berlin under Allied control of certain German ministries. Attaches also a report of 23 June (Annex 4 to No. 74) on these proposals from the Chairman of the A.C.A.O. committee supporting proposal for German ministries but warning on the Field-Marshal's alternative of a separate administration for Western Germany: this 'would involve a final break with Russia on German matters and should not be considered except as a last resort'. F.O. covering memo. concludes that early establishment of a central German Government would be premature: ideal seems to be to continue building-up from below and to establish some central ministries as proposed by F.M. Montgomery and approved by the Prime Minister [C 3786/267/18].

ii   (a) *3 July 1945   Annex 5 to No. 74: F.O. memorandum on dismemberment of Germany.* Progress of the tripartite Committee on Dismemberment set up by Crimea Conference [C 3786/267/18]. (b) *12 July 1945   Memorandum by Mr. Troutbeck.* Replies to Mr. Eden's enquiry why departmental work on dismemberment has been suspended. Mr. Eden minuted: 'We should take this note with us to Berlin conference. (I cannot remember its code name) . . . P.M. who has in the past always favoured dismemberment is likely to complain

[8] See No. 114.

quite a little that we have made no progress even in our own examination and the knowledge that F.O. has always been against it will hardly provide a sufficient answer. A. E. July 14' [C 4618/292/18].

iii *7 July 1945   (a) Annex 6 to No. 74: F.O. memorandum on Trades Unions and Political Activity in Germany. Summarizes British, American and Russian directives.* [C 3786/267/18]. *(b) Note by Sir F. Leggett (Deputy Secretary, Ministry of Labour and National Service) on Trades Unions in Germany:* problem of cooperation with Russians over trade unions [C 3815/156/18].

iv *2 July 1945   Annex 7 to No. 74: F.O. memo. on co-ordination of propaganda and information services to Germany:* danger of a propaganda war between the Powers [C 3786/267/18].

No. 75

Memorandum by Viscount Hood

[*U 5595/11/70*]

FOREIGN OFFICE, *10 July 1945*

Zones of Occupation in Austria

(O.R.C.(45)8)[1]

This Agreement[2] has been long in the making. The zones of occupation were settled without much difficulty but a long wrangle ensued about the area of joint occupation at Vienna and its sub-division. The British, U.S. and French Delegations favoured the Gau[3] as providing the necessary airfields and elbow-room for our troops and officials in Vienna. The Russians favoured the City limits ostensibly on the grounds that the Gau was a Nazi creation and must therefore be destroyed.

As a result of the visit to Vienna by British, U.S. and French missions we abandoned our claim to the Gau, partly because it was found that it did not provide the necessary airfields. We thus accepted the City limits but have obtained facilities outside for recreation, training and accommodation and two airfields under British and American control respectively. We have thus carried out the Prime Minister's injunctions that we should obtain equal treatment with the Americans in the matter of airfields. We have agreed to accommodate the French on our airfield as it proved impossible to persuade the Russians to make a third airfield available.

It is desirable that His Majesty's Government should signify their approval of both this Agreement and the one on the Control Machinery for Austria,[2] as we want them to be put into effect at once. The War Office have authorised General McCreery to try to arrange a meeting with his colleagues to this end.

HOOD

[1] Annex below.
[2] See No. 56, note 1.
[3] District of German administration.

Memorandum by United Kingdom Representative on the European Advisory Commission

O.R.C. (45)8

Secret   FOREIGN OFFICE, *10 July 1945*

Zones of Occupation in Austria

I attach as Annexes A[2] and B[4] the texts of the Agreement and Covering Report signed at the E.A.C. on 9th July.

2. When this subject was last discussed at the A.P.W. Committee (A.P.W.(45) 10th Meeting of 13th April, Item 1)[5], the outstanding question was the area of joint occupation at Vienna and its sub-division between the Four Powers. In view of the deadlock at the E.A.C. arrangements were made for British, American and French missions to visit Vienna and to report on the actual conditions there. On receipt of the missions' reports discussions were resumed at the E.A.C. and agreement has now been reached.

3. We have accepted the Soviet desire that the City of Vienna should be the area of joint occupation. The British sector within the City is in two pieces. This, though inconvenient, should not prove a serious disability. It includes the good and undamaged residential area around Schönbrunn.

4. The Innere Stadt[6] is to be occupied jointly by the Four Powers and the Russians have conceded two good aerodromes outside the City for American and British/French use respectively. It is also agreed that arrangements will be made for free movement of persons, transit of goods, common use of the facilities in Vienna, and for facilities outside the City for training, recreation and, in special cases, living accommodation.

5. I recommend that I should be authorised to inform my colleagues that His Majesty's Government approve the Agreement and the Covering Report.[7]

R. I. CAMPBELL

CALENDAR TO NO. 75

i *10–11 July 1945*   To and from Sir A. Clark Kerr *(Moscow) Tels. Nos. 3866 and 3089.* (a) Following Soviet acceptance of satisfactory formula on Austria (cf. No. 35), and E.A.C. agreement and report of 9 July, instructions to request Soviet agreement to meeting of four Commanders-in-Chief for prompt implementation. (b) Has spoken as instructed to M. Molotov who thought suggestion very sensible but must consult Marshal Stalin [U 5354, 5391/11/70].

[4] See No. 56, note 2.
[5] Not printed.
[6] Inner city.
[7] Notification of approval of the agreements of 4 and 9 July 1945 was given by H.M. Government on 12 July, by the French Government on 12 and 16 July, by the Soviet Government on 21 July and by the U.S. Government on 24 July.

No. 76

Memorandum by Viscount Hood

[U 5496/473/70]

FOREIGN OFFICE, *10 July 1945*

Russian shortcomings at the E.A.C.

After a year's work, the European Advisory Commission had only completed two agreements—the Instrument of Surrender and the Occupation Protocol.[1] In answer to the remonstrance which the Secretary of State delivered to M. Molotov at the second Moscow Conference we received a reply from the Soviet Government which gave hope of better things.[2] These hopes were not fulfilled:–

1. The failure in spite of repeated undertakings to send to London the Russian Element of the Control Commission made it impossible to discuss or make any preliminary plans for the establishment and operation of Control Machinery.

2. M. Gousev's refusal to discuss any of the British and U.S. Directives has meant that there is no agreed Allied policy in any specialised field.

3. Even on the subjects which the Soviet Government stated to be in their view of primary importance, the Commission was unable to make any progress. Committees were set up to deal with two of them—repatriation of prisoners of war and internees and the detailed measures for the disarmament and demilitarisation of Germany. The Russians either failed to nominate a representative or refused to meet. In both cases it was thus necessary to take unilateral action when the emergency arose. No discussion has ever taken place in the E.A.C. on the other two subjects specified by the Russians: the abolition of the Hitlerite régime and the handing over of war criminals; and the control of German economy. War criminals are now being discussed through other channels and the control of German economy is now, of course, under discussion by the Reparation Mission in Moscow.

4. Agreements have now been concluded on Control Machinery in Germany and on the Control & Occupation of Austria, but even on the main subjects which have been discussed at the E.A.C. the Russians have been dilatory and obstinate. The General Order (or Additional Requirements) tabled by us in August, 1944, only began to be discussed in May of this year. It was several months before M. Gousev was in a position to discuss our papers on Austria. The French amendments to the basic E.A.C. documents, which in the case of the Instrument of Surrender and the Control Agreement were purely formal, were tabled in January, but not agreed until May. The Agreement about the French zone in Germany is now being held up by M. Gousev because of difficulties about the French sector in Berlin. The proposals for a Restitution Commission tabled by the U.K. Delegation in November, 1944, were only discussed this Summer and were turned down flatly by the Russians. The British paper on the Disposal of Enemy War Material tabled in August, 1944, has never been discussed, nor

---

[1] The Agreement of 25 July 1944 on the Instrument of Surrender for Germany and the amendments thereto of 1 May 1945 are printed in *F.R.U.S. 1944*, vol. i, pp. 256–61 and *F.R.U.S. 1945*, vol. iii, pp. 258–9. The Protocol of 12 September 1944 on the Zones of Occupation in Germany and the Administration of Greater Berlin and the amendments thereto of 14 November 1944 are printed in Cmnd. 1552 of 1961, pp. 27–30.

[2] See Sir L. Woodward, *op. cit.*, vol. v, pp. 257–9.

has our paper on Foreign Representation in Berlin tabled this spring.[3]

HOOD

CALENDARS TO NO. 76

i   *10 July 1945   Brief No. 48 for U.K. Delegation on the Work and Future of the European Advisory Commission.* Time has come to wind up the E.A.C. Any need for a standing four-power body with wider terms of reference than the Allied Control Commissions could be met by setting up the suggested Council of Foreign Ministers. If this proposal is not accepted, E.A.C. should not, however, be abolished hastily [U 5500/473/70].

ii *13 July 1945   Minute by Sir R. Campbell to Mr. Eden, E.A.C. Summary No. 101.* Continued Soviet objections to concluding agreement on French zone in Germany. Soviet delegation still without authority to sign Agreement on Additional Requirements from Germany [U 5522/473/70].

[3] The memorandum of 1 August 1944 by the U.K. delegation on Ownership and Disposal of German War Material is not printed. The British paper of 30 April 1945 on Representation of Foreign Countries in Germany after Surrender is printed in *F.R.U.S. 1945*, vol. iii, pp. 1084–7.

No. 77

Minute from Mr. Eden to Mr. Churchill
No. P.M./45/322 [*F.O. 800/416/63*]

FOREIGN OFFICE, 10 July 1945

As you know, the Foreign Office have been considering, with a view to discussions at Terminal, what cards we hold for a general negotiation with the Russians, in the shape of things which the Russians want from us and which it is in our power to give or to withhold.[1] The following is the best list we have been able to make.

2. *Credits.* The Russians would not be interested in any credits from us of a size that we could afford to give. But they have approached the Americans for very large credits. The Americans have told the Russians that such a proposal would require special legislation and that this is at the moment out of the question.

3. *Germany.* Here again we hold a certain number of assets which the Russians require such as the merchant navy and a substantial part of the industry and industrial resources of Germany. For instance, 70% of German steel making capacity is situated in the British zone. Physical control of these assets gives us an advantage which we could turn to account in securing acceptable reparation and other settlements.

4. We and the Americans hold jointly the greater part, possibly the whole, of the German diplomatic archives. The Russians are pressing us for access

[1] The preceding passage is cited by Sir L. Woodward, *op. cit.*, vol. v, p. 353, where this document is summarized.

to them. Our intention had been to grant this on a basis of reciprocity, though this would be largely a formality as we doubt if the Russians hold anything of importance to us. In view however of recent Russian behaviour to us I would not give access to these documents until we are met on other issues.

5. The Russians may also want information from us about German secret devices. This, however, is a card we would not wish to play.

6. Finally, there is the German fleet, the major part of which is in our control. The Admiralty are submitting a Cabinet Paper about this, which seems to be a good card in our hand. The Russians want badly their share of the ships and we hold all that are seaworthy. We ought not to meet their demands without getting a settlement of our requirements on other outstanding issues.

7. *The Italian fleet*. The Russians have claimed the following Italian warships: 1 battleship, 1 cruiser, 8 destroyers and 4 submarines, together with 40,000 tons of merchant shipping. We have many claims on the Russians which are at least as well founded as their claim to the Italian ships. I hope, therefore, that we shall not agree without a *quid pro quo*.

8. *The Straits*. We have expressed willingness to consider sympathetically Russian proposals for the modification of the Straits Régime, but we are not committed to accepting them. This is a valuable asset, since modification of the régime is not possible without our consent. Furthermore, any new régime they wish to establish would probably require reference to the World Organisation, where again our consent is necessary. Similar considerations would apply to any Russian proposals about access to the Baltic and control of the Kiel Canal, though here we are even less committed.

9. *The Baltic States*. If the Russians request our recognition of their annexation of these little countries we have numerous demands to make in return, in particular in regard to our interests in those countries themselves.

10. *Tangier*. The Russians have asked to participate in discussions on this subject, and presumably in any future international regime. We should certainly not agree to this without a *quid pro quo*.

Anthony Eden[2]

[2] Mr. Eden had minuted on the draft of this paper: 'Good. I will also talk to Mr. Winant on these lines. A. E. July 9.'

No. 78

Sir A. Clark Kerr (Moscow) to Mr. Eden (Received 17 July)
No. 468 [N 8674/165/38]

MOSCOW, *10 July 1945*

Sir,
Elsewhere I have discussed the phase of mutual suspicions and disappointments and at times of severe strain through which Anglo-Soviet relations

passed during the weeks which followed the Crimea Conference and, more particularly, in the days before and after the end of the war in Europe. Abroad the fresh confidence, now confirmed by victory, which the Russians feel in themselves was reflected in blundering unilateral action, which took little or no account of the interests or prestige of their major allies, and shook the faith of even the hardiest believers in continued collaboration after the war. The omens for the next meeting of the three heads of governments seemed therefore to hold no promise. During the past month, however, the horizon has cleared and many of the darkest clouds that threatened to burst upon that meeting have been dissipated.

2. At home this confidence is without measure. It has expressed itself recently in a Victory Parade in honour of the triumph of Soviet arms, at which the efforts of the allies got but the scantiest notice; and in not only the bestowal of high ranks, decorations and more substantial gifts of villas, *etcetera*, upon the successful Soviet military leaders, but in the revival of the old title of Generalissimo for Stalin himself. In the midst of this military exuberance Stalin has however found time to declare that the efforts of himself and his marshals would not have been 'worth a damn' without the little civilian cogs in the great State machine. As I have said, this gush of self-praise has left little room to the allies of the Soviet Union for a share in the credit for victory. In a recent leader dealing with Stalin's new title *Red Star* claimed that the Soviet State (apparently single-handed) had 'saved civilisation from fascist obscurantism and barbarism, and had emerged from the war more mighty, still more monolithic and with still greater vitality'. Another Moscow newspaper in the same connexion used these words: 'Our position in world affairs is unshakeable. We are particularly aware of the firmness of the ground we stand upon and of our confidence in ourselves and in our future'. At the same time, however, the Soviet public is being encouraged to look with new hope to durable peace and universal security in the years of undisturbed development ahead.

3. This pride of achievement has been fostered in recent weeks by outward signs of Moscow's new importance as a great world capital. The Reparation Commission has taken up its work here. It has been here that the Polish negotiations have taken place.[1] Hardly a week has passed without some visit to Moscow by leading foreign statesmen. Moscow again has been the scene of fevered, though fruitless, talks between the Czechs and the Poles about Teschen, and, as a result of concurrent Russian-Czechoslovak negotiations, Sub-Carpathian Ruthenia has passed to the Soviet Union as Trans-Carpathian Ukraine. So thickly do the visiting statesmen crowd upon one another that photographs of the Czechoslovak Prime Minister's departure and of the Chinese Prime Minister's arrival appeared side by side in the

---

[1] The Yalta Declaration on Poland (see No. 45, note 6) had authorized M. Molotov, Mr. Harriman and Sir A. Clark Kerr as a commission to consult in Moscow with Polish leaders for the reorganization of the Polish Provisional Government; conversations with Polish representatives were accordingly held there in June 1945: cf. Sir L. Woodward, *op. cit.*, vol. iii, pp. 490f.

Moscow press on July 1st. No less publicity has been given to the presence in Moscow during the past fortnight of large and distinguished delegations of foreign scientists for the celebration of the 220th anniversary of the Russian Academy of Sciences.

4. All this might seem somewhat reminiscent of the pilgrimages to Berlin which marked the heyday of Hitler's power before the war. Fortunately, however, the Soviet authorities, while encouraging the pride and self-confidence of their people and sustaining in them a spirit of vigilance, have now found it possible to begin demobilisation on a substantial scale and thus to restore much needed manpower to the vocations of peace, and to declare an amnesty covering a wide field.

5. This relaxation in tension within Russia, welcome though it be, would be of little significance had it not been accompanied by the marked improvement in relations with her allies to which I have referred. At the end of May there was hardly one of the many vital international problems requiring urgent solution on which we were not at loggerheads with the Soviet Union. During the past month, however, the veto difficulty which threatened the San Francisco Conference with disaster has been overcome, thanks to a Soviet concession; the new World Organisation has been established with full Soviet support and is being presented to the Soviet people as a great and constructive achievement. In Germany, agreement has at last been reached on the execution of the decisions about zones of occupation and control. The British, American and French contingents are now moving into Berlin. This has been accompanied by friendly meetings and exchanges of decorations between British, American and Soviet commanders, which have been played up in the Soviet press and form a welcome change from the previous weeks of bitter invective about alleged shortcomings and tenderness towards Fascists and war criminals on our part and on that of the Americans. The problem of Vienna seems also to be on the way to a solution. The greatest single source of friction between the Soviet Union and her western allies—the Polish question—has been disposed of on the lines of the Crimea Agreement. Even at Trieste, a provisional agreement has been reached. Here the Soviet Government clearly did not wish to be a party to a trial of strength. Although we still have cause for serious dissatisfaction over our own position and internal developments in Roumania, Bulgaria and Hungary, there has been a definite easing in the situation in recent weeks, and the Soviet Government have themselves taken the initiative in proposing a return to more normal relations. This relatively cheerful picture is completed by the beginning of the work of the Reparation Commission in Moscow and the meeting in London of representatives of the major allies, including the Soviet Union, to settle policy in regard to war criminals.

6. It must be recognised nevertheless that the above list of happy events does not include a single instance in which the Soviet Government have given way substantially on any issue affecting their vital interests. We must however reckon it as a definite gain that they are gradually substituting the technique of international negotiation for that of unilateral action, even

though their methods may still be rough and ill-mannered. A great effort was needed to bring about the above results. One of the main reasons for the unaccommodating and even hostile attitude previously taken up by the Soviet Government on almost every problem of common concern was their suspicion that their British and American allies were combining to deprive them of some of the fruits of victory. The Russians had become so used to the steady stream of praise of Soviet policy and activities, more particularly in Britain, that a disproportionate importance was attributed here to signs of British displeasure and to open criticism in the British press of certain aspects of Soviet policy in eastern Europe. At one stage the United States Government clearly took fright at what they conceived to be a widening gulf between their two allies. To bridge this gulf and to restore a happier relationship between the three major allies Mr. Harry Hopkins[2] was sent to Moscow at the end of May as President Truman's personal emissary. Mr. Hopkins evidently went a long way to persuade the Soviet Government that for the present at any rate American policy tended to follow the lines laid down by President Roosevelt. At the same time he seems to have moved Stalin to see that the behaviour of the Soviet Government, before and after the end of the war in Europe, had seriously disturbed public opinion in America, and that a more forthcoming attitude was needed on the Soviet side if the new President were to carry the American public behind him in a policy of continued friendship between the two countries. The outstanding results of Mr. Hopkins' mission were the Soviet concession on the veto question and the agreement with Stalin on the list of persons to be invited to the Polish consultations, which enabled the Moscow Commission to get to work again. But while these were the direct results of Mr. Hopkins' talks the indirect result was the whole improvement in the international situation during the month of June.

7. This renewed American-Soviet flirtation of course means more than a mere attempt to break a temporary deadlock. The Americans and the Russians alike are probably hoping to establish a direct relationship with one another which would avert the dangers of an Anglo-American *bloc* on the one hand or an Anglo-Soviet *bloc* on the other. The Russians have recently shown more irritation on account of British than American criticisms; they find us standing in their way more often than the Americans, while at the same time it is possible that they feel that British policy may be largely discounted during the election period. They also realise that it is to America that they must look for economic assistance now that wartime lend-lease has ceased. In preparation for this the Moscow press is allowing itself a mixture of blandishments and of warnings about the danger of large-scale American unemployment. Finally, as the Russians turn their eyes more and more towards the Far East, so their preoccupation with America also tends to increase.

8. I think, therefore, that in the months immediately ahead we must

[2] Special Adviser and Assistant to President Truman.

expect to see the Russians and the Americans getting closer together, and we may if we are not careful, find ourselves playing a more modest role than we deserve in the exchanges between the three major allies. In so far as this may have limits and may lead to a relacation [*sic*] of international tension, as it has done during the past month, we can only welcome a development, from which we shall benefit more than anyone else.

9. The most disquieting feature of Soviet policy at present so far as we are concerned is, however, to be found in Greece and Turkey. The far-reaching demands upon Turkey which seem to have been made in complete disregard of the understanding reached between the Prime Minister and Marshal Stalin at Yalta, suggest a threat to our position in the Middle East. As regards Greece, the Soviet press has now cast aside restraint, and its efforts to damage the position of the Greek Government are combined with scarcely veiled attacks upon British policy. Meanwhile, Yugoslav and Bulgarian territorial ambitions concerning Greece are being encouraged. The Dean of Canterbury is being used by Soviet propaganda to assist Soviet claims against Turkey much as similar naïf British visitors to Berlin were once used by Dr. Goebbels.[3] The strident complaints in the Soviet press about the sufferings of the unfortunate Slav inhabitants of Greek Macedonia are almost identical with the complaints in the German press before Munich about the sad lot of the Sudeten Germans. So far, however, this undermining of our position in the Middle East has not gone deep. For example, the Soviet Government have been careful not to embarrass us in the Levant, where we have had full American support and where they are in any case faced by the obvious difficulty of choosing between their British and French allies and their potential Arab friends. There is therefore still time in which to show the Soviet Government that, while we are very ready to consider reasonable demands, such as a revision of the Montreux Convention, we are not prepared to abandon the interests of our Greek and Turkish allies, or indeed to contemplate a gradual encroachment upon our own vital interests throughout the Middle East.

10. One lesson to be drawn from the events of the past month, and in particular from the successful solution of the Trieste crisis, is the importance of securing full and unquestioned American support on any question likely to involve trouble with the Russians. It was clear from the outset that the United States Government were prepared, if necessary, to contemplate military operations in opposition to Marshal Tito's Trieste adventure. The result, as we know, was salutary. If we are also to make the Russians pause in Greece and Turkey it is equally essential to obtain full American backing there.

[3] Dr. Hewlett Johnson, Dean of Canterbury, on a visit to Moscow had been received by Marshal Stalin on 6 July 1945. (Mr. F. K. Roberts reported on this visit in Moscow despatch No. 529 of 31 July, received on 11 August: on N 10166/744/38, not printed.) Dr. Joseph Goebbels had been German Minister for Public Enlightenment and Propaganda, 1933–45.

11. Despite the trials of the war the Soviet Union is teeming with vitality and bent upon making her influence felt, even far from her own frontiers. The most recent example of this is the insistence upon participation in the Tangier negotiations. She remains indifferent to arguments about the unwisdom of stirring up fresh troubles in a troubled world. Her propaganda is active against countries such as Portugal, Spain, Argentina and even democratic Switzerland, with all of whom we have certain ties, whatever the internal régimes of the moment may be. I do not suggest that in all these cases the Soviet Union is consciously opposing our interests. Her actions are, I think, mainly a symptom of a state of mind to which I have from time to time called your attention. It is of high importance and I may perhaps be forgiven if I again remind you that Russia of to-day is rejoicing in all the emotions and impulsions of very early manhood that spring from a new sense of boundless strength and from the giddiness of success. It is immense fun to her to tell herself that she has become great and that there is little or nothing to stop her making her greatness felt. Why resist therefore the temptation to put a finger into every pie? Why be patient of correction? Untroubled by the pricks of public opinion at home, she is as often as not oblivious to its influence abroad, until a sharp reaction to some major blunder brings it home to her that there are others in the world than she who have a sense of greatness. When this happens she tends, more expecially of late, to lend a readier ear to voices that come from across the Atlantic than to those that reach her from the United Kingdom, for ultimately she feels safer with our people. Despite the visit of Mr. Hopkins the Russians clearly remain in a state of doubt about the new President of the United States and his policy. Of Mr. Roosevelt they were sure, but Mr. Truman is something fresh and unknown that still calls for gingerly treatment. This uncertainty and the approach of the meeting at *Terminal* may well explain the slight restraint which has marked Soviet policy in recent weeks. Meanwhile it is a melancholy truth that the Russians are still uncertain about ourselves. I mean how far we are ready to go to back our friends and to stand up in good time for our principles and what we conceive to be our vital interests. About this I feel that we should leave them in no doubt, for when they are in doubt they tend to be a danger. What would therefore serve us best is a progressive forthright and clear-cut policy aimed at those areas for which we have long been primarily responsible—our colonial empire and the Middle East—and above all where our new responsibilities lie—in the British zones in Germany and Austria. Here we must be at pains to show that we are not going to fall short of our Soviet allies in the task of uprooting fascism and punishing war criminals. This is of the utmost importance. At the same time we may base our policy in all tranquillity upon our own conception of democracy without too nice a regard for what to us may seem to be inadmissible Soviet susceptibilities. And, in doing this, it would be prudent in us to pass speedily on to enlighten our own public opinion, soberly and with forethought, about what is distasteful to us in some aspects of Russian democracy.

I am sending a copy of this despatch to His Majesty's Ambassador at Washington.[4]

I have, &c.,

ARCHIBALD CLARK KERR

CALENDARS TO No. 78

i   *9–10 July 1945*   *Letters to Chancellor of Exchequer from Minister of Production and Sir A. Cadogan:* postwar trade with Soviet Union. Agreement on formal withdrawal of previous British offer of credits; but question of further credits in event of Soviet interest [N 8420, 7645/1/38].

ii   (a) *19 July 1945*   *Mr. Roberts (Moscow) No. 498,* without enclosure: celebration of 220th anniversary of Russian Academy of Sciences; successful Anglo-Soviet scientific contacts despite some irritation over British refusal of exit permits to eight British scientists required for work on the Japanese war [N 9421/6021/38];   (b) *22–26 July 1945 Correspondence between Mr. Warner and Sir A. Clark Kerr:* Anglo-Soviet student-exchange; question of including science students [N 9100, 8938/174/38].

iii   *23 July 1945   Memorandum A.S.E. (45) 29 by Mr. O. Lyttelton for the Allied Supplies Executive Committee of the Cabinet on exchange of scientific information with the Russians,* with reference to minutes previously exchanged with Prime Minister. Records action by Chiefs of Staff [W 10295/1520/49].

---

[4] This despatch was minuted as follows by Mr. J. E. C. Hill and other members of the Northern Department of the Foreign Office, by Mr. W. Ridsdale, Head of News Department, by Sir O. Sargent and by Mr. Ernest Bevin after he had succeeded Mr. Eden as Foreign Secretary on 28 July 1945: 'This is a very valuable despatch, bringing out the confident state of mind with which the Soviet Govt. approaches international affairs. The following conclusions emerge: (1) In the immediate future the Soviet Govt. is likely to be much more anxious to conciliate the U.S. Govt. than to conciliate ourselves (paras. 7 & 8). (2) It is therefore important to be sure of full & unquestioned American support on any question likely to involve trouble with the Russians (para. 10). (3) It is also important that we should have a clear policy towards Germany & Austria & should establish the fact that we are determined to uproot fascism & punish war criminals (para. 11). ? Print Soviet Union D. J. E. C. Hill 19/7.' 'Another important recommendation is that made in the last sentence of the penultimate paragraph—that we should pass on speedily to enlighten our own public opinion, soberly and with forethought, about what is distasteful to us in some aspects of Soviet democracy. The *Manchester Guardian* has already published one or two good leaders of the type suggested by H.M. Ambassador at Moscow. Could News Department say whether any guidance is being given to the press along these lines? T. Brimelow 20/7/45.' 'This excellent despatch confirms the line on Russian policy we have been taking for some time past in the News Dept. with all suitable clients. W. R. R[idsdale] 24/7'. 'This despatch is in line with feeling here. Print & resubmit. C. F. A. Warner 25/7.' 'This despatch should be given K[ing and] C[abinet] D[istribution] O. G. Sargent Aug. 8.' 'A. C[adogan] Aug. 9, 1945.' 'A good summary. E. B.'

No. 79

Letter from Sir A. Clark Kerr (Moscow) to Sir O. Sargent (Received 20 July)
No. 406/4/45 [N 8935/2/38]

Personal and Secret   MOSCOW, *10 July 1945*

My dear Moley

    I think that I should draw your attention to a paper [i], dated July 6th, which General Gammell has sent to General Nye,[1] and of which you may hear more in London. It sums up his first impressions of Russia and of Soviet policy, and you may hear of it from the War Office or from the War Cabinet Offices.

2. General Gammell consulted me about this paper, which inevitably deals with political as well as military topics. I told him that I had not the slightest objection to his sending it to London, and that I welcomed all contributions to our study of the Russian problem. In fact, I think that this is a very sensible contribution which should prove helpful in removing many of the misconceptions which have grown up about Russia in recent months. His recommendations on future policy are also on sound lines, although I think that he underestimates the difficulties of persuading the Soviet Government to agree to grant better facilities for the publication to the outside world of full and accurate information about conditions in the Soviet Union.

3. There are one or two passages in the General's paper to which I should not myself subscribe. For example, he mentions once or twice the absorption of its neighbours into the Soviet Union as being one of the objectives of Soviet policy if it can be achieved without undue international complications. Hitherto, the Russians have only claimed neighbouring territory to which they had a good historical or ethnical claim, and there is no evidence to suggest that they intend to go further than this. I should also myself have gone further than the General does in demolishing the disastrous theory that soon we shall have to fight this country. The General preferred simply to state the case and to leave his readers in London to draw the moral. These are however only small points of criticism, and do not affect the balance of the paper.

4. The General has made a good start and is standing up well to the usual frustrations and disappointments. But the Russians have dropped a broad hint in a recent note that in their view the days of Military Missions here and in London are numbered.

Yours ever

A. C. K.

CALENDAR TO No. 79

i 6 July 1945 General Sir J. Gammell (Moscow): Note on Russia—July 1945. Considers factors in Soviet policy in relation to British policy [N 8935/2/38].

[1] Lieutenant-General Sir J. Gammell was Head of the British Military Mission in Moscow. Lieutenant-General Sir A. Nye was Vice-Chief of the Imperial General Staff.

No. 80

Letter from Mr. Roberts (Moscow) to Mr. Warner (Received 19 July)
[N 9073/558/38]

MOSCOW, 10 July 1945

Dear Christopher,

There is, I think, a certain amount of misunderstanding about Soviet policy towards Germany, arising out of the apparent contrast between Russian criticisms of the alleged tenderness of their allies towards the Germans and their own policy and propaganda in the Soviet zone, which appears distinctly less severe towards the Germans than our own.

Soviet policy towards Germany has however recently been summarised very conveniently by M. Maisky at the opening meeting of the Reparation Commission on June 21st. As the minutes of these meetings may tend to remain within the circle of reparation experts, I thought it might be useful to draw your special attention to M. Maisky's statement, of which I enclose a copy.

Yours ever
Frank K. Roberts

Enclosure in No. 80

As representative of the U.S.S.R. on this Commission I will permit myself a few words to describe the attitude of the Soviet people to the problem which lies before us. The Soviet people have made immeasurable sacrifices in this war which has been imposed on it by the cruel and treacherous enemy. In our country we have no family which has not suffered in some manner as a result of the war. Humanly, it would be understandable and even pardonable that the Soviet people should seek vengeance for the sufferings which they have undergone. However, the Soviet people, at the liquidation of the war, does not seek vengeance but seeks only two things: *justice* and *security*. From this it may be seen that the Soviet people consider that Germany should be compelled to compensate to the maximum extent of her capabilities for the whole of this damage which she has caused to peace-loving nations—that is justice. At the same time the Soviet people considers that Germany, which in the course of one generation has twice cast the world into all the horrors of war, should be *deprived of the possibility once again to threaten other nations—this is the most important contribution to the work of international security.* The Soviet people has never aspired, and does not now aspire, to destroy the German people. However, bearing in mind the experience of the last thirty years, the Soviet people cannot and does not intend to subject itself again to mortal risk. Let Germany live, but she must be made harmless once and for all.[1]

Calendar to No. 80

i *11 & 20 July 1945* Letters (*without enclosures*) *from Mr. Roberts* (*Moscow*) *to Mr. Warner, from Mr. Warner to Mr. Dixon* (*Berlin*). Views of Soviet commentators on democracy and the international situation. M. Ermashev against dismemberment of Germany. Observations by MM. Maisky and Litvinov [N 9568, 9416/18/38].

[1] This statement was minuted as follows in the Northern Department of the Foreign Office: 'The clearest statement we have yet had of Soviet policy towards Germany, & even in this ambiguities still remain. It sounds like "de-industrialization"; but it is not incompatible with allowing a certain economic recovery under strict political control. J. E. C. Hill 26/7.' 'T. Brimelow 26/7.' 'This is not very illuminating as regards what is of most importance (but will naturally not be precisely formulated) viz. Soviet policy as regards the treatment of the German people & future German political institutions. C. F. A. W. 5/8.'

No. 81

Letter from Sir M. Peterson (Istanbul) to Sir O. Sargent (Received 19 July)
No. 171/115/45 [R 12179/4476/44]

Secret & Personal   ISTANBUL, *10 July 1945*

Dear Moley,

Moscow telegram No. 3008[1] of July 8th to you.

I don't like the way Archie is handling this.

In the first place is it really necessary for him to *write* to Molotov? I know the Russians are hard to get hold of but the effect of a letter seems to me to be likely to be absolutely nil.

In the second place by substituting 'discussed question' for 'demands' Archie seems to me greatly and unfortunately to weaken the whole démarche.

In the third place his para 3 is quite inconsistent with what he said before in the first para of his No. 2825[2] of June 30th to you. Possibly the Turkish Ambassador is inconsistent but I should be happier if Archie showed some consciousness of his inconsistency.

My own view is that the eastern frontier is by far the more dangerous place at the moment.[3]

Yours ever

MAURICE PETERSON

---

[1] Not printed. This telegram (received at 9.30 a.m. on 9 July 1945) explained the action recorded in No. 19. In this telegram Sir Archibald Clark Kerr explained that in his letter to M. Molotov, in view of a previous suggestion that the Turkish Ambassador in Moscow 'may have been manoeuvred into raising the subject himself, I have ventured to say that Soviet Government "discussed question" not that they made "demands" ' in regard to bases in the Straits. Sir A. Clark Kerr added, in paragraph 3 of his telegram No. 3008: 'Turkish Ambassador has been informed of my representations to Molotov. He considers that the Soviet Government attach at least as much importance to their territorial demands in the East as to their requirements concerning the Straits. In his view frontier revision in the East would be only the first step in a long term policy of expansion towards the Mediterranean and the Persian Gulf, but his evidence of this was flimsy.'

[2] Not printed. Sir A. Clark Kerr had there reported: 'I went over the ground with Turkish Ambassador this morning. He had nothing new to tell and his speculations did not amount to much. He seemed to hope that question of 1921 frontier [cf. No. 3, note 9] had been raised as part of "softening" process and would be dropped if Soviet Government got concessions about the Straits.'

[3] On 21 July 1945 Sir O. Sargent replied in a letter to Sir M. Peterson: 'I think that Archie's idea in writing to Molotov was all right. . . . We merely wanted to enter a caveat with them [the Russians] and to warn them that we should raise the question at Terminal . . . I agree with you that . . . "discussed question" instead of "made demands" weakens our démarche in a sense, but I think it was necessary in order to forestall' likely Russian rejoinder that subject was raised by Turkish Ambassador. 'I should be interested if you could develop the view you put forward in your last paragraph.'

Brief for the United Kingdom Delegation to the Conference at Potsdam
No. 2 [R 11596/81/67]

FOREIGN OFFICE[1]

Peace Treaties with Soviet-controlled Balkan countries

At the beginning of June, we asked for the views of the United States Government on the proposal that we should as soon as possible conclude peace treaties with Roumania, Bulgaria and Hungary.[2] We could see no prospect of persuading the Soviet Government to agree to the formation of more representative Government in these countries in accordance with our interpretation of the Yalta Declaration on Liberated Territories. We were also dissatisfied with the treatment accorded to our Representatives on the Control Commissions and with the manner in which our direct commercial interests were ignored or damaged with apparent deliberation by the Soviet authorities. Several attempts to remedy these grievances by direct negotiation had failed. We, therefore, decided that our best course was to work for the conclusion of peace treaties, which would give some chance of the withdrawal of the Red Army and the relaxation of the Soviet control in these countries, thus creating conditions in which the emergence of democratic Governments might be possible. By this means it would be possible to withdraw our Representatives on the Control Commissions without loss of prestige and without proclaiming a serious divergence between ourselves and the Russians.

2. Simultaneously with our approach to the United States Government, Stalin informed the Prime Minister that he considered the time ripe for the exchange of diplomatic representatives with Roumania and Bulgaria, similar action to be taken with Hungary in the near future.[3] The Prime Minister replied that we hoped to put before the United States and Soviet Governments comprehensive proposals to determine our relations with these States. Stalin later repeated his suggestion, and it is believed that he will exchange diplomatic representatives, at any rate with Roumania, on or about the 15th July.

3. The comprehensive proposals which the Prime Minister promised to send to Stalin were our proposals for the conclusion of peace. The United States Government, however, informed us at the end of June that they could give no more than qualified support to these proposals. They preferred instead to pursue the proposals they had themselves made in Moscow and London for the reorganisation of the Control Commission in the three countries

---

[1] This brief is undated. An explanatory minute by Mr. D. Stewart is dated 10 July 1945.

[2] See *F.R.U.S. 1945*, vol. iv, pp. 827–8.

[3] See No. 40, note 3.

concerned (a separate brief is submitted on this point).[4] Simultaneously, the United States Government hoped to secure the broadening of these three Governments by direct negotiation with the Soviet Government and His Majesty's Government.

4. After further consultation with their representatives in Sofia, Bucharest and Budapest, the United States Government have altered their position. On 9th July they informed us[5] that, far from supporting our proposals on the conclusion of the Peace Treaties, they would feel bound to oppose them and would at the same time oppose the establishment of diplomatic relations with the present Governments in these three countries. Nevertheless, we remain convinced that our proposals give the best chance of successful action in the Soviet-controlled Balkan countries and do not believe that the United States Government will make any progress on the lines they are now following. The lengthy delay which is likely to result from the inevitably fruitless argument with the Russians upon which the Americans propose to embark will be to our disadvantage since, in the meantime, the present Governments of the three countries concerned are entrenching their position by terrorising their opponents. Our proposals for the conclusion of the Peace Treaties should, therefore, be put forward at the earliest suitable opportunity and it is suggested that we should not feel bound to wait until the Americans are disillusioned and show greater readiness to accept our point of view. Nor should we be frightened by the prospect of finding ourselves on this occasion in agreement with the Russians against the Americans.

[4] This undated brief on the 'Status of British and American Representatives on the Control Commission in the Soviet-controlled Balkan countries' (entered on R 11654/81/67 under date of 10 July 1945) is not printed.

[5] In a letter from the American Embassy in London in pursuance of the instructions printed in *F.R.U.S. Berlin*, vol. i, pp. 399–400: *v. ibid.*, pp. 409–10 for the reply of 12 July from Sir O. Sargent. Lord Halifax had been correspondingly instructed in Foreign Office telegrams Nos. 7266 and 7376 to Washington of 8 and 11 July respectively, not printed.

No. 83

Mr. Stevenson (Belgrade) to Mr. Eden (Received 7 August)
No. 152 [R 13196/447/92]

BELGRADE, *10 July, 1945*

Sir,

With reference to my despatch No. 119[1] of June 21st, I have the honour to enclose a copy of my Press Attaché's report[2] for the month of June.

2. A most encouraging feature is the success of the English Reading Room;

[1] Not printed.

[2] This report, with an annex on Foreign Propaganda in Yugoslavia, is not printed. The Press Attaché reported in particular that during the period 11–30 June 1945 the British Information Centre and Reading Room in Belgrade had been used by 10,681 persons.

and I am confident that as it becomes more widely known and appreciated, the attendance figures, which are already satisfactory, will go even higher. There is a growing demand for reading matter that is free from political propaganda.

3. The appendix to the report was also prepared in the Press Section. It is perhaps hardly surprising that the Russians are not making any special efforts of their own in the way of propaganda as this is largely done for them by the present régime, not merely on the obvious grounds of race and ideology, but also to give the firm impression that the whole might of Soviet Russia is behind them. Against this preponderance of Russian influence, it is somewhat uphill work for the Western Democracies to make much headway, in spite of their far higher technical standards; and it is certainly to be hoped that France will start to play a part before long.

4. I do not think that anything is likely to shake the hard core of the present régime out of their conviction that Mother Russia is another Caesar's wife, and that Great Britain, America and even France are reactionary capitalist states; but I am hopeful that if we continue projecting ourselves, as we are doing now, we shall gradually make a deeper impression on the Yugoslav consciousness and that our influence, and that of America and France, will be able to soften some of the rigours of the present régime, and to show that the liberty of the people has been known and practised elsewhere in the world.

I have, &c.,
R. C. SKRINE STEVENSON

CALENDAR TO NO. 83

i [7] *July 1945 Brief No. 13 for U.K. delegation: British press representation in Eastern Europe.* Requirement for cessation of policy of excluding British correspondents from Soviet-controlled countries, and for some reciprocity for the complete freedom of movement and expression permitted to Soviet correspondents in Italy and Greece [F.O. 934/6].

No. 84

Mr. Caccia (Athens) to Mr. Churchill (Received 18 July)
No. 353 [R 12094/100/19]

ATHENS, *10 July 1945*

Sir,

I have the honour to send you herewith a report on economic conditions in Greece which has been compiled by the Economic Adviser.[1] The object of the report is to show the economic problems with which Greece was con-

---

[1] This report of 19 June 1945, comprising 160 paragraphs, by Mr. E. R. Lingeman is not printed.

fronted at the end of May, 1945, against the background of her pre-war position, and the devastation resulting from the war.

2. An understanding of these problems is particularly necessary at the present time in Greece. The policy of His Majesty's Government has been described as the establishment as soon as possible of a stable and friendly Greece. To this end a considerable effort is being made to restore the Greek fighting services. Equipment and guidance is also being made available in the re-formation of the Greek police and Gendarmerie. In addition the British army is not only giving Greece a guarantee of external and internal security, but also providing innumerable services in transport and engineering works. As a result of these efforts the Greek state is beginning once again to be something more than a geographic expression. The Writ of the Government is steadily becoming more effective in the provinces and Greek administration is starting to function on something like normal lines, both in the capital and outside.

3. But all these efforts may be frittered away unless at the same time Greek economy can be set on its own feet. This was understood from the first and the work done by Military Liaison was the proof. That work is being carried on by UNRRA, and the Greek Government itself are now addressing themselves earnestly to the problem in the new economic programme laid down by Monsieur Varvaressos.[2] The value of the enclosed report lies in showing how hard a path Greece will have to follow in order even to achieve some measure of economic stability on a very low standard of living. But the task is by no means hopeless and there are many ways in which we should be able to help with economic as well as political advantage to ourselves, a point which is brought out in the Conclusion.

4. Finally, I would like to draw attention to the amount of hard work entailed for Mr. Lingeman, in compiling this report. In present conditions statistics are either non-existent or hard to come by, and the Greek Government Departments are still sadly lacking in information about actual conditions in the country as a whole. Nevertheless, the outline which Mr. Lingeman has drawn is a clear one, and the material which he has provided will not only be most useful to all British authorities on the spot, but will I trust be of assistance to the Home Departments concerned.

I have, &c.,

Harold Caccia

CALENDARS TO No. 84

i *6 July 1945 F.O. Note on British Police and Prisons Mission to Greece*, under Sir Charles Wickham [R 11598/1918/19].

ii [*10*] *July 1945 Brief No. 25 for U.K. delegation on Greek Internal Affairs.* Varkiza Agreement is being implemented. Martial law has been raised, with an amnesty, and complete freedom of the press established. Prospective plebiscite and elections [R 11690/4/19].

[2] Greek Deputy Prime Minister and Minister of Supply.

iii [*10*] *July 1945   Brief No. 14 for U.K. delegation on Albania.* H.M.G. do not favour recognition of government under Enver Hoxha pending free elections [R 11661/46/90].

iv *12 July 1945   To Sir A. Clark Kerr (Moscow) Tel. No. 3885.* Bulgarian reparations to Greece. Mr. Eden minuted to Mr. Dixon on this telegram: 'Please keep by me. We ought to have a file of examples of Russian bad faith for Terminal. A. E.' [F.O. 934/5/55(1)].

v *12 July 1945   To Mr. Caccia (Athens) No. 418.* Future of Greek armed forces and status of British Military Mission [R 10199/8172/19].

No. 85

Brief for the United Kingdom Delegation to the Conference at Potsdam No. 26 [U 5399/5399/70]

FOREIGN OFFICE, *10 July 1945*

Question of Procedure for a General European Settlement

It is to our interest to clear up as soon as possible by a definite settlement the aftermath of the war. Continued uncertainty will make it impossible for Europe to settle down, and in particular, if territorial disputes are left open, there will be a constant risk of local fighting and direct action by minor States as happened last time. Delay will be greatly to the disadvantage of ourselves and the Americans, who must demobilise while still faced with the Japanese war.

2. The questions to be settled fall broadly under the following five heads:

(i) Germany;

(ii) Austria;

(iii) Italy;

(iv) The Axis Satellites (Roumania, Bulgaria, Hungary and Finland);

(v) Differences between the Allied and 'associated' countries (Poland and Czechoslovakia, Greece and Yugoslavia, Albania).

3. There are great differences between the situation of the various enemy countries and in the attitude of the Allies towards them. Disputes between the Allies must obviously be handled separately from those involving enemies. The unfortunate experience of the Versailles Conference after the last war gives a warning against embarking on a general Conference until the ground has been fully prepared.

4. Our experience in this war of drawing up the terms of surrender for the enemy countries has shown the advantages of the Major Allies taking the lead, securing the concurrence of the interested lesser Allies at a comparatively late stage in the proceedings.

4. [*sic*] Consideration at the official level in the Foreign Office of the problems involved has led to the conclusion that we ought to aim at:

(a) Dealing with each enemy country separately and in the manner and with the timing appropriate to each case;

156

(b) Establishing some regular body representing the four principal European Allies to do the preparatory work and draft the actual terms for subsequent ratification by the other Allied States concerned at a general Conference or by whatever means might be found expedient.

5. The United States Ambassador has now sent the Secretary of State an advance copy of the proposal which President Truman intends to table at Terminal. A copy of this document, which has also been communicated to the Soviet Government, is at *Annex A*.

6. The Americans have been thinking on the same lines as ourselves. They discount the idea of any general Conference until definite proposals have been worked out by the principal Allies, and for this purpose they propose to establish a Council of the Foreign Ministers of the *five* big Powers. Each Minister would appoint a deputy to take his place if necessary and a joint secretariat would be formed. According to oral explanation by the State Department, it is intended that the Council should first meet on the Continent; it is not clear whether it is suggested that it should thereafter be peripatetic. The first task of the Council should be to draw up Treaties of Peace with Italy and the Satellites (less Finland with which the United States are not at war) and to propose settlements of other territorial questions and of any other European problems of an emergency character. The Americans contemplate that later, if a suitable German Government emerged, the Council might also draw up a Peace Treaty with Germany. Lesser States directly interested in the matter could be invited to send representatives to the Council's discussion. Eventually the results of the Council's work would be submitted to the United Nations as a whole, possibly at a general Conference.

7. In discussing this proposal the State Department have made it plain that they contemplate the winding up of the European Advisory Commission as redundant.

8. This American proposal would, it is submitted have the following important advantages:–

(i) It would secure the principle that the essential preparatory work should be done by the Great Powers;

(ii) The Council of Foreign Ministers would have the necessary status and prestige to handle the great problems involved. The importance of this has been shown by the difficulties and delays of the 'official' European Advisory Commission.

(iii) The provision for the appointment of deputies would enable work to go on continuously, and the deputies could tackle complicated details— the sort of work which the E.A.C. was designed for—with the authority and backing of the Foreign Ministers to carry the work along smoothly and rapidly.

(iv) We and the Americans would have a better chance to obtain an effective voice in drawing up the Treaties with the Satellites;

(v) The Council would be available to deal, if necessary at short notice, with any dangerous territorial or other disputes which might arise between the Allies as a legacy of the war, here again doing with greater authority work which we hoped might be done by the E.A.C.

(vi) Although it will surely be necessary for the Council to have a regular seat somewhere convenient (e.g. London), there would be advantage in leaving the venue of its main meetings flexible as it would no doubt reconcile the proposal to the Russians if the meetings to deal with the Satellites were held at Moscow or somewhere in Eastern Europe. (Monsieur Maisky suggested to Mr. Roberts some time ago that the 'Peace Conference' should be held in Prague.)

9. As against these advantages must be set the following points:–

(a) The introduction of China into the detail of European peace making is very questionable. Although Article 106 of the Charter of the new World Organisation provides that the five Great Powers shall, in accordance with the Moscow Declaration on general security of October 1943,[1] continue to take joint action to keep the peace pending the coming into full operation of the world security system, Article 107 of the Charter preserves the belligerent rights of the principal Allies to take action against enemy States. China is not a party to the Four Power assumption of supreme authority over Germany and she is not at war with any of the Satellites. The Soviet Government are unlikely to agree to her inclusion as a principal party on the Council for all purposes.

(b) If, as appears to be implied, the American proposal is to await the emergence of a German Government capable of signing a Treaty before settling German problems, the delay might be dangerous and it would certainly give rise to many difficulties.

(c) The Soviet Union and China would be brough[t] from the outset into the preparatory work of the Italian Treaty, whereas our policy has been to agree the draft settlement first with the Americans and only at the second stage with the French and Russians.

10. It is suggested, however, that these difficulties could be overcome. With regard to (a), it might be arranged that, while China would be nominally a member of the Council, she would not join in treaty making in the case of the Satellites, with whom she is not at war; and while she would have the right to participate in discussions about Germany, any action taken in respect of Germany in advance of the final settlement would continue to be taken by the four Powers in virtue of their assumption of supreme authority over Germany. With regard to (b), it is suggested in the separate note in *Annex B*[i] to this paper that we ought to avoid the delay and other objections in waiting for a German Government to emerge and that urgent questions affecting Germany should be finally settled by further Declarations imposed by the four Powers, (e.g. as regards Germany's new frontiers with Poland and Czechoslovakia). If this procedure were agreed, the Council of Foreign Ministers could work out the terms of the Declara-

---

[1] This declaration on the establishment and maintenance of international peace and security, issued on 30 October 1943 by the United Kingdom, China, Soviet Union and United States of America, is printed in *B.F.S.P.*, vol. 154, pp. 362–3.

tions in the same way as they would Treaties with the other enemy States, leaving the assent of the other interested United Nations to be obtained by Conference or any other suitable means in the light of circumstances. With regard to (c), it is suggested that we could accept the disadvantages of a closer Soviet intervention in arrangements for Italy, which is offset (as mentioned in paragraph 8 (iv) above) by the advantage we should derive if the Council were to take charge of treaty making with the Satellites.

11. The formation of the new Council would in fact render the E.A.C. superfluous, The latter has virtually completed the main plans for Germany and Austria and subsidiary matters can now best be discussed by the Four Power Commissions at Berlin and Vienna. Other current questions which might in theory have gone to the E.A.C., could obviously best be handled by the Council of Foreign Ministers.

12. The question of the arrangements to be made in respect of the various countries, as grouped under the five heads in paragraph 2 above, is examined in more detail in the separate note at *Annex B*, which was written before we had received the American proposal. At *Annex C* is a list of outstanding territorial problems.

13. The following *Conclusions* are suggested:

(i) We should welcome the American proposal;

(ii) We should point out the difficulties about China (paragraph 8[9] (a) above) and suggest that she should be admitted as a sort of 'sleeping partner' as suggested in paragraph 10 above;

(iii) We should emphasise the advantage of the new body having a permanent seat, particularly for its secretariat, although it might as occasion required meet elsewhere. We might recommend London (provided this did not mean M. Gousev), but could agree to Prague if the Russians insisted;

(iv) We should agree to the dissolution of the E.A.C. on the understanding that the new Council would meet regularly and deal not only with policy but also with the inevitable detailed preparatory work on frontiers, etc.

(v) We should urge strongly the need for the Deputies to be specially appointed, since theirs will be a full-time job which could not be performed adequately by local Ambassadors, least of all by Monsieur Gousev.

(vi) We suggest that the Council ought to deal with the peace treaty for Finland as well as the other Satellites, the United States representative becoming, like his Chinese colleague, a 'sleeping partner' on this occasion.

Reconstruction Department

ANNEX A TO No. 85

Letter from Mr. Winant to Mr. Eden[2]

Embassy of the United States of America,
1 Grosvenor Square, W.1.

Secret   *8 July 1945*

Dear Mr. Eden,

In connexion with the first item of the suggested list of topics for discussion at

[2] This letter is printed in *F.R.U.S. Berlin*, vol. i, p. 289.

the forthcoming meeting of the Heads of Government transmitted in my letter of July 7, 1945, I have been requested to communicate to you the proposal enclosed herewith[3] which the President plans to present to Prime Minister Churchill and Marshal Stalin at an early stage in their forthcoming conversations.

This document is being communicated in advance to the British and Soviet Governments in the belief that they may wish to be giving the matter some thought prior to the meeting.

Sincerely,
JOHN G. WINANT

ANNEX C TO No. 85
List of Outstanding Territorial Problems in Europe

Germany
(a) *Western Frontier*
(i) Dutch claims to frontier rectification on the Ems River and possibly elsewhere;
Dutch claims of territory to compensate for German flooding of the Netherlands.
(ii) Possible Belgian and Luxembourg claims for minor rectifications.
(iii) Franco-German frontier and the question of a special régime for 'Rheno-Westphalia'
(b) *Southern Germany*
Rectification of German-Czechoslovak frontier.
(c) *Eastern Germany*
(i) Russian annexation of part of East Prussia.
(ii) German-Polish frontier.
(iii) Poland's acquisition of Danzig.

Austria
(i) Fixing of German-Austrian frontier.
(ii) Yugoslav claims on Carinthia.
(iii) Austro-Italian frontier, including disposal of South Tyrol.

Italy
(i) Disposal of Italian islands in the Mediterranean.
(ii) Italo-Yugoslav frontier in North-East Italy.
(iii) Disposal of former Italian territory on the Dalmation [sic] coast.
(iv) Possible rectifications of Franco-Italian frontier.
(v) Disposal of the Dodecannese [sic].

Roumania
(i) Final allocation of Transsylvania [sic].
(ii) Regulation of session [cession] of Roumanian territory to Soviet Union under the Armistice.

Bulgaria
Formal redefinition of Bulgarian frontiers with Greece, Yugoslavia and Roumania.

---

[3] This 'Proposal for the establishment of a Council of Foreign Ministers', not here printed (cf. paras 5-7 above), is printed *ibid.*, pp. 286-7: cf. p. 289, note 3.

Hungary

General rectification of frontiers with Czechoslovakia, Yugoslavia and Roumania.

Finland

Regularisation of new frontiers between Finland and the Soviet Union as provided in the Armistice.

Albania

Rectification of frontiers with Yugoslavia and Greece.
Yugoslav-Greek frontier in Macedonia

CALENDAR TO No. 85

i *July 1945   Annex B to No. 85: F.O. Note:* considerations affecting procedure for a peace settlement for Germany, Austria, Italy, Axis satellites; Inter-Allied territorial questions [U 5399/5399/70].

No. 86

Brief for the United Kingdom Delegation to the Conference at Potsdam
No. 33 [Z 8318/16/28]

FOREIGN OFFICE, *10 July 1945*[1]

Tangier

The Soviet Government have asked to be invited to take part in the preliminary conversations about Tangier which it was original[l]y contemplated should be held in Paris between the United States, the United Kingdom and French Governments; and eventually to participate in the administration of the Tangier zone.[2]

The Chiefs of Staff have agreed that Russian participation may be accepted and the Cabinet have given blanket approval to the Russian request being agreed to at Terminal.

The Soviet Ambassador in London has spoken twice on the subject during the last week and begged for an early reply. There is, therefore, good reason to anticipate that the Soviet Delegation will bring the matter up themselves at Terminal.

Although there are obvious objections to Russian participation in Tangier, it is not very easy to find good reasons for turning down their request, since:

---

[1] Date of initialing by Mr. Harvey of this undated brief.

[2] For the British communication of 30 June 1945 informing the Soviet Government of the proposal to hold conversations to concert an approach to the Spanish Government for the withdrawal of its troops and administration from Tangier, which had been unilaterally occupied by Spain since June 1940, and to discuss the re-establishment of an international régime in Tangier on a provisional basis see *F.R.U.S. Berlin*, vol. i, p. 988. For the Soviet request on 2 July 1945 to participate in the conversations and for a British proposal on 9 July for their deferment *v. ibid.*, pp. 989–90, 1003.

(a) Once Russia by the San Francisco decisions has been put on an equal footing with the United States, the United Kingdom, France and China,[3] it seems difficult to exclude her from any international organisation. And as a major European Power, Russia has at least as much interest in Tangier as Sweden, Belgium and Holland.[4]

(b) Russia has in theory just as much right as the United States to participate in Tangier since although neither of them was a party to the 1923 Convention, both signed the Act of Algeciras.[5]

(c) The United States are in favour of acceding to the Russian request and the French are equally prepared to agree, though they hope to get something out of the Russians in return. If we resist we may therefore find ourselves alone in doing so.

Furthermore, to refuse the U.S.S.R. the right to participate in the administration of Tangier would not keep Russia out of North Africa. The Soviet Government could quite well establish a Consulate-General in Tangier without being party to the international regime (as indeed the U.S. do at the present moment), and could equally well set up posts in French Morocco if they wished.

For all these reasons it seems likely that the Russian request will have to be granted at Terminal. It would, however, seem highly desirable that we should only make this concession to the Russians in return for some kind of concession by them,[6] and that we should sell our agreement about Tangier for the highest possible price. What this price should be will presumably depend upon developments at Terminal and on the Russian attitude to our various *desiderata*. The French have suggested that they may try to make their assent to the Russian request about Tangier conditional upon the Soviet Government agreeing to French participation in the Moscow Reparations Conference. If no better counter concession of more importance to purely British interests offers itself, it might be to our advantage also to bargain Russian participation in Tangier against French participation in the Reparations talks. We want to get the French into the Reparations Conference and by helping them in this way, we might make them more

[3] Under articles 23 and 27 of the Charter of the United Nations the Soviet Union was one of the five permanent members of the Security Council, with right of veto: see No. 1, note 5, and No. 42, note 5.

[4] These three Powers had acceded to the convention of 18 December 1923 between Great Britain, Spain and France regarding the organisation of the Statute of the Tangier Zone, printed (Cmd. 2203 of 1924) in *B.F.S.P.*, vol. 117, pp. 499–517.

[5] The General Act of the International Conference relating to the affairs of Morocco, concluded at Algeciras on 7 April 1906, is printed with annexed documents in *B.F.S.P.*, vol. 99, pp. 141–71.

[6] On 10 July 1945 the Cabinet approved Mr. Eden's proposal that 'while it would be impossible to exclude the Russians from the discussions, it would be preferable to defer giving a definite reply to their request until the Three Power Meeting. It might then be found that our willingness to invite them to participate in these discussions could be used to secure some concession from them on another subject' (C.M. (45) 13th Conclusions, minute 4).

amenable over Tangier where they are showing signs of being difficult.

It would not seem desirable to go further at Terminal than simply to agree, insofar as His Majesty's Government are concerned, to Russian participation in Tangier. It would only lead to complications to try to discuss at this stage what the next step should be and what new arrangements for Tangier should be made. Indeed it would really be impossible to discuss such matters in the absence of the French. The most that could be said would be that on the assumption that not only we but also the U.S. and the French Governments agreed to Russian participation, then the next step would seem to be the assembly in Paris of an informal meeting of representatives of the four Governments. It would be for this meeting to consider what steps should be taken to summon an early conference of all the Tangier Powers (presumably excluding Italy in the present circumstances) plus the U.S. and the U.S.S.R.; and to discuss what arrangements can best be made, pending the summoning of such a conference, to get the Spaniards out of Tangier and to provide for the interim administration of the zone.

CALENDARS TO No. 86

i *6 July 1945   Mr. Holman (Paris) Tels. Nos. 344–6 Saving.* French views on revision of the convention of 1923 and on Soviet participation in conversations concerning Tangier [Z 8129, 8135/16/28].

ii *6 July 1945   Viscount Cranborne to Governments of Canada, Australia, New Zealand, South Africa, Tel. D. No. 1174.* Soviet, Dutch and Portuguese claims to participate in discussions on Tangier [Z 8019/16/28].

No. 87

Earl of Halifax (Washington) to Mr. Eden (Received 11 July, 6.50 p.m.)
No. 4810 Telegraphic [F 4181/584/61]

Secret. Important   WASHINGTON, *11 July 1945, 12.8 p.m.*

My immediately preceeding telegram.[1]
Following is text of covering letter received from Grew.
(Begins)
As of possible interest I am enclosing a copy of a statement made today to the press on the subject, of alleged Japanese peace offers. My purpose in making this statement was to try to put an end to the current speculation by the public and in the press that a *bona fide* peace offer has really come from Japan and that we have paid no attention to it. The facts are that such peace feelers as have been reported to us have come from sources which have given no satisfactory evidence that they speak with authority and we

---

[1] Not printed. This telegram of even date transmitted the text of a press-statement made on 10 July 1945 by Mr. J. C. Grew; cf. Sir L. Woodward, *op. cit.*, vol. v, p. 505.

believe that they have been purely fishing expeditions on the part of individuals. I hope that my statement may serve to clear the air. (Ends).

No. 88

Sir A. Clark Kerr (Moscow) to Mr. Eden (Received 11 July, 4.30 p.m.)
No. 59 Victim Telegraphic [*UE 2730/624/77*]

MOSCOW, *11 July 1945, 1.33 p.m. G.M.T.*

Repeated to Washington, Paris.

From United Kingdom Delegation Moscow.

Your telegram No: 43.[1]

I conveyed your decision to Pauley with the explanation (. . . ? put)[2] out in your telegram. He was extremely pleased.[3]

Foreign Office please repeat to Washington and Paris as my telegrams Victim 44 and 45 respectively.

[1] No. 50.

[2] The text is here uncertain.

[3] Mr. Eden minuted against this, 'What by? A. E.' Mr. Coulson explained in a minute of 13 July that 'Mr. Pauley had made it very clear that he would insist on a share of reparation for the United States equal to our own. This question was considered by the Ministerial Committee on Reparation and although, on the basis of effort plus losses, we do not agree that they are entitled to it, Ministers decided that we must accept Mr. Pauley's contention', subject to the proviso in No. 50. Further minuting followed: 'I don't know why we gave way to Americans on this. It is not the truth. Did P.M. approve? A. E. July 17.' 'The decision of the Ministerial Committee was not submitted to the P.M. It was only taken on July 9th and I think he had already left for France. J. E. Coulson 17/7.' 'A. C. July 18, 1945.' 'There is no real basis in fairness for this decision. I don't know who Ministers are who took it without ref. to P.M. or myself. They will have to defend it. A. E. July 19.'

No. 89

Sir A. Clark Kerr (Moscow) to Mr. Eden (Received 11 July, 4.40 p.m.)
No. 3017 Telegraphic [*K 12990/2648/238*]

Confidential   MOSCOW, *11 July 1945, 1.46 p.m. G.M.T.*

My telegram No. 2407.[1]

When he saw Stalin on July 7[6]th[2] the Dean of Canterbury, at my request, described to him the plight of our Soviet wives. Stalin showed considerable

[1] In this telegram of 13 June 1945 Sir A. Clark Kerr had reported: 'I raised yesterday with Molotov the question of Soviet wives. I reviewed our reiterated appeals in the past and his reasons for rejecting them of which the principal one was that Supreme Presidium was too busy in war-time to consider such matters. . . . The Anglo-Soviet alliance warranted a strong claim by us upon 15 or 16 young Soviet citizens now waiting eagerly to join their British husbands. . . . I therefore made a formal claim upon them.'

[2] Cf. No. 78, note 3.

surprise and, turning to Molotov, asked if the Dean's story was true. Molotov confessed with some slight embarrassment that it was. Stalin said that there was clearly something wrong that he would be able to put right. He then corrected himself, saying that he would 'probably' be able to put it right.

No. 90

Mr. Houstoun-Boswall (Sofia) to Mr. Eden (Received 11 July, 9.50 p.m.)
No. 801 Telegraphic [R 11851/21/7]

Confidential   SOFIA, *11 July 1945, 7.6 p.m. G.M.T.*

My telegram No. 793.[1]

Cabinet met again yesterday when Minister Petkov reiterated his attitude: if the Government wanted to relieve itself of his presence it must resign and reform.

2. If that occurred it might have repercussions on composition of Regency Council, as Regent Ganev[2] in particular, feels that as he has been associated closely with Petkov since 1940, he would find it impossible to carry on if Petkov were to be left out of any new Government.

3. There are even those who fear the possibility of a fake *coup d'état* (staged by Obbovists[3] and communists) in order to give the Russians a pretext to step in and restore order under a Government still more Communist-controlled than the present one. Far-fetched as any provocation of this sort may seem, I would not be prepared to discount it entirely. Things cannot go on very much longer in this atmosphere of uncertainty and apprehension.[4]

---

[1] This telegram of 10 July 1945 had summarised a 'very courageous and forthright circular issued by Minister N. Petkov and others to the presidents of local agrarian associations throughout Bulgaria' in protest against interference in the Bulgarian Agrarian National Union. Included among items of the programme of the Union were: 'close friendship with Soviet Union, sincere friendship with Western democracies'; 'restoration of constitutional liberties of Bulgarian people'; 'closer and more real collaboration with Patriotic Front and especially with communist party'; 'really free elections'. Mr. Houstoun Boswall further reported that M. Petkov had told him on 7 July that he had refused a call on him and his two agrarian Cabinet colleagues to resign since 'there was not a word in the circular which conflicted with the programme of the Patriotic Front as originally laid down . . . If they were no longer required in the Government it was for the Government to get rid of them by resigning and reforming. . . . 7. Cabinet crisis cannot be concealed much longer, and, in my opinion, this act of resistance, belated though it may be, on the part of true agrarians to communist pressure will have a wholesome effect (though it may well lead to a great many arrests). Patriotic Front Government is thus proved publicly to be no more than a marionette directed by ill-concealed hand of the communist party.'

[2] Upon the assumption of power in Bulgaria on 9 September 1944 by the Patriotic (Fatherland) Front, Professor V. Ganev had been appointed a member of the Regency Council constituted on behalf of the infant King Simeon II after the death of King Boris III on 28 August 1943.

[3] Adherents of M. A. Obbov, who had replaced M. Petkov as Secretary of the Bulgarian Agrarian National Union in June 1945.

[4] Mr. Eden minuted on this telegram: 'Can we give any help, by a little judicious publicity or any other means? A. E.'

i *20–26 July 1945 Mr. Houstoun-Boswall (Sofia) Tels. Nos. 834, 840 & 852.*
Grave cabinet crisis continues; concern of Exarch Stephan (tel. 840 of 21 July)
at deteriorating situation in Bulgaria; summary (tel. 852 of 26 July) of letter
from M. Petkov and associates to Bulgarian Prime Minister, whose resignation
they are trying to force [R 12276, 12347, 12616/21/7].

No. 91

Sir R. Bullard (Tehran) to Mr. Eden (Received 11 July, 7.55 p.m.)
No. 691 Telegraphic [E 5045/20/34]

Immediate   TEHRAN, *11 July 1945, 4.35 p.m. G.M.T.*

Repeated to: Moscow, Government of India, M.E. Min[ister] Saving, Bagdad
for P.A.I.C.[1] Saving.

There are many signs that Russians are making a tremendous effort to
obtain virtual mastery over this country before the moment of evacuation
arrives.[2]

2. Violent article in *Pravda* mentioned in my telegram No. 689[3] suggests
that action is being justified before the event by manufacture of evidence
which, as the Russians are well aware, no one on the other side can expose
for lack of means of publicity.

3. Efforts of Tudeh[4] backed by Russians to stir up industrial unrest are
now to be backed powerfully by strong Russian Trades Union Delegation
which has arrived in Tehran and is already holding out to Persian Trade
Unionists the hope of a seat and a vote on Paris Trades Union International.
Delegates are beginning tour with Isfahan, where the chief opponent of
Tudeh was recently murdered in the street and where Persian authorities are
already much too terrified of the Russians to pursue enquiry into the murder
seriously.

4. There is no doubt that in parts of Northern Kurdistan to which Russians
do not allow Persia to send troops, Kurdish independence movement is
being encouraged.

5. Tudeh emissaries are working hard in the villages in the north and
north west often, if not always, urging non-payment of rent, and opposition
to them is paralysed by fear. I am obliged to accept at least in part evidence
that if emissaries are not actually accompanied by Red Army soldiers, such
soldiers often happen to be in the vicinity at the critical moment.

6. Local officials in the north have no control whatsoever over Tudeh.
I have as yet no confirmation of recent reports that Tudeh are forming

---

[1] Persia and Iraq Command of British Forces (Paiforce) in the Middle East.
[2] Mr. Eden minuted against this paragraph: 'What action do we take? A. E.'
[3] This telegram of 10 July is not printed.
[4] An Iranian radical party of reform.

Soviets in Resht, Tobriz [Tabriz] and elsewhere in the north but their complete independence of control is shown by the fact, witnessed recently by our Press Attaché in more than one place in the north, that Tudeh agents wearing arm bands setting out their functions search all vehicles leaving for the south and confiscate all rice found in them. Excuse given is that rice is being exported but if the Russians had managed to induce Millspaugh[5] to agree to another Russian barter scheme it is unlikely that Tudeh would have stopped export of rice to Russia.

7. The Russians are using Radio Tehran for violent political propaganda. One recent broadcast was against Fascists in United States. Another comprised items on British elections (objective but not their business) one item against anti-Soviet influences in various countries, violent attack on Swedish Government and highly critical items about the Doenitz Government.

8. Newspapers closely associted with Russians have appeared more openly anti-British. 'Rastakhizi-Iran' published a series of scurrilous articles accusing the British of having murdered Middle East statesmen including Faisal[6] and engineered not only murder of the United States Consul who was lynched by a fanatical crowd in Tehran twenty years ago but also execution of Persian pilgrim who was put to death in Mecca in 1943 on a charge of sacrilege. (It was with the greatest difficulty that I secured suspension of this paper though Persian authorities suspended at once on demand of Soviet Embassy a paper which had published serious article questioning the claim of Russia to be any sort of democracy.) Even *Rahbar* which is regarded as direct voice of the Soviet Embassy alleged that when three British officials were touring in Bakhtiari country recently they planned to have Tudeh headquarters in Shiraz burnt. It has now referred to a tale published by another pro-Russian newspaper that during his recent visit General Paget[7] had a secret meeting with Saed Zia[8] and in an article studded with ironical notes of exclamation has expressed hope that General Paget did not come here as he went to Syria 'merely to restore order.'

9. It seems improbable that the Russians will try to bring off some violent coup, though in the absence of publicity[9] even this cannot be entirely excluded. Most probable explanation is that they are determined to force upon the electors so many of their candidates that even if Tudeh has not a majority in the Majlis[10] it will in fact be able to run it.

10. No one could blame the Persian Government if they refused to hold elections until after the withdrawal of foreign troops but in that case the

---

[5] Dr. A. Millspaugh, head of an American financial mission in Iran, had been Administrator General of Finances in Iran, 1942–February 1945.

[6] King Feisal I of Iraq had died in 1933 while taking a cure in Switzerland.

[7] British Commander-in-Chief, Middle East Force.

[8] Leader of the recently formed Iradé-i-Milli, National Will Party, in Iran.

[9] Mr. Eden minuted in the margin 'Cannot we publicise? A. E.'

[10] Iranian Legislative Assembly.

Russians would almost certainly cause elections to be held for Soviet or provincial councils in the north. Possible remedies are

(1) visit of a party of journalists who would be able and not afraid to publish their views and in view of servile attitude of English press towards Russia as reported in a recent Foreign Office telegram, they must be American or

(2) admission of foreign observers to all parts of Persia at the time of the elections (in view of our policy in Greece suggestion to this effect would not be unreasonable).

11. Withdrawal of British and Russian troops from considerable area of Persia would, of course, have an excellent effect. Even withdrawal from Tehran alone would put heart into the Government and administration. And I again repeat my conviction that if the Russians refuse to evacuate even Tehran it would pay us to leave the city immediately. Apart from the effect on Persia this would make it extremely difficult for the Russians to convince the world of the genuineness of the elections resulting in their favour in areas dominated by their troops.[11]

Foreign Office please pass to Government of India as my telegram No. 179.

[11] Mr. Eden minuted on this telegram: 'P.M. should see Persian telegrams at once.' With reference to Mr. Eden's marginal minutes above, Mr. L. F. L. Pyman of Eastern Department stated in a minute of 13 July 1945: 'The only radical cure for the situation is to secure as big a Russian troop withdrawal as possible. The Secretary of State is sending a minute to the Prime Minister about this [No. 129], with a view to settling the matter at Terminal. With regard to publicity, . . . owing to the Soviet censorship, resident correspondents in Tehran find it impossible to send out messages critical of Soviet policy in Persia. Moreover, even when messages are got out of Persia, by various means, British papers are reluctant to use them lest the publication of articles hostile to the Soviet Government leads to that Government refusing the let the paper concerned send correspondents to Russia or Russian-controlled areas.' For consequential action see No. 323.

No. 92

Sir R. Bullard (Tehran) to Mr. Eden (Received 11 July, 8.40 p.m.)
No. 695 Telegraphic [E 5046/20/34]

Immediate   TEHRAN, *11 July 1945, 5.40 p.m. G.M.T.*

Repeated to Moscow, Government of India, M.E. Min, Bagdad (for P.A.I.C.).

My telegram No. 691.[1]

Last night several grenades, one of which exploded, are said to have been thrown at the house of Dr. Keshavarz, one of the the leading Tudeh deputies.

2. Tehran is living in a state of deep anxiety awaiting the next move of the Russians expecially since the news of the Russian demands on Turkey and all the inhabitants except presumably Tudeh want the Russians to remove their troops and are anxious not to give them any pretext for remaining in

[1] No. 91.

the country. In these circumstances it is difficult to believe that the grenades with one convincing explosion between them were thrown by an opponent of Dr. Keshavarz. No moment is so convenient from the Tudeh point of view. The explosion might be expected to prove that the dangers depicted by Pravda only two days ago are real. Finally the Soviet Trade Union delegation are in Tehran at the moment when the outrage is committed and can see for themselves under what a reign of terror freedom-loving people live in Persia.[2]

Foreign Office please pass to Government of India as my telegram No. 181 and to Bagdad for PAIC as my telegram No. 41.

[2] Mr. Eden minuted on this telegram: 'Are we bringing Persia up at Terminal? Are we still reluctant to withdraw ourselves A. E.,   even from Teheran?'

No. 93

Sir R. Bullard (Tehran) to Mr. Eden (Received 11 July, 9.5 p.m.)
No. 692 Telegraphic [E 5053/20/34]

Important   TEHRAN, *11 July 1945, 5.52 p.m. G.M.T.*

Repeated to Moscow, Government of India, M.E. Min Saving, Bagdad (for P.A.I.C.) Saving.

My telegram No. 622.[1]
Soviet Trade Union delegation are leaving for Isfahan July 12th. They will presumably visit all towns where they can do most harm to stability of Persian Government.[2]

2. We have no guarantee that they will not take action which might endanger Anglo-American military measures against Japan. I suggest General Officer Commanding-in-Chief Paiforce should request Soviet General Officer Commanding in Persia to ensure that delegation should not visit Ahwaz or any other place in oil area where their efforts might be misunderstood and cause interruption in supply of oil for prosecution of the war against Japan. I could, of course, make this request of Soviet Embassy but I think that purely military treatment of the problem is more appropriate.

Foreign Office please pass to Government of India as my telegram No. 180.

[1] Of 22 June 1945, not printed.
[2] Sir R. Bullard further reported in Tehran telegram No. 34 Saving of 13 July (received, 5.55 p.m. on 19 July): 'Minister for Foreign Affairs informs me that when the Persian Ambassador in Moscow hesitated to grant visas to the Soviet Trade Union Delegation without reference to the Persian Government he was told by the Commissariat for Foreign Affairs that the delegates would go with or without visas, but that if the visas were refused this would be noted as yet another proof of the inveterate hostility of the Persian Government to the Soviet Union. Thereupon the Persian Ambassador granted the visas.'

i *13 & 17 July 1945   To Sir R. Bullard (Tehran) Tel. No. 417; Sir J. Grigg to General Paget (Cairo) Tel. No. 60420.* Foreign Office and War Office views on possible visit by Soviet trades union delegation to Iranian oil area [E 5053, 5172/20/34].

No. 94

Earl of Halifax (Washington) to Mr. Eden (Received 12 July, 8.55 a.m.)
No. 4842 Telegraphic [E 5096/420/89]

Immediate. Secret   WASHINGTON, *11 July 1945, 11.21 p.m.*

Your telegram No. 7304[1] and my telegram No. 4797.[2]

The considerations in paragraph 2 to paragraph 4 of your telegram have been put to Mr. Henderson with a strong appeal for American assistance in equipping and training the Syrian and Lebanese gendarmerie.[3] It was pointed out to him that whilst we appreciate the difficulties which the United States Government feel in sending a token force or warships to the Levant States, the assistance over M.I.R.A. and the gendarmerie for which we are now asking, much more modest though they be, are none the less of great importance and urgency in the present difficult situation.

2. Mr. Henderson said that he personally took the view that the United States Government must be prepared to take some share of the burden. He could foresee possible difficulties over the supply of equipment for the gendarmerie since the Levant States are not (repeat not) entitled to lend-lease and cannot pay cash. There was also the traditional American reluctance to assume responsibilities of this kind which he was doing his best to overcome. He would have the matter examined at once and would let us know further as soon as possible. But he could not (repeat not) say off-hand whether the decision would be favourable.

3. I believe it would be of assistance if the United States representative in Beirut could recommend to the State Department that early and favourable consideration be given to our request for American assistance. If, however, the matter were broached with Mr. Wadsworth and his recommendations to the State Department were unfavourable, it would of course do more harm than good here. Mr. Shone[4] will be the best judge of the desirability of putting the matter to him at this stage.

4. Foreign Office please pass important to Beirut and Paris as my telegrams Nos. 56 and 239 respectively.

---

[1] No. 66.
[2] Not printed. This telegram of even date reported instructions from the State Department to American representatives at Cairo and Beirut to discuss with British authorities there the question of American technical help requested in No. 66.
[3] An American record of this conversation is printed in *F.R.U.S. 1945*, vol. viii, pp. 1199–1200.
[4] Mr. T. A. Shone was H.M. Ambassador at Beirut.

No. 95

Mr. Eden to Sir M. Peterson (Angora)
No. 209 [R 11820/4476/44]

Top Secret   FOREIGN OFFICE, 11 July 1945

Sir,

The Turkish Foreign Minister[1] came to see me to-day, accompanied by the Turkish Ambassador.

2. They were at pains to impress on me the sinister motives which, in their opinion, underlay the recent requirements formulated by M. Molotov to the Turkish Ambassador as necessary before there could be any revival of the Turco-Russian Treaty. They suspected that the fourth Russian requirement, which had not been defined, would turn out to be nothing less than a demand that Turkey should enter Russia's orbit in respect of both her domestic and foreign affairs. In any case, Turkey would fight rather than cede territory or give bases.

3. They were aware of the caveat which we have put in at Moscow, but they were anxious to know whether the question would be discussed at the forthcoming meeting at Berlin. I told them that it certainly would be, but I could not foretell how the discussion would develop. At any rate, the Turkish Government would in no circumstances be faced with a joint *fait accompli*. I pointed out that a clear distinction could be made between the revision of the Montreux Convention by international agreement, which had been foreshadowed for a considerable time, and the Russian demand now made for the first time for territorial changes and the grant of bases. I observed that the Soviet Government might well, for tactical reasons, be putting forward extreme demands whilst prepared in the long run to accept something much less and more reasonable. The Foreign Minister did not demur to this.

4. I advised the Foreign Minister to see the United States Ambassador while he is in London and explain to him the anxieties of his Government. Mr. Winant has since agreed to receive him.

I am, &c.,
ANTHONY EDEN

CALENDARS TO No. 95

i *11 July 1945* Record by Sir A. Cadogan of conversation with Greek Ambassador, who expressed apprehension in regard to Russian policy in the Balkans and Turkey [R 11998/4476/44].

ii *13 July 1945* Record of a private conversation between Mr. Eden and the Turkish Foreign Minister and Ambassador: further discussion of Turkish anxieties in regard to Soviet policy, and reassurances by Mr. Eden [R 11820/4476/44].

iii *12 July 1945* Extract from 175th Meeting of Chiefs of Staff. Report by General Ismay on annexed minutes of 17 and 22 June from and to Mr. Churchill on supply of war-material to Turkey [R 12196/43/44].

[1] M. Hasan Saka was returning from the United Nations Conference at San Francisco.

No. 96

Brief for the United Kingdom Delegation to the Conference at Potsdam
No. 38 [W 10343/22/13]

FOREIGN OFFICE, *11 July 1945*

European Economic Co-operation

The Americans have put on their agenda for Terminal 'Co-operation in solving European economic problems.' They have pointed out, in explanation, that everything should be done to ensure that the Soviet Government should not merely join such bodies as the Emergency Economic Committe for Europe, the European Coal Organization and the European Central Inland Transport Organization, but should also effectively co-operate in making them a success.

2. Separate briefs on each of these European Organizations, and the position taken by the Soviet Government towards them, are attached.[1] The salient points, with reference to discussion at Terminal, are:

United Maritime Authority

3. There is reason to believe that the Soviet Government will not join this body and their participation is not, in our view, essential. Nothing about Soviet participation in it need therefore be said at Terminal.

European Central Inland Transport Organisation

4. We have suggested to the United States and French Governments that we should invite the Soviet Government to resume participation in the conference, which has discussed the formation of this body, as soon as a delegation representing the new Polish Government can arrive in London and take part in it. It is recommended that Marshal Stalin and Monsieur Molotov should be pressed at Terminal to agree to give favourable consideration to this proposal.

Emergency Economic Committee for Europe

5. The Americans are likely to press the Soviet Government to join this organization.[2] If so, it is recommended that we should support them on the grounds that:–

(1) Great Power solidarity on this as on other matters is highly desirable.

(2) The majority of the European Allies clearly desire such a body.

(3) The problems with which this body will deal are so urgent that we cannot as the Russians suggested await the full fruition of the Economic and Social Council[3] which will anyhow be concerned with much longer-term problems.

---

[1] Not printed: cf. below.

[2] In Washington telegram No. 4775 of 10 July 1945 Lord Halifax had reported 'that the State Department are determined to do everything open to them to ensure the success of the E.E.C.E. With this in view, they have given very careful thought to their representative on the Committee.'

[3] Under chapter X of the United Nations Charter: see No. 1, note 5.

(4) The Emergency Committee may well pave the way for the operations of the Economic and Social Council when it is in a position to begin functioning.

6. It may be (though there is no particular reason to suspect it) that suggestions may be put forward at Terminal for the creation of a Supreme Economic Council. It is submitted that any such suggestion should be opposed. We have already created, with considerable difficulty, the Emergency Economic Committee for Europe and it would be pointless to start a new organization for much the same purpose. If special economic collaboration between the Four Powers is required in regard to Europe, then the representatives of these Powers on the Emergency Economic Committee can meet together without formality and act as a sort of steering Committee. Moreover, if the economic questions involved are of sufficient importance, they can be discussed at any regular meetings of Foreign Secretaries which may take place, and their representatives on the Committees would join them there.

European Coal Organization

7. The Americans are likely to press the Russians to join the European Coal Organization. If so, we should support them on the grounds that:

(*a*) Without Russian membership there is likely to be a serious impairment of our policy of treating Germany as an economic whole;

(*b*) Russian membership is necessary because the Control Council as a whole must determine the existence of exportable surpluses and decide on any outside help which may be needed for the successful exploitation of the German Mining Industry in the common interest.

(*c*) In a matter of this sort, of such overriding concern to the economies of so many European allies, Three Power solidarity is in the highest degree desirable.

8. In pressing the Russians to join, there are three important points to secure:

(*a*) Arrangements should be concerted for ensuring that the Polish Government also joined.

(*b*) The European Coal Organization should allocate, according to need and not necessarily with reference to reparation percentages, any coal which the Control Commission may declare to be surplus and available for export.

(*c*) German Silesian coal should be regarded as part of the resources of Germany and not of Poland.

9. Discussion on the European Coal Organization may prove a convenient opportunity of explaining to the Russians the directive to be issued to the Zone Commanders, of which details are contained in another brief[4] (German Coal Production). If so, it is important not to ignore the dilemmas created by this problem:

---

[4] No. 114.ii.

(*a*) If the export of coal from Germany is subordinated to the retention in Germany of the minimum of coal necessary to maintain order, this export is likely to be much reduced and may have disastrous effects on the economy of the liberated countries.

(*b*) Too rapid a rate of redeployment of the allied forces in and out of Germany may make it impossible to reach the target figure for exports.

No. 97

Memorandum by Mr. Hasler

[*UR 2334/9/850*]

FOREIGN OFFICE, *11 July 1945*

Russia and UNRRA

We have to-day received information most confidentially that the Chief Russian representative in London on UNRRA matters has told Commander Jackson[1] that the Soviet Ambassador has gone back to Moscow with a strong recommendation that the U.S.S.R. should now apply to UNRRA for free relief. He said that U.S.S.R. had paid for imports before the war by concentrating on the export of certain commodities. This export had ceased during the war years and his country had now insufficient foreign exchange to pay for relief supplies which were vital to her. He said that U.S.S.R. had hoped to obtain credits in the United Kingdom and United States in order to finance emergency imports, but these credits had not been provided and that, therefore, UNRRA seemed to be the only source of finance. He added that when he raised in January, 1944, the question of UNRRA assistance for the Soviet Union, he had been told that this could not be provided without interference with protocol supplies[2] which absorbed all the shipping available for supplies to Russia. Now that the war was over it seemed logical to re-consider the matter.

The statement by the Soviet representative to Commander Jackson was intended as a forewarning of something that might be raised in a big way by his Government. There does not seem to be any action we can take over it at the present stage in relation to UNRRA. If the Soviet Government accept this suggested change of policy, however, it may very well affect their attitude towards other matters such as membership of various European institutions dealing with economic matters.

---

[1] Commander R. G. A. Jackson, Senior Deputy Director General of U.N.R.R.A., was Acting Head of the U.N.R.R.A. European Regional Office in London as Personal Representative of the Director General, Governor H. Lehman.

[2] i.e. Anglo-American-Canadian military supplies to the Soviet Union as provided for in the Third Lend Lease Protocol of 19 October 1943, printed in *Soviet Supply Protocols* (Department of State Publication No. 2759 in *European Series 22*: Washington, 1948), pp. 51–2.

i *15 July 1945 Mr. Caccia (Athens) Tel. No. 1540.* Transmits views of Governor Lehman, then visiting Greece, on possibility of Soviet application for relief: clearly in order to apply and, subject to usual procedures, U.N.R.R.A. must stand ready to give aid requested within resources available. Considers possible timing of Soviet request which could entail drastic revision of present U.N.R.R.A. programmes. Seeks British and U.S. views; question of ability to pay [UR 2391/9/850].

No. 98

Memorandum by Mr. Hasler
[UR 2394/1590/851]

FOREIGN OFFICE, *11 July 1945*

Allocation of Food Supplies to Liberated Areas

A meeting has been called for 3 p.m. to-morrow (Thursday) on this question. Mr. Ronald will preside and Ministry of Food and Ministry of Production, and possibly War Office and Treasury will be there.

2. There is a host of telegrams on the subject. Every hour a new one arrives in a new series. I think that we shall do best if we concentrate on No. 942 from Paris on the French position in relation to the Argentine contract, on No. 4693 from Washington on Danish surpluses and No. 4718 from Washington on the Argentine contract and Danish surpluses.[1]

3. I suggest that the policy which we should wish to see adopted is as follows:

Argentina

Two suggestions have been made. First, that we should propose a joint purchasing mission with U.K. and French and perhaps another Allied representative: that this should be blessed in some way by E.E.C.E. and that E.E.C.E. should recommend an allocation of the proceeds. H.M. Embassy in Washington think that this would be objected to by the Americans and I agree. We must, I think, concentrate on getting the allocation of Argentine surpluses squarely in C[ombined] F[ood] B[oard]. Telegram No. 4718 from Washington, paragraph 6, suggests that we should agree with the French, the Belgians and the others on a fair share of Argentine supplies and then have this share blessed by C.F.B. We should then make a contract with Argentina on terms which are agreeable to the French and other claimants. This seems the most sensible course, and I think we should push for its adoption.

---

[1] These three telegrams, respectively of 29 June, 6 and 7 July 1945, are not printed: see below.

Denmark

There are two problems:

(i) How should we enlist the aid of the State Department in order to get the U.S. War Department into a more reasonable frame of mind about the share which they should have? It is suggested in telegram No. 4693 from Washington that we should propose that each army should reduce its claim to one-sixth of the total Danish surplus, leaving two-thirds to the Allies. This has been complicated by the fact that SHAEF Main[2] have decided that two-thirds of Danish surpluses should go to the armies and one-third to Civil Affairs, and that of the two-thirds to the armies the British and American forces should share on a *per capita* basis, thus giving the Americans a much greater proportion. This arrangement is to run until October 1st, which is the date at which Civil Affairs shipments cease to arrive. If we now propose to the Americans a reduced share for the armies we shall have to set aside the SHAEF Agreement. I suggest that we should try to do this on the grounds that after July 13th SHAEF ceases to exist and that therefore any directives about using surpluses in the SHAEF area for military purposes cease to have effect. On grounds of administrative convenience we might agree that the arrangement agreed by SHAEF should continue until the end of July, but no longer. After the end of July it seems to me that the share of the armies should be much reduced and that we should push for a declaration to be made on behalf of the U.S. and the U.K. that they would not ask for *any* supplies from Denmark for their armies (except for the British troops actually in Denmark) and that if on grounds of supply convenience any Danish supplies were allocated to these armies equivalent supplies would be made good to the Allies. The declaration should say that this arrangement ran until, say, the end of the year, and was a self-denying ordnance to assist the Allied Governments. If Departments are not ready to be as virtuous as this we should fall back on the suggestion in the Washington telegram that the armies should take one-sixth of the Danish supplies each.

(ii) Procedure for allocation. Telegram No. 4718 from Washington, paragraph 7, suggests that E.E.C.E. should arrange an agreement between its members on the share of Danish surpluses between the Allied Governments on one hand and the British and American armies on the other. This means, presumably, that whatever policy was agreed on the question in (i) above should be put forward at E.E.C.E. It is then suggested that E.E.C.E. should proceed to recommend an allocation between the Allied Governments which would then be sent to C.F.B. for review in the light of the total world position and the allocations made or being made by C.F.B. I think we should adopt this procedure. This gives E.E.C.E. full right to recommend allocations, but it also gives C.F.B. the right to make amendments in these in the light of the additional knowledge of allocations and the technical considerations which they have in mind, but which will

[2] i.e. S.H.A.E.F. Main Headquarters at Frankfurt am Main.

not be available to E.E.C.E. If we had made a declaration on the lines suggested in (i) above I am sure that the Allied Governments would accept this proposal.

3[*sic*]. The Ministry of Food on the official level seem ready to contemplate arrangements of the sort indicated above. It also seems likely that their Minister is less obstructive on the subject than he was a few weeks ago. How far he will go without a new Cabinet decision I do not, however, know. We may also run into difficulties with the War Office in relation to the agreement reached at SHAEF.[3]

W. J. HASLER

CALENDARS TO No. 98

i   *11 July 1945   Record by Sir A. Cadogan of conversation with the Netherland Ambassador*, in handing him aide-mémoire on relief for Holland after the termination of S.H.A.E.F. [Z 8434/74/29].

ii   *13 July 1945   Mr. A. W. G. Randall (H.M. Minister, Copenhagen) Tel. No. 337:* deadlock over food prices and Anglo-American reluctance to permit free Danish disposal of produce to Europe; advances possible compromise solution. [UR 2339/1590/851].

iii   *13 July 1945   Lord Halifax (Washington) Tel. No. 4877:* atmosphere in Washington, aggravated by Danish controversy, is unfavourable to general discussion regarding extension of purchasing agreements. Advises caution in presenting to U.S. any new, even relatively mild, proposal regarding Argentine meat contract, and a British review of existing commodity arrangements [UE 2995/2641/53].

iv   *13 July 1945   Minutes of 4th meeting of E.E.C.E. Sub-Committee on Food and Agriculture.* Discussion of proposals for modifying co-ordinated purchasing and allocation of foodstuffs in short supply: relations between C.F.B. and E.E.C.E. [UR 2155/1600/53].

[3] At the interdepartmental meeting on 12 July 1945, attended by representatives of all the departments mentioned in the first paragraph above, it was agreed: (i) that the Foreign Office, in consultation with the other interested departments, should prepare a memorandum for the consideration of the Minister of Food in making any proposal to the Cabinet on the Argentine negotiations; (ii) 'to invite the War Office to send a signal to S.H.A.E.F. with regard to the date of termination of S.H.A.E.F. responsibility in respect of Danish surpluses and endeavour to secure agreement to a change to 1st September'; (iii) 'to invite the Ministry of Food to consider whether we could state that from the time that S.H.A.E.F. ceased to be responsible for the allocation of Danish surpluses until the end of 1945, the United Kingdom would not make any prior claim on those surpluses for its armed forces.'

No. 99

Minute by Mr. Hoyer Millar
[*U 5474/5397/70*]

FOREIGN OFFICE, *11 July 1945*

There are really two aspects of this question[1]:

(*a*) How big a fleet is to be left to the Italians, and

[1] The present minute related to No. 99.i.

177

(b) What is to happen to the ships that are taken away from the Italians.

As regards (a), Sir Noel Charles, Admiral Stone, the American head of the Allied Commission, and—though not so insistently—Field-Marshal Alexander have all represented that as few ships as possible should be taken away from the Italians in the Peace Treaty. They point out that the Italians have always been very proud of their fleet and that from the psychological point of view a heavy cut in the fleet will have a very depressing effect on them and make them less inclined to accept the other clauses in the Peace Treaty. Furthermore, since the armistice the Italian navy have done good work for us against the Germans. On the other hand, it seems quite clear that a very considerable cut must be made in the fleet under the Peace Treaty. Public opinion in this country and still more in the lesser Allied countries will demand this, and there are good strategic reasons why the Italians should not be left in possession of what would for the next five years be the strongest fleet on paper in the Mediterranean. Nor is it really in Italy's own interest to have too big a fleet since this would only encourage her to waste money on it. Furthermore our own policy towards Italy is, while helping her on the way to recovery, not to allow her once again to suffer from the illusion that she is a Great Power. Finally, there is the complication arising from the claims of other countries against Italian ships. On the whole, therefore, I do not think that we can quarrel with the general lines of the Admiralty's proposals (which, incidentally, though it is not made clear in their paper, include a provision in the Peace Treaty that the Italians may not build any additional ships for five years). The figures suggested in paragraph 9 seem, however, in some respects rather on the low side, i.e. Italy is only to be allowed to keep two destroyers, whereas she has at present ten, most of which I believe have recently done good work with our own navy. For political reasons, we would, I think, welcome it if Italy could be left with a few more[2] destroyers and still more so if the Admiralty's tentative suggestion of leaving Italy with the two new Littorio[3] battleships instead of two old ones could be adopted.

As regards (b) and the question of what is to be done with the ships that are taken away from the Italians, it seems rather difficult not to let the French have any ships if they really put in a strong claim for them. After all, the French did suffer considerably more at the hands of the Italians than did the Russians, and their building yards have been badly bombed during the war. Could not they perhaps be given two or three of the destroyers destined for the Russians? If, however, this cannot be done then it will be all the more important to ensure that the French get a reasonable allocation out of the German ships. As regards Russia, it certainly seems that their quota of Italian ships is excessive, especially if they are going to be allowed to keep the British ships which have been lent to them in the meantime.[4] Could not

[2] Mr. Eden noted here: 'Yes'.
[3] Mr. Eden noted here: 'Surely not. A. E.'
[4] Mr. Eden minuted on this paper: 'If the Russians keep Royal Sov. etc. they have less claim on Italian fleet. A. E.'

the Russians be persuaded to take a few less destroyers in view of the fact that they will be retaining seven British destroyers? The resultant Italian destroyers could then be divided between the Italians themselves and the French.

It is not clear whether or not the question of the Italian fleet will come up at Terminal, though since the German fleet is on the agenda it may also be brought up. Since, however, the ultimate settlement regarding the Italian fleet will have to be dealt with in the peace settlement and since it is not contemplated that we should discuss any details of the proposed Peace Treaty at Terminal, it would be better if possible that the question should not be put on the agenda. If, however, it does come up, it would be desirable to confine the discussion to ascertaining whether the Russians intend to maintain their claim for the Italian ships and if possible to persuade them to be somewhat less exigent. Perhaps, too, some indication of the views of the United States Government on the general question of the future of the Italian fleet might be obtained. On their usual form the United States authorities will probably take a more lenient attitude towards the Italians then we are inclined to do.

F. R. Hoyer Millar

Calendar to No. 99

i *11 July 1945 Memorandum (C.P. (45) 74) by First Lord of the Admiralty on disposal of the Italian fleet.* Proposes policy designed to meet Allied claims and reduce Italian navy to an acceptable size without permanently estranging Italy [U 5553/5397/70].

No. 100

Minute by Lord Dunglass[1] to Mr. Eden
[N 8896/6/55]

FOREIGN OFFICE, 11 July 1945

I see that the subject of 'Poland' has been taken off the version of the agenda for 'Terminal' which was sent to the Russians and I hope this will not prevent you from raising the question of the organisation of Free Elections in Poland.

I cannot see the House of Commons being ready to accept a pledge by this Provisional Government as sufficient and we do not want to start off the new Parliament with our own side making a very critical attack, which in the light of the Yalta debate,[2] would be difficult to meet.

---

[1] Lord Dunglass (later Earl of Home) was Joint Parliamentary Under-Secretary of State for Foreign Affairs.

[2] In the House of Commons on 27 February to 1 March 1945, in which Lord Dunglass had spoken on 27 February: *Parl. Debs., 5th ser., H. of C.*, vol. 408, cols, 1267–1345, 1416–1516 and 1579–1672.

Could you have a shot at getting the Russians and Americans to join with us in a request to the Provisional Government that, when the time comes, they will consult with the three Governments as to the adequacy of the machinery prepared for carrying out the Yalta decisions? It is possible that the Russians (doubtless with many mental reservations) might agree to such a request at this stage. I am sure that we should not be content with the present position and that we should press some such addition to the pledge with great force and good reason. (I feel we can afford not to press for hurried elections if we can secure the right to consultation when the time comes.)

There are other points which you may perhaps consider to be matters for direct approach to the Polish Government, a favourable solution to which would go far towards creating a better atmosphere for a House of Commons discussion:

(1) The vacancy caused by Thugutt's refusal[3] must be filled by a Mikolajczyk nominee of standing and influence in London.

(2) A pledge of personal security from the Provisional Government publicly given (if possible underwritten by the Russians) would have a great influence in inducing Poles in London and in the forces to return home.

(3) An announcement of an orderly scheme for the repatriation of Polish exiles in Russia. This seems to be beginning but it may not cover deported Poles in concentration camps.

(4) Freedom for our press to go into Poland, to circulate in the country and to send back uncensored news.

I may have an opportunity for a word on this this evening.

D.

[3] M. Mieczyslaw Thugutt, a member of the Polish Peasant Party, had refused to hold office in the Polish Provisional Government of National Unity.

No. 101

Record by Sir R. Campbell of a conversation with Mr. Halpern

[AN 2245/22/45]

FOREIGN OFFICE, 11 July 1945

Mr. Halpern,[1] who left the United States about a week ago, came to see me this morning.

He said that anti-British feeling in the United States was less of a political factor than heretofore. It was, of course, endemic and varied in degree from group to group (the Germans and the Irish would never like us), but, while it was a permanent element of American psychology, now weaker, now stronger, it was not so important as it used to be in Anglo-American relations.

[1] Mr. Eden enquired here: 'Who is this? A. E.' Mr. N. M. Butler explained on 13 July 1945 that Mr. A. J. Halpern had been working 'for Sir William Stephenson, our chief Security Officer in New York', and was 'considered a man of some penetration and good judgement.'

What was important was that an assumption now prevailed, even amongst some of our best friends, whether in the Administration or private individuals, that Great Britain was now definitely a second rate Power.[2] There was a feeling that political relations between members of the Commonwealth were not strengthening the United Kingdom (South Africa, Mr. Evatt) any more than the strengthening of economic ties between Canada and the United States.

The Americans also were beginning to believe that the position of the United Kingdom in Europe was weakening; we were losing friends rather than increasing their number. On this point Mr. Halpern referred to European and especially Belgian criticism which was to the effect that we were not assuming as we should the leadership of Western Europe, and that our policy was a hand-to-mouth opportunist one without central direction or object.

With regard to Italy, Mr. Halpern feared that we were allowing the United States to make use to our detriment with the Italians of the idea that they were the friends and we the enemies of Italy. This was made more easy by the existence of a large Italian element in the United States to which the Administration had to play up, making promises which were effective even if they could not in the event be fulfilled. Our publicity about our attitude towards Italy was also poor and if better might improve the situation he had mentioned. He heard that there was hostility in the British army towards the Italians. We would do much better to deflect educators from the re-education of German prisoners-of-war to the task of re-educating British soldiers in their attitude towards the Italians.[3]

Mr. Halpern can be reached by telephone at Central 9945. Sir Orme Sargent might find it worth while to spare him half an hour some time. He also had some things to say about Franco-British relations.

R. I. CAMPBELL[4]

[2] Mr. Butler minuted against this: 'What does he mean by this? N. B.'
[3] Mr. Eden commented here: 'You can hardly expect British soldiers to love Italians. Americans forget they came late into this war! A. E.'
[4] Sir R. Campbell addressed this record to Sir O. Sargent with the note: 'This may be useful in connection with your memo.', i.e. No. 102.

No. 102

Memorandum by Sir O. Sargent

[U 5471/5471/70][1]

Secret   FOREIGN OFFICE, *11 July 1945*

Stocktaking after VE-Day[2]

The end of the war in Europe leaves us facing two main problems, neither

[1] The filed texts of this memorandum and annexes are final versions in Confidential Print. Passages from this memorandum are cited by C. Thorne, *Allies of a Kind: The United States, Britain and the war against Japan, 1941–1945* (London, 1978), pp. 538, 648, 660, and by V. Rothwell, *Britain and the Cold War 1941–1947* (London, 1982), pp. 144–7 *passim*.
[2] The day of the Allied Victory in Europe on 8 May 1945.

of which has any resemblance to the problems with which we were faced at the end of the last war. They are (*a*) the military occupation by Soviet troops of a large part of Eastern Europe, and the Soviet Government's future policy generally; and (*b*) the economic rehabilitation of Europe so as to prevent a general economic collapse.

2. Our own position, too, in dealing with these problems is very different from what it was at the end of the last war, when we and France shared and disputed, and eventually lost, control of Europe. This time the control is to a large degree in the hands of the Soviet Union and the United States, and neither of them is likely to consider British interests if they interfere with their own and unless we assert ourselves.

3. For this very reason it suits us that the principle of co-operation between the three Great Powers should be specifically accepted as the basis on which problems arising out of the war should be handled and decided. Such a co-operative system will, it is hoped, give us a position in the world which we might otherwise find it increasingly difficult to assert and maintain were the other two Great Powers to act independently. It is not that either the United States or the Soviet Union do not wish to collaborate with Great Britain. The United States certainly find it very convenient to do so in order to fortify their own position in Europe and elsewhere; and the Soviet Union recognise in Great Britain a European Power with whom they will certainly have to reckon. But the fact remains that in the minds of our big partners, especially in that of the United States, there is a feeling that Great Britain is now a secondary Power and can be treated as such, and that in the long run all will be well if they—the United States and the Soviet Union—as the two supreme World Powers of the future, understand one another. It is this misconception which it must be our policy to combat.

4. For this reason and because we are numerically the weakest and geographically the smallest of the three Great Powers, it is essential that we should increase our strength in not only the diplomatic but also the economic and military spheres. This clearly can best be done by enrolling the Dominions and especially France, not to mention the lesser Western European Powers, as collaborators with us in this tripartite system. Only so shall we be able, in the long run, to compel our two big partners to treat us as an equal. Even so, our collaboration with the United States and the Soviet Union is not going to be easy in view of the wide divergence between our respective outlooks, traditions and methods.

5. To take the Soviet Union first. It is particularly dangerous to assume that the foreign policies of totalitarian governments are opportunist and fluctuating, like those of liberal governments (using the term 'liberal' in its widest sense as representing all that is opposed to totalitarianism, whether to the Right or to the Left). All totalitarian governments—and Russia is certainly no exception—are able to conduct a consistent and persistent foreign policy over long periods because the government is not dependant on public opinion and changes of government. And precisely because totalitarian

governments need not explain or justify their policy to their own people it is much more difficult for the foreigner to analyse the governing principles which underlie it. It is true that in the case of Nazi Germany Hitler kindly explained in *Mein Kampf* both his objectives and methods. We were thus duly warned, but did not heed the warning. Again, Mussolini, by crudely imitating Hitler, revealed to us the secrets of his long-term policy. But in the case of the Soviet Union Stalin is not likely to be as obliging. We shall have to try and find out for ourselves what is his plan of campaign and to anticipate the tactics which he intends to employ from time to time to carry it through. And this is not going to be easy, nor shall we always be able, even among ourselves in this country, to agree on the conclusions to be reached.

6. Without attempting on this occasion to analyse Russia's foreign policy and foretell its future course, it is worth calling attention to one factor in the policy of modern totalitarian governments which seems to be fairly constant, namely, their desire to obtain for their régime the maximum degree of security both at home and abroad. As a result of the defeat of 1918 the Nazis feared encirclement by the rest of Europe and sought security by means of territorial conquest. Hence their demand for Lebensraum.[3] Mussolini resented the encirclement of the Mediterranean by France and Great Britain and tried to break out into Africa. Soviet Russia now fears a world coalition of the liberal Powers ('liberal' again being used in its widest sense), and the revival of Germany as a 'liberal' Power; for Stalin knows even better than we do that it was the material strength and wealth of the liberal Powers, combined with the belief in their own philosophy of life, which really won the war, and he probably has fewer illusions than we and the Americans have about the capacity of Germany to recover first her economic, then her political, and lastly her military power in Europe. Stalin, however, does not necessarily intend to obtain his security by territorial conquest, as Hitler wanted to. He may well prefer to obtain it by creating what might be termed an ideological Lebensraum in those countries which he considers strategically important. If he eventually is convinced that the danger of a liberal coalition is not going to materialise he may relax somewhat his search for security, or rather change its nature so as to apply only to Germany. It must be remembered, too, that, unlike Hitler, he fortunately has not the motive of revenge to spur him on.

7. At the present moment the Soviet Union has been so weakened by the war that Stalin is hardly in a position to force through ruthlessly his policy of ideological penetration against definite opposition. For instance, in the case of Greece, Venezia Giulia, and to a certain extent Poland, he has not pressed matters to extreme and has actually compromised, though it may well be that he has only made a temporary retreat. But at the present moment it can surely be assumed that he does not want and could not afford another war in Europe, and it is also doubtful whether he aims at further territorial

---

[3] Living-space.

expansion. At Annex I[4] will be found a memorandum by Sir R. Bruce Lockhart on Soviet policy and the best means of reacting to it.

8. The economic strength of the United States has certainly impressed Stalin no less than the potentiality of the Western Air Forces. He has seen what has happened to Germany from the air and what is happening to Japan. No doubt Stalin feels that now before his troops have been withdrawn from the countries which they are now occupying and before their demobilisation has begun he must seize the opportunity to reap the fruits of victory to the full, since if he delays or hesitates there may be some which later on he will no longer be able to grasp. As for ourselves, though economically we shall grow stronger as time goes on, militarily our strength in Europe will soon decline from its present peak—even quicker than the Russian strength. For this reason we must take a stand in the immediate future if we are to prevent the situation crystallising to our permanent detriment. This means in practice that we must keep our foot firmly in Finland, Poland, Czechoslovakia, Austria, Yugoslavia and Bulgaria, even though we may have to abandon perhaps for the moment Roumania and Hungary as beyond our reach.

9. If there is to be a trial of strength between us—that is to say a diplomatic trial of strength—now is the time for us to take the offensive by challenging Russia in these six countries, instead of waiting until the Soviet Government threatens us further west and south in Germany, in Italy, in Greece, and in Turkey. This is what inevitably will happen if we let Stalin pocket for good these six countries which at present he controls by a combination of political force and military pressure. Further reasons for this change of policy and the tactics to be employed in applying it are examined in Annex II.

10. We must, of course, also be prepared for the Soviet Government to make an effort to establish their influence in Germany, Italy, Greece and and Turkey. In the three latter countries we ought to be able to maintain our position, and our object must be to build them up as bastions of 'liberalism', even though this may involve us in responsibilities and commitments of which we otherwise would be only too glad to be rid. But the struggle for Germany, if it is engaged, will not only be much harder, but the result will be decisive for the whole of Europe, for it is not overstating the position to say that if Germany is won over to totalitarianism this may well decide the fate of liberalism throughout the world.

11. In every country of Europe the Soviet Government will have the great advantage of being able to exploit for their own ends the economic crisis which in the coming months may well develop into a catastrophe capable of engulfing political institutions in many European countries and paralysing all orderly government in a large part of the Continent. It is the existence of this economic crisis which makes it so important to obtain the wholehearted

---

[4] Not printed. This memorandum of 11 April 1945 (cf. note 5 below) is printed in *The Diaries of Sir Robert Bruce Lockhart 1939–1965*, ed. K. Young (London, 1980), pp. 420–2.

co-operation of the United States, who alone have the material means of coping with it.

12. If the United States realise both the political and economic implications of the European situation it will not be too difficult for us to perform the double task of holding the Soviet Government in check in Europe and at the same time amicably and fruitfully co-operating with the United States and Soviet Governments in the resettlement of Europe. But we must be prepared for the United States to falter from time to time when called upon to pull their weight in Europe, and to prefer the more agreeable and less arduous rôle of mediator in European affairs generally and in particular in any disputes between Great Britain and Russia, even threatening maybe that only on such terms will they be prepared to make their indispensable contribution in the economic sphere.

13. Unfortunately the foreign policy of the United States is, like that of the Soviet Union, difficult to forecast, but not because, as in Russia, it is secret, but because the 'liberalism' of the United States constitution makes it fluctuating, uncertain, and emotional. But if we accept the view that after this war the United States Government is going to be very much in the same position as Great Britain was after the last war, it may be easier to guess the general tendency of American policy in Europe. Just as we considered France troublesome, quarrelsome and reactionary after the last war, so the United States will consider us to be so now. If they tend to act as conciliators between us and Russia (and Germany), if they try to free themselves from what they consider to be British tutelage in European affairs, they will be following the same line as we took after the last war, when we tried to reconcile France and Germany at the expense of France's policy of weakening Germany in every way possible. This policy of ours gradually broke the spirit of France, and final disillusionment came with the reoccupation of the Rhineland in 1936. We must take care that United States policy does not have the same effect upon us now. France felt that she could not rely upon Great Britain and at the same time could not stand up to Germany without us. We must not allow ourselves to get into the same defeatist mood in dealing with post-war Europe. We must have a policy of our own and try to persuade the United States to make it *their own*. But failing that, we must be prepared to stand by it, even if the United States refuse to support us and insist upon mediating instead. We must face the fact that they will feel that being the richest and strongest Power they must also be the wisest and the most fair-minded, and will therefore resent any contradiction by us. In particular, they may suspect our political motives to be reactionary when we, rather than they, intervene in the countries which the Soviet Government is intent on controlling. They will, however, be more ready to co-operate in solving the economic problems of Europe, and once their interest and prestige is engaged in these questions it is to be hoped that they will find it difficult to disinterest themselves in the political development of the countries whom they are saving materially. An estimate of the outlook of the men who will

be responsible for United States policy in the immediate future will be found in Annex III.

14. At present our problems, as far as they are political, are concerned with the Soviet Government rather than with Germany. But Germany will shortly have it in her power to play an important and dangerous part. She will have a still greater incentive than in 1918 to seek revenge, and it would be wise not to under-estimate her innate capacity for recuperation and reconstruction. Against this there is this time nothing left of her administration and institutions, and she will have to evolve a new political and economic system without being able, as after 1918, to use the Army with its traditions, and big business with its machinery, as the nucleus around which to build. Thus the process of reconstruction will be slower, but it is likely, for the same reason, to be more carefully thought out and planned. After the last war Germany was hamstrung until 1933 by having a liberal form of government alien to her temperament. This will not happen this time, unless we make very great efforts to impose such a régime on Germany, for her natural tendency will be to strive to return to some form of authoritarianism. If we hesitate or allow our German policy to be at the mercy of the emotions and ignorance of the people of the United States we shall be lost, for it will give Germany the opportunity not only to decide and plan her own future but also, when the times come, to put herself up to the highest bidder so as to play off each of the three Great Powers one against the other. Once such a competition begins the Soviet Government has the best chance of carrying off the prize, and, as already said, the winning of this prize may well decide the future of Europe and of 'liberalism' throughout the world.

15. The problems we have considered have been primarily those of post-war Europe. It is too early to make a similar analysis of the corresponding problems which will face us in the Far East. So long as the war there still continues it is impossible to foresee what will be the relative positions of both victors and vanquished when victory has been achieved. It is, however, fairly safe to suppose that British interests will again be best served by a policy of co-operation between the three Great Powers, for in isolation we should be in a weaker position even than in Europe. For the same reason we shall probably find it useful to organise under our leadership the lesser colonial Powers who have a stake in the Far East; in other words, France, the Netherlands and Australia. For the rest, the United States are more likely to be more aggressive and pertinacious in the Far East than they will be in Europe, while the Soviet Government may well be less security-haunted than it is in Europe. If so, its Asiatic policy may be less coldly realistic and more opportunist. But all will in the last resort depend on the state in which Japan and China are left by the war, and what part they will be able to play in Far Eastern politics after it is over. It seems almost inevitable that the United States and the Soviet Union will eventually struggle for the body and soul of China unless the latter can acquire in time such a degree of national unity as is necessary to enable her to develop her latent resources in manpower and economic resources in defence of her national independence. In

the course of such a struggle it seems almost inevitable that Japan would sooner or later be called in to help by one of the protagonists.

16. To sum up:–

(*a*) We must base our foreign policy on the principle of co-operation between the three World Powers. In order to strengthen our position in this combination we ought to enrol the Dominions and especially France not to mention the lesser Western European Powers, as collaborators with us in this tripartite system.

(*b*) We must not be afraid of having a policy independent of our two great partners and not submit to a line of action dictated to us by either Russia or the United States, just because of their superior power or because it is the line of least resistance, or because we despair of being able to maintain ourselves without United States support in Europe.

(*c*) Our policy, in order not to be at the mercy of internal politics or popular fashion, must be in keeping with British fundamental traditions and must be based on principles which will appeal to the United States, to the Dominions, and to the smaller countries of Europe, especially in the West. It must be definitely anti-totalitarian, and for this purpose be opposed to totalitarianism of the Right (Fascism, &c.), as much as to the totalitarianism of the Left (Communism, &c.). In pursuance of this policy of 'liberalism' we shall have to take risks, and even live beyond our political means at times. We must not, for instance, hesitate to intervene diplomatically in the internal affairs of other countries if they are in danger of losing their liberal institutions or their political independence. In the immediate future we must take the offensive in challenging Communist penetration in as many of the Eastern countries of Europe as possible, and we must be ready to counteract every attempt by the Soviet Government to communise or obtain political control over Germany, Italy, Greece or Turkey.

(*d*) We must not desist from this course or be discouraged even if the United States give us no help and even if they adopt a policy of appeasement towards Russian domination, as well they may.

(*e*) We must exert every effort to grapple with the economic crisis in Europe—not only in our own interests (a prosperous Europe is Great Britain's best export market) but in order to use the material resources at our and America's disposal as a makeweight throughout Europe against Communist propaganda, which the Soviet Government will use for their own ends wherever possible.[5]

O. G. Sargent

[5] Sir O. Sargent submitted this memorandum to Sir A. Cadogan under the following minute: 'The S[ecretary of] S[tate] when he was still down in the country, said he would like to have a "Stock-Taking" Memo on the general political situation at the end of the European war. The attached is a rather hurried attempt to get something down on paper before the S/S leaves. I have sent a copy to the Private Secretary. O. G. Sargent July 11.' Sir A. Cadogan and Mr. Eden minuted as follows: 'This seems to me a most useful paper. I entirely endorse conclusion (*a*) in para. 16—all of it. As regards conclusion (*b*), I think

Till our invasion of France, that is to say, till the Second Front had been opened, our attitude was, and indeed had to be, defensive and almost apologetic. Even since then, during the spectacular advances of the Russian armies last year, the Soviet Union seemed in Europe to be establishing a military predominance which would show its full force at the Peace Settlement and which it would be folly to ignore. Indeed, it looked until the other day that it would be the Russian armies which would invade and occupy the heart of Germany, including Berlin, before the British and Americans had penetrated the German defences in the West.

In these circumstances it was only prudent that we should in our diplomatic dealings with the Soviet Government set ourselves to humour and to propitiate our Russian Ally. The policy was, no doubt, the right one at the time, and though it produced no spectacular results, and indeed, very little response from the Soviet Government, who can say that the situation would not have been very much worse if we had during this period asserted our rights on every occasion by the various means of pressure open to us, such as retaliation in kind, denial of material help, and isolated action in those parts of Europe where our interests and those of the Soviet Union appeared to conflict?

But with the sudden, almost unexpected, break-through in the West, involving the collapse of the German armies and the opening of the heart of Germany to invasion by British and American armies, the situation had radically changed. Instead of the Russians being in the position in Germany to dictate their terms to their Allies, these latter are meeting them on equal terms in that country and,

it is right, in any hypothesis, to speak frankly to the Soviet and show no subservience. Sir O. Sargent, in § 8, assumes that, from now on, our military strength in Europe will decline at a greater rate than that of Russia, and that there is therefore no time to lose in taking a firm stand. I think this is probably right (though I am a little chary of the "show-down" referred to several times in Annex II! [Annotation by Sir O. Sargent: 'This has been altered in the final version as printed O. G. S.']). Sir R. Bruce Lockhart, in Annex I, seems to take a somewhat different view. The last 4 paras. of that Annex deal with the crux of the matter. Sir R. Bruce Lockhart there says "Anglo-American military strength is at its peak; *Russia's has long since passed it.* In 1941 we made the mistake of under-estimating Russia's military strength. We must be careful today to avoid the error of exaggerating it . . . [*sic*] Of all countries that dare not risk a prolongation of war, Russia must be very nearly first." (This may be shortly disproved.) "Stalin is faced with great problems of reconstruction which he cannot hope to solve without Anglo-American aid." I have often heard this said but I have never heard it argued in any detail. Can it be accepted as true, without any qualification? [Annotation by Mr. Eden: 'I fear not. A. E.'] It is true that Russia during the war has received enormous material aid from us, but is it not also true that her own production is proof of an astonishing rate of development which, if maintained, might lead her almost anywhere?   Sir R. Bruce Lockhart's conclusion corresponds with Sir O. Sargent's: "The moment is therefore highly favourable for a bolder diplomacy". As I have said, I do not quarrel with that, but if Sir R. Bruce Lockhart is right, there is not such great urgency about it as Sir O. Sargent wd. maintain, and time might be expected to work on our side.   I hesitate to accept this, and therefore rather endorse Sir O. Sargent. A. C. July 11, 1945.' 'I think that this is an excellent paper and the Annexes are all valuable. I should like P.M. to see them & I am tempted to let Cabinet have a look also. I am most grateful for the guidance they give and agree wholeheartedly. A. E. July 12.'

indeed, the terms on which they meet may end by being more favourable to the Western Allies than to the Russians.

One might suppose that this would make the Soviet Government more anxious to humour us and the Americans, but, unfortunately, their reaction may take quite a different form, especially if they think, as they no doubt do, that we and the Americans intend to rehabilitate Germany as we have undertaken to rehabilitate Italy so as to save her from Communism. Thus they may well decide that there is not a moment to be lost in consolidating their *cordon sanitaire*, not merely against a future German danger, but against the impending penetration by the Western Allies. In such a mood they might not stop to count in terms of Allied co-operation, the cost of destroying the last vestiges of *bourgeois* rule and sovereign independence in the countries to be sacrificed for this purpose.

This may be a too gloomy view of the situation, but given the Russian character it is sufficiently possible to warrant our considering whether our present diplomatic technique in dealing with the Soviet Government is the best calculated to divert them from this policy, or at least to minimise its effects.

Has not the moment come to speak plainly to the Soviet Government, to show our resentment, and to formulate what we consider our rights? To propitiate Stalin when we were weak he would understand, but for us to do so now when we are strong would surely appear to him as a cunning manœuvre intended to put him off his guard. He is much more likely to understand if we insist on clearly stating our case at this juncture because our respective positions in the European scene have altered.

It would, no doubt, be easy to strike a bargain with the Soviet Government if we were prepared to recognise their exclusive interests in certain countries. But it is inconceivable that we should adopt this course. Not only would we never be sure that the Soviet Government would observe such a bargain, but it would appear in the eyes of the world as the cynical abandonment of the small nations whose interest we are pledged to defend; and for ourselves it would represent the abdication of our right as a Great Power to be concerned with the affairs of the whole of Europe, and not merely with those parts in which we have a special interest.

If, however, we cannot found our policy of co-operation on a system of spheres of influence, we must confine ourselves to making it abundantly clear to the Soviet Government that the policy of Anglo-Soviet co-operation must apply fully in Central and South-Eastern Europe as in the rest of the world, and that, indeed, we are not prepared to work the policy on any other basis.

It is difficult to foresee what would be the Soviet Government's reaction to such a summons. It would largely depend on the value they attach to the continuance of co-operation with Great Britain and the United States after the war; on the extent to which they fear the prospect of Great Britain and the United States organising an anti-Russian and anti-Communist *bloc* in Europe; and lastly, on the material difficulties they may foresee in embarking after an exhausting struggle on a policy of political expansion which might easily develop into a military occupation. In any event the Soviet Government's reaction could not very well be worse than a continuance of the present state of uncertainty and drift which is operating all the time to our disadvantage.

We should, of course, have to demonstrate that this plain-speaking was, in our view, necessary in order to establish in the changed circumstances of to-day a new basis on which to continue and develop Anglo-American-Soviet co-operation during the difficult times ahead of us, and we should be at pains to show that it is precisely because of the importance that we attach to this co-operation that we feel it necessary to tackle this difficult and disagreeable subject in such a frank, realistic and comprehensive manner.

In such a discussion with the Soviet Government we should be well advised not to lay too much stress, as the United States Government are inclined to do, on the outward forms of Parliamentary Government, such as free elections, party administrations, &c., which are probably unattainable in present circumstances, and are, in any case, not in keeping with the traditions and outlook of the peoples concerned. We had better instead concentrate on essentials which will enable those countries to develop their own institutions as best suit their conditions and traditions, so long as these involve no persistent persecution of any political parties, or individuals in the interests of Communism, and provided that the individual can in one way or another enjoy that degree of liberty of action and speech and elementary justice to which he was accustomed before the war and before the advent of the Communist conception of the totalitarian State.

Annex III to No. 102

The following opinions about Mr. Byrnes have recently been expressed by Mr. Tom Finletter and General Macready. Mr. Tom Finletter served for several years as a temporary official in the State Department where he dealt with economic matters and showed himself extremely co-operative, broad-minded, friendly and resourceful. He is by profession a lawyer in the firm of Coudert Brothers. Mr. Finletter said he did not think that the appointment of Mr. Byrnes as Secretary of State would be a good one. Byrnes had both the Liberal and Conservative elements of public opinion against him on the basis of his voting record when in Congress as Representative and Senator. For Conservatives and for Republicans in general he was the Southern Democrat and therefore suspect on grounds of liberalism (in other than questions to do with the Negro). By the Conservative elements represented by the Roman Catholic hierarchy and Roman Catholic circles in general he was mistrusted as a renegade from his religion. Liberal opinion was opposed to him because he was a regular Southern statesman with all that that meant in the way of reactionary tendencies. Negro and Liberal sentiment had misgivings about him because of his regular Southern Democrat attitude towards the Negro. Both the Labour movements, the C.I.O. and the A.F. of L.,[6] were united against him. For these reasons, in Mr. Finletter's opinion Mr. Byrnes's path as far as internal sentiment was concerned would not be likely to be smooth, notwithstanding the fact that he stood well with Congress. (Mr. Finletter gives perhaps rather more than their due weight to the above factors.)

General Macready has been Head of our Army Mission in Washington for several years, has pretty wide contacts and knows the Washington scene pretty well. He, like Mr. Finletter, feels misgivings about Mr. Byrnes. His two chief grounds are that Mr. Byrnes, having by the nature of his offices concentrated on internal American affairs (his last office was Director of War Mobilisation), has had no time to become acquainted with foreign affairs or the world outside the United States. He is therefore entirely ignorant in respect of such matters. Moreover, Mr. Byrnes's concern with practical internal questions has inclined

---

[6] The Congress of Industrial Organisations and the American Federation of Labour.

to make him look at external questions overmuch from the point of view of their effect on immediate American interests in the first place. *I.e.*, his view of what are American interests is too parochial.

The opinions of Mr. Finletter and General Macready on President Truman may also be of interest. Mr. Finletter, while saying that the President had up to the present done extremely well, and that his stock was high, stated that it should be remembered that as far as Congress was concerned he was in the honeymoon period. We should not assume that Mr. Truman would enjoy Congressional goodwill indefinitely. There was a sort of Congressional truce as long as the war with Japan continued, but the need for this truce would cease to be felt as soon as the war ended. Even then, as long as President Truman merely continued to follow Rooseveltian policies things might go on all right; but the moment the President began to put forward policies and measures of his own trouble with Congress should be anticipated. (It is none the less reasonably certain that the personal popularity that President Truman won in the Senate will militate in his favour and will keep the temperature low in any possible disputes.)

General Macready considers that the President, while an honest, friendly and co-operative man has, like Mr. Byrnes, an outlook to some extent limited by concern with the home scene of the United States. He is much in the hands of his advisers. A particular aspect of this is his relationship with the American Chiefs of Staff. Whereas President Roosevelt was independent of these, and whereas they had always to expect that the President might at any moment overrule them, this was no longer the case. If a suggestion was made by the Prime Minister to President Truman that the opinion of their advisers should in a given instance be overruled, President Truman's reply merely repeated and endorsed the opinion of his Chiefs of Staff.

Mr. Finletter mentioned Mr. Stettinius's speech of the 28th May in which he made his reference to 'mediation.'[7] Mr. Finletter said that the intention of this remark had been misunderstood in this country. So far from its portending American aloofness and a germ of isolationism, and so far from it being dictated by a mere fear of appearing to gang up with us against others, its intention had been quite different. It was meant to convey that though American interests would not be so intimately engaged in, say, Syria as in, say, Mexico, yet in areas in which the United States were less closely interested they would play their part, on the principle that all nations should act helpfully everywhere. The phrase was really used with the intention of removing foreign apprehensions that the United States might behave again as they had in the case of Greece in December last, *i.e.*, tell this country that as far as they were concerned it was free to go ahead and act as it thought best, and then come out and criticise its actions and dissociate themselves therefrom. The Americans had been rather disappointed at our first reaction about the phrase 'mediation'.

CALENDARS TO NO. 102

i   *19 July–5 Aug. 1945   Foreign Office minutes on No. 102*, including comments on postwar policy by Mr. Jebb, Mr. Troutbeck, Mr. Harvey, Mr. D. Howard,

---

[7] In a broadcast on 28 May 1945 Mr. Stettinius had declared: 'The interests of the United States extend to the whole world. We maintain those interests in our relations with other great Powers, and we must mediate between them when their interests conflict among themselves.'

Mr. Warner, Mr. J. C. Sterndale Bennett, Mr. N. M. Butler, Sir R. Campbell [U 5471/5471/70].

ii *11 July 1945 Memorandum by Sir O. Sargent on 'Stocktaking after V.E.-Day'.* Revised version, without annexes, under original date of No. 102, taking account of i above [U 5471/5471/70].

No. 103

Sir W. Strang (*Lübbecke*) to Mr. Eden (*Received 13 July*)
No. 1 [*C 3858/3086/18*]

LÜBBECKE, *11 July 1945*

Sir,

Before I left London on June 26th to resume my duties as Political Adviser to the Commander-in-Chief, British Forces of Occupation in Germany, it was intimated to me by your Department that they would welcome a political report on Germany at an early date. I also understood from the War Office that they would like to receive a copy of any such report.

2. Having arrived in Germany and established my residence at Lübbecke, the prospective seat of the headquarters of the British Element of the Control Commission, and my office at Headquarters, 21st Army Group, Bad Oeynhausen, pending the opening of the offices at Lübbecke, I decided, with the Commander-in-Chief's concurrence, to make a tour of the British zone in order to visit the Commanders of the three Corps districts, to see for myself the operations of some of our military government detachments, and to come to what judgment I could, even in so short a time, of the state of Germany and of the character of the problems facing our forces of occupation and our Control authorities.

3. Major-General G. W. R. Templer, who is in charge of the Civil Affairs/Military Government Branch at H.Q., 21st Army Group, was kind enough to draw up a programme for my tour. I made the journey by car, accompanied by Lieut. Colonel Goronwy Rees, of the Political Division of the Control Commission. Colonel Rees kept a diary of the tour and I cannot do better than enclose it as it stands.[1] The reader will, I hope, find that Colonel Rees' chronicle conveys the keen interest with which both he and I heard the stories of our pioneer military government teams in Germany, and our sympathy with the single-minded devotion which they are bringing to their unprecedented task. I have seldom met a body of men who are more obviously enjoying the work in which they are engaged, though they have to do it with inadequate staff, working long hours, and often in the absence of the requisite instructions. The skill, good humour and commonsense with which they are guiding the local German administrations which are growing up under their care may derive from a traditional aptitude for government, but they also reflect credit upon those who planned and conducted the

[1] Not printed.

courses of instruction under which our military government officers were trained.

4. We traversed the British zone from Essen to Kiel. We visited and were kindly entertained by military government detachments at each level—Province, Regierungsbezirk, Kreis and Stadtkreis[2]—each of them composed of a group of experts under a Commanding Officer of the Regular Army or territorial forces. We inspected camps for displaced persons and ex-prisoners of war, the control of which is, in the present phase, one of the more arduous duties of the forces of occupation themselves. We saw the North German Coal Control at Essen and the wireless station and the Information Control detachment at Hamburg. We enjoyed the hospitality of the Commanders of the three Corps districts—Lieut. General S. C. Kirkman, Commanding I Corps (Province of Westphalia and Northern Rhine Province); Lieut. General B. G. Horrocks, Commanding 30 Corps (Province of Hannover); and Lieut. General Barker, Commanding 8 Corps (Province of Schleswig-Holstein, and Hamburg)—all of whom were good enough to give me generously of their time and the benefit of their experience.

4[sic]. I find it difficult to sum up my impressions, and I could wish that time permitted the preparation of a less superficial and more finished report than this can be.

5. First, the general aspect of the country. A smiling countryside, beautifully farmed with bountiful crops growing to the roadside and hedgerows: villages and small towns off the main roads quite intact: towns and villages at important communication points badly smashed. Larger centres like Münster or Osnabrück, half or three-quarters devastated; industrial cities like Dortmund almost totally in ruins, except round the outer fringes. The population more healthy looking, better dressed, and showing less sign of strain than one would have expected, even in the more heavily damaged urban areas. The official ration is low, but in the country it is at present supplemented from stocks and garden produce. The position in the large towns is difficult, and the workers certainly do not receive enough to sustain heavy labour. We were told at Dortmund that signs of mal-nutrition are beginning to appear, and that administrative staffs are beginning to show signs of over-work, bad temper and tiredness, from shortage of food. But I cannot say that, even in the Ruhr, from a casual inspection, we saw obvious or widespread signs of acute distress. What the winter may bring is another story; and what the position may be in the Soviet zone is also another story. It is strange to see people going serenely and even cheerfully about their business in their ruined towns and cities. I asked the Commander of the military government detachment at Dortmund where the 400,000 inhabitants of Dortmund found place to live. He said that they had moved out to the less devastated periphery, several families to a house. I asked how, if that was so,

---

[2] The Prussian provinces and certain other German states (Länder) were administratively divided into Regierungsbezirke. The Stadt (urban) and Land (rural) Kreise were subordinate units of German administration.

it came about that the main streets in the centre were thronged with people. He explained that although Dortmund is in ruins, the life of the city goes on in cellars and on ground floors. Some factories are working; some banks are open; some shops are doing business; exchange of goods and services goes on. Roads still lead in and out of Dortmund (though it is like threading a maze to find one's way about them), and where those roads meet the life of the community continues to spring and begins to reorganise itself. I asked whether he thought that Dortmund would ever be re-built. He said certainly, sooner or later. The city authorities were already thinking ahead and actively debating alternative schemes: he himself had been brought into consultation.

6. The Germans in the British zone have not the appearance of a broken people, Except during recent months, it might be argued that, generally speaking, they have suffered less from the continued strain of war than our own people. They have had the material resources of Europe to draw upon and have had the profit of slave labour. There are still substantial, though diminishing, private stocks of food. Their women have not, in any degree comparable to our own, had to go into the Services or the factories. (The owner of the house at Lübbecke which I now occupy—a modern villa with six bedrooms—after nearly six years of war still employed a cook, two young housemaids, a laundry maid and a gardener.) Their sufferings are still to come. Unless the mines of the Ruhr and the Saar can find the minimum of coal for Germany over and above the essential requirements of the liberated territories, and unless substantial imports of grain can be made available for Germany, there is likely to be widespread mal-nutrition and something near starvation in many places, with the possibility of disorder and a general breakdown. This will be the test both of the German people and of the forces of occupation, and—apart from the acute but passing problem of the Russian displaced persons (most of these should have gone within the next three months)—it is this prospect which chiefly dominates the minds and sharpens the anxieties of our Commanders and military government authorities, and indeed of the local German administrations and the population as a whole. But looking at them now, in the favourable light of summer, one would think that the German people still have some reserve of toughness and endurance.

7. It is fortunate that we entered upon the occupation of Germany in the early summer. It has given us a favourable season in which to take hold; to begin the purge of Nazi officials; to start to re-staff the administrative machine at each level—Kreis, Regierungsbezirk and Province; to promote the restoration of communications and the revival of commerce and industry, at any rate on a local basis, in a measure sufficient to maintain the economy in being, if only on a hand-to-mouth basis, and so to be in as good a position as possible to meet the crises of the coming winter. To this extent our military government authorities and the local German administrations have a common interest, and in that common interest, and at the present stage, the collaboration of the German officials is fully forthcoming. The victorious British Army, after the battle, now finds itself charged with a task of reconstruction; and I am assured that it finds this task congenial. One of the Corps Commanders

told me that he had never been prouder of the men of his Corps than since they became the forces of occupation in Germany. Heavy though their duties are, the men are, he said, in good heart and showing the usual British good humour, practical ingenuity and common-sense in tackling the new and strange jobs they now have to do. Indeed, he said that the occupation of Germany is an excellent school of citizenship. Among others he told of the platoon sergeant and 20 men who were suddenly charged with the care of 10,000 displaced persons and within a few weeks had made them into a well-ordered community. We ourselves visited a camp near Arnsberg, in Westphalia, where 22,000 Russians, part ex-prisoners of war and part displaced persons, including women, lived. We were taken round it by the young Company Commander of the Gloucestershire Regiment who has it in his charge with no more than 60 men to help him.

8. Those who feared that there would be persisting disorder and a breakdown in the administration after the capitulation and that the Germans would decline to collaborate with the occupying forces have not so far been justified in their misgivings. German economy is certainly shattered, but the political structure up to the provincial level has survived the defeat and the purge, and is now gaining coherence and self-confidence. In the view of most of those concerned with military government, the time is ripe to begin to erect a central administration, which the Germans themselves are beginning to reach out for, and without which the country cannot be efficiently governed. The Germans have a strong will to survive, and to revive their strength. In so far as this may serve to carry the country through the perils of next winter and to bring Germany up above the danger line, both politically and economically, this is a good thing. But many of those with whom I have talked assert that there is in the Germans not only a will to survive, but also still a formidable will to rebuild the power of Germany which, if not contained, would again become dangerous. Another of the Corps Commanders said that if our military government officers had a fault, it was that some of them were so keen on getting their areas into working order that they tended to forget that the people they were dealing with were Germans. The officer in charge of trade and industry in one of the provinces told us that industrial activity, excluding agriculture, in his province, which includes half the Ruhr, was at present about 25% of the normal; but a far smaller proportion of the industrial equipment of Germany had been destroyed than was generally supposed and, if given a free hand, the Germans could restore their industrial potential in the matter of equipment to something approaching 75% of the normal without very great difficulty. But for the present, of course, the lack of coal governed everything. In other ways, too, there is a darker side to the picture. While it is true that there are still apparently no subversive movements directed against the occupying powers there are in some places, though not in all, a growing hostility and a good deal of passive resistance, the return to their homes of the members of the armed forces, particularly those from overseas prisoner of war camps, may foster these tendencies. Nazi elements still continue to

exercise influence: if there are requisitions, it is the anti-Nazi who is apt to suffer, and in shops the Nazis tend to get better service than the others. Fear of the party régime has not yet been eradicated, and there are some Germans who do not believe that we intend to uproot Nazism.

9. Even the 'good' Germans are Germans still and have a German way of looking at things. The Commander of the military government detachment at Hamburg was anxious that I should meet the Burgomaster, and he invited him to join us one evening after dinner. The Burgomaster, Dr. Petersen, is a member of an old Hamburg family which has produced more than one Burgomaster in the past. He talks excellent English, is a man of culture, widely travelled and possessed of a strong sense of public duty. If there are 'good' Germans, this should be one of them. He is, and has been, sincerely anti-Nazi. Though he has much support in the city he is thought by some to be reactionary. He admitted that Germany had behaved with incredible folly, both in making war and in the conduct of the campaign. Though he spoke of folly rather than guilt, he recognised also that Germany must pay the penalty. But Germany must not be tried too hard. After the inexpressible relief of being out of the war and freed from the Nazis, the Germans were now beginning to feel disillusioned and disappointed. They sincerely wished for friendship with England, but the policy of the occupying powers seemed to be one of grinding Germany in the dust. Unless more help was speedily forthcoming, German economy would collapse next winter. At the very least, the Germans ought now to be given some hope, if not for the immediate future, at any rate for an ultimate future. Without some prospect of betterment, they might well decide, in despair, to turn to communism.

10. When Mr. Petersen had spoken for some time on this theme and was about to enlarge upon the Russian danger and the need for British leadership in Europe. I thought it was time to correct some of his impressions. The essential fact was that twice within a generation there had been destructive wars in Europe for which Germany was responsible. We were determined that this should not happen again. This was the purpose of our alliance with the Soviet Union, which was one of the foundations of our policy. It was for this object that the Allies had occupied Germany and were now proceeding jointly to her complete disarmament and demilitarisation, and to the complete uprooting of the Nazi Party. It was not the primary purpose of the occupation to promote Anglo-German friendship, or to bring about the economic revival of Germany. On the other hand, deliberately to bring about complete economic collapse in Germany, would hardly be in our own interest. But the Burgomaster was under an illusion if he thought, as he seemed to do, that in order to help Germany, all that would be necessary would be to turn on a tap to draw upon the abundance of the outside world. These five years and more of war had brought tremendous destruction in Europe and dislocation in the world. It was not only Germany but other countries too which would pass through a crisis next winter. If there was not enough to go round, and there certainly was not, the needs of the liberated territories which had suffered under German occupation must first be met, and among others from

Germany's resources. Our military government was doing its best to place the German administration and economy upon a tolerable basis. But the sufferings of the coming winter would have to be faced. As for the more distant future, there was no reason why the German people should not take a worthy place among the peoples of Europe: but it would be for the German people to deserve such a place, and for that a long apprenticeship might well be required. Meanwhile, the four Powers were united in their determination to prevent another German war, and it was our policy that 4-Power collaboration for this purpose should be long maintained. As for communism, it was no use talking as though we were still in the 1920's. The world, including Russia, had learnt much since then. Meanwhile, the Burgomaster was in the best position to know how humane and constructive was the approach of our military government to the immediate problems of Germany.

11. To this latter theme I now revert. It was the almost unanimous view of the military government detachments that the time was now ripe to mitigate somewhat the austerity of our regulations. Events, in their view, have rather outrun a policy which was undoubtedly wise in its original conception. Administratively and psychologically, the Germans are making a more rapid recovery than was expected. It might therefore help to take their minds off their economic anxieties and to lead them into healthier ways of thought if we gave them more with which to exercise their minds—more newspapers with more news in them, and comment as well as news; liberty, within reason and with due regard to security, to meet for political discussions and to combine in trade unions; if we began to open the schools, the theatres and the cinemas, to provide them more vital and more varied wireless programmes, and to allow more concerts. The Commander-in-Chief has himself made recommendations on these lines.[3]

12. I found our interlocutors, from the Corps Commanders downwards, deeply interested in the broad political scene in which the German problem is situated and in our long-term objectives in Germany. I did my best to answer their enquiries and I can only hope that they found my replies one half as satisfactory as theirs were to me.

13. From what I have said above, it will be clear that the military government of the British Zone under 21 Army Group through Major-General Templer's Civil Affairs/Military Government Branch has made an excellent start. But the machinery is still far from complete. The deployment of the British Element of the Control Commission is yet in its early stages. The integration of the headquarters staff of the Control Commission with the directing staff of the military government at H.Q. 21 Army Group is still to be effected. While there has been some consultation with the Americans and, in a lesser degree, with the French at Frankfurt, the projected 4-Power Control Machinery has not yet been set up in Berlin, though representatives of the British and U.S. commands have had a few preliminary meetings there

---

[3] Mr. Eden minuted in the margin of the immediately preceding passage: 'I agree with all this & have said so elsewhere. How can we get it done? A. E.'

with Marshal Zhukov. It is to these problems that the Chief of Staff, British Zone, is still giving his main attention.

14. I am glad to record that the members of the Political Division of the Control Commission have established the happiest relations with General Templer's staff, who have found their advice to be of real assistance.

15. Ideally speaking, what the executive agents in the field would wish to have from the directing authority in London would be (1) clear instructions on broad lines of policy; (2) reasonable latitude as to their application to current problems; (3) reasonably prompt decisions on requests for instructions. The directing authorities are, I would think, entitled, in their turn, to expect the executive agents in the field (a) to keep them supplied with a clear picture of the situation; (b) to give timely warning of new problems likely to call for decisions in the future. Members of the Intelligence Branch at headquarters are already giving attention to the problem of their situation reports. In the past their duty has been to assess the disposition and strength of enemy forces and to divine his intentions. Since what is now being conducted is a politico-military operation, they have had to turn their hands, among other things, to the description and assessment of a political situation. They are in consultation with members of the Political Division who have experience in political reporting, and this will lay the basis of a collaboration which will be useful to both sides.

16. I cannot close this despatch without a grateful tribute to the kindness and cordiality with which I have been received here by the Commands and staff, from the Commander-in-Chief downwards. They have spared no pains to make my conditions of life agreeable and to place at my disposal the facilities required for the fulfilment of my duties.

17. I should have preferred, before submitting the present despatch to you, to have shown it to General Weeks and General Templer. But circumstances of time and place have not permitted. I have, however, given an oral account of my impressions to the Commander-in-Chief, and I do not think that they will be found to be out of harmony with his views. But, of course, they engage no one's responsibility but my own.

18. I have given a copy of this despatch to the Chief of Staff, British Zone, and have sent a copy to the War Office.

I have, &c.,
WILLIAM STRANG[4]

[4] On 19 July 1945 Mr. Harvey minuted that he found this report disturbing because (1) the German people had suffered less in the war than inhabitants of liberated territories and therefore faced the coming winter with a considerable initial advantage; (2) the British and American military governments found ground for rapprochement with Germans in hostility to displaced persons, overlooking German moral responsibility for their sufferings; (3) an apparent German demand for clearer and swifter denazification; (4) inadequate numbers in Allied Military Government service; (5) hesitancy regarding trade unions; (6) the danger that the British and American zones of Germany would recover quicker than the liberated territories or Italy, which lacked trained personnel, communications and political tranquility to enable them to get a fair share of Allied resources, especially

i *18 July 1945* Sir W. Strang (Lübbecke) No. 2. Encloses report on the achievement of Military Government in British zone [C 4274/24/18].

ii *18 July 1945* Mr. Roberts (Moscow) Tel. No. 3201. Attention paid in Soviet press to alleged British and American failure to suppress Nazis and German industrialists while denying democratic expression [C 4031/2069/18].

iii *20 July 1945* Memorandum by Sir R. Bruce Lockhart to Mr. Eden. Comments on No. 103, paragraph 11 in regard to information policy in British zone [C 4131/3086/18].

after the relaxation of the non-fraternisation rule. He suggested that these comments, except for the last, should be sent to Sir W. Strang. On 21 July Sir O. Sargent minuted his agreement. See No. 421.

No. 104

Mr. Randall (Copenhagen) to Mr. Eden (Received 12 July, 11.20 a.m.)
No. 324 Telegraphic [N 8589/9/15]

Secret   COPENHAGEN, *12 July 1945, 7.58 a.m.*

Your telegram No. 19 Saving.[1]

Withdrawal from Denmark has at no time been discussed with the Danish Government but yesterday[2] Danish Minister for Foreign Affairs referring to dissolution of S.H.A.E.F. Mission asked me whether I thought it possible to establish a relation between the ultimate withdrawal of British force and that of Russian forces from Bornholm and what I thought of the possibility of arriving at an understanding on the subject at the forthcoming conference of the Big Three. In regard to the latter I gave him no encouragement and on the former I said it depended on what functions the respective forces still had to perform, and what exactly the term withdrawal comprised; for example mine sweeping which was as of much importance to the Danes as to anybody, might necessitate a fairly long stay by ce[r]tain British forces. I also had in mind, although I did not mention it, the possibility that continued presence here of British air or military or naval mission might be so interpreted by the Russians as to justify their remaining in Bornholm indefinitely.

2. Danish Ministe[r] for Foreign Affairs made it clear that he would very much like His Majesty's Government to assist the Danish Government in taking the initiative with the Russians. I did not respond to this, but . . .[3] perhaps we might know more about Bornholm after Admiral Holt and

[1] This telegram of 30 June 1945 concerning withdrawal of British forces from Denmark had outlined plans to reduce land and naval forces upon completion of their tasks (disposal of enemy war-material, etc.), probably by mid-October unless the Danish Government should raise the question of earlier withdrawal.
[2] The present telegram was drafted on 11 July.
[3] The text is here uncertain.

General Dewing[4] had paid their informal visit to the Governor. I added, in reply to suggestion that I might go to Bornholm, that as there were no British residents there I did not think that the visit by me at the present juncture would be justifiable or advisable.

3. On the assumption that the Russian stay in Bornholm will be determined by their own interpretation of their interests, I think it would be a mistake to allow the Danish Government to use the withdrawal of our forces as a lever. In their eagerness to get Russians out, they might be led to press for termination of activities by our military naval or air services here, which are as much in the Danish interests as our own. The case might be altered if we could reach understanding with the Russians, and Danes about synchronising withdrawal of fighting units, but the plain truth is, I think, that the Danish Government is prepared to accept the unostentatious presence of the British here for a long time, but does not, despite the excessively cordial remarks made by the Minister for Foreign Affairs on various occasions, want any Russians at all in Bornholm and wishes anyone but himself to ask them how much longer they propose to stay.

[4] Vice-Admiral R. V. Holt was British Flag Officer, Denmark. Major-General R. H. Dewing was British member of the S.H.A.E.F. Mission to Denmark.

No. 105

United Kingdom Delegation (Berlin) to Mr. Eden (Received 12 July, 2 p.m.)
No. 2 Comms Telegraphic [U 5410/3628/70]

Important   BERLIN, *12 July 1945, 11.17 a.m. G.M.T.*

Please pass following to Mr. Tompkins from Mrs. Gibbs.[1] Personal.

Your letter of July 10th[2] thanks about brandy which will be met[*sic*]. It has not been possible to communicate sooner as conditions here are somewhat . . . [3]

2. Monckton, Waley, Turner and Berry[4] arrive here to-day. If Theakstone is to be available for Foreign Office and Berlin is coming too it can be agreed that Berry need not stay as accommodation is very difficult. Please instruct me.

3. Cabinet Office here inform me Brand may also be added to the Foreign Office party. Can you confirm this.

[1] Mr. E. E. Tomkins and Mrs. E. S. Gibbs were temporarily employed, in the Foreign Office and at Berlin respectively, on administrative arrangements for the Conference at Potsdam.

[2] Untraced in Foreign Office archives.

[3] The text is here uncertain.

[4] Mr. G. W. Berry was designated to act as interpreter for the Foreign Office together with Major L. M. Theakstone and Mr. I. Berlin. On 13 July 1945 Mr. Tomkins informed Mrs. Gibbs that Mr. Berlin would not be going to Berlin.

4. Extra bodies are appearing on all sides and the Delegation is swelling rapidly. There is now no spare accommodation and any further additional staff will have to be squeezed into the houses and offices already full.

5. Stationary [*sic*] supplies are insufficient and must be increased almost immediately especially writing paper, envelopes and ink. Real ink not the dried variety please also pens, pencils red and blue.

6. It will be wise if you can make arrangements for the Foreign Office to send daily newspapers direct to the Foreign Office Delegation here in fairly large supplies, as was done at San Francisco.[5]

[5] In Berlin telegrams Target Nos. 71 and 78 of 18 July Colonel Sir Eric Crankshaw, Secretary of the Government Hospitality Fund, asked Mr. M. W. Stanley, Staff Officer at the Treasury, to arrange for the despatch from London over the period 20–25 July of itemized quantities of provisions [CAB 21/867].

No. 106

Mr. Eden to Earl of Halifax (Washington)
No. 7378 Telegraphic[1] *[U 5822/5202/70]*

Important   FOREIGN OFFICE, *12 July 1945, 3.27 a.m.*

As you are aware, one of the documents signed at San Francisco was entitled 'Interim Arrangements concluded by the Governments represented at the United Nations Conference on International Organisation'.[2] This document established a Preparatory Commission (which held its first meeting the day following signature of the Charter) and an Executive Committee of fourteen States which will exercise the Commission's functions when it is not in session. It was also agreed that the seat of the Commission and the Committee should be located in London and that His Majesty's Government in the United Kingdom should as soon as possible inform the other members of the Executive Committee when it would be desirable for the latter to hold its first meeting.

2. An examination of the practical considerations involved has now been made and His Majesty's Government feel that all the necessary arrangements can be concluded in time for a meeting of the Committee on Thursday 9th August at Church House, Deans Yard, Westminster.[3]

3. Please therefore inform Government to which you are accredited of this tentative date and report as soon as possible whether it is agreeable to

[1] This circular telegram was also sent as No. 3893 to Moscow, No. 737 to Chungking, No. 1232 to Paris, No. 259 to Rio de Janeiro, No. 135 to Mexico City, No. 13 to the Hague, No. 140 to Prague, No. 1012 to Belgrade, No. 115 to Santiago and No. 413 to Tehran.

[2] This agreement of 26 June 1945 is printed in Cmd. 6669 of 1945.

[3] Lord Halifax reported in Washington telegram No. 4905 of 10.51 p.m. on 13 July (received, 5.57 a.m. on 14 July) that the arrangements proposed in this paragraph were agreeable to the American Government.

them. You should at the same time enquire who their representative is likely to be and what staff will be attached to him.

4. It was also agreed at the first meeting of the Preparatory Commission referred to above that His Majesty's Government in the United Kingdom would appoint an 'Interim Administrative Officer' who would be responsible for making all the necessary preliminary arrangements. Mr. Gladwyn Jebb, C.M.G.[4] has now been appointed to this post and will be available in London for consultations regarding the establishment of the Executive Committee which any Government concerned may wish to set on foot. Government to which you are accredited should be informed accordingly.

CALENDAR TO NO. 106

i *Undated Brief No. 42 for U.K. Delegation.* Suggested organisation of Executive Committee of the United Nations, for informal discussion at Potsdam [F.O. 934/6].

[4] Companion of the Order of St. Michael and St. George.

No. 107

Mr. Duff Cooper (Paris) to Mr. Eden (Received 12 July, 8.20 p.m.)

No. 988 Telegraphic [Z 8352/16/28]

PARIS, *12 July 1945, 5.32 p.m. G.M.T.*

Repeated to Tangier, Madrid, Washington, Moscow.

My immediately preceding telegram.[1]

Following from Peake.

I then explained to Meyrier your point of view and the reasons why it would be impossible for you to deal with Tangier so soon as the French Government wished. You were, I said, as anxious as he . . . [2] that there should be no undue delay and I thought you would be prepared to see conversations resumed not later than the first week in August. I thought it most unlikely that they could proceed before then. I further said that should the French Government wish to approach the Soviet Government as indicated in their note (Paris despatch No. 720)[3] you would certainly see no objection and that it was also your intention as soon as you had been able to give further consideration to the question, to make communication to the

[1] Not printed. In this telegram Mr. Peake reported that on the afternoon of 11 July 1945 he had, together with his American colleagues, seen M. Meyrier, Director-General in French Ministry of Foreign Affairs, 'and found him in a state of considerable agitation. He began by reading me the text of the Note which he had prepared (copy by bag [not printed: cf. *F.R.U.S. Berlin*, vol. 1, pp. 1004–5]) in reply to your intimation that the Tangier conversations had better be deferred': see No. 86, note 2.

[2] The text is here uncertain.

[3] Of 6 July, not printed: see No. 86.i.

Soviet Government, and that you agreed that they would have to be invited to take part in conversations. M. Meyrier asked whether he might address a frank question to me which was, did you intend to speak to the Soviet Government about Tangier at the forthcoming Berlin Conference? I said that while I could not say I thought you might well find this the quickest and most convenient method of disposing of the invitation to Russia. Meyrier then said that speaking with the utmost frankness he felt bound to say that the French Government were very sensitive on the point that they had not been invited to the Three-Power Conference and that they did not relish the thought of His Majesty's Government and Soviet Government doing a deal about Tangier behind the back of the French Government.

I told Meyrier that I would speak with equal frankness and tell him that his aspersion was unworthy and that in any case he was exaggerating the importance of Tangier. The fact was that you had far more important questions to consider at Berlin than that of Tangier. The only aspect of the question which might be discussed there was the circumstances in which the invitation would be issued to the Soviet Government.

Meyrier said that I had greatly relieved his mind and that this put a new complexion on the question of delay. Minister for Foreign Affairs had, however, been much disturbed by a report in the *Herald Tribune* which he showed me in which it was stated that the Foreign Office spokesman in London had specifically said that Tangier was to figure on the agenda of Berlin Conference. If it was merely a point of invitation to Russians being discussed there, he thought the French Government would agree to delay of conversations till the first week in August as I had suggested. It would, however, greatly assist if the Ambassador would himself tell the Minister for Foreign Affairs that the future Tangier régime would not be discussed with the Russians at Berlin. I said I would ask His Excellency to do this.

To this conversation which lasted more than an hour the only contribution made by the Americans was to change their minds about the date of conversations and to join the French in pressing me that they should begin at once.[4]

[4] In Washington telegram No. 4873 of 9.45 p.m. on 12 July (received 5.20 a.m. on 13 July: repeated to Paris, Madrid, Tangier and Moscow) Lord Halifax reported: 'State Department have confirmed that they do not (repeat not) agree to postponement of Paris conversations on the future of Tangier. They would not (repeat not) wish to exclude U.S.S.R. if the latter wishes to take part in the discussions. A delay of a few days might however be necessary to allow the Soviet delegates time to reach Paris.' Foreign Office telegram No. 7452 of 1.55 p.m. on 14 July to Washington (repeated as above) replied: 'Please inform State Department that we regret that we are not in a position to resume Paris conversations immediately, and that we shall only be in a position to take a final decision on the Soviet request at 3 Power meeting. If we are eventually able to agree to Soviet participation, we should be ready to resume the talks in the first week of August.' In Foreign Office telegram No. 1244 of 11.25 p.m. on 14 July to Paris Mr. Duff Cooper was instructed to make a similar communication to the French Ministry of Foreign Affairs and to 'explain that His Majesty's Government have no intention of discussing any aspect of the Tangier question at Terminal other than question of Russian participation and that they will of course only speak for themselves in this last respect.'

Foreign Office please repeat to Tangier and Moscow as my telegrams Nos. 15 and 38.[5]

[5] Mr. Eden minuted in Berlin on this telegram: 'Mr. Peake makes heavy weather. We don't propose to discuss anything about Tangier here save Russia joining such discussions. A. E.'

No. 108

Letter from Mr. J. T. Henderson to M. Francfort[1]

[*E 4801/8/89*]

FOREIGN OFFICE, 12 July 1945

My Dear Francfort,

Your letter No. 377[2] of 29th June was addressed to Robin Hankey, but he is now immersed in Polish affairs, and though you were kind enough to say that no answer was required, I feel that such a friendly and generous letter really calls for some reply.

I read the articles and I am struck by their reasonable and sympathetic tone. It is indeed sad that two countries which have a deep and lasting regard for one another, based on an exchange of civilisation, even on chivalrous quarrels in the past, should hurt one another as much as we hurt you by our apparent heavy-handedness, as you hurt us by your suspicions. But even in the bitterness one finds some comfort, because, though one may be angered by an adversary, one can only be hurt by a friend.

To-day I had a talk with a Frenchman, and in his first sentence he referred to Syria and the Lebanon as 'colonies'. Of course he knew they were mandates, and possibly ceased even to be mandates when France granted them their independence on 8th June, 1941, but the *feeling* which lay behind the mistaken expression was that we were taking away from France something that belongs to her. And that we are doing so in a brutal fashion. So we seem to be doing this in order to humiliate France. And that is disappointing, from a friend. Or is he a friend?

[1] Mr. J. T. Henderson was a member of Eastern Department of the Foreign Office. M. P. Francfort was a Counsellor at the French Embassy in London.

[2] Not printed. This letter enclosed copies of two articles in *Le Figaro*, of 21 June 1945 by M. François Mauriac and of 22 June by M. Georges Duhamel respectively, on Anglo-French relations. M. Francfort wrote that he believed that these authors 'traduisent l'unanime émotion et tristesse qu'a provoqué l'affaire de Syrie dans les milieux de tradition libérale les plus ouverts à la raison et à la compréhension. Je sais que vous n'avez pas besoin de ces articles pour comprendre nos sentiments, mais je souhaiterais qu'ils puissent vraiment convaincre des personnes plus importantes que nous, du retentissement des évènements de Syrie et de la bonne foi de la plupart des Français dans la façon dont ils interprètent l'attitude des autorités militaires britanniques au Levant. Les sentiments des Français sont d'autant plus touchés que s'était accrue au cours de ces dernières années la profondeur de leur amitié pour l'Angleterre qui poursuivait fraternellement une lutte commune dont dépendait leur libération; ce sont ces sentiments d'amitié et d'enthousiasme qu'avec tristesse beaucoup de Français craignent de voir s'affaiblir.'

We do not feel we are taking anything from France, because we do not regard the mandate as property, especially since the grant of independence, which we guaranteed. We do not wish to humiliate France. We are not that kind of people, and anyway it could not do us any good. We do not wish to stay in the Levant, or to come back after leaving. We need our man-power elsewhere. I am sure you know these facts, and understand that we did sadly what we felt compelled to do. I hope Frenchmen will give us credit for good motives and will not believe that we have ceased to feel affection and respect for them, even if we must sometimes disagree.

Yours very sincerely,
JIM HENDERSON

No. 109

Meeting of the British Chiefs of Staff Committee held at the Cabinet Office on 12 July 1945 at 10.30 a.m.[1]

C.O.S. (45) 175th Meeting [E 5141/15/31]

1.[2] *Policy in the Middle East*

J.P.(45) 167 (Final) [i]

(Previous Reference: C.O.S.(45) 153rd Meeting, Minute 16)[3]

THE COMMITTEE considered a report [i] by the Joint Planning Staff covering a draft reply to a minute[4] by the Prime Minister about future policy regarding Palestine.

THE COMMITTEE:—

Approved the terms of the draft minute, as amended in discussion, and instructed the Secretary to submit[5] it to the Prime Minister.

2. *Montreux Convention and Security of the Baltic*

J.P.(45) 170 (Final)[6]

C.O.S.(45) 447 (O) and 444 (O)[7]

(Previous Reference: C.O.S.(45) 170th Meeting, Minute 2)[8]

THE COMMITTEE considered a report[6] by the Joint Planning Staff on

---

[1] The following members of the Committee were present: Field-Marshal Sir A. Brooke, Chief of the Imperial General Staff; Marshal of the Royal Air Force Sir C. Portal, Chief of Air Staff; Admiral of the Fleet Sir A. Cunningham, First Sea Lord and Chief of Naval Staff; and General Sir H. Ismay, Chief of Staff to Minister of Defence.

[2] Relevant items from this record were entered in Foreign Office files as separate extracts. Minutes 2 and 3 are supplied from R 12919/44/44 and F 4445/1057/23 respectively. See also No. 95.iii.

[3] Of 15 June 1945, not printed.

[4] *Note in filed copy:* 'M.679/5 [No. 15], circulated under cover of Secretary's minute C.O.S. 992/5', not printed.

[5] *Note in filed copy:* 'Annex I'.

[6] Annex II below, supplied from R 11962/44/44.

[7] Of 7 July (respectively on R 11554/44/44 and U 5906/443/70), not printed.

[8] Of 5 July (on R 11695/44/44), not printed.

possible Russian demands for the revision of the Montreux Convention and on draft briefs[7] prepared by the Foreign Office for use at 'Terminal' on this question and on the security of the Baltic.

As regards a possible Russian request for a base in the Dardanelles area, it was generally agreed that such a base would be unnecessary to secure for Russia free passage through the straits in peace and war, though it might be used by the Russians to prevent ships of other nations entering the Black Sea.

SIR ANDREW CUNNINGHAM thought that it was important that, if the question were referred to the World Organisation, discussion should hinge on the question of whether it was necessary for Russia to have a base in this area and not as to how such a base should be provided. He suggested amendments to paragraph 10 of the report.

THE COMMITTEE:–

Approved the report by the Joint Planning Staff, subject to amendments agreed in discussion, and instructed the Secretary to circulate it over their signatures[9] and to send a copy to the Foreign Office.

3. *Possible Russian participation in the war against Japan*
J.P.(45) 140 (Final)[10]
THE COMMITTEE considered a report by the Joint Planning Staff on the possible participation in the war on Japan by the Russians.

[9] *Note in filed copy:* 'Circulated as C.O.S. (45) 459 (O).' This report of 12 July 1945 (on R 11962/44/44: not printed) was identical with Annex II below subject to the omission of the first two words of paragraph 1, the omission of paragraph 11 and the following additions to paragraph 10: '(d) . . . raised by us and if raised by others, we should point out that the occupation of Germany removes any urgency from this question and that it is suitable for discussion by the World Organisation . . . . (f) The early conclusion of Special Agreements concerning bases holds no immediate advantages for us. It is, therefore, better to avoid even appearing to commit ourselves to the principle that Special Agreements for the entrances to the Baltic and Dardanelles are necessary. We shall be in more favourable position to decide this question some months hence when Russian intentions in Europe become clearer.'

[10] Not printed. The conclusions of this report of twentyseven paragraphs on 'Possible Russian participation in the war against Japan', under date of 10 July 1945 and the same signatories as in Annex II below, were:

'(a) The earliest possible declaration of war by the Russians would be to our advantage.

'(b) Russian action is likely to be directed to the capture of Manchuria and Korea with the port of Dairen.

'(c) The two main lines of Russian approach are:

A. An attack from the Lake Baikal area through Mongolia and the Gobi Desert directed against the Pekin area.

B. An attack across the Amur River and from the Maritime Province into Manchuria and Korea.

Russia is likely to use both simultaneously if she can. If she cannot do so, she is likely to favour Course A, but we would prefer Course B.

In addition, the invasion of Southern Sakhalin (Karafuto) with a threat to Hokkaido to tie down Japanese forces in that area to be timed with Coronet [see No. 232, note 8], would be of value.

'(d) Since Russian action is unlikely to be influenced by our requirements and as the

Sir Alan Brooke said he did not agree with the Directors of Plans that the most likely line of a Russian advance was that through the Gobi Desert or that they were likely to launch an attack against Manchuria from the Vladivostok area. In his view the most likely course to be adopted by the Russians was an advance towards Harbin from the Manchouli and Heiho areas in Northern Manchuria, with a view to protecting the railway on which their forces in the maritime provinces depended. It was possible that such an advance would be supported by moving a small force through the Gobi Desert. It had been estimated that it would take the Russians some 8–11 months to clear the Japanese from Manchuria and reach the Korean frontier. While this estimate might be somewhat pessimistic, he thought it quite possible that the Russians would take so long.

Sir Andrew Cunningham suggested that in view of the limited transportation facilities across Russia, the Russians might well ask for a guarantee that a sea route would be opened to the maritime provinces within a specified period. Should the Russians make such a demand, he did not see any very great difficulty in meeting it, though it would be necessary to provide convoys with carrier escort and some losses would undoubtedly be incurred.

The Committee:

Took note of the report by the Joint Planning Staff and of the views expressed in discussion . . .[2]

Annex I to No. 109

Minute from General Ismay to Mr. Churchill

No. C.O.S. 1006/5

Copy   *12 July 1945*

Reference your minute M. 679/5,[11] the Chiefs of Staff have examined the strategic implications of your suggestion that the Americans should be asked to relieve us of the Palestine Mandate.

2. In the first place, the Chiefs of Staff entirely agree with you that the presence of the United States in Palestine would be an insurance to our general strategic position in the event of a breakdown of the World Security Organisation. Not only would it deter unwanted Powers from pursuing their aims in the Middle East itself, but it would go some way towards ensuring the early intervention of the United States in a general European war, if that occurs.

Russians are likely to take advantage of any requests by us to obtain promises of political support for their aims in the Far East, we would prefer, on political grounds, that the Russians should take the initiative in proposing their strategy.
'(e) Should the Russians need to deploy forces above those now in the Far East or should their L[ines] of C[ommunication] be seriously interrupted, it would probably be necessary to open a sea route for further supplies from Allied sources. Unless the Russians captured a port in Manchuria, this would involve a major commitment.'
[11] No. 15.

3. On the other hand, the Chiefs of Staff see grave disadvantages in the suggestion. The Middle East remains of high strategic importance to us because of its oil supplies, sea and air communications and as a base for the Imperial Strategic Reserve. Palestine is the key to the internal security of the Middle East area;[12] its internal troubles are immediately reflected outside. To yield up our responsibility for it might well have two main effects:

(a) We should be adjudged to have abandoned our predominant position in the Middle East. This abrogation of responsibility would have evil consequences, not only in Middle East countries but in India and beyond.

(b) The safeguarding of our strategic interests in the Middle East would virtually depend upon the policy pursued by the United States in Palestine. If that policy, over which we should have little if any control, were inimical to our interests, we should be faced with an increased internal security commitment in the Middle East and an embarrassing conflict of policy with the United States.

4. The effect upon Russia of American control in Palestine can only be guessed. The Foreign Office advise us that Russia might see in this change of responsibility some covert threat to herself. Moreover, the Russians might be ready to set themselves up as champions of the Arabs if in the event the Americans pursued a Zionist policy in Palestine and we felt obliged to acquiesce in it.

5. The Chiefs of Staff conclusion is, therefore, that while we would in general welcome a distribution of responsibilities in Europe and the Middle East, which imposed a permanent commitment upon the United States, they would not, on strategic grounds, recommend the transfer to the Americans of the Palestine Mandate.

6. A copy of this has been sent to the Secretary of State for the Colonies, who is submitting to you a separate paper.[13]

ANNEX II TO No. 109

Report by the Joint Planning Staff

J.P. (45) 170 (Final)

CHIEFS OF STAFF COMMITTEE, JOINT PLANNING STAFF, *11 July 1945*

Top secret

Montreux Convention and security of the Baltic

As instructed,[14] we have examined the demands which the U.S.S.R. have made to the Turkish Government prior to negotiating a new Russo-Turkish Treaty together with the views of the Foreign Office on this subject.[15] We have also examined a brief[16] for Terminal written by the Foreign Office on the security side of future arrangements for the entrances to the Baltic and Kiel Canal, together with a minute[16] by Mr. Jebb of the Foreign Office commenting on this brief.

---

[12] The preceding clause is cited by N. Bethell, *The Palestine Triangle*, p. 201.
[13] Untraced.
[14] *Note in filed copy:* 'C.O.S. (45) 170th Meeting', not printed.
[15] *Note in filed copy:* 'C.O.S. (45) 447(O)', not printed.
[16] *Note in filed copy:* 'C.O.S. (45) 444(O)', not printed.

2. The Baltic and the Dardanelles constitute the two main ocean gateways for the Russians. In dealing with one alone, there is a risk that a solution in one case may be used as an argument against us in the other. We have, therefore, considered these two problems together.

Account must also be taken of the two main Mediterranean gateways, namely, the Straits of Gibraltar and the Suez Canal. The Russians have already shown an interest in the former by expressing a wish to take part in the Tangier discussions. So far, they have shown no signs of raising the question of control of the Suez Canal, but we must take into account the possibility that they may do so.

Foreign Office Views

3. As described below, the briefs and comments put forward by the Foreign Office lay a slightly differing emphasis on the desirability of raising at Terminal the question of the entrances to the Baltic and Kiel Canal.

In their brief on the Dardanelles, the Foreign Office suggest that it might be wise at Terminal to associate the question of bases in this area with the rather similar problem of the entrances to the Baltic. Presumably, they feel that if we raised the question of the Baltic, we should be more likely to obtain Russian agreement to some arrangement providing for international control of bases in the Dardanelles area.

In their brief on the entrances to the Baltic and the Kiel Canal, the Foreign Office do not suggest that this question should be raised at Terminal, but they point out that if the Russians raise it, some international arrangement for these areas would be possible under the charter of the World Organisation. The precise form of the arrangement would be a matter for discussion amongst the powers concerned.

In his comment on this brief, Mr. Jebb suggests that the emphasis should be slightly shifted and concludes that there is everything to be said in favour of the general staffs of the Great Powers discussing the preparation of a scheme for the Baltic and the Kiel Canal as soon as possible.

Military Implications

4. We examine in Annex I and Annex II[17] the strategic implications of the acquisition by the Russians of additional facilities in the Dardanelles and the Baltic respectively and the justification for their demands.

5. From these examinations, we conclude that:

(*a*) It is in our wider interests to support the Russian proposals for free passage in peace and war through the Straits, although it would be detrimental to our local strategic interests in the E. Mediterranean.

(*b*) Russian demands for bases should be resisted.

(*c*) Similarly, the establishment of Russian influence at the entrance to the Baltic is even more undesirable and we should strongly resist any demands they may make for bases in that area.

(*d*) It is in our interests, therefore, to retain the *status quo* as regards bases in both these areas.

6. It is also most important that we should retain our present control of the Straits of Gibraltar and Suez Canal.

[17] Not printed.

Possible Solutions

7. If the Russians will not accept the retention of the *status quo* as regards bases, particularly in the case of the Dardanelles and the Baltic, there appear to be two possible solutions under the charter of the World Organisation:

A — Control by two or more great powers.

B — Control by a single great power.

Course A

8. This course would allow the Russians to increase their influence in the Baltic and Dardanelles areas and it might be politically difficult to restrict the extension of their influence. It would, however, allow us to retain some measure of control.

The danger of this Course is that it might lead to a suggestion that the Suez Canal and Straits of Gibraltar should be treated similarly. This would be entirely contrary to our interest.

Course B

9. If the control of the gateways were left to one great power, the Russians would inevitably state that they were the great power most concerned with the entrances to the Baltic and the Dardanelles and it would be difficult for us to resist this claim. This would clearly be most disadvantageous from a strategic point of view. It should, however, allow us to retain our position in the Straits of Gibraltar and the Suez Canal.

Conclusions

10. We conclude that:

(*a*) The Russian demands for right of passage through the Dardanelles in time of war is a reasonable one. They already have right of passage through the Baltic entrances in time of war.

(*b*) Russian bases in these areas to secure these passages are not really necessary on military grounds and Russian demands should be strongly resisted.

(*c*) From our strategic point of view, the best solution would be the maintenance of the *status quo* regarding bases covering sea gateways, particularly in view of the effect that any change may have on our position in Gibraltar and the Suez Canal.

(*d*) We should, therefore, prefer that the range of the discussions at Terminal should be limited as far as possible. The question of entrances to the Baltic should not be raised by us.[18]

(*e*) If the Russians persist in their demands for bases in the Dardanelles, the question must be referred for discussion by the Four Great Powers or the World Organisation, rather than settled bilaterally between Russia and Turkey.[18]

Recommendation[18]

11. We recommend that a copy of this paper should be sent to the Foreign Office.

G. Grantham
G. S. Thompson
W. L. Dawson

Offices of the Cabinet and Minister of Defence, S.W.1. 11th July, 1945

[18] Cf. note 9 above.

i *10 July 1945 Report by the Joint Planning Staff, J.P.(45) 167 (Final)* on future control of Palestine [E 5141/15/31].

No. 110

Minute from Lord Cherwell [1] to Mr. Churchill
[PREM 3/139/9]

Top secret   GREAT GEORGE STREET, S.W.I., *12 July 1945*
                    T[ube] A[lloys] [2]

The Americans have met us on all the points which we raised about the statements [ii] which the President and Stimson propose to make after the operational test. It is especially satisfactory that all references to the processes used are to be deleted.

No doubt, however, Truman will still raise the question of what is to be said to the Russians at Terminal.

The two alternative courses are:

(1) Not to say anything and face the fact that when, a few weeks after Terminal, concealment is no longer possible Stalin may claim that our lack of candour in not mentioning such an important matter justifies him in going back on any engagements he may have made.

(2) To say, in broad general terms, that we have done a great deal of work on T.A. and hope shortly to make an operational test, but to refuse to say anything further. This might spoil the atmosphere at Terminal if the Russians demanded further information. But they have no right to any and I am sure the Americans will not give it.

The arguments are fairly closely balanced. But as the Americans have contributed such an overwhelming proportion of the effort, I do not think it would be easy to oppose Truman strongly, if he seems anxious to take the second course.

In any event the issue may be forced by Stalin asking point blank what the position is. [3]

CHERWELL

---

[1] Paymaster-General.

[2] Code-name for research and development of atomic energy. For British accounts of the development of the atomic bomb and the decision to use it, cf. John Ehrman, *Grand Strategy*, vol. vi (H.M.S.O., 1956), pp. 275–299; M. Gowing, *Britain and Atomic Energy 1939–45* (London, 1964), pp. 367–378.

[3] This document was minuted as follows by Mr. Rowan: 'Prime Minister. 1. You said you would write to the President on Sunday evening [15 July] about this. 2. You will see from the Chancellor's note [ii] . . . that *if* statements are made, the U.S. authorities have asked to see what you propose to say—as we have seen what the President and Mr. Stimson propose to say. T. L. R. 14.7.45.' On 16 July Mr. Rowan noted: 'P.M. decided not to write to President but to speak to him if possible during meeting at 11 a.m. today.' No record of this meeting on 16 July has been traced in Foreign Office archives: cf. W. S. Churchill, *op. cit.*, vol. vi, p. 545; *F.R.U.S.Berlin*, vol. ii, pp. 10 and 35; Charles Mee, *Meeting at Potsdam* (London, 1975), pp. 74-7.

i *29 June 1945 Minute from Sir J. Anderson to Mr. Churchill:* 'Notes on T.A. for "Terminal" '. Sir J. Anderson, as Minister with responsibility for questions of atomic energy, advises early discussion with President Truman since Americans now think that he should mention topic to the Russians during the Conference; discusses possible statement; suggests that Mr. Churchill should express the hope to the President 'that full and effective cooperation based upon an interchange of information and personnel will be continued both until the end of the Japanese war and subsequently' [PREM 3/139/8A].

ii *6 July 1945 Minute from Sir J. Anderson to Mr. Churchill.* Attaches with comments (a) first draft of draft statement to be made by Mr. Stimson on atomic fission bombs, with interleaved British comments (PREM 3/139/8A fos. 279–94); (b) draft statement to be made by President Truman with proposed British amendments (PREM 3/139/9 fos. 666–671); (c) preliminary draft of statement to be issued by Mr. Churchill (PREM 3/139/8A fos. 273–278). Most important point on U.S. statements is their 'proposal to reveal so much about the technical processes used in the production of the material': see *F.R.U.S. Berlin*, vol. ii, pp. 1376–8, and *Documents on American Foreign Relations*, vol. viii (Princeton, 1948), pp. 413–9, for final texts of U.S. statements issued on 6 August 1945 [PREM 3/139/9 fos. 663–4].

No. 111

Minute from Mr. Eden to Mr. Churchill

No. P.M./45/324 [U 6125/3628/70]

FOREIGN OFFICE, *12 July 1945*

On my return to the Foreign Office I have been considering the agenda and procedure at Terminal. I find world outlook gloomy and signs of Russian penetration everywhere.[1]

2. *Agenda.* You will have seen the telegrams exchanged between London and Washington. I enclose copies.[2] The State Department agree generally

---

[1] This finding by Mr. Eden is cited by Sir L. Woodward, *op. cit.*, vol. v, p. 355.

[2] Attached to the original were the following telegrams: Foreign Office telegrams Nos. 6972–3 to Washington, transmitting to Lord Halifax on 30 June 1945 the British list of subjects for discussion at Potsdam and comments thereon (see *op. cit.*, vol. v, pp. 343–5); Washington telegram No. 4620 of 4 July, transmitting a report of a conversation on 3 July between Mr. J. Balfour, Minister in H.M. Embassy in Washington, and Mr. Matthews on the British agenda for Potsdam (see *F.R.U.S. Berlin*, vol. i, pp. 206–9); Washington telegrams Nos. 4708–9 (see 21, note 9); Washington telegram No. 4759 (No. 21.i), and Foreign Office telegram No. 3861 to Moscow of 10 July, instructing Sir A. Clark Kerr to communicate to the Soviet Government an amended version of the list in Foreign Office telegram No. 6973. This revised list, transmitted accordingly to M. Molotov on 11 July (also, in Washington, to Mr. Dunn), was the same, subject to minor verbal variation, as that printed in No. 171, section A: cf. *Sovetskiy Soyuz na mezhdunarodnykh konferentsiyakh perioda Velikoy Otechestvennoy voyny, 1941–1945 gg* (Moscow, 1978 f.), tom vi, *Berlinskaya (Potsdamskaya) konferentsiya rukovoditeley trekh soyuznykh derzhav—SSSR, SShA i Velikobritanii (17 iyulya—2 avgusta 1945 g): sbornik dokumentov*, pp. 304–5 (Moscow, 1980: The Soviet Union at international conferences at the time of the Great Patriotic War 1941–1945: volume vi, the Conference of Berlin (Potsdam) between the leaders of the three Allied powers—U.S.S.R., U.S.A. and Great Britain—17 July–2 August 1945—: collection of documents, hereafter cited as *Berlinskaya konferentsiya*).

that our list (Foreign Office telegram to Washington No. 6973) represents the topics which should be raised at the meeting, and we and the Americans have communicated our lists to the Soviet Government. But it cannot be said that there is an agreed agenda for the meeting. We do not know the views of the new American Secretary of State, and the two State Department high officials (Dunn and Matthews) whose views we have ascertained, each give a somewhat different emphasis to the order of importance of the subjects to be discussed.

3. I should have liked a preliminary exchange of views with Byrnes like the useful exchange which Stettinius and I had at Malta before the Crimea Conference.[3] But this is not possible since it seems that the President and Byrnes will not arrive at Terminal until the opening day. Cadogan is however planning to arrive twenty-four hours early in order to meet Dunn at Terminal for a preliminary exchange of views.

4. This being so, I think that we can only leave it until we get to Terminal to decide in what order to raise the various topics in our list. (Foreign Office telegram to Washington No. 6973). I enclose copies of briefs[4] which have been prepared in the Foreign Office. You may care to glance in particular at the following:

    2. Peace Treaties with Balkan Countries.[5]
    3. Transfer of German populations from Poland and Czechoslovakia.[6]
    5. Germany (Political Questions).[7]
  10. Turco-Soviet Relations.[8]
  17. Situation in Yugoslavia.[9]
  18. Persia.[10]

Briefs on procedure for a general European settlement,[11] on the Polish Western Frontier,[12] on Italy[13] and on the Straits[14] will be sent to you as soon as they are ready.

5. *Procedure.* You will remember that at the Crimea the Conference was rather slow in getting down to business, and that on the second day I suggested to you (P.M.(A) 5 of February 5th)[15] that the Heads of Government should decide the items which they wished to discuss at the Conference and how they were to be dealt with. I suggested that on some of them preliminary work could well be done by the Foreign Secretaries who could forward the results or differences for decision by the Heads of Government. Other major questions should first be the subject of direct treatment by the Heads of Government. You agreed with this proposal, and the Conference worked conveniently under the following procedure: the three Foreign Secretaries met in the mornings and the three Heads of Government in the afternoons, the Foreign Secretaries dealing with subjects which had been

[3] See No. 4, note 2.   [4] Not attached to filed copy.   [5] No. 82.
    [6] No. 59.i.   [7] No. 74, annex.
    [8] No. 19.i.   [9] No. 3.iv(c).
    [10] No. 129.i.   [11] No. 85.
    [12] No. 115.   [13] No. 138.
    [14] Not printed: see No. 109, note 7.   [15] Not printed.

remitted to them by the Heads of Government and reporting the results of their deliberations for consideration by the Heads of Government.

6. I think that a similar procedure might be followed at Terminal. If you agree with this, perhaps you would raise the question of procedure at the first meeting of the Big Three.

ANTHONY EDEN

CALENDAR TO No. 111

i *12 July 1945 Minute by Mr. Hayter.* Suggestions for topics for discussion at preliminary meeting with the Americans at Potsdam, and procedure in accordance with No. 111. 'We might also make to Mr. Dunn the point about not playing too early the *cards* we have in our hands. . . . Even if the Russians should make reasonable requests we should not grant them except in return for their agreement to reasonable requests on our part' [F.O. 800/416/63].

No. 112

Letter from Mr. Eden to Field-Marshal Sir B. Montgomery (Bad Oeynhausen)

[C 3787/24/18]

FOREIGN OFFICE, *12 July 1945*

I was most interested to read the notes on the present situation in the British zone which you were good enough to send me under cover of your letter of the 8th July.[1]

I think your ideas coincide very largely with our own. The most difficult part of your problem will, as I see it, be winning the 'battle of the winter' on the economic front. I was gratified to see from earlier reports that everything possible is being done to extract the maximum out of the soil, and arrangements are of course in hand to bring in some imports of food if, as seems likely, they prove necessary. But in other respects the position is of course most difficult. The whole of Western Europe is in desperate straits for coal and Germany is the only important source on which to draw. It is not going to be easy to reconcile the minimum requirements of the Western Allies in this respect with the minimum requirements of Germany. I will not go further into this problem now beyond saying that it is one which I have very much in mind.

I hope we shall get some agreement at Terminal on the political matters discussed in the latter part of your paper. Our object is to get broad agreement on such questions as the establishment of political parties and trade unions, fraternisation, and the establishment of essential central German ministries. Incidentally, I think it important to keep a close watch on

[1] No. 43.

214

meetings when they are allowed to take place. I also hope that something may be done at Terminal to break down the wall between the Russian zone and the zones of the Western Allies by getting it agreed that Germany is to be treated as an economic whole and also by persuading the Russians that the Control Council must start working without further delay as an effective body.

I am particularly interested in propaganda and information to the German people. I agree with you that very energetic action is required. I have discussed the matter with our authorities at the Political Intelligence Department and find that they are only too eager to give every assistance, in their power, as in fact they are doing already by, for example, supplying a full broadcasting service to Germany through the European Service of the B.B.C. and a daily World Press News Service, which provides the material for both the British and American newspapers in the British and American zones. But they themselves need assistance, particularly in the following respects:

(1) They would like to feel assured that the importance of the information services is fully appreciated by all commanders in the British zone;

(2) They hope that all possible action will be taken to establish good communications between London and the British zone and to provide adequate accommodation and transport facilities for such P.I.D. personnel as can be transferred to Germany;

(3) They would like to see the establishment for the Information Branch of the British Element increased as soon as possible;

(4) They hope that everything will be done to maintain the fullest co-operation between the authorities in our zone and the Americans;

(5) They would like to get formal War Office recognition of P.I.D. as the Office responsible for supplying the necessary material for information services to Germany;

(6) They hope that the Treasury may be persuaded to give immediate facilities for dealing with an emergency situation without awaiting approval of final establishments.

We are taking up vigorously such of the foregoing points as must be handled in London. I am sure we can rely on you to help us with them in Germany.[2]

CALENDARS TO NO. 112

i *13 July 1945 Letter from Mr. Eden to Sir J. Grigg.* Comments on American proposals on the status of foreign correspondents in Germany: 'We want to secure the greatest possible freedom of discussion and information about what goes on in all parts of Germany' [C 3974/2492/18].

ii *16 July 1945 Minutes of 2nd Meeting of the Cabinet European Control Committee (E.C.C.):* propaganda to the German people, and policy with regard to German establishments for research and development [C 4073/3943/18].

---

[2] Signature lacking on filed copy.

No. 113

Minute by Mr. Hall-Patch

[C 4022/1/18]

FOREIGN OFFICE, *12 July 1945*

Germany: Location of Control Commission

It is generally recognised that the work of the Control Commission cannot be efficiently discharged without the active help of the German administrative machine.

While the reconstitution of this machine is proceeding apace in provincial centres in the Western Zones of occupation (and we understand in the Russian Zone) the reconstitution at the centre has still to take place. Until it does the task of administering Germany as an economic unit by the Control Commission will be almost insuperable.

For the purposes of the Control Commission it is essential that the central German administrative machine should be situated side by side with the Control Commission.

This raises the problem of accommodation in Berlin. In General Weeks' view there is only just sufficient room to house the military. He feels it will be impossible to provide accommodation in Berlin for the large numbers of German officials which will be required under a year or eighteen months. This is the critical period of the occupation, when rapid decisions, and rapid action on these decisions, will be required. It is during this period when the German administrative machine will be of the greatest use to the Control Commission.

In these circumstances, now that we know the physical possibilities of Berlin, there may well be a case for having the control of Germany centred elsewhere. This raises large issues of policy, but these may have to be faced if it proves impossible for the Control Commission to discharge its duties efficiently from Berlin.

E. L. HALL-PATCH[1]

---

[1] Sir W. Strang and Sir A. Cadogan minuted on this: 'At the meeting between Marshal Zhukov, General Weeks and General Clay at Berlin on July 10th it was decided that representatives of the three Delegations should reconnoitre Berlin in order to find accommodation for the central services of the Control Council, the Coordinating Committee and other organs of the Allied Control Authority for Germany. General Weeks suggested to Marshal Zhukov that Potsdam and its neighbourhood, which is outside Greater Berlin and in the Soviet zone, might be suitable for this purpose. Marshal Zhukov at first demurred but afterwards said he would think about it. In the meantime General Weeks is finding accommodation in the British sector of Berlin for that part of the British Element of the Control Commission which will need to work in Berlin in the near future. This includes headquarter offices and living accommodation for members of the staff. It is difficult to see a solution of the problem. We shall probably require to accommodate within easy reach of each other:

'(1) that part of the British, American, Russian and French Elements of the Control Commission which will require to be at the centre;

'(2) the international Secretariat and headquarter services of the Control Commission and other organs of the Allied Control Authority;

'(3) the Allied military missions, anything between ten and twenty in number, accredited to the Control Council: some of these missions will very probably be quite large;

'(4) the offices and staffs of such central German departments as we decide to set up.

'Whether these could be accommodated in Berlin plus Potsdam I have no idea: but I should think it doubtful. W. Strang, 12th July, 1945.'

'There were political objections to establishing central control in Berlin. If in fact Berlin proves not to afford the necessary physical accommodation, that wd. appear to be decisive! But I don't know where it cd. be located. A. C. July 13, 1945.'

No. 114

Brief for the United Kingdom Delegation to the Conference at Potsdam
No. 44 [UE 3046/2100/53]

FOREIGN OFFICE, *12 July 1945*

Germany: Economic Aspects

1. The political issues, for all their importance, cannot be considered in isolation. Their solution will be conditioned by economic considerations. Workable solutions will not emerge if the German population have empty stomachs and no coal. Field-Marshal Montgomery calls for a good short term plan to tackle the battle of the winter.

2. In certain respects this is in train. Plans are in hand for providing some imports of food, though on a minimum scale, and encouragement is being given to the greatest possible use of the soil. But in other respects our plans will inevitably make the Field-Marshal's task more difficult.

3. Firstly the Hyndley-Potter Report, which has been endorsed by President Truman and the Cabinet, is based on the idea of removing the maximum quantities of coal from Germany for the benefit of Western Europe. This idea also underlies the draft directive to the Commanders of the Western Zones forwarded to the Prime Minister by the President and already accepted by General de Gaulle. In commenting on this draft we have made certain reserves which have, in substance, been accepted by the State Department. The reserves were designed to permit the retention in Germany of sufficient coal to provide essential services and to enable the Control Commission to function. But even these minimum requirements make the drastic recommendations of the Hyndley-Potter Report inoperable. To that extent there will be less coal available from Germany for export and the liberated areas will suffer. But the choice must be made; either a coal famine in Germany with the consequent difficulties of maintaining order and of effecting re-deployment, or less German coal for our Allies.

4. Secondly it is our policy, agreed with our Allies, to enforce draconian measures of economic disarmament, to impose heavy reparation deliveries (though not necessarily in the immediate future) and to countenance large levies of reparation labour. This policy, however desirable in itself, will add

to the existing economic dislocation in Germany, as will the large movement of German populations from Poland and Czechoslovakia which seem to be contemplated.

5. The control of Germany will be difficult, if not impossible, in the absence of a minimum of food and fuel. There is a world shortage of both. To the extent Germany's needs are met, our Allies, and perhaps ourselves, will go short. The fact is that by her action Germany has placed all the liberated countries in a condition of serious fear and want. Her population can now only be saved from the most dire consequences at the expense of the political and economic needs of our Allies. This fact is inescapable. No workable solution can be reached in Germany, and no useful guidance can be given to Field-Marshal Montgomery, without taking into account these economic factors which are part and parcel of the political problems with which we are faced.

6. Briefs on the main economic issues in Germany have been prepared and are listed below:
(a) Industrial Disarmament of Germany [iii].
(b) Treatment of Germany as an Economic Unit.[1]
(c) Coal Production in Germany [ii].
(d) Economic Assets in the British Zone [i].
(e) Reparation; briefs on various outstanding points.[2]

E. L. HALL-PATCH

CALENDARS TO NO. 114

i *10 July 1945 Brief No. 37 for U.K. Delegation on the Economic Assets of the British Zone of Occupation in Germany.* Lists principal resources in which British zone is markedly superior (coal, steel, etc), or inferior (food, timber, etc.), to others. Economic bargaining potential of the British zone in relation to others [F.O. 934/6].

ii *11 July 1945 Brief No. 22 for U.K. Delegation on Coal Production in Germany.* Refers to Hyndley-Potter report, correspondence on draft coal directive and meeting of 7 July in Berlin (see No. 58), and to Field-Marshal Montgomery's notes of 6 July (see No. 43). Lists main points to be ensured in any discussions at Potsdam [F.O. 934/6].

iii *12 July 1945 Brief No. 57 for U.K. Delegation on Industrial Disarmament of Germany.* Recommends that, if the subject is raised, British delegation at Potsdam should aim to secure four-power agreement to a provisional programme of certain limited and urgent measures of economic disarmament to be imposed in the four zones [F.O. 934/6].

[1] No. 125.
[2] The reference was probably to No. 116 and to the following briefs, not printed: (a) brief No. 23, on French representation on the Reparation Commission, concluding that His Majesty's Government had made considerable efforts to secure French representation and that no further initiative should be taken for the present: should the U.S. delegation at Potsdam raise the question the British delegation would support them; (b) brief No. 24 on the Moscow Reparation Commission and the Control Council in Germany.

No. 115

Brief for the United Kingdom Delegation to the Conference at Potsdam
No. 43 [N 8810/6/55]

FOREIGN OFFICE, *July 1945*[1]

Poland's Western Frontiers

The Position of the Three Major Allies

At the Moscow Conference in October, 1944, His Majesty's Government discussed with the Soviet Government the draft of a statement of the views of the two Governments concerning a general settlement of the Polish question.[2] This draft was never accepted by the Polish Government but it indicates the extent to which His Majesty's Government were at that time prepared to commit themselves in regard to the acquisition by Poland of former German territory. The relevant passage of the draft statement is as follows:

'Upon the unconditional surrender of Germany, the territory of Poland in the West will include the free city of Danzig, the regions of East Prussia west and south of Konigsberg, the administrative district of Oppeln in Silesia, and the lands desired by Poland to the east of the line of the Oder. It is further agreed that possession of these territories shall be guaranteed to Poland by the Soviet and British Governments. It is understood that the Germans in the said regions shall be repatriated to Germany and that all Poles in Germany shall at their wish be repatriated to Poland.'

2. The declaration on Poland issued at the Crimea Conference contained the following passage:

'The three Heads of Government . . .[3] recognise that Poland must receive substantial accessions of territory in the North and West. They feel that the opinion of the new Polish Provisional Government of National Unity should be sought in due course on the extent of these accessions and that the final delimitation of the Western frontier of Poland should thereafter await the Peace Conference.'

The Attitude of the Polish and Soviet Governments

3. After the Crimea Conference evidence continued to accumulate that the Polish Provisional Government in Warsaw were, in fact, continuing to extend their administration over former German territories in East Prussia

---

[1] This undated brief was probably prepared on 12 July 1945. On 11 July Mr. D. Allen had minuted that he proposed to embody a draft telegram to Washington with a few opening historical paragraphs in a memorandum which could be handed to the American delegation at Berlin. Telegram No. 7412 to Washington, approved by Mr. Eden and despatched on 12 July, corresponded closely to paragraphs 8–12 below. For the resultant memorandum of 13 July from H.M. Embassy at Washington to the State Department see *F.R.U.S. Berlin*, vol i, pp. 778–81: also Sir L. Woodward, *op. cit.*, vol. v, pp. 412–3.

[2] *V. op. cit.*, vol. iii, pp. 228 f.

[3] Punctuation as in original, quoting from section VI of the report of the Conference at Yalta: see *B.F.S.P.*, vol. 151, p. 228.

and also in Silesia, Brandenburg and Pomerania up to the line of the Rivers Oder and Western Neisse. It was to be assumed that the transfer of these territories to Polish administration could only take place with the Soviet Government's consent.

4. His Majesty's Embassy at Moscow were instructed to seek elucidation of the attitude of the Soviet Government in the matter. A letter addressed by Monsieur Molotov to Sir A. Clark Kerr on the 2nd April, contained assurances to the effect that the entrusting of the civil administration of former German territory conquered by the Red Army to Polish administration in no way conflicted with the agreement reached between His Majesty's Government and the United States Government and the Soviet Government concerning the occupation of Germany and the control machinery in Germany; and also that the organisation in existing circumstances of Polish administration in Silesia could in no way be connected and certainly not identified with the question of Poland's future frontiers.

5. On 14th May Mr. Roberts, on instructions from the Foreign Office, addressed a further letter to Monsieur Vyshinski, taking note of Monsieur Molotov's assurances but drawing attention to the agreement reached in the European Advisory Commission on the occupation of Germany, which created zones out of 'Germany within her frontiers as they were on the 31st December, 1937', and to the further agreement of control machinery in Germany[4] which laid down that members of the Control Council will jointly exercise supreme authority on matters affecting Germany as a whole. Mr. Roberts stated that in these circumstances His Majesty's Government assumed that local administration in the areas of Germany concerned was being entrusted by the Soviet Authorities to Polish officials simply on grounds of convenience and that such officials were merely the agents of the Soviet Government as the occupying power and in no way responsible to any Polish authority. His Majesty's Government assumed that the authority of the Control Council would extend to the above mentioned areas within the 1937 frontiers of Germany as much as to the British and United States zones or to any other part of the Soviet zone. Mr. Roberts also enquired whether the Soviet Government accepted responsibility for measures enacted by Polish officials in the territories in question and whether the Soviet Government agreed that in view of the Crimea declaration none of the measures enacted by the Polish authorities could be understood as establishing the incorporation of such territory into the Polish State. Finally Mr. Roberts requested information about the position in the free city of Danzig and about the extent of the areas within the 1937 frontiers of Germany in which Polish officials had been entrusted with administrative responsibility.

6. A reply to Mr. Robert's letter was received in a letter from Monsieur Vyshinski dated the 1st June. The following were the chief points in this Russian reply.

---

[4] Cf. No. 76, note 1 (protocol of 12 September 1944), and No. 8, note 3.

(1) In the view of the Soviet Government the supreme authority of the Allies in Germany (i.e. the Control Council) extends over the separate zones of occupation only in respect of questions common to the whole of Germany.

(2) The Polish administration in former German territory is operating under the direction of the Polish Provisional Government and is not responsible to the Soviet Government.

(3) The activities of the Polish authorities in these territories cannot, however, be taken as prejudging the question of the Polish-German frontier which remains for settlement at the Peace Conference.

7. A note has now been received by His Majesty's Embassy in Moscow[5] from the Polish Ambassador in Moscow setting forth in detail the claim of the Polish Provisional Government of National Unity to all territories up to the line of the Oder and Western Neisse including the port of Stettin.[6]

Argument

8. His Majesty's Government have reconsidered this whole question in the light of these communications and of the new situation created by the establishment of the Polish Provisional Government of National Unity. Certain arguments operate in favour of reaching a provisional agreement among the three major Allies in regard to Poland's Western frontier at the forthcoming meeting of Heads of Governments. The Poles and the Russians appear now to have committed themselves to regarding the line of the Oder-Western Neisse as the Western Frontier of Poland and the passage of time will only assist the Poles, with Russian support, in consolidating their hold over all territory to the East of this line. If we allow the permanent settlement of the frontier to be postponed, indefinitely, only putting our views on record for the present, the difficulties of settlement at a later date will be aggravated; and meanwhile we shall be permitting the Soviet Government to flout the authority of the Allied Council Control over Germany, and hence to establish a precedent for creating all manner of difficulties at a later date.

9. On the other hand, there are serious objections to accepting the Oder-Neisse line here and now as the frontier between Poland and Germany. So precipitate a concession of the maximum Russian claims might be regarded as a sign of weakness and provoke other excessive demands elsewhere. We have always doubted whether British public opinion would lastingly support a settlement involving the amputation of about one-fifth of the total area of Germany normally inhabited by over ten million persons of undisputably German stock, and such a settlement might prove a formidable obstacle to

---

[5] Moscow telegram No. 3081 of 11 July 1945 had reported receipt of this undated memorandum, transmitted to the Foreign Office in Moscow despatch No. 477 of even date (received on 20 July): printed in *F.R.U.S. Berlin*, vol. i, pp. 757–77.

[6] Mr. Warner minuted on Moscow telegram No. 3081: 'It is interesting that the Polish memo. includes a claim to Stettin which we have understood the Russians to have claimed for themselves. C. F. A. W. 12/7.'

the maintenance of European peace. Moreover, the immediate transfer of these territories to Poland would withdraw them from the authority of the Allied Control Council in Germany, and also from the fields of German reparation and supply and from the total area from which the British and United States authorities might hope to obtain food supplies for the feeding of Western Germany, thus giving a proportionat[e] advantage to Russia and Poland in excess of their fair share. In this connexion it is noteworthy that at the Tripartite Military Meeting to discuss the military government of Berlin held at Marshal Zhukov's Headquarters on the 7th July, Marshal Zhukov stated, when the question of food supplies was under discussion, that territory East of the Oder and the Neisse was under Polish control and not in his zone, and again, in regard to fuel supplies, that Silesia was not available to him as the Eastern Frontier of his zone was the Oder and the Neisse 'as agreed at the Crimea Conference' (*sic*).[7]

10. In these circumstandes [*sic*] the assurance in M. Vyshinsky's letter summarised in paragraph 6 above, to the effect that the presence of Polish administration does not prejudice the fate of German territory, which is for discussion at the Peace Conference, is of little practical value. That assurance is in any case rendered nugatory by the preceding passages in M. Vyshinsky's letter, the effect of which is to place the territories in question completely in the hands of the Polish authorities without supervision by, or responsibility to the Soviet Government, and without the agreement of any other of the Allied Governments represented on the Control Council for Germany. While we can agree that there are certain matters in each zone in Germany in which the Allied authority in that zone may act independently, we can neither accept the claim made in M. Vyshinsky's letter that the supreme authority of the Allies in Germany extends over the separate zones only in respect of questions common to the whole of Germany, nor admit the right of the Soviet Government to place a part of their zone outside the authority not only of the Control Council, but also of the Soviet Commander in-Chief in that zone. The Soviet Government would indeed certainly object were His Majesty's Government and the United States Government to hand over the Ruhr or the Rhineland to the French on similar conditions.

11. H.M.G. therefore consider that, if the United States Government agree, we should make it plain at 'Terminal' that we cannot acquiesce in the Soviet Government's interpretation of the situation. For the reasons stated in para. 8 above, however, we should not be content with merely going on record as withholding our consent to the present situation. It is therefore proposed that we indicate our willingness:

(i) to reach an understanding with the Soviet Government on a reasonable Western Frontier for Poland (which will necessarily be well short of her present claims and should in the view of H.M.G. not exceed the free city of Danzig, East Prussia south and west of Koenigsberg, Oppeln Silesia and the most eastern portion of Pomerania), and;

7 Cf. No. 58.i.

(ii) to agree, subject to the necessary concurrence of the French Provisional Government, to the transfer of the Polish territories to the east of such a frontier to permanent Polish administration, subject to ratification when the final peace settlement on this question is made.

12. It is further proposed that if we fail to reach agreement with the Soviet Government on an acceptable compromise on these lines, we should indicate:

(i) that we shall be willing to give our formal consent to the transfer to the administration of the Polish Provisional Government of National Unity only of such German territories as all four controlling Powers are prepared to allow Poland to acquire permanently;

(ii) that, if the Soviet Government insist nevertheless upon handing over parts of Germany to Poland without our consent, thus reducing the capacity of Germany as a whole to pay reparations, we shall be obliged to insist upon the proportionate reduction in Russia's share of reparations from Germany. H.M.G. would if necessary, be prepared to inform the Soviet Government that we shall not allow them any reparations deliveries from the American and British zones in Germany, unless these issues are settled to our satisfaction.

CALENDAR TO No. 115

i *13 July 1945 Lord Halifax (Washington) Tel. No. 4908.* When memo. of 13 July (cf. note 1) was communicated to Mr. Durbrow, Chief of the Division of East European Affairs of the State Department, he said State Department agreed with conclusions in paragraph 4 (see paragraph 11 above) but had not considered points raised in paragraph 5 (see paragraph 12 above). 'His own feeling was that your suggestions were eminently sound and he considered that the United States delegation should have no difficulty in giving you their full support' [N 8588/6/55].

No. 116

Brief for the United Kingdom Delegation to the Conference at Potsdam
No. 40 [F.O. 934/6]

FOREIGN OFFICE, *12 July 1945*
Statement of Principles on Reparation

The United Kingdom Delegation to the Moscow Reparation Commission reported on 16th [11th] July (Victim 58)[1] that it was of cardinal importance to Mr. Pauley that the Statement of Principles (on Raparation [*sic*]) prepared by the Moscow Commission should be approved by the Heads of Governments at Berlin. We ourselves would prefer the statement to be settled in the Moscow Commission, but we cannot prevent the Americans from raising it at Terminal.[2]

[1] Not printed: see below.
[2] In this connexion Mr. Eden minuted: 'No harm in discussing if time can be found. A. E. July 18.'

2. The Statement of Principles as contained in Victim 46 from Moscow (copy attached)[3] was approved by all three Delegates in Moscow on 6th July *ad referendum*.

3. Subsequently the Russians maintained that in the Text which they had agreed paragraph 4 referred to 'the Governments (in the plural) concerned' and not to 'the Government concerned'. They said that they could not agree to a form of words that would enable a zone Commander to suspend reparation deliveries from his zone except as a result of a decision by the Control Council.

4. We have approved the Statement of Principles and have authorised the Solicitor General to agree to its publication. In communicating our approval to Moscow (Victim 41[1] of 9th July) the following points were made:

(*a*) We admit the logic of the Russian contention in paragraph 3 above. We recognize that paragraph 4 of the Statement of Principles contains general principles to be observed in drawing up the reparations plan which is necessarily a matter for agreement between the three, and later four, Governments. The opinion of any one Government or Commander-in-Chief is not relevant at this stage. We would prefer to omit the words 'in the opinion of the Government(s) concerned' altogether, but if matters have advanced too far to permit of this, we would accept 'Governments' (in the plural). This does not mean that we do not attach the greatest importance to protecting the position of our Commander-in-Chief in the application of the plan, but this is a question of execution, not of principle. The Delegation have accordingly been instructed to make it clear that in drawing up the plan it will be necessary to provide machinery whereby the Commander-in-Chief of any zone may be able to secure the suspension of the Reparation Plan, pending reference to the Control Council, in any case where he is of the opinion that its execution would be prejudicial to his task.

(*b*) It had been suggested that paragraph 7 of the Statement of Principles by omitting any reference to a minimum standard of living for Germany would, in view of the known Russian intention of making the fullest possible use of German capital equipment, automatically commit us to extensive deindustrialisation of Germany to the point of provoking starvation and chaos in Germany and so adding immeasurably to the burden of control. The Delegation have accordingly been instructed to make it clear that we do not regard this paragraph of the Statement as committing us to any particular formula for deindustrialisation. The latter is a question of high policy which will depend on agreements still to be reached on the extent of the destruction of German industries and on once-for-all-deliveries, and also on specific decisions of the Control Council. At present we are merely concerned to see that justice is done to our Allies and in particular that Germany's economy does not rise to a higher level than that of our Allies by reason of Germany retaining resources which might otherwise be used to assist them.

[3] Annex below.

5. It is therefore recommended that, if the Americans put forward the Statement of Principles in that [the] form at Annex A,[3] we should accept it, but should put on record a statement in the sense of the passage marked 'X' in paragraph 4(*b*) above.[4]

ANNEX TO NO. 116

Sir A. Clark Kerr (Moscow) to Mr. Eden (Received 7 July, 2.45 p.m.)
No. 46 Victim Telegraphic

Immediate   MOSCOW, *7 July 1945, 12 a.m. G.M.T.*

Repeated to Washington, Paris, Sir W. Strang, 21st Army Group.

From United Kingdom Delegation Moscow.

Following is text referred to in my immediately preceding telegram.[5]

1. Removals of property for reparations shall be primarily such as to assist in bringing to an end the war-making power of Germany by eliminating that part of Germany's industrial capacity which constitutes war potential.

2. Reparations shall be such as will speed recovery and reconstruction in countries devastated at German hands.

3. For the purposes of making a reparations plan Germany will be treated as a single economic unit.

4. Any plan of reparations shall be avoided which necessitates external financial assistance either to enable reparations deliveries to be made or to facilitate economic reconstruction required for reparation purposes, or which might, in the opinion of the Government concerned, prejudice the successful execution of the task entrusted to the armies of occupation.

5. To (. . . ? a maximum)[6] extent, reparations shall be taken from the existing national wealth of Germany. While, for convenience, claims may be stated in terms of money, it is necessary to bear in mind that, in contrast to the reparations after World War No. 1 which were assessed and exacted in money, this time reparations will be assessed and exacted in kind in the form of things such as plants, machines, equipment, stocks, foreign investments, etc.

6. In order to avoid building up German industrial capacity and disturbing the long term stability of the economies of the United Nations, long run payment of reparations in the form of manufactured products shall be restricted to a minimum.

7. In justice to the countries occupied by the enemy, reparations shall be calculated on the basis that the average living standards in Germany, during the reparations period, shall not exceed the average of the standards of living of European countries. (Note: 'European countries' means all countries of Europe excluding the United Kingdom and the U.S.S.R.).

8. After payment of reparations enough resources must be left to enable the German people to subsist without external assistance. In working out the economic

[4] i.e. the third sentence, beginning 'The latter', in paragraph 4(*b*).

[5] Not printed. This telegram of even date had reported that the statement of principles here following had been approved *ad referendum* on 6 July 1945 by the three delegates on the Allied Commission on Reparations in Moscow: 'Words about first charge on current deliveries to pay for approved imports were carried after a strenuous battle.'

[6] The wording in this uncertain text was correct: cf. the text printed, with minor verbal variation, in *F.R.U.S. Berlin*, vol. i, p. 528.

225

balance of Germany the necessary means must be provided for payment for imports approved by the governments concerned before reparation deliveries are made from current production or from stocks of goods.

Foreign Office please repeat to Washington, Paris and Sir W. Strang, 21st Army Group as my telegram No. 34 Victim.

No. 117

Letter from Sir W. Monckton (Moscow) to Sir J. Anderson[1]
No. RCM(45)C48 [F.O. 934/1/4(2)]

Copy   MOSCOW, *12 July 1945*

My dear Chancellor of the Exchequer,

I have read with much interest the Minutes[2] of the meeting of the Ministerial Committee on Reparations held on the 9th July. First of all, I should like to thank you most warmly for the very speedy and helpful replies which you and your colleagues have been sending to our telegrams. This has been all the more valuable since the trouble with the Russians about aeroplanes has made the bag service so ineffective up to the present.

The particular point on which I feel I can usefully write to you at the moment is that of de-industrialisation. I will try to set out what is happening at this end so that you may give the Delegation here further guidance by telegram if you think it is necessary.

When we first arrived, Maisky told us in conversation that the Russians think that the German metallurgical industry should be reduced by 80% and that the German chemical industry should be eliminated 100%. (Probably this was an 'opening bid'.) This, of course, is in addition to the removal of specialised armament factories. He said nothing at the time about shipbuilding, but it appeared at a Committee meeting yesterday that the Russians consider that some part of the German shipbuilding industry should be retained, since otherwise the payment of freight in foreign currencies would involve too heavy a burden on the German balance of payments.

It is clear that there must be some considerable removal of industrial plant and equipment, since Germany's territory has been reduced and her

---

[1] The date of receipt is uncertain.
[2] No. 50.i.

working population will be reduced still more in war casualties, the departure of foreign workers and reparation labour. A great deal of the existing plant and equipment (or at any rate of what existed before we destroyed it by air attacks) was installed since 1933 and represents the building up of war potential. Everyone would agree that all or a great part of this additional plant and equipment is available for removal. Thus, of course, the question is not whether industrial plant and equipment should be removed, but to what degree this process should be carried out.

The Russians have shown no desire to reduce the German standard of living out of motives of revenge. Their motives in proposing de-industrialisation on so drastic a scale are:

(*a*) that all the plant and equipment of this kind is in some degree war potential and

(*b*) that they themselves want to obtain plant and equipment up to the amount provided for in the Russian Reparation Plan.[3]

They are, of course, making a post-war economic plan and wish to include these reparation deliveries as part of their Plan. They therefore argue that all plant and equipment in these metallurgical and chemical and co-ordinate industries should be available for reparation deliveries, except what is needed to enable Germany to maintain the approved standard of living, either by producing in Germany for Germany's own consumption, or by producing sufficient exports to pay for the necessary imports. (The scale of imports has not yet been discussed in detail, but the Russians have mentioned that they contemplate imports to the value of about $1\frac{1}{2}$ billion marks.)

Owing to the unexplained delay in the production of the Russian Reparation Plan, our Delegation has not, until recently, had to take up any position. Now, however, the expert Committee on Once-and-for-all deliveries has begun to meet, the Russian experts express their own ideas as to the amount of plant and equipment to be removed in each industry and invite the views of the American and British experts.

The Russian method of approach appears to us to be in itself logical and reasonable. As regards economic security, we have said that a good deal of the thinking in London has been on the lines of a draconian attack on selective industries rather than on any all-round de-industrialisation. But the general proposition that all industry of this kind constitutes to some

---

[3] Sir A. Clark Kerr had reported in Moscow telegram No. 6 Victim of 23 June 1945 that at the first formal meeting of the Reparation Commission on 21 June M. Maisky had submitted the Russian reparation plan, which followed 'closely Russian plan put forward at Crimean Conference [cf. Sir L. Woodward, *op. cit.*, vol. v, p. 280] except that a division of the total of 20 billion dollars as between once-for-all and current deliveries was left open for discussion and its proposed discussion should begin with once-for-all deliveries since decisions on this subject will affect extent of current deliveries and also amount and type of reparation labour available. Maisky said that Russian proposal would be open to criticism and discussion with a view to reaching agreed conclusions. He promised to supply detailed calculations and data on which the total of 20 billion dollars is based. Mr. Pauley and I [Sir W. Monckton] agreed to take the Russian plan as basis for discussion.'

degree war potential is one which it is not easy to dismiss. Still less can we raise any objection to the Russian view that their need for industrial plant and equipment is so great that we ought to make available for reparation deliveries all the plant and equipment which is surplus to what is required to maintain the approved standard of living in Germany. The Russians are confident that they can make good use of everything for which they are asking and if we were to express doubts whether other countries could really make use of plant and equipment on so large a scale, the Russians will, of course, merely ask for their share to be increased.

Thus, if we proceed industry by industry to discuss what plant and equipment is available for removal and deal with the matter on an expert and objective basis, we shall inevitably be led to recognise the justification for a high degree of de-industrialisation. Our experts are, of course, careful to express their views in a tentative way, but once it appears that at the technical expert level we raise no serious objection to the Russian proposals it will become very difficult indeed for H.M.G. to object to them as a matter of high policy. We cannot successfully argue that a high degree of de-industrialisation will cause a great deal of permanent unemployment for all the experts think that Germany will be very short of labour and the first call on German manpower will necessarily be the agricultural production to supply food for Germans to live on. We can, of course, argue and will not fail to do so, that de-industrialisation will cause a vast amount of dislocation and of, at any rate, temporary frictional unemployment. We can also argue that these expert calculations must contain a very wide margin of error and that if our proposals are too drastic, commonsense indicates that the result may well be economic chaos and political trouble. The Russians, however, are deliberately taking a short view. They urgently want plant and equipment to improve their own standards of living. They know that it can be removed and they are not concerning themselves over-much with what is going to happen to Germany in the years to come.

My own feeling is that we must at all costs avoid giving the impression that we have come here in order to see that Russia obtains a small rather than a large amount of once-and-for-all deliveries. I think therefore that we shall have to discuss the various industries on the lines on which they are being discussed by the Russians. We shall always try to moderate their proposals when it seems to us necessary, but we shall end up by the experts contemplating the removal of plant and equipment from these industries on a very large scale indeed. We shall not then at any later stage or at any higher level be able to reduce the degree of de-industrialisation much below what emerges as the degree justified by these expert discussions. It may be that this will lead to troubles for our Army of Occupation in future, but at best any solution of the reparation problem must be a choice of evils and I think we shall have to face these future difficulties, if and when we come to them.

If you and your colleagues dissent from these views, no doubt you will send a telegram direct to the Delegation during my absence in Berlin.

[Yours sincerely,][4]

WALTER MONCKTON

CALENDAR TO NO. 117

i *14 July 1945   Note by Mr. Mark Turner (Moscow) of an informal conversation between members of the Allied Reparation Commission (GEN 72/14 of 17 July).* Explanation by M. M. Z. Saburov of Soviet views [UE 3096/624/77].

[4] Supplied from another copy (UE 3113/624/77) as circulated with No. 313 to the Ministerial Committee on Reparations on 20 July.

No. 118

Conclusions of a Meeting of the Cabinet held at 10 Downing Street, S.W.1., on Thursday, 12 July 1945, at 3 p.m.[1]

C.M.(45) *14th Conclusions* [U 5472/5397/70]

Disposal of the German and Italian fleets

(Previous Reference: W.M.(44) 40th Conclusions, Minute 3[2])[2]

1. The Cabinet had before them Memoranda by the First Lord of the Admiralty (C.P.(45) 67 and 74)[3] on the disposal of the German and the Italian Fleets.

THE FIRST LORD OF THE ADMIRALTY proposed that, so far as concerned the German fleet, we should strongly support the American view that there should be a wholesale scrapping of combat units with the exception of vessels which were required for experimental or immediate operational purposes or were capable of being converted to civilian use. If, however, the Russians refused to accept this proposal, we should suggest a division of the German fleet on the lines indicated in paragraph 11 of C.P.(45)67, the main effect of which was to give the Russians the minimum number of U-boats. Dominion Governments were not likely to raise any objection, provided that the policy was explained to them in advance; and, although the proposals might lead to some disappointment among our minor Allies, they had not any real grounds of complaint in view of the generous treatment which they had received from us during the war. The proposals in C.P.(45)

[1] Members of the Cabinet present for items 1 and 3 were: Mr. Eden (in the Chair); Sir J. Anderson; Viscount Cranborne; Colonel O. Stanley; Mr. H. Macmillan, Secretary of State for Air; Mr. O. Lyttelton; Mr. L. S. Amery; Mr. Brendan Bracken; Lord Rosebery, Secretary of State for Scotland; Mr. R. S. Hudson, Minister of Agriculture and Fisheries. Also present were Sir A. Cadogan, Marshal of the Royal Air Force Sir C. Portal, Admiral of the Fleet Sir A. Cunningham, Field-Marshal Sir A. Brooke, and Mr. M. S. McCorquodale, Parliamentary Secretary, Ministry of Labour and National Service.

[2] This record of 27 March 1944 is not printed.

[3] Nos. 10.i and 99.i respectively.

67 had been informally communicated to Admiral King,[4] who had indicated that in principle he fully agreed with them.

With regard to the Italian fleet, it had been agreed at Teheran that the Russian share should be one battleship, one cruiser, eight destroyers and four submarines.[5] Subsequently, in view of the objection to the immediate transfer of Italian ships to Russia, it was agreed to lend to the Soviet Navy a United States cruiser, the British battleship 'Royal Sovereign', eight old 'Town' class destroyers and four submarines. We ourselves had originally claimed two 'Littorio' class battleships, while France, Greece and Yugoslavia had also put forward claims for a share of the Italian fleet. The problem was to find a settlement which, without estranging Italy, would meet inescapable Allied claims and reduce the Italian Navy to a size acceptable to her neighbours. With this object it was proposed that the original Russian claim to one Cavour battleship, one six-inch cruiser, eight destroyers and four submarines should be met in full. In addition, Greece should receive two six-inch cruisers and one further damaged six-inch cruiser for cannibalisation. There should be no transfer of Italian ships to France, whose claims should be met by the allocation of German ships; and Yugoslavia should at most receive one or two torpedo boats. Although we did not require either of the two 'Littorio' class battleships, we should claim both (or one, if the United States desired to claim the other) and should appropriate these ships at the Peace settlement unless ultimately it was considered necessary to be more lenient with regard to the Italian fleet, in which case the two 'Littorios' might be left in Italian hands instead of the two old 'Cavour' class ships which would otherwise compose the Italian battleship force.

In discussion it was suggested that if there was no practical advantage in recovering the ships which we had lent to Russia it might be expedient, subject to agreement with the Americans, to propose to the Russians in the first instance that they should retain the ships which had been lent to them in respect of their original claim to ships from the Italian fleet. If the Russians accepted this proposal, we should be in a position to treat Italy more leniently should this seem desirable, e.g. by increasing the number of destroyers to be retained by her. If, on the other hand, the Russians insisted on securing their share of the Italian ships, they should be only allowed to retain the British ships in return for some financial consideration or some other countervailing advantage, e.g. in the negotiations over the German Fleet.

The Cabinet:
(1) Invited the First Lord of the Admiralty to consider whether the proposals in paragraphs 7 (*a*) and 11 of C.P.(45) 74 should be amended in the light of the suggestion made in the discussion.

[4] Admiral E. J. King was Commander-in-Chief of the U.S. Fleet.
[5] For discussion on the disposal of the Italian fleet at the Conference of Tehran cf. W. S. Churchill, *op. cit.*, vol. v, pp. 347–8, and Sir L. Woodward, *op. cit.*, vol. ii, pp. 604–5.

(2) Subject to the preceding conclusion, agreed that the proposals in C.P.(45) 67 and 74 should be adopted as a basis for any negotiations at the Three Power Meeting with regard to the disposal of the German and Italian fleets . . .[6]

Italy: Peace Treaty

(Previous Reference: W.M.(45) 35th Conclusions, Minute 2)[7]

3.[6] The Cabinet had before them a Memorandum (C.P.(45) 64)[8] by the Secretary of State for Foreign Affairs to which were appended proposals for the political clauses of a possible Peace Treaty with Italy. This draft had been prepared with a view to its communication first to the Dominions, and then to the United States Government, who had for some time been anxious to terminate the Armistice régime in Italy.

THE FOREIGN SECRETARY said that at the Three Power Meeting there would be discussions about Italy, both with the United States and with the Soviet delegations. He hoped that the Cabinet would be ready to endorse the broad lines proposed in C.P.(45) 64 as a basis for those discussions; and, in addition, to agree upon the following outline of our general policy towards Italy:

(*a*) We should aim at building up Italy into a useful member of the European comity of nations, and should lead her to look to the west rather than to the east. To this end she should be encouraged to provide herself with a government elected on western democratic principles.

(*b*) Such a policy being as much in the interests of the United States as of the United Kingdom, we should do all we could to encourage continuing American interest in Italy. We should not mind their taking the lead, more particularly in economic matters, in which we were less well placed to make a contribution.

(*c*) To give effect to this policy we would have to help Italy politically and economically, and might have to undertake some additional obligations in regard to personnel or supplies.

To implement such a policy the following steps would be desirable:

(i) The conclusion of an early Peace Treaty.

(ii) The encouragement of early elections for the Constituent Assembly, though that might not be possible before next spring.

(iii) A decision as regards the number of Allied troops to be retained in Italy. From the political point of view the Foreign Office would see advantage in retaining Allied troops in Italy, at any rate until after the elections, and thought it desirable to keep there United States troops as well as British.

(iv) The Italian Government should be enabled to maintain armed forces adequate to preserve internal security and defence against local

---

[6] Relevant numbered conclusions of this meeting were entered in Foreign Office files as separate extracts. Conclusion 3 is supplied from a copy on U 5518/50/70.

[7] This record of 22 March 1945 is not printed.

[8] See No. 31, note 1.

aggression. We should be ready to assist with material and the training of personnel and, in particular, should aim at the establishment for a limited period of a Military Mission—preferably Anglo-American—to help to train the Italian Army.

(v) A Police Mission should be considered. It was of great importance to get the Italian Police reorganised. It might not be easy for us to find the personnel, and there would be some political disadvantages in a British Mission. Perhaps we might therefore encourage the United States to take the lead in this matter.

(vi) We should step up our propaganda in Italy so as to convince the Italians of the advantages of a western democratic way of life. That might mean the provision of more staff for the Ministry of Information.

(vii) The sooner arrangements could be made for the repatriation of Italian prisoners of war the better.

(viii) U.N.R.R.A. should be encouraged to take over supply responsibilities for Italy as soon as practicable from the Allied Commission; and, if SACMED concurred, the remaining economic functions of the Commission should then be transferred to some other form of Anglo-American advisory machinery.

(ix) Italy would continue to need much assistance over supplies, particularly coal. It was in our interest and that of the United States to make every effort to prevent a breakdown. It would be desirable to clear this point at the Three Power Meeting.

(x) Our general policy should be gradually to reduce the other activities of the Allied Commission over as wide a field as possible.

After discussion the Cabinet:-

(1) Gave general approval, subject to conclusions (3) and (4) below, to the proposals in C.P.(45) 64 and to the statement of policy outlined by the Foreign Secretary.

(2) Took note that the Secretary of State for the Colonies would communicate with the Foreign Secretary on one or two technical points on the draft Treaty annexed to C.P.(45) 64.

Return of Italian Prisoners of War

A discussion followed as regards the repatriation of Italian prisoners of war.

THE MINISTER OF AGRICULTURE AND FISHERIES said that he was most anxious to retain 30,000 prisoners for work in the U.K. on a wage-earning basis, but for legal reasons arrangements would have to be made which would allow them to retain the technical standing of prisoners of war. If the Cabinet approved his proposal in principle, detailed arrangements could be worked out at the official level.

Attention was drawn to the possible political objections to retaining Italian prisoners of war on a wage-earning basis if this should coincide with unemployment in this country. It was pointed out, on the other hand, that there was unlikely to be unemployment in agriculture; and no difficulty should arise so long as we honoured the guarantees given to the Trade

Unions that prisoners of war would not be employed where British labour was available.

THE SECRETARY OF STATE FOR INDIA said that the Government of India were employing 5,350 Italian officers and men on ship repairs, and were obtaining 2,750 skilled and some hundreds of unskilled workers from East Africa and the Middle East. They would certainly want provision made in the Treaty to cover the retention of these men. It was suggested that the need for ensuring that Italians should retain the status of prisoners of war would not arise in India, where they could be treated as collaborators, enlisted by their own Government and disciplined by their own officers.

After discussion the Cabinet:–

(3) Agreed that it was desirable to retain some 30,000 Italian prisoners of war on a wage-earning basis in agriculture in this country, and invited the Minister of Agriculture and Fisheries to arrange for the Departments concerned to consider how these prisoners could be retained with the technical status of prisoners of war.

(4) Invited the Secretary of State for India to consult the Government of India on the arrangements to be made for retaining essential Italian prisoner of war labour in India.

Consultation with Dominion Governments

THE DOMINIONS SECRETARY suggested that he should immediately communicate to Dominion Governments the text of the draft Peace Treaty appended to C.P.(45)64;[8] inform them that the matter was likely to be raised at the Three Power Meeting; that we would avoid entering into detail, or taking any final decisions without further consultation with them, and ask for their immediate comment.

The Union of South Africa had asked[9] that formal provision should be made for the Three Powers to consult South Africa before any final decision was taken as to the allocation of the Italian Colonies. This raised a difficult point of general procedure which would require further study. He suggested ['X'], however, that if matters went faster at the forthcoming Conference than was expected, we might meet the point by putting it on record that we would consult South Africa, on behalf of the Three Powers, as to the allocation of these territories.

The Cabinet:–

(5) Agreed that the Secretary of State for Dominion Affairs should consult Dominion Governments as proposed, and endorsed his suggestion at 'X' above regarding the point raised by the Union of South Africa. . . .[6]

[9] In a letter of 9 July 1945 (received 11 July: U 5402/50/70) from the South African High Commissioner in London, Mr. G. Heaton Nicholls, to Mr. P. V. Emrys-Evans, Parliamentary Under-Secretary of State for Dominion Affairs. This letter concluded: 'As we have a considerable stake in Africa and in view of our contribution towards the defeat of Italy, we desire that formal provision should be made under which the four Powers concerned would consult with the Government of the Union of South Africa before any decision is reached regarding the future status and disposal of the Italian territories in Africa.'

233

No. 119

Brief for the United Kingdom Delegation to the Conference at Potsdam
Unnumbered [U5419/445/70]

FOREIGN OFFICE, *12 July 1945*

Franco-British Treaty and Policy in Western Europe[1]

1. The idea of a 'Western Group' has been suggested in connexion with a 'regional association of Western Europe', within the framework of the World Organisation, (Chapter VIII of the Charter). A bilateral Franco-British Treaty of Alliance would provide the foundation and the small Allied countries of North-Western Europe would be attached in some way to the Franco-British Treaty, whether by a multilateral treaty or by arrangements made separately by the small countries with the United Kingdom and France. The question of admitting to such a system neutrals like Portugal or Sweden would be left to the future.

2. No decision has been taken by His Majesty's Government. The Prime Minister has expressed misgivings about the burdens which a Western association would impose on the United Kingdom, but has said that the matter should be discussed in Cabinet at the proper time.

3. Public opinion in the United Kingdom and France appears generally in favour of a Franco-British Treaty, and also of a wider European association, although opinion in neither country would accept the leadership being vested exclusively in the other. The present Ministers for Foreign Affairs of Belgium, the Netherlands and Norway are closely in favour of a 'Western Group' under British leadership, although there might be some opposition in their countries (particularly from Communists). It is not clear how they

---

[1] This document and annex 1 below were submitted to Sir A. Cadogan under the following minute: 'I attach a brief on the question of a Franco-British Treaty of Alliance and the formation of a Western Group which has been prepared as a result of a departmental meeting. The question is not on the agenda of the Conference, and I think the brief should only be held in reserve in case the subject comes up of its own. In view of the Prime Minister's attitude it is not proposed to circulate the brief throughout the delegation, but Mr. Ward will have copies with him in case they are required. O. C. Harvey. July 12th, 1945.'

would look upon a 'Western Group' in which the leadership was shared between the United Kingdom and France. But it is clear that a Western Group without the United Kingdom would have no attraction for them.

4. The Charter of the World Organisation is favourable to regional associations, and its signature definitely facilitates any scheme upon which we may finally decide, subject to care being taken to reconcile the wording with the Charter.

5. The final attitude of the Soviet Union cannot be predicted, but both Stalin and Molotov have in the past appeared to see no objection in principle to a western association provided it were clearly directed against Germany. The American attitude would be coloured by the Soviet reaction, but if the 'Western Group' were closely integrated with the Charter of the World Organisation, they would not be able to object. Both the Soviet Union and the United States of America are in any case actively building up their own 'regional associations' and they are not in a logical position to contest our doing the same.

6. No progress can be made towards the constitution of a 'Western Group' until a Franco-British Treaty has been concluded.

7. There is no item on the British and American agendas for Terminal which would directly raise the question of the 'Western Group'. However, it is possible that the matter might arise in the course of discussion about the future of Europe generally, or in connexion with the Soviet policy of going ahead with the conclusion of treaties of alliance with the small Slav countries of Eastern and Southern Europe. If the question did come up, it is suggested that we might explain frankly our interest in improving the organisation of security in Western Europe to guard against the renewal of German aggression. We could draw upon the lessons of this war, where the Continental countries were destroyed 'one by one', and point to the provisions of the new Charter, which give us both authority and encouragement to go ahead with our scheme.

ANNEX 1 TO No. 119

Brief for United Kingdom Delegation at Terminal
The 'Western Group' and Franco-British Treaty
I. Past History

In June 1944, in preparation for the Dumbarton Oaks Conference,[2] the Foreign Office began to give serious consideration to the possibilities of some regional grouping in Western Europe for security purposes and a paper was brought before the Chiefs of Staff. It was suggested that it would be for many reasons in the interest of the United Kingdom to begin to work towards the creation of some regional security system covering Western Europe, as part of the machinery necessary to

[2] From 21 August to 7 October 1944 conversations between British, American, Soviet and Chinese officials had been held at Dumbarton Oaks, Washington. The resultant Statement of Tentative Proposals for the establishment of a General International Organisation is printed in Cmd. 6560 of 1944.

make effective a general system of European security under a World Organisation. Such a regional system of this character would also be a reinsurance against the possible failure of the World Organisation. The arguments in favour of the scheme are listed in the extract from the Foreign Office paper at *Annex A*.

2. The interim reply of the Chiefs of Staff was extremely favourable (*Annex B.*), but the Foreign Office made all reserves about the suggestion that Germany might have to be included in the system.[3]

3. Meanwhile, various hints and suggestions for perpetuating the war-time association between their countries and the United Kingdom had been received from the Belgian, Dutch and Norwegian Foreign Ministers. In July 1944, the Secretary of State saw the three Ministers separately and told them that the fact that their approaches had so far gone unanswered did not mean that H.M.G. were uninterested. But in the existin[g] state of international relations they had felt it better to[4] enter into discussions about collaboration in any one part of Europe, and in particular they felt it would be advisable to postpone discussions until after the Dumbarton Oaks Conference on the World Organisation. (A copy of the recording despatch is at *Annex C*).[5] The Secretary of State also spoke on the same lines to Monsieur Viénot, then French Representative in London, and later to Monsieur Massigli when he came to London as French Foreign Minister towards the end of August. Monsieur Massigli, however, turned the discussion away to his own set idea that Western security should be guaranteed by definite political and military arrangements in the Rhine area ('Rheno-Westphalia') to hold down Germany.

4. At the Dumbarton Oaks conference the United Kingdom Delegation secured the insertion of satisfactory provisions authorising 'regional associations' within the World Organisation (these have since been expanded in the Charter see paragraph 17 below). Sir Alexander Cadogan took the occasion to mention to the United States and Soviet Delegations the inclination of His Majesty's Government towards forming a closer association with the Western European countries and no objection was raised.

5. In October [September] 1944 the Secretary of State met a rising interest in the House of Commons by informing the House that he agreed with the need for close collaboration with our neighbours in Western Europe, and that certain informal discussions with them about our future relations would be pursued in due course.[6] A close association with these states would, he suggested, serve as a buttress for the general world structure and as a guarantee of future peace. As a result of this speech the matter was again examined with the Chiefs of Staff, who confirmed their support on military grounds for a scheme covering France, Belgium, Holland, Denmark, Norway and Iceland—with the possible later addition of Sweden, Spain and Portugal.

6. When Monsieur Spaak[7] came to London in November he communicated a paper giving the suggestion of his government for Anglo-Belgian co-operation

[3] This clause (from 'but the Foreign Office') was deleted in another copy of this document on Z 9639/13/17.

[4] On Z 9639/13/17 it was suggested that before this word the word 'not' had been omitted.

[5] Not printed. For this despatch of 19 July 1944, on U 6468/180/70, from Mr. Eden to H.M. Ambassadors to the Belgian, Netherland and Norwegian Governments, cf. Sir L. Woodward, *op. cit.*, vol. v, pp. 191–2.

[6] Cf. *Parl. Debs.*, 5th ser., H. of C., vol. 403, cols. 705–6.

[7] Belgian Minister for Foreign Affairs.

within a Western European regional entente and in harmony with the Dumbarton Oaks proposals. This gave specific proposals for co-operation in the military, political & economic spheres. A translation of this paper is in the print at *Annex D*. The Prime Minister did not agree that the time had come to discuss these matters with our Western Allies, & the talks with Monsieur Spaak were restricted to generalities. They had however the positive result of producing agreement on a concrete scheme for British assistance in the equipment and training of the Belgian forces.

7. By this time a lot had been written about the idea of a 'Western bloc' in the *Times* and other journals, stimulated by Field Marshal Smuts' famous speech[8] in which he advocated such a bloc under British control as an antidote to the relative weakness of the United Kingdom in man-power and resources compared with the U.S.A. and the Soviet Union. The Communist parties in liberated France[9] and Belgium began to attack the 'Western bloc' as anti-Soviet, and the Soviet Embassy in London made various soundings on the subject in connexion with Mr. Spaak's visit to London and displayed considerable suspicion.

8. In order to counter this suspicion the Secretary of State instructed His Majesty's Ambassador at Moscow on the 26th November to explain to M. Molotov the position and the true attitude of His Majesty's Government, recalling the remark which Marshal Stalin had spontaneously made to the Secretary of State in Moscow in December 1941 about the desirability of Great Britain taking the lead in organising Western security. The explanation made it clear that the idea of a Western security group was subordinate in the mind of His Majesty's Government to the establishment of a World Organisation; that they intend to rely upon the Anglo-Soviet Treaty as the primary instrument for preventing the renewal of German aggression; and that any detailed regional defence proposal would be discussed in detail with the Soviet Government. The text of this instruction is at *Annex E*, and Sir A. Clark Kerr's telegram reporting M. Molotov's not un-satisfactory reaction is at *Annex F*.[10]

Immediately before this demarche the Prime Minister had himself mentioned to Marshal Stalin in a personal telegram that he had not yet considered the idea of a 'Western bloc' as discussed in the Press, and that he trusted first of all to the Anglo-Soviet Treaty and close collaboration with the United States to form the mainstays of a World Organisation to ensure peace.

9. Arising out of the message to Stalin, the Prime Minister minuted to the Secretary of State at the end of November that while he thought the 'Western bloc' should be discussed in the Cabinet, he was apprehensive of the proposal in view of the hopeless weakness of the Allied countries and feared that it would lead to an impossible commitment for the United Kingdom to defend these countries, while the French Army was likely to take many years to regain its strength. The Prime Minister thought that the scheme would involve a large British Army on the Continental model; that this would not be acceptable to Parliament; and that, if threatened with renewed aggression in the West, our policy should be to maintain

---

[8] Field-Marshal J. C. Smuts, Prime Minister of South Africa and Minister of External Affairs and Defence, had delivered an address on 'Thoughts on the New World' at a meeting in London of the United Kingdom Branch of the Empire Parliamentary Association on 25 November 1943: cf. text in *The Times* of 3 December 1943, p. 5.

[9] This word was a tentative manuscript insertion to supply a gap in the original typescript.

[10] For the documents in annexes E and F (not printed) cf. Sir L. Woodward, *op. cit.*, vol. v, pp. 196–7.

the defences of our island and rely upon our strength in the air and on the sea. The Secretary of State replied to the Prime Minister in a minute of 29th November (copy at *Annex G*) laying stress upon the advantages of a 'Western group':

    (*a*) to avoid the Western countries being again eaten up 'one by one'

    (*b*) to avoid the Western countries turning to Russia for their salvation;

    (*c*) to provide depth to the defences of the U.K.;

    (*d*) to prevent a European ag[g]ressor again obtaining the use of the man-power of Western Europe for slave labour.

The Secretary of State pointed out that the Western group would clearly have to be pursued within the framework of the proposed World Organisation, as sketched out at Dumbarton Oaks; that France was the key to the situation and that we should wait and see what came of General de Gaulle's visit to Moscow.

10. The Franco-Soviet conversations at Moscow in December did not, however, advance matters, for, rejecting our suggestion for a tripartite Anglo-Franco-Soviet instrument, General de Gaulle concluded with the Soviet Government a purely bilateral Treaty.[11] In his rejoinder of the 31st December to the Secretary of State's minute, the Prime Minister, while maintaining his general view, agreed that the first step towards a 'Western group' now depended upon proposals for a Franco-British Treaty. He felt strongly that it was for the French to take the initiative.

11. Contrary to M. Molotov's suggestion in November (see paragraph 3 of Moscow telegram at *Annex F*)[10] none of these questions came up at the Crimea Conference in February.

II. *Latest Developments of Present Position*

12. The realisation of a 'Western group' still seems to depend upon the prior conclusion of a Franco-British Treaty or equivalent mutual defence arrangements. If this can be achieved it should not now be difficult to fit it within the framework of the Charter for the World Organisation.

13. There is abundant evidence that the idea of a Franco-British Treaty still lends[12] itself very widely to public opinion in both the U.K. and France, despite General de Gaulle's antics[13] and our many troubles with the French. It is noteworthy that recently, in the very midst of the humiliation suffered by France in Syria, the French Consultative Assembly passed a resolution that the French Government 'should increase their efforts towards drawing up a Franco-British Treaty which, with the Franco-Soviet Treaty, would be one of the European foundations for the building of world peace.' Unfortunately, the French Government themselves, although at various moments wobbling on the brink, have never brought themselves to make a straightforward proposal to us for a Treaty. When M. Bidault came to see the Secretary of State at Binderton in February he was consumed with grievance over France's exclusion from the Crimea Conference. M. Bidault, echoing General de Gaulle himself, in a public speech on 5th February said that while the French Government wanted a treaty with H.M.G. they thought it necessary first to reach general agreement about the Levant and Germany.

[11] The text of the Franco-Soviet Treaty of Alliance and Mutual Assistance signed on 10 December 1944 is printed in *B.F.S.P.*, vol. 149, pp. 632–5.

[12] It was suggested on the original that this word should read 'commends'.

[13] Extracts from this and later paragraphs of this document are cited by V. Rothwell, *op. cit.*, pp. 412–3.

14. On the eve of the San Francisco Conference, we received a rather excited proposal from the Quai d'Orsay whereby M. Chauvel[14] would come to London immediately to conclude a short Treaty in general terms, relegating the French 'preliminary' questions to subsidiary exchanges of letters. We welcomed immediate discussion, but doubted whether it was possible or desirable to conclude a formal Treaty in the few days before the Conference began. In the event, the visit never materialised and it seemed that M. Bidault and his officials had outrun General de Gaulle.

15. During the San Francisco Conference M. Bidault, in the Secretary of State's words, 'only muttered vaguely' on the subject of a Treaty. The crisis over the Levant, and the offensive attitude taken by General de Gaulle towards this country, has in any case ruled out any progress. Nevertheless, the French are clearly still hankering after a treaty. For example, the resolution of the French Assembly quoted in paragraph 13 above and M. Bidault's remark to Mr. Duff Cooper on 28th June that he was as anxious as ever for a Franco-British Treaty, which should be followed by a tripartite Treaty with Soviet Russia (M. Bidault even admitted that he had been wrong in rejecting our proposal for a tripartite Agreement at the time of General de Gaulle's visit to Moscow).

16. For our part, we are at least ready with a model draft Treaty, the text of which is at *Annex H*. The Secretary of State saw and liked this draft as a whole, but it has not yet been shown to the Prime Minister or to other Ministers, nor, of course, has it ever been seen by the French. The idea behind this draft was to recognise that a Franco-British Treaty must form the essential basis of a Western Group, since to be of real military value the group would require France and her armed forces, and the French would only participate on terms of equality. In order to marry the bilateral Treaty with the eventual Group we inserted Article 5(ii) in the draft, expressing a joint determination to form a regional association of Western Europe directed against Germany and within the framework of the World Organisation (as a supplement to the bilateral Treaty) and the intention to make joint arrangements. The Secretary of State was doubtful of this article, observing that the Prime Minister's attitude at present would prevent him from putting it forward.

17. Meanwhile the evolution of the new *World Organisation* has been favourable to the conclusion of a Franco-British Treaty and of a Western European Security Group. Chapter VIII of the Charter signed at Francisco deals with 'regional arrangements' and specifically recognises 'regional arrangements or agencies' as instruments for handling 'such matters relating to the maintenance of international peace and security as are appropriate for regional action, provided that such arrangements or agencies and their activities are consistent with the Purposes and Principles of the United Nations'. The text of this Chapter, and other relevant Articles, is contained in *Annex I*.[15] The upshot of these provisions seems to be:

(*a*) As the Chapter now recognises, and indeed welcomes, regional arrangements, it would be entirely consistent with the World Organisation for the U.K. to take the lead in establishing a western regional association, based upon the

---

[14] Secretary-General of the French Ministry of Foreign Affairs.

[15] Not printed. This annex, entitled 'Articles relevant to the question of a Regional Association of Western Europe', comprised the texts of articles 1–2, 43, 51–4, 102–3 and 106–7 of the Charter of the United Nations (Cmd. 7015 of 1946).

Franco-British Alliance, provided (which should not be difficult) that care were taken in the drafting to keep the terms consistent with the 'purposes and principles' of the Charter.

(b) Both a Franco-British Treaty and a wider regional arrangement should be specifically directed against a renewal of German aggression. Direct military action could be taken under these instruments against Germany:–

(i) In the event of Germany making an armed attack;

(ii) For holding down Germany under the 'transitional arrangements', pending the assumption by the World Organisation of responsibility for preventing renewed aggression by the enemy States.

(c) Subsequently, when the Security Council has assumed full responsibility, it would still be possible to use these Western regional arrangements as agencies for keeping the peace, but acting under the directions of the Security Council.

18. Meanwhile, we have made inconspicuous progress in what must nevertheless be a very important part of any eventual 'Western Group', that is to say the rebuilding of the Allied armed forces with British assistance in equipment and training. Comprehensive offers of help covering all three Services have been made to the Belgian, Dutch and Norwegian Governments; we have undertaken to form a small Luxembourg land force; and a comprehensive offer of help to Denmark has been agreed with the Service Departments and is awaiting the Secretary of State's approval. The French are a special case as in time they should again be able to equip their forces from their own industry. However, the War Office are providing obsolescent equipment to help the French in training their Army and, in addition to maintaining eleven existing French air squadrons, we have offered to equip, and train the air crews for, a further ten squadrons. The Belgians have accepted our offer and six brigades are already either complete or in training. The Norwegians have also accepted and technical discussions are beginning. The Dutch seem likely to accept, but have not yet given their minds to the matter. The French seem attracted by our air force proposal and technical discussions with them should shortly begin. These offers have been made on their own merits, as a continuation of the help we have given the Allies during the war, and we have been careful not to connect them with long-range political and strategic policy. However, it is obvious that these schemes, involving a continuing close connexion between our forces and the Allied forces, would facilitate the formation of any 'Western Group'. One of the express objects of the offers made to the small countries is to build up Allied contingents to take part under British command in the occupation of the British zone in Germany, and this would accustom the small Allies to serving under British command in peace as well as in war.

19. The 'Western Group' has also its advocates on purely economic grounds. There would undoubtedly be very great advantages in close economic association between the countries of Western Europe, but the difficulties are formidable, as to make a successful job, it would be necessary to have a customs union, which would present difficulties from the point of view of the Dominions and would be certain to arouse opposition in the U.S.A. However, it is possible that, as suggested by the Belgian Government in their paper at *Annex D*, a start could be made on the economic side by mutual arrangements connected with war industry and a joint coordinated scheme for developing the war potential of the Western countries.

20. Finally, a note may be useful upon the latest indications as to the attitude

which the Soviet and United States Governments are likely to take towards any concrete proposal for the 'Western Group', which may emerge.

21. The *Soviet Government* have never officially objected to the idea and indeed in December 1941 Marshal Stalin encouraged it. Monsieur Molotov reacted quite favourably to the explanation given to him in November 1944. (*Annexes E and F*).[10] No comment was made upon information given about our offers made to re-arm the Belgian, Dutch and Norwegian forces. On the other hand, the 'Western Group' has been assailed in the Communist press in France and Belgium and recently the Moscow press has hotly attacked articles in the *Economist* advocating a regional association of Western Europe on the ground that the proposal was Anti-Soviet and would lead to strife between Eastern and Western Europe. These attacks however, no doubt derive from the belief in Russia that the *Economist* is fundamentally anti-Soviet. Probably the truth is that the Soviet Government are pursuing their usual policy of keeping an open mind so as to be free to determine policy in the light of any specific plan which may eventually emerge, and in this connexion our future policy towards Germany would be a powerful factor. The whole question of the Russian attitude is analysed in a memorandum by His Majesty's Embassy at Moscow at *Flag* (*Annex*) *J*. This was written in November 1944, and its favourable forecast of the Soviet Government's attitude must therefore be qualified to some extent by the recent press denunciation of the *Economist* articles.

22. Meanwhile, the Soviet Government have, without seeking our consent, made Treaties of Alliance with Czechoslovakia, Yugoslavia and Poland, and there is now talk of their making formal alliances with Roumania and Finland. They have thus in fact taken long steps towards creating an 'Eastern Group'; but this would certainly not prevent them from opposing a 'Western Group' if they thought it in their interests to do so.

23. The *United States Government* will probably take a very cautious attitude towards any proposal for a 'Western Group', particularly in their present mood of giving the Soviet Union 'the benefit of the doubt' and considering themselves as 'mediators' between the rival camps in Europe. There would inevitably be in America people who saw in the 'Western Group' the cause of a third world war, by splitting Europe into two hostile camps, and such people would fear that the U.S.A. would again be called in to pull Western Europe's chestnuts out of the fire. Others no doubt would also be apprehensive of the economic implications. However, like the Soviet Union, the U.S.A. are not really in a position to object, since they are at great pains to build up their own regional association in the Western Hemisphere (cf. the recent 'Act of Chapultepec'). Lord Halifax in September 1944 took the view that American opinion 'would not necessarily be opposed' to a 'Western Group' comprising Allied States provided it were brought within the framework of the World Organisation. He pointed out, however, that the United States were very anxious to keep on good terms with Russia and that their attitude would be influenced considerably by the view taken by the Soviet Government.

Reconstruction Department, Foreign Office, S.W. 1, 10th July, 1945

ANNEX 1A TO NO. 119

There are a number of political and economic arguments which favour the establishment of a West European regional system. These can be summarised as follows:–

241

(*a*) It can be argued that the United Kingdom could play a much more effective role in the World Organisation if she were associated with her Western neighbours for purposes of defence, particularly against Germany. Such an association might serve to refute suggestions which have been made in the United States and the Union of Soviet Socialist Republics casting doubt upon the will and capacity of the United Kingdom to play its part adequately and make an effective contribution equal to that of the other two World Powers.

(*b*) Marshal Stalin, late in 1941 expressed himself in favour of Great Britain assuming certain defence obligations in Western Europe, and similar views have been put forward by influential persons in the United States.

(*c*) The Anglo-Soviet Treaty lies at the base of our whole European policy, and we should try to reinforce it by all means in our power. The formation of some Western European security system would, however, reinforce rather than detract from the Anglo-Soviet Treaty, more especially if the Russians, with our approval, constructed some similar security system in Eastern Europe—and they will almost certainly do so whether we approve it or not.

(*d*) This country, if it is to maintain itself after the termination of the war and of Lend-Lease, will have many calls on its limited man-power. A Western European system might serve to ease the manpower situtation.

(*e*) Active French co-operation will be essential for the purposes of restraining Germany, and a strong and friendly France is essential to us. A Western European system would serve to strengthen and consolidate France.

(*f*) The association for security and for political purposes could be buttressed by economic association prepared in such a way as not to be hostile to any wider scheme of economic collaboration.

It is suggested that some of the results which might flow from a Western European regional system would be:–

(*a*) The lay-out and stationing of forces throughout the system to the best general advantage of the constituent nations.

(*b*) The equipment of the national forces of the constituent nations, on a common model.

(*c*) An arrangement of war industries in Western Europe with an eye to reducing their vulnerability to air attack.

(*d*) The joint use and protection of important economic resources, such as shipping, skilled manpower, and so on. The obligations of one member State would not of course extend to the oversea dependencies of another.

The immediate advantages from a military point of view might be added depth to our defence, increased resources, greater flexibility and a common defence plan concerted in advance with the countries of Western Europe. The corresponding disadvantages might be an increased risk of being involved in the defence of Western European countries against continental attack, and of having to maintain and tie up substantial manpower in land forces on a continental scale. These military considerations, which arise primarily in the event of the failure of the World Organisation to achieve success, ought to be assessed, so that we may know whether or not, from a military point of view, our interests would be served by extending our commitments to include France, the Low Countries and Norway, and possibly other seaboard countries. The matter is one of importance, and the Chiefs of Staff are asked to consider it and express their views on the whole proposal.

Comments by the Chiefs of Staff on policy towards Western Europe

Top secret

In a letter dated 22nd June 1944[16] we have been asked by the Foreign Office for our views on the proposal that once agreement on the principle of a World Organisation has been achieved, we should begin to work towards the creation of some regional security system to cover Western Europe, and to include the United Kingdom.

2. Taking a long term view, this proposal raises issues of the greatest importance for the future of this country, upon which we are not yet ready to give our considered views. Though in the immediate future our security will depend upon preventing the resurgence of Germany, in the long run the most important factor will be our relationship with Russia. It may be that a successful world organisation will emerge, which will be capable of resolving disputes between the major Powers. Should this not be so, we shall sooner or later be faced with a clash of interests between ourselves and Russia, and in that event the attitude and power of Germany becomes of vital importance.

3. We are setting on foot a further examination of our long term military position, which will have a considerable bearing upon the action which should be taken towards Germany when defeated. In the meantime, from the military point of view, we see great advantage in adopting the proposal put forward by the Foreign Office, which would at any rate be a start in the[17] building up of a strong association of nations in Western Europe to provide us with the depth which is becoming increasingly necessary to our defence. That this group can possibly be strong enough or give us sufficient depth, without the incorporation at a later stage of all or part of Germany, seems to us to be unlikely, though it is difficult to be definite at the present time.

4. We realise that we must on no account antagonise Russia by giving the appearance of building up the Western European block against her, and that for this reason the immediate object of a Western European Group must be the keeping down of Germany; but we feel that the more remote, but more dangerous, possibility of a hostile Russia making use of the resources of Germany must not be lost sight of, and that any measures which we now take should be tested by whether or not they help to prevent that contingency ever arising.

27th July, 1944

ANNEX ID TO No. 119

(Translation from the French)   8th November, 1944

Suggestions relating to the Organisation of Co-operation between Great Britain and Belgium within the Framework of a Western European Regional Entente.

I. The organisation of co-operation between Great Britain and Belgium should take account of the following considerations:–

(*a*) It should be inspired by the proposals contained in the report on general international organisation published as a result of the Dumbarton Oaks Conference;

---

[16] Not printed: cf. Sir L. Woodward, *op. cit.*, vol. v, pp. 187–9.
[17] The rest of this sentence is cited *ibid.*, p. 195.

(*b*) it should be harmonised with the contemplated co-operation, on a regional basis, with the Netherlands and France; it should at the same time take account of existing relations between Belgium and Luxemburg, especially in the economic sphere;

(*c*) it should extend to the military, political and economic fields;

(*d*) it should be based on the co-operation which the war has already developed between Great Britain and Belgium, and steps to bring it about should begin forthwith.

II. Chapter VIII(C) of the Dumbarton Oaks report envisages the conclusion of regional agreements.

It specifies that nothing in the proposed pact is to constitute an obstacle to the existence of regional agreements or bodies.

It defines their object as:

'Dealing with such matters relating to the maintenance of international peace and security as are appropriate for regional action'.

It lays down the conditions which they are to fulfil; such agreements or bodies must be:

'Consistent with the purposes and principles of the organisation.'

On the other hand Chapter VIII(B) provides that:

'In order that all members of the organisation should contribute to the maintenance of international peace and security, they should undertake to make available to the Security Council, on its call and in accordance with a special agreement or agreements concluded among themselves, armed forces, facilities, and assistance necessary for the purpose of maintaining international peace and security. Such agreement or agreements should govern the numbers and types of forces and the nature of the facilities and assistance to be provided. The special agreement or agreements should be negotiated as soon as possible, and should in each case be subject to approval by the Security Council and to ratification by the signatory States in accordance with their constitutional processes.'

Thus regional groups figure as the executive organs charged by the Council with ensuring the maintenance of peace and security within the regional framework.

III. The part to be played by regional agreements and bodies implies in the first place co-operation in the military sphere. This co-operation in Anglo-Belgian relations should be inspired by the co-operation achieved during the war and would involve more especially:–

(*a*) Measures with a view to standardising armaments and war material;

(*b*) co-ordination of plans for the organisation of land, sea and air forces;

(*c*) co-ordination and as far as possible unification of the tactics of land, sea and air forces;

(*d*) co-ordination of training by means of the exchange of pupils in military schools and the reciprocal organisation of officers' courses;[18]

(*e*) exchange of information;

(*f*) co-ordination of industry important to national defence and of national mobilisation;

(*g*) establishment in Great Britain of depôts and other installations of the Belgian army and air force;

(*h*) reciprocal organisation of air bases;

[18] *Note in filed copy:* ' "stages réciproques d'officiers" in the original French.'

(i) setting up of a permanent Chiefs of Staff Committee charged with ensuring military and air co-operation.

Certain items on this programme have already been partially put into effect during the Belgian Government's stay in Great Britain; the achievement of others could be set about immediately if effect were given to the Belgian Government's proposals regarding the equipment and training of the new units which it intends to create.

IV. Co-operation in the military sphere cannot be thought of without co-operation in the political sphere, which implies a guarantee of territorial integrity and political independence.

(*a*) According to the Dumbarton Oaks report such co-operation would involve in the regional sphere–

(i) Pacific settlement of disputes.

(ii) Organisation of concerted action with a view to preventing and suppressing aggression. The Dumbarton Oaks report suggests in this connexion that 'no enforcement action should be taken under regional arrangements or by regional agencies without the authorisation of the Security Council.' It would seem that an exception from this rule should be made, as was done by the Rhineland pact of Locarno,[19] for cases in which arrangements for ensuring peace are flagrantly violated in such a manner as to necessitate immediate action.

(*b*) The more immediate implications of co-operation in the political sphere are as follows–

(i) Decision upon the obligations to be imposed on Germany to prevent any possible further aggression;

(ii) Measures to be taken to ensure the carrying out of these obligations, and particularly arrangements concerning the occupation of Germany.

(iii) The régime for Western Germany and particularly the Rheno-Westphalian area.

The above questions, as well as all those which may directly or indirectly concern the peace and security of Western Europe, should be subject to standing consultation and exchange of information; for this purpose an appropriate procedure ought to be established.

V. The economic sphere cannot be dissociated from the military and political spheres. The effectiveness of any action for the purpose of preventing or suppressing aggression is the function of economic power. On the other hand close political co-operation could not develop under a system which did not ensure the harmonising and co-ordination of economic interests.

The foundation of co-operation in the economic field is laid by the Anglo-Belgian Monetary Agreement of the 5th October, 1944[20] which provides for:

(*a*) Co-operation in the immediate future with a view to restoring Belgian economic potential (re-supplying and re-equipment of the principal branches of production and the public services);

(*b*) co-ordination of programmes of development of agricultural and industrial production with a view to meeting in the first place the demands of the war

---

[19] The Treaty of Mutual Guarantee between the United Kingdom, Belgium, France, Germany and Italy, initialed at Locarno on 16 October 1925, is printed (Cmd. 2525 of 1925: Annex A) in *B.F.S.P.*, vol. 121, pp. 923–6.

[20] Printed in Cmd. 6557 of 1944.

effort and subsequently peace-time requirements; co-operation is particularly necessary in respect of those rapidly developing industries of which Germany was tending to secure a monopoly;

(*c*) co-ordination of measures to ensure full employment;

(*d*) co-ordination of transport policy, particularly in the field of civil aviation.

Contacts on these various points should be organised forthwith, in accordance with a programme to be drawn up by the two Governments, and should be placed on a permanent footing.

ANNEX 1G TO NO. 119

Minute from Mr. Eden to Mr. Churchill

No. P.M./44/732

Secret   FOREIGN OFFICE, 29 November 1944
Copy

Your minute M.1144/4[21] of 25th November.

I agree that we must have an early talk about the so-called 'Western Bloc'.

2. Let me say at the outset that I entirely agree with you that it would be both absurd and highly dangerous for us to enter into any commitments for the defence of Norway, Denmark, Belgium or Holland except in conjunction with the French and as part of some general plan for containing Germany evolved under the aegis of a World Organisation. On these two points the Foreign Office has never had any doubts and I have repeatedly made them clear myself.

3. I further agree with you that the Western European countries behaved very foolishly between the two wars and were grossly unprepared to meet the blow when it fell. But our own record in this period was not entirely praiseworthy and we only escaped their fate by the skin of our teeth and thanks to the Channel. It has always seemed to me that the lesson of the disasters of 1940 is precisely the need to build up a common defence association in Western Europe, which would prevent another Hitler, whencesoever he may come, pursuing what you have so aptly called the policy of 'one by one'. The best way of creating such an association would obviously be to build up France and we can only hope that during the period of the occupation of Germany such a build up will be possible. It is, in fact, only when we evacuate Germany that the desirability of any regional defence organisation of Western Europe arises in a concrete form.

4. Nevertheless, there seems every reason to start thinking about it now, since if our Western European allies and more especially the French have the impression that we are not going in future to accept *any* commitments on the Continent it may well be (as you suggest) that they will come to the conclusion that their only hope lies in making defence arrangements, not with us, but with the Russians. And surely the development of long range missiles proves that somehow or other, if we are to retain our independence, we must obtain some kind of 'defence in depth'?

5. As I see it, then, a properly organised Western Europe can provide us with depth for defence and large resources of manpower which would greatly ease our burden and enable us to avoid a huge standing army which would cripple our economy. Hitler's strategy of 'one by one' not only gave him ideal bases from

---

[21] Not printed. Cf. paragraph 9 of annex 1 above, also Sir L. Woodward, *op. cit.*, vol. v, pp. 193–4: *ibid* for the present document.

which to bombard us and assault our sea communications, but also deprived us of a manpower pool of over sixty millions. Consequently, we have once again had to strain ourselves to the utmost to raise a large army as well as a powerful Air Force and Navy, and even then we could not have hoped for victory without the manpower of Russia and America. Meanwhile, Hitler has himself had the labour of millions of these Western Europeans, which has greatly helped him to keep up the numbers of the German Army. This situation might be avoided in the future if we have some system whereby France in the first instance and the smaller Western European Allies in the second agree to organise their defences together with us according to some common plan. I see no reason to suppose that such an arrangement would result in the maintenance by us of a huge standing army, though I think we should have to reconcile ourselves to making a rather larger land contribution than the famous two divisions which was all we had to offer last time.

6. You asked how the idea of 'what is called the Western Bloc got around in the Foreign Office and other influential circles.' I think the idea was first mooted in connexion with the preparatory work for the World Security Organisation talks at Dumbarton Oaks. Concurrently, the Foreign Ministers of Norway, Belgium and the Netherlands were all spontaneously telling me that their countries had learned the bitter lesson of 1940 and were determined in future to collaborate closely with us for the joint security of Western Europe and in particular to continue and expand the arrangements by which, during the war, we have trained and equipped their reconstituted national forces. I also had some correspondence with Duff Cooper on the subject which was circulated to the War Cabinet (W.P. (44) 409 of 25th July).[22]

7. In view of all this, on my instructions the Foreign Office invited the Chiefs of Staff in June to consider the question of some regional security system to cover Western Europe as part of the machinery necessary to make effective a general system of European security under a World Organisation. (A copy of the Foreign Office memorandum is attached at Annex A).[23] While reserving their considered views on the whole question of the future security of the United Kingdom, the Chiefs of Staff replied that from the military point of view they saw great advantage in the proposal for a special regional association in Western Europe, which would 'be a start in building up a strong association of nations in Western Europe to provide us with the depth which is becoming increasingly necessary to our defence.'

8. As the outcome of this favourable opinion of the Chiefs of Staff, our representatives at the Dumbarton Oaks conversations were able to play their part in securing the provisions contained in Section VIII of the agreed scheme of recommendations which looks forward to the establishment of regional security associations within the framework of the World Organisation. I attach the text in question (Annex B),[24] and also that of another provision (Annex C)[25] which would permit the establishment of regional sub-committees of the Military Staff Committee. During the discussions at Dumbarton Oaks neither the United States and Soviet Delegations appeared to have any objection to the possible development of a Western European association under these provisions.

[22] Not printed: cf. Sir L. Woodward, *op. cit.*, vol. v, pp. 190–1.
[23] Not annexed to the present copy: cf. *ibid.*, pp. 187–9.
[24] Not annexed to the present copy: see chapter VIII C of the Dumbarton Oaks proposals in Cmd. 6560 of 1944.
[25] Not annexed to the present copy: see chapter VI D (2) *ibid.*

9. The key to the matter is at present the attitude of the French, and we must wait to see what comes out of General de Gaulle's talks at Moscow. In December 1941 Stalin spontaneously urged that we should, in our own interest, take charge after the war of security in Western Europe (see marked passage on page 1 of record of interview with Marshal Stalin on December 16th, 1941, Annex D),[26] and I cannot believe that he would oppose the creation of a special regional association in Western Europe provided this were an integral part of the general system of world security, under the control of the World Organisation, and that it were made perfectly clear that it was directed against a resurgence of Germany.

ANNEX 1H TO No. 119

Top Secret

Draft Treaty of Alliance and Mutual Assistance
between the United Kingdom and the French Republic

His Majesty's Government in the United Kingdom etc. and the Provisional Government of the French Republic;

(1) Desiring to confirm in a formal Treaty of Alliance the cordial friendship and close association of interests between the United Kingdom and France;

(2) Determined to continue together until a victorious conclusion the common war against Germany and thereafter to collaborate in measures to prevent a renewal of German aggression;

(3) Determined to collaborate closely with one another as well as with the other United Nations in order to create an international organisation to ensure the effective maintenance of general peace and the welfare of mankind in accordance with the undertakings which they have each assumed in the Declaration by the United Nations made at Washington on 1st January, 1942;

(4) Having regard to the Treaties of Alliance and Mutual Assistance which they have respectively concluded with the Soviet Union;

Have decided to conclude a treaty with these objects and have nominated as their plenipotentiaries:

(insert names)

Who, having communicated their Full Powers, found in good and due form, have agreed as follows:

Article 1

The Contracting Parties mutually undertake to continue until final victory, together with the other United Nations, the common struggle against Germany and to afford one another military and other assistance and support of all kinds for this purpose.

Article 2

The Contracting Parties undertake not to (enter into negotiations with any Government or authority in Germany which does not clearly renounce all aggressive intentions, or to) negotiate or conclude except by mutual consent any armistice or peace treaty with Germany.

---

[26] Not annexed to the present copy: cf. Earl of Avon, *op. cit.*, *The Reckoning*, p. 290.

Article 3

(i) The Contracting Parties declare their desire to join with the other United Nations in establishing a world organisation to preserve peace and resist aggression in the post-war period.

(ii) Pending the establishment of such a world organisation and the assumption by it of full responsibility for rendering impossible the repetition of aggression or violation of the peace by Germany, the Contracting Parties will, after the termination of the present hostilities with Germany, concert together in order to take all the measures in their power to render impossible such action on the part of that State.

Article 4

Should either of the Contracting Parties become again involved in hostilities with Germany in consequence of an attack by that State against that Party, or as a result of measures taken against Germany by the Contracting Parties in concert under Article 3 (ii) above, or by the World Organisation mentioned in Article 3 (i), the other Contracting Party will at once give the Contracting Party so involved in hostilities all the military and other support and assistance in its power.

Article 5

(i) It is the intention of the contracting parties that the present treaty should operate within the framework and in strict accordance with the principles and regulations of the World Organisation mentioned in Article 3 (i). On the establishment of the said Organisation they will consult together with a view to making any adjustments to the present treaty which may be required for this purpose.

(ii) The contracting parties desire in particular to form, in concert with other neighbouring Allied Governments, a regional military association in Western Europe, within the framework of the Organisation referred to in Article 3 (i) and under its supreme authority, for the purpose of mutual assistance in preventing or suppressing any renewal of German aggression. Pending the establishment of the said Organisation the contracting parties will invite the other Governments concerned to preliminary consultations with this object.

Article 6

The Contracting Parties agree to render one another, after the conclusion of hostilities with Germany, all economic assistance in their power and to work together in close and friendly collaboration for the organisation of economic prosperity throughout the world.

Article 7

Each Contracting Party undertakes not to conclude any alliance and not to take part in any coalition directed against the other Contracting Party.

Article 8

The present Treaty is subject to ratification and the instruments of ratification shall be exchanged in

as soon as possible.

It shall come into force immediately on the exchange of the instruments of ratification and shall remain in force for a period of twenty years. Thereafter, unless twelve months notice has been given by either party to terminate the Treaty, it shall continue in force until twelve months after either Contracting Party shall have given notice to the other in writing of its intention to terminate it.

Memorandum

*Observations on the attitude of the Soviet Government towards possible formation
of a group of Western European Democracies*

1. The Russians regard our post-war attitude towards Germany as the touchstone of our good faith as an ally.

2. They will look to us to collaborate closely with them in enforcing on Germany the maximum possible measures of economic disarmament.

3. At a time when the Russians themselves are concerned to build up in Southeastern and Central Europe a bulwark of military and economic power against a renewal of German aggression, there seems to be no reason to suppose that they would find it abnormal if we on our side were to promote security measures of our own designed to extend British military and economic power into Western Europe. Indeed, during the Moscow talks[27] Marshal Stalin seemed to agree with the Prime Minister when the latter remarked that it would be an advantage for British industry if German heavy industry were to be kept under control after the war. So, too, during his visit to London in 1942 M. Molotov suggested to the Secretary of State that Britain might wish to acquire bases for herself across the Channel.

4. Whilst the Russians interpret any British inclination to deal leniently with a regenerated Germany as dictated by anti-Soviet motives, they have throughout the period of our association as allies shown no jealousy of Britain's strength as a great power, and their propaganda has abandoned almost all criticism of us on the score of imperialist designs.

5. So long as His Majesty's Government pursue an anti-German policy in collaboration with the Soviet Government the attitude just described is likely to persist, and the Russians will welcome all evidence that Great Britain is ready to play a vigorous part in containing Germany. Indeed, throughout the Moscow talks, Marshal Stalin frequently went out of his way to stress the need for the peace-loving powers to be constantly in readiness to assert their strength. He repeatedly argued that the weakness of these powers, including Great Britain, had enabled the agressors to score their initial successes in Europe and the Far East. He developed the same theme in his broadcast speech on the 6th November.

6. The Russians think of the future world order in terms of a concert of the three major allies. They are opposed to independent regional federations of smaller states, which they expect to move in the orbit of the great power situated nearest to them. In so far as can at present be judged, the Russians are aiming at the creation in Central and South-eastern Europe of a bailiwick of more or less independent countries. Their object is to build up a military and economic security zone which will make it impossible to revive any of the pre-war makeshift plans of a *cordon sanitaire* against the Soviet Union.

7. On present showing moreover the Soviet Government are disposed to admit that, just as they are themselves entitled to organise a continental orbit of power in regions adjacent to their borders, so His Majesty's Government are at liberty to claim the right to pursue a similar policy along the Atlantic and Mediterranean seaboards—subject always to the proviso that the primary aim is to immobilise

[27] For the Anglo-Soviet conversations held in Moscow on 9–17 October, 1944, see W. S. Churchill, *op. cit.*, vol. vi, pp. 197–209; also Sir L. Woodward, *op. cit.*, vol. v, pp. 229–31.

Germany. In return for the recognition by His Majesty's Government of their special interests in Roumania and Bulgaria the Soviet Government have done the like for us as regards Greece. During the Moscow talks they spontaneously acknowledged that the Adriatic Coast had a special importance for Britain. They have followed Anglo-American leadership in the recognition of the Provisional Government of France.

8. The readiness of the Russians to support, and even to encourage, moves on our part calculated to contain Germany, seems to be reinforced by a belief that it would not redound to their military and economic advantage if Britain were so weak as to leave world power to be divided between the U.S.A. and the U.S.S.R. As was clearly shown during the presidential campaign, the Kremlin has deep misgivings as to whether the U.S.A. may be permanently counted upon to pursue a policy of international collaboration.

9. All present indications go to show that the Soviet Government are convinced that the future of Germany, and with it the future of European security, must be decided within the months immediately following the collapse of the *Reich*, whilst memories of German barbarism are still fresh in the minds of the victims. As the Russians see it, common enmity to Germany is at present the only really solid bond between the United Nations, who will tend to fall apart unless new links can be forged in the first glow of victory.

10. The Russians themselves are apparently taking time by the forelock in so far as concerns the organisation of Central and South-eastern Europe. From the foregoing analysis of their attitude it would seem to follow that, if we on our side wish to safeguard our interests in the manner suggested, we must take action before the Russians can have ground for thinking that our policy is dictated by other than anti-German motives. It would incidentally seem advisable to deal with the problem whilst the political conditions in Western Europe are favourable to a closer alignment with us and, if need be, with the Americans.

11. In the absence of concerted action to stimulate closer association between ourselves and the countries of Western Europe, there is a risk that the latter will conclude that a war-weary Britain has abdicated her continental power. Left wing elements in those countries would then inevitably be driven to place an even greater reliance than they do already on Soviet power and influence. The Soviet Government themselves, confronted with a security vacuum, would be tempted to exploit the situation to their own exclusive advantage. The resulting increase in the domestic strains and stresses of Western European countries needs no emphasis.

12. The preceding paragraphs may seem to have placed undue stress upon Germany as the predominant factor in the future of Anglo-Soviet relations. So far as concerns the immediate future, an examination of the problem certainly suggests that the initial basis for European concord must take the form of international arrangements somewhat akin to Bismarck's *Drei Kaiserbund*,[28] a main purpose of which was to prevent the resurrection of Poland. At the same time this initial basis of collaboration seems to offer the only practicable point of departure for that wider Anglo-Soviet understanding which is essential for the maintenance of world peace.

His Majesty's Embassy, Moscow, 19th November, 1944

[28] A League of the Three Emperors of Germany, Austria and Russia had been concluded in 1881.

No. 120

Mr. Duff Cooper (Paris) to Mr. Eden (Received 13 July, 6.55 p.m.)

No. 992 Telegraphic [*E 5138/8/89*]

Most Immediate. Top secret   PARIS, *13 July 1945, 6.40 p.m. G.M.T.*

Personal for Secretary of State.

I saw Prime Minister last night July 12th[1] and discussed with him the possibility of his staying in Paris on his way to Berlin in order to have a friendly talk with De Gaulle.

2. When I left him he had agreed to my putting forward the proposal but on my arrival here at mid-day I received his instructions to take no further action. I regret this because I believe that it might now be possible to solve the problem of the Levant by such informal discussion. The French have handed over special troops and may be willing to withdraw all their own troops if we would do the same. The Prime Minister said that he would have no objection to doing so.

3. My own view, which I put before him, is that if this agreement were reached and our troops were withdrawn we should make it plain to the States that we did not intend to interfere with their affairs again and that as independent powers it was their privilege if they had difficulties with . . .[2] and other powers to appeal to the World Organisation but not to us. This would be solution of the problem which would avoid difficulties and delays of international conference and interference by less interested but not dis-interested powers. It seems to me that the moment has arrived when such a solution is practicable.

4. If it were possible for either you or the Prime Minister to stay here for 24 hours on your way back from Berlin much might be accomplished.

[1] Cf. No. 1, note 1.
[2] The text is here uncertain.

No. 121

Mr. Broad (Caserta) to Mr. Eden (Received 14 July, 12.30 a.m.)

No. 1346 Telegraphic [*R 11905/4/19*]

Secret   CASERTA, *13 July 1945*[1]

Repeated to Athens, Belgrade, Washington, Moscow.

Athens telegram No. 1430 to you.[2]

Field Marshal Alexander has recently been considering military implications of the situation which would arise in Greece in the event of small-scale incursions into Greek territory by local Yugoslav, Albanian or Bulgarian armed bands.

[1] The time of despatch is not recorded.
[2] This telegram of 24 June 1945 (R 10860/100/19) is not printed.

2. In view of the territorial claims by these three countries against Greece and Greek counter claims Field Marshal Alexander considers incidents on Greece's northern frontier are a distinct possibility. He has therefore reported to Combined Chiefs of Staff that he has felt it necessary to clarify the position of commander of the land forces of Greece[3] and has asked their approval for the following policy.

a. Greek forces should be made entirely responsible for guarding their own frontier.

b. Primary task of commander of land forces of Greece is stil[l] to support the Greek Government in maintenance of law and order but in the event of violations of Greek frontier he should be prepared to support the Greek Government by concentrating maximum force possible in affected area.

c. Commander of land forces of Greece should take all precautionary steps to avoid hostilities and unless directly attacked should consult Field Marshal Alexander before using force.

3. Field Marshal Alexander has already informed Combined Chiefs of Staff that in his opinion in the event of frontier incidents in Greece a strong line should be adopted as in the case of Venezia Giulia.

4. In order to lessen the risk of incursions he has recommended that a warning be given now by Principal Allied Powers to Greece, Yugoslavia, Bulgaria and Albania condemning means by which they are apparently trying to anticipate peace settlement.

Foreign Office please repeat to Moscow as my telegram No. 161.

CALENDAR TO NO. 121

i *16 July 1945   Mr. Caccia (Athens) Tel. No. 1545.* Considers warning proposed in No. 121, para. 4 would be indignantly rebutted by Greece; fears a loss of Greek confidence if impartiality between them and their northern neighbours is carried too far [R 12013/4/19].

---

[3] The corresponding passage of Field-Marshal Alexander's telegram NAF 1037 of 12 July (R 11875/11875/19: not printed), which made the report here summarised, referred to the 'Commander Land Forces Greece', i.e. Lieut.-General Sir Ronald Scobie.

No. 122

Mr. Eden to Mr. Bowker (Madrid)[1]
No. 563 Telegraphic [Z 8075/16/28]

FOREIGN OFFICE, *13 July 1945, 6.20 a.m.*

Repeated to Tangier No. 171, Washington No. 7375, Moscow No. 3891, Paris No. 1629 Saving.

---

[1] Mr. R. J. Bowker was British Chargé d'Affaires at Madrid.

Your telegram No. 515 (of the 5th July: Tangier).[2]

Spanish Ambassador called on Sir A. Cadogan on July 6th on instructions but did not leave any written communication.

2. His Excellency began by enquiring whether there was any prospect of a purely Spanish administration being allowed to continue in Tangier, to which Sir A. Cadogan replied that this was out of the question. He then enquired whether it would not be possible to have an international régime confined to the United Kingdom, France, Spain and the United States. Sir A. Cadogan explained that we were anxious to return to something more like the 1923 régime.

3. His Excellency then expressed the distrust which his Government felt for any participation by the Soviet Government in Tangier administration, and enquired whether any decision had been taken in regard to the latter's request to this effect. Sir A. Cadogan replied that the matter was still under consideration, adding that of course if the Spanish Government had not themselves upset the international régime in 1940 the problem would not have arisen.

4. The Ambassador said that his Government had always maintained that their action in 1940 had been taken by agreement with His Majesty's Government in order to preserve the neutrality of Tangier. He expressed no surprise, however, when Sir A. Cadogan said there was no foundation for this view.

[2] Not printed. Mr. Bowker had there reported that the Spanish Under Secretary of State for Foreign Affairs had told him that the Spanish Ambassador in London had been instructed 'to inform His Majesty's Government that Spanish Government were ready to reach an agreement regarding restoration of an international régime in Tangier by discussion with Great Britain and the United States but not with any other power. Under Secretary of State said that Spanish Government were still strongly opposed to a return to the *status quo* and considered that a four power administration . . . was the only practical solution. He added that present instructions . . . were a distinct advance in that specific mention was made of Spain's readiness to agree to a return to an international administration and these instructions had been approved by General Franco.'

No. 123

Mr. Kirkpatrick (Frankfurt am Main) to Mr. Eden
(Received 13 July, 6.50 a.m.)

No. 150 Telegraphic [C 3908/24/18]

FRANKFURT AM MAIN, *13 July 1945*[1]

Supreme Commander has decided to dissolve SHAEF at 0000[2] hours on July 14th. I shall close British Political Office on July 14th and leave for England.

[1] The time of despatch is not recorded.

[2] Annotation on filed copy: '(There is no such time)'.

Mr. King will remain behind and will become Economic Liaison Officer to Economic[3] Political Division on the strength of our Control Commission's Special Echelon at Frankfurt.

It will be for Political Division to determine permanent political establishment here and make the necessary staff and accommodation arrangements.

CALENDAR TO NO. 123

i *11 July 1945 Extracts from 174th Meeting of Chiefs of Staff:* consideration of U.S. proposal for the transaction, after termination of S.H.A.E.F., of business concerning Germany and Austria previously handled by Combined Committees in Washington. Approval of proposal to defer until after Potsdam Conference decision on dissolution of A.F.H.Q., which should, however, be reduced: cf. *F.R.U.S. Berlin*, vol. i, pp. 710–11 [C 3900/3899/18; U 5446/3276/70].

[3] It was suggested on the filed copy that this word should read 'British'.

No. 124

Mr. Eden to Mr. Labouchere (Stockholm)[1]
No. 252 Arfar Telegraphic [UE 3033/1579/77]

FOREIGN OFFICE, *13 July 1945, 6.20 p.m.*

Repeated to Washington No. 735 Arfar, Moscow No. 17 Arfar, Paris No. 68 Arfar.

Safehaven[2]

The United States Government propose, and we agree, that a formal communication should be made to neutral Governments warning them that the four Allied Powers claim title to or control over Axis-owned or controlled companies. The four Powers must ask therefore that no action should be taken by neutral Governments which could conflict with this title which must be recognised as having come into existence.

2. As soon as your United States colleague receives similar instructions please join him in making above communication to the Government to which you are accredited.

3. For your own information and guidance. We are anxious that no mention should be made at present of vesting enemy assets in the Control Council or any other allied body, since it may eventually prove more convenient to vest them in a German body under allied control.

[1] Mr. G. P. Labouchere was Chargé d'Affaires at H.M. Legation in Stockholm. This telegram was also sent as No. 244 Arfar to Lisbon, No. 570 Arfar to Madrid and No. 623 Arfar to Berne.

[2] Codename for the programme to forestall any German attempt to conceal assets and looted property in neutral countries, adopted under resolution VI of the Final Act of the United Nations Conference at Bretton Woods: cf. No. 42, note 10, also W. N. Medlicott, *The Economic Blockade* (H.M.S.O., 1952 f.), vol. ii, pp. 622–9.

i *1 Aug. 1945 Mr. Ashley Clarke (Chargé d'Affaires, Lisbon) Tel. No. 236 Arfar.*
Following execution of instructions in No. 124, Portuguese Foreign Ministry
has indicated that if intention were to claim an absolute right to control
tangible assets, especially real estate, in Portuguese territory, it would be
resisted 'tooth and nail' [UE 3476/1579/77].

No. 125

Brief for the United Kingdom Delegation to the Conference at Potsdam
No. 58 [UE 3042/2100/53]

FOREIGN OFFICE, *July 1945*[1]

Treatment of Germany as an Economic Unit

Summary

It is highly desirable to reach Anglo-American-Soviet agreement on the
treatment of Germany as an economic whole. The main objects of such an
agreement will be the free exchange of foodstuffs, goods and services between
zones, so as to minimise the need for imports and facilitate administrative
arrangements, and the uniform application of economic measures of all
kinds to Germany. Without such agreement the administration of Germany
will be wasteful of resources and manpower and productive of Allied
disunity.

2. An illustration of the need for such agreement is provided by the
recent discussions in the Control Council on the feeding and fueling of
Berlin.

3. It is recommended that we should:

(*a*) try to secure the agreement of President Truman and Marshal Stalin
to a statement of policy on this subject which should be referred to the
Commanders-in-Chief to translate into an administrative agreement, or

(*b*) failing this, to remit to the Control Council the task of drawing up
such a formula and basing their arrangements upon it.

Treatment of Germany as an Economic Unit

The treatment of Germany as an economic whole is on both the United
States and United Kingdom Agenda for Terminal. The United States
Government are known to favour the proposition, and the French would, no
doubt with certain lapses in practice, probably enter into the spirit of an
agreement that Germany should be treated in this way. The Russians have
accepted the principle for the purposes of a reparation settlement, and might
well accept in the case of foodstuffs, although the amount likely to be
available from Eastern to Western Germany in the immediate future is
inconsiderable. Even so, the Russians will try to drive the hardest bargain.

---

[1] This brief, amended from a draft by Mr. Lincoln, was approved by Sir A. Cadogan
on 13 July 1945.

2. It is suggested that the matter might be discussed by the Heads of Governments on the basis of the draft formula attached.

3. It is the policy of His Majesty's Government that, during the period of occupation, Germany should be administered in obedience to common policies worked out by the four Controlling Powers which might well, however, in certain fields involve a high degree of decentralisation. But though Germany may not for all purposes be treated as a political unit, it is of the highest importance that she should be treated as an economic unit.

4. In our view the treatment of Germany as an economic unit in accordance with agreed policies for the purposes of the occupation should entail the following:–

(*a*) Free inter-Zonal exchange of foodstuffs, and other goods essential to the economic existence of the German people, which would enable local deficiencies to be met from national sources instead of by imports from outside Germany; and make it possible to draw up a co-ordinated national import programme in a period of continuing supply and shipping shortages.

(*b*) Free inter-Zonal exchange of services, e.g. public utilities, transport.

(*c*) The absence of artificially stimulated disparities in wages, rationing, price levels and standards of living.

(*d*) The existence of a unified currency and banking system; of uniform taxation and a central budget.

(*e*) Uniform visitation upon the German people of the economic penalties which a war of aggression has brought upon their nation.

5. The treatment of Germany as an economic unit in accordance with agreed policies need and should not, in our view, entail the following:–

(*a*) The preservation and perpetuation in an undesirable form or to an undesirable degree of Germany's economic strength. Indeed, the uniform application of agreed measures of industrial disarmament would have the opposite effect.

(*b*) Unreasonable curtailment of the executive authority of the command of the Commanders in Chief in their zones.

6. It appears, therefore, to be in the essential interest of the Controlling Powers to agree as a measure of policy, that Germany should be treated as an economic unit and that any agreement to secure this should be carried out in the letter and in the spirit. A negative demonstration of the necessity of doing this arises from a consideration of some of the consequences of not treating Germany as an economic unit but upon a zonal basis.

(*a*) An overall loss of efficiency. If Germany is not to be treated as a unit, the only logical alternative is that each zone should be treated as completely autonomous. In that way it might be possible to secure a self contained unit, but only at the price of an incommensurate expenditure of the resources in goods and man-power, of the Occupying Power. To establish economic autonomy in the zones would delay once-for-all deliveries and economic disarmament, since some installations would have to be kept in existence, however uneconomically, in order that economic life might go on. Again one zone might be obliged to import grain from overseas for cattle food because the surplus fodder in an adjoining zone was not available.

(*b*) In the chaotic state of Germany, anarchy can only be prevented by the maintenance of certain economic controls. These controls cannot be abandoned at present, and would depend for their efficient continuation upon the fact that they were national and not local.

(*c*) Certain German industries are closely integrated, e.g. the textile and chemical industries. It is desirable in the interests of meeting Germany's minimum requirements and aiding the rehabilitation of Europe that the German textile industry should not cease to function because of the creation of artificial barriers between its component parts. It will probably be important in the interests of industrial disarmament substantially to reduce the German chemical industry; but any measures to this end will fail if they are applied in one zone and not in another.

7. Apart from the general interest, it is of outstanding importance to the British zone that the policy of treating Germany as an economic whole should be adopted and enforced. This is of particular importance in the case of food supplies of which only the Soviet zone normally has a surplus, while both the British and American are deficient, the former to a greater extent than the latter. The British zone, moreover, includes the highly industrialised, thickly populated and heavily devastated Ruhr area. If we cannot look to Eastern Germany for supplies, we must either make use of shipping to import food, which in the present supply situation can be done only at the expense of liberated countries, or face widespread disorder and the impediment of essential industries e.g. coal mining.

8. The administrative difficulties and the danger to the relations of the Controlling Powers which the absence of policy on this question may cause us, was recently illustrated in Berlin. On the 7th July Marshal Zhukov made it clear to the British and United States representatives, when discussing problems of the administration of Berlin, that the Russians had assumed that each of the powers occupying Berlin would be responsible for feeding the Germans in its own sector. In the case of coal, the Russians expected that out of an estimated requirement for public utilities of 7,500 tons a day, 5,000 would be supplied from the Ruhr, despite the fact that in 1936/1937 between 40 and 50% of the hard coal consumed in Greater Berlin came from the Ruhr and almost all the remainder from German Upper and Lower Silesia.

9. Had this situation been allowed to continue, the Berlin Conference would have been sitting at a time when the 900,000 odd Germans in the British Sector might have been without food and public utilities were running down or had stopped. General Weeks was given provisional instructions to join with General Clay of the United States Sector in providing one month's supply of certain foodstuffs to the British and United States Zones, pending discussion of the problem at Terminal. He was also authorized to explore the possibility of supplying some coal; and to propose

the immediate appointment of the quadripartite hard fuel Committee recommended in the Potter-Hyndley Report upon the Coal Situation in North-West Europe. (C.P.(45) 35).[2]

10. These instructions were endorsed by the Cabinet at their meeting on the 10th June.

11. It thus seems essential that fuel for Berlin should be supplied from the resources of Germany as a whole including German Silesia. It is suggested that quotas from the various German sources of supply e.g. Ruhr, German Silesia should be in the same proportions as they were on an average during the two years before the war. Similarly an equitable arrangement must be made for the provision of food for Berlin from its normal sources of supply. These suggestions are in line with a Cabinet decision taken on the 10th July.

12. There are two methods of securing the adoption of this policy by the other three Controlling Powers. The first is by convincing them of the necessity for it on its merits. The second is by a threat to withhold the resources of the British zone from the other zones. The first course would probably prevail with the French and the Americans; it remains to be seen whether it would prevail with the Russians. Probably they would only accept such a formula if it were based on a substantial overall reduction of the German standard of living and consequent increase in available loot. The second course involves the question how strong are our bargaining assets and how do we wish to use them? In relation to the French and United States zones our bargaining position would be fairly strong especially since we control the Ruhr coal. In relation to the Soviet Government we have a strong short-term bargaining position in that there are situated in British zone very considerable capital installations and equipment which the Russians are probably anxious to obtain as once-for-all deliveries in reparation.

13. We must obviously if possible pursue the first course in preference to the second. We should take the line that the treatment of Germany as an economic unit is so obvious a consequence of the joint undertaking of the Four Powers in occupying Germany, that there can be no question of bargaining.

14. Once we admit the possibility of bargaining, we may be obliged to barter our short-term strength against long-term formulas which the Russians may never observe. We know how little value it is to agree formulas with the Soviet Government, when they do not intend to carry them out—especially formulas which, from their very generality, cannot be so drafted as to be unassailable by a determined and litigious defaulter. We should therefore reserve our capital assets in the zone for bigger and more advantageous bargains.

15. It is suggested that the aims of our Delegation should be:

[2] This memorandum of 14 June by Mr. Lyttelton (UR 2108/1590/851) covering the Hyndley-Potter report (cf. No. 58.ii) is not printed.

(*a*) To secure the agreement of President Truman and Marshal Stalin to a statement of policy on the lines of the attached draft; and to the remission of the formula to the four Commanders-in-Chief with an instruction that they should jointly translate it into an immediate administrative agreement, applying to Germany (including Greater Berlin). This statement should be published.

(*b*) If it proves impossible to secure agreement on the terms of the formula for lack of time, to secure agreement that the drawing up of a formula and arrangements to embody the determination of the three powers to treat Germany as an economic unit shall, at the earliest opportunity, be undertaken by the Control Council.

ANNEX TO NO. 125

Germany to be treated as an economic unit

In the exercise of control over German economy for the purpose of carrying out the objectives of the occupation, Germany will be treated as far as possible as a single economic unit. This policy will apply in particular to the production, collection and distribution of foodstuffs and other goods essential to the economic existence of the German people and to the maintenance and use of services necessary for this purpose. The freest possible interchange of goods and services between the zones will be permitted. Germany's standard of living will be based on her minimum essential needs, which shall be calculated on the basis that the average living standards in Germany during the Reparation period shall not exceed the average of the standards of living of all European countries other than the United Kingdom and the Union of Soviet Socialist Republics. These minimum needs shall be taken into account in determining what exports of material from Germany can be made, whether by way of reparation or otherwise. For this purpose a surplus of foodstuffs shall only be deemed to exist where the supplies available until the next harvest are clearly in excess of minimum essential needs for the same period.

2. Austria also shall, as far as possible, be treated as a single economic unit for the purpose of carrying out the objectives of the occupation.

No. 126

Minute from Mr. Eden to Mr. Churchill

No. P.M./45/325 [*U 5467/19/70*]

FOREIGN OFFICE, *13 July 1945*

Last year the Chiefs of Staff worked out a comprehensive scheme for British assistance to our small Allies of Western Europe in rebuilding their armed forces after the end of the German war. The object of this scheme was to continue the assistance we have given to the Allies during the war and generally to capitalize our close co-operation and good relations with them. At the same time it would enable them to raise enough troops to

keep order in their own countries and—which is very important to us—
to provide contingents towards the garrison of the British zone of occupation
in Germany.

2. We communicated our scheme to the Americans and were told by the
State Department that the United States Government had no objection to
our going ahead.

3. With your approval, I have made offers of help to the Belgian, Netherlands and Norwegian Governments. The Belgians and the Norwegians
have warmly accepted and I think the Dutch will also when they can apply
their minds to such matters.[1] The Belgian scheme is now well advanced and
a first Belgian contingent is already in our zone in Germany.

4. The Danes are very keen to have our help in rebuilding their forces.
This is a healthy sign and from every point of view I am convinced that it
is to our interest to encourage them to abjure their past pacifism and to
look to us for equipment and training. The Service Departments agree
and have worked out with us the scheme in the attached note [iii], which I
have instructed His Majesty's Minister at Copenhagen to address to the
Danish Foreign Minister.[2]

5. In accordance with our practice in the case of the offers to the other
Allies, we will inform the United States and Soviet Governments as soon
as we know that the Danish reaction is favourable.[3]

ANTHONY EDEN

[1] On 20 July 1945 the Netherland Ambassador in London handed Sir O. Sargent an
aide-mémoire of 19 July stating that the Netherland Government 'gladly accept the offer
of His Majesty's Government to give all possible assistance in the equipment and training
of the Netherlands Armed Forces', and expressing a desire for staff talks at the earliest
opportunity.

[2] Mr. Randall addressed this note to the Danish Foreign Minister on 18 July 1945. On
20 July M. Christmas Möller stated in his reply to Mr. Randall: 'I shall revert to this
matter as soon as the suggestions of the interested Departments are at hand. I hasten,
however, to assure you that this generous offer is warmly welcomed by the Danish Government.'

[3] Foreign Office telegrams No. 4238 to Moscow and No. 1313 to Paris of 4.40 p.m. on
31 July 1945 instructed H.M. Representatives to inform the Soviet and French Provisional
Governments respectively, in general terms, of British plans for assistance to Danish forces
as indicated in No. 126.iii: 'You should explain that these proposals are intended to give
effect to policy of encouraging the smaller Allies to play their part in the general system of
post-war European security. We had intended to inform the Soviet and French Governments of specific proposals for assistance to Danish forces as soon as these had been agreed
with the Danish Government. In view however of premature reports . . . we are informing
them at once of position in order to prevent any misunderstanding.' Foreign Office telegram
No. 7989 of 5 p.m. on even date to Washington, conveying corresponding instructions,
commented: 'Premature disclosure of our offer is embarrassing . . . You should emphasise
[to U.S. Government] that we have made it clear to the Danes that execution of programme
(in which United States Government have concurred in principle) is subject to Combined
Munitions Assignment machinery and that United States Government are to be kept
informed.'

i 6 *July 1945   Minute from Mr. Harvey to Mr. Dixon* enclosing draft minute to Mr. Churchill concerning British equipment for the French Air Force. F.O. 'support strongly the Air Ministry's view that we should not allow the Syrian imbroglio' to impede this. On 10 July Mr. Eden minuted his approval [U 5389/19/70].

ii 6 *July 1945   Letter from Mr. J. G. Ward (F.O. Reconstruction Dept.) to Group Captain MacArthur (Air Ministry).* Confirms that it is not British policy to disband the Italian Air Force and hopes that material aid can be continued [ZM 3563/243/22].

iii 10 *July 1945   To Mr. Randall (Copenhagen) No. 64* Explains progress of scheme for British assistance to Allied armed forces of Western Europe; instructions for offer to Danish Govt. of such assistance in equipping and training their armed forces for internal security and for an occupation contingent in British zone of Germany. It should be suggested orally to M. Möller that if the offer is accepted Soviet Govt. should be informed through Danish channels in addition to their being informed as usual by H.M.G. [U 5152/19/70].

iv 9 *July 1945   Brief No. 27 for U.K. Delegation on Re-armament of the European Allies.* Review of scheme offered to Belgium, the Netherlands, Norway, France, Luxembourg and Denmark. Special considerations in regard to Poland, Czechoslovakia, Greece and Yugoslavia [U 5396/19/70].

v 10 *July 1945   War Office to Field-Marshal Montgomery.* To British strategic interest that forces of smaller Allies of North-West Europe should participate in British zone of occupation in Germany: would foster formation of a Regional Association of Western Europe under the World Organisation if this eventually became a British objective [U 5303/20/70].

vi 18 & 31 *July 1945   Correspondence between Mr. Falla (F.O. Reconstruction Dept.) and Air Ministry.* Allocation of places at R.A.F. Staff College, Bulstrode, for Allied staff training [U 5523, 5989/19/70].

No. 127

Mr. Eden to Mr. Stevenson (Belgrade)
No. 266 [R 12068/190/92]

Confidential   FOREIGN OFFICE, *13 July 1945*

Sir,

On my instructions Mr. Howard called to-day on King Peter of Yugoslavia.

2. King Peter began by handing Mr. Howard a letter addressed to me covering a letter which he had sent to the Prime Minister on the 6th July. I enclose a copy of the latter [i].

3. King Peter then said that he was becoming daily more concerned over the situation in Yugoslavia and the policy which Tito is adopting. The internal situation was highly unsatisfactory inasmuch as Tito was not carrying out the terms of the Tito–Subasić Agreement or of the Yalta Declaration. King Peter had been persuaded by His Majesty's Government to accept that

agreement—which he had finally done in the hope that His Majesty's Government would use their influence to see that it was properly carried out. Tito continued to ignore the terms of the agreement and the King felt he had the right to ask His Majesty's Government to bring this to the notice of the Russians and Americans. Externally, Tito was making many blunders. The Yugoslavs had a good claim to Venezia Giulia and Istria. Tito had gone about it all in the wrong way and annoyed His Majesty's Government and the United States Government and had finally had to give in, having meanwhile done considerable harm to the Yugoslav cause. Having muddled that issue, Tito was now doing his best to make an enemy of Greece, previously one of Yugoslavia's best friends. Tito was, in fact, according to King Peter, a public menace to Yugoslav interests. For all these reasons he felt bound to draw the attention of the Prime Minister and myself to the situation and to beg us to do our best for Yugoslavia at 'Terminal'.

4. King Peter was told that the Prime Minister and I were fully aware of the situation in Yugoslavia and that this subject figured on our agenda for discussion at 'Terminal.' King Peter was not given to think that great results were expected from any approach that might be made to the Russians at 'Terminal'; but he was assured that the intention was to raise the matter if possible. King Peter was relieved to hear this and said that he would take no further action until he heard the result of the forthcoming Conference.

I am, &c.,
ANTHONY EDEN

CALENDAR TO No. 127

i 6–13 July 1945 Letters from King Peter II of Yugoslavia to Mr. Churchill and to Mr. Eden expressing his concern at non-implementation of Tito-Subasic Agreement [R 12068/190/92].

No. 128

Letter from Sir D. Gainer (Rio de Janeiro) to Mr. Perowne[1] (Received 26 July)
[R 12595/4476/44]

Confidential   RIO DE JANEIRO, *13 July 1945*

My dear Perowne,

With reference to my letter of 3rd July[2] and Greenway's of the 5th July[3]

---

[1] Sir D. Gainer was H.M. Ambassador at Rio de Janeiro. Mr. J. V. T. W. Perowne was head of the South American Department of the Foreign Office.

[2] In this letter (on R 12378/4476/44, received 23 July 1945) Sir D. Gainer had reported an after-dinner conversation on 29 June with Mr. Adolf Berle, U.S. Ambassador at Rio de Janeiro, who 'felt quite certain that the Turkish/Soviet contretemps was of itself only the initial stage of a Soviet policy which eventually contemplated control not only of the Straits but also even of Suez. . . . He envisaged the Soviet eventually working round from the Straits through the middle East—where she was undoubtedly behind the Arab League—to Suez and we might be faced with her demands also in that area. . . . His view was that the Soviet should be resisted from the start.'

[3] This letter from Mr. J. D. Greenway, Acting Counsellor at Rio de Janeiro, is untraced.

on the subject of conversations with Mr. Berle about the Russian Turkish situation, it may be of interest to tell you that the Turkish Minister came to see me a few days ago and said he was convinced that the Soviet long term objective was to eliminate Great Britain from the near and middle East. She would never apparently have a better opportunity than now and unless we were prepared to resist and to assist Turkey in so doing we were lost— in any case the Soviet Government were to some extent bluffing.

Yesterday evening (12th July) Adolf Berle tackled me again on the same question. He had also seen the Turkish Minister and considered the situation grave. He had advised the State Department that they must support Turkey in resisting the Soviet demands even though the effect might be to bolster up the British Empire in that area—a thing which no American could contemplate in the ordinary way with any pleasure. But at least the British and Americans spoke more or less the same language and the British would discuss matters reasonably frankly whereas the Russians would not.

He then waved a large 'highball' at me and said that he thought the United States of America would be justified in asking us a price 'for defending the Empire'. For reasons purely selfish we were working against the United States of America and were refusing to allow American air lines to operate in that area for the benefit of the British Overseas Airways Corporation or other British air lines and opposing United States tele-communication for the benefit of Cables and Wireless—if we wanted United States support and we might want it badly why did we annoy the United States by our dog in the manger attitude? I challenged his allegations and he replied that he knew well enough what he was saying; he had had personal experience of our attitude and 'as for Lord Swinton,[4] he should be painted bright green and hung up in the House of Lords as an awful warning'.

I said that he kept telling me that the United States people disliked the British Empire and would like to see an end of it and at the same time they wanted to make use of it for air line bases &c., if it were true, which I was not prepared to admit, that we wanted to freeze the United States of America out of our spheres of interest, this might not be due as he alleged solely to commercial reasons but also to sound political reasons. Why should we facilitate the entry into our Empire of people whose professed desire was to break it up? In any case, we had had experience of Yankee trading methods and we did not like them.

The conversation was pretty frank but quite friendly, but there is no doubt that Adolf Berle is strongly anti-British though quite willing to make use of us for United States interests.

I am sending a copy of this letter to the Chancery at Washington.

Yours ever,

D. St. Clair Gainer

---

[4] Minister of Civil Aviation.

P.S.   Berle in referring to the British Empire also said that we did not really understand the relation of the United States to the South American countries which was that of a friendly neighbour always ready with good advice. 'Lord Halifax', he said, 'once said to me "please tell the Brazilian Government to do something" and I replied we cannot *tell* Brazil to do anything, we can only offer them advice and cannot do what you do e.g. in India'.[5]

[5] This letter was minuted as follows by Mr. McDermott and Mr. Pumphrey: 'I think there may be a good deal of truth in the views expressed in para. 1, & by Mr. Berle (see also R 12378), about Russia's long-term intentions. It is up to us to make the term long indeed; & at Potsdam the further moves in the game have not gone all in our disfavour . . . G. L. McDermott. 31/7.' 'Soviet demands on Turkey & Soviet infiltration into Persia bear all the hall-marks of a pincer movement; & Mr. Molotov made some tendentious remarks at Terminal about the different British attitudes to the Straits & the Suez Canal. J. L. Pumphrey. 2/8.'

No. 129

Minute from Mr. Eden to Mr. Churchill
No. P.M./45/326 [F.O. 954/19: Per/45/18]

FOREIGN OFFICE, *13 July 1945*

Troop Withdrawals from Persia

Sir Alexander Cadogan's minute P.M./45/316 of the 5th July.[1]

2. You will have seen from Bullard's latest telegrams[2] that the Russian grip on Persia is becoming tighter. The remedy is to secure a complete withdrawal of Russian forces as soon as possible. We can only do this, if we are prepared to offer a complete withdrawal of our own forces.

3. I want to get this settled at Terminal. I should like to offer complete joint withdrawal in three stages:–

(1) Both Allies to withdraw their forces completely from Tehran at once.

(2) The next stage would be withdrawal from the whole of Persia except the Abadan and southern oilfield area, in return for the Russians withdrawing from the whole of Persia except for a zone in either the North-East or the North-West.

(3) When the second stage has been completed, we would withdraw from the oil area and the Russians would withdraw from their remaining zone.

4. If we can get the Russians to accept this proposal at Terminal, we can leave the demarcation of the withdrawal zones to be worked out afterwards.

[1] For this minute, not printed, see Sir L. Woodward, *op. cit.*, vol. iv, p. 474, also *ibid.*, for the present document.
[2] See Nos. 91–93.

5. At present, our military authorities are not ready to carry out our part in any of the withdrawal stages which I have described above. They are prepared to withdraw a battalion stationed at Tehran but wish to keep a headquarters there to supervise the disposal of assets etc. I should hardly have thought this would be essential. They also wish to retain summer camps near Kermanshah. I can understand that it may be impossible to interrupt the arrangements made for this year, but after then it should not be difficult to make alternative arrangements. Finally, they are not prepared to entrust the protection of the oil fields to the Persians but in my view the supremely important thing is to get the Russians out of Persia and there will be much more risk to the oil fields if we fail in this than in leaving their protection to the Persians, as in years gone by.

ANTHONY EDEN

CALENDARS TO No. 129

i *9 July 1945   Brief No. 18 for U.K. Delegation on Persia: possible agreed withdrawal of Allied troops* [E 5043/103/34].

ii *11 July 1945   To Sir R. Bullard (Tehran) Tel. No. 410:* British object to relax Russian grip on North Persia by securing mutual withdrawals [E 4719/103/34].

No. 130

Brief for the United Kingdom Delegation to the Conference at Potsdam No. 52 [*U 5497/51/70*]

FOREIGN OFFICE, 13 July 1945[1]

Future of the Italian Colonies and the Italian Mediterranean Islands

1. We have a strategic interest in ensuring that these Italian overseas possessions do not come under the control of potential enemy states as they flank our sea and air communications through the Mediterranean and the Red Sea, and provide bases from which Egypt, the Sudan and Kenya could be attacked. At the same time we have no wish to annex these possessions and indeed could not do so compatibly with the Atlantic Charter. They are economic liabilities and we do not want to incur the additional expense and responsibilities. Moreover we do not want to lay ourselves open to accusations of British Imperialism. The best way of providing for the future of these territories would appear to be to bring them within the scope of international trusteeship.

2. The American ideas on the future of these territories are set out in the State Department memorandum (Annex A).[2] Ideas about international trusteeship have now been carried a stage further in Chapters XI–XIII of

---

[1] Date on which the draft of this brief was initialed by Lord Hood.
[2] Annexes to this brief are not attached to filed copy.

the San Francisco Charter[3] (Annex B). Under our draft heads of treaty with Italy,[4] we provide for cession of these possessions by Italy to the Four Powers. It will be for the Four Powers to formulate recommendations, for approval by the United Nations, for the future of these territories. Such recommendations might consist either (a) in allotting these territories to individual powers who might then announce their intention of classifying them as 'strategic areas' or 'trusteeship areas', in which case the necessary terms of a 'mandate' would be negotiated between the recipient and the United Nations; or (b) in allotting these territories to individual powers with the condition attached that they must be classified as 'strategic areas' or 'trusteeship areas' and the terms of the 'mandate' would be worked out as a preliminary to the transfer of the territory concerned to the ultimate recipient.

3. The following possible ways of dealing with the individual territories are the results of examination at the official level and have not been agreed interdepartmentally nor approved by Ministers.

Italian North Africa

4. We see no reason to maintain the unity of Libya which is a purely artificial creation.

Cyrenaica

5. We have given an undertaking to Sheik Seyyid el Idris that the Senussi in Cyrenaica will not again fall under Italian domination.[5] Cyrenaica might be made into a nominally independent arab emirate under the Sheik, with a status comparable to Transjordan, under international trusteeship, with Great Britain as a trustee. In view of its strategic importance parts of Cyrenaica might be classified as a 'strategic area'. On subsidiary points we might recommend (a) that the frontier between Cyrenaica and Tripolitania should run at least as far West as from the Wadi Harawa southwards, so as to include the oasis of Zella in Cyrenaica; (b) that there should be no alteration of the existing frontier between Egypt and Cyrenaica; (c) that French claims to Kufra should be resisted; (d) that the Oweinat oasis should be returned to the Sudan.

Tripolitania

6. This territory might be placed under international trusteeship with Italy as administrator. No other power is likely to be particularly interested in this territory, and there will be advantages in permitting Italy to retain a direct interest in one of her former Colonies. Such an arrangement could only become effective once Italy has been elected to the World Organisation. It may be desirable to make some frontier rectification in favour of France who has aspirations to the Fezzan and the Oases near the Tunisian frontier.

---

[3] See No. 1, note 5.
[4] See No. 31, note 1.
[5] See the statement made by Mr. Eden in the House of Commons on 8 January 1942: *Parl. Debs.*, 5th ser., *H. of C.*, vol. 377, cols. 77–8.

Eritrea

7. Eritrea is an artificial creation and might be dismembered along ethnic lines, giving the Western Lowlands to the Sudan and the remainder to Ethiopia. The cessation of this major portion of Eritrea would be conditional on:

(i) the acceptance by Eritrea either of international trusteeship obligations, or at least those suggested by the Americans in their memorandum (Annex A);

(ii) satisfactory arrangements for the use of Massawa and access to the Asmara Plateau in the event of our requiring these facilities in time of war. [The establishment of a United Nations Base at Massawa, has in the past been considered unnecessary by the Chiefs-of-Staff. It may, however, be desirable to consider whether it ought now to be classified as a strategic area];[6]

(iii) further rectifications between Ethiopia on the one hand and the Somali areas in South East Kenya near Moyale and the Sudan on the other hand all of which are in the interests of the local inhabitants;

(iv) Cession of the Ogaden.

Italian Somaliland

8. The elimination of Italy provides an opportunity for unifying all Samali [sic] inhabited territories and this is to be recommended in principle both as a progressive and forward-looking step, and because it would eliminate constant boundary troubles and friction. Unless however the Ogaden were included the unification of all Samali inhabited territories would not be achieved, and the unification of British and Italian Somalilands only, would involve the maintenance of a frontier with Ethiopia which is bound to cause friction. If a greater Somalia is established, one individual power should assume responsibility for its administration and that power must be strong enough to provide for the security of the state, both in time of peace or war. His Majesty's Government are reluctant to assume that responsibility themselves, and if by any chance the United States of America felt able to themselves assume responsibility for Italian Somaliland and the Ogaden, His Majesty's Government will welcome this. Furthermore if the British Somali tribes express a wish to be included in a greater Somalia under United States administration, His Majesty's Government would for their part certainly not stand in the way of a transfer. If however, the United States of America are not prepared to accept responsibility, then His Majesty's Government in view of their interest in these territories, which flank one of their main sea communications, might be forced to accept responsibility.

9. It is however by no means certain that Ethiopia can be induced to cede the Ogaden and the United States Government may well sympathize

---

[6] Square brackets in original.

with this attitude. From the British Somaliland point of view, the main concern is to secure from Ethiopia certain grazing lands which are used by the British solalis [Somalis] and essential to the efficient administration of British Somaliland. If the greater Somalia scheme is ruled out, we should press for the necessary frontier rectification between British Somaliland and the adjacent Ethiopian territory. Italian Somaliland could be placed as a separate unit under international trusteeship with the United States of America, France or in the last resort, ourselves as trustee.

10. If either Greater Somalia or Italian Somaliland is under non-British administration, it would be desirable to restore the Kenya frontier to the line of the river Juba thus taking back the territory ceded to Italy in 1924 and restoring a workable frontier. If on the other hand His Majesty's Government are forced to accept responsibility, then it may be administratively convenient to include in the Somali administrative unit, not only Jubaland but also part of the present Northern frontier district of Kenya.

Pantellaria and the Pelagian Islands

These islands might be treated in the same way as the Japanese islands in the Pacific and be classified as a 'strategic area', in which case Great Britain might be the responsible power. There may however be advantage in allowing Italy to continue to administer the islands. In that case they might be made 'a trusteeship area' with arrangements for inspection to make sure that their demilitarization is maintained.[7]

---

[7] This brief was minuted as follows in the Reconstruction and Egyptian Departments of the Foreign Office: 'This brief was produced at the last moment in order to give our representatives at Terminal some of the background in case this subject is raised. Although the future of the Italian Colonies has been frequently discussed at the official level, we have so far been unable to formulate definite recommendations for Ministerial approval. With the end of the war in Europe and the probability of an early Peace Treaty with Italy it is time that we arrived at some firm conclusions. An essential peice of back-ground which was previously lacking is now available in the shape of the Trusteeship chapters in the San Francisco Charter. I have suggested on another paper that the future of Cyrenaica ought now to be taken up and I think it is equally desirable that we should straighten out our ideas on the future of the other Italian African possessions. As a first step we might send the enclosed brief to the Colonial Office with a view to an early interdepartmental meeting, with the object of preparing a paper for submission to the Chiefs of Staff and the Cabinet. Hood 19th July, 1945.' 'Yes. But it will be useless to pursue the C.O.'s idea of a Greater Somaliland including the Ogaden unless we have first brought the Americans round to our way of thinking. Perhaps the C.O. can suggest how to do this. Mere logic will not be enough. A. V. Coverley Price 18/7.' 'Presumably this sort of problem will hereafter be dealt with by the Foreign Ministers' Committee. Our representative on it will have to be instructed by the O.R.C. As soon as Terminal is over, therefore, we should prepare a paper for submission to O.R.C. This paper will not only have to contain proposals for solving the various problems, but also discuss possible tactical lines for adoption e.g. the possibility of squaring the Americans on this or that before the matter reaches the Committee. My own personal feeling is that, judging by the behaviour of the Americans before and during Terminal, we have small hope of involving them in preliminary bilateral discussions on anything. N. B. R[onald] 23.vii.'

No. 131

Minute from Mr. Eden to Mr. Dixon
[U 6051/51/70]

FOREIGN OFFICE, *13 July 1945*

We should be giving careful thought to our whole Middle Eastern position. I have Cyrenaica particularly in mind. We are likely to have trouble with Egypt later on, and events in Levant may accelerate this. Cyrenaica seems to have obvious advantages.

(1) Less local political difficulty.

(2) Good training ground.

(3) Good place from which to keep an eye on canal from a distance in time of peace.

I thought that Sir E Grigg or his predecessor promised us something on all this long ago.[1] At least we should consider what arrangement we should require, presumably from Senussi, to give us what we need. I should hope that it could all be done by a Treaty.[2]

A.E.

[1] Mr. P. S. Scrivener, Head of Egyptian Department, stated in a minute of 15 July 1945 that 'Sir E. Grigg has in fact put in a paper [of 28 May on E 3977/571/65: not printed] emphasising the importance of Cyrenaica strategically and politically.'

[2] Mr. Pierson Dixon minuted on this on 13 July to Sir R. Campbell: 'I have ascertained from the S. of S. that the kind of arrangement he has in mind under the attached minute is the creation of an independent state of Cyrenaica (preferably not to be a member of the United Nations) which w[oul]d be linked closely with Great Britain by a treaty. No doubt you will be sending the S. of S. the results of your consideration of his suggestions.' Consideration was given to this question in the Foreign Office but action on it was deferred till after the Conference at Potsdam.

No. 132

Letter from Mr. Dening (Kandy)[1] to Mr. Sterndale-Bennett (Received 21 July)
No. 1652 [F 4541/47/23]

HEADQUARTERS, SUPREME ALLIED COMMANDER, SOUTH EAST ASIA, *13 July 1945*

Top secret. Personal

Dear Sterndale-Bennett,

I arrived on 10th July[2] just in time to have a brief conversation with the Supreme Commander before he left on the following morning to visit General MacArthur. Since then I have been asked to explain to the Chief

[1] Mr. M. E. Dening was Political Adviser to Admiral Lord Louis Mountbatten, Supreme Allied Commander, South East Asia (S.A.C.S.E.A.).

[2] Mr. Dening had returned to Kandy via London from a visit to Washington.

of Staff, the Assistant Chief of Staff and also the Joint Planning Staff the general position as I found it in Washington and London.

2. There is undoubtedly considerable resentment here at the way S.E.A.C. has been treated, particularly in respect of Python.[3] All the senior staff are agreed that, if it is decided to mount an assault force for Japan from India, it will put a complete stop on all S.E.A.C. operations after Mailfist.[4] I think they feel that they and India should have been consulted as to the practicability of the scheme before it was put up. There was some tendency to try to propagand against it by last minute telegrams, but I told the Chief of Staff that, in view of Cossea 331[5] and of the fact that I knew the Prime Minister had already given his decision, I thought it would make the worst possible impression to send any telegrams at all. I further advised complete silence on all except routine matters until the Supreme Commander goes home and can talk to people himself.

3. Quite a number of the staff are to go home at or about the same time as the Supreme Commander, and I gather that he will take his Planners with him. I do not know how this invasion from S.E.A.C. will go down in London, but on the other hand I think it is a good idea that the Supreme Commander is going with his Planners, as there is a good deal to be said on the side of S.E.A.C. even if they don't manage to put it over very well in telegrams.

4. If the offer of the assault force is accepted by the Americans and if it is true that mounting of it in India will put a stop to all S.E.A.C. operations for many months, then I am afraid the political consequences may well be serious. For we cannot afford a long hiatus, the more so as any enthusiasm which exists for the war against Japan is likely to wane rather than to wax. We may find that the liberation of territories other than Malaya cannot take place until the latter half of 1946 and even well on into 1947. Either the Japanese will have given in before then and we shall have failed to attain the military objectives which to my mind are essential to the restoration of our political position south of the Tropic of Cancer, or we shall drag on wearily with a growingly unpopular war while the general economy of the Far East grows worse and worse. It is not an inviting prospect.

5. I gather that the Planners here are not in favour of an attack on Siam because they consider it uses up certain resources which could be better employed elsewhere. They point out that Indo-China also has a large rice surplus and that it would be more profitable to cut off the Japanese in Siam by an assault on Indo-China, and they like to think that then the Siamese could finish off the Japanese by themselves. I mention this because it may come up. The Supreme Commander and the Chief of Staff, as well as the Planners, are quite well disposed towards my idea of a staging post in

[3] Codename for the procedure for the repatriation of British troops after a fixed period of service overseas.

[4] Codename for the projected British operation for the recapture of Singapore, after landings in Malaya (Operation Zipper).

[5] *Note on original:* 'not rec'd'.

Indo-China followed by the opening of the Pearl River and the capture of Hongkong.

6. I hope that the decisions at Terminal may prove more favourable to S.E.A.C. than there is reason to suppose at present. The trouble is that the Chiefs of Staff have always been against S.E.A.C. strategy and that they cannot realise that *politically* it has been and must remain the most important part of our war in the Far East. Militarily it is an American party anyway.[6]

Yours ever,

M. E. DENING

[6] Mr. B. W. A. Plunket, a member of the Far Eastern Department of the Foreign Office, minuted on this letter: 'The problems raised here seem to boil down to one vital question. Is it more important militarily and politically for H.M. Forces to participate in the final assault on Japan than for S.E.A.C. to liberate the territories in that command? We cannot do both. B. W. A. Plunket 26/7.'

No. 133

Mr. Roberts (Moscow) to Mr. Eden (Received 14 July, 2.25 p.m.)

No. 3133 Telegraphic [F.O. 934/3/12(5)]

Important. Secret　　　　　　　　　　　MOSCOW, *14 July 1945, 11.30 a.m.*

Repeated to Chungking (Foreign Office please repeat unnumbered).

Soong left Moscow this morning and expects to be in Chungking on July 16th. He intends to return to Moscow and resume his conversations with Stalin after Terminal. Meanwhile Doctor Victor Hoo[1] is staying in Moscow for further talks with Soviet officials in preparation for Soong's return visit.

2. Doctor Hoo told me this morning at the airfield that Soong might then go straight to London from Moscow although he had not yet been able to make definite plans.

3. Greatest discretion is being maintained here about Soong's visit on which His Majesty's Ambassador is reporting personally at Terminal.[2]

[1] Chinese Administrative Vice-Minister for Foreign Affairs.

[2] This telegram was forwarded from the Foreign Office to the British Delegation in Berlin on 16 July 1945.

No. 134

Earl of Halifax (Washington) to Mr. Eden (Received 15 July, 4.45 a.m.)

No. 4925 Telegraphic [W 9589/1520/49]

Immediate. Secret　　　　　　　　　　WASHINGTON, *14 July 1945, 10.10 p.m.*

My telegram No. 4330.[1]

The British Air Commission has communicate[d] to me a memorandum received from the State Department by the joint aircraft committee signed by the chairman of the 'Committee for Technical Information Security

[1] Of 22 June 1945, not printed.

Controls of the State, War and Navy Departments Coordinating Committee'. After referring to the exchange of information which has taken place under the Lend Lease agreement this memorandum goes on to say that insofar as existing procedures (of the joint aircraft committee) require or authorise the disclosure to representatives of the British Commonwealth of United States technical information classifying [classified][2] 'confidential' or higher which meant they are to be considered[3] usable in the prosecution of the war against Japan before the first of January, 1(?9)47 [they][2] are contrary to the policy of the United States Government. The memorandum requests that the procedures be modified accordingly. (British Aircraft Commission have reported this to M.A.P. in Briny 78.)[4]

2. Meanwhile the British Central Scientific Office received a communication on 6th July, from the director of the 'New Developments Division' of the War Department refusing a request for the 'United States Arm[y] Air Forces report on guided missiles' on the ground that the information requested was primarily of significance for post-war development and was not considered 'usable in connexion with the provision of articles which have developed to such a point that they will be produced for the war against Japan' within the meaning of the Lend Lease agreement.

3. I am not aware of the decision reached by His Majesty's Government on the joint staff missions report MM(S) (45–50) final of the 15th June [i], referred to in paragraph 1 of my telegram under reference but it is clear that instructions have now been issued on the United States side not to disclose information on research and development in the defence field which cannot be applied in the war against Japan. I am informed that United States service departments are not happy about these instructions and may well try to circumvent them or minimise their effect as far as they can. But you will appreciate that the position as regards exchange of information with the United States will now steadily deteriorate unless corrective action on the lines proposed by the joint staff mission in their report referred to above is taken without delay.

4. Please repeat to Terminal.[5]

[2] Supplied from an amended version of this sentence sent in Washington telegram No. 4963 of 16 July.

[3] In Washington telegram No. 4963 the preceding phrase read 'which may not (repeat not) fairly be considered'.

[4] This telegram to the Ministry of Aircraft Production is untraced in Foreign Office archives.

[5] This telegram, repeated as No. 17 Onward of 15 July to Berlin, was minuted there by Mr. Churchill to Mr. Eden: 'This is of high importance. W. S. C. 16.7.' Mr. Eden replied: 'I agree. I do not suppose that President gave this directive himself. It would probably therefore be salutary if you had a word about it with Truman yourself while we are here. A. E. July 16.' On 17 July Mr. Churchill sent a letter to General of the U.S. Army George C. Marshall enclosing a copy of the present telegram, 'which rather worried me. As you said you had not heard about this point, I send you a copy. I should be glad if you would let me have it back as soon as you have read it' (PREM 4/17/16/1527). This telegram was read and returned by General Marshall without comment.

i *15 June & 10 July 1945   British Joint Staff Mission (Washington) Report M.M. (S)* *(45) 50 Final on collaboration with the United States on research and development;* *Minute from General Sir H. Ismay to Mr. Churchill.* Aim should be to reach agreement with U.S. to continue collaboration for an indefinite period aftet the end of the war against Japan. It is suggested that Mr. Churchill should approach President Truman: cf. H. Duncan Hall, *North American Supply* (H.M.S.O., 1955), pp. 464–5 [W 9942/1520/49, PREM 4/17/16].

ii *14 July 1945   Memorandum by Joint Staff Mission, C.C.S. 864/2, on allocation* *policy on samples of secret weapons.* British Chiefs of Staff agree that where supplies are inadequate U.S. requirements should receive preferential treatment over those of U.K. provided this constitutes best contribution to development of weapons for use in Japanese war. Proposes joint consultations before removal from Germany to U.S. or U.K. of scientific personnel, equipment etc: encloses draft message to S.C.A.E.F. [UE 3465/818/53].

iii *14 & 16 July 1945   Notes, E.C.C. (45) 3, by Major-General E. I. C. Jacob* *(Cabinet Office, Military Staff) and Mr. Lincoln.* Mr. Churchill has sent telegram to F.M. Montgomery instructing that no research establishments in Germany should be destroyed without further instruction. Mr. Churchill requests urgent report from European Control Committee on such policy. Briefing note of 16 July by Mr. Lincoln for committee meeting that afternoon of the E.C.C. (cf. No. 300) [UE 3123/3123/53].

No. 135

Mr. Eden to Earl of Halifax (Washington)
No. 7443 Telegraphic [UR 2230/1590/851]

Important   FOREIGN OFFICE, *14 July 1945*, *5.40 a.m.*

Following for Ambassador from Ministry [Minister] of Food.

I understand that a full reply is being prepared to the various points raised in your telegram No. 4718.[1] In the meantime however, I want to thank you personally for your advice and to say how much I agree with you in the need for insuring that our attempts at closer co-operation with our European Allies do not endanger the supplies of food coming to us from North America.

Nevertheless I feel that the difficulties we are experiencing here may not be fully appreciated in Washington. The Governments of France, Belgium and other European countries are growing increasingly restive under impression that the United States, United Kingdom and Canada are carving up the world food supplies without regard to the needs of liberated countries. They would value the assurance that they are to have a fair share, and in any event while supplies are short, they want to know the facts. I feel that we should do something to prevent their discontents from gaining

---

[1] See No. 98, note 1.

ground and that one immediate step to this end would be to bring them at once into the deliberations of the combined machinery. I should be most grateful therefore if you could use your influence to impress upon the American Administration the wisdom of acting quickly in inviting our European Allies to join various committees of the C.F.B. along the lines which we have already suggested to them.

I discussed this topic with Clayton during my recent visit[2] and understood that he was of the view that we could not hope to maintain C.F.B. machinery unless we widened the circle of membership of its main committees. I do not know what has occurred since to prevent United States Administration from accepting our proposal. It is certain that action will have to be taken if the combined machinery is to be maintained. The sooner therefore a favourable decision is communicated to the Governments concerned the better.

[2] Colonel J. J. Llewellin and Mr. Oliver Lyttelton had in March-April 1945 led a mission to Washington to discuss food supplies and allocations: see R. J. Hammond, *Food* (H.M.S.O. 1951 f.), vol. i, pp. 251–4.

No. 136

Mr. Houstoun-Boswall (Sofia) to Mr. Eden (Received 14 July, 5.15 p.m.)
No. 815 Telegraphic [R 12309/5063/67]

Immediate   SOFIA, *14 July 1945, 1.59 p.m. G.M.T.*

Repeated to Washington, Moscow, Bucharest, Budapest, Paris, Athens Saving Resmed Caserta Saving.

Your telegram No. 7376 to Washington.[1]

It seems to me that the attitude of United States Government in pressing for reorganisation of control Commissions, has met with some success in Bulgaria at any rate (see Military Mission's telegrams Nos. 1443 and 1444 to War Office).[2] In these circumstances would it not be unfortunate to give them an opportunity to *oppose* in the presence of Russians your proposal to establish diplomatic relations with this Government.

2. From my experience of the Russians (which is, I admit, confined only to Sofia) I feel that any such disagreement between His Majesty's Government and United States Government would be grist to their mill.

[1] See No. 82, note 5.
[2] These telegrams of 12 July 1945 respectively reported receipt of, and transmitted a translated text of, a communication of 11 July concerning reorganization from the Soviet Assistant Chairman of the Allied Control Commission in Bulgaria to the British Commissioner, Major-General W. H. Oxley, in the same terms as that to the American representative, printed in *F.R.U.S. Berlin*, vol. i, pp. 405–6. Similar Soviet communications were sent in respect of Hungary on 11 July (see No. 197.i), of Finland on 12 July (cf. *F.R.U.S. 1945*, vol. iv, pp. 617–8) and of Roumania on 16 July (see No. 259).

Should we not therefore do our utmost to avoid giving them such a chance to exploit?

3. I submit too that the present would be a most inauspicious moment to confer on this parody of 'United and democratic' patriotic front government the prestige which would accrue to them from recognition (see my telegrams Nos. 709[3] and 793[4] especially paragraph 7). Let us rather leave them to stew in their own juice and in the knowledge that so long as they behave badly they will not be recognised.[5]

Foreign Office please pass important to Washington as my telegram No. 94 and no priority to Paris as my telegram No. 5.

CALENDAR TO No. 136

i *12 & 14 July 1945 British Military Mission (Bulgaria) Tels. Nos. M. 1448 & M. 1457.* British Acting Commissioner counsels 'utmost caution' in accepting Soviet proposals for A.C.C. Recent experiences indicate there is no real ground for satisfaction, and current British effort to establish rights and privileges in Bulgaria on a just basis should not be deflected. Subsequent comments (M. 1457) from Major-General Oxley in general agreement [F.O. 934/2/9(26)].

[3] Of 12 June, not printed.
[4] See No. 90, note 1.
[5] Mr. Eden here minuted: 'Much to be said for this. A. E.'

No. 137

Mr. Caccia (Athens) to Mr. Eden (Received 14 July, 10.5 p.m.)
No. 1536 Telegraphic [R 11909/210/19]

Immediate   ATHENS, *14 July 1945, 7.8 p.m. G.M.T.*

Repeated to Washington, and Saving to Moscow, Belgrade, Rome, Sofia, Resmed's Office Caserta.

I have just received your despatch No. 1395 [395][1] about Greek territorial claims. Before carrying out your instructions to tell the Greek Government 'that they should not put forward official claims to Yugoslav or Bulgarian territory' and that they 'might be well advised not to press their claims against Albania', I respectfully request that the following points should receive further consideration.

2. The present Government is a service Government and rightly regards itself as nothing more than a caretaker Government until the plebiscite and election can be held. I should not despair, therefore, of persuading them to accept this unpalatable advice about their claims on their northern neighbours provided that I could at the same time tell them that the possibility of Greece presenting such claims at the proper time and place

[1] Of 28 June 1945, not printed.

was not thereby being prejudiced. Even this would not be easy for the present Greek Government, for they are subject to pressure not only from public opinion but also from the Greek Foreign Affairs Committee of ex-Prime Ministers and ex-Foreign Secretaries. An example of this over Southern Albania is contained in my telegram No. 1535[2] of July 13th. But they might reasonably resist this pressure on the ground that Greek national claims should be presented by an elected rather than a caretaker Government. Can I therefore have some indication of what the proper time and place will be for the presentation of national claims which in the case of Greece will certainly include the Dodecanese?

3. I am not only concerned about the effect on the stability of the present Government of our advice on these matters. It is a subject which will be bound to have a lasting effect on our relations with and standing in Greece in the future. May I therefore ask whether His Majesty's Government prefers to act entirely alone over this or whether it might not be to our advantage to try to get the United States Government to act on parallel lines? From my conversations with the United States Ambassador in recent days I know that he, for one, thinks it would be extremely unwise for Greece to put forward claims against their northern neighbours *at present* and that in private conversation he has already given certain political leaders his personal advice to wait for the proper time and place. In his personal view the Greek Government (. . . ? even then)[3] would probably be well-advised to make no territorial claims on Bulgaria, and certainly on (. . . ? Yugoslavia).[3] But he does not exclude the possibility that a Greek claim for (. . . ? rectification)[3] in Southern Albania might not have the sympathetic support of the United States Government. In view of this and the fact that the United States Government are not prepared to join with us in the supervision of the Greek plebiscite and election, I would urge strongly from the local point of view that we should not act alone with the Greek Government but should concert our advice with the United States Government.

4. If, despite the above considerations, you still wish me to act as instructed in your despatch I would ask two things: firstly, that I may be allowed to restrict my objective to that contained in Sir O. Sargent's letter of June 1st to the Greek Chargé d'Affaires,[4] namely, to advise them 'not to emphasise at present their territorial claims against their northern neighbours': or that I may have discretion to abstain

(a) from mentioning any rewards which they may reap at this stage of a policy of self-abnegation, e.g. in their relations with Albania: and

(b) from suggesting that the justice of Greek claim in Southern Albania is still more doubtful now than it was after the last war.

The mention of possible rewards as at (a) would appear to them derisory in the light of what they feel they have suffered as a result of the decision of the

[2] Not printed (R 11904/322/19).
[3] The text is here uncertain.
[4] Not printed.

Ambassador's [*sic*] Conference in 1921.[5] It will be remembered that this was the decision which belied the proposals previously made by all the major Powers including His Majesty's Government for granting to Greece most of the territory which she now claims. The suggestion at (*b*) would seem to the Greeks cynical in the extreme in view of their sacrifices and successes in the 1940–1941 Albanian campaign as well as of the measures taken by the Albanians since 1921 and particularly in the last two years to reduce the Greek population in the area. In a small country and with people as quick-witted as the Greeks, an argument based on the present balance of forces in the Balkans should be quite sufficient.[6]

CALENDAR TO NO. 137

i *16 July 1945 Letter from Mr. Houstoun-Boswall (Sofia) to Mr. Hayter.* Views of Regent Ganev on Bulgaro-Greek relations. Greek intransigence towards Bulgaria could deter Bulgarians from looking to the West [R 12472/4443/7].

[5] By a decision of 9 November 1921 (printed in *League of Nations, Official Journal, 1921*, part ii, p. 1195) the Albanian frontiers established in 1913 were confirmed, subject to the further delimitation of certain portions in the north, by the Allied Conference of Ambassadors for the interpretation and execution of the peace treaties concluded at the Conference of Paris.

[6] Action on this telegram was suspended and was not subsequently taken up.

No. 138

Brief for the United Kingdom Delegation to the Conference at Potsdam
No. 54 [ZM 3830/1/22]

FOREIGN OFFICE, 14 July 1945[1]

Italy

The United States having put Italy on their agenda for Terminal, the matter will presumably come up for tripartite discussion. Although it is not difficult to prepare a brief on Italy for purely Anglo-American discussion, tripartite discussion is more difficult since in fact our present policy towards Italy is largely directed to trying to ensure—and trying to get the Americans similarly to ensure—that Italy does not fall under Russian influence, that she looks towards the West rather than the East and that she becomes a kind of outpost of democracy and a stabilising influence in the Mediterranean rather than yet another 'police state' under Communist domination and with a government which in no way really represents the popular will.

The best way out of the difficulty would therefore seem to be to prepare two briefs on Italy, the first for Anglo-American-Russian discussion and the second for purely Anglo-American discussion. These briefs are attached. (Annexes A and B[2].)

[1] Date of covering minute of instruction for entry by Mr. Hoyer Millar.
[2] Annex B is not printed. For this annex, which referred to Nos. 12.i and 118, see Sir L. Woodward, *op. cit.*, vol. iii, pp. 487–9.

Italy

Brief for Anglo-American-Russian discussion

His Majesty's Government are anxious to help Italy recover her position as a useful member of the European comity as soon as possible. This objective is not only desirable from the point of view of the Italian people themselves but is in the general interest since it is clearly important that Italy should become a stabilising influence in Europe and in the Mediterranean rather than a focus of trouble and disorder. Clearly, the Italian people should be encouraged to stand on their own feet as soon as possible and to work out their own salvation to the greatest possible extent. At the same time they will clearly want much assistance from the Allied Governments in the near future if their return to stability is not to be unduly delayed. It is in the interests of the Allied Governments themselves to give Italy this support.

Support for Italy can take two forms—political and economic. On the political side His Majesty's Government attach great importance to the elections for the Constituent Assembly being held at the earliest possible moment so that Italy can be provided with a governmental machine—both local and central—based firmly on popular elections and the will of the people freely expressed. The new Italian Government are showing every sign of wishing to proceed along these lines and to hold the elections at an early date. It might, however, be helpful if some public statement were to be made by the three Governments welcoming the new Italian Government's programme, reaffirming the Moscow Declaration[3] and definitely stating that the three Governments for their part hope that the elections will be held as soon as practicable.

It is equally very desirable that the elections should be held in a calm atmosphere so that all sections of the population can vote freely and without fear of the consequences. The new Italian Government will no doubt do their utmost to maintain order during the interval preceding the elections, but the coming months are likely to be very difficult and some reference to the necessity of the Italian people keeping calm and co-operating with each other might usefully be included in any statement by the three Governments.

The corollary to any such statement about the elections is, of course, that the three Governments will strictly abstain from endeavouring in any way to influence the outcome of the elections. His Majesty's Government for their part are only concerned that the elections should be conducted farily [fairly] without intimidation from any side and in such a way as to enable the great mass of the population to express their views candidly. There is no truth in the suggestion that His Majesty's Government are anxious to insist on the return of the monarchy. They regard the decision on this point as entirely one for the Italian people and a matter in which no foreign power should attempt directly to intervene. It is incorrect to say that His Majesty's Government (and the United States Government) have insisted on the Italian Government giving the pledge not to raise the 'institutional question' for reasons of their own and in order to further the cause of the monarchy. The obligation on the Italian Ministers not to raise the institutional question was in fact imposed by the Italian Government themselves in the decree law of June,

---

[3] *Note in filed copy:* 'see copy attached', not here printed. The Anglo-American-Soviet Declaration regarding Italy, issued at Moscow on 1 November 1943, is printed in *F.R.U.S. 1943*, vol. i, pp. 759–60.

1944, which stated: 'The Ministers and Under-Secretaries of State swear on their honour . . . [4] until the convocation of the Constituent Assembly not to commit acts which in any way will prejudice the solution of the institutional question'. Furthermore, it is clearly not in the interests of the Italian people that the institutional question should be pronounced on until the population as a whole (as opposed to the political parties) can express a view on the question at duly constituted elections.

A further way in which the new Italian Government could be greatly helped and its authority strengthened would be if the three Governments were to state that they were in favour of the early conclusion of a Peace Treaty.

On the economic side, Italy will require much assistance and advice during the coming months, although at the same time the Italians should be encouraged to stand on their own feet as much as possible. If serious unemployment, with the consequent risk of internal disorders (which might react unfortunately on the elections) is to be avoided, more particularly in North Italy, considerable supplies, especially of coal, will have to be made available to Italy in the near future. Some public assurance by the three Governments that Italy's needs in this respect will be given sympathetic consideration would be useful.

The draft of a possible tripartite for the statement[5] on Italy is attached.

[4] Punctuation as in original quotation.
[5] Typed in error for 'tripartite public statement'. This draft, not here printed, was attached to annex B: see note 2 above and, for an amended text, annex 3 to No. 212.

No. 139

Minute by Viscount Hood
[U 5598/20/70]

FOREIGN OFFICE, *14 July 1945*

The French zone of occupation in Germany extends up to the northern boundary of the districts of Trier and Koblenz. This means that the French zone will march with the Belgian frontier up to the neighbourhood of St. Vith.

I believe the Belgian Ambassador raised this orally with the Secretry of State yesterday and was informed as above. May I take it that no further reply is required?[1]

HOOD

[1] Mr. Harvey minuted: 'The Secretary of State showed the Belgian Ambassador the northern boundary of the French zone on the map yesterday. The Ambassador was somewhat concerned to see that it confirmed his fears. The Secretary of State did his best to reassure him on the subject, adding that he could not believe that the French harboured any of the designs which he attributed to them. O. C. H. 14th July, 1945.' That day Sir Hughe Knatchbull-Hugessen, H.M. Ambassador in Brussels, expressed the opinion in his despatch No. 226 (Z 8484/8433/4: received 18 July) that 'the accusation against my French colleague for conducting propaganda in Wallonia is not lacking in foundation. Complaints have been made to me on several occasions during the last few months to this effect. I am also aware that he has expressed himself as strongly opposed to the return of King Leopold the III.'

i *14 July 1945   Letter from Mr. Harvey to Sir H. Knatchbull-Hugessen (Brussels).* Disadvantages of retaining British forces in Belgium considered greater than those of possible disturbances arising from King Leopold's stand against abdication [Z 7919/3172/4].

ii *16 July 1945   Sir H. Knatchbull-Hugessen (Brussels) Tel. No. 470.* Belgian Prime Minister reports fluctuating attitude of King Leopold towards abdication [Z 8422/3172/4].

iii *21 July 1945   To Sir H. Knatchbull-Hugessen (Brussels) No. 417.* Conversations on 12–13 July with members of the French Embassy in London: British impartiality and non-intervention in Belgian constitutional question; refusal in the Foreign Office to credit reports of French intervention [Z 8602/3172/4].

No. 140

Mr. Norton (Berne)[1] to Mr. Eden (Received 9 August)
No. 2656 [U 6108/16/73]

BERNE, *14 July 1945*

His Majesty's Minister at Berne presents his compliments to His Majesty's Principal Secretary of State for Foreign Affairs and has the honour to transmit to him the under-mentioned documents.

Reference to previous correspondence:
F.O. telegram No. 1158 of 22.6.1945[2]

Description of Enclosure

Name and Date	Subject
From: H.M. Consulate, Geneva.	Conditions in German concentration
Date: 12th July 1945	camps and 'slave' labour in Germany.

ENCLOSURE IN No. 140

Letter from Mr. Armstrong (Geneva) to M. MacKillop (Berne)[3]

Copy
GENEVA, *12 July 1945*

Dear MacKillop,

With reference to Foreign Office telegram 1158[2] of June 22nd concerning information to be obtained from the I[nternational] R[ed] C[ross] C[ommittee] on Conditions in German Concentration Camps and 'slave' labour in Germany, I wrote at once to the IRCC enquiring whether they would put any of their

---

[1] Mr. C. J. Norton was H.M. Minister at Berne.
[2] Annotation on original: 'Wrong ref. No trace.'
[3] Mr. R. A. L. Armstrong was H.M. Vice-Consul at Geneva. Mr. D. Mackillop was Counsellor in H.M. Legation at Berne.

material at our disposal. Having received no reply by July 6th I mentioned the matter to President Huber[4] at the Red Cross luncheon in honour of Lady Limerick.[5] He was extremely evasive, though kind and courteous as usual. He promised, however, to let me have an answer of some sort, but hinted that very often Red Cross statistics were of an entirely confidential nature. On July 11th, being still without a definite reply, I telephoned to his secretary, Baron de Graffenreid, who this morning gave me verbally a message from President Huber to the following effect:

The IRCC have no information on the Concentration camps in their possession at present other than that already in the hands of the Allied Governments, since their delegates were never able to enter these camps until a few days before the Allies took them over. Though they expect some reports from their people, most of these have not yet come in. The IRCC, however, propose to publish in about two months time a White Book[6] giving a complete account of all their endeavours since 1939 to 'get the powers to do something about Concentration Camps'.

As to 'slave' labour, de Graffenreid stated categorically that this matter was quite outside the province of the IRCC.

I have the feeling that nothing more can be extracted.

Yours ever,
RONALD ARMSTRONG

CALENDAR TO No. 140

i *19 July 1945   Mr. Norton (Berne) No. 2678.* Transmits I.R.C.C. letter of 13 July confirming message of 11 July [U 6201/16/73].

[4] Dr. Max Huber was President of the International Red Cross.
[5] The Countess of Limerick was Deputy Chairman of the British Red Cross Society.
[6] Untraced. Cf., however, *Rapport du Comité international de la Croix-Rouge sur son activité pendant la seconde guerre mondiale (1er septembre 1939–30 juin 1947)* (Geneva, 1948).

No. 141

Minute from Sir R. Campbell to Mr. Dixon
[*Campbell Papers*]

Top secret and Personal   FOREIGN OFFICE, *14 July 1945*
T[ube] A[lloys]

Sir A. Cadogan and I thought it better to spare the Foreign Office delegation to Terminal the responsibility of having any papers with them on this subject, especially since the Prime Minister will have all that seems necessary for the meeting.

The papers[1] the Prime Minister will have are:

[1] The listed papers are not attached to the filed copy and are untraced in Foreign Office archives: cf., however, notes 2–4 below.

(1) Notes prepared for him by the Chancellor[2] (already seen by the Secretary of State). These include the text of what President Truman has been advised to say to U. J. spontaneously, and also what both Governments have agreed should be said if any mention of the subject were to be left for a possible enquiry from U. J. without any spontaneous statement from our side.

(2) A minute with the texts of the proposed statements to be issued by the President and Mr. Stimson after the project has been put into effect. These texts contain our suggested amendments interleaved.[3]

With these texts is also the text of the proposed statement to be issued by the Prime Minister just after the issue of the American statements.

(3) The latest state of the texts of the two statements resulting from further counter amendments by H.M.G. and the American proposals for meeting these. The Prime Minister will have spare copies of these texts for the Secretary of State and Lord Cherwell.

(4) A note by Lord Cherwell[4] for the Prime Minister on the subject of speaking to U. J. This sets out the pros and cons (a) of taking the initiative, (b) of saying anything at all to U. J., in case the matter comes up in one way or the other. The note also refers to the difficulty of rejecting the American wish to initiate some statement to U. J. since the vastly major proportion of effort has been put in by the United States.

You might remember that an approach has been made to van Kleffens[5] with a view to an agreement for the control of thorium in the Netherlands East Indies. This approach was made on July 12th in very general terms with due injunctions about secrecy and the importance of speedy action. Van Kleffens had no doubt that the attitude of his Government would be entirely cooperative. He would have to mention the matter to his Prime Minister and the Minister for Overseas Territories but only to these. He would do this immediately on his return to The Hague on July 17th and would propose the designation by his Government of somebody competent to deal with the matter who would come to London possibly (but not certainly) next week. Van Kleffens would probably attend the next conversations on this matter.

Will you please tell Sir A. Cadogan of the foregoing?

R. C.

CALENDARS TO No. 141

i *10 July 1945 J.S.M. (Washington) Tel. No. 334 Ancam.* Mr. Byrnes has instructed that negotiations with the Netherlands and Sweden for agreements on thorium and uranium be pressed on. (For the subsequent Anglo-American

[2] Cf. No. 110.i.
[3] See No. 110.ii.
[4] No. 110.
[5] Dr. E. van Kleffens was the Netherland Minister for Foreign Affairs: see ii below.

approach to the Swedish Government cf. *F.R.U.S. 1945*, vol. ii, pp. 24 f. and M. Gowing, *op. cit.*, p. 314) [Campbell Papers].

ii *12–13 July 1945 Minute from Sir R. Campbell to Mr. Eden; to J.S.M. (Washington) Tel. No. 358 Canam.* Meeting between Sir J. Anderson and Mr. Winant on approach to Netherland Government and ensuing meeting between Sir J. Anderson and Dr. van Kleffens: cf. *F.R.U.S. 1945*, vol. ii, pp. 30–1 (cf. *ibid.*, pp. 32–3 for further meeting of 30 July) [Campbell Papers].

No. 142

Record of a preliminary meeting with the United States Delegation held at Berlin on the afternoon of 14 July 1945[1]
[*F.O. 934/2/8(1)*]

Secret   BERLIN, *15 July 1945*

Present

British SIR A. CADOGAN, Mr. Hayter, Mr. Coulson.

U.S. MR. HARRIMAN,[2] Mr. Clayton, Mr. Joseph Davies, Mr. Moseley [Mosely], [Mr. Dunn].

Procedure for the Conference

SIR A. CADOGAN mentioned the Secretary of State's proposal to the Prime Minister that the procedure adopted at Yalta should be followed at this meeting.[3] MR. DUNN said he did not know the views of the President and Mr. Byrnes, but he thought that this would be all right.

2. MR. HARRIMAN brought up the question of the chairmanship of the Conference. He mentioned that Mr. Roosevelt had presided at Tehran and Yalta, as the only Head of State present. He did not know what Mr. Truman's views would be, but the U.S. Delegation proposed to ask him about this as soon as he arrived.

3. *Procedure for European Settlement*

SIR A. CADOGAN mentioned that this was first on our agenda, but that he thought that the question of Germany should take precedence over it. MR. DUNN agreed and asked what Sir A. Cadogan thought of the American proposals for a Council of Five Foreign Ministers.[4] SIR A. CADOGAN said that

---

[1] The American record of this meeting is printed in *F.R.U.S. Berlin*, vol. i, pp. 155, 242–3, 295–6, 320, 417, 505–6, 552, 596, 700, 781, 958, 971, 1009, 1052. No record of its discussion on reparations, the Levant or Tangier has been traced in Foreign Office archives.

[2] Mr. W. A. Harriman was American Ambassador at Moscow.

[3] Cf. No. 111, paragraphs 5–6.

[4] Mr. J. G. Ward, a member of the British Delegation at Potsdam, subsequently recalled in a minute of 8 October 1945 (U 7856/5559/70) that 'when introducing their first draft of the Terms of Reference for the Council of Foreign Ministers at Potsdam, the American Delegation told us privately that they had included China because they were very anxious to have France in on an equal footing with the three big Allies. They felt it was most important to build up France as a Great Power (a startling change from the policy of

His Majesty's Government were in general agreement, subject to a few points of detail. He thought that the Council of Five would need to have a Secretariat, and that the Secretariat would have to have a fixed location; but there was no reason why Foreign Ministers should not be peripatetic.

4. MR. HARRIMAN mentioned that, on receiving the American communication about the Council of Five, M. Molotov had raised his eyebrows on learning of the proposal to include the Chinese. M. Molotov had added, however, that he was not opposed to it. Mr. Harriman did not expect any trouble about the inclusion of the French, but thought the Russians might suggest adding Poland and Yugoslavia. MR. DUNN thought that the Security Council had set the precedent for a Committee of Five.

Germany

5. MR. DUNN and MR. CLAYTON emphasised the importance of the early institution of the Control Council. As soon as this was done the European Advisory Commission should be wound up. SIR A. CADOGAN suggested that the European Advisory Council might form the nucleus of the Deputies of the Council of Foreign Ministers.

6. MR. DUNN thought that the economic treatment of Germany was more important than political questions affecting Germany, but asked whether we had any political questions to bring up. SIR A. CADOGAN mentioned our proposal for the institution of a limited number of centralised ministries.[5] MR. DUNN agreed on the necessity for centralised machinery, though he thought it undesirable to use the word 'ministries' at the present stage.

8.[*sic*] SIR A. CADOGAN pointed out that the question of treating Germany as an economic whole was bound up with the question of the Polish Western frontier, since it was important to secure that Silesian coal was available. MR. COULSON emphasised the importance of maintaining a lien on the coal in Oppeln Silesia. If the principle of treating Germany as an economic whole was to be established, German Silesian coal must be available for meeting German needs. For this reason it was undesirable to come to a formal agreement at an early stage on the incorporation of Oppeln Silesia into Poland. Sir A. Cadogan gave Mr. Dunn a copy of a telegram to Washington[6] giving the views of His Majesty's Government on the Polish Western frontier, and MR. DUNN said that the United States Government did not like the Western Neisse line. SIR A. CADOGAN pointed out that the question of the Western frontier was linked up with that of the transfer of populations. If the full Polish claims were accepted there might be ten or more million Germans from Poland and Czechoslovakia who would have to

President Roosevelt). They thought that they could only get France admitted without the Russians pressing claims for Poland, Yugoslavia, etc., if they modelled the membership of the Council upon the five Permament [*sic*] Members of the Security Council of the UNO.'

[5] See No. 74.
[6] See No. 115, note 1.

find a place in the reduced Reich. MR. DUNN thought that the transfer of populations would need to be regulated and take place over a period of five years. It must be subject to the decisions of the Control Council.

9. MR. HARRIMAN thought that the best way of dealing with the two connecting questions of the Western frontier and the transfer of populations was not to make a flat statement of our own views, but to ask Marshal Stalin what his intentions were in regard to the Polish territorial claims (Mr. Harriman mentioned that these claims were now endorsed by all the Poles, including Mr. Mikolajczyk, on the grounds that Poland needed extra agricultural land to settle the displaced persons from Germany and from Poland east of the Curzon Line[7]). If Marshal Stalin supported the Polish proposals, he should then be asked how he proposed to deal with the inevitable consequences, namely the influx of ten or more million Germans, who would need to be fed and housed. The removal of labour for work in the Soviet Union would not solve the problem, but would even aggravate it, since their dependents would be left behind as useless mouths. MR. DUNN felt that the question of the Polish Western frontier, unlike other frontier questions, would have to come up for decision at this meeting.

10. Mr. Dunn agreed with our proposals about the encouragement of political parties and activities in Germany, and on the co-ordination of propaganda,[5] which he thought might also include re-education.

11. Mr. Dunn mentioned the French proposals about the internationalisation of the Ruhr and political control of the West bank of the Rhine.[8] The exact intention of these French proposals was obscure, and it was agreed that they were unlikely to come up for discussion at the meeting.

12. Mr. Dunn felt that the less said about the dismemberment of Germany the better. SIR A. CADOGAN said that our view had always been that dismemberment would be desirable if it came about of itself, but that it was useless to attempt to force it. The question was now in suspense and had perhaps better remain so until we saw how conditions in Germany developed.

Italy

13. SIR A. CADOGAN said that we were anxious to conclude a Treaty of Peace with Italy. MR. DUNN said that he thought the meeting should review tripartite policy on Italy, should consider the revision of the Surrender

---

[7] i.e. the line proposed by H.M. Government to the Soviet Russian Government as the basis of an armistice between Poland and Soviet Russia in a telegram sent by Lord Curzon, Secretary of State for Foreign Affairs, on 11 July 1920: see *Parl. Debs.*, 5th ser., H. of C., vol. 131, cols. 2372–3. For the trace of this line, cf. *ibid*: also *Documents on British Foreign Policy 1919–1939* (hereafter cited as *D.B.F.P.*), First Series, vol. viii, Nos. 57 and 59.

[8] Cf. Sir L. Woodward, *op. cit.*, vol. v, pp. 239–42.

Terms and the abolition of the Advisory Council,[9] and should agree on the desirability of concluding a Peace Treaty. The Peace Treaty could be dealt with by the proposed Five Power Committee. Sir A. Cadogan said that we appeared to be in agreement in regard to our objectives. He thought that we wanted Italy to look West rather than East. For this she would require economic help, which must come mainly from the United States. It was desirable that elections should take place as soon as possible. Finally, Italy must be enabled to maintain adequate armed forces. Mr. Dunn expressed his general agreement with these ideas. He also agreed that it would be desirable that the Conference should issue some statement about Italy.

14. Mr. Clayton said that the United States Government had been unable to think of any way of giving further economic help to Italy after the end of the present year, except through UNRRA. Mr. Coulson said that what was preventing Italian recovery was lack of coal.

The Balkans

15. Mr. Dunn mentioned that peace treaties with the Balkan countries was the one subject on which we seemed to be in disagreement. Mr. Harriman suggested that peace treaties with the Balkans might well be referred to the Five Power Council.

16. Sir A. Cadogan mentioned the necessity for bringing up at the Conference the question of Russian treatment of our oil interests in Roumania.[10]

17. Sir A. Cadogan referred to Mr. Stevenson's proposal for a tripartite declaration about the fulfilment of the Tito-Subasic Agreement,[11] and Mr. Dunn agreed that this would be desirable.

Turkey

18. Sir A. Cadogan said it was necessary to remind Marshal Stalin of his promise to communicate to us his proposals about the Straits[12] and to ask him what his intentions were. Mr. Dunn thought that, of the demands made by the Russians on the Turks, the territorial question was the most important, then bases, and then the question of the Straits, which in the light of modern warfare seemed to have lost some of its importance. He thought that the right line was to suggest that all these topics were unsuitable for bilateral handling and should be referred to the World Organisation.

Persia

19. Sir A. Cadogan explained our proposals for a *pari passu* withdrawal.[13] Mr. Dunn said he was in general agreement. The U.S. would not withdraw

---

[9] The Allied Advisory Council in Italy, comprising British, American, French and Soviet representatives, had been constituted in accordance with a decision of the Conference of Foreign Ministers at Moscow in October 1943.

[10] Cf. No. 48.

[11] See No. 3.iv(*a*).

[12] Cf. No. 7.

[13] i.e. a simultaneously staged withdrawal: cf. No. 129.

their troops from Persia until a general agreement had been reached. The policy they favoured was the withdrawal of all forces whose presence was not essential for the prosecution of the Far Eastern War. If they could not all go at once, there should be *pari passu* withdrawal.

Yalta Declaration

20. MR. DUNN said the President took considerable interest in this question and in that of the situation of our representative on the Control Commissions in Balkan countries. Mr. Truman thought it ridiculous that now that the war was over we should continue to have so little say in what went on there. Mr. Dunn was sure that the President would bring this up at the meeting. SIR A. CADOGAN expressed some doubts about the possibility of achieving anything, but said that we would give the Americans such support as we could.

21. The U.S. Delegation were given copies of a number of our briefs, some of which had been appropriately edited.

CALENDAR TO No. 142

i *15, 16 & 18 July 1945 Minute by Mr. Hayter (Berlin) and letters from Mr. Hayter to Mr. Howard.* List of briefs given to U.S. Delegation at meeting. In view of Mr. Dunn's statement in No. 142, para. 15, a copy of No. 82 was not given to U.S. Delegation. Receipt of American briefs. 'The Americans have all the right ideas about Turkey.' Berlin 'looks like a set for a film about the destruction of modern civilisation' [F.O. 934/6; R 12309/5063/67; F.O. 934/2/9(2)].

No. 143

Earl of Halifax (Washington) to Mr. Eden (Received 15 July, 9.30 a.m.)

No. 4929 Telegraphic [R 11919/81/67]

Important   WASHINGTON, *15 July 1945, 2.10 a.m.*

Repeated to Moscow, Sofia, Bucharest, Budapest, Paris Saving, Athens Saving, Resmed Caserta Saving.

Your telegram No. 7376[1] first paragraph.

We have had some further discussion with the State Department regarding the attitude which the United States delegation at Terminal are likely to adopt towards His Majesty's Government's proposals regarding peace treaties with ex-satellites.[2] Whilst it is clear that in principle State Department favour the concluding of peace treaties at an early date they are definitely opposed to negotiating with the present Government of Roumania

---

[1] See No. 82, note 5.
[2] For this conversation of 14 July 1945, cf. *F.R.U.S. Berlin,* vol. i, pp. 413–4.

and to a somewhat lesser extent Bulgaria and Hungary, and will take this line at the Conference.[3]

2. We have done our best but without success to extract some indication of the attitude which the United States delegation would adopt if they should fail to get satisfaction of their own proposals from the Russians and if the question of peace treaties were then brought up by His Majesty's Government . . .[4] The State Department do not appear to have considered what they would do in this event and the United States representatives at Terminal may in fact be expected to make up their minds on the spot.

3. Foreign Office please pass to Sofia, Bucharest and Budapest as my telegrams Nos. 52, 64 and 12 respectively and to Paris as my telegram No. 113 Saving.

---

[3] Mr. Eden here minuted: 'They are right. A.E. Dept. should be told so' (cf. Sir L. Woodward, *op. cit.*, vol. v, p. 353, note 1). Sir O. Sargent minuted: 'Dept. Should we argue this with the S/S [?].' Mr. D. L. Stewart observed in a minute of 21 July: 'It is clear that opinion in the Delegation is hardening against our peace proposals and that they are unlikely to be put forward; but we can bring them forward for further consideration a month or six weeks after the conclusion of Terminal when we shall be able to see clearly the practical effect of any concessions which we or the Americans may secure there. I do not think that a delay of this length would make any very serious difference and if at the end of it we discover that any concessions wrung from the Russians at Terminal are in practice valueless, the arguments for concluding peace treaties would be very much stronger and we might have much less difficulty in persuading the Americans.' Sir O. Sargent countersigned this minute that day.

[4] The text is here uncertain.

No. 144

United Kingdom Delegation (Berlin) to Sir J. Anderson[1]
(Received 15 July, 2.57 p.m.)

No. 14 Comms Telegraphic [U 5456/3628/70]

Immediate   BERLIN, 15 July 1945, 4.47 p.m. G.M.T.

Mr. Eden and party arrived safely at three-thirty local time.[2]

---

[1] Sir J. Anderson, who was presiding over the Cabinet during the absence of Mr. Churchill and Mr. Eden, was also in charge of the Foreign Office. Incoming communications from diplomatic missions abroad continued to be formally addressed to Mr. Eden. In the Foreign Office Sir O. Sargent deputized for Sir A. Cadogan during his absence at Berlin.

[2] In Berlin telegram No. 22 Target of 4.50 that afternoon Mr. Rowan reported: 'Prime Minister and party arrived safely after a good flight.'

No. 145

Mr. Roberts (Moscow) to Mr. Eden (Received 15 July, 8.30 p.m.)
No. 3149 Telegraphic [W 9608/142/803]

MOSCOW, *15 July 1945, 6.45 p.m. G.M.T.*

Repeated to Bucharest No. 76.

Your telegram No. 759 to Bucharest.[1]

In his despatch No. 483,[2] Sir A. Clark Kerr sent you the translation of interim reply dated July 11th to letter which he addressed to Vyshinsky on the receipt of your telegram No. 2826.[3] Vyshinsky merely says that question of creation of Danube Commission is under study, by Soviet authorities and that he will be able to inform us of the results of this study as soon as it is completed.

2. I assume that[4] in view of the French and American attitude reported in Paris telegram No. 987[5] and in Washington telegram No. 4873[6] that the Soviet participation in preliminary Tangier talks is now probable. Our case for participation in the Danube Commissions is much stronger than the Soviet case over Tangier and I suggest that if and when Tangier talks have begun with Soviet representatives, we should return to the charge over the Danube Commissions, quoting the Tangier precedent.

[1] This telegram of 12 July 1945 had observed: 'We are glad to note that Roumanian Government regard any present arrangements designed to maintain and control navigation on the Danube as purely provisional and recognise claims of His Majesty's Government to representation on both Commissions when eventually reconstituted. We are however by no means certain that attitude of Soviet Government is equally favourable to our interests. They would be much more likely to desire our exclusion from the Danube altogether ... Air Vice Marshal Stevenson should leave Susaikov in no doubt that we deplore his failure to inform us of appointment of Soviet representatives to Iron Gates Administration.'

[2] This covering despatch of 12 July with enclosure as indicated below (received, 30 July) is not printed.

[3] Of 25 May, not printed.

[4] It was suggested on the filed copy that this word should be omitted.

[5] See No. 107, note 1.

[6] See No. 107, note 4.

No. 146

Sir J. Anderson to Mr. Broad (Caserta)
No. 2219 Telegraphic [R 11769/24/92]

Important　　　　　　　　　　　　FOREIGN OFFICE, *15 July 1945, 5.25 p.m.*

Repeated to Washington No. 7466, Rome No. 1842, Belgrade No. 1026.

Your telegram No. 1326[1] (of July 10th: Venezia Giulia).

Please report steps being taken to remedy this unsatisfactory situation.

2. In my[2] opinion Allied Military Government should be very energetic and firm in rounding up these Yugoslav *agents provocateurs* and repressing their activities by drastic sentences. Only chance of holding the situation seems to be to demonstrate at once that Allied Military Government is capable of coping with and countering Tito's policy of sabotage and obstruction.

3. I also hope that Allied Force Headquarters will keep Allied correspondents well informed of the Yugoslav misdemeanors and of Allied counter-measures.

CALENDARS TO No. 146

i   *14 July 1945   To Mr. Hopkinson (Rome) Tel. No. 1841.* Question of retention of Allied Military Government in Udine [ZM 3893/3/22].

ii *21 July 1945   To Mr. Broad (Caserta) Tel. No. 2256.* Requests report from Allied Force Headquarters on alleged oppression of Italians in Fiume, Zara and other Italian territory under Yugoslav occupation [R 11884/24/92].

[1] This telegram (received at 12.10 a.m. on 11 July 1945) had transmitted from Allied Force Headquarters a summary of events in Venezia Giulia during the preceding week. This summary reported in particular: '2. Yugoslav civil administration and "stay behind" organisations are, as predicted, pursuing a policy of passive obstruction coupled with widespread propaganda aimed at discrediting Western Allies and Allied Military Government.   3. "Stay behind" numbers are estimated at 5,500 including many Yugoslav ex-soldiers lately employed in Guardia Del Popolo civil administration and workers' committees. This number is probably increasing due to present lack of frontier control on Morgan line.   4. The Guardia del Popolo, although officially abolished, is reported to be still functioning clandestinely and 2,000 are said to have been absent from disbanding parade on June 24th. All these and also pro-Yugoslav elements in Friuli area are believed to receive directions from Ljubljana which is the seat of Slovene Government and headquarters of . . . [text uncertain:? Yugoslav] 4th Army.   5. Since the abolition of Guardia del Popolo no civil police force has existed in occupied area but considerable numbers are now volunteering for the new Allied Military Government Police.' Mr. Eden had minuted on this telegram 'Not good.'

[2] This telegram had been drafted on 13 July as from Mr. Eden.

No. 147

Mr. Roberts (Moscow) to Mr. Eden (Received 15 July, 8 p.m.)
No. 3143 Telegraphic [N 8661/7765/55]

MOSCOW, *15 July 1945, 6.15 p.m. G.M.T.*

My immediately preceding telegram.[1]

In conversation this afternoon the Ambassador made it clear that the

[1] This telegram of even date, reporting a communication from M. Modzelewski on Polish shipping, is not printed.

last sentence of the communication in my telegram under reference refers to direct shipping routes between United Kingdom and Poland which the Polish Provisional Government wish to see resumed as soon as possible.

2. The Ambassador who is taking up his new post at the Polish Ministry of Foreign Affairs[2] next week added that he would work for the resumption and increase of commercial exchanges between the United Kingdom and Poland as this would provide a solid basis for good political relations.

3. He again said that as soon as current problems were on the way to solution his Government would want to discuss with us the renewal of the Anglo-Polish alliance in a form suited to the new situation.

Please pass to Warsaw.

[2] As Deputy Minister.

No. 148

Sir J. Anderson to Mr. Shone (Beirut)
No. 527 Telegraphic [E 5144/14/89]

Important   FOREIGN OFFICE, *15 July 1945, 7.15 p.m.*

Repeated to Paris No. 1248 Important, M.E. Min. No. 1230.

My telegrams Nos 523 and 524.[1]

At further interview with French Ambassador today, I[2] asked him whether he had any suggestions to make as a contribution to the solution of the Franco-Levant States problem, making it clear I wished our conversation to be regarded as an informal exchange of thoughts and suggestions.

2. With regard to the French-Levant States aspect of the question, M. Massigli suggested that you should:

(i) urge on the Syrians and Lebanese that they should expedite the conclusion of the arrangements for the transfer of the Troupes Spéciales so that the matter should not fail to be concluded within the forty-five days.

(ii) urge on them to try within the same period to reach a settlement of the other outstanding matters (except question of a French base which the Ambassador thought could best be reserved for a later stage and possibly for settlement by the World Organisation).

[1] These Foreign Office telegrams of 14 July 1945 (on E 5144/14/89 and E 4866/8/89 respectively) had reported that on 11 July M. Massigli had called and had, in particular, 'complained that advent of British troops in any region was often signal for outbreaks against French or pro-French persons. He may have been building too much on outbreak at Derbissiye in Jezireh, which occurred on night 28/29 June after arrival in Jezireh of British troops on June 25 . . . It is also possible (*a*) that local inhabitants do think they can attack French with impunity on arrival of British, whom they regard as being anti-French, and (*b*) that sometimes British troops may not arrive in time completely to prevent disturbances which would have taken place in any case, and would have been worse but for their arrival.' Cf. further paragraph 4 below.

[2] This telegram, drafted on 13 July, had been initialed by Mr. Eden on 14 July.

I informed His Excellency of the advice you had not ceased to press upon the two local Governments but undertook to request you to continue your efforts. I told him I would send him a note[3] setting out what you had done in this direction.

3. With regard to what he called the Franco-British aspect, the Ambassador said that the events surrounding and following the intervention of British troops made it appear that the Lyttelton-de Gaulle Agreement[4] (as far as it recognised the French responsibilities) was no longer being applied and that this lent to our actions the appearance (which he knew to be false) of being dictated by an intention to supplant the French. He urged the desirability of some action which would demonstrate to doubters the falsity of any such deduction, and suggested, with special reference to incident at I think, Deirezzor or perhaps Derbissiye, that before British forces took precautionary action in the interests of order, the necessity of such action and the form which it was proposed it should take should whenever possible be discussed and agreed with the French authorities. Co-operation of this sort would do much to avoid giving material for allegations that all our actions demonstrated an intention to supplant the French. In general, M. Massigli wondered whether the Anglo-French Commission dealing with military measures could not be given a more really consultative character rather than only having the form of machinery through which orders decided by the British Commander were conveyed to the French. I undertook to put this to you.

4. The Ambassador again referred to the suggestion he made on July 11th for the re-association of the French in the administrative field particularly where there had been no disturbances; with special reference to M.I.R.A. and the O.C.P., he threw doubt on the effects we anticipated for any such participation by the French, especially as far as the Lebanon was concerned, and considered that there was a good deal of blackmail on the part of the States in this as in other aspects of the whole situation. He suggested that, if the British grain collecting authorities associated Frenchmen with their operations and the Syrians refused to produce the grain, they would only have themselves to blame for any resulta[n]t food shortage. I told him that our local authorities were convinced that French participation would result in the grain being withheld and, with regard to the question of responsibility, that the matter was a practical one which needed to be looked at from the point of view that shortage of bread would cause disorder. I told him however, that I had already referred to you his earlier suggestion about re-associating the French in the administrative field, and would inform you of what he had just said with a recommendation that if anything could be done in this direction it should, if possible, be devised. At the same time I said that I noticed that the local press was already beginning to talk of us and the French as the two Imperialistic Powers. With regard to

[3] This note of 13 July is not printed.
[4] See No. 64.i.

possible Levantine blackmailing tactics, I said that we were all fully alive to this factor.

5. In general, I stated our anxiety for an early solution and for the withdrawal of British troops, and that we were fully conscious of the potential effect on our interests in Egypt and Iraq (to which the Ambassador had referred) of a solution based either on extreme French claims or of an exaggerated attitude on the part of the Levant States.

6. I then told M. Massigli that I had a very tentative suggestion to make which I asked him to turn over in his mind. I referred to M. Paul Boncour's proposal[5] for a fact-finding commission of three disinterested Governments, and wondered whether the terms of reference of such a commission might not be expanded to include making recommendations, perhaps to the World Organisation, for a solution. I thought that such an expedient might at any rate reduce the tension. The Ambassador, while not rejecting my suggestion, said that he hoped that there was now some prospect that a bilateral arrangement might be reached between the French and the Levant States and that if this was possible it was probably the best solution. At the same time if a deadlock was reached a commission of the kind I had mentioned might be very useful. He promised to think it over and asked again that you should deploy yet further efforts to induce the States now to begin negotiations on other outstanding matters. I repeated my promise to ask you to do so, and, while pointing out that it would be necessary to overcome the unwillingness of the States to negotiate in advance of the withdrawal of French troops, gave my opinion that we should do our best to overcome this which seemed to me unreasonable.

[5] M. Jean Paul-Boncour had been French delegate to the Conference at San Francisco. For his proposal in June 1945 see Sir L. Woodward, *op. cit.*, vol. iv, p. 340.

No. 149

Sir J. Anderson to Earl of Halifax (Washington)
No. 7499 Telegraphic [ZM 3829/1/22]

Immediate　　　　　　　　　　　FOREIGN OFFICE, *15 July 1945, 10.45 p.m.*

Repeated to Rome No. 1849, Resmed.'s Office Caserta No. 2226, Terminal No. 19 Onward (En clair by bag).

Rome telegram No. 1137 (of July 14th:[1] Italian declaration of war on Japan).

[1] In this telegram (received at 8.20 p.m. that day) Mr. Hopkinson had reported that the Secretary General of the Italian Ministry of Foreign Affairs had that evening communicated the decision of the Italian Government to declare war on Japan as from 15 July 1945: 'Signor Prunas explained that the Italian Government had been prompted to make this gesture by the imminence of the Big Three meeting in Berlin. They hoped it would make a good impression on public opinion, particularly in the United States and China, and would be interpreted as showing a sincere desire for solidarity with the United Nations.'

This morning we received following message from United States Embassy:

'The State Department was recently told by the Italian Ambassador at Washington that Italy had decided to declare war on Japan and that her declaration would be published on July 15th (to-day). The State Department would accordingly announce on July 17th (Tuesday) the intention of the United States Government to support officially Italy's admission in due course to the World Security Organisation. The United States Embassy was instructed to inform the Foreign Office and to express the hope that His Majesty's Government would feel able to support the United States' decision.'[2]

2. After considering matter, we asked member of United States Embassy to call this afternoon and informed him that State Department's communication had created somewhat unfortunate impression on us, both as regards method of procedure and substance.

3. As regards method of procedure, Italy's intention to declare war on Japan had been known for several weeks. There was therefore no reason why State Department should present us with this statement of their intentions at such short notice and on a more or less take it or leave it basis. To expect us to give a snap decision on an important question of principle at a time when the Prime Minister and Secretary of State were known to be out of the country was bad enough. It was even worse when a matter concerning Italy was at stake. We had always been at pains to try to co-operate most closely with the United States Government on all questions of principle concerning Italy, and we thought that in view of all we had had to put up with from Italy during the war, we were entitled to more consideration from the United States authorities.

4. As regards the substance of the State Department's proposals, it seemed in the first place that they were attaching altogether too much importance to Italy's declaration of war on Japan.

In the second place, question of Italy's admission to the World Security Organisation was closely connected with question of making a Peace Treaty with Italy. His Majesty's Government had consistently maintained in their discussions with the United States Government that it would be a mistake to make a preliminary Peace Treaty, merely giving Italy all the jam and none of the powder. They were still of this opinion and were convinced that it would be most unfortunate to make any definite concessions or promises to Italy about her future status until it was possible to agree among ourselves on the complete Peace Treaty. We therefore saw serious objections to giving Italy a formal undertaking here and now that her candidature for admission to the World Security Organisation would be supported by the Allied Governments.

5. On the other hand, His Majesty's Government were as anxious as United States Government to proceed to conclusion of Italian Peace Treaty

[2] This message and the communication below is summarized with citations by Sir L. Woodward, *op. cit.*, vol. v, pp. 467–8.

as soon as possible. We were also disposed to think that public statement by United States, United Kingdom and Soviet Governments at Terminal that they were in favour of early conclusion of Peace Treaty and intended to recommend this course to other interested Allied Powers would be desirable and have useful effect in Italy. We had, therefore, already suggested that in any tripartite discussions on Italy at Terminal, United Kingdom Delegation should propose that some such statement should be issued at the end of the Conference. We felt, however, that it was highly important that any such statement about desirability of early conclusion of Italian Peace Treaty should be made in the names of all three Governments and that any unilateral statement by one of the Governments—and *a fortiori* any unilateral statement on the lines suggested by the State Department—would be most unfortunate.

6. We hoped, therefore, that the State Department would agree to take no further action in the matter until the question had been discussed at Terminal and until it had been decided whether any statement would be issued there on the subject of the conclusion of the Peace Treaty.

We would inform United Kingdom Delegation at Terminal of position and we hoped United States Delegation might be similarly informed by State Department.

7. Please speak urgently to State Department in similar terms.[3]

[3] Cf. *F.R.U.S. Berlin*, vol. i, pp. 303–4, also vol. ii, pp. 621–2 and 1079–80 for the British *aide-mémoire* of 16 July accordingly remitted to State Department. In Foreign Office telegram No. 23 Onward of 16 July to Berlin Mr. Harvey informed Mr. Dixon with reference to the present telegram: 'We think it would be useful if United Kingdom Delegation could speak in similar terms to United States Delegation.'

No. 150

Memorandum by the British Chiefs of Staff [1]

C.C.S. 884/2 (*Terminal*) [CAB 99/39]

Top secret   BABELSBERG, *15 July 1945*

Information for the Russians concerning the Japanese War

(*References:* C.C.S. 884 and 884/1.)[2]

1. The British Chiefs of Staff have considered the reply by the United States Chiefs of Staff (C.C.S. 884/1)[2] to their Memorandum (C.C.S. 884)[2] concerning the information which should be given to the Russians if they enter the war against Japan.

2. The British Chiefs of Staff cannot agree that this is an inappropriate matter for combined agreement.

[1] Printed in *F.R.U.S. Berlin*, vol. i, pp. 935–6.
[2] See No. 52, notes 2–3.

3. Hitherto throughout the war against Germany, it has been customary, although not obligatory, for the United States and British Chiefs of Staff to consult together as to the measure and means of our dealings with the Russians. The British Chiefs of Staff consider that on the whole this policy has been wise and profitable, and they see no reason now that Germany has been defeated and Russia is not yet at war with Japan, to depart from it. They are not aware that it has aroused resentment on the part of the Russians, who nevertheless must have been aware of our joint collaboration.

4. If the British and American Staffs now take an independent and quite possibly divergent line as regards passing information to the Russians, it seems possible that the Russians will be tempted to play one of us off against the other.

5. For the above reasons the British Chiefs of Staff would be grateful for an opportunity of discussing this matter further with the United States Chiefs of Staff at 'Terminal'.

No. 151

Memorandum by the British Chiefs of Staff[1]
C.C.S. 891 (Terminal) [CAB 99/39]

Top secret   BABELSBERG, *15 July 1945*
Combined Chiefs of Staff Machinery after the War with Japan
(Reference: C.C.S. 880/1.)[2]

1. We should like at 'Terminal' to discuss with our United States colleagues the question of the continuation of machinery for combined United States/British collaboration in the military sphere after the defeat of Japan.

2. Since 1941 the machinery of the Combined Chiefs of Staff and its associated committees has worked smoothly and effectively. For the reasons which follow, we consider that it would be a retrograde step to allow this machinery to fall into disuse merely because Germany and Japan have been defeated and there are no supreme allied commanders to receive the instructions of the Combined Chiefs of Staff.

3. As we see it, the world, all too unfortunately, is likely to remain in a troubled state for many years to come. Major problems will constantly arise affecting both American and British interests. In many cases these interests may well be closely identified, and in many cases also they will have important military implications.

4. For these reasons we consider that some machinery for the continuation of joint and combined United States/British collaboration is desirable. For example, it may be to the great advantage both of the United States and

---

[1] Printed *op. cit.*, vol. i, p. 825.
[2] Printed *ibid.*, pp. 193–4.

ourselves that some machinery should exist for the mutual exchange of information. Some measure of uniformity in the design of weapons and in training may also be mutually beneficial.

5. It is not our intention in this paper to attempt to fashion the form or the structure of the machinery which may be found necessary for the above purpose after hostilities have ended. All that we suggest at this stage is that we[3] should now recommend to our respective Governments that they should approve the maintenance of the framework of the Combined Chiefs of Staff organisation after the war with Japan, and the principle of consultation on matters of mutual interest.

6. We do not think that the maintenance of the Combined Chiefs of Staff machinery after the end of hostilities need in any way cut across or impinge upon the Military Staff Committee of the World Security Organisation. There is plenty of room and work for both.

[3] Annotation on filed copy of uncorrected proof on AN 2627/38/45: 'i.e. C.C.S.'

No. 152

Note by Sir W. Monckton (Berlin)[1]
[F.O. 934/1/4(1)]

[BERLIN,] *15 July, 1945*

Reparations

The object of this Note is to suggest what questions the U.S. Delegation are likely to wish the Conference to discuss, which of these questions we think can usefully be discussed and in brief outline our views about these questions.

(1) *The Reparation Plan*

It was agreed at Moscow to take the Russian plan as the basis of discussion,[2] but the Russians have not yet produced their plan and there is therefore clearly nothing which calls for any decision by the Conference on this aspect. We believe that when the Russian plan is produced we may find it more drastic in some respects and less drastic in other respects than would accord with our own views. The Russians want to prevent Germany producing tanks and guns and will want the German metallurgical industry to be very drastically reduced, while we also want to prevent Germany in future producing submarines and rockets and want to eliminate German ship-building and certain branches of the German chemical industry. The relevant point is that there may be serious differences of opinion between the Russians and ourselves and we do not want at this stage to make concessions which we shall wish to use in negotiations later.

[1] This note was addressed to Mr. Eden.
[2] See No. 117, note 3.

(2) *The allocation of Reparation Receipts as between Russia, the U.K. and the U.S.A.*

The attached paper marked 'A'[3] has been agreed *ad referendum* by the Moscow Commission. It means that if the other Powers jointly receive a 10% share, the shares of the Big Three will be

Russia	50%
U.K.	20%
U.S.A.	20%

while if the other Powers receive more than 10% (which, in fact, Russia will strongly oppose) the three Big Powers will all contribute rateably.

The Americans said at the Crimea Conference that they did not want to take reparations other than German interests and possibly raw materials. (Our private record says: 'Stettinius recalled that the President had stated that the U.S. were interested in no reparations other than German investments and possibly raw materials; he himself would be surprised if the total share required by the U.S. would approach anything like one half of the allotment which the Russians had made to the U.S.A. and the U.K.'.[4]) At Moscow we failed to obtain any satisfactory assurance as to whether the Americans would put back into the pool that part of their share which they did not want to take, or any information as to the stage of negotiations at which they would offer to give up any of their share. It would be useful if these two points could be further explored.

The original instructions to the U.K. Delegation Moscow were that reparation labour should be brought into the account so that Russia would receive less than 50% of deliveries. Mr. Pauley gave us no support on this and we received amended instructions that labour should not be brought into the account so that Russia would receive her full share of 50% of deliveries subject to rateable reduction if the other Powers receive more than 10% of the total. Our belief (and it will certainly also be the Russian belief) is that Mr. Pauley definitely proposed that reparation labour should *not* be brought into the account and that we agreed to the proposal. The State Department proposed to us this morning that 'the net value of labour services rendered by Germans outside Germany (i.e. the portion of the workers' wages, allowances and maintenance provided by Germany or paid in marks) should be credited to reparation account' [i]. Mr. Pauley now says that the point was left unsettled at Moscow. We cannot honestly support him in this view. We would hope to clear up the point before the paper marked 'A' comes for formal approval before the Conference.

(3) *Procedure for bringing the other Powers into the Negotiations*

The attached paper marked 'B'[3] was approved by the Moscow Commission *ad referendum*. It is in accordance with the instructions received

---

[3] The texts of papers 'A' and 'B' (see paragraph 3 below), not here attached, are printed in *F.R.U.S. Berlin*, vol. ii, pp. 834–35.

[4] Mr. Stettinius made this statement at the meeting of Foreign Ministers on 7 February 1945: cf. *F.R.U.S. The Conferences of Malta and Yalta 1945*, pp. 703 and 706.

by us from London and should need only formal endorsement by the Conference.

(4) *The first charge on exports from Germany to pay for imports into Germany*

The Statement of Principles set out in document 'C'[5] was approved *ad referendum* by the Moscow Commission after we had received authority from Ministers in London. But at the last moment the Russian Delegation objected to the second sentence in paragraph 8 which sets out the principle that imports into Germany must be a first charge on exports from Germany. It is estimated that in order to prevent starvation in the western zones, imports between February and November 1945 will be necessary which will cost at least £10,000,000 involving payment in U.S. dollars or Canadian dollars. Both we and the Americans regard it as essential that there should be no free reparation deliveries from current production or stocks of goods until payment of these necessary minimum imports has been covered. The American Delegation in Berlin will press this very strongly and we can give them the fullest support.

(5) *France*

We believe that the Americans will press that France should be made a member of the Moscow Commission at an early stage and before the shares of the other Powers are settled. The proper time would seem to be after the three Big Powers are agreed in principle at any rate upon a reparation plan. The Russians will not bring them in before this since they might otherwise find themselves in a minority of one to three. The need to bring the French in arose from the practical consideration that they are one of the four Powers controlling Germany and can (and will) torpedo everything if they are not brought in before the minor Powers.

(6) *Full accounting*

The Americans will propose that the Russians should be debited on reparation account with everything that they have taken or may take from the Russian zone and that the other three Powers should be allowed free movement in the Russian zone in order to verify what the Russians take. For example, there might be a four-Power inventory of Russian factories etc. in all the zones and a four-Power customs control of everything which goes out of Germany of any frontier. We can certainly support the Americans on this but it will be difficult to secure what we want.[6] It is no good to us at all[7] that the Russians should accept the principle of full accounting but refuse the other three Powers any possibility of moving about in the Russian zone to find out what has really happened or is really happening.

(7) *Austrian Reparations*

The Americans consider that Austria should be called upon to pay no reparations other than plant and equipment from German war plants put

---

[5] The text of document 'C', not here attached, was the same as that in the annex to No. 116.

[6] Mr. Eden here noted in the margin: 'We must support Americans on this. A. E.'

[7] This phrase was ticked by Mr. Eden.

up after the incorporation of Austria into Germany and productive capacity superfluous to a healthy peacetime economy (e.g. aircraft factories). The Russians maintain that in principle Austria should pay reparations and we believe that by now[8] the Russians have removed from Austria a very great deal of plant and equipment. In general the view of His Majesty's Government coincides with the view of the Americans.

(8) *Restitution*

His Majesty's Government have placed before the European Advisory Commission their proposed definition of restitution which provides for the return to any country of articles which existed before it was occupied by the enemy and still exist and can be identified.[9] In our view where the identical article no longer exists there should be no claim for it to be replaced by a similar article (except in the case of works of art) since claims in respect of articles which no longer exist are claims to reparation and not claims to restitution. The Russians have proposed a somewhat wider definition and the Americans a somewhat narrower one.[10] The Americans may want the matter settled at the Conference but we think that the matter should not be brought before the Conference because (*a*) it is too technical and complicated; (*b*) it is a matter of particularly vital interest to France which is represented on the European Advisory Commission but is not represented at the present Conference. If the Americans want to propose a definition different from ours it seems that their right course would be to bring their proposal before the European Advisory Commission.

(9) *War Booty*

The Russians undertook to produce a paper on this but have hitherto failed to do so. They will probably propose that everything which is included in the scope of reparation removals under the Crimea Conference decision (e.g. plant and equipment) should be treated as reparation and not be treated as war booty.[11] The instruction which we had received from London would enable us to accept a narrower definition of war booty and the Americans seem ready to do so. But unless we can obtain the right to move freely in the Russian zone the result may well be that we shall have to treat all the factories, plant and equipment in the western zones as available for reparation of which the Russians will have a share while the Russians will remove the factories, plant and equipment in the Russian zone and tell us nothing about it. It seems therefore that if we are to accept a narrower definition of booty, this should come at a later stage of the negotiations as it would represent a major concession to the Russians. Subject to this a narrow definition would suit us insofar as it would mean that the gold found

[8] Mr. Eden sidelined the ensuing passage to the end of this paragraph with the annotation 'Yes. A. E.'

[9] Cf. *F.R.U.S. 1945*, vol. iii, pp. 1171–2.

[10] For the Russian and American definitions of restitution see *F.R.U.S. Berlin*, vol. i, pp. 542–3 and 549 respectively.

[11] Mr. Eden here noted: 'I don't quite follow argument here. A. E.'

by the Americans at the Merkers mine[12] would not be treated as booty but as subject to restitution in kind if it is identifiable as property of an Ally or as reparation if it is no[t] so identifiable. The matter seems too technical and complicated to bring before the Conference and should, for the reasons suggested above, be dealt with at a later stage rather than now.

(10) *Interim Deliveries*

It is our policy that interim deliveries should normally be confined to raw materials and consumption goods urgently needed by liberated territories. The one negotiating weapon which we have is that the Russians want to remove capital goods from the western zones.[13] If we allow them to do so before agreement is reached on a reparation plan, the Russians will have no motive to reach agreement and the negotiations will drag on for ever. Moreover, arrangements to remove capital goods will require a rather elaborate executive machinery which has not yet been set up. We hope that we have convinced the American Delegation of the wisdom of the above view, but unfortunately at Moscow Mr. Pauley advocated a system of interim deliveries which would cover capital goods[14] and thus made a very false move in the negotiations. In our view, the question of interim deliveries should certainly not be brought before the Conference. It would however, be useful if without bringing the matter before the Conference we could get a common policy with the Americans on interim reparation deliveries of raw materials and consumption goods and interim deliveries for restitution of identifiable objects including works of art.[15] The essential point is that we should not allow the Russians to take capital goods out of the western zones until the main details of the reparation plan have been agreed between the three Powers and this is not likely to happen for say six to eight weeks from now.[16]

WALTER MONCKTON

CALENDARS TO NO. 152

i *15 July 1945 Record of Anglo-American meeting on reparations:* restitution, war booty, interim deliveries, territorial zones. On question of labour Sir W. Monckton said that American proposal was not his understanding of agreement reached at Moscow: 'we had agreed to Russia receiving five [fifty] percent of reparations excluding labour'. Consensus that with certain exceptions Austria should not pay reparations and that France should be invited to join the Moscow Reparation Commission as soon as possible [F.O. 934/1/4(4)].

[12] In April 1945 the American Third Army had discovered an important German hoard of gold bullion, foreign currency and works of art in a salt mine at Merkers.

[13] Mr. Eden here noted: 'I agree emphatically. A. E.'

[14] See *F.R.U.S. Berlin*, vol. i, pp. 544–6: also No. 3.i(*a*) above.

[15] Mr. Eden sidelined the latter part of this sentence and noted 'Yes' against it.

[16] Mr. Eden here noted: 'I would go further. Nothing from the west except *pari passu* with meeting of our requirements elsewhere, A. E.'

No. 153

Letter from Mr. Harrison (Berlin) to Mr. Troutbeck[1]
[C 4043/24/18]

Copy   [BERLIN,] *15 July 1945*

My dear Jack,

Document 'A'[2], enclosed, is Monty's[3] interpretation of treating Germany
as an administrative and economic whole.

Document 'B' is our version as amended at a meeting attended by the
Reparation boys from Moscow (Monckton, Waley, Turner), John Coulson,
Tommy Brand and Fred French.[4]

We assume it is for Monty's guidance, but we have amended it with an
eye to the possibility that we may be challenged by the Russians or Americans
to say what we mean by 'treating Germany as an administrative and
economic whole'.

This should be on your desk on Monday morning. If you have any
comments, try and let me know by one of the bags in the course of the day.
Germany comes, in all probability, very early on the agenda.[5]

Yours ever,

GEOFFREY HARRISON

---

[1] Received by Monday, 16 July 1945: see No. 164.

[2] Text supplied from F.O. 934/1/2(1).

[3] i.e. Field-Marshal Montgomery's.

[4] Mr. T. H. Brand was Chairman of the Official Committee on Supplies for Liberated
Areas (S.L.A.O.). Brigadier F. G. French was Deputy Director of Civil Affairs in the War
Office.

[5] On 16 July Mr. Troutbeck further received from Mr. Harrison a 'first revise' of a
draft personal message (on C 4063/24/18) from Field-Marshal Montgomery to the German
people. On 16 July Sir A. Cadogan minuted: 'F.M. Montgomery agreed with me yesterday
evening that there was no great hurry about the issue of this message, and that in fact it
must in some respects await the outcome of Terminal. A. C. July 16/45.' On 18 July
Mr. Eden stated: 'This seems in order to me.' Sir A. Cadogan further minuted on 20 July:
'Pres. Truman asked the P.M., after the meeting this afternoon [see No. 208], that all
declarations shd. await the result of Terminal. P.M. agreed. A. C. July 20, 1945.' See
No. 563.i.

Enclosure A in No. 153

Memorandum by Field-Marshal Montgomery

One Germany—or Two

A decision is required at Terminal as to whether Germany is to be treated as one administrative and economic whole.

If the answer is in the affirmative, it carries with it the following implications and repercussions, amongst others, which must be faced up to:

1. Free circulation of allied nationals in all zones, by land and air, subject to normal regulations.

2. Central administration of many forms of German governmental machinery; including in particular Finance, Transportation, Communications.

3. Consequential on central finance, common policies as regards currency, servicing the German debt, and central taxation.

4. Common policies as regards the reconstruction of industries, wage rates, price control.

5. Transfer and exchange of resources and services, including food, between zones so as to preserve a balanced economy throughout Germany.

6. Consequential on No. 5, global demands from outside sources to make up deficits.

7. Common policies as regards the method of treatment of the German civil population.[6]

B.L.M.

13-7-45

Enclosure B in No. 153[7]

One Germany—or Two

A decision is required at Terminal as to whether Germany is to be treated as one administrative and economic whole.

If the answer is in the affirmative it carries with it the following implications and repercussions, amongst others, which must be faced up to:

1. Subject to normal regulations, free circulation, *on a basis of reciprocity*, of *British, U.S., Soviet and French* nationals in all zones by land and air.

2. Common policies as regards the method of treatment of the German civil population.

3. Central administration of *a number of* forms of German governmental machinery; including in particular finance, *including customs;* transportation, communications; *and to the extent required to ensure common policies as regards the subjects set out in this note as follows:*

(*a*) Currency, servicing the German debt, and central taxation.

(*b*) *Payment of compensation claims to German nationals including those in regard to requisition, war damage, reparation, deliveries and removals.*

(*c*) *Industrial production*, wage rates, price control *and rationing*.

(*d*) *Reparations and removal of industrial war potential.*

---

[6] A variant text of this memorandum is printed in *The Memoirs of Field-Marshal the Viscount Montgomery of Alamein, K. G.* (London, 1958), p. 392.

[7] A copy of Document B was handed to General Weeks, for communication to Field-Marshal Montgomery, by Sir W. Strang on 16 July 1945.

(*e*) Transfer and exchange of resources and services, including food, between zones so as to preserve a balanced economy throughout Germany *and reduce the need for imports*.

(*f*) German imports and exports.

15th July, 1945

CALENDARS TO NO. 153

i [? *15*] *July 1945 Memorandum by U.K. Delegation at Berlin on One Germany—or Two*: variant, possibly earlier, version of enclosure B in No. 153 [F.O. 934/1/2 (1)].

ii *16 July 1945 Letter from Mr. Troutbeck to Mr. Harrison (Berlin)*, without enclosure. Refers to Nos. 153 and 164. Suggests that issue of individual statements by Commanders-in-Chief as proposed by F.M. Montgomery (see note 5 above) might make it more difficult to 'get the Control Council working effectively' under an allied policy [C 4063/24/18].

No. 154

Record of a Meeting held at Berlin at 9.30 p.m. on 15 July 1945
[*F.O. 934/1/2(4)*]

Secret

Present:
SIR W. MONCKTON (in the Chair), Sir A. Cadogan, Lt. Gen. Sir R. Weeks, Sir W. Strang, Sir D. Waley, Brigadier French, The Hon. T. H. Brand, Mr. Mark Turner, Mr. Hayter, Mr. Harrison, F/Lt. Greenwood, Mr. Coulson.

Industrial Disarmament

It was explained that, at a meeting held on July 14th,[1] the Americans had thought that Germany should come up on the agenda as one of the first items at the 3-Power meetings and that economic subjects would be of prime importance. The Foreign Office had certain briefs on the subject and so had General Weeks. It was desired to hand these briefs over and exchange views upon them.

SIR W. MONCKTON said that one of the problems that exercised them most in the Moscow Commission was the degree of de-industrialisation which should be applied in Germany. The Russian idea was to decide what measures of de-industrialisation were needed to produce in Germany a standard of living corresponding roughly to the middle European standard. All the industry surplus to that would be regarded as reparation. It might be that the standard of living of neighbouring countries would improve in a few years' time, in which case the Russians would have no objection to the German standard of living rising correspondingly.

MR. TURNER added that the Russians regarded a drastic cut in the heavy steel and engineering industries as being essential, but they did not appear

[1] See No. 142.

to mind the light engineering industries, or such industries as synthetic rubber continuing in existence.

GENERAL WEEKS said that he thought the Control Commission would be able to state in a short time what was necessary to maintain the minimum economy of the British Zone, but they had not yet all the necessary data. The Economic Division felt considerable anxiety about the possibility of financial and industrial chaos being produced. The coal situation was critical. Whereas in the Hyndley-Potter Report a target figure of 25,000,000 tons of coal had been mentioned for export by the end of April, it now seemed likely that no more than 8,000,000 tons could be achieved. 38,000,000 tons could be produced; of this only 28,000,000 could be moved. 20,000,000 tons were needed for military and domestic purposes. This was on the assumption that only the barest minimum should be used for German industry. A report[2] on this had been prepared and would be circulated. He would also be able to circulate on the following day the observations of Field-Marshal Montgomery on the proposals about industrial disarmament which had been sent to him for comment after the Cabinet had considered the matter.[3]

At this point of the meeting a memorandum, which had been forwarded to the War Office by General Weeks, on German economy was read to the meeting by Sir D. Waley. This report is attached as an annex[4] to these minutes.

SIR D. WALEY said that there appeared to be a misunderstanding both here and in London about the nature of the problems which the Reparation Commission in Moscow were facing. So far they had not received the Russian plan, which had long been promised, and they were therefore able to defer their views on some points. It was quite clear, however, that the Russians were not so much interested in continuing deliveries out of current production as in taking away from German[y] once-for-all deliveries. The Moscow Commission wanted to make a plan, but it was difficult for the British Delegation to co-operate. They knew they must stall until the General Elections were over, but they could not go on stalling. They must in fact soon express a view on how much plant was to remain in Germany in order to maintain a modest standard of living and how much could go in the form of reparation. It was impossible to separate dis-industrialisation from reparation. It was of course possible to consider how much industry had been established in Germany for purely war-like purposes; it was only a matter of arithmetic to decide how much to remove. Nevertheless, such arithmetical sums might be wrong. It was unrealistic to assume that, when the 4-Power machinery had hardly started in Germany, the same degree of control could be exercised as in Russia or in Hitlerite Germany. The Moscow

[2] See No. 191.i.

[3] The comments of the British element of the Control Commission for Germany, dated 15 July 1945, upon the interim directive to Field-Marshal Montgomery and proposals by the Armistice and Post-War Committee are not printed.

[4] Not printed. This paper was entitled 'Future of German Industry'. For the full report to which it was appended see ii below.

Commission were therefore most anxious to know what guidance the Control Commission could give them.

SIR A. CADOGAN added that the transfer of German populations from Poland and Czechoslovakia, which we estimated at something like 10,000,000 people, would seriously aggravate the problems facing the Control Commission.

GENERAL WEEKS said that any serious influx would be out of the question, though if it were spread over a fair period, it might be acceptable.

SIR D. WALEY said that there would be advantages in the Moscow Commission having a practical liaison with the Control Commission so that they could obtain the help of food and industrial experts when they needed them.

GENERAL WEEKS promised to look into this and also said that he had made arrangements for the appropriate experts to be in Berlin for the Conference.

There was some discussion about the possibility of making interim deliveries of goods from Germany, before a reparation plan had been agreed. The danger was that, if we embarked on such a scheme, the Moscow Commission might sit indefinitely. This would particularly apply if we permitted the removal of capital goods. In any case, this was a complicated matter and required continuing expert supervision. It would be impossible to start a scheme of this kind in the absence of the necessary executive machinery. (GENERAL WEEKS remarked that large-scale movements would be impossible; it was difficult enough to move the necessary coal.) It was pointed out that the Reparation, Restitution and Deliveries Division of the Control Commission might be able to arrange for any deliveries. This was the view which the Russians normally held, though the London view had always been that it was not a proper function of the Control Commission to decide between different claimants. If, however, a further body had to be set up to make such decisions, there might be an awkward interval before we could collect the necessary staff.

GENERAL WEEKS pointed out that this problem was intimately connected with the problem of treating Germany as an economic unit.

It was agreed to pursue this subject further at a meeting to be held the following afternoon with Sir P. Mills[5] at 3.30 p.m. if he had arrived in time.

Feeding and Fuelling of Berlin

GENERAL WEEKS said that they had had some further discussion of this and that he was circulating a report on the subject. They were in a difficult position over meat and General Clay was not ready to contemplate the procurement of further supplies of foodstuffs after October.

French Sector in Berlin

SIR W. STRANG said that at present the Russians had refused to surrender

[5] President of the Economic Sub-Commission of the British Element of the Control Commission for Germany. Cf. No. 154.iii.

any space to the French and it had been left to the British and Americans to find room for them. The object of the Conference should be to get the Russians to give something up; once this decision of principle had been reached the detailed arrangements could be referred elsewhere.

GENERAL WEEKS said that he had not yet received a full report from Brigadier Lyne, the preliminary indications were that we should be able and ready to give up Reinickendorf. This might not be big enough for the French; on the other hand, they might be prepared to accept it.

SIR A. CADOGAN said that, if this arrangement proved possible, it would no longer be necessary for us to raise the question. We would have made our contribution and, if it were not big enough, it would be up to the French to obtain some further contribution from the Americans and Russians. We might, however, hold this offer in reserve and use it at an appropriate moment.

CALENDARS TO No. 154

i *14 July 1945   Report by General Weeks (Berlin) on provision of food and coal for Berlin*: Berlin should be fed from the Russian zone and any coal from the Ruhr should be kept to a minimum. In view of gravity of the problem of feeding the British zone, 'a continuing liability to feed and fuel the British share of Berlin is really alarming and should be avoided if it is politically possible'. A firm decision by the Potsdam Conference is essential [F.O. 934/1/2(2)].

ii *17 July 1945   Note by the secretariat of the European Control Committee of the Cabinet, E.C.C.(45)4: annexing comments by Field-Marshal Montgomery on the agenda for the Potsdam Conference*: difficulties of receiving a massive transfer of population from Poland and Czechoslovakia; non-fraternisation order should be modified and appropriate political activity permitted. Appendices on treatment of Germany as an economic whole and on future of German industry [C 4096/267/18].

iii *16 & 18 July 1945   Correspondence between Mr. Coulson (Berlin) and Mr. Lincoln.* Transmits No. 154. A further British meeting on 16 July suggested that if industrial disarmament is raised it should if possible be referred to Reparation Commission with object of holding 'our position as regards plant and machinery in our zone until a full reparation plan has been produced'. Transmits also No. 154.i, appendix A to No. 154.ii, and No. 191, annex. [F.O. 934/1/2(4 & 12).]

No. 155

Mr. Roberts (Moscow) to Mr. Eden (Received 16 July, 3 p.m.)
No. 3158 Telegraphic [N 8677/6/55]

Immediate   MOSCOW, *16 July 1945, 1.6 p.m.*

Repeated to Washington, Paris No. 90, Terminal, Warsaw.

Washington telegram No. 5,008.[1]

Anglo-American journalists who have just returned from a tour of Silesia,

---

[1] Subsequently amended to '4908': see No. 115.i.

308

received the impression that the Soviet authorities might now be less inclined to support extreme Polish claims. They said that the Poles were prevented by the Russians from expelling the Germans from Breslau and Lausitz on the pretext that the harvest had to be gathered in. Many Poles whom they met doubted whether the Poles would now receive any territory in Lower Silesia beyond Oppeln district. They alleged that the German inhabitants were being encouraged by the Russians to return to the districts formerly inhabited by them and complained of alleged Soviet tenderness towards the Germans. On the other hand in Oppeln district and in former Polish districts of Silesia expulsion of German inhabitants had been completed by the Poles.

2. Official Soviet standpoint was however expressed by M. Molotov at Moscow Commission Meeting with the Poles[2] on June 21st when he said that the Soviet Government still regarded the Polish Provisional Government's claims to the line of the Oder and Western Neisse as well founded and fully justified. While therefore the Soviet Government might agree that the Poles should not have Stettin or even Breslau they would certainly regard the frontier suggested in paragraph 4(1) of your telegram No. 7,412 to Washington[3] as inadequate and would probably try to gain popularity amongst the Poles at our expense by contrasting their generosity with our niggardly attitude.

3. The Polish Ambassador told me on July 14th that his Government's claims were most moderate having regard to Polish losses in the east and that on this issue at least they could count on solid support of Polish public opinion. He admitted that there was still a good deal of criticism of his Government, who must therefore conciliate national sentiment by showing that they were adequately defending Poland's vital interests. He claimed that Polish stand over Teschen had done much to increase the Government's popularity. Skladkowski[4] who had been a member of the pre-war Pilsudskist Governments, had visited the Ambassador recently on his return from Roumania and told him that he and many of his friends were prepared to support the new Government precisely because it was pursuing a strong line of policy in the west. We must therefore expect action proposed in your telegram No. 7412 to Washington[3] to be exploited against us and to handicap our efforts to restore our influence in Poland, despite return to Warsaw of His Majesty's Embassy and of Mikolajczyk.

4. While we are fully entitled to insist upon a proportionate reduction in Russian share of reparations as suggested in first sentence of paragraph 5 (2) of your telegram No. 7412 to Washington[3] and so automatically to reduce deliveries to the Soviet Union from our zones the further threat to withhold altogether reparations deliveries from our zones might be difficult to defend. It would arouse strong Soviet resentment and would be regarded as a punish-

[2] Cf. No. 78, note 1.
[3] See No. 115, note 1 and paragraph 11.
[4] General F. Slawoj-Skladkowski had been Polish Minister of the Interior and Prime Minister (1936-39).

ment disproportionate to the crime. I hope therefore that it will not be necessary to make this further threat which might only provoke awkward Soviet reactions on other equally important issues.

CALENDAR TO No. 155

i *16 July 1945 Memorandum by Mr. D. Allen (Berlin) on Polish control over the 'Regained Territories'.* Polish Government claim a western frontier on Western Neisse and Oder, including Stettin. Discusses extent of Polish administration and settlement in 'Regained Territories' [F.O. 934/2/10(5)].

No. 156

Mr. Nichols (Prague) to Mr. Eden (Received 16 July, 6.55 p.m.)
No. 227 Telegraphic [N 8668/207/12]

Secret   PRAGUE, *16 July 1945, 5.21 p.m.*

Repeated to Washington.

My telegram No. 204.[1]

The President informed me recently that Russian withdrawals were definitely taking place and exceeded his expectations in Bohemia and Moravia, though the position was not so good in Slovakia. You will remember that withdrawal and regroupings should have been completed by July 15th (my telegram No. 169).[2]

2. The President intimated that it would be well received if the Americans were to withdraw from[3] frontier regions as the Russians were doing, thus freeing Pilsen and other towns.

3. My United States colleague, who tells me that American troops are being reduced by further two divisions who are destined for the Pacific, leaving therefore only three divisions in the American zone, has also informed me that for administration reasons it would be difficult for Americans to withdraw to frontier regions. There are 180,000 displaced persons in American area and it was necessary to remain in Pilsen and other towns in order to deal with this problem as long as (. . . ? it)[4] existed.

Please pass to Washington as my telegram No. 14.

CALENDARS TO No 156

i *23 July 1945 Mr. Nichols (Prague) No. 65.* According to American Ambassador in Prague, Mr. L. A. Steinhardt, American military authorities had been taking steps to withdraw all U.S. troops from Czechoslovakia until position

---

[1] Of 12 July (N 8575/207/12), not printed.
[2] Of 3 July (N 7925/28/12), not printed.
[3] Marginal annotation on filed copy: '? surely *to*'.
[4] The text here is uncertain.

reversed 'as a result of the opposition displayed by the State Department, by His Majesty's Government and himself, the final decision being taken by President Truman' [N 9632/7395/12].

ii *29 July 1945 Mr. Nichols (Prague) Tel. No. 282.* Visit of General Patton to Prague. Mr. Nichols believes that presence of U.S. troops until Russian withdrawal is favoured by all Czechoslovak parties except Communists [N 9406/207/12].

No. 157

Sir J. Anderson to Mr. Stevenson (Belgrade)
No. 1033 Telegraphic [R 11967/24/92]

FOREIGN OFFICE, *16 July 1945, 3.45 a.m.*

Repeated to Athens No: 1516, Caserta No: 2227, Washington No: 7501, Moscow No: 3960, Sofia No: 696.

Your telegrams Nos. 995 and 1093[1] (of June 23rd and July 10th Yugoslav press campaigns on Greek Macedonia, Carinthia and Venezia Giulia.)

I[2] am not prepared to let Tito's speech of July 7th pass without notice. I think you should now seek an interview with Tito himself and take up with him the recent conduct of the Yugoslav propaganda machine on the following lines.

2. *Greek Macedonia.* For some weeks the Belgrade press and radio have been conducting what appears to be a deliberate and inspired campaign to inflame Yugoslav opinion against Greece. Now that the President of the Yugoslav Government has given in a public speech the weight of his authority to the campaign of more irresponsible elements, His Majesty's Government feel obliged to express to the Yugoslav Government their concern at the course which they are following. Any complaints which Yugoslavia has to make against Greece should be addressed to the Greek Government. The sooner therefore that Ambassadors (or Ministers) are exchanged between Athens and Belgrade the better. Until then His Majesty's Government would be glad to act as intermediaries and to lend their good offices in seeing that the complaints are properly investigated and suitable measures taken to redress any abuses. The report of firing across the Yugoslav frontier, if well-founded, seems to require representations of this kind. So

---

[1] These telegrams (respectively on R 10758, 11763/11/67) are not printed. Belgrade telegram No. 1093 (received 11 July) had reported that in a speech on 7 July Marshal Tito had claimed that 'thousands and thousands' of Macedonians and Greeks had fled to Yugoslavia as refugees. 'The Marshal maintained that in spite of all the wishes of the Yugoslavs' to remain on good terms with Greece, 'EDES troops on Greek frontier were firing from mortars and machine guns on Yugoslavs without any provocation.' Mr. Eden had minuted to Mr. Dixon on this telegram: 'P.D. Do we say and do nothing about this. Should not Jug. here be sent for or Stevenson told to speak to Jugs. in Belgrade. It is dangerous to let this grow unchecked & I presume it is not true.   A.E.'

[2] The draft of the present telegram had been initialed by Mr. Eden on 13 July.

far as we are aware however, there is no foundation whatever for this report. This course should surely be welcome to the Yugoslav Government if their object is to remove the causes of grievance and restore the cordial relations which should subsist with their neighbour and fellow Member of the United Nations, an object which cannot be attained either by irresponsible vociferations in the press or by the inflammatory utterances of responsible Yugoslav statesmen.

3. *Venezia Giulia and Carinthia.* His Majesty's Government have also noted with displeasure the efforts of the Belgrade press and radio to mislead Yugoslav opinion on the conduct of A.M.G. in Venezia Giulia and Carinthia. The Yugoslav Government have several established channels open to them to inform the Allied military authorities or the British Government of any complaints or grievances which they may have. In this case also the only effect of the press and radio campaign must be to alienate Yugoslavia from a country with whom it is in her interest to maintain friendly relations. His Majesty's Government would be content to ignore the vulgar abuse which has been addressed against them, but for the consideration that it is in the interests of Yugoslavia that there should be no further indulgence of spiteful feelings.

4. I should like you also to take the opportunity to hint that Tito's attempt to appeal to the great British public over the head of His Majesty's Government was ill-advised. There has been no complaint from any quarter here that the Agreements about Venezia Giulia have been unfair to Yugoslavia; Yugoslav conduct during the incident has on the other hand been very generally blamed.

5. Yugoslav Ambassador here will be spoken to in a similar sense.[3]

[3] See No. 317.

No. 158

Draft record of a Meeting between Mr. Eden and M. Molotov at 30, Kaiserstrasse near Potsdam on 16 July 1945 at 6.20 p.m.[1]

[*F.O. 934/2/8(3)*]

Present:

SECRETARY OF STATE, Sir Alexander Cadogan, Major L. H. Theakstone (*Interpreter*).

M. MOLOTOV, M. Vyshinsky, M. Pavlov (*Interpreter*).

1. *Date of opening of Conference*

After an exchange of greetings, it was agreed that the talks should begin on July 17th 1945.

[1] The authorship of this draft record is not indicated, but the present text includes amendments in the handwriting of Mr. Eden, Sir A. Cadogan (who initialed it on 17 July 1945) and Mr. Dixon. Mr. Eden noted to Mr. Dixon: 'This is such a poor record that it is not worth keeping. The Turkish part in particular is hopeless & I can't write it all again.' Mr. Hayter, Secretary-General of the British Delegation, was accordingly instructed that it was not to be circulated or treated as a record. No other record of the conversation has, however, been traced in Foreign Office archives.

2. *Agenda*

The question of additions to the Agenda was discussed. The Secretary of State had no additions to make, but M. Molotov suggested the following:

(*a*) Disposal of German Navy and Merchant Marine.

(*b*) Reparations.

(*c*) Territorial Trusteeship and the role of the U.S.S.R.

The Secretary of State pointed out that addition (*c*) w[oul]d be a continuation of the conversations in San Francisco. M. Molotov agreed.

(*d*) Poland.

M. Molotov remarked that the Arciszewski Government and the Polish Army abroad still existed. The Secretary of State replied that the Polish Government in London was gradually being liquidated while the Warsaw Government was gaining prestige abroad. We should also wish to discuss the fulfilment of the Yalta declaration.

(*e*) Diplomatic relations with the Satellite countries.

(*f*) Spain.

The Secretary of State did not resist an exchange of opinion though he did not think there was much to be done under this head. M. Molotov agreed.

(*g*) Tangier.

(*h*) Syria and Lebanon.

3. *Yugoslavia*

At this point the Secretary of State brought up the question of Yugoslavia observing that Marshal Tito had been rude to the British and that the Tito-Subasic agreement had hardly begun to work. M. Molotov explained that Yugoslavia was almost the worst devastated country in Europe: its economic life had been paralysed; there could be a comparison only with the destruction in the U.S.S.R. and even Poland had not suffered as much.

The Secretary of State pointed out that there had not been much fighting in Yugoslavia, to which M. Molotov replied that the fighting had been of a partisan nature.

The Secretary of State went on to say that the Skupshchina (Parliament) had not yet been summoned. M. Molotov replied that the Skupshchina had not met because the majority of its members had been pro-German and that all anti-German elements had left it. However, he had read in the Press that a meeting of some sort was to be called for the 23rd July 1945.

4. *Czechoslovakia*

The Secretary of State and M. Molotov agreed that there was no Czechoslovak problem, M. Molotov remarking that Czechoslovakia was more fortunate than Yugoslavia from the economic point of view, because the Germans had moved many of their own industries during the war to Czechoslovakia and much of the equipment had fallen into Czechoslovak hands.

5. *Procedure*

It was agreed that the Crimean procedure with regard to the Talks should be adopted. Plenary Meetings to be held daily at 5 p.m.

6. *San Francisco*

It was agreed that despite many difficulties, the San Francisco Conference had done its work remarkably well.

It was felt that Mr. Byrnes w[oul]d prove a good colleague in the place of Mr. Stettinius who was now, M. Molotov said, the 'peacemaker'.

7. *Turkey*

The Secretary of State said that the Turks had been to see him in London.[2] M. Molotov observed that the Turks had come also to the Soviet Ambassador in Ankara and had approached the Soviet Government in Moscow on the question of a Treaty of Alliance.[3] The Secretary of State said that M. Molotov had failed to calm them, whereupon M. Molotov said that the Russians were not less anxious than the Turks. He said that the Russians, and especially the Armenians, had been unfairly treated in 1921[3] and moreover the Montreux Convention did not suit the Russians. M. Molotov said: 'I know that the Turks have informed you of these talks. All I need do is to tell you what the Turks told me. But read Yalcin's articles!'[4]

The Secretary of State said that the Turks were ready to discuss the Montreux Convention. Was there anything more to the Turkish question?[5]

M. Molotov replied that there was the question of Armenians living under Turkish rule, the Turks being guilty of massacring Armenians and Georgians.

The Secretary of State said that this had not been discussed at Yalta.[5]

M. Molotov said that the question of a Treaty of Alliance had been raised by the Turks and that the Russians had replied that, if the Armenian question was settled, there would be no obstacle to making such a Treaty.

The Secretary of State said that the British would not object[5] to such a Treaty, but he expressed doubt as to the Russian territorial claim!

M. Molotov though that the Turks were not prepared to cede any territory.

The Secretary of State said that the Turks had already ceded to the Russians Batum which had been occupied by them during the last war.

M. Molotov observed that the Turks had kept Kars and Ardahan, both formerly Russian. He had quoted to the Turks the example of Poland: a similar territorial adjustment could be made with mutually satisfactory results.

M. Molotov concluded his argument by mentioning that the Dean of Canterbury's opinion was identical with his.

As to the Armenian population, M. Molotov said that one million people were in the Armenian Republic and over one million in the rest of the world, including 300,000 in Turkey. He suggested that if Armenia were united there would be a tendency for all Armenians to return to their home land.

[2] See No. 95.
[3] See No. 3, note 9.
[4] M. Yalcin was the editor of the Turkish newspaper *Tanin*.
[5] Mr. Eden put an exclamation remark in the margin against this sentence. Cf. note 1 above.

No. 159

Letter from Mr. Eden[1] to Mr. Byrnes (Berlin)
[N 8885/6/55]

[My dear Secretary of State,]

On the 5th July, at the time of our recognition of the new Polish Provisional Government of National Unity, His Majesty's Ambassador at Washington informed the United States Government that His Majesty's Government had sought from the Polish Provisional Government certain explanations and assurances as to their attitude in regard to the participation of 'all democratic and anti-Nazi parties' in free elections in Poland in accordance with the Crimea decisions.[2] In seeking such assurances, His Majesty's Government had had in mind that, of the four main parties which throughout the war had supported the Polish Government in London and their resistance movement in Poland, only two are represented in the present Provisional Government. The settlement of the Polish question which has now been reached would be criticised in the United Kingdom if it were found that only the parties now included in the Provisional Government were to take part in the elections as a Government bloc without any effective opposition.

In reply to our enquiries, Sir A. Clark Kerr obtained from the Polish Ambassador in Moscow assurances in writing that the Government coalition 'leaves freedom of choice to the former elements of the Democrat or Christian Labour Parties which are democratic and anti-Nazi to take part in the elections or in any other way'. The Polish Ambassador's communication stated, however, that the National Democratic Party no longer existed in its pre-war form. In an oral communication to Sir A. Clark Kerr, the Polish Ambassador stated that the Democratic and Christian Labour Parties would 'have complete freedom of action in regard to the elections and in all other respects'. The Polish Ambassador also indicated that political leaders who wished to start or revive other democratic parties would be free to do so and that such parties would participate in the elections either independently or in blocs as they saw fit.

M. Popiel, the leader of the Christian Labour Party, recently left London for Warsaw to discuss co-operation with the new Government at their invitation; but the Government have made, so far as we know, no move towards any National Democrats. In the circumstances we felt bound to inform the United States and Soviet Governments that we were not satisfied with the assurances which we had so far received on this question and reserved the right to raise it at the present Conference as affecting the

---

[1] The draft of this undated letter was approved by Mr. Eden on 16 July 1945, and the present copy was sent to the Foreign Office that day (received 17 July): cf. the text printed in *F.R.U.S. Berlin*, vol. ii, pp. 1107–9, whence the opening and concluding formulations have been supplied. Cf. also No. 100 above.

[2] See No. 6, note 2, and No. 45, sixth paragraph.

implication of the Crimea decisions. The Polish Provisional Government were informed that we had made this communication to the United States and Soviet Governments.

I do not now think that it would in fact be desirable to discuss this matter in detail at the present Conference. It would be arguable that the question is one which should properly be pursued in direct discussion with the Polish Provisional Government, and it is perhaps unlikely that we should find common ground with the Russians such as would enable effective international action to be taken at the time of the elections. I therefore consider that we should aim rather at securing the insertion in the Communiqué to be issued at the end of this Conference of a reference to the Polish question. This might take the form of a statement on the following lines:

The Three Powers have taken note with pleasure of the agreement reached among representative Poles from Poland and abroad which has made possible the establishment in accordance with the Crimea decisions of a Polish Provisional Government of National Unity recognised by the Three Powers and pledged to the holding of free and unfettered elections as soon as possible on the basis of universal suffrage and secret ballot in which all democratic and anti-Nazi parties shall have the right to take part and to put forward candidates. It is the confident hope of the Three Powers that the elections will be so organised as to enable all sections of Polish opinion to express their views freely and thus play their full part in the restoration of the country's political life. The Three Powers will further expect that representatives of the Allied Press shall enjoy full freedom to report to the world upon developments in Poland before and during the elections. Finally, they are anxious to assist the Polish Provisional Government in facilitating the orderly return to Poland as soon as practicable of all Poles abroad who wish to go; the Polish Provisional Government could itself greatly assist in this task by giving specific undertakings that those Poles who return will do so with full assurance of their personal security, freedom and livelihood.

A statement on these lines seems to us desirable. It would help His Majesty's Government in securing the full support of Parliament in the Polish statement and also in dealing with the very difficult practical problems arising out of the presence of some 250,000 Poles on British soil and in the armed forces under British command.

If you agree that some statement of this sort would be useful I would propose to take an appropriate opportunity of raising it at a meeting of Foreign Ministers and I would hope that I might then count on your support.

[Yours sincerely]
ANTHONY EDEN

No. 160

Sir J. Anderson to Mr. Hankey[1] *(Warsaw)*

No. 389 [N 8615/211/55]

Confidential   FOREIGN OFFICE, *16 July 1945*

Sir,

I desire, on your departure to Warsaw as the first representative of His Majesty's Government to the new Polish Provisional Government of National Unity, to give you, in the following paragraphs, a picture of the situation consequent upon the recognition by His Majesty's Government of the new Government established in accordance with the Crimea Agreement on Poland, as it appears to me, and general guidance as to the attitude you should adopt in your relations with the new Government.

2. Accurate information of the state of affairs in Poland has been scanty, but there is little doubt that the so-called Polish Provisional Government, which preceded the present Government, were, whether by desire or by force of circumstances, puppets of the Soviet Government. They were certainly quite unrepresentative and, although nominally based upon the Communist, Socialist, Peasant and Democratic parties, members of the Government who nominally represented the last three of those parties could not be accepted as in fact doing so and the genuine party organisations and machinery of those three parties were not in fact permitted to operate. On the other hand, although the administration was long ago nominally handed over to the 'Government,' the authorities of the Red army or of the Soviet Government appear, in fact, by one means or another, to have been running the country. The Red army seems to have been running riot, living on the country and despoiling it. Air and rail communications—and probably to a large extent road communications, too—appear to have been all controlled by the Russian authorities and the same applies to radio and telegraphic communications.

3. It is not to be supposed that all this has been changed by the appointment of the new Government, which amounts in fact to the reappointment of the old Government with the addition of M. Mikolajczyk, M. Kiernik, M. Stanczyk, M. Wyciech and I assume a substitute for M. Thugutt chosen by M. Mikolajczyk and the appointment of the elderly M. Grabski and possibly the more elderly M. Witos to the Presidium of the National Council (it is not clear whether M. Witos has in fact accepted the appointment). Also M. B[i]erut, originally appointed President by the Russians, remains

---

[1] Mr. R. M. A. Hankey had arrived in Warsaw on 14 July 1945 to take up his appointment there as British Chargé d'Affaires. On 13 July Mr. Eden had approved the draft of this despatch.

President until a new Diet is elected.[2] On the other hand, there appears to have been little doubt that only some five to ten per cent. at most of the population supported the previous Government, and it may be that the Government and the Soviet Government came to the conclusion that for a variety of reasons it was desirable to secure a greater measure of popular support for the régime. Be that as it may, M. Mikolajczyk informed Mr. Winch during his recent passage through Warsaw that no attempt was being made to prevent him from taking steps to revive and invigorate the peasant party and establish his own influence with the rank and file of the people. Mr. Winch also reports that he received the impression that many of the Ministers of the previous Government, including M. Osobka Morawski, the Prime Minister, are patriotic Poles according to their lights rather than mere Russian puppets, that they are restive under Russian domination, that they look forward to renewing their contacts with the West and to receiving representatives of as many foreign countries as possible.

4. It appears, therefore, that there is a possibility that the reorganisation of the Government and its recognition by the Powers may mark the opening of a new phase. It is clear, of course, that the Soviet Union will retain a predominant influence in Polish affairs. Even were they not to retain puppets in the Government and Russian representatives in various guises scattered throughout the Polish Administration, even were they to relax their direct hold on communications and to withdraw the bulk or the whole of the Red army, the Soviet Government would be able to dictate to the Polish Government on major matters of policy and it is difficult to see how or when, in practice, this would cease to be. If so, it will be for His Majesty's Government to decide in the light of the European political situation as a whole whether and by what methods to challenge the Soviet Government's position in this matter or attempt to constitute themselves the champions of the Poles in trying to reduce the extent of Russian domination. You will be careful not to be influenced by any section of the Polish Government or people into taking up at the present juncture a definite position in regard to this very delicate question. In point of fact, it is very unlikely that M. Mikolajczyk or other members of the Polish Government who share his views would attempt to force your hand at this early stage; for they may doubt whether it is in fact in the power of His Majesty's Government or the United States Government to effect a change of policy in present circumstances, and they may feel that to attempt any such thing might result in the Russians taking steps to circumscribe the activities of the foreign representatives and foreign press in the case of Poland as they have in the case of Roumania and Bulgaria. Thus your task—at the outset at least—

[2] MM. W. Kiernik, J. Stanczyk and C. Wycech were respectively the Ministers of Public Administration, Labour and Public Welfare, and Education in the Polish Provisional Government of National Unity. Professor S. Grabski and M. B. Bierut were respectively Deputy President and President of the Praesidium of the Polish National Council of the Homeland.

will be limited to judging whether the Soviet authorities are preparing to allow the new Polish Government a greater degree of freedom, and whether and how the latter, and especially M. Mikolajczyk, wish to make use of it.

5. The arrangements reached between the Poles in Moscow and accepted by the Commission of Three[3] are by no means all that His Majesty's Government would have desired, either as regards the composition or probable policy of the Government or as regards the conditions under which the elections provided for in the Crimean decision are likely to be held. The crux of the matter will, it seems, be to what extent M. Mikolajczyk and his friends will be able to play an effective part in the Government and be able to extend their influence in the country through the intermediary of peasant and socialist parties strong enough for their voices to be heard and listened to. If M. Mikolajczyk and his friends are able to achieve this and if other members of the new Government are anxious to decrease the degree of Poland's servitude to the Soviet Union, His Majesty's Government will no doubt be ready to consider whether and if so in what way they can help the Polish Government in their task of re-establishing an independent Poland and will give any proposals sympathetic consideration provided that what is suggested takes a reasonable account of the real position of Poland *vis-à-vis* of the Soviet Union.

6. As you are aware, His Majesty's Government are most anxious to see the establishment of such political and administrative conditions as will be most conducive to the holding of free and unfettered elections. I shall be glad to receive a report from you on the best course to pursue in order to further this end, so soon as you have been able to have a conversation on the subject with M. Mikolajczyk. It is in this connexion that the treatment of the press is most important and I shall be glad if you will keep me informed as to how far the principle of a free press is being applied in practice. It is clearly difficult to judge from London whether to favour early elections, or whether is is desirable to await the return of the maximum number of Poles who have been in contact with the West, and also to wait until there has been some progress towards the re-establishment of a strong party system. As regards the latter aim, I shall be glad to know as soon as possible what is the outcome of the discussions regarding the future rôle of the Christian Labour Party in which M. Popiel was to take part on his return to Warsaw. You are aware of the correspondence with the Polish Government which has recently passed through His Majesty's Ambassador in Moscow on the subject of the parties which are not to be considered, in the terms of the Crimea decision, anti-Nazi and democratic.[4] It appears to me that the intention of the Polish Provisional Government is to dissolve the National Democrat party but—ostensibly at least—to allow the formation of new *bourgeois* parties and to aim at the absorption of the members who support the National Democrat party into the small 'Democratic' party which is represented in the Government by the Ministry of Foreign Affairs.

[3] Cf. No. 78, note 1.   [4] Cf. No. 159.

On the other hand it has been the aim of His Majesty's Government to secure, if possible, that the Left wing of the National Democrat party at least (*i.e.*, the supporters of that section of the party which did not withdraw from General Sikorski's Government at the time of the Stalin-Sikorski Agreement)[5] should be enabled to participate as a separate entity in the political life of the new Poland. You should discuss this point, as soon as possible after your arrival, with M. Mikolajczyk and report the result by telegram.

7. On all the matters dealt with in the three preceding paragraphs I shall expect to receive from you full and frequent reports. I should wish you, therefore, to watch the situation, to acquire all the information you can by legitimate means of the true state of affairs in Poland. For this purpose you should also attempt discreetly to establish a close contact with M. Mikolajczyk, and to encourage him to confide in you, taking care of course not to compromise him.

8. Meanwhile your first duty, of course, will be the protection of British interests. You are aware of the facilities for communication, &c., which M. Berut promised in Moscow that His Majesty's Embassy and British correspondents should enjoy. You should at once report if you are not in practice able to exercise any of these facilities. You should pursue at an early date the question of the establishment of consular posts. It might, however, be that the Soviet authorities, who are understood, according to M. Garreau, to have allowed him considerable freedom from restrictions, will take steps on the arrival of representatives from the numerous countries who may be expected to recognise the new Government, to restrict the Diplomatic Corps. You will realise that if the Soviet Government so wish, they can in fact do so by using such means as they have used in Roumania and Bulgaria. It would be wise, therefore, while not abating at all your claims to all normal facilities of movement, &c., to exercise some discretion in the use to which you put them.

9. You should also do all you can to ensure that British correspondents, who it is hoped will shortly proceed to Warsaw, are given adequate facilities to travel in the country, to interview those they wish to question, and to send reports to their newspapers in this country without their being so censored as to render them valueless. The same applies to British business men and representatives of British firms who will, I hope, be visiting Poland in due course.

I have, &c.,
J. ANDERSON

CALENDAR TO No. 160

i *16–24 July 1945   Communications with H.M. Embassy at Warsaw: (a) correspondence of 16–19 July between Foreign Office, Mr. Hankey (Warsaw), British Delegation at Berlin and Sir W. Strang regarding road convoy to H.M. Embassy* [Y 7549,

[5] See No. 45, note 5.

7564, 7619/7218/652; F.O. 934/2/10(4)]; (b) *letters of 20 & 24 July from Sir A. Clark Kerr to M. Vyshinski (Berlin)* concerning facilities through Soviet Zone for road convoy, and clearance for twice-weekly air service between London and Warsaw [F.O. 934/2/10(30); F.O. 934/4/31(2–3)].

No. 161

Mr. Hankey (Warsaw) to Mr. Eden (Received 16 July, 11.30 p.m.)
No. 5 Telegraphic [N 8688/211/55]

WARSAW, *16 July 1945, 9.12 p.m. G.M.T.*

We were met on arrival at Warsaw airfield by political director of Ministry of Foreign Affairs and other officials and by Soviet Counsellor and Secretary. Adequate arrangements were made by Ministry of Foreign Affairs for temporary accommodation of His Majesty's Embassy at Hotel Polonia the relative comfort of which is in striking contrast to the ruin, desolation, and misery on every hand. Warsaw is unrecognisable. Many streets are still not cleared and work is proceeding slowly. The people all show signs of their sufferings and many look hungry and ill. Ministry of Health are concerned in containing the number of typhus and typhoid cases.

2. The arrival of our Embassy is most evidently welcome. Even before I had unpacked, the Chef de Protocole took me to the French Ambassador's reception for July 14th, when I was presented to President Bierut, Minister for Foreign Affairs, M. Mikolajczyk, M. Stanczyk and other personalities. All were most cordial, the President somewhat reserved. Minister for Foreign Affairs complained of the extreme difficulty of communicating with London at present. Had not yet heard of the name proposed for His Majesty's Ambassador. I took the opportunity to say we were installing radio transmitter in our hotel. He welcomed this. Members of the Ministry of Foreign Affairs (including the political director who is of very Left wing type) all said they regarded relations with Western Europe as essential to avoid Poland looking solely to the East. I had to decline with some difficulty pressing invitation to leave during the same night to attend Slavonic victory celebrations at Grunwald in East Prussia.

3. With Mikolajczyk I made an immediate private understanding to keep friendly but quite unostentatious contact and in any case not more than he felt wise at any time. M. Stanczyk is less cautious.

4. People of every class come to our offices quite freely and do not seem to feel compromised thereby. I have met many former acquaintances, most of them among the lower classes. Most people express the opinion that it is too soon for Poles abroad to come back especially if they were connected in any way with . . .[1] army. General opinion that N.K.V.D. still operate but only by arresting individuals mostly at night. It is impossible as yet to

---

[1] The text is here uncertain.

confirm or deny these allegations but there is evidently some fire behind the smoke. This applies to the south and centre of Poland as well as to Warsaw.

5. The Government offices seem to be in considerable chaos. The telephone does not work and we are greatly hampered by absence of transport until our cars arrive.

No. 162

Sir J. Anderson to Sir L. Collier (Oslo)

No. 292 [N 8052/90/30]

Top secret   FOREIGN OFFICE, *16 July 1945*

Sir,

In Your Excellency's telegram No. 92[1] of the 4th July you reported that the Norwegian Minister for Foreign Affairs had informed you that the Storting, during a secret session, had authorised negotiations regarding the Russian demands concerning Spitzbergen and Bear Island on the basis offered to M. Molotov at San Francisco.

2. The Norwegian Minister for Foreign Affairs informed me[2] in the greatest secrecy at the end of last year that during his visit to Moscow last November M. Molotov had raised with him the question of the status of Spitzbergen and Bear Island, the sovereignty over which was conferred upon Norway under a treaty of the 3rd February, 1920, to which Great Britain, Denmark, France, Italy, Japan, Norway and Sweden were parties[3], and to which the Russians adhered in 1935. M. Molotov proposed, on the grounds of safeguarding Russian economic and strategic interests, that Spitzbergen could be placed under a condominium of Norway and the U.S.S.R. and also that Bear Island which had originally been Russian should be returned to the Soviet Union. When M. Lie showed himself unresponsive, M. Molotov

---

[1] Not printed. This telegram (received 10.50 p.m. on 4 July 1945) regarding Soviet demands concerning Spitzbergen and Bear Island had reported in particular that the Norwegian parliament or Storting, 'although much disturbed, had authorized negotiations on basis offered to M. Molotov at San Francisco: viz: joint defence arrangements with recognition of Norwegian sovereignty.' With reference to this telegram Sir O. Sargent had stated in Foreign Office telegram No. 110 of 15 July to Oslo: 'At the request of M. Lie the Secretary of State and I have treated the information he has given us on this subject as being of the utmost secrecy. Please ask M. Lie if this is still his wish' in view of his having reportedly spoken of it to Sir L. Collier's 'United States colleague. If the subject is mentioned to us by the Americans or by the Russians are we to pretend that we know nothing about it?' Sir O. Sargent further requested in Foreign Office telegram No. 114 of 19 July to Oslo: 'Please expedite reply. Matter has been raised by Americans with Sir A. Cadogan at Potsdam.': see No. 299.

[2] Mr. Eden.

[3] This treaty of 9 February 1920, to which the United States and the Netherlands were also signatories, is printed with annex in *B.F.S.P.*, vol. 113, pp. 789–97.

adopted a somewhat harsh tone and said that it was better to settle such matters amicably.

3. The Norwegian Government were somewhat alarmed by these Russian demands and communicated to the Soviet Government in reply a reasoned statement claiming that Russian economic interests were adequately safeguarded under the international treaty of 1920, and suggesting that the Norwegian and Soviet Governments should jointly approach the other interested Allied Powers with a view to securing their agreement to the militarisation of Spitzbergen and Bear Island, such militarisat[ion][4] to form part of a world-wide or a regional security arrangement. The Soviet Government replied that this Norwegian offer did not go far enough.

4. On the 7th March last, the Norwegian Minister for Foreign Affairs came to see Sir Orme Sargent and informed him that the Norwegian Minister in Moscow had received a note from the Soviet Government stating that they agreed to later proposals of the Norwegian Government to the effect that they should negotiate with the Soviet Government on the joint military defence of Spitzbergen and Bear Island and then consult the Allied Governments concerned about the proposals worked out between the Norwegian and Soviet Governments. M. Lie mentioned that his Government proposed to reply that [they][4] would be very glad to enter into negotiations with the Sovie[t][4] Government as soon as they had returned to Norway, but that they would find it difficult to start negotiations before the liberation of Norway, as, while the Norwegian Government were in London, they had no access to the necessary documents and maps which they would require to carry on the discussions. M. Lie begged, as he had already previously, that we should in no way reveal the fact that His Majesty's Government were aware of the exchange of view which had been proceeding between the Norwegian and Soviet Governments.

5. You should know for your personal information only that the view of the Chiefs of Staff as regards a Soviet occupation of Spitzbergen and Bear Island is that the naval and air base facilities which could be developed at Spitzbergen are very limited and their use would be severely restricted by the weather. It is unlikely that any bases could be established in Bear Island. The islands are of small commercial value to Norway and their loss, if the Soviet Union should prove hostile to her, would not seriously embarrass her economy. Is is considered that in any case Soviet bases there would not threaten our own interests or those of Norway, and that we ourselves would not need bases further north than Norway. The Chiefs of Staff therefore see no strategic objections to the Russians establishing bases in these islands. From a practical point of view, neither we nor the Norwegians could hold the islands against a hostile Soviet Union.

6. As there is therefore no British strategic interest in Spitzbergen or in Bear Island, His Majesty's Government's attitude towards any Soviet insistence regarding this matter can be governed by political considerations

[4] The text is here defective.

alone. No alteration however in the present status of these islands can be effected except in agreement with all the signatories of the Treaty of 1920.

I am, &c.,

(For Sir John Anderson)

ANTHONY HAIGH[5]

[5] Signature of Mr. A. A. F. Haigh, a member of the Northern Department of the Foreign Office, is supplied from the filed draft.

No. 163

Letter from Mr. Dean (Berlin) to Mr. Pink (Lübbecke)[1]

[U 5604/16/73]

Immediate   BRITISH DELEGATION, BERLIN, *16 July 1945*

In connection with the discussions about war criminals I keep being asked whether the British military authorities in 21 Army Group Zone have actually held any trials of minor German war criminals and if not, why not. I have been told on more than one occasion that now that the Royal Warrant[2] has been issued, everything is ready to begin trials as soon as the necessary instructions are received from London and Francis Brown[3] tells me that this is his impression also.

There are two classes of criminals concerned, viz:

(*a*) those who have committed violations of the rules of war against British subjects and in particular British soldiers (e.g. shooting parachute troops or maltreating prisoners);

(*b*) those who have committed war crimes against Allied nationals in British zones, but whom we are prepared to try because it would be difficult to hand them over to the Allies. The best examples of this class are the Commandants and guards of concentration camps, particularly at Belsen.

From our point of view we should like some of these trials to begin as soon as possible as it is likely to be some time still before we can stage any trials of the major criminals and now that the risk of reprisals is over, there seems no reason why people like Kramer[4] should not be dealt with as soon as possible.

[1] This letter was copied to Mr. R. D. J. Scott Fox in the Foreign Office.

[2] The Royal Warrant of 14 June 1945 on Regulations for the Trial of War Criminals had been issued as Special Army Order No. 81 on 18 June: printed in *War Crimes Trials*, vol. ii (London, 1949), pp. 647–51.

[3] Mr. F. D. W. Brown, a member of the Political Division of the Control Commission for Germany (British Element), was attached to the staff of Military Government at 21st Army Group Headquarters.

[4] Hauptsturmführer Josef Kramer had been commandant of Bergen-Belsen concentration-camp.

Could you please let me know what the position is either via the Foreign Office or direct here if that is possible. If the matter is still held up on some technical point of procedure, can anything be done to move the necessary authorities to take action at once?[5]

This is a delightful place though exceedingly hot and we have not yet begun to do any real work.

P. DEAN

[5] Mr. Pink replied to Mr. Dean in a letter of 20 July 1945 that the War Crimes Section of the British 21st Army Group 'are only awaiting certain written evidence . . . still in the hands of the J[udge] A[dvocate] G[eneral] in London who is having photostatic copies made. It is hoped, however, that the first batch of war criminals, numbering about 49, will be brought to trial about the middle of next month. I understand that Kramer will be among these.'

No. 164

Letter from Mr. Troutbeck to Mr. Harrison (Berlin)
[F.O. 934/1/2(31)]

Immediate   FOREIGN OFFICE, *16 July 1945*

My dear Geoffrey,

Many thanks for your letter of the 15th July[1] enclosing a copy of your amended interpretation of the implications of treating Germany as an economic whole. We think the result is a stout effort in the way of compressed drafting and the alterations we suggest below are advanced in a spirit of admiration! They are the upshot of a rather hurried meeting between myself, Lincoln, Ritchie, Playfair, Stopford, Trevaldwyn,[2] and Rugman of of the Control Commission.

2. We note that the rubric has now been extended from the treatment of Germany as an economic whole to the treatment of Germany 'as an administrative and economic whole'. We imagine there is no particular significance in this and assume it to mean in effect the treatment of Germany as an economic whole, and the administrative measures necessary to secure that end.

3. We attach for your consideration a redraft of your document 'B'. This redraft contains the following features:

(*a*) We have omitted your paragraph 1. This is not because we do not think free circulation of Allied nationals highly important. Solely from the aspect of treating Germany as an economic whole it would undoubtedly be useful, since by that means each Controlling Power could see through

[1] No. 153.
[2] Mr. W. Ritchie was an Assistant Secretary in the Economic Advisory Branch of the Foreign Office. Mr. R. J. Stopford was an Assistant Secretary in the Directorate of Civil Affairs in the War Office, and Mr. J. R. Trevaldwyn was on the Financial Staff there.

its own representatives what was actually occurring in the zones of its neighbours. All the same, we would not regard a stipulation of this kind as springing directly out of the treatment of Germany as an economic whole; and since the subject may cause controversy, we think it might be better to keep it out of the present context, lest by raising it here we endanger reaching agreement about the treatment of Germany as an economic whole. It seems really more a political question and is bound up with press correspondents.

(*b*) As they stand, paragraphs 2 and 3 seems to us rather to confuse the different objectives of securing agreement in matters of policy and agreement upon methods of administration. We have, therefore, recast these two paragraphs to keep the questions of policy and the questions of machinery apart.

(*c*) We have added a sentence to your paragraph 3(*e*). While the Zone Commander must clearly retain discretion, at any rate for the time being, to permit or not permit specific movements of goods out of his zone, we should like to aim at getting a free exchange of goods between the zones without administrative interference from the central control machinery.

4. Two other comments. The first is that we have not attempted to include in our revise of your formula any provision about the responsibility, which should be common to the four Occupying Powers, for the provision of goods for Germany from sources outside Germany. No doubt this point will be borne in mind in any discussion of supply arrangements for Germany. The second point is to remind you that the formula attached to the brief which we have given the Delegation[3] differs in one respect from the formula which was laid before Field-Marshal Montgomery. The difference consists in the substitution for the fourth sentence of the formula submitted to the Field-Marshal of the fourth sentence appearing in the draft formula attached to the Delegation brief. This latter sentence is based upon paragraph 7 of Moscow telegram No. 46 Victim.[4]

5. We note that your draft has been prepared with an eye to the possibility that we may well be asked what we mean by the treatment of Germany as an economic whole. You will no doubt want to decide yourselves on the spot whether, having regard to the progress of the conversations, you wish to use it only for this negative purpose or whether it will be desirable to incorporate some or all of it as an interpretative supplement to the formula itself.

6. I enclose a copy of your own letter, since it was in manuscript and you may not have kept a copy. I also enclose an extra copy of this letter for John Coulson.

Yours ever
JACK TROUTBECK

[3] No. 125.
[4] Annex to No. 116.

One Germany—or Two

A decision is required at *Terminal* as to whether Germany is to be treated as one administrative and economic whole.

If the answer is in the affirmative it carries with it the following implications and repercussions, amongst others, which must be faced:

1. Common policies as regards the method of treatment of the German civil population particularly in respect of the following subjects:

(*a*) Currency, servicing the German debt, and central taxation.

(*b*) Payment of compensation claims to German nationals including those in regard to requisition, war damage, reparation, deliveries and removals.

(*c*) Industrial production, wage rates, price control and rationing.

(*d*) Reparations and removal of industrial war potential.

(*e*) Transfer and exchange of resources and services, including food, between zones so as to preserve a balanced economy throughout Germany and reduce the need for imports. The aim should be the maximum movement of goods, without administrative restriction, between the zones.

(*f*) German imports and exports.

2. Central administration of a number of forms of German governmental machinery, including particularly finance (including customs), transportation, communications, and generally to the extent required for carrying out the policies referred to in paragraph 1.

CALENDAR TO No. 164

i *17 July 1945 Minutes by Mr. Harrison and Mr. Coulson* covering redraft of No. 164, enclosure, under title, by Sir W. Strang, of 'Treatment of Germany as an Economic Whole' [F.O. 934/1/2(31)].

No. 165

Memorandum by Mr. Playfair (Treasury)[1]
OF 213/3/2 [UE 3048/624/77]

Secret   *16 July 1945*

Reparations

This note is designed to give an account of the Moscow negotiations up to the departure of Sir Walter Monckton and Mr. Pauley for Terminal on the 14th July.

2. The negotiations have been proceeding for nearly a month, without making very much progress. One reason for this is that Mr. Pauley did not hide the fact that his desire was to leave Moscow for Terminal, carrying with him as much as he could by way of results. His desire to score a quick

---

[1] A copy of this memorandum was sent to Mr. Dent of the Economic Relations Department of the Foreign Office by Mr. Playfair under cover of a letter of 17 July 1945 wherein he explained that he had prepared the memorandum for Sir E. Bridges.

personal success made him an obvious victim for delaying tactics, and Mr. Maisky did not hurry. The Russians, from the start, promised to produce a detailed plan for discussion, but so far they have produced nothing more than what they presented at Yalta, (the reason for the delay is not quite clear to the delegation: Mr. Pauley's impatience scarcely seems sufficient), and very little in conversation.

3. Mr. Pauley determined to reach agreement, before Terminal, on the following important points:

(a) the allocation between the Three Big Powers to be subject later to proportionate reduction to meet the claims of the others;

(b) principles and procedures whereby percentages of other claimant nations may be determined;

(c) the definition of 'reparation', 'restitution' and 'war booty';

(d) providing a speedy programme of interim reparations for all countries entitled thereto.

He also put forward, and hoped to get agreed, a set of 'general principles' governing reparation.

4. Of all this, only (a) and (b) above have been agreed; and the agreement on (b) deals with procedure rather than principle. As regards the general principles, the Russians have declined to agree with what is to us the most important part of it—paragraph 8, which lays down the first charge in favour of exports (see paragraph 20 below). The rest of the text (see Annex I)[2] is agreed.

5. The meetings have been well conducted. Mr. Maisky is an excellent chairman and a first-rate (and tough) negotiator. Practically everything has been done in a small steering committee, where there have been serious and useful discussions on all the important questions (it has the advantage that its proceedings are all in English). Numerous sub-committees have been decided upon, but only one of them, it seems, has so far functioned. On it there have been some useful discussions on economic security. Relations with the Americans are good; with the Russians not close, but not unsatisfactory.

6. *Allocation.* At Yalta the Russians proposed a division of physical deliveries (leaving out of account reparation labour for which they will be much the biggest claimants) as follows:

U.S.S.R.	50%
U.S.A. and U.K.	40%
The others	10%[3]

Statistical studies in London showed that, while it was impossible to translate

[2] Not printed. This text was the same as that included in the annex to No. 116 except that, in accordance with an agreement reached by the Moscow Reparation Commission and reported in Moscow telegram No. 72 Victim of 14 July, paragraph 6 included the words 'which may contribute to the regeneration of German militarism' after the words 'German industrial capacity'.

[3] Cf. Sir L. Woodward, *op. cit.*, vol. v, pp. 278–82.

the Yalta formula exactly into figures, something like the following would be a justifiable allocation for all reparations (i.e. including labour):

U.S.S.R.	50%
U.K.	27%
U.S.A.	12%
The others	11%

The respective proportions of the U.S.A. and ourselves were based on the assumption that our war efforts could be regarded as roughly equal, but that our losses were far greater.

7. When these ideas were discussed with the Americans, we came up against strong opposition. They were in no way inclined to dispute the Russian claim to 50% excluding labour; they did not think it was unjustified, and they thought that any attempt to contest it would only lead to an acrimonious deadlock. Sir Walter Monckton inclined to agree with this view and thought he would find it very hard, on the basis of the data available, to argue against the Russian claim. As regards the United States share, Mr. Pauley declared that as a matter of personal pride he declined on any account to agree to accepting a smaller share than our own; he would rather resign. Further, though the United States did not want much reparation for themselves, they wanted as large a share as possible to distribute among other countries, so as to reduce the credits they might otherwise have to give and to enable them to guide the reconstruction of Europe.

7. [*sic*] The United States Ambassador at Moscow strongly urged Sir Walter Monckton to give way on both points. As regards the American share, he said that Mr. Pauley had great influence on President Truman. If we insisted on this matter, which was not of inherently great importance, we might well affect adversely our relations with him at the time of Terminal. In the light of these representations, and of Sir Walter Monckton's own views on the Russian share, Ministers decided to give way on both points, provided that it was made clear that our agreement on the American share was based on broad and general considerations of Anglo-American relations, and not on any precise calculation of effort and loss such as appeared to be contemplated in the Yalta agreement.[4]

8. At Mr. Pauley's suggestion, a different formula has been adopted for expressing the allocation between the big three from that which was originally contemplated. Pending consideration of the shares of the other countries (which Mr. Maisky at first said might be anything up to 25%, but now seems to think should be 10% or at most 12½%), they have allocated nothing to them, but have given only the proportions between the big three (working out at 56:22:22), and have stipulated that these percentages shall be abated proportionately to meet the agreed claims of the other countries. The agreed text of the Commission's recommendation is attached as Annex II.[5]

[4] Cf. Nos. 50 and 88.

[5] Not printed. Annexes II and III were respectively the same as Annexes A and B to No. 152: *v. ibid.*, note 3.

329

9. *Procedure for determining shares of the other allies.* A formula was agreed *ad referendum* immediately before Sir W. Moncktons' departure for Terminal. The text is shown in Annex III.[5]

10. *Definition of 'reparation'.* There is no sign that this topic of Mr. Pauley's has been discussed as such. This is perhaps not surprising, as it seems to contain in itself the sum of the Commission's work. Some progress has been made towards it in the statement of general principles.

11. *Definition of 'restitution'.* We have put in a paper on the general principles,[6] and the Russians have also put in a text, which does not differ very widely from our views, though there is one important point of difference.[7] No final agreement has yet been reached.

12. Meanwhile Mr. Pauley, with the President's authority, has put into action in the American zone a scheme for the restoration of looted works of art found in that zone; he only consulted us after telegraphing to General Eisenhower.[8] This procedure is lamentable, but the scheme itself is not ill-founded, though it could be improved. We agree in regarding the matter as one of great urgency; the military authorities are overwhelmed with requests from the Allies for urgent restitution, which have been held up by the constant refusal over about eight months of the Russians on the EAC to discuss our proposals for an inter-allied Restitution Commission. About the time of Mr. Pauley's action, the matter was at last discussed, and our proposals turned down flat by the Russians. We are therefore following Mr. Pauley's lead, and attempting to get agreement at Moscow on a slightly improved version of Mr. Pauley's scheme. We should like to extend it beyond works of art.

13. *Definition of 'war booty'.* The Americans and ourselves are agreed that we must have a precise definition of booty, since the Russian conduct in the satellite countries, where they have seized everything and anything under the name of booty, shows that without a clear understanding they might drive a coach and four through any arrangements. We were not clear, when the delegation went out, whether we should aim at a wide or narrow interpretation of the word, and had hoped to defer a decision till after Terminal; but Mr. Pauley's haste made earlier discussion necessary, though his own ideas are not fully formed. Mr. Maisky seems to favour a narrow definition (having started from the position that no definition is necessary), and says (for what it is worth) that the Russians will gladly account for all they have taken outside the definition. Ministers have now agreed that we should work for a narrow definition.

14. *Interim deliveries.* Side by side with his restitution scheme, Mr. Pauley set on foot a scheme for urgent interim deliveries from the American

---

[6] See *F.R.U.S. Berlin*, vol. i, p. 539, note 5, and vol. ii, p. 848.

[7] The British Delegation at Moscow had reported on 14 July in Moscow telegram No. 73 Victim that they had objected to the words 'as well as property which came into existence on the said territory during the period of enemy occupation' in the Russian text referred to in No. 152, note 10, as extending restitution to goods already paid for.

[8] Cf. No. 3.i(*a*).

330

zone. It was sound in principle, but rather half-baked. At the moment of his departure for [? from] Moscow, a scheme was being discussed but no agreement had been reached; it was a development from Mr. Pauley's scheme, with ideas of our own and of the Russians inserted. It is an urgent matter, but extremely difficult, and the fact that the Russians have rejected the idea of the first charge[9] will probably make agreement still more difficult. We had attempted to get the first charge firmly written in by suggesting that payment should be made for current deliveries.

15. *Statement of general principles.* This is, from our point of view, an excellent document; the Americans and ourselves would be glad to see it published. Mr. Pauley is determined that it should be agreed at Terminal. The only real trouble about it is that the Russians do not agree to it as it stands. Some points in it have proved contentions and deserve special comment.

16. *Paragraph 1—economic security.* All three delegations are agreed on the importance of economic security as a determinant of the kind of plant to be removed. Some preliminary discussions have taken place on the kind of economic security programme which should be pursued, but no conclusions have yet been reached.

17. *Paragraph 3—treatment of Germany as an economic unit.* In its more general context, this will be on the agenda of Terminal. At Moscow, the Russians refrained from comment.

18. *Paragraph 4—the Commander's veto.* The last limb of this article was inserted by ourselves; at the first stage it stood in a more definite form, providing that each Commander, in his zone, should have the right to suspend the operation of the plan if he felt that it jeopardised in any case the fulfilment of his mission. The Russians objected to this, and Ministers felt that in the present context they were justified. The idea was important, but it was a matter not of principle but of procedure. However, we shall have trouble over this in the future; the Russians want to make the fulfilment of reparation an overriding principle; we do not give it the same absolute priority.

19. *Paragraph 7—the German standard of living.* This phrase, as it stands, is fairly harmless, and looks just. But we have agreed to it with some foreboding. The delegation have advised us that the Russians may seek to use this to drive the reparation plan beyond the limits of common sense. Our feeling is that we must watch its application; if it is properly interpreted, it should not have that effect; and we can only agree to it on the understanding that it means no more than it says. At the same time, it would be very hard to say no to such a principle.

20. *Paragraph 8—the first charge.* This paragraph contains a principle to which we attach the highest importance, as do the Americans: namely, that the cost of imports ranks as a first charge on German exports, above reparations (we exclude from the operation of this charge once-for-all

[9] See No. 152, paragraph (4).

331

deliveries of German plant etc.). The Russians, at the last moment, have declined to agree to it. Their view is that the plan must give first priority to reparation, while allowing for some exports to pay for imports. If the Germans do not earn enough for imports they must do without. We cannot agree to this, and it will doubtless have to be discussed at Terminal, where Mr. Pauley is certain to ask the President to bring it up.

21. The foregoing paragraphs deal with the questions which Mr. Pauley has pushed forward with a view to getting them settled in time for Terminal. The following paragraphs deal with other questions which have been, or will be, discussed.

22. We have throughout urged that France ought to be an original member of the Moscow Commission. She is one of the controlling powers, and the scheme will not work without her. We do not think much of Mr. Maisky's argument that it does not much matter what the French do in their little zone. Unfortunately the matter was not settled in that sense at Yalta. We tried again afterwards, but the Russians would only agree on condition that Poland and Yugoslavia were made original members too. We were prepared to stick out, but Mr. Pauley left for Moscow and we felt bound to follow him. He and Sir W. Monckton have constantly pressed for the French to be admitted, but have met with no signs of yielding at all from the Russians. Mr. Pauley proposes to raise the question again at Terminal.

23. *Continuing machinery.* The Russian idea seems to be that the plan should be carried out by the Control Commission, the Moscow Commission being kept alive but dormant to deal with big questions of principle. Our view is that, while the Control Commission must carry out the executive functions in Germany, there should be a separate body, sitting in Germany, and representative of all the interested powers, which should deal with all questions which arise between the different claimants. The Americans appear to agree more or less with the Russians. This matter has yet to be discussed.

24. *The amount of reparation.* The Russians are still sticking to their contention that the Moscow Commission should, *a priori*, fix a total figure for reparation. They have not departed from their figure of $20 billion, though they emphasise that the figure remains for discussion, and Mr. Maisky, in conversation, has referred to the possibility of the figure coming as low as $12 million. Mr. Pauley and Sir W. Monckton have both spoken strongly against this view, and they may have made some impression, but the matter will not really come up for discussion till the Russians produce their plan.

25. *Labour.* There have been no discussions yet. Mr. Maisky, in conversation, has confirmed that they have in mind a figure of about 4 million workers—the figure which was mentioned at Tehran. The Americans are inclined towards picking reparation labour from among 'war criminals'—this phrase being interpreted in its widest sense.

26. *Safehaven.* Apart from a flurry at the beginning, which led nowhere, German assets in neutral countries have not yet been discussed. But it is

worth mentioning that we shall soon hear plenty of it, since the Americans are more interested in that than in anything else.

27. *Ships.* This subject has not yet been discussed. Some time ago Marshal Stalin staked out a claim for German naval and merchant ships to the Prime Minister and the President. He was told that this should be discussed at Terminal. The question of naval ships (which was discussed last week at the Cabinet)[10] will doubtless be settled there; but the question of merchant ships should, in the view of the Ministry of War Transport, be referred back to the Moscow Commission as a reparation question. This may give rise to difficulty, as our view is that reparation ships should be divided in accordance with shipping losses, which would mean that we should get half and the Russians next to none.

28. *Austria.* Our line on Austrian reparations is that there is no reason of principle why she should not pay any, but that, after taking into account the first charge for imports (on which Austria greatly relies) and the fact that we are committed to setting her up as an independent state, it is most unlikely that she can in fact pay any. The Americans support this view. The Russians say that she ought to pay reparations, whether she can on these conditions or not; and they have already started to strip their zone.

29. This came up, on a side-wind, at the EAC. A deadlock was reached, and we hoped to get the question remitted by the EAC to Moscow, where it belonged. But the French on the EAC naturally refused to remit it to a body on which they are not represented. Sir W. Monckton discussed with Mr. Pauley whether they should raise it independently at Moscow, but they came to the conclusion that they could only reach a deadlock there. They suggested that it should be raised at Terminal, but we see little better hope for it there. The whole question is in a state of unsatisfactory suspense.

[10] See No. 118.

No. 166

Letter from Mr. Harrison (Berlin) to Mr. Troutbeck[1]
[F.O. 934/1/2(1)]

Personal BRITISH DELEGATION, BERLIN, *16 July 1945*

My dear Jack,

It may be useful to you to have a few first impressions of Berlin.

First of all as regards accommodation we are for once being treated royally. We have a row of high class villas along the shore of one of the many narrow lakes in the German suburbs. The rooms are comfortably furnished and we practically all have one to ourselves. Our office accommodation is also spacious and comfortable. A real contrast to Yalta!

We flew into Germany low over Essen, Brunswick and Magdeburg with a

[1] The date of receipt is uncertain.

final sweep in over the centre of Berlin. I have driven the route in peace time. Much of it lies through (or over) thickly populated areas with masses of railways and roads. People swarm all over the place. The overwhelming impression we got flying in on Saturday[2] was of the total devastation and stillness of all the built-up areas. In the whole flight over Germany I did not see a single train moving though in the Ruhr area there were many trucks and carriages in sidings. One saw a few chimneys smoking but they were noticeably the exception. There were hardly any people moving about at all; where they have all got to God alone knows. In a word the built-up areas on our route were still as death.

The countryside presented a considerable contrast. Not that one saw many people moving about but the smaller provincial towns and villages were practically untouched. Acres and acres of corn-fields stretched below us. As we got further east they gave place to large woods, many of which had large areas burnt, whether as a result of incendiaries or by accident I do not know.

It was a staggering sight sweeping in low over Berlin. We came in over the Grunewald, round by the Potsdamer Strasse, along the Wilhelm Strasse, over the Unter den Linden and right up the Charlottenburger Chaussee to our air field at Gatow. The Tiergarten looked like those pictures of battle-fields in France and Belgium after the last war, nothing but skeletons of trees, and I don't think it is an exaggeration to say that we did not see a single house with a roof on it. And hardly a soul in the streets.

On Sunday morning we took a car into Berlin (we are about ten miles out) and spent a couple of hours sight-seeing. You will remember that we were told that there were 900,000 odd Germans in our sector of Berlin. Our first impression was that this figure must have been exaggerated nine-fold by the Russians in order to get extra supplies in. One hardly saw a soul about except here and there long queues stretching round the corners at an odd food shop. Our impression from the air was confirmed that there is literally hardly an untouched building in Berlin. We stopped by the Brandenburger Tor where the French and United States Embassies are derelict. We walked round the corner into the Wilhelm Strasse and poked about in the ruins of the British Embassy (incidentally I found the remains of my old Vauxhall car in the garage). Not a thing has survived intact except the iron-work on the main entrance with the British coat of arms. If we get a opportunity we are going to suggest that they might be retrieved as a curio to be placed in the new Embassy when it is built. We went on down the Wilhelm Strasse and spent three-quarters of an hour poking about in the Reichskanzlerei [sic][3], a building into which I never succeeded in getting in the course of my two years in Berlin before the war. Iron Crosses were littered all over the place and we all carried off a chunk of Hitler's marble desk. There was a Russian sentry on the door and one or two Russians

---

[2] 14 July 1945.   [3] The Reich Chancellery.

living inside, but they made no difficulty about our going inside. I really felt that was the crown of my work on German affairs covering on and off the last eight years!

I hope the above will give you some idea of the total material devastation in great German cities like Essen and Berlin. I cannot give you any real picture of the German people because I doubt whether I have so far seen more than fifty all told since I have been here and I have spoken to none. Those that I did see still looked comparatively well-fed and well turned out, but that of course means nothing as it takes three or four months for shortened rations to reduce health and of course much longer to build it up again. There were a certain number of urchins running round the streets, a few young women and a few old people, but I saw no young men.

The Conference still has not got into its stride. I expect they will be exchanging formal visits today and that we shall really get started tomorrow. Germany will be first on the list, I believe. My guess is that the political subjects will go through without great difficulty. The whole centre of gravity has shifted on to the economic side and the general view seems to be that the problems here are insoluble. We had a most useful meeting last night with Weeks,[4] who seems to have a first class grip on affairs. He said they had been working out coal figures and reckoned that even allowing not a ton for German industry they would not have a surplus of more than 8,000,000 tons for export during the winter and that very likely they could not even move that.

The point we really reached was this. If the Russians stand on their view that all German territory east of the Oder-Neisse line is outside their control; if they strip their zone of all industrial plant and agricultural machinery; if, as we understand, they are making no plans for lifting the harvest in that part of their zone from which we and the Americans have withdrawn; then indeed, as General Weeks put it, we have bought a pup. None the less I think the general view is that anyhow on the long term we must still aim at uniform treatment of Germany as an administrative and economic whole. But on the short term we shall have to try to make the Russians pay our price for recognition of Polish claims, i.e. we must try to ensure that over the coming year German territory in the east, whether or not it is occupied by the Poles, should contribute a percentage of the coal and food which it contributed before the war.

As regards transfers of population Weeks said categorically that there could be no question of taking in a single extra mouth to feed during the coming winter.

By and large we have had an extremely pleasant two days settling in. The sun is shining brilliantly and the Rhine wine is beginning to come in; spirits flow freely. It will be rather a blow when we really have to get down to work.

Yours ever,
G. W. Harrison

4 See No. 154.

No. 167

Letter from Mr. Eden to Lord Killearn[1] (Cairo)

[E 5164/8/89]

Copy   FOREIGN OFFICE, *16 July 1945*[2]

Thank you very much for your manuscript letter of the 29th June.[3] It was very good of you to write, and I was touched by the kind things which you said.

As regards the Levant, while I can understand your feelings about our apparent excessive patience with the French, I think that we have to consider more than the local situation and I am sure that from the wider angle we could not have acted a moment sooner. We have many critics, even in this country, who are on the look-out for any sign that we are aiming to supplant the French in Syria. We had to give the French in Syria the opportunity of coming to a settlement or of bringing the situation to such a pass that our intervention would be regarded as being inevitable. Nor can we altogether leave out of account the state of opinion in France where in fact there seems to be some realisation of the fact that de Gaulle and their own officials were possibly at fault. By waiting until the last moment, as we did, we have obtained a more [much] more objective frame of mind in France—and after all we have to live next door to France, if possible in amity.

In the United States also, where there are always enthusiastic critics lying in wait to suspect British policy of imperialist aims, we had a reasonably good press, which meant that the Administration were able to co-operate with us much more openly than they could have done had we acted sooner. The United States Government have been helpful and will, I hope, continue to be, which has made our task less difficult. We are still trying to take the French along with us and to obtain an agreed settlement, because, as the French have shown, force will not provide a final answer. But I confess that I have never seen a more intractable problem and cannot even catch a glimpse of a solution.

Yours ever

ANTHONY EDEN

CALENDARS TO No. 167

i *16 July 1945   Minute from Mr. Eden to Mr. Churchill (Berlin) No. P.M./45/1T.*
Submits memorandum of 15 July on British policy in the Levant States: whole position in the Levant should eventually be considered by World Security Council, where French case on bases should be supported, having in mind British position in Egypt; British aim should be to obtain complete and

---

[1] H.M. Ambassador at Cairo.

[2] Date of despatch from the Foreign Office of this letter drafted on 12 July 1945 and initialed by Mr. Eden before his departure for Berlin.

[3] Not printed.

immediate withdrawal of French and British troops, without differentiation between Syria and the Lebanon [F.O. 954/15: Me/45/108; E 5171/8/89].

ii *Undated   Minute by U.K. Delegation on the Levant States.* Any detailed discussion on the Levant States at Potsdam with Soviet Delegation undesirable in the absence of the French. Discusses procedure [F.O. 934/5/44(1)].

iii *21 July 1945   Letter from Mr. G. MacKereth (H.M. Consul-General at Rabat) to Mr. Scrivener:* effects on Arab world of situation in Levant; U.S. interest in 'native welfare' in Morocco [Z 8761/900/69].

No. 168

Memorandum by Mr. Foulds (Berlin)

[F.O. 934/3/14(4)]

Top secret   BERLIN, *16 July 1945*

According to information given to Lord Halifax by Admiral King, Marshal Stalin is 'likely to raise a question of some further interpretation being provided for the Japanese of the meaning of unconditional surrender'.[1]

A brief on this subject, prepared in the Far Eastern Department, is attached [i]. It suggests that we should leave the initiative in raising this issue to the Americans (or the Russians). If it is raised we might put forward the view that the Japanese attitude suggests that it is of more immediate importance for the Allies to state what 'unconditional surrender' does *not* imply, than what it does imply. It need not necessarily imply the imposition of any particular form of government, or the abolition of the Imperial system, or any intention to destroy the basis of Japanese economic life.

The brief recommends that China should be consulted before any public statement is made.[2]

L. H. FOULDS

CALENDARS TO No. 168

i *12 July 1945   Unnumbered Brief for U.K. Delegation on Surrender Terms for Japan.* Evidence that Allied insistence on unconditional surrender is chief obstacle to acceptance of defeat by Japanese people. Considers American attitude on this (cf. No. 87). Sir A. Cadogan minuted, and Mr. Eden agreed, against any British initiative on this while being 'very chary of *dropping* "unconditional surrender" ' [F 4216/584/61].

ii *19 July 1945   Letter No. 2 from Mr. Sterndale Bennett to Mr. Foulds (Berlin):* indications from U.S. media that 'should unconditional surrender be modified, we may be faced with another legend in the United States that this was due partly, if not wholly,' to British agitation [F.O. 934/3/14(5)].

[1] Cf. No. 4, note 1.
[2] 'Yes. A. E.': marginal comment here by Mr. Eden, who initialed this paper on 18 July 1945.

No. 169

Note for First Plenary Meeting
[F.O. 934/2/8(4)]

Procedure might be settled first. It would be desirable to follow the Yalta precedent and arrange for meetings of the Foreign Secretaries in the morning and of the Big Three[2] in the afternoons.

The agenda is now a long one. All Three Powers have suggested topics for discussion. We have been slow in getting started, and we should probably be wise to reckon on having to finish our work by July 25th. That being so, it is probably hopeless to consider plodding through the agenda item by item as at a regular international meeting.

There is, however, one topic that is very urgent and requires detailed discussion and, if possible, decision. This is Germany.

Of the German problems the economic questions are undoubtedly more important and more difficult than the political questions. The Big Three ought perhaps to begin their work by preliminary discussion of Germany's economic problems. Meanwhile, the political problems, in regard to which there is a good prospect of general agreement, might be referred at once to the Foreign Secretaries. These political problems include:

Setting up of the Control Council.

Central Administration for Germany.

Attitude towards political parties and activities.

Co-ordination of propaganda.

There is, however, one political problem whose economic repercussions are so considerable that it needs to be discussed as soon as possible by the Big Three. This is the question of the Polish Western frontier. This should be discussed before the Big Three come on to the treatment of Germany as an economic whole and the economic problem generally, important aspects of which are reparations and the supply of food and fuel for Berlin.

Another German problem which the Big Three should discuss is the transfer of German populations from Poland and Czechoslovakia. This is partly a political and partly an economic question.

The Russian Delegation has raised the question of the German fleet. There is no great urgency about the settlement of this problem as compared with those of the administration of Germany, but it is certainly one which merits discussion.

For the rest we hope that we may be able to obtain at the meeting clarification of Russian policy on a number of points. These include in particular Turkey, the Balkans and Persia. The Russians have suggested putting on the agenda the questions of Tangier, Levant and Spain. We

---

[1] This undated, unsigned brief, which bears a correction apparently in Mr. Hayter's hand, was probably written on 16 or 17 July 1945.

[2] President Truman, Mr. Churchill and Marshal Stalin.

should be glad to know what the Russian proposals are in regard to these questions and to give any explanation they may wish about our own policy.

It may well be that in the course of a general discussion of this character the position in other countries including,[3] Yugoslavia and Italy, may come up. We are particularly anxious that the Conference should make a statement re-affirming the validity of the Tito-Subasic Agreement. There may also be points in regard to Poland which will need examination.

We may hope that when we have got a general indication of the views and policy of the Soviet Government on these questions their further detailed discussion may be fitted into the framework of the proposals which the American Delegation are making for dealing with European questions as a whole.

[3] Punctuation as in original.

CHAPTER II

Earlier proceedings of the Conference at Potsdam
17 — 26 July 1945

No. 170

*Record of First Plenary Meeting held at Cecilienhof,
Potsdam, on Tuesday, 17 July 1945 at 5 p.m.*

P.(*Terminal*)*1st Meeting* [*U 6197/3628/70*]

Top secret

Present:

PREMIER STALIN, M. V. M. Molotov, M. A. Ya. Vyshinski, M. A. A. Gromyko,
M. F. T. Gousev, M. K. V. Novikov, M. A. A. Sobolev, M. B. F. Podtzerob,
M. V. N. Pavlov (*Interpreter*).

PRESIDENT TRUMAN, Mr. J. F. Byrnes, Mr. Joseph E. Davies, Fleet-Admiral W. D.
Leahy, Mr. W. A. Harriman, Mr. E. W. Pauley, Mr. J. C. Dunn, Mr. H. F.
Matthews, Mr. C. E. Bohlen (*Interpreter*).

MR. CHURCHILL, Mr. Eden, Mr. Attlee, Sir A. Cadogan, Sir A. Clark Kerr,
Sir W. Strang, Sir E. Bridges, Mr. N. Brook, Mr. P. J. Dixon, Major A. Birse
(*Interpreter*).

Contents

Minute	Subject
1.	Chairmanship.
2.	Subjects for Discussion.
3.	Council of Foreign Ministers.
4.	Procedure for Consideration of Matters Listed for Discussion.

1. Chairmanship of the Conference

PREMIER STALIN proposed that President Truman should take the Chair
at Plenary Meetings during the Conference.

MR. CHURCHILL supported this proposal.

PRESIDENT TRUMAN, in accepting this invitation to act as Chairman,
said that he was deeply conscious of the great honour thus bestowed upon
him. He had come to this Conference with a keen sense of the great

responsibilities resting upon the leaders of the three Allied Powers, who had such grave decisions to take at this critical juncture in the world's history. He was conscious, too, of his difficulties in following his predecessor in office, President Roosevelt, who had forged such strong links of personal friendship with both Mr. Churchill and Premier Stalin. He hoped that, before the present Conference ended, he would have been able to make some progress in forming similar bonds of friendship with the leaders of the great Allied Powers.

MR. CHURCHILL, on behalf of the United Kingdom Delegation, expressed his sincere thanks to President Truman for undertaking the Chairmanship of the Conference. He extended a most cordial welcome to the President. Both he and Premier Stalin had entertained the warmest feelings of regard, and even affection, for President Roosevelt. They both looked forward to forming a similar bond of friendship with President Truman. They were glad to welcome him to their deliberations, and it was their earnest desire to continue to pursue in his company the high aims which the three great Allied Powers had sought to achieve throughout the bitter years of the war in Europe. He confidently believed that their mutual understanding and friendship would grow closer and more firm as they went forward together in common study of the difficult problems which awaited their consideration.

PREMIER STALIN said that the sentiments which Mr. Churchill had expressed were fully shared by himself and all members of the Russian Delegation.

2. *Subjects for discussion at the Conference*

PRESIDENT TRUMAN said that it would be useful if at this first Meeting each delegation indicated the main subjects which they desired to bring forward for discussion at the Conference. It would be understood that the list of subjects mentioned at the outset would not be exhaustive: each Delegation would retain the right to bring forward further subjects at a later stage. It would, however, be useful at this first Meeting to run through the main topics for discussion and to formulate a provisional Agenda for the Conference.

President Truman indicated the principal topics which the United States Delegation wished to bring forward (shown in the list circulated separately as P. (Terminal) 1).[1] The President handed in memoranda on these subjects (circulated separately as P. (Terminal) 2–5).[2]

---

[1] No. 171.

[2] Not printed. Of these American memoranda of 17 July 1945, P. (Terminal) 2 and 3, relating respectively to the establishment of a Council of Foreign Ministers and to Germany, are respectively printed in *F.R.U.S. Berlin*, vol. ii, pp. 609–10, and vol. i, p. 240. Appendix A to P. (Terminal) 3 was the Proposed Agreement on the Political and Economic Principles to govern the treatment of Germany in the initial control period, printed *op. cit.*, vol. ii, pp. 775–78, with an additional antepenultimate paragraph 13 which read: 'A suitable programme for the restitution of identifiable property looted by Germans from Allied

PREMIER STALIN referred to the main subjects which the Russian Delegation wished to bring forward (shown in the list circulated separately as P. (Terminal) 1)[1].

MR. CHURCHILL said that the British list of subjects (also set out in P. (Terminal) 1), had already been notified to the United States and Soviet Governments through the diplomatic channel.

In the course of a preliminary discussion on some of these subjects, the following points were raised:

(a) Italy

PRESIDENT TRUMAN said, as Italy had now declared war on Japan, he would be glad if the present Conference could agree that Italy be admitted to association with the United Nations. If this could be agreed, a public announcement to this effect might be made before the end of the Conference.

MR. CHURCHILL said that this was a matter which would require careful consideration. The British people would not easily forget Italy's conduct in declaring war on the British Commonwealth in the hour of her greatest peril, when French resistance was on the point of collapse; nor could they forget the long struggle which we had had against Italy in North Africa in the period before the United States came into the war. We had also suffered severe Naval losses in the Mediterranean. We had, however, the greatest goodwill to Italy, as was shown by the fact that we had provided 14 out of the 15 ships lent to Russia against Russia's claim to an immediate share of the Italian Fleet.

(b) Spain

PREMIER STALIN said that, in the Russian view, the present political régime in Spain had not sprung from the free will of the Spanish people but had been imposed upon them by Germany and Italy. This régime harboured great dangers for the United Nations, who would be well advised to seek to create conditions in Spain which would enable the Spanish people to establish the political régime which they themselves would choose.

(c) Tangier

MR. CHURCHILL said that this was not a question on which any final decision could be taken at a Conference which included no representative of the French Government. PREMIER STALIN said that, none the less, it would

---

territory shall be carried out promptly.' Annex 1 to appendix A to P. (Terminal) 3— circulated separately as P. (Terminal) 6—comprised an American proposal on German reparations printed *ibid.*, pp. 832–35, with an American paper on the German import programme, printed *op. cit.*, vol. i, p. 499. P. (Terminal) 4 and 5, relating respectively to the proposed implementation of the Yalta Declaration on Liberated Europe and to policy towards Italy, are printed respectively *op. cit.*, vol. ii, pp. 643–44, and in No. 208, minute 4, below.

be useful to clarify the views of the three major Allies on this question.[3]

(d) Poland

MR. CHURCHILL said that in recent weeks there had been a substantial improvement in the Polish situation; but he thought that various aspects of that problem ought to be discussed. Thus, he attached great importance to the early holding of free elections in Poland which would truly reflect the wishes of the Polish people. He also recognised that it would be desirable to exchange views about the disposal of the Polish Government in London. In this matter, however, the United Kingdom Government had a more difficult task than the other two Governments represented at the Conference, for the United Kingdom had been the base from which Polish resistance to Germany had been organised since 1940, and the United Kingdom Government were confronted with various secondary problems of some difficulty about the future treatment of the Poles who had fought with the United Nations under the protection of the British Government.

(e) German Fleet

PREMIER STALIN asked why Mr. Churchill did not agree that Russia should have a third of the German Fleet.

MR. CHURCHILL said that this was not the position. It was, however, for consideration whether the German Fleet should be divided up, or whether it would be sunk.

PREMIER STALIN said that in his view the German Fleet should be divided up. If other countries wished to sink the ships which made up the share allotted to them they could do so, but he did not intend that the ships allotted to Russia should be sunk.

3. Proposal for establishment of a Council of Foreign Ministers

A preliminary discussion took place on the document handed in by President Truman (P. (Terminal) 2)[2] for the establishment of a Council composed of the Foreign Ministers of Great Britain, Russia, China, France and the United States, and having as its immediate task the drawing-up, with a view to their submission to the United Nations, of treaties of peace with Italy, Rumania, Bulgaria and Hungary, and the preparation of settlements of territorial questions outstanding on the termination of the war in Europe.

PREMIER STALIN said that he was not clear why it was proposed that China should be a member of this body, more particularly if it was the intention that it should deal primarily with European questions. He also asked whether he was right in assuming that, if the Council was set up, it

---

[3] According to Soviet and American records of this meeting Marshal Stalin here suggested that there should also be discussion of Syria and the Lebanon: *The Tehran, Yalta & Potsdam Conferences: Documents* (Moscow, 1969: hereafter cited as *Conferences: Soviet Documents*), p. 152; *F.R.U.S. Berlin*, vol. ii, pp. 55, 61: cf. No. 171, section C below.

would take the place of the permanent machinery for regular consultation between the three Foreign Secretaries to which the three Great Powers had agreed at Yalta,[4] and also of the European Advisory Commission.

PRESIDENT TRUMAN said that the reason why he had proposed that the Foreign Minister for China should be included in the proposed Council was because China was a member of the Security Council of the World Organisation.

As regards Premier Stalin's second question, the proposed Council was to be set up to perform certain specific tasks; nevertheless, he thought that if this proposal was accepted, there would be little scope for separate meetings of the three Foreign Secretaries.

MR. CHURCHILL said that at Yalta it had been agreed that the Foreign Secretaries of the three Great Powers should meet every three or four months and that they should advise on a number of matters of current importance in Europe. It would add a needless complication to make an arrangement whereby China had to be brought into discussions about the detailed settlements in Europe. When the time came to decide the terms of the world peace settlement, China should be brought in; but in the meantime there were many matters which could not be properly handled by telegram, and for which meetings with the Foreign Secretaries would be of great use.

PREMIER STALIN asked whether it would be for the proposed Council to deal with the question of reparations. He also asked whether, seeing that the Council was to prepare matters for a future Peace Conference, any indication could be given as to when that Conference would be held.

PRESIDENT TRUMAN said that the Peace Conference should be held as soon as it could be held successfully, but not before.

MR. CHURCHILL said that the date of the Peace Conference would depend on the course of events in Europe and also on the progress made by the proposed Council of Foreign Ministers.

Continuing, Mr. Churchill said that he thought that the objective in the President's proposal could be reconciled with his own point of view if it were agreed that the appointment of the new Council would not interfere with the European Advisory Commission or with existing arrangements for meetings at regular intervals of the three Foreign Secretaries. He would be sorry to see these existing organisations done away with : But arrangements could be made to bring China in on matters which concerned world peace. He suggested that the three Foreign Secretaries might be asked to consider the matter in the light of the discussion which had taken place and to report back.

PREMIER STALIN suggested that the three Foreign Secretaries should also consider whether it was necessary to retain the permanent arrangements for meetings of the three Foreign Secretaries and the European Advisory

---

[4] See article XIII of the protocol of the proceedings of the Yalta Conference: *B.F.S.P.*, vol. 148, p. 88.

Commission in addition to the proposed Council of Foreign Ministers of the five Powers.

These suggestions were agreed to, and the matter was accordingly remitted for consideration by the three Foreign Secretaries.

4. *Procedure for consideration of matters listed for discussion*

After a short discussion it was agreed that the three Foreign Secretaries should meet at 11 a.m. on the following day (18th July) and should consider the lists of matters submitted for discussion by the Three Powers.

The Foreign Secretaries were asked to select three or four items which would be suitable for discussion at the next Plenary Session, which would be held at 4 p.m. 18th July.

It was also suggested that the Foreign Secretaries might indicate which of the items listed for discussion in their view called for consideration in the first instance at a Plenary Session and which might be remitted forthwith for examination by the Foreign Secretaries.

Cabinet Office, Potsdam, 17th July, 1945

CALENDAR TO No. 170

i *July 1945 Covering Note F.O.(E.R.)1 by Mr. Lincoln* circulating paper from F.O. Delegation at Potsdam expressing general agreement with P. (Terminal) 3 and 6 of 17 July: see note 2 above [UE 3110/2100/53].

No. 171

List of subjects submitted for discussion
P.(Terminal)1 [U 6197/3628/70]

Top secret   *17 July 1945*[1]

A—*List communicated by the United Kingdom Government*[2]

1. *General*

(*a*) Question of procedure for a general European settlement.
(*b*) Application of Yalta Declaration on Liberated Europe.
(*c*) Permission for representatives of the Press to function freely in countries of Eastern Europe.
(*d*) War Crimes.

---

[1] The final texts in Confidential Print of P.(Terminal) memoranda (cf. Preface, p. xiv) did not include the locations usually given in the typescript drafts. These designations were usually, for British, American and Soviet memoranda respectively, 'Cabinet Office, Potsdam', 'U.S. Delegation, Terminal' and 'Soviet Delegation, Terminal'.

[2] See No. 111, note 2.

2. *Germany*

(*a*) Polish Western Frontier. Status of Polish administration in the former German territory.

(*b*) Transfer of German populations from Poland and Czechoslovakia.

(*c*) Exchange of views about setting up a central German administration in Berlin to co-ordinate transport, &c.

(*d*) Attitude towards political parties and activities.

(*e*) Treatment of Germany as an economic whole.

(*f*) Co-ordination of propaganda and information services to Germany.

3. *Italy*

4. *Balkans*

(*a*) Internal situation in ex-satellite countries.

(*b*) The question of eventual peace treaties with these countries.

(*c*) The status of the British and American representatives on the Control Commissions pending the conclusion of peace treaties.

(*d*) The removal as booty of Allied industrial equipment, especially in Roumania.

(*e*) The situation in Yugoslavia and the implementation of the Tito-Subasic Agreement.

(*f*) The assurance of free elections in all the Balkan countries.

5. *Turkey*

The question of the Straits and Russo-Turkish relations generally.

6. *Persia*

Question of mutual withdrawal of troops.

B—*List of Subjects Mentioned by President Truman at the 1st Plenary Meeting*

1. Establishment of a Council of Foreign Ministers.
2. Policy with regard to Germany.
3. Yalta Declaration on Liberated Europe.
4. Policy towards Italy.
5. German Reparations.

C—*List of Subjects Mentioned by Premier Stalin at the 1st Plenary Meeting*

1. German Fleet and Merchant Navy.
2. Reparations
3. Territories to be placed under Trusteeship.
4. Diplomatic Relations with Satellite States.
5. Régime in Spain.
6. Tangier.

7. Syria and Lebanon.[3]
8. Poland.

[3] See No. 170, note 3.

No. 172

Minute from General Sir H. Ismay to Mr. Churchill (Berlin)[1]
C.O.S. (Terminal) 2nd Meeting:annex [CAB 99/39]

Top secret   BABELSBERG, *17 July 1945*
Copy

1. The Combined Chiefs of Staff at their first meeting[2] had under consideration a paper prepared by the Combined Intelligence Staffs on the enemy situation, in which it was suggested that if and when Russia came into the war against Japan, the Japanese would probably wish to get out on almost any terms short of the dethronement of the Emperor. This led to a discussion on the interpretation to be placed on the term 'Unconditional Surrender'. It was generally agreed that, if this involved the dissolution of the Imperial dynasty, there would be no-one to order the cease fire in outlying areas, and fighting might continue in various British and Dutch territories, and also in China for many months or even years. Thus from the military point of view, there was a good deal to be said for the retention in Japan of some central authority who would command obedience.

2. The United States Chiefs of Staff said that they had had considerable discussion on this point among themselves, and suggested that it ought to be considered at the highest level during 'Terminal'. They asked whether you yourself would be prepared to raise the point with the President.

3. We replied that, as the Americans were so very much the predominant partner in the war against Japan, you might feel reluctant to take the lead in this matter; but we agreed to inform you at once of what had taken place.

---

[1] This minute, printed by J. Ehrman, *op. cit.*, vol. vi, p. 291, had been agreed by the British Chiefs of Staff Committee at its second meeting at Babelsberg, held at 39–41 Ring Strasse at 10.30 a.m. on 17 July 1945 (C.O.S. (Terminal) 2nd Meeting). This meeting, and the first, held at 25 Ringstrasse at 10.30 a.m. on 16 July, (C.O.S. (Terminal) 1st Meeting) had mainly considered the military prosecution of the war against Japan.

[2] *Note in filed copy:* 'C.C.S. 193rd Meeting, Minute 2 (b).' This record of the first meeting of the Anglo-American Combined Chiefs of Staff held in connection with the Conference at Potsdam, at 25 Ring Strasse in Babelsberg at 2.30 p.m. on 16 July, is printed in *F.R.U.S. Berlin*, vol. ii, pp. 35–8. The record of the second meeting (C.C.S. 194th Meeting), held at 2.30 p.m. on 17 July and also concerned with the war against Japan, is printed *ibid.*, vol. ii, pp. 48–51. At this meeting, in particular, the Combined Chiefs of Staff 'agreed in principle to the participation of a British Commonwealth land force in the final phase of the war against Japan, subject to the satisfactory resolution of operational problems and to the clarification of certain factors which the United States Chiefs of Staff believe will be controlling': see J. Ehrman, *op. cit.*, vol. vi, p. 269.

347

No. 173

Record of a private talk between the Prime Minister and Generalissimo Stalin after the plenary session on 17 July 1945 at Potsdam[1]

[*F.O. 800/417/64*]

Top secret

THE GENERALISSIMO said that as his party was leaving Moscow, an unaddressed message was delivered to the Generalissimo through the Japanese Ambassador Sato. It was assumed that the message was intended for either the Generalissimo or President Kalinin or other members of the Soviet Government. It was from the Emperor of Japan who stated that 'unconditional surrender' could not be accepted by Japan, but if it was not insisted upon Japan might be prepared to compromise with regard to other terms. The Emperor was making this suggestion in the interests of all people concerned.[2]

The Generalissimo had not spoken of the message to anyone except the Prime Minister, but he wanted to bring it up at the next session of the Conference.

THE PRIME MINISTER thought the Generalissimo should send the President a note on the subject in order to warn him before the next Session.

THE GENERALISSIMO pointed out that he did not wish the President to think that the Soviet Government wanted to act as an intermediary, but he would have no objection if the Prime Minister mentioned it to the President.

THE PRIME MINISTER agreed to do so, pointing out that he also did not wish the President to feel that we were not at one with the United States in their aim of achieving complete victory over Japan. America had helped us enormously in the war against Germany and we intended to help her now to the full.[3] At the same time, people in America were beginning to doubt the need for 'unconditional surrender'. They were saying: was it worth while having the pleasure of killing ten million Japanese at the cost of one million Americans and British?

THE GENERALISSIMO remarked that the Japanese realised our strength and were very frightened. Unconditional surrender in practice could be seen here in Berlin and the rest of Germany.

THE PRIME MINISTER asked: Where was Germany?

---

[1] Major Birse minuted to Mr. Rowan on 17 July 1945: 'The attached notes of the Prime Minister's private talk with Generalissimo Stalin had to be written from memory, as I was unable to make notes during the talk. They may therefore be incomplete, but I think they contain the gist of what was said' (PREM 3/430/7). Cf. W. S. Churchill, *op. cit.*, vol. vi, p. 555.

[2] This message further proposed the despatch to Moscow of Prince Konoye as a special Japanese envoy. Cf. the translation of M. Sato's report of his delivery of the message at 5 p.m. on 13 July in *F.R.U.S. Berlin*, vol. i, pp. 879–80.

[3] The preceding portion of this paragraph and the two previous paragraphs are cited by J. Ehrman, *op. cit.*, vol. vi, p. 302.

THE GENERALISSIMO said Germany was nowhere and everywhere.

The Generalissimo went on to say that he could not understand German up-bringing. The Germans were like sheep and had always needed a man who could give them orders. They never thought for themselves.

THE PRIME MINISTER agreed and said that the Germans had always believed in a symbol. If a Hohenzollern had been allowed to reign after the last war, there would have been no Hitler. They certainly were like sheep.

THE GENERALISSIMO observed that the need for a symbol applied only to the Germans.

To illustrate the German sense of justice, the Generalissimo then spoke of an incident which had recently occurred in Berlin. An S.S. man had fired at a Russian soldier from a house. Soviet troops immediately surrounded the house. A crowd of Germans approached the troops and said they had heard that, in retaliation, their rations would be stopped for a week. Instead of stopping their rations, they offered 40 or 50 hostages. When the Russians refused the hostages, the Germans immediately entered the building and seized the S.S. man and handed him over.

The Generalissimo observed that there were several questions he would like to discuss with the Prime Minister and it was agreed that they should meet at the Generalissimo's house at 8.30 p.m. on July 18th.

The Generalissimo told the Prime Minister that he had taken to smoking cigars.

THE PRIME MINISTER replied that if a photograph of the Generalissimo smoking a cigar could be flashed across the world, it would cause an immense sensation.

On the subject of working late hours, the Generalissimo said he had become so accustomed to working at night that now that the need had passed, he could not get to sleep before 4 a.m.

The Prime Minister thanked the Generalissimo for the welcome which Mrs. Churchill had received during her visit to Russia.[4]

THE GENERALISSIMO replied that the visit had been a great pleasure to him.

THE PRIME MINISTER spoke of the women workers in Stalingrad whom Mrs. Churchill had seen and who had said they were glad to work hard as they were reconstructing the city for their husbands who would soon be coming home.

THE GENERALISSIMO appeared to be touched.

THE PRIME MINISTER said that Britain welcomed Russia as a Great Power and in particular as a Naval Power. The more ships that sailed the seas the greater chance there was for better relations.

THE GENERALISSIMO replied that he also wanted good relations. As regards Russia's fleet it was still a small one, nevertheless, great or small, it could be of benefit to Great Britain.

---

[4] Mrs. Churchill had visited Russia as a guest of the Russian Red Cross and Red Crescent Society in April–May 1945.

THE PRIME MINISTER asked Marshal Stalin whether in future he should call him Premier, Marshal or Generalissimo. Stalin replied that he hoped the Prime Minister would call him Marshal as he always had done in the past.

No. 174

Minute from Mr. Rowan to Mr. Churchill (Berlin)
[PREM 4/17/15]

[BERLIN,] *17 July 1945*

1. Attached is a memorandum[1] which the President sent over after luncheon today with the request that you should see it as soon as possible.

2. Paragraph 1 of the memorandum seems to meet the difficulty raised by the Chiefs of the Staff about the cutting down of the provision of military supplies to us under Lend-Lease agreed in the Autumn of last year.[2] With regard to paragraph 2, in which the President says that it does not necessarily follow that either the munitions or non-munitions programme for the present year will be equal in total or individual items to the amounts agreed last Autumn, you should know that on the munitions side, the figure has in fact been cut by us from 2.8 to 1.8 billion dollars.

3. In the third paragraph, the President raises the very important question of the level of our gold and dollar resources which, as you will recall, has been raised on several occasions previously by the Americans. This gives you an excellent opportunity to make the point which the Chancellor wished made, namely, would it not be a good thing to suggest to the Americans that there should be high level Anglo-American discussions in the Autumn about all these questions, namely, the winding up of Lend-Lease and what is to follow after.

4. I have sent a copy of the President's paper home for the Chancellor of the Exchequer, and you may wish to send him a telegram asking him, in conjunction with other Ministers concerned, to consider the matter and advise you on the reply you should send. In the meantime, a copy of the document could, if you agree, be sent to the Chiefs of the Staff to ask them to what extent the point made in their minute of July 13 (Flag 'C')[2] is met by the President's assurance.

T. L. R.

ANNEX TO No. 174
Memorandum for the Prime Minister[3]

Copy   THE WHITE HOUSE, WASHINGTON

I have gone into the question that you raise in your telegram of May 28[4] in

---

[1] Annex below supplied from UE 3074/32/71.

[2] See No. 26, note 7, and No. 26.iv.

[3] A text of this memorandum is printed in *F.R.U.S. Berlin*, vol. ii, pp. 1179–80.

[4] A text of this message is printed *op. cit.*, vol. i, p. 807. Cf. also H. Duncan Hall, *op. cit.*, p. 456.

regard to Lend-Lease during the Japanese War. We intend to furnish Lend-Lease generally in accord with the schedules of requirements for the first year following the defeat of Germany and other terms worked out between British and American supply representatives in October and November 1944.

You, of course, realize that the policy I have indicated does not necessarily mean that either the munitions or the non-munitions program for the present year will be equal in total or individual items to the Lend-Lease requirements as estimated in the meetings of last fall. Those estimates were subject to changing strategic demands as well as to supply, procurement, and allocation considerations, and to the provision of the necessary funds by the Congress. Individual requisitions are of course handled by the usual administrative and allocation channels, with full discussion between our supply representatives.

In connection with the foregoing, it has come to my attention that the British gold and foreign exchange holdings are now considerably higher than was anticipated at the time of the Phase II discussions. I do not wish to propose re-opening the Phase II discussions on this account. However, I would like to request that your Government relax its position with respect to permitting dollar payments on certain items, particularly those where the unwillingness of your Government to make payments leads to political criticism in the United States. For example, it would be of considerable assistance if your Government relaxed its restrictions on dollar payments for the proceeds of property sales in the Middle East and elsewhere; if the United Kingdom continued to take its share of the burden of the military relief and UNRRA programs in Europe; and if dollar payments were allowed on other items which arise from time to time in our relationships. I urge that you provide this flexibility in the long-term interests of both your country and mine.

HARRY S. TRUMAN

Berlin
July 17, 1945.

CALENDARS TO No. 174

i *17 July 1945   Mr. Eden (Berlin) Tel. No. 65 Target.* Message in pursuance of a minute on No. 174 by Mr. Churchill: requests comments by telegraph. He will speak to Mr. Truman on the subject on 18 July but 'will try to keep the position open' [UE 3074/32/71].

ii *18 July 1945   Minute from Mr. Churchill (Berlin) No. D (T) 3/5 to Chiefs of Staff.* Enquires effect of No. 174, annex, on British requirements of supplies from the U.S.A. in directions not directly connected with the prosecution of the war against Japan [UE 3300/32/71].

No. 175

Minute from Sir D. Waley to Mr. Dixon (Berlin)

[F.O. 934/1/4(10)]

[BERLIN,] *17 July 1945*

We have just had a long talk with the American Reparation Group.[1] They

---

[1] Cf. No. 152.i.

351

told us that the draft letter[2] from President Truman to the Prime Minister and Marshal Stalin has not been sent since the President preferred to raise reparation in general terms.[3]

I said that if there were any points which Mr. Byrnes would like to discuss with our Secretary of State in the way of a preliminary exchange of views, Mr. Eden would be very glad to do so.

I will report our exchange of views later. In brief we told them why we thought it would be a mistake to ask the Conference to define Booty and Restitution and they explained to us what underlies their own proposals.

D. Waley

Calendar to No. 175

i *17–21 July 1945 Correspondence, mainly between the British Delegation at Potsdam and the Treasury, concerning deliveries of reparations and definition of booty in regard to Germany. (a) 17 July Sir D. Waley to Mr. Playfair. Interim deliveries and booty. (b) Mr. Turner to Mr. Lincoln, enclosing copy of No. 152.i, minute of 17 July by Sir W. Monckton on President Truman's draft letter, and letter from Mr. Pauley about relationship between reparation and ceded German territory (not here reproduced: see F.R.U.S. Berlin, vol. ii, p. 831). (c) 18 July Mr. Playfair to Mr. I. C. Mackenzie (F.O.). (d) Sir D. Waley to Mr. Playfair. (e) Mr. Playfair to Sir D. Waley and to Mr. Dent. (f) 20 July C.C.S. Tel. FAN 603 to Field Marshals Alexander and Montgomery, and General Eisenhower:* captured enemy material: cf. *op.cit.,* pp. 162, 836. *(g) Mr. C. H. M. Waldock (Admiralty) to Mr. Playfair. (h) 21 July Mr. Dent to Mr. Playfair* [F.O. 934/1/4 (5) (4) (3); UE 3220, 3165, 3166/624/77; UE 3210/2615/77; U 5727/251/70].

[2] Printed in *F.R.U.S. Berlin,* vol. i, pp. 548–50.
[3] See No. 170, note 2.

No. 176

Minute from Mr. Eden to Mr. Churchill (Berlin)[1]

No. P.M./45/2.T. [F.O. 954/26:SU/45/136]

[BERLIN,] *17 July 1945*

You mentioned in conversation yesterday that the Russian policy was now one of aggrandisement. This is undoubtedly true. And, considering in this light the additions which Molotov told me yesterday[2] he wished to make to our Agenda, I find them disquieting. Russia has no direct interest in such matters as Tangier and the Levant, nor in countries to be placed under trusteeship. This last is, in any event, a matter for the new World Organisation and not for us here. We had much difficulty with the Russians about

[1] This minute is printed with slight verbal variation by the Earl of Avon, *The Eden Memoirs: The Reckoning,* pp. 546–7.
[2] See No. 158.

trusteeship at San Francisco. The truth is that on any and every point, Russia tries to seize all that she can and she uses these meetings to grab as much as she can get.

2. At previous meetings such as Tehran and Yalta we have met in the knowledge that Russia was bearing a heavy burden in this war and that her casualties and the devastation of her country were worse than anything that we or the Americans were suffering. But now all this is over. Russia is not losing a man at the present time. She is not at war with Japan and yet she is doing her utmost to demand more of China than was agreed.

3. To meet this situation we have not many cards in our hand. One of them, however, is the possession of the German Fleet. I agree with the Admiralty view that it would be best if this Fleet were sunk. But, in any event, we must not, I am sure, yield a single German ship in our possession until we have obtained satisfaction for our interests, which the Russians are treating with contempt in all the countries where their authority holds sway. Our oil interest in Rumania is one example of this. On the political side there are many subjects with which I have troubled you in earlier minutes, but most urgent is to get agreement over the withdrawal of troops from Persia. The independence of that country is important to us. Unless we can begin the withdrawal soon, it is clear from Bullard's telegrams[3] that North Persia will be completely sovietised.

4. All this brings me to the question of Russian access to the great seas. I know that you feel that her demands in this respect are just, and personally I agree with you that there is no reason why Russia should not be allowed free access to the Mediterranean. At the same time, I feel that it would be unwise to speak about this to the Russians at this meeting. We told them before that we were in favour of revising the Montreux Convention. What has been their response? To make other demands on Turkey which would result in placing Constantinople under Russian guns and would probably be the first stage in the subjection of Turkey to Russia. One must also remember that while we agree that the Russians should be free to enter the Mediterranean, they have not yet freedom to get out of it. Having achieved what they desire about Turkey, Russia's next request may be for a position at Tangier where they may give us much more trouble. And is their interest in the Lebanon a first stage to an interest in Egypt, which is quite the last place where we want them, particularly since that country with its rich Pashas and improverished fellahin would be a ready prey to Communism? If we were to talk generously to the Russians this time about access to the wider oceans, I fear that they would only regard it as an indication that we had not been shocked by their demands on Turkey and would proceed to make more and more demands on Persia and other countries in the Middle East.

5. Forgive this sermon, with all of which I feel sure you will agree. But reading through our briefs and documents again last night I am deeply

[3] Cf. Nos. 91–3.

353

concerned at the pattern of Russian policy, which becomes clearer as they become more brazen every day.[4]

A. E.

CALENDARS TO No. 176

i *20 July 1945 F.O. memorandum on political developments in Soviet-occupied and controlled territories* [N 10672/10672/38].

ii *27 July–5 Aug. 1945 F.O. letter to Cairo,* enclosing memo. on effect of U.N. Charter on Anglo–Egyptian Treaty of Alliance of 26 August 1936 (Cmd. 5360 of 1937): favours its early revision; Chiefs of Staff asked for views. Comments from Lord Killearn [U 5678/12/70, J 2789/3/16].

[4] Copies of this minute were sent to Mr. Attlee and to General Ismay for the Chiefs of Staff.

No. 177

Minute from Mr. Eden to Mr. Churchill (Berlin)
No. P.M./45/3.T. [*F.O. 934/1/5(2)*]

[BERLIN,] *17 July 1945*

War Crimes

The discussions in London[1] to set up the Four Power Military Tribunal to try the principal Nazi leaders and organisations still continue but they are likely to be concluded soon. I attach for your consideration the latest drafts[2] of the Agreement and the Charter for the Court, together with a copy of the Moscow Declaration, upon which they are based.

2. The Attorney General has been conducting the negotiations on behalf of His Majesty's Government and may require authority to sign at an early date. On May 30th the War Cabinet gave authority to the Attorney General to conduct the negotiations on the basis of an earlier American draft and I do not think the matter need go back to the Cabinet again. The Attorney General, however, will require your authority before he can sign on behalf of His Majesty's Government.

3. I regard the draft Agreement and Charter as satisfactory and recommend that you should give your approval to the Attorney General to sign if necessary, provided that the drafts remain substantially in their present form.

4. I would draw your attention to the following points:

(*a*) The members of the Court will be drawn from the Four Powers responsible for the control of Germany. Although it might be attractive

[1] See No. 14, note 1.

[2] Not attached to filed copy. These British drafts of 11 July 1945 (on PREM 4/100/12) are printed in *Report of Robert H. Jackson,* pp. 202–10. Cf. *ibid.,* pp. 11–12, for a text of the Moscow Declaration regarding atrocities, issued by President Roosevelt, Mr. Churchill and Marshal Stalin on 1 November 1943.

to have a fifth member to represent the smaller Allies, I am satisfied that the practical objections to doing so outweigh any advantage this would have.

(*b*) The charges to be brought are set out in Article 6 of the Charter and I understand it is intended to proceed primarily under Article 6(d). (The brackets around this article indicate that final Russian approval has not yet been obtained). This, I am advised, is sound in law, though it is a new departure to apply it in the international sphere.

(*c*) In Article 23 the place of trial is left blank. I am strongly opposed to the trial being held at any place under Soviet control and I understand the Americans are very firm on this point. Nuremberg or possibly Munich seems to me the right place and, as we and the Americans hold almost all the prisoners, the Russians may have to agree.

(*d*) We intend to keep the list of defendants in the first instance as short as possible and the names we have suggested are the following:

Goering, Hess, Ribbentrop, Ley, Keitel, Kaltenbrunner, Rosenberg, Hans Frank, Frick and Streicher.

5. I have personally some doubts about Keitel and would like to know more of the reasons for his inclusion. It also seems rather rough to drag Hess out after all these years to face a trial but Russians will include him anyway and if we leave him out we shall increase their suspicions that we favour him for some sinister reason.

6. I would be grateful if you would give your authority to the Attorney General to sign or to initial the Agreement, though the place of trial may have to be left blank and settled during our meeting here.[3]

A. E.

CALENDARS TO NO. 177

i   *18–20 July 1945 Correspondence between Mr. Dean (Berlin) and Mr. Scott Fox; minute by Mr. E. J. Passant (F.O. Research Dept.)*, without enclosures. Progress of London discussions on trial of war criminals. Case of Field-Marshal Keitel [U 5655/29/73; F.O. 934/1/5(3 & 6); U 5972/16/73].

ii   *19 July 1945 Texts of Draft Agreement for the prosecution and punishment of major war criminals and Charter on the Constitution of the International Military Tribunal* [U 5614/29/73].

iii   *21–2 July 1945 Minutes by Mr. Dean, Sir. A Cadogan and Sir W. Monckton.* Disquiet expressed over re-drafting of articles VI and XV(1) of draft Charter in ii above. Sir W. Monckton accordingly proposes to go to London for discussion with Attorney General. Mr. Eden minuted: 'I agree without,

---

[3] On 20 July 1945 Mr. J. H. Peck, Assistant Private Secretary to Mr. Churchill minuted to Mr. J. N. Henderson: 'The Prime Minister has approved the Foreign Secretary's minute P.M./45/3.T about War Crimes. With regard to the last paragraph of Mr. Eden's minute, the Prime Minister's approval gives the Attorney General the authority to sign or initial the Agreement, and I presume that you will take the necessary action on this. You may like to know that the Prime Minister has put a marginal tick against points 4 (*a*) and 4 (*c*) of the Foreign Secretary's minute. J. H. P. 20.7.45.'

I confess, understanding what it is all about. I hope that Solicitor General's absence will only be very short. A. E. July 23' [F.O. 934/1/5(6–7)].

iv 22–4 July 1945 (a) Tels. from and to Mr. Eden (Berlin) Nos. 150 Target and 183 Onward with minute by Sir B. Newton; (b) Letter from Mr. Scott Fox to Mr. Dean (Berlin) (a) Mr. Eden cannot agree to redrafts of articles VI and XV (1), which would require Cabinet authority. Substantial reversion to original article VI is reported in Tel. 183 Onward of 24 July (Soviet representative stated on 23 July 'that it was *not* his Government's intention to try many criminals'). Agreement reached on article XV. (b) Attorney General anxious to avoid reference to the Cabinet: dangers of delay [U 5637,5737/29/73].

v 25 July 1945 Minute by Mr. Dean. Outstanding drafting points on articles VI, XV and XXII [U 5815/29/73].

No. 178

Record of First Meeting of Foreign Secretaries held at Cecilienhof, Potsdam, on Wednesday, 18 July 1945 at 11 a.m.

F.(Terminal) 1st Meeting [U 6197/3628/70]

Top secret

Present:

M. V. M. Molotov, M. A. Ya. Vyshinski, M. A. A. Gromyko, M. F. T. Gousev, M. K. V. Novikov, M. A. A. Sobolev, M. B. F. Podtzerob, M. V. N. Pavlov (*Interpreter*).

Mr. J. F. Byrnes, Mr. W. A. Harriman, Mr. J. C. Dunn, Mr. H. F. Matthews, Mr. W. L. Clayton, Mr. C. E. Bohlen, Mr. B. V. Cohen, Mr. E. Page (*Interpreter*).

Mr. Eden, Sir A. Cadogan, Sir W. Strang, Mr. N. Brook, Mr. P. J. Dixon, Mr. W. Hayter, Major L. M. Theakstone (*Interpreter*).

Contents

Minute   *Subject*

1. *Chairmanship of Foreign Secretaries' Meetings*

M. Molotov proposed that Mr. Byrnes should act as Chairman of the present meeting. This was agreed to.

It was further agreed that at subsequent meetings of Foreign Secretaries during the Conference each of the three Foreign Secretaries should preside in turn, Mr. Eden taking the Chair at the next meeting. The Chairman for the day would act as *rapporteur* to the Plenary Meeting.

2. *Council of Foreign Ministers*

(Previous Reference: (P. (Terminal) 1st Meeting,[1] Minute 3.)

Mr. Byrnes invited the views of the Russian and United Kingdom Delegations on the proposals for the establishment of a Council of Foreign Ministers which were outlined in the Memorandum by the United States Delegation (circulated as P. (Terminal) 2).[2]

Participation of China. M. Molotov said that if this Council was to deal, not only with European problems, but also with other problems, there would be no objection in his view, to the inclusion of China.

Mr. Byrnes suggested that the Council might in form consist of the Foreign Secretaries of Great Britain, U.S.S.R., United States, France and China; but the representative of China might take an active part in the work of the Council only when it was discussing 'matters of Asiatic interest or matters of world-wide concern.' The reasons which had led the United States Delegation to include China were:

(*a*) If the war with Japan were to end soon, the proposed Council would be available to deal with the problems that would arise and the Chinese could at once join in discussions with the other Powers;

(*b*) China was one of the permanent members of the Security Council of the World Organisation.

Mr. Eden said that if the proposed Council were to be concerned solely with European affairs he would favour the exclusion of China. As he saw it, the work which at Yalta was remitted to the three Foreign Secretaries, could conveniently be done by the proposed Council; and, in any case, with the probable disappearance of the European Advisory Commission, a forum for Four-Power discussions, and a Four-Power Secretariat, would certainly be needed. If, however, the scope of the proposed Council was to be widened to cover world-wide problems, then he agreed that provision should be made for China to participate in this part of the Council's work.

The Task of the Council. M. Molotov pointed out that according to the American draft the first task of the Council would be to draft peace treaties with Italy, Roumania, Bulgaria and Hungary. He asked whether the Council should not also be authorised to prepare a draft peace treaty with Finland.

> It was agreed that Finland should be added to the list of countries in respect of which draft treaties should be prepared by the proposed Council.

Mr. Eden asked whether it was suggested that the Council should also deal with day-to-day problems as they arose.

Mr. Byrnes explained that the reason why the scope of the Council had been limited, in the American draft, to the preparation of peace treaties was to avoid delaying the completion of this work by burdening the Council with current problems. He would, however, be prepared to consider adding words which would enable the Council to consider other matters referred to

---

[1] No. 170.　　　　　[2] See No. 170, note 2.

it by the five Governments, provided that it was made clear, that the attention of the Council was not to be diverted thereby from the primary tasks set out in the American draft.

MR. EDEN said that he was anxious to be clear about the relation between the proposed Council and the meetings of the three Foreign Secretaries which had been agreed to at Yalta. He hoped that the proposed Council might take over the tasks assigned to the three Foreign Secretaries by the Yalta decision.

MR. BYRNES said that, as he saw it, the present proposal did not affect the Yalta decision. The three Foreign Secretaries would continue to meet to discuss current problems of common interest, and the meetings of the proposed Council would provide opportunities for this. The three Foreign Secretaries would be free, as before, to discuss all matters of common concern to their Governments.

M. MOLOTOV thought it would be better to abide by the present American proposals and consider later in the light of experience whether it would be wise to widen the scope of the Council to include discussion of current problems.

MR. EDEN said that he had hoped that the meetings of the three Foreign Secretaries might have become, by the inclusion of France, meetings of four. In view, however, of the trend of the discussion he must accept the views of his two colleagues on this point.

Participation of France. M. MOLOTOV pointed out that the primary tasks of the proposed Council included the preparation of peace treaties with countries with which France had not signed any Armistice. France ought not, in his view, to participate in the preparation of these peace treaties. He suggested, therefore, that there should be added to Section (1) of the American draft words such as: 'which will perform its functions with a composition corresponding in character to the questions under discussion.'

MR. EDEN said he would prefer to leave the first paragraph as it stood. The proposed amendment would invoive discussing how the Council should be composed in relation to each question that came before it. If the substance of M. Molotov's suggestion were accepted he would prefer that the terms of reference should state explicitly that, in the preparation of peace treaties, the Council should be composed of representatives of those States which had signed armistices with the countries concerned.

MR. BYRNES pointed out that the United States Government had never been at war with Finland; nevertheless, due weight would, no doubt, be given to any views which the United States might express in the preparation of the peace treaty with Finland. Would there not be a case for giving similar weight to the views of France in the preparation of peace treaties with Roumania, Bulgaria, Hungary and Finland, even though she had not been a signatory to the Armistices with these countries? Could the point be met by empowering the Council to appoint Committees of the States primarily concerned with particular matters?

M. MOLOTOV thought this would make the structure of the Council too complicated. It was not the Russian intention to exclude France from any discussion at the Peace Conference of matters affecting these countries. His point was that the peace treaties with these countries should be prepared by representatives of the States which had signed Armistice terms with them.

MR. BYRNES said he would accept this, if a suitable formula agreeable to all three parties could be worked out. A drafting committee was accordingly appointed to prepare such a formula.

Later in the meeting, the report[3] of this drafting committee was received and considered.

It was agreed that the draft constitution appended to the Memorandum by the United States Delegation (P (Terminal) 2)[2] should be accepted subject to the following amendments in paragraph (3):

(a) In the fourth line, for 'and Hungary' substitute 'Hungary and Finland.'

(b) At the end of the paragraph insert: 'For the discharge of each of these tasks the Council will be composed of the members representing those States which were signatories to the Terms of Surrender imposed upon the enemy State concerned.

Other matters may from time to time be referred to the Council by agreement between the States members thereof.'

Position of European Advisory Commission. M. MOLOTOV suggested that, when the proposed Council had been established, there would be no need to retain the European Advisory Commission.

MR. EDEN and MR. BYRNES agreed that the Control Councils for Germany and Austria could take over the remaining tasks of the European Advisory Commission.

MR. EDEN pointed out, however, that a final decision to wind up the European Advisory Commission could not be taken at the present Conference in the absence of the French who were members of the Commission.

M. MOLOTOV agreed that the winding up of the European Advisory Commission was a matter for a separate decision, to be taken after consultation with the French Government.

3. *Agenda for Second Plenary Meeting*

MR. BYRNES recalled that the Foreign Secretaries had been invited to select a number of subjects for discussion at the Second Plenary Meeting, which was to be held that afternoon.

He asked whether it would be convenient to discuss the proposals of the United States Delegation regarding the admission of Italy to membership of the United Nations.

M. MOLOTOV said that the Russian Delegation had not yet had sufficient time to consider these proposals; and he suggested that discussion of them might be deferred for a day or two. It seemed to him that the most urgent questions for discussion at the Conference were those relating to Germany.

[3] Printed in *F.R.U.S. Berlin*, vol. ii, pp. 611–2.

After some further discussion, it was agreed that the following subjects should be put forward for discussion at the Second Plenary Meeting:

(a) *Preparation for the Peace Settlement: proposed establishment of a Council of Foreign Ministers.* Memorandum by the United States Delegation: P (Terminal) 2.[2]

(b) *Policy towards Germany: authority of the Control Council for Germany in political matters.* Memorandum by the United States Delegation: P (Terminal) 3.[2]

(c) *Poland:* in particular, the position of the Polish Government in London, and the possibility of further measures being taken in Poland to implement fully the agreement reached at the Crimea Conference.

M. MOLOTOV suggested that some further matters might be set down for discussion at the Second Plenary Meeting. The disposal of the German Fleet might, he thought, be added to the subjects already mentioned.

MR. EDEN said that this was not a specially difficult issue and could conveniently be left till later in the Conference.

M. MOLOTOV suggested that, if the issue was simple, there was much to be said for disposing of it without delay. After some further discussion, it was agreed that the question of the German Fleet should not be put forward for discussion at the Second Plenary Meeting, on the understanding that it would be taken at a Plenary Meeting fairly soon.

> It was agreed that Mr. Byrnes, as Chairman of this meeting of Foreign Secretaries, should put forward for discussion at the Second Plenary Meeting the three subjects listed at (a)—(c) above.

4. *Germany: Authority of Control Council in Political Matters*

M. MOLOTOV suggested that, although this question was to be considered at the Plenary Meeting later in the day, the present meeting might with advantage hold a preliminary discussion on certain points raised in the memorandum by the United States Delegation (P (Terminal) 3)[2] on the Political Principles which should govern the treatment of Germany in the initial control period.

His first point was that the wording of paragraph 1 (on the Authority of the Control Council) differed somewhat from that of the corresponding paragraph in the agreement on Control Machinery in Germany which had been approved by the four Governments.[4] Was it the wish of the Americans that control should be more centralised than had previously been agreed?

MR. BYRNES said that no change was intended. M. MOLOTOV then suggested that the text should be remitted to a drafting Committee for comparison with the original agreement and for settlement of any differences which might emerge. This was agreed to.

On paragraph 2(i)(a), M. MOLOTOV said that the Soviet Government held a large number of German prisoners-of-war, whom they did not regard as subject to demobilisation.

[4] See No. 8, note 3.

MR. Byrnes said that the paragraph was not intended to affect the status of prisoners-of-war and it was agreed that the drafting Committee should make the necessary amendment to make this clear.

For paragraph 3, M. Molotov suggested the following alternative wording:

'In addition to the measures already adopted, all Fascist laws, decrees, orders and instructions shall be abolished as directed against the rights and civil liberties of the German people. Discrimination on grounds of race, creed or political opinion established by Nazi laws shall be liquidated. No such discriminations, whether juridical, administrative or any other, shall be tolerated.'

MR. Byrnes said that he had no objection in principle to this suggestion, which could be considered by the drafting Committee.

As regards paragraph 5, M. Molotov thought that the last sentence should be deleted, since he considered that it might offer a loophole for the retention of Nazis in office.

MR. Byrnes explained that these posts would be entrusted only to non-Nazis or to persons who had been forced to serve in the Nazi administration against their will. It should be made clear to them that they could only hold their posts during good behaviour.

MR. Eden thought that the phrase should be deleted from paragraph 5, where it might be misunderstood, but that there would be advantages in making it clear somewhere else in the document that Germans would hold office only during good behaviour.

M. Molotov continued to press for the deletion of this sentence; and it was finally agreed that the balance of advantage lay on the side of deleting it.

On paragraph 7 (i), M. Molotov suggested that it was too soon for the Governments of the three major Allies to commit themselves to holding elections.

MR. Byrnes said that it would be for the Control Council to decide when the situation was such that elections could properly be held. Paragraph 7 (iii) made it clear that the responsibility for holding elections would rest with the Control Council, who were the most suitable body to decide when the time was ripe.

M. Molotov maintained his view that it was too soon to contemplate elections in Germany at present and that it would be a mistake to include in the document any statement which contained a promise that elections would be held.

MR. Eden said that they were all agreed (i) that it was too soon to hold elections now but (ii) that it was their intention to hold elections eventually. He therefore thought that the qualification in paragraph 7 (iii) should also be included in paragraph 7 (i).

M. Molotov then suggested that the words 'on democratic principles, with due regard to safeguarding the military and civil security of the Allied Forces' might be substituted for the words 'through elective councils,' in paragraph 7 (i).

MR. BYRNES said he was prepared to adopt Mr. Eden's suggestion by merging sub-paragraphs (i) and (iii). Since elections were the pre-requisite of democratic government, he thought there could be no objection to including some reference to the holding of elections. In any case he wished to make it clear to the Control Council that the timing of any elections which might be held was their responsibility. He agreed with a suggestion by Mr. Eden that the words 'at the discretion of the Control Commission' should be added to paragraph 7 (i), and M. MOLOTOV also agreed to this. It was decided to invite the drafting Committee to consider the wording of paragraph 7 in the light of the points raised in the discussion.

MR. BYRNES then said that it might be possible to hold elections in one zone sooner than in the other zones. He thought that the zone commander was therefore the best person to judge when the time was ripe to hold an election in his zone, and wished to reserve some discretion in this matter to the authorities responsible for the several zones.

MR. EDEN and M. MOLOTOV thought that in this matter it was important to adhere to the principle of joint action, and that on this account the decision should be taken by the Control Council.

It was agreed that Mr. Byrnes' point should be borne in mind by the Drafting Committee and brought up for later decision.

As regards paragraph 7 (iv), M. MOLOTOV suggested that the word 'political' should be omitted. This was agreed.

On paragraph 8, MR. EDEN suggested that the words 'any existing restrictions would be progressively relaxed' should be added in the first sentence after the word 'permitted'. He said that full freedom could obviously not be given all at once. This was agreed.

> It was agreed that the following should be appointed as a Drafting Committee:
> United States Delegation: Mr. F. Matthews, Mr. B. Cohen;
> United Kingdom Delegation: Sir William Strang, Mr. Harrison;
> Russian Delegation: M. Vyshinski, M. Semionov[Semenov];
> to consider the points which had been raised in discussion and such other drafting points as might be referred to them on behalf of the three Delegations.

5. *Germany: Consideration of Economic Problems*

MR. BYRNES said that, although he had recommended (see Minute 3 above) that the Second Plenary Meeting should discuss the authority of the Control Council for Germany in political matters, he did not think that a Plenary Meeting could make satisfactory progress at this stage with the discussion of the complex and technical questions which were arising in connection with Germany's economic problems. In the economic field he thought that further preparatory work must be done before a Plenary Meeting was invited to take final decisions. He therefore suggested that a small Committee should be appointed—consisting of a small number, say two, from the staff of each Delegation—to survey the problems which would confront the

Control Council for Germany in the economic field and to define the issues on which agreement could not be reached among members of the Delegation staffs. These issues might then be considered by the Foreign Secretaries' Meeting, who could in turn select those major questions which must be put forward for decision by the Plenary Meeting. By this means it should be possible to reduce substantially the amount of time which the Plenary Meeting would have to spend on Germany's economic problems.

Mr. Byrnes gave, as examples of the kind of problem which would have to be reviewed by this Committee, restitution, Germany's import programme, and the proposal that German exports required to pay for necessary imports should be treated as outside reparations deliveries. He explained that, while the Committee would be largely concerned with problems relating to the reparations question, they would not be confined to reparations only, but would review the whole field of Germany's immediate economic problems.

After discussion:

> It was agreed to appoint a Committee to carry out a review of Germany's economic problems, on the lines suggested by Mr. Byrnes. The following have been nominated to act on this Committee:
>
> On behalf of the United States Delegation: Mr. W. Clayton, Mr. E. W. Pauley.
>
> On behalf of the United Kingdom Delegation: Sir Walter Monckton, Sir David Waley, Mr. J. Coulson, Mr. M. Turner.
>
> On behalf of the Russian Delegation: M. Maisky, M. Artumyan, M. Sobolev.

Cabinet Office, Potsdam, 18th July, 1945

CALENDARS TO No. 178

i [?*18*] *July 1945   Note for F. (Terminal) 1st Meeting on proposed Council of Foreign Ministers.* Welcomes American proposal but favours limitation to the four Foreign Secretaries [F.O. 934/3/16(2)].

ii *18 July 1945   Memorandum by Mr. Dixon (Berlin) on Italy:* discussions with Mr. Matthews and Mr. Dunn of U.S. Delegation: much common ground but two new American proposals [F.O. 934/2/6(8)].

No. 179

Minute from Mr. Attlee to Mr. Eden (Berlin)

[*U 6311/2600/70*]

[BERLIN,] *18 July 1945*

I have read your note to the Prime Minister on Russian policy[1] and agree with you as to the need for countering the increasing pressure from

---

[1] No. 176.

this source, but there seems to me to be a danger of our getting into a position where we and the Russians confront each other as rival great powers at a number of points of strategic importance.

If we take our stand on the basis of our own particular interests in such areas as the Western and Eastern exits from the Mediterranean, we are, I think, fighting on weak ground. We ought to confront the Russians with the requirements of a world organisation for peace, not with the needs of the defence of the British Empire.

I think that the views expressed in Brief 50,[2] 'Security Arrangements for the Baltic Sea Gateways and the Kiel Canal' are very short term and seem to envisage a world of potentially warring great powers rather than a world organised for peace. San Francisco is not in the picture. The attitude towards the defence of Gibraltar and the Suez Canal seem[s] to me to be unrealistic in view of air warfare and to be based on an obsolete conception of imperial defence derived from the naval era. The concept of the special interest of Great Britain in the strategic areas and the acceptance of responsibility for them involves us in a continuing heavy burden of defence expenditure. Similarly the conception of the paramount interest of Russia in the Baltic and Black Sea exits are based on the old conception of naval defence. Later we shall be faced with the question of the future of Singapore. I am afraid of us undertaking responsibilities which we shall be a little [sic] fitted to undertake in the economic conditions of the post-war period. If we really believe and intend to operate a world organisation for peace we ought, I think, to get away from old conceptions. In my view the only realistic policy is that of placing all these strategic areas under international control, not the control of one or two powers, but of the United Nations. I am a little afraid lest the discussions here should prejudice the larger issues which must be dealt with when the San Francisco Charter is taken up by the United Nations.

C. R. A.

[2] Not printed. For this brief of 13 July 1945 see No. 109, annex II.

No. 180

Minute from Sir A. Clark Kerr to Mr. Eden (Berlin)
[F.O. 800/303:45/22]

FOREIGN OFFICE [*sic*], *18 July 1945*

Here is a memorandum about my talk with T. V. Soong.[1]

You will, I am sure, remember that I promised him that it would be for no other eyes than yours and the Prime Minister's.

A. C. K.

[1] Cf. No. 133.

Top Secret

Foreign Secretary.

At Moscow on the 10th of July I had a long talk with Dr. T. V. Soong about his negotiations with Stalin.

He began by saying that he wanted to get something off his heart to me as an old friend and to ask for my advice. But before he told his story he must get a pledge from me that I would pass it on to no one but the Prime Minister and yourself. He did not want it to become a cabinet paper. I pledged myself.

He was in gloomy mood and full of doubts about the future and what contribution he should make to its shaping. His responsibilities were clearly heavy on him and he was sore about the terms of the Yalta Agreement on the Far East[2] and about China's not having been consulted. But his approach to the whole matter was calm and practical. He has certainly increased in stature since I knew him in China between 1938 and 1942.

I asked him when he had first learned of the Yalta Agreement. To my surprise he said that Mr Truman had communicated the text to him in Washington in June. I had understood from Averell Harriman that General Hurley[3] was to have 'sold' it to Chiang Kai shek in Chungking. Indeed General Hurley, when he was in Moscow on his way back to China in the middle of April, told me that this was to be the chiefest of his preoccupations in Chungking.

Dr Soong said that the Agreement had come to him, and subsequently to Chiang Kai shek, as a great shock. But they were realists enough to recognise that it had been done and signed by the three Heads of Governments, and that China would have to face it or, at any rate, some form of it.

He had had five talks with Stalin at all of which Molotov had been present. These talks had shown that the Russians were trying to expand the text of the Agreement to their own advantage.

A. *Outer Mongolia*

For instance, point A, which provided for the preservation of the *status quo* in Outer Mongolia. Here the Russians were asking him to recognise the so-called Republic of Outer Mongolia, whereas, under the *status quo* China's sovereign rights were admitted. The province was, he confessed, of no material value to China, for it was nothing but a sandy waste, over which there wandered some 600,000 nomads with their dromadaries [*sic*] and their shaggy ponies. China could live at ease without this province. But since it came into being, the Republic of China had never willingly yielded up an inch of its territories, and its prestige with its own peoples demanded that this policy should be maintained. It was important therefore that China should emerge as whole as when she went into it. Nevertheless he saw that he must be practical about it and, if the worse came to the worst, he would be prepared to consider the recognition of the Republic of Outer Mongolia, provided that he got a satisfactory general agreement and certain specific commitments from Russia that were of first class importance to

[2] This agreement concerning the entry of the Soviet Union into the war against Japan, signed in the Livadia Palace at Yalta on 11 February 1945 by President Truman, Mr. Churchill and Marshal Stalin, is printed (Cmd. 6735 of 1946) in *B.F.S.P.*, vol. 148, pp. 88-9.

[3] Major-General P. J. Hurley was U.S. Ambassador at Chungking.

China. I asked what he had in mind. He said that the first commitment was the complete and genuine recognition by Russia that the Province of Sinkiang was Chinese. Even though the Russians had withdrawn from Sinkiang they were still interfering and putting obstacles in the way of the Chinese efforts to quell risings by the Moslem tribes. That would have to stop and Sinkiang must be brought back into the body of China. The second was that Russia should give to China a solemn undertaking that she would render no help, either material or moral, to the Chinese 'Communists'.

Dr. Soong said that he thought that Stalin was disposed to give him what he wanted on both these points.

B. [(i)] *Restoration of Russian rights lost in 1904*

    (ii) *Dairen and Port Arthur*

He was not concerned with point B (i) about Southern Sakhalin, *etcetera*. But (ii)—the internationalisation of Dairien [*sic*] and the lease of Port Arthur—touched China very painfully. As regards Dairien the words 'with safeguards for the pre-eminent interests of the U.S.S.R.' disturbed him. Could I tell him what the word 'pre-eminent' meant to a Russian mind? I had to confess that it probably had a wide and important meaning. He said that he too feared that this was so, for the Russians were demanding the posts of mayor and harbour master for their nominees. They were indeed offering him Chinese deputies, but he could not persuade himself that a régime in which the two principal jobs were to be permanently in Russian hands could ever be called 'international'. I was bound to agree with him. Then there was another thing that seemed to him to make the genuine internationalisation of Darien impossible. The only access to it from the land side would, if the Russian claims were met, lie through a Soviet military area. This would mean that the passage of every railway truck and every traveller would be subject to the issue of a Soviet pass. This made the whole plan of internationalisation absurd. I asked for some explanations about this and he showed me a map of the peninsula upon which Port Arthur and Darien lie. He said that in Tsarist times the lease of Port Arthur had included a substantial hinterland. The peninsula was a waisted affair. North of the waist was a region known formerly as the 'Neutral Zone'. This Stalin was ready to see handed back to China. South of the waist lay the tip of the peninsula with the ports of Port Arthur to the South and Darien to the east. Stalin was claiming the whole of this tip on the ground that this bit of hinterland was necessary for purposes of defence. It was to be occupied by the Russian Army. Dr. Soong pointed out to me that, if China had to consent to a lease of Port Arthur, the addition of this little chunk of territory would not matter much, were it not for the fact that, as I have said, the only access to Dairen passed through it. He thought therefore that the Russians should be confined to an area immediately round the fortress and that the railway should be left free.

    (iii) *The Chinese Eastern and the South Manchuria Railways*

The Yalta Agreement provided for the *joint* operation of these two railways by a Soviet-Chinese company. Here again the disturbing words 'the pre-eminent interests of the U.S.S.R.' emerged. Dr. Soong thought that the admission of anything like pre-eminence for the Russians might, in course of time, end in the domination of Manchuria by the Soviet Union. In virtue of the words quoted Stalin was claiming for Russia four seats out of a board of directors of seven. Dr. Soong said that this was unacceptable. There was nothing 'joint' about a management with a Russian majority. He would have to fight it. At the same time about this question he had obtained from Stalin an assurance that the joint operation would be restricted to the main lines, branch lines being excluded, and that the policing of the railways would be in purely Chinese hands. This he felt to be something of an achievement.

In the rest of the Yalta Agreement Dr. Soong said he was not interested, although he said that he would welcome a Soviet-Chinese alliance against Japan.

Dr. Soong was in two minds whether to clinch with Stalin or to claim that he must go home to consult Chiang Kai shek. It looked to me a little as if someone had suggested to him that he would incur the enduring ill will of Stalin if he did not clinch in Moscow. It seemed to me however that he could most reasonably claim the right to consult the Head of his government on a matter of such high importance and when he asked for my advice I suggested that he would be wise to tell Stalin frankly that he felt bound to take Chiang Kai shek's opinion. The meeting at *Terminal* was about to take place. The matter would be bound to arise there and I felt pretty sure that China could count upon British and American support against Russian attempts to go beyond what was agreed to at Yalta. I gather from the newspapers that Dr. Soong left Moscow on July 13th and, as no announcement of an agreement was made, it is to be assumed that he decided that he must consult Chiang Kai shek.

A. C. K.

July 18. 45

No. 181

Summarized note of the Prime Minister's conversation with President Truman at luncheon on 18 July 1945
[PREM 3/430/8]

Top secret   23 RINGSTRASSE, BERLIN, *18 July 1945*

No others present.

The following subjects were touched upon:–

1. *T[ube] A[lloys]*

The President showed me telegrams about the recent experiment,[1] and asked what I thought should be done about telling the Russians. He seemed determined to do this, but asked about the timing, and said he thought that the end of the Conference would be best. I replied that if he were resolved to tell, it might well be better to hang it on to the experiment, which was a new fact on which he and we had only just had knowledge. Therefore he would have a good answer to any question, 'Why did you not tell us this before?' He seemed impressed with this idea, and will consider it.

On behalf of His Majesty's Government I did not resist his proposed

[1] For telegrams reporting the successful testing of the atomic bomb at Alamogordo on 16 July 1945, cf. *F.R.U.S. Berlin*, vol. ii, p. 81, note 7.

disclosure of the simple fact that we have this weapon. He reiterated his resolve at all costs to refuse to divulge any particulars.[2]

2. The President asked how I thought we should handle the Russian request for the division of the German Fleet. I said, speaking personally, my view was that we should welcome the Russians on to the broad waters and do it in a manner which was wholehearted and gracious. This would affect the view we took of the Dardanelles, Kiel Canal, the mouth of the Baltic, and Port Arthur. I found it hard to deny the Russians the right to keep their third of the Fleet afloat if they needed it. We British should not have any use for our third of the warships. The President said the Americans would take their share, but it would be of no use to them.

I made it clear that the case of the U-boats must be considered separately, as they were nasty things to have knocking about in large numbers. He seemed to agree.

I said I thought this matter should be handled in connection with the general layout in Central Europe. Were all these States which had passed into Russian control to be free and independent, or not? Of course they could not pursue a policy hostile to Russia. The President attached great importance to this, and evidently intends to press with severity the need of their true independence in accordance with free, full and unfettered elections. He seemed to agree with my point that everything should be settled as a whole, and not piecemeal.

When I mentioned Persia, Turkey and Greece, he seemed to be in full accord.

3. I then got on to finance, Lease-Lend, etc. I told the President that I had sent his paper[3] for comment to the Chancellor of the Exchequer, and would send him a short note upon it in a day or two.

I spoke of the melancholy position of Great Britain, who had spent more than one-half her foreign investments in the time when we were all alone for the common cause, and now emerged from the War the only nation with a great external debt of £3,000 millions. I explained to him the way in which this had grown up for war purposes through buying supplies from India, Egypt, etc. with no Lease-Lend arrangement; and that would impose upon us an annual exportation without any compensatory import to nourish the wages fund. He followed this attentively and with sympathy.

The President then spoke of the immense debt owed by the United States to Great Britain for having held the fort at the beginning. 'If you had gone down like France, we might well be fighting the Germans on the American coast at the present time'. This justified the United States in regarding these matters as above the purely financial plane. I said I had

[2] Minute 1 was circulated only to Mr. Eden (F.O. 800/417/64), Sir J. Anderson, Lord Cherwell and General Ismay for the Chiefs of Staff Committee. This minute is printed by W. S. Churchill, *op. cit.*, vol. vi, p. 552. For other parts of this conversation cf. *ibid.*, pp. 546–8, J. Ehrman, *op. cit.*, vol. vi, pp. 302–3, Thomas G. Patterson, *On Every Front: the Making of the Cold War* (New York, 1979), p. 99.

[3] Annex to No. 174.

told the Election crowds that we were living to a large extent upon American imported food, etc., for which we could not pay, and we had no intention of being kept by any country, however near to us in friendship. We should have to ask for help to become a going concern again. Until we got our wheels turning properly once more, we could be of little use to world security or any of the high purposes of San Francisco. The President said he would do his very utmost; but of course I knew all the difficulties he might have in his own country. His attitude was most warm and comforting in these matters.

Naturally I spoke of Article 7,[4] reminding him of the late President's message to me about our not being committed about Imperial preference,[5] and saying that if not wisely handled it might cause a split in the Conservative Party. I had heard that America was making great reductions in her Tariff. He replied that he understood my difficulties, and that the American Tariff had been reduced by 50 cent. He now had authority to reduce it by another 50 per cent, leaving it at one-quarter of its pre-war height. I said of course this was a great factor, and would have a powerful influence on our Dominions, especially Canada and Australia. I made it clear we would discuss this matter in the full spirit of Article 7.

4. I said that the Japanese war might end much quicker than had been expected, and that the eighteen months period which we had taken as a working rule required to be reviewed. Also, Stage III[6] might be upon us in a few months, or perhaps even earlier.

I imparted to the President the disclosure, about the offer from the Mikado, made to me by Marshal Stalin the night before; and I told him he was quite free to talk it over with the Marshal, as I had informed him at the Marshal's express desire. (See my conversation recorded by Birse.)[7]

The President also thought the war might come to a speedy end.

Here I explained that Marshal Stalin had not wished to transmit this information direct to him for fear he might think the Russians were trying to influence him towards peace. In the same way I would abstain from saying anything which would indicate that we were in any way reluctant to go on with the war against Japan as long as the United States thought fit. However I dwelt upon the tremendous cost in American life and, to a smaller extent, in British life which would be involved in enforcing 'unconditional surrender' upon the Japanese. It was for him to consider whether this might not be expressed in some other way, so that we got all the essentials

[4] Of the Anglo-American Agreement of 23 February 1942 on Principles applying to Mutual Aid in the prosecution of the War against Aggression: see No. 26, note 2. Article 7 related to expansion of production and the elimination of discriminatory treatment in international commerce.

[5] This message of 11 February 1942 from President Roosevelt to Mr. Churchill is printed in *F.R.U.S. 1942*, vol. i, pp. 535–6.

[6] The envisaged period of reconversion from war to peace after the defeat of Japan: cf. No. 26, note 7.

[7] No. 173.

for future peace and security, and yet left the Japanese some show of saving their military honour and some assurance of their national existence, after they had complied with all safeguards necessary for the conqueror. The President countered by saying that he did not think the Japanese had any military honour after Pearl Harbour. I contented myself with saying that at any rate they had something for which they were ready to face certain death in very large numbers, and this might not be so important to us as it was to them. He then became quite sympathetic, and spoke, as Mr. Stimson had to me two days earlier,[8] of the terrible responsibilities that rested upon him in regard to unlimited effusion of American blood.

My own impression is that there is no question of a rigid insistence upon the phrase 'unconditional surrender', apart from the essentials necessary for world peace and future security, and for the punishment of a guilty and treacherous nation.

It has been evident to me in my conversations with Mr. Stimson, General Marshall,[9] and now with the President, that they are searching their hearts on this subject, and that we have no need to press it. We know of course that the Japanese are ready to give up all conquests made in this war.

5. The President raised the subject of Air and Communications. He had great difficulties to face in regard to airfields in British territory, especially in Africa, which the Americans had built at enormous cost. We ought to meet them on this, and arrange a fair plan for common use.

I said I was very sorry that there had been a breakdown at Chicago,[10] and that, if I continued to be responsible, I should like to re-open the Air question as regards communications with him personally. He welcomed this. It would be a great pity, I said, if the Americans got worked up about bases and Air traffic, and set themselves to make a win of it at all costs. We must come to the best arrangements in our common interest. As to the airfields and other bases, President Roosevelt knew well that I wished to go much farther, and would like to have a reciprocal arrangement, including naval and Air, all over the world between our two countries. Britain, though a smaller Power than the United States, had much to give. Why should an American battleship calling at Gibraltar not find the torpedoes to fit her tubes, and the shells to fit her guns deposited there? Why should we not share facilities for defence all over the world? We could add 50 per cent. to the mobility of the American Fleet.

The President said that all this language was very near his own heart. Any plan would have to be fitted in, in some way, as a part of the method of carrying out the policy of the United Nations.

I said that was all right so long as the facilities were shared between

---

[8] The reference, however, would appear to be to a conversation between Mr. Churchill and Mr. Stimson on the afternoon of 17 July 1945, of which no official record has been traced: cf. W. S. Churchill, *op. cit.*, vol. vi, pp. 551–2, and *F.R.U.S. Berlin*, vol. ii, p. 47.

[9] Cf. W. S. Churchill, *op. cit.*, vol. vi, p. 552.

[10] For the proceedings of the Conference on International Civil Aviation held at Chicago from 1 November–7 December 1944, see *F.R.U.S. 1944*, vol. ii, pp. 355–613.

Britain and the United States. There was nothing in it if they were made common to everybody. A man might make a proposal of marriage to a young lady, but it was not much use if he were told that she would always be a sister to him. I wanted, under whatever form or cloak, a continuation of the present war-time system of reciprocal facilities between Britain and the United States in regard to bases and fuelling points in their possession.

The President seemed in full accord with this, if it could be presented in a suitable fashion, and did not appear to take crudely the form of a military alliance à deux. These last were not his words, but are my impression of his mind.

Encouraged by this, I went on with my long-cherished idea of keeping the organization of the Combined Chiefs of Staff in being, at any rate until the world calmed down after the great storm and until there was a world structure of such proved strength and capacity that we could safely confide ourselves to it.

The President was replying to this in an encouraging way, when we were interrupted by his officers reminding him that he must now start off to see Marshal Stalin.

He was good enough to say that this had been the most enjoyable luncheon he had had for many years, and how earnestly he hoped the relations I had had with President Roosevelt would be continued between him and me. He invited personal friendship and comradeship, and used many expressions at intervals in our discussion which I could not easily hear unmoved. He seems a man of exceptional character and ability, with an outlook exactly along the lines of Anglo-American relations as they have developed, simple and direct methods of speech, and a great deal of self-confidence and resolution.

Let us hope that further developments at this Conference and hereafter will vindicate these hopeful notes.

No. 182

Memorandum by the British Chiefs of Staff[1]
C.C.S. 890/2 [CAB 99/39]

Top secret   BABELSBERG, *18 July 1945*

Control and Command in the War against Japan

1. The British Chiefs of Staff have considered the memorandum by the United States Chiefs of Staff (C.C.S. 890/1)[2] on Control and Command in the War against Japan. They have the following comments to make:

2. They fully understand that it will ultimately be necessary to obtain the

---

[1] This memorandum is printed in *F.R.U.S. Berlin*, vol. ii, pp. 1315–6.
[2] This memorandum of 17 July 1945 is printed *op. cit.*, vol. ii, pp. 1313–5.

agreement of the Generalissimo[3] to the inclusion of Indo-China in South-East Asia Command. They are anxious, however, that the United States Chiefs of Staff should support them in recommending to the President and the Prime Minister that they should press the Generalissimo to agree to this transfer.[4] They suggest, therefore, that a recommendation to this effect should be included in the final report of the 'Terminal' Conference.

3. The British Chiefs of Staff note that the United States Chiefs of Staff consider it necessary to retain control of the Admiralty Islands. They, therefore, withdraw their proposal for the inclusion of these Islands in the Australian command. They also agree not to press for the eastward extension of the present boundary of the South-West Pacific Area until United States activities are cleared from the area. They note that the United States Chiefs of Staff would offer no objection to British operations against Ocean and Nauru Islands.

4. The British Chiefs of Staff realise the advantage of an early transfer of the South-West Pacific Area but are up against two difficulties. The first is in fact that Admiral Mountbatten is now fully engaged on planning further operations The assumption of further responsibilities at this particular stage must inevitably embarrass him. Secondly, we have no idea what degree of assistance the United States Chiefs of Staff are at present providing to the Borneo operations[5] nor when those operations are due to be completed. On present information, therefore, we cannot assess the commitment we should be undertaking if we agree to the transfer on any particular date. We should like, therefore, to discuss this further with the United States Chiefs of Staff.

5. On the question of the higher strategic control of the war against Japan, the British Chiefs of Staff wish to reiterate and amplify their view that they should now be given a larger share of control of strategy on the lines suggested in C.C.S. 890.[6] They desire to bring to the notice of the United States Chiefs of Staff the following particular considerations:

(a) The United States and Great Britain are the two major Powers allied against Japan, and thus jointly responsible for the prosecution of the war. It is most desirable that they should consult freely on all matters of major strategic importance relating to the conduct of the war.

(b) The British Chiefs of Staff have an inescapable responsibility to advise His Majesty's Government on the use to which British Forces are put in all theatres of war.

(c) Although the United States are, of course, providing the major share, the war against Japan like that against Germany is being fought with pooled United States and British resources, particularly shipping. It is

---

[3] Generalissimo Chiang Kai-shek.   [4] From the Chinese theatre of operations.
[5] For Allied operations in Borneo following Australian landings in May 1945, cf. S. V. Woodburn Kirby, *The War against Japan* (H.M.S.O., 1957f.), vol. v, pp. 134–7.
[6] This memorandum of 9 July by the Representatives in Washington of the British Chiefs of Staff is printed *op. cit.*, vol. i, pp. 921–4.

right, therefore, that the British should have full understanding and knowledge of the proposed methods of applying these resources.

6. The British Chiefs of Staff wish to make it clear that the full extent of what they are asking is that they should be consulted on major strategic policy. They have no intention of suggesting interference with the operational control now accorded to General MacArthur and Admiral Nimitz, in whom they have the utmost confidence.

The British Chiefs of Staff ask, therefore, that the United States Chiefs of Staff should reconsider their attitude on this question.

No. 183

Minutes of a Meeting of the Combined Chiefs of Staff Committee held in the Conference Room at 25 Ringstrasse, Babelsberg, on Wednesday, 18 July 1945 at 2.30 p.m.[1]

C.C.S. 195th Meeting [CAB 99/39]

Top secret

Present:

GENERAL OF THE ARMY G. C. MARSHALL, USA, Fleet Admiral E. J. King, USN, General of the Army H. H. Arnold, USA.

FIELD-MARSHAL SIR ALAN F. BROOKE, Marshal of the Royal Air Force Sir Charles F. A. Portal, Admiral of the Fleet Sir Andrew B. Cunningham.

Also Present:

General B. B. Somervell, USA, Lieut.-General J. E. Hull, USA, Vice-Admiral C. M. Cooke, Jr., USN, Major-General L. Norstad, USA, Captain H. R. Oster, USN, Captain A. S. McDill, USN.

Field-Marshal Sir Henry Maitland Wilson, General Sir Hastings L. Ismay, Lieut.-General Sir Gordon Macready, Major-General R. E. Laycock, Major-General L. C. Hollis.

Secretariat: Brig.-General A. J. McFarland, USA, Brigadier A. T. Cornwall-Jones, Captain C. J. Moore, USN, Lieut.-Colonel T. Haddon.

1. *Approval of the Minutes of the C.C.S. 194th Meeting*[2]

THE COMBINED CHIEFS OF STAFF–

Approved the conclusions of the C.C.S. 194th Meeting and approved the detailed report of the meeting subject to the substitution in the 2nd paragraph on page 177[3] of the words 'dispatch of a corps commander and staff to the Pacific' for 'above' and subject to any later minor amendments.

---

[1] This record is printed in *F.R.U.S. Berlin*, vol. ii, pp. 82–6; cf. *ibid. et passim* for text or annotations of the documents cited in minutes 2 and 3 below. See further No. 249, paragraphs 15, 17 and appendix E.

[2] See No. 172, note 2.

[3] Cf. *op. cit.*, vol. ii, p. 50, fifth paragraph.

2. *French and Dutch participation in the War against Japan*
    (C.C.S. 842, 842/1, and 842/2.)[1]
THE COMBINED CHIEFS OF STAFF—
    Approved the memorandum in the enclosure to C.C.S. 842/2 and
    directed the Secretaries to forward it separately to the French and
    Netherlands Representatives to the Combined Chiefs of Staff.

3. *Staff Conversations with Portugal*
    (C.C.S. 462/25 and 462/26.)[1]
THE COMBINED CHIEFS OF STAFF—
    Approved the letter to the Department of State and Foreign Office in
    the enclosure to C.C.S. 462/25, as amended in C.C.S. 462/26.

4. *The South-East Asia and South-West Pacific Area*
    (C.C.S. 890/2.)[4]

The Combined Chiefs of Staff considered paragraphs 2, 3, and 4 of
C.C.S. 890/2.

In regard to paragraph 2, GENERAL MARSHALL asked the British Chiefs
of Staff if they would express their reaction to dividing Indo-China into
two parts, leaving the northern part in the China Theatre.

SIR ANDREW CUNNINGHAM pointed out that the line dividing Indo-China
would be dependent to some extent on contemplated operations through
Thailand.

ADMIRAL KING stated that the division of Indo-China along the latitude
of 15 degrees north was an arbitrary division and might be changed to suit
contemplated operational requirements.

THE BRITISH CHIEFS OF STAFF expressed the view that they should like to
study the question of the dividing line before making any proposals in
regard to the matter.

The proposals contained in paragraph 3 were accepted by the Combined
Chiefs of Staff without discussion.

In the discussion of paragraph 4, SIR ALAN BROOKE explained that the
British Chiefs of Staff were in doubt as to the commitment which they would
be undertaking if they agreed to the transfer on a particular date. They did
not know when the operations in Borneo were scheduled to be completed
nor what sort of liability they would be accepting in the form of maintenance
and support for those operations.

In reply, GENERAL MARSHALL referred to the United States Chiefs of
Staff reply to the questionnaire which the British Chiefs of Staff had submitted (C.C.S. 852 and 852/1),[5] and described the extent to which the
United States Chiefs of Staff were proposing to support operations in the
new British command. He said that most of the United States troops had been
withdrawing from the area of the proposed new British command and that
no further operations were scheduled in Borneo. He added that in any

[4] No. 182.   [5] Not printed: cf. No. 249, appendix D.

event there would be no question of 'leaving the Borneo operations in the lurch.'

GENERAL MARSHALL then went on to point out that it would be a great advantage to the United States Chiefs of Staff if the transfer of the area to Admiral Mountbatten could take place at an early date. General MacArthur is fully occupied with operations to the northward and it would be a considerable benefit to him if he could be relieved of these responsibilities as soon as possible.

SIR CHARLES PORTAL said that Admiral Mountbatten also was fully occupied in his present and contemplated operations in the South-East Asia Command, and since General MacArthur was familiar with and is dealing with the Australians at the present, it might be best to continue that procedure until Admiral Mountbatten was in a better position to undertake these new responsibilities.

THE BRITISH CHIEFS OF STAFF agreed that it was desirable to effect a transfer of command in the South-West Pacific Area at an early date, but considered that it would be necessary for them to study the matter before a definite time could be agreed upon.

GENERAL MARSHALL suggested that as Admiral Mountbatten was about to visit General MacArthur in Manila, that he and General MacArthur might discuss the timing of the transfer of command.

THE COMBINED CHIEFS OF STAFF–

(a) Agreed in principle that that part of the present South-West Pacific area lying south of the boundary proposed in paragraph 2 of C.C.S. 852/1[5] should pass from United States to British command as soon as possible.

(b) Took note that the British Chiefs of Staff would investigate and report to the Combined Chiefs of Staff the earliest possible date on which the transfer of the above area could be effected.

(c) Took note that the British Chiefs of Staff would consider where the dividing line might lie in the event that approximately half of French Indo-China should be included in the new British command.

(At this point the Combined Chiefs of Staff went into closed session.)[6]

5. *Command and Control in the War against Japan*
(Paragraphs 5 and 6, C.C.S. 890/2.)[4]

GENERAL MARSHALL said that he wished to explain the point of view of the United States Chiefs of Staff.

He pointed out that the general concept of operations in the Pacific had been approved by the Combined Chiefs of Staff and that the control of operational strategy lay with the United States Chiefs of Staff. He recognised that in the past the British Chiefs of Staff had not had all the information that

[6] It would appear probable that in this unrecorded session General Marshall reported to the Combined Chiefs of Staff the successful test of the atomic bomb: cf. Lord Ismay, *The Memoirs of General the Lord Ismay* (London, 1960), p. 401; Admiral of the Fleet Viscount Cunningham of Hyndhope, *A Sailor's Odyssey* (London, 1951), p. 646.

they wanted and assured them that this would be remedied in the future. He felt, however, that the operational strategy in the Pacific must remain the responsibility of the United States Chiefs of Staff. He explained the extensive difficulties in the conduct of the strategy of the Pacific arising from the great distances involved and the enormous land, sea and air forces employed. He said that the United States Chiefs of Staff felt that they could not, in addition to these problems, shoulder the burden of debating the pros and cons of operational strategy with the British Chiefs of Staff.

The United States Chiefs of Staff would be glad to give the British Chiefs of Staff timely information of United States plans and intentions and to hear their comments. But they felt bound to retain freedom to decide ultimately what should be done. If then the British Chiefs of Staff felt that they could not commit British troops to the operations decided upon, then they would of course be at liberty to withdraw British forces from those operations; but he desired to make it clear that if this were done, it would be necessary for the United States Chiefs of Staff to be given ample warning of British intentions so that plans of United States Chiefs of Staff could be adjusted accordingly.

SIR ALAN BROOKE said that the British Chiefs of Staff had felt that they had been rather left out of the picture, but confirmed that the British Chiefs of Staff entirely supported the strategy which the United States Chiefs of Staff had so far developed. For the future, they hoped that they would be consulted on the further development of strategy but had no wish to suggest that they should interfere in any way with the operational strategy.

SIR ANDREW CUNNINGHAM asked if the British Chiefs of Staff would be consulted in regard to the strategy that would be adopted in the event of the Russians coming into the war.

GENERAL MARSHALL said that the strategy to be adopted in these circumstances would be considered on a tripartite basis.

ADMIRAL KING said that the United States Chiefs of Staff would consult with the British Chiefs of Staff, of course, but must reserve the final decision to themselves.

GENERAL MARSHALL said that in the event of any disagreement, the British Chiefs of Staff would certainly be given the opportunity of convincing the United States Chiefs of Staff that they were wrong.

THE COMBINED CHIEFS OF STAFF—

Agreed that with respect to the strategic control of the war against Japan:

(a) The control of operational strategy in the Pacific theatre will remain in the hands of the United States Chiefs of Staff.

(b) The United States Chiefs of Staff will provide the British Chiefs of Staff with full and timely information as to their future plans and intentions.

(c) The United States Chiefs of Staff will consult the British Chiefs of Staff on matters of general strategy, on the understanding that in the event of disagreement, the final decision on the action to be taken will lie with the United States Chiefs of Staff.

(*d*) In the event the British Chiefs of Staff should decide that they cannot commit British troops in support of a decision made by the United States Chiefs of Staff as indicated in (*c*) above, the British Chiefs of Staff will give to the United States Chief of Staff such advance notice of their decision as will permit them to make timely rearrangements.

(*e*) In the event the U.S.S.R. enters the war against Japan, the strategy to be pursued should be discussed between the parties concerned.

CALENDARS TO No. 183

i *16 July 1945 Sir H. Seymour (Chungking) Tel. No. 699.* Advice of General Carton de Wiart, British special representative with Generalissimo Chiang Kai-shek, on consulting the Generalissimo on transfer of Siam and Indo-China to South-East Asia Command [F 4281/47/23].

ii *19 July 1945 Memo. by Mr. Foulds (Berlin):* 'Background to French Indo-China in relation to South-East Asia Command' [F.O. 934/3/12].

No. 184

Record of Second Plenary Meeting held at Cecilienhof, Potsdam, on Wednesday, 18 July 1945 at 5 p.m.

P. (*Terminal*) *2nd Meeting* [U 6197/3628/70]

Top secret

Present:

PREMIER STALIN, M. V. M. Molotov, M. A. Ya. Vyshinski, M. F. T. Gousev, M. A. A. Gromyko, M. K. V. Novikov, M. A. A. Sobolev, M. B. F. Podtzerob, M. V. N. Pavlov (*Interpreter*).

PRESIDENT TRUMAN, Mr. J. F. Byrnes, Mr. Joseph E. Davies, Fleet-Admiral W. D. Leahy, Mr. W. A. Harriman, Mr. J. C. Dunn, Mr. H. F. Matthews, Mr. B. V. Cohen, Mr. L. E. Thompson, Mr. C. E. Bohlen (*Interpreter*).

MR. CHURCHILL, Mr. Eden, Mr. Attlee, Sir A. Cadogan, Sir A. Clark Kerr, Sir W. Strang, Sir E. Bridges, Mr. P. J. Dixon, Mr. W. Hayter, Major A. Birse (*Interpreter*).

Contents

Minute	Subject
1.	Relations with the Press
2.	Subjects for Discussion. Report by the Three Foreign Secretaries
3.	Proposal for Establishment of a Council of Foreign Ministers
4.	Policy with regard to Germany
5.	Poland

1. Relations with the Press

MR. CHURCHILL said that there was one matter outside the Agenda of the meeting which he would like to mention, and which was of immediate local interest. At the Teheran Conference, it had been very difficult for the Press to get near the meeting place, and at Yalta it had been impossible. But now, immediately outside the Delegation area there were 180 journalists prowling around in a state of furious indignation. They carried very powerful weapons, and were making a great outcry in the world Press about lack of facilities accorded to them.

In reply to a question by Premier Stalin as to who had let all these journalists in, the Prime Minister said they were not within the Delegation area, but were mostly in Berlin.

Continuing, the Prime Minister said that the Conference could only do its work in quiet and secrecy, which must be protected at all costs. If Premier Stalin and President Truman so wished, he would be willing, himself, to see the Press representatives, and explain to them in a friendly manner why the Press had to be excluded, and why nothing could be divulged to them until the end of the Conference. Possibly President Truman would be willing to see the Press. The plumage of the Press needed to be smoothed down; but he thought that, if the importance of secrecy and quiet for those engaged in the Conference was explained to them, the Press would accept their exclusion from the Conference with a good grace.

PREMIER STALIN enquired what it was that the journalists wanted.

PRESIDENT TRUMAN said that each of the Heads of Government had his own Press representative to stand between him and the Press. He thought that the matter should be left to these representatives, and that the Conference should proceed, the Press being excluded, as had already been agreed.

MR. CHURCHILL said that he was quite happy to leave the matter on that basis, if that was felt to be best. But he thought that some statement should be given to the Press explaining the reason for their exclusion from the Conference.

2. Subjects for Discussion. Report by the Three Foreign Secretaries

PRESIDENT TRUMAN said that in accordance with the decision taken at the 1st Plenary Meeting,[1] the three Foreign Secretaries had met that morning[2] to recommend the subjects for discussion at the Plenary meeting. He asked the Secretary of State to read out the agreed recommendations of the Foreign Secretaries.

MR. BYRNES then read out the following Report, which was accepted:

'The Foreign Ministers agreed that they would recommend to the Heads of Governments that the subjects for discussion at the meeting this afternoon, the 18th July, should be the following:

'(1) *Procedure and machinery for peace negotiations and territorial settlements*

---

[1] *Note in filed copy:* 'P. (Terminal) 1st Meeting, Minute 4': see No. 170.
[2] See No. 178.

'(2) *Authority of the Control Council for Germany in political questions*

'(3) *The Polish question*, particularly the problems having to do with the liquidation of the former London Polish Government and with the implementation of the Yalta Agreement on Poland.'

3. *Proposal for Establishment of a Council of Foreign Ministers*

(*Previous Reference:* F. (Terminal) 1st Meeting,[2] Minute 2.)

Mr. Byrnes read the following report from the Meeting of Foreign Secretaries:

'*Procedure for Peace Settlements*

'The draft proposal[3] for the establishment of a Council of Foreign Ministers, presented by the United States was approved in principle.

'The following redraft of paragraph 3 of the United States draft was approved:

"(3) As its immediate important task, the Council would be authorized to draw up, with a view to their submission to the United Nations, treaties of peace with Italy, Roumania, Bulgaria, Hungary and Finland, and to propose settlements of territorial questions outstanding on the termination of the war in Europe. The Council shall be utilized for the preparation of a peace settlement for Germany to be accepted by the Government of Germany when a government adequate for the purpose is established.

For the discharge of each of these tasks the Council will be composed of the Members representing those States which were signatory to the Terms of Surrender imposed upon the enemy State concerned.

Other matters may from time to time be referred to the Council by agreement between the States Members thereof."

'The Soviet Delegation reserved the right to suggest a change in the first paragraph of the United States draft.

'It was agreed that the meetings of the three Foreign Ministers approved at the Yalta Conference would not be affected by the establishment of the new Council of Foreign Ministers, though they might at times be held simultaneously with meetings of the Council.

'It was agreed that the functions of the European Advisory Commission would, after agreement with France, be transferred to the Allied Control Councils (for Germany and Austria).'

Premier Stalin said that the Soviet Delegation withdrew their objection to the first paragraph of the United States Draft. The document was acceptable to the Soviet Government.

Mr. Churchill asked the exact meaning of the words in paragraph 3 of the Draft proposal 'with a view to their submission to the United Nations.' If that meant that all members of the United Nations had to be consulted, it would be a very lengthy and laborious process, and he would be sorry to agree to it.

---

[3] *Note in filed copy:* 'P. (Terminal) 2': see No. 170, note 2.

Mr. Byrnes said that the intention was that after agreement between the Five Powers on any matter brought before the Council of Foreign Ministers, the recommendations should be submitted to the United Nations in accordance with the terms of the United Nations Declaration.[4] It was not intended that there should be any submission at any earlier stage in the discussions.

Mr. Churchill said that if the paragraph ran 'with a view to their ultimate submission to the United Nations,' he would be happy. Would this amendment be acceptable?

Premier Stalin said that his understanding was that the procedure would be as described by Mr. Byrnes. The Great Powers would take on themselves the responsibility of representing the interests of all. He thought the actual addition of the word 'ultimate' was unnecessary.

Mr. Churchill said that he agreed to the report provided that there was an understanding on record that the intention was 'ultimate submission to the United Nations.' He thought that the three Foreign Secretaries had done an excellent piece of work in producing this report.

The Report of the Foreign Secretaries on this matter was accepted by the Conference.

4. Policy with regard to Germany

(*Previous References*: F. (Terminal) 1st Meeting,[2] Minutes 4 and 5.)

Mr. Byrnes read the following report from the Committee of Foreign Ministers:

'*Political Authority of the Control Council for Germany.*—The political section of the proposed agreement, presented by the United States,[5] on the political and economic principles to govern the treatment of Germany in the initial control period was discussed by the Foreign Ministers. A number of amendments were suggested which were referred to a drafting sub-committee named by the Foreign Ministers. The sub-committee has not yet completed its work, but the Foreign Ministers agreed that it would be desirable for the Heads of Governments at this afternoon's meeting to have a preliminary and exploratory discussion of the authority of the Control Council for Germany in political matters.

'*Economic Principles.*—The Foreign Ministers agreed that the economic questions connected with Germany are of such a difficult nature that they should be referred in the first instance to a sub-committee of experts. This sub-committee will at the earliest possible time report back to the Foreign Ministers those questions upon which the sub-committee is unable to reach agreement. The Foreign Ministers will then determine which of these questions they will recommend that the Heads of Governments will discuss and decide.

'*German Fleet.*—The Foreign Ministers agreed that, while they would

---

[4] This declaration of 1 January 1942 is printed in *B.F.S.P.*, vol. 144, pp. 1070–2.

[5] *Note in filed copy:* 'P. (Terminal) 3': see No. 170, note 2.

not discuss to-day the question of the disposition of the German fleet and merchant ships, they would take up this question at an early date.'

Mr. Churchill asked what was meant by 'Germany' in this report. If pre-war Germany was meant, then he was in general agreement.

Premier Stalin said that Germany was what she had become *after* the war. There was no other Germany. The term 'Germany' certainly did not include Austria.

President Truman suggested that the Germany of 1937 should be taken as a basis.

Premier Stalin said he thought that the territory lost by Germany in 1945 should be deducted from the 1937 Germany. It would be best to regard Germany as a geographical section.

President Truman said that it was essential to have an agreed definition of 'Germany' from which discussions could start.

Premier Stalin said that it was impossible to get away from the results of the war. For instance, was it intended to restore Sudetenland to Germany? Again, if a German administration appeared in Konigsberg [*sic*], he would expel it.

President Truman said that at Yalta it had been agreed that the final settlement of frontiers must be decided at the Peace Conference.

Premier Stalin suggested that the Conference should first define the Western frontier of Poland and the matter would then become much clearer.

President Truman said this would be done after we had settled what to do with the territories taken away from Germany.

Premier Stalin said he saw great difficulty in settling what Germany was to-day. The country no longer existed. There were no definite frontiers and there were no frontier guards or troops. The country had been broken up into four occupied zones.

President Truman said that he still thought the right plan would be to take 1937 Germany as a starting point.

Mr. Churchill said that he agreed with this suggestion.

Premier Stalin said that as a starting point, or hypothesis, he would accept the 1937 frontiers of Germany.

The Conference:

> Agreed to proceed on the basis that the 1937 frontiers of Germany would be taken as a starting point.

Further discussions ensued about the section of the United States Memorandum (P. (Terminal) 3)[6] dealing with the political authority of the Control Commission for Germany.

Mr. Byrnes explained that although certain drafting amendments were being considered by a sub-committee, there was no reason why points of substance should not be discussed that afternoon.

Premier Stalin said that the Russian Delegation accepted all the main points in the political section of the Memorandum. They had, however, one

[6] See No. 170, note 2.

amendment to suggest to paragraph 5, the last sentence of which they would propose should be omitted. This read as follows:

'Those Germans who are permitted to remain in or are appointed to official posts (*e.g.*, in the Police or the administration) should understand they hold office only during good behaviour.'

MR. BYRNES said the Foreign Secretaries had agreed to omit this sentence.

PREMIER STALIN said that he agreed the rest of the document, but would like another chance of going through the draft.

MR EDEN said that the Foreign Secretaries would take the matter up on the following morning and would report to the Plenary session in the afternoon.

PREMIER STALIN agreed to this course.

MR. CHURCHILL referred to paragraph 2(i)(*b*) which dealt with the destruction of arms, ammunition and implements of war and all specialised facilities for their production. He said that there were a number of experimental establishments in Germany which were of great value. He instanced great wind tunnels for testing aircraft. Such establishments should not be destroyed unless it was decided that the Allies had no use for them.

It was explained that at the meeting of Foreign Secretaries it had been arranged that the Drafting Committee should consider an amendment of this paragraph.

Later in the meeting Mr. Churchill again referred to the weight of the political principles embodied in the United States draft. He would like to be sure that it was the intention that there should be a uniform system throughout the four zones, rather than different practices prevailing in each zone.

PREMIER STALIN said the understanding of the Soviet Government was that all the three Great Powers favoured the adoption of a uniform policy.

MR. CHURCHILL said that he only wished to emphasise this matter because of its great importance.

The Conference:

Adopted the Report of the Committee of Foreign Ministers quoted at the beginning of this minute, subject to the conclusion recorded above that the 1937 frontiers of Germany would be taken as a starting point.

5. *Poland*

MR BYRNES read the following report from the Foreign Secretaries:

'The Foreign Ministers agreed that they would recommend that the Heads of Governments discuss at this afternoon's meeting the Polish question. They suggested two aspects of this question as requiring consideration: (1) all of the various problems connected with the liquidation of the former London Polish Government; and (2) the questions connected with the continued implementation of the Yalta Declaration on Poland, especially the arrangements for the early holding of free and unfettered elections.'

PREMIER STALIN handed in a draft 'Statement of the Heads of the three

Governments on the Polish Question' prepared by the Soviet Delegation.[7]
This read as follows:

'In view of the setting up on the basis of the decisions of the Crimea Conference of the Provisional Polish Government of National Unity and in view of the establishment by the United States of America and by Great Britain of diplomatic relations with Poland, which previously already existed between Poland and the Soviet Union, we agreed that the Governments of Great Britain and the United States of America as well as the Governments of other United Nations shall sever all relations with the Government of Arzishevsky [Arciszewski]. We deem it imperative to render to the Provisional Polish Government of National Unity the necessary assistance in the immediate transmission to it of all stock, assets, and all other property belonging to Poland, which still is at the disposal of the Government of Arzishevsky and its organs, in whatever form this property may be and no matter where or at whose disposal this property may prove to be at the present moment. The transfer of this property to any institution of any kind or to private persons is forbidden.

'We also found it necessary that the Polish armed forces, including the Navy and the Merchant Marine, now subordinated to the Government of Arzishevsky, should be subordinated to the Provisional Polish Government of National Unity, which will determine the further measures to be taken in respect of these armed forces, men-of-war and merchant ships.'

MR. CHURCHILL said that the burden of this matter lay on British shoulders. When their homeland had been overrun and they had been driven from France, the Poles had sheltered upon our shores. There was no property of any worthwhile size belonging to the Polish Government in London; there was, however, he believed, about £20,000,000 in gold in London and Canada. This had been frozen by us since it was an asset of the Central Bank of Poland. The question of unfreezing this sum and moving it to a Central Polish Bank must follow the normal channels for such transfers. This sum was not in the possession of the Polish Government in London who had had no power to draw upon it. Mr. Churchill added that there was, of course, the Polish Embassy in London which had been vacated by M. Raczynski and which was open and available for use by a Polish Ambassador as soon as the new Polish Government cared to send one—and the sooner the better.

In view of this, one might well ask how the Polish Government had been financed during their 5½ years in London. The answer was that this had been done by the British Government; we had paid the Poles about £120,000,000 to finance their Army and Diplomatic Service, and to enable them to look after Poles who had sought refuge on our shores from the German scourge. When the Polish Government in London was disavowed by His Majesty's Government, and the new provisional Polish Government recognised, it

[7] Printed in *Berlinskaya konferentsiya*, pp. 318–9.

was arranged that three months' salary should be paid to all employees and that they should then be dismissed. It would have been improper to have dismissed them without this payment, and the expense of this measure fell upon Great Britain.

Mr. Churchill then asked the indulgence of the President to unfold an important matter, because our position with regard to it was unique—namely, the liquidation or transfer to their homeland of the Polish forces that had fought with us in the war. On the fall of France, we had evacuated from France all those Poles who wished to come (some 40,000–50,000), and built up from these men, and from others who had come through Switzerland and elsewhere, a Polish Army, which in all had reached finally the strength of some 5 divisions. There were now about 30,000 Polish troops in Germany, and a Polish Corps of 3 divisions in Italy in a highly excited state of mind and grave mental and moral distress. This Army, totalling, from front to rear, some 180,000–200,000 men, had fought with great bravery and good discipline, both here in Germany and, on a larger scale, in Italy. These latter had suffered severe losses and had held their positions with as much steadfastness as any troops employed on the Italian front. Mr. Churchill, therefore, made it perfectly clear that this matter involved the honour of His Majesty's Government. These troops had fought gallantly side by side with ours, at a time when trained troops had been scarce. Many had died by our side, and even if he had not given pledges in Parliament, which he had, we would wish to treat them honourably.

Premier Stalin said he agreed.

The Prime Minister continued that these men had taken oath to President Raczkiewicz,[8] whom we had, of course, ceased to recognise. It was, therefore, necessary for Mr. Churchill to state what the policy was that we were pursuing towards them.

Our policy was to persuade as many as possible, not only of the soldiers but also of the civilian employees of the late Polish Government, to go back to Poland. Mr. Churchill had been disturbed to learn General Anders had announced to his troops in Italy[9] that, if they went back to Poland, they would probably be sent to Siberia. Disciplinary action would be taken against this officer and he would certainly not be allowed to make such prejudicial statements to his troops. We must, however, have a little time to get over our difficulties.

He took this opportunity to rejoice in the great improvements in Poland over the last two months, and to express his cordial hopes for the success of the new Government, which, although not all that we could wish, had been a great advance and was the result of the patient work of the three Great

[8] President of the Polish Republic, 1939–45.

[9] General Wladyslaw Anders had been commander of the Polish forces in the Middle East and Italy, 1942–45, and Commander-in-Chief of the Polish armed forces, February–June 1945. The reference was apparently to General Anders' order of the day of 6 July 1945 printed in General W. Anders, *An Army in Exile* (London, 1949), pp. 276–8.

Powers. He had said in the House of Commons[10] that if there were Polish soldiers who had fought at our side and did not want to go back, we would take them into the British Empire. Of course, the better conditions were in Poland, the more Poles would go back. It would assist if the new Polish Government could give an undertaking that those who did return to Poland would do so with the assurance of their livelihood and freedom, and that they would not be victimised for their former allegiance.

Mr. Churchill's hope was that with continued improvement in Poland, the bulk of these people would return and become good citizens of the land of their fathers which had been liberated by the bravery of Russian armies. He suggested that the meeting might discuss this aspect of the question.

PREMIER STALIN asked whether Mr. Churchill had read the draft circulated by the Russian Delegation.

MR. CHURCHILL answered that he had, and that subject to what he had just said, he agreed with it in principle. He suggested that it should be remitted to the Foreign Secretaries.

PREMIER STALIN said that he appreciated the difficult position in which the British Government were situated. He knew that the British Government had sheltered the former rulers of Poland in England and that in spite of this hospitality they had caused the British Government many difficulties. He would like Mr. Churchill to believe him when he said that the Russian draft statement was not designed to make those difficulties greater. The Government of M. Arzishevski, however, continued to exist in London; they had means to continue their activities with the Press and elsewhere, and they had their agents. This made a bad impression on all Allied countries. The object of the draft put forward by the Soviet Delegation was to put an end to this. If Mr. Churchill thought that some items of the draft would complicate the issue he was quite prepared to omit them.

MR. CHURCHILL said that we were in entire agreement with the Marshal. The former Polish Government was non-existent and liquidated in the official diplomatic sense; we had severed all connection with them and they would get no help from us. Nevertheless when a Government is dissolved it is not possible in England to prevent its individual members living and talking to people, to for instance, journalists, and their former contacts. Moreover, we had to be careful about the Army, for if the situation was mishandled, there might be mutiny. Our purpose was exactly the same as that of the Marshal. His Majesty's Government asked for the Marshal's trust and confidence and a reasonable time for making the necessary arrangements. He also asked that everything possible should be done to make Poland an encouraging place for the Poles to return to.

In conclusion the Prime Minister said that we should be quite willing for the draft of the Soviet Delegation to be examined by the three Foreign Secretaries in the light of this discussion, and in the light of a paper in more detail that the Foreign Secretary would circulate.

[10] On 14 March 1945: *Parl. Debs., 5th ser., H. of C.,* vol. 409, cols. 224–5.

Summing up, PRESIDENT TRUMAN said that he saw no fundamental difference of opinion: the Prime Minister was asking for a reasonable amount of time and Premier Stalin had undertaken to omit any item on his draft which might complicate the issue. He was therefore of the opinion that if the Foreign Secretaries looked the document through, there would be no difficulty.

Turning to the second aspect of the Polish question for discussion, The President said that he was most anxious for the principle of the Yalta Agreement to be implemented as soon as possible.

PREMIER STALIN suggested that the whole matter should be referred to the Foreign Secretaries.

MR. CHURCHILL said that the Foreign Secretaries might deal with the question of elections also.

PRESIDENT TRUMAN agreed that the Foreign Secretaries should deal with the whole matter.

MR. CHURCHILL suggested that the Foreign Secretaries might try to produce a new draft, covering all the essential points.

PREMIER STALIN said that the Provisional Polish Government had never refused to hold free elections.

The Conference–

Accordingly agreed to refer the whole matter to the Foreign Secretaries.

Cabinet Office, Potsdam, 18th July, 1945

CALENDARS TO NO. 184

i   *18–19 July 1945   Brief for Prime Minister for above meeting:* proposed Council of Foreign Ministers; representation of France and China. Minutes by Mr. Ward and Sir A. Cadogan [F.O. 934/3/16(3–4)].

ii   *18 July 1945   Briefs for Prime Minister on Poland: (a)* Fulfilment of the Crimea decisions; the three Powers should place on record their views on free elections in Poland. *(b)* Liquidation of Polish Government in London [F.O. 934/2/10 (6–7)].

iii   *18 July 1945   Letter from Sir O. Sargent to General Sir A. Nye, Vice-Chief of the Imperial General Staff.* Encloses translation of the order of the day referred to in note 9 above. Prevention of issue of such Polish orders of the day to be considered [N 8419/123/55].

No. 185

Record of a private talk between the Prime Minister and Generalissimo Stalin at dinner on 18 July 1945 at Potsdam[1]

[F.O. 181/1009/6]

Top secret

The following is a very fair summary of some of the salient points. The

[1] This record, amended by Mr. Churchill (on PREM 3/430/6), was made by Major Birse: for this conversation see W. S. Churchill, *op. cit.*, vol. vi, p. 548 f., also J. Ehrman, *op. cit.*, vol. vi, p. 303.

conversations lasted from 8.30 p.m. till 1.30 a.m., and were thoroughly informal and genuinely friendly. It did not seem that any notes were taken by M. Pavlov to help him in his translations.

1. *General Election in England.* MARSHAL STALIN suggested that the Prime Minister would have a majority of about 80. He thought the Labour Party would receive 220–230 votes. The Prime Minister was not sure how the soldiers had voted, but the Marshal said that an Army preferred a strong Government and would therefore vote for the Conservatives.

Marshal Stalin asked why King George was not coming to Berlin, and the Prime Minister replied that it was because his visit would add to the security problem.

Marshal Stalin then volunteered the following: that no country needed a Monarchy so much as Great Britain, because the Crown was the unifying force throughout the Empire, and that no one who was a friend of Britain would do anything to weaken the respect shown to the Monarchy.

2. THE PRIME MINISTER said he would be going home[2] for one day after the meeting on July 25.

The Prime Minister asked what Marshal Stalin thought of President Truman as Chairman of the Conference. He himself thought the President was doing well. MARSHAL STALIN replied that it was too early to say.

3. *Japan.* Marshal Stalin showed the Prime Minister the Soviet Government's reply[3] to the Mikado's message. In their reply, the Soviet Government stated that as the Mikado's message had been in general terms and contained no concrete proposals, the Soviet Government could take no action.

From Marshal Stalin's further statements, it was evident that Russia intends to attack Japan soon after August 8. (The Marshal thought it might be a fortnight later.)

4. THE PRIME MINISTER said that it was his policy to welcome Russia as a great power on the sea. He wished to see Russian ships sailing across the oceans of the world. Russia had been like a giant with his nostrils pinched: this referred to the narrow exits from the Baltic and the Black Sea.

The Prime Minister brought up the question of Turkey and the Dardanelles. He said the Turks were very frightened. MARSHAL STALIN explained what had happened: the Turks had approached the Russians with regard to a treaty of alliance. In reply the Russians had said that there could be a treaty only if neither side had any claims. Russia however claimed Kars and Ardahan, which had been taken away from her at the end of the last War. The Turks then said that they could not discuss this claim. Russia then raised the question of the Montreux Convention. Turkey said she could not discuss it, so Russia replied that she could not discuss a treaty of alliance.

THE PRIME MINISTER said that he personally would support an amendment

---

[2] In connection with the declaration of the results of the British general election.
[3] A text of this Soviet note of 18 July 1945 is printed in *F.R.U.S. Berlin*, vol. ii, p. 1251.

to the Montreux Convention, throwing out Japan and giving Russia access to the Mediterranean. He repeated that he welcomed Russia's appearance on the oceans, and this referred not only to the Dardanelles but also to the Kiel Canal, which should have a régime like the Suez Canal, and to the warm waters of the Pacific. This was not out of gratitude for anything Russia had done, but his settled policy.

THE MARSHAL brought up the question of the German Fleet. He said that a share of it would be most useful for Russia, who had suffered severe losses at sea. He was grateful to the Prime Minister for the ships delivered in connection with the surrender of the Italian Navy, but he would like his share of the German ships.

5. Marshal Stalin spoke of Greek aggression on the Bulgarian and Albanian frontiers. He said there were elements in Greece which were stirring up trouble.

THE PRIME MINISTER said that the situation on the frontier was confused, and that the Greeks were grievously alarmed at the Yugoslav and Bulgarian attitude. He had not heard of any fighting worthy of the name. He thought that the Conference should make its will plain to these small Powers, and that none should be allowed to trespass or fight. They should be told this plainly and that any alteration in the frontier lines could only be settled at the Peace Conference. Greece was to have a plebiscite and free elections, and he suggested that observers should be sent to Athens by the Great Powers. MARSHAL STALIN thought that the presence of observers would show a want of confidence in the honesty of the Greek people. He thought that the Ambassadors of the Great Powers should report on the elections.

6. Marshal Stalin asked what were the Prime Minister's views about Hungary? THE PRIME MINISTER replied that he was not sufficiently informed upon the subject to give a view on the immediate situation, but he would enquire of the Foreign Secretary.

MARSHAL STALIN said that in all the countries liberated by the Red Army, the Russian policy was to see a strong, independent, sovereign State. He was against Sovietization of any of those countries. They would have free elections, and all except Fascist parties would participate.

7. *Yugoslavia.* THE PRIME MINISTER spoke of the difficulties in Yugoslavia, where we had no material ambitions, but there had been the 50–50 arrangement.[4] It was now 99–1 against Britain. Marshal Stalin protested that it was 90 per cent. British, 10 per cent. Yugoslavian, and 0 per cent. Russian interests. In reply to the Prime Minister's remarks, he said that Marshal Tito had the partisan mentality and had done several things he ought not

[4] At Anglo-Soviet conversations in Moscow in October 1944 Mr. Churchill and Marshal Stalin had reached a rough agreement on a percentage basis for a division of Allied predominance in the Balkans. The proportions were to be on a 'fifty-fifty basis' in Yugoslavia and Hungary, 90 percent to Russia in Roumania, 90 percent to Great Britain in Greece and 75 percent to Russia in Bulgaria: cf. W. S. Churchill, *op. cit.*, vol. vi, pp. 198 and 201–4, and Sir L. Woodward, *op. cit.*, vol. iii, pp. 150–3, for subsequent modification of certain of these numerical approximations.

to have done. The Soviet Government often did not know what Marshal Tito was about to do.

8. *Roumania.* MARSHAL STALIN said that he had been hurt by the American demand for a change of Government in Roumania and Bulgaria.[5] He was not meddling in Greek affairs, so he thought it was unjust of the Americans to make the present demand. The Prime Minister said he had not before seen the American proposals. Marshal Stalin explained that in the case of countries where there had been an émigré government, he had found it necessary to assist in the creation of a home government. This of course did not apply in the case of Roumania and Bulgaria. Everything was peaceful in those two countries. THE PRIME MINISTER asked why the Soviet Government had given an award to King Michael. THE MARSHAL thought King Michael had acted bravely and wisely at the time of the *coup d'état.*[6]

9. THE PRIME MINISTER spoke of the anxiety felt by some people with regard to Russia's intentions. He drew a line from the North Cape to Albania, and named the capitals east of that line which were in Russian hands. It looked as if Russia were rolling on westwards. MARSHAL STALIN said he had no such intention. On the contrary, he was withdrawing troops from the West. Two million men would be demobilized and sent home within the next four months. Further demobilization was only a question of adequate railway transport.

10. MARSHAL STALIN mentioned that Russian losses during the War had amounted to 5 million killed and missing. The Germans had mobilized 18 million men apart from industry, and the Russians 12 million.

11. THE PRIME MINISTER hoped that agreement would be reached both as regards the questions connected with frontiers of all the European countries as well as Russia's access to the seas, including the division of the German Fleet, before the Conference ended. He said that the Three Powers gathered round the table were the strongest the world had ever seen, and it was their task to maintain the peace of the world.

It was agreed that, although satisfactory to us, the German defeat had been a great tragedy. But the Germans were like sheep. The Prime Minister told the story of young Lieutenant Tirpitz.[7] MARSHAL STALIN spoke of his experience in Germany in 1907, when two hundred Germans missed a Communist meeting because there was no-one to take their railway tickets at the station barrier.

12. Marshal Stalin apologised for not having officially thanked Great Britain for her help in the way of supplies during the War. This would be done.

---

[5] See No. 82, paragraphs 3–4.

[6] King Michael of Roumania was presented with the Soviet Order of Victory by Marshal Tolbukhin in Bucharest on 19 July 1945. For the *coup d'état* of February 1945 in Roumania, cf. No. 62, paragraph 7.

[7] The reference is uncertain.

13. Marshal Stalin, in reply to a question, explained the working of Collective and State farms. It was agreed that both in Russia and Britain there was no fear of unemployment. The Marshal said that Russia was ready to talk about Anglo-Russian trade. THE PRIME MINISTER said that the best publicity for Soviet Russia abroad, would be the happiness and well-being of her people. The Marshal spoke of the continuity of Soviet policy. If anything were to happen to him, there would be good men ready to step into his shoes. He was thinking thirty years ahead.

No. 186

Report by the British Joint Planning Staff
J.S. (Terminal) 9 (Final) [CAB 99/39]

Top secret   BABELSBERG, *18 July 1945*

Basic Objectives and Undertakings

As instructed,[1] we have redrafted the proposed memorandum by the British Chiefs of Staff.[2] We have consulted the Ministry of War Transport and we understand that Lord Leathers approves the memorandum in this form.

G. GRANTHAM
G. S. THOMPSON
W. L. DAWSON

ANNEX TO No. 186

Memorandum by the British Chiefs of Staff
Basic Objectives, Strategy and Policies

We have considered the latest proposals of the United States Chiefs of Staff in C.C.S. 877/2.[3] In the attached schedule we have set out in one column the

---

[1] *Note in filed copy:* 'C.O.S. (Terminal) 3rd Meeting', not printed. This third meeting at Babelsberg of the British Chiefs of Staff Committee, held at 39–41 Ringstrasse at 10.30 a.m. on 18 July 1945, had in particular approved the circulation of No. 182 and had 'had under consideration a memorandum by the Minister of War Transport in which he [Lord Leathers] stated that he did not agree that the version of the basic objectives and undertakings suggested by the British Chiefs of Staff in C.C.S. 877/3 [see note 2 below] adequately protected the British position. He pointed out that the question to be settled was whether the new basic objectives and undertakings should or should not include civil programmes and that when that point had been decided consequential amendments should be made. The Committee also had under consideration a minute from the Prime Minister in which he insisted that the United Kingdom import programme should be protected in the list of basic undertakings' (cf. No. 218, note 8). In the light of the above the Chiefs of Staff Committee instructed the Joint Planning Staff, in consultation with the Ministry of War Transport, to prepare a revised list of basic objectives and undertakings.

[2] *Note in filed copy:* 'C.C.S. 877/3'. This proposed memorandum of 16 July 1945 is not printed.

[3] Not here printed. This memorandum of 10 July 1945 is printed in *F.R.U.S. Berlin*, vol. i, pp. 913–4.

document as proposed by the United States Chiefs of Staff, together with the amendments which we should like to see introduced. In the right-hand column we set out our comments.

2. We recommend that the Combined Chiefs of Staff adopt the basic objectives, strategy and policies as amended in the attached, and incorporate them in the Final Report of the 'Terminal' Conference.

ENCLOSURE

Basic Objectives and Undertakings

Memorandum by United States Chiefs of Staff with Proposed Amendments by British Chiefs of Staff	*Comments by British Chiefs of Staff*
The agreed summary of broad principles regarding the prosecution of the war, set forth in C.C.S. 776/3.[4] was based upon the agreed concept that Germany was the prinicipal enemy. The unconditional surrender of Germany, and the vital importance of rapidly reorienting strength so that the maximum possible effort may now be brought to bear against Japan, make it desirable that this summary of broad principles be revised in consonance with the changed situation. Acceptance now of these principles will establish appropriate emphasis on the war against Japan, while taking cognizance of the changed situation in the European Theatre. Accordingly, the United States Chiefs of Staff recommend that the Combined Chiefs of Staff approve the following statements of basic objectives, strategy and policies.	

I.—*Overall Objective*

In conjunction with other Allies to bring about at the earliest possible date the unconditional surrender of Japan.

II.—*Overall Strategic Concept for the Prosecution of the War*

2. In co-operation with other Allies to establish and maintain, as necessary, military control of Germany and Austria.

---

[4] This report by the Combined Chiefs of Staff of their agreed summary of conclusions reached at the Yalta Conference, submitted to President Roosevelt and Mr. Churchill on 9 February 1945, is printed in *F.R.U.S. The Conferences at Malta and Yalta 1945*, pp. 827–33.

3. In co-operation with other Allies to bring about at the earliest possible date the defeat of Japan by: lowering Japanese ability and will to resist by establishing sea and air blockades, conducting intensive air bombardment, and destroying Japanese air and naval strength; invading and seizing objectives in the Japanese Home Islands as the main effort; conducting such operations against objectives in other than the Japanese Home Islands as will contribute to the main effort; establishing absolute military control of Japan; and liberating Japanese-occupied territory if required.

III.—*Basic Undertakings and Policies for the Prosecution of the War*

4. ~~The following basic undertakings are considered fundamental to the prosecution of the war.~~[6]

The following established basic undertakings will be a first charge against resources:

~~A.—Maintain the security of the Western Hemisphere and the British Commonwealth.~~

~~B.—Maintain the war-making capacity of the United States and the British Isles in so far as it is connected with the prosecution of this war.~~[6]

A. *Maintain the capacity of the Western Hemisphere and the British Commonwealth successfully to prosecute the war against Japan and to enforce the military control of Germany and Austria, and enable them to fulfil their obligations for world security.*

B. ~~C.~~[6] Support the war-making capacity of our forces, in all areas, with first priority given to those forces in *or destined for* combat areas.

C. ~~D~~[6] Maintain vital overseas lines of communication.

We fully agree that the first priority should be given to the main operations against the Japanese Islands.

We trust, however, that other operations in the Outer Zone,[5] which will achieve the secondary object of evicting the Japanese from all occupied territories, will receive the fullest possible consideration.

Our proposed wording is based on paragraph 6 of C.C.S. 776/3.[4]

The wording of paragraph 4B as proposed by the United States Chiefs of Staff does not allow for the maintenance of the war-making capacity of such countries as Canada, India or Australia, all of which are making an important contribution towards the prosecution of the war. War-making capacity cannot be confined solely to that required for the defeat of Japan, since it is also necessary to meet the requirements for military control of Germany and Austria, as stated in the overall strategic concept for the prosecution of the war, and for the preservation of world security.

If first priority is given only to the support of the war-making capacity of forces in the combat areas, this might lead to the withholding of priority from the forces destined to relieve or support

[5] The area comprising those territories still under Japanese occupation outside the Japanese home islands.

[6] Deletion as in filed copy.

D. *Restore the capacity of European liberated areas to fulfil their obligations for the prosecution of the war against Japan, for the military control of Germany and Austria, and for the creation and maintenance of European order in the interests of the war effort.*

5. In order to attain the overall objective, first priority in the provision of forces and resources of the United States and Great Britain, including re-orientation from the European Theatre to the Pacific and Far East, will be given to meeting requirements of tasks necessary to the execution of the overall strategic concept and to the basic undertakings ~~fundamental to the prosecution of the war.~~[6]

The invasion of Japan and operations directly connected therewith are the supreme operations in the war against Japan; forces and resources will be allocated on the required scale to assure that invasion can be accomplished at the earliest practicable date. No other operations will be undertaken which hazard the success of, or delay, these main operations.

6. The following additional tasks will be undertaken in order to assist in the execution of the overall strategic concept:

A. Encourage Russian entry into the war against Japan. Provide such aid to her war-making capacity as may be necessary and practicable in connection therewith.

B. Undertake such measures as may be necessary and practicable in order to aid the war effort of China as an effective ally against Japan.

them. For example, the forces in India are required for maintaining the forces in active operations and providing reinforcements. As is known, many installations supporting the operations in S.E.A.C. are outside those areas which can strictly be termed combat areas. Unless these requirements are recognised, the war-making capacity of forces in combat areas will be jeopardised.

This is consequential upon the amendment suggested to the first sentence of paragraph 4 above.

393

C. Provide assistance to such of the forces of liberated areas as can fulfil an active and effective role in the present war—*or are required to maintain world order in the interests of the war effort*. Within the limits of our available resources assist co-belligerents to the extent they are able to employ this assistance in the present war.

~~Having regard to the successful accomplishment of basic undertakings, to provide such supplies to the liberated areas as will effectively contribute to the capacity of the United Nations to prosecute the present war.~~ [6]

D. In co-operation with other Allies conduct operations, if required, to liberate enemy-occupied areas.

The present wording would appear to limit this assistance strictly to those forces which can take part in the war against Japan. We feel, however, that the necessity for the maintenance of world order, particularly in Europe, must be recognised. Having brought about the liberation of Europe, it would be illogical to allow unrest to occur owing to lack of forces in the liberated areas to keep order.

The last sentence is unnecessary as it is already covered by the proposed 4D.

No. 187

Minutes of a Meeting of the British Chiefs of Staff Committee held at 39/41 Ring Strasse, Babelsberg, on Thursday 19 July 1945 at 10.30 a.m.

C.O.S.(*Terminal*)4*th Meeting* [*CAB 99/39*]

Top secret

Present:
FIELD-MARSHAL SIR ALAN F. BROOKE, Chief of the Imperial General Staff (*in the Chair*), Marshal of the Royal Air Force Sir Charles F. A. Portal, Chief of the Air Staff, Admiral of the Fleet Sir Andrew B. Cunningham, First Sea Lord and Chief of Naval Staff, General Sir Hastings L. Ismay, Office of the Minister of Defence.

The following were also present:
The Right Hon. Lord Leathers, Minister of War Transport (*for Item 1*). Field-Marshal Sir Henry Maitland Wilson, Major-General R. E. Laycock, Chief of Combined Operations, Lieut.-General Sir James Gammell (*for Item 2*), Lieut.-General Sir Gordon Macready, Major-General N. G. Holmes, War Office.

Secretariat:
Major-General L. C. Hollis, Brigadier A. T. Cornwall-Jones, Lieut.-Colonel G. Mallaby, Lieut.-Colonel T. Haddon.

1. *Basic Objectives and Undertakings*
(J.S. (Terminal) 9 (Final).)[1]
(Previous Reference: C.O.S. (Terminal) 3rd Meeting, Minute 3.)[2]

THE COMMITTEE had under consideration a revised draft by the Joint Planning Staff of the memorandum on basic objectives and undertakings.

LORD LEATHERS explained that though he himself was satisfied with the wording suggested by the Joint Planning Staff, he could not guarantee that it would meet the requirements of the Prime Minister. He stated that at the request of the Treasury he had called a meeting for 2.30 p.m. that afternoon at which Lord Cherwell would be present and also a representative of the Treasury. He hoped that as a result of this meeting, he would be able to say whether it would be correct for the Chiefs of Staff to table the proposed memorandum.

SIR ALAN BROOKE pointed out the difficulty in which the Chiefs of Staff were being put. They would have preferred to have confined the paper to military requirements only, but now it was apparently being widened to embrace the requirements of various non-military departments, including the Treasury. He said the Chiefs of Staff could not have sufficient knowledge of the various interests involved to defend the British version of this document adequately in Combined Chiefs of Staff discussion, and it was evident from the proposed wording that it would be difficult to get American agreement.

SIR ANDREW CUNNINGHAM suggested that if the paper were to cover such wide issues, it would be better if it were sponsored by the civilian departments.

LORD LEATHERS explained that demands on shipping came from both military and non-military departments and it was desirable that all shipping requirements should be covered by the proposed document. In any case, it was the Prime Minister's instruction that the United Kingdom import programme should be protected. This was particularly important in view of the increase in the import programme which was likely to take place.

SIR CHARLES PORTAL pointed out that whereas before the defeat of Germany it had been possible to protect civil requirements by the comprehensive phrase 'maintain the war-making capacity, &c.,' this was no longer the case, and there was now a sharp cleavage between what was required for the prosecution of the war against Japan and what was required for the revival of Europe. The Chiefs of Staff had not sufficient knowledge to argue the latter requirement.

SIR ALAN BROOKE entirely agreed and pointed out as an example that this was the first occasion on which the Chiefs of Staff had heard anything about an increase in the United Kingdom import programme.

Turning to the actual wording of the proposed draft, LORD LEATHERS said he had only two suggestions to make:

(*a*) To change the wording of paragraph 4A to make it clear that it was

---

[1] No. 186.　　　　[2] See No. 186, note 1.

the Western Hemisphere and the British Commonwealth who were required to fulfil their obligations for world security.

(b) To substitute the word 'establishment' for 'preservation' in the last sentence of the Chiefs of Staff comment on paragraph 4A.

SIR ALAN BROOKE asked why it was necessary to return to the 'Argonaut'[3] wording in the lead-in sentence to paragraph 4 and suggested that the wording proposed by the Americans was more in line with the heading of this section of the paper.

LORD LEATHERS said that although he thought the American wording too limiting, he was prepared to admit it if necessary. He said that he would let the Chiefs of Staff know the result of his afternoon meeting and whether it was acceptable to circulate the memorandum.

SIR HASTINGS ISMAY said that as the Treasury and Lord Cherwell now proposed to take a hand in this question, it would be desirable for the Chiefs of Staff to be represented at their meeting and he proposed, if Lord Leathers had no objection, that General Macready should represent the Chiefs of Staff.

LORD LEATHERS concurred.

THE COMMITTEE–

Instructed the Secretary to withhold the proposed memorandum from circulation until Lord Leathers reported the result of his meeting with Lord Cherwell, the Treasury and General Macready. If no substantial amendments were required as a result of that meeting, the report should be issued as a memorandum by the British Chiefs of Staff. If substantial amendments were required, the question should be referred again to the Chiefs of Staff Committee.

2. *Future of No. 30 Military Mission*
(C.O.S. (45) 462 (O).)[4]
(Previous Reference: C.O.S. (45) 176th Meeting, Minute 3.)[4]

THE COMMITTEE considered an aide-mémoire by the War Office on the future of No. 30 Military Mission in Moscow. This aide-mémoire pointed out that there were three possible methods of dealing with this question:

(a) To withdraw the Mission leaving it to the Russians to follow whatever they liked regarding their own Mission in London.

(b) To secure a mutual withdrawal of Missions from Moscow and London, and arrange for the exchange of senior officers for specific purposes if and when the need arose.

(c) To maintain the Mission in Moscow, leaving General Gammell free to make any temporary reduction he may think desirable.

SIR ALAN BROOKE asked General Gammell whether he knew what attitude the Americans were adopting with regard to their Mission.

[3] Code-name of the Conference at Yalta: see No. 186, note 4.
[4] Not printed.

General Gammell said that he believed the Americans would have withdrawn their Mission but for the chance of Russia entering the war against Japan. He said they had been examining a reorganisation of their Military Attaché's Department, in case the Mission were withdrawn. He pointed out, however, that the American Mission in Moscow handled lend-lease business and, therefore, had more responsibility than the British Mission. He suggested that one of the reasons for the suspicion with which the Russians regarded the British Mission was their lack of activity. They could not understand why highly-placed British officers should be kept in Moscow.

Sir Alan Brooke said that if the Americans withdrew their Mission and reverted to the conduct of business by Military Attachés, we could do the same but not otherwise.

Sir Charles Portal agreed with this view and felt sure that if we took the lead in withdrawing our Mission, the Americans would not follow it. He enquired at what stage the Americans thought it would be acceptable to withdraw their Mission.

General Gammell said that he thought there was no question of withdrawing the American Mission until either the end of the war against Japan or the cessation of lend-lease arrangements.

Sir Andrew Cunningham said it was most important that we should continue to be represented by a Mission in Moscow for the duration of the Japanese war.

General Gammell explained the difficulties the Mission had in making either official or personal contacts and emphasised that it was only to transient visitors that the Russians were at all forthcoming.

Sir Alan Brooke said that while the Chiefs of Staff appreciated the difficulties and the sense of frustration which the Mission had, it was essential to retain it as long as the Americans kept their Mission.

The Committee–

Decided to maintain the Mission in Moscow, leaving General Gammell free to make any small reductions he thought desirable without informing the Russians.[5]

3. *Move of Dutch Forces to the Far East*
(Previous Reference: C.O.S. (Terminal) 3rd Meeting, Minute 4.)[4]

Sir Hastings Ismay reported that he had received a telegram[6] from General Galloway repeating a message from the Head of S.H.A.E.F.

[5] A copy of this minute (on N 9159/2/38) was minuted in the Foreign Office as follows: 'It does not look as if S/S took action on our memo.[N 8681/2/38] suggesting that the advantages of reverting to Attachés shd. be pressed on the C.O.S. I see no reason why we shd. retain a useless Mission just because the Americans do. However—it is not of the first importance. C. F. A. Warner. 21/7.' 'O. G. Sargent July 21.'

[6] *Note in filed copy:* 'Annex', not printed. This undated telegram from General A. Galloway, Commander of Netherlands District of 21st Army Group, was as indicated below, with reference to the Dutch Minister-President, Professor W. Schermerhorn, who had recently succeeded Dr. P. S. Gerbrandy.

Mission to the Netherlands to the effect that the Dutch authorities were most anxious to send Dutch reinforcements to the Far East and that the Dutch Minister Resident [President] and Doctor Gerbrandy were anxious to come to 'Terminal' to plead the case personally with the Prime Minister and the President.

THE COMMITTEE–

Invited General Ismay to reply to General Galloway pointing out that the Head of the S.H.A.E.F. Mission to the Netherlands should not handle such questions but should advise that they should be dealt with by diplomatic channels.

4. *Command in Indo-China*
(Previous Reference: C.O.S. (45) 158th Meeting, Minute 2.)[4]

THE COMMITTEE were informed that the Joint Planning Staff were examining the suggestion of the United States Chiefs of Staff, that Indo-China should be divided into two parts for the purpose of operational command and would report.

5. *British Participation in the War against Japan*
(C.C.S. 889/2.)[7]
(Previous Reference: C.O.S. (Terminal) 2nd Meeting, Minute 6.)[8]

THE COMMITTEE instructed the Joint Planning Staff to examine and report on a memorandum by the United States Chiefs of Staff[9] giving extracts of a message from General MacArthur concerning British participation in the war against Japan.

6. *Lend-Lease in Stage II*
(C.O.S. (Terminal) 2.)[10]
(Previous Reference: C.O.S. (45) 177th Meeting, Minute 11.)[11]

THE COMMITTEE had under consideration the following papers:
(*a*) A Minute by the Prime Minister, Serial No. D (T) 3/5.[12]
(*b*) Extract from a Memorandum by the President dated 17th July, 1945.[13]
(*c*) Extract from a letter from General Jacob dated 17th July, 1945[i].
(*d*) A brief prepared in accordance with C.O.S. (45) 176th Meeting, Conclusion 2(*b*) [ii].

---

[7] Not here printed. This memorandum of 18 July 1945 by the United States Chiefs of Staff is printed in *F.R.U.S. Berlin*, vol. ii, pp. 1336–7.

[8] Not printed. Cf. No. 172, note 1.

[9] *Note in filed copy:* 'C.C.S. 889/2': see note 7 above.

[10] Not printed. In this covering 'Note by Secretary', dated at Babelsberg on 18 July 1945, Major-General L. C. Hollis had circulated as annexes I—IV the four documents listed below.

[11] Of 16 July 1945, not printed. This short minute recorded that the Chiefs of Staff Committee had taken note of President Truman's directive of 5 July: see No. 26, note 4.

[12] No. 174.ii.

[13] This extract comprised the first two paragraphs of the annex to No. 174.

THE COMMITTEE—

Instructed a special sub-committee consisting of General Macready, Brigadier Cornwall-Jones and Colonel Norman, to examine these papers and to prepare for their approval a minute to the Prime Minister covering a revised memorandum to President Truman.

7. *Approval of Minutes of C.C.S. 195th Meeting*[14]

SIR ANDREW CUNNINGHAM recalled that the United States Chiefs of Staff had recommended at the meeting of the Combined Chiefs of Staff on the 18th July[15] that the word 'above' in the first line of page 3 of these minutes should be amended to read 'despatch of a corps commander and staff to the Pacific.' The minutes then went on to say that this despatch was acceptable to the United States Chiefs of Staff and that General MacArthur would be informed accordingly. Since it was recorded in Conclusion (*b*) on page 3 of the minutes[16] that appropriate commanders and staff should visit General MacArthur and Admiral Nimitz, there might be some doubt, in view of the United States Chiefs of Staff amendment, as to whether the appropriate staffs should discuss details with Admiral Nimitz. He (Sir Andrew Cunningham) undertook to consult Admiral King on this matter.

THE COMMITTEE—

(*a*) Took note that Sir Andrew Cunningham would discuss the matter with Admiral King.

(*b*) Approved the minutes of C.C.S. 195th Meeting.

8. *Directive to S.A.C.S.E.A.*
(J.S. (Terminal) 8 (Final) [iii].)

THE COMMITTEE had before them a draft Memorandum covering a draft directive to S.A.C.S.E.A. in the form of a paper for submission to the Combined Chiefs of Staff. A number of amendments were agreed upon.

THE COMMITTEE—

Approved the draft directive as amended, and instructed the Secretary to submit it for the Prime Minister's approval prior to reference to the Combined Chiefs of Staff.

Babelsberg, 19th July, 1945

CALENDARS TO NO. 187

i *17 July 1945 Extract from letter from General Jacob to General Sir H. Ismay.* Encloses ii below which should not 'be lightly tabled to the Americans'. Refers to recognition by U.S. War Department in Nov. 1944 of 'the necessity of giving us assignments for the task of occupying Axis countries in Europe': a statement 'clearly inconsistent with the idea either that Lend-Lease should

[14] No. 183.
[15] *Note in filed copy:* 'C.C.S. 195th Meeting, Minute 1': see No. 183, note 3.
[16] *Note in filed copy:* 'C.C.S. 194th Meeting, Minute 2': see No. 172, note 2.

be confined to what is required for direct use against Japan or that we should be forced to denude our forces of occupation of equipment that could be used against Japan before obtaining supplies on Lend-Lease' [CAB. 99/39].

ii *Undated draft brief for the Chiefs of Staff on Lend-Lease:* effect on British armed services of new U.S. lend-lease policy. Army and RAF likely to be most affected, particularly through dislocation of British aircraft production resulting among other things in 'grave shortage' of military transport aircraft for occupational forces in Europe and lines of communication in Middle East [CAB. 99/39].

iii *18 July 1945 Report by Joint Planning Staff J.S.(Terminal)8(Final).* Attaches draft C.O.S. memorandum covering draft directive to S.A.C.S.E.A. for circulation to C.C.S. Since views of Australian Government on proposed new organisation of command have not yet been received regrets it is not possible to suggest that directive be sent in draft to S.A.C.S.E.A. at once. (C.O.S. memorandum, as amended in minute 8 above, circulated as C.C.S. 892/1 of 20 July—see *F.R.U.S. Berlin*, vol. ii, pp. 1317–8, 1338–9—amended that day at C.C.S. 197th Meeting—*op. cit.*, p. 162—and re-circulated as C.C.S. 892/2: see *op. cit.*, pp. 1338–9, notes 5–9) [CAB. 99/39].

No. 188

Memorandum by the United Kingdom Delegation (Berlin)
[*F.O. 934/4/22(3)*].

[BERLIN,] *19 July 1945*

The Foreign Secretaries at their meeting this morning[1] have the following subjects on their agenda:

(1) *Germany—political questions.* The drafting Committee met last night and has virtually reached agreement.

(2) *Poland.* We have produced a paper[2] which incorporates the Russian draft[3] and the Secretary of State's letter to Mr. Byrnes.[4]

The Committee on German Economic Questions could not meet yesterday afternoon as arranged, since the Russians failed to turn up. Consequently German economic questions cannot figure on the agenda of the Foreign Ministers or the Big Three meeting today. It would probably be a mistake to raise the Polish western frontier or the transfer of German populations from Poland and Czechoslovakia until we are ready with the German economic question.

We have discussed with the Americans at the official level what other subjects might be suggested by the Foreign Ministers this morning for placing on the agenda of the Big Three in the afternoon. We have agreed with them the following order of priority:

[1] See No. 189.   [2] See No. 189, minute 4.
[3] See No. 184, minute 5.   [4] No. 159.

(3) *Yalta Declaration on liberated Europe.* This will be raised in connection with the paper put in by the President on July 17th (copy attached).[5] This paper raises the whole question of Russian behaviour in Eastern Europe. The Americans are willing to take the lead and it is very advantageous that they should. We might confine ourselves to supporting them in general terms. We have always been doubtful about the possibility of taking effective action under the Yalta Declaration, especially in view of the American interpretation that all three Governments must agree before action under it can be taken. But this does not prevent us from giving general support. We could also mention two further points:

(*a*) Russian depredations on our oil interests in Roumania.

(*b*) since we are in the Balkan area, Tito's behaviour in Yugoslavia and his non-fulfilment of the Tito-Subasic agreement.

(4) *Turkey.* The American delegation have not been able to put the case to Mr. Byrnes, though up to that level they are in full agreement with our views as expressed in the briefs[6] and would support us. It might therefore be better merely to hold this in reserve.

The Russians will probably again suggest putting the German fleet on the agenda. We might continue to stall. The Americans would probably support this.

CALENDARS TO No. 188

i   *19 July 1945   U.K. Delegation memorandum.* Variant version of No. 188 [F.O. 934/4/22(3)].

ii   *19 July 1945   Memorandum by Sir W. Strang (Berlin)* on German political questions: points raised in Drafting Committee on 18 July [F.O. 934/4/20(3)].

iii   *19 July 1945   Letter from Mr. Harrison (Berlin) to Mr. Troutbeck.* Political principles for Germany. Explains background to No. 190: good atmosphere at Drafting Committee [C 4150/24/18].

iv   *18 July 1945   Letter from Mr. Coulson (Berlin) to Mr. Hall-Patch.* Encloses brief giving British reactions to American proposals in P. (Terminal) 3: see No. 170, note 2. Explains difficulties in making progress on economic questions; reparation tends to take priority [F.O. 934/4/20(2)].

v   *19 July 1945   Minute from Sir D. Waley to Mr. Dixon (Berlin).* Reports on progress in Economic Sub-committee, and indicates likely disagreements. Attaches British memo. on programme of minimum required imports for Germany as a whole [F.O. 934/1/2(35)].

vi   *18 July 1945   Brief for Mr. Eden* on transfer of German populations from Poland and Czechoslovakia. Suggests Mr. Eden should ascertain the U.S. and Soviet attitudes to this problem (cf. No. 59), and indicate the desirability of effecting any transfers in as orderly and humane manner as possible. Field-Marshal Montgomery considers that Germany cannot receive large numbers of Germans from outside for many months [F.O. 934/5/43(1A)].

[5] Not attached to filed copy: see No. 170, note 2.
[6] Cf. No. 19.i.

No. 189

Record of Second Meeting of Foreign Secretaries held at Cecilienhof, Potsdam, on Thursday, 19 July 1945 at 11 a.m.

F. (Terminal) 2nd Meeting [U 6197/3628/70]

Top secret

Present:

M. V. M. Molotov, M. A. Ya. Vyshinski, M. A. A. Gromyko, M. F. T. Gousev, M. K. V. Novikov, M. V. S. Semenov, M. S. A. Golunski (*Interpreter*).

Mr. J. F. Byrnes, Mr. W. A. Harriman, Mr. J. C. Dunn, Mr. H. F. Matthews, Mr. C. E. Bohlen, Mr. B. V. Cohen, Mr. E. Page (*Interpreter*).

Mr. Eden, Sir A. Cadogan, Sir A. Clark Kerr, Sir W. Strang, Mr. N. Brook, Mr. P. J. Dixon, Mr. W. Hayter, Major L. M. Theakstone (*Interpreter*).

Contents

1. *Council of Foreign Ministers*

(Previous Reference: P. (Terminal) 2nd Meeting,[1] Minute 3.)

Mr. Byrnes asked that further consideration should be given to the revised draft of paragraph (3) of the proposed constitution of the Council of Foreign Ministers, which had been approved at the Second Plenary Meeting on the previous day. The present wording would have the effect that a member State which had been at war with an ex-enemy State but had not been a signatory of the Terms of Surrender would be excluded from participation in the preparation of a treaty of peace with that ex-enemy State. For example, France had been at war with Italy, but was not a signatory of the Terms of Surrender imposed on Italy; and the present wording would not allow France to take part in preparing the terms of a peace settlement with Italy. Mr. Byrnes suggested that States represented on the Council should be able to participate in the preparation of peace treaties with any ex-enemy country with which they had been at war, whether or not they had been signatories of the Terms of Surrender.

It was agreed that the drafting Committee which had prepared (F. (Terminal) 1st Meeting,[2] Minute 2) the revised draft constitution of the proposed Council should consider how the point raised by Mr. Byrnes could best be met and should report back to the Meeting of Foreign Secretaries.

[1] No. 184.   [2] No. 178.

2. *Germany: Authority of Control Council in Political Matters*
(Previous References: F. (Terminal) 1st Meeting,[2] Minute 4; P. (Terminal) 2nd Meeting,[1] Minute 4).

MR. EDEN invited Sir William Strang to submit the report of the drafting Committee which the Foreign Secretaries had appointed on the previous day to revise, in the light of their discussion and of any further drafting suggestions which might be made by the three Delegations, the draft statement of the Political Principles to govern the treatment of Germany in the initial control period (P. (Terminal) 3).[3]

SIR WILLIAM STRANG said that the drafting Committee had reached unanimous agreement on the terms of a revised statement (since circulated as P. (Terminal) 7)[4] and this had been communicated to all three Delegations. This statement would form the political section of the proposed Agreement on the Political and Economic Principles to govern the treatment of Germany in the initial control period. He drew attention to various amendments and additions which had been made to the original draft. The main changes were as follows:

In *paragraph 1* the Committee had restored the wording used in the original Four-Power Agreement on control machinery in Germany. The sub-title 'Authority of the Control Council' had been deleted; and paragraph 1 thus became the first of the political principles.

In the revised *paragraph 2* (i) (*a*), use had been made of the wording used in the draft General Order[5] recommended to the Four Governments by the European Advisory Committee.

In *paragraph 5* a new second sentence had been inserted, to indicate the type of person to be appointed to public offices and other positions of responsibility in Germany.

Paragraph 7 contained new material about the reorganisation of the German judicial system.

Paragraph 7 of the original draft had been revised to give effect to the views expressed at the Foreign Secretaries' Meeting about the need for caution in referring to the holding of elections in Germany. The new version (*paragraph 8* of the revised draft) brought out more clearly the conditions which must be satisfied before elections could be held. Thus, the new sub-paragraph (i) provided that 'local self-government shall be restored throughout Germany on democratic principles and in particular through elective councils as rapidly as is consistent with military security and the purposes of military occupation.' And sub-paragraph (iii) had been amplified so as to make it clear that representative and elective principles were not to be applied in wider areas until such a course was justified by the successful application of these principles in local self-government.

The three Foreign Secretaries agreed that the original draft had been

[3] See No. 170, note 2.
[4] No. 190.
[5] Cf. No. 29, note 5.

substantially improved by the amendments and additions made, and expressed their appreciation of the work of the drafting Committee.

It was agreed that the revised draft (P. (Terminal) 7)⁴ should be submitted to the Plenary Meeting for final approval.

3. *Germany: Consideration of Economic Problems*
(Previous Reference: F. (Terminal) 1st Meeting,² Minute 5).

MR. EDEN recalled that at the Foreign Secretaries' Meeting on the previous day it had been agreed to appoint a small sub-committee of experts to survey the problems which would confront the Control Council for Germany in the economic field and to report back those issues on which agreement could not be reached on the sub-committee. It had been contemplated that the Foreign Secretaries' Meeting would then determine which of those issues should be submitted to the Plenary Meeting.

Mr. Eden said that a meeting of the sub-committee had been called the previous afternoon; but the representatives of the Russian Delegation had not been able to attend. There was therefore no report from this sub-committee available for consideration by the Foreign Secretaries' Meeting.

4. *Poland*
(Previous Reference: P. (Terminal) 2nd Meeting,¹ Minute 5.)

MR. EDEN recalled that this matter had been referred to the Foreign Secretaries by the Second Plenary Meeting. He presented a revised draft of the proposed statement on Poland, in the following terms:

'(1) We⁶ have taken note with pleasure of the agreement reached among representative Poles from Poland and abroad which has made possible the formation, in accordance with the decisions reached at the Crimea Conference, of a Polish Provisional Government of National Unity recognised by the Three Powers. The establishment by the British and United States Governments of diplomatic relations with the Polish Provisional Government has resulted in the withdrawal of their recognition from the former Polish Government in London, which no longer exists.

'(2) The British and United States Governments express their willingness to discuss with properly accredited representatives of the Polish Provisional Government the orderly transfer to it of Polish State property, including the Polish Embassies in London and Washington, in regard to which measures of conservation have been taken by the two Governments. They assume that such discussions would embrace also the questions of the acknowledgement by the Polish Provisional Government of liability for the credits advanced to the late Polish Government and other outstanding debts, and the relation of such advances to any assets of the Polish State available abroad.

'(3) The Three Powers are anxious to assist the Polish Provisional Government in facilitating the return to Poland as soon as practicable of

---

⁶ This revised draft is printed by Sir L. Woodward, *op. cit.*, vol. v, pp. 417–8.

all Poles abroad who wish to go, including members of the Polish Armed Forces and Merchant Marine. It is their desire that as many of these Poles as possible should return home, and they consider that the Polish Provisional Government could itself greatly assist in this regard by giving specific undertakings that those Poles who return will do so with full assurance of their personal security, freedom and livelihood.

'(4) The Three Powers note that the Polish Provisional Government is pledged to the holding of free and unfettered elections as soon as possible on the basis of universal suffrage and secret ballot, in which all democratic and anti-Nazi parties shall have the right to take part and to put forward candidates. It is the confident hope of the Three Powers that the elections will be so organised as to enable all sections of Polish opinion to express their views freely, and thus play their full part in the restoration of the country's political life. The Three Powers will further expect that representatives of the Allied Press shall enjoy full freedom to report to the world upon developments in Poland before and during the elections.'

In discussion of this revised draft the following points were raised:

(a) *Paragraph 1.*—M. MOLOTOV and MR. BYRNES said that they saw no objection to this paragraph.

(b) *Paragraph 2.*—M. MOLOTOV did not think that the first sentence sufficiently emphasised the urgency of the problem. It was essential that immediate steps should be taken to prevent the transfer of Polish State property to private persons or institutions.

MR. EDEN said that he had just received from London an account[7] of the measures already taken by the British Government. The whole machinery of the former Polish Government in London was being rapidly liquidated. Control over civil and military expenditure was in the hands of a Committee appointed by the British Treasury. As soon as recognition had been transferred, all diplomatic privileges had been withdrawn from members and servants of the former Polish Government in London; all Polish State property, with the exception of the Embassy, had been taken over and all Ministries had been closed down, except for work necessary to complete the process of liquidation. A War Office Mission had been established to supervise the Polish General Staff and all recruiting for the Polish Armed Forces had ceased. The Polish Merchant Navy was already under British charter. It was clear that the British Government had done, and were doing, a very great deal in the direction desired by the Russian Government; and they were ready to enter into the discussions referred to in the draft statement as soon as the Polish Provisional Government sent a representative to London for the purpose. Mr. Eden was quite willing to insert 'immediately' after 'willingness to discuss' in the first sentence of paragraph 2 of the draft.

M. MOLOTOV said that he would prefer that the first sentence of the paragraph should state that the British and United States Governments agreed in principle to the immediate transfer of Polish State property to

---

[7] *Note in filed copy:* 'Onward 69': see i below.

the Polish Provisional Government and that they were willing to discuss the method and timing of such a transfer with representatives of that Government.

Mr. Eden said that he would be willing for the draft to be revised on these lines, if the United States Delegation agreed.

Mr. Byrnes said that he would accept such an amendment. He added that in Washington an attempt had been made to transfer the Polish Embassy and other Polish property to a corporation to be established for the purpose, but this had been stopped on the intervention of the United States Government.

M. Molotov recalled that the Russian draft submitted to the Second Plenary Meeting had contained an explicit statement forbidding the transfer of Polish State property to any institution of any kind or to private persons. It was accepted that measures to prevent such transfer had been taken in London and Washington; but there was Polish State property in other places also, such as Canada, Italy and North Africa. He thought therefore that the draft should contain a reference to the prohibition of such transfer.

Mr. Eden pointed out that the taking of such measures in the countries referred to by M. Molotov would be for the Governments concerned; it should be possible, however, to insert a sentence to meet the point M. Molotov had in mind.

M. Molotov then referred to the second sentence of paragraph 2, regarding the liability of the Polish Provisional Government for the credits advanced to the late Polish Government and other outstanding debts. He could not say whether this would be acceptable to the Polish Provisional Government without knowing what the total liability was likely to be.

Mr. Eden explained that there was no intention to ask the Polish Provisional Government to accept in advance liability for these debts. The purpose of the sentence was to indicate that this point would have to be covered in the discussions.

M. Molotov suggested that in that case some word other than 'acknowledgment' should be used in this sentence.

(c) *Paragraph 3.* M. Molotov asked whether the last word of this paragraph implied that the Polish Provisional Government must guarantee a *livelihood* to all Polish nationals who were willing to return to Poland. In present circumstances few countries in the world would be in a position to give such a guarantee. Was it reasonable to ask that these Poles should be in a more privileged position than their fellow citizens already in Poland?

Mr. Eden agreed that the word 'livelihood' might be omitted from this sentence, and suggested that words might be added to show that what was here intended was that there should be no discrimination between Poles returning to Poland and their fellow citizens already in Poland.

Mr. Eden suggested, and it was agreed, that the three Delegations were in sufficient agreement on the substance of the revised draft to warrant its being remitted to a drafting Committee for further examination of the wording.

It was agreed that the following should be appointed as a drafting Committee:

United States Delegation: M. A. Harriman, Mr. F. Bohlen;
United Kingdom Delegation: Sir A. Clark-Kerr, Mr. P. Dean;
Russian Delegation: M. Vyshinski, M. Golunski;

to prepare a revised text of the draft statement in the light of the discussion, and to report to their respective Foreign Secretaries with a view to the submission of the revised text to the Plenary Meeting.

5. *Agenda for the Third Plenary Meeting*

MR. EDEN said that the Third Plenary Meeting, which was to be held later that day, could be invited to approve the revised draft of the proposed agreement on the Political Principles to govern the treatment of Germany in the initial control period (see Minute 2 above). They could also consider the draft statement on Poland, if the drafting committee which had been appointed that morning were able to complete their revision of the draft before 4 p.m. that afternoon (see Minute 3[4] above). If the revised draft were not available by then, this subject could be held over for discussion by the Plenary Meeting on Friday, the 20th July.

MR. BYRNES suggested that the Third Plenary Meeting might discuss the Yalta Declaration on Liberated Europe, on the basis of the statement submitted by President Truman (P. (Terminal) 4).[3]

M. MOLOTOV said that he was anxious that there should be an early discussion of the two papers which he had handed in earlier in the Meeting, on the disposal of the German Navy and Merchant Marine[8] and on the political régime in Spain.[9] Mr. EDEN said that he was not in a position to discuss these papers that morning: on the question of the German Navy, in particular, he would wish to consult with the Naval Staff and had not yet had an opportunity of doing so. MR. BYRNES said that these were both subjects which could be considered by a Plenary Meeting, without preliminary discussion by the three Foreign Secretaries, and he suggested that both should be placed on the Agenda for the Third Plenary Meeting. MR. EDEN agreed.

Mr. Eden suggested that two further subjects might be added to the Agenda: (a) The situation in Yugoslavia and the implementation of the Tito–Subasic Agreement; and (b) Removal as booty of Allied Industrial Equipment, particularly from Roumania. He undertook to prepare memoranda on both of these subjects for consideration at the Third Plenary Meeting.

It was agreed that the following subjects should be put forward for discussion at the Third Plenary Meeting:

---

[8] This paper P. (Terminal) 9 of 19 July 1945 (not printed) comprised the text of the Soviet memorandum cited in No. 194, minute 6. The Russian text is printed in *Berlinskaya konferentsiya*, p. 322.

[9] This paper P. (Terminal) 8 of 19 July (not printed) comprised the text of the Soviet memorandum cited in No. 194, minute 7. The Russian text is printed *op. cit.*, pp. 322–3.

(*a*) *Germany: Authority of Control Council in Political Matters* (P. (Terminal) 7).[4]
(*b*) *Poland* (if revised draft statement was available by 4 p.m. that day).
(*c*) *Disposal of German Navy and Merchant Marine* (P. (Terminal) 9).[8]
(*d*) *Political Régime in Spain* (P. (Terminal) 8).[9]
(*e*) *Yalta Declaration on Liberated Europe* (P. (Terminal) 4).[3]
(*f*) *Yugoslavia* (P. (Terminal) 22).[10]
(*g*) *Removal as booty of Allied Industrial Equipment, especially from Roumania* (P. Terminal) 10).[11]

Cabinet Office, Potsdam, 19th July, 1945

CALENDARS TO NO. 189

i *18–19 July 1945 From and to Mr. Eden (Berlin) Tel. No. 81 Target and No. 69 Onward.* With reference to No. 184, minute 5, position on liquidation of affairs of Polish administration in London, and arrangements for Polish armed forces [N 8854/6/55].

ii *19–20 July 1945 Letters from Mr. Allen (Berlin) to Mr. Warner:* discussions on Poland at conference; question of Poland's western frontier not yet raised, largely because of American priorities on economic questions [N 9253/6/55].

iii *20 July 1945 Brief for Mr. Eden for No. 208 below.* Attaches British revised draft statement on Poland (see minute 4 above) and text at No. 215; explains reasons for differences between British and Soviet delegations [F.O. 934/2/10(34)].

[10] Not printed. The text of this British memorandum of 19 July was as cited in No. 194, minute 9.
[11] Not printed. The text of this British memorandum of 19 July was as cited in No. 194, minute 10.

No. 190

Proposed Agreement on the Political and Economic Principles to govern the treatment of Germany in the initial control period
Text as approved by the Foreign Secretaries[1]
P. (*Terminal*) 7 [U 6197/3628/70]

Top secret   *19 July 1945*
Political Principles

1. In accordance with the agreement on Control Machinery in Germany, supreme authority in Germany is exercised, on instructions from their respective Governments, by the Commanders-in-Chief of the armed forces of the United Kingdom, the United States of America, the Union of Soviet

[1] This document is printed in *F.R.U.S. Berlin*, vol. ii, pp. 784–6. Cf. also Sir L. Woodward, *op. cit.*, vol. v, pp. 440 f.

Socialist Republics, and the French Republic, each in his own zone of occupation, and also jointly, in matters affecting Germany as a whole, in their capacity as members of the Control Council.

2. The purposes of the occupation of Germany by which the Control Council shall be guided are:

(i) the complete disarmament and demilitarisation of Germany and the elimination or control of all German industry that could be used for military production. To these ends:

(a) All German land, naval and air forces, the S.S., S.A., S.D. and Gestapo,[2] with all their organisations, staffs and institutions, including the General Staff, the Officers' Corps, Reserve Corps, military schools, war veterans' organisations and all other military and quasi-military organisations, together with all clubs and associations which serve to keep alive the military tradition in Germany, shall be completely and finally abolished in such manner as permanently to prevent the revival or reorganisation of German militarism and Nazism;

(b) all arms, ammunition and implements of war and all specialised facilities for their production shall be held at the disposal of the Allies or destroyed. The maintenance and production of all aircraft and all arms, ammunition and implements of war shall be prevented.

(ii) To convince the German people that they have suffered a total military defeat and that they cannot escape responsibility for what they have brought upon themselves, since their own ruthless warfare and the fanatical Nazi resistance have destroyed German economy and made chaos and suffering inevitable.

(iii) To destroy the National Socialist Party and its affiliated and supervised organisations, to dissolve all Nazi institutions, to ensure that they are not revived in any form, and to prevent all Nazi and militaristic activity or propaganda.

(iv) To prepare for the eventual reconstruction of German political life on a democratic basis and for eventual peaceful co-operation in international life by Germany.

3. All Nazi laws which provided the basis of the Hitler régime or established discriminations on grounds of race, creed, or political opinion shall be abolished. No such discriminations, whether legal, administrative or otherwise, shall be tolerated.

4. War criminals and those who have participated in planning or carrying out Nazi enterprises involving or resulting in atrocities or war crimes shall be arrested and brought to judgment. Nazi leaders, influential Nazi supporters and high officials of Nazi organisations and institutions and any other persons dangerous to the occupation or its objectives shall be arrested and interned.

5. All members of the Nazi Party who have been more than nominal participants in its activities and all other persons hostile to Allied purposes

[2] Geheime Staats-Polizei (Secret State Police).

shall be removed from public and semi-public office, and from positions of responsibility in important private undertakings. Such persons shall be replaced by persons who, by their political and moral qualities, are deemed capable of assisting in developing genuinely democratic institutions in Germany.

6. German education shall be so controlled as completely to eliminate Nazi and militarist doctrines and to make possible the successful development of democratic ideas.

7. The judicial system will be reorganised in accordance with the principles of democracy, of justice under law and of equal rights for all citizens without distinction of race, nationality or religion.

8. The administration of affairs in Germany should be directed towards the decentralisation of the political structure and the development of local responsibility. To this end–

(i) local self-government shall be restored throughout Germany on democratic principles and in particular through elective councils as rapidly as is consistent with military security and the purposes of military occupation;

(ii) all democratic political parties with right of assembly and of public discussion shall be allowed and encouraged throughout Germany;

(iii) representative and elective principles shall be introduced into regional, provincial and state (Land) administration as rapidly as may be justified by the successful application of these principles in local self-government;

(iv) for the time being no central German Government shall be established.

9. Subject to the necessity for maintaining military security, freedom of speech, press and religion shall be permitted, and religious institutions shall be respected. Subject likewise to the maintenance of military security, the formation of free trade unions shall be permitted.

CALENDAR TO NO. 190

19 July 1945 Minute from Sir W. Strang to Sir A. Cadogan (Berlin). French acceptance of No. 190 necessary in order to validate instructions to Four-Power Control Council [F.O. 934/4/20(14)].

No. 191

Minute from Mr. Eden to Mr. Churchill (Berlin)
No. P.M./45/5.T. [F.O. 934/1/2(16)]

[BERLIN,] *19 July 1945*

I attach a note on the treatment of Germany as an economic whole. This note has been discussed with General Weeks and other members of the

British Element of the Control Commission.[1] They are in general agreement.

3. [*sic*] I suggest that we should take as our objectives under this item of the agenda the points made in this note.

A. E.

Annex to No. 191

Germany as an economic whole

By the 'treatment of Germany as an economic unit' we mean broadly speaking:

(*a*) Unified control of German economic life;

(*b*) The free interzonal exchange of goods and services, in such a way as to minimise imports into Germany and facilitate administrative efficiency.

2. In the long run this policy is obviously advantageous in the interests of order and harmony. The arguments have been developed at length in the brief on this question.[2]

3. In the short run, however, it would present certain dangers unless the necessary safeguards are secured:

(*a*) The Russians have allowed the Poles to take complete possession of German Silesia.[3] Thus, according to Marshal Zhukov, German Silesian coal is out of his control and cannot be used to meet Germany's requirements.[4] If this were accepted, and at the same time we had an agreed policy of treating Germany as an economic unit, we should be forced to meet all Germany's requirements from the Ruhr and Saar. This would mean hardly any export of coal from Germany to the Western European countries.

(*b*) The Russians have stripped their zone of almost everything. It normally has a food surplus but now has none. Indeed it almost certainly has a deficit. The Western zones have no surplus either, indeed a deficiency even in peace time, but the Russians might call for other kinds of economic help from us for their zone.

4. These dangers have been thrown up during the last week by the problem of feeding and fuelling Berlin; a temporary solution for only one month has been found.[5] A further difficulty is illustrated by the Hyndley-Potter report, which recommended that at least 25 million tons by the end of next April must be exported from the Ruhr and Saar to Western Europe.

5. In spite, however, of the short term dangers to us of treating Germany as an economic whole, it seems clear that we cannot go back on this policy. To administer Germany centrally and to apply a common policy generally towards Germany would be totally impossible if the same principle were not applied economically. There is no dividing line between economic and political administration.

6. In this situation we might aim at the following:

(*a*) Until production in Western Germany reaches a more normal figure, we should secure the use of German Silesian coal sufficient to meet that portion of Germany's requirements which it normally supplied. It is essential that, in

[1] Cf. No. 154.iii.

[2] No. 125.

[3] This sentence is cited by Ian Colvin in *The Daily Telegraph* of 25 March 1975, p. 6.

[4] See Nos. 58 and 70.

[5] See No. 70, and No. 125, paragraph 9.

the political discussions on the Polish western boundary, this point should not be given away. Even if we should have to recognise Poland's right to administer the disputed territory or part of it at once, the use of the resources of that territory must be reserved. How they could be brought into the general pool, so that they were available for Germany, would be a matter for further discussion depending on how the political talks had gone.

(*b*) In the absence of special reasons to the contrary, each of the zones of occupation, including the Greater Berlin area, should draw its supplies from the areas on which it had drawn before the war.

(*c*) The strongest pressure should be brought on the Russians to improve production of food and fuel in their own zone and refrain from living on the country. A plain warning might at this point be given them that we shall not be able to supply the Russian zone or any part of Eastern Europe with food, owing to the serious world shortage.

(*d*) The first charge on German exports should be the sum needed to pay for German imports, i.e. *free* deliveries of German goods on reparation account, from the current production or from stocks, can only come after Germany[6] has obtained enough money from her exports to pay for her essential imports. (This point may be more conveniently dealth [*sic*] with when reparation is discussed, though it is relevant to the general organisation of Germany's economy.)

(*e*) We should obtain agreement on the particular forms of German governmental machinery which should be centrally administered and or [on] the various economic matters on which a common policy is required. (Field Marshal Montgomery has produced some notes[7] on these which will be available when the time comes.)

Calendars to No. 191

i *17 July 1945 Memo. by Mr. Brand (Berlin) on coal for Germany*, without enclosure: British estimates and objectives. Soviet agreement to a Silesian contribution of coal necessary for treatment of Germany as an economic whole. Desirability of Soviet cooperation with E.C.O., and of Polish membership [F.O. 934/1/2(11)].

ii *16–18 July 1945 Exchange between Mr. N. B. Ronald and Mr. Coulson (Berlin)*: timing, in relation to Soviet attitude, of invitation to Poland to join E.C.O. [F.O. 934/1/2(10)].

iii *16 July 1945 Letter from Mr. A. H. Lincoln to Mr. Coulson (Berlin)* enclosing memo. by Mr. Ronald on points for any discussion at Potsdam of President Truman's directive on coal [UE 3052/607/53].

iv *17 July 1945 To Mr. Eden (Berlin) Tel. No. 39 Onward minuted by Mr. Coulson, Sir A. Cadogan and Mr. Eden*: withdrawal of War Office objections to U.S. draft directive on coal clears way for its acceptance: see further No. 233.ii [UR 2398/2109/851; F.O. 934/1/2(6)].

---

[6] The Prime Minister amended the preceding passage (F.O. 954/10) to read ' . . . to pay for essential German imports. No free deliveries of German goods on reparation account, from current production or from stocks, can come until Germany' &c.

[7] Cf. No. 43, enclosure, and No. 43.ii.

No. 192

Minute from Mr. Eden to Mr. Churchill (Berlin)
No. P.M./45/4.T. [*E 5908/103/34*]

[BERLIN,] *19 July 1945*

Troop Withdrawals from Persia

My minute No. P.M./45/326[1] of the 13th July.

I am most anxious to get this matter settled at Terminal. The presence of the Soviet forces in Persia is an excellent example of their methods of penetration[2] and is causing me much concern.

2. Since I wrote my minute of the 13th July I have received a copy of the Chiefs of Staff report No. C.O.S.(45) 460 (o)[3] on the protection of the South Persian oilfields. An analysis of this paper is attached at flag B.[4]

3. I think you will agree with me that the report of the Chiefs of Staff shows that the danger is very small of an interruption in our oil supplies if British troops are withdrawn from the oilfields area in the third stage and the protection of that area entrusted to Persian troops. Attached at flag A is a brief[5] in support of our proposal for the complete joint withdrawal in three stages of British and Soviet troops from Persia. I am anxious to circulate a paper on this to the Conference at an early date and should be grateful to have your concurrence.[6]

A. E.

ANNEX TO No. 192

Analysis of the Chiefs of Staff Report No. COS (45)460(o).[3]

This paper analyses the causes which might possibly lead to an interruption in the supply of oil from Persia between now and the end of the war with Japan, as follows:

---

[1] No. 129.

[2] The preceding seven words are cited by Ian Colvin in *The Daily Telegraph* of 25 March 1975, p. 6.

[3] Not printed. For this report of 12 July 1945 see annex below.

[4] Annex below.

[5] Not printed. The first three paragraphs of this undated brief were substantially an earlier draft of No. 220 with the addition, after the words 'worked out afterwards', of the sentence: 'Even under this proposal, unless the Japanese war ends very soon, it is unlikely that British troops will, in fact, have all been withdrawn from Persia by the time the war ends'. The brief further adduced considerations advanced in No. 129.i.

[6] Mr. Churchill minuted to Mr. Eden on 20 July: 'By all means circulate your paper': see No. 220.

'(*a*) *Sabotage*
This is extremely difficult to carry out and is considered to be unlikely.
(*b*) *Tribal Unrest*
Inter-tribal clashes are more likely to affect communications and the safety of the workers than to be directed against the actual oilfields themselves. Tribes are generally well disposed towards the Anglo-Iranian Oil Company from which they derive employment and financial benefit.
(*c*) *Labour Unrest*
This is the most probable source of trouble. However, it is unlikely to assume serious proportions until some time after our troops have been withdrawn, since the Tudeh party (left wing organisation supported by Russia) has not yet tried to gain any influence in South Persia.'
After examining various alternative means of providing protection for the oilfields if British troops were withdrawn, the report declares that the units of the Persian army now stationed in Southern Persia should, on their present standard of efficiency, be able to compete with such troubles as may arise before the conclusion of the war with Japan. The Chiefs of Staff, however, maintain that if the protection of the oilfields were left to the Persian army a high degree of security could not be guaranteed and accordingly recommend that militarily it is undesirable to withdraw the British-Indian forces.

CALENDAR TO NO. 192

i *17–21 July 1945 Sir R. Bullard (Tehran) Tel. No. 716 minuted by Mr. Eden; from and to Mr. Eden (Berlin) Tels. Nos. 122 Target & 128 Onward.* Question of press reporting on proposed British and Soviet evacuation of Persia [F.O. 934/3/15(4 & 6); E 5330/103/33].

No. 193

Minutes of a Meeting of the Combined Chiefs of Staff Committee held in the Conference Room at 25 Ringstrasse, Babelsberg, on Thursday, 19 July 1945 at 2.30 p.m.[1]
C.C.S. 196th Meeting [*CAB 99/39*]

Top secret

Present:
GENERAL OF THE ARMY G. C. MARSHALL, USA, Fleet Admiral E. J. King, USN, General of the Army H. H. Arnold, USA.
FIELD-MARSHAL SIR ALAN F. BROOKE, Marshal of the Royal Air Force Sir Charles F. A. Portal, Admiral of the Fleet Sir Andrew B. Cunningham.

Also present:
General B. B. Somervell, USA, Lieut.-General J. E. Hull, USA, Vice-Admiral C. M. Cooke, Jr., USN, Major-General L. Norstad, USA, Captain H. R. Oster, USN, Captain A. S. McDill, USN.

[1] This record is printed in *F.R.U.S. Berlin*, vol. ii, pp. 112–5.

Field-Marshal Sir Henry Maitland Wilson, General Sir Hastings L. Ismay, Major-General R. E. Laycock, Major-General L. C. Hollis.

Secretariat: Brigadier-General A. J. McFarland, USA, Brigadier A. T. Cornwall-Jones, Captain C. J. Moore, USN, Lieut.-Colonel T. Haddon.

1. *Approval of the Minutes of C.C.S. 195th Meeting,*[2] *18th July, 1945*

THE COMBINED CHIEFS OF STAFF—

(*a*) Approved the conclusions of the C.C.S. 195th Meeting[2] subject to the following amendments:

(1) Change item 4 (*a*) to read:
'Agreed in principle that that part of the present South-West Pacific Area lying south of the boundary proposed in paragraph 2 of C.C.S. 852/1,[3] should pass from United States to British command as soon as possible.'

(2) Change item 5 (*e*) to read as follows—
'In the event the U.S.S.R. enters the war against Japan, the strategy to be pursued should be discussed between the parties concerned.'

(*b*) Approved the detailed report of the meeting subject to later minor amendments.

2. *Participation of Two French Colonial Infantry Divisions in Far Eastern Operations* (C.C.S. 895, C.C.S. 895/1, C.C.S. 895/2.[4])

THE COMBINED CHIEFS OF STAFF—

Approved the reply to the Chief of the French Military Mission in the United States in the Enclosure to C.C.S. 895/2.

3. *Combined Chiefs of Staff Machinery after the War with Japan* (C.C.S. 891,[5] C.C.S. 891/1.[6])

SIR ALAN BROOKE said that the British Chiefs of Staff had considered the memorandum by the United States Chiefs of Staff in C.C.S. 891/1.[6] The British Chiefs of Staff were prepared to discuss the matter or to take note of the views of the United States Chiefs of Staff as the latter desired.

GENERAL MARSHALL said that the United States Chiefs of Staff were not in a position to discuss at this date the post-war relationship between the respective military staffs.

[2] No. 183.

[3] Not printed: cf. No. 249, appendix D.

[4] These documents, not here printed, are printed *op. cit.*, vol. ii, pp. 1341–6 *passim*.

[5] No. 151.

[6] This memorandum of 19 July 1945 by the United States Chiefs of Staff, printed *op. cit.*, vol. ii, p. 1202, read as follows: 'With reference to C.C.S. 891, the political relationship of the United States with other nations in the period following this war is not yet sufficiently defined to permit the United States Chiefs of Staff to discuss at this date the post-war relationships between the respective military staffs. The United States Chiefs of Staff will bring up for consideration the problem of the most effective military machinery to be used from now forward and prior to the end of the Japanese war.'

Admiral King said that the second paragraph of C.C.S. 891/1 was meant to refer to the procedure envisaged in the changed conclusion under 5 (*e*) of the minutes of the Combined Chiefs of Staff 195th Meeting.[2]

The Combined Chiefs of Staff–

Took note of C.C.S. 891 and 891/1.

4. *Information for the Russians Concerning the Japanese War*
(C.C.S. 884,[7] C.C.S. 884/1,[7] C.C.S. 884/2.[8])

Sir Alan Brooke said that the British Chiefs of Staff felt that it was desirable that the policy adopted in imparting information concerning the Japanese war to the Russians should be co-ordinated with the policy of the United States Chiefs of Staff.

General Marshall said that the United States Chiefs of Staff had considered the matter raised in the memorandum by the British Chiefs of Staff and had come to the following conclusion:

(*a*) The United States Chiefs of Staff desired to retain freedom of action regarding the passing of purely operational information and intelligence to the Russians.

(*b*) On matters of information and intelligence which were not purely operational, the United States Chiefs of Staff would agree not to pass such information to the Russians without consulting the British Chiefs of Staff.

(*c*) As regards information and intelligence from purely British sources, this would not be passed without permission of the British Chiefs of Staff.

Sir Charles Portal said that there was considerable technical information which had been developed by joint effort, and he asked whether this information would be handled the same as operational information.

Admiral King said that information on technical equipment was not included in purely operational information. Operational information or intelligence included information on such matters as weather and the composition and disposition of enemy forces. The technical information referred to by Sir Charles Portal would not therefore be handled under (*a*) above.

General Marshall said that it was the policy of the United States Chiefs of Staff to pass purely operational information and intelligence freely to the Russians and not to withhold it for bargaining purposes. If such information contributed to the efficiency of the Russian armies or aided in the prosecution of the war the United States Chiefs felt that it should be given to the Russians regardless of whether or not the Russians reciprocated.

Sir Alan Brooke said that this policy would be agreeable to the British Chiefs of Staff as they felt it would be better for the British and United States Chiefs of Staff to pursue the same policy in this matter since both countries have military missions in Moscow.

---

[7] See No. 52, notes 2–3. [8] No. 150.

THE COMBINED CHIEFS OF STAFF—
Agreed:

(a) *Operational Information and Intelligence*
That the United States and British Chiefs of Staff will pass to the Russians such operational information and intelligence regarding the theatres in which they are respectively responsible as either may wish and without bargaining.

(b) *Information and Intelligence other than Operational*
The United States and British Chiefs of Staff will consult together before passing to the Russians any information and intelligence other than operational. Neither party will pass to the Russians information or intelligence derived wholly or in part from the other party's sources without their consent.

5. *Planning Date for the End of Organised Resistance by Japan*
C.C.S. 880/8.)[9]
THE COMBINED CHIEFS OF STAFF—
Agreed that for the purpose of planning production and the allocation of man-power, the planning date for the end of organised resistance by Japan be the 15th November, 1946; that this date be adjusted periodically to conform to the course of the war.

6. *Appointment of Colonel Douglas to Allied Commission in Italy*
FIELD-MARSHAL WILSON reported that he had attended that afternoon a meeting between the United States Secretary of War, the United States Assistant Secretary of War and Field-Marshal Alexander at which the appointment of Colonel Douglas as Chief Commissioner to the Allied Commission in Italy had been discussed.[10]

It was proposed at that meeting that Colonel Douglas should visit Italy for a month or so to examine the situation on the spot. He could then take over the appointment from Admiral Stone in September, when all Italian territory, excluding Venezia Giulia, would have been handed back to the Italian Government and a change in the status of the Control Commission to more of a civilian basis would take place.

This proposal had been accepted by the United States and British representatives present at the meeting, and subject to approval by Colonel Douglas which was being requested from Washington, it was decided to adopt the above suggestions provided the State Department and the Foreign Office agreed.

THE COMBINED CHIEFS OF STAFF—
Took note of Field-Marshal Wilson's statement.

[9] *Note in filed copy:* 'See J.S.M. 953'. This memorandum of 7 July 1945 by the United States Chiefs of Staff is printed *op. cit.*, vol. i, p. 915.
[10] For this meeting cf. *op. cit.*, vol. ii, pp. 111–2.

No. 194

*Record of Third Plenary Meeting held at Cecilienhof, Potsdam,
on Thursday, 19 July 1945 at 4 p.m.*
P. (Terminal) 3rd Meeting [U 6197/3628/70]

Top secret

Present:

PREMIER STALIN, M. V. M. Molotov, M. A. Ya. Vyshinski, M. I. M. Maisky
(*for part of Meeting*), M. F. T. Gousev, Admiral N. G. Kuznetsov, M. A. A.
Gromyko, M. K. V. Novikov, M. A. A. Sobolev, M. B. F. Podtzerob, M. V. N.
Pavlov (*Interpreter*).

PRESIDENT TRUMAN, Mr. J. F. Byrnes, Mr. Joseph E. Davies, Fleet-Admiral
W. D. Leahy, Mr. W. A. Harriman, Mr. E. W. Pauley, Mr. J. C. Dunn, Mr. H. F.
Matthews, Mr. B. V. Cohen, Mr. L. E. Thompson, Mr. C. E. Bohlen (*Interpreter*).

MR. CHURCHILL, Mr. Eden, Mr. Attlee, Lord Leathers (*for Item 6*), Sir A.
Cadogan, Sir A. Clark Kerr, Sir W. Strang, Sir E. Bridges, Mr. P. J. Dixon,
Mr. W. Hayter, Major A. Birse (*Interpreter*).

Contents

1. *Greece*

MR. CHURCHILL said that immediately prior to the Plenary Meeting on
the previous day, Premier Stalin had mentioned a report of trouble on the
Greek frontiers with Albania, Yugoslavia, and Bulgaria.[1] He had made
enquiries and no evidence of such trouble could be found. There might, of
course, have been some sniping. There were no Greek field divisions in
Northern Greece, but only 7,000 National Guards on all the three frontiers.
These National Guards were equipped and deployed only for an internal
security rôle. On the other side of the frontiers, however, there were said
to be 30,000 Albanian, 30,000 Yugoslav and 24,000 Bulgarian troops. He
only mentioned this matter because he felt that the Three Great Powers
assembled at the Conference should make it clear to the smaller States that

---

[1] Cf. No. 185, minute 5.

they would not tolerate marauding across frontiers. Any frontier adjustments would be settled at the Peace Conference, and it should be made abundantly clear that any marauding adventures would be detrimental to the marauders.

PREMIER STALIN said that he had mentioned this matter privately to Mr. Churchill. It did not concern the Conference.

MR. CHURCHILL agreed that Premier Stalin had raised the matter across the table the previous day before the arrival of President Truman. He would, however, put it formally on the Agenda of the Conference if this was found necessary.

2. *Council of Foreign Ministers*
(Previous Reference: F (Terminal) 2nd Meeting,[2] Minute 1.)

MR. EDEN reported[3] that Mr Byrnes had informed the Foreign Secretaries at their meeting that morning that the United States Government desired to propose an amendment to the redraft, accepted by the Conference on the previous day,[4] of paragraph (3) of the draft constitution of the Council of Foreign Ministers. The Foreign Secretaries had agreed to refer this point to a drafting Committee.

THE CONFERENCE:
Noted the position.

3. *Germany: Authority of Control Council in Political Matters*
(Previous Reference: F (Terminal) 2nd Meeting,[2] Minute 2.)

MR. EDEN reported that the Foreign Secretaries had given further consideration to the political section of the proposed statement of political [and economic] principles to govern the treatment of Germany in the initial control period, circulated by the United States delegation.[5]

Preliminary consideration had been given to this draft by Heads of Governments at their meeting the previous day, and the Foreign Secretaries had been asked to submit a Report, which had now been circulated to the Conference.[6] Besides clarifying the text, the Foreign Secretaries had supplemented it in a few places with new material. They now recommended it for acceptance by the Heads of Governments. When the section on economic principles had been discussed and agreed upon, it would be for consideration by the Conference whether the whole statement should be made public.

[2] No. 189.
[3] The text of a report (untraced in Foreign Office archives) to the third Plenary Meeting at Potsdam by Mr. Eden as rapporteur of the second Meeting of Foreign Ministers is printed *op. cit.*, vol. ii, pp. 108–9. The main substance of this report is covered by the present record of statements by Mr. Eden: and similarly for other untraced texts of reports from meetings of Foreign Ministers.
[4] *Note in filed copy:* 'P (Terminal) 2nd Meeting [No. 184], minute 3'.
[5] *Note in filed copy:* 'P (Terminal) 3'. See No. 170, note 2.
[6] *Note in filed copy:* 'P (Terminal) 7', No. 190.

THE CONFERENCE:
Accepted the text submitted by the Foreign Secretaries[6] on the political principles to govern the treatment of Germany in the initial control period.

4. *Poland*
(Previous Reference: F (Terminal) 2nd Meeting,[2] Minute 3.)

MR. EDEN reported that the United Kingdom Delegation had put forward a redraft of the draft 'Statement by the Heads of the Three Governments on the Polish Question' put forward by Premier Stalin at the Plenary Meeting the previous day.[7] The Foreign Secretaries, after a valuable discussion, had remitted this redraft to a drafting Committee.

THE CONFERENCE:
Agreed to consider this redraft as soon as it had been approved by the Foreign Secretaries.

5. *Subjects for Discussion: Report by the Three Foreign Secretaries*

MR. EDEN reported that the Foreign Secretaries had agreed to submit the following further questions for discussion at the Plenary Meeting that afternoon:
(*a*) The Germany [*sic*] Navy and Merchant Marine.
(*b*) Spain.
(*c*) The Yalta Declaration on Liberated Europe.
(*d*) Yugoslavia.
(*e*) Roumania: Removal, as booty, of Allied industrial equipment.
It was agreed to proceed with the discussion of these matters.

6. *The German Navy and Merchant Marine*

THE CONFERENCE considered the following Memorandum by the Soviet Delegation (circulated as P. (Terminal) 9)[8]:

'1. One-third of the total German navy, including the ships which at the beginning of unconditional surrender of Germany were under construction or in repair shall be handed over to the Soviet Union.

2. One-third of reserve armaments, ammunition and supplies of the German navy in accordance with the classes of ships shall be handed over to the Soviet Union.

3. One-third of the German merchant marine shall be handed over to the Soviet Union.

4. The transfer and receipt of the ships of the German navy and merchant marine shall begin 1st August and shall be completed by 1st November, 1945.

5. There shall be established an expert commission the strength of which shall be determined by the Naval Commands of the three Allied

---

[7] *Note in filed copy:* 'P (Terminal) 2nd Meeting [No. 184], minute 5'.
[8] Cf. No. 189, note 8.

countries to transfer and take the ships of the German navy and merchant marine located in the ports and bases of the Allied Commands as well as the ports and bases in Germany and other countries.'

PRESIDENT TRUMAN said that the first step was to decide what was 'booty' and what was 'reparations.' Material defined as booty should belong to the nation whose forces captured it. Material defined as reparations should be divided up in agreed proportions. He thought that the Conference would have at some time to reach agreement on a precise definition of these two terms. In his opinion, the German Merchant Fleet should fall under 'reparations,' and should be divided up. He was most interested in the Merchant Fleet, as he was anxious that it should remain under the present control until the end of the Japanese war.

PREMIER STALIN said that the German battle fleet and all its weapons was booty, and should therefore belong to those who accepted the German surrender, in the same way as the weapons of the surrendered German armies. It had been stipulated in the Surrender Terms imposed on Germany that the Fleet should surrender. It was therefore booty. As regards the German merchant shipping, however, he thought that it might be possible to discuss whether this should be treated as booty or reparations. He mentioned that in the case of Italy, both the Fleet and the merchant shipping were treated as booty, and no one had raised the question of reparations.

MR. CHURCHILL said that he did not want to approach the question of the German Fleet from any juridical standpoint with exact definitions, but rather to try and reach a fair and friendly agreement between the three Powers as part of a general settlement of the problems before them. The major part of the German Fleet was now in British hands; and, assuming that the Three Powers came to a friendly general settlement of the affairs before the Conference, he would not oppose a fair division of the German Fleet. He did not propose to discuss the question of the Italian Fleet at this meeting, as this was part of the general policy which we should pursue towards Italy.

Continuing, Mr. Churchill said that in these matters the question of replacement of losses was, of course, very relevant. The British Fleet had suffered immense losses—speaking from memory, some 10 capital ships (battleships or first-class carriers), some 20 cruisers, and hundreds of smaller craft. It seemed to him that the disposal of the German U-boats was in a rather different position from the other vessels. U-boats had a limited war use. An International Convention, of which Germany had been a signatory, prohibited the use of U-boats in the way in which the Germans had employed them during the war,[9] and which we had been forced to follow up to a point.

---

[9] Cf. the procès-verbal relating to the rules of submarine warfare in Part IV of the Naval Limitation Treaty of 22 April 1930 (printed in *B.F.S.P.*, vol. 132, pp. 603–19), signed in London on 6 November 1936, between the United Kingdom, the United States of America, France, Italy and Japan, with German accession thereto on 23 November 1936: printed *op. cit.*, vol. 140, pp. 300–2

He considered that the U-boats should be destroyed or sunk. However, some of the most modern U-boats had devices of interest to all Three Powers, and these should be shared. He therefore suggested that, as part of a final settlement, most of the U-boats should be sunk, and the small balance required for research should be shared.

As regards the other units of the German Fleet, if the Conference came to a friendly general settlement of their problems, he was prepared to divide them equally, for he would welcome the appearance of the Russians on the seas of the world.

Mr. Churchill then dealt with the German Merchant Navy. So long as the war against Japan continued, all merchant ships captured from the enemy should be used for the war. The power of waging war was limited by merchant shipping. Man-power, aircraft and men-of-war were plentiful, but the movement of large armies over vast spaces made a great call on shipping. The problem of feeding Great Britain and liberated Europe also called for every ton of available shipping during this critical time. All the Allies had put their shipping into a common pool, and he would be very sorry if any merchant shipping captured from the enemy did not play its part in the defeat of Japan and the distribution of the supplies to the liberated areas.

Mr. Churchill said that we understood that Finland had had 400,000 tons of merchant shipping, which had passed into the control of Russia. The Roumanians had also some ships, including one or two which would be very valuable for trooping purposes; and troopships were specially wanted.

If, therefore, there was to be a division into thirds as a result of this meeting, these Finnish and Roumanian ships should come into this division into three.

PREMIER STALIN said that the Russians had not taken a single ship from the Finnish Fleet and had only taken one from Roumania. This was a troopship which was being used to carry wounded.

MR. CHURCHILL said that there was also the question of participation of other nations besides the three Great Powers. Norway had suffered terrible losses. Their oil tanker fleet constituted a considerable part of Norway's national life. We had had free use of it, and it had suffered a grievous proportion of loss. Other nations, too, had suffered very heavy losses. It was for consideration whether the German merchant navy should be divided into four parts, the fourth part being allocated to meet the needs of other nations not represented at the table.

Mr. Churchill said he threw out these points as needing careful consideration; but he would deprecate a hard-and-fast decision being reached that day.

PRESIDENT TRUMAN said that the subject was one of great interest from the United States point of view. He would be happy to see a division of the German merchant fleet, but would not like this division to take place until the end of the Japanese war. Shipping was greatly needed in the Pacific and also to send supplies for rehabilitation. We should need all the shipping we could lay our hands on, and even so would only be able to do a part of what needed to be done.

PREMIER STALIN asked for President Truman's views about the German Merchant Navy.

PRESIDENT TRUMAN said that he would be ready to dispose of it, provided that agreement was reached. He added that after the war the United States would have plenty of merchant ships and naval ships for sale. He did not want to upset the apple-cart before the Japanese war was over.

PREMIER STALIN asked whether the Russians were to wait until the Japanese war was over.

PRESIDENT TRUMAN said that he thought they would have to. But if Russia came into the war against Japan we should, of course, want Russia to come into the pool with us and share in the allocation of resources.

PREMIER STALIN said that the principle was important.

MR. CHURCHILL said that, on the assumption that a general agreement was reached, merchant ships could be earmarked as belonging to a particular country, but could continue to be used for the purposes of the Japanese war so long as it lasted. If they were damaged or lost before they were handed over, some arrangement could be come to as to their replacement. He himself, on merits, supported Premier Stalin's desire that Russia should, in principle, receive a share of Germany's merchant vessels and navy. The only alternative course was the wholesale sinking of the warships. But this was a hard thing to do when one of the Allies expressed a strong desire to keep their share. In principle, therefore, he ranged himself with Premier Stalin.

PRESIDENT TRUMAN said that the three Great Powers were not apart.

PREMIER STALIN asked which ships it was intended should be earmarked.

MR. CHURCHILL said the merchant ships, not the warships.

PREMIER STALIN said that it was not, of course, possible to depict Russia as a people who had any wish to stand in the way of a successful prosecution of the war against Japan. Russia had no such intention. Nor could the matter be expressed by saying that Russia was going to receive a gift from the other Allies. (MR. CHURCHILL interposed that he had certainly not intended to imply this.)

PREMIER STALIN said that he did not say that Mr. Churchill had said this. He would, however, like matters to be cleared up and he wanted to know whether Russia had the right to claim one-third of Germany's battle fleet. He thought they had this right, and anything they received, they should receive as a matter of right. If his colleagues thought otherwise, then they should say so and he would accept their decision.

PRESIDENT TRUMAN indicated that he did not differ from Premier Stalin.

PREMIER STALIN said that he only aimed at clarity. If it was recognised that Russia had a right to a third of the German battle fleet, then Russia would be satisfied. As to the use to which the German merchant fleet would be put, he would have no objection to the Russian third being used in the Allied war effort against Japan.

Premier Stalin then proposed that the matter should be formally settled at the end of the Conference as Mr. Churchill had proposed. But there was one thing he would like to see settled. The Russians had set up a special Naval

Commission, but members of the Commission had not been allowed to see the ships of the German Fleet. They had not even been given the particulars of the ships. Could not this ban be lifted so that the Russian Naval Commission could inspect the German Fleet?

MR. CHURCHILL said that this was a perfectly proper request. But he asked that reciprocal facilities should be given to our people to see German weapons and installations in the Baltic ports. He understood that there were 45 U-boats at Gdynia, some of which were probably of the latest types.

PREMIER STALIN said he was prepared to grant facilities to any British authorities. The U-boats at Gdynia were, however, all damaged.

MR. CHURCHILL said that we only wanted equality and fair-play.

PRESIDENT TRUMAN said that so far as the United States were concerned Premier Stalin was at liberty to see all the German ships they had got. But they would like information to be reciprocal.

MR. CHURCHILL said that he had made a distinction which he regarded as important between the German surface fleet and the U-boats. He knew that Premier Stalin would appreciate the sensitiveness of the people of an island like Great Britain, which grew far less than two-thirds of its food. We had suffered greatly from U-boats in two wars, in a way that no other nation had suffered. Twice we had been brought to the brink of disaster by U-boat campaigns, and the U-boats were not a popular weapon with the British people. He would strongly urge that a considerable portion of the U-boats should be sunk, and that the rest should be shared alike: the number kept by the Three Powers should be a token; more in order to spread technical knowledge than to keep large numbers in existence. As Great Britain had been subjected to terrible assaults by U-boats, we did not welcome any nation expanding in this form of naval construction. He hoped that Premier Stalin and President Truman would pardon his emphasising our special position in this matter.

PREMIER STALIN said that he also favoured sinking a large proportion of the German U-boats and was in agreement with this view.

PRESIDENT TRUMAN indicated that he also was in agreement.

It was accordingly agreed that this matter should be left over with a view to its settlement at the end of the Conference on the lines indicated in the discussion recorded above.

7. *Spain*

The Conference then discussed the following memorandum[10] by the Soviet Delegation about Spain:

'The Soviet Government present for consideration by the Conference the following suggestion:

In view of the fact:

1. that the régime of Franco originated not as a result of the development of the internal forces in Spain, but as a result of the intervention

---

[10] *Note in filed copy:* 'P (Terminal) 8': cf. No. 189, note 9.

by the principal axis-countries[11]—Hitler Germany and Fascist Italy, which imposed upon the Spanish people the Fascist régime of Franco;

2. that the régime of Franco consistutes a grave danger to the freedom-loving nations in Europe and South America;

3. that in the face of brutal terror instituted by Franco the Spanish people have repeatedly expressed themselves against the régime of Franco, and in favour of the restoration of democratic government in Spain,

the Conference deems it necessary to recommend to the United Nations:

1. to break off all relations with the Government of Franco;

2. to render support to the democratic forces in Spain and to enable the Spanish people to establish such a régime as will respond to their will.'

PREMIER STALIN said that he had nothing to add to the paper.

MR. CHURCHILL said that both the present and previous British Government had a strong distaste for General Franco and for the Government of his country. He had himself been misrepresented as being friendly to this gentleman, although all he had ever said was that there was more in Spanish politics than drawing rude cartoons of General Franco. He regarded the continued cold-blooded executions of men who had lain in Spanish prisons for over six years, and other cruelties perpetrated by the Franco régime, as wholly distasteful and undemocratic. When General Franco had sent him a letter suggesting that we should line up with him against the grave menace of Soviet Russia he had sent him, with the full approval of the Cabinet, a very chilling reply, and he sent copies of the correspondence to Premier Stalin and the President.[12]

PREMIER STALIN said that he had received this correspondence.

MR. CHURCHILL continued that there was therefore no question but that he disliked, and indeed, detested, the present Spanish régime.

Where he saw some difficulty in the proposal put forward by Marshal Stalin was in the recommendation that the United Nations should break off all relations with the Government of Franco, which was now the Government of Spain.

It seemed to him that to follow this suggestion might, given the proud and touchy nature of the Spanish people, have the effect of rallying around General Franco those elements which were now deserting him and which were making his position more precarious than ever. Moreover breaking off relations with a country was not altogether a simple business; the actual rupture of relations might give some satisfaction, but once it had been done

[11] The Rome-Berlin axis was a term for the cooperation of Fascist Italy and Nazi Germany. Cf. *D.B.F.P.*, Second Series, vol. xvii, No. 345, note 9.

[12] For the letter of 18 October 1944 from General Franco, delivered to Mr. Eden by the Spanish Ambassador in London on 21 November, and for the British reply of 20 December 1944, handed by Mr. Eden to the Spanish Ambassador on 16 January 1945, see Sir L. Woodward, *op. cit.*, vol. iv, pp. 33 f.

there was no contact at all. Ambassadors were needed, especially in time of difficulty. The result would be to strengthen General Franco's position. He had an army, although probably not a very good one, and a mountainous country easily defended. We should, therefore, either have to take a rebuff or to use heavy forces, and that he would be opposed to.

He did not think that we should interfere with the internal affairs of another country; although of course in the case of a country which had fought against us, or of a country we had liberated, we could not countenance a system of government which was repugnant to us. But here we had a country which had neither fought against us, nor been liberated by us, and he would, therefore, deprecate doing what was suggested. The Franco régime, it was to be hoped, would soon pass away and in all proper diplomatic ways we should speed the parting guest. Breaking off relations, however, was a dangerous practice in world affairs. Moreover he would find still more difficulty in countenancing any action that would lead to a renewal of the Civil War. That had been a terrible war; of a population of 18 million people, 2 million had been killed in the wide and stony peninsula of Spain.

There was the additional point that the World Organisation set up at San Francisco made provision against interference by one country in the domestic affairs of another. While we were preparing to ratify the Charter it would be inconsistent to take action which it would prohibit. He would, therefore, be reluctant to interfere, especially when things looked as if they might improve.

THE PRESIDENT said that he had no love for General Franco and no desire to get involved in another Spanish Civil War. He would, however, be most happy to recognise a government other than General Franco's; but it would be for Spain to settle that.

PREMIER STALIN said that meant that nothing would be changed.

PRESIDENT TRUMAN said not necessarily.

PREMIER STALIN said that in his opinion the Franco régime was gaining strength and feeding semi-Fascist organisations in other countries. His colleagues would know that this régime had been imposed upon the Spanish people by Hitler and Mussolini, and that they were in process of destroying the work of these men. He believed that his colleagues had no love for Franco, but this should be proved in deeds. The fact that we had liberated Europe meant something. What the Soviet Delegation were suggesting was, not military intervention, nor that civil war should be let loose in Spain. But he wished the Spanish people to know that we, representing democratic peoples, were against the Franco régime. They might say that, since we did not denounce the Franco régime, we supported it. Diplomatic means could be used to show the Spanish people that we were on the side of democratic principles. On the assumption, however, that breaking off relations was too severe a measure, could not the Conference think of a more flexible democratic means to let the Spanish people know that we do not sympathise with Franco? It seemed dangerous to leave the situation as it was, and wash our hands. Public opinion in Europe and in the United States, as shown by the press, was in no sympathy with Franco, and if we were to let this cancer in Europe pass in silence, it would mean that we sanctioned it—a very grave charge and one he would not like to be accused of.

Mr. CHURCHILL interjected that the Soviet Union had no diplomatic relations with Franco.

PREMIER STALIN agreed, but said that he did have means to settle with Franco.[13] Moreover the 'Big Three,' and he was one of them, had sufficient power. Were they to remain silent about what was going on in Spain? It would be a blunder to shut our eyes to the great danger which the Franco régime represented to the whole of Europe.

Mr. CHURCHILL said every Government was free to express its own opinion. The Soviet, British and United States press were speaking their views very freely about Spain, and in a manner very similar to those expressed by Premier Stalin. This movement of thought was bringing about a mitigation of the situation in Spain. Speaking for His Majesty's present Government he would not like, unless he were very sure of the favourable result, to take the step of breaking off all relations. There was also the consideration that we had very important trade relations by which we secured oranges, iron ore and wine and received a market for our manufactures.

He quite understood, however, how the Marshal felt about it; there had been the question of the Blue Division on the Russian front which had inflicted an injury. At a time, however, when Spain could have done us great injury during the 'Torch' operation,[14] when our forces were concentrated in Algeciras Bay, she had taken no action.

PREMIER STALIN interposed to say that this was because they were afraid and would have been doomed to failure.

Mr. CHURCHILL explained that he had only mentioned this point in order to show that, while Soviet Russia had been personally injured by Spain we had not. But the point was not of importance.

PREMIER STALIN mentioned that Great Britain had also suffered at the hands of Franco Spain, since bases had been provided for German submarines; in fact, all the Powers had suffered in this or other ways.

He would not, however, like the matter to be viewed from this angle; what mattered was the grave danger that the Franco régime represented for Europe, and he thought that some steps should be taken. All that it was necessary to do was to say that we were not in sympathy with the Franco régime, and that the aspirations of the Spanish people towards democracy were just. He, therefore, suggested that the Foreign Secretaries should try to find a milder and more flexible method than that suggested in the Soviet Delegation paper to make this clear.

[13] The Soviet record here read: 'Stalin: But I do have the right and the possibility of raising the question and settling it': *Conferences: Soviet Documents*, p. 177; cf. *F.R.U.S. Berlin*, vol. ii, p. 124.

[14] The code-name for the Anglo-American landings in French North Africa in November 1942.

PRESIDENT TRUMAN said that he was perfectly prepared to follow this course.

MR. CHURCHILL said that he would deprecate this course and that the matter must be settled round the present table.

PREMIER STALIN agreed that the matter should be decided here, but suggested that the Foreign Secretaries should give it preliminary study.

MR. CHURCHILL said that he really did not think this advisable, since it was a question of principle: non-intervention in the internal affairs of another country.

PREMIER STALIN contended that it was not a domestic affair but an international danger.

MR. CHURCHILL suggested that that could be said about almost any country.

PREMIER STALIN maintained that no such régime remained in any country in Europe.

MR. CHURCHILL suggested that Portugal might be an example of a dictatorship.

PREMIER STALIN pointed out that the Government in Portugal resulted from an internal development, whereas that of Franco came from outside by the intervention of Hitler and Mussolini. Moreover, the behaviour of Franco was most provocative, as he was giving shelter to Nazis. Portugal and Spain were, therefore, not on the same level.

MR. CHURCHILL, returning to the main subject, said that he would not be prepared to advise a House of Commons in which he had a majority, that His Majesty's Government should take the action suggested. He would be very glad, speaking personally, if a change took place in Spain resulting in a constitutional monarchy on democratic lines, and an amnesty for political prisoners. If, however, this view was announced openly, all Spain would turn against it, since no country disliked intervention more than Spain. He believed that Franco was moving to his finale, and that the combined action suggested would only serve to rivet him in place. On the other hand, of course, the British Government would not lift a finger to support him.

PRESIDENT TRUMAN then repeated that he would very much like the matter referred to the Foreign Secretaries so that some decision could be reached.

PREMIER STALIN said that he too would like that course. He fully appreciated, however, the difficulties about questions in Parliament. He therefore, in order to facilitate this matter, would make an alternative proposal, namely, that the Foreign Secretaries should be instructed to prepare an appraisal of the Régime of Franco, making it clear to public opinion that we did not support him; and that this appraisal should be included in a Declaration at the end of the Conference, since he supposed there would be some general Declaration on the lines of that issued after the Yalta Conference. This would not be binding in any way, but would merely represent a short statement of the situation prevailing in Spain.

From it, however, public opinion would know that our sympathy was against Franco. This suggestion was the most mild form of action that could be taken, and indeed milder than that applied to Greece, Yugoslavia or Poland. He therefore suggested that the Foreign Secretaries should think the matter over on these lines.

Mr. Churchill said that he was not aware that he had agreed in principle to any Declaration about Spain being made, nor, he thought had the President.

Premier Stalin interposed to say that he had not meant the Declaration to cover Spain alone.

Mr. Churchill repeated that the line he had taken was that we should not interfere in the domestic affairs of a country which had not been involved in war against us, and which we had not liberated. There was therefore a difference between the question of Spain and for instance that of Yugoslavia, Bulgaria and Roumania, where frankly there were things which he did not like. Moreover, although he had a great admiration for declarations on general principles, he felt that if we laid them down with special application to Spain, we should find ourselves in deep water. He felt, too, that the Spanish people were already moving away from Franco, and he would therefore like to give that movement a chance. He did not therefore see what there was for the Foreign Secretaries, who were already very busy, to do in this matter.

At the suggestion of President Truman, who thought that there was no chance for agreement at the present time, it was decided to leave the topic for the moment and to go on to the next item on the agenda.

8. *Yalta Declaration on Liberated Europe*

President Truman said that he recommended for discussion at the present Meeting the Memorandum by the United States Delegation (P. (Terminal) 4).[15]

At the request of Premier Stalin, who said that the Soviet Delegation had another document on this subject to submit, the Conference agreed to discuss it at a later date.

9. *Yugoslavia*

The following memorandum[16] had been circulated by the British Delegation:

'At the Crimea Conference on the 10th February the Heads of the three Governments discussed the Yugoslav question and agreed to recommend to Marshal Tito and Dr. Subasic that the agreement between them be put into effect and a new Government formed on the basis of the agreement.

2. The three Governments have thus endorsed the Tito-Subasic Agreement, with its guarantees of the basic principles of democratic

[15] See No. 170, note 2.
[16] *Note in filed copy:* 'P (Terminal) 22'.

liberties, in particular personal freedom, freedom from fear, freedom of religion and conscience, freedom of speech, press meetings and associations, and the right of property and private initiative, and with the promise of a democratic election within three months of the Yugoslav liberation.

3. Doubtless owing to war conditions, the principles set out in the Tito–Subasic Agreement have not been fully carried out. In view of the declaration issued at Yalta,[17] it is desirable that, at the close of the present meeting, the three Heads of Governments should issue a statement recalling the fact that they had given recognition to the Yugoslav Government on the basis of the Yalta agreement and the Tito–Subasic Agreement, which they expect to be fully carried out in the near future.'

PREMIER STALIN said that it was not possible to discuss this matter without inviting representatives of the Yugoslav Government. Without this no results could be achieved.

MR. EDEN pointed out that the original declaration made at the Yalta Conference had been agreed to by the representatives of the three Great Powers without the hearing of representatives from Yugoslavia.

PREMIER STALIN said that at the time of the Yalta Conference the position had been different. There had then been two Governments of Yugoslavia which could not agree. But now a legitimate Government was in existence, and accusations made against that Government could not be settled in their absence.

MR. CHURCHILL asked if it was intended to invite Marshal Tito and Dr. Subasic.

PREMIER STALIN said that he did not mind who was invited.

MR. CHURCHILL said that the two parties in the Government were in extreme disagreement.

PREMIER STALIN said that he had no such information. This was the first time he had heard anything of the kind: that was why he suggested summoning representatives and hearing what the position was.

PRESIDENT TRUMAN asked whether the information was sufficiently serious to make it necessary to send for representatives of the Yugoslav Government.

MR. CHURCHILL said that at Yalta the Tito–Subasic Agreement had been endorsed, but this Agreement had not yet been carried out. No electoral law had been published; the Avnoj had not been enlarged; ordinary judicial procedure had not been restored in any part of the country; Tito's administration had imposed a strictly controlled party organisation backed by political police; and the press almost as closely controlled as in Fascist countries. The proposal which he, Mr. Churchill, was making was, therefore, a very modest one, namely, that we should renew the declaration which we had made at Yalta.

PREMIER STALIN said that Mr. Churchill had passed to the question of

---

[17] As article VIII of the Protocol of the Conference at Yalta: *B.F.S.P.*, vol. 148, pp. 86–7.

430

substance and had not answered President Truman's question how far the matter was worth pursuing. The information which Mr. Churchill had given about the Yalta decision was not known to the Russian Government. Mr. Churchill might be right or he might not. But if we were to deal with the substantive accusations we must have representatives of the Yugoslav Government.

MR. CHURCHILL said that he would prefer to speak of complaints rather than of accusations.

PREMIER STALIN said that he still did not see how complaints against the Yugoslav Government could be dealt with in their absence.

MR. CHURCHILL said he had only had a moment or so to think over the suggestion that we should send for representatives of the Yugoslav Government; but it might be useful if Marshal Tito and Dr. Subasic were to be invited to come to the Conference. It might well be that these difficulties could be overcome as a result of discussion. Anyhow an opinion could be formed from discussion with these gentlemen. Did Premier Stalin think they would be willing to come?

PREMIER STALIN said that he did not know, but we could send an enquiry.

PRESIDENT TRUMAN said that he wished to make a statement before a decision was reached. He had come to Berlin for a discussion of world affairs with Premier Stalin and Mr. Churchill. He did not want, so to speak, to sit on a court which would hear complaints dealing with the affairs of various small States. His purpose was to discuss matters, as between three Heads of Government, on which they could come to an agreement. If he did otherwise, he would be wasting his time.

PREMIER STALIN said that this was a correct observation.

MR. CHURCHILL said that he thought the United States was much interested in this matter, because of the paper which they had submitted about the Yalta Declaration on Liberated Europe. Of course great allowances could be made for Tito on account of the difficult condition of his country. Nevertheless, the Yalta Declaration, in which the United States had played so large a part, ought to be renewed and enlarged.

PRESIDENT TRUMAN said that it was certainly his intention to carry out his obligations to the letter. From time to time he had heard a number of complaints as regards Yugoslavia, but he thought it would be best to show some patience with the Yugoslav Government for a while.

MR. CHURCHILL said that as the British Delegation's paper had not obtained the support which he had expected, he was willing not to press the matter further at the moment. But the question of Yugoslavia could not be dropped.

PRESIDENT TRUMAN suggested that the matter should be postponed for a day or so.

MR. CHURCHILL said that he would like to thank Premier Stalin for his patience in this discussion; but if they could not express their minds freely to each other round this table, when could they do so?

PREMIER STALIN thanked Mr. Churchill for what he had said, and

431

agreed that the matter could be talked over. But complaints could not be settled in the absence of those against whom the complaints were made. Complaints were made against the heads of the Yugoslav Government, and his answer was that the heads of the Government should be heard.

MR. CHURCHILL said he was ready to agree to this course, but President Truman did not agree to it.

PREMIER STALIN said that it seemed, therefore, that the question would have to be dropped for the time being.

10. *Roumania: Removal of Industrial Equipment*

The Conference had before it the following paper[18] by the United Kingdom Delegation:

'1. Large sums of British capital are invested in companies producing oil in Roumania. In October 1944 the Soviet authorities in Roumania removed large quantities of equipment from these British companies and from other Allied-owned companies, on the grounds that it was war booty.

2. The resulting damage to British interests was very considerable. Furthermore, the action taken has reduced the total output of Roumanian oil wells by one million tons a year, at a time of grave oil shortage. As a result, Roumania's capacity to pay reparations and the revenue-earning capacity of British and other Allied capital was diminished.

3. In January 1945 the Soviet Government agreed to discontinue removals of equipment. But the equipment already removed was not returned, nor did the Soviet Government agree to regard it as deliveries on account of reparations.

4. Further oil equipment was removed from a British-controlled company in April.

5. His Majesty's Government ask that the equipment which has been removed from these British companies shall be returned as soon as possible. Furthermore, they ask that no further action damaging to these British companies shall be taken by the Soviet authorities, and that the consent of the British representative on the Allied Control Commission in Roumania shall be sought before any action in their regard is undertaken.'

MR. CHURCHILL said that the British Delegation had circulated this paper as it seemed that sort of question which the Foreign Secretaries might discuss together, and on which they might reach agreement. In any case the Plenary Meeting should have the benefit of their advice, especially as the matter was one of great complexity.

PREMIER STALIN thought that this was a trifling matter which could be settled through the usual diplomatic channel, and need not be raised at this Conference. Since it had been brought up, however, he would like to correct one of two inaccuracies in the paper. No British property had been taken by Russia from Roumania. What had happened was that certain

---

[18] *Note in filed copy:* 'P (Terminal) 10'.

British oil companies had purchased tubes from Germany. These tubes had been seized by Germany during the war and had been proclaimed by them as being their own property. The Russians had removed some quantity of these tubes to make good the devastation done by the Germans to the Russian oil industry in the Caucasus.

Having made this observation Premier Stalin said he had no objection to the three Foreign Secretaries examining the matter, though it was so trifling that it could be settled by the ordinary diplomatic channels without troubling the Conference.

MR. CHURCHILL said that the matter was not quite trifling, and we had suffered loss. If this matter had been included in reparations, we should have been able to recover the cost. We had only brought it up at the Conference because we had not been able to obtain satisfaction through the ordinary channels.

PRESIDENT TRUMAN said that certain American-owned companies were also concerned, and he suggested that the three Foreign Secretaries should see what progress they could make with the matter.

PREMIER STALIN agreed with this proposal.

Cabinet Office, Potsdam, 19th July, 1945

CALENDARS TO No. 194

i *18 July 1945   U.K. Delegation brief on the Eastern Frontier of Germany as it affects the principles governing the treatment of Germany and the authority of the Control Council.* Refers to Nos. 115 and 184, minute 5. Concludes that H.M.G., 'while fully supporting Poland's right to accessions of territory, regard the present claim to the Oder-Neisse line, including Stettin, as excessive': printed in *F.R.U.S. Berlin*, vol. ii, pp. 1136–8 [F.O. 934/2/10(8)].

ii *19 July 1945   Letter from Mr. Hayter (Berlin) to Mr. Howard.* Reports discussion in minutes 9 and 10 above of British papers on Yugoslavia and Roumania respectively; these topics, coming after 'a rather heated debate' on Soviet proposal to break off relations with Spain, 'did not get very far' [F.O. 934/2/8(5)].

iii *19–24 July 1945   To Mr. Eden (Berlin) Tel. No. 71 Onward, minuted by Mr. Ward.* Repeats Moscow telegram No. 3200 of 18 July reporting Russian refusal of British request to charter some Finnish merchant ships: discussed in relation to minute 6 above [F.O. 934/4/24(1)].

No. 195

Minute from Mr. Hoyer Millar to Sir A. Cadogan (Berlin)
[F.O. 934/4/26(2)]

[BERLIN,] *19 July 1945*

I understand from this afternoon's discussion that the question of Spain and the Russian suggestion of some kind of anti-Franco resultion [*sic*] being adopted may be brought up again at any time in the future.[1] Judging by what Marshal Stalin said it seems more than likely that the Russian Delegation will in fact press the matter further.

There are of course obvious objections to the Russian proposals as originally drafted;[1] the suggestion that we should break off relations with Franco's Government will lead us nowhere, while the proposal that we should 'render support to the democratic forces in Spain to enable the Spanish people to establish such a régime as will respond to their will' is equivalent to direct intervention in Spanish internal affairs. Clearly therefore we cannot in any circumstances accept the Russian proposals in their original form. Nor, it was clear, would the U.S. Delegation be prepared to accept them. On the other hand from Marshal Stalin's remarks it seemed fairly clear that he would be prepared to accept some alternative form of wording provided always that this made it clear that the three Governments definitely disapproved of Franco and his régime. While we have always taken the line that the question of any alternative régime to Franco was a matter for the Spanish people to decide themselves, and any suggestion that the Three Powers felt themselves entitled to dictate to the smaller ex-enemy countries the kind of government they should have must be avoided, there is, I think, something to be said in favour of trying to find some fairly anodyne form of anti-Franco resolution. If we continue to resist we shall make the Russians more obstinate on points to which we attach importance and we run the risk of creating a suspicion in the minds of the Americans that we are pro-Franco and reactionary. Furthermore, it is definitely the case that H.M.G. would welcome Franco's disappearance. At the moment he seems to have gained rather than lost influence in Spain during the last six months and the speech he made two days ago[2] indicates that he himself has every intention of remaining in power and keeping the Falange[3] on with him as long as possible. On the other hand the action taken at San Francisco on the Mexican resolution which suggested that Spain would be ineligible for the membership of the World Organisation[4] had quite an effect in Madrid—so much so that it has caused the Spanish Government to ask several foreign Governments including H.M.G. how they interpreted the resolution [i].

That being so, it might be possible both to satisfy the Russian Delegation and effectively to indicate our dislike of the Franco régime without at the same time appearing directly to intervene in Spanish internal affairs by passing a resolution somewhat on the following lines:

'The Three Governments, while recognising that it rests with the Spanish people themselves to choose the type of government under which they wish to live, feel bound to make it clear that insofar as they them-

[1] See No. 194, minute 7.
[2] Cf. *The Times* of 18 July 1945, p. 3, and *F.R.U.S. 1945*, vol. v, pp. 681–2.
[3] General Franco was the leader of the Spanish nationalist movement of the Falange Española Tradicionalista.
[4] See No. 65, note 3.

selves are concerned, they will find it difficult to place their own relations with Spain on a better footing so long as General Franco and the Falange régime remain in power.[5] In particular as long as the present régime in Spain remains unaltered, the Three Governments will feel unable to support any application from the Spanish Government for membership of the World Organisation.'[6]

F. R. Hoyer Millar

Calendar to No. 195

i *17 July 1945 To Mr. Bowker (Madrid) Tel. No. 575.* Oral reply from Sir A. Cadogan on 13 July to Spanish request for views on Mexican Declaration: H.M.G. 'regard the Declaration as expressing the general view of the Commission concerned' but question of applying principle expressed therein would be for the U.N.O. itself to decide. Sir A. Cadogan had commented that 'Spain under the Franco régime had no chance whatever of being admitted to the World Organisation' [U 5284/12/70].

[5] Sir A. Cadogan, who initialed this minute on 20 July 1945, noted against the preceding clause: 'I think this is going a little far towards interference in domestic affairs. A. C.' At foot he noted: 'I have submitted in outline an alternative formula': see No. 196, note 3.
[6] This proposed resolution is printed by Sir L. Woodward, *op. cit.*, vol. v, p. 471.

No. 196

Minute by Mr. Hayter (Berlin)
[*F.O. 934/4/26(2)*]

[Berlin,] *20 July 1945*

Spain and Yugoslavia

These two subjects were adjourned yesterday without any decision.[1] It might perhaps be possible to link them.

I understand that Mr. Hoyer Millar thinks an anodyne statement saying that we do not like Franco would be unobjectionable.[2] The Secretary of State might think it worth while saying to Molotov that he believed that it might be possible to convince the Prime Minister that a statement about Spain would be desirable, but that he would find it easier to do so if the Russians for their part would agree to something being said about Yugoslavia in the final protocol. This might merely be to the effect that the Three congratulated Yugoslavia on her final liberation from the enemy, and expressed the confident expectation that, as recommended by the Yalta

[1] See No. 194, minutes 7 and 9.
[2] See No. 195.

435

Conference, the Tito-Subasic agreement would continue to form the basis for the Yugoslav State.[3]

W. G. HAYTER

[3] Sir A. Cadogan minuted at foot: 'As regards Spain, I put it to Mr. Byrnes last night that it might be possible to have a declaration to the effect that the 3 Powers were disposed to support at the proper time Italy's candidature for admission to the World Organisation: they w[oul]d also be prepared to examine the candidature of neutral countries though this could *not*, in present circumstances and in the light of the San Francisco resolution, apply to Spain. Mr. Byrnes seemed receptive. A. C. 20 July, 1945.'

No. 197

Minute from Mr. Eden to Mr. Churchill (Berlin)
No. P.M./45/6.T. [F.O. 934/5/36(1)]

[BERLIN,] 20 July 1945

In your minute [i] on the telegram from the British Military Mission in Hungary BMM/565 of July 14th, you asked what we want about Hungary.

2. We want nothing specific about Hungary at the present Conference, apart from the questions which we hope the Americans will raise about the improvement of the status of our Control Commissions and the implementation of the Yalta Declaration on liberated areas, which of course apply to Hungary as well as to Bulgaria and Rumania.

3. There may be a few small points about British controlled factories in Hungary, but, so far as we know, there is no need to take these up with the Russians at the present.[1]

A. E.

CALENDARS TO No. 197

i *13–14 July 1945 Mr. Gascoigne (Budapest) Tel. No. 231; Major-General Edgecumbe (British Commissioner, A.C.C. Hungary) Tel. No. B.M.M. 565.* Summarizes and comments on arrangements for A.C.C. in Hungary proposed by Marshal Voroshilov in letter of 11 July to General Edgecumbe (cited under date of 12 July in No. 518, minute 7). In cordial conversation on 13 July (in tel. B.M.M./565) General Edgecumbe told Marshal Voroshilov that he was 'very pleased' with these principles, and explained British interest in economic future of Hungary. Mr. Churchill minuted on this telegram 'Foreign Office. What do we want about Hungary? W.S.C. 19.vii' [F.O. 934/2/9(26); F.O. 934/5/36(1)].

ii *15–16 July 1945 To and from Mr. Gascoigne (Budapest) Tels. Nos. 239 and 234.* Differences between Soviet communications of 11 July on A.C.C.s. in Bulgaria (cf. No. 136, note 2) and Hungary [R 11915, 11989/84/21].

[1] This minute was initialed by Mr. Churchill on 23 July 1945.

No. 198

Minutes of a Meeting of the British Chiefs of Staff Committee held at 39/41 Ringstrasse, Babelsberg, on Friday, 20 July 1945 at 10.30 a.m.

C.O.S. (Terminal) 5th Meeting [CAB 99/39]

Top secret

Present:

FIELD-MARSHAL SIR ALAN F. BROOKE, Chief of the Imperial General Staff (*in the Chair*), Marshal of the Royal Air Force Sir Charles F. A. Portal, Chief of the Air Staff, Admiral of the Fleet Sir Andrew B. Cunningham, First Sea Lord and Chief of Naval Staff, General Sir Hastings L. Ismay, Office of the Minister of Defence.

The following were also present:
Field-Marshal Sir Henry Maitland Wilson, Major-General R. E. Laycock, Chief of Combined Operations, Lieut.-General Sir Gordon Macready, Major-General N. G. Holmes, War Office (*for Items 1, 2 and 3*).

Secretariat: Major-General L. C. Hollis, Brigadier A. T. Cornwall-Jones, Lieut.-Colonel G. Mallaby, Lieut.-Colonel T. Haddon, Lieut.-Colonel M. R. Norman.

1. *Basic Objectives and Undertakings*
(C.O.S. (Terminal) 6)[1]
(Previous Reference: C.O.S. (Terminal) 4th Meeting,[2] Minute 1.)

THE COMMITTEE had under consideration a revised edition of the draft paper on Basic Objectives, Strategy and Policies.

MAJOR-GENERAL HOLMES explained that he had attended the meeting the previous afternoon with Lord Leathers, Lord Cherwell, a representative of the Treasury, Sir Edward Bridges and General Macready, and that he had subsequently discussed the question with General Somervell. As a result of this last discussion, he had suggested the inclusion of a new paragraph 7 and the inclusion of this paragraph made unnecessary certain of the amendments proposed by the Joint Planning Staff on the previous day. He informed the Committee that Lord Leathers had agreed the paper as

---

[1] Not printed. Under this covering note dated at Babelsberg on 19 July 1945 Major-General Hollis had circulated as an annex a revised text of the annex to No. 186. This revised annex was subsequently circulated as a memorandum of 20 July by the British Chiefs of Staff (C.C.S. 877/4: see note 3 below), and is printed in *F.R.U.S. Berlin*, vol. ii, pp. 1299–1304. In his covering note, C.O.S. (Terminal) 6, General Hollis had stated in particular: 'It will be recalled that the Prime Minister directed that the United Kingdom import programme was not to be removed from this paper and was to be adequately safeguarded. Paragraph 4 A of this draft secures the United Kingdom import programme in so far as it is part of the war-making capacity of the United Kingdom. The programme is further safe-guarded by the fact that the total shipping required to meet it up to the end of June 1946 has been agreed in the Cargo Shipping Review and paragraph 7 of the attached provides that no interference in the tonnages therein allotted can be made without reference to Governments.'
[2] No. 187.

now drafted, and later in the meeting a message was received saying that Lord Cherwell agreed on behalf of the Prime Minister.

GENERAL MACREADY said that although it was possible that the United States Chiefs of Staff would agree with the inclusion of a new paragraph 7, there was almost certain to be opposition from them on the suggested amendments to paragraphs 4B and 6C. He thought, however, that the amendment to paragraph 4B, which was only designed to ensure that forces being despatched to the war against Japan arrived there properly equipped, might be accepted. There was a danger that the Americans would feel that the amendment to paragraph 6C was in direct conflict with the President's directive on the subject of lend-lease. It could, however, be argued that all we were seeking to do was to state the purposes for which the resources of both Great Britain and the United States should be used and to allow ourselves a free hand to use our own equipment for the areas in which we had responsibility.

SIR ALAN BROOKE agreed that there might be difficulty over the second of these two amendments and felt that logically the Combined Chiefs of Staff should not consider the paper on basic objectives until the matter of lend-lease had been settled.

After further discussion on this point, the Committee agreed that if the United States Chiefs of Staff raised objections to the inclusion of the amendments to paragraph 4C[?6C], the British Chiefs of Staff would suggest reserving a decision on the paper until the outcome of any negotiations between the President and the Prime Minister on lend-lease was known.

THE COMMITTEE–
Instructed the Secretary to circulate the memorandum as a C.C.S. paper.[3] . . .[4]

[3] *Note in filed copy:* 'Subsequently circulated as C.C.S. 877/4': cf. note 1 above.
[4] The rest of these minutes, concerning other questions, are not printed: cf. No. 199, note 1, and No. 211, note 1: also S. V. Woodburn Kirby, *The War against Japan*, vol. v, p. 225.

No. 199

Report by the British Chiefs of Staff to Mr. Churchill (Berlin)[1]
C.O.S. *(Terminal) 5th Meeting: annex* [CAB 99/39]

BABELSBERG, *20 July 1945*
Cabinet Office, 'Terminal'

1. Reference your Minute Serial No. D. (T) 3/5, we have examined the first two paragraphs of the President's Memorandum of the 17th July about Lend-Lease.[2]

[1] This report (cf. No. 187, minute 6) had been approved on 20 July 1945, without recorded discussion (cf. note 7 below), by the Chiefs of Staff Committee at its fifth meeting at Babelsberg: minute 3 of C.O.S. (Terminal) 5th Meeting: cf. No. 198, note 4.
[2] See No. 187, notes 12–13.

2. We should first point out that as far as the supply of military material is concerned the whole basis of the arrangements made between Lord Keynes and Mr. Morgenthau last autumn,[3] was that equipment and stores would be made available under Lend-Lease, not only to assist us in meeting the needs of our forces directly engaged in the war with Japan, but also the forces supporting these operations and occupying Europe.

3. The first paragraph of the President's Memorandum is not clear. We fear, however, that it must be interpreted as meaning that the supply of Lend-Lease equipment will only be made available to such of our forces as are engaged in the prosecution of the war against Japan, because:

(a) The President issued a Directive to the War and Navy Departments on the 5th July, in the following terms:

'Approval of the issue to Allied Governments of Lend-Lease munitions of war and military and naval equipment will be limited to that which is to be used in the war against Japan, and *it will not be issued for any other purpose.*'[4]

The War and Navy Departments are very naturally rigidly adhering to this Directive, and assignments to us of military material are suffering seriously in consequence.

(b) The Lend-Lease Continuation Act,[5] which was passed by Congress last month, states that Lend-Lease military supplies can only be provided for *direct use* in the prosecution of the war against Japan.

So far as we are aware, there are no practical difficulties in the actual production of our requirements in the United States, except perhaps in the case of clothing and textiles. The alternative seems to be:

Either (a) That the President should be persuaded to cancel the Directive quoted in paragraph 3 (a) above and instruct the War and Navy Departments to work on the wider basis of the arrangements made last autumn;

Or (b) That some method other than Lend-Lease should be found for financing the supplies required for those forces not actually engaged in the war against Japan.

5. [*sic*] You asked for an explanation of what were our requirements of lend-lease supplies not directly connected with the prosecution of the war against Japan, and why we needed them.

6. British Commonwealth Forces all over the world are partially equipped with United States equipment. We are reducing the scales and reserves of all such equipment to the greatest extent possible, so as to make available a maximum quantity for use in the Far East. The remaining United States equipment however must be maintained by a constant flow of spare parts. Otherwise the equipment would become useless and we cannot replace it

[3] Cf. No. 26, note 7.
[4] See No. 26, note 4.
[5] Of 16 April 1945, printed in *Documents on American Foreign Relations*, vol. vii (Princeton, 1947), p. 138.

by comparable British equipment within any reasonable time and without increasing the United Kingdom munitions programmes.

7. The three Services are also dependent in varying degrees on supply from the United States of components required for equipment manufactured in the United Kingdom and Canada.

8. At Flag 'A' (Enclosure 1)[6] are set out some examples of equipment and components which the three Services require from the United States and the effect on the position of our Forces all over the world if these needs are not met.

9. In view of the situation described above, we submit at Flag 'B' (Enclosure 2) a revised memorandum in the form in which we earnestly hope you will feel able to take the matter up with the President.

A. F. BROOKE
C. A. PORTAL
A. B. CUNNINGHAM

ENCLOSURE 2 IN NO. 199

Draft Memorandum from the Prime Minister to the President[7]

1. Thank you for your memorandum of the 17th July[8] about Lend-Lease. I am very gratified to see that you intend to furnish us with Lend-Lease for the prosecution of the war against Japan generally in accord with the schedules of requirements for the first year following the defeat of Germany, and other terms worked out between our respective supply representatives last autumn. I should, however, be grateful if you would confirm that this means that troops of occupation and other forces carrying out essential tasks now holding American equipment, will be entitled to such maintenance as they require, in addition to what will be assigned to those forces directly engaged in the war against Japan. Also that our other requirements for components, &c., needed for manufacturing programmes in the United Kingdom and Canada, which were included in the autumn agreement, will also be made available to us.

2. I mention this because our requirements are at present only being accepted by your agencies if they are needed for direct use against the Japanese, apparently as the result of a directive which has been given to them. In addition, the United States members of the Combined Munitions Assignment Board are questioning and often rejecting bids which are within the requirements accepted in principle last autumn, on the grounds that the equipment in question can be made in the United Kingdom. These seem to me to be questions of governmental policy which were covered by the agreements made last autumn, and the discussion of them is, in my opinion, quite outside the province of the Combined Munitions Assignment Board.

---

[6] Not printed. This undated memorandum, entitled 'Effect upon the three Services if supply of certain lend-lease equipment is limited to forces actually fighting the Japanese', was an abbreviated version of No. 187.ii.

[7] In approving the draft of this document on 20 July (cf. note 1 above) the Chiefs of Staff Committee had 'suggested a few small amendments'.

[8] No. 174, annex.

3. The reason that we need continuing assignments of Lend-Lease equipment not only for our forces directly engaged against Japan is that the Commonwealth forces all over the world, in occupied territory and on the lines of communication to the Far East, are partly equipped with American equipment for which we cannot ourselves provide spare parts and which could not be replaced in a reasonable time by new British equipment.

4. Further, unless we can obtain the components we were counting on from the United States for equipment being made in the United Kingdom and Canada, our own production programmes will be seriously dislocated.

5. Again, certain types of completed aircraft are required in connection with our redeployment and inter-communication services. At the moment we do not manufacture comparable types in the United Kingdom and our general military efficiency would suffer if these aircraft were withheld from us.

6. In paragraph 2 of your memorandum you refer to the changed situation since the Lend-Lease arrangements were made in the autumn of 1944. I am not quite clear to what you refer, since we have now arrived at the very situation which was envisaged when the arrangements were made last autumn, namely, the end of hostilities in Europe. It was certainly agreed at that time that adjustments should be made to our requirements in the light of the actual date of the defeat of Germany, and the military requirements which we are now putting forward have accordingly been rigorously pruned. On our calculations they represent, for the twelve months ended the 30th June, 1946, rather less than two-thirds of the value of the requirements which were accepted in the negotiations last autumn, *i.e.*, some 1.8 billion dollars, as compared with 2.8 billion.

7. I earnestly hope that you will find it possible to let it be known to your administration that these requirements which are now in process of being stated to the Departments in Washington, resting as they do upon the whole assessment of our position which was agreed at that time, should be accepted and that the necessary financial and production provision should be made to meet them.

8. I hope that you will also agree that once these requirements have been accepted for procurement, they should also be accepted as a valid basis for assignment. By valid basis I mean that if the items are not in short supply our bids within these totals should be accepted without argument. It would be understood, of course, that items which are in short supply would be assigned with due regard to operational priorities. Our request for assignments would fall within the total of our accepted requirements, except for any items which may become urgently necessary for unforeseen operational reasons. Even if we give British equipment to Allied forces, such as those which will assist in the occupation of the British Zone in Germany, or are necessary for purposes of internal security, we should do so at the expense of our own troops, and would not seek to increase the total of our requirements on this account.

9. I therefore ask that you cause to be issued to all those in the War and Navy Departments dealing with these matters a directive on the lines suggested in paragraphs 7 and 8. All our present plans are based on the principles underlying the agreements reached last autumn and unless procurement and assignment operate on these lines, the fulfilment of our obligations in the war against Japan, and in the pacification of Europe, will be gravely prejudiced.[9]

[9] General Ismay stated in a minute of 20 July (on PREM 4/17/15) to Mr. Rowan concerning No. 199: 'I have had a talk with Lord Cherwell who tells me that he and you and Sir Edward Bridges thought that the suggested draft memorandum from the Prime Minister

to the President was too long and detailed for the Prime Minister to sign as his own, and that the better course would be for the Prime Minister to send a short minute to the President in very general terms, annexing the suggested draft as a staff paper. Personally, I entirely agree with this idea.' See further No. 232, note 26.

No. 200

Record of Third Meeting of Foreign Secretaries held at Cecilienhof, Potsdam, on Friday, 20 July 1945 at 11 a.m.
F. (Terminal) 3rd Meeting [U 6197/3628/70]

Top secret

Present:

M. V. M. Molotov, M. A. Ya. Vyshinski, M. A. A. Gromyko, M. F. T. Gousev, M. K. V. Novikov, M. V. S. Semenov, M. S. A. Golunski (*Interpreter*).

Mr. J. F. Byrnes, Mr. W. A. Harriman, Mr. J. C. Dunn, Mr. H. F. Matthews, Mr. W. L. Clayton, Mr. C. E. Bohlen, Mr. B. V. Cohen, Mr. E. Page (*Interpreter*).

Mr. Eden, Sir A. Cadogan, Sir A. Clark Kerr, Sir W. Strang, Mr. N. Brook, Mr. P. J. Dixon, Mr. W. Hayter, Major L. M. Theakstone (*Interpreter*).

Contents

Minute	Subject
1.	Outstanding Business
2.	Council of Foreign Ministers
3.	Subjects for Discussion
4.	Italy and Spain
5.	Reparations: Liability of Italy and Austria
6.	Balkans: Yalta Declaration on Liberated Europe
7.	Agenda for Fourth Plenary Meeting

1. *Outstanding Business*

M. Molotov said that reports from Sub-Committees were outstanding on (*a*) Germany: Consideration of Economic Problems, and (*b*) Poland.

It was agreed that both Committees should be instructed to report to the Foreign Secretaries' Meeting the following morning.

2. *Council of Foreign Ministers*
(Previous Reference: P. (Terminal), 3rd Meeting,[1] Minute 2.)

It was recalled that the amendment to the draft constitution of the Council which had been suggested by Mr. Byrnes at the previous Meeting had been referred to the Committee which had prepared the first revised draft of the constitution (F. (Terminal) 1st Meeting,[2] Minute 2). It had not been possible

---

[1] No. 194.　　　　　　　　　　[2] No. 178.

for this Committee to hold more than one short meeting, since M. Sobolev was fully occupied on the Committee on Economic Policy towards Germany.

MR. BYRNES said that a number of suggestions had already been put before the Committee. The quickest procedure might be for each member of the Committee to submit these to his Foreign Secretary and for the Foreign Secretaries to meet at 3.45 p.m., so that, if they could agree, the draft constitution might be brought before the Plenary Meeting for final approval that afternoon.

It was agreed that the procedure suggested by Mr. Byrnes should be adopted.

3. *Subjects for Discussion*

M. MOLOTOV suggested that the Meeting might now proceed to consider:
(a) Yalta Declaration on Liberated Europe. (P. (Terminal) 4).[3]
(b) Western Frontier of Poland.
(c) Territorial Trusteeship.
(d) Agenda for the Plenary Meeting that afternoon.

The Soviet Delegation had prepared memoranda on the first three of these questions.

MR. EDEN said that he would prefer that the Foreign Secretaries should, as far as possible, dispose of the matters already referred to them by the Plenary Meeting, before undertaking new subjects, and asked whether they should not first discuss the Roumanian question, which had been remitted to them by the Plenary Meeting on the previous day (P. (Terminal) 3rd Meeting,[1] Minute 10).

MR. BYRNES agreed. Another matter which he wished to have considered was Policy towards Italy, on which he was ready to make a further proposal affecting the question of Spain (P. (Terminal) 3rd Meeting,[1] Minute 7).

M. MOLOTOV agreed that these subjects might be considered; but he suggested that, although the Yalta Declaration on Liberated Europe had not been specifically referred to the Foreign Secretaries, it might be helpful for them to give some preliminary consideration to the memorandum which the Soviet Delegation had prepared.

It was agreed that the following subjects should be discussed:
(a) Italy and Spain.
(b) Yalta Declaration on Liberated Europe.
(c) Roumania: Removal of Industrial Equipment.

4. *Italy and Spain*
(Previous References: P. (Terminal) 1st Meeting,[4] Minute 2 (a) and 3rd Meeting[1], Minute 7.)

MR. BYRNES recalled that in submitting his memorandum on Italy (P. (Terminal) 5)[5] President Truman had suggested that a public announcement might be made at the end of the Conference foreshadowing the admission of Italy to association with the United Nations.

[3] See No. 170, note 2.   [4] No. 170.   [5] See No. 208, minute 4.

Mr. Byrnes now wished to put the further suggestion that in this announcement it might be indicated that the three Great Powers would not favour the admission of Spain to association with the United Nations, so long as she remained under the control of the present régime. He proposed the appointment of a drafting committee to prepare a statement on these lines for submission to the Plenary Meeting.

MR. EDEN said that he was attracted by Mr. Byrnes' suggestion. He wondered whether such a statement would not be strengthened if it included a reference to other neutral countries in the same position as Italy. Would not this emphasise still further the contrast with Spain?

MR. BYRNES agreed. He believed that a statement on these lines would meet the suggestion regarding Spain made by Premier Stalin at the last Plenary Meeting.

In answer to a question by M. Molotov, MR. EDEN said that the other neutral States which he had in mind were Sweden, Switzerland and Portugal. He was not, however, proposing that the statement should contain a definite promise that named neutral States would be admitted to association with the United Nations: what he had in mind was that the Great Powers should declare themselves in favour of considering the eventual admission of Italy and States which had been neutral in the war with Germany, with a specific proviso that Spain could not be regarded as eligible for admission so long as she remained under the control of the present political régime.

M. MOLOTOV asked whether reference would also be made to the admission of ex-enemy States who had become co-belligerents.

MR. EDEN said that this might be considered. It must, however, be borne in mind that the conclusion of a peace settlement must precede admission to association with the United Nations in the case of all countries (including Italy) which had waged war against the United Nations. For this reason he had thought it would be simpler to contrast the position of Spain with that of other neutrals.

It was agreed that the following should be appointed as a Committee:
United States Delegation:
Mr. H. F. Matthews, Mr. C. W. Cannon;
United Kingdom Delegation:
Mr. F. Hoyer Millar, Mr. P. Dean;
Russian Delegation:
M. I. M. Maisky, M. F. T. Gousev;
to prepare a draft statement on the lines suggested in the discussion recorded above.

5. *Reparations: Liability of Italy and Austria*

In the course of the discussion recorded in the preceding Minute M. MOLOTOV asked whether it was intended that Italy should pay reparations and how it was suggested that the question should be considered.

MR. BYRNES said that he doubted whether in practice Italy could pay reparations. The United States Government had already advanced some

444

200 million dollars to Italy and would probably have to advance a further 400 or 500 million dollars. They were not, therefore, expecting any benefit from Italian reparations; and he wished to make it clear that the United States were not prepared to advance money to Italy, or to any other ex-enemy country, for the purpose of enabling her to pay reparations.

M. Molotov pointed out that Finland was paying reparations. It would not be just, nor would it be acceptable to world opinion, that a large country like Italy should be allowed to go free while a small country like Finland had to pay.

Mr. Eden agreed that in principle Italy was liable to pay reparations. The extent to which this liability was to be enforced was a matter which should be considered when the Peace Treaty with Italy was prepared. He inclined to agree with Mr. Byrnes's view of Italian ability to pay. The question of Italy's admission to association with the United Nations (see Minute 4 above) would not be affected by this point. Italy's liability to reparations would be defined in the Peace Treaty, and her subsequent admission to association with the United Nations would be conditional upon her compliance with the obligations imposed on her by that Treaty.

M. Molotov said that he regarded the two questions as connected: for members of the United Nations would not pay reparations. In any case the question whether Italy should pay or not had to be considered urgently: perhaps it would be appropriate to refer that question to the Committee appointed to draft the statement on Italy and Spain.

Mr. Byrnes doubted whether this Committee should deal with such a matter. On the other hand, he agreed that the question of Italian reparations must be settled before a Peace Treaty with Italy could be concluded, and the United States Delegation wished to be able to proceed with the preparation of that Treaty as soon as possible. Would it not be preferable to refer the question of Italian reparations to the Committee which was already considering reparations from Germany and other economic problems affecting Germany, and to instruct that Committee to deal also with the payment of reparations by Austria?

It was agreed that the Committee appointed to review Germany's economic problems (F. (Terminal) 1st Meeting,[2] Minute 5) should also consider the liability to reparations of Italy and Austria.

6. *Balkans: Yalta Declaration on Liberated Europe*
(Previous Reference: P. (Terminal) 3rd Meeting,[1] Minute 8.)

M. Molotov submitted a memorandum by the Soviet Delegation on the Yalta Declaration on Liberated Europe (P. (Terminal) 11).[6]

After studying this, Mr. Eden said that he must point out at once that the description which it contained of the situation in Greece was a complete travesty of the facts. The Soviet Government had no official representative in Greece nor, as far as he knew, any source of information save a correspondent of the Tass Agency. The Soviet Government were, therefore, not in a

[6] No. 201.

position to know what the true situation was. There were, on the other hand, British troops in Greece; and their commander, Field-Marshal Alexander, was here in Berlin and would be able to assure M. Molotov that there was in fact no 'terrorism' in Greece. The Press of the world were free to go to Greece and see for themselves what conditions were like and they were free to telegraph full and uncensored reports of what was going on. The same could not be said of Roumania and Bulgaria. Further, elections were about to be held in Greece in which all parties would be entitled to take part. The Greek Government had invited the Allied Powers to supervise the elections to satisfy themselves that they were free and unfettered. Here again there was no comparable situation in Roumania and Bulgaria.

M. MOLOTOV replied that both the United States and Great Britain had missions in Bulgaria and Roumania and representatives on the Control Commission. MR. EDEN agreed that this was so, but said that no facilities were accorded to these official representatives to see or do anything, and the representatives of the Press had no facilities either to see or to report what was going on. M. MOLOTOV said that the British representatives in these countries were more numerous than the Soviet civil representatives, and they were quite numerous enough to keep the British Government informed of the situation. Now that the war in Europe was at an end, the Soviet representatives on the Control Commissions in Bulgaria and Roumania, as well as in other countries under armistice régimes, had made suggestions with a view to modifying the status of Allied representatives on the Control Commissions in such a way as to adapt it to present conditions and to provide increased facilities.[7] MR. EDEN said that he hoped that these suggestions would lead to some improvement.

MR. BYRNES said the United States Government had hoped that the spirit of the Yalta Declaration would be carried into effect. In Bulgaria and Roumania this hope had certainly been disappointed. The Governments of these countries had restricted the movements of United States representatives: members of the United States staff on the Control Commission had been delayed in Italy for a month or six weeks before being permitted to enter Bulgaria. The Press, too, had been denied entry. And there was no sign of fulfilment of the promise of the Yalta Agreement that elections would be held at the earliest possible date. All this had been a source of great irritation to the people of the United States. It was not right that one of the three Great Powers should decide alone what should be done to meet this situation. The burden should be shared between the three Powers and steps should be taken to see that there was no discrimination against either of them. In view of the attitude of the Governments of Roumania and Bulgaria, it was not possible for the United States at this time to recognise those Governments. It had been agreed at Yalta in the Declaration on Liberated Europe that interim governmental authorities should be formed which were broadly representative of all democratic elements in the

[7] See No. 136, note 2.

populations; and the signatories to that Declaration were pledged to the holding of free elections at the earliest possible date. If such elections were held, the United States Government would gladly recognise any Government resulting from these elections. But the United States could not recognise the existing Governments so long as they denied to the official representatives of the United States and to the Press of the United States an opportunity to observe and report the situation in these countries.

M. MOLOTOV said that in Roumania and Bulgaria he knew of no disorders such as those which had taken place in Greece. The nature and extent of those disorders could be judged by reading the British and United States Press. At one time the situation in Bulgaria and Roumania had been difficult, but all that was past.

M. Molotov added that no elections had been held in Italy, who had come out of the war long before Bulgaria and Roumania and whose contribution to the victory over Germany had been far less than that made by Bulgaria and Roumania. Elections would be held in Bulgaria on the 26th August, and in Roumania very shortly. In each country all parties would be free to nominate representatives. The Soviet Government felt they could no longer delay the establishment of diplomatic relations with those two countries.

MR. BYRNES said that the United States Government had been invited by the Greek Government to supervise the elections in Greece, and he had sent that morning a letter[8] to M. Molotov inviting the Soviet Government to join in this supervision.

MR. EDEN said that the United Kingdom Delegation had, independently, sent a similar invitation.[9] As regards Bulgaria, according to his information

[8] Printed in *F.R.U.S. Berlin*, vol. ii, pp. 1042–3.

[9] Mr. Hayter had stated in a minute of 19 July 1945, approved that day by Mr. Eden, concerning this invitation: 'There is a small snag about this. The draft communication to the Russians, which the Foreign Office have drafted, speaks of supervision of the plebiscite and the election. The communication which the British and American Ambassadors in Athens made to the Greek Government, which the latter have approved, speaks only of supervising the "Greek national elections". The United States Delegation here say that they have not enough information on the subject to be able to recommend to Mr. Byrnes that he should include supervision of the plebiscite as well as the elections when he writes to M. Molotov, and would have to refer the matter to Washington. On the other hand, if the communication refers only to the Greek national elections they are prepared to go ahead at any time. I think the point is at this stage academic. The object of our communication to the Russians here is to elicit from them an expected refusal to take part in supervision. We can subsequently discuss with the Americans whether or not they join in supervising the plebiscite; it is in any case uncertain which will take place first or whether they will be simultaneous. In view of the time factor, I think we should go ahead on the lines of the communication made by our two Ambassadors to the Greek Government.' Mr. Eden stated in his letter of 20 July 1945 to M. Molotov (printed in *Berlinskaya konferentsiya*, pp. 327–8) that in view of the Allied obligations to Greece, the Yalta Declaration on Liberated Europe and article 9 of the Varkiza Agreement, 'His Majesty's Government, in agreement with the United States Government and with the full approval of the Greek Government, wish to propose to the Soviet and French Governments that the approaching Greek National Elections be held under the supervision of the four Allies.' Corresponding British and American notes were addressed to M. Bidault on 21 July.

447

the elections would be so conducted that people would have to vote for a list. That was not our understanding of what free elections should be, nor did it correspond to our idea of democracy.

M. MOLOTOV said that many people had serious doubts how far there was democracy in Greece. MR. EDEN replied by inviting M. Molotov to send representatives to Greece to go and see for themselves. He denied M. Molotov's assertion that the freedom of the Soviet representatives would be restricted by British control in Greece, and emphasised that there was complete freedom of the Press in Greece, as M. Molotov must know from the reports of the *Tass* correspondent there. There were no corresponding facilities in Bulgaria and Roumania, and our journalists had been forced to leave since they could not do their work.

MR. BYRNES said that the United States Government had no interest in seeing any particular type of Government established in Bulgaria and Roumania: they merely wished to be satisfied that such Governments would be representative and would permit United States officials and the Press to move about the country and to report on conditions. If elections were held in these countries without a previous request for Soviet, British and United States supervision, the Government resulting from such elections would be distrusted by the American people. Such a situation would affect American relations with the Governments in Bulgaria and Roumania. They wished to be assured that the Governments established in these countries would be friendly to all the three Great Powers, not least the Soviet Union.

Mr. Byrnes said that the United States Government were not anxious to supervise elections anywhere and regretted that it should be necessary to do so. Because they were satisfied that it was necessary in order to improve conditions, they were willing to co-operate with the Soviet Union and with the British Commonwealth in supervising elections in Italy, Greece, Bulgaria, Roumania and Finland. The world would then know that the United States Government meant what they said at Yalta when they went on record as favouring free and unfettered elections.

M. MOLOTOV said that the Soviet Government had no reason to fear that elections in Bulgaria and Roumania would be unduly delayed, nor that they would not be free. That was not so in Greece, where terrorism raged against the most democratic elements in the country and against those who had contributed most towards the defeat of Germany. Moreover, warlike speeches against the neighbours of Greece were being made. This did not happen in Bulgaria and Roumania.

MR. EDEN said that for some time past, the Yugoslav press and wireless had been imputing aggressive designs to Greece. The same charge appeared in the memorandum circulated by M. Molotov, viz., that 'the Greek Government were breaking the peace with their neighbours.' At the meeting of the Plenary Committee the previous day (P. (Terminal) 3rd Meeting,[1] Minute 1) the Prime Minister had given figures of the Greek forces stationed on the Greek frontier and had proved that the Greeks were not in a position

448

to attack anyone, quite apart from the fact that there were British troops in the country. Since the Soviet document had been handed in after the Prime Minister made his statement, Mr. Eden could only suppose that the Soviet Delegation did not accept the figures furnished by the Prime Minister. The fact was, however, that the Greek Government had no aggressive intentions and, even if they had, they had not the forces to give effect to them.

Mr. Byrnes then said that he knew little about the situation in Greece, but he thought it would be unwise to believe everything that was said in the Press, whether about Greece or about any other country. Nor should undue importance be attached to 'warlike speeches' for, as long as there were orators, there would always be speeches, some of which would cause trouble. And orators were not confined to one country only. What impressed him about Greece was that they were all free to send representatives to find out for themselves the accuracy of the press reports. This they were not able to do in Bulgaria and Roumania and, in consequence, all sorts of rumours grew which could not be checked.

M. Molotov asked what increased facilities the British and United States Governments desired in Bulgaria and Roumania, adding that it was in the power of the Soviet Government to see that further facilities were granted.

Mr. Byrnes said that official representatives of the British and United States Governments and Press correspondents should be free to go where and when they pleased, and should be free to send reports out of the country without censorship.

M. Molotov said that the official representatives already had these rights. Now that the war in Europe was over, he considered that the facilities accorded to Press correspondents should be broadened—subject, of course, to military censorship by the occupying authorities such as applied in Italy. In general he thought that the position of Allied representatives in Hungary, Bulgaria, Roumania and Finland could be assimilated to that obtaining in Italy.

Mr. Byrnes said that if they could accomplish that they would have made great progress.

M. Molotov said that it would be good to have a common understanding. It would also be good if they were able to get the Greek Government to take a more objective view of the democratic elements in the country and to behave in a less warlike manner. People in Greece were not satisfied with the position. The agreement of Varkize was a good agreement, but it was not being carried out.

Mr. Eden said that he must take exception to these statements, which constituted a serious reflection on the British Government. He must also take the gravest exception to the memorandum submitted by the Soviet Delegation, particularly in view of the statement made by the Prime Minister yesterday.

After some further discussion Mr. Eden asked whether it would be helpful if the United Kingdom and United States Delegations submitted memoranda setting out what they wanted to see done in these countries as regards:

(i) The rights of the Control Commission.

(ii) Freedom of Elections.

(iii) The Freedom of the Press.

M. Molotov said that the Soviet Delegation had already expressed their views. He saw no reason to supervise elections in Bulgaria and Roumania, but pointed out that the situation was somewhat different in Italy and Greece. He agreed that more freedom should be given to the Press. He thought it would be useful to have the written suggestions of the British and United States Delegations.

> It was agreed that the discussion should be adjourned, and that meanwhile the British and United States Delegations should submit memoranda on the lines suggested by Mr. Eden, which might serve as a basis for further discussion at a subsequent meeting.

7. Agenda for the Fourth Plenary Meeting

M. Molotov said that, if the Foreign Secretaries were able to reach agreement at their meeting at 3.45 that afternoon (see Minute 2 above), it would be possible to invite the Plenary Meeting which was to be held at 4 p.m. to give final approval to the draft constitution for the proposed Council of Foreign Ministers.

M. Molotov asked whether it would be possible for the Plenary Meeting to discuss the question of Italy and Spain (see Minute 4 above). Mr. Byrnes said that it would be preferable to await the Report of the drafting committee which had been appointed to consider the terms of the proposed declaration on this subject. President Truman was anxious, however, that the Plenary Meeting should consider the proposal, made in the Memorandum which he had submitted on the 17th July (P. (Terminal) 5),[5] that the short terms of surrender[10] for Italy and the obsolete clauses of the long terms of surrender should be terminated and replaced by certain undertakings by the Italian Government which would meet the requirements of the existing situation. He suggested, and it was agreed, that this proposal should be brought forward for discussion at the Plenary Meeting that afternoon.

Mr. Eden said that the Prime Minister wished to raise a point about the situation in Austria, particularly in Vienna, on which he would give the Plenary Meeting information derived from recent telegrams which he had received.

M. Molotov submitted a Memorandum (and map) on the Western

[10] The conditions of an armistice between the United Nations and Italy signed in Sicily on 3 September 1943, together with additional conditions signed on 29 September 1943 (Instrument of Surrender of Italy) and protocol of 9 November 1943 in amendment of the additional conditions, are printed in *B.F.S.P.*, vol. 145, pp. 278–93. The conditions of 3 September and those of 29 September were known respectively as the short and the long terms of surrender.

Frontier of Poland,[11] and a Memorandum on Territorial Trusteeship.[12] He suggested, and it was agreed, that both these Memoranda should be placed on the Agenda for the Fourth Plenary Meeting.

MR. EDEN said that the United Kingdom Delegation also wished to discuss at that meeting the position in relation to Turkey.

It was agreed that the following subjects should be put forward for discussion at the Fourth Plenary Meeting:

(a) *Council of Foreign Ministers.*
(b) *Policy towards Italy* (P. (Terminal) 5).[5]
(c) *Situation in Austria.*
(d) *Western Frontier of Poland* (P. (Terminal) 12).[11]
(e) *Territorial Trusteeship* (P. (Terminal) 13).[12]
(f) *Turkey.*

Cabinet Office, Potsdam, 20th July, 1945

CALENDARS TO NO. 200

i *21 & 22 July 1945 Bulgarian elections.* (a) *Letter from Mr. Howard to Mr. Hayter (Berlin).* In addition to any action by U.K. Delegation on lines suggested in No. 62. ii, it is proposed that Mr. Houstoun-Boswall should inform Bulgarian Govt. that H.M.G. will be unable to recognise as representative any government elected by these means. This communication should then be given maximum publicity. (b) *To Mr. Eden (Berlin) Tel. No. 142 Onward* in support of the above. Mr. Eden minuted in favour of such action, with American co-operation [F.O. 934/2/9(5–6)].

ii *19–26 July 1945 Correspondence on supplies to Greece.* (a) *19 July Mr. Caccia (Athens) Tel. No. 718.* Political importance of winter clothing for Greek army; minuted by Mr. Eden: 'This is really important. Anything I can do to help! A. E.' (b) *20, 21 & 26 July To Mr. Eden (Berlin) Tel. No. 96 Onward* (minuted by Mr. Eden); *F.M. Alexander to Sir J. Grigg Tel. No. F. 26046; Sir O. Sargent to Sir A. Cadogan (Berlin) Tel. No. 242 Target.* Instructions by F.M. Alexander for releasing lorries for Greece; discussions with U.N.R.R.A. and Americans on such releases for Greece and Yugoslavia [R 12243/1941/19; F.O. 934/1/1(10); UR 2368/200/850].

[11] No. 202.
[12] No. 203.

No. 201

Memorandum by the Soviet Delegation (Berlin)[1]
P.(*Terminal*)11 [*U 6197/3628/70*]

Top secret   20 July 1945

The Yalta Declaration 'on Liberated Europe'

1. In connection with the note[2] of the United States delegation regarding the Yalta declaration on liberated Europe, the Soviet Government deem it

[1] Note on copy filed on F.O. 934/3/17(2): 'Translation from Russian by S. Golunsky.' The Russian text is printed in *Berlinskaya konferentsiya*, pp. 330–1.
[2] *Note in filed copy:* 'P. (Terminal) 4': see No. 170, note 2.

necessary to declare that they cannot agree to the statements regarding Rumania and Bulgaria expounded in the above-mentioned note.

2. The Soviet Government feel obliged to draw the attention of the United States Government to the fact that in Rumania and Bulgaria as well as in Finland and Hungary since the signature of the instruments of surrender by the Governments of these States, due order exists and legal power in acting, which has authority and is trusted by the population of these States. The Governments of these States faithfully carry out the obligations assumed by them under their respective instrument of surrender. Rumania and Bulgaria gave the United Nations serious assistance by their armed forces in the struggle against German troops, having put out against our common enemy 10–12 divisions each. Under these circumstances the Soviet Government see no reason for interfering in the domestic affairs of Rumania or Bulgaria.

3. But there is one country—Greece—in which no due order still exists, where law is not respected, where terrorism rages directed against democratic elements which have born[e] the principal burden of the fight against German invaders for the liberation of Greece. Moreover, the present Greek Government is breaking the peace with their neighbours and threatening Albania and Bulgaria with military action. All those circumstances create the necessity of taking urgent measures to eliminate such a situation in Greece.

4. In accordance with the aforesaid the Soviet Government consider it necessary:

(1) to restore in the nearest days diplomatic relations with Rumania, Bulgaria, Finland and Hungary, as further delay in this respect could not be justified;

(2) to recommend to the Regent of Greece to take immediate measures towards the establishment of a democratic Government in the spirit of the agreement reached at Varkize, the 12th February, 1945, between the representatives of the then existing Government of Greece and the representatives of Greek democracy.

The Soviet Government express their assurance that the above-mentioned measures will find the support of the Governments of Great Britain and the United States and will be carried out.

No. 202

Memorandum by the Soviet Delegation (Berlin)[1]
P.(Terminal)12 [U 6197/3628/70]

Top secret   *20 July 1945*
Western frontier of Poland

We have considered the question of western frontier of Poland and have, taking in consideration ethnographical and historic conditions, recognised it

[1] Printed in *Berlinskaya konferentsiya*, pp. 331–2.

necessary and equitable, pending the final settlement of territorial questions at the Peace Congress, to fix the western frontier of Poland along the line marked on the attached[2] map, viz., west of Swinemünde to the river Oder leaving Stettin on the Polish side, further up the river Oder to the estuary of the river West.[3] Neise and from there along the West.[3] Neise to the Czechoslovakian frontier.

[2] *Note in filed copy:* 'Copies not available'. This map is untraced in Foreign Office archives: cf. note 2 to the text of this document printed in *F.R.U.S. Berlin*, vol. ii, p. 1138.

[3] Apparently an abbreviation for 'Western'.

No. 203

Memorandum by the Soviet Delegation (Berlin)[1]
P.(Terminal)13 [U 6197/3628/70]

Top secret   20 July 1945

Trust Territories

In connection with the fact that the Charter of the United Nations Organisation provides for bringing into effect the trusteeship system, the Conference deems necessary to lay down in conformity with the Charter measures for settlement, in the nearest future, of the question of the trust territories. By this are understood categories of territories defined in decision of the Crimea Conference[2] and in the above-mentioned Charter of the International Security Organisation.

For the purpose of elaborating practical measures in order to bring into effect provisions on trusteeship system provided in the Charter, the Conference deems necessary to authorise the Council of Foreign Ministers to consider in detail this question and work out practical proposals. In considering the question of preparing such proposals on category of territories which are detached from enemy States, the Council of Foreign Ministers shall be guided by the necessity of solution in the nearest future of the problem relating to the terms of trusteeship on the former colonial possessions of Italy in Africa and in the Mediterranean, having in view herewith the possibility of establishing the trusteeship system exercised by individual States or by U.S.S.R., U.S.A. and Great Britain jointly on the above-mentioned former colonial possessions of Italy.

The Council of Foreign Ministers shall also work out practical measures for reaching agreements on trusteeship system provided by the Charter of

[1] Printed in *Berlinskaya konferentsiya*, p. 332.

[2] i.e. article 1 of the Protocol of the Proceedings of the Conference at Yalta: see No. 30, note 2.

the United Nations, including proposals on the further régime of territories now held under mandate of the League of Nations.[3]

[3] In the Foreign Office Lord Hood and Mr. Jebb minuted on this memorandum (U 5768/191/70): 'It seems quite suitable that the new Council of Foreign Ministers should work out proposals for trusteeship territories in general, and the ex-Italian colonies in particular. There is another noteworthy exclusion of France at the end of para. 2. Hood 21/vii.' 'Yes indeed. Gladwyn Jebb 21/7.'

No. 204

Memorandum by Major Theakstone (Berlin)

[F.O. 934/1/2(15)]

[BERLIN,] *20 July 1945*

During lunch today with M. Molotov, at which the following persons were present, Sir Alexander Cadogan, Sir Archibald Clark Kerr, M. Vyshinsky, M. Maisky, M. Gousev, ? M. Molochkov[1] and two interpreters, Mr. Eden answered a number of questions addressed to him by M. Molotov and M. Maisky on the subject of the Ruhr.

M. Molotov started by saying that the People's Commissariat for Steel Production had visited the Ruhr and reported that only about ten per cent. of the industrial plant had been put out of commission as the result of air bombardment.

Sir Alexander Cadogan, who had also joined in the conversation, remarked that the chief effect of bombing was the dispersal of labour and that the chief value of the Ruhr was its coal-mining industry.

Pursuing his enquiries, M. Molotov was informed by Mr. Eden that after reparations questions had been settled, the Ruhr industry, in his opinion, should be placed under joint control of the Allies. M. Molotov appeared to be anxious that the joint control should be introduced forthwith. M. Eden said that he hoped that the period of control would be a long one. He personally would prefer a control in perpetuity. Mr. Eden said that the main British interest in the Ruhr was its coal. He said that the United Kingdom was called to provide coal for France and other countries on the continent. Many British miners were still in the Army and the United Kingdom was quite unable to supply all the coal needed. He further said that it was expected that about a quarter of the industries of the Ruhr would shortly resume production.

[1] M F. F. Molochkov was Head of the Protocol Department of the Soviet Ministry of Foreign Affairs.

Another subject discussed was the proposed site for the United Nations Organisation. Sir Alexander Cadogan favoured Copenhagen as being near London. There was an argument between M. Molotov and Mr. Eden as to whether it would be preferable to select an American or a European city. M. Molotov's view was that if the Organisation had its headquarters in America, it would enjoy a greater popularity in the New World than if the headquarters were in Europe. He gave as his reason the existence in America of an isolationist movement.

L. M. THEAKSTONE

CALENDARS TO No. 204

i *11 July 1945 Letter from Mr. Harvey to M. Paris (French Embassy).* Refers to French Govt.'s wish for association with any organs set up in the Ruhr by the British Commander-in-Chief in Germany. Understands that question of control of German coal-production as a whole has now been raised in message from President Truman to General de Gaulle and approach to H.M.G. [C 3437/22/18].

ii *21 July–2 Aug 1945 Minute from Sir W. Monckton to Mr. Eden (Berlin), and Foreign Office minutes.* At meeting of Economic Committee on 20 July M. Maisky suggested internationalising the Ruhr district with object of controlling Germany's war potential. Sir W. Monckton stated, with regard to the wide political implications, that this idea was beyond the committee's terms of reference. Americans took similar line [C 4112/22/18].

iii *20 & 21 July 1945 (a) Lord Halifax (Washington) Tel. No. 5061.* Confidential information from Mr. Stettinius that Soviet, Chinese, Australian, New Zealand and other governments have indicated to U.S. Govt. their preference for Pacific Coast of U.S. as permanent seat of the U.N. Americans inclined to favour Assembly's meeting in different countries. (*b*) *Minute from Mr. Jebb to Mr. Ronald and Sir O. Sargent:* discusses the above. Sir A. Cadogan stated in a minute of 22 July: 'M. Molotov indicated to me that he thought San Francisco wd. be a good centre, in many ways. Horrified, I trotted out Copenhagen. But I don't flatter myself that I made much impression. The U.S. (or Mr. Stettinius) have got fantastic ideas on the manner in which the World Organisation will function' [U 5617/12/70].

No. 205

Letter from M. Molotov to Mr. Eden (Berlin)

[*F.O. 934/2/10(42)*]

Translation BERLIN, *20 July 1945*

Dear Mr. Eden,

I am sending you herewith a message addressed by M. B[i]erut, President of the Polish National Council, and M. Osubka-Moravski [*sic*], Prime Minister of the Polish Provisional Government, to the Prime Minister, Mr. Churchill, with a request to forward it to him. I received this letter

455

through the headquarters of Marshal Rokossovski's Military Command.[1]

Expressing in advance my gratitude for carrying out my request I beg of you to accept my assurances of very high esteem.

M. V. MOLOTOV

ENCLOSURE IN No. 205

MM. Bierut and Osobka-Morawski to Mr. Churchill[2]

His Excellency, Winston Churchill, Prime
Minister of His Majesty's Government

On behalf of the Polish Provisional Government of National Unity we address ourselves to Your Excellency desiring to call the attention of Your Excellency to the problem of Western frontier of the Polish Republic, a problem that is of a vital importance to the Polish Nation.

Expressing the unanimous and inflexible will of the whole Nation, the Polish Provisional Government of National Unity are convinced that only the boundary line that follows, beginning in the south, the former frontier between Czechoslovakia and Germany, then the Lausitzer Neisse river, then runs along the left bank of the Oder, and leaving Stettin for Poland reaches the sea west of the town of Swindemunde, can be considered a just frontier that guarantees successful development to the Polish Nation, security to Europe, and a lasting peace to the world.

The Polish Nation, which suffered such enormous losses in the war against the Germans, would consider any other solution of the problem of their Western boundary as harmful and injurious and endangering the future of the Polish Nation and State.

Simultaneously we transmit identical note to Generalissimo Stalin, Chairman of the Council of the Peoples Commissars of the USSR, and to Mr. Truman, President of the United States of America, and we are convinced that the problem of Poland's Western frontier will find a positive solution during the present debates that are of such a far reaching momentum.

We avail ourselves of this opportunity to assure Your Excellency of our highest consideration.

BOLESLAW BIERUT, President of National Council
EDWARD OSOBKA-MORAWSKI, Prime Minister

Warsaw, July 20, 1945.

[1] Marshal K. K. Rokossovski was Commander-in-Chief of Soviet forces in Poland.

[2] Texts of this note as also addressed to President Truman and Marshal Stalin are printed respectively in *F.R.U.S. Berlin*, vol. ii, pp. 1138–9, and *Berlinskaya konferentsiya*, p. 329.

No. 206

Letter from M. Molotov to Mr. Eden (Berlin)[1]

[*F.O. 934/1/1(10)*]

Translation   BERLIN, *20 July 1945*

Dear Mr. Eden,

In acknowledging receipt of your letter of 20th July,[2] containing a

[1] Printed in *Berlinskaya konferentsiya*, p. 328.
[2] See No. 200, note 9.

proposal to institute an Allied Control in connexion with the Greek national elections, I wish to state that the point of view of the Soviet Government on the question of the situation in Greece has been explained by me on 20th July during the meeting of the Foreign Ministers.[3] Thus you are now aware that the Soviet Government, while adopting a negative attitude to the practice of the control by foreign states of national elections, had its own proposals in connexion with the state of affairs in Greece, which, as I hope, we will examine again.[4]

Sincerely yours,

V. MOLOTOV

[3] See No. 200, minute 6.

[4] Mr. Eden, in his telegram No. 136 Target of 21 July 1945, informed Sir J. Anderson of this letter from M. Molotov and commented: 'Matter will no doubt come up again during further discussion of the question of free elections in the Balkan countries.' For the corresponding letter from M. Molotov to Mr. Byrnes see *F.R.U.S. Berlin*, vol. ii, pp. 1043-4.

No. 207

M. Molotov to Sir A. Clark Kerr (Berlin)
[R 12851/4476/44]

Translation BERLIN, *20 July 1945*

Dear Mr. Ambassador,

In reply to your note of 7th July,[1] I have the honour to inform you that some time ago the Turkish Government had, on its own intiative, approached the Soviet Government with a proposal to conclude with it a treaty of alliance which would also contain provisions for the solution of the question of the Straits.

In reply to this proposal, the Turkish Government was informed that the conclusion of such a treaty was conceivable on condition of the solution, apart from the question of the Straits, also of the question of the territories which were seized from the Soviet Union and incorporated in Turkey in 1921.

In this manner there did actually take place, on the initiative of the Turkish Government, an exchange of opinion on the possibility of, and the conditions for, the conclusion of a treaty of alliance.

At the same time, I consider it necessary to add that the Soviet Government had every reason to believe that the Turkish Government, being the initiator of the above mentioned questions, had fully and in due time informed the British Government of the exchange of opinion which had taken place in Moscow. The Soviet Government in its turn had in view a discussion of this problem at the Berlin Conference.

[1] No. 19, enclosure.

I request you, Mr. Ambassador, to accept my assurances of very high esteem.[2]

V. MOLOTOV

[2] A copy of this note was sent to Mr. Brimelow in the Foreign Office under cover of a letter of 25 July 1945 from Captain P. J. Bolton, Private Secretary to Sir A. Clark Kerr, at Potsdam. Captain Bolton commented: 'You will see that Auntie has taken it upon herself to reply to H[is] E[xcellency, Sir A. Clark Kerr] here to a letter that he wrote from Moscow.'

No. 208

Record of Fourth Plenary Meeting held at Cecilienhof, Potsdam, on Friday, 20 July 1945 at 4 p.m.

P.(*Terminal*)4th Meeting [U 6197/3628/70]

Top Secret

Present:

PREMIER STALIN, M. V. M. Molotov, M. A. Ya. Vyshinski, M. I. M. Maisky, M. F. T. Gousev, M. A. A. Gromyko, M. K. V. Novikov, M. A. A. Sobolev, M. B. F. Podtzerob, M. V. N. Pavlov (*Interpreter*).

PRESIDENT TRUMAN, Mr. J. F. Byrnes, Mr. Joseph E. Davies, Fleet-Admiral W. D. Leahy, Mr. W. A. Harriman, Mr. E. W. Pauley, Mr. J. C. Dunn, Mr. H. F. Matthews, Mr. B. V. Cohen, Mr. L. E. Thompson, Mr. C. E. Bohlen (*Interpreter*).

MR. CHURCHILL, Mr. Eden, Mr. Attlee, Sir Walter Monckton, Sir A. Cadogan, Sir A. Clark Kerr, Sir W. Strang, Sir E. Bridges, Mr. P. J. Dixon, Mr. W. Hayter, Major A. Birse (*Interpreter*).

Contents

Minute	Subject
1.	Report from Meeting of Foreign Secretaries
2.	Procedure: Hour of Plenary Meetings
3.	The Establishment of a Council of Foreign Ministers
4.	Italy
5.	Austria
6.	Western Frontiers of Poland
	Trust Territories
	Turkey

1. *Report from Meeting of Foreign Secretaries*

M. MOLOTOV reported the proceedings of the morning's meeting of the Foreign Ministers[1] as follows:

(1) *Outstanding Business:*

[1] See No. 200.

Reports from Sub-Committees were outstanding on (*a*) Germany: consideration of economic problems; (*b*) Poland. Both Committees had been instructed to report to the Foreign Secretaries meeting on the following morning.

(2) *Council of Foreign Ministers:*

The Foreign Secretaries had met at 3.45 p.m.[2] Their Report on this subject is given in Item 3 below.

(3) *The Yalta Declaration on Liberated Europe:*

The Foreign Secretaries had considered the memorandum submitted by the Soviet Delegation (P. (Terminal) 11).[3]

The views of the Foreign Secretaries showed some divergence about the situation in Roumania, Bulgaria and Greece. Mr. Byrnes had proposed an agreement by the Three Powers for the supervision of the elections in all Balkan countries, and for the free entry and movement of Press representatives in these countries. Mr. Eden had associated himself with these views. M. Molotov, on the other hand, had seen no reason for special supervisors in Bulgaria and Roumania, and he had therefore suggested that this matter should be discussed further with Mr. Eden and Mr. Byrnes. As to Greece, the Soviet Government's view was set out in the paper which they had circulated.

At this point MR. BYRNES interposed to say that it was his understanding that M. Molotov had expressed agreement with his proposals, subject to the terms of any announcement being agreed by representatives of the three Governments.

M. MOLOTOV replied that what he had said was that, inasmuch as Mr. Eden and Mr. Byrnes wanted to submit proposals, he was ready to discuss them; but these proposals had not yet been submitted.

MR. EDEN said that his understanding was that M. Molotov had agreed that more liberty for the Press was probably necessary, but that he had not agreed on the supervision of elections.

M. MOLOTOV said that his views on Roumania, Bulgaria and Greece were fully expounded in the document he had presented at the morning's meeting (P. (Terminal) 11).[3] Moreover, he recognised that the Allied Press in these countries might have more opportunities. He had understood, however, that Mr. Byrnes and Mr. Eden would submit their proposals in writing.

MR. CHURCHILL thought that would be best. He wanted, however, to comment on the word 'supervision' that had crept in. He had not considered *control*, which was what supervision meant, and he suggested 'observation' as a better word. He wanted to make it clear that these observers should not have responsibility, but should be in a position to find out what was going on.

M. MOLOTOV was asked to proceed with his report.

(4) *Italy.*

Mr. Byrnes had suggested that the proposed announcement about Italy

[2] No minutes of this meeting have been traced.
[3] No. 201.

should include an indication that the three Great Powers, while supporting the association of Italy with the United Nations, were not prepared to support the association of Spain with the United Nations, so long as that country was under its present régime. Mr. Eden had said that he was attracted by this proposal, but that if any declaration was worked out, he would deem it expedient for the three Powers to support also the entry of neutrals such as Switzerland, Sweden and Portugal.

The question of the entry of ex-enemy States who had become co-belligerents to association with the United Nations had also been raised, but Mr. Eden had thought that while it should be discussed, it could only be implemented after the conclusion of the peace treaties. A Sub-Committee, consisting of:

United States Delegation: Mr. H. F. Matthews, Mr. C. W. Cannon.
United Kingdom Delegation: Mr. F. Hoyer Millar, Mr. P. Dean.
Russian Delegation: M. I. M. Maisky, M. F. T. Gousev.
had therefore been appointed to consider the matter. In this connection it had been agreed to ask the Committee dealing with reparations and Germany's economic problems (F. (Terminal) 1st Meeting,[4] Minute 5) to consider the question of *Reparations from Italy and Austria*.

(5) *Western Frontier of Poland*
(6) *Trusteeship*

The Soviet Delegation had submitted memoranda (P. (Terminal) 12 and P. (Terminal) 13)[5] on these matters, for discussion at the Plenary Meeting that afternoon.

(7) M. MOLOTOV then read out the following Agenda which the Foreign Ministers suggested should be taken at the present meeting:

(1) *Council of Foreign Ministers.*
(2) *Policy towards Italy.*—Memorandum submitted by the United States Delegation on the 17th July (P. (Terminal) 5).[6]
(3) *The Situation in Austria and Vienna*, upon which Mr. Churchill wished to speak.
(4) *The Western Frontiers of Poland.*—Memorandum by the Soviet Delegation (P. (Terminal) 12).
(5) *Territorial Trusteeship.*—Memorandum by the Soviet Delegation (P. (Terminal) 13).

2. Procedure: Hour of Plenary Meetings

MR. CHURCHILL said that he had a small point to raise as regards procedure. The Foreign Ministers met daily together, and did a tremendous morning's work. There was scarcely time, however, for the important documents resulting from the morning's meeting to be read: nor time for the Heads of Governments to understand fully what had passed at the

[4] No. 178.
[5] Nos. 202 and 203 respectively.
[6] See minute 4 below.

morning meetings before they themselves met at 4 p.m. He wondered, therefore, whether it would not be better to meet a little later in the day, say at 5 p.m.

PREMIER STALIN and PRESIDENT TRUMAN said that they agreed, and the President added that he would like to suggest to the Foreign Ministers that they should report not later than 3.30 p.m.

3. *The Establishment of a Council of Foreign Ministers*
(Previous Reference: F. (Terminal) 3rd Meeting,[1] Minute 2.)

The Conference accepted the following additional text for the second part of paragraph 3 of the enclosure to the United States Delegation memorandum on this subject (P. (Terminal) 2)[7]:

'For the discharge of each of these tasks the Council will be composed of the members representing those States which were signatory to the terms of surrender imposed upon the enemy State concerned. For the purposes of the peace settlement for Italy, France shall be regarded as a signatory to the terms of surrender for Italy.

Other members will be invited to participate when matters directly concerning them are under discussion.'

PRESIDENT TRUMAN said that the only thing left to settle was the question of time and place for the first meeting of the Council.

MR. CHURCHILL said that, with the indulgence of the President and Premier Stalin, he would say that he had a strong view that London should be the permanent home of the Secretariat and the place at which the first meeting at any rate should be held. This did not mean that meetings might not be held in other capitals from time to time. London had been the capital most under fire, and longest in the war. It had claims to be the largest city in the world and one of the oldest; and, moreover, it was more nearly half-way between the United States and Russia than any other place in Europe.

PREMIER STALIN agreed that this counted more than any other factor.

MR. CHURCHILL went on to say—and PREMIER STALIN interposed to say that he agreed—that it was also London's turn. He had crossed the Atlantic six times to have the honour of meeting the late President, and twice had had the pleasure of going to Moscow. On the other hand, except for the journey which M. Molotov made to London when the 20 Years' Treaty was so successfully concluded,[8] we had had no such meeting in London. A feeling was growing up in England that it was London's turn. He asked Mr. Attlee to say a word on this subject.

MR. ATTLEE said that he entirely agreed with the reasons given by Mr. Churchill. The people of London had a right to see some of these

[7] *Note in filed copy:* 'The revised text of the approved document has been circulated as P. (Terminal) 14': No. 209.
[8] Cf. No. 39, note 2.

distinguished people, and moreover the geographical argument was very strong.

PRESIDENT TRUMAN said that he agreed with Mr. Churchill's view. The United States felt that they had had their share at San Francisco, and that therefore London should be the place. He added that this would not, of course, prevent the President of the United States inviting other Heads of Governments to the United States.

PREMIER STALIN said that he also agreed with Mr. Churchill.

MR. CHURCHILL wished to express to the President and to Premier Stalin the thanks of the British Delegation for this generous acceptance of his suggestion.

PRESIDENT TRUMAN invited the Foreign Secretaries to consider at their meeting on the following day what procedure should be adopted for informing France and China of the decision to set up this Council, and inviting them to join it, and the timing of any action recommended by them.

This was agreed.

4. *Italy*
(Previous Reference: F. (Terminal) 3rd Meeting,[1] Minute 4.)

The Conference had before them the following document, which the President had handed round at the first Plenary Meeting[9] (P. (Terminal) 5):

'The objectives of the three Governments with regard to Italy are directed towards her early political independence and economic recovery, and the right of the Italian people ultimately to choose their own form of government.

Italy's present status as co-belligerent and unconditionally surrendered enemy is anomalous, and hampers every effort both by the Allies and by Italy herself, to improve Italy's economic and political situation. This anomaly can be finally solved only through the negotiation of a definitive peace treaty which would at best require some months. The preparations of such a treaty should be one of the first tasks of the suggested Council of Foreign Ministers.

Meanwhile, however, improvement in the Italian internal situation would be greatly facilitated by some immediate interim arrangement whereby the Italian Government would have some tangible recognition of Italy's contribution toward the defeat of Germany.

It is therefore recommended that the short terms of surrender and the numerous obsolete clauses of the long terms of surrender be terminated, and replaced by certain undertakings on the part of the Italian Government to meet the requirements of the existing situation.

These undertakings should provide:

1. That the Italian Government will refrain from any hostile action against any of the United Nations pending the conclusion of the treaty of peace.

[9] Cf. No. 170, minute 2.

462

2. That the Italian Government will maintain no military, naval or air forces or equipment, except as authorised by the Allies, and will comply with all instructions on the subject of such forces and equipment. Under this interim arrangement, control of Italy should be retained only so far as is necessary:

A. To cover Allied military requirements, so long as Allied forces remain in Italy or operate therefrom.

B. To safeguard the equitable settlement of territorial disputes.'

PREMIER STALIN said that he wanted to see Italy's position improved but thought it would be well for the three Foreign Secretaries to discuss this paper, since certain drafting amendments and improvements might be called for.

He also thought that it would be a good thing to ask the Foreign Secretaries to consider a question which was parallel to that of Italy, namely, the position of other satellite countries such as Roumania, Finland, Hungary and Bulgaria. The Conference had no grounds for singling out Italy from among the other satellites. Italy, it was true, had been the first satellite to surrender. Her forces had since fought on our side, although in small numbers. Moreover, she now proposed to come into the war against Japan.

Other satellites, such as Roumania and Bulgaria, were in a similar position, and had done much to help us. For instance, Bulgaria had provided 8 or 10 divisions, and Roumania 10 or 12, in the last stages of the war against Germany. These armies had fought well. Finland, although she had given no serious help against Germany, was behaving all right, and was carrying out the Armistice Terms[10] satisfactorily. Her position also should therefore be alleviated. The same applied to Hungary.

He therefore thought it would be well, in discussing how we were to ease the situation of Italy, also to consider easing that of the other satellite countries, treating them all as part of one single question. If his colleagues agreed, then the three Ministers for Foreign Affairs might be instructed to consider all these satellites together.

PRESIDENT TRUMAN explained that his reason for singling out Italy in the document he had circulated was that she had surrendered first, and that the Armistice Terms imposed on her were harder and more binding than those imposed upon the others. He agreed, however, that the position of these countries also should be referred to the three Foreign Secretaries.

MR. CHURCHILL said that our position in the Italian story was not quite the same as that of either of his two colleagues present. We had been attacked by Italy in June 1940. We had suffered very heavy losses in the Mediterranean fighting, especially that on the North African shore, to which Italy had brought German troops, and in Egypt. We had also had grievous losses in warships and merchant ships in the Mediterranean. Unaided, we

[10] The Armistice Agreement between the United Nations and Finland, signed at Moscow on 19 September 1944, is printed (Cmd. 6586 of 1945) in *B.F.S.P.*, vol. 145, pp. 513–25.

had had to undertake the Abyssinian campaign, and had replaced the Emperor on his throne.

Special detachments of Italian aircraft had been sent to bomb London, and it must also be remembered that Italy had made a most dastardly and utterly unprovoked attack upon Greece. Moreover, just before the war began, she had seized Albania by a most lawless act. All these things had happened while we had been alone. It could not therefore be denied that we had suffered grievously at the hands of the Italian State. Nor could we acquit the Italian people entirely of their responsibility for these acts, any more than we could acquit the German people for the actions taken by them under the yoke of Hitler. Nevertheless, we had endeavoured to keep alive the idea of a revival of Italy as one of the important powers of Europe and the Mediterranean. When he had gone there a year ago, he made proposals to President Roosevelt, the bulk of which, with some improvements, had been included in a joint Declaration[11] made soon afterwards. When the question of dividing the Italian fleet into three parts had been raised,[12] it had been agreed between the three Powers that if this division could not be made immediately, the Soviet Government should receive a number of Allied ships corresponding to the Italian ships that they would have received. Of the 15 Allied ships so provided, 14 had come from Great Britain.

He only said this to show on the one hand the injuries we had received at Italian hands, and on the other the broad manner in which we approached the future of Italy, and in order to show that we were not hostile to the Italian people. He therefore came forward now on behalf of His Majesty's Government to make it clear that we wished to do what was best for the future. He was anxious to join, in principle, with President Truman and Premier Stalin in making a gesture of friendship and comfort to the Italian people, who had suffered terribly and had aided the Allies in expelling the Germans from their land. The British Delegation did not oppose the suggestion for preparing a peace treaty with Italy. This work of preparation would take several months and he wondered whether the general Peace Conference would be very far off when this work of preparation was completed.

He noticed that the present Italian Government had no democratic foundations, founded on free, fair and unfettered elections. They were simply politicians who called themselves leaders of political parties. He understood it was the intention of the Italian Government to hold elections before the winter. While, therefore, he agreed that the Council of Foreign Ministers should start work on the preparation of a Peace Treaty, he did not think it would be advisable to come to final conclusions with the Italians until their Government stood on a recognisable democratic foundation.

He did not find himself in complete agreement with the memorandum by

[11] For the Anglo-American declaration of 26 September 1944 on Italy see Sir L. Woodward, *op. cit.*, vol. iii, pp. 447-53.

[12] Cf. *op. cit.*, vol. ii, pp. 604-11.

the United States Delegation, where it was suggested that some immediate interim arrangement should be made for the replacement of the short Terms of Surrender and the numerous obsolete clauses of the long Terms of Surrender by certain undertakings on the part of the Italian Government. The present Italian Government, dependent on political parties of twenty years ago, stood on a basis which might be repudiated by the electorate. If we sacrificed our existing rights under the Terms of Surrender, and if there was a long interval before the peace settlement, then we should have lost our power to secure our requirements from Italy, save by the exercise of force, which no one wished to use. A gap between the existing Terms of Surrender and the final peace terms, covered only by undertakings from a Government which stood on so uncertain a footing, was dangerous.

The United States memorandum listed certain undertakings to be accepted by the Italian Government, but these did not cover such vital questions as the future of the Italian Fleet, the future of the Italian Colonies, or the payment of reparations. Therefore, we should lose our rights under the Terms of Surrender without having made any satisfactory arrangements to take their place.

Finally, he must remind the Conference that the Terms of Surrender were signed on behalf of many other nations besides the three Great Powers, including the Dominions. Australia, New Zealand and South Africa had suffered great losses at the hands of the Italians in this war, as had other countries who had signed the Terms. He did not think we could go further than to assent in principle to steps being taken to prepare a peace treaty with Italy, and to agree that this matter should receive priority at the hands of the Council of Foreign Ministers.

Mr. Churchill then referred to the other countries which had been mentioned in discussion. He said that Bulgaria had no claim on Great Britain. Bulgaria had struck a deadly blow in the last war and it was not for him to describe the sufferings of Russia at her hands. During this war Bulgaria, crouching in the Balkans and fawning upon Germany, had inflicted great injuries to Yugoslavia and Greece and had been a constant threat to Turkey. Bulgaria was still armed—he understood with 15 divisions. No arrangements had been made for the payment of reparations by Bulgaria. He felt much more favourably inclined to start preparations for a peace treaty with Italy than with Bulgaria.

In conclusion, Mr. Churchill said that he regretted to have to differ from the views expressed by Premier Stalin and President Truman, and expressed his appreciation for their attention to his statement.

PREMIER STALIN said that he thought that these questions about Italy and the satellite countries generally were questions of high policy. The purpose of this policy was to separate the satellites from Germany in order to reduce her power. There were two methods of achieving this policy. First, by the use of force against the satellites. This method was successfully applied during the war by the Allies against Italy and by the Russians against the satellites. But the use of force alone was not sufficient to separate the satellites from Germany. If we confined ourselves to the use of force, there was a danger that we should create conditions which favoured the association of the satellites with Germany and thereby drive them into the German camp. He therefore considered it expedient to supplement force by alleviating the position of the satellites. This seemed to him the only means to rally the satellites around us and to detach them for ever from Germany.

In comparison with these considerations of high policy, all other considerations, of complaints or revenge, must lapse. It was in the light of these considerations that he had considered the United States memorandum, and he felt that it was in full harmony with the policy of detaching the satellites from Germany by easing their position. He therefore had no objection in principle to the United States memorandum, although no doubt some drafting improvement would be necessary.

Continuing, Premier Stalin said that there was another aspect to which Mr. Churchill had referred in the second part of his statement. Italy had, of course, committed great sins against Great Britain, and also against Russia although to a lesser degree. Russia had had to fight the Italians in the Ukraine, on the Don and on the Volga—that was a long way into Russian territory. But it seemed to him that it would be wrong to be guided by memories of injuries or by feelings of retribution. The spirit of revenge or redress for injuries was a very bad adviser in politics. It was not for him to teach his colleagues in this matter, but in politics one should be guided by the calculation of forces.

The question was, did we wish to have Italy on the side of the United Nations so as to isolate all possible forces which might join with Germany? In his view, we did, and that was the determining factor. The same considerations must be applied also to the other satellites.

Many difficulties and sacrifices had been caused by these satellites. Roumania had thrown in against the Russians 22 divisions; Hungary 26 divisions; and even greater sacrifices and defeats had been caused by Finland, who had mobilised 24 divisions against her. If it had not been for Finnish help, Germany could not have blockaded Leningrad. Fewer difficulties and injuries had been caused by Bulgaria. She had helped Germany to conduct offensive operations against Russia, but had not joined in the war or sent troops. On the other hand, Bulgaria had done considerable harm to our Allies in Yugoslavia and Greece, and Bulgaria must be punished for this.

Under the Armistice Terms[13] Bulgaria was required to pay reparations, and Russia, together with the other Great Powers, would see to this. There need be no doubt on this matter.[14] Also under the Armistice Bulgaria had

[13] The Armistice Agreement between the United Nations and Bulgaria, signed at Moscow on 28 October 1944, is printed (Cmd. 6587 of 1945) in *B.F.S.P.*, vol. 145, pp. 526–30.

[14] With reference to the two preceding sentences Mr. Houstoun-Boswall was informed in Foreign Office telegram to Sofia No. 748 of 2 August 1945: 'You and His Majesty's Chargé d'Affaires in Moscow are authorised to make such use of this remark as you think fit for discussion of Greek reparations claims.'

been required to provide troops to fight against Germany. The terms had also provided that, after the German war was over, Bulgarian forces would be demobilised to peacetime strength. The three Great Powers, who signed these Armistice Terms, would see that they were carried out.

These were the sins which Bulgaria had committed against the Allies generally and against Russia in particular. We might start by taking revenge on account of her brazen behaviour, but he did not favour that policy. Allied Control Commissions were functioning in the satellite countries, and it was high time to pass to the other policy of alleviating their position—although not to the same extent as in Italy. He was convinced that this was the only means to make a gulf between Germany and the satellites, and to bring them into our own camp.

As to the specific proposals in the American memorandum, he understood that President Truman did not propose that a Peace Treaty with Italy should be immediately prepared, but rather that the way should be cleared for this. In the meantime, the President wanted an intermediate stage between the conditions imposed by the Terms of the Surrender and the Peace Treaty. It was difficult to oppose this. Such a proposition was practical and right.

As regards the other satellites, it was not proposed that a Peace Treaty should be signed, nor even that there should be the same intermediate stage. But he thought that we should resume diplomatic relations.

Referring to the statement that there was no freely elected Governments in the satellite countries, Premier Stalin said that the same conditions applied in Italy and yet diplomatic relations had been resumed with her. Nor, indeed, were there yet freely elected Governments in France or Belgium.

MR. CHURCHILL interjected that these two countries were our Allies.

PREMIER STALIN said he agreed, but the principles of democracy were the same everywhere, whether in Allied or satellite countries.

PRESIDENT TRUMAN mentioned that the Italian Armistice Terms had been signed only by the three Great Powers, and PREMIER STALIN said that the Dominions had not signed.

MR. EDEN explained that the three Great Powers had signed the Terms on behalf of all the Allies, including the Dominions, who had associated themselves with the signature.

PRESIDENT TRUMAN suggested that the question of relations with Italy and with other satellites should be referred to the Foreign Secretaries for examination. He agreed most cordially with Premier Stalin's remarks that peace could not be made on the basis of revenge. Sinners must be punished, but revenge was the wrong start.

Referring to the question of reparations from Italy, President Truman said that the United States must provide between ¾ and 1 billion dollars to feed Italy this winter. The United States was a rich country but they could not continue on this basis without the prospect of any relief from this burden of expenditure. Countries like Italy must be set on their own feet, so that they could look after themselves. The United States had shown that they were prepared to play their full part in assistance to Europe, but steps must be taken to limit this burden.

Mr. CHURCHILL thought that there was general agreement that the preparation of an Italian Peace Treaty should be remitted to the Council of Foreign Ministers. He only deprecated abolition of the Surrender Terms because this would remove our sole right to ensure that our requirements from Italy were met. The Terms of Surrender could be enforced and, as at present advised, he was reluctant to give them up too soon.

Continuing, Mr. Churchill said that he cordially agreed with the views expressed by Premier Stalin and President Truman about the importance of not governing the future by a spirit of revenge. It gave him great pleasure to hear these sentiments expressed with such solemnity and authority. He added that His Majesty's Government had great sympathy for Italy. We were not thinking of any reparations from Italy for ourselves but rather in connection with the claims of Greece. Perhaps, in the communique to be issued at the end of the Conference, some public reference could be made to the preparation of an Italian Peace Treaty.

PRESIDENT TRUMAN suggested that the whole problem of easing the situation of Italy and the other satellites should be referred to the Foreign Secretaries for examination and report.

Mr. CHURCHILL said that he was prepared to agree now that the preparation of an Italian Peace Treaty should be referred to the Council of Foreign Ministers. He thought that the question of interim arrangements with Italy should be referred to the Foreign Secretaries.

PREMIER STALIN suggested that the Foreign Secretaries should also consider relations with the other satellites.

This was agreed to.

THE CONFERENCE:

Agreed that the Foreign Secretaries should examine and report on interim arrangements, pending the conclusion of Peace Treaties with Italy and also with the other satellite countries.

5. *Austria*

Mr. CHURCHILL said that he much regretted that it seemed that he had to argue against the Soviet point of view at this meeting. But he felt that the situation in Vienna and in Austria was very unsatisfactory. It had been agreed in principle a long time ago that Austria and Vienna should be divided into zones of occupation. More than two months ago we had asked that British officers should be allowed to go to Vienna to see what accommodation we wanted and to arrange about airfields and so forth. A visit had been paid but no satisfactory arrangements had been arrived at. The Mission which we had sent had had to leave and we still had no representative in Vienna. We had not been allowed to take up the area allotted to us in Vienna, nor had the British troops been allowed to occupy Styria and a request to this effect had been specifically refused.[15] Altogether

[15] See No. 35.

468

three or four months had passed since discussions on this matter had started, and he did not understand why so much difficulty should attend so simple a matter. Moreover, we had had very unsatisfactory reports of the position from Field-Marshal Alexander.[16]

Continuing, Mr. Churchill said that it was high time that we were allowed to occupy our zone and move into Vienna.

Mr. Churchill reminded the Conference that, on the previous day, the Russian Delegation had asked to send a Mission to view the German warships in our possession.[17] He thought it was important that the procedure in such matters should be reciprocal. At present they had reached a deadlock. In Germany we and the Americans had retired long distances into the allotted zones; but we were still prevented from moving into ours in Austria.

PREMIER STALIN said that general agreement had been reached on the zones of occupation in Austria but not in Vienna. It had taken some time to negotiate this matter but he had approved the recommendations of the European Advisory Council[18] on the previous day.

PRESIDENT TRUMAN said that he had done the same.

PREMIER STALIN said there had also been the question of arrangements for airfields round Vienna, on which agreement had not been reached. However, the French—they were always late—had yesterday agreed to the proposals. The way was therefore now free to fix the date for the entry of the British and American troops into their zones in Vienna. As far as he was concerned this could start at once. The Prime Minister seemed to be indignant, but there were no grounds for this. He had said that the British could not enter their Austrian or Vienna zones, but such language was not permissible. The Russians had not been admitted to their zones in Germany for a month, but had raised no complaint. The Soviet Government had no intention of violating the agreement about zones in Austria. It was not their practice to fail to carry out their agreements. Wiser action had been taken as regards the position in Berlin, which had been settled more quickly. Field-Marshal Alexander had, it seemed, acted less skilfully and this was one of the factors which led to delay. He had behaved as though the Russian troops were under his command. That attitude only had the effect of delaying things. In Germany, on the other hand, the British and United States Commanders had behaved well and all had proceeded satisfactorily.

There was no objection to the Allied armies now occupying the zones allotted to them in Vienna and Austria. Indeed, agreement had only been finally reached the previous day.

MR. CHURCHILL said that he was glad to know that this matter had now at last been settled, and that we could be allowed to move into our allotted zone. As to what had been said about Field-Marshal Alexander, he (Mr. Churchill) doubted whether it had been possible for the Field-Marshal to

[16] Cf. No. 314.
[17] See No. 194, minute 6.
[18] See No. 56.

attend personally to all the details for which he was responsible.

PREMIER STALIN said that he had no complaint against Field-Marshal Montgomery, but that his people had complained about Field-Marshal Alexander, although he, himself, had not checked up on the matter.

MR. CHURCHILL said that he would like to have particulars of any complaints.

PREMIER STALIN said he did not wish to institute an investigation. He had not spoken as a public prosecutor, but had made a political speech.

MR. CHURCHILL said that he must put on record that Field-Marshal Alexander had the complete confidence of His Majesty's Government and that they had approved the actions he had taken.

PREMIER STALIN said that he had made no complaints; he had only stated what he had been told by his Commanders and had pointed to this as one of the factors which had caused delay.

MR. CHURCHILL said that we were not the only people concerned. The British and United States representatives had gone together to Vienna. It was on record in his correspondence with President Truman that the United States authorities had also been greatly dissatisfied with the position.[19] He did not stand alone in this matter.

PRESIDENT TRUMAN agreed that this was the case. As Premier Stalin reported that the zones in Austria and Vienna could now be occupied, no decision was called for from the Conference, which could now pass to the next item.

6. *Western Frontiers of Poland*
   Territorial Trusteeship
   Turkey

Discussion of these items was postponed, it being agreed that 'Western Frontiers of Poland' and 'Territorial Trusteeship' should appear on the Agenda for the Plenary Session on the following afternoon.

Cabinet Office, Potsdam, 20th July, 1945

[19] Cf. *F.R.U.S. 1945*, vol. iii, pp. 132–7.

No. 209

Proposal for the establishment of a Council of Foreign Ministers
Text agreed by United Kingdom, United States and Soviet Delegations

P. (*Terminal*) *14* [*U 6197/3628/70*]

Top secret   *20 July 1945*

1. There shall be established a Council composed of the Foreign Ministers of Great Britain, the Union of Soviet Socialist Republics, China, France, and the United States.

2. The Council shall meet at . . .[1] and its first meeting shall be held on . . . [2] Each of the Foreign Ministers shall be accompanied by a high-ranking deputy, duly authorised and capable of carrying on the work of the Council in the absence of his Foreign Minister. He will likewise be accompanied by a small staff of technical advisers suited to the problems concerned and to the organisation of a joint secretariat.

3. As its immediate important task, the Council would be authorised to draw up, with a view to their submission to the United Nations, treaties of peace with Italy, Roumania, Bulgaria, and Hungary,[3] and to propose settlements of territorial questions outstanding on the termination of the war in Europe. The Council shall be utilised for the preparation of a peace settlement for Germany to be accepted by the Government of Germany when a Government adequate for the purpose is established.

For the discharge of each of these tasks the Council will be composed of the members representing those States which were signatory to the terms of surrender imposed upon the enemy State concerned. For the purposes of the peace settlement for Italy, France shall be regarded as a signatory to the terms of surrender for Italy.

Other members will be invited to participate when matters directly concerning them are under discussion.

Other matters may from time to time be referred to the Council by agreement between the States Members thereof.

4. Whenever the Council is considering a question of direct interest to a State not represented thereon, such State should be invited to send representatives to participate in the discussion and study of that question. It is not intended, however, to fix hard and fast rules, but rather to permit the Council to adapt its procedure to the particular problem under consideration. In some cases it might desire to hold its own preliminary discussions prior to the participation of other interested States. In other cases, the Council might desire to convoke a formal conference of the States chiefly interested in seeking a solution of the particular problem. It is so authorised.

CALENDAR TO NO. 209

i   *20 July 1945   Brief for Mr. Eden for No. 214: Council of Five Foreign Ministers.*
Annexes variant text of No. 209 (cf. notes 1–3 above) and suggests procedures for inviting French and Chinese Govts. to join Council, for its first meeting and for secretariat [F.O. 934/3/16(6)].

---

[1] Thus on filed copy. The text annexed to No. 209.i here included 'London': cf. *F.R.U.S. Berlin*, vol. ii, pp. 612–3.

[2] Thus on filed copy. The text annexed to No. 209.i here included '(? September 1st)'.

[3] The text annexed to No. 209.i here read, presumably correctly (cf. No. 178, minute 2), '. . . Bulgaria, Hungary and Finland.'

No. 210

Report of the Economic Sub-Committee to the Foreign Secretaries[1]
P. (*Terminal*) 15 [U 6197/3628/70]

Top secret   *20 July, 1945*

We have considered the proposals in a memorandum by the United States Delegation on the Economic Principles to govern the treatment of Germany in the initial control period, together with the Annex dealing with reparations.[2]

We have unanimously agreed to recommend the adoption of the Economic Principles set out in the attached clauses[3] for incorporation in the proposed Agreement.

On one matter, which relates both to the Economic Principles and to Reparations, we have to report that agreement has not been reached.

The United Kingdom and United States representatives consider that it is essential that such necessary imports into Germany as are approved by the Governments controlling Germany shall constitute a first charge against exports from Germany whether of capital equipment or current production and stocks of goods. They therefore recommend the adoption of the text attached hereto as Annex II[4] for incorporation in the Agreement on Economic Principles. The Soviet Representatives do not accept this principle and express the view that reparation deliveries should have priority and that imports into Germany, should, if necessary, be confined to the amount that can be paid for by exports from Germany after reparation schedules have been met.

The United Kingdom and United States representatives point out that the provisions of paragraph 18 (to the effect that it shall be the general principle, that in the absence of special reasons to the contrary, each of the zones of occupation, including the Greater Berlin area, will draw its supplies, so far as practicable, from the areas in Germany on which it had drawn before the war) apply to the territory of Germany as it existed on the 31st December, 1937, whether or not any part of such territory is administered by or ceded to another State.

The Soviet representative thinks that any decision on this point at the present time is premature, pending a decision by the Conference on the future boundaries of Germany.

The United Kingdom and United States representatives point out that there are two matters in addition to those mentioned in paragraph 13 on which a common policy is essential in the treatment of Germany as a single economic unit:

[1] This report with appendices is printed in parts with some verbal variation in *F.R.U.S. Berlin*, vol. ii, pp. 795–9 and 845–6.
[2] See No. 170, note 2.
[3] See the Appendix below.
[4] To the Appendix below.

(1) Uniform method of treatment of the German civilian population;

(2) Subject to normal regulations, free circulation of nationals of United Kingdom, United States, U.S.S.R. and France in all zones by land and air.

The Soviet representative takes the position that these two points, while having economic significance, have a wider political application, and that they should therefore not be considered by the Economic Sub-Committee.

The Allied Commission on Reparations has agreed on seven basic principles. The Sub-Committee recommend that these principles (Annex I)[5] should be accepted.

The Allied Commission on Reparations failed to reach agreement on the underscored[6] last clause of an eighth principle:

'After payment of reparations, enough resources must be left to enable the German people to subsist without external assistance. In working out the economic balance of Germany, the necessary means must be provided for payment of imports approved by the Governments concerned *before reparation deliveries are made.*'

As stated above, the Sub-Committee have been unable to reach agreement on this point.

The Sub-Committee at the request of the Soviet representative has postponed discussion of definitions of reparations, restitution and war booty.

The Sub-Committee were informed that the Allied Commission on Reparations had agreed on a formula for allocation of reparations between the U.S.S.R., United Kingdom and United States and a procedure for settling the division of reparations among other countries, the texts of which are attached as Annexes III and IV.[7]

The United States representatives feel that the definition of restitution, war booty and reparations are so interrelated with the formulæ for allocation of reparations that agreement must be reached on all of these matters simultaneously. The Sub-Committee therefore make no recommendations on these matters at the present time.

APPENDIX TO NO. 210

Proposed Agreement on the Political and Economic Principles to govern the treatment of Germany in the initial control period
Text as submitted to the Foreign Secretaries by Economic Sub-Committee

Economic Principles

10.[8] In order to eliminate Germany's war potential, the production of arms, ammunition and implements of war, as well as all types of aircraft and sea-going

---

[5] Not here printed. The text in Annex I was the same, subject to minor verbal variation, as principles 1 to 7 in the Annex to No. 116 except that paragraph IV referred to 'Governments concerned' in the plural. A note to Annex I read: 'Additional items still under discussion in the Economic Sub-Committee.'

[6] Here italicized.

[7] Not printed. Cf. No. 152, note 3.

[8] This paragraph numbering is consecutive to that in No. 190.

ships, shall be prohibited and prevented. Production of metals, chemicals, machinery and other items that are directly necessary to a war economy shall be rigidly controlled and restricted to Germany's approved post-war peace-time needs to meet the objectives stated in paragraph 14. Productive capacity not needed for permitted production shall be destroyed, or shall be removed in accordance with the reparations plan recommended by the Allied Commission on Reparations and approved by the Governments concerned.

11. At the earliest practicable date, the German economy shall be decentralised for the purpose of eliminating the present excessive concentration of economic power as exemplified in particular by cartels, syndicates, trusts and other monopolistic arrangements. Notwithstanding this, however, and for the purpose of achieving the objectives set forth herein, certain forms of central administrative machinery, particularly in the fields of Finance, Transportation and Communications, shall be maintained or restored.

12. In organising the German economy, primary emphasis shall be given to the development of agriculture and peaceful domestic industries.

13. During the period of occupation Germany shall be treated as a single economic unit. To this end common policies shall be established in regard to:

(a) mining and industrial production and allocation;
(b) agriculture, forestry and fishing;
(c) wages, prices and rationing;
(d) import and export programmes for Germany as a whole;
(e) currency, central taxation and customs;
(f) reparation and removal of industrial war potential.

In applying these policies account shall be taken, where appropriate, of varying local conditions.

14. Allied controls shall be imposed upon the German economy, but only to the extent necessary:

(a) to carry out programmes of industrial disarmament and demilitarisation, of reparations, and of approved exports and imports;
(b) to assure the production and maintenance of goods and services required to meet the needs of the occupying forces and displaced persons in Germany and essential to maintain in Germany average living standards not exceeding the average of the standards of living of European countries. (European countries means all European countries excluding United Kingdom and U.S.S.R.);
(c) to ensure in the manner determined by the Control Council the equitable distribution of essential commodities between the several zones so as to produce a balanced economy throughout Germany and reduce the need for imports;
(d) to control German industry and all economic and financial international transactions, including exports and imports, with the aim of preventing Germany from developing a war potential and of achieving the other objectives named herein. For the same purpose no grant of credit to Germany or Germans by any foreign persons or Governments shall be permitted except with the approval of the Control Council;
(e) to control all German public or private scientific bodies, research and experimental institutions, laboratories, &c., connected with economic activities.

15. In the imposition and maintenance of economic controls established by the Control Council, German administrative machinery shall be created and the German authorities shall be required to the fullest extent practicable to proclaim and assume administration of such controls. Thus it should be brought home to

the German people that the responsibility for the administration of such controls and any breakdown in these controls will rest with themselves. Any German controls which may run counter to the objectives of occupation will be prohibited.

16. The principles and conditions governing the exaction of reparations from Germany are set forth in Annex I[5] to this agreement.

17. Measures shall be promptly taken:
  (a) to effect essential repair of transport;
  (b) to enlarge coal production;
  (c) to maximise agricultural output; and
  (d) to effect emergency repair of housing and essential utilities.

18. In securing the objective mentioned in paragraph 14 (c) it shall be the general principle that, in the absence of special reasons to the contrary, each of the zones of occupation, including the Greater Berlin Area, will draw its supplies so far as practicable from the areas in Germany on which it had drawn before the war.

ANNEX II TO APPENDIX TO No. 210

19. The Control Council shall formulate as soon as possible a programme of minimum required imports for Germany as a whole. Such a programme shall include provision for equitable inter-zonal distribution of supplies available within Germany, so as to minimise the net deficit for, and imports into, Germany as a whole. Responsibility for the procurement and financing of approved imports for Germany as a whole shall be shared on a basis to be negotiated in the Control Council. Reimbursement for all the net advances made for approved imports into Germany shall be a first charge against the proceeds of both exports of capital equipment, and of current production and stocks from Germany.

No. 211

Letter from Major-General Hollis to Sir A. Cadogan (Berlin)[1]
[F.O. 934/3/12(7)]

Top Secret   CABINET OFFICE, 'TERMINAL', *20 July 1945*

Dear Sir Alexander Cadogan,

The Chiefs of Staff are most anxious to get some agreement with the United States Chiefs of Staff during this Conference on the vexed question

---

[1] This letter was sent in accordance with a decision of the Chiefs of Staff Committee at its sixth meeting at Babelsberg, held at 39–41 Ringstrasse at 6 p.m. on 20 July 1945: minute 2 of C.O.S. (Terminal) 6th Meeting, not printed. At that meeting the Chiefs of Staff were informed that in accordance with instructions given at their meeting that morning (minute 4 of C.O.S.—Terminal—5th Meeting: cf. No. 198, note 4) the memorandum enclosed below by General Hollis to Sir A. Cadogan had been circulated but 'that it had not been possible to obtain the agreement of the Foreign Office on a high level to the issue of this memorandum. The opinion of the Foreign Office was understood to be in favour of leaving the situation in Indo-China as it was, on the grounds that it was undesirable to impose an awkward decision on the Generalissimo [Chiang Kai-shek] unless it was absolutely necessary. The present proposal to divide Indo-China in two had, in the opinion of the

of the area of command in which Indo-China should be. They had hoped that the United States Chiefs of Staff would agree to a recommendation that the Prime Minister and the President should ask the Generalissimo to transfer the whole of Indo-China to South East Asia Command. The Americans, however, have now proposed that, for the purpose of command, Indo-China should be divided into two, the northern half remaining in the China Theatre and the southern half being transferred to South East Asia Command.[2] The British Chiefs of Staff would like to agree with this proposal and table the attached paper for consideration by the Combined Chiefs of Staff.

The Chiefs of Staff realise that the Foreign Office would prefer that the present situation with regard to command in Indo-China should continue, although the Prime Minister has already agreed with the Chiefs of Staff paper on Control and Command in the War against Japan (C.O.S. (45) 423(O))[3] with the British proposal that the whole of Indo-China should be transferred to South East Asia Command.

They hope, therefore, that the Foreign Office would not oppose a recommendation to the President and the Prime Minister on the lines of that in the attached memorandum. They feel that apart from strictly military reasons, it is most desirable to put an end to the conflict of personalities which has arisen out of this question.

Would you, therefore, let me know if the Foreign Office have any objection to the Chiefs of Staff tabling the attached paper as proposed?

Yrs sincerely
L. C. HOLLIS

Foreign Office, the additional disadvantage of being unpopular with the French. Nevertheless, a letter had been written to Sir Alexander Cadogan requesting that, in spite of this, the Foreign Office should not oppose the proposal of the United States Chiefs of Staff to divide Indo-China which had been agreed by the British Chiefs of Staff.

'*Sir Hastings Ismay* thought that there might be considerable difficulty in proceeding with the memorandum already circulated by the British Chiefs of Staff without the concurrence of the Foreign Office. He, therefore, suggested that the memorandum should be withdrawn and the letter to Sir Alexander Cadogan should be amended into a request to the Foreign Office to agree to the circulation of the memorandum proposed by the British Chiefs of Staff. He thought that, if there was delay in receiving the reply from the Foreign Office, it would be quite acceptable to omit the question of Indo-China from the Final Report of the Conference and to deal with it through normal channels.

'*Sir Charles Portal* recalled that the Prime Minister had already agreed with the Chiefs of Staff proposal that the whole of Indo-China should be transferred to South-East Asia Command and thought that the Foreign Office might be impressed with this point.

'*The Committee*—

Instructed the Secretary—

(*a*) to withdraw the memorandum on Command in Indo-China.

(*b*) to write to Sir Alexander Cadogan on the lines suggested in discussion.'

[2] See No. 183, minute 4.

[3] Of 30 June 1945 (F 4056/69/23), not printed.

Memorandum by the British Chiefs of Staff[4]

Top Secret

Command in Indo-China

We agree that as a first step in re-organising command in Indo-China, there is advantage in dividing the country into two, leaving the northern portion in China theatre and allotting the southern portion to South East Asia Command. This organisation of command should be subject to review in the light of the development of operations in that area.

2. We have examined the run of communications in Indo-China and suggest that the most satisfactory dividing line would be latitude 16°N.

3. We, therefore, recommend that the Combined Chiefs of Staff should include in their final report to the Prime Minister and President, a statement on the following lines:

'We consider it important that there shall be unity of control of major operations in the Indo-China–Siam area when they develop and of previous subversive and para-military operations. As the first step in securing this unity of control, we are agreed that the best arrangement would be to include that portion of Indo-China lying south of latitude 16° North in South East Asia Command. This arrangement would continue General Wedemeyer's control of that part of Indo-China which covers the flank of projected Chinese operations in China, and would enable Admiral Mountbatten to prepare the ground in the southern half of Indo-China where any initial operations by him would develop.

We recommend that the President and the Prime Minister should approach the Generalissimo to secure his agreement to this arrangement.'

[4] This memorandum, circulated as C.C.S. 890/3 on 22 July, is printed in *F.R.U.S. Berlin*, vol. ii, p. 1319.

No. 212

Minute from Mr. Hoyer Millar to Mr. Eden (Berlin)

[*F.O. 934/2/6(4)*]

[BERLIN,] *20 July 1945*

The American paper about policy towards Italy (P Terminal 5)[1] is to be considered at the meeting of Foreign Secretaries tomorrow, July 21st.

The objections to this paper as it stands are set out at length in the attached copy of a minute given to the Prime Minister today.[2] There are really two main points to which we take exception:

(*a*) We do not like the American proposal formally to terminate the bulk of the armistice provisions and replace them by *ad hoc* agreements with the Italian Government. In the first place this greatly weakens our legal position both now and later on in connection with the peace

[1] See No. 208, minute 4.

[2] Annex 1 below.

negotiations; and in the second place *ad hoc* arrangements with the Italian Government might take quite a time to negotiate.

(*b*) In the second place it seems doubtful wisdom to try here to lay down how the transfer of responsibilities from the Allied Commission to the Italian authorities (which has in fact already gone pretty far) should be effected. It seems wiser simply for the three Governments to lay down certain general principles and to invite the Allied Commission to suggest the way in which these principles can best be implemented.

I have discussed the matter with the Americans and have tried to convince them that there is no real disagreement with us on the principle involved; where we differ is on the practical steps to put this principle into effect. The Americans suggested that it might be possible to find some compromise wording based on their original resolution which they could accept. I accordingly attach the draft[3] of a possible revise of the American paper which I have cleared with Brigadier French of the War Office. Under this redraft the practical results which the Americans wish to secure would, I think, be obtained without any wide abrogation of the armistice terms and without our position at the peace settlement being prejudiced.

If this redraft meets with your approval perhaps it could be handed round at tomorrow's meeting. The redraft is, I think, applicable *mutatis mutandis* to the satellite countries with only slight changes.

Under the redraft certain duties are placed on the Allied Commission in Italy. There is a Russian member of the Commission though he has not hitherto taken any active part in its work. I do not think, however, that his intervention at this stage should cause much complication as the Commission in its present form is moribund. And if the Russian does take an increasing part in the work of the Commission in Italy it strengthens the case for the British and American representatives taking a larger part in the Control Commissions in the satellite countries. But we do not want to go out of our way to encourage Russian interest in Italy.

As a pendant to our redraft of the American paper I also attach the draft of a possible statement[4] about Italy to be issued at the end of the Conference.[5] This on the face of it should be relatively uncontroversial and acceptable to the Americans. You will see that in the statement there is included a passage saying that once the Italian peace treaty is concluded it will be possible for the three Governments to support an application from Italy to join the World Security Organisation. This would cover the first part of the suggestion made by President Truman this morning[1] and would make it easier to deal with the question of the exclusion of Franco quite separately from that of the inclusion of Italy. It would then be possible to link Franco simply with the neutrals and not with Italy or the satellites. The draft of the

[3] Annex 2 below.

[4] Annex 3 below.

[5] Note in original by Mr. Hoyer Millar: 'If our paper is approved, something general could be added to the statement about withdrawing obsolete Armistice terms.'

statement on this point[6] which we thought of trying to get the Drafting Committee to consider is also attached.

F. R. HOYER MILLAR

[P.S.] I have since shown the draft of our paper to F. M. Alexander, who approved it, & to Mr. Dunn of the U.S. Delegation, who seemed fairly happy with it[7].

ANNEX 1 TO No. 212

His Majesty's Government are in full agreement with the objects of this United States paper[1]—i.e. to help Italy recover her position as a useful member of European society as soon as possible and to facilitate the early holding of elections so as to ensure the establishment of a properly representative Government.

2. His Majesty's Government are too in entire agreement with the United States Government in wishing to see Italy's present anomalous position as a co-belligerent but not a member of the United Nations terminated as soon as possible. They feel that much the most satisfactory way of achieving this is by the early conclusion of the peace treaty which should be all inclusive and which in addition to making Italy eligible for membership of the United Nations, etc., would dispose of the various Allied claims against Italy—e.g. territorial revision, colonies, size of Italian armed forces, etc. Now that the new Council of Foreign Ministers is to be set up the machinery for dealing with such a peace treaty will be in existence. It would therefore be possible to refer the question of the Italian peace treaty to the Council of Foreign Ministers in the very near future. H.M.G. would hope in fact to be in a position to communicate their proposals on the subject to the Council of Foreign Ministers in the course of the next few weeks. Admittedly it will take some time before the consultations with the various other interested Governments are completed and the treaty is finally agreed on but given goodwill and energy it should not, one would hope, take more than a few months to complete the negotiations.

3. Apart from any other considerations there is every advantage in pushing on with the matter quickly as it would be most desirable to conclude the Italian peace treaty before the Italian Constituent Assembly meets. Otherwise the treaty may become involved with the internal Italian politics.

4. It is suggested therefore that H.M.G.'s policy should be to press hard for the earliest possible conclusion of the Italian peace treaty and in the meantime to carry on with the plans already envisaged for the progressive handing over to the Italian authorities of the responsibilities of the Allied Commission. It is expected that by the end of September all Italy will have been handed back to the Italian Government except Venezia Giulia and Boltzano [sic]. Outside these two areas the political and administrative functions of the Allied Commission will, in virtue of the Macmillan directive of February last,[8] be limited to advisory duties.

---

[6] Not attached to filed copy: see, however, No. 225.i.

[7] Mr. Eden minuted on this paper: 'All this is ingenious & if we can come out at anything like this we shall do well—I have made one or two changes [cf. notes 9, 12–13 below]. We must be careful not to be fulsome to Italians; it don't do them any good. A. E. July 21.'

[8] For this directive, received by Field-Marshal Alexander from the Combined Chiefs of Staff on 31 January 1945, and explanatory aide-mémoire of 24 February to the Italian Government from Mr. Harold Macmillan, then Acting President of the Allied Commission for Italy, cf. respectively C.R.S. Harris, *op. cit.*, pp. 236–9, and *F.R.U.S. 1945*, vol. iv, pp. 1244–8.

It is also contemplated that the economic functions of the Allied Commission should be handed over at an early date and a great deal more responsibility be given to the Italian authorities.

5. The U.S. Government however contemplate introducing interim arrangements pending the conclusion of the peace treaty which seemed to amount to the formal termination of large parts of the armistice and their replacement by some kind of *ad hoc* agreement with the Italian Government partly to cover matters connected with the rights of Allied troops in Italy (such as those normally covered by Civil Affairs agreements) and partly in some way to leave the Allied Governments in power at some subsequent date to dispose of the outstanding territorial and other questions. This American suggestion is designed expressly to strengthen the position with the Italian Government. We have every sympathy with this objective but it seems at least doubtful if the American plan would do much to achieve it. What the Italian Government want is to be recognised as an ally and as a member of the United Nations. This cannot happen until the peace treaty is signed. Merely to do away with the existing armistice and substitute some other form of agreement, sanction for which would still in fact rest upon the armistice and upon the fact that the Allied troops were in occupation of Italy does not seem likely to help the Italians very much. Nor would the American proposals alter the present situation in Italy in fact to any great extent. Finally the negotiation of the different *ad hoc* agreements suggested by the United States Delegation might take some considerable time.

6. Much the best way of helping the Italians would seem to be to stick to our own plan of pressing on with the peace treaty and making some public statement at the end of Terminal to that effect. There is still, however, advantage in keeping to this plan of leaving things as they are and having two [*sic*] outstanding questions settled at the Peace Conference in that it would prevent the Russians pressing for immediate decisions on various questions connected with the Italian peace settlement—such as the future of Trieste. The proper place for this to be handled is the Council of Foreign Ministers.

7. It is suggested therefore that the attached revised draft[3] of the United States paper would be greatly preferable from our point of view. It is also suggested that the attached public statement[4] might usefull[y] be given at the end of Terminal.

ANNEX 2 TO NO. 212

*Redraft of United States Memorandum[1] on Policy
towards Italy*

The objectives of the Three Governments with regard to Italy are directed towards her early political independence and economic recovery, and the right of the Italian people ultimately to choose their own form of Government.

Italy's present status as co-belligerent and unconditionally surrendered enemy is anomalous, and hampers every effort both by the Allies and by Italy herself to improve Italy's economic and political situation. This anomaly can be finally solved only through the negotiation of a definitive Peace Treaty which would at best require some months. The preparation of such a Treaty should be one of the first tasks of the suggested Council of Foreign Ministers which should be invited to[9] press on with the matter with the utmost expedition.

[9] After this word Mr. Eden bracketed the rest of the sentence and substituted 'take this as their first task.'

In the meanwhile some steps should be taken to afford the Italian Government some tangible recognition of Italy's contribution towards the defeat of Germany.

As a first step in this direction the Three Governments should publicly announce their intentions as to the early conclusion of a Peace Treaty; coupled with an undertaking to provide Italy with such economic assistance as is practicable and reiterating the desirability of early elections in Italy.

As a second step, the Allied Commission in Italy should be invited to accelerate and intensify the steps already taken (in accordance with the statement communicated to the Italian Government by the acting President of the Allied Commission on February 24th)[8] to hand over increasing responsibilities to the Italian Government. The Allied Commission should aim at reducing their own activities to the greatest practicable extent compatible with the safeguarding of Allied military requirements, and without prejudicing those points requiring to be dealt with in the eventual Peace settlement. The Allied Commission should be invited to make concrete recommendations to this end as soon as possible.

Finally the Allied Commission should be invited to indicate which of the provisions of the armistice terms can now be considered obsolete, in order that the Italian Government can be notified that these provisions can now be regarded as no longer in force.

Annex 3 to No. 212

Draft Statement regarding Italy

At their meeting in Moscow in November, 1943, the three Governments declared *inter alia* that 'Allied policy towards Italy must be based upon the fundamental principle that Fascism and all its evil influence and emanations must be utterly destroyed and that the Italian people shall be given every opportunity to establish governmental and other institutions based upon democratic principles.'[10] Similar views were expressed in the tripartite declaration issued at the time when the Italian Government was recognised as a co-belligerent.[11] In this declaration it was stated that; 'The three Governments acknowledge the Italian Government's pledge to submit to the will of the Italian people after the Germans had been driven from Italy, and it is understood that nothing can detract from the absolute and untrammelled right of the people of Italy by constitutional means to decide on the democratic form of government they will eventually have.'

In the light of these declarations the three Governments naturally welcome the recent announcement by the new Italian Government that they intend to take steps to assemble a Constituent Assembly, based on popular election, as soon as possible. They welcome also the declared intention of the Italian Government to reconstitute the communal and provincial administrations and to take steps to promote regional autonomy. They feel confident that all these measures will be taken with the object of setting the Government of Italy—local as well as central—on a sound democratic basis, resting on the freely expressed will of the people as a whole. For their part, the three Governments hope that the elections will be held at the earliest practicable moment, and they call on the Italian people in the meantime during the interval before the elections to show a spirit

[10] See No. 138, note 3.   [11] See No. 12, note 3.

481

of clamness [calmness] and resolution and to co-operate in the task of the moral and material reconstruction of their country. Only through the combined efforts of all sections of the Italian people can this object be achieved.

The Three Governments further consider that the time has come to terminate the present anomalous position of Italy and to recognise the valuable[12] contribution made by the Italian people to the final defeat of Germany. They therefore feel that very early steps should be taken to conclude a Peace Treaty with Italy, thus enabling her to play a full part in World society. One consequence of such a Peace Treaty will be to make it possible for the Three Governments to support an application from the Italian Government for membership to the World Security Organisation. Another consequence will be finally to supersede the terms of the armistice, many of which are already obsolete and the application of which has moreover already been substantially modified in Italy's favour during recent months.

The Three Governments will therefore recommend to the other interested Allied Governments that the necessary steps to proceed to the conclusion of a Peace Treaty with Italy should be taken at the earliest practicable moment. They therefore propose that the question of the Peace Treaty should be placed on the agenda of the first meeting of the Council of Foreign Ministers[13] and they hope that the latter will deal with the question with the utmost expedition.

The Three Governments recognise that Italy will require much[12] assistance in the economis [sic] sphere to enable her to overcome the great difficulties with which she is faced. They will do all in their power to help Italy in this direction, bearing in mind the overriding necessity of carrying on the war against Japan to the full, the overall supply difficulties with which the world is faced at the present time and the pressing claims of the liberated countries in Europe and the Far East.

[12] This word was bracketed by Mr. Eden.

[13] After this word Mr. Eden bracketed the rest of the sentence and noted 'I am not very fond of this adjuration. We don't want to have to work under a threat & I would prefer to omit. A.E.'

No. 213

Notes by Sir D. Waley (Berlin) on the Report of the Economic Sub-Committee P. (Terminal) 15[1]

[F.O. 934/1/2(35)]

[BERLIN,] *21 July 1945*

1. The first charge on exports from Germany must be to pay for approved necessary imports into Germany. This is a fundamental point, both to the Americans and to ourselves. We offered as a concession to the Russians that the first charge should apply only to current deliveries, and not to capital goods in which the Russians are mainly interested. We withdrew this

[1] No. 210.

concession last night as no agreement was reached. It is important that the point should not be shelved. The President will certainly press it strongly at the Plenary.

2. *The provision of food and fuel for Eastern Germany, including the Greater Berlin Area*

The point here is that German territory which is administered by or ceded to Poland must, at any rate for the time being, continue to supply food and coal to Berlin. We reluctantly agreed to supply the British Zone in Berlin with food for a month, since otherwise 900,000 people would have starved while the Conference is sitting. We cannot continue to do so and food must come from the East as it has done in the past. The Foreign Secretaries, in submitting the Economic Principles to the Big Three, could include the following recommendation:

'The Berlin Kommendatura should submit to the Control Council a plan for providing food and fuel for the Greater Berlin Area. These supplies should be drawn, so far as they are available, from the areas in Germany (as it existed on December 31, 1937) on which the Greater Berlin Area had drawn before the war.'

This point should be settled before the Big Three conclude their discussion on Poland. The attached extract from the note which the Foreign Secretary sent to the Prime Minister on the Eastern Frontier of Germany[2] shows how the argument can be put forward.

3. *Uniform method of treatment of the German civilian population and free circulation in all Zones of British, American, Russian and French nationals*

Field-Marshal Montgomery has drawn attention to these points as an essential part of treating Germany as a single unit.[3] Agreement on these points should be reached and recorded and the political experts should be instructed to agree on a text. Probably these clauses should not be included in the Political and Economic Principles, but kept separate.

4. *The Eight Basic Principles of Reparations*

Seven Principles have been agreed. The eighth Principle cannot be agreed until the Russians accept the British and American view that payment for approved imports into Germany must constitute a first charge against exports (see above). We cannot, of course, agree to the Seven Principles being accepted as the basis for the Reparation Plan, or to the Seven Principles being published until the eighth Principle is settled in a form satisfactory to us.

5. *Other Reparation Questions*

The Russians refused to discuss this last night and the Sub-Committee is to meet again at 8 p.m. tonight. We should prefer most of these questions to

[2] Not printed. The extract comprised the introductory line and sub-paragraphs (1) and (2) of the fourth paragraph of No. 194.i.
[3] See No. 153, enclosure A.

be referred back to the Moscow Commission. The Russians want to force through the Conference a Plan for Interim Deliveries so that they can get capital goods out of the Western Zone. We think that this is almost the only Joker in our pack and we do not want to play it until agreement has been reached on a Reparation Plan as a whole. The Americans told us that they agreed in our view, but without warning changed their tactics last night and offered to discuss a Plan for Interim Deliveries.

6. *Restitution*

We submitted our proposal to the European Advisory Commission[4] on which the French are represented. The French will want a wider definition than ours and the Americans have now put forward a much narrower definition[5] confined to works of art and other cultural objects. A fourth definition is favoured by the Russians.[6] We think that the Conference cannot settle this:-

(a) because it is too complicated and

(b) because the French are not represented here.

7. *Procedure for Bringing in the Other Powers*

This document (Annex IV)[7] was agreed at Moscow. We should like it approved by the Conference because it is important to invite the other Powers to formulate their claims without delay.

8. *France*

Before we started the talks in Moscow and ever since, we have pressed that the French should be brought in as soon as possible and at any rate before the minor Powers are brought in. The Americans take the same view. It would be a great help if a decision on this point could be reached by the Conference.[8]

S. D. WALEY

CALENDAR TO NO. 213

i *25 July 1945 To Mr. Roberts (Moscow) Tel. No. 67 Victim.* Summary of meeting of Economic Sub-Committee at Potsdam on 21 July. Russians put forward wide definition of war booty [UE 2982/624/77].

[4] See No. 152, note 9.
[5] Circulated as annex II to P. (Terminal) 6: see No. 170, note 2.
[6] Cf. No. 152, note 10.
[7] See No. 210, note 7.
[8] On 19 July 1945 Mr. Coulson had written from Berlin to Mr. J. S. Dent in the Foreign Office concerning reparation: 'Mark Turner tells me that our delegation are in fact keeping the French pretty fully informed. I think therefore we can let things be, and if the French revert to us again, we can tell them what is actually happening.'

No. 214

Record of Fourth Meeting of Foreign Secretaries held at Cecilienhof,
Potsdam, on Saturday, 21 July 1945 at 12 noon

F.(Terminal)4th Meeting [U 6197/3628/70]

Top secret

Present:

M. V. M. Molotov, M. A. Ya. Vyshinski, M. I. M. Maisky, M. A. A. Gromyko,
M. F. T. Gousev, M. A. A. Sobolev, M. V. S. Semenov, M. S. A. Golunski
(*Interpreter*).

Mr. J. F. Byrnes, Mr. W. A. Harriman, Mr. J. C. Dunn, Mr. H. F. Matthews,
Mr. W. L. Clayton, Mr. C. E. Bohlen, Mr. B. V. Cohen, Mr. E. Page (*Interpreter*).

Mr. Eden, Sir A. Cadogan, Sir A. Clark Kerr, Sir W. Strang, Mr. N. Brook,
Mr. P. J. Dixon, Mr. W. Hayter, Major L. M. Theakstone (*Interpreter*).

Contents

Minute	Subject
1.	Council of Foreign Ministers
2.	Germany: Economic Problems
3.	Poland
4.	Peace Treaties—Interim Arrangements with ex-enemy Satellite States
5.	European Oil Supplies
6.	Agenda for Fifth Plenary Meeting

1. *Council of Foreign Ministers*

(Previous Reference: P. (Terminal) 4th Meeting,[1] Minute 3.)

Mr. Byrnes suggested that the Council of Foreign Ministers should hold
their first meeting in London not later than 1st September, 1945. Their first
task would be to organise the work of the Council and settle their procedure.
It followed that all the five States Members of the Council should be represented at this first meeting.

Mr. Eden said that the British Delegation were grateful to the other two
Delegations for falling in with the suggestion that the Council should
normally meet in London. He recognised, however, that there would be
occasions when his colleagues on the Council would find it more convenient
to meet elsewhere. It might be advisable to make this clear in the
constitution of the Council and he suggested the following formula: 'The
Council shall normally meet in London, which will be the permanent seat
of its Secretariat. Meetings may, however, be held in other capitals as may
be agreed from time to time.'

It was agreed that the first meeting of the Council should be held in
London not later than 1st September, 1945; and that the constitution of

---

[1] No. 208.

the Council should include a provision about its normal place of meeting in the terms suggested by Mr. Eden.

MR. BYRNES recalled that at the Plenary Meeting on the previous day[1] the Foreign Secretaries had been invited to consider the procedure and timing for informing the Governments of France and China of the decision to establish this Council and inviting them to join it. He suggested that a telegram should be sent to these Governments from the Conference.

It was agreed to appoint a Committee consisting of:
United States Delegation: Mr. F. Matthews.
United Kingdom Delegation: Mr. J. Ward.
Soviet Delegation: M. Gromyko.
to prepare and submit to the three Foreign Secretaries the draft of such an invitation to the Governments of France and China.

MR. EDEN said that there were still one or two points to be cleared up in connection with the establishment of the Council. Some further consideration would have to be given to the procedure and timing for terminating the European Advisory Commission. There were also a few minor drafting amendments which the British Delegation wished to suggest in the draft constitution of the Council. At Mr. Eden's suggestion:

It was agreed that the drafting committee which had prepared the revised draft constitution for the proposed Council of Foreign Ministers should be asked to consider these issues and report to the three Foreign Secretaries.

2. Germany: Economic Problems

(Previous References: F. (Terminal) 2nd Meeting,[2] Minute 3, and F. (Terminal) 3rd Meeting,[3] Minute 1.)

MR. BYRNES said that the report of the sub-committee on Germany's Economic Problems had been received (P. (Terminal) 15)[4] and circulated to the three Delegations with a view to its being discussed at the present meeting.

M. MOLOTOV said that the report had not been completed until late on the previous evening, and he would like to have a further opportunity of studying it.

It was agreed that this report should be discussed as the first item on the Agenda at the meeting of Foreign Secretaries on 22nd July.

3. Poland

(Previous Reference: P. (Terminal) 3rd Meeting,[5] Minute 4).

It was recalled that at their second meeting the Foreign Secretaries had appointed a drafting Committee to prepare a revised text of the draft statement on Poland.[6] M. Vyshinski, Chairman of the Committee, was now ready to report.

---

[2] No. 189.
[3] No. 200.
[4] No. 210.
[5] No. 194.
[6] See No. 189, minute 4.

M. Vyshinski explained that the Committee had held three meetings, at which a number of points of difference, some of them serious, had been satisfactorily settled. As a result a revised text of the statement had been prepared (subsequently circulated as P. (Terminal) 17).[7] There were, however, five main points outstanding on which the Committee had been unable to agree, together with one subsidiary point which concerned only the Soviet and British Delegations.

The meeting proceeded to deal with these points *seriatim*, as follows:

(a) *Assets and Liabilities* (paragraph 2 of P. (Terminal) 17).[7]

M. Vyshinski explained that the Soviet members of the Committee desired to omit from the end of the third sentence the words 'and the question of the liability of the Polish Provisional Government for the credits advanced to the late Polish Government and other outstanding debts, and the relation of such advances to any assets of the Polish State available abroad'. They regarded this as a separate matter, which should not be dealt with in the statement since (i) it was a matter for bi-lateral discussion between the Polish Provisional Government on the one hand and, on the other, the British Government or the United States Government; (ii) the Polish Provisional Government had no representatives at the Conference with whom it might be discussed; and (iii) the amount and character of the liabilities referred to were not known to the Governments represented at the Conference.

Mr. Byrnes pointed out that the reference to assets, which the Soviet Delegation desired to include, was on the same footing as the reference to liabilities. The United States Government, on recognising the Polish Provisional Government, had at once taken steps to protect its property. This was not disputed by the Polish Provisional Government, and there was, therefore, no reason why the United States Government should make any statement about it. He could not in any case agree to any statement about the transfer of assets which did not also explain how the question of liabilities would be dealt with. Whatever debts might be due to the United States Government from the Polish Government, he was sure that the Polish Government were in no doubt that the attitude of the United States would be sympathetic, as it had always been. He would have much preferred to make no statement at all about the transfer of assets, which followed automatically on the recognition of the Polish Provisional Government; but, if some reference to it was desired by the other two Delegations, he suggested that paragraph 2 should be redrafted as follows:

'The British and United States Governments have already taken measures to protect the interests of the Polish Provisional Government, as the recognised Government of the Polish State, in the property belonging to the Polish State located in their territories and under their control, whatever the form of that property may be. They have further taken measures to prevent the alienation to third parties of such property. All

[7] No. 215.

proper facilities will be given to the Polish Provisional Government for the exercise of the ordinary legal remedies for the recovery of any property belonging to the Polish State which may have been wrongfully alienated.'

Mr. Byrnes added, however, that he would feel bound to advise President Truman that, if a declaration was made which included a paragraph on these lines, the President should also make it public that the Polish Provisional Government had never questioned the readiness of the United States Government to transfer to it the property which became due to it on recognition.

MR. EDEN agreed with Mr. Byrnes. He did not know the extent of the liabilities of the Polish Provisional Government, nor the extent of their assets; but the Soviet Government could be assured that the British Government would not drive a hard bargain with the Polish Government. Their position was the same as that of the United States Government, that any public statement referring to the assets of the Polish Government must also refer to their liabilities. In the circumstances, he rather agreed with Mr. Byrnes that the best course might be to omit paragraph 2 altogether. If, however, M. Molotov would accept the new paragraph proposed by Mr. Byrnes, which seemed to go a long way to meet the Russian view, he also would accept it.

    (1) It was agreed that this matter must be submitted for decision to the Plenary Meeting.

(b) *The Position of Polish Repatriates* (Paragraph 3 of P. (Terminal) 17).[7]

M. VYSHINSKI said that three points had been made in this paragraph:

    (i) the hope that as many Polish exiles as possible would return home;
    (ii) the suggestion that the Polish Provisional Government could assist in this by giving certain assurances; and
    (iii) the expectation that the repatriates should enjoy equal rights with the rest of their fellow citizens.

The Soviet Delegation entirely accepted (iii). They objected, however, to the implication in (i) and (ii) that if fewer Poles than was hoped were willing to return home, this would be the fault of the Polish Provisional Government.

MR. EDEN explained that the intention of the British Government in this part of the statement was to encourage Poles abroad to return home. He did not understand why it should be regarded as offensive to the Polish Provisional Government to refer to the assistance which he was sure they would be willing to give. Would it meet the Soviet Delegation if the words 'they consider that the Polish Provisional Government could itself greatly assist' were altered so as to read 'they are confident that the Polish Provisional Government will itself assist'?

M. MOLOTOV said he did not understand why the British Delegation were so insistent on this paragraph. All three Delegations were agreed on the need for complete equality of personal rights and rights of property as between the repatriates and their fellow citizens: this was, however, covered by the last sentence of the paragraph, which was accepted by the Soviet Delegation.

Mr. Eden said that, in the light of M. Molotov's explanation, he would agree to the omission of the second sentence.

(2) It was agreed that the second sentence of paragraph 3 of P. (Terminal) 17[7] should be omitted, and that the third sentence should should read: 'They expect that those Poles who return home shall be accorded personal rights and rights of property on the same basis as all Polish citizens.'

(c) *Powers of Arrest* (paragraph 4 of P. (Terminal) 17).[7]

M. Vyshinski explained that this was the subsidiary point on which there was a difference of view only between the Soviet and the British Delegations. It was the desire of the former that a paragraph should be included in the statement to the effect that the British Government would prevent on British territory and on territories controlled by British authorities, the arrest of Poles wishing to return to Poland.

Mr. Eden said that he could on no account accept this suggestion. The Soviet Delegation were presumably thinking of the powers conferred by war-time legislation on the Polish Government in London (as on other refugee Governments in the United Kingdom) to exercise disciplinary powers over members of their Armed Forces. With the transfer of recognition the legal power to exercise discipline over the members of the Polish Forces who recognised the authority of the Provisional Government would pass to that Government. The late Government did not exist and could not therefore exercise any such power.

M. Molotov said that, in the light of Mr. Eden's explanation, he would not press for the inclusion of this paragraph.

(3) It was agreed that paragraph 4 of P. (Terminal) 17[7] should be omitted.

(d) *The 'pledge' of the Polish Provisional Government regarding the holding of Elections* (P. (Terminal) 17[7]: paragraph 5, first sentence).

M. Vyshinski explained that in the first sentence of this paragraph the Soviet Delegation objected only to the use of the word 'pledge' in connection with the holding of free and unfettered elections.

The declaration on Poland, issued as a result of the Crimea Conference, had contained the phrase: 'the Polish Government of National Unity should pledge itself to the holding of free and unfettered elections.' It was well known that the Polish Provisional Government had accepted the decisions of the Crimea Conference; and in the view of the Soviet Delegation it would be sufficient to say that 'the Three Powers note that the Polish Provisional Government, in accordance with the decisions of the Crimea Conference, has agreed to the holding of free and unfettered elections. . . .'[8]

Mr. Eden and Mr. Byrnes accepted this suggestion.

[8] Punctuation as in original quotation.

(4) It was agreed that the first sentence of paragraph 5 of P. (Terminal) 17[7] should be amended as suggested by the Soviet Delegation.

(e) *Conduct of Elections and Freedom of the Press* (P. (Terminal) 17[7], paragraph 5, second and third sentences).

M. Vyshinski pointed out that in the second sentence of paragraph 5 reference was made to the free expression of opinion by *all* sections of Polish opinion. This was objectionable to the Soviet Delegation, in so far as it implied freedom for Fascist or Nazi organisations. He had, therefore, suggested that 'sections of opinion' should be limited by the words 'democratic and anti-Nazi'; but this qualification would, in the view of the Soviet Delegation, have the result that this sentence added nothing to the first sentence of the paragraph. He had also urged that the last sentence of the paragraph should be omitted. During the aftermath of hostilities in Poland it had not been possible to grant unlimited freedom to the Press; but, as conditions improved, the Soviet Government hoped that wider facilities would be afforded. This, however, was a purely domestic matter for the Polish Provisional Government, which it was not possible to settle in the absence of their representatives. Further, it did not seem necessary, in a statement on Poland, to make a special reference to the provision of wide facilities for Press representatives, since it had already been agreed at the Plenary Meeting the previous day[1] that these should be provided in all the countries of Eastern Europe, including the ex-enemy countries.

Mr. Eden said that he would be prepared to agree to the omission of the second sentence of paragraph 5, as desired by the Soviet Delegation, if they would in turn agree to the retention of the last sentence dealing with the Press.

Mr. Byrnes said that the policy of the United States Government was that the Press should be free in all countries. With the end of war in Europe the position had changed and the progress made in Poland in the last few weeks had given great comfort to Poles in the United States. As M. Vyshinski had said, Premier Stalin had accepted the United States point of view in principle; and the United States Government thought it particularly important that it should be publicly recognised that the Press in Poland was free.

M. Molotov said that he had two questions to ask:
(i) Were the Polish Provisional Government obstructing the entry of Press representatives into Poland?
(ii) Had the Press representatives already in Poland made any complaints of their treatment?

Mr. Byrnes said that he was not aware that any complaints had been made, but conditions had been such that there were at present no regular representatives of the United States Press in Poland. That, however, was not the point. The intention of the sentence was simply to express the hope that the Press would henceforth enjoy full freedom in Poland.

M. Molotov said that in so far as the sentence implied some censure of the Polish Provisional Government, he was not prepared to accept it.

MR. EDEN pointed out that in the circumstances he should not be regarded as having agreed to the omission of the second sentence of paragraph 5.

(5) It was agreed that the questions arising on these two sentences should be submitted to the Plenary Meeting.

4. Peace Treaties
Interim Arrangements with Ex-Enemy Satellite States.
(Previous Reference: P. (Terminal) 4th Meeting,[1] Minute 4).

MR. BYRNES recalled that at the Plenary Meeting on the previous day it had been agreed that the Foreign Secretaries should consider and report what interim arrangements could be made, pending the conclusion of Peace Treaties, with ex-enemy satellite States. As a basis for this discussion he handed in two memoranda prepared by the United States Delegation on 'Policy towards Italy' (P. (Terminal) 20) and 'Policy towards Roumania, Bulgaria, Hungary and Finland' (P. (Terminal) 19).[9]

M. MOLOTOV said that at the Plenary Meeting on the previous day Premier Stalin had expressed the view that the problem of alleviating the armistice conditions imposed on Italy was closely parallel with that of alleviating the conditions of the other ex-enemy satellite States, and had suggested that the problem of interim arrangements for all these satellite States, pending the conclusion of treaties of peace, should be considered as a single problem. Neither President Truman nor Mr. Churchill had raised any objection to this suggestion. M. Molotov therefore proposed that the two memoranda submitted by the United States Delegation should be referred to a sub-committee with instructions to combine them into a single statement covering all the ex-enemy satellite States.

MR. BYRNES said, that, as had been recognised at the Plenary Meeting the previous day, there was some difference between Italy on the one hand and, on the other, Roumania, Bulgaria, Hungary and Finland. For example, the armistice terms imposed on Italy had been very different from those imposed on the other countries. The United States Delegation had two further reasons for dealing with Italy separately: (i) the United States Government had not yet recognised the Governments of Roumania, Bulgaria and Hungary; and (ii) the United States had never been at war with Finland.

M. MOLOTOV recognised that there were some differences between Italy and the other countries, but these were not differences of substance and they could be taken into account in the preparation of the draft declaration. The points of similarity were, in his view, much greater than the points of difference; and he thought there should be no difficulty in preparing a single declaration covering both Italy and the other countries. The two memoranda submitted by the United States Delegation would afford good material for such a declaration and he was sure that, if these two papers

[9] Not here printed. These two American memoranda are printed in *F.R.U.S. Berlin*, vol. ii, pp. 1085 and 699 respectively.

were remitted for consideration by a sub-committee, there would be little difficulty in finding a common point of view between the three Delegations.

M. Molotov said that he must place it on record that the Soviet Delegation adhered to their view that the time had now come when the British and United States Governments should extend diplomatic recognition to the existing Governments of Roumania, Bulgaria and Hungary.

It was agreed that the question whether there should be a single declaration on this subject, covering both Italy and the other ex-enemy satellite States, should be remitted for decision by the Plenary Meeting.

5. *European Oil Supplies*

MR. BYRNES handed in a memorandum by the United States Delegation (P. (Terminal) 18)[10] recommending that the Governments of the Three Great Powers should agree that as from 1st September, 1945, crude oil or refined oil products should be provided from southern and eastern Europe for shipment into western Europe at the rate of at least 50,000 barrels a day. At Mr. Byrnes' suggestion:

It was agreed that the Sub-Committee on Economic Problems should be invited to consider this memorandum and report to an early meeting of Foreign Secretaries.

6. *Agenda for Fifth Plenary Meeting*

It was agreed that the following subjects should be put forward for discussion at the Fifth Plenary Meeting that afternoon:

(*a*) *Western Frontier of Poland.* (P. (Terminal) 12.)[11]
(*b*) *Territorial Trusteeship.* (P. (Terminal) 13.)[12]
(*c*) *Poland.* (P. (Terminal) 17.)[7]
(*d*) *Turkey.*

Cabinet Office, Potsdam, 21st July, 1945

CALENDAR TO No. 214

i *Undated Draft paper by U.K. Delegation:* summary consideration of policy towards Bulgaria, Roumania and Hungary [F.O. 934/2/9(4)].

[10] Not here printed. This American memorandum is printed *ibid.*, pp. 1382–3.
[11] No. 202.
[12] No. 203.

No. 215

Draft Statement[1] *on the Polish question as submitted by Drafting Committee to Meeting of Foreign Ministers on 21 July*
P.(*Terminal*)*17* [U 6197/3628/70]

Top secret   21 July, 1945

Note: The Soviet Members of the drafting Committee would omit passages in italics.

[1] Printed in *F.R.U.S. Berlin*, vol. ii, pp. 1120–1, and *Berlinskaya konferentsiya*, pp. 342–3.

The United Kingdom members would omit passages in square brackets.[2]

1. We have taken note with pleasure of the agreement reached among representative Poles from Poland and abroad which has made possible the formation, in accordance with the decisions reached at the Crimea Conference, of a Polish Provisional Government of National Unity recognised by the Three Powers. The establishment by the British and United States Governments of diplomatic relations with the Polish Provisional Government has resulted in the withdrawal of their recognition from the former Polish Government in London, which no longer exists.

2. The British and United States Governments have already taken measures to prevent the alienation to third parties of property (including merchant vessels) belonging to the Polish States located on their territory and under their control, whatever the form of this property may be. They are ready to take immediate measures to arrange for the transfer in accordance with the requirements of the law of such property to the Polish Provisional Government. To this end they are prepared to discuss with properly accredited representatives of the Polish Provisional Government the manner and time of such transfer *and the question of the liability of the Polish Provisional Government for the credits advanced to the late Polish Government and other outstanding debts and the relation of such advances to any assets of the Polish State available abroad.* All proper facilities will be given to the Polish Provisional Government for the exercise of the ordinary legal remedies for the recovery of any property belonging to the Polish State which may have been wrongfully alienated.

3. The Three Powers are anxious to assist the Polish Provisional Government in facilitating the return to Poland as soon as practicable of all Poles abroad who wish to go, including members of the Polish armed forces and merchant marine. *It is their desire that as many of these Poles as possible should return home and they consider that the Polish Provisional Government could itself greatly assist in this regard by giving suitable assurances.* (They expect) that those Poles who return home shall be accorded personal and property rights on the same basis as all Polish citizens.

4. (The British Government will at the same time take measures in order to prevent on British territory and on territories controlled by British authorities arrests of Poles who wish to return to Poland).

5. The Three Powers note that the Polish Provisional Government is pledged to the holding of free and unfettered elections as soon as possible on the basis of universal suffrage and secret ballot in which all democratic and anti-Nazi parties shall have the right to take part and to put forward candidates. *It is the confident hope of the Three Powers that the elections will be conducted in such a way as to make it clear to the world that all* (democratic and anti-Nazi) *sections of Polish opinion have been able to express their views freely, and thus to play their full part in the restoration of the country's political life. The Three*

[2] Here printed in round brackets.

Powers will further expect that representatives of the Allied Press shall enjoy full freedom to report to the world upon developments in Poland before and during the elections.

CALENDAR TO NO. 215

i *Undated Brief for Prime Minister for No. 219.* Attaches revisions of No. 215 [F.O. 934/2/10(35)].

No. 216

Memorandum by the United Kingdom Delegation (Berlin)
[*F.O. 934/2/10(28)*]

[BERLIN,] *21 July 1945*

Polish-German Frontier

The blue line on the attached map[1] shows a possible line which His Majesty's Government could support in the light of their past statements on this subject.

The red line shows the frontier now claimed by the Polish Provisional Government and supported by the Soviet Government.

His Majesty's Government have never proposed or agreed to any definite frontier line. The general effect of their past declarations on the subject is, however, that they are committed, on the assumption that Poland is to lose all territory east of the Curzon Line, to support the transfer to Poland of Danzig, East Prussia West and South of Königsberg, and the Oppeln district of Silesia. There would also be good grounds for agreeing to the transfer to Poland of the Eastern parts of Pomerania up to some such line as that shown on the attached map.

Whilst His Majesty's Government are not committed beyond this, they have agreed in general terms that Poland shall have the right to claim further territories up to the line of the Oder (though not up to the Western Neisse now claimed by the Polish Provisional Government).

Before formulating any final views we shall no doubt wish to have some indication of Soviet views in regard to the authority of the Control Council over the territories to the East of the Oder and Western Neisse and the availability of food and fuel supplies from this area for the provisioning of Germany and for reparations.

Any understanding reached here among the Three Powers would in any case not constitute a final settlement and would be subject to ratification by all the Powers concerned at some later date.

Foreign Office

[1] Untraced in Foreign Office archives.

494

i *22 July 1945 U.K. Delegation Brief* on economic aspects of Polish western
frontier [F.O. 934/2/10(43)].

No. 217

Memorandum by the United Kingdom Delegation (Berlin)[1]
[*F.O. 934/5/41(1)*]

[BERLIN,] *21 July 1945*

Turkey

We suggested yesterday that Turkey should be on the agenda of the Big
Three.[2] The Russians put it off until today.

Our line about this might be to ask the Russians what their intentions are.
We should recall that at the beginning of July we asked our Ambassador in
Moscow to take this question up with the Soviet Government, and to warn
them that it would need to be discussed at Terminal.[3] Our line here should
be not to make any proposals ourselves but to ask the Russians to elucidate
their intentions.

The Russians have put three requests to the Turks:

(1) They have asked for the return of the Provinces of *Kars and Ardahan*,
which except for the period between 1878 and 1918 have always been
part of Turkey.

The Americans regard this as the most important of the issues between
Russia and Turkey, and we might throw the lead to them on this point.
Our own view is that while this is primarily a matter between the Soviet
and Turkish Governments, nevertheless it concerns the Powers responsible
for World Organisation. Moreover, Marshal Stalin agreed at Yalta that
appropriate assurances should be given to Turkey regarding the maintenance
of her independance [*sic*] and integrity.

(2) The Russian request for *bases in the Dardanelles*. The Americans have
told us that they cannot object to bilateral negotiations for bases since they
themselves have concluded numerous bilateral agreements on this subject,
notably with ourselves. Nevertheless, they feel that such bilateral negotiations
must be with the free consent of both parties, and that if the party from whom
bases are requested objects, the matter can only be settled through the
World Organisation. We might take a rather stronger line on this point
and ask what they want them for. They are not necessary for free transit;
they would dominate Turkey's largest city.

(3) The *Montreux Convention*. The Russians raised the question of
revision of the Convention at Tehran, at Moscow and at Yalta. They made

---

[1] Annotation on filed copy: 'Corrected copy sent to P.M.'
[2] See No. 208, minute 6.
[3] See No. 19.

no concrete suggestions for revision, but gave it to be understood that they would let us have their views. This they have never done, but they have now made suggestions to the Turks for an agreement between the two of them on this subject. We should remind the Russians of their promise[3] to let us know their views, and express some surprise that they should broach the matter with the Turks before telling us what their intentions were. We should say that we have always been willing to discuss the revision of the Convention but that no progress could be made until we knew the Russian *desiderata*, and that these are still undefined. We should emphasise that the Montreux Convention is a multilateral one, and its revision is not a matter which can be settled between any two parties to the Convention.

Finally we might say that in view of Marshal Stalin's promise at Yalta that the Turks should be reassured about the maintenance of their independance and integrity as a preliminary to the Montreux Convention, we are surprised at the recent Soviet press and radio campaign against Turkey, which we feel is making the Turks nervous and less likely to be receptive to reasonable proposals for revision.

Foreign Office

No. 218

Minutes of a Meeting of the British Chiefs of Staff Committee held at 39/41 Ringstrasse, Babelsberg, on Saturday, 21 July 1945 at 2.30 p.m.
C.O.S.(*Terminal*) 7th Meeting [CAB 99/39]

Top secret

Present:
FIELD-MARSHAL SIR ALAN F. BROOKE, Chief of the Imperial General Staff (*in the Chair*), Marshal of the Royal Air Force Sir Charles F. A. Portal, Chief of the Air Staff, Admiral of the Fleet Sir Andrew B. Cunningham, First Sea Lord and Chief of Naval Staff, General Sir Hastings L. Ismay, Office of the Minister of Defence.

The following were also present:
The Right Hon. Lord Leathers, Minister of War Transport, Lieut.-General Sir Gordon Macready, Major-General N. G. Holmes, War Office.

Secretariat: Major-General L. C. Hollis, Brigadier A. T. Cornwall-Jones, Lieut.-Colonel G. Mallaby, Lieut.-Colonel T. Haddon.

1. *Basic Objectives and Undertakings*
(C.O.S. (Terminal) 8.)[1]
(C.C.S. 877/5.)[2]

---

[1] Not printed. In this note dated at Babelsberg on 20 July 1945 Major-General Hollis forecast the amendments likely to be (but not in fact fully so) proposed by the United States Chiefs of Staff (cf. note 2 below) to memorandum C.C.S. 877/4: see No. 198, note 1.

[2] Not here printed. This memorandum by the United States Chiefs of Staff is printed in *F.R.U.S. Berlin*, vol. ii, pp. 1304–8.

(Previous Reference: C.O.S. (Terminal) 5th Meeting,[3] Minute 1.)

THE COMMITTEE had under consideration a note[1] by the Secretary forecasting the amendments likely to be proposed by the United States Chiefs of Staff to the Basic Objectives paper and a memorandum[2] by the United States Chiefs of Staff setting out their proposed amendments in full.

LORD LEATHERS said that he had hoped, from private conversations he had been having, that the paper by the United States Chiefs of Staff would have gone considerably further to meet the British point of view. In point of fact, the paper now before the Committee showed a much wider divergence of view than in any previous drafts.

SIR ALAN BROOKE said that it was now clear that it would be quite impossible to get an agreement on this subject amongst the Combined Chiefs of Staff. In the first place, the United States Chiefs of Staff were clearly tied by the President's latest directive on lend-lease. Secondly, the British Chiefs of Staff were obliged, by the Prime Minister's instructions, to cover the United Kingdom import programme and they had not the necessary information with which to defend, against United States objections, the proposed paragraph on cargo shipping.

SIR CHARLES PORTAL said there were only two courses open on this question, either to attempt to argue the case without sufficient information, or to admit that agreement was impossible at Chiefs of Staff level and would continue to be impossible until the two outstanding points on lend-lease and cargo shipping had been settled on Government level. He suggested that the latter was the right course to adopt.

LORD LEATHERS agreed that, since all efforts had failed, it was now necessary to leave the outstanding questions to Governments. He undertook to explain the cargo shipping point to the Prime Minister.

THE COMMITTEE decided—

    (a) To inform the United States Chiefs of Staff that they were not prepared to discuss C.C.S. 877/5[2] and to explain their reasons.[4]

'X'   (b) To explain to the Prime Minister that it was not possible for the Combined Chiefs of Staff to make any progress with the paper on Basic Objectives until there had been governmental agreement on lend-lease and on the inclusion of the United Kingdom import programme in the basic undertakings.

THE COMMITTEE—

    (a) Instructed the Secretary to submit a minute[5] to the Prime Minister on the lines of 'X' above.

    (b) Took note that Lord Leathers would explain the cargo shipping point to the Prime Minister.

---

[3] No. 198.

[4] Field-Marshal Sir Alan Brooke made this communication at the 198th meeting of the Combined Chiefs of Staff held at 25 Ringstrasse, Babelsberg, at 3.30 p.m. on 21 July 1945 (minutes printed *op. cit.*, vol. ii, pp. 201–2): cf. Annex I below.

[5] *Note in filed copy:* 'Annex I.'

2. *Oral Report by the Secretary for Procedure for Dealing with Outstanding Business*

THE COMMITTEE were informed that there were now three subjects outstanding which it had been hoped to include in the Final Report:–

(a) *Basic Objectives and Undertakings*

This subject now awaited the result of the action called for in Minute 1 above.

(b) *Command in Indo-China*

This subject awaited the concurrence of the Foreign Office.

(c) *Disposition of Captured German Passenger Ships and British Troopship Employment in United States Transatlantic Programmes in the First Half of 1946.*

This paper[6] was awaiting the approval of the Prime Minister.

It seemed to the Committee unlikely that Basic Objectives would be cleared in time for inclusion in the Final Report, but there was a good chance that the papers referred to in (b) and (c) above might be ready for consideration by the Combined Chiefs of Staff on Monday, the 23rd July, 1945.

THE COMMITTEE therefore decided to work to the following programme:–

Monday

    10.30 a.m.—Meeting of the British Chiefs of Staff.

    11.30 a.m.—Meeting of the Combined Chiefs of Staff, with a provisional agenda as follows:–

        (i) Indo-China.

        (ii) Disposition of Captured German Passenger Ships and British Troopship Employment in United States Trans-Atlantic Programmes in the First Half of 1946.

        (iii) Draft Report to the Prime Minister and the President.

Tuesday

    11.30 a.m.—Plenary Meeting to discuss the Report to the President and the Prime Minister. If it were not possible to include everything necessary in the report by this time, then it should be submitted in the form of an interim report.

THE COMMITTEE thought that it was most desirable that they should have a discussion with the Prime Minister before the Plenary Meeting and invited General Ismay to take his instructions.[7]

Babelsberg, 21st July, 1945

ANNEX I TO No. 218

Minute from General Sir H. Ismay to Mr. Churchill (Berlin)

Copy   *21 July 1945*

In accordance with the instructions contained in your minute No. D (T) 2/5,[8] the Chiefs of Staff, keeping in close touch with Lord Leathers, have pressed for the inclusion of the United Kingdom import programme in the list of basic objectives. Up till to-day, there was ground for hoping that we would get our

[6] Circulated as C.C.S. 679/8 of 22 July 1945: printed *op. cit.*, vol. ii, pp. 1199–1200.
[7] *Note in filed copy:* 'Annex II.'
[8] For this minute of 17 July see No. 186, note 1.

way with the United States Chiefs of Staff. They have, however, now put in the attached paper,[9] which not only refuses to include anything about cargo shipping in the list of basic objectives, but also raises issues connected with lend-lease which cannot be discussed until the President has replied to your minute[10] on this subject. The passages sidelined on pages 1[11] and 3[12] will show you the impasse that has been reached.

2. The British Chiefs of Staff considered this paper at a meeting this afternoon, in consultation with Lord Leathers. They came to the conclusion that the differences between ourselves and the United States Chiefs of Staff can be resolved only on the level of Governments. They so informed the United States Chiefs of Staff at their meeting with them later in the day. The United States Chiefs of Staff agreed.

3. The position is therefore as follows:–
(a) As regards the lend-lease issues in the Basic Objectives paper, nothing can be done till we know the President's reaction to your approach:
(b) As regards the inclusion of the United Kingdom import programme in the list of basic objectives, Lord Leathers has said that he will send you a separate minute.

ANNEX II TO No. 218

Minute from General Sir H. Ismay to Mr. Churchill (Berlin)

Copy   *21 July 1945*

We informed the United States Chiefs of Staff to-day that you had agreed to a Plenary Meeting at 11.30 a.m. on Tuesday, 24th July. They told us that the President has also agreed to this. May I have your instructions as to the venue of the Meeting—presumably either your house or the President's?

2. The only paper which the Combined Chiefs of Staff have to place before the meeting is their customary formal report of business done. It is hoped to complete this by Monday morning the 23rd July. It will be little more than a summary of conclusions which have already been reported to, and approved by you; and it will not include the usual section on basic objectives unless you are able to resolve the lend-lease problem with the President during the week-end.

3. The Chiefs of Staff wonder whether you could have a meeting with them before the Plenary. If so, about 3 p.m. on Monday the 23rd or about 10 a.m. on Tuesday the 24th would seem to be the best, if not the only, times that you could manage?

[9] *Note in filed copy:* 'C.C.S. 877/5': see note 2 above.
[10] Cf. No. 251, annex I.
[11] *Note in filed copy:* 'Paragraph 1.'
[12] *Note in filed copy:* 'Paragraph 5, line 5 to line 15.'

No. 219

Record of Fifth Plenary Meeting held at Cecilienhof, Potsdam, on Saturday, 21 July 1945 at 5 p.m.
P.(Terminal)5th Meeting [U 6197/3628/70]

Top secret

Present:

PREMIER STALIN, M. V. M. Molotov, M. A. Ya. Vyshinski, M. F. T. Gousev,

M. A. A. Gromyko, M. K. V. Novikov, M. A. A. Sobolev, M. B. F. Podtzerob, M. V. N. Pavlov (*Interpreter*).

PRESIDENT TRUMAN, Mr. J. F. Byrnes, Mr. Joseph E. Davies, Fleet-Admiral W. D. Leahy, Mr. W. A. Harriman, Mr. J. C. Dunn, Mr. H. F. Matthews, Mr. B. V. Cohen, Mr. L. E. Thompson, Mr. C. E. Bohlen (*Interpreter*).

MR. CHURCHILL, Mr. Eden, Mr. Attlee, Sir Walter Monckton, Sir A. Cadogan, Sir A. Clark Kerr, Sir W. Strang, Sir E. Bridges, Mr. P. J. Dixon, Mr. W. Hayter, Major A. Birse (*Interpreter*).

Contents

Minute	Subject

1. *Report from Meeting of Foreign Secretaries*

MR. BYRNES submitted a report from the meeting of the Foreign Secretaries held that morning.[1] This report[2] is set out in Minutes 2–7 below.

2. *Council of Foreign Ministers*

The Meeting of Foreign Secretaries reported as follows:

'The Foreign Secretaries discussed the date of the formal establishment of the Council and agreed that it should be set up not later than the 1st September. It was also agreed that telegrams of invitation to participate in the work of the Council should be despatched to the Government of China and the Provisional Government of France before public announcement of the establishment of the Council is made. At the request of the British Delegation, the drafting committee which has been dealing with this question was asked to make a few minor changes in the present text of the proposal.'

The Conference accepted this Report.

3. *German Economic Questions*

The Meeting of Foreign Secretaries reported as follows:

'Since the report[3] of the sub-committee on this question had only just

---

[1] See No. 214.

[2] The text of this report is printed with verbal variation in *F.R.U.S. Berlin*, vol. ii, pp. 195–7.

[3] *Note in filed copy:* 'P. (Terminal) 15', No. 210.

been presented and the various delegations have not had an opportunity to give it adequate study, it was agreed to delay the discussion of this subject until to-morrow.'

4. *Polish Question—Liquidation of the London Government and Implementation of the Yalta Declaration*

The Meeting of Foreign Secretaries reported as follows:

'The Chairman of the sub-committee which has been dealing with this subject presented the sub-committee's report. Since the sub-committee have been unable to reach full agreement, the points of disagreement were discussed at length. The Foreign Ministers were able to reach an understanding on several of these points, but the following were referred to the Heads of Governments for final decision:

(*a*) The paragraph relating to the transfer of assets and the recognition of liabilities by the Provisional Government. (P. (Terminal) 17[4]— paragraph 2.)

(*b*) The paragraph relating to the holding of elections and to freedom of the press. (P. (Terminal) 17[4]—paragraph 5.)'

MR. BYRNES said that as regards the paragraph relating to the *transfer of assets and the recognition of liabilities* (P. (Terminal) 17—paragraph 2) the British and United States Delegations were ready to accept the following alternative draft:

'The British and United States Governments have taken measures to protect the interests of the Polish Provisional Government, as the recognised Government of the Polish State, in the property belonging to the Polish State located in their territory and under their control whatever the form of this property may be. They have further taken measures to prevent alienation to third parties of such property. All proper facilities will be given to the Polish Provisional Government for the exercise of the ordinary legal remedies for the recovery of any property belonging to the Polish State which may have been wrongfully alienated.'

Mr. Byrnes said that there had been much discussion on the penultimate sentence of the drafting Committee's paragraph dealing with assets and liabilities. The position of the United States Government was that this was a matter for determination directly between the United States Government and the Polish Provisional Government. Obviously the question of liabilities must be discussed at the same time as that of assets. The United States Government would transfer to the Polish Provisional Government any assets to which it was entitled under the law. The redraft of the paragraph quoted above gave effect to this view.

PRESIDENT TRUMAN said that in law it was impossible for the United States Government to transfer any assets without taking liabilities also into consideration. As he had stated the previous day, the nations of Europe must be made to stand on their own feet. It was therefore impossible to

[4] No. 215.

hand over to the new Polish Government the assets of the London Government without also taking into account the liabilities.

MR. CHURCHILL said that he was content with the paragraph as redrafted. In particular, he agreed with the President's statement that assets could not be released without taking liabilities into account. He was not, however, quite clear as to how it was proposed that the question of assets and liabilities was to be covered.

MR. BYRNES pointed out that the new wording made no specific mention of either. The position of the United States Government was that the settlement of property rights was one which the United States Government should settle direct with the Provisional Polish Government. The same direct settlement would of course apply to the Soviet and British Governments. There was no need for a public declaration by the three Governments to the effect that assets which belonged to the Polish Provisional Government would be transferred to it.

MR. CHURCHILL said that the result of this redraft would be that we had abandoned the idea of making arrangements at this Conference about Polish assets and liabilities. This was, of course, a more serious question for us than for the Americans, as our own credits to the Poles had been so much greater.

PRESIDENT TRUMAN said that he did not like to have to single out the United States and British Governments as having to make a public statement that they would meet their obligations.

PREMIER STALIN enquired whether the British Government proposed to exact from the new Polish Government settlement for all advances made to the former Polish Government.

MR. CHURCHILL said that this was a matter for discussion with the Poles.

PREMIER STALIN said that Russia had granted credits to Sikorsky, and to the Polish Government (Lublin) in the early days. He considered, however, that these credits had been redeemed by the action of the Polish forces, and that the whole matter was now closed. He thought that the paragraph proposed by the Americans was satisfactory, subject to minor drafting amendments. He suggested that the final sentence might read:

> 'All proper facilities will be given to the Polish Provisional Government in accordance with the requirements of law for the recovery of any property belonging to the Polish State . . .'[5]

The sentence as it now stood might result in lengthy juridical procrastination, and his amendment was designed to ensure quick action under the law.

After some discussion, and at PRESIDENT TRUMAN's request, PREMIER STALIN agreed to accept the redrafted paragraph proposed by the United States Delegation.

MR. BYRNES said that it had been agreed that paragraph 3 should read as follows:

> 'The Three Powers are anxious to assist the Polish Provisional Govern-

---

[5] Punctuation as in original quotation.

502

ment in facilitating the return to Poland as soon as practicable of all Poles abroad who wish to go, including members of the Polish armed forces and Merchant Marine. They expect that those Poles who return home shall be accorded personal rights and rights of property on the same basis as all Polish citizens.'

Mr. Byrnes said that it had been agreed that paragraph 4 of the drafting Committee's statement should be omitted.

Mr. Byrnes then referred to paragraph 5 of the drafting Committee's statement, which dealt with *freedom of the Press and elections*, and asked Mr. Eden to explain his compromise proposal.

MR. EDEN said that at the Foreign Secretary's meeting that morning he had suggested as a compromise:

The omission of the second sentence of this paragraph, reading as follows:

'It is the confident hope of the Three Powers that the elections will be conducted in such a way as to make it clear to the world that all democratic and anti-Nazi sections of Polish opinion have been able to express their views freely, and thus to play their full part in the restoration of the country's political life.'

and the retention of the final sentence, which read:

'The Three Powers will further expect that representatives of the Allied Press shall enjoy full freedom to report to the world upon developments in Poland before and during the elections.'

PREMIER STALIN said that he was glad that Mr. Eden was meeting the interests of the dignity of Poland by putting forward this compromise, but would he take one more step, and agree also to the omission of the final sentence about freedom of the Press? He felt that the first sentence of paragraph 5, with its added reference to the decision of the Crimea Conference, provided all that was necessary. The Allied Press had come into Poland, and there had been no complaints. The Poles were very touchy on the freedom of the Press, and he thought it would be much wiser to confine this paragraph to the first sentence only.

MR. CHURCHILL pointed out that this proposal of Premier Stalin's was no compromise at all.

PREMIER STALIN said that it was a compromise in regard to the Polish Government.

MR. CHURCHILL said he had hoped to strengthen the final sentence of this paragraph by adding that the Allied *Governments* as well as the Allied Press should enjoy full freedom.

PREMIER STALIN said that everyone in Poland was enjoying freedom to report what they wished. So why rub this in to the Poles?

PRESIDENT TRUMAN said that there were many Poles in the United States, and he was therefore very interested in ensuring that there would be free elections in Poland. The retention of the sentence about the Press would greatly help him.

PREMIER STALIN then suggested the following wording for this paragraph:

'The Three Powers note that the Polish Provisional Government, in accordance with the decisions of the Crimea Conference, has agreed to the holding of free and unfettered elections as soon as possible on the basis of universal suffrage and secret ballot in which all democratic and anti-Nazi parties shall have the right to take part and to put forward candidates; and that the representatives of the Allied Press will enjoy full freedom to report to the world upon developments in Poland before and during the elections.'

This was agreed.

THE CONFERENCE:

Approved the statement on the Polish question as amended in discussion (see P. (Terminal) 23).[6]

5. *Implementation of the Yalta Agreement on Liberated Europe and Satellite States*

The report of the Foreign Secretaries was as follows:

'The U.S. Delegation circulated a paper (P. (Terminal) 21)[i] on this question at the meeting, but it was decided to postpone discussion of the paper in order to allow time for further study.'

6. *Italy and the other Satellite States*

The Report of the Foreign Secretaries was as follows:

'The United States Delegation presented in this connection two papers: one on policy towards Italy[7] and one on policy towards Rumania, Bulgaria, Hungary and Finland.[8] The Foreign Ministers agreed to refer these papers to a drafting sub-committee. A point of difference arose, however, as to whether the drafting sub-committee should be instructed to deal with policy toward all these States in a single paper or to deal separately with Italy on the one hand and with Bulgaria, Rumania, Hungary and Finland on the other. The Soviet Delegation favoured a single paper and the United States favoured two separate papers. It was agreed that, since the question of policy toward Italy and the other satellites had been referred to the Foreign Ministers by the Heads of Governments, the Heads of Governments should be asked to decide at to-day's meeting whether or not the drafting sub-committee should be instructed to prepare a single paper on all of these countries or two papers based on the United States drafts.'

PRESIDENT TRUMAN said that, on the first day of the Conference, the United States Delegation had presented two papers, one on Policy towards

---

[6] Not printed. This paper, amended from No. 215 as agreed in minute 4 above, corresponded, subject to minor variation, to the final text of the statement in article VIIIA of the Protocol of the Proceedings of the Berlin Conference: see No. 603. For a slightly variant text of the statement as approved at the present meeting see *F.R.U.S. Berlin*, vol. ii, pp. 1123–4, and *Berlinskaya konferentsiya*, pp. 343–4 for the Russian text.

[7] *Note in filed copy:* 'P (Terminal) 20': see No. 214, note 9.

[8] *Note in filed copy:* 'P (Terminal) 19': see No. 214, note 9.

Italy (P. (Terminal) 5)[9] and one on the Yalta Declaration on Liberated Europe, which concerned Rumania and Bulgaria (P. (Terminal) 4).[9] The reason for having two separate papers was that Italy had been the first satellite to surrender, and that the Italian Terms of Surrender had been much more drastic than the terms for the other satellites. There was already a United States Ambassador in Italy and, although there was no more hurry over the development of policy towards Italy than towards the other satellites, he felt that these countries could best be dealt with in a separate paper.

PREMIER STALIN referred to the recently circulated Memorandum by the United States on Policy towards Rumania, Bulgaria, Hungary and Finland (P. (Terminal) 19),[10] and suggested that there should be added to paragraph 2 a sentence to the effect that, at the present time, the three Governments found it possible to resume diplomatic relations with these countries.

PRESIDENT TRUMAN said that the United States Government had not recognised the satellite Governments (except Finland, with which the United States had not broken off relations); so that it would be quite impossible to accept Premier Stalin's amendment.

PREMIER STALIN said that, in these circumstances, he was not in a position to discuss the policy either towards Italy, or towards the satellites. He, therefore, suggested that the discussions should be adjourned.

MR. CHURCHILL supported the views expressed by President Truman. He regretted that decision on these matters must be delayed as time was passing.

THE CONFERENCE:

Agreed to defer further consideration of these matters.

7. *Further Subjects for Discussion at the Plenary Meeting*

MR. BYRNES reported that the Foreign Secretaries had recommended the following subjects for discussion that afternoon:

(a) *Polish Western Frontier.* (P. (Terminal) 12.)[11]
(b) *Territorial Trusteeship.* (P. (Terminal) 13.)[12]
(c) *Turkey.* It was understood that the British Delegation wished to raise this question orally.

THE CONFERENCE:

Agreed to proceed with discussion of these matters.

8. *Western Frontier of Poland*

The Conference had before them a memorandum by the Soviet Delegation on the Western Frontier of Poland (P. (Terminal) 12).[11]

PRESIDENT TRUMAN said that it had been agreed that Germany should

[9] See No. 170, note 2.
[10] See No. 214, note 9.
[11] No. 202.
[12] No. 203.

be divided into four zones of occupation. It had also been agreed at Yalta that the Eastern frontier of Poland should, broadly speaking, follow the Curzon Line; that Poland should receive substantial accessions of territory in the North and West; that the opinion of the new Polish Government of National Unity should be sought in due course on the extent of these accessions; and that the final delimitation of the Western frontier of Poland should thereafter await the Peace Conference.[13]

At the second meeting of the present Conference, it had also been agreed that we should proceed on the basis that the 1937 frontiers of Germany would be taken as a starting point (P. (Terminal) 2nd Meeting,[14] Minute 4).

The boundaries of the zones of occupation in Germany had been settled together by the three Governments. The United States had moved their troops back into their own zone in an orderly fashion according to this agreement, and so had the British. It now appeared, however, that the Soviet Government had given a zone to the Poles without consultation with the other two Governments. It seemed to him that this should have been agreed beforehand between the three Powers. Moreover, he could not say how the question of reparations and everything else connected with Germany could be settled until it had been made clear that the part of the Soviet zone occupied by Poland was part of Germany. He was, however, very ready to help Poland so far as possible.

PREMIER STALIN recalled that, at the Crimea Conference, it had been agreed that the Heads of Government felt that the eastern frontier of Poland should follow the Curzon Line; as regards the western frontier it had been decided that Poland should receive accessions of territory in the north and west. The three Heads of Government had gone on to say that the opinion of the Polish Provisional Government should be sought at the appropriate time on the question of the size of these accessions of territory, but that the final settlement should be put off until the Peace Conference.

PRESIDENT TRUMAN interposed to say that that was the right interpretation and that it was for that reason that he thought the Conference had no right to settle the question of Poland's western frontier.

PREMIER STALIN said that, on the basis of the Crimea decision, the Polish Government had already expressed their view.

PRESIDENT TRUMAN said that, so far as he knew, this had not yet been formally expressed to the United States Government but he understood that the Secretary of State had received a communication[15] the previous day from the Polish Government which he (President Truman) had not yet seen.

PREMIER STALIN said that the proposal of the Soviet Delegation was that they should express their opinion at the present Conference in sympathy with the proposals of the Polish Government. It did not, however, make any difference whether this was done to-day or to-morrow, in any case, since the final settlement would have to be left until the Peace Conference.

[13] See No. 115, paragraph 2.
[14] No. 184.
[15] See No. 205, note 2.

As regards the suggestion that they had given Poland a zone of occupation without agreeing it beforehand with the other two Powers, he said that this was not quite accurate. The Soviet Government had received proposals in various Notes from the United States and British Governments[16] that they should not admit Polish administration into Western Poland until the frontier problem had been settled. The Soviet Government had not been able to accept these proposals because the German population had retreated to the west with the German Armies, and the Polish population alone had remained. At the same time, the Soviet Armies had needed in their rear areas a local administration, since they were not accustomed to fight and clear the territory as they advanced and, at the same time, set up the necessary administration. The Soviet Government had accordingly replied on these lines to their American and British friends. They were the more ready to allow the Polish Government and administration to function since they felt sure that Poland would secure an accession of territory to the west of her former frontier. He did not see what harm there was in allowing the Poles to administer territories in which they were to remain.

PRESIDENT TRUMAN said that he was not objecting to the Conference expressing an opinion on this matter, but he wished it clearly to be understood that Germany should be occupied in accordance with the zones stated at Yalta. If this were not done, it would make things very difficult, both as regards reparations and other matters.

PREMIER STALIN interposed to say that the Soviet Government were not worried about the reparations issue.

PRESIDENT TRUMAN added that the United States would get no reparations anyhow but would try, as they had before, to avoid paying anything.

PREMIER STALIN said that nothing had been decided at the Crimea Conference about the western frontier of Poland, and that the President must only be speaking of the interpretation of what had been said there, since nothing definite had been fixed and only a vague provision made. The question therefore remained open and the Powers were not bound by any decisions.

MR. CHURCHILL and PRESIDENT TRUMAN assented.

PRESIDENT TRUMAN asked Mr. Churchill if he had anything to say.

MR. CHURCHILL replied that he had a good deal to say about the boundary line which was now put forward, but that he understood from President Truman that the time had not yet come to discuss this.

PRESIDENT TRUMAN said that he did not think it was possible to settle here and now things that must be settled at the Peace Conference.

PREMIER STALIN observed that it was still more difficult to restore the German administration in the areas in question.

PRESIDENT TRUMAN said that he would raise no objection if the Soviet Government wanted to use a Polish administration in its own zone of occupation in Germany.

[16] Cf. No. 115, paragraphs 4–6, and F.R.U.S. Berlin, vol. i, pp. 743–5, note 4.

PREMIER STALIN said that he would like the President to understand the Russian fashion of fighting during war. While a war was on, the Army was engaged in fighting; it did not care for anything except winning the war; in order to enable it to advance, the Army required a quiet rear area, since an Army cannot wage war both on its front and on its lines of communication. An Army would fight well if its rear areas were quiet, and better still if those areas were actually friendly to it. Even if the Germans had not fled out of the areas in question, it would have been difficult to set up a German administration since the majority of the people were in fact Poles. He asked the Conference to imagine a situation where the Germans either fled or shot the Russian Armies in the back, while the Poles received these Armies in a friendly manner; it was natural that, in such a situation, both the Government and the Military Authorities should set up an administration in sympathy with the Armies.

PRESIDENT TRUMAN entirely agreed.

PREMIER STALIN went on to say that there had in fact been no other way out, but that that did not mean that they themselves were determined on any particular line for the frontier. If the Conference did not agree on a particular boundary line, surely this issue could remain in suspense.

MR. CHURCHILL said that he wondered whether the line could in fact remain unsettled. There was the question of supplies, since these regions were a very important source from which Germany had to be fed.

PREMIER STALIN apologised for interrupting, but asked who would work these regions in order to produce the grain, since there was nobody but the Poles left to plough the land.

PRESIDENT TRUMAN said that it was not a question of who occupied these areas, but of how the three Powers stood on the question of the occupation zones of Germany. He had always understood that each of the four Powers would occupy a zone; there was, therefore, no question of settling boundaries in this particular instance, since the whole region was part of the Soviet zone.

PREMIER STALIN said that formally, on paper, the region in question was German, but that in practice it was Polish.

MR. CHURCHILL and PRESIDENT TRUMAN asked what had become of the Germans.

PREMIER STALIN said that they had fled.

MR. CHURCHILL replied that if that was the case, how was it possible for the Germans who had fled to be fed in the regions to which they had gone, since according to Premier Stalin's view, the produce of the regions which they had left would no longer be available for feeding Germany as a whole. He had been told that if the plan of the Polish provisional Government, which he understood was being put forward by the Soviet Government, were carried out in full, one quarter of the arable land available within the 1937 frontiers of Germany would be alienated. This was important from the point of view of food supply and of reparations. As for the population question, he understood that there were some 3–4 million Poles who would have to be moved into the suggested area of Poland from east of the Curzon Line; whereas if the full Polish plan for Poland's western frontier were implemented, there would be some 8¼ million (he thought the figure given by the United States Delegation was 9 million) Germans who would have to be moved out into Germany. Apart from the question of the wholesale movement of population, he thought that this figure would mean bringing a wholly disproportionate number of Germans into a greatly reduced Germany.

PRESIDENT TRUMAN agreed, and wondered what would happen if we gave the Saar and the Ruhr to France, as had been suggested in some quarters.

PREMIER STALIN replied that the claims of France had not been decided, whereas on the question of Poland a decision in principle had been arrived at.

MR. CHURCHILL continuing, referred to the Marshal's statement that all Germans were out of the region in question, and said there were other figures to show that some 2½ million remained. Evidently this was a matter where the data would have to be explored.

PREMIER STALIN said that the Conference had begun by discussing the western frontier of Poland, but had now switched to discussion of Germany's food supplies. He raised no objection to this.

MR. CHURCHILL said that one of the reasons why we were so interested in this point was because of the burden which would be cast upon us if food supplies were not available conformably with the population.

PREMIER STALIN said that he fully appreciated the point of view of the President and the Prime Minister, and he was ready to admit that difficulties would arise in the question of supplying the Germans in Germany. The Germans, however, were the principal people to be blamed for these difficulties. Mr. Churchill had just quoted the figure of 8¼ million Germans who were said to have populated the area in question. But it should be remembered that the Germans had several times called up men from those districts, and that, in fact, the Germans had, for the most part, left the area. For example, Stettin now had a population of some 8,000, compared with a population of some 500,000 [*sic*] before the war. Most of these Germans had fled to the west of the German lines during the battle, and some of them to the Koenigsberg area. They had got wind of the rumour that the Russians were in Koenigsberg, and they preferred Russian to Polish rule. Not a single German, therefore, remained in the area from which it was suggested that Poland should get her accessions of territory; there only remained Poles. The Germans had quit their lands between the Oder and the Vistula, and the Poles were cultivating them. It would, therefore, be unlikely that the Poles would agree to the Germans returning to cultivate these lands. This peculiar situation should be borne in mind.

PRESIDENT TRUMAN said that he wished to make it clear again that the zones of occupation in Germany should be occupied as had been agreed. He did not think that we should settle the question of the western frontiers of Poland at this conference, but should leave it for the Peace settlement.

MR. CHURCHILL said that he was deeply concerned to support compensation for Poland, at the expense of Germany, for what was being taken from her (in his view quite properly) east of the Curzon Line. But he thought that there should be a balance between what Poland lost and received. Poland was now claiming vastly greater compensation than what she had been called upon to give up. He could not feel that [?it] would be for the good of Europe that such an exaggerated movement of population should take place. If there were now three to four million Poles east of the Curzon Line, then room should be made for three or four million Poles to occupy territories to the west of Poland's pre-war frontiers. A movement of population even on this scale would cause a great shock to the people of Great Britain. But a move of 8¼ million people would be more than he could defend. Compensation should bear some relation to loss. Nor would it be good for Poland itself to acquire so much additional territory. If the Germans had run away from the territory in question, they should be allowed to go back. The Poles had no right to pursue a policy which might well involve a catastrophe in the feeding of Germany.

Mr. Churchill explained that the resulting position might seriously affect our own responsibilities. He was anxious that the Marshal should understand our difficulties as we wished to understand his. We did not want to be left with a vast German population on our hands deprived of the sources of supply on which they had previously depended for food. The vast population of the Ruhr was in the British zone. If enough food could not be found to feed this population, we should be faced with conditions in our zone of occupation such as had existed in the German concentration camps, only on a scale a thousand times greater.

PREMIER STALIN said that Germany had never managed to do without importing grain in the past and would not be able to do so in future. Germany should buy food from Poland.

MR. CHURCHILL said that His Majesty's Government did not admit that territory in the east of Germany overrun during the war could now be regarded as having become Polish territory.

PREMIER STALIN said that these territories were now inhabited by Poles who were cultivating the land and producing bread. It was impossible to compel the Poles to produce bread and to give it away to the Germans.

MR. CHURCHILL said that conditions in the great area to which the Poles had been introduced were most peculiar. He was told that the Poles were now selling to Sweden coal from the Silesian mines. All this at a time when the people in Great Britain were faced with a greater shortage of fuel in the coming winter than at any time during the war. We took our stand on the general principle that the supplies of food and fuel available from the Germany of the 1937 frontiers should be available to the whole of the German people within those frontiers, irrespective of the particular zone in which they lived.

PREMIER STALIN asked who was to produce the coal? The Germans were not producing coal from Silesia, but the Poles were. The German proprietors of the Silesian coal field had fled. They would be reluctant to come back because they had tormented the Poles and had bad consciences. If they were to come back now the Poles would probably hang them.

MR. CHURCHILL said that he had been deeply impressed by what Premier Stalin had said at the previous meeting[17] about not allowing our policy to be governed by memories of injuries or by feelings of retribution. He thought that Premier Stalin should endeavour to meet the case put to him which was that we were faced with having a large number of Germans dumped in our area, who could not be fed unless they got food from the area which the Poles had occupied.

PREMIER STALIN said that the remarks he had made on the previous day did not apply to war criminals.

MR. CHURCHILL said that not all the 8¼ million who had fled from eastern Germany were war criminals.

PREMIER STALIN said that in speaking of war criminals he referred to the proprietors of the coal mines who had fled from Silesia. The Russians were themselves purchasing coal from Poland, since they were short of coal in Western Russia and the Baltic countries.

PRESIDENT TRUMAN said it seemed to be an accomplished fact that the eastern area of Germany had been given to Poland. His position was that, from the point of view of reparations and supplies, these areas could not be treated as having been detached from Germany. He was perfectly willing to talk over what should be the future western frontier of Poland, although the question of boundaries was one which could only be settled at the Peace Conference. But he would not be prepared to see sections of Germany given away piecemeal.

PREMIER STALIN said that no one except the Poles could exploit these regions. The Russians were short of labour and there were no Germans in the area. The alternatives were, either to stop all production, or to let the Poles do the production. The Poles had lost a valuable coal basin to Russia, and had taken the Silesian coal basin which they were now working.

MR. CHURCHILL said that there had always been Polish workers in the Silesian Mines and he did not object to their working the mines as agents for the Russian Government. But he did object to Silesia being treated as though it was already part of Poland.

PREMIER STALIN said that it was not possible to upset the present state of affairs. He would like to call Mr. Churchill's attention to the following peculiar facts. The Germans themselves had been short of labour. As the Russians had advanced into Germany they had found enterprises employing forcibly-deported Italians, Bulgarians and other nationalities including Russians and Ukrainians. As the Russian troops had advanced, these foreign labourers had felt free to return to their homes. It must be remembered that vast numbers of men had been mobilised in Germany and that most of them had either been killed or were in captivity. The vast German industry had

[17] See No. 208, minute 4.

had few German workers, but had depended on foreign labour which had now melted away. Either therefore these enterprises would be closed down, or Poles must be given a chance to work them. What happened was not a result of deliberate policy, but of a spontaneous course of events. And only the Germans were to blame for this.

Premier Stalin referred to what Mr. Churchill had said about the frontier question. He agreed that the Polish Government's proposals would make difficulties for Germany.

MR. CHURCHILL interjected, and for the British too.

PREMIER STALIN said that he was not averse to making additional difficulties for the Germans; indeed it was our policy to make difficulties for them and to make it impossible for them to aggress again. It was better to make difficulties for the Germans than for the Poles. Moreover, the less industry there was in Germany the more markets would be open to British trade. The Germans were dangerous competitors in trade because their standard of living was so low.

MR. CHURCHILL said that we did not wish to be faced with masses of starving people in Germany.

MR. ATTLEE said that he would like to approach this question from the point of view of the Powers occupying Germany, and to leave over the question of the future western frontier of Poland. We were faced with a country in chaos; a country which was formerly an economic unit and which depended partly for food and largely for coal on its eastern territories. It seemed to him that, pending final settlement, the resources of the whole of Germany within the 1937 frontiers would have to be treated as available for distribution, as might prove necessary, to the existing population of 1937 Germany. If a part of Germany was now arbitrarily annexed to Poland, the result would be to put a very heavy burden on the countries occupying the western and southern zones of Germany. The resources of the eastern area should be made available for the population in the west, particularly the labour demobilised from the armies in Western Germany, which must be found employment unless an impossible burden was to be placed on the occupying Powers.

PREMIER STALIN said that perhaps Mr. Attlee would bear in mind that Poland was also an ally, and should not be put in a very stupid position.

PRESIDENT TRUMAN said that, put briefly and frankly, he could not agree to parts of eastern Germany being regarded from the point of view of reparations and supplies as having been detached from the rest of Germany.

It was agreed to adjourn discussion on this subject. The Conference accordingly adjourned until 5 p.m. the following day.

Cabinet Office, Potsdam, 21st July, 1945

CALENDAR TO No. 219

i *21 July 1945* U.S. Delegation memo. P. (*Terminal*) 21, and commenting U.K. Delegation memo., on *Yalta Declaration on Liberated Europe:* American memo. (printed in *F.R.U.S. Berlin*, vol. ii, pp. 646–7) entirely acceptable to U.K.

Delegation, but likely to be rejected by Soviet Govt. Question of reminders to Greek Govt. of Varkiza agreement and to Yugoslav Govt. of Tito–Subasic agreement [U 6197/3628/70; F.O. 934/3/17(5)].

No. 220

Memorandum by the United Kingdom Delegation (Berlin)[1]

P. (Terminal) 16 [U 6197/3628/70]

Top secret   *21 July 1945*

Persia

His Majesty's Government and the Soviet Government are maintaining their troops in Persia by virtue of the Anglo-Soviet-Persian Treaty of the 29th June [January], 1942,[2] under Article 5 of which these forces are to be withdrawn from Persia '*not later than* six months after all hostilities between the Allied Powers and Germany and her Associates had been suspended.' His Majesty's Government have suggested to the Soviet Government that the Allied forces should be withdrawn from Persia *pari passu* and in stages before the final treaty date is reached. The Soviet Government have not, however, replied.

2. In His Majesty's Government's view the time has now come for the complete joint withdrawal of Allied forces from Persia, and they propose that this should take place in three stages as follows:–

(1) British and Soviet forces would be withdrawn completely from Tehran at once;

(2) After the completion of the first stage, British and Soviet troops would be withdrawn from the whole of Persia except that British troops would remain in Abadan and the southern oilfields area and Soviet troops would remain in a zone in either north-east or north-west Persia;

(3) On the completion of the second stage, British troops would be withdrawn from Abadan and the oilfields area in south Persia, and Soviet troops would be withdrawn from the last area in which their troops were stationed in either north-east or north-west Persia.

3. If this proposal is accepted the demarcation of the withdrawal zones can be worked out afterwards.

CALENDAR TO NO. 220

i *22 July 1945   Revised Brief for Persia.* Additional points to No. 220 on withdrawal of allied troops; pending this 'there is no chance of Persia returning to a normal state of affairs' [F.O. 934/3/15(9)].

[1] Printed in *F.R.U.S. Berlin*, vol. ii, pp. 1391–2.
[2] Printed in Cmd. 6335 of 1942.

No. 221

Minute from Mr. Eden to Mr. Churchill (Berlin)
No. P.M.|45|8.T. [F.O. 934|3|14(9)]

[BERLIN,] *21 July 1945*

I think we must accept this American draft.[1] I hope however that the Americans can be asked to consider the amendments in the attached memorandum.[2]

2. The purpose of the Amendments is to convert the document from a proclamation to the Japanese people to a communication to the Japanese Government. It seems to me that we are unlikely to secure Japanese acceptance of defeat if at this stage we attempt to appeal to the people over the head of the lawfully constituted Government. There is no reason why this declaration should not be made openly over the radio in the form we prefer.

3. I presume that, as China,[3] is mentioned in the document, it is your and the President's intention to consult Chiang Kai Shek before it is issued.[4]

A. E.

[1] Mr. Foulds noted on this file on 24 July 1945: 'The American draft to which this paper refers is with the P.M. We have no copy.' For the communication of this American draft (printed in *F.R.U.S. Berlin*, vol. ii, pp. 1275–6) see No. 231.

[2] This tabular memorandum, not here printed, is printed *ibid.*, p. 1277. For these British amendments see No. 231, annex.

[3] Punctuation as in original.

[4] With reference to the present document Mr. Rowan minuted to Mr. Dixon on 22 July 1945: 'The Prime Minister saw the President this morning and handed him the enclosure to the Foreign Secretary's minute suggesting amendments to the American draft. I understand from the Prime Minister that the President will now consider these and will produce a revised draft. In the meantime, I am finding out from the Prime Minister the reply to paragraph 3 of the Foreign Secretary's minute. T. L. R. 22.7.45.' No official record of the meeting between Mr. Truman and Mr. Churchill at 12.15 p.m. on 22 July has been traced; for this meeting, which apparently considered use of the atomic bomb, cf. *F.R.U.S. Berlin*, vol. ii, p. 243, and W. S. Churchill, *op. cit.*, vol. vi, pp. 552–3. On 23 July Mr. Churchill minuted to Mr. Rowan: 'The President did not consider it necessary to consult Chiang Kai Shek. I should greatly deprecate the delay in sounding him. I should much prefer that the appeal should be signed by the President and me alone. I presume arrangements are made to keep the Cabinet informed of what is passing here. W. S. C. 23.7.45' (PREM 8/34/1872).

No. 222

Minute from Mr. Eden to Mr. Churchill (Berlin)
No. P.M.|45|9.T. [U 6116|20|70]

[BERLIN,] *21 July 1945*

French sector in Berlin

You will have seen from Foreign Office telegram No. 89 Onward [i] of July 19th that the Soviet Delegation in the European Advisory Commission have proposed the following formula:

'The Commission recommends that the question of the delimitation of the French area in Greater Berlin, which will have to be allotted from the American and British areas of Greater Berlin as a consequence of the greater destruction in the Soviet area of the city, should be referred to the Control Council in Berlin for consideration'.[1]

2. The U.S. Delegation have been authorised to accept this formula.[2]

3. I understand that Field-Marshal Montgomery is perfectly ready to hand over to the French, out of the British sector, the districts of Reinickendorf and Wedding (these are both populous districts containing altogether some 400,000 Germans), subject to certain facilities remaining available to us.

4. I have some doubts whether the French zone in Berlin should come entirely out of ours. Berlin is a responsibility, but we and France do not want to appear inferior to the Russians and the Americans.

5. None the less, if Field-Marshal Montgomery is content to hand over this area of the British sector to the French, I think we should agree rather than try to insist—probably unsuccessfully—on the Russians contributing towards the French sector.

Do you agree?[3]

A. E.

CALENDAR TO No. 222

i *18–21 July 1945 General Weeks (Control Commission, Germany, British Element) to War Office Tels. Nos. 2 & 5 Argus; to and from Mr. Eden (Berlin) Tels. Nos. 89 & 124 Onward and No. 138 Target.* Anglo-American military discussions on area for French sector. In view of impending demise of E.A.C., Foreign Office would like to conclude without delay two outstanding draft agreements on (*a*) Zones of occupation in Germany (early instructions requested) and (*b*) additional requirements (cf. No. 76): would be very helpful if Mr. Eden would speak to M. Molotov about signature: see further No. 253 [U 5575, 5619/20/70].

[1] For this formula and discussions thereon in the European Advisory Commission on 12 July 1945, cf. *F.R.U.S. Berlin*, vol. i, pp. 601–3.
[2] Cf. *op. cit.*, vol. ii, p. 1002.
[3] Mr. Churchill signified agreement by initialing this minute on 23 July 1945.

No. 223

Minute from Mr. Hoyer Millar to Mr. Eden (Berlin)
[*F.O. 934/4/26(11)*]

[BERLIN,] *22 July 1945*

Tangier

The Soviet Delegation may at some time raise the question of their participation in the suspended Paris talks about Tangier—which implies, of course, eventually Soviet participation in the new Tangier régime.

It has been agreed that we cannot resist such Soviet participation, and we should therefore indicate that we for our part agree to the Soviet Government taking part in the Paris talks (which it is hoped would then be able to start again early in August). It has also been agreed, however, that in giving our acceptance we should try to secure some counter-concession from the Russians. Unfortunately, however, our concession to the Russians in respect of Tangier is not worth very much—more especially as both the French and the Americans have let it be known in the papers that they are in favour of Russian participation. It is important that, having once agreed to Russian participation in the Paris talks, we should not allow any further discussion of the Tangier problem to take place or any discussion upon what are the future arrangements for Tangier. Not only are these the very questions which the Paris meeting is to consider, but we have given a definite pledge to the French Government[1] that the only aspect of the Tangier question which will be considered at Terminal is whether or not the Russians should take part in the Paris talks This undertaking to the French has been given more than once quite categorically. We should have the greatest difficulty with the French if we did not stick to it.

F. R. Hoyer Millar

CALENDAR TO No. 223

i *22 July 1945 Minutes from Mr. Hoyer Millar to Mr. Eden (Berlin).* Further arguments against wider discussions on Tangier at Potsdam Conference, and against any Russian complaint at not being spontaneously invited to proposed Paris talks [F.O. 934/4/26(11)].

[1] See No. 107, note 4.

No. 224

Record of Fifth Meeting of Foreign Secretaries, held at Cecilienhof, Potsdam, on Sunday, 22 July 1945, at 11 a.m.
F.(*Terminal*)*5th Meeting* [U 6197/3628/70]

Top secret

Present:

M. V. M. Molotov, M. A. Ya. Vyshinski, M. I. M. Maisky, M. F. T. Gousev, M. K. V. Novikov, M. A. A. Sobolev, M. B. F. Podtzerob, M. S. A. Golunski (*Interpreter*).

Mr. J. F. Byrnes, Mr. W. A. Harriman, Mr. E. W. Pauley, Mr. J. C. Dunn, Mr. H. F. Matthews, Mr. W. L. Clayton, Mr. C. E. Bohlen, Mr. B. V. Cohen, Mr. E. Page (*Interpeter*).

Mr. Eden, Sir W. Monckton, Sir A. Cadogan, Sir W. Strang, Lieut.-General Sir R. Weeks, Sir D. Waley, Mr. N. Brook, Mr. P. Dixon, Mr. W. Hayter, Major L. M. Theakstone (*Interpreter*).

Contents

1. *Subjects for Discussion*

MR. EDEN suggested that the Meeting might begin by reviewing the subjects awaiting discussion by the Foreign Secretaries and noting how each of these now stood. The outstanding items were:

(i) *Council of Foreign Ministers*

The report from the drafting committee might be received during the course of the morning: if so, it might be possible to dispose of this subject.

(ii) *Italy and Spain: Proposed Declaration regarding the admission of certain countries to association with the United Nations*

The work of the drafting committee had not yet been completed.

(iii) *Germany: Economic Problems*

The report of the Committee (P. (Terminal) 15)[1] had been brought up at yesterday's meeting of the Foreign Secretaries and deferred at the request of the Soviet Delegation.[2] This might perhaps be discussed at the present meeting.

(iv) *Yalta Declaration on Liberated Europe*

The memorandum by the United States Delegation (P. (Terminal) 21)[3] might be discussed at the present meeting.

(v) *Roumania: Removal of Allied Industrial Equipment*

Mr. Eden proposed that the memorandum on this subject which had been submitted by the British Delegation (P. (Terminal) 10)[4] should be discussed at the present meeting.

M. MOLOTOV suggested that the meeting might also discuss:

(vi) *Reparations:* from Germany, Austria and Italy.

MR. BYRNES suggested two further subjects:

(vii) *Austria:* Date and other arrangements, for entry of Allied Troops into their respective zones of occupation in Vienna.

(viii) *International Co-operation in solving immediate Economic Problems in Europe.*

In the course of discussion M. MOLOTOV referred to other subjects on which the Soviet Delegation wished to see some further progress made at an early date. These were: *Spain, Tangier* and the disposal of the *German Fleet and Merchant Navy.* It was pointed out that the question of the German Fleet was one for discussion by the Plenary Meeting, and MR. BYRNES indicated that the United States Delegation intended to put forward proposals on this subject.

[1] No. 210.   [2] See No. 214, minute 2.
[3] See No. 219.i.   [4] See No. 194, minute 10.

It was agreed to discuss at the present meeting the subjects noted at (iii), (iv), (v) and (vii) above; and to leave for consideration at a later meeting the other subjects mentioned in the discussion recorded above.

2. *Yalta Declaration on Liberated Europe*

(Previous Reference: P[F]. (Terminal), 3rd Meeting,[5] Minute 6.)

At the meeting of Foreign Secretaries on the 20th July the British and United States Delegations had been invited to submit memoranda indicating the measures which they wished to see adopted in ex-enemy satellite countries as regards:

    (*a*) the powers of Allied representatives on the Control Commissions;
    (*b*) the freedom of the Press;
    (*c*) the freedom of Elections.

The United States Delegation had submitted a memorandum (P. (Terminal) 21)[3] in response to this request.

MR. EDEN said that the British Delegation had not thought it necessary to submit a separate memorandum of their own, since they were in complete agreement with the proposals put forward in the memorandum by the United States Delegation.

M. MOLOTOV said that he had now been able to study the memorandum by the United States Delegation. He himself thought it a mistake to group Greece, which was a member of the United Nations, with the other countries, which were ex-enemy satellites—they were so grouped together in paragraph 1 of the memorandum—but he was ready to discuss the proposals in the memorandum as they stood.

(*a*) *Powers of Allied Representatives on Control Commissions*

The memorandum by the United States Delegation proposed that the Control Commissions in Roumania, Bulgaria and Hungary should operate henceforth 'on a tripartite basis under revised procedures providing for tripartite participation, taking into account the interests of responsibilities of the three Governments which together presented the terms of armistice to the respective countries.'

MR. BYRNES said that, in the view of the United States Delegation, all the Allied representatives on the Control Commissions should meet together to exchange views and suggestions; and the Soviet representatives should not take action without consultation with their Allied colleagues. According to his information, this course had not been followed hitherto; the Soviet High Command had taken unilateral action without such consultation.

M. MOLOTOV said that, as had been indicated in earlier discussions, the Soviet Government were willing to consider modifying the powers and rights of the British and United States representatives on the Control Commissions, to meet the changed conditions resulting from the end of the war in Europe. Indeed, in all the countries where they had the initiative on the Control Commissions, the Soviet representative had already put forward suggestions

[5] No. 200.

for such modifications. Such proposals had recently been communicated by Marshal Voroshilov to the British and United States representatives on the Control Commission in Hungary,[6] and these proposals were understood to be acceptable to the British and United States representatives. M. Molotov said that he was willing to circulate to the three Foreign Secretaries a note of the suggestions which had been made, so that they might have an opportunity to comment on them. Alternatively, these suggestions might be considered by the British and United States representatives on the various Control Commissions, and any amendments which they might wish to suggest could then be considered by the three Governments.

MR. EDEN said that, on his present information, he could not judge how far the suggestions put forward by the Soviet representatives on the Control Commissions would meet the view of the British and United States Delegations. It would, therefore, be useful if M. Molotov could circulate particulars of these proposals, which might be referred for examination by a sub-committee.

M. MOLOTOV then drew attention to the fact that paragraph 3 of the memorandum by the United States Delegation referred only to Roumania, Bulgaria, and Hungary, and contained no mention of Italy—though Italy was mentioned in paragraph 1 of the memorandum. Yet there was Allied control machinery in Italy.

MR. BYRNES explained that no mention had been made of Italy in this paragraph, because, so far as he knew, there had been no complaints about the working of the Allied Control machinery in Italy.

M. MOLOTOV said that, according to his information the Soviet representative on the Allied Council in Italy was not given an opportunity to take an effective part in the work of the Council and was not consulted before action was taken. Indeed, he had not been informed of the proposal to transform the Control Commission into an Allied Council, and the Soviet Government had only learned of this change from reports in the Press.

MR. BYRNES and MR. EDEN said that this was the first complaint they had heard about the working of the Allied Control machinery in Italy. If M. Molotov would indicate in what respects the Soviet Government were not satisfied with the present arrangements, the British and United States Delegations would be glad to consider during the present Conference what changes could be made to meet the views of their Russian Allies.

MR. BYRNES said that the United States Government were ready to agree that the Soviet representative on the Allied Council in Italy should have the same rights and duties as were proposed for the United States representatives on Control Commissions in Roumania, Bulgaria and Hungary.

It was noted that M. Molotov would submit a memorandum containing
(i) particulars of the suggestions already made on behalf of the Soviet Government for modifying the powers and rights of British and United States representatives on the Control Commissions in Roumania,

[6] Cf. No. 197.i.

Bulgaria and Hungary; and (ii) his comments on the position of the Soviet representative on the Allied Council in Italy.

(b) Freedom of the Press

The memorandum by the United States Delegation proposed that, as the war in Europe was now over, measures should be taken to facilitate the entry of representatives of the world's Press and radio into all liberated or ex-enemy satellite States, and to afford them freedom of movement and adequte opportunities for the despatch of their reports without restriction by reasons of political censorship. The memorandum also suggested the removal of such restrictions on the freedom of the Press as had been imposed, in these countries, to prevent access to news from abroad.

Mr. BYRNES said that hitherto representatives of the United States Press had been denied both freedom of movement within these countries and freedom to despatch their reports without political censorship. The Soviet Delegation had now agreed, in earlier discussions at the Plenary Meetings (P. (Terminal) 4th Meeting,[7] Minute 1), that as the war in Europe was now over increased facilities should be given to the world's Press in these countries. The United States Delegation asked that the improvements to which Premier Stalin had assented in principle should be carried into effect without delay.

M. MOLOTOV said that the end of the war in Europe had produced a new situation; and he had no doubt that everything practicable would be done to afford increased facilities to Press correspondents in these countries, subject only to the needs of military censorship. In these circumstances, he doubted whether it was necessary to make any public declaration on this point.

Mr. EDEN emphasised that it was not only freedom of movement for Press correspondents that was in question: it was also important that they should be free to despatch their reports without political censorship. He hoped, therefore, that the Soviet Government would feel able to accept the specific proposals set out in paragraph 2 of the memorandum by the United States Delegation. If, as it appeared, the Soviet Delegation felt unable to accept this paragraph without further examinatior it would be useful to appoint a sub-committee to consider in detail what facilities could now be accorded to correspondents of the world's Press and radio in these countries.

(c) Freedom of Elections

The memorandum by the United States Delegation proposed that the three Governments should inform themselves of the proposed electoral procedures in Italy, Greece, Bulgaria, Roumania, and Hungary, and should arrange for the observation of elections in these countries 'for the choice of Governments responsive to the will of the people.'

Mr. BYRNES said that the United States Government did not like the idea of having to supervise the conduct of elections in these countries; but they were persuaded that this was necessary in order to allay the suspicions of world opinion about the manner in which those elections were likely to be

[7] No. 208.

conducted. The elections might be conducted in the fairest possible manner; but, if official representatives of the United States could not see for themselves what was going on, and if the world's Press were not free to publish full and uncensored reports, public opinion in the United States would not be satisfied. The only way to remove such suspicions, which would cause great harm, was to have observers of the three Great Powers at these elections, as had been agreed at Yalta.

Mr. EDEN agreed. The British Government would also have preferred to avoid assuming this responsibility, but they were satisfied that the three Governments could not fulfil the spirit of the Yalta Declaration unless they arranged to have observers at these elections.

M. MOLOTOV said that the Soviet Delegation could not approve this proposal for sending observers to these elections. They considered such a procedure to be unnecessary. The only justification which had been put forward for it was the suspicion that the elections would not be fairly conducted. As against this, he cited the example of Finland—the only ex-enemy satellite country in which elections had so far been held. There had been no complaints about the conduct of the elections in Finland. Why then should there be any suspicion that the elections to be held in the other satellite countries would not be conducted fairly?

Mr BYRNES said that public opinion in the United States had been satisfied as to the conduct of the elections in Finland because representatives of the United States Government and correspondents of the world's Press had been there to observe and to report on events. The United States had not been at war with Finland and had not severed diplomatic relations with the Finnish Government.

M. MOLOTOV then said that he would be more ready to discuss the questions raised in the memorandum by the United States Delegation if the other Delegations were willing to discuss at the same time the restoration of diplomatic relations with ex-enemy satellite States.

Mr. EDEN said that there was some force in the last point made by M. Molotov. If elections were held in these countries under the conditions recommended by the United States Delegation, it would be much easier to consider the recognition, in some form, of the Governments established as a result of those elections. He said 'in some form' because the British Government could not entertain normal diplomatic relations with countries with which they were still nominally at war. We should, however, be ready to consider establishing relations analogous to those which we had with Italy, which amounted in practice to something very close to ordinary diplomatic relations.

Mr. BYRNES said that he had already made clear the position of the United States Government in this matter. If elections were held in these countries under the conditions which he proposed, the United States Government would at once recognise any Government established as a result of those elections. Under existing conditions, however, there could be no question

521

of the United States Government recognising the Governments in those countries.

M. MOLOTOV indicated that he could not accept, even in principle, the suggestion that elections in these ex-enemy satellite countries should be 'supervised' by observers nominated by the three Great Powers.

It was therefore agreed that Mr. Eden should report to the Plenary Meeting that afternoon that the meeting of Foreign Secretaries had failed to agree on the proposals (in paragraph 1 of the memorandum by the United States Delegation) for Three-Power 'observers' of elections in the ex-enemy satellite countries. Mr. Eden should, however, report that the Foreign Secretaries had decided to refer the proposals (in paragraph 2 and 3 of the memorandum by the United States Delegation) regarding (i) the powers of Allied representatives on Control Commissions and (ii) the freedom of the Press, in the ex-enemy satellite countries, to a sub-committee composed as follows:

United States Delegation: Mr. Cannon, Mr. Russell.
Soviet Delegation: M. Sobolev, M. Golunski.
United Kingdom Delegation: Mr. Hayter.

3. *Germany: Economic Problems*
(Previous Reference: F. (Terminal) 4th Meeting, Minute 2.)[2]

MR. BYRNES said that it appeared from their Report (P. (Terminal) 15)[1] that the Committee on Economic Problems had reached unanimous agreement on certain of the economic principles which should govern the treatment of Germany in the initial control period. The Committee had not, however, been able to reach agreement on certain other questions, which raised important issues connected directly or indirectly with the problem of reparations.

Mr. Byrnes said that he was not prepared to discuss at the present meeting questions involving reparations; and he proposed that the present discussion should be confined to the Statement of Economic Principles, on which the Committee had been in agreement. It would be useful to ascertain whether the three Foreign Secretaries could endorse this Statement. If so, it could be reported to the Plenary Meeting, who had already approved (P. (Terminal) 3rd Conclusions,[8] Minute 3) the corresponding Statement of Political Principles which should govern the treatment of Germany in the initial control period.

The following points were raised in discussion of the Statement of Economic Principles annexed to P. (Terminal) 15[1]:

Paragraph 10.—At M. MOLOTOV's suggestion, it was agreed that the last sentence of this paragraph should be amended so as to read:

'Productive capacity not needed for permitted production shall be removed in accordance with the reparations plan recommended by the

[8] No. 194.

Allied Commission on Reparations and approved by the Governments concerned or, if not so removed, shall be destroyed.'

Paragraph 13.—The first sentence of this paragraph read: 'During the period of occupation Germany shall be treated as a single economic unit.'

M. Molotov suggested that, as was clear from other parts of the document, Germany could not at once be treated as an economic unit to the same extent for all purposes; and he thought it would be necessary for the Control Council to issue detailed instructions from time to time regarding the extent to which Germany could be treated as an economic unit for particular purposes. He therefore suggested that at the end of this sentence there should be inserted some such words as: 'according to detailed instructions to be issued by the Control Council in conformity with the principles set out in this Agreement.'

Mr. Byrnes doubted whether it should be made possible for the statement of principle contained in this sentence to be whittled away by detailed directives issued by the Control Council. The amendment proposed might have the effect that Germany could be treated as a single economic unit only in so far as the Control Council were agreed on the application of that principle. If this amendment were adopted, he feared that the Control Commission would discuss from day to day the extent to which the principle should be applied.

M. Molotov said that in his view the statement of principle in the Agreement should be the basis for the work of the Control Council, but it should be supplemented by more detailed instructions issued by the Control Council from time to time regarding the application of that principle. He contemplated that the Control Council would issue its first directive in the near future, and this might remain in force for several months. The Council might then review the position in the light of experience and issue an amended directive. He believed that this procedure would be found necessary in practice, even if it were not explicitly provided for in the Agreement.

Mr. Byrnes said that he could not at present accept the amendment proposed. He would consider the wording, in the light of M. Molotov's explanation, and would indicate his final views at a later stage.

Paragraph 16.—It was pointed out that this paragraph, which referred to the principles governing the payment of reparations by Germany, could not be included in the draft Agreement until the recommendations on reparations had been approved.

Paragraph 18.—M. Molotov suggested that this paragraph should be omitted. In many parts of Germany, particularly in eastern Germany, the war had produced very serious economic changes; and, as Premier Stalin had stated at the Plenary Meeting on the previous day (P. (Terminal) 5th Meeting,[9] Minute 8), it would not be practicable to restore the pre-war economic structure throughout Germany. Having regard to the discussions which were proceeding in the Plenary Meetings on such matters as the

[9] No. 219.

Western Frontier of Poland, it would be impracticable for the Foreign Secretaries to discuss at this stage how far the various zones of occupation should draw their supplies from the areas in Germany on which they had drawn before the war.

MR. EDEN said that it was noted in the fifth paragraph of the Report of the Committee that this was a matter on which the Committee had not been able to reach agreement. It followed that paragraph 18 of the Statement of Economic Principles must be reserved for later discussion.

> It was agreed that the Statement of Economic Principles annexed to the Report of the Economic Committee (P. (Terminal) 15)[1] might be approved, for eventual submission to the Plenary Meeting, subject to: (i) the amendment of paragraph 10 noted above; (ii) further consideration of the proposed amendment of paragraph 13; and (iii) the omission at this stage of paragraphs 16 and 18.

4. Roumania: Removal of Allied Industrial Equipment
(Previous Reference: P. (Terminal) 3rd Meeting, Minute 10.)[4]

MR. EDEN recalled that the Plenary Meeting had referred to the Foreign Secretaries the British Memorandum on this matter (P. (Terminal) 10).[4] As he saw it, the position was that the British and American oil companies in Roumania were the owners of certain equipment which they had bought and paid for. Some of it had come from Germany and some from elsewhere. When the Germans invaded Roumania, they had seized the equipment. The British Government had naturally assumed that, when Roumania fell into Allied hands, the equipment would be restored to its owners. They were, therefore, concerned to hear that it had been seized by the Russians.

Asked by M. Molotov to explain the matter from the point of view of the Soviet Delegation, M. VYSHINSKI said that it had two aspects, economic and legal; and he would show that, under both, the complaints against the Soviet action were without foundation.

(a) Economic aspect

In 1939, the oil borings in Roumania totalled 256,000 metres, for which 18,000 tons of tubing were required. In 1943, the peak year of Roumanian oil production, the borings had totalled 342,000 metres, requiring 24,000 tons of tubing, When, on the occupation of Roumania by the Red Army, some of this tubing had been exported to Russia, there remained in Roumania 62,000 tons, i.e., enough for 4 years' output on the pre-war basis, or 3 years on the 1943 basis. This showed that the removal of the tubing did not account for the fall in Roumanian oil production; this was no doubt due to the course of military operations in Roumania during 1944. Moreover, the Soviet Government had taken positive steps to protect the interests of the British and American oil companies and of Roumanian oil production. When the question had been raised of the removal of a certain 100-octane plant, which might properly have been regarded as booty, the Soviet Government, in order not to interfere with the production of 100-octane fuel and to comply with the wishes of the British Government, had ordered that the plant should not be removed.

(b) Legal aspect

This was a question of ownership. The tubing had been made in German factories and imported into Roumania by the Germans, not only for oil boring in Roumania, but also for the construction of a pipe-line to convey Soviet oil from Batum across the Black Sea to Constanza. It had been argued that the tubing had been bought by the British and American companies and was therefore their property. The question was whether it had been paid for and, if so, how. An entry in a banking account was not evidence. The oil companies concerned had been seized by the Germans, who transferred to them German tubing in order to produce oil for the German war machine. If they chose to regard the oil as payment for the tubing, that did not make the transaction a purchase by the companies in the proper sense of the term. The only connection between the tubing and the companies was that it had been found on their land. On these grounds, the Control Commission had decided that the property was German; and under Article 7 of the Roumanian Armistice Terms, as defined by Section 2 of the Protocol,[10] had decided to treat it as booty.

MR. BYRNES said that, as he understood it, the question was, not whether the Soviet Government had the right to take as booty German property used for war purposes, but whether the property of United States citizens might be so taken. He was sure that the Soviet Government would sympathise with the American owner of an oil well in Roumania who had had some of his oil removed by the Germans and did not wish to see the rest of it taken by the Russians. If it was established that a given pipe-line was German property, then he would agree that the Soviet Government might remove that pipe-line or make some equivalent arrangement. The root of the matter was the question of ownership. This was a question of fact and its determination in each case ought, in his view, to be referred to some body like the Reparations Commission: it could not be settled at the present meeting. He would, however, like to suggest now that the three Powers should agree in principle that the property of their nationals should not be treated as booty. This would be in accord with Article 13 of the Roumanian Armistice Terms.[11]

---

[10] *Note in filed copy:* 'Article 7 reads: "The Roumanian Government and High Command undertake to hand over as trophies into the hands of the Allied (Soviet) High Command all war material of Germany and her satellites located on Roumanian territory, including vessels of the fleet of Germany and her satellites located in Roumanian waters." Paragraph 2 of the Protocol reads: "That the term 'war material' used in Article 7 shall be deemed to include all material or equipment belonging to, used by, or intended for use by, enemy military or para-military formations or members thereof." ' Cf. No. 48, note 9.

[11] *Note in filed copy:* 'Article 13 reads: "The Roumanian Government undertakes to restore all legal rights and interests of the United Nations and their nationals on Roumanian territory as they existed before the war and to return their property in complete good order." '

M. Vyshinski said that the present discussion concerned the equipment of oil companies and not the oil itself. The oil which the Soviet Government was obtaining from Roumania was provided by the Roumanian Government as reparations. As to the equipment, the Soviet contention was that it was not the property of any Allied national but of the Germans.

Mr. Eden said that he emphatically rejected M. Vyshinski's contention as to ownership. It seemed clear, however, that the present meeting could not investigate this complicated question in detail. He suggested, therefore, that it should be examined fully by a Committee of experts from the three Delegations. Meanwhile, he must make the following comments on M. Vyshinski's statement:

(i) M. Vyshinski had referred chiefly to tubing; the British case con-concerned other equipment as well.

(ii) The tubing in question had been bought and paid for before the war and was indisputably British or American property.

(iii) Objection had never been raised to the removal of equipment which was surplus; our complaint was that the removal had been indiscriminate and the expert British representatives had not been consulted.

(iv) Much of the trouble had arisen from the fact that unilateral decisions of the Soviet High Command, about which the British and American representatives had not been consulted, had been represented as the decisions of the Allied Control Commission.

Mr. Byrnes doubted whether a committee of the Conference could determine the question of ownership in particular cases. It might, however, be useful for such a Committee to consider whether an agreed statement of principle could be drafted, or whether the principle already enunciated in Article 13 of the Armistice Terms had been violated. It would surely be helpful to have the matter examined on these lines, in order to remove this source of friction between the Governments of the three Powers.

M. Molotov said that he regarded M. Vyshinski's explanation as satisfactory; he did not see what more a committee could do. Naturally every oil company wanted as much tubing as it could get, and no doubt the British and American companies could make good use of it; that, however, was not the point.

Mr. Eden said that, if agreement could not be reached, he would have no alternative but to explain publicly to the British Parliament the position as he saw it. That much was due to the owners of the equipment in England and America. He had, however, hoped that it might be possible to avoid a public statement of this kind.

M. Molotov said that he saw no reason for a public statement. If the owners complained, it should be sufficient to give them the facts as set out by M. Vyshinski.

Mr. Eden said that he must reserve his position. He would consider the matter further and see whether he had any suggestions to make.

It was agreed that further consideration of this matter should be deferred.

5. *Agenda for Sixth Plenary Meeting*
Subjects for discussion at Plenary Meeting

MR. EDEN suggested, and it was agreed, that he should propose for discussion at the Plenary Meeting that afternoon the following subjects, which had been previously brought up for discussion at the Plenary Meeting but had not been disposed of:

   (a) *Western Frontier of Poland.*   (P. (Terminal) 12.)[12]
   (b) *Territorial Trusteeship.*   (P. (Terminal) 13.)[13]
   (c) *Turkey.*

M. MOLOTOV suggested that, in connection with the proposed discussion on the Western Frontier of Poland, it would be convenient if the Plenary Meeting also considered a proposal which the Soviet Delegation wished to put forward on:

   (d) *Minor adjustments of the Western Frontier of the U.S.S.R.*

M. Molotov explained that the Soviet Delegation did not wish to re-open the decisions reached at the Crimea Conference about the Curzon Line. They wished, however, to propose certain minor adjustments near Koenigsberg and East Prussia. It was agreed that this question should be put forward for discussion at the Plenary Meeting that afternoon.

MR. EDEN suggested, as a further subject of discussion:

   (e) *Persia: Withdrawal of Troops.*   (P. (Terminal) 16.)[14]

It was agreed that the subjects noted above should be brought forward as subjects for discussion by the Plenary Meeting that afternoon.

Subjects for Reference to Foreign Secretaries

It was further agreed that certain other subjects might be mentioned at the Plenary Meeting in order that they might be referred for consideration by the Foreign Secretaries' meeting.

MR. BYRNES said that President Truman would suggest that this course should be followed in respect of:

   (a) *International Co-operation in Solving the Immediate Economic Problems of Europe*
   (b) *Directive to be issued by Governments Responsible for the Control of Germany to their respective Commanders of Occupation Forces in Germany.* (P. (Terminal) 24.)[15]

---

[12] No. 202.   [13] No. 203.   [14] No. 220.
[15] This document, dated 22 July 1945, is not here printed. This draft of a directive, proposed in a memorandum of 21 July by the United States Delegation, is printed in *F.R.U.S. Berlin*, vol. ii, pp. 806–7. Mr. Harrison and Sir A. Cadogan minuted on this document as follows (F.O. 934/4/20(12)): 'The attached document, which has been circulated by the United States Delegation, purports to be a draft directive for issue to the four Allied Zone Commanders in Germany. It is understood to have been drafted by General Clay, General Eisenhower's number 2.
'It is incomprehensible why the Americans have circulated this document, which parallels

M. Molotov said that Premier Stalin would suggest that this course should be followed in respect of:

(c) *Tangier*

(d) *Syria and the Lebanon*

It was agreed that Mr. Eden should report to the Plenary Meeting that afternoon in the sense indicated above.

Cabinet Office, Potsdam, 22nd July, 1945

CALENDARS TO No. 224

i *22 July 1945   Minute from Mr. Hoyer Millar to Mr. Hayter (Berlin)*. Objections to Soviet suggestion in minute 2 above that paragraph 3 of P (Terminal) 21 (see No. 219.i) concerning Control Commissions in Roumania, Bulgaria and Hungary be applied also to Italy [F.O. 934/2/6(33)].

22 July 1945   Memorandum by Mr. Ward (Berlin): the two drafting committees have reached agreements on three drafts on the establishment of a Council of Foreign Ministers (annexes I, II, III to No. 244). Discusses procedure for presentation of the drafts [F.O. 934/3/16(6)].

their own paper on "political and economic principles" [cf. No. 170, note 2] on which a large measure of agreement has already been obtained. One can only assume it is another instance of jealousy between the military and civil departments.

'Apart from the fact that the document is written in horrible English, it differs in many respects from the paper on "political and economic principles". The order is different, the language is different, new points are made, other points are omitted. The only result of the Conference accepting both documents can be the creation of muddle and confusion.

'It is suggested that when Mr. Byrnes proposes his paper, the Secretary of State might take the following line:

' "I am not quite clear as to the purpose Mr. Byrnes has in mind in circulating this paper, which seems to have many points of resemblance with that on "political and economic principles". My understanding has been that the latter document would be communicated to the Allied Control Council for Germany, who would apply the principles set out in it. I cannot see the purpose of addressing to the Zone Commanders a further set of principles in the form of a directive. The only effect, so far as I can see, would be to create confusion. The two documents differ in many respects both in substance, form and wording. I should much prefer therefore to limit ourselves to the document on 'political and economic principles,' on which we have already reached a large measure of agreement."

'(Sir W. Strang has agreed the line of this minute, though he has not seen the actual text of it.)   G. W. Harrison, 22nd July, 1945.'

'Surely, if the Conference agree on the text of principles, that text is the effective document. It only needs to be sent to the Commanders under a short coverer. Otherwise, we shall either have to waste the Conference's time in going through this document word by word, or risk complete muddle and confusion.   A. C. July 23, 1945.'

No. 225

Minute from Mr. Eden to Mr. Churchill (Berlin)
No. P.M./45/10.T. [*F.O. 934/5/48(10)*]

[BERLIN,] *22 July 1945*

You will remember that the drafting committee was set up to prepare a resolution to cover the question of Italy's admission to and Spain's exclusion from the United Nations Organisation.[1] It is to be hoped that the Soviet Delegation will accept some such resolution on the subject of Spain in substitution for the paper which they put forward[2] earlier in the proceedings suggesting that we break off relations with Franco and generally interfere in Spanish internal affairs.

2. The drafting committee had its first meeting yesterday and agreed that the best way of dealing with the problem would be to have two separate resolutions, one covering the admission of Italy to the United Nations Organisation and the other dealing with the question of Spain and indicating that though the three Governments would welcome applications for membership from neutral countries in general, they would not support an application from Franco's Government.

3. I attach a copy of the first draft prepared by the drafting committee and should be glad to know if you are prepared to agree to it.[3] It is, of course, definitely anti-Franco but I understand it is much less so than Maisky originally wished.

ANNEX TO No. 225[4]

Admission to the United Nations

Whereas Article IV of the Charter of the United Nations declares that:
1. membership in the United Nations is open to all other peace-loving States who accept the obligations contained in the present Charter and, in the judgment of the organisation, are able and willing to carry out these obligations;
2. the admission of any such State to membership in the United Nations will be effected by a decision of the General Assembly upon the recommendation of the Security Council.

The three Governments so far as they are concerned will support applications for membership from those States which have remained neutral during the war and which fulfil the qualifications set out above.

The Three Governments feel bound however to make it clear that they for their part would not favour any application for membership put forward by the present Spanish Government, which, having been founded on the support of the Axis Powers, does not, in view of its origins, its nature, its record and its close association with the aggressor states, possess the qualifications necessary to justify such membership.

---

[1] See No. 200, minute 4.

[2] See No. 194, minute 7.

[3] Mr. Churchill minuted 'I agree. W. S. C. 23.vii.' Attached to another copy of the present document (on PREM 8/123) was also a separate resolution on Italy (printed in *F.R.U.S Berlin*, vol. ii, p. 626). It would appear that this was the Anglo-American draft which was subsequently superseded: cf. ii below.

[4] This draft had been annexed to a report by Mr. Hoyer Millar of 21 July 1945, upon which No. 225 was based. On the morning of 22 July Mr. Eden had commented on Mr. Hoyer Millar's report: 'This is not too bad. Our representatives must have argued well.'

i [?*21*] *July 1945*   First British draft of No. 225, annex, with minutes [F.O. 934/5/48 (10)].

ii *22–3 July 1945*   *Minutes by Mr. Hoyer Millar and Sir A. Cadogan (Berlin):* on 21 July the drafting committee agreed *ad referendum* the resolution regarding Spain at annex above. After the meeting the British and American Delegations prepared a draft resolution regarding Italy (cf. note 3 above). However, a new American draft now combines the two proposed resolutions [F.O. 934/5/48(1–2)].

No. 226

Record of Sixth Plenary Meeting held at Cecilienhof, Potsdam, on Sunday, 22 July 1945, at 5 p.m.

P.(Terminal)6th Meeting [U 6197/3628/70]

Top secret

Present:

PREMIER STALIN, M. V. M. Molotov, M. A. Ya. Vyshinski, M. F. T. Gousev, M. A. A. Gromyko, M. K. V. Novikov, M. A. A. Sobolev, M. B. F. Podtzerob, M. V. N. Pavlov (*Interpreter*).

PRESIDENT TRUMAN, Mr. J. F. Byrnes, Mr. Joseph E. Davies, Fleet Admiral W. D. Leahy, Mr. W. A. Harriman, Mr. J. C. Dunn, Mr. H. F. Matthews, Mr. B. V. Cohen, Mr. L. E. Thompson, Mr. C. E. Bohlen (*Interpreter*).

MR. CHURCHILL, Mr. Eden, Mr. Attlee, Sir A. Cadogan, Sir W. Strang, Sir E. Bridges, Mr. P. J. Dixon, Mr. W. Hayter, Major A. Birse (*Interpreter*).

Contents

Minute	Subject
1.	Austria
2.	Report from Meeting of Foreign Secretaries[1]
3.	Yalta Declaration on Liberated Europe
4.	Germany: Economic Problems
5.	Roumania: Removal of Allied Industrial Equipment
6.	Agenda for the Plenary Meeting
7.	The Western Frontier of Poland
8.	Territorial Trusteeship
9.	Turkey
10.	Poland: Invitation to Representatives of the Polish Government to Attend the Conference
11.	Ukrainians in a British Prisoner of War Camp in Italy

[1] This heading is supplied from the draft on F.O. 934/3/18(6). In the present filed copy this heading reads in error 'Yalta Declaration on Liberated Europe'.

1 *Austria*
(Previous Reference: P. (Terminal) 4th Meeting,[2] Minute 5.)

PREMIER STALIN said that the withdrawal of Soviet troops in Austria had begun,[3] and would be completed by the 24th July. They would have to go back some 100 kilometres. Advanced units of British and American troops had already entered Vienna.

MR. CHURCHILL and PRESIDENT TRUMAN said that they were greatly obliged to the Soviet Government for having acted so promptly on the ratification of the Occupation Agreement.

PREMIER STALIN said it was the duty of the Russians to withdraw.

2. *Report from Meeting of Foreign Secretaries*

MR. EDEN submitted the report[4] from the meeting of the Foreign Secretaries held that morning. This report is set out in Minutes 3–6 below.

3. *Yalta Declaration on Liberated Europe*
(Previous Reference: F. (Terminal) 5th Meeting,[5] Minute 2.)

The Meeting of Foreign Secretaries reported as follows:

'The meeting had before it a memorandum submitted by the United States delegation on the 21st July (P. (Terminal) 21).[6] This Memorandum dealt with three questions:

　　1. The observation of elections in certain European countries.

　　2. Facilities for press representatives in liberated and former Axis satellite States.

　　3. Procedure of Control Commissions in Roumania, Bulgaria and Hungary.

The British Delegation has expressed agreement with the United States Memorandum.

The Soviet Delegation was unable to agree with the proposal in regard to the observation of elections. As regards the second and third questions it was agreed that these should be referred to a sub-committee for discussion. This committee consisted of:

　　United States: Mr. Cannon and Mr. Russell.

　　Soviet Union: M. Sobolev and M. Golunski.

　　United Kingdom: Mr. Hayter.

The Soviet Delegation undertook to provide a Memorandum showing recent improvements in the status of the British and American representatives on the Control Commissions in Roumania, Bulgaria and Hungary. The Soviet Delegation also agreed to prepare a Memorandum showing

---

[2] No. 208.

[3] The corresponding Soviet and American records here included the word 'today': *Conferences: Soviet Documents*, p. 214; *F.R.U.S. Berlin*, vol. ii, p. 244.

[4] The text of this report is printed with verbal variation in *F.R.U.S. Berlin*, vol. ii, pp. 240–3.

[5] No. 224.

[6] No. 219.i.

the changes which they felt desirable in regard to the procedure of the
Allied Council in Italy.'

4. *Germany: Economic Problems*
(Previous Reference: F. (Terminal) 5th Meeting,[5] Minute 3.)
The Meeting of Foreign Secretaries reported as follows:
'The Foreign Secretaries had before them a report by the Economic
Sub-Committee (P. (Terminal) 15).[7] The United States delegation asked
for discussion on reparations to be postponed to a subsequent meeting, and
the Soviet delegation asked that discussion should be confined to the
economic principles which had been agreed by the Sub-Committee. The
Foreign Secretaries therefore decided to discuss the agreed principles and
not the principles in dispute or reparations questions. It was agreed that
reparations should figure as the first item on the Agenda of the Foreign
Secretaries for their meeting on the 23rd July.
Paragraphs 11, 12, 14, 15 and 17 of the principles were agreed, subject
to agreement on the points remaining in dispute.
As regard the remainder:
Paragraph 10.—It was agreed to amend the last sentence to read as
follows:
'Productive capacity not needed for permitted production shall be
removed in accordance with the reparations plan recommended by the
Allied Commission on Reparations and approved by the Governments
concerned [or], if not so removed, shall be destroyed.
Paragraph 13 was still under discussion.
Paragraphs 16 and 18 were reserved.'

5. *Roumania: Removal of Allied Industrial Equipment*
(Previous Reference: F. (Terminal) 5th Meeting,[5] Minute 4.)
The Meeting of Foreign Secretaries reported as follows:
'A general discussion took place on this question on the basis of a
Memorandum (P. (Terminal) 10)[8] submitted by the United Kingdom
delegation on the 19th July. No agreement was reached and the question
was adjourned for further consideration.'

6. *Agenda for the Plenary Meeting*
The Meeting of Foreign Secretaries reported as follows:
'The Foreign Secretaries agreed to recommend as the agenda for this
afternoon's meeting the following items:
1. *The Western Frontier of Poland* (resumption of discussion—P. (Terminal)
12).[9]

[7] No. 210.
[8] See No. 194, minute 10.
[9] No. 202.

2. *Territorial Trusteeship* (adjourned from yesterday's Plenary Meeting —P. (Terminal) 13).[10]

3. *Turkey* (adjourned from yesterday's Plenary Meeting).[11]

4. *Minor adjustments of the Western Frontier of the Soviet Union* (proposal of the Soviet delegation).

5. *Persia: Withdrawal of troops* (memorandum submitted by the United Kingdom delegation on the 21st July—(P. (Terminal) 16).[12]

Certain further topics were proposed for remission to the Foreign Secretaries Meeting on the 23rd July. These were as follows:

International co-operation in solving immediate economic problems of Europe (proposal of United States delegation—P. (Terminal) 32).[13]

Directive to be issued by Governments responsible for the control of Germany to their respective Commanders of Occupation Forces in Germany (proposal of United States delegation—P. (Terminal) 24).[14]

Tangier (proposal of Soviet delegation—P. (Terminal) 28).[15]

Syria and Lebanon (proposal of Soviet delegation).

It is hoped that it might be agreed to refer these at once to the Committee of Foreign Secretaries without discussion at this stage by the Plenary Meeting.'

Mr. Churchill said that, before it was decided to refer Syria and the Lebanon to the Foreign Secretaries' Meeting, he would be very interested to learn what the Soviet Government proposed about Syria and Lebanon. This was a matter which affected the British Government more than either the United States or Russia, because it was only British troops that were concerned. Moreover, we had experienced great difficulty with France there. We were perfectly prepared to withdraw our troops from Syria and Lebanon, but if we were to do so at the present time the French would be massacred.

M. Molotov said that the Russian position was as follows:[16]

---

[10] No. 203.

[11] See No. 219, minute 7.

[12] No. 220.

[13] No. 245.

[14] See No. 224, note 15.

[15] This Soviet proposal of 22 July 1945 (Russian text printed in *Berlinskaya konferentsiya*, p. 351), read as follows:

'*International Zone of Tangier: Draft submitted by the Soviet Delegation*

'Having considered the question of the zone of Tangier, we have agreed that this zone which includes the city of Tangier and the area adjacent to it, shall, owing to its specific strategic importance, remain international.

'Representatives of the states chiefly concerned, viz., Great Britain, the United States of America, the Union of Soviet Socialist Republics and France, which will be invited to join this declaration will work out an appropriate status of this international zone corresponding to the new conditions that have resulted from the victory over Hitler Germany.

'Spain will be invited to adhere to the new status after the re-establishment of a democratic régime in the country.'

[16] This statement is ascribed to Marshal Stalin in the Soviet record, *Conferences: Soviet Documents*, p. 216.

Syria had asked the Soviet Government to intervene in this matter. It was common knowledge that the Soviet Government had addressed a Note[17] on the subject of Syria and Lebanon to the British, United States, and French Governments. He would like to be given some information on this subject, as Russian interests were concerned. He therefore suggested that the Foreign Secretaries should have a preliminary discussion. The Soviet Government had no proposals for the removal of any troops from Syria and Lebanon.

MR. CHURCHILL said that he would like the Soviet proposals on Syria and Lebanon to be considered by the Heads of Governments, either on the following day, or on some convenient date. He was quite agreeable that the other three matters should be remitted to the Foreign Secretaries for consideration.

There was general agreement with this arrangement.

7. *Western Frontier of Poland*

(Previous Reference: (P. (Terminal) 5th Meeting,[18] Minute 8).)

PRESIDENT TRUMAN suggested that the Conference should continue the discussion begun the previous day. He had already stated the position of the United States Government, to which he had nothing to add.

MR. CHURCHILL said that he, too, had nothing to add at the present time.

PREMIER STALIN inquired whether his colleagues had seen the Polish statement addressed to Mr. Churchill on the 20th July by M. Bierut, and M. Osobka-Morawski.[19]

MR. CHURCHILL and PRESIDENT TRUMAN said that they had seen this statement.

PREMIER STALIN inquired whether each delegation still maintained its views.

PRESIDENT TRUMAN and MR. CHURCHILL said that that was the position.

PREMIER STALIN said that in that case the question seemed unsettled and in suspense.

MR. CHURCHILL asked whether that meant that nothing further would be done about the matter.

PRESIDENT TRUMAN said that that was not necessarily the position. The question could be discussed again at any time.

MR. CHURCHILL expressed the hope that it would become ripe for discussion again before the Conference parted. It would be most unfortunate if this matter were discussed by all the Parliaments of the world, before the three Heads of Governments had bridged the gap between them.

PREMIER STALIN said that in that case he proposed that the Polish request contained in their statement should be complied with.

MR. CHURCHILL said that this was quite unacceptable to His Majesty's Government.

[17] See No. 64, note 2.
[18] No. 219.
[19] Enclosure in No. 205.

Premier Stalin inquired why.

Mr. Churchill said that he had given several reasons at the meeting on the previous day. The most important of these were:

(i) The final decision on all boundary questions could only be reached at the Peace Conference itself.

[Premier Stalin said that he agreed with this.][20]

(ii) It would not be advantageous for the Polish nation to take over so large an area as they were now asking for.

(iii) It would rupture the economic unity of Germany, and throw too heavy a burden on the Powers occupying the Western zones, particularly in food and fuel.

(iv) The British had grave moral scruples about vast movements of population. We could accept a transfer of Germans from Eastern Germany, equal in number to the Poles from Eastern Poland transferred from East of the Curzon Line—say 2 to 3 millions. But a transfer of 8 or 9 million Germans, which was what the Polish request involved, was too many and would be entirely wrong.

(v) The information about the number of Germans in the disputed areas was not agreed. The Soviet Government said that they had all gone. The British Government believed that great numbers, running into millions, were still there. We, of course, had not had the opportunity of checking these figures on the spot, but we must adhere to our own figures until they were shown to be wrong.

Mr. Churchill said that he could give further reasons in support of his views. But he did not wish to burden the Conference.

Premier Stalin said that he could not undertake to reply now to the Prime Minister on all points, but he would deal with the two most important:

Fuel.—Germany would have fuel resources in the Ruhr and the Rhineland, so no great difficulty would be created for Germany if the Silesian coalfields were taken from her. Her main coal resources were in the West.

Movements of populations.—There were neither eight, nor six, nor three, million Germans in these areas. There had been several call-ups from the population of these areas, and many Germans had been killed in the armed services. Very few Germans had remained, and even these had fled when the Russians approached. These figures could, of course, be checked.

Premier Stalin suggested that it might be arranged for the representatives of the Polish Provisional Government to come to the Conference, and for their views to be heard.

Mr. Churchill said that he would hesitate to agree to this proposal on account of the strong views expressed by President Truman the other day about inviting the representatives of the Yugoslav Government.

Premier Stalin then suggested that the Council of Foreign Ministers to be set up in London should invite representatives of the Polish Provisional Government and hear their views.

---

[20] Square brackets as in filed copy.

PRESIDENT TRUMAN agreed to this proposal.

Considerable discussion ensued as to whether these matters should be referred to the meeting of the Council of Foreign Ministers in London, or whether the resulting delay would jeopardise the position.

MR. CHURCHILL thought that it would be a pity to refer this matter to a body of less authority than the present Conference.

PRESIDENT TRUMAN said that he could not understand the urgency of the matter. It could not be finally settled until the Peace Conference. There had been a most useful and helpful discussion here, and he thought that further consideration of the matter should be remitted to the Council of Foreign Ministers.

PREMIER STALIN said that if the matter was not urgent, then it should be referred to the Council. All matters for settlement at the final Peace Conference would have to be discussed by the Council of Foreign Ministers.

MR CHURCHILL said that, with great respect to the President's views, he would like to emphasise the urgency of this matter. The local position would remain unremedied. The Poles, who had assigned to themselves, or had been assigned, this area, would be digging themselves in and making themselves masters. He therefore very much hoped that some decision could be reached at the Conference, or at least that we should know just where we stood in this matter. He could see no advantage in the Poles being invited to the Council of Foreign Ministers in London to discuss this matter, if the Three Powers had been unable to agree at the present Conference. In the meantime, the whole burden of the fuel and food problems would remain, and would fall particularly on the British, as their zone had poor supplies of food and the largest population to sustain.

Suppose that the Council of Foreign Ministers, after hearing the Polish views, could reach no agreement—and from the views expressed round the table it appeared unlikely that they would—the winter would be coming on with its attendant difficulties and it would be found impossible to settle the matter without a further meeting of the Heads of Governments. He was most anxious to meet the practical difficulties put forward by Premier Stalin on the previous day. These had been brought about by the movement of armies and by the march of events.

The British Delegation would be ready to suggest a compromise proposal, for consideration by the Conference, which would cover the interim period. He would suggest a line which might be provisionally occupied by the Polish authorities as Poles, and west of that line any Poles would be working as the agents of the Soviet Government, in accord with the agreement already reached on the occupation of Germany.

Continuing, Mr. Churchill said that he had had the advantage of previous discussion with Premier Stalin at Tehran on this subject, and he thought there was broad agreement between them that the new Poland should advance its western frontier to what might be called the line of the Oder.[21] The

[21] Cf. No. 73, note 5.

difference between Premier Stalin and himself was not that we did not recognise that the Poles should have a large extension westwards, but rather as to how far this extension should reach. The words 'line of the Oder' had been used at Tehran. This was not an exact expression, but the British Delegation had a line which could be considered in some detail by the Foreign Secretaries. He hoped that his colleagues would agree to consider such a provisional line to cover the interim period.

Mr. Churchill repeated that he had only used the words 'line of the Oder' as a general expression and that of course the proposal he had made could only be put forward satisfactorily on a map. In places the line fell short of the Oder, and at one part it went over to the Western side.

He appealed to the Conference to persevere in this matter, if not at that meeting then at another, and he asked them to consider the position they would be in if the Foreign Secretaries met in September and discussed Poland, and again reached a deadlock, just when the winter was upon them. As an example, he took Berlin's fuel supply next winter, of which part had in the past come from the Silesian mines.

Premier Stalin interjected to say that Zwickau in Saxony was where Berlin got its coal. Although this was not hard coal, the briquettes were useful enough.

Mr. Churchill replied that before the war some forty per cent. of the hard coal for Berlin had come from Silesia.

President Truman asked the indulgence of the Conference to state the case again. At Yalta it had been agreed:

'The three Heads of Government consider that the Eastern frontier of Poland should follow the Curzon Line with digressions from it in some regions of 5 to 8 kilometres in favour of Poland. They recognise that Poland must receive substantial accessions of territory in the North and West. They feel that the opinion of the new Polish Provisional Government of National Unity should be sought in due course on the extent of these accessions and that the final delimitation of the Western Frontier of Poland should thereafter await the Peace Conference.'[22]

That had been the agreement reached by his predecessor, President Roosevelt, and by the Marshal and Mr. Churchill; he was himself in complete accord with it. His point of view was that five countries were now occupying zones in Germany instead of the four that had been agreed upon. It would have been easy enough to have agreed upon a zone for Poland, but he did not like the way that the Poles had occupied this area without consultation of any sort with the 'Big Three'. He appreciated the difficulties to which the Marshal had referred the day before, and which Mr. Churchill had mentioned to-day; he had been thinking just as they had about these difficulties. That, however, did not matter. It was the way in which this action had been taken that mattered. Summing up, he said that that was his position yesterday, to-day, and to-morrow.

[22] Cf. No. 115, note 3.

Premier Stalin said that if the meeting were not bored with the question of frontiers, he would like to speak. He referred again to the Yalta Declaration, quoted a moment before by the President. According to the exact meaning of the decision then taken, the Powers were bound, after the Polish Government of National Unity had been founded in Poland, to seek the views of that Government on the question of the Western frontier. That Government had now come forward with its views. There were therefore two possibilities. The first was to approve the proposals put forward by the Polish Government; if this were done it would, of course, not be necessary to summon the Poles to the Conference. The second was that, if the Conference were not prepared to agree to those proposals, it would be necessary to summon the Poles and to hear their views. He had thought that it would be expedient to settle this question at the present Conference. As therefore it had appeared that they were not in agreement, he had suggested that representatives of the Polish Government should be brought in. The view had, however, been expressed just before that this was not worth while. He therefore suggested now that the whole question should be submitted to the Council of Foreign Ministers.

He would like to remind Mr. Churchill and others who had been at Tehran, that the view held at that time by President Roosevelt and Mr. Churchill—with which he did not himself agree—was that the Western frontier of Poland should begin at the estuary of the River Oder, and follow the line of the Oder to where the Eastern Neise joined it. He, for his part, had insisted on the line of the Western Neise. Under the plan of President Roosevelt and Mr. Churchill, the town of Stettin was to have been left on the German side of the line, as also was Breslau and the area to the West of it.

The question to be settled was one of frontiers, not of a merely temporary demarcation line. That question could either be settled or put off.

Premier Stalin then referred to the President's remarks that a fifth country had been brought in to occupy Germany, and his displeasure at the manner in which the Poles had done this. If the President thought that anybody was to blame, then it was not so much the Poles who were to blame as the Russians and circumstances.

President Truman said that he understood Premier Stalin's point, and that was in fact what he had meant.

Mr. Churchill said that he now withdrew the doubts which he had expressed on behalf of His Majesty's Government to representatives of the Polish Government being invited to come to the Conference, and to the Conference making one more effort to reach a decision without waiting for the Peace Settlement.

President Truman said that he had no objection to the Poles being invited, and to the meeting of Foreign Secretaries hearing their views.

PREMIER STALIN agreed that that was the right course.[23]

MR. CHURCHILL added that after the Polish representatives had been heard by the Foreign Secretaries, the results could be brought up to a Plenary Meeting.

The Conference agreed that the Chairman should send the necessary invitation to the Polish Government to send representatives to attend the Conference.

8. *Territorial Trusteeship*

The Conference had before it a Memorandum by the Soviet Delegation (P. ('Terminal') 13).[10]

M. MOLOTOV explained that the Soviet Delegation's Memorandum arose out of the decisions made at the San Francisco Conference. As the question of principle had been settled by the Charter of the United Nations, the Soviet Government now wished to raise the specific question of territories. He did not think that it would be possible for the Conference to have a detailed discussion on the matter, but it was possible to make some progress.

First of all he wished to discuss the question of the Italian Colonies in Africa and the Mediterranean area. The Soviet Memorandum put forward two alternatives and he suggested, if Mr. Churchill and the President agreed, that it should be referred to the meeting of the Foreign Ministers.

The second question which the Soviet Government wished to raise was that of territories mandated under the League of Nations.

MR. EDEN asked what mandated territories M. Molotov had in mind, since there were now only a few left, held by England and France.

M. MOLOTOV replied that the question in general deserved attention on the part of the Conference in accordance with the San Francisco decisions.

There was one more point, namely, that the Conference should exchange views on the question of Korea.

MR. CHURCHILL said that it was possible for the Conference to exchange views on almost any subject, but if these views were diametrically opposed to one another, all that would have been achieved would be an agreeable and interesting discussion. He was under the impression that the question had been dealt with at San Francisco.

PRESIDENT TRUMAN said that if the Conference would bear with him, he would read the Article of the Charter of the United Nations on trusteeship, namely, Article 77:

'1. The trusteeship system shall apply to such territories in the following categories as may be placed thereunder by means of trusteeship agreements:

(*a*) Territories now held under mandate;

---

[23] For a further interjection attributed to Marshal Stalin, possibly in connection with the present discussion, cf. *F.R.U.S. Berlin*, vol. ii, p. 252, note 26. No record of this possibly apocryphal interjection ('How many divisions has the Pope?') has been traced in British archives or in the published Soviet records of the Potsdam Conference.

(*b*) Territories which may be detached from enemy States as a result of the Second World War; and

(*c*) Territories voluntarily placed under the system by States responsible for their administration.

2. It will be a matter for subsequent agreement as to which territories in the foregoing categories will be brought under the trusteeship system and upon what terms.'

He imagined that it was under Section (*b*) that the Soviet Government wished to raise their point.

PREMIER STALIN said that that was so.

PRESIDENT TRUMAN continuing, said that he quite agreed that the matter should go to the Foreign Secretaries meeting.

MR. CHURCHILL was inclined to doubt whether, since the matter was in the hands of the Word Organisation, the opinions round the present table would be required.

PRESIDENT TRUMAN thought that it was just as appropriate to discuss this matter, as for instance, Poland.

PREMIER STALIN said that he had learnt from the Press that Mr. Eden had said in Parliament that Italy had lost her Colonies once and for all.[24] He wondered who had settled that, and where in fact the colonies had got to. Who had found them?

MR. CHURCHILL replied that he could answer that question. The British Army through heavy losses and indisputable victories had conquered them.

PREMIER STALIN interjected to say that Berlin also had been taken by the Red Army.

MR. CHURCHILL continuing said that Italian Somaliland, Eritrea, Cyrenaica and Tripolitania had been captured by our Armies. We had suffered heavy losses, although these were nothing like so great as had unhappily been those of the valiant Soviet Armies. We came out of this war as the greatest debtor in the world; there was, also, no possibility of ever regaining sufficient Naval equality with the United States. During the war we had only built one capital ship in spite of the fact that so far as he could remember, we had lost 10 or 12. Nevertheless, in spite of these losses, we had made no territorial claims. For us there was no Königsberg, no Baltic States, nothing.

It was, therefore, with a sense of perfect rectitude and complete disinterestedness that we approached this matter. As to the Italian Colonies, we had said in the House of Commons that Italy had lost them. That meant that she had not claim of right, but it did not at all preclude that at the final peace settlement Italy should have some of her Colonies restored to her on certain conditions. He did not say that he favoured that proposal, but as far as we were concerned, it was entirely open for discussion in the Council of

[24] Cf. statements made by Mr. Eden in the House of Commons on 4 October 1944, 17 January and 30 May 1945: *Parl Debs.*, 5th ser., *H. of C.*, vol. 403, col. 908; vol. 407, col. 137; vol. 411, col. 192.

Foreign Ministers and, of course, at the final Peace Conference. Having visited Tripolitania and Cyrenaica, he must say he had seen Italian work of reclamation of an admirable character and, while we did not declare ourselves in favour of restoration, neither did we say that this should be precluded. At present we held these Colonies. He wondered who wanted them; if there were claimants at the table they should come forward.

PRESIDENT TRUMAN said that the United States certainly did not want them, nor did they want trusteeship for them; they already had enough poor Italians in the United States.

MR. CHURCHILL said that we had wondered if any of these countries would do for the Jews, but it appeared that the Jews were not very smitten with this suggestion. Great Britain had, of course, great interests in the Mediterranean, and any change in the *status quo* would require long consideration on our part.

M. MOLOTOV remarked that the Soviet Delegation had submitted their proposals in writing, and that they would like the Conference to give them preliminary discussion.

MR. CHURCHILL said that he was afraid that he was unable to see exactly what was desired. Did M. Molotov wish to put forward claims for some of these Colonies, or for trusteeship of them?

M. MOLOTOV[25] replied that they would like to learn whether we considered it advisable for Italy to lose her Colonies. If it were advisable, then to what States should they be given, or what States should have trusteeship over them?

MR. CHURCHILL replied that we had not yet reached a conclusion on this matter.

PREMIER STALIN said that if the Conference thought that it was premature, they could postpone the discussion; nevertheless, it would have to be brought up sooner or later.

MR. CHURCHILL said that he had not before considered the possibility of the Soviet Government wanting large tracts of the North African shore. If that were the case, it would have to be considered in relation to many other factors.

PREMIER STALIN replied that the Soviet Delegation at San Francisco had stated that they were anxious to secure the mandates for certain territories; this had been stated in a letter[26] to Mr. Stettinius.

MR. CHURCHILL said that we were not seeking territory.

PREMIER STALIN asked how then they were to be disposed of.

MR. CHURCHILL replied that the question of what Italian Colonies were to be taken away was for the Peace Conference, and that the question of the ultimate administration of any Colonies that were taken away was for the World Organisation.

[25] This statement is ascribed to Marshal Stalin in the Soviet record, *Conferences: Soviet Documents*, pp. 226–7.

[26] Of 20 June 1945, printed in *F.R.U.S. Berlin*, vol. ii, p. 633.

PREMIER STALIN asked if Mr. Churchill was to be understood as saying that the present Conference was not qualified to settle this question.

MR. CHURCHILL replied that they were not qualified finally to settle this question—that was for the Peace Conference—although, of course, if the three Heads of Governments now present were to agree it would make things much easier.

PREMIER STALIN said that he had not meant that the Conference should settle the matter definitely, but merely that they should consider it. Why was this objection to it being raised?

MR. CHURCHILL said that if the Marshal would state precisely what his questions were, he would address himself to them.

PREMIER STALIN replied that he had already submitted his questions to the Conference in writing.

PRESIDENT TRUMAN reminded the Conference that Premier Stalin's suggestion had been that the Foreign Secretaries should discuss these questions at their meeting; to this he saw no objection.

MR. CHURCHILL said that he saw no objection either, but there were many more urgent matters to discuss. Moreover, it had been agreed that the problems of the Italian peace settlement would have priority at the Conference of Foreign Secretaries to be held in September. At that Conference the question would immediately come up whether Italy was to lose her Colonies and, if so, it would then immediately be asked what was to be done with them. He suggested that the matter might be dealt with by the Foreign Secretaries here, provided that this did not hold up more urgent business.

PREMIER STALIN thought that it should be referred without reservation; if the Foreign Secretaries had no time to discuss the matter they would say so.

MR. CHURCHILL then said that if his colleagues thought this worth while, he would agree.

> The Conference agreed accordingly to refer the matter to the Foreign Secretaries.

9. *Turkey*

MR. CHURCHILL said that he had told Premier Stalin at Tehran that we were in favour of the revision of the Montreux Convention, but that such revision could only be carried out with the consent of all the signatories, except Japan. The revision of the Convention was necessary, if only to expel the Japanese from their participation in the Convention rights. He had also already told Premier Stalin that we should welcome the free movement of Russian warships or merchant ships in and out of the Black Sea. Therefore, this discussion could be started on a basis of friendly agreement. At the same time, he had impressed upon Premier Stalin the importance of not alarming Turkey.

Turkey had undoubtedly been very much alarmed by the strong concentration of Bulgarian and Russian troops in Bulgaria, by the continuous

542

attacks made on Turkey in the Soviet Press and Radio, and by the turn of the conversations between M. Molotov and the Turkish Ambassador, at which modifications of the Turkish Eastern frontier were mentioned, including Kars and Ardahan as well as a Russian military base in the Black Sea Straits. All this had led Turkey to fear for the integrity of her Empire, and to doubt her power to defend Constantinople.

He understood, however, that these were not demands made by Russia on Turkey, but that Turkey had asked for an alliance with Russia, and M. Molotov had then stated the conditions on which such an alliance would be considered. He could quite understand that if Turkey asked Russia to make an offensive and defensive alliance, it would be for Russia to say what improvements she would like to see in the Turkish position. Nevertheless, Turkey had been alarmed by the conditions stated by the Russians. As he did not know what had happened since these conversations, he would be very glad to hear a statement of the present Russian position in this matter.

M. Molotov said that he would hand to Mr. Churchill and President Truman a written statement of the Russian point of view, but first he would explain how this matter had arisen.

The Turkish Government had taken the initiative through their Ambassador in Moscow in suggesting a Treaty of Alliance. This question had first been raised with the Russian Ambassador in Ankara, and then through the Turkish Ambassador in Moscow on his return there in May. In early June there had been two conversations between himself (M. Molotov) and the Turkish Ambassador in Moscow. In reply to the Turkish proposal for an alliance, he had said that Russia had no objection, subject to certain conditions. He had pointed out that before concluding an alliance, there were certain mutual claims which must be settled. On the Russian side there were two points:

(i) The conclusion of a Treaty of Alliance meant that Russia and Turkey jointly undertook to defend all the frontiers of Turkey and Russia. He had explained that Russia could not undertake to defend certain sections of the Turkish frontier, because they were unjust. In 1921 the well-known areas of Kars and Ardahan had been torn from the Soviet family. He had said that, before the conclusion of any Treaty, this question must be settled by the restoration of the alienated territory.

(ii) The Black Sea Straits. Russia had repeatedly informed the Allies that she was dissatisfied with the Montreux Convention, which she did not regard as correct. The rights which Russia enjoyed under this Convention were the same as those of the Japanese Emperor. This did not correspond to the present situation. Russia knew that both the President and the Prime Minister, as Allies, admitted the necessity for correcting this position; therefore certain proposals had been prepared by the Soviet Government which were set forth in the paper, copies of which were then handed in (P. (Terminal) 26).[27]

Continuing, M. Molotov said that at the same time he had pointed out to the Turkish Ambassador that, if they were prepared to settle these two points, Russia would be ready to make an alliance. He also said that Russia would be prepared to settle any questions which Turkey wished to raise. He had added that if Turkey was not prepared to settle the two points raised by Russia, Russia would still be ready to make an agreement about the Straits. In making this communication to the Turkish Ambassador, he had put forward the proposals now being handed to the Conference.

MR. CHURCHILL and PRESIDENT TRUMAN then read these proposals.

MR. CHURCHILL said that this was a very important document, which went far beyond anything discussed between Premier Stalin and himself.

M. MOLOTOV pointed out that at the time of those discussions there was no question of a treaty of alliance with Turkey.

MR. CHURCHILL said that he was not speaking of any treaty, but of the paper just circulated.

Referring to paragraph 1 of these proposals, Mr. Churchill said that he presumed the words 'abrogated in the proper regular procedure' would mean that all signatories except Japan would be consulted.

PREMIER STALIN agreed to this.

MR. CHURCHILL said that the Russian paper raised the entirely fresh issue of a Russian military base in the Straits. It was also proposed that no one was to have anything to do with the passage of vessels through the Straits except Russia and Turkey. He felt certain that Turkey would never agree to such a condition.

M. MOLOTOV said that such treaties had previously existed between Russia and Turkey.

MR. CHURCHILL asked what previous treaties there had been which gave Russia military bases in the Straits.

M. MOLOTOV mentioned the Russian-Turkish Treaties of 1805 and 1833.

MR. CHURCHILL said that he must ask for the opportunity to look up these ancient treaties.[28] He would only say for the present that the Russian proposals went far beyond his earlier discussions with Premier Stalin, and he would not be prepared to press their acceptance on Turkey.

[27] No. 227.

[28] The Russo-Turkish treaty of defensive alliance of 21 September 1805 is printed in French translation in *The Consolidated Treaty Series*, ed. C. Parry (New York, 1969 f.), vol. 58, pp. 215–224. The treaty of Unkiar Skelessi of 8 July 1833 is printed in *B.F.S.P.* vol. 20, pp. 1176–80. In this connection Sir O. Sargent minuted on 29 August 1945 to the Foreign Office Research Department: (U 5681/3628/70): 'Your memorandum "The Régime of the Straits" (R 9068/3795/44) of November 23rd, 1943, does not bear out M. Molotov's statement that these treaties gave Russia military bases in the Straits. Could you let us have a memorandum on this point, since M. Molotov is quite likely to raise it again at the forthcoming meeting of Foreign Ministers.' The resultant Foreign Office memorandum of 3 September 1945 stated in particular: 'M. Molotov's statement on this point is not borne out by anything in the texts of the treaties or their secret annexes. There

M. Molotov said that no proposals had been put forward. It had been intended to submit them to the meeting of Foreign Secretaries which was to be held in London in June, but which in fact never took place owing to the San Francisco Conference.

Mr. Churchill said that he would stand by his agreement with Premier Stalin to press for the revision of the Montreux Convention. His undertaking to do this still stood, but he felt himself quite free on these new Russian proposals.

Premier Stalin said that of course Mr. Churchill was quite free in this matter.

President Truman said he too would like time to consider the Russian proposals before further discussion.

The Conference agreed to defer consideration of the Russian proposals to Turkey until a later meeting.

10. *Poland: Invitation to Representatives of the Polish Government to attend the Conference*

President Truman referred to the decision to invite representatives of the Polish Government to attend the Conference. (See Minute 7 above.) This information was sure to become public and he thought that the right course would be to issue a communiqué.

Mr. Churchill thought that it was undesirable that the communiqué should indicate the purpose for which the representatives of the Polish Government were being invited to attend the Conference.

The Conference agreed that a communique should be issued, stating that representatives of the Polish Government had been invited to attend the Conference, but not stating the purpose for which they were invited to attend.

11. *Ukrainians in a British Prisoner of War Camp in Italy*

M. Molotov had said that he was anxious to make a statement about a camp in Italy under British control in which prisoners of war, who were

is no question of any Turkish territory being leased to Russia or otherwise placed at her disposal for use as a military base or for any other purpose, and in the treaty of 1805 the parties expressly foreswear aggrandisement and guarantee one another's territorial integrity. (Arts 11 and 13).' In submitting this memorandum Dr. A. J. Toynbee, Director of the Research Department, minuted on 3 September: 'My conclusion is, as you will see, that the Research Dept. memorandum on "The Régime of the Straits" was right about the facts, but that the Russians at Potsdam were sly.' Sir O. Sargent countersigned this minute on 4 September. That day Mr. Hayter further minuted: 'I do not think that the Potsdam record is accurate at this point. M. Molotov's claim, to the best of my recollection, was that the 1805 and 1833 Treaties laid down that no one was to have anything to do with the passage of vessels through the Straits except Russia and Turkey. The inaccuracy comes in the report of Mr. Churchill's remark.' Mr. Hayter suggested that this point would be cleared up if the sentence in minute 9 of the record reading 'Mr. Churchill asked what previous treaties there had been which gave Russia military bases in the Straits' were altered to read 'Mr. Churchill asked what previous treaties there had been of this kind.' No such alteration to the record has been traced.

Soviet subjects, were being held. With the approval of the Chairman a statement was made at the conclusion of the meeting.

M. Molotov said he referred to Camp No. 5 at Cesenatico in Italy. The camp was under British control and chiefly Ukrainian subjects were concerned. The first statement which had been received stated that there were 150 prisoners of war in the camp. But when the Soviet representative had visited the camp he had found instead 10,000 persons.

MR. CHURCHILL asked from whom this information had been received and at what date.

M. MOLOTOV said he would obtain additional particulars on this point.

MR. CHURCHILL said the dates were of importance as large numbers had been dealt with in connection with the German surrender. He was sure that M. Molotov would agree that we would not deliberately pass on untrue information.

M. MOLOTOV, continuing, said that the British authorities had formed a whole division of 10,000 strong consisting of Ukrainian subjects. The division was organised in 12 regiments, including Engineer and Signal units. Officers had been selected from those who had served in the ranks of the German Army. When the Russian representatives had visited the camp 665 men had stated that they were willing to return to their native country. This was the substance of the information which had been received from General Golikov who was in charge of repatriation arrangements in Moscow.

MR. CHURCHILL said that he would call for a special report by telegram.[29] He thought it might be found that some of those in the camp were Polish citizens.

M. MOLOTOV said that no Poles were concerned, but only Ukrainians who were Soviet citizens. In reply to a further question, M. Molotov said that the information had been contained in a telegram which had been received that day.

Cabinet Office, Potsdam, 22nd July, 1945

CALENDARS TO No. 226

i *22–23 July   U.K. Delegation briefs* on (a) Korea, (b) Russian interest in trusteeship for former Italian colonies, (c) Trusteeship and present Mandates [F.O. 934/4/30(3 & 6)].

ii *23 July 1945   Memorandum by Mr. Hoyer Millar (Berlin):* proposed British line on Soviet memorandum on Tangier in note 15 above [F.O. 934/4/26(11)].

---

[29] Field-Marshal Sir H. Alexander accordingly telegraphed that day from Potsdam (tel. Target No. 157) to inform General Sir F. Morgan at Caserta of the above representation by M. Molotov. Field-Marshal Alexander concluded: 'No doubt camp visited was organised for obvious administrative but not tactical reasons, and it seems possible that it may have included a number of Poles. Prime Minister has ordered enquiry to enable this charge to be answered. Signal urgently necessary information in particular organisation of prisoners of war or surrendered personnel held there together with their nationality and status. Urgent and not detailed reply required on general lines indicated above.'

No. 227

Draft submitted by the Soviet Delegation (Berlin)[1]
P.(Terminal)26 [U 6197/3628/70]

Top secret   *22 July 1945*

The Black Sea Straits

With regard to the Régime of the Black Sea Straits the Conference found necessary that–

1. The International Straits Convention signed in Montreux shall be abrogated in the proper regular procedure, as it no longer corresponds to the present time conditions.

2. The determination of the régime of the Straits—the only sea passage from and to the Black Sea shall fall within the province of Turkey and the Soviet Union as the States chiefly concerned and capable of ensuring the freedom of commercial navigation and the security in the Black Sea Straits.

3. In addition to other measures, the new Straits régime should also provide for the following:–

In the interests of their own security and maintenance of peace in the area of Black Sea, Turkey and the Soviet Union shall prevent by their common facilities in the Straits the use of the Straits by other countries for the purposes inimical to the Black Sea Powers (in addition to Turkish military bases the establishment of Soviet military bases in the Straits).

[1] Printed in *Berlinskaya konferentsiya*, p. 350.

No. 228

Memorandum by Mr. Churchill (Berlin)[1]
P.(Terminal)25 [U 6197/3628/70]

Top secret   *22 July 1945*

Greece

In view of the reference to Greece in the Soviet Memorandum,[2] I circulate the following two papers to the Conference. The first[3] is the

[1] Printed in *F.R.U.S. Berlin*, vol. ii, p. 1045.
[2] No. 201.
[3] *Note in filed copy:* 'Annex I'.

547

report of Field-Marshal Sir Harold Alexander. The second[4] is the report on the visit of the British Trade Union Delegation to Greece, which was headed by Sir Walter Citrine and composed of leading Trades Unionists. This I believe gives a true picture of the rights and wrongs of the Greek position.

I am puzzled at the reference on paragraph 4, sub-section 2 of the Soviet Memorandum to 'the representatives of Greek democracy.' According to the information I have, the E.A.M.-E.L.A.S. elements in Greece in no way represent Greek democracy or the vast majority of Greeks. Their conduct in Athens during their attempt to seize and dominate the city have made a gulf between them and the Greek people which will last for many years. The report of the Trades Union Delegation should be read in this connection.

W. S. C.

ANNEX I TO No. 228

Report by Field-Marshal Sir Harold Alexander[5]

With reference to the Soviet Memorandum on Greece, the following points are submitted for the Prime Minister:–

1. The general feeling of the great mass of the Greek people is one of relief from terror, due to the presence of British troops.

2. We have in Greece a Headquarters under General Scobie, and two British Empire Divisions, *i.e.*, the 4th British and 4th Indian, spread about throughout the country for the purpose of keeping law and order, and, as is well known, British troops do their duty.

3. U.N.R.R.A. is now functioning in Greece, which they were unable to do during the E.L.A.S.-E.A.M. terror.

4. As regards the alleged Greek threat to Albania and Bulgaria, I must point out that the Greeks have so far only one Division, and this Division does not finish its training until October: while the 2nd and 3rd Divisions are only in cadre form and have not yet been formed. They will be ready in March, 1946. The National Guard are in process of being disbanded and are gradually being replaced by a gendarmerie. Against this, the Yugoslavs have 52 divisions, of which some 8 are in the area of Skoplje and the Greek frontier. The Bulgarians have an Army of some 18 Divisions, and the Albanians have 7 Divisions, of which 2 appear to be in Yugoslav Macedonia in close proximity to the Greek frontier. With regard to the relative forces facing each other, any suggestion of a Greek threat is unfounded.

5. The situation however is aggravated by a strong propaganda campaign by Press and radio emanating from Yugoslavia, Albania and Bulgaria.

H. R. ALEXANDER, F.-M.

21st July, 1945

---

[4] *Note in filed copy:* 'Annex II', not here printed. This report is printed in *What we saw in Greece: Report of the T.U.C. Delegation* (London, Trades Union Congress, 1945), pp. 3–20.

[5] This report is printed in *F.R.U.S. Berlin*, vol. ii, pp. 1064–5.

No. 229

Draft submitted by the Soviet Delegation (Berlin)[1]

P.(Terminal)27 [U 6197/3628/70]

Top secret   *22 July 1945*

Western Frontier of U.S.S.R.

On shaping the decision of the Three Heads of Governments regarding the transfer to the Soviet Union of the Koenigsberg area,

The Conference approved the proposal of the Soviet Union that pending the final settlement of territorial questions at the Peace Congress, the part of the western border of U.S.S.R. adjoining the Baltic Sea should follow the line from the point on the eastern shore of the Danzig Bay indicated on the map, annexed hereto,[2] eastward—north of Braunsberg–Goldap to the junction of the frontiers of the Lithuanian S.S.R., the Polish Republic and the former East Prussia.

[1] Printed in *Berlinskaya konferentsiya*, p. 351.
[2] Not annexed to filed copy.

No. 230

Brief by the United Kingdom Delegation (Berlin)[1]

[F.O. 934/2/10(46)]

[BERLIN,] *23 July 1945*

Königsberg

The Soviet draft[2] is not acceptable in its present form. The draft would commit H.M.G. to some extent to:

(i) admitting that East Prussia no longer exists;

(ii) admitting that the Königsberg area is not under the authority of the Allied Control Council in Germany;

(iii) recognising the incorporation of Lithuania in the U.S.S.R. as the Lithuanian Soviet Socialist Republic.

2. We could not accept any of these commitments:–

(i) In article 1 of the Agreement on the occupation of Germany reached in the European Advisory Commission,[3] the Province of East Prussia was mentioned as forming part of the Soviet zone within the 1937 frontiers of Germany. Pending a final settlement of territorial questions it should continue to be treated as such. If convenient parts of East Prussia south and west of Königsberg may be administered by the Poles as agents for the Soviet authorities.

[1] *Note in filed copy:* 'Top copy with P.M.'
[2] No. 229.
[3] See No. 76, note 1.

But there is no justification for including any part of East Prussia within the borders of the Soviet Union in advance of the final settlement.

(ii) It is the view of His Majesty's Government that the authority of the Control Council should extend to the whole of the Soviet zone to the same extent as to the British and United States zones. This view is based upon the Agreement on control machinery in Germany[4] which has been accepted by the three Governments.

(iii) His Majesty's Government have always taken the view that the question of the recognition of the incorporation of the Baltic States in the U.S.S.R. must await the peace settlement.

3. We might explain our point of view to the Russians on the foregoing lines and leave it to them whether or not to pursue their proposal.

CALENDAR TO No. 230

i *22–3 July 1945   U.K. Delegation Brief and Memorandum by Mr. Allen (Berlin) on Königsberg:* Soviet claim thereto; suggests deferment of discussion if raised by Marshal Stalin in connection with No. 226. Mr. Allen's memorandum, prepared after discussion with Mr. Harrison and Mr. Dean, was broadly similar to (possibly an earlier version of) No. 230 [F.O. 934/2/10 (44 & 37)].

[4] See No. 8, note 3.

No. 231

Minute from Mr. Rowan to Sir E. Bridges (Berlin)
[*F 4767/364/23*]

Top secret   BERLIN, *23 July 1945*
Copy

The United States Secretary of State recently handed the Prime Minister a draft proclamation to be addressed to Japan, stating the terms on which war could be brought to an end.[1]

This was considered by the Foreign Secretary who suggested certain amendments.[1] These are now incorporated (and underlined)[2] in the draft attached. I understand that the President felt no difficulty in accepting our amendments[3] and that he might himself re-write certain passages. Furthermore the President did not consider it necessary to consult Chiang Kai Shek and, as I understand the position, the present intention is to issue the proclamation over the signature of the President and the Prime Minister only.

I asked the Prime Minister about bringing this matter to the notice of the Cabinet at home, and he said that he presumed arrangements are made to

[1] See No. 221.
[2] Here italicised.
[3] Cf. No. 221, note 4.

keep the Cabinet informed of what is passing here. You told me that the Chancellor of the Exchequer is receiving copies of the minutes and papers here, and I assume that I can tell the Prime Minister that he informs the Cabinet. Perhaps you will also have the matter dealt with in this minute brought to the notice of the Chancellor so that he may do the same in this case.[4] I have sent a copy of this minute to Dixon.

T. L. ROWAN

ANNEX TO NO. 231

Draft Proclamation by the Heads of Government

United States . . . United Kingdom . . . [U.S.S.R. . . . China][5]

(1) We, —The President of the United States, and the Prime Minister of Great Britain, representing the hundreds of millions of our countrymen, have conferred and agree that *Japan* shall be given an opportunity to end this war.

(2) The prodigious land, sea and air forces of the United States, the British Empire and of China, many times reinforced by their armies and air fleets from the west have now been joined by the vast military might of the Soviet Union, and are poised to strike the final blows upon Japan. This military power is sustained and inspired by the determination of all the Allied nations to prosecute the war against Japan until her capitulation.

(3) The result of the futile and senseless German resistance to the might of the aroused free peoples of the world stands forth in awful clarity as an example to the people of Japan. The might that now converges on Japan is immeasurably greater than that which, when applied to the resisting Nazis, necessarily laid waste to the lands, the industry and the method of life of the whole German people. The full application of our military power, backed by our resolve, will mean the inevitable and complete destruction of the Japanese armed forces and just as inevitably the utter devastation of the Japanese homeland.

(4) The time has come for *Japan* to decide whether *she* will continue *to be controlled by* those self-willed militaristic advisers whose unintelligent calculations have brought the Empire to the threshold of annihilation, or whether *she* will follow the path of reason.

(5) Following are our terms. We will not deviate from them. There are no alternatives. We shall brook no delay.

(6) There must be eliminated for all time the authority and influence of those who have deceived and misled the people of Japan into embarking on world conquest, for we insist that a new order of peace, security and justice will be impossible until irresponsible militarism is driven from the world.

(7) Until such a new order is established and until there is convincing proof that Japan's war-making power is destroyed, *points* in Japanese territory *to be designated by the Allies* shall be occupied to secure the achievement of the basic objectives we are here setting forth.

(8) The terms of the Cairo Declaration[6] shall be carried out and Japanese

---

[4] Sir John Anderson circulated the amended draft to the Cabinet on 25 July.

[5] Punctuation and square brackets as in filed copy.

[6] This Anglo-American-Chinese Declaration of 1 December 1943 on future military operations against, and policy concerning, Japan is printed in *B.F.S.P.*, vol. 154, pp. 363–4.

sovereignty shall be limited to the islands of Honshu, Hokkaido, Kyushu, Shikoku and such minor islands as we determine.

(9) The Japanese military forces, after being completely disarmed, shall be permitted to return to their homes with the opportunity to lead peaceful and productive lives.

(10) We do not intend that the Japanese shall be enslaved as a race or destroyed as a nation, but stern justice shall be meted out to all war criminals, including those who have visited cruelties upon our prisoners. *The Japanese Government shall remove all obstacles to the revival and strengthening of democratic tendencies among the Japanese people.* Freedom of speech, of religion, and of thought, as well as respect for the fundamental human rights shall be established.

(11) Japan shall be permitted to maintain such industries as will sustain her economy and permit the exaction of just reparations in kind, but not those which would enable her to re-arm for war. To this end, access to, as distinguished from control of, raw materials shall be permitted. Eventual Japanese participation in world trade relations shall be permitted.

(12) The occupying forces of the Allies shall be withdrawn from Japan as soon as these objectives have been accomplished and there has been established in accordance with the freely expressed will of the Japanese people a peacefully inclined and responsible government.

(13) We call upon the *Government of Japan* to proclaim now the unconditional surrender of all the Japanese armed forces, and to provide proper and adequate assurances of their good faith in such action. The alternative for Japan is prompt and utter destruction.[7]

[7] On 24 July 1945 a redraft of the present annex with variations underlined (an identic text without underlinings is printed in *F.R.U.S. Berlin*, vol. ii, pp.1280–1) was received by Mr. Churchill from President Truman. In sending a copy of this redraft to Mr. Dixon, Mr. Rowan stated in a covering minute of even date: 'I was informed by the United States Secretary of State, when I received this paper, that a copy of it had been sent to General Hurley with a request that he should place it before Generalissimo Chiang Kai Shek and ask for his concurrence. This, as you will see, is different from the procedure which I understood was proposed, and the document is now apparently to be issued in the names of the President, Chiang Kai Shek and the Prime Minister.'

No. 232

Minutes of a Meeting of the British Chiefs of Staff Committee held at 39/41 Ringstrasse, Babelsberg, on Monday, 23 July 1945 at 10.30 a.m.
C.O.S. (Terminal) 8th Meeting [CAB 99/39]

Top secret

Present:

FIELD-MARSHAL SIR ALAN F. BROOKE, Chief of the Imperial General Staff (*in the Chair*), Marshal of the Royal Air Force Sir Charles F. A. Portal, Chief of the Air Staff, Admiral of the Fleet Sir Andrew B. Cunningham, First Sea Lord and Chief of Naval Staff, General Sir Hastings L. Ismay, Office of the Minister of Defence.

The following were also present:
Major-General R. E. Laycock, Chief of Combined Operations, Lieut.-General Sir Gordon Macready, Major-General N. G. Holmes, War Office.

Secretariat: Major-General L. C. Hollis, Brigadier A. T. Cornwall-Jones, Lieut.-Colonel G. Mallaby, Lieut.-Colonel T. Haddon.

1. *British Participation in the War against Japan*
(C.C.S. 889/3)[1]
(Previous Reference: C.O.S. (Terminal) 4th Meeting,[2] Minute 5.)

THE COMMITTEE took note of a memorandum by the United States Chiefs of Staff to the effect that General MacArthur and Admiral Nimitz would welcome the visit of a British Corps Commander and accompanying officers who should arrive at an early date and, if practicable, by the 1st August, 1945.

SIR ANDREW CUNNINGHAM pointed out that it would be the Naval Force Commander who would be visiting General MacArthur and Admiral Nimitz, that he could not be described as an 'accompanying officer' of the British Corps Commander. No action was, however, necessary on this memorandum as the position was correctly stated in the Joint Report to the President and Prime Minister.[3]

THE COMMITTEE–
> Agreed that no answer was required to the memorandum by the United States Chiefs of Staff.

2. *Future Business*
(Previous Reference: C.O.S. (Terminal) 7th Meeting,[4] Minute 2.)

THE COMMITTEE was informed that the Plenary Meeting would take place at the President's house at 11.30 A.M. on Tuesday, 24th July; and that the Prime Minister wished to discuss the Final Report with the Chiefs of Staff at luncheon on Monday, 23rd July.

3. *Return of Staffs to the United Kingdom*
THE COMMITTEE was informed that the Prime Minister would be returning to the United Kingdom on Wednesday to hear the results of the Election and that if these results allowed he would probably return to 'Terminal' on Friday.

THE COMMITTEE decided–
> (*a*) That they would return to the United Kingdom with the Prime Minister and would take his instructions on the subject of returning to 'Terminal' later.

[1] Not here printed. This American memorandum of 21 July 1945 (printed in *F.R.U.S. Berlin*, vol. ii, p. 1339) was as indicated below.
[2] No. 187.
[3] See No. 249, enclosure, paragraph 11.
[4] No. 218.

(*b*) That the Staffs of the three Service Ministries should return to the United Kingdom on Wednesday or Thursday as administrative arrangements allowed.

(*c*) That office and living accommodation should be retained in case the Chiefs of Staff with their staffs returned to 'Terminal' later in the week.

4. *Internationalisation of the Danube River*
(C.C.S. 896)[5]
(Previous Reference: C.O.S. (45) 168th Meeting, Minute 5.)[6]

Reference was made to a memorandum[5] by the United States Chiefs of Staff recommending that the Combined Chiefs of Staff should send a letter to the Department of State and the Foreign Office on the question of creating a Danube Navigation Agency.

SIR ANDREW CUNNINGHAM informed the Committee that the Admiralty would be submitting a paper on this subject.

5. *The War against Japan—Australian Views*

THE COMMITTEE had under consideration a telegram from the Prime Minister of Australia to the Prime Minister,[7] giving the views of the Australian Government on the proposals for participation in 'Coronet'[8] and for reorganisation of command in the South-West Pacific Area.

THE COMMITTEE were informed that the Joint Planning Staff were examining this telegram and would circulate, during the course of the day, a report recommending what further action was required.

6. *Lend-Lease in Stage II*
(Previous Reference: C.O.S. (Terminal) 5th Meeting,[9] Minute 3.)

THE COMMITTEE considered a minute by the Secretary giving the reply of the Prime Minister[10] to the memorandum[11] submitted to him on the 20th July on the subject of lend-lease.

THE COMMITTEE were informed that a telegram had been sent to London asking for the additional information required to answer the Prime Minister's minute. General Jacob had replied to this telegram by telephone to the effect that representatives of the War Office and Air Ministry would fly out to 'Terminal' that afternoon with as much information as possible.

---

[5] This American memorandum of 21 July with enclosures, not here printed, is printed *op. cit.* vol. ii, pp. 651–4. Mr. N. J. A. Cheetham of the General Department of the Foreign Office commented on this in a minute of 25 July (W 10047/142/803): 'The Americans are showing an unexpected but, I imagine, not an unwelcome interest in the question of European international rivers.'

[6] Of 4 July, not printed.

[7] *Note in filed copy:* 'Onward 114', No. 250.i.

[8] Code-name for an American plan to invade Honshu.

[9] No. 198.

[10] *Note in filed copy:* 'Annex I'.

[11] *Note in filed copy:* 'Annex II'.

General Jacob might himself accompany them. General Jacob had pointed out that it was almost impossible to get the information necessary to answer the question in paragraph 3 (*b*) of the Prime Minister's minute.

THE COMMITTEE–

> Instructed a Sub-Committee consisting of General Macready, General Holmes, Brigadier Cornwall-Jones, the representatives of the War Office and Air Ministry and General Jacob to examine the Prime Minister's minute and to prepare a draft reply for submission to the Chiefs of Staff by the evening of Tuesday, the 24th July.[12]

> **Note:* Subsequently the Prime Minister talked to the Chiefs of Staff at luncheon and arranged for a revised memorandum[13] to be submitted to him by dinner that day.

7. *Employment of Captured Enemy Ocean-going Passenger Shipping and British Troopship Employment in U.S. Trans-Atlantic Programmes in the First Half of 1946*

(C.O.S. [C.C.S.] 679/8[14] and 679/9.[15])

(Previous Reference: C.O.S. (Terminal), 6th Meeting[16], Minute 1.)

A memorandum by the United States Chiefs of Staff (C.C.S. 679/9)[15] in reply to the suggestions of the British Chiefs of Staff (C.C.S. 679/8)[14] was circulated at the meeting. In this memorandum, the United States Chiefs of Staff asked that the Combined Chiefs of Staff should allocate the total lift of the *Caribia, Patria, Vulcania, Potsdam, Pretoria* and *Milwaukee* to the United States until the 30th June, 1946. The United States Chiefs of Staff pointed out that these ships would be used in the Pacific and that it would be uneconomical to remove them from the Pacific after the one trip which they would be able to complete before the 31st December, 1945.

GENERAL HOLMES advised the Chiefs of Staff that it would be better to adhere to the British draft and make no promise of this lift beyond the 31st December, 1945, pending the results of the review of personnel shipping to be completed by mid-September.

SIR CHARLES PORTAL agreed with this view and thought that it was unacceptable to remove these six ships out of the shipping review by committing them up to the 30th June, 1946, especially as the United States Chiefs of Staff were suggesting no compensation beyond the lift for 16,000 Canadians up to the end of 1945. The fact that these ships were in the Pacific would naturally be taken into account in the shipping review and it was indeed very probable that the shipping review would recommend that they should stay in the Pacific but it would be wrong to prejudge this at this stage.

---

[12] *Note in filed copy:* 'Annex III'.

[13] *Note in filed copy:* 'Annex I' [? III].

[14] See No. 218, note 6.

[15] Not here printed. This American memorandum of 23 July (printed with enclosure, *op. cit.*, vol. ii, pp. 1201–2) was as indicated below.

[16] Not printed: cf. No. 211, note 1.

THE COMMITTEE:

(a) Agreed to stand by the wording suggested in the memorandum by the British Chiefs of Staff (C.C.S. 679/8).[14]

(b) Agreed in discussion with the United States Chiefs of Staff to follow the line of argument proposed by Sir Charles Portal.[17]

8. *Provision of Personnel Shipping for the Requirements of Allied Governments* (C.C.S. 897.)[18]
(Previous Reference: C.O.S. (45) 166th Meeting, Minute 11.)[19]

THE COMMITTEE had under consideration a report by the Combined Military Transportation Committee suggesting a method of ensuring the efficient co-ordination of the demands for personnel shipping submitted by Allied Governments, other than British and American military movements, and providing a machinery for dealing with essential personnel movements other than those already approved.

GENERAL HOLMES explained that the British members of the Combined Military Transportation Committee were in agreement with the recommendations in this memorandum.

SIR ANDREW CUNNINGHAM enquired what was the meaning of the words 'the appropriate agencies of the United Kingdom and United States' referred to in paragraph 4 (c) of the report.

GENERAL HOLMES explained that whereas decisions on the movement of American civilians were within the power of the United States Chiefs of Staff, in the case of British civilians, the British Chiefs of Staff had not the same jurisdiction and the question was one for His Majesty's Government.

SIR CHARLES PORTAL suggested that in that case, it would be better to substitute the word 'authorities' for 'agencies.'

SIR ALAN BROOKE proposed certain further minor amendments to the enclosure of the report.

THE COMMITTEE–

Agreed with the amendments proposed by Sir Charles Portal and Sir Alan Brooke.[20]

9. *Command in Indo-China*
(C.C.S. 890/3.)[21]
(Previous Reference: C.O.S. (Terminal) 6th Meeting,[16] Minute 2.)

THE COMMITTEE were informed that the Foreign Office had now replied[22]

[17] See the statement made by Sir Alan Brooke at the 199th meeting of the Combined Chiefs of Staff held at 11.30 a.m. on 23 July: *op. cit* vol. ii, pp. 292–4.

[18] Not here printed. This report of 21 July by the Combined Military Transportation Committee of the Combined Chiefs of Staff (printed *ibid.*, vol. ii, pp. 1194–8) was as indicated below.

[19] Of 3 July, not printed.

[20] Cf. further No. 249, paragraph 22.

[21] See enclosure in No. 211.

[22] *Note in filed copy:* 'Annex IV'.

to the letter[23] from the Secretary annexed to C.O.S. (Terminal) 6th Meeting. In view of the reply, the memorandum by the British Chiefs of Staff had been circulated as C.C.S. 890/3.[21]

10. *Report to the President and the Prime Minister*
(C.C.S. 900[24] and 900/1.)[25]

THE COMMITTEE went through the draft of the report of the 'Terminal' Conference to the President and the Prime Minister and agreed to certain minor amendments.

THE COMMITTEE were informed that the United States Chiefs of Staff were now proposing a more accurate definition of the boundary between the British and United States areas of command in the South-West Pacific (C.C.S. 900/1).[25] The Committee decided that this definition was acceptable to them.

Babelsberg, 23rd July, 1945

ANNEX I TO No. 232

Minute from Mr. Churchill to General Sir H. Ismay (Berlin)

No. D. (Ter.) 4/5

Personal

The C.O.S. Memorandum[11] is not at all convincing to me. It is, of course, a good argument to say that our troops are supplied with American equipment and must be permitted to draw upon American spares to keep it up. It should, however, be possible to change over to British equipment, of which there must be large reserves, in a short time.

2. I am afraid also that the requests for transport aircraft will be regarded as an attempt on our part to improve our civil aviation position. Is this so?

3. Before I could send such a paper forward, I should have to know–

(*a*) The total value of munitions and military stores we are asking for;

(*b*) The amount the Americans consider qualify for issue because they are being used against Japan;

(*c*) The character of the principal items, composing the difference between the two. This last should be set forth in considerable detail, covering at least one page.

4. I do not wish to go into action on a bad case. When I have these facts, I will re-draft the letter in my own words.

W. S. C.

22.7.45.

---

[23] No. 211.

[24] Not printed. This draft report of 21 July was an earlier version of the draft report in the enclosure in No. 249.

[25] This American memorandum of 23 July, not here printed, is printed *op. cit.*, vol. ii, p. 1320.

Annex II to No. 232

Memorandum from the British Chiefs of Staff to Mr. Churchill [26]

Lend-Lease

We have seen President Truman's memorandum of the 17th July about Lend-Lease.[27] We note that the President intends to furnish us with lend-lease for the prosecuting of the war against Japan generally in accord with the schedules of requirements for the first year following the defeat of Germany and with other terms worked out between our respective supply representatives last autumn. We should, however, be grateful to know whether this means that troops of occupation and other forces carrying out essential tasks now holding American equipment will be entitled to such maintenance as they require, in addition to what will be assigned to those forces directly engaged in the war against Japan. Also that our other requirements for components, &c., needed for manufacturing programmes in the United Kingdom and Canada, which were included in the autumn agreement,[28] will also be made available to us.

2. We mention this because our requirements are at present only being accepted by United States agencies if they are needed for direct use against the Japanese, apparently as the result of a directive which has been given to them. In addition, the United States members of the Combined Munitions Assignment Board are questioning and often rejecting bids which are within the requirements accepted in principle last autumn, on the grounds that the equipment in question can be made in the United Kingdom. These seem to us to be questions of governmental policy which were covered by the agreement made last autumn and the discussion of them is, in our opinion, outside the province of the Combined Munitions Assignment Board.

3. The reason that we need continuing assignments of lend-lease equipment not only for our forces directly engaged against Japan is that the Commonwealth forces all over the world, in occupied territory and on the lines of communication to the Far East, are partly equipped with American equipment, for which we cannot ourselves provide spare parts, and which could not be replaced in a reasonable time by new British equipment.

4. Further, unless we can obtain the components we were counting on from the United States for equipment being made in the United Kingdom and Canada, our production programmes will be seriously dislocated.

5. Again, certain types of completed aircraft are required in connection with British redeployment and intercommunication services. At the moment the British do not manufacture comparable types in the United Kingdom and our general military efficiency would suffer if these aircraft were withheld.

6. In paragraph 2 of the President's memorandum, reference is made to the changed situation since the Lend-Lease arrangements were made in the autumn of 1944. We are not quite clear to what this refers, since we have now arrived at the very situation which was envisaged when the arrangements were made last autumn, namely, the end of hostilities in Europe. It was certainly agreed at that time that adjustments should be made to our requirements in the light of the

---

[26] *Note in filed copy:* 'This memorandum was substituted for the one originally proposed, and annexed to C.O.S. (Terminal), 5th Meeting': see No. 199.

[27] Annex to No. 174.

[28] Cf. No. 26, note 7.

actual date of the defeat of Germany, and the military requirements which we are now putting forward have accordingly been rigorously pruned. On our calculations, they represent for the twelve months ended the 30th June, 1946, rather less than two-thirds of the value of the requirements which were accepted in the negotiations last autumn, *i.e.*, some 1.8 billion dollars, as compared with 2.8 billion.

7. We earnestly hope that the President will find it possible to let it be known to the United States Administration that these requirements which are now in process of being stated to the Departments in Washington, resting as they do upon the whole assessment of our position which was agreed at that time, should be accepted and that the necessary financial and production provision should be made to meet them.

8. We hope that the United States authorities will also agree that once these requirements have been accepted for procurement, they should also be accepted as a valid basis for assignment. By valid basis we mean that if the items are not in short supply our bids within these totals should be accepted without argument. It would be understood, of course, that items which are in short supply would be assigned with due regard to operational priorities. Our request for assignments would fall within the total of our accepted requirements, except for any items which may become urgently necessary for unforeseen operational reasons. Even if we give British equipment to Allied forces, such as those which will assist in the occupation of the British zone in Germany, or are necessary for purposes of internal security, we should do so at the expense of British troops, and would not seek to increase the total of our requirements on this account.

9. The Chiefs of Staff therefore ask that the President may be invited to cause to be issued to all those in the War and Navy Departments dealing with these matters a directive on the lines suggested in paragraphs 7 and 8. All our present plans are based on the principles underlying the agreements reached last autumn and unless procurement and assignment operate on these lines, the fulfilment of our obligations in the war against Japan, and in the pacification of Europe will be gravely prejudiced.

A. F. Brooke
C. Portal
Andrew Cunningham

Annex III to No. 232

Memorandum by the British Chiefs of Staff
Lend-Lease

The Chiefs of Staff have seen President Truman's minute of the 17th July about Lend-Lease.[27] We note that the President intends to furnish us with Lend-Lease for the prosecution of the war against Japan. We earnestly hope that it is also his intention:–

(*a*) That troops of occupation and other British forces carrying out essential tasks, who now hold American equipment, will continue to receive such equipment and maintenance as they require.

(*b*) That American components needed for equipment manufactured in the United Kingdom and Canada will continue to be made available.

559

(*c*) That these United States items on which, under the Agreement reached at Quebec last autumn,[28] we are counting to supplement our own manufacturing programme of the same articles, will be supplied to us.

2. For (*a*) above our case is as follows:–

By agreement between the two Governments, British forces throughout the world are equipped with certain items of American equipment for which there is no British counter-part and no possibility of maintenance from British sources. Consequently, in the absence of American spares and replacements, such equipment is a wasting asset with the resultant loss of efficiency. Take for example the Jeep. There is no British counterpart, and therefore we have to rely on United States production not only to maintain our Jeeps in Europe and the Middle East, but also to recondition those which are required to be sent from Europe to South-East Asia Command to take part in the war against Japan. At present, numbers of these are held up here because spare parts to refit them cannot be shipped from America owing to the freezing of Lend-Lease equipment. As regards the Royal Air Force, the Dakota is a good example. We ourselves do not produce any transport aircraft comparable to this machine, and therefore 15 squadrons in Europe and the Mediterranean, which are, or are planned to be, equipped with this type of aircraft would be gradually demobilised or, alternatively, forced to use obsolescent Halifaxes. It is only by the use of transport aircraft that we can to some extent make good the acute shortage of our manpower in relation to our world-wide military commitments. After the war with Japan, we will be perfectly prepared to return to the Americans any United States-type transport aircraft which it could be established by agreement were surplus to our military needs. The Navy are not greatly affected, since so much of the Fleet is, or will be, operating against Japan. But here, again, the lack of maintenance stores for ships and equipment of United States type, which are now being used for minesweeping and other duties around Europe, would hit us hard.

3. The case for (*b*) is perhaps best illustrated by the Royal Air Force. The Canadian Mosquito is designed to take a Packard engine, while the Sunderland IV is equipped with American turrets. The necessity for the continuance of the supply of these and similar components requires no emphasis.

4. We now turn to (*c*). In accordance with the agreement reached at Quebec last autumn, our plans have been based on the assumption that we could count on the supply from America of certain articles of equipment, such as clothing, telephone cables, &c., to supplement the flow of similar articles manufactured by ourselves. Unless the Quebec Agreement, as we read it, is implemented in this respect, we are informed that all the above plans will have to be entirely recast.

5. We beg you to take up these matters with the President as a matter of urgency. In doing so, we hope that you will make it clear that the issue to us of this American equipment should not militate against our issuing our own British equipment to Allies and others in various parts of the world in pursuance of our world-wide interests.

A. F. BROOKE
C. PORTAL
ANDREW CUNNINGHAM

23rd July, 1945

Letter from Sir A. Cadogan to Major-General Hollis (Berlin)

Copy

22 *July 1945*

* * *29

Thank you for your letter[30] of the 20th July about the American proposal that French Indo-China should be divided between the China and South-East Asia theatre.

As you say, the Foreign Office would prefer that the present situation with regard to command in Indo-China should continue and we cannot pretend to be happy about the present proposal. We foresee that, when the French hear of it, they will be likely to raise objections.

We have, however, no desire to raise difficulties over the submission of the proposal to the President and Prime Minister if the Combined Chiefs of Staff consider it to be of military advantage.

* * *29

CALENDARS TO NO. 232

i *22 July 1945 Mr. Eden (Berlin) Tel. No. 146 Target.* Message from General Hollis to General Jacob requesting material in reply to Annex 1 above [UE 3298/32/71].

ii *23 July 1945 Mr. Eden (Berlin) Tel. No. 170 Target.* Favours proposal in minute 4 above, as an American initiative for three-power co-operation in Central Europe [W 9977/142/803].

[29] Thus in filed copy, from which the superscription and signature of this letter are omitted.

[30] *Note in filed copy:* 'Annex II to C.O.S. (Terminal), 6th Meeting': No. 211.

No. 233

Record of Sixth Meeting of Foreign Secretaries held at Cecilienhof, Potsdam, on Monday, 23 July 1945, at 11 a.m.
F.(Terminal)6th Meeting [U 6197/3628/70]

Top secret

Present:

M. V. M. MOLOTOV, M. A. Ya. Vyshinski, M. I. M. Maisky, M. A. A. Gromyko, M. F. T. Gousev, M. K. V. Novikov, M. A. A. Sobolev, M. B. F. Podtzerob, M. S. A. Golunski (*Interpreter*).

MR. J. F. BYRNES, Mr. W. A. Harriman, Mr. J. C. Dunn, Mr. H. F. Matthews, Mr. W. L. Clayton, Mr. C. E. Bohlen, Mr. B. V. Cohen, Mr. E. Page (*Interpreter*).

MR. EDEN, Sir W. Monckton, Sir A. Cadogan, Sir A. Clark Kerr, Sir W. Strang, Lieut.-General Sir R. Weekes [*sic*], Sir D. Waley, Mr. N. Brook, Mr. P. J. Dixon, Mr. W. Hayter, Major L. M. Theakstone (*Interpreter*).

Contents

1. *Subjects for Discussion*

M. MOLOTOV proposed the following Agenda for the present meeting:

(a) *Reparations: Germany, Austria and Italy.*

(b) *Germany: Economic Principles.* (Further consideration of P. (Terminal) 15.)[1]

(c) *Council of Foreign Ministers:* Revised draft of Constitution and Consequential Matters.

(d) *Territorial Trusteeship.* (P. (Terminal) 13.)[2]

(e) *Directive to Allied Commanders in Germany.* (P. (Terminal) 24.)[3]

(f) *Co-operation in solving the immediate economic problems of Europe.*

(g) *Tangier.* (P. (Terminal) 28.)[4]

(h) *Agenda for Seventh Plenary Meeting.*

This Agenda was adopted.

2. *Reparations: Germany, Austria and Italy*

M. MOLOTOV said that the Soviet Delegation had prepared two memoranda:

(a) Plan of Reparations from Germany. (Subsequently circulated as P. (Terminal) 29.)[5]

(b) Draft, for consideration by the Economic Committee, on 'once for all' deliveries from Germany. (Subsequently circulated as P. (Terminal) 30.)[6]

The memoranda had only just been submitted, and he recognised that his colleagues would need time to study them. He therefore suggested that formal consideration of them might be postponed until the following day. Meanwhile he would be willing to hold informal preliminary discussions, if either of his colleagues thought this would be helpful, to clarify any points

---

[1] No. 210.
[3] See No. 224, note 15.
[5] No. 242.

[2] No. 203.
[4] See No. 226, note 15.
[6] No. 243.

which might be obscure, *e.g.*, the connection between reparations and booty.

Mr. Eden and Mr. Brynes [*sic*] said they would prefer to study the memoranda and open discussion of them at the meeting of Foreign Secretaries on the following day.

It was agreed that the memoranda submitted by the Soviet Delegation (P. (Terminal) 29[5] and 30[6]) should be considered at the Meeting of Foreign Secretaries on the following day.

3. *Germany: Economic Problems*
(Previous Reference: F. (Terminal) 5th Meeting,[7] Minute 3.)

(*a*) *Statement of Economic Principles*

M. Molotov said that he was prepared to withdraw the suggestion which he had made at the meeting of Foreign Secretaries on the previous day for amendment of paragraph 13 of the Statement of Economic Principles annexed to P. (Terminal) 15.[1] He hoped that his colleagues would be willing to delete paragraph 18 of that Statement.

Mr. Byrnes thought that it would be difficult to omit paragraph 18 altogether.

Mr. Eden agreed. He pointed out that this was linked with the fifth paragraph of the Committee's Report, which specifically raised an issue for decision at a higher level.

M. Molotov then drew attention to the fact that, unlike paragraph 18 of the Statement, the fifth paragraph of the Report referred to Germany as it existed on the 31st December, 1937. The Soviet Delegation considered that, in order to achieve practical results, the Conference must take into account the changes which the war had brought about in the German political and economic system. The Soviet Delegation were unable to discuss this problem on the basis of 1937 frontiers. In M. Molotov's view there were two questions which required settlement. The first was the frontiers of Germany, which could only be settled by the Plenary Meeting, and the second was the question of the source of supplies for the various zones of occupation in Germany. M. Molotov thought that it would not be possible for the present meeting to decide the second question. In his view, it was not a matter on which a binding decision could be reached in general terms. In any event, the meeting had not the necessary data on which to reach conclusions. He considered that the question should be examined by the Control Council. The Council should endeavour to reach agreement on the basis of the factual information available to them about requirements and supplies, and any points of disagreement could be referred to the three Governments for decision.

Mr. Eden said that, in his view, there was nothing to be gained by referring the problem back to the Control Council. In support of this view, he cited the difficulty of the Control Council in reaching agreement on the

[7] No. 224.

problem of providing food and fuel for Berlin: a temporary arrangement had had to be made to tide over the period of the Conference and it was important that a solution to the problem should be found by the Conference before it broke up. He agreed that the Control Council had the factual information needed for an informed decision; but they required guidance from higher authority as to the lines along which they should seek a solution of their practical problem. If the Conference could agree on general principles, it could be left to the Control Council to apply them.

MR. BYRNES pointed out that the Committee had not proposed an absolute rule that each of the zones of occupation, including Berlin, should draw its supplies from the areas in Germany on which it had drawn before the war. They had recommended this as a general principle which should be applied so far as practicable. It was not, therefore, a question of a hard and fast ruling; but the Control Council must have some principles to guide them in determining the areas from which supplies should be drawn.

As agreement could not be reached:

> It was decided that the issue raised in paragraph 18 of the Statement of Principles annexed to P. (Terminal) 15 must be referred to the Plenary Meeting for decision.

(b) Reparations and Exports from Germany

M. MOLOTOV said that the Drafting Committee had not been able to reach agreement on the question whether priority should be given to reparations over exports in the matter of goods and raw materials produced in Germany. He therefore suggested a new formula[8] which might be embodied as paragraph 19 of the Statement of Principles. Under this formula any short-fall on estimated production would be divided so as to fall equally on exports and reparations deliveries. He gave the following example to illustrate how the formula would work:

> Suppose 2 million tons of coal are produced in any given month to meet a programme of 2,200,000 tons for export, reparations and internal consumption, i.e., there is a deficit of 10 per cent. In this case the allocations of coal for export, reparations and home consumption would each be reduced by 10 per cent. The Germans should try to make good the deficit in the next month and in the subsequent months if necessary. It might or it might not be found that the deficit would be balanced in the course of a year. If there was a deficit over the whole year then the allocations for the year would be reduced correspondingly by 10 per cent. and compensated when conditions permitted.

M. Molotov thought this was fair and he went on to say that, if coal were produced in excess of planned requirements, the reparation claim would stand unchanged. The surplus, however, would be allocated either to exports, home consumption or stocks.

---

[8] Russian texts of this draft formula and of the alternative draft formula submitted by M. Molotov below are printed in *Berlinskaya konferentsiya*, pp. 357–8. Cf. No. 495, minute 5(d).

MR. EDEN said that, as he saw the position, either payment for imports or reparations must be a first charge on exports: or they should rank together, as the Soviet draft suggested. The effect of this last proposal was that, if there was no coal or insufficient coal for export as payment for necessary imports, then somebody would have to supply imports without payment. To avoid such a situation priority should therefore be given to exports required to pay for the minimum programme of necessary imports.

MR. BYRNES said that if the minimum import and export programmes had been agreed, they must be fulfilled. He could not agree that either should be cut down merely in order that reparations should be met. Nor did he think that the demand for reparations justified a reduction in the internal consumption once the scale had been approved. Imports were therefore the first charge, and until they had been paid in full not a dollar from the United States Zones would be paid for reparations.

MR. EDEN said that cuts in a minimum agreed import programme could only be made at the expense of exports which were designed to pay for them. For instance, if less food were imported into Germany less coal would be mined. In order to avoid this it would be necessary to import more food. Who was to pay for this food?

M. MOLOTOV said that if coal exports were insufficient, the deficit should be compensated by some other export, such as chemicals or textiles. He then suggested that, if his first proposal was not acceptable, an alternative[8] might be considered. This was that exports from Germany should have the first priority to the extent previously agreed by the Control Council. Beyond that point, reparations should have priority. He gave the following example to illustrate his alternative proposal:

An export programme of 500,000 tons of coal to cover payment for imports had been agreed. Production had been planned for 2 million tons. If then, for instance, the British authorities insisted on exporting 700,000 tons instead of the agreed 500,000 tons, it would have to be decided by the Control Council whether the additional 200,000 should be made available. If the Control Council agreed that the additional quantity should be exported, it would rank ahead of reparations, but if this was not agreed, or until it was agreed, the 200,000 tons would be treated as a reparation delivery.

Further discussion suggested that it was unlikely that agreement on this point could be reached between the Foreign Secretaries at this meeting.

It was therefore agreed to refer the matter to a Plenary Meeting for decision.

4. *Council of Foreign Ministers*
(Previous Reference: P. (Terminal) 5th Meeting,[9] Minute 2.)

M. MOLOTOV reported that the Drafting Committee had prepared an agreed text (subsequently circulated as P. (Terminal) 31)[10] of the

[9] No. 219.　　　　　　　　　　[10] No. 244.

Constitution of the Council of Foreign Ministers. For his part he was prepared to accept this text.

Mr. Eden and Mr. Byrnes said it was acceptable to them also.

(1) It was agreed that the Constitution of the Council of Foreign Ministers should be as set out in P. (Terminal) 31.[10]

M. Molotov said that a report had also been received from the Committee appointed on the 21st July (F. (Terminal) 4th Meeting,[11] Minute 1) to consider the procedure for inviting the Governments of France and China to join the Council of Foreign Ministers. The Committee had agreed upon the terms of a telegram to be sent separately by each of the three Governments to the Governments of China and France.

As regards the timing of this invitation, Mr. Byrnes pointed out that, if these telegrams were sent at once, information about the proposed establishment of the Council might reach the Press before the release of the official communique which would be issued at the end of the present Conference. He therefore suggested that the despatch of the telegrams might be deferred until the day before the final communique was issued.

Mr. Eden said that the Governments of China and France might feel aggrieved at receiving such short notice; and on this account it might be preferable to despatch the telegrams 48 hours before the issue of the communiqué, even though this involved some slight risk of premature disclosure of this part of the conclusions reached at the Conference.

(2) It was agreed that telegrams in the terms proposed by the Drafting Committee should be despatched by each of the Governments of the Three Great Powers, separately, to the Governments of China and France 48 hours before the release of the final communiqué to be issued at the conclusion of the present Conference.

5. *Territorial Trusteeship: Former Italian Colonies*
(Previous Reference: P. (Terminal) 6th Meeting,[12] Minute 8.)

M. Molotov said that the Soviet Memorandum (P. (Terminal) 15[13])[2] dealt with the former colonial possessions of Italy in Africa and the Mediterranean. It suggested that either separate trusteeships should be set up for each territory or all should be under the joint trusteeship of the Three Great Powers.

Mr. Eden said that in his view there were two questions: first, should Italy lose all her former colonies or not? All that the British Government had said on this point up to now was that they did not regard Italy as having any right to recover any of her former colonies. In his view, the time to consider whether any and, if so, which of these territories should be restored to Italy was when the Peace Treaty with Italy was under consideration by the Council of Foreign Ministers. When that first question had been decided, it could be considered—and perhaps the proper body to do this was the

[11] No. 214.   [12] No. 226.

World Organisation—what form of trusteeship would be appropriate for those colonies which it was decided not to restore to Italy.

MR. BYRNES agreed. The position of the United States Government was as stated by President Truman at the Plenary Meeting on the previous day.[12] At the President's suggestion it had been tentatively agreed that the peace settlement with Italy should be the first business of the new Council of Foreign Ministers. In discussing the terms of that settlement the Council would have to consider all territorial questions affecting Italy, including the future of her colonies. This being so, he did not see how these questions could profitably be discussed now.

M. MOLOTOV said that he had hoped that the British Government, as the Power occupying the colonies in question, would find it possible to give at the present meeting their views on the next steps to be taken in disposing of these colonies. He had also hoped to hear the views of the United States Government, who had themselves raised the question of trusteeship at Dumbarton Oaks and San Francisco as well as in Moscow.[13] If, however, neither of these Governments was ready to express a view, he was quite content to leave the matter over. It could be dealt with at the first meeting of the Council of Foreign Ministers in September.

MR. BYRNES pointed out that at Dumbarton Oaks and San Francisco, the United States had expressed views on the general question of territorial trusteeship; they had not then attempted to deal with any specific trusteeship arrangements for particular territories.

M. MOLOTOV agreed. Might the Soviet Memorandum then be referred to the first meeting of the Council of Foreign Ministers?

MR. EDEN pointed out that this matter would arise automatically when the Council considered the terms of the peace settlement with Italy. There was, therefore, no particular need to refer the Soviet Memorandum to the Council.

> It was agreed to take note that the Soviet Government would raise this matter at the first meeting of the Council of Foreign Ministers in September, 1945.

6. *Germany: Directive to Allied Commanders*
(Previous Reference: P. (Terminal) 6th Meeting,[12] Minute 6.)

MR. BYRNES said that the United States Memorandum (P. (Terminal) 24)[3] had been submitted because, in the opinion of the United States representative on the Control Council, it was desirable that there should be a uniform directive to each of the Commanders of Occupying Forces in Germany, conveying to them those decisions of the Conference which affected them. He suggested that the United States draft should be referred to a Committee which could consider any suggestions the British and Soviet Delegations might wish to make.

MR. EDEN said that the Conference had already agreed on a statement of

[13] Cf. Sir L. Woodward, *op. cit.*, vol. v, pp. 312–9.

the political principles which should govern the treatment of Germany in the initial control period and were considering a corresponding statement of economic principles. These, when finally approved, would no doubt be communicated to Allied Commanders. The present memorandum seemed to cover much the same ground, and he was doubtful about the need for a further document of this kind.

M. MOLOTOV agreed. It would be undesirable that a document purporting to convey to the Commanders the decisions of the Conference should be worded differently from the decisions themselves. If, however, it was identically worded, it appeared to be unnecessary. Perhaps, however, there were other matters which it was intended to cover in such a directive.

MR. BYRNES agreed that the wording of both documents should be identical. It was likely, however, that before the Conference ended it would reach other decisions affecting the Allied Commanders, apart from those embodied in the documents mentioned by Mr. Eden. His purpose in submitting this memorandum was to secure a procedure for ensuring that the Commanders would be informed of all the decisions of the Conference which were of concern to them. Would his colleagues agree to the appointment of a Committee to prepare such a directive on the basis of the memorandum which he had submitted?

MR. EDEN entirely agreed that decisions of the Conference affecting the Commanders should be conveyed to them officially. He would accept the appointment of a Committee for preparing such instructions; it might conveniently deal also with the question of consulting the French Government, the Commander of whose zone would also require instructions.

It was agreed to appoint a Committee consisting of:

Soviet Delegation: M. Gousev, M. Sobolev;
U.S. Delegation: Mr. R. Murphy, Mr. J. W. Riddleberger;
U.K. Delegation: Sir William Strang, Mr. [G.] W. Harrison;

to report on the best means of (*a*) informing the Soviet, United States and British Commanders in Germany of all decisions of the Conference affecting them, and (*b*) securing similar action on the part of the French Government.

7. *Immediate Economic Problems of Europe: International Co-operation*

MR. BYRNES said that he was circulating to the other Delegations a memorandum on International Co-operation in solving the immediate economic problems of Europe (subsequently circulated as P. (Terminal) 32).[14] He proposed that this memorandum should at once be referred to a Committee of experts. It might perhaps be convenient to refer it to the Committee which had already been constituted to consider Germany's Economic Problems.

M. MOLOTOV said that he would prefer a separate Committee for this

[14] No. 245.

purpose, as the Soviet representatives concerned with these wider issues would be different from those on the existing Committee.

It was agreed to appoint the following Committee:

United States Delegation: Mr. W. Clayton, Mr. E. W. Pauley;
United Kingdom Delegation: Mr. T. Brand, Mr. J. Coulson;
Soviet Delegation: M. Artumyan, M. Gerostchenko;

to consider and report to the Foreign Secretaries' meeting on the issues raised in this Memorandum by the United States Delegation.

8. *Tangier*

(Previous Reference: P. (Terminal) 6th Meeting,[12] Minute 6).

The meeting had before them a memorandum by the Soviet Delegation (P. (Terminal) 28)[4] on the international zone of Tangier. This proposed (i) that the Three Great Powers should agree that, on account of its strategic importance, Tangier should continue to remain an international zone; (ii) that representatives of the Governments of Great Britain, the United States, the U.S.S.R. and France should meet to work out a new constitution for this international zone; and (iii) that the Spanish Government should not be invited to adhere to the new constitution of Tangier until a democratic régime had been re-established in Spain.

MR. EDEN said that he agreed in principle with the first of the three proposals put forward by the Soviet Delegation. The Tangier zone should remain international, and the existing Spanish occupation of the zone should be brought to an end as soon as possible. As regards the second proposal, it had already been suggested that the Governments primarily concerned should send representatives to Paris in the near future for a preliminary discussion on the reconstitution of the international zone. He would welcome the participation of the Soviet Government in these preliminary discussions. While it was desirable that there should be preliminary discussions between the four Powers, the interests of the other Governments concerned must not be overlooked; and before the new constitution could be finally decided, there would have to be further discussion at a larger meeting attended by representatives of all the Governments which had been signatories of the Act of Algeciras. He hoped that this larger conference would be convened before very long.

In the light of the explanation which he had given, he hoped that the other delegations would not wish to pursue this matter further at the present Conference. It was of close concern to France; and the British Government had in fact given the French Government an assurance that they would not discuss the substance of this question at any meeting at which France was not represented.

As regards the third proposal in the memorandum by the Soviet Delegation, Mr. Eden said that the position of Spain would have to be considered in the forthcoming discussions in Paris, and he did not think it necessary to say anything on this point at the present meeting.

MR. BYRNES asked whether, in view of the explanation which Mr. Eden had given, the Soviet Delegation wished to press for any public announcement indicating that the question of Tangier had been discussed at the present Conference.

M. Molotov said that if, as he understood, the first paragraph of his memorandum was accepted in principle and it was agreed that the Soviet Government would be invited to participate in the forthcoming discussions in Paris, he did not ask that any public announcement should be made on this subject at the present time.

The meeting took note:

(a) that the Governments of the Three Great Powers were agreed in principle that the Tangier zone, in view of its strategic importance, should continue to be administered as an international zone; and

(b) that arrangements would be made for representatives of the Soviet Government to participate in the preliminary discussions which were to be held in Paris in the near future about the reconstitution of the international zone of Tangier.

9. *Italy and Spain: Admission to the United Nations*
(Previous Reference: F. (Terminal) 3rd Meeting,[15] Minute 4.)

At their meeting on the 20th July the Foreign Secretaries had appointed a Committee to prepare the draft of a statement regarding the eventual admission of Italy to association with the United Nations. This statement was to cover, in addition to Italy, States which had been neutral in the war with Germany; but was to contrast the position of those neutral countries with that of Spain and make it clear that Spain could not be regarded as eligible for admission to association with the United Nations so long as she remained under the present political régime.

Mr. Byrnes said that according to his information the Committee were finding difficulty in completing this draft statement. It seemed that the Committee could not reach agreement; and he suggested that the matter might be brought up for further discussion by the Foreign Secretaries.

It was agreed that the Committee should meet that afternoon and make an effort to reach agreement on the terms of the draft statement; but that, whether agreement was reached or not, the matter should be reported to the Foreign Secretaries on the following day.

10. *Greece*
(Previous Reference: F. (Terminal) 3rd Meeting,[15] Minute 6.)

Mr. Eden said that, in view of the statements about conditions in Greece contained in the memorandum by the Soviet Delegation (P. (Terminal) 11),[16] Mr. Churchill had thought it advisable to submit a memorandum on this subject.

Mr. Eden handed copies of this memorandum to Mr. Byrnes and M.

[15] No. 200.　　　　　　　　[16] No. 201.

Molotov for the information of the United States and Soviet Delegations. The memorandum has since been circulated as P. (Terminal) 25.[17]

11. *Agenda for Seventh Plenary Meeting*
    It was agreed that the following subjects should be put forward for discussion at the Seventh Plenary Meeting that afternoon:
    (*a*) *Turkey* (P. (Terminal) 26).[18]
    (*b*) *Western Frontier of U.S.S.R.* (P. (Terminal) 27).[19]
    (*c*) *Syria and the Lebanon.*
    (*d*) *Persia: Withdrawal of Troops* (P. (Terminal) 16).[20]
    M. MOLOTOV undertook to include, in his report on the Foreign Secretaries' meeting, a reference to the conclusions reached about *Tangier* (see minute 8 above).
    It was further agreed that the Plenary meeting should not at this stage be invited to discuss *Reparations* or *Germany's Economic Problems*. Discussion of both these subjects should be resumed at the meeting of Foreign Secretaries on the following day.
Cabinet Office, Potsdam, 23rd July, 1945

CALENDARS TO No. 233

i   *23 July 1945*   *Minute from Sir D. Waley to Mr. Dixon (Berlin)*. Briefing on report of the Economic Sub-Committee (No. 210) and on reparations for discussion in minute 2 above. British views on definitions of restitution and booty [F.O. 934/1/2(35)].

ii   *23 July 1945*   *Letter from Mr. Eden to Mr. Byrnes (Berlin)*. Gives British agreement to U.S. draft directive on coal production: cf. No. 191. iv ('Coal remains one of the most dangerous world shortages and in our view it is important that we should obtain Russian support for the European Coal Organisation.') [F.O. 934/1/2(19)].

iii   *23 July 1945*   *Minute by Mr. Hoyer Millar (Berlin)* : lack of progress on drafting of resolutions on Italy and Spain referred to by Mr. Byrnes in minute 9 above. Attaches suggested amendments [F.O. 934/5/48(1)].

[17] No. 228.   [18] No. 227.
[19] No. 229.   [20] No. 220.

No. 234

Mr. Eden (Berlin) to Sir J. Anderson (Received 23 July, 10 a.m.)
No. 163 Target Telegraphic [*F.O. 954/30:US/45/162*]

Immediate   BERLIN, *23 July 1945, 11.55 a.m.*
Following for The King from the Prime Minister.
Begins.
    With humble duty. The President of the United States informed me yesterday of the deep regret he felt that he would not be able to accept

Your Majesty's invitation to visit England before returning to the United States.[1] Mr. Truman is sending Your Majesty a letter of regret which will be delivered through the United States Ambassador.

2. Mr. Churchill thinks the Conference here may well last until the end of the first week in August, and Mr. Truman has to get back at the earliest moment to his own country on account of internal affairs.

Ends.

[1] See No. 1.

No. 235

Minutes of a British Staff Conference held in No. 23, Ringstrasse, Babelsberg, on Monday, 23 July 1945 at 1.30 p.m.
C.O.S. (Terminal) 9th Meeting [CAB 99/39]

Top secret

Present:

THE RIGHT HON. WINSTON S. CHURCHILL, Prime Minister and Minister of Defence (in the Chair), The Right Hon. Anthony Eden, M.P., Secretary of State for Foreign Affairs (for part of the Meeting), Field-Marshal Sir Alan F. Brooke, Chief of the Imperial General Staff, Marshal of the Royal Air Force Sir Charles A. Portal, Chief of the Air Staff, The Right Hon. Lord Leathers, Minister of War Transport, Admiral of the Fleet Sir Andrew B. Cunningham, First Sea Lord and Chief of Naval Staff, General Sir Hastings L. Ismay, Office of the Minister of Defence, Major-General L. C. Hollis, Secretary.

1. *Lend-Lease in Stage II*
(Previous Reference: C.O.S. (Terminal) 8th Meeting,[1] Minute 6.)

THE PRIME MINISTER said that he did not think the Memorandum[2] by the Chiefs of Staff on lend-lease was sufficiently convincing. The case required simplification. Examples of where the shoe was pinching should be included.

It was explained that the answers to the questions asked in the Prime Minister's minute[3] Serial (D. (Ter.) 4/5) would take some time to prepare.

THE PRIME MINISTER said that if the Chiefs of Staff could revise their memorandum and include some examples he would put in the paper to the President that evening.

The Chiefs of Staff undertook to revise their memorandum[4] as requested by the Prime Minister.

2. *Basic Objectives*
(Previous Reference: C.O.S. (Terminal) 7th Meeting,[5] Minute 1.)

It was explained that no agreement had been reached between the Combined Chiefs of Staff on the Basic Objectives paper.

[1] No. 232.
[2] *Note in filed copy:* 'Annex II to C.O.S. (Terminal), 8th Meeting': No. 232.
[3] *Note in filed copy:* 'Annex I to C.O.S. (Terminal), 8th Meeting.'
[4] *Note in filed copy:* 'For revised memorandum see Annex III to C.O.S. (Terminal), 8th Meeting.'
[5] No. 218.

LORD LEATHERS said that the difficulty arose over the United Kingdom Import Programme. For the first time it was proposed to exclude this programme from the paper, and this might result in military requirements squeezing out vital civil needs. The Prime Minister was informed that it had been decided to set out in an annex to the Final Report the proposals of the United States Chiefs of Staff alongside those of the British Chiefs of Staff. Further than that, it was not possible to go at present.

THE CONFERENCE took note of the position.

Babelsberg, 23rd July, 1945

No. 236

Minute from Mr. Churchill to Mr. Eden (Berlin)
No. M.(Ter)11/5 [F.O. 954/7:FE 45/69]

Top secret [BERLIN,] *23 July 1945*

Mr. Byrnes told me this morning that he had cabled to T.V. Soong advising him not to give way on any point to the Russians[1], but to return to Moscow and keep on negotiating pending further developments.

It is quite clear that the United States do not at the present time desire Russian participation in the war against Japan.[2]

W. S. C.

---

[1] The filed copy of this minute carried at foot the following reference: 'Ref: Record of a conversation between Sir A. Clark-Kerr and Dr. T. V. Soong on 10.7.45 [No. 180, annex] about the latter's negotiations with Marshal Stalin in connection with the Livadia agreement on the Far East.' Cf. *F.R.U.S. Berlin*, vol. ii, p. 1241, for a message of 23 July from Mr. Truman to Generalissimo Chiang Kai-shek.

[2] The above minute is printed by J. Ehrman, *op. cit.*, vol. vi, p. 292.

No. 237

Minute from Mr. Attlee[1] to Mr. Churchill (Berlin)
[U 6311/2600/70]

[BERLIN,] *23 July 1945*

Montreux Convention and the Straits

The Russian intention of getting control of the exits from the Black Sea by concluding an agreement with Turkey and of obtaining a military base therein seems to us a crude exercise of power politics, but it is necessary for us to look at the matter from the Russian angle. The facts of geography have denied Russia an unimpeded approach to the oceans except in the icebound north and the far east. Her weakness in the past has placed her at the mercy

---

[1] For Mr. Attlee's authorship of this unsigned minute cf. No. 459, paragraph 2.

of other powers who controlled the gateways. Denmark formerly and then Germany controlled the Baltic exits. The gateways from the Black Sea were in the hands of Turkey, for the last century a weak country buttressed against Russia by the western powers. We, in our own interests, have for long controlled the Mediterranean route which we considered vital to our interests. For this reason we hold Gibraltar and have taken part in the international control of Tangier. We, with the French as junior partner, have had in our hands the Suez Canal. Egypt from the Russian point of view is a British satellite. Russia in the time of her weakness was not invited to share responsibility for keeping open these fields. The gates were held by the interested powers. Our claim that we occupy these positions as trustees for the rest of the world that can trust our disinterestedness is not likely to be generally accepted. I fear that our assertion of our intention of seeking nothing for ourselves out of this war does not carry much weight and the subconscious retort by the Russians is 'Why should you, you have got all you want'.

To the Russians the present position not unnaturally appears to be the result of the power politics of the past. Now that they are strong they do not intend to live on the sufferance of others. It appears to me that the present demand on Turkey, the possible request for a share of the Mandate in the former Italian colonies in North Africa, the raising of the Tangier question and perhaps also the interest displayed in Syria and the Lebanon and Russian policy in Persia are all expressions of the determination of Russia to assert an equal right to have free access to the oceans and to be in a strategic position to enforce this right if necessary. This is not unnatural in the second greatest power in the world. For us to claim a voice in the settlement of the regime in the Straits is to invite a demand by Russia for a share in the control of the Mediterranean exits and for strategic bases in those areas. It is, in my view, useless to argue these cases on past precedents or old treaties or to assert for ourselves special interests, however valid they appear to us. We are facing a new situation. I doubt whether we shall get much support from the U.S.A. although they would no doubt be stiff enough over their own control of the Panama Canal zone. In my view, the occupation and holding of particular strategic areas have today only a relative importance in the light of modern war conditions now that air power transcends all frontiers and menaces all home lands. I therefore consider that the only effective way of meeting these claims and dealing with these problems is as part of the general world organisation for peace. I do not think that we are in a position effectively to oppose these claims in detail. For instance whether or not Russia obtains a strategic base in the Dardanelles, Turkey today militarily is at the mercy of Russia as indeed without the support of other powers she has been for decades. I suggest therefore that we should take the line that the whole question of the control of strategic areas should be taken up when the United Nations organisation comes into being and that we should be ready with constructive proposals suitable to the new conditions of the world in which we have to live.

No. 238

Minute from Mr. Eden to Mr. Attlee (Berlin)[1]
[F.O. 954/22:Pwp/45/60]

Top secret   [BERLIN,] 23 July 1945

Many thanks for your minute of the 18th July about strategic policy and
the particular question of the security régime for the Baltic and other sea
passage[s].[2] I read your minute with interest and am sorry that owing to
pressure of work I have not sent you an earlier reply.

2. I should explain first that the Foreign Office brief No. 50[3] about
'security arrangements for the Baltic sea gateways and the Kiel Canal' is
only a planners study. It has no Ministerial authority and was only prepared
to give a basis for consideration of the Baltic question if it happened to come
up at Terminal, by association of ideas with the problem of the future
régime of the Straits. We have never had any intention ourselves of raising
the Baltic question here and I certainly hope that it will not be brought up
by anyone else as I believe it would be premature to do so.

3. I quite agree with you that our broad policy must be to bring the
future régime for all the important sea passages within the world-wide
system of security which we hope will be established by the World
Organisation. I think that the brief No. 50[3] in fact brings this out. It is
suggested in the brief that the security arrangements for the Baltic passages
will fall to be considered by the Military Staff Committee of the World
Organisation, in preparation for the conclusion of the proposed 'special
agreements' between the Security Council and member States defining
their respective military contributions to the maintenance of international
peace.

4. The Chiefs of Staff are nervous lest the consideration of this question by
the Security Council and its Military Staff Committee may lead to proposals
for exclusively Russian bases in the small 'riparian countries'. I certainly
agree with them that this would be a dangerous development, as we cannot
unfortunately assume that Russian policy has developed to the point where
they are prepared to participate in a genuinely international security
system rather than to pursue their own national interests. You will notice,
however, from the annex to the brief that the Chiefs of Staff agree that
the question of the defence of these sea passages must be a matter for the
World Organisation to consider.[3]

5. You express the fear that we may run ourselves into an intolerable
burden of defence expenditure by seeking to maintain our special interest
in places like Gibraltar and the Suez Canal area. It does not seem to me
that, on the showing of this war which has proved them vital to our national

---

[1] This correspondence was copied to Mr. Churchill.
[2] No. 179.
[3] Cf. No. 109, note 7 and annex II.

existence, it is unrealistic to hold that we should continue to maintain our special position in these two areas. I should be sorry to think that we could not undertake to maintain the necessary minimum forces for this purpose, particularly in these days when aircraft go so far to make up our deficiency in manpower.

6. The Baltic sea passages, of course, are another question, and there has never been any suggestion that we should attempt to maintain British bases in that area. To do so would be an invitation to the one thing we want to avoid, namely a Russian claim to have their national bases in the Scandinavian countries.

7. The Russian attitude is, I think, the key to the whole question. We may know more about that when the Conference has discussed the question of the Straits and the Montreux Convention.

ANTHONY EDEN

No. 239

Minute from Mr. Eden to Mr. Attlee (Berlin)
[F.O. 934/1/2(21)]

Confidential   [BERLIN,] *23 July 1945*

You asked me the other day whether we had any definite line with regard to the ownership of German industry by Krupps, Thyssens, etc.

We have given a good deal of thought to the ownership of German industry, and I enclose a note which will, I hope, give you the information you want.

ANTHONY EDEN

ENCLOSURE IN NO. 239

The Ownership of German Industry

The Economic and Industrial Planning Staff recently prepared a Paper on the control and ownership of German industrial concerns. The conclusions reached were that from the security aspect control through ownership (i.e. by virtue of majority shareholding) was less advantageous than control exercised by powers enforced under a peace treaty. There would be less chance of political conflict if control consisted of rights of inspection of Germany [*sic*] industry with powers to take over direct control should inspection reveal that a company was engaged in illicit practices.

2. As regards ownership for the purpose of obtaining reparation the report suggested that this was undesirable for the following reasons:–

(1) Difficulties of allocating industries between claimants and dangers of political conflict if industries were owned jointly by all claimants.

(2) Conflict between reparations and economic security. The former would look for industrial expansion; the latter for contraction.

576

(3) Profits in marks would be of little or no value. Conversion of marks into foreign currencies would only add to the already difficult transfer problem.

(4) Permanent ownership would be contrary to the principle of getting reparation settled in a reasonably short period; temporary ownership presupposes an eventual German purchaser. Even if one was forthcoming there would still be the same transfer difficulties referred to in (3) above.

3. A Ministerial Committee recently considered these recommendations and gave them their approval.

4. As regards the fate of Krupps, Thyssens, Hermann Goering [Werke], etc. many of these will virtually disappear under a reparations plan. It is true that the owners of the capital would receive compensation on this account from the German Government and that this would theoretically be available to recreate the companies. In practice, however, this is unlikely to happen since it seems probably that the German Government will have to introduce some form of capital levy to avoid the inflationary effects of the enormous increase in credit consequent upon their defeat.

5. As a temporary measure and in order to ensure that industrial disarmament is effectively carried out, the Americans have recently taken over control of I. G. Farben. They have done this not by acquiring the share capital but under the powers conferred by the terms of surrender. We understand that similar action in regard to Krupps and Hermann Goering is contemplated in the British Zone.

No. 240

Note of an informal meeting held in the President's room at the Cecilienhof, Potsdam, on Monday, 23 July 1945 at 4 p.m.[1]

[UE 3238/86/77]

Present:

MR. BYRNES, Mr. Pauley, Mr. Clayton, Mr. Bohlen (*Interpreter*).

MR. EDEN, Sir W. Monckton, Sir D. Waley, Mr. Turner, Mr. Coulson, Major Theakstone (*Interpreter*).

M. MOLOTOV, M. Maisky, M. Golunsky (*Interpreter*).

MR. BYRNES said he had suggested[2] this informal meeting because he did not see at present how we could reconcile our differences on reparation and supply questions. He referred to the definition of war booty which M. Maisky had submitted on 21st July,[3] and asked whether it was correct that this would cover such things as plant, machinery, coal mines, etc.

M. MOLOTOV said that they had devised a new formula, which he handed round. A copy is annexed.

MR. BYRNES asked whether plant and machinery had already been removed from the Soviet zone. He was hearing daily reports of furniture, silver,

[1] This record was circulated to the British Delegation on 25 July 1945 as P. (Terminal) 38.

[2] In a conversation with M. Molotov at 10.30 a.m. on 23 July: see *F.R.U.S. Berlin*, vol. ii, p. 275.

[3] See No. 213.i.

plumbing and even mortgages from banks being removed. If this sort of thing was happening, he did not see how there could be any proper system of accounting.

M. MOLOTOV suggested that, rather than complicate the question, the Russian reparation account might be reduced. Perhaps 300 million dollars worth had been removed, although the Russians had claims for billions of dollars. They would be ready to reduce their claims by that amount, so that the whole question could be dismissed, though they could not of course forget their large losses.

MR. BYRNES pointed out that all the Allies had large losses. He quoted the figures of United States war expenditure. He said that they did not wish to discuss this; all they were concerned with was to consider how they might remove the difficulties which might arise between us.

M. MOLOTOV suggested that if they attempted to make an exact account of all these items they would merely lose time and produce no practical result. The Russians had asked for 10 billion dollars. They would be ready to take 9 billion and finish with it.

MR. BYRNES then said that, according to Marshal Stalin's statement on the previous day, the coal mines in Silesia were now in the possession of the Poles and the Russians had no control over them.[4] He asked if this was also true of the copper, zinc and other resources in that part of former German territory.

M. MOLOTOV said that the Germans could not be sent back there.

There was then some discussion of the value of the disputed territory which was now being administered by Poland.

M. MOLOTOV maintained that it was only 16% of the national wealth of 1937 German territory, whereas MR. PAULEY maintained that it was approximately 20%.

M. MOLOTOV said that it had been decided at the Crimea Conference that Poland should receive a substantial accession of territory in the west and north. She had in fact received roughly what had been there decided on. But they had not had in mind at that Conference that this territory should be stripped for reparations before it was handed over to Poland. Nevertheless, a certain amount of what was contained in the territory should be included in Poland's share of reparation.

MR. BYRNES pointed out that this would mean that 20% of what was thought at Yalta to be available for general reparation purposes was given away to Poland.

M. MOLOTOV asked what we had in mind when we decided to make these accessions of territory to Poland. Did we mean to take away the resources of the territory?

MR. EDEN pointed out that what was said at Yalta was that the accession of territory should not take place until the peace treaty. Moreover we were

[4] See No. 219, minute 8.

anxious that Germany should in the meantime be treated as an economic whole.

M. MOLOTOV again referred to the contradiction between the promise of compensating Poland by new territory and the removal of wealth from that territory. He had always had in mind that, since this territory was to be handed over, it could not be treated the same as all the rest of Germany.

MR. EDEN said this was a fundamental point. The Russians had in mind that part of German territory should be exempted from reparation. We on the other hand had never contemplated this.

M. MOLOTOV said he had contemplated it only to some extent. The Russians were ready to reduce their demands by 1 billion dollars though this was about three times as much as they had removed from their zone.

MR. BYRNES queried the figure of 9 billion dollars which the Russians claimed and said that such figures were quite meaningless. In answer to M. Molotov's statement that the United States delegation had not objected to the figure of 20 billion dollars at the Crimea Conference, he pointed out that, since that time, all our armies had moved into Germany and we had destroyed billions of dollars of property by air bombardment. The whole picture was now changed. They had only agreed to the 20 billion dollar figure as a basis of discussion. It must now be discussed in the light of the situation as it exists today.

M. MOLOTOV said that he was ready to discuss. He had already proposed 9 billion instead of 10 billion dollars as the Russian share. He might even agree to 8 billion.

MR. BYRNES said that the principal concern of the United States was the amount of money which would have to be taken from their people in food and coal to pay reparation for someone else. By driving the Germans out of Silesia, the United States now had some 4 million extra population in the whole of their zone and about 800 thousand more in their Sector in Berlin. This was a terrible problem.

Mr. Byrnes continued that, according to United States estimates, the Russian zone (including the territory now administered by Poland) included about 50% of German resources. If the Russians collected their reparation from their own zone, and if the British, French and Americans did likewise from their area and undertook to pay out of it any reparation claims to Belgium, Holland and other United Nations, we should then at least avoid having to discuss the sort of questions that were now being raised, and which would cause great irritation in the days to come. The United States did not want the machinery in their zone. They would like to give it to Poland in return for coal or to Russia for something in the Soviet zone which could be used for helping the liberated countries.

M. MOLOTOV objected that reparation should not be paid for and that Russia wanted to receive supplies from other zones as reparation. He also asked what would happen to the resources of the Ruhr and asked whether, under Mr. Byrnes' scheme, Russia would not get any of this as reparation. If so, this was unacceptable. They could only consent to any scheme of this kind provided they received a certain amount of machinery from the Ruhr. They might agree to a total of 9, perhaps 8½ or even 8 billion dollars if 2 or 3 billions of this amount came from the Ruhr, all the rest to come from their own zone. This might be a basis for discussion.

M. Molotov then queried Mr. Byrnes' statement that 50% of German resources were in the Russian zone, and it was agreed that the figure could not be reconciled at present, as the Russians maintained that their zone contained less than 40%.

Mr. Eden said he had listened with great interest to this conversation. The real difficulty which worried him was that, owing to the allocation of large areas to Poland, there was no contribution from the Russian zone towards the feeding and fuelling of the large areas of Germany which used to be supplied from these sources. These supplies must therefore be made good from somewhere, but it was difficult to see how. If we had to supply to Berlin the percentage of coal which used to come from Silesia, we could only do so at the expense of France, Holland or Belgium, to whom the U.K. could not send any more after 1st August. He was interested in Mr. Byrnes' ideas, because they did seem to offer the possibility of our getting some supplies from the east in return for supplies from the west. He was anxious, however, lest this scheme might seem an apparent departure from Four Power unity.

M. Molotov at this point made some attempt to discuss the possible internationalisation of the Ruhr and asked what plans there were for this.

Mr. Eden said this was a big political question which might well be discussed, but the immediate problem was the difficult economic situation to be faced this winter. We simply could not go on sending food and coal to Berlin, when this only meant cutting down supplies for France and other Allied countries.

Mr. Byrnes remarked that there was another thing of which he was afraid. Any reparation which the Russians wished to receive from the British or American zones could be secured only from production over and above what the Germans must spend to import food and coal. He feared there would always be an argument with the Russians about the amount of food and other supplies which must be left to the Germans. If they evolved a plan which made the Russians get their reparation from the Germans and not from the Americans and the British, this would remove a constant source of irritation which might otherwise affect the peace.

M. Molotov said he was ready to agree to a limited amount of reparation from the Ruhr, but Russia could not do without this.

Mr. Eden replied by asking what help Russia could supply in the way of food and coal, and M. Molotov said this question must be discussed.

War Trophies[5]

Under the 'war trophies' is understood:

(1) All military property of Germany, including all military property, which belongs, is being used or was intended to be used by the military and para-military units of the enemy or by the members of these units;

(2) Property which was used by the enemy for military purposes and which in the course of the war was removed from Germany to serve the military needs of the Allies.

[5] This document is printed in slightly variant text *op. cit.*, vol. ii, p. 888; for the Russian text see *Berlinskaya konferentsiya*, p. 361.

No. 241

Record of Seventh Plenary Meeting held at Cecilienhof, Potsdam, on Monday, 23 July 1945 at 5 p.m.

P.(*Terminal*)7th Meeting [U 6197/3628/70]

Top secret

Present:

PREMIER STALIN, M. V. M. Molotov, M. A. Ya. Vyshinski, M. F. T. Gousev, M. A. A. Gromyko, M. K. V. Novikov, M. A. A. Sobolev, M. B. F. Podtzerob, M. V. N. Pavlov (*Interpreter*).

PRESIDENT TRUMAN, Mr. J. F. Byrnes, Mr. Joseph E. Davies, Mr. W. A. Harriman, Mr. J. C. Dunn, Mr. H. F. Matthews, Mr. B. V. Cohen, Mr. L. E. Thompson, Mr. C. E. Bohlen (*Interpreter*).

MR. CHURCHILL, Mr. Eden, Mr. Attlee, Sir A. Cadogan, Field-Marshal Sir H. Alexander (*Item 14*), Sir A. Clark Kerr, Sir W. Strang, Sir E. Bridges, Mr. N. Brook, Mr. P. J. Dixon, Mr. W. Hayter, Major A. Birse (*Interpreter*).

Contents

Minute	Subject
1.	Foreign Secretaries' Report
2.	Reparations: Germany, Austria and Italy
3.	Germany: Economic Problems
4.	Council of Foreign Ministers
5.	Territorial Trusteeship: Former Italian Colonies
6.	Germany: Directive to Allied Commanders
7.	Immediate Economic Problems of Europe: International Co-operation
8.	Tangier
9.	Agenda for Plenary Meeting
10.	Turkey
11.	Western Frontier of U.S.S.R.
12.	Syria and the Lebanon

13. Persia: Withdrawal of Troops
14. Austria
15. Future Meetings of the Conference

1. *Foreign Secretaries' Report*

M. MOLOTOV submitted the report of the Meeting of the Foreign Secretaries held that morning. This is set out in Minutes 2–9 below. The report was accepted by the Meeting.

2. *Reparations: Germany, Austria and Italy*
(Previous Reference: F. (Terminal) 6th Meeting,[1] Minute 2.)

M. MOLOTOV said that he had submitted to his colleagues two memoranda:

(*a*) Plan of reparation from Germany (P. (Terminal) 29).[2]
(*b*) Draft for consideration by the Economic Committee on 'once for all' deliveries from Germany (P. (Terminal) 30).[3]

It had been decided that the Economic Committee should give preliminary consideration to these memoranda and that they should be considered at the Meeting of the Foreign Secretaries on the following day.

3. *Germany: Economic Problems*
(Previous Reference: F. (Terminal) 6th Meeting,[1] Minute 3.)

M. MOLOTOV said that the Foreign Secretaries had resumed the discussion of P. (Terminal) 15.[4] He had indicated that he was prepared to withdraw his amendment to paragraph 13; and had suggested that paragraph 18 should be deleted, on the understanding that the matters affected by this paragraph would be considered by the Allied Control Commission for Germany and that any point on which the Commission could not agree would be referred to the three Governments for decision. No agreement had been reached between the three Foreign Secretaries on this matter and it had been decided to refer it for decision at a Plenary Meeting.

He had proposed a new paragraph 19, which Mr. Byrnes had said was unacceptable to the United States Government. He had then suggested an alternative formula, under which exports from Germany approved by the Control Commission would be given priority over everything else, but in all other cases priority would be given to reparation deliveries. No agreement had been reached on this matter, which it had been decided to refer to a Plenary Meeting.

4. *Council of Foreign Ministers*
(Previous Reference: F. (Terminal) 6th Meeting,[1] Minute 4.)

M. MOLOTOV said that the Foreign Secretaries had approved the constitution of the Council of Foreign Ministers as set out in a revised draft submitted by the Drafting Committee (P. Terminal) 31).[5]

[1] No. 233.   [2] No. 242.   [3] No. 243.
[4] No. 210.   [5] No. 244.

The Committee had also approved the terms of the telegrams to be despatched to the Governments of France and China, and had agreed that these communications should be despatched 48 hours before the release of the final communiqué issued at the end of the present Conference.

5. *Territorial Trusteeship: Former Italian Colonies*
(Previous Reference: F. (Terminal) 6th Meeting,[1] Minute 5.)

M. Molotov said that the Memorandum submitted by the Soviet Government (P. (Terminal) 13)[6] had been discussed.

Mr. Eden had said that in his view there were two stages. First, it should be settled which Italian colonies Italy should lose. This was a question which should be settled when the Peace Treaty with Italy was being drawn up. When this question had been decided, it would be for the World Organisation to settle what form of trusteeship would be appropriate for any colonies which it might be decided not to restore to Italy.

Mr. Byrnes had proposed to postpone settlement of this matter until the Peace Treaty with Italy, when all territorial questions affecting Italy would be settled.

The Foreign Secretaries had agreed to take note that the Soviet Government would raise this matter at the first meeting of the Council of Foreign Ministers in September 1945.

6. *Germany: Directive to Allied Commanders*
(Previous Reference: F. (Terminal) 6th Meeting,[1] Minute 6.)

M. Molotov said that the United States Delegation had submitted a draft directive (P. (Terminal) 24)[7] to the Commanders-in-Chief of the occupying forces in Germany conveying to them the decisions of the Conference which affected them. The Foreign Secretaries had agreed that an arrangement of this kind would be desirable and had appointed a Committee consisting of:

Soviet Delegation: M. Gousev, M. Sobolev;
United States Delegation: Mr. R. Murphy, Mr. J. W. Riddleberger;
United Kingdom Delegation: Sir William Strang, Mr. W. Harrison;

to report on the best means of (*a*) informing the Soviet, United States and British Commanders in Germany of all decisions of the Conference affecting them, and (*b*) securing similar action on the part of the French Government.

7. *Immediate Economic Problems of Europe: International Co-operation*
(Previous Reference: F. (Terminal) 6th Meeting,[1] Minute 7.)

M. Molotov reported that it had been decided to appoint the following Committee:

United States Delegation: Mr. W. Clayton, Mr. E. W. Pauley;
United Kingdom Delegation: Mr. Brand, Mr. J. Coulson;
Soviet Delegation: M. Artumyan, M. Gerostchenko;

to consider and report to the Foreign Secretaries' meeting on the issues

[6] No. 203.　　　　　　　　[7] See No. 224, note 15.

raised in a Memorandum by the United States Delegation on this subject (P. (Terminal) 32).[8]

8. *Tangier*

(Previous Reference: F. (Terminal) 6th Meeting,[1] Minute 8.)

M. MOLOTOV said that on the Soviet Memorandum (P. (Terminal) 28)[9] the following conclusions had been reached:

(*a*) that the Governments of the Three Great Powers were agreed in principle that the Tangier zone, in view of its strategic importance, should continue to be administered as an international zone; and

(*b*) that arrangements would be made for representatives of the Soviet Government to participate in the preliminary discussions which were to be held in Paris in the near future about the reconstitution of the international zone of Tangier.

9. *Agenda for Plenary Meeting*

The Foreign Secretaries recommended that the following subjects should be discussed at the present meeting:

(*a*) *Turkey.*
(*b*) *Western Frontier of the U.S.S.R.*
(*c*) *Syria and the Lebanon.*
(*d*) *Persia: Withdrawal of Troops.*

10. *Turkey*

(*Previous Reference:* P. (Terminal) 6th Meeting,[10] Minute 9.)

PRESIDENT TRUMAN suggested that the Conference should resume the discussion of this matter, and asked Mr. Churchill whether he had any further remarks.

MR. CHURCHILL said that he had made it clear on the previous day that he could not support the fortification of the Straits by a Russian base, and he could not press the Turks to agree to this.

PREMIER STALIN said that on the previous day Mr. Churchill had said that Russia had frightened Turkey, and that one of the main reasons was the concentration of too many Russian troops in Bulgaria. The information cited by Mr. Churchill was out of date. He did not know how he had been informed by the Turks, but he was bound to say that Russia had far fewer troops in Bulgaria than the British had in Greece.

MR. CHURCHILL asked how many British troops Premier Stalin thought were in Greece.

PREMIER STALIN said 5 Divisions.

MR. CHURCHILL said that we had only 2 Divisions—the 4th British and the 4th Indian Divisions.

PREMIER STALIN enquired whether there were any armoured divisions.

MR. CHURCHILL said there was none. Speaking from memory, we had about 40,000 men in Greece. Field-Marshal Alexander was here, and would

[8] No. 245.   [9] See No. 226, note 15.   [10] No. 226.

be able to give a more accurate figure, if his own had been mistaken. (Later in the meeting Field-Marshal Alexander confirmed Mr. Churchill's statement.)

PREMIER STALIN said that he entirely accepted Mr. Churchill's figures. The Russians had 30,000 men in Bulgaria. If required, the Chief of the Russian General Staff would make a report on this. There was therefore nothing for the Turks to be afraid of, particularly as the Turks had 20 to 23 Divisions on the frontier.

Continuing, Premier Stalin referred to the question of the rectification of frontiers which Mr. Churchill thought had frightened the Turks. Perhaps the suggested restoration of the pre-war frontier of Czarist Russia might have frightened them. He (Premier Stalin) bore in mind that Kars was part of Armenia, and Ardahan was part of Georgia. These questions of the restoration of frontiers would not have arisen if the Turks had not asked for an alliance. An alliance meant that Russia undertook to defend the Turkish frontiers in the same way as Turkey undertook to defend the Russian frontiers. Russia considered the existing frontier in the area of Kars and Ardahan to be incorrect, and had told Turkey that this must be rectified. If the Turks did not want this rectified then the question of an alliance would be dropped.

Premier Stalin asked what there was in this for the Turks to be afraid of?

Premier Stalin then referred to the question of the Straits. The position for such a great State as Russia was desperate. The Montreux Convention in all its aspects was directed against, and inimical to, Russia. Under the Convention Turkey had the right to block the Straits against any ships—not only if Turkey was at war with a State but also if it seemed to Turkey that there was a threat of war. It was also left for Turkey to decide when a threat existed. This was an impossible situation. Turkey could always block the Straits as soon as she thought there was a threat. Moreover, Russia had the same rights under the Convention as the Japanese Emperor. This was ridiculous but a fact.

The result of this situation was that a small State (Turkey), supported by Great Britain, held a great State (Russia) by the throat. Imagine what a commotion would be raised in Great Britain if a similar régime existed at Gibraltar or the Suez canal, and in the United States in the case of the Panama Canal!

Therefore the point at issue was how to give Russia the right to pass freely to and from the Black Sea. As Turkey herself was too weak to guarantee the passage of the Straits in case of complications, Russia would like to see it guaranteed by force.

MR. CHURCHILL asked whether Premier Stalin suggested that it should be guaranteed by force or by law?

PREMIER STALIN said that the right must be guaranteed by force, as it was in the Panama Canal by the United States Navy and in the Suez Canal by the British Navy. He enquired whether the Prime Minister thought a naval base in the Straits would be unacceptable to Turkey.

MR. CHURCHILL said that he thought it would be unacceptable.

PREMIER STALIN said that in that case Russia should be given a base in some other place, where the Russian Fleet could be repaired and refuelled, and, together with its Allies, keep order in that area. It would be ridiculous to allow the present situation to continue.

PRESIDENT TRUMAN said that the view of the United States Government was that the Montreux Convention ought to be revised. The Straits should be a free waterway for all, and guaranteed by the Great Powers. After much study he had come to the conclusion that all the wars in the last 200 years had originated in the area bounded by the Baltic Sea and the Mediterranean on the North and South and by the Eastern border of France and the Western border of Russia. In the last two wars the peace of the world had been overturned first by Austria and then by Germany. It should be the business of the present Conference and of the coming Peace Conference to see that this did not happen again. To a great extent this object could be accomplished by securing freedom for the passage of goods and intercourse in that part of Europe which he had just mentioned, in the same way as in the United States.

President Truman said that he would table an additional paper setting out his proposals. He wished to see everyone with free access to all the seas of the world. President Truman then read out his paper (subsequently circulated as P. (Terminal) 33)[11] entitled: 'Free and Unrestricted Navigation of International Inland Waterways.'

President Truman said that these proposals should apply to the Kiel Canal and to the Straits. He had no wish to have another war in 25 years starting perhaps on the Danube. The ambition of the United States Government was to see a Europe which was self-supporting, and which would make the United Kingdom, Russia and France prosperous and satisfied. The United States Government also wanted a prosperous Europe with which they could do business on equal terms. The proposals he had just read out were a step in this direction.

He thought that the territorial matters between Russia and Turkey should be settled direct between them, but that this question of the Straits and of other international waterways was a matter which concerned the whole world, and must be settled by the Great Powers.

MR. CHURCHILL said that he strongly supported Premier Stalin's wish to revise the Montreux Convention, with the object of securing to Russia free and unrestricted navigation through the Straits between the Black Sea and the Ægean Sea—by both merchant ships and warships, whether in peace or war. He entirely agreed with the President that this freedom of navigation should be guaranteed by all concerned. A guarantee by the Great Powers and by the other interested Powers would certainly be effective. He hoped that Premier Stalin would consider this alternative rather than press for a Russian base near Constantinople.

[11] No. 246.

With regard to the other waterways mentioned by the President, Mr. Churchill said that he was in full accord with the general line of the proposals. The Kiel Canal should certainly be free and open, and guaranteed by the Great Powers. He also attached great importance to the freedom of navigation on the Rhine and the Danube.

In conclusion, he felt that there was a very large measure of agreement on these matters between the three Powers.

PRESIDENT TRUMAN said that there was no disagreement about the revision of the Montreux Convention.

MR. CHURCHILL added that neither was there any doubt about the purpose for which it should be revised.

PREMIER STALIN said that it would be necessary to examine the President's proposals carefully.

Discussion on this matter was therefore adjourned.

11. *Western Frontier of U.S.S.R.*

The Conference discussed the Memorandum submitted by the Soviet Delegation (P. (Terminal) 27).[12]

PREMIER STALIN said that this question had been discussed at the Tehran Conference. It had been raised because all the existing Russian ports in the Baltic froze during the winter for a shorter or longer period. He had stated that it would be necessary for Russia to have one ice-free port at the expense of Germany. His arguments in favour of this course had been—first, Russia had shed so much blood and gone through untold suffering during the present war. Secondly, Russia was anxious to secure some piece of German territory, so as to give some small satisfaction to the tens of millions of her people who had suffered in the war.

Neither President Roosevelt nor Mr. Churchill had raised any objection to this proposal, which he therefore regarded as agreed between the three Great Powers. He now wanted the matter confirmed by the present Conference.

PRESIDENT TRUMAN said that in principle the United States Delegation were ready to agree to this proposal, though they thought that some examination of it on ethnological grounds might prove necessary. But he raised no objection to Russia acquiring a piece of German territory.

MR. CHURCHILL said that Premier Stalin was right in saying that this matter had been raised at Tehran. It had been referred to again in October 1944 at the Moscow Conference, in connection with the talks about the Curzon Line.

PREMIER STALIN confirmed that this was so.

Continuing, MR. CHURCHILL said that on 15th December, 1944, he had made a speech in the House of Commons, in which he had mentioned that the Soviet Government desired to have the ice-free port of Königsberg, and that the Polish frontier would run to the south of this port.[13] He had made it clear that His Majesty's Government were in sympathy with this wish.

[12] No. 229.
[13] See *Parl. Debs.*, 5th ser., *H. of C.*, vol. 406, col. 1483.

The only question which now arose was what he might describe as the legal question of transference. At present the Soviet draft involved an admission by us all that East Prussia no longer existed, and that Königsberg and the territory around it was [not] under the authority of the Allied Control Commission for Germany, and that Lithuania was now one of the Soviet Republics. All these were really matters for the final peace settlement. But so far as His Majesty's Government were concerned, we were ready to support the Soviet wish that the Peace Treaty should make provision for the U.S.S.R. acquiring the port of Königsberg.

Mr. Churchill said that he had made this statement as one of principle. He had not examined the exact line on the map, and this would be a question which would have to be examined at the Peace Conference. But he would like to assure Premier Stalin of our continuing support of the Russian position in this part of the world when the Peace Conference came.

Premier Stalin said that he suggested nothing more at the present time. A final settlement of this question would be made at the Peace Conference. He was satisfied with the assurances given by the British and United States Governments.

Mr. Churchill said that some redrafting of the Russian statement would be necessary if it was proposed to incorporate it in any communiqué issued at the end of the Conference. The matter would have to be dealt with in somewhat more general terms. Meanwhile the understanding of the three Great Powers would be recorded in the conclusions of the present Conference.

12. *Syria and the Lebanon*

(Previous Reference: P. (Terminal) 6th Meeting,[10] Item 6).

Premier Stalin handed round a memorandum[14] by the Soviet Delegation proposing that, subject to prior consultation with the French Government, the situation in the Levant States should be discussed at a conference attended by representatives of the Governments of Great Britain, the United States, the U.S.S.R. and France.

Mr. Churchill said that at the present time the burden of maintaining peace and order in Syria and the Lebanon had fallen upon our shoulders. We had no intention or desire to gain any advantages in these countries except those enjoyed by other Powers. At the time when we had entered Syria and the Lebanon, in order to throw out the Germans and the troops of Vichy France, we had made arrangements with the French by which both Powers recognised the independence of the Syrians and the Lebanese. In consideration of the very long historical connection of France with these countries, we had said that we would not object to France having a favoured position there, if that were satisfactorily arranged with the new independent Governments of Syria and the Lebanon. We had told General de Gaulle that the moment he made a treaty with Syria and the Lebanon which was

[14] This brief memorandum of 23 July 1945, which was as indicated below, is printed in *Berlinskaya konferentsiya*, p. 361.

satisfactory to France and to those countries, we would withdraw our troops. To do so before that would probably lead to the massacre of the French civilians and the small number of French troops there. We should not like to see that happen since it would lead to very great excitement throughout the Arab world, which would increase our difficulties in maintaining order in Palestine and Iraq. A great outbreak of turbulence and warfare in this part of the world might also affect Egypt. There could not be a worse moment for such a disturbance in the Middle East, since it would endanger the lines of communication through the Suez Canal, through which large reinforcements of troops and supplies, both British and American, were passing to sustain the Forces engaged in the war against Japan. Those lines of communication were of great importance at the present time to the United States, as well as to Great Britain.

General de Gaulle had acted very unwisely in this region. Against all our advice and entreaties he had sent about 500 troops to Syria in a ship of war, and it had been this which had led to the outbreak which even now had hardly died away. How foolish this was, for what could 500 men do? They had, however, been a spark which had fired the uprising against the French. The Government and people of Iraq had wished to go at once to the help of the Syrians; and the whole of the Arab world, including Egypt, had been convulsed with excitement.

Lately, however, General de Gaulle had agreed to hand over the *Troupes Spéciales* to the local Governments. This afforded some hope that we should now be able to reach—he would not say an agreement—but a settlement with General de Gaulle that would guarantee the independence of Syria and the Lebanon and secure for France some recognition of the cultural and commercial interests which she had built up there over so many years.

Mr. Churchill said that he would like to repeat before the present Conference that Great Britain had no wish to remain in these countries one day longer than was necessary. We should be delighted to withdraw from what had been a thankless task, which we had undertaken in the interests of our Allies. As, however, this matter rested between ourselves, the French and the Governments of Syria and the Lebanon, we did not welcome the proposal put forward by the Soviet Delegation for a conference in which the United States and the Soviet Union would join with France and Great Britain and come to decisions. The whole burden had rested upon us; nobody had helped us—although we had received the diplomatic support of the United States—and we should not therefore welcome a conference of the kind suggested. If the United States were prepared to take our place that, of course, would be a different situation.

President Truman said that the United States Government had no desire to assume this responsibility.

The President said that, at the outset of the disorder in the Levant, he had been assured by Mr. Churchill that the British Government had enough troops in that area to prevent the outbreak of war in the Middle East; and it was with his full agreement that British troops were ordered to intervene so as to safeguard the lines of communication for the war against Japan. He must, however, make it clear that on one point the United States Government were not in full agreement with the policy of the British Government. They did not consider that France deserved to retain any special privileges in Syria and the Lebanon, especially after the troubles which they had provoked in that part of the world. In any event, it was the considered view of the United States Government that no country should have special privileges in the Levant States—or indeed elsewhere. They stood for equal rights for all, with special privileges for none.

PREMIER STALIN asked whether he could assume from what had been said that his colleagues did not claim that the French had any privileged position in Syria and the Lebanon.

PRESIDENT TRUMAN said that this was so, as far as the United States Government was concerned.

MR. CHURCHILL said that the British Government, for their part, would like to see some special privileges conceded to the French in Syria and the Lebanon by the Governments of those countries. The British Government had not, however, undertaken to make any serious exertions to procure these privileges for the French. Their position was that, if the French could obtain them, they would not object; indeed, they would smile benignly on their achievement. The French had schools and archæological establishments in these countries; many French people lived there; and the French claims to special interests in these areas went back as far as the Crusades. They even had in France a popular song: 'Partant pour la Syrie.' At the same time, the British Government would not embark on any serious dispute in order to secure these privileges for the French: they would go no further than give them their friendly backing in their negotiations with the Governments of the two Levant States.

In reply to questions by Premier Stalin, Mr. Churchill made it clear that it was the view of the British Government that the French would have to secure these concessions, in negotiation, from the Governments of Syria and the Lebanon.

PRESIDENT TRUMAN said that the position of the United States Government was that they stood for equal rights for all, and special privileges for none. They would do nothing to prevent the Governments of Syria and the Lebanon from conceding special privileges to the French; but he did not think it likely that these Governments would, in fact, make such concessions.

PREMIER STALIN said that he shared the President's view on this point.

Premier Stalin said that in view of Mr. Churchill's statement, for which he was most grateful, he would withdraw his proposal that the position in the Levant States should be the subject of discussion between representatives of the Governments of Great Britain, the United States, the U.S.S.R. and France.

MR. CHURCHILL and PRESIDENT TRUMAN thanked Premier Stalin and said that they were much obliged to him for withdrawing this proposal.

13. *Persia: Withdrawal of Troops*

Mr. Churchill said that the United Kingdom Delegation had submitted a memorandum (P. (Terminal) 16)[15] proposing a joint programme for the progressive withdrawal of Allied forces from Persia. He invited the views of his colleagues on the proposals set out in this memorandum.

Premier Stalin said that these proposals seemed to be based on the assumption that the period during which Allied forces might remain in Persia, by virtue of the Anglo-Soviet-Persian Treaty of the 29th June [January], 1942, had already expired. The view of the Soviet Government was that it had not yet expired, and should not be regarded as expiring until after the end of the war with Japan. Article 5 of the Treaty provided that these forces should be withdrawn 'not later than six months after all hostilities between the Allied Powers and Germany and her associates had [have] been suspended.' Japan was one of Germany's associates and, strictly speaking, the time-limit in the Treaty would not expire until six months after the end of the Japanese war. Nevertheless, the Soviet Government accepted the proposal in paragraph 1 of the Memorandum by the United Kingdom Delegation that the Allied forces should be withdrawn from Persia *pari passu* and in stages before the final Treaty date was reached; and they were further prepared to agree that the first of the three stages proposed by the United Kingdom Delegation—the withdrawal of British and Soviet Forces from Tehran—should be put into force at once.

Mr. Churchill said that the British Government had been anxious to secure agreement that the two further stages which they proposed should follow immediately upon the first, so that the whole operation could be completed well within the time-limit assigned by the Treaty. They had assured the Persian Government that British troops would be withdrawn from Persia after the war with Germany was over. More than two months had passed since the end of hostilities with Germany; and the British Government would have wished, not only to carry out the first stage of withdrawal, but also to agree on the second and third stages so that the whole process of withdrawal might take place in an orderly manner within the time prescribed by the Treaty.

Premier Stalin said that he was unwilling to commit himself at this stage to anything beyond the immediate withdrawal of British and Soviet troops from Tehran. The time-limit under the Treaty was still some way ahead and the proposals for further withdrawals could be considered later on.

Mr. Churchill suggested that the Conference should approve the immediate withdrawal of Allied troops from Tehran and should agree that the further stages of the withdrawal should be considered at the first meeting of the Council of Foreign Ministers, which was to be held in London in September, 1945.

Premier Stalin said that he would be prepared to accept this suggestion.

President Truman said that the United States Government, for their

[15] No. 220.

part, did not propose to delay the withdrawal of the whole of their troops from Persia, since these troops were required elsewhere for the prosecution of the Japanese war. It was possible that the withdrawal of all the United States forces in Persia might be completed within 60 days.

PREMIER STALIN said that, in case the United States Government had any anxieties on this point, he could assure the President that the Soviet Government had no intention of taking any action against Persia.

It was agreed that the British and Soviet Forces should be withdrawn from Tehran at once; and that the Council of Foreign Ministers at their first meeting in September 1945, should consider the further stages in the withdrawal of Allied forces from Persia.

14. *Austria*

(Previous Reference: P. (Terminal) 6th Meeting,[10] Minute 1.)

MR. CHURCHILL said that he had a question to raise about the feeding of the civil population in the zones of occupation in Vienna. There were some 500,000 civilians in the British Zone. As the food supplies for Vienna had always come from the east of the city, we were not able to undertake the feeding of these 500,000. The suggestion which he wished to make was that Russia should continue to provide food supplies for civilians in the British Zone until a more permanent arrangement could be worked out. He asked Field-Marshal Alexander to explain the position in further detail.

FIELD-MARSHAL ALEXANDER said that the situation was as Mr. Churchill had stated. There were some 500,000 civilians to be fed. He had not got the necessary food to send from Italy. There was a small reserve in the Klagenfurt area; but it would last no more than three weeks to a month at the most. It therefore appeared that, if we were to undertake the feeding of the civil population in the British Zone of Vienna, the food would have to come from the United States.

PRESIDENT TRUMAN said that there were about 375,000 civilians in the United States Zone. In view of the many calls on shipping and transport, it would be impossible for the United States to undertake any further commitment in connection with the supply of food to Vienna.

PREMIER STALIN said that he would like to discuss the position with Marshal Koniev, who would know what supplies would have to be provided to tide over until the harvest.

MR. CHURCHILL repeated that the difficulty was that this 500,000 people in the British Zone and 375,000 in the United States Zone had always drawn their food from the east and would have to continue to do so even after the harvest.

PREMIER STALIN explained that the Soviet Government had agreed with Dr. Renner's Government to provide food for Vienna[16] until the harvest had been gathered in, viz., until August or September. He would discuss

---

[16] According to the Soviet record (*Conferences: Soviet Documents*, p. 239) the Soviet Government had agreed to provide the Austrian Government with 'some food in return for goods'.

the matter with Marshal Koniev either that evening or the following day and would report to the Plenary Meeting without delay.

MR. CHURCHILL said that Field-Marshal Alexander had been reluctant to take up occupation of the British Zone in Vienna until this food problem had been settled. FIELD-MARSHAL ALEXANDER said that, if Premier Stalin could help him with this food problem, he would like his troops to go forward into their Zone at once.

PREMIER STALIN repeated that he would be able to give his answer on the following day.

MR. CHURCHILL thanked the Marshal for his reply.

PREMIER STALIN then made the further suggestion that it would be helpful if the British and United States Governments would recognise that the authority of the Renner Government extended to their Zones of occupation in Vienna. This would facilitate the provision and distribution of this food. It would not imply the recognition of the Renner Government nor involve establishing diplomatic relations.

PRESIDENT TRUMAN and MR. CHURCHILL undertook to consider this suggestion.

15. *Future Meetings of the Conference*

MR. CHURCHILL said that it would be necessary for him and Mr. Attlee to return to London on Wednesday, 25th July, so that they might be there when the results of the General Election were announced on 26th July. Mr. Eden would also wish to return to London at the same time. Subject to the views of the President and Premier Stalin, he proposed that they should leave soon after midday on 25th July and return during the afternoon on 27th July. It would be possible, therefore, to hold a Plenary Meeting during the morning on 25th July; and representatives of the British Government should be back in time to attend a Plenary Meeting in the late afternoon of 27th July.

Mr. Churchill further suggested that the Foreign Secretaries' meetings might continue during the period while Mr. Eden was away, if the President and Premier Stalin were content that during this time Mr. Eden should be represented by Sir Alexander Cadogan.

PRESIDENT TRUMAN and PREMIER STALIN said that they were glad to accept the proposals put forward by Mr. Churchill.

It was agreed that the Plenary Meeting on Wednesday, 25th July, should be held at 11 a.m.; and that during the period 25th–27th July Sir Alexander Cadogan should represent Mr. Eden at Foreign Secretaries' Meetings.

Cabinet Offices, Potsdam, 23rd July, 1945

CALENDARS TO NO. 241

i *24–27 July 1945 Minutes by Mr. McDermott and Mr. Howard* on plenary discussions at Potsdam on Turkey and the Straits. *U.K. Delegation briefs of 24 July on (a) Turkey and the Straits.* Discussion will doubtless begin with

President Truman's proposal in minute 10 above. 'Stalin will probably try a diversion by alluding to *Suez* (he may well not allude to Panama, so as to divide us from the Americans)'; (*b*) *Régime for international inland waterways.* Proposes support for American proposal in application to the Danube, Rhine, Kiel Canal and the Straits [R 12516/44/44; F.O. 934/5/41(5); F.O. 934/5/38 (2)].

ii *24 July 1945 U.K. Delegation briefs on* (*a*) *feeding Vienna:* important that Russians should continue responsibility for supply of food and coal until quadripartite machinery set up, when treatment of Austria as an economic whole is an essential British interest; (*b*) *question of recognition of Renner Government* [F.O. 934/4/25(9)].

No. 242

Memorandum submitted by the Soviet Delegation (Berlin)[1]
P.(Terminal)29 [U 6197/3628/70]

Top secret   *23 July 1945*

Plan of reparations from Germany

1. The total sum of Reparations 20 billion dollars which is accepted for consideration has to be covered approximately 50 per cent. by the way of once for all removals from the national wealth of Germany within two years after the capitulation and approximately 50 per cent. by the way of the annual deliveries in kind within 10 years after the capitulation.

2. The once for all removals from the national wealth of Germany are to be exacted from the following branches of her economic life:–

	Billion dollars
(1) War and chemical industries (aircraft production, tank production, naval shipbuilding, arms and ammunition production, production of power and explosives, synthetic rubber and fuel, artificial fibre, cellulose, koke-chemie)	2.0 – 2.2
(2) Iron and steel, non-ferrous metals, engineering (including electrical industry), coal, power stations ..	2.3 – 2.7
(3) Building industry, textiles, food industry, printing, transport (including water transport), communications (radio, telephone, telegraph), equipment of ports, warehouses, &c.	1.8 – 2.0
(4) Foreign investments and claims of Germany ..	1.1 – 1.4
(5) Shares of the German enterprises (railways, ports, canals, &c.), foreign currency, precious metals ..	1.9 – 2.3
(6) Miscellaneous	0.9 – 1.2
	10.0 – 11.8

[1] Printed in *Berlinskaya konferentsiya*, pp. 354–5.

For the purposes of removals German property is property situated on the territory of Germany in 1937 frontiers as well as German property abroad.

3. To fix the following approximate list of goods with which the post-war Germany has to pay her annual deliveries in kind:–

Coal, brikets.

Chemicals (drugs, dyes, potassium, &c.).

Machinery, tools.

Cement, building materials.

Timber, paper.

Sugar.

Cattle, agricultural produce.

Ceramics.

Medical instruments, optical apparatus.

River shipbuilding.

4. To fix the total sum of annual deliveries in kind, 1 billion dollars per annum or 10 billion dollars in 10 years. To ask Allied Commission on Reparations to make more detailed calculations concerning these deliveries.

5. The basis of calculations are prices of 1938 plus 15 per cent. on equipment and 10 per cent. on raw materials and finished goods.

6. The rate of exchange: 1 dollar = 3.5 marks.[2]

[2] This memorandum was minuted in the Foreign Office as follows: 'The effect of para 5 is to render the Russian figure of 20 billion dollars more realistic than if a more reasonable basis of valuation were adopted. In that it enables the Russians to quote for internal public purposes a handsome figure for reparation—a point the importance of which they have always emphasised—there is something to be said for adopting inflated values for reparation. Others besides the Russians may find the practice convenient politically.   Categories 1 to 3 deserve no particular comment. Category 4 should in our view be excluded, but as our view seems to have met with no enthusiasm from either the Americans or the Russians we may have to give way. It remains to be seen what difficulties are presented by category 5. We are not particularly anxious to take over German enterprises as reparation, and I should doubt if others will want to either. The last sentence of para 2 is interesting in view of the fuss the Russians have made over reparation delivery to other powers from the eastern territories that they want to transfer to Poland. John S. Dent 26/7.'
'Shares in German enterprises, at best, will only give us marks which are no good to us. I hope we shall not be forced into the position of having to agree. E. L. H[all] P[atch] 30/7.'
'This was discussed by the Economic Subcommittee on July 24th (Gen 72/24 [No. 266]). Criticisms were directed at the excessive values of categories 1, 2 & 3, (according to the Americans they equal the total moveable assets in these categories) at the inclusion of category 3 at all, and at the effrontery of the Russians in delaying over a month in producing it, and then in expecting it to be discussed immediately and in the absence of any explanation of the bases on which it was compiled.   It is now overtaken by events, and particularly by the proposal to allocate once for all deliveries so far as possible by zones. J. S. D. 1/8.'

No. 243

Memorandum submitted by the Soviet Delegation (Berlin)[1]

P.(Terminal)30 [U 6197/3628/70]

Top secret

23 July 1945

Advance deliveries from Germany

1. Pending the establishment of a permanent allied reparation agency, advance deliveries (removals) should be based upon the urgency of need of

[1] Printed *op cit.*, pp. 356–7.

suffered Nations for rehabilitation purposes, and should be made as advance deliveries with subsequent accounting of these deliveries as reparations or restitution, or for purchase account of the recipient nations.

2. With respect to advance deliveries of capital goods to all United Nations, the following procedure should be adopted:–

(a) Immediate establishment of a sub-commission of the Allied Commission on Reparations to be situated in Berlin, and to be composed of representatives of the nations participating in the Allied Commission on Reparations. This sub-commission should keep in constant consultation with the Control Council, and should keep the Control Council informed of all its activities.

(b) The Allied Commission on Reparations will transmit to its sub-commission a list of industries from which advance deliveries of equipment will be allowed.

(c) Advance deliveries (removals) of capital equipment from those industries up to an agreed percentage of the movable assets, expressed in physical terms, may be made upon the approval or recommendation of the sub-commission. Shipping documents covering such advance deliveries (removals) shall include notification to the receiving country that in the final accounting such deliveries (removals) may be deemed by the Allied Commission on Reparations to be on account of reparations or restitution.

(d) Each of the occupying Powers may remove or permit to be removed from its zone of occupation, plant and equipment from any industries in such list, subject to the following conditions:–

(1) With respect to any removal by an occupying Power for its own account, the respective zone commander shall notify the sub-commission of the contemplated removal, giving the sub-commission an opportunity to enter such removal in the plan of advance deliveries.

(2) With respect to any removal from the zone of one occupying Power for the account of another United Nation (whether or not such United Nation be an occupying Power) such removal shall only be permitted upon the approval or recommendation of the sub-commission.

3. With respect to advance deliveries to all United Nations of raw materials out of current production or inventories, such deliveries may be made upon the approval or recommendation of the sub-commission on the basis of the need of the claimants after due regard to the supplies available and the requirements of the occupation forces. Shipping documents covering such advance deliveries shall include notification to the receiving country that, in the final accounting, such deliveries may be deemed by the Allied Commission on Reparations to be on (1) export account to be paid for in acceptable currencies, (2) reparation, or (3) restitution.

4. Adequate and uniform accounting shall be instituted with respect to all deliveries effected under the above proposed plan.

5. Claimant nations should be notified of the establishment of the foregoing procedures for effecting urgently needed advance deliveries.

6. It shall be mutually agreed that each of the occupying Powers shall submit, within six months of the date hereof, a statement of all property removed from Germany after the termination of war with Germany.

CALENDAR TO NO. 243

i *25 July 1945   Letter from Mr. Dent to Mr. Playfair (Treasury).* Since No. 243 substantially accepts unfortunate proposals by Mr. Pauley (cf. No. 55), foresees unnecessary difficulty in getting them sufficiently altered [UE 3254/624/77].

No. 244

Note by the British Secretariat (Berlin)
P.(Terminal)31 [U 6197/3628/70]

Top secret   *23 July 1945*

Council of Foreign Ministers

(Circulated to the United Kingdom Delegation only)

Annexed are:–

(*a*) The constitution of the Council of Foreign Ministers—Annex I.[1]

(*b*) The telegram of invitation to be sent to the Governments of China and France—Annex II.[2]

(*c*) A draft passage on this matter for inclusion in the final protocol and published report of the Conference—Annex III.

Annexes I and II have been approved by the Conference (F. (Terminal) 6th Meeting,[3] Minute 4, and P. (Terminal) 7th Meeting,[4] Minute 4). Annex III has not been considered by the Foreign Secretaries.

ANNEX III TO NO. 244

Draft passage for inclusion in the final Protocol and published Report of the Conference

The Conference reached the following agreement for the establishment of a Council of Foreign Ministers to do the necessary preparatory work for the peace settlements:

[Here insert final text, *i.e.*, Annex I.][5]

---

[1] Not printed. This annex, headed 'The establishment of a Council of Foreign Ministers', was the same as section IA (1) – (4) of No. 603.

[2] Not printed. This annex, headed 'Draft for identical invitation to be sent separately by each of the three Governments to the Governments of China and France', corresponded to the text in inverted commas immediately following this heading in section IB of No. 603.

[3] No. 233.

[4] No. 241.

[5] Square brackets as in filed copy.

It was agreed that the three Governments should each address an identical invitation to the Governments of China and France to adopt this text and to join in establishing the Council.

It was understood that the establishment of the Council of Foreign Ministers for the specific purposes named in the text would be without prejudice to the agreement of the Crimea Conference that there should be periodical consultation between the Foreign Secretaries of the United States, the Union of Soviet Socialist Republics and the United Kingdom.

The Conference also considered the position of the European Advisory Commission in the light of the Agreement to establish the Council of Foreign Ministers. It was noted with satisfaction that the Commission had ably discharged its principal tasks by the recommendations that it had furnished for the terms of surrender for Germany, for the zones of occupation in Germany and Austria, and for the inter-Allied control machinery in those countries. It was felt that further work of a detailed character for the co-ordination of Allied policy for the control of Germany and Austria would in future fall within the competence of the Allied Control Commission at Berlin and the Allied Commission at Vienna. Accordingly the Conference agreed to recommend to the Member Governments of the European Advisory Commission that the Commission might now be dissolved.

No. 245

Memorandum by the United States Delegation (Berlin)[1]
P.(Terminal)32 [U 6197/3628/70]

Top secret   *23 July 1945*

Co-operation in solving immediate European economic problems

The urgent tasks of European relief and reconstruction can be most effectively carried out only if supported by the combined efforts of the United States, the Soviet Union, and the United Kingdom. It is, therefore, recommended that the three Governments agree to participate fully in the Emergency Economic Committee for Europe (E.E.C.E.), European Coal Organisation (E.C.O.) and the European Central Inland Transport Authority (E.C.I.T.O.). It should be the aim of the three Governments to assist in making these organisations effective agencies for handling the problems of relief and reconstruction by day-to-day co-operation in their activities.

CALENDAR TO No. 245

i *24 July 1945 Letter from Mr. Coulson (Berlin) to Mr. Ronald.* Describes meetings of the subcommittee to consider No. 245. Attitude of the Soviet representatives [W 10226/22/13].

[1] Printed in *F.R.U.S. Berlin*, vol. ii, p. 1160.

No. 246

Memorandum by the United States Delegation (Berlin)[1]

P.(Terminal)33 [*U 6197/3628/70*]

Top secret   *23 July 1945*

Free and unrestricted navigation of international
inland waterways

The United States Government proposes that there be free and unrestricted navigation of such inland waterways as border on two or more states and that the regulation of such navigation be provided by international authorities representative of all nations directly interested in navigation on the waterways concerned.

As an initial step there should be set up as soon as possible interim navigation agencies for the Danube and the Rhine. The functions of the interim navigation agencies should be the restoration and development of navigation facilities on the river concerned, the supervision of river activities in the interest of equal treatment for various nationalities and the establishment of uniform regulations concerning use of facilities, rules of navigation, customs and sanitation formalities, and other similar questions. Membership on these agencies should include the United States, the United Kingdom, the U.S.S.R.,[2] France, and the sovereign riparian states recognised by these Governments.

CALENDAR TO NO. 246

i   *24–26 July 1945   From and to Lord Halifax (Washington) Tels. Nos. 5170 & 7846; Minute by Mr. R. A. Gallop (Head of F.O. General Dept.)* Action on three U.S. memoranda on Danube and inland waterways, minuted by Mr. Gallop on 25 July as 'complete confusion'. Circulation of No. 246 to Soviet delegation 'can hardly fail to kill any chance there might have been of getting the Russians to agree to a Danube agency at Terminal except in return for membership of the Rhine Agency': on which further information requested from Washington with instruction to discuss the general question urgently with State Department: possible negotiation after the Potsdam Conference [W 10042, 10046, 10047/142/803].

[1] Printed *op. cit.*, vol. ii, p. 654.
[2] Mr. N. J. A. Cheetham here annotated on another copy (W 10046/142/803): 'Do we want the Russians on the Rhine?'

No. 247

Minute from Mr. Churchill to Mr. Eden (Berlin)

No. M.(T)14/5 [*F.O. 934/3/13(4)*]

Secret   BERLIN, *23 July 1945*

I am much disturbed by what I read in the papers about the expulsion of the Germans from Czechoslovakia. Ought this topic not to be raised?

Of course there must be an exodus, but it should be conducted with due regard to the repercussions in other countries.[1]

W. S. C.

CALENDAR TO NO. 247

i *23 July 1945 Memorandum by Mr. Harrison (Berlin).* Attitude of Dr. Benes in regard to expulsion of Germans from Czechoslovakia. Press report of such expulsions [F.O. 934/3/13(4)].

[1] Earlier, apparently, on the day of 23 July 1945 Mr. Rowan had minuted to Mr. Dixon in Berlin: 'The Prime Minister has asked whether he may have a report regarding the expulsion of Germans from Czechoslovakia. Among other things, he would like to know the numbers involved, the conditions under which the expulsion has been carried out (for example the time allowed etc.), and also information about the zones into which these Germans are going.' In reply Mr. J. N. Henderson on 23 July sent Mr. Rowan a brief minute covering an explanatory memorandum [i] from Mr. G. W. Harrison. Next day Mr. Henderson noted that this had crossed the present minute from Mr. Churchill to Mr. Eden. On 24 July Mr. Rowan informed Mr. Henderson that Mr. Churchill had minuted on i: 'Surely the matter should be raised at the Conference'. This minute was communicated that day to Mr. Eden.

No. 248

Minute from Mr. Rowan to Mr. Dixon (Berlin)
[F.O. 934/5/42(2)]

BERLIN, *23 July 1945*

1. Before we left London, Millard[1] sent Colville a minute, reference K.11837/2648/328,[2] on the question of 'Soviet' wives of British subjects. The Prime Minister has now seen this, but his present view is that it would not be appropriate for him to raise this matter himself with Marshal Stalin.

2. On the other hand, he[3] has expressed the view that some change should be made in our present policy of [*sic*] regarding the return of Soviet Nationals who are in our hands. The proposal he made was that we should take the line that we do not require the return of any British subjects in Soviet hands against their will. They should be quite free to choose whether they return or not to this country. It would follow from this that Soviet Nationals in our hands would be treated in the same way, i.e. they would not be forced to return to the U.S.S.R. against their will.

3. Perhaps you could consider this and let me have your comments.

T. L. ROWAN

[1] Mr. G. E. Millard was Assistant Private Secretary to Mr. Eden.
[2] This Foreign Office memorandum of 29 June 1945, explaining the case of twenty-one Soviet wives wishing to join their British husbands, is not printed: cf. No. 89, note 1.
[3] The rest of this paragraph and selections from i below are cited by N. Tolstoy, *op. cit.*, p. 418.

i *25 July 1945 Minute by Mr. Dean (Berlin).* Attaches No. 430 in draft with comments on the balance of considerations [F.O. 934/5/42(2)].

No. 249

Note by the Secretaries of the Combined Chiefs of Staff
C.C.S. 900/2 (Terminal) [CAB 99/39]

Top secret   BABELSBERG, *23 July 1945*
Report to the President and Prime Minister

The attached draft of the final report of the Combined Chiefs of Staff is circulated for consideration by the President and Prime Minister.[1]

A. J. McFarland,
A. T. Cornwall-Jones,

Combined Secretariat

ENCLOSURE IN No. 249

Draft Report to the President and Prime Minister of the
agreed summary of conclusions reached by the Combined
Chiefs of Staff at the 'Terminal' Conference

1. The agreed summary of conclusions reached at the 'Terminal' Conference is submitted herewith.

I.—*Over-all Objective*

2. In conjunction with other Allies, to bring about at the earliest possible date the unconditional surrender of Japan.

II.—*Over-all Strategic Concept for the Prosecution of the War*

3. In co-operation with other Allies, to bring about at the earliest possible date the defeat of Japan by: lowering Japanese ability and will to resist by establishing sea and air blockades, conducting intensive air bombardment, and destroying Japanese air and naval strength; invading and seizing objectives in the Japanese home islands as the main effort; conducting such operations against objectives in other than the Japanese home islands as will contribute to the main effort; establishing absolute military control of Japan; and liberating Japanese occupied territory if required.

4. In co-operation with other Allies to establish and maintain, as necessary, military control of Germany and Austria.

III.—*Basic Undertakings and Policies for the Prosecution of the War*

(The respective views of the United States and British Chiefs of Staff are set out in parallel columns in Appendix 'A.')

---

[1] This draft had been approved by the Combined Chiefs of Staff at their meeting at 11.30 a.m. that day (C.C.S. 199th Meeting: cf. No. 232, note 17).

IV.—*The War against Japan*
Strategic Direction of the War

8. We have discussed[2] the strategic direction of the war against Japan and have agreed as follows:

(*a*) The control of operational strategy in the Pacific theatre will remain in the hands of the United States Chiefs of Staff.

(*b*) The United States Chiefs of Staff will provide the British Chiefs of Staff with full and timely information as to their future plans and intentions.

(*c*) The United States Chiefs of Staff will consult the British Chiefs of Staff on matters of general strategy on the understanding that in the event of disagreement the final decision on the action to be taken will lie with the United States Chiefs of Staff.

(*d*) In the event the British Chiefs of Staff should decide that they cannot commit British troops in support of a decision made by the United States Chiefs of Staff as indicated in (*c*) above, the British Chiefs of Staff will give to the United States Chiefs of Staff such advance notice of their decision as will permit them to make timely [re]arrangements.

(*e*) In the event the U.S.S.R. enters the war against Japan, the strategy to be pursued should be discussed between the parties concerned.

Operations in the Pacific

9. We have taken note[3] of the plans and operations proposed by the United States Chiefs of Staff in Appendix 'B.'

10. We have considered[4] the scope and nature of British participation in operations in the Pacific area. Our conclusions are as follows:

(*a*) The British Pacific Fleet will participate as at present planned.

(*b*) A British very long-range bomber force of 10 squadrons, increasing to 20 squadrons when more airfields become available, will participate. There is little prospect that airfield space for more than 10 squadrons of this force will become available before the 1st December, 1945 at the earliest.

(*c*) We have agreed in principle that a Commonwealth land force and, if possible, a small tactical air force, should take part in the final phase of the war against Japan, subject to the satisfactory resolution of operational and other problems. In addition, some units of the East Indies Fleet may also take part.

11. In connection with paragraph 10 (*c*) above, we have agreed that the appropriate British commanders and staff should visit Admiral Nimitz and General MacArthur and draw up with them a plan for submission to the Combined Chiefs of Staff.

Operations in South-East Asia Command

12. We have discussed[5] the instructions that should be issued to the Supreme Allied Commander, South-East Asia, and have agreed upon the terms of the directive in Appendix 'C.'

[2] See No. 183.
[3] At C.C.S. 193rd meeting: cf. No. 172, note 2.
[4] At C.C.S. 194th meeting: cf. *ibid.*
[5] At C.C.S. 197th meeting at 2.30 p.m. on 20 July 1945 : printed in *F.R.U.S. Berlin,* vol. ii, pp. 161–2.

Reallocation of Areas and Command in the South-West Pacific and South-East Asia Areas

13. We have agreed[2] in principle that that part of the South-West Pacific Area lying south of the boundary described in Appendix 'D' should pass from United States to British command as soon as possible. The British Chiefs of Staff have undertaken to obtain the agreement of the Australian, New Zealand and Dutch Governments to these proposals and to investigate and report the earliest practicable date on which the transfer can be effected.

14. We consider it desirable that initially Admiral Mountbatten control operations undertaken in Southern Indo-China since these are more closely related to those of South-East Asia Command than to those of the China Theatre. We are agreed that the best arrangement would be to include that portion of Indo-China lying south of latitude 16° North in South-East Asia Command. This arrangement would continue General Wedemeyer's control[6] of that part of Indo-China which covers the flank of projected Chinese operations in China, and would enable Admiral Mountbatten to prepare the ground in the southern half of Indo-China where any initial operations by him would develop.

We recommend that an approach to the Generalissimo be made by our two Governments to secure his agreement to this arrangement.

At a later date it may prove to be desirable to place all or part of the remainder of Indo-China within the sphere of operations of the South-East Asia Command.

French and Dutch Participation in the War

15. We have considered[2] the arrangements which can be made for French and Dutch participation in the war against Japan and our conclusions are as follows :–

(*a*) While it is at present impracticable, due chiefly to logistical difficulties, for French or Netherlands armed forces to take a major part in the immediate operations in the Far East, the provision of such assistance which may be synchronised with operations will be taken into account. The use of such forces will depend solely on military considerations. French or Netherlands forces so accepted must operate under the complete control of the commander in chief concerned.

(*b*) The French–Netherlands Representatives will be given timely information of our intentions in respect of any operations that will directly affect French–Netherlands territories or armed forces in the Far East.

16. We have considered[7] an offer by the French of a French corps of two infantry divisions to serve in the Pacific war and have agreed on the following reply :–

'(*a*) Whether the corps will serve under United States or British command and the area in which it will operate will be determined later.

'(*b*) Final acceptance of the corps will involve an agreement with the Government concerned on basic matters, including command, combat efficiency, replacements and logistical support.

'(*c*) Maximum use will be made of equipment provided under the North African and Metropolitan Rearmament Programmes.

'(*d*) The time of movement will be in accordance with the priority of the operations in which it is to be used. Pressing shipping and other requirements

---

[6] Lieutenant-General A. C. Wedemeyer was Commanding General of United States forces in the China theatre and Chief of Staff to the Supreme Commander there, Generalissimo Chiang Kai-shek.

[7] See No. 193.

for operations in the Pacific make certain that the corps cannot be moved from France for at least several months. Whether used in the main effort or in the South China Sea area, it will not be possible to commit it to operations prior to the spring of 1946.'

Portuguese Participation in the War

17. We have examined[2] a report by an Anglo-American Military Mission which discussed with the Portuguese military authorities Portuguese proposals for participation in such operations as may eventually be conducted to expel the Japanese from Portuguese Timor. We have informed the State Department and the Foreign Office of our views, which are set out in Appendix 'E.'

Information for the Russians concerning the Japanese War

18. We have discussed[7] the policy to be followed by the British and the United States Chiefs of Staff in passing to the Russians information and intellgience concerning the Japanese war and have agreed as follows:–

(*a*) The United States and British Chiefs of Staff will pass to the Russians such operational information and intelligence regarding the theatres in which they are respectively responsible as either may wish and without bargaining.

(*b*) The United States and British Chiefs of Staff will consult together before passing to the Russians any information and intelligence other than operational. Neither party will pass to the Russians information or intelligence derived wholly or in part from the other party's sources without their consent.

Planning Date for the End of Organised Resistance by Japan

19. We recommend[7] that for the purpose of planning production and the allocation of man-power, the planning date for the end of organised resistance by Japan be the 15th November, 1946, and that this date be adjusted periodically to conform to the course of the war.

V.—*Miscellaneous*

Personnel Shipping

20. We have considered[8] the employment of certain captured enemy ocean-going passenger shipping and have agreed that the total lift of the *Europa, Caribia, Vulcania, Patria, Potsdam, Pretoria* and *Milwaukee* should be allocated for United States employment up to the 31st December, 1945. We have taken note that the United States Chiefs of Staff will allocate to the United Kingdom a lift of 16,000 during the remainder of 1945 for the movement of Canadians.

21. We have directed[8] the completion by the 15th September, 1945, of a study of the combined requirements and combined resources, including captured enemy troop lift, for the first half of 1946.

Personnel Shipping for the Requirements of Allied Governments

22. We have considered[8] the best means of insuring the efficient co-ordination of the demands for personnel shipping submitted by Allied Governments, other than British and American military movements, and of providing a machinery for dealing with essential personnel movements other than those already approved. We have forwarded to the Combined Shipping Adjustment Board the memorandum contained in Appendix 'F.'[9]

[8] At C.C.S. 199th meeting: see note 1 above. Cf. also No. 232, minute 8.
[9] Not here printed: see *F.R.U.S. Berlin*, vol. ii, pp. 1472–3.

III—*Basic undertakings and policies for the prosecution of the war*[10]

United States Proposals	British Proposals
4. [*sic*] The following basic undertakings are considered fundamental to the prosecution of the war:–	
A. Maintain the security of the Western Hemisphere and the British Commonwealth.	Delete A and B and substitute:–
	A. Maintain the security and war-making capacity of the Western Hemisphere and the British Commonwealth as necessary for the fulfilment of the strategic concept.
B. Maintain the war-making capacity of the United States and the British Commonwealth in so far as it is connected with the prosecution of the war against Japan.	
C. Support the war-making capacity of our forces in all areas, with first priority given to those forces in or designated for employment in combat areas in the war against Japan.	Delete C and substitute the following as B:–
	B. Support the war-making capacity of our forces in all areas, with first priority given to those forces in or destined for combat areas.
D. Maintain vital overseas lines of communication.	

5. In order to attain the over-all objective, first priority in the provision of forces and resources of the United States and Great Britain, including reorientation from the European Theatre to the Pacific and Far East, will be given to meeting requirements of tasks necessary to the execution of the over-all strategic concept and to the basic undertakings fundamental to the prosecution of the war.

The invasion of Japan and operations directly connected therewith are the supreme operations in the war against Japan; forces and resources will be allocated on the required scale to assure that invasion can be accomplished at the earliest practicable date. No other operations will be undertaken which hazard the success of, or delay, these main operations.

6. The following additional tasks will be undertaken in order to assist in the execution of the over-all strategic concept:–

---

[10] This document is printed *op. cit.*, vol. ii, pp. 1310–2.

A. Encourage Russian entry into the war against Japan. Provide such aid to her war-making capacity as may be necessary and practicable in connection therewith.

B. Undertake such measures as may be necessary and practicable in order to aid the war effort of China as an effective ally against Japan.

C. Provide assistance to such of the forces of liberated areas as can fulfil an active and effective role in the present war. Within the limits of our available resources assist co-belligerents to the extent they are able to employ this assistance in the present war. Having regard to the successful accomplishment of basic undertakings, to provide such supplies to the liberated areas as will effectively contribute to the capacity of the United Nations to prosecute the war against Japan.

Add at the end of the first sentence: 'or are required to maintain world order in the interests of the war effort.'

Delete the last sentence of 6 C because this is dealt with in paragraph 7 below.

D. In co-operation with other Allies conduct operations, if required, to liberate enemy-occupied areas.

7. The inclusion under Basic Undertakings of terms concerning a specific resource such as cargo shipping is undesirable.

It is agreeable, however, to include in the text of the report the following paragraph:–

Cargo Shipping

Present estimates of the requirements for cargo shipping indicate the position to be sufficiently manageable to provide for the maximum effort in the prosecution of the war against Japan, for the maintenance of the war-making capacity of the British Commonwealth of Nations and the Western Hemisphere, in so far as it is connected with the prosecution of the war against Japan, and for an additional amount for civilian requirements. Should a substantial conflict arise, the shipping situation will be a matter for examination by the two Governments at the time and in the light of changed conditions.

7. Present estimates of the requirements for cargo shipping indicate the position to be sufficiently manageable to provide for the maximum effort in the prosecution of the war against Japan, for the maintenance of the war-making capacity of the British Commonwealth of Nations and the Western Hemisphere in so far as it is connected with the prosecution of the war against Japan, for an additional amount for the reconstruction and rehabilitation of the United Kingdom, for supplies to liberated areas and for essential programmes of the Western Hemisphere.

Should substantial conflict arise, the shipping situation will be a matter for examination by the two Governments at the time and in the light of changed conditions.

Plans and operations in the Pacific
(See paragraph 9 of the Report.)

1. In conformity with the over-all objective to bring about the unconditional surrender of Japan at the earliest possible date, the United States Chiefs of Staff have adopted the following concept of operations for the main effort in the Pacific:–

(*a*) From bases in Okinawa, Iwo Jima, Marianas, and the Philippines to intensify the blockade and air bombardment of Japan in order to create a situation favourable to:

(*b*) An assault on Kyushu for the purpose of further reducing Japanese capabilities by containing and destroying major enemy forces and further intensifying the blockade and air bombardment in order to establish a tactical condition favourable to:

(*c*) The decisive invasion of the industrial heart of Japan through the Tokyo Plain.

2. We have curtailed our projected expansion in the Ryukyus by deferring indefinitely the seizure of Miyako Jima and Kikai Jima. Using the resources originally provided for Miyako and Kikai, we have accelerated the development of Okinawa. By doing this, a greater weight of effort will more promptly be brought to bear against Japan and the risk of becoming involved in operations which might delay the seizure of southern Kyushu is avoided.

3. In furtherance of the accomplishment of the over-all objectives, we have directed:–

(*a*) The invasion of Kyushu.

(*b*) The continuation of operations for securing and maintaining control of sea communications to and in the western Pacific as are required for the accomplishment of the over-all objective.

(*c*) The defeat of the remaining Japanese in the Philippines by such operations as can be executed without prejudice to the over-all objective.

(*d*) The seizure of Balikpapan. (This operation is now approaching successful completion.)

(*e*) The continuance of strategic air operations to support the accomplishment of the over-all objective.

4. Planning and preparation for the campaign in Japan subsequent to the invasion of Kyushu are continuing on the basis of meeting the target date for the invasion of Honshu. This planning is premised on the belief that defeat of the enemy's armed forces in the Japanese homeland is a prerequisite to unconditional surrender, and that such a defeat will establish the optimum prospect of capitulation by Japanese forces outside the main Japanese islands. We recognise the possibility also that our success in the main islands may not obviate the necessity of defeating Japanese forces elsewhere; decision as to steps to be taken in this eventuality must await further developments.

5. We are keeping under continuing review the possibility of capitalising at small cost, without delaying the supreme operations, upon Japanese military deterioration and withdrawals in the China Theatre.

6. We have directed the preparation of plans for the following:–

(*a*) Keeping open a sea route to Russian Pacific ports.

(*b*) Operations to effect an entry into Japan proper for occupational purposes in order to take immediate advantage of favourable circumstances, such as a sudden enemy collapse or surrender.

Appendix 'C'

Directive to the Supreme Allied Commander, South-East Asia
(See paragraph 12 of the Report.)

The following directive has been approved by the Combined Chiefs of Staff on the understanding that the British Chiefs of Staff will obtain the agreement of the Australian, New Zealand and Dutch Governments to the proposed reallocation of areas and command set-up in South-West Pacific and South-East Asia.

1. Your primary task is the opening of the Straits of Malacca at the earliest possible moment. It is also intended that British Commonwealth land forces should take part in the main operations against Japan which have been agreed as the supreme operations in the war; and that operations should continue in the Outer Zone to the extent that forces and resources permit.

2. The eastern boundary of your command will be extended to include Borneo, Java and the Celebes.

Full details of this extension are contained in the Annex hereto.[11]

3. Further information will be sent to you regarding Indo-China.

4. It is desirable that you assume command of the additional areas as soon as practicable after the 15th August, 1945. You will report to the Combined Chiefs of Staff the date on which you expect to be in a position to undertake this additional responsibility.

5. From that date, such Dominion and Dutch forces as may be operating in your new area will come under your command. They will, however, continue to be based on Australia.

6. The area to the east of your new boundary will be an Australian command under the British Chiefs of Staff.

7. It has been agreed in principle that a British Commonwealth land force of from three to five divisions, and, if possible, a small tactical air force, should take part in the main operations against Japan in the spring of 1946. Units of the East Indies Fleet may also take part. Certain important factors relating to this are still under examination.

8. You will be required to provide a proportion of this force together with the assult lift for two divisions. The exact composition of this force and its rôle and the mounting and supporting arrangements will be discussed between Admiral Nimitz, General MacArthur and the British force commanders, and will receive final approval by the Combined Chiefs of Staff.

9. The requirements for the force taking part in the main operations against Japan must have priority over all the other tasks indicated below.

10. Subject to the fulfilment of the higher priority commitments given above,

---

[11] This annex, headed 'Eastern Boundary of Southeast Asia Command', read: 'Beginning on the coast of Indo-China at 16° north; thence to intersect at 7 degrees 40 minutes north latitude 116° east longitude, the boundary between the Commonwealth of the Philippine Islands and British North Borneo; thence along the 1939 boundary line of the Philippines to latitude 05° north longitude 127° east; thence south-westward to 02° S. 123° E; thence south-eastward to 08° S. 125° E; thence south-westward to 18° S. 110° E.'

you will, within the limits of available resources, carry out operations designed to:
- (a) Complete the liberation of Malaya.
- (b) Maintain pressure on the Japanese across the Burma–Siam frontier.
- (c) Capture the key areas of Siam.
- (d) Establish bridgeheads in Java and/or Sumatra to enable the subsequent clearance of these areas to be undertaken in due course.

11. You will submit a programme of operations to the British Chiefs of Staff as soon as you are in a position to do so.

12. You will develop Singapore and such other bases as you may require to the extent necessary for operations against the Japanese.

Appendix 'D'

Boundary between the British and United States Areas of Command in the South-West Pacific[12]

(See paragraph 13 of the Report.)

Beginning on the coast of Indo-China at 16° north; thence to intersect at 7° 40′ north latitude 116° east longitude, the boundary between the Commonwealth of the Philippine Islands and British North Borneo; thence along the 1939 boundary line of the Philippines to latitude 05° north longitude 127° east; thence east to 05° north 130° east; thence south to the equator; thence east to 140° east; thence generally south-east to 02° 20′ south 146° east; thence east to 02° 20′ south 159° east; thence south.

Appendix 'E'

(See paragraph 17 of the Report.)

The Combined Chiefs of Staff have communicated to the Department of State and the Foreign Office the following views on Portuguese participation in the war against Japan:–

(a) The Combined Chiefs of Staff are agreed on the acceptance of Portuguese assistance in such operations as may be conducted eventually to expel the Japanese from Portuguese Timor. While they have made no agreement with the Portuguese military authorities as to the direct use of Portuguese forces, they have recognised the possibility of such use and agreed that plans will be worked out as a result of the studies conducted in staff conversations in Lisbon.

(b) As between the two military forces offered by Portugal (a regimental combat team of 4,000 or a battalion combat team of 2,200, both including 400 native troops), the larger force is likely to be the more acceptable. Steps are being taken to allocate a suitable training area.

(c) The air component offered by Portugal should under no circumstances be included in the acceptance of the Portuguese offer in view of the small number of planes available and the state of the training of the pilots, mechanics and radio specialists.

(d) There is no objection from the military viewpoint to Portugal receiving munitions when they can be spared but negotiations as to the basis for transfer is an action to be taken on a governmental level.

(e) The Combined Chiefs of Staff in accepting Portuguese participation do not intend to enter into a commitment for the retaking of Portuguese Timor.

[12] Printed *op. cit.*, vol. ii, p. 1471.

Neither is acceptance to be construed as a commitment to use Portuguese troops in any other area.

(*f*) Military operations against Portuguese Timor must for the present await the completion of operations against higher priority Japanese-held objectives. The Combined Chiefs of Staff will notify the Portuguese military authorities of impending operations against Portuguese Timor in time for them to prepare their troops for participation therein. Details as to the assembly, shipment, training and equipping of the Portuguese force will be decided by the Combined Chiefs of Staff at the appropriate time.

They have informed the State Department and the Foreign Office that they have no objection to the disclosure of any of the above information to the Portuguese if the Department of State or Foreign Office deem it necessary in diplomatic conversations.[13] The participation of Portuguese forces in the liberation of Portuguese Timor is considered of little military importance in the war against Japan.

CALENDAR TO No. 249

i *23–30 July 1945   Correspondence on Portuguese participation in recapture of Timor: (a) 23 July Record by Sir O. Sargent of conversation with Portuguese Ambassador and attached Portuguese note; (b) 29–30 July Letters from Mr. Garran to Mr. H. Ashley Clarke (Lisbon) and Col. C. R. Price, War Cabinet Offices:* refer to annex E above and favour despatch of Portuguese warships [Z 8732/50/36].

[13] The preceding part of this document is printed *op. cit.*, vol. ii, pp. 1471–2.

No. 250

Report by the British Joint Planning Staff
J.S.(Terminal) 11 (Final) [*CAB 99/39*]

Top secret   BABELSBERG, *23 July 1945*

The War against Japan—Australian views

We have considered a telegram[1] from the Prime Minister of Australia to the Prime Minister. This telegram raises various points of difficulty on the formation of a British Commonwealth force to participate in 'Coronet,' and on the creation of a British Commonwealth Command in the South-West Pacific Area.

2. We suggest that most of these difficulties will not be satisfactorily resolved by a series of telegrams between the Prime Ministers. We believe, however, that they are capable of solution by consultation and that the proper procedure, therefore, should be to ask the Prime Minister to send a reply on the lines of the telegram annexed.[2] This telegram:–

(*a*) Gives the Australian Government the relevant decision reached at 'Terminal.'

[1] *Note in filed copy:* 'Onward 114' : i below.
[2] Not printed: see No. 251, note 8, and enclosure in annex II to No 251.

(*b*) Invites the Australian Government to nominate an Australian officer to accompany British Force Commanders to General MacArthur's Headquarters.

(*c*) Invites the Australian Government to appoint a representative to take part in discussions with Admiral Mountbatten in London on the reorganisation of Command in the South-West Pacific Area.

(*d*) Suggests that when agreement on command has been reached between the British and Australian Governments, an approach should be made to the Dutch Government.

3. If the Chiefs of Staff agree with this suggested procedure, we will, on return to London, prepare a full brief for discussion with Admiral Mountbatten and the Australian representative.

G. Grantham
G. S. Thompson
W. L. Dawson

CALENDAR TO No. 250

i   *21 July 1945*   To Mr. Eden (Berlin) *Tel. No. 114 Onward* transmitting tel. No. 197 of 20 July from Mr. J. B. Chifley, Australian Prime Minister, for Mr. Churchill. Concentration in the Pacific of Australian military effort and participation in main offensive against Japan are of vital importance. However, doubts practicability of present proposals for formation of British Commonwealth force for operations against Japan and creation of British Commonwealth Command in S.W. Pacific Area. Right of Australian Government to refuse use of forces is reserved. Cf. No. 251, annex II [F 4622/69/23].

No. 251

*Minutes of a Meeting of the British Chiefs of Staff Committee
held at 39/41 Ringstrasse, Babelsberg, on Tuesday, 24 July 1945
at 10.30 a.m.*

C.O.S.(Terminal) 10th Meeting [*CAB 99/39*]

     Top secret

Present:

FIELD-MARSHAL SIR ALAN BROOKE, Chief of the Imperial General Staff (*in the Chair*), Marshal of the Royal Air Force Sir Charles F. A. Portal, Chief of the Air Staff, Admiral of the Fleet Sir Andrew B. Cunningham, First Sea Lord and Chief of Naval Staff, General Sir Hastings L. Ismay, Office of the Minister of Defence.

The following were also present:

Field-Marshal Sir Henry Maitland Wilson, Lieut.-General Sir Gordon Macready, Major-General R. E. Laycock, Chief of Combined Operations.

Secretariat: Major-General L. C. Hollis, Brigadier A. T. Cornwall-Jones, Lieut.-Colonel G. Mallaby, Lieut.-Colonel T. Haddon.

611

1. *Lend-Lease in Stage II*
(Previous Reference: C.O.S. (Terminal) 9th Meeting,[1] Minute 1.)

THE COMMITTEE were informed that the Prime Minister had now agreed the report submitted to him the previous evening on Lend-Lease with two small amendments and had signed the memorandum to the President.[2]

2. *Tripartite Military Conversations*

THE COMMITTEE were informed that Tripartite Meeting between United States, British and Russian Chiefs of Staff had been arranged for that afternoon at 2.30 p.m. at the Cecilienhof. It was hoped that Admiral Leahy would be able to give further particulars at the Plenary Meeting.

3. *Move of Dutch Forces to the Far East*
(Previous Reference: C.O.S. (Terminal) 4th Meeting,[3] Minute 3.)

THE COMMITTEE considered a draft telegram circulated personally to each Chief of Staff which the Foreign Secretary proposed to send regarding the wish of the Netherlands Prime Minister for Foreign Affairs to pay a visit to 'Terminal' [i].

THE COMMITTEE:–

Agreed with the terms of the draft telegram and instructed the Secretary to inform the Foreign Office accordingly.

4. *Internationalisation of the Danube River*
(C.O.S. (Terminal) 10 [ii]).
(Previous Reference: C.O.S. (Terminal) 8th Meeting,[4] Minute 4.)

THE COMMITTEE had under consideration a memorandum by the First Sea Lord commenting on proposals put forward by the United States Chiefs of Staff on the Internationalisation of the Danube.[5] The report recommended that the Chiefs of Staff should agree with the memorandum by the United States Chiefs of Staff.

THE COMMITTEE:–

(*a*) Instructed the Secretary to inform[5] the United States Chiefs of Staff that the British Chiefs of Staff agreed with the draft letter at Enclosure A to C.C.S. 896.[6]

(*b*) Instructed the Secretary to send copies of the memorandum by the First Sea Lord to the Foreign Office and Ministry of War Transport Delegations at 'Terminal.'

[1] No. 235.
[2] *Note in filed copy:* 'Annex I'.
[3] No. 187.
[4] No. 232.
[5] *Note in filed copy:* 'Circulated as C.C.S. 896/1', printed in *F.R.U.S. Berlin*, vol. ii, p. 655.
[6] See No. 232, note 5.

5. *The War against Japan—Australian Views*
(J.S. (Terminal) 11 (Final).[7]
(Previous Reference: C.O.S. (Terminal) 8th Meeting,[4] Minute 5.)

THE COMMITTEE had under consideration a report by the Joint Planning Staff suggesting a reply from the Prime Minister to the Prime Minister of Australia on the questions of the participation of a British Commonwealth Force in 'Coronet' and on the creation of a British Commonwealth Command in the South-West Pacific Area.

The Committee agreed with the reply proposed by the Joint Planning Staff, subject to one small amendment in paragraph 6 of the telegram.

THE COMMITTEE–
Instructed the Secretary to submit the telegram attached to the Report by the Joint Planning Staff to the Prime Minister.[8]

6. *Approval of Minutes of C.C.S. 199th Meeting.*[9]
THE COMMITTEE approved the Minutes of the 199th Meeting of the Combined Chiefs of Staff.

Babelsberg, 24th July, 1945

ANNEX I TO No. 251
Letter from Mr. Churchill to President Truman (Berlin)[10]

Copy   *24 July 1945*
My dear Mr. President,
I thank you for your memorandum of the 17th July.[11] I am pleased that you say the Agreement made in Washington last autumn stands. We have never, of course, regarded the munitions schedules as absolutely rigid. Indeed, I am told that our munitions requirements have already been scaled down from the 2.8 billion dollars agreed last autumn for the first year of Stage II to 1.8 billion, and that all these items are within the terms then arranged. Unfortunately the Departments in Washington have recently been insisting that nothing can be delivered save what is needed for direct use against Japan, and interpreting this in the narrowest possible sense; this has reduced munitions supplies almost to vanishing point, and has put us in a very difficult position.

Much as I dislike troubling you with technical questions of this kind at the present time, it is urgently necessary for us to find a solution. I attach a note[12]

---

[7] No. 250.

[8] *Note in filed copy:* 'Annex II' below. With reference to the above-mentioned small amendment, paragraph 6 of the initially proposed reply had read: 'I have not yet received any answer from the New Zealand Government.'

[9] Cf. No. 232, note 17.

[10] This letter is printed *op. cit.*, vol. ii, pp. 1180–1.

[11] Annex to No. 174.

[12] *Note in filed copy:* 'Enclosure', not here printed. This memorandum was the same as annex III to No. 232 subject to the following amendments: addition to the end of third sentence from the end of paragraph 2 of 'as one of the Occupying Powers'; replacement of second sentence of paragraph 3 by 'For example the Sunderland IV is equipped with American turrets'; replacement of last sentence of paragraph 5 by 'The mere fact that some American equipment has been or is being issued to us should not limit our ordinary

on the position by the Chiefs of Staff, and very much hope that you will find it possible to let me know whether their reading of your intentions, as expressed in paragraph 1 of the note, is correct. If so, I earnestly hope you will be able to see your way to issue the necessary directive to your agencies.

The important financial questions mentioned in your last paragraph are, of course, of a somewhat technical character, and I should hesitate to enter into them deeply at this stage. But I am told that our present gold and dollar balances (1.8 billion dollars) do not exceed what was agreed as reasonable last autumn in Washington by the United States Administration; on the other hand our external liabilities, owing to the prolongation of the war, have increased to 13 billion dollars.

The Chancellor asks me to add that, both in the matter of sales of surplus in the Middle East and elsewhere and in the matter of relief to Europe, he has, in an earnest endeavour to meet your wishes, already authorised proposals to the State Department which go a long way beyond what he could have justified on any other ground. In particular we have told the State Department that we are willing to continue relief during the military period in Italy until U.N.R.R.A. takes over relief there in the early autumn, and to make a further contribution to the general work of U.N.R.R.A. for next year. Both of these proposals are at present under discussion with the State Department, though the Chancellor has not yet any Parliamentary authority for this further relief expenditure.

All these questions, of course, are linked up closely with the general post-war economic arrangements which will have to be worked out before the war ends. For this purpose, I should be very glad if you would agree to our sending a special delegation to Washington as soon as convenient—say in September. It will, I am sure, be in our common interest to achieve as soon as possible agreement on these vital post-war issues, so that we can view the economic picture as a whole.

Yours very sincerely,
WINSTON S. CHURCHILL

ANNEX II TO NO. 251
Minute from General Sir H. Ismay to Mr. Churchill (Berlin)

Copy

25 July 1945

Reference Telegram No. 197[13] from the Prime Minister of Australia

The Chiefs of Staff have examined Telegram No. 197 from the Prime Minister of Australia about Australian participation in 'Coronet,' and on the proposed creation of an Australian Command in the South-West Pacific Area.

2. Mr. Chiffley's main points are as follows:—

(a) He is anxious lest agreement to join in the British Commonwealth Force for 'Coronet' should result in the Australians taking no part in the main operations at all. This anxiety arises from his not knowing the progress of discussions at 'Terminal,' or the target date for the main operations.

(b) He says that if the Australians take part in the main operations, they will not have sufficient resources to undertake the additional responsibility of an

freedom in regard to the use and disposal of British equipment; providing, however, that we do not seek American equipment in order to give us more latitude in the disposal of the British equipment.' Cf. *op. cit.*, vol. ii, pp. 1181–2, for a variant text.

[13] See No. 250.i.

exclusively Australian command. It is, therefore, necessary, in his view, that the Americans should continue to provide a portion of the necessary forces for the new Australian area which is to take over part of the South-West Pacific Area. He does not realise that the Americans have already moved nearly all their troops out of the area in question and will move the rest before 'Coronet,' irrespective of whether or not the British take over responsibility for the South-West Pacific Area.

3. The Chiefs of Staff suggest that you should reply to Mr. Chiffley on the lines of the attached draft.[14]

4. A copy of this minute has been sent to the Secretary of State for the Dominions.

25th July, 1945

ENCLOSURE TO ANNEX II TO No. 251

Draft Telegram

From the Prime Minister to the Prime Minister of Australia.

1. Your telegram No. 197[13] reached me here just as Combined Chiefs of Staff had agreed in principle that a Commonwealth Land Force and assault shipping and, if possible, a small Tactical Air Force should take part in the main operations against Japan subject to the satisfactory resolution of operational and other problems. They had also agreed that in order to resolve these problems, appropriate British Commanders and Staff should visit Admiral Nimitz and General Mac-Arthur and draw up with them a plan for submission to the Combined Chiefs of Staff.

2. We have all had in mind the practical difficulties to which you refer. We hope, however, that the appointed British Commanders in consultation with General MacArthur and Admiral Nimitz will be able to formulate a practical and acceptable plan. The United States Chiefs of Staff are anxious that the British Commanders should reach General MacArthur at a very early date. The Chiefs of Staff will proceed with the appointment of Force Commanders as early as possible, and in order that Australian views may be fully represented at the consultations with General MacArthur, I suggest that you should appoint an Australian officer to join the British Commanders at General MacArthur's Headquarters. This officer would then be able to return to Australia to explain in full detail all the arrangements proposed. I hope and believe that you will then find it possible to join with us in this enterprise. The time and details of the visit of the British Commanders will, of course, be notified to you as soon as possible.

3. I have noted the various problems and difficulties which would, in your view, arise from the organisation of command suggested in my telegram No. 219,[15] and I fully accept that the Australian Government must be the sole arbiter of the extent of their own war effort and allocation of man-power and material resources. I believe, however, that a satisfactory solution of the command arrangement and a proper distribution of effort in the present South-West Pacific Area and in South-East Asia Command could be achieved by consultation between us.

[14] *Note in filed copy:* 'Enclosure', below.

[15] Of 4 July (F 4622/69/23), not printed: cf. G. Long, *The Final Campaigns*, vol. vii (Canberra, 1963), p. 548, in Series I (Army) of *Australia in the War of 1939–1945.*

4. Admiral Mountbatten is due to visit us in London in the near future and will undertake discussions with the Chiefs of Staff on future operations in S.E.A.C. and on possible extensions of his Command. I suggest that it would be most helpful if you could appoint a representative to take part in these discussions, represent your views and keep you fully informed. No final decision will, of course, be taken without your concurrence.

5. I agree that we are under obligation to bring the Dutch Government into this question and I suggest the proper course would be to approach them when we have reached agreement.

6. I have not received the answer from the New Zealand Government.

7. I, therefore, propose:–

(a) That you should appoint an Australian officer to be ready to meet British Force Commanders for discussions at General MacArthur's Headquarters.

(b) That you should appoint a representative to take part in London in discussions with the Chiefs of Staff and Admiral Mountbatten on the question of the re-organisation of the South-West Pacific Area. These discussions should start on about the 1st August.[16]

CALENDARS TO No. 251

i *20–5 July 1945   To and from Mr. Eden (Berlin) Tels. Nos. 104 Onward & 235 Target.* Reasons why requested Dutch visit to Conference is found impracticable [F.O. 934/5/53(1–2)].

ii *23–5 July 1945   International régime for the Danube:* (a) *23 July   Memo. by Admiral Sir A. Cunningham: C.O.S. (Terminal) 10;* (b) *24 July   U.K. Delegation brief No. 60 and covering minute by Mr. Cheetham;* (c) *25 July   Letter from Major-General Hollis to Sir A. Cadogan* [CAB 99/39; F.O. 934/6; W 9978, 10353/142/803].

[16] This telegram was despatched as Dominions Office telegram No. 260 to Canberra on 26 July at 1.30 p.m.

No. 252

Memorandum by Sir W. Monckton (Berlin)[1]
[UE 3221/624/77]

[BERLIN,] *24 July 1945*
German Reparations

1. We have hitherto been proceeding on the basis that the Moscow Commission would decide that all of the plant and equipment from certain key industries (e.g. synthetic oil) and part of the plant and equipment from other industries (e.g. metal and chemical industries), should be available for removal as once-for-all deliveries; that all of the powers entitled to reparation would have a right to their agreed share in the once-for-all deliveries from all of the four Zones and that Russia would account for the

[1] This memorandum was circulated by Sir J. Anderson to the Reparations Committee of the Cabinet under his covering note R.M.(45)11 of 25 July 1945.

plant and equipment which she has already removed or handed over to Poland.

2. We have felt, however, that this system involves great difficulties. Russia would be unwilling to account for all that she has taken and it would not be possible for us to check up on her statements of what she has taken, even if she allowed us to make inspections in her Zone. Russia would probably want to de-industrialise Germany to a greater extent than we thought wise. Finally, there might be competing claims between Russia and ourselves for the most valuable steel plants, etc. in our Zones and this would lead to a series of squabbles.

3. We have failed to reach agreement that approved imports should be a first charge on German exports, but even if we succeeded we should be faced with the difficulty that Russia might, as a member of the Control Council, be unwilling to approve imports into our Zone which we regard as essential, so that either the population of the Zone would starve, or we should import more than the amount approved by the Control Council and the first charge for approved imports would not help us.

At a private meeting with the Foreign Ministers yesterday[2] Mr. Byrnes put forward a proposal which was intended to overcome these difficulties. He said that 50% of Germany's industrial wealth is in the Russian Zone. The Russians have either handed this over to Poland or removed plant and equipment or will be in a position to remove both plant and equipment and current production in future. Russia, therefore has taken, or is in a position to take the 50% share which she claims. She should be at liberty to take whatever she likes out of the Russian Zones and should get nothing out of the Western Zones and the Commander-in-Chief of each of the Western Zones should decide what reparation deliveries to the Powers entitled to reparation other than Russia are to be made from his own Zone.

The Russians did not reject this idea out of hand, but said they could consider it, provided that they got plant and equipment from the Ruhr to the value of U.S.$3 billion. At this point the meeting adjourned.

4. In the evening we had a private talk with the Americans at which Sir Walter Monckton, Sir David Waley and Mr. Mark Turner were present on our side and Mr. Will Clayton, Mr. McCloy and Mr. Pauley on the American side. Mr. Clayton said that he believed that a bargain could be made and that he thought that now is the time to make it. He was not prepared to talk in terms of dollars. He would concede that what the Russians have in their own Zones, including what they handed over to Poland, amount to only 45% of what is available in Germany as a whole, so that they will be justified in taking from the Ruhr enough to make up their share from 45% to 50%. He would offer them a further share of what is available in the Western Zones in return for an undertaking to supply food, coal etc. of an equivalent value from the Russian Zone to the Western Zones. He recognised that we might have as part of our offer to guarantee

[2] See No. 240.

that it would amount to the plant and equipment needed for the production of some definite number of tons of steel and so on.

Apart from this special deal, each Zone Commander would decide what deliveries, whether once-for-all or from current production are to be made from his Zone and what is to be imported into his Zone and what is to be exported to pay for such imports.

Mr. Clayton asked us to consider whether we would agree to an attempt to clinch a bargain on these lines.

5. The advantages in a bargain of this kind are obvious. It is suggested that we should agree to the matter being explored in this way subject to the following conditions:–

(1) the burden of allowing Russia to take deliveries from the Western Zones should be shared equally between ourselves and the Americans and later the French should be brought in to take a proportionate share. Thus, if, in fact, the Russians want to take everything from the Ruhr which is in our Zone, the adjustments required to equalise the burden should be made between ourselves and the Americans (and eventually the French). Mr. Clayton fully recognises this and we would anticipate no difficulties.

(2) we cannot commit ourselves as to the extent to which de-industrialisation will be carried in our Zone until we have consulted the Commander-in-Chief and the Cabinet in London. We cannot therefore take any snap decision as to how much we can offer Russia.

(3) we should make a genuine attempt to treat Germany as a single economic unit. This means that the programme of imports must be approved for Germany as a whole and that the exports from all four Zones must be available to pay for these approved imports before they are available for reparation deliveries. If the Russian member of the Control Council will not agree to a programme of imports which our Commander-in-Chief regards as necessary, the attempt to treat Germany as a single unit will, in fact, have broken down and there will have to be a separate programme of imports and a separate ration scale for the Russian Zone. This must have far-reaching economic and political results and we should not abandon the attempt to treat Germany as a single unit unless and until we are forced to do so owing to the four Governments being unable to agree on what we regard as essential in our Zone.

(4) the Americans, as stated above, propose that we should swop some once-for-all deliveries from the Western Zones for the supply of food and coal from the Russian Zone to the Western Zones. It would be better that the question of the supply of food and coal from the Russian Zone and from Silesia should be tied up with the question of the Western frontier of Poland and that we should swop capital goods from the Western Zones for timber and potash from the Russian Zone.

If some bargain with Russia is made on the lines which the Americans suggest and each Zone Commander decides what reparation deliveries are to be made from his own Zone, there is no longer much point in working out an elaborate Reparation Plan with the Russians at Moscow. The Russians will take what they can from their own Zone and no longer be interested in what happens in the Western Zones. A Reparation Plan would require to be worked out between ourselves, the Americans and the French and subsequently between all the powers entitled to reparation. It would be much more sensible to work this out at Berlin in close touch with the Control Council rather than at Moscow. It may now [?not], however, be easy to persuade the Russians of this and we ought not to press it.

6. In the course of our talk with the Americans two very interesting points emerged:–

(*a*) The Americans said that their views about de-industrialisation had completely changed. Their present feeling is that it would be foolish to carry de-industrialisation further than is required for a policy of economic security based on dealing drastically with a few selected key industries and leaving the rest more or less alone. At the same time they may recognise that a disarmed Germany will require for peace-time production a very considerably smaller metal and chemical industry than that which existed in 1944. It is clear that General Clay has been speaking to the Americans in much the same terms as General Weeks has been speaking to us and has made a great impression on them.

(*b*) the Americans are also now greatly impressed with the need for leaving each Commander-in-Chief the final word about matters in his own Zone. They put forward the view that if the Control Council fail to reach agreement on any matter, each Commander-in-Chief is entitled in his own Zone to carry out his own ideas.

W. Monckton

No. 253

Letter from Mr. Eden to M. Molotov (Berlin)
[*U 5784/20/70*]

BRITISH DELEGATION, BERLIN, 24 July 1945

As you know, we have agreed in principle that the European Advisory Commission should be dissolved.

I should like to remind you that there are still before the Commission two outstanding draft Agreements, which I think should be concluded before the Commission is dissolved.

The first is the draft Agreement on Zones of Occupation in Germany. I understand that agreement in regard to the French sector in Berlin, which was holding up the main agreement, is now in sight and I hope this matter will soon be disposed of.

The second is the draft 'Agreement . . .'[1] on certain additional requirements to be imposed on Germany'. You will be aware that, when the
United Kingdom Representative on the European Advisory Commission
agreed to abandon the British draft comprehensive long 'Terms of
Surrender for Germany',[2] he did so on the understanding that His Majesty's
Government could accept the shorter 'Instrument of Surrender' proposed
by the Soviet Representative only if the Commission would go on to prepare
a further document to cover those additional subjects which were dealt
with in the longer British draft armistice.

The Commission duly prepared such a document, which supplements
the Declaration signed at Berlin on June 5th last and sets out the requirements of the Allies in the fields not mentioned in the Declaration.

His Majesty's Government attach great importance to securing agreement
to this document and the United Kingdom Representative on the
European Advisory Commission has been instructed to press his colleagues
to recommend it for approval to their Governments. The United States and
French Representatives accept it, but hitherto the Soviet Representative
has not been authorised to do so.

I write to ask you therefore whether the Soviet Representative on the
Commission may now be authorised to sign the Agreement in order that
this matter may be disposed of before the Commission is dissolved.[3]

A. EDEN

[1] Punctuation as in original quotation.
[2] Submitted by Sir W. Strang to the European Advisory Commission on 15 January
1944: printed in *F.R.U.S., 1944*, vol. i, pp. 116–139.
[3] M. Vyshinski informed Sir A. Cadogan in a letter of 28 July 1945 that the Soviet
representative had been so instructed on 23 July: see No. 406.

No. 254

Record of Seventh Meeting of Foreign Secretaries, held at
Cecilienhof, Potsdam, on Tuesday, 24 July 1945 at 11 a.m.

F.(*Terminal*)7th Meeting [U 6197/3628/70]

Top secret

Present:

M. V. M. MOLOTOV, M. A. Ya. Vyshinski, M. I. M. Maisky, M. A. A. Gromyko,
M. F. T. Gousev, M. K. V. Novikov, M. A. A. Sobolev, M. B. F. Podtzerob,
M. S. A. Golunski (*Interpreter*).

MR. J. F. BYRNES, Mr. W. A. Harriman, Mr. E. W. Pauley, Mr. J. C. Dunn,
Mr. H. F. Matthews, Mr. W. L. Clayton, Mr. C. E. Bohlen, Mr. B. V. Cohen,
Mr. E. Page (*Interpreter*).

MR. EDEN, Sir W. Monckton, Sir A. Cadogan, Sir A. Clark Kerr, Sir W. Strang,
Sir D. Waley, Mr. N. Brook, Mr. P. J. Dixon, Mr. W. Hayter, Major L. M.
Theakstone (*Interpreter*).

Contents

1. *Outstanding Business*

MR. BYRNES suggested that the meeting should begin by reviewing the business at present outstanding.

(i) *Western Frontier of Poland*

The representatives of the Polish Provisional Government had now arrived in Potsdam. He suggested that they should be asked to attend the present meeting of Foreign Secretaries at 12.30 p.m. This was agreed to. (See Minute 4 below.)

(ii) *Reparations from Germany, Austria and Italy*

(iii) *Germany: Economic Problems*

On both these matters reports were awaited from the Economic Committee who were meeting that evening.

M. MOLOTOV said that the Soviet Delegation had now prepared memoranda on reparations from Austria and Italy. (Subsequently circulated as P. (Terminal) 36 and 37.)[1]

MR. BYRNES suggested that these papers should be remitted to the Economic Sub-Committee, and that meanwhile consideration of both (ii) and (iii) above should be postponed.

This was agreed to on the understanding that the reports would be ready for consideration at the next meeting of Foreign Secretaries.

(iv) *European Oil Supplies.* (P. (Terminal) 18.)[2]

The Economic Committee had discussed this memorandum, but the Soviet representative had asked for more time to consider it. It was agreed that, on this question also, the views of the Economic Committee should be reported to the next meeting of Foreign Secretaries.

(v) *Yalta Declaration on Liberated Europe*

It was recalled that this question fell into three parts—(a) Elections; (b) Powers of Allied representatives on the Control Commissions; and (c) Facilities for Press Representatives.

MR. BYRNES said that the Committee appointed to consider (b) and (c) had not met since the 22nd July, when the Soviet member had promised further proposals from the Soviet Delegation. These had not yet been considered by the Committee.

M. MOLOTOV said that memoranda setting out the views of the Soviet

[1] Nos. 261 and 262 respectively.
[2] See No. 214, note 10.

Delegation on both these points were now available. The Committee could, therefore, proceed with its business.

2. *Neutral and Ex-Enemy States: Admission to United Nations*
(Previous Reference: F. (Terminal) 3rd Meeting,[3] Minute 4.)

MR. BYRNES recalled that the Foreign Secretaries had appointed a Committee to consider the suggestion that the proposed statement on the admission of Italy to association with the United Nations should also indicate that Spain would not be regarded as eligible for such admission so long as she remained under the control of the present political régime. As the Committee were unable to agree on a report, he suggested that the Foreign Secretaries should themselves discuss the matter now, on the basis of a draft statement prepared by the United States Delegation with which the British Delegation were understood to be in general agreement. This was as follows:

'1. The three Governments consider that the time has come to terminate the present anomalous position of Italy. Italy was the first of the Axis Powers to break with Germany, to whose defeat she has made a material contribution, and has now joined with the Allies in the struggle against Japan. Italy has freed herself from the Fascist régime and is making good progress towards the re-establishment of a democratic government and institutions. She gives promise of becoming a firm supporter of a policy of peace and resistance to aggression.

'2. The three Governments have therefore resolved that very early steps should be taken to conclude a peace treaty with Italy and have included the preparation of this among the immediate important tasks to be undertaken by the new Council of Foreign Ministers. The conclusion of such a peace treaty will make it possible for the three Governments to fulfil their desire to support an application from Italy for membership of the United Nations organisation.

'3. As regards the admission of other States, Article IV of the Charter of the United Nations declares that:

'(1) membership in the United Nations is open to all other peace-loving States who accept the obligations contained in the present Charter and, in the judgment of the organisation, are able and willing to carry out these obligations;

'(2) the admission of any such State to membership in the United Nations will be effected by a decision of the General Assembly upon the recommendation of the Security Council.

'4. The three Governments so far as they are concerned will support applications for membership from those States which have remained neutral during the war and which fulfil the qualifications set out above.

'5. The Three Governments feel bound however to make it clear that they for their part would not favour any application for membership put

[3] No. 200.

forward by the present Spanish Government, which, having been founded on the support of the Axis Powers, does not, in view of its origins, its nature, its record and its close association with the aggressor States, possess the qualifications necessary to justify such membership.'

MR. EDEN said that he had two drafting suggestions to make. First, he thought that the last sentence of paragraph 1 should be omitted. Secondly, paragraph 2 should take account of the fact that Governments other than the three responsible for the statement would also be concerned with the Peace Treaty. For this reason he suggested that paragraph 2 should be re-worded as follows:

'2. The Three Governments have therefore resolved that it is desirable that very early steps should be taken to conclude a peace treaty with Italy, and they trust that the other interested Allied Governments will share their views. They have, therefore, included the preparation of the treaty as the first among the immediate important tasks to be undertaken by the new Council of Foreign Ministers. The conclusion of such a peace treaty will make it possible for the three Governments to fulfil their desire to support an application from Italy for membership of the United Nations Organisation.'

M. MOLOTOV said that he was not prepared to consider drafting suggestions until a question of principle had been decided. The Soviet objection to the American draft was that it contained no reference to the position of Bulgaria, Roumania, Hungary and Finland, who had done more than Italy had done to help in bringing about the eventual defeat of Germany.[4] The Soviet Delegation had proposed that the British and United States Governments should enter into diplomatic relations with the Governments of these States. Unless it was agreed that there should be some reference to them in the proposed statement he could not discuss its wording.

MR. BYRNES recalled that President Truman had already explained the attitude of the United States Government towards the resumption of diplomatic relations with the satellite States (P. (Terminal) 5th Meeting,[5] Minute 6). They were unwilling to recognise these Governments because they did not regard them as sufficiently representative. If M. Molotov raised this question, it must be submitted to the Plenary Meeting. For his part, he was willing to accept both the amendments which Mr. Eden had suggested. It could, therefore, be reported to the Plenary Meeting that afternoon that the draft was accepted by the British and United States

---

[4] Mr. W. Hayter minuted at Potsdam on 24 July 1945 (F.O. 934/5/48(3)): 'The Russians may raise the question of admission of the Balkan satellites to the United Nations in connexion with the draft resolution about the admission of Italy. If so, it might be possible to agree to the insertion of something on the following lines:

"After the conclusion of peace with Italy the next task of the Council of Foreign Ministers is the consideration of peace treaties with Finland, Roumania, Hungary and Bulgaria. When these peace treaties have been concluded the Three Powers will be prepared to consider the question of the admission of these countries into the World Organisation." '

[5] No. 219.

Delegations, but not by the Soviet Delegation, who desired that it should contain a reference to the position of the satellite countries.

M. MOLOTOV said that it should also be reported that the Soviet Delegation had been unable to discuss the wording of the draft because the British and United States Delegations had declined to discuss the question of establishing diplomatic relations with these countries. If he had to choose between referring in the statement to neutral countries such as Switzerland and Portugal, or to co-belligerent countries such as Roumania and Bulgaria, he would prefer to mention the latter. They had helped in the war, and it would be unjust to give a more privileged position to neutral States or to Italy.

MR. EDEN said that the British Government were not ready to recognise the Governments of those satellite States, particularly Roumania and Bulgaria, because they did not regard them as sufficiently representative. While the Government of Italy was composed of representatives of the main political parties, the Governments of Roumania and Bulgaria were minority Governments, drawn chiefly from the Communist Party.

M. MOLOTOV said that in that case it was strange that they were trusted by the people. The fact was that the representatives of the Communist Party in both these Governments formed a small minority.

At this point the following exchange took place:

M. MOLOTOV: M. Tatarescu[6] is not a Communist.

MR. EDEN: No. But he has a past—of a different kind—as M. Vyshinski knows.

M. MOLOTOV: But not, at any rate, a Communist past. And does Mr. Eden suggest that King Michael is a Communist?

MR. EDEN: He is not a member of the Government.

M. MOLOTOV: He is above the Government. He appointed it.

MR. EDEN: With a little help from M. Vyshinski?

M. VYSHINSKI: And from many other people besides me.

MR. BYRNES said that he had been considering the Soviet proposal and suggested that the following paragraph might be added to the draft statement:

'The three Governments also hope that the Council of Foreign Ministers may, without undue delay, prepare peace treaties for Bulgaria, Roumania, Hungary and Finland. It is also their desire, on the conclusion of peace treaties with responsible democratic Governments in these countries, to support their application for membership of the United Nations Organisation.'

He would also suggest, in order to go further to meet M. Molotov's point of view, that the last sentence of paragraph 2 of the draft, as amended by Mr. Eden, should read:

'The conclusion of such a peace treaty *with a responsible and democratic Italian Government* will make it possible for the three Governments to

[6] Roumanian Minister for Foreign Affairs.

fulfil their desire to support an application from Italy for membership of the United Nations Organisation.'
The addition of the words in italics would make the language used of Italy correspond to that used of the satellite countries.

M. MOLOTOV said that such a draft, while still requiring some improvement, might form a good basis for consideration if the United States and British Delegations would agree, as a matter of principle, that Roumania, Bulgaria, Hungary and Finland should be put in a position no worse than that of Italy.

MR. BYRNES said that he had no authority to modify the attitude of the United States Government towards the recognition of the present Governments of these countries, He was, however, satisfied that the statement as now amended would place these countries in the same position as Italy in the matter of their association with the United Nations. Could not the Soviet Delegation accept the draft on this basis?

M. MOLOTOV said that the question was a complicated one affecting a number of neutral and ex-enemy countries. But the question of substance was whether they could agree that the satellite countries should be in no worse a position than Italy. If so, it should not be difficult to express their agreement in words.

MR. EDEN said that, in his view, it was always a mistake to use words to paper over cracks. In fact there was, in his mind, a difference between Italy and some at least of the four satellite countries in which the Soviet Government were specially interested. The British Government would be ready to make a peace treaty and renew diplomatic relations with the present Government in Italy, but not, on their present information, with the existing Governments in Bulgaria and Roumania.

M. MOLOTOV said that the whole matter should be referred to the Plenary Meeting as one on which the Foreign Secretaries were unable to reach agreement.

It was agreed that this matter should be submitted to the Plenary Meeting for consideration.

3. *Roumania: Removal of Allied Industrial Equipment*
(Previous Reference: F. (Terminal) 5th Meeting,[7] Minute 4.)

MR. EDEN handed in a memorandum[8] re-stating the case put forward by the United Kingdom Delegation regarding the removal of Allied industrial equipment from Roumania, and suggesting that the ownership of the disputed property should be made the subject of impartial and expert investigation by a Committee of three Allied nationals drawn from States not interested in the dispute. He proposed that, if this Committee found that the property belonged to Germany, it should be retained by the Russians: if the Committee found that it belonged to one of the British companies, the Soviet Government should return it or pay compensation to the company.

[7] No. 224. [8] No. 264.

Mr. Byrnes said that he supported this proposal.

M. Molotov said that he must ask for time to consider this proposal, since the memorandum by the United Kingdom Delegation had not yet been translated into Russian.

It was agreed that consideration of this proposal should be deferred.

4. Western Frontiers of Poland
(Previous Reference: P. (Terminal) 6th Meeting,[9] Minute 7.)

At the Plenary Meeting on the 22nd July, President Truman had been asked to invite the Polish Provisional Government to send representatives to attend the Conference to put forward their views on the question of Poland's Western Frontier.

Mr. Byrnes introduced to the meeting the following representatives of the Polish Provisional Government, who had come to Potsdam for this purpose:

M. Bierut	Marshal Rota [Rola] Zymierski[10]
M. Mikolajczyk	M. Gomulka
M. Rzymowski	M. Modzelawski [sic]
M. Grabski	M. Osobka-Morawski

The views of the Polish Provisional Government were put forward by MM. Bierut, Mikolajczyk and Rzymowski. A full record of their statements is contained in the Annex to these Minutes.

At the conclusion of these statements, Mr. Byrnes said that the question of Poland's Western Frontier had been mentioned in the following terms in the communiqué issued at the end of the Crimea Conference:

'The Three Heads of Governments . . .[11] recognise that Poland must receive substantial accessions of territory in the North and West. They feel that the opinion of the new Polish Provisional Governments of National Unity should be sought in due course on the extent of those accessions and that the final delimitation of the western frontier of Poland should thereafter await the Peace Conference.'

It was in accordance with this declaration that the Heads of Governments assembled at the present Conference had sought to ascertain the views of the Polish Provisional Government on this question; and the Foreign Secretaries would report to the Heads of Governments the statements which had been made that morning. If any of the representatives of the Polish Provisional Government wished to supplement what had been said that morning, they might send to him in writing any further statements which they wished to make and they could be assured that these would receive due consideration by the Heads of Governments.

M. Molotov said that he would like to state the views of the Soviet Delegation. The question of Poland's Western Frontier was an issue of grave historical importance, not only to Poland, but to the whole of Europe. It

---

[9] No. 226.
[10] Minister of National Defence and Commander-in-Chief of the Polish armed forces.
[11] Punctuation as in original quotation.

was of special concern to the Soviet Government. The question of Poland's Eastern Frontier had been decided at the Crimea Conference—with the friendly participation of Great Britain and the United States but, perhaps even more important, in full agreement between the Soviet Government and her Polish neighbours. By this decision certain territory in the east of pre-war Poland had been handed over to the U.S.S.R.; and it had been agreed that Poland could look for compensation through the accession of territory in the North and West. It was for this reason that the Soviet Government had a special responsibility in connection with Poland's Western Frontier. On that question the views of the Soviet Government were known to the Polish Provisional Government. It was, however, his duty to say at this Conference that, in the view of the Soviet Government, the request which was now put forward by the Polish Provisional Government was a just and timely request. Justice required that this territory should be taken from Germany and handed over to Poland. Such an adjustment would be in the interests of the peace of Europe and of the world. It would substantially reduce the risk of further aggression by Germany; and it would substantially assist in establishing a strong and independent Poland. If this territory were ceded to Poland, she would be one of the pillars of peace in Europe. This adjustment would make it possible for all Poles to be brought together into a single homogeneous State. Within these boundaries a new Poland could be built up which could be strong and independent, both economically and politically. It was, therefore, the sincere hope of the Soviet Government that the Conference would feel able to give sympathetic consideration to the request put forward by the Polish Provisional Government.

Mr. Byrnes said that, in this matter, the duty of the Foreign Secretaries was limited to ascertaining the views of the Polish Provisional Government and reporting them to the Heads of Governments, who would consider the matter in Plenary Conference.

Mr. Eden agreed. As this matter was before the Plenary Meeting, he did not think it right that he should make any statement at the present meeting about the views of the British Government.

M. Molotov said that the Soviet Government was in a somewhat different position from the British and United States Governments. The U.S.S.R. was a neighbour of Poland and had special obligations towards the Polish people.

Mr. Byrnes remarked that the United States had always been friendly to Poland; and Mr. Eden recalled that it was on Poland's behalf that the British Commonwealth had declared war on Germany in 1939.

5. *Agenda for the Eighth Plenary Meeting*

Mr. Byrnes proposed that the following subjects should be put forward for discussion at the Eighth Plenary Meeting that afternoon:

(a) *Turkey*

The Plenary Meeting on the previous day had not disposed of this question and would wish to discuss the Memorandum submitted by the United States Delegation on the Navigation of International Inland Waterways (P. (Terminal) 33).[12]

(b) Neutral and ex-enemy States: Admission to United Nations.

It had been agreed earlier in the present meeting that it should be reported to the Plenary Meeting that the Foreign Secretaries had been unable to reach agreement on this question (see minute 2 above).

(c) Western Frontier of Poland

It might be reported to the Plenary Meeting that the Foreign Secretaries had heard the views of representatives of the Polish Provisional Government.

M. MOLOTOV asked when it was proposed that the Plenary Meeting should resume further discussion on the disposal of the *German Fleet and Merchant Navy.* MR. EDEN recalled that it had been agreed at the Plenary Meeting on the 19th July[13] that this question should be left over for settlement at the end of the Conference. It was suggested that the Plenary Meeting might be asked, at their meeting the following day, to consider what would be an appropriate day on which to resume discussion of this question.

M. MOLOTOV suggested that the Plenary Meeting might consider those of the recommendations of the Moscow Commission on *Reparations* on which agreement had been reached.

MR. BYRNES thought there was little prospect of securing agreement between the three Delegations on the outstanding points of disagreement; and he favoured bringing the whole matter direct to the Plenary Meeting. Some of these issues were, however, to be considered by the Economic Committee at their meeting that evening. He suggested that, if the Committee were able to reach agreement, their Report might be referred direct to the Plenary Meeting on the following day. If, on the other hand, they failed to agree, he thought it unlikely that the Foreign Secretaries would find a solution of these problems, and the position might be reported to the same Plenary Meeting.

It was agreed that Mr. Byrnes should suggest, for discussion at the Plenary Meeting that afternoon, the three subjects noted at *(a)* to *(c)* above.

Cabinet Office, Potsdam, 24th July, 1945

ANNEX TO No. 254

(F.(Terminal)7th Meeting Minute 4)[14]

Statement made to meeting of Foreign Secretaries on 24 July 1945 by representatives of the Polish Provisional Government on Western frontier of Poland

M. BIERUT said that he was grateful to the three Heads of Governments for giving him and his colleagues this opportunity of stating their views on the question of Poland's Western Frontier.

[12] No. 246.
[13] See No. 194, minute 6.   [14] See above.

The problem of Poland's Eastern Frontier had been settled at the Crimea Conference, but no decision had yet been taken with regard to the Western Frontier. The Polish Delegation asked that in the settlement of this matter the present Conference should bear in mind the vital interests of Poland. Poland had suffered great losses in the war, both in human life and in property. The war, which had been declared in the first instance on account of Poland, had shown that Poland was a very important factor in the peace of Europe. She recognised this and was prepared, like other belligerents, to make some sacrifices for the common good.

In the east, Poland had had to cede 180,000 square kilometres. The Polish Provisional Government thought, however, that this was a just settlement and one which was in accordance with the principle of nationality. They considered, however, that their loss in the east should be compensated by an equivalent accession of territory in the west, which should be regulated according to considerations of security and economics. They proposed that the line of Poland's Western Frontier should run from a point on the Baltic west of Swinemünde, leaving Stettin to Poland, and should then follow the line of the Oder and the western Neisse as far as the Czechoslovak frontier. If this line were adopted it would bring to Poland less territory than she had lost in the east, but since the Western territories were more closely integrated from an economic point of view than the Eastern they should provide the necessary guarantees for Poland's economic development. By such a settlement the total area of Poland would be reduced from 388,000 square kilometres to 309,000. The population of the new Poland would fall from 34 millions to 26 millions, but it would be more homogeneous than before the war. It would present no minorities problem. The great majority of the German residents had already fled from the areas claimed by Poland under this proposal. It was estimated that between one and [one and] one-half millions remained; but it was believed that many of these would be ready to leave the country. As regards the population of the territories East of the Curzon Line, the great majority were Ukrainians, White Russians and Lithuanians.

The density of population of pre-war Poland was 83 inhabitants per square kilometre. In order to maintain the same density, Poland would need 314,000 square kilometres of territory. Only 309,000 square kilometres were being claimed and the density of population would therefore rise. Since, however, the territories in the west were of greater economic value than those in the east, the population could be settled more satisfactorily in this smaller area, and there would be no need for Poles to emigrate, as they had done before the war, to the United States or to western Germany. There was the further point that before the war hundreds of thousands of Poles had been in the habit of going to Germany every year to work for the Germans, mostly in agriculture. It was just that Poland should acquire the land on which so many Polish workers had been employed, so that in future the Polish nation could enjoy the fruits of this Polish labour.

M. Rzymowski said that Poland had been the first victim of German imperialism. The war had begun in Poland and Poland had remained under German occupation for longer than any other Allied country. German economic policy during the war had shown that the Germans had intended to destroy Poland and incorporate it in the German *lebensraum*. When they reached Cracow, the heart of Poland's cultural life, they had arrested the University professors and had sought to destroy the cultural life of the country. As it had been the German aim to exterminate the Polish nation and Polish culture, so it should be the aim of the Allies to create a Polish State capable of resisting German aggression and of maintaining Polish life and traditions. For the sake of friendship with the Soviet Union a settlement in the east had been made which left 4 million Poles outside the frontiers of Poland. These Poles had the right to return to Poland and to find the means of earning a decent living there. The new democratic Poland must be able to absorb them. It must also provide a home and a livelihood for all those Poles who before the war had been forced to emigrate to Germany and to France in search of work.

It was just that, for the territory which she had ceded to the U.S.S.R. in the East, Poland should be compensated by these territories in the West. It was in the interests of maintaining peace that Poland had ceded these eastern territories; and it was appropriate that in the West territory should be given to Poland which had in the past been the fortress of German aggression. It was in the interests of peace in Europe that Germany should lose this territory, which had been a *place d'armes* on her eastern border.

Within the new boundaries proposed, Poland could establish a strong State which would be a unity economically, ethnologically and culturally. It would be a State without national minorities, and it could look forward with confidence to a healthy national development.

The claim of the Polish Provisional Government was moderate: it involved a loss of 80,000 kilometres of territory, as compared with pre-war Poland; but within this smaller area the Poles would have conditions more favourable to the economic and cultural development of their country.

Poland had special justification for laying claim to Silesia. Even before the war the bulk of the population in Silesia had been Polish, and as soon as the administrative pressure of Germany was removed the whole population in that area would feel and act like Poles.

The line of the Oder and the Neisse had not been lightly chosen. It represented the boundaries of an age-old Polish State, which was the cradle of the Polish nation. It was the shortest boundary and the easiest to defend against any future aggression by Germany. This was the only side on which the new Polish State was likely to be threatened by aggression; and if she could obtain a secure frontier to the West she would be a strong guarantee of peace and security in Europe.

Finally, the acquisition of a long coastline on the Baltic, together with the industrial area in Silesia, would give Poland a fair opportunity to reconstruct her social and economic life. Before the war a large proportion of the Polish population had lived in rural areas; over-population of the rural areas and under-development of the towns had been one of the main characteristics of Poland's social and economic structure. There had been an average of 4 million unemployed in the villages, for whom there was no room for these numbers in the towns. The inclusion of Silesia within the Polish borders would make it possible to provide industrial employment for the surplus population in the rural areas. The claim to Stettin was, of course, closely linked to the claim to Silesia; for Stettin was the natural outlet to the sea for the product of Silesian industry.

M. Mikolajczyk said that it was the interest of all that Germany should be unable to undertake any new aggression. German imperialism had been founded on her industrial war potential and on her commercial position as an intermediary with other countries in Eastern Europe.

One of the main bases of Germany's industrial war potential was in the territory claimed by Poland. The greater part of Germany's zinc production, and a large part of her coal production, was centred in Silesia. It was in the interests of world peace that these natural resources should not remain under German control.

Before the war, the value of German foreign trade was enormous. Very large quantities of goods have been transported across Germany from Czechoslovakia, Hungary, Roumania and Yugoslavia, apart from the goods transported from Poland itself. Although the natural route for these goods to reach the outside world was through Stettin, the Germans sent them through Hamburg. If Stettin were under Polish control they would find their natural outlet. Stettin and the whole Oder Basin was necessary to Poland because she would have to build up a large export and import trade to provide employment for her citizens and make good the damage she had suffered. The outlet provided by the Vistula was not sufficient.

The River Oder was not, however, naturally navigable, and in order to make it so the whole water resources of the Oder Basin had to be controlled. The sources of water for the purpose lay between the Oder and the western Neisse. If these were not in Polish hands the water could be cut off and navigation of the Oder could be seriously impeded. To give Poland what she claimed would not only contribute to the security of Poland and the whole world, but would also create a new economic and commercial system in eastern Europe, with Poland taking on the rôle of intermediary with the U.S.S.R. to the east and Czechoslovakia, Roumania and Hungary to the south.

Relatively speaking, Germany, who lost the war, would lose less territory than Poland. If the Polish claims were satisfied, she would still be losing 20 per cent. of her territory, while Germany would lose only 18 per cent.

The possibility of exchanging the German and Polish populations had been questioned. But it was the Germans who began these transfers, and the aim of Poland was to bring back the Poles who had lived in all parts of Germany before the war. In his view, the whole world would regard this as right.

In conclusion, he asked for a speedy and satisfactory decision. The repatriation of Polish citizens from the U.S.S.R. and other countries was an absolute necessity for the speedy reconstruction of Poland, and the territory claimed was required to provide homes for them in Poland.

No. 255

Minutes of the First (and only) Plenary Session between the United States and Great Britain, held at 2 Kaiserstrasse, Babelsberg, on Tuesday, 24 July 1945 at 11.30 a.m.
(Prepared by the British Secretaries)
[CAB 99/39]

Top secret

Present:

THE PRESIDENT, Fleet Admiral W. D. Leahy, General of the Army G. C. Marshall, Fleet Admiral E. J. King, General of the Army H. H. Arnold, General B. B. Somervell.

THE PRIME MINISTER, The Right Hon. Lord Leathers, Field-Marshal Sir Alan F. Brooke, Marshal of the Royal Air Force Sir Charles F. A. Portal, Admiral of the Fleet Sir Andrew B. Cunningham, General Sir Hastings L. Ismay, Field-Marshal Sir Henry Maitland Wilson, Major-General R. E. Laycock.

Secretariat:
Major-General L. C. Hollis, Brigadier-General A. J. McFarland, Brigadier A. T. Cornwall-Jones.

1. *Arrival of the Supreme Allied Commander, South-East Asia*

THE PRIME MINISTER said that Admiral Mountbatten was about to arrive in Potsdam. He suggested that the Combined Chiefs of Staff might take the opportunity of his presence to hear an account of the latest situation in South-East Asia. A considerable situation seemed to be developing in Lower Burma.

2. *Report to the President and the Prime Minister*
(C.C.S. 900/2)[1]

THE MEETING had before them the draft of the final report to the President and the Prime Minister containing the results of the Combined Chiefs of Staff 'Terminal' discussions (C.C.S. 900/2).[1]

THE PRESIDENT and THE PRIME MINISTER proceeded to examine the report paragraph by paragraph.

Coming to paragraph 4 FLEET ADMIRAL LEAHY explained that there was a divergence of view on two or three points in regard to the basic undertakings and policies for the prosecution of the war, and the Prime Minister and the President then turned to examine the respective views of their Chiefs of Staff as set out in Appendix 'A.'[2]

Appendix 'A', Paragraph 4.

Fleet Admiral Leahy explained that the United States Chiefs of Staff proposed to include the following:–

'A. Maintain the security of the western hemisphere and the British Commonwealth,

'B. Maintain the war-making capacity of the United States and British Commonwealth in so far as it is connected with the prosecution of the war against Japan.'

The British Chiefs of Staff on the other hand wished to amalgamate these two paragraphs in one and express them as follows:

'Maintain the security and war-making capacity of the western hemisphere and the British Commonwealth as necessary for the fulfilment of the strategic concept.'

The difference between the two was that the United States Chiefs of Staff felt that the basic commitment in this respect should be confined to the maintenance of war-making capacity in so far as it was connected with the

[1] No. 249.
[2] To the enclosure in No. 249.

prosecution of the war, whereas the British Chiefs of Staff felt that it should be extended to include the occupation of Germany and Austria, as provided in the strategic concept.

THE PRIME MINISTER said that he supported the British Chiefs of Staff and suggested that the holding down of Germany and Austria was certainly a very vital matter. He felt therefore that this commitment should be embraced in this particular section of the basic undertakings.

The Prime Minister then drew a picture of the extent to which the British industrial effort had been interwoven with that of the United States, as a result of agreements reached earlier in the war and his own discussions with President Roosevelt at Quebec.[3] As a result of these agreements many British units were equipped with United States equipment and no provision had been made to replace this equipment from British sources. To make such provision would take time and he hoped very much that the President would be able to make it possible for him to pass smoothly from this position of dependence on the United States to one in which British forces could be independent. He feared that a rigid interpretation of an undertaking to maintain the British war-making capacity only in so far as it was connected with the prosecution of the war against Japan, would place him in great difficulties. He hoped also that the rules applied to the supply of Lend-Lease equipment would not be held to limit British sovereign rights over British equipment. He must be free to give British equipment, for example, to the Belgians, if His Majesty's Government felt that this was desirable, and he hoped that this would not result in the drying up of equivalent supplies from the United States.

THE PRESIDENT explained that he was handicapped in his approach to this matter by the latest renewal of the Lend-Lease Act. As Vice-President, he had worked out its clauses together with Senator George, who had explained to the Congress that the Act was intended to be a weapon of war only. The President was now striving to give to the Act the broadest interpretation possible and he had no intention of causing the British any embarrassment in the matter of furnishing supplies to British troops or the maintenance thereof. However, he must ask the Prime Minister to be patient as he wished to avoid any embarrassment with Congress over the interpretation of the Act and it might be necessary for him to ask for additional legislation in order to clear the matter up.

With respect to the basic undertaking under discussion, The President said that he thought that the holding down of Germany and Austria was quite definitely a part of war. After all, we were technically still at war with Germany and Austria.

GENERAL OF THE ARMY MARSHALL said in view of the foregoing that the United States Chiefs of Staff accepted the paragraph proposed by the British Chiefs of Staff.

[3] Cf. No. 26, note 7.

Appendix 'A', Paragraph 4 C

THE PRIME MINISTER said that he did not see there was very much difference between the two sub-paragraphs proposed. He suggested that the proposal of the United States Chiefs of Staff should be accepted.

THE PRESIDENT agreed.

Appendix 'A', first sentence of paragraph 6 C

FLEET ADMIRAL LEAHY explained that the British Chiefs of Staff were anxious to add a clause at the end of the first sentence of this paragraph which would extend the combined liability to provide assistance not only to such of the forces of the liberated areas as could fulfil an active and effective rôle in the present war, but also to such of those forces as were 'required to maintain world order in the interests of the war effort.' Thus, in his view, the issue before the meeting was whether or not the United States were prepared to undertake a commitment to equip and supply forces of occupation other than American.

THE PRIME MINISTER asked what the British Chiefs of Staff had in mind in proposing this clause.

FIELD-MARSHAL BROOKE instanced the Belgian and Dutch forces, and ADMIRAL OF THE FLEET CUNNINGHAM suggested that such French divisions as were not going to the Far East would also fall into this category.

In the light of this explanation, THE PRIME MINISTER felt that the point had already been covered under the discussion over Appendix 'A,' paragraphs 4A and B above, where it had already been agreed that occupational forces should be included in that particular basic undertaking.

It was agreed that the point would be adequately covered if the words 'in accordance with the over-all strategic concept,' were added to the first sentence of paragraph 6C, in lieu of the clause proposed by the British Chiefs of Staff.

Appendix 'A', Paragraph 7

At this point Lord Leathers entered the meeting.

THE PRIME MINISTER explained that he attached great importance to the United Kingdom import programme and would not wish to see it lose its status in a document of this nature.

THE PRESIDENT said that he was not quite clear how far he could accept liability for reconstruction and rehabilitation of the United Kingdom under existing United States law. If, therefore, this paragraph were intended to indicate any such liability, his acceptance of it would have to be on the understanding that the necessary authority did exist.

FLEET ADMIRAL KING and GENERAL OF THE ARMY MARSHALL explained that the United States Chiefs of Staff felt that this paragraph was out of place as a basic undertaking. General of the Army Marshall drew attention to paragraphs 20, 21 and 22 of the Report and suggested that the proper place for this paragraph would be at the end of the Report under the heading 'Miscellaneous.' If this particular item on Cargo Shipping were to be included as a basic undertaking, then there would be other subjects which also ought to be included.

LORD LEATHERS pointed out that the inclusion of the United Kingdom import programme had been implicit in the basic undertakings at previous conferences. In consonance with the changed situation, a major change was now being made in the presentation of the basic undertakings. As shipping requirements for military and civilian needs were closely interlocked, his view was that the United Kingdom import programme would be more properly associated with military requirements if it were linked to them in the basic undertakings.

GENERAL OF THE ARMY MARSHALL said that he did not consider that any great change had been made in the presentation of the basic undertakings. He still felt that the matter would be more properly included at the end of the Report under the heading 'Miscellaneous.'

THE PRIME MINISTER enquired whether this would result in the United Kingdom import programme being swept aside.

THE PRESIDENT suggested that General of the Army Marshall's proposal should be accepted and the paragraph incorporated at the end of the Final Report. The Prime Minister could take his word for it that the United Kingdom import programme would not suffer from this change.

THE PRIME MINISTER said that on this understanding he would certainly agree that the paragraph should be included at the end of the Report.

Appendix 'A', last sentence of paragraph 6 C

LORD LEATHERS suggested that as it had now been agreed that paragraph 7 should be removed from the basic undertakings and placed at the end of the Report, the last sentence of paragraph 6C would more properly be deleted. However, if it were held that this sentence merely referred to supplies and not to shipping, he thought it might remain.

THE PRESIDENT and THE PRIME MINISTER agreed that the last sentence of paragraph 6C should stand.

The Prime Minister referred to paragraph 8d of the Report, in which it had been agreed that 'In the event the British Chiefs of Staff should decide that they cannot commit British troops in support of a decision made by the United States Chiefs of Staff, the British Chiefs of Staff would give to the United States Chiefs of Staff such advance notice of their decision as would permit them to make timely rearrangements.' The Prime Minister said that he hoped it would not be thought the British Chiefs of Staff would wish to take advantage of this arrangement. What was good enough for the United States would certainly be good enough for the British.

FLEET ADMIRAL KING said that the United States Chiefs of Staff did not expect that the British Chiefs of Staff would have to invoke this paragraph and GENERAL OF THE ARMY MARSHALL explained that it had been put in at his suggestion. After 'Olympic'[4] for example, if the British Chiefs of Staff

---

[4] Code-name for the American plan to invade Kyushu.

did not agree with the action proposed by the United States Chiefs of Staff, they would by this paragraph be free to take such action as they thought fit. The paragraph was the result of an attempt on his part to cover both sides.

THE PRIME MINISTER thanked the United States Chiefs of Staff for their explanation and the spirit in which this provision had been made.

THE PRESIDENT and THE PRIME MINISTER accepted and approved the report as amended in the above discussion, and directed that copies of the revised version be submitted to them for signature. (The report in its approved form was subsequently circulated as C.C.S. 900/3.)[5]

[5] This report, not here printed, was the enclosure in No. 249 as revised by the amendments above; this revise is printed in *F.R.U.S. Berlin*, vol. ii, pp. 1462–73.

No. 256

Record of First Tripartite Military Meeting held at the Cecilienhof on Tuesday, 24 July 1945 at 2.30 p.m.

M.(*Terminal*)1 [*CAB 99/39*]

Top secret

Present:

ADMIRAL OF THE FLEET KUZNETSOV, Army General Antonov, Marshal of Aviation Falaleev, Lieut.-General Slavin, Major-General Vaviliov, Captain (1st rank) Kushkov, Captain (3rd rank) Sobolev, Major Evsekov (*Interpreter*).

FLEET ADMIRAL W. D. LEAHY, USN, General of the Army G. C. Marshall, USA, Fleet Admiral E. J. King, USN, General of the Army H. H. ARNOLD, USA, Brigadier-General A. J. McFarland, USA, Captain C. J. Moore, USN, Lieut. J. Chase, USNR (*Interpreter*).

FIELD-MARSHAL SIR ALAN F. BROOKE, Marshal of the Royal Air Force Sir Charles F. A. Portal, Admiral of the Fleet Sir Andrew B. Cunningham, General Sir Hastings L. Ismay, Major-General L. C. Hollis, Lieut.-Colonel G. Mallaby, Major H. A. Lunghi (*Interpreter*).

Russian Participation in the War against Japan

At the suggestion of Army General Antonov and with the concurrence of Field-Marshal Sir Alan Brooke, Fleet Admiral Leahy took the chair.

FLEET ADMIRAL LEAHY enquired what information the Russian Chiefs of Staff could now give on their plans and intentions against Japanese-held areas in the Far East.

ARMY GENERAL ANTONOV said that Soviet troops were now concentrating in the Far East and would be ready to begin operations on a certain date (communicated very secretly to the Conference).[1] The actual date for the start of operations would depend upon negotiations with China, which were still in progress. He said that the object of Russian operations would be to destroy Japanese troops in Manchuria and to advance to the L[i]aotung Peninsula. He added that after the defeat of Japan the Soviet Armies would withdraw from Manchuria.

He gave the Soviet estimate of Japanese forces in Manchuria as about 30 divisions, together with about 20 Manchurian divisions. He pointed out that in order to enable the Soviet operations to achieve success, it was important that the Japanese should not reinforce Manchuria from China and the Japanese islands. The Soviet Staff had calculated that the Japanese might bring as many as ten divisions from China and seven divisions from Japanese islands, and considering the lack of communications through Eastern Russia, where there was only one railway line, it was essential that Japanese reinforcements should be continuously impeded.

He asked whether the United States Chiefs of Staff would now outline their view of the situation in the war against Japan.

General of the Army Marshall gave an outline of the situation in the Western Pacific and showed how in areas not yet occupied by United States forces the Japanese were withering away through lack of supplies and through disease. He thought there might be about a million Japanese in China, though some had lately moved away to Kyushu. He emphasised the enormous development of bases which was taking place in order to allow the full employment of forces against Japan. Already, by naval and air action, Japanese communications between the main islands and the mainland were very much interfered with, and he doubted now if any troop movements could take place from the main islands to Manchuria. He thought that towards the end of this year it would be almost impossible for cargo shipping to move along this route.

With regard to China, he said that a general withdrawal of Japanese was taking place from South China except for Japanese garrisons in particular places such as Canton and Hong Kong. Air attacks on railways and sabotage had made this movement a difficult problem for the Japanese and these difficulties would increase when General Wedemeyer's operations developed, since the capture of Fort Bayard would permit a much more economical introduction of supplies of aviation fuel. The 10th and 14th Air Forces would then be fully equipped to operate against the railway communications in China.

Fleet Admiral King gave a summary of the naval situation in the Pacific and outlined the operations that had taken place since the Yalta Conference. He said that the Japanese Fleet had been reduced to a third of

[1] In the fuller American record of this meeting printed in *F.R.U.S. Berlin*, vol. ii, pp. 344–53, the corresponding sentence read: '*General Antonov* said that Soviet troops were now being concentrated in the Far East and would be ready to commence operations in the last half of August.'

its strength and that, apart from suicide attacks, the remainder were of doubtful value.

GENERAL OF THE ARMY ARNOLD explained the limitations on the deployment and operation of air forces against Japan and the steps that were being undertaken to overcome these limitations. He said that the performance of the B.29 had exceeded expectations and that with increasing experience of weather conditions and the continuous weakening of Japanese opposition, he thought that the weight of bombs which could be dropped on Japanese industries and communications both in the main islands and in Manchuria would be most formidable.

ARMY GENERAL ANTONOV enquired again whether the United States Chiefs of Staff thought it would be possible for the Japanese to bring reinforcements into Manchuria either from China or Japan.

GENERAL OF THE ARMY MARSHALL repeated that it was unlikely that movements of troops from Japan to Manchuria could now take place and that the operations now being developed would make it a difficult and slow process to bring in large reinforcements overland from China into Manchuria.

ARMY GENERAL ANTONOV then put forward two questions:–

(a) Would it be possible to operate against the Kuriles to secure communications to Soviet ports?

(b) Would it be possible to mount amphibious operations against Korea in support of Russian operations against the Laotung Peninsula?

FLEET ADMIRAL KING said that it would not be necessary to conduct operations against the Kuriles in order to maintain sea communications to Soviet ports.

GENERAL OF THE ARMY MARSHALL said that the United States Chiefs of Staff were not contemplating any amphibious operations against Korea in the near future. All available assault shipping and craft were already earmarked for operations against Kyushu. He realised the importance to the Soviet Armies of operations against Korea but said that it would be necessary to examine the situation again after the attacks upon Kyushu.

FLEET ADMIRAL KING pointed out that after the capture of Kyushu, it should be possible to open sea communications to Vladivostok.

ARMY GENERAL ANTONOV enquired whether the United States Chiefs of Staff had any suggestions to make about possible Russian courses of action.

GENERAL OF THE ARMY MARSHALL said that the United States Chiefs of Staff had prepared some written questions[2] for the Soviet Staff which he asked General Antonov to consider in due course.

FLEET ADMIRAL KING recalled the conversations with the Russians at Yalta and asked whether the Soviet Staff thought operations against Southern Sakhalin were possible.

---

[2] Note in filed copy: 'Annex', not printed. This American questionnaire comprising five operational questions respecting the war in the Far East is printed op. cit., vol. ii, pp. 1327–8.

ARMY GENERAL ANTONOV explained that they had examined operations against Southern Sakhalin but they involved large movements of Soviet forces and, therefore, could not be undertaken as early as operations against Manchuria. It was for that reason that the Soviet Staff had decided that the first step should be operations against Manchuria.

GENERAL OF THE ARMY MARSHALL then handed two books to General Antonov:–

(a) A book summarising United States experiences of their operations against the Japanese.

(b) A book giving the United States estimate of the present Japanese situation.

FLEET ADMIRAL LEAHY then asked the British Chiefs of Staff to outline the present position in South-East Asia Command.

SIR ALAN BROOKE outlined the present situation in Burma and the preparations now being made for the clearance of Malaya, the opening of the Malacca Straits and the recapture of Singapore. He pointed out that these operations would shorten the sea communications by which we could send help to the Americans in their main operations against the Japanese main islands. The limitation on the size of assistance we could send was availability of shipping.

SIR ANDREW CUNNINGHAM said that since the destruction of two Japanese 8-inch cruisers, there was little of the Japanese Fleet left west of Singapore.

SIR CHARLES PORTAL said that Anglo-American Air Forces in South-East Asia Command enjoyed complete superiority over the Japanese Air Force which in Burma, Siam, Malaya and Sumatra was estimated on the 15th July to amount to 260 aircraft, a figure which was not likely to be increased.

ARMY GENERAL ANTONOV, in conclusion, stated that the Soviet Staff would now study the questions addressed to them by the United States Chiefs of Staff and would then ask for a further meeting.[3]

Cabinet Office, Potsdam, 24th July, 1945

[3] The Soviet reply to the American questionnaire remitted to General Antonov was given at a meeting of the United States and Soviet Chiefs of Staff held in the Cecilienhof Palace at 3 p.m. on 26 July 1945: cf. *op. cit.*, vol. ii, pp. 408–17.

No. 257

Record of a Meeting at the Prime Minister's Residence, Potsdam, on 24 July 1945 at 3.15 p.m.

[*F.O. 934/2/10(52)*]

Present:

THE PRIME MINISTER, The Foreign Secretary, Sir A. Clark Kerr, Field-Marshal Alexander, Mr. Rowan, Mr. Allen, Captain Leggett (*Interpreter*).

PRESIDENT BIERUT, M. Osóbka-Morawski, M. Mikolajczyk, M. Gomólka, M. Rzymowski, Marshal Rola Zymiesski[*sic*], Professor Grabski, M. Modzielewski [*sic*].

THE PRIME MINISTER, after welcoming the Polish delegation, said that Great Britain had entered the war on the occasion of the invasion of Poland and in consequence of her treaty engagements. We had always taken the greatest interest in Poland and would not be satisfied unless Poland emerged from the war strong and independent with worthy territory to live in. We had exerted ourselves greatly during the last year to ensure that Poland should enjoy such a position. Our relations with Soviet Russia were warm and friendly. We wanted Poland to be friendly to the Russians but also independent of them. We could not tolerate a Poland that plotted against Soviet Russia who had the right to have a friendly Poland on her frontiers. A hostile Poland would be a disaster for Russia. There was, however, little danger of that. Although many Poles hated Russia the great majority were now agreed that it was essential to them to live in friendship with their eastern neighbour.

There was therefore a broad basis of agreement from which we could start the present discussions. His Majesty's Government had always been the champions of a strong and independent Poland. But they were not supporters of the frontiers which Poland had now been offered and apparently wished to take. We had thought in terms rather of a frontier that might extend to the Oder in some places but would not follow its whole length. Now Poland was claiming a frontier on the western Neisse. It was a mistake for countries to be guided purely by territorial appetite. The frontiers now claimed by Poland would involve the loss by Germany of one-quarter of the arable land she possessed in 1937. It would mean the movement of from eight to nine million persons, whereas the total number of Poles displaced from east of the Curzon Line amounted to only three to four millions. The idea of such great shiftings of population came as a shock to the western democracies. The Poles should keep within the limits necessary to give Poland an adequate home. Their present claims would not constitute a lasting and final arrangement. They would not receive the blessing of Great Britain nor probably of the western democracies as a whole. It was dangerous for a country to bite off more than it could chew.

Great Britain also had an interest in this question. Poland, and to some extent Russia too, were taking the large feeding grounds on which Germany had always drawn for supplies, particularly of food and coal. This part of Germany was the most productive of food, whereas the British zone produced less, and had in addition to support the people who had sought refuge there. The result was that the Poles and the Russians had the food and the fuel, while we had the mouths and the hearths. We should oppose such a division particularly when the question of reparations had also to be taken into account. We were discussing all this in great detail with our Russian friends. We were not moved in any way by ill will towards Poland, but we were convinced that there was a danger the Poles might go too far in pressing towards the west just as they had once pressed too far to the east.

There were other matters which troubled us. If British opinion were to be reassured about developments in Poland it was essential that the elections that were to be held should be genuinely free and unfettered and that all the main democratic parties should have full opportunity to participate and to make their programmes known. It would be asked what was the definition of democratic parties. He did not take the view that only Communists were democrats. It was easy to call everyone who was not a Communist a Fascist beast. But between these two extremes there lay great and powerful forces which were neither one or the other. Surely it was to Poland's advantage that the basis of political life should be widened to include as many as possible of these moderate elements instead of branding with the stigmas of war all those who did not fit the pre-conceived definitions of the extremists.

Anyone with power could now in the present distracted state of Europe strike at his opponents and condemn them, but the result was merely that the moderate elements were excluded from political life. It took all sorts to make a country. Could Poland afford to divide herself? She should seek a unity as broad as possible so that she might join hands with the west as well as with her Russian friends.

For example, it would be important that the Christian Democrat Party and all those sections of the National Democrat Party not compromised by active collaboration with the enemy should take part in the elections. M. Popiel should be given full opportunity to revive his party and to take part in the restoration of Polish political life.

We should also expect that the press, and naturally our Embassy, should enjoy full freedom to see and report what was happening in Poland before and during the elections.

Only by pursuing a policy of tolerance and even, on occasion, mutual forgiveness could Poland preserve the regard and support of the western democracies and especially of Great Britain, who had something to give and also something to withhold.

M. BIERUT, after thanking the Prime Minister for his invitation and for his frank statement, said that it would be a terrible mistake if Great Britain, after having entered the war for the sake of Poland, did not show understanding for Poland's claims, which were modest and took account of the needs of peace in Europe. Poland did not claim more than she had lost. To satisfy her claims it would be necessary to shift only one and a half million Germans (inclusive of those in East Prussia) who were all that remained. Poland needed new territory to settle four million Poles from east of the Curzon Line and some three million who would return from abroad. She would have less territory than before the war. She had lost valuable agricultural land round Vilna and valuable forests (Poland was always poor in timber) as well as the oil-fields of Galicia. Before the war some eight hundred thousand Polish farm hands had always migrated as seasonal workers to eastern Germany. A majority of the population in the areas claimed, especially in Silesia, were really Poles though attempts had been made to Germanise them. These territories were historically Polish. East Prussia still retained a large Polish population in the Masurians.

THE PRIME MINISTER interjected to say that there was no dispute about the cession to Poland of East Prussia south and west of Königsberg.

M. BIERUT continued that, whereas Germany, who had lost the war, would lose eighteen per cent of her territory, Poland would on balance lose twenty per cent. The density of population in Poland before the war (an average of eighty-three per square kilometre) was such that the Poles had had to emigrate.

The Poles asked only that their claims should be closely examined. It would be found that the boundary they proposed was the shortest possible frontier line between Poland and Germany. It would give Poland just compensation for her losses and her contribution to Allied victory. The Poles believed that the British people would sympathise with their wish that Poland's wrongs should be righted.

THE PRIME MINISTER pointed out that hitherto it had been impossible for us to find out for ourselves how matters stood in Poland, since it was a closed area. Could we not send people with full freedom to move about in Poland and tell us what was happening there?

In conclusion, the Prime Minister repeated his warning that though he was in favour of ample compensation for Poland he thought the Poles were ill-advised to ask for as much territory as they were now seeking.

No. 258

Record of Eighth Plenary Meeting held at Cecilienhof, Potsdam, on Tuesday, 24 July 1945 at 5 p.m.

P.(*Terminal*)*8th Meeting* [U 6197/3628/70]

Top secret

Present:

PREMIER STALIN, M. V. M. Molotov, M. A. Ya. Vyshinski, M. F. T. Gousev, M. A. A. Gromyko, M. K. V. Novikov, M. A. A. Sobolev, M. B. F. Podtzerob, M. V. N. Pavlov (*Interpreter*).

PRESIDENT TRUMAN, Mr. J. F. Byrnes, Mr. Joseph E. Davies, Fleet-Admiral W. D. Leahy, Mr. W. A. Harriman, Mr. J. C. Dunn, Mr. H. F. Matthews, Mr. B. V. Cohen, Mr. L. E. Thompson, Mr. C. E. Bohlen (*Interpreter*).

MR. CHURCHILL, Mr. Eden, Mr. Attlee, Sir A. Cadogan, Field-Marshal Sir Harold Alexander (*for items 5–7*), Sir A. Clark Kerr, Sir W. Strang, Sir E. Bridges, Mr. T. L. Rowan, Mr. P. J. Dixon, Mr. W. Hayter, Major A. Birse (*Interpreter*).

Contents

Minute	Subject
1.	Foreign Secretaries' Report
2.	Western Frontier of Poland
3.	Neutral and ex-Enemy States: Admission to United Nations
4.	Turkey

5. Ukrainians in British Prisoner of War Camp in Italy
6. Austria: Supply of Food to the British and United States Zones
7. Austria: Authority of Dr. Renner's Government
8. Procedure: Issue of a Communiqué at the End of the Conference

1. *Foreign Secretaries' Report*

MR. BYRNES submitted the Report of the meeting of the Foreign Secretaries held that morning[1] as follows:

(i) *Reparations from Germany, Austria and Italy.*
(Previous Reference: F. (Terminal) 7th Meeting,[1] Minute 1 (iii).)

MR. BYRNES said that the committee dealing with Germany's economic problems and German reparations was not yet ready to present a further report on these matters. M. Molotov had pointed out that this committee had also been asked to consider the question of Austrian and Italian reparations. He had presented two brief papers[2] in regard to reparations from these two latter countries. It had been agreed that these papers should be referred to the Economic Committee for study.

It had also been agreed that discussion of German reparations and German economic questions, and of Italian and Austrian reparations, should be postponed until the following morning. The Economic Sub-Committee would meet that night in the hope of completing their Report, or at least of making some further progress.

(ii) *European Oil Supplies.*
(Previous Reference: F. (Terminal) 7th Meeting,[1] Minute 1 (iv).)

MR. BYRNES said that he had inquired whether a report was ready on the United States paper on this subject which had been presented on the 20th July.[3] He had ascertained that this paper was still before the Economic Committee and it had been agreed that discussion of this subject should be postponed until that committee had reported.

(iii) *Yalta Declaration on Liberated Europe.*
(Previous Reference: F. (Terminal)7th Meeting,[1] Minute 1 (v).)

The committee dealing with this subject was not yet ready to report and it had been agreed to postpone discussion until their report was available.

(iv) *Roumanian Oil Equipment.*
(Previous Reference: F. (Terminal) 7th Meeting,[1] Minute 3.)

The British Delegation had circulated a new paper[4] regarding the disposition of British and United States oil equipment in Roumania. The Soviet delegation had asked for time to study this paper and discussion of this question had therefore been adjourned.

[1] See No. 254.
[2] Nos. 261 and 262.
[3] See No. 214, note 10.
[4] No. 264.

(v) *Agenda for Present Meeting.*

Mr. Byrnes proposed the following:

(a) *Western Frontier of Poland*—Report of statement made to the Foreign Secretaries' Meeting by representatives of the Polish Provisional Government.

(b) *Neutral and Ex-enemy States: Admission to the United Nations*—The paper presented to the Foreign Ministers that morning[5] was available to the Heads of Government as a basis for discussion.

(c) *The Black Sea Straits and Free and Unrestricted Navigation of International Inland Waterways*—Discussion of this question had been adjourned at the Plenary Meeting the previous day in order to afford an opportunity for study of the paper on Free and Unrestricted Navigation of International Inland Waterways which President Truman had circulated.[6]

(vi) *Agenda for Plenary Meeting on 25th July.*

Mr. Byrnes proposed the following subjects for discussion at the Plenary Meeting on the 25th July:

(a) Disposition of the German fleet and merchant marine.

(b) Reparations.

2. *Western Frontier of Poland*

(Previous Reference: F. (Terminal) 7th Meeting,[1] Minute 4.)

MR. BYRNES said that a delegation representing the Polish Provisional Government and headed by President Bierut had stated their views to the Foreign Secretaries' Meeting that morning. He assumed that each Foreign Secretary had reported the principal points covered in the statements made by the Polish Delegation, but he would summarise these if this was desired.

PREMIER STALIN said this would be very useful.

MR. BYRNES said that the Polish Delegation considered that the Western frontier of Poland should run from a point on the Baltic, west of Swinemünde, leaving Stettin on the Polish side, and should then follow the line of the River Oder and the Western Neisse as far as the Czechoslovakian frontier. The principal arguments put forward by the Polish Delegation in support of this frontier were as follows:

(a) Poland would lose 180,000 sq. kilometres of territory in the East, and should receive some compensation in the West.

(b) The territory under consideration was a single economic unit.

(c) Under this proposal Poland would receive less territory in the West than she had given up in the East. The area of Poland would be reduced from 388,000 sq. kilometres to 309,000. Her population would be reduced from 34 million to 26 million, but it would be more homogeneous.

(d) From 1 to 1½ million Germans were left in the area, but in the opinion of the Polish Delegation these would be willing to leave the country and

[5] See No. 254, minute 2.
[6] See No. 241, minute 10, and No. 246.

to return to Germany. This territory in the West would enable Poland not only to support her population, but also to employ those Poles who had formerly been in the habit of going every year to work in Germany.

(e) From the point of view of security, the frontier proposed was the shortest possible line and the easiest to defend.

(f) Germany had tried to destroy the Polish nation and to ruin Polish culture. It would be an expression of justice to compensate Poland in this way.

(g) Poland had ceded territory in the East for the sake of preserving peace, and it would be right for Germany to cede territory in the East which had been a fortress of German aggression.

(h) This transfer of territory would reduce Germany's capacity for war production in the East. It would leave Poland without any problem of national minorities.

(i) Before the war, a large proportion of Poles had lived in rural areas, and there had been an excess of rural population which could not be absorbed in urban centres. The acquisition of the new territory would enable this excess population to be employed in Poland, and Poles who had been forced to emigrate would be able to return to Poland.

(j) The area in question had been one of the bases of the German armament industry. It contained an important coal basin and had been one of the centres of German Imperialism. The loss of this territory would also deprive Germany of potash.

(k) Before the war, Germany's foreign trade had been very large and great quantities of goods had been transported across Germany from Czechoslovakia, Hungary, Roumania and Yugoslavia, apart from the goods transported from Poland itself. The natural route for these goods to reach the outside world was through Stettin, but Germany had sent them through Hamburg. With Stettin in Polish control, these would find their natural outlet.

(l) The whole Oder Basin was necessary to Poland in order that the whole water resource of the Oder Basin could be controlled, since the river was not naturally navigable.

(m) If the proposed transfer of territory was agreed, Poland would still lose, as a result of the war, a larger proportion of her territories (20 per cent) than would Germany (18 per cent).

(n) A speedy decision of this question by the Great Powers was very necessary, so as to promote the return from abroad of the Poles who must participate in the rebuilding of Poland.

The question was raised whether there was time for discussion of this matter at the present meeting.

Mr. Churchill said that he hoped to see M. Bierut shortly and thought the discussion should be postponed to a later Meeting.

This was agreed to.

3. *Neutral and Ex-Enemy States: Admission to United Nations*
(Previous Reference: F. (Terminal) 7th Meeting,[1] Minute 2.)

MR. BYRNES said that at the Meeting of Foreign Secretaries that morning he had suggested that, as the Committee dealing with this matter had not been able to come to any agreement, the question should be considered by the Foreign Secretaries on the basis of the document on which the Committee had been working. M. Molotov had then said that the Soviet Delegation would not be able to take part in the discussion of this document since it omitted reference to the admission to the United Nations of Bulgaria, Hungary, Roumania and Finland. Mr. Eden had suggested that the last sentence of the first paragraph of the paper in question be dropped, and Mr. Byrnes had agreed. Mr. Eden had proposed a redraft of paragraph two of the paper which would take into account the interest of other countries concerned with the peace treaty with Italy. The amended paragraph was embodied in the revised draft. (See P. (Terminal) 35.)[7]

Mr. Byrnes said that he had then proposed the following additional paragraph in order to meet the point which M. Molotov had raised:

'The three Governments also hope that the Council of Foreign Ministers may, without undue delay, prepare peace treaties for Roumania, Bulgaria, Hungary and Finland. It is also their desire, on the conclusion of the peace treaties with responsible democratic Governments of these countries, to support their application for membership in the United Nations Organisation.'

M. Molotov had urged that it should be agreed in principle that Roumania, Bulgaria, Hungary and Finland should not be put in a worse position in this matter than Italy. Mr. Byrnes had suggested that, with the language offered, which was identical with that for Italy, M. Molotov's purpose would be fulfilled. After some further discussion, however, it had been agreed that, since full agreement could not be reached, the problem should be referred to the Plenary Meeting that afternoon.

Mr. Byrnes said that he understood there was agreement between the British and United States Delegations on the text of the paper which had been circulated to the Meeting, including amendments proposed by the United States Delegation.

MR. EDEN said he had some doubts about the amendment which proposed the insertion of the words 'with a responsible and democratic Italian Government' in paragraph 2 of the draft after the words 'conclusion of such a Peace Treaty.' This would make it look as though we thought that the Italian Government must be reconstructed before a Peace Treaty could be negotiated with Italy.

MR. BYRNES said that this amendment had been suggested in the hope that it would meet the view, expressed by M. Molotov at the Foreign Secretaries Meeting that morning, that invidious comparison between Italy and the other satellites should be avoided. The amended wording

[7] No. 260.

646

would mean that Italy would be supported for membership of the United Nations only when we were satisfied with the character of the Italian Government. The United States had already shown their satisfaction by resuming diplomatic relations with Italy.

MR. EDEN said that, in view of this explanation, he would not resist the proposed amendment.

PREMIER STALIN said that, if the point at issue was to ease the position of the satellites, then all the satellites should be mentioned in paragraph 2. The position of Italy would be eased under the proposed statement, and he did not object to that. On the other hand, an abnormal position was being created for the other satellites. This artificial distinction drawn between the different satellites compelled him to think that Roumania, Hungary, Bulgaria and Finland were being treated as lepers.[8] In this he saw an intention to discredit the Soviet Union and the Soviet Army. What were the deserts of Italy in comparison with the other satellites? Italy had been the first to surrender, but otherwise her behaviour had been worse than any of the others. None of the other satellites had done so much harm to the Allies as Italy had. He questioned whether the Italian Government was really more democratic or more responsible than the other Governments. No democratic elections had been held in Italy, or in the other satellite States, so that in this respect they were equal. He was, therefore, not clear as to the cause of such a benevolent attitude to Italy in comparison with the others. The first step towards easing Italy's position had been taken when diplomatic relations had been resumed. Now it was proposed to take a second step. He was in favour of this. But, at the same time, let us take the first step towards the other satellites by resuming diplomatic relations with them. This would be just.

MR. CHURCHILL said he was in general agreement with the United States Delegation's proposals. (As in P. (Terminal) 35.)[7]

PRESIDENT TRUMAN said the reason for the different attitude towards Roumania, Hungary and Bulgaria was that we had been seriously hampered in our efforts to get free access to these countries and information from and about them. This was not the case in Italy, where everyone was free to come and go. As he had said at the Conference the other day, when satisfactory Governments had been set up in these countries, and freedom of movement and communications had been established on a proper basis, the United States Government would be willing to recognise them as they had recognised Italy. It was for this reason that the paper attempted to deal with Roumania, Bulgaria, Hungary and Finland on exactly the same basis as Italy.

M. MOLOTOV[9] said that the United States Government had already re-established diplomatic relations with Italy.

[8] Parts of this sentence, and of other passages in the present minute, are cited by Sir L. Woodward, *op. cit.*, vol. v, p. 477.

[9] This observation and the further statement below in the name of M. Molotov are ascribed to Marshal Stalin in the Soviet record, *Conferences: Soviet Documents*, pp. 245-7.

PRESIDENT TRUMAN said that the other satellites could have the same recognition when they had complied with the United States Government's requirements, but this they had not so far done.

PREMIER STALIN said that none of these satellites could, since the war was over, hamper the Allied representatives from moving freely and getting any information.

PRESIDENT TRUMAN repeated that nevertheless they had done so.

PREMIER STALIN said that restrictions had also been placed on the Russian representatives in Italy.

PRESIDENT TRUMAN said he was asking for the reconstitution of the satellite Governments on democratic lines, in accordance with the Yalta Declaration.

PREMIER STALIN said that he could give an assurance that the satellite Governments were more democratic and nearer to the people than was the Italian Government.

PRESIDENT TRUMAN said that he had already made it quite plain that the United States Government would not recognise the satellite Governments until they had been reconstituted on a democratic basis.

PREMIER STALIN said that the words 'responsible and democratic' should be deleted, both with reference to the Governments of Bulgaria, Finland, Hungary and Roumania and with reference to the Italian Government, since these words only served to discredit the Governments concerned.

PRESIDENT TRUMAN said that he could only support these Governments if he was satisfied that they were both responsible and democratic.

PREMIER STALIN said that these Governments were not Fascist—in fact, much less Fascist than the Government of the Argentine, which had been admitted to the World Organisation. If they were not Fascist, then they must be democratic. He thought that the word 'responsible' reflected discredit on them. He must ask that the resumption of diplomatic relations should be mentioned in the document. This should be regarded as the first step in preparation of Peace Treaties for these States.

M. MOLOTOV proposed that there should be added to the paragraph dealing with Bulgaria, Roumania, Hungary and Finland, the words 'Each of our Governments will consider separately, in the near future, the resumption of diplomatic relations with these countries.' This did not mean that they would all have to be recognised at the same time. He pointed out that in Italy the United States and Soviet Governments had ambassadors, but France and the United Kingdom had only political representatives without the status of ambassadors.

MR. CHURCHILL said that we regarded our political representative in Rome as being to all intents and purposes a fully accredited ambassador. The only difference arose because we were still technically at war with Italy. In reply to further questions by Premier Stalin, Mr. Churchill said that he regarded our political representative in Rome as 90 per cent. an ambassador.

PREMIER STALIN asked whether the British Government could not accredit to Roumania someone who was 90 per cent an ambassador. All this, however, related to the past. The difficulty for the Soviet Government was that the effect of the document as it stood was to disparage the Governments of Roumania and Bulgaria, and thus to throw discredit on the Soviet Government.

PRESIDENT TRUMAN said that there was no such intention.

MR. CHURCHILL said that there was no desire to issue any statement from the Conference which would have such an effect. He put in a plea for Italy. She had been the first of the Axis satellites out of the war. It was indeed nearly two years since the Italian surrender, whereas it was only a very short time since these other satellite countries had ceased fighting against us—some four to five months.

Since Italy had left the war, she had had troops fighting on our side. Also, for some time past, our representative had been living in Italy and knew all about the conditions there. This was certainly not the case as regards Roumania and Bulgaria. Again, the North of Italy had, until recently, been under the enemy. We had always recognised that until North Italy had been liberated, Italy could never have a completely solid democratic Government. Meanwhile, the Italian Government had been recovering. We had established close relations with them. There had been no political censorship in Italy and he (Mr. Churchill) had frequently been the subject of attacks in Italian newspapers, even in the months immediately following the Italian surrender. There had thus been a considerable growth of political liberty in Italy, and it had been decided to have elections and set up a new Government before Christmas. He therefore could not see any reason why we should not start discussing the terms of a Peace Treaty with Italy. But about Roumania, and still more Bulgaria, we knew almost nothing. Our Missions in Bucharest were hemmed in so closely as almost to amount to internment.

PREMIER STALIN asked whether it was necessary to make these statements without their being verified.

MR. CHURCHILL said that he knew his facts, which had been reported officially by our military mission and diplomatic representative. Premier Stalin would be astonished to read the catalogue of incidents to our missions in Bucharest and Sofia. They were not free to go abroad. An iron curtain had been rung down.

PREMIER STALIN said that these were fairy tales.

MR. CHURCHILL said that they were not fairy tales, and he had confirmed them from our diplomatic representative and our military representative (Air Vice-Marshal Stevenson) at Bucharest, whom he had known personally for many years. The conditions of our mission there had been most painful, and had caused great distress. It was not for him to say what were the experiences of the United States representatives. But when our people went out in motor cars, they were closely followed wherever they went, and every movement they made was supervised. Moreover, great delay had been imposed upon the aircraft used for our Mission. Complaints

649

had been made by the Soviet Government of the size of our Mission, although it was small enough. Again, the Control Commission was supposed to consist of three members, but nearly always the meetings consisted of two members: that was to say that the Soviet member sometimes saw the United States member and sometimes the British member, but rarely saw them both together.

The situation in Italy, on the other hand, was different. There the Soviet authorities were welcome to come whenever they liked. For example, M. Vyshinski had been to Italy.

PREMIER STALIN said that this was not so. The Soviet Government had no rights in Italy and, indeed, wanted none. M. Vyshinski had never been a member of the Allied Control Commission for Italy.

M. VYSHINSKI said that he had been a member of the Advisory Council.

MR. CHURCHILL said that Premier Stalin was free to send anyone to Italy and that they could go wherever they liked. The Russians had been welcomed even when the fighting was going on in Italy. Therefore, he did not think that Italy was in the same position as all these other countries.

PRESIDENT TRUMAN said that very great difficulties had been imposed on the United States missions in Roumania and Bulgaria. In saying this he did not mean to cast any reflection on the Soviet Government or their representatives at the Conference, and he was sure that Mr. Churchill would agree with him.

MR. BYRNES referred to the amendment to which Premier Stalin objected and suggested that instead of 'responsible and democratic Governments' there should be substituted 'recognised and democratic Governments.'

PREMIER STALIN said that this was more acceptable, but he would still like the addition proposed by M. Molotov[10] to be added at the end of the paragraph about the four satellite countries. The addition might be as follows: 'The three Governments agreed to consider, each separately, in the immediate future, the question of the establishing of diplomatic relations with Finland, Roumania, Bulgaria and Hungary.' This was only another way of putting the object which they all had in mind, namely, that peace treaties should be prepared with these States. But one could not conclude a peace treaty with a country until one recognised its Government.

PRESIDENT TRUMAN said he saw no objection to this proposed addition.

PREMIER STALIN said if this amendment was accepted the Soviet Government would accept the draft as a whole as amended.

MR. CHURCHILL said that he was not sure that he understood where we stood in this matter. Was there not a risk that we were covering up with words a real difference of view between us? He had understood President Truman to say that he was not prepared to recognise the present Governments of Roumania and Bulgaria. Had he understood the position correctly?

PRESIDENT TRUMAN said that the present amendment committed them to examine separately the question of the recognition of these countries.

[10] Cf. note 9 above.

MR. CHURCHILL feared that verbal agreement would make for difficulties, if the underlying difference was not resolved. An impression would be created that we intended to recognise these countries speedily.

PRESIDENT [*sic*] STALIN suggested that the President himself should say which Governments he was prepared to recognise. He did not accept Mr. Churchill's point of view. The fact that it was intended to prepare Peace Treaties with these countries (as shown in the new paragraph suggested by the United States Delegation at the Foreign Secretaries' Meeting) meant that recognition of these countries was imminent. If the proposed addition to the paragraph could not be accepted, then the whole paragraph ought to be struck out.

MR. CHURCHILL asked whether President Truman contemplated that he would recognise the representatives of Roumania and Bulgaria and invite them to come to the Council of the Foreign Secretaries in September in order to discuss the preparation of Peace Treaties.

PRESIDENT TRUMAN said that the only Governments which would be so invited would be the Governments which the United States Government would recognise.

MR. CHURCHILL said that he was sorry to press the point, but the paragraph would be made public and would have to be explained and defended in the Parliaments. The Governments of the countries concerned would appeal to the terms of the paragraph and would expect that they would be shortly recognised.

PRESIDENT TRUMAN suggested that it should be left to the Foreign Secretaries' Meeting to look at the draft again in the light of a discussion which had taken place.

In a further discussion it was pointed out that there was an important difference between speaking (in the suggested new paragraph 3) of the preparation of Peace Treaties *for* Bulgaria, Finland, Hungary and Roumania and the preparation of Treaties *with* Bulgaria, Finland, Hungary and Roumania.

It was agreed that the meeting of the Foreign Secretaries should be invited to examine the draft in the light of the discussion that had taken place, and to report back to the Plenary Meeting.

4. *Turkey*
(Previous Reference: P. (Terminal) 7th Meeting, Minute 10.) [6]

PRESIDENT TRUMAN said that he would be glad of the views of his colleagues on the paper which he had circulated about International Inland Waterways, including the Straits. (P. (Terminal) 33.) [6]

PREMIER STALIN observed that the paper circulated by the President did not deal specifically with Turkey and the Straits, but rather with the Danube and the Rhine. What the Soviet Delegation wished to discuss was the question of the Straits and bases in the Straits for Russia.

PRESIDENT TRUMAN replied that he wished to see both these questions considered together.

Premier Stalin feared that the meeting would not reach agreement on the question of the Straits, since their views differed too widely. He suggested, therefore, that consideration of the question should be postponed.

Mr. Churchill said that, if memory served him right, the President had said the previous day that he favoured the view that the freedom of the Straits should be approved and guaranteed by an international authority, including the Three Great Powers. This was a remarkable, indeed a tremendous fact.

President Truman agreed that the Prime Minister had summarised fairly what he had said the day before.

Premier Stalin also agreed that as regards freedom of passage, this statement was correct. The Soviet Government were in favour of this. But they thought that it would also be necessary to have bases in the Straits.

Mr. Churchill said that we had hoped, of course, that an international guarantee would be more than a substitute for the erection of fortifications.

M. Molotov interposed to ask what would be done about the Suez Canal according to that same principle. Would there be the same international regulation and the same international agreement?

Mr. Churchill replied that the Canal was open in peace and war, and we already had an agreement which had served all parties well for some sixty or seventy years.[11]

M. Molotov said that there had been quite a lot of complaints. He thought that Egypt's views on this would be interesting.

Mr. Churchill replied that Egypt was, of course, a party to the Treaty, as was also France.

M. Molotov said that the Prime Minister had asserted that the principle of an international guarantee was better than a treaty; the Soviet Government had also suggested a treaty with Turkey.

Mr. Churchill said that he quite agreed that Russia should have complete freedom for her ships to come and go through the Straits. His Majesty's Government would be prepared to join with other nations in guaranteeing that passage and would be prepared to press Turkey to accept this arrangement. Was it to be supposed that Turkey would resist an arrangement providing for such a guarantee by the United Nations when thay knew that the Three Great Powers were taking a great interest in the matter? Perfect freedom of passage could be obtained without either trouble with Turkey or expense. He quite agreed that if Premier Stalin so wished the discussion could be put off; but he earnestly hoped that the tremendous fact heard round that table the day before would not be forgotten by our Russian friends, since a guarantee such as that mentioned gave every security to Russia.

President Truman said that he wished again to make clear his position

[11] The Convention of 29 October 1888 between Great Britain, Austria-Hungary, France, Germany, Italy, the Netherlands, Russia, Spain and Turkey, respecting the free navigation of the Suez Maritime Canal is printed in *B.F.S.P.*, vol. 79, pp. 18–22.

in this matter; he was prepared to support an international guarantee of the freedom of the Straits for all nations without reservation. He contemplated no fortifications at all.

MR. CHURCHILL said that he fully agreed and sympathised with Premier Stalin's view that it was not suitable, in time of war, or just because Turkey saw a threat of war, for a Great Power like Russia to have to go cap in hand to a small country like Turkey. He was not opposing Premier Stalin's wishes in this matter.

PREMIER STALIN pointed out that this question had been brought up by the United Kingdom Delegation; it had become evident that the opinions at the table differed; therefore, considering that there were a great many questions which were more urgent, he thought that discussion of this matter could be put off.

MR. CHURCHILL replied that it was quite true that this matter had been brought up by the United Kingdom Delegation, but only because conversations with the Soviet Government made it clear that they wanted a revision of the Montreux Convention, a course which we supported.

PREMIER STALIN said that he quite understood the position. But he thought the question was not yet ripe and that some talks should take place on the subject.

PRESIDENT TRUMAN said that he had stated his position.

PREMIER STALIN said that the Soviet Government had interrupted their talks with the Turks but only for the time being. They could resume their talk with the Turks and ascertain the Turkish views. Great Britain could do the same. He was not certain whether Turkey would be prepared to agree to an international guarantee.

MR. CHURCHILL said that they were more likely to agree to an international guarantee than to a large fort being erected near Constantinople.

PREMIER STALIN said very likely, but he was not sure.

PRESIDENT TRUMAN said that the United States Government would try to make the Turkish Government see the advantages of International Control.

Discussion of this item was adjourned.

5. *Ukrainians in British Prisoner of War Camp in Italy*
(Previous Reference: P. (Terminal) 6th Meeting,[12] Minute 11.)

MR. CHURCHILL informed the meeting that he had now received a report on this matter.

It was quite true that there were some 10,000 men in this camp. It must be remembered, however, that we had just taken about a million prisoners of war in Italy. These 10,000 were in the process of being sifted by the Russian Mission at Rome and that Mission had been given full access to the camp. The personnel in the camp were said to be mainly non-Soviet Ukrainians and included numbers of Poles who, so far as we could find out had not been

[12] No. 226.

domiciled within the 1939 frontiers of Russia. 665 of these prisoners wished to return to Russia and their wish would immediately be fulfilled. We would also hand over immediately any others who would go without the use of force. The question how much force could be used was one that must be fully considered and very carefully handled.

This body of 10,000 men had surrendered almost intact as an enemy division. We had therefore retained the original regimental groups under their own commanders, but this was exclusively for administrative reasons.

We should have been very glad if General Golikov had made his complaint to Field-Marshal Alexander's Headquarters, since the Field-Marshal would like to have received that complaint himself and to have answered it.

FIELD-MARSHAL ALEXANDER said that he only wished to add one thing to what the Prime Minister had said. Everybody at the present table should know that he had always given the Russian representatives in Italy complete freedom of movement and every facility and assistance to see anything, anywhere and at any time. He had done this because in questions of this sort it was a great help to him to have the advice of responsible Russian representatives. He hoped, therefore, that if Premier Stalin agreed he might be allowed to continue to give those facilities, as he had done in the past.

PREMIER STALIN observed that under the treaty which they had signed[13] each side was bound to grant the other admission to all camps and not to raise any obstacle to the return to their native land of anybody who wished to go.

MR. CHURCHILL suggested that Premier Stalin should send the General who was concerned with these matters to discuss them at Field-Marshal Alexander's Headquarters.

PREMIER STALIN agreed, and said that the matter could be regarded as disposed of.

6. *Austria: Supply of Food to the British and United States Zones*
(Previous Reference: P. (Terminal) 7th Meeting,[14] Minute 14.)

PREMIER STALIN said that he had talked to Marshal Koniev as a result of Mr. Churchill's remarks the previous day. Marshal Koniev had reported that he had not ceased to issue rations to the people of Vienna, irrespective of the zone to which they belonged, and that he would not cease to do so, at any rate until alternative arrangements had been made.[15]

[13] See No. 44, note 2.
[14] No. 241.
[15] The preceding five words were an amendment of 'the matter could be fully discussed' in the typescript text, apparently made at the suggestion of Mr. Harrison, who informed Mr. Troutbeck in a letter of 25 July 1945 that in his view the original text of minutes 6 and 7 was inaccurate. Mr. Harrison's 'understanding of item 6 was that Marshal Koniev had agreed to continue to provide food for the whole of Vienna until "the British and Americans were able to undertake something else" ': Allied Force Headquarters had been so informed in telegram No. Target 210, [i] below (C 4308/317/3).

PRESIDENT TRUMAN and MR. CHURCHILL thanked Premier Stalin very much for this report.

7. *Austria: Authority of Dr. Renner's Government*
(Previous Reference: P. (Terminal) 7th Meeting,[14] Minute 14.)

MR. CHURCHILL referred to the question, mentioned on the previous day, of the recognition of the Government of Dr. Renner in Vienna as having administrative control in the American and British zones of Vienna.[16] The British and United States Delegations had undertaken to furnish their views on this suggestion. Mr. Churchill proposed that this was one of the first questions to be tackled by the Control Council when we occupied our zone in Vienna. In principle it was desirable to have a single Austrian administration and we wanted to disturb local administrative arrangements as little as possible.

The Conference approved the proposal made by Mr. Churchill.

8. *Procedure: Issue of a Communiqué at the end of the Conference*
PRESIDENT TRUMAN said that he wished to make a suggestion as regards the procedure of the Conference. When the Conference was finally concluded in, say, a week or ten days' time, a communiqué containing the results achieved would be required. He therefore suggested that as the Prime Minister was going away to England for two days, the Foreign Secretaries should now be asked to appoint a Committee to work on that communiqué as far as the Conference had gone up to date.

MR. CHURCHILL, commenting that it was wise to put the fish in the basket as they were caught, agreed.

> It was agreed that the Foreign Secretaries should appoint a Committee to begin work on the preparation of a draft communiqué.[17]

Cabinet Office, Potsdam, 24th July, 1945

CALENDARS TO No. 258

i *24 July 1945 Mr. Eden (Berlin) Tel. No. 210 Target.* Message for Gens. Morgan and McCreery summarizing Marshal Stalin's statement in minute 6 above, with instruction from F.M. Alexander to take up British occupational responsibilities in Vienna [F.O. 934/4/25(6)].

[16] The rest of this minute had been amended (cf. note 15 above) from the typescript, which read '. . . zones of Vienna, upon which the British and United States Delegations had undertaken to furnish their views. He said that this was one of the first questions to be tackled by the Control Council when we occupied our zone in Vienna. In principle it was desirable to have a single administration and we wanted to destroy local administrative arrangements as little as possible. This suggestion was agreed.' Mr. Harrison commented in his letter of 25 July: 'This was one of the few items on which the Prime Minister has read straight from one of his briefs': No. 241. ii; Mr. Harrison proceeded to cite Mr. Churchill's statement as cited in paragraph 2 of No. 411.

[17] Upon rising from this plenary meeting Mr. Truman, in accordance with his earlier discussion with Mr. Churchill concerning the atomic bomb (cf. No. 181), had a brief and officially unrecorded conversation with Marshal Stalin wherein the President informed him of possession of a new weapon of unusual destructive force: cf. Harry S. Truman, *Year of Decisions, 1945* (London, 1955), p. 346, and W. S. Churchill, *op cit.*, vol. vi, pp. 579–80.

ii *25 July 1945 A.C.A.O./P (45) 74.* Directive issued by Secretary of State for War to Commander-in-Chief, British armed forces of occupation in Austria [C 4452/317/3].

iii *23 & 25 July 1945 To Mr. Eden (Berlin) Tels. Nos. 171 and 205 Onward.* Information from Gen. Morgan on Ukrainian prisoners as requested (see No. 226, note 29) and as indicated in minute 5 above: U.K. Delegation minute comments that above is 'complete defence' against Soviet allegations, discusses use of force and suggests protest against Gen. Golikov's 'untrue' accusations [F.O. 934/5/42(6 & 3)].

No. 259

Soviet note handed to the representatives of the Governments of the U.S.A. and Great Britain on the Allied Control Commission in Roumania

P.(Terminal)34 [U 6197/3628/70]

Top secret   *24 July 1945*[1]

Roumania: system of work for the Allied Control Commission

In view of the changed circumstances, now that the war with Germany has come to an end, the Soviet Government considers it essential to establish the following system of work for the Allied Control Commission in Roumania:

1. The President (or President's deputy) of the Allied Control Commission, at regular intervals, calls a meeting for the British and American representatives to discuss the most important questions concerned with the work of the Allied Control Commission. Meetings are called once every ten days, and in case of necessity even more often.

2. Directives for the Allied Control Commission on questions of principle are issued by the President (or President's deputy) of the Allied Control Commission after preliminary discussion of the projects of these directives with British and American representatives.

3. British and American representatives take part in the general meetings of the Heads of Departments and plenipotentiaries of the Allied Control Commission, which are summoned by the President (or President's deputy) of the Allied Control Commission, and which must be regularised. The British and American representatives likewise may personally, or through their representatives, in corresponding circumstances take part in mixed commissions, which are formed by the President (or President's deputy) of the Allied Control Commissions, on questions connected with the fulfilment by the Allied Control Commission of its functions.

4. The British and American representatives are allowed freedom of movement through the country on condition that the Allied Control

---

[1] Date of British circulation, as P. (Terminal) 34 under the heading below, of this translation of a note of 16 July 1945 from General I. Z. Susaikov. A variant translation is printed in *F.R.U.S. Berlin*, vol. ii, pp. 691–2.

Commission is warned in advance of the time and route of their journeys.[2]

5. The British and American representatives in the Allied Control Commission have the right to determine the numbers and composition of their own representatives.

6. The British and American representatives in the Allied Control Commission receive and despatch by air their mail, stores and diplomatic couriers in accordance with the periods and regulations laid down by the Allied Control Commission, and in special circumstances in accordance with preliminary agreement with the President (or President's deputy) of the Allied Control Commission.

I consider it necessary to add to this that on all other points the 'statement on the Allied Control Commission in Roumania,' which was brought to the notice of the Governments of Great Britain and the United States on the 20th September, 1944,[3] must remain in force in the future as well.

(*Translator's Note*[4]—It is clear from the Russian text that when 'the British and American representatives' are referred to, one British and one American representative is meant.)

CALENDAR TO NO. 259

i   *17–26 July 1945*   (a) *Mr. Le Rougetel (Bucharest) Tel. No. 715;* (b) *Air Vice-Marshal Stevenson (Bucharest) Tels Nos. RAC 2032–4/165 to War Office.* Conversation on 16 July between Air Vice-Marshal Stevenson and General Susaikov upon his remission of above note. Local British and American reactions [F.O. 934/2/9(26, 30); R 12686/217/37].

[2] On 24 July Mr. Peck asked Mr. Rowan at Potsdam in a minute (on R 12768/217/37) on this paragraph: 'Does this mean that no journey can be undertaken until the Allied Control Commission have approved it, or does it mean that prior notification only is required? The distinction seems important as one of the chief difficulties encountered by our representatives in Eastern Europe has been the long delays in obtaining Russian approval for any request made to them. If it means that prior notification only is required, should not the time limit be considered, e.g. provided three days' notice is given, approval should be assumed unless the would-be traveller hears to the contrary? If you do not have a time limit, requests will be held up on the ground that the notice given was too short.' Mr. Rowan minuted to Mr. Dixon on 26 July that the Prime Minister wished the Foreign Secretary to see Mr. Peck's minute. Mr. V. G. Lawford replied in a letter of 31 July to Mr. Rowan: 'On the face of it paragraph 4 of this paper means that only prior notification is required. I doubt if we need consider a time limit in the way Peck suggests, since the form would be for our representatives to notify the Russians that they proposed to go to such and such a place on such and such a date, and the Russians would have to object in time. To be absolutely safe we should have to confirm that the Russians interpreted "warn" in the same sense as we do, since the document is a translation, but I think that in practice we need not bother further about this paragraph. General Oxley who is now in this country, tells us that there has been a great improvement. He now simply tells the Russians that he is going to a certain place and goes there.'

[3] In a letter from M. Vyshinski to Sir A. Clark Kerr, enclosing 'Regulations concerning the Allied Control Commission in Roumania' (R 16203/14264/37 of 1944: not printed. Cf. *F.R.U.S. 1944*, vol. iv, pp. 240–1).

[4] The translator was Major H. A. Lunghi.

No. 260

Memorandum by the United Kingdom Delegation (Berlin)

P.(*Terminal*)*35* [*U 6197/3628/70*]

Top secret   *24 July 1945*

Ex-enemy States: admission to the United Nations
(Circulated to the United Kingdom Delegation only)

Annexed is a draft statement on this matter in the form in which it was presented by the American Delegation to the Plenary Meeting to-day. (P. (Terminal), 8th Meeting,[1] Minute 3.)

It may be convenient to have on record the amendments proposed in the course of discussion at that Meeting.

(*a*) By the United States Delegation–

In paragraph 2, line 11[8] and paragraph 3, line 5[3]:
Delete 'responsible,' and
Substitute 'recognised.'

(*b*) By the Soviet Delegation–

Add to the end of paragraph 3:

> 'The three Governments agree to consider, each separately, in the immediate future, the question of establishing diplomatic relations with Bulgaria, Finland, Hungary and Roumania.'

ANNEX TO No. 260

Admission to the United Nations[2]

1. The Three Governments consider it desirable that the present anomalous position of Italy, Bulgaria, Finland, Hungary and Roumania should be terminated by the conclusion of Peace Treaties, so that as soon as possible thereafter relations between them and the ex-enemy States can, where necessary, be re-established on a normal footing. They trust that the other interested Allied Governments will share these views.

2. For their part the Three Governments have included the preparation of a Peace Treaty with Italy as the first among the immediate important tasks to be undertaken by the new Council of Foreign Ministers. Italy was the first of the Axis Powers to break with Germany, to whose defeat she has made a material contribution, and has now joined with the Allies in the struggle against Japan. Italy has freed herself from the Fascist régime and is making good progress towards the re-establishment of a democratic Government and institution. The conclusion of such a Peace Treaty with a responsible and democratic Italian Government will make it possible for the Three Governments to fulfil their desire to support an application from Italy for membership of the United Nations.

3. The Three Governments have also charged the Council of Foreign Ministers with the task of preparing Peace Treaties with Bulgaria, Finland, Hungary and Roumania. The conclusion of Peace Treaties with responsible democratic

---

[1] No. 258.
[2] A revised draft of this statement is printed in *F.R.U.S. Berlin*, vol. ii, pp. 627–9.

Governments in these States will also enable the Three Governments to support applications from them for membership of the United Nations.

4. As regards the admission of other States, Article IV of the Charter of the United Nations declared that:

1. Membership in the United Nations is open to all other peace-loving States who accept the obligations contained in the present Charter, and in the judgment of the organisation, are able and willing to carry out these obligations;

2. The admission of any such State to membership in the United Nations will be effected by a decision of the General Assembly upon the recommendation of the Security Council.

The Three Governments, so far as they are concerned, will support applications for membership from those States which have remained neutral during the war and which fulfil the qualifications set out above.

5. The Three Governments feel bound, however, to make it clear that they for their part would not favour any application for membership put forward by the present Spanish Government, which, having been founded on the support of the Axis Powers, does not, in view of its origins, its nature, its record and its close association with the aggressor States, possess the qualifications necessary to justify such membership.

CALENDARS TO No. 260

i *24 July 1945 F.O. Delegation Minute to Mr. Churchill (Berlin).* Comments on (*a*) American draft statement (not here reproduced) cited in No. 254, minute 2, and (*b*) British re-draft [F.O. 934/5/48(2)].

ii *25–6 July 1945 Minutes by Mr. Hoyer Millar (Berlin).* Annex above is an almost verbatim reproduction of i(*b*) above which was circulated to U.S. Delegation in advance of 8th Plenary Meeting (No. 258). Proposes alternatives to Soviet amendment in No. 258, minute 3 [F.O. 934/5/48(12)].

No. 261

Note handed by Soviet representatives to the United States and United Kingdom representatives (Berlin)[1]
P.(Terminal)36 [U 6197/3628/70]

Top secret   *24 July 1945*
Reparations from Austria

1. The total sum payable by Austria in reparations to be fixed at 250 million dollars, payable in equal instalments during the six years beginning on the 1st July, 1945.

2. Reparations mainly to be exacted in the form of deliveries of goods produced by the Austrian industry.

3. Reparations are exacted with the object of compensating for the damage inflicted by the war on the Soviet Union, Great Britain, the United States of America and Yugoslavia.

[1] Printed in *Berlinskaya konferentsiya*, p. 364.

No. 262

Note handed by Soviet representatives to the United Kingdom and United States representatives (Berlin)[1]
P.(Terminal)37 [U 6197/3628/70]

Top secret   24 July 1945

Reparations from Italy

1. The total sum payable by Italy in reparations to be fixed at $600 million.

2. The sum fixed for reparations from Italy must be paid in the course of six years by means of deliveries of goods produced by the Italian industry and agriculture.

3. The reparations imposed upon Italy must serve as a compensation for the damage inflicted on the Soviet Union, Great Britain, the United States of America, Yugoslavia, Greece and Albania as a result of Italy's participation in the war.

[1] Printed *op. cit.*, p. 364.

No. 263

Memorandum by the United Kingdom Delegation (Berlin)
P.(Terminal)39 [U 6197/3628/70]

Top secret   24 July 1945[1]

Germany: Political Principles

The report of the Economic Sub-Committee to the Foreign Secretaries included the following passage, which was not considered when the report was taken by the Foreign Secretaries:–[2]

'The United Kingdom and United States representatives point out that there are two matters in addition to those mentioned in paragraph 13 on which a common policy is essential in the treatment of Germany as a single economic unit:

(1) Uniform method of treatment of the German civilian population;

(2) Subject to normal regulations, free circulation of nationals of the United Kingdom, United States, U.S.S.R. and France in all zones by land and air.

The Soviet representative takes the position that these two points, while having economic significance, have a wider political application, and that they should therefore not be considered by the Economic Sub-Committee.'

The United Kingdom Delegation attach importance to agreement on these two matters being recorded. They would accordingly propose:–

[1] Date of initialing by Mr. Eden.
[2] See No. 224, minute 3.

(*a*) that a new paragraph be inserted after paragraph 1 of the text on 'Political principles' which has been approved by Heads of Governments as follows:–

'So far as is practicable, there shall be uniformity of treatment of the German population throughout Germany.'

(*b*) that a new paragraph be added after paragraph 9 as follows:–

'Subject to normal regulations, there shall be free circulation of nationals of the Powers represented on the Control Council in all zones by land and air.'

No. 264

Note by the Secretary of State for Foreign Affairs (Berlin)[1]
P.(Terminal)40 [U 6197/3628/70]

Top secret   *24 July 1945*

Removal of Allied industrial equipment, especially in Roumania

Our case can, I think, be stated simply as follows:–

There are only two articles in the Roumanian Armistice under which property can be removed from Roumania.

One of these is Article 11 which provides for the payment of reparations. The Soviet Government do not claim that the oil equipment was removed under this Article, but that it was taken as booty.

The second is Article 7, which provides that the Roumanian Government should hand over as 'trophies' war material of Germany and her Satellites located on Roumanian territory. (It is clear from Article 1 that Satellites here exclude Roumania.)

It is clear, therefore, that the only property which can be claimed as booty is German property or the property of another Satellite of Germany.

The question is whether any of the property now in question is German property. The Soviet Delegation have not claimed that any equipment acquired by Allied nationals before the war can be regarded as German property, and I cannot understand why this property has not been returned at once without further argument.

The more difficult case is that of property acquired by the companies during the war when they were under German management. But even this is clear if we examine it carefully. The companies at the time when they were seized by the Germans had certain assets (money, equipment, oil concessions). When under German management, they parted with some of these assets (money or oil) and received from Germany other assets in return (equipment). Thus the equipment was indubitably the property of the company at the time of liberation.

---

[1] Printed in *F.R.U.S. Berlin*, vol. ii, pp. 743–4.

If any British company had on its premises property which clearly belonged to Germany and had merely been deposited there for custody, its removal as booty would of course be justified.

As a means of settling this question I now propose that the ownership of the disputed property should be subject to impartial and expert investigation. This might be entrusted to a Committee of three allied nationals drawn from States not interested in this dispute. If the property is found to belong to Germany we would agree that it should be retained by the Russians. If it is found to belong to one of the British companies the property should be returned by the Soviet Government or compensation paid to the company.

No. 265

Minutes of a Meeting of the Combined Chiefs of Staff Committee held in the Conference Room at 25 Ring Strasse on Tuesday, 24 July 1945 at 5.30 p.m.[1]

C.C.S. 200th Meeting [CAB 99/39]

Top secret

Present:

GENERAL OF THE ARMY G. C. MARSHALL, USA, Fleet Admiral E. J. King, USN, General of the Army H. H. Arnold, USA.

FIELD-MARSHAL SIR ALAN F. BROOKE, Marshal of the Royal Air Force Sir Charles F. A. Portal, Admiral of the Fleet Sir Andrew B. Cunningham.

Also present:

General B. B. Somervell, USA, Lieut.-General J. E. Hull, USA, Vice-Admiral C. M. Cooke, Jr., USN, Major-General L. Norstad, USA, Captain A. S. McDill, USN, Captain H. R. Oster, USN.

Admiral the Lord Louis Mountbatten, Supreme Allied Commander, South-East Asia, Field-Marshal Sir Henry Maitland Wilson, General Sir Hastings L. Ismay, Lieut.-General Sir Gordon Macready.

Secretariat: Major-General L. C. Hollis, Brigadier-General A. J. McFarland, USA, Brigadier A. T. Cornwall-Jones, Lieut.-Colonel G. Mallaby.

1. *200th Meeting of the Combined Chiefs of Staff*

The Combined Chiefs of Staff took note that this was their 200th meeting.

2. *Operations in South-East Asia Command*

GENERAL MARSHALL said that the United States Chiefs of Staff would like to extend a welcome to Admiral Mountbatten and take this opportunity of congratulating him personally on the conclusion of his great campaign in Burma.

[1] Printed *op. cit.*, vol. ii, pp. 375–8.

Admiral Mountbatten thanked the United States Chiefs of Staff and then proceeded to give an account of past, present and future operations in his command.

In recounting the broad tale of events in South-East Asia, from the Sextant Conference[2] in 1943 to the capture of Rangoon in May 1945, he emphasised two points of importance–

(*a*) Air transport was the lifeblood of all operations in his command. They had saved the day when things looked black in the spring of 1944 and had enabled him to complete successfully the great overland campaign to recapture Burma, which had previously been thought impracticable. The Dakota was far and away the best transport aircraft for his purposes.

(*b*) The tremendous steps in the reduction of casualties made possible by preventive medicine.

In describing the current situation in Burma Admiral Mountbatten explained that–

(*a*) He had some 56,000 Japs still to destroy. At the moment seven divisions were employed on the job, three of which would soon be withdrawn to take part in forthcoming operations. Considerable fighting was still going on.

(*b*) He had a big problem in getting supplies through to the native population in the face of one of the worst monsoons in history. He was being forced to use some air transport for this as well as for the maintenance of the troops.

(*c*) His air transport squadrons were some 20 per cent. under strength.

As regards future operations, the Supreme Commander paid tribute to the immense effort being put forward by the India Command to organise India as a base for these operations, which were the largest that had ever been undertaken from the country. He drew a picture of the problem of mounting operation 'Zipper'; the vast distance over which the forces would have to converge on the objective; the fact that they would have to rely on carrier-borne air support for the landing; and the degree of opposition they were likely to meet. Risks were involved, but these were calculated risks which he was prepared to accept.

Finally, he paid tribute to the morale of the troops and the high degree of inter-Allied co-operation that had been built up in the past two years. This spirit, he felt, would carry the command through forthcoming operations in spite of the disappointments inevitably involved in the acceptance of a second priority in the war as a whole.

Sir Alan Brooke then invited the United States Chiefs of Staff to put any questions they would like to Admiral Mountbatten, observing that the British Chiefs of Staff would have the opportunity at subsequent discussions in London.

[2] Codename of the Allied Conferences held at Cairo on 22–26 November and 2–7 December 1943.

GENERAL MARSHALL suggested that it might be possible to use more submarines to prevent the infiltration into Malaya of further Japanese reinforcements.

SIR ANDREW CUNNINGHAM said that no specific demand for further submarines for this purpose had been made from the theatre and that within reason there was no limitation on the number that might be employed. There were, however, very few worthwhile targets left in the area.

ADMIRAL MOUNTBATTEN said that he felt that the present distribution of submarines, balanced as it was to meet the various tasks to be carried out, was satisfactory.

GENERAL MARSHALL asked the Supreme Commander how soon he thought he would be able to take over the new command, explaining that the United States Chiefs of Staff were very anxious to relieve United States commanders in the Pacific of their responsibilities for the area at the earliest possible moment.

ADMIRAL MOUNTBATTEN said that he had not expected to be called upon to assume these new responsibilities until 'Mailfist'[3] had been completed. He would like a little further time to consider the idea of taking them on earlier, but assured the United States Chiefs of Staff that he would do his best to meet them. When assured by General Marshall that the forces now in the area would be left there, he said that this certainly made things easier. It appeared that the problem would be merely a matter of assuming the higher direction of operations in the area.

GENERAL MARSHALL asked what Admiral Mountbatten thought of the idea of splitting French Indo-China into two and placing the southern half, south of 16° N., in the South-East Asia Command.

ADMIRAL MOUNTBATTEN said that he had just heard of the proposition and that his first reactions were favourable. He would have liked some latitude in the actual northern limit of the area in case his operations were to develop either to the north or to the south of the degree of latitude suggested, but did not feel very strongly on the point. He thought the French might find the proposition a little less agreeable.

GENERAL MARSHALL explained the background to the French offer of two French divisions for operations in the war against Japan, and said that the Combined Chiefs of Staff were agreed that the best place to employ these divisions would probably be in French Indo-China. One of these two divisions had had battle experience and had done well. Both were composed of white men and the French proposal specifically provided that they would arrive with corps supporting and service units. He asked Admiral Mountbatten's opinion as to the acceptance of these two divisions in South-East Asia Command. They could not be moved out for several months and it would probably be the late spring of 1946 before he could expect to get them.

ADMIRAL MOUNTBATTEN said that, subject to the views of the British Chiefs of Staff, he would certainly welcome these two French divisions provided they came with a proper proportion of service and supporting units. The obvious place to employ them would be in French Indo-China where he would be relieved of the necessity of dealing with a problem which could be satisfactorily handled only by Frenchmen.

GENERAL HULL said that General MacArthur had drawn up a list of the supporting and service units which these two divisions would require if they came out to the Pacific, and this list had been communicated to the French. He undertook to provide Admiral Mountbatten with this list.

No. 266

Record of a Meeting on German Reparations held at the Cecilienhof, Potsdam, on 24 July 1945 at 8 p.m.

[*UE 3332/624/77*]

Present:

Russia MR. MAISKY, Mr. Sobolev, Mr. Sobourov [Saburov], Mr. Varga, Mr. Arkadiev, Mr. Sokirkin, Mr. Artumyan, Mr. Golunski.

U.S. MR. CLAYTON, Mr. Pauley, Mr. Murphy, Mr. McCloy, Dr. Lubin, Mr. Despres, Mr. Collado, Col. Fogelson, Mr. Parton, Mr. Moseley [*sic*].

U.K. SIR WALTER MONCKTON, Sir David Waley, Mr. Coulson, Mr. Turner.

The items on the agenda for the meeting were German, Italian and Austrian Reparations, and shipments of oil from south-east to western Europe. After some discussion it was decided to start by discussing German reparations.

MR. MAISKY asked whether the U.S. and U.K. Delegations had had an opportunity of considering the Russian Plan.[1] SIR WALTER MONCKTON said that he would be interested to hear from the Russians how they arrived at the estimates of the value of once-for-all deliveries under the six categories set out in paragraph 2 of their Plan. MR. MAISKY replied that he was not in a position to give any detailed break-down of these figures but would like to know whether his British and American colleagues agreed that they were reasonable. If the figures seemed too high, had they any alternative figures to put forward? SIR WALTER MONCKTON said that it was inconceivable to him how Mr. Maisky could make such a proposal. The Allied Reparation Commission had waited four weeks in Moscow for the submission of the Russian Plan which was to have been a basis for the Commission's discussions. We had now had the Plan for two days in the broadest of outlines with no explanation of how the figures were arrived at, and were expected to give a quick answer as to what the amount of reparations should be. MR. PAULEY supported Sir Walter Monckton's statement and added that the Soviet definition of booty on the one hand

---

[1] No. 242.

665

and their statements in regard to the cession of territory to Poland on the other hand made it quite impossible to discuss reparations except on a zonal basis.

Mr. Clayton elaborated Mr. Pauley's statement and pointed out that Category III of once-for-all deliveries in the Russian Plan consisted of plant and equipment from industries which would not be subject to restriction on security grounds; the extent of the removals of these industries would be impossible to estimate in advance of careful examination; and in any case he thought that the Russian estimates were very much too high; according to a very rough estimate which the American Delegation had made the amounts of removals for the first three categories in the Russian list was equal to the total movable assets of the industries concerned. He therefore thought it was better to try and arrive at a simple formula without reference to money values. He would like Mr. Maisky carefully to consider the proposal already put forward by the Americans that the Russians should take as reparations or booty the equipment that they needed from their own zone, which, according to his calculations, contained about 50% of the movable wealth of Germany. The Russians should bear in mind that this was a favourable proposition from their point of view, since in the territories ceded to Poland and Russia all the assets in the area would be removed and not merely those categories scheduled as reparation deliveries.

In reply to Mr. Maisky, Mr. Pauley stated that he had arrived at his figure of 50% by taking into account the capital equipment in the area together with the current production of mineral and agricultural products as well as manufactured goods.

Mr. Sobourov stated that the metallurgical, chemical and heavy engineering and mining industries in Russia had suffered very severely. The Soviet Government wished to replace these from Germany but these industries did not exist in the Russian zone. How therefore were they to be obtained? Mr. Pauley replied that the Russians could obtain this plant by exchanging it for the surplus products in the Russian zone.

Mr. Maisky said that he was prepared in principle to consider the American Plan but that he must point out at the outset that it had one very serious defect. According to the estimates of Mr. Varga, only 30% of the removable wealth in Germany was in the Russian zone and there was very little that the Russians had to exchange for capital equipment from the west. The Russians would therefore require about $3 billion of equipment free as reparations from the Russian zone.

Mr. Varga said that he thought that the Americans had based their estimates of movable wealth on the 1939 edition of *Deutsche Industrie*. The real figure for the movable wealth in the Russian zone, according to his calculations, was 32.3%, including an allowance for half of the province of Saxony. Therefore a considerable proportion of the assets in the western zone would have to be delivered free to the Russians as reparations. Mr. Pauley said he would rather not talk in terms of money but in terms of things. He would certainly be prepared to let the Russians have things out of western Europe but only on an exchange basis. MR. CLAYTON added that the Russians' calculations seem to have ignored the additional values that Russia would receive in respect of ceded territories.

MR. SOBOLEV said that Mr. Clayton's proposals suggested that a different method of reparation should be applied in the Russian zone from that applied in the British and American zones. The reason for transferring territory to the Russian zone was security, not reparations. Categories of goods available for reparation in territories ceded to Poland and Russia should be taken into account in the same way as they had been taken into account for non-ceded territory, but only on the basis of prepared reparation schedules. The proposal to take $3 billion from the western zones was an attempt to even up the differences in national wealth between the two zones. The greater part of heavy industries in Germany were in the British and American zones, and these industries had to be removed or destroyed for security purposes. Neither the U.K. nor the U.S. had expressed a desire to remove equipment of a military character. The Russians and Poles on the other hand wished to remove these industries in order to build up their own industrial potential. Mr. Maisky's proposal therefore appeared to fit in with Mr. Pauley's Plan.

MR. CLAYTON again suggested to Mr. Maisky that the conversation should be confined to things and not to money. For example, what ideas had the Russians about the German steel industry?

MR. SOBOUROV said that he would be prepared to give an exposition of the Russian statistical case. In south Russia 80% of the steel industry had been destroyed as well as many coal mines, which required new equipment. If part of the iron and steel industry were taken from Germany, less coal would be wanted and some of the mining equipment would be available. Heavy machinery, plant making such things as electrical generating equipment, presses, blast furnaces, etc. had also been destroyed and the same was true of the chemical and other industries. Having lost so much of her heavy capital equipment, Russia was unable to restore her own industries without assistance. The assistance she needed was the removal of similar industries from Germany; but all these industries were located in the Rhineland-Westphalia districts of Germany. Russia had suffered more industrial damage than any other country and the British and American Delegations should agree that she should have immediate and substantial deliveries from Germany. MR. CLAYTON said he was in no doubt that Russia needed German equipment and that the American Delegation were very sympathetic to their claim. He was trying, however, to get some idea as to what Russia needed in one particular industry. Could they give some idea of the need of steel plant capacity expressed in terms of ingot steel production? MR. MAISKY said that the pre-war steel production of Germany was about 23 million tons, and that in the opinion of the Russian Delegation she would not require more than one-third of this capacity after the war to satisfy her peacetime needs. Did the British and American Delegations agree with this view? SIR WALTER MONCKTON said that he was not in a position to express an opinion on this point. A special Sub-Committee had been appointed by the Allied Reparation Commission to examine how far German industrial capacity can be reduced. He did not think it profitable for the matter to be considered at the meeting.

The discussion then reverted to the question of the comparative wealth of the Russian zone on the one hand and the rest of Germany on the other. MR. PAULEY said that according to his calculations 38.3% of the industry and 48% of the agriculture of Germany was situated in the Russian zone. By weighting these percentages he had arrived at an average of 43% of the wealth of Germany in the Russian zone in 1939. Since then, however, there had been a shift in the location of German economy, according to his information, and an increase of 5% had taken place both in industry and agriculture, making a total of 48%. Under the formula allocating reparations agreed between the three Delegations in Moscow the Soviet Government would receive 50% of the reparation claim, but this would probably be reduced to 47½% when the claims of the minor Allies were taken into account But even if their claim was 50%, they would only have 2% deficiency to make good from the American zone and that would have to be made good in exchange for food and other requirements of western Germany.

MR. MAISKY said he would like to get down to principles. Article X of the Political and Economic Principles[2] provided for the destruction of German war potential. The heart of Germany's war potential was her iron and steel and heavy engineering industry situated in the Ruhr. What was the British view about the fact of this industry?

SIR WALTER MONCKTON said that the application of Principle X to the Ruhr would involve a large scale reduction in the industry in that area. The extent of that reduction would, however, require careful investigation. There would be a number of claimants for the plant in that area and some of it would be wanted in the U.K. His understanding of Mr. Pauley's Plan was that the difference between the agreed national wealth of the eastern zone and the percentage share of reparations to which Russia was entitled would be received as reparations from the west, any balance that Germany required being exchanged for current deliveries such as potash and timber. MR. MAISKY asked whether Sir Walter Monckton thought that $3 billion reparation deliveries from the western zone was too great. SIR WALTER MONCKTON said that what the meeting would like to know was how much equipment the Russians wanted out of western Germany and we could then examine on the basis of Mr. Pauley's Plan how much they would obtain free and how much against exchange of goods from the Russian zone. MR. MAISKY asked whether Mr. Pauley thought that the Soviet Government would get $5 billion of once-for-all deliveries and $5 billion of current deliveries out of its own zone. MR. PAULEY replied that he could not express

[2] See appendix to No. 210.

668

an opinion in regard to this without associating himself with the Russian Plan. He did not pointed [*sic*] out that the American Plan referred only to removable plant and equipment.

MR. MAISKY then asked how the needs of the other Allies would be met. MR. PAULEY said that as far as the Americans were concerned they were prepared to meet them out of their own zone, with the exception of Poland which had already received compensation by transfer of territory in the east. SIR WALTER MONCKTON associated himself with Mr. Pauley's statement. M. Maisky then asked whether the British and American Delegations had had an opportunity of considering his proposal to internationalise the Rhineland.[3] MR. CLAYTON and SIR WALTER MONCKTON reported that they had both reported Mr. Maisky's proposal to their respective Foreign Secretaries but were unable to say what the latter thought about the matter. In any case the problem was mainly a political one.

MR. MAISKY then summarised the American Plan as follows:

(1) The Soviet Government would collect reparations from its own zone.

(2) The U.S., U.K. and France would collect their reparations from their zones.

(3) No industrial equipment would go to the U.S.S.R. from the western zone on reparations account but industrial plant and equipment from the Ruhr might be exchanged for agricultural and other products from the Soviet zone.

(4) Reparations claims of countries other than Poland would be met from the U.S. and British zones.

The only point on which he was still rather obscure was the British plan for the liquidation of war potential in the Ruhr. Mr. Maisky went on to say that the figure of $20 billion in the Russian Plan was not sacrosanct: in fact, at the previous day's meeting of Foreign Secretaries[4] Mr. Molotov had agreed to reduce the Russian claim. He was not, however, prepared to consider the American Plan unless there were substantial free deliveries to Russia from the western zones.

MR. CLAYTON then suggested that statistical experts should leave the meeting and endeavour the reach an agreement in regard to the percentages of wealth in the two parts of Germany. Mr. Varga, Mr. Sobourov, Dr. Lubin and Mr. Despres then retired.

On their return MR. VARGA said that without allowances for shifts in industry calculated by Mr. Pauley at 5%, 42% of German wealth was in the Russian zone and 58% in the other three zones. This was an overall percentage including industry and agriculture. Taking industry separately, the percentages were 35% for the Russian zone and 65% for the remainder. MR. MAISKY said that on the basis of these figures he considered that the statement that the wealth was equally divided between the two parts was not accurate. The Russian zone had more agriculture proportionately to

[3] Cf. No. 204, ii and No. 240.
[4] See No. 233, minute 3.

the area, and this was not a very satisfactory basis for reparation deliveries; agriculture in fact would have to develop rather than contract and would need machinery for this purpose. As regards industry, the Soviet zone contained less than the other zones and was predominantly of a light character. The possibilities of removals from the Russian zone for the purpose of destroying German industrial war potential were much less than in the west. The restoration of her iron and steel industry was much more important than anything else to the Soviet Government and if they adopted the American Plan they must obtain substantial free deliveries from western Germany.

In reply to a request by Mr. Pauley, MR. SOBOLEV stated that the Russian claim to $3 billion from the western zone was arrived at as follows. Taking $10 billion as the amount of once-for-all deliveries and assuming that 35% of the industry was in eastern Germany and 65% in the west, $3½ billion would be available from the Russian zone and $6½ billion from the British, American and French zones. The west, however, contained far more heavy industry (which would have to be eliminated for security reasons) than the east. It was unlikely, in fact, that Russia could obtain more than $2 billion deliveries from her zone. Therefore the balance of $8 billion would have to come from the west. If Russia was to obtain 50% of once-for-all deliveries she would therefore require $3 billion of free deliveries from the British, American and French zones. SIR WALTER MONCKTON pointed out that even the Russian Plan did not assume $10 billion of deliveries of plant and equipment. Of the $10 billion of once-for-all deliveries set out in paragraph 2 of their Paper, about $4 billion consisted of German foreign assets, shares in German industrial concerns and miscellaneous items. There were therefore only $6 billion of plant and equipment to be removed and not $10 billion. The Russian Delegation made no comment.

MR. PAULEY then reverted to the statistical position. His original principle, he explained, had been to weight agriculture equally with industry and to allow 5% for the additional industry and agricultural development that had taken place in eastern Germany since 1939. If a lower weighting was given to agriculture and industry, the proportion of wealth in the Russian zone would work out at 45%. If the Russian figure of $10[billion] were taken as a basis for discussion, this would only entitle them to $500 million of once-for-all deliveries. MR. MAISKY said that the bulk of the war potential which we had determined to destroy was in the U.K. zone. For this reason he thought the Russian claim to $3 billion was well-founded. MR. PAULEY repeated that the best case he could make out for the Russians was $500 million, but, as he had said before, he would much prefer not to talk in money but in things, e.g. tons of steel capacity, machine tools, etc. MR. MAISKY agreed that there was no point in talking in terms of money. Would Mr. Pauley be prepared to consider removals from the western zone as reparations, i.e. as free reparation deliveries? MR. PAULEY said he did not want to preclude discussion but he wanted Mr. Maisky to realise that the Americans needed food and fuel for their zone of occupation. It seemed to him ridiculous that the U.S. should be transporting food and fuel across the Atlantic into Berlin, which should draw its supplies from surrounding areas. Mr. Maisky agreed that it was necessary for Europe to be more self-supporting and that that problem could be more easily solved after the reparations problem had been got out of the way. He was quite ready to discuss the question of arriving at a balanced economy for Germany and he thought that it would be possible to make certain arrangements. He thought, however, that the two problems should be discussed separately. They should at least be discussed simultaneously.

Mr. Maisky said that for the Soviet Union the problem of reparations was more urgent than the question of food and fuel. As a practical politician, he believed the solution of the latter problem depended on friendly co-operation between the three Powers. Once reparations were out of the way a favourable atmosphere would be created for solving these problems. If reparations were not satisfactorily solved, the solution of other problems would be much more difficult.

Mr. Clayton said that everyone agreed that Russia needed, and should receive, heavy equipment, but that from the point of view of the wealth-producing potential of western Germany the eastern zone contained a share equivalent to that to which Russia was entitled. At Yalta the Russian share was provisionally fixed at 50%, but taking the claims of other countries into account she would be unlikely to receive more than $47\frac{1}{2}\%$, which was precisely the American estimate of the wealth of the Russian zone. He appreciated that not in every case would this wealth be in the form of goods which Russia needed. Nevertheless, the Russian zone contained surpluses of freely marketable goods such as food, zinc, potash and coal. Would it not be possible, therefore, to work out a satisfactory exchange? He thought it might be possible to proceed on the following lines:

First, an agreement of the percentage of plant to be left in Germany.

Secondly, agreement on how the plant scheduled for removal would be divided.

Finally, a swop of commodities from the Russian zone with plant and equipment from the western zone.

He thought that the meeting might start with the assumption that 50% of German pre-war steel and heavy engineering capacity should be allowed to remain. How did that strike the Russians? Mr. Maisky thought that this was too much. One-third would be better. But he pointed out that Mr. Clayton had turned the conversation back to the question of exchanges; it seemed to him (Mr. Maisky) that Mr. Pauley had been ready to consider certain free deliveries from the western zones. Mr. Pauley said he was not aware that he had taken a commitment on this point and Mr. Clayton suggested that they should start on the basis of exchange and consider later whether some part of what the Russians needed should not be received as reparations. Mr. Maisky said that he hoped that the meeting would reach certain conclusions then and there and he wanted a direct answer to his question as to whether his U.S. and U.K. colleagues were prepared to make certain reparation deliveries free from the western zone. In other words, leaving aside the question of exchanges, did the Russians receive certain Ruhr equipment free or did they not? THE AMERICAN DELEGATION said that as the bulk of the equipment to be removed from the western zone was situated in the Ruhr, this question should be answered by Sir Walter Monckton.

SIR WALTER MONCKTON said that for his part he had been examining during the course of the evening a new American Plan.[5] This Plan had been based on the assumption that the Russian claim would be satisfied out of their zone and other claimants, excluding Poland, out of the western zone and that anything which either party wanted from the other zones would be obtained on the basis of an exchange of goods between the zones. He had not been considering the matter from the point of view of free deliveries from one zone to another. MR. PAULEY added that so far as the Americans were concerned they were not going to import food and fuel into Europe and let other people receive reparations. To get paid for their food and fuel they would have to allow Germany to export goods and this might mean a smaller degree of deindustrialisation than had at one time been contemplated. MR. MAISKY said that the meeting had obviously been unable to reach agreement on the American Plan and must report accordingly to the Foreign Secretaries. He suggested that the Sub-Committee should turn its attention to the Russian Plan and discuss it either at that meeting or at a later date. MR. PAULEY said as U.S. representative he wished to state that he declined to accept the Russian Plan or treat it as a basis of discussion.

MR. CLAYTON then intervened and suggested that rather than report disagreement to the Foreign Secretaries on the following day, they should ask for a further 24 hours to consider the matter. He did not think that there was really any fundamental disagreement between the two parties and that after sleeping on the problem for a night they might be able to reach agreement. A meeting was provisionally fixed for 3 o'clock on the following afternoon.

CALENDAR TO NO. 266

i *24 July 1945 Minute from Sir D. Waley to Mr. Rowan (Berlin).* Summary of above meeting [PREM 8/48].

[5] Cf. the American position-paper of 24 July 1945 on reparations printed in *F.R.U.S. Berlin,* vol. ii, pp. 867–9: the proposal annexed thereto was circulated in the British Delegation on 29 July as P. (Terminal) 50.

No. 267

Record of a discussion on Poland at the Secretary of State's House at Potsdam on 24 July 1945 at 11 p.m.

[*F.O. 934/2/10(67)*]

Present:
SECRETARY OF STATE, Sir A. Cadogan, Sir A. Clark Kerr, Mr. Allen, Captain Leggett (*Interpreter*).

M. Bierut, M. Mikolajczyk, M. Gomulka, M. Rzymowski, M. Zebrowski (*Interpreter*).

Western Frontiers

Monsieur Bierut said it was important for the Poles, who trusted England, that the British people should take account of Poland's needs. Some misunderstandings must be removed. According to the Polish Provisional Government's frontier proposals Germany would cede a hundred and five thousand square kilometres out of a total area before the war of six hundred thousand square kilometres. Poland's net loss would be even greater. The territory claimed by the Poles could not be divided; it was closely knit geographically, economically and demographically.

No other frontier could secure for Poland the same natural advantages from the military and strategic points of view. It would be a mistake to create again the situation reached in 1918 under which Poland could be destroyed in a few hours.

Economically the whole territory was closely bound up with a whole river system of which Stettin formed the outlet to the sea. By possessing this river system Poland would serve the needs of other countries such as Austria, Hungary and Czechoslovakia, and the solution would be closely linked with economic conditions and the problem of security in the whole of Central Europe.

The great Powers had a moral obligation to see that Poland should not, as a result of the war, be diminished territorially, economically or in population. The war had in part been due to the reaction of the great Powers to the injury done to Poland by Germany. If further injury were now to be done to Poland by those whom she trusted most the effect in Poland would be disastrous.

The Secretary of State said that we had no wish to do Poland harm. If we had any doubts they were the doubts of friends. We feared that Poland was taking more territory than for the future of Poland was wise. We had always visualised something else—at Moscow in October, 1944, we had spoken of 'the lands desired by Poland up to the line of the Oder'.[1] We had always foreseen that Poland should have, besides Danzig and East Prussia, South and West of Konigsberg [*sic*], Upper Silesia and possibly some of Pomerania, but not the lands west of the Oder up to the Western Neisse. Moreover, the present Polish proposals would make German–Polish relations very difficult. After the last war we had told the Poles that in our view they were laying up trouble for themselves with Russia in pushing so far East. Now we had the same feeling about their going too far West. Our present doubts arose purely from concern for Poland. If we had no such doubts nothing would be easier for the British people than to say to Poland 'take as much of Germany as you would like.'

Monsieur Bierut said that to leave a wedge of German territory between

[1] See Sir L. Woodward, *op. cit.*, vol. iii, p. 230.

Poland and Czechoslovakia would be a cause of constant conflict. Possession of the whole industrial core contained in these territories was essential if Poland was to be strong. If left to Germany this territory would be a base for the development of armaments. Whereas in Polish hands it would form the basis of the industrialisation of Poland. A largely agricultural country of twenty-six million people could only live in the modern world if industrialised. There was no present parallel with the advance to the East after the last war, since that advance into territory populated largely by non Polish people had been based upon the idea of the development of Poland as an agricultural country.

In reply to a question why Poland needed an area that before the war held eight million people in order to find a place for four million, Monsieur Bierut explained that Central Poland before the war had been over-populated and there had been both seasonal migration into Eastern Germany, two million of whose inhabitants were of Polish stock anyway, and more permanent emigration to other foreign countries. The Poles had a very high rate of increase whereas even the German statistics showed that the Germans were withdrawing from their eastern territories before the war. The German figures also showed that the Oder was in no sense essential to Germany's economic prosperity as it was to Poland's.

Monsieur Mikolajczyk said that he wished to make two points. First with regard to Mr. Eden's doubts about the effect of the present proposals upon Polish-German relations in the future he felt that German feeling would in any case be the same whether Poland held only East Prussia and Danzig or whether she held Stettin as well. The main point was that Germany was now beaten and must continue to be held down in the future.

Secondly, the settlement of the Western frontier had a direct bearing upon the question of elections. If no settlement of Poland's Western territories were reached, the elections could only be organised in a part of Polish territory, possibly not more than one third.

Political Parties

Monsieur Bierut said that there must be some misunderstanding on this question due perhaps to our lack of understanding of the changes which had taken place in Poland. Neither the former nor the present Governments in Poland was Communist. They wished to remove certain absurdities that hampered Polish political life and to eliminate those movements that were modelled upon Hitler's Germany. The present Polish Government had, therefore, returned to and intended to enforce the principles of the 1921 Constitution which had followed the ideas current in Western countries. He was frankly astonished that the Poles were ex[h]orted to hold free and secret elections since the 1921 Constitution clearly guaranteed that elections would be held under the most liberal and progressive rules. The present Government did not renounce these ideas and stood by the five principles of free, secret, equal, universal and proportional elections.

Mr. Eden explained that people in England knew little about Polish political parties, but they cared greatly about Poland. They would expect His Majesty's Government to see that the elections in Poland were held in a way that gave the country its best chance of expressing its wishes. They knew the names of the five main parties in Polish political life and would ask whether all these parties would be allowed to have candidates in the elections.

MONSIEUR BIERUT said that the election would be open to no less than twenty-three parties, that is to say all except groups such as the N.S.Z. or the O.N.R.,[2] which were supporters of the Fascists and Hitlerites.

MR. EDEN asked whether that part of the National Democrat Party which did not collaborate in this way would be able to put forward candidates.

MONSIEUR BIERUT replied that theoretically if we followed the principles of the 1921 Constitution all existing parties, whether there were twenty-three or two hundred and thirty would be able to participate. But in practice the present Government were favouring the tendency to consolidate the small parties into major political groups such as were contained in the present Four Party Coalition. He was confident that within these major groups all shades of opinion could find expression for their views. These principles would apply when conditions had returned to normal, but for the election period all parties would be able to participate and express their opinions. But if the great Allies carried their interest in Polish affairs to the extent of bringing pressure to bear upon the Poles that would constitute an encroachment upon Polish sovereignty.

MR. EDEN said that we had no wish to encroach but that he was putting the questions which he would inevitably be asked as the Foreign Secretary responsible for recognising the present Polish Government.

Press

Mr. Eden said that he would, for instance, be asked whether foreign press correspondents would be allowed to move about and report freely or whether there would be a severe political censorship.

MONSIEUR BIERUT replied that conditions had been exceptional during the war but that now foreign correspondents in Poland had the same privileges as Polish correspondents in other countries. British correspondents had already been to Poland and had travelled as far as Silesia and had expressed themselves as satisfied with the facilities accorded to them.

Trials

MR. EDEN referred to the report in *The Times* on the 24th July that three hundred trials were taking place and that six thousand more were pending. This was a very large figure.

MONSIEUR BIERUT wondered whether in proportion to the total population this figure was larger than that in other liberated countries. Traitors must

[2] Narodowe Siły Zbrojne (National Armed Forces) and Obóz Narodowo-Radykalny (National Radical Camp).

be punished. The rate of punishment might be greater than in normal times, but it would not be excessive considering the abnormal conditions brought about by the war.

At the last session of the National Council on the 22nd July a resolution had been passed to introduce a bill for a general amnesty. Even before this many detained persons had been released following the end of the war. Other recent resolutions provided for the cancellation of further war-time restrictions such as the state of emergency. Much that was being said abroad about Poland was based upon the unfriendly propaganda of the Arciszewski Government.

THE SECRETARY OF STATE said that he wished to be able to tell Parliament the truth. The more information we could get the better we could counter unfriendly propaganda.

European Coal Organisation

Mr. Eden said that he understood that the competent British authorities were anxious that Poland should join the European Coal Organisation. He did not ask for an immediate decision but he hoped the Polish Government would consider this suggestion sympathetically.

Poles in Germany

MONSIEUR RZYMOWSKI said that the Polish Government wished to bring back Poles from Germany and hoped that they might be permitted for this purpose to attach a mission to the Allied Control Commission in Germany.

MR. EDEN said that he would welcome such a step if it would help the return of Poles to Poland.

Reparations Commission

MONSIEUR RZYMOWSKI said that the Polish Government wished to be represented on the Reparations Commission. In Germany there were many works of art, tram-cars, locomotives, etc., which had been looted by the Germans from Poland. In addition to claiming the return of such property the Poles demanded satisfaction for the destruction by the Germans of monuments of art and libraries in Poland and above all for the complete destruction of Warsaw.

MONSIEUR BIERUT said that Germany was richer than Poland. The Poles had no books, not even enough elementary text-books for the schools. Could not the Germans print books for Poland?

THE SECRETARY OF STATE said that the position of France raised difficulties in connexion with Poland's representation on the Reparations Commission. He saw, however, no reason why Poland should not present her claims to the Commission. In any case, she had an absolute right to the restitution of her property. But as regards reparation he personally doubted whether anyone would get much out of Germany; the wealth was not there. The Secretary of State suggested that the Poles might have a word with the Solicitor General about these problems.

Transfer of Polish Merchant Fleet

MONSIEUR RZYMOWSKI asked that arrangements be made to have the Polish merchant ships brought back to Polish waters. Poland at present had no ships whatever. They had none in which to bring iron ore from Sweden.

MR. EDEN said that we wanted the merchant fleet as well as the armed forces to return to Poland. As confidence grew this would be easier. Opinion must first be got moving in the right direction. The Polish ships were at present in the Allied Shipping Pool but he thought we would certainly consider the possibility of the early release of some of them.

MONSIEUR GOMULKA said that the present state of affairs could not continue, in which control of the armed forces lay in other than Polish hands in complete disregard of Polish sovereignty. The Polish Government would like to reach an agreement with His Majesty's Government about taking over the armed forces.

MR. EDEN said that we wanted the armed forces to go home but we must allow them a little time. Now that the new Government in Warsaw had been recognised information would circulate in the Polish army and there would be an increased desire among the men to return. If we were to order them prematurely to return there would be trouble. They had fought very gallantly. When they heard the other side of the story they would want to go back. But it would be better that they should go willingly than by force. Some would never return but they would be few.

Interim Treasury Committee

MONSIEUR GOMULKA said that it was for His Majesty's Government to facilitate the return of Poles abroad. What was now happening was certainly not helping. A Commission had been formed of members of the former Polish Government in London which was bending its energies towards preventing Poles from going back. To encourage the return of Poles abroad His Majesty's Government should be in close touch with the Polish Government in Warsaw, particularly over questions such as the liquidation of the former Government in London. Yet the Commission which had been sent to London from Warsaw had been given no facilities to carry on its work.

SIR ALEXANDER CADOGAN explained that the Interim Treasury Committee was a British official organisation which had been set up to supervise the winding up of the Polish Government's affairs, and the continuation under proper control of only such activites as were indispensable. The Warsaw Government's Commission had been received unofficially in the Foreign Office,[3] but until agreement had been reached as to the scope of its activities, it could not be accorded official status. Matters would be greatly helped by the early appointment of a Polish Ambassador in London.

July 25th, 1945

[3] See No. 61.

i *24 July 1945 Note from Polish Provisional Government*, communicated to Mr. Eden. Requests representation on Reparation Commission, on Allied Commission in Berlin in connection with repatriation of Poles from abroad, and return as soon as possible of Polish merchant fleet [F.O. 934/2/10(58)].

No. 268

Record of a Meeting between Mr. Churchill and M. Bierut at the Prime Minister's house, Potsdam, on 25 July 1945 at 10 a.m.

[N 9536/6/55]

Poland

The Prime Minister saw M. Bierut alone. After M. Bierut had thanked the Prime Minister for sparing so much of his valuable time the Prime Minister opened the conversation by remarking that he and M. Bierut had hitherto been on opposite sides but that he was very glad that an arrangement had now been reached.

M. BIERUT said that he would like to explain how the present Polish leaders envisaged the future development of Poland. War, he said, provided an opportunity for new social developments.[1]

THE PRIME MINISTER asked whether this meant that in the chaos caused by war Poland was to plunge into Communism. He was opposed to that but it was of course a purely Polish affair. M. BIERUT said that Poland, according to his ideas, would be far from Communist. Poles wished to live on friendly terms with the Soviet Union and wished to profit by the Soviet Union's experiences, but did not wish to copy the Soviet system. The Polish nation would not consent to such a system since they had different traditions. Even if any attempt were made to impose such a system by force the Polish nation would probably resist. Poland would develop on lines of her own.

THE PRIME MINISTER suggested that the democratic development of Czechoslovakia before the war had been on sound lines. Internal developments in Poland would be for the Poles to decide but they would affect relations between our two countries. He agreed however that there was room for reform in Poland especially in the matter of the great landed estates.

M. BIERUT said that Poland's development would be based on the principles of Western democracy. The Great Powers who have the responsibility for building up the system of peace in Europe will also be responsible for laying the foundations upon which Poland will develop in the future. Poland is not small geographically, it occupies a central position in Europe, and will have twenty-six million Polish inhabitants. The Great

[1] The last three words, and other phrases in this record, are cited by W. S. Churchill, *op. cit.*, vol. vi, pp. 575–7.

Powers could not be indifferent to the development of such a country. If Poland were to develop on Western democratic lines, particularly on the English model, some changes would be inevitable.

THE PRIME MINISTER said that he attached particular importance to free elections. Not only one side must be able to put up candidates. There must be free speech so that everyone can argue matters out and everyone can vote. That has recently been happening in Great Britain. He hoped that Poland too would have such free elections and take pride in them.

The Prime Minister continued that he would do all in his power to persuade Poles abroad to return to Poland at the right time. But the Polish Provisional Government must encourage them. The Poles returning from abroad must be enabled to start their life again on honourable terms with their fellow-countrymen. He was certainly not satisfied with the way some Polish officers had been behaving in suggesting that all Poles who returned would be sent to Siberia, though it was true that many Poles had been deported in the past.

M. BIERUT interposed to say that none were being deported now.

THE PRIME MINISTER continued that Poland must have courts of law independent of the executive. The latest phase of development in the Balkan countries had been not towards Sovietisation so much as in the direction of police government. The political police carried out arrests on the orders of the government. The Western democracies viewed such happenings with aversion. He hoped that there would be an improvement in such matters in Poland. Was for instance the N.K.V.D. leaving the country?

M. BIERUT stated that generally speaking the whole Russian army was leaving. The N.K.V.D. played no role in Poland at present. The Polish Security Police were independent and under the control of the Polish Government. The Soviet Union could not now justifiably be accused of attempting to impose such forms of assistance upon Poland. Conditions there were returning to normal now that the war was over.

M. Bierut continued that he shared the Prime Minister's views on elections and democratic political life. Poland would be one of the most democratic countries in Europe. The Poles were not in favour of police regimes though exceptional measures had had to be taken to heal the serious rifts in Polish politics resulting from the war.

In reply to a further question by the Prime Minister M. Bierut stated that some 99 per cent of the population of Poland were Catholics. There was no intention to limit the development of Catholic sentiments. The clergy generally speaking were satisfied with the present conditions.

THE PRIME MINISTER said that Great Britain wanted nothing for herself in Poland but only to see Poland strong, happy, prosperous and free. There had been no progress after Yalta but matters had improved greatly in the last few weeks. There was now a recognised Polish Government. He hoped that it would make itself as broad as possible or at least ensure that the elections were as broad as possible. Not all people had been equal to the

679

terrible events of the German occupation. The strong resisted but many average people bowed their heads. Not all people could be martyrs or heroes. It would be wise now to bring all back into the main stream of political life. Why, for instance, was M. Bierut so afraid of the revival of M. Popiel's party?

M. BIERUT said that no-one was afraid; M. Popiel was busy recreating his party.

In reply to a question by the Prime Minister whether the elections would be based upon proportionate representation M. Bierut said that the Polish Government did not wish to prevent the expression of political views but that they were anxious to avoid a multiplicity of small parties. In the elections as many small parties as wished could participate but in normal times there would be only a few major groups, probably not more than four or five. The present trend was in that direction. M. Popiel at first tried to form a small group of his own. During the war, however, supporters of the Christian Democrat Party had been active in Poland. M. Popiel had now joined forces with these and had given up trying to form his own exclusive group. That was the way in which parties could be prevented from splitting up into fractions without their political leaders necessarily being hampered.

M. Bierut continued that the elections in Poland would in his view be even more democratic than those in England. The 1921 Constitution had come into being at a time of awakening and alertness and was therefore genuinely liberal and progressive. The 1935 Constitution had been put aside. Internal political relations would now develop more and more harmoniously following the general lines of English political life.

THE PRIME MINISTER said that he wished the Poles all success. M. Bierut had suggested that the Great Powers must not stand in the way of Poland's development and that this question was closely linked with the frontier problem. The Prime Minister said that there was no question of our standing in the way but that the frontier question was tangled up with the problems of reparation and supply. We had had a great mass of Germans thrown upon our hands but the Poles had the rich territories from which these Germans had been fed.

M. BIERUT said that they were mostly Poles in those territories.

THE PRIME MINISTER said that he had been ready to support Polish claims up to the Oder at some points but not along its whole length. Now the Poles were asking too much. In consequence there might be failure to reach agreement. We and the Americans might pursue one policy on our side and the Russians another. That would have serious consequences.

In conclusion the Prime Minister expressed the hope that M. Bierut was getting on well with M. Mikolajczyk. He had always pressed M. Mikolajczyk to return. We wanted all Poles to return. He looked to M. Bierut to make the most of his present opportunities to encourage Poles abroad to go back and help to build the free, happy and prosperous Poland which we wished to see.

Foreign Office, 25th July, 1945

i *25 July 1945   Letter from Mr. Allen (Berlin) to Mr. Warner, with minutes of 27 July by Mr. Warner and Sir O. Sargent.* Encloses copies of Nos. 267 and 268 with comments. Mr. Warner fears that 'tussle between our friends in Poland and the Communists' is 'reaching a crucial stage . . . If we can get nothing at Potsdam I am afraid M. Mikolajczyk will have lost the game': suggests possible sanctions in Polish negotiations [N 9536/6/55].

No. 269

Record by Sir A. Clark Kerr of a conversation between Mr. Eden and M. Mikolajczyk at the Secretary of State's house at Potsdam on 25 July 1945 at 10.30 a.m.

[F.O. 934/2/10(73)]

M. Mikolajczyk called on the Foreign Secretary at 10.30 this morning.[1]

He began by saying that all that M. Bierut had told us last night[2] about twenty-three political parties in Poland was nonsense, as was also much of what he had said about the freedom that would be given to the expulsion [*sic*] of popular opinion at the elections. Ten days or so ago when I had been in Warsaw he (Mikolajczyk) had been able to give me a good account of the way things were shaping.[3] That was no longer possible, for there had been a marked change in the attitude of Bierut, who had gone back upon many of the undertakings he had given to Mikolajczyk in Moscow.[4] For instance: it had been agreed

(1) that the Peasant party should have full freedom to work. This had now been denied him. He had been prevented from issuing his party programme and from restarting the party newspaper.

(2) that one third of the National Home Council[5] should be drawn from the Peasant Party. When however the time had come, his nominees had been rejected. For this reason he had refused to take the oath.

(3) that the distribution of under-secretaryships should be on the same basis as that of the seats in the Cabinet. Upon this too Bierut had gone back.

In reply to a question by the Foreign Secretary M. Mikolajczyk said

---

[1] '25 July' was here pencilled in on the filed copy (cf. the dating at foot).
[2] See No. 267.
[3] See No. 319.i.
[4] Cf. No. 78, note 1.
[5] Polish general assembly of nominated delegates.

that he did not regret his return to Poland. It had been his duty to go back and he was going to see the struggle for independence through.

He went on to say that it was clear that Bierut had been aiming at setting up the one party system. He had had some success in the towns, but he had failed in the country where the peasants were determined to preserve their party intact. For this reason Bierut was afraid of the peasants and was putting obstacles in the way of Mikolajczyk's efforts to organise them, accusing Mikolajczyk of splitting the party instead of uniting it, because Mikolajczyk had been reluctant to absorb the members of the bogus Peasant's Party which had grown up at Lublin during his absence in London. Mikolajczyk thought that his best course would probably be to admit these people in the hope that the real peasants would be able in due course to digest them.

Here Mikolajczyk repreated much of what he had told me at Warsaw about the failure of the Lublin agrarian policy to catch the fancy of the peasants, who were now returning their title deeds to the Ministry and asking for work instead of land. He described the plight of the landlords, who were not even allowed to live in the houses on their confiscated estates. He hoped to be able to right some of their wrongs after the elections. Meanwhile he could do little to help them without laying himself open to the charge of trying to restore landlordism.

After saying a few words about the difficulties Popiel was having in his efforts to build up the Christian Democrat Party, he passed on to talk about the industries. Morawsky [*sic*] had been in favour of wide nationalisation, Gomalko [*sic*] had opposed it and Mikolajczyk had good reason to hope that a sound industrial system would emerge.

He then turned to the elections and said that if they had been held some weeks ago the Communists would have got some twenty per cent of the votes. Today he would not put that vote at more than one per cent, so great had become the public hatred of the government and its secret police. It was of the first importance to get rid of the N.K.V.D. Once that was done the Polish people would know how to deal with their own secret police.

He went on to speak of the large numbers of people still in the woods and afraid to come out. In the Lublin district for instance half the population was in hiding. Although the Red Army was withdrawing, 250,000 Cossacks were now being brought into Lublin to deal with the people in the woods.

(At this point the Foreign Secretary had to break off the conversation and go to a meeting and he asked me to listen to what Mikolajczyk had to say. The following[6] is a record of our conversation made by Captain Leggett.)

A. C. K.

July 24 [*sic*] 45

[6] No. 270.

No. 270

Record of a conversation between Sir A. Clark Kerr and
M. Mikolajczyk at the Secretary of State's house at Potsdam,
on 25 July 1945 at 11 a.m.[1]

[*F.O. 934/2/10(73)*]

M. Mikolajczyk continued[2] on the subject of

The Soviet Forces and N.K.V.D. in Poland

Conditions were tolerable in Central Poland and the Krakow district, and in the south. They had deteriorated recently in the Poznan and Pomerania areas. They were particularly difficult in the Lublin district.

Arrests were nothing out of the ordinary, and it frequently happened that a Polish *starosta* or *wojewoda* (local administrative officials) was apprehended and subsequently released.

A typical instance of Soviet behaviour in Poland was quoted by M. Mikolajczyk as occurring in the Jarocin district, where:

80% of the original livestock and machinery had been left after the German withdrawal;

whereas 8% now remained after receiving the attentions of the Red Army.

Conditions were extremely difficult in the territories west of Poland's 1939 German frontier; Polish authorities did exist in these territories, but their control was a mere fiction.

100,000 Poles had been transferred there, as these lands stood empty.

Violence, raping, arbitrary requisitioning were going on; there were shooting affrays between the Soviet Army and that of General Zymierski, as the soldiery was undisciplined and the Armies lived on the land. There was no regular provisioning; the normal practice consisted of wholesale commandeering on a short-term basis regardless of damage and cost.

M. Mikolajczyk had called on Pavlov the Chief Quartermaster of the Soviet Army and had signed an agreement with him on the above issue, but to no practical purpose. Next M. Mikolajczyk had visited Marshal Rokossovsky, in whose area matters had improved, but Koniev's and Zhukov's zones were independent of Rokossovsky's command.

So much for the economic side.

As regards the political aspect, M. Mikolajczyk pointed out three dangers:

(*a*) The Soviet Army;

(*b*) The N.K.V.D.

(*c*) The Polish Security Police.

In M. Mikolajczyk's view it would not be possible to hold free elections whilst (a) and (b) were still in the country, as they exercised a general

---

[1] This record was noted at head as a 'Resumé of Conversation' held at 21 Ringstrasse, Babelsberg, and lasting till noon.

[2] See No. 269.

terror. When they quitted, the Poles would know how to deal with remaining N.K.V.D. elements that have infiltrated the Polish Security Police.

In reply to the Ambassador's question, Mr. Mikolajczyk said that a withdrawal of Soviet forces from Poland was in progress, but it was a very painful process as these forces took everything away with them whilst in other parts there was a reverse movement, for instance ten newly arrived Cossack troops in the Lublin district.

In the western areas (west of the 1939 Polish/German frontier) there was an area of 2,000,000 hectares to be cultivated. Of these, 400,000 hectares are already being cultivated by the Poles whilst it would be necessary to cultivate a further 700,000 hectares in this area if the Polish population were to be fed.

The Poles did not grudge the Soviet forces the use of arable land west of the 1939 frontier, but they resented and opposed Soviet encroachments east of this frontier.

The Soviets regarded all machinery and livestock outside the Polish 1939 frontiers as war booty, and this attitude extended even to livestock raised since 1939 *inside* pre-1939 Polish territory; e.g.—stud horses.

The withdrawing Soviet forces would leave a desert behind them.

If genuine elections were to be held, they should be held swiftly, as soon as possible, after the evacuation by Soviet forces of clearly delimited areas where the Polish population could live and settle.

The Polish Forces and Return of Emigres

All appointments from major upwards in the present Polish army were held in fact by Russians in Polish uniform; some of these were very loyal to Poland but the majority could not speak Polish and maltreated their Polish subordinates, many of whom took to the woods. The feeling of national pride and self-respect in Poland was thereby greatly impaired.

To restore the nation's and army's dignity it was essential to bring back the Polish armed forces now abroad so as to create a genuine national army, independent of foreign control.

M. Mikolajczyk referred to the hesitancy with which M. Bierut had replied to Mr. Eden's query on Tuesday night[3] as to whether the Poles desired the transfer of the Polish navy from British to Polish waters. (Mr. Bierut had previously specified the Merchant Navy in his request). M. Mikolajczyk indicated that it was the intention of M. Bierut's government to allow the Soviets to form a new navy for Poland, whereby the Soviets would establish themselves firmly on the Baltic coast. The Soviets were giving Poland a few old trawlers for their fleet.

The Polish Merchant Navy and fleet must return to Polish waters, if the Poles were to recover their sense of dignity and independence and if they were to avert the threat of Soviet control of their navy.

M. Mikolajczyk declared that he would personally guarantee the safety

[3] Cf. No. 267.

of Poles returning to their native land; some of them might be arrested. But most of them would be safe, and in the coming struggle for Polish independence, M. Mikolajczyk considered that a few would have to be sacrificed for the sake of the many, even as soldiers going into battle.

Both Generals Zymierski and Spychalski[4] showed understanding and willingness to receive back Polish forces from abroad. Prompt action was necessary if they were to return in time to contribute Polish independence.

Of course there could be no question of forcing them to return, but ways of setting about the problem might be considered.

The best sort of approach to them was a frank and sincere one, and a good impression had been created in London by Drozniak and Kolodziejski, since they had painted a realistic picture of conditions in Poland, giving both the good and the bad aspects of the situation.

Elections

In order to postpone the elections in Poland, 'they' (presumably the Bierut party) were putting forward the following excuses:
(1) The emigrés must first return home from East and West (however nothing serious was being done about it);
(2) The frontiers of Poland must first be drawn.
An agreement had already been signed[5] for the repatriation of 4,000,000 Poles from territories east of the Curzon Line. However only 300,000 had so far been transferred. In general the agricultural population was showing little sign of moving and the peasants were slow to shift. M. Mikolajczyk said that Poland now risked the danger of losing not only the territories in the east, but the *ethnic* Polish population as well. At present there was no propaganda to encourage these Poles to move west. Such encouragement could only be offered by a definition of Poland's frontiers.

At the moment only a small proportion of pre-war Polish territory was recognised as Polish. Some authoritative pronouncement, some legal formula, must be devised to indicate the Polish territories in which elections were to be held.

Freedom of Political Expression

The Communist Party were hated; they were not averse to violence.

The Socialist Party were clearing up their house and making progress.

The Peasant Party were being hampered in their activities. An attempt was being made to bring Communist stooges into the Peasant Party, against which tendency warning has been uttered by the orthodox Peasant Party leader, Witos.

[4] Brigadier Marjan Spychalski was serving in the Political Division of the Polish Army under Marshal Rola-Zymierski.

[5] Following agreements in September 1944 between the Polish National Committee in Lublin and the Ukrainian, Byelorussian and Lithuanian Soviet republics for reciprocal exchanges of population, a Polish-Soviet Agreement regarding repatriation and nationality had been signed in Moscow on 6 July 1945: cf. *B.F.S.P.*, vol. 155, pp. 840–3.

The Christian Democratic Party were also meeting with difficulties.

The National Democrats had no freedom at all, and theirs was a lost cause. But they would probably vote with the Christian Democrats if the latter were given enough freedom.

M. Mikolajczyk added (à propos of Mr. Eden's previous remark that His Majesty's Government did not wish to interfere in Polish internal affairs,) that after all His Majesty's Government was a party to the Yalta decisions and therefore had a right to see to it that those decisions were implemented.

As regards the 1921 Constitution, M. Mikolajczyk believed that in spite of all his assurances, M. Bierut did not intend to use this Constitution as a basis for the coming elections. In actual fact M. Bierut had packed the National Home Council with his supporters to the number of 100, in spite of the agreement reached in Moscow that each party should be represented by one third. M. Mikolajczyk's followers numbered only fifty. M. Bierut's excuse had been that the extra delegates represented various professional and social organisations and factions,—an electorate trick practised elsewhere in Europe.

The Frontier Question

M. Mikolajczyk attributed much of the popular acclaim which he had experienced to the fact that many Poles still thought and hoped that certain areas such as Lwow would yet return to Poland. His had been the unpleasant but necessary task of disillusioning them.

In some territories west of the Curzon line, the local Ukrainian population had remained, and was living under its own administration, in the expectation that the Soviet frontier would be expanded westwards to include them. They must be moved out of Polish territory.

The crux and keypoint of the whole matter, said M. Mikolajczyk, was that the difficulties over territory and frontiers were complicating the question of elections.

M. Mikolajczyk realised that the Prime Minister had said that vis-à-vis Poland His Majesty's Government were in a position different from that in which they stood as regards Yugoslavia and Czechoslovakia, for the reason that, in the case of Poland, there was a belt of intervening Soviet territory (occupied German territory). If the belt were indeed to be regarded as Soviet territory, as suggested by Mr. Eden and the Prime Minister, and M. Mikolajczyk thought that this was right, then the point in question was not the line along which the German frontier would lie in the east, but whether this 'belt of Soviet territory' should be allowed to stretch east of the Oder and the Neisse.

Yesterday Mr. Truman had said that this was not the time or place to fix the frontiers, which should be left to the Peace Conference.[6] But if the

---

[6] See the record of a conversation at 4.30 p.m. on 24 July between President Truman and the Polish Delegation: *F.R.U.S. Berlin*, vol. ii, pp. 356–7; cf. also No. 219, minute 8 above.

door were not opened to the Poles now, said M. Mikolajczyk, then Poland might well lose her independence and succumb to Soviet influence. The lot of the peasants was meanwhile deteriorating.

M. Mikolajczyk then declared 'It is for you to decide. But as for myself, as a Pole who has come out to Poland, I say Poland will be independent if we have speedy elections; the elections in turn are dependent on the fixing of the frontiers and the removal of Soviet troops from Polish territory'. When the Ambassador asked how best we could help him, M. Mikolajczyk stressed that it was essential to negotiate trade agreements at once. At the moment there was much talk and little action in Poland, for instance as regards the reconstruction of Warsaw, where little was being done.

M. Mikolajczyk then returned to the question of the delimitation of Poland's western frontier which was his chief anxiety. He feared that as a result of His Majesty's Government and the United States Government's negative attitude to Polish claims, Soviet propaganda would paint M. Molotov as Poland's only true friend and protector, whilst Mikolajczyk and Stanczyk would be discredited as having no pull with the Western Democracies.

In M. Mikolajczyk's view, Poland should acquire all the territory now claimed by her, so as to control the Neisse and Oder navigation systems, which were essential to the Polish nation for various reasons as a transit area for trade with Czechoslovakia and South-East Europe, as a natural boundary, etc.

In reply to the Ambassador's question, why the Poles wished to acquire an area capable of holding eight to nine million people when they have to resettle only four million Poles from the east, M. Mikolajczyk gave the following reasons:

(1) The Central Area of Poland had already previously been over-populated, so that living space had to be found for the surplus;

(2) Among the eight million to the west of the 1939 Polish/German frontier were two million Poles;

(3) A million seasonal labourers had before the war annually crossed into this territory from Poland proper;

(4) There was an extremely high birth-rate and natural increase in population in Poland;

(5) Even German statistics had shown a *Drang nach Westen*[7] of the German population from these disputed areas into industrial Germany.

M. Mikolajczyk realised that there was strong opposition to Poland's territorial claims, but he foresaw that if no Tripartite agreement were reached, then the Soviets would probably enforce some sort of solution of their own in this area.

Meanwhile the Soviets regarded all persons in the territories west of the 1939 Polish/German frontier as *Reichsdeutsche* or *Volksdeutsche*,[8] and as

---

[7] Drive to the West.   [8] German nationals or ethnic Germans.

such they even deported them on forced labour to the Baltic States. There was at present no Polish administration to look after them in these areas.

The Ambassador then summed up the proposed points for action as follows:

(a) Obtain a provisional delimitation of Poland's frontiers;

(b) His Majesty's Government to send a representative to negotiate a trade agreement with Poland;

(c) A resourceful British firm to undertake contracts in Poland in order to show what private enterprise could do;

(d) Arrange for an immediate and regular air communication between London and Warsaw.

M. Mikolajczyk said that there was a crying need for the 11,000 trained Polish pilots and ground staff now in the United Kingdom. In Poland there were only eighteen Polish aeroplanes received from the Russians, but even these were manned by Russians and were Polish in name only.

M. Mikolajczyk was satisfied that Soviet Russia was genuinely unable to send any supplies to Poland owing to her own shortages. Here was a wonderful opportunity to enter into trade agreements with other states before the Soviets could get going.

M. Mikolajczyk's opinion of M. Molotov's speech of the day before[9] was that it had been so much propaganda, and that its only effect had been to provoke the British and United States delegates into an attitude of opposition. In so far as propaganda was concerned it would be a precious instrument in the hands of those Poles who leaned towards the Soviet Union rather than towards the west.

The Polish Embassy

M. Kot and M. Strasburger[10] had been considered for the post of Ambassador to Washington, the Washington establishment had now been filled as follows:

Ambassador — *Barcikowski*, a lawyer, an honest man with leftish sympathies, but no Communist.

1st Secretary — *Kulerski*.

2nd Secretary — *Fialkiewicz*, to work with the Communists.
Drohojowski

Paris: The Communists had insisted on the appointment of *Strzeszewski*, a Communist to be Ambassador, but had now agreed to send one of M. Mikolajczyk's men, *Kuzniacz*, as 1st Secretary.

The Polish Foreign Office

Rzymowski wielded no influence at all, and the real controller of policy was *Berman*,[11] who was in close touch with Bierut.

---

[9] See No. 254, minute 4.

[10] Former Polish Delegate in the Middle East.

[11] M. Jacob Berman was Head of the Political Department in the Polish Ministry of Foreign Affairs.

There was some slight rivalry between Bierut and *Osubka-Morawski* [*sic*] about each other's prerogatives.

The Amnesty

A resolution had been submitted to the President but Mikolajczyk had forced Osubka-Morawski to make a proclamation regarding the Amnesty, which had annoyed Bierut.

M. Mikolajczyk thought that there was a growing understanding and appreciation of the A[rmia] K[rajowa] (the Underground Movement) who were regaining their natural rights. M. Mikolajczyk was maintaining contacts with the A.K. and had obtained a promise that they would dissolve altogether. What they asked for was security.

M. Mikolajczyk's suggestions regarding the role of His Majesty's Ambassador in Warsaw were that he should not overtly interfere in Polish affairs, but should gather information and in the course of his conversations with Polish Government representatives he should show that he was aware of what was happening whilst showing a desire to help in practical ways on a business level.

The Russians were taking everything, but simultaneously they were running a propaganda campaign designed to present them as the friends and supporters of the Polish state. Some people were giving evidence to this propaganda. It would be useful to have a British counter balance—for instance a British sponsored newspaper in Polish would have a very good circulation in Warsaw.

Restrictions of press correspondents

M. Mikolajczyk suggested that the first consideration should be to establish the representatives of the main newspapers and press agencies in Warsaw who would at a later stage acquire increasing liberty in their activities.

Foreign Office, 26th July 1945

No. 271

Record of Ninth Plenary Meeting held at Cecilienhof, Potsdam, on Wednesday, 25 July 1945 at 11 a.m.
P.(Terminal)9th Meeting [*U 6197/3628/70*]

Top secret

Present:

PREMIER STALIN, M. V. M. Molotov, M. A. Ya. Vyshinski, M. F. T. Gousev, M. A. A. Gromyko, M. K. V. Novikov, M. A. A. Sobolev, M. V. N. Pavlov (*Interpreter*).

PRESIDENT TRUMAN, Mr. J. F. Byrnes, Mr. Joseph E. Davies, Mr. J. C. Dunn, Mr. H. F. Matthews, Mr. E. W. Pauley, Mr. W. L. Clayton, Mr. C. E. Bohlen (*Interpreter*).

Mr. Churchill, Mr. Eden, Mr. Attlee, Sir W. Monckton, Sir A. Cadogan, Sir W. Strang, Sir E. Bridges, Mr. N. Brook, Mr. T. L. Rowan, Mr. P. J. Dixon, Mr. W. Hayter, Major A. Birse (*Interpreter*).

Contents

Minute	Subject
1.	German Fleet and Merchant Navy
2.	Transfers of Population
3.	Western Frontier of Poland
4.	Future Procedure and Subjects for Discussion

1. *German Fleet and Merchant Navy*
(Previous Reference: P. (Terminal) 3rd Meeting,[1] Minute 6.)

Mr. Churchill said that the British Delegation had been preparing concrete proposals on the lines of the general understanding reached at the previous discussion. He hoped to have a Memorandum ready for circulation shortly.

President Truman said that the United States Delegation had also been going into the details. While he was willing to discuss the matter, if that were generally desired, he would prefer to have some further time to study detailed proposals.

Premier Stalin agreed that this matter might be postponed.

It was agreed that further consideration of this matter should be deferred until detailed proposals were available.

2. *Transfers of Population*

Mr. Churchill said that at some stage the Conference should consider the problems involved in the large-scale transfer of populations across national frontiers, *e.g.*, the transfer into Germany of the large numbers of Germans now in Czechoslovakia and Poland. He understood that of the 3¼ million Sudeten Germans about 2½ million were to be transferred from Czechoslovakia into Germany; and the Czechoslovak Government would also wish to return to Germany a further 150,000 Reich Germans, who had been evacuated into Czechoslovakia to escape Allied air raids. According to his information only a few thousand of these had been moved so far, under an agreement between the Soviet and Czechoslovak Governments. It would be a large problem to move these great numbers. Were they all to go into the Russian Zone?

Premier Stalin said that most of them would come into the Russian Zone. He believed that many had already been moved, having been evicted at short notice by the Czechs. On the east the Poles were retaining about 1½ million Germans to work on the harvest in the areas claimed by the Polish Provisional Government: as soon as the harvest was in, they would evict them. The Polish and Czechoslovak Governments were proceeding with

[1] No. 194.

690

these transfers on their own initiative without consulting the Soviet Government. He had never heard of the agreement mentioned by Mr. Churchill.

MR. EDEN said that President Benes had suggested to the British Government that the question of the transfer of Germans from Czechoslovakia should be discussed at the present Conference. He had understood that President Benes had made this suggestion to each of the three Great Powers.[2] Could it be referred to the Foreign Secretaries to consider?

PREMIER STALIN asked whether this would involve inviting representatives of the Czech Government to the Conference. MR. CHURCHILL said that, if that became necessary, he would be glad to welcome Dr. Benes, who was an old friend of his as well as of Premier Stalin's.

PREMIER STALIN wondered whether it was not already too late to consider this question. He believed that most of the Germans had already left Czechoslovakia.

MR. CHURCHILL said that he doubted whether this could be so, in view of the very large numbers involved. There were also the transfers from Poland to be considered, and some question—though on a much smaller scale—of the transfer of Germans from Hungary. He therefore suggested that the Foreign Secretaries should look into these matters and establish the facts.

> It was agreed that these questions should be referred to the Foreign Secretaries for consideration.

3. *Western Frontier of Poland*
(Previous Reference: P. (Terminal) 8th Meeting,[3] Minute 2).

MR. CHURCHILL said that he and Mr. Eden had now had an opportunity for further discussion with M. Bierut and other representatives of the Polish Provisional Government. It was clear that the question of Poland's Western Frontier could not be settled without taking into account the large number—about 1½ millions—of Germans still in the area claimed by the Poles and also the questions of reparations, occupational zones, &c., which were still undecided.

PRESIDENT TRUMAN agreed. He and Mr. Byrnes had also met the Polish representatives[4] and Mr. Byrnes was to have further conversations with them. The best course, therefore, seemed to be to postpone further consideration of this matter until the next Plenary Meeting. Meanwhile, however, he must make plain to his colleagues how he stood in this matter. At present there were in theory four occupational zones in Germany and four occupying Powers; but Poland seemed to be gradually acquiring the status of a fifth. If this were to be so, the position should be regularised. The Polish Government should be made properly responsible for the administration of this area as an occupational zone, while the final delimitation of the frontiers was left, as it must be, for settlement at the Peace Conference and incorporation in the Peace Treaty. He wished to be as helpful as he could,

[2] Cf. No. 59, note 8.
[3] No. 258.
[4] Cf. No. 270, note 6.

both to the Soviet Government and to the Polish Government, but he must make clear the position of the United States Government in this matter.

He must also make clear to his colleagues at the Conference his powers as President of the United States. Under the constitution of the United States, a Treaty of Peace could be ratified only with the consent and advice of the Senate. When he gave his assent to a proposal put forward at this Conference, he would use his best endeavours to secure its acceptance by the Senate. But his assent should not be taken as a guarantee of subsequent acceptance by the Senate; nor should it preclude his coming back to his colleagues and informing them that, because of public opinion in America, he could not secure acceptance of a particular decision of the Conference without endangering their common interest in obtaining a stable settlement which would have the continuing support of the three Great Powers. He was not suggesting any alteration in the basis on which he, and President Roosevelt before him, had entered into these discussions between Heads of Governments but he wished them clearly to understand the limits of his constitutional authority. He was at the Conference to present the point of view of the people of the United States; and the Polish question now under consideration was of particular interest to them. He had the greatest sympathy for the point of view of the Polish and Soviet Governments, but the most important point was that the decision reached should be one which he could honestly recommend to the Senate and which it would be likely to accept. This limitation of his powers applied, of course, only to matters which would be dealt with in Peace Treaties. His wartime powers were unrestricted, but he was not prepared to abuse those powers by invoking them for purposes for which they were not intended. It was essential to the future peace of the world that, in all he did at this Conference, he should be able to command the continuing support of public opinion in the United States.

MR. CHURCHILL said that he wished to emphasise how important for the success of the Conference was the settlement of the Polish question and the other questions bound up with it, such as reparations and the feeding of Germany. If the Poles were allowed to assume the position of a fifth occupying Power, without arrangements being made for spreading the food produced in Germany equally over the whole German population and without agreement being reached on a reparations plan or a definition of war booty, it must be admitted that the Conference would have failed. It was his earnest hope that a broad agreement would be reached on this net-work of problems lying at the very heart of their work. So far, however, no progress had been made towards such an agreement.

PRESIDENT TRUMAN agreed. Much progress had been made at the Conference, but not on these questions.

PREMIER STALIN said he thought that even more important than the question of food supplies was that of obtaining for the rest of Germany supplies of coal and metals from the Ruhr.

MR. CHURCHILL said that supplies from the Ruhr for the Russian zone of Germany or for Poland would have to be bartered against food from these areas. He could not accept a position whereby all supplies in the Russian zone and to the east of it were disposed of by the Soviet Government unconditionally, while the right of the Soviet Government was admitted to obtain a proportion of products from the other zones.

Premier Stalin said that, if the Ruhr was to remain within the boundaries of Germany, then the whole of Germany should draw on it for supplies. There were two factors in the problem: supplies from the Ruhr and food.

Mr. Churchill said that, if the miners in the Ruhr did not get food, they could not produce coal. Where was the food to come from?

Premier Stalin said that Germany had always imported food and must do so again. Mr. Churchill asked how then could they pay reparations. Premier Stalin said there was still a good deal of fat left in Germany.

Mr. Churchill said he could not agree to an arrangement under which there would be starvation in the Ruhr during the coming winter, while the Poles disposed of all the products of the food producing areas in the east.

Premier Stalin said that the Poles were short of food. Only recently they had asked the Soviet Government for food grain to tide them over until the harvest.

Mr. Churchill said he was ready to recognise the difficulties of the Soviet Government, and he hoped that Premier Stalin would recognise his. Great Britain would have the most fire-less winter of the war this year, because of the shortage of miners to produce the necessary coal.

Premier Stalin suggested that the British Government should use German prisoners of war in the mines. The Soviet Government were doing so: indeed they could not have produced enough coal without them. There were, he understood, 400,000 German troops still in Norway who had not yet been disarmed. Here was a source of man-power for coalmining.

Mr. Churchill said that we had been exporting coal to France, Holland and Belgium since their liberation, and while we were thus denying ourselves we found it strange that the Poles should be selling to Sweden and other countries coal obtained from mines in territory which we had not yet recognised as Polish.

Premier Stalin said that this coal had been obtained, not from the former German territories, but from the Dabrowa basin. The Soviet Government had to face a situation even more difficult than the British. They had lost over 5 million men in the war and were desperately short of labour. He did not, however, wish to dwell unduly on the difficulties of the Soviet Union.

Mr. Churchill said that the British Government would be glad to send coal from the Ruhr to Poland or elsewhere provided they received in exchange food for the German miners who produced the coal.

Premier Stalin said that the whole problem needed careful consideration before a decision was reached.

Mr. Churchill agreed that a decision could not be taken at once. His only desire was to make clear to his colleagues the difficulties that lay ahead.

It was agreed to defer further consideration of this matter until a later meeting.

4. *Future Procedure and Subjects for Discussion*

PRESIDENT TRUMAN said that the next Plenary Meeting would be held at 5 p.m. on Friday, 27th July. He suggested that meanwhile the Foreign Secretaries should prepare material for consideration at that meeting.

The President suggested that one subject with which the Foreign Secretaries might deal was his Memorandum on:

(*a*) *Free and Unrestricted Navigation of Inland Waterways* (P. (Terminal) 33).[5]

PREMIER STALIN agreed that this should be studied by the Foreign Secretaries.

M. MOLOTOV said that he was proposing to submit two Memoranda for consideration by the Foreign Secretaries:

(*b*) *Obstacles to the return of Soviet Citizens from Austria and Germany.*

(*c*) *German Troops in Norway.*

MR. CHURCHILL recalled that this second subject had been mentioned by Premier Stalin earlier in the Meeting (see Minute 3 above). It had always been our intention that these German troops in Norway should be disarmed at once; and he was not aware that they had not been disarmed. We certainly had no intention of using them as an armed force. He would have enquiries made and would submit a report on the facts.

It was agreed that the subjects listed at (*a*) and (*c*) above should be considered by the Foreign Secretaries, who should also prepare an agenda for the next Plenary Meeting.

Cabinet Office, Potsdam, 25th July, 1945

CALENDARS TO No. 271

i *25 July 1945 F.O. Delegation minute on supplies from Silesia to Prussia.* Arrangements for supplies of coal and foodstuffs are essential as a condition of British agreement to Polish western frontier. Discusses means of achieving this [F.O. 934/2/10(66)].

ii *24–5 July 1945 Letter from Mr. Brand (Berlin) to Mr. Hasler; minute from Mr. Brand to Mr. Coulson (Berlin)* without first enclosure: latest position at Potsdam on coal [UR 2483/2109/851; F.O. 934/1/2(29)].

[5] No. 246.

Letter from President Truman to Mr. Churchill (Berlin)[1]
[*F 4767/364/23*]

THE WHITE HOUSE, WASHINGTON, AT BABELSBERG (BERLIN), *25 July 1945*

Top secret
Copy

My dear Mr. Prime Minister:

In reply to your letter of the 24th,[2] the Secretary of State is preparing a copy of the memorandum directive to the Joint Chiefs of Staff on the issuance of Lend Lease material. It is my intention to abide strictly by the law as passed by the United States Congress on Lend Lease, as I explained to you yesterday, although a liberal construction will be given to the distribution of those items referred to in your memorandum from your Chiefs of Staff.[3]

I am making every effort to get a construction of the new Lend Lease renewal act so as to cause the least difficulty and embarrassment to our Allies. As soon as the memorandum to our Chiefs of Staff is finally prepared, I shall send you a copy.

We sent you last night a copy of our telegram to Chiang Kai-shek.[4] I am hoping that we will receive a concurrence from him, and that we may be in a position to issue the Proclamation at the earliest possible moment. I shall inform you, as soon as I hear from him, and we will issue the Proclamation jointly from here, if that is satisfactory to you.

Very sincerely yours,
HARRY S. TRUMAN

[1] This letter is printed in extracts in *F.R.U.S. Berlin*, vol. ii, pp. 1183 and 1279.
[2] No. 251, annex I.
[3] See No. 251, note 12.
[4] See *op. cit.*, vol. ii, p. 1278: also No. 231, note 7 above.

No. 273

Letter from Mr. Churchill to President Truman (Berlin)[1]
[*F 4767/364/23*]

Most secret   BERLIN, *25 July 1945*

My dear Mr. President,

I thank you for your letter of July 25,[2] and I await the Memorandum on Lend-Lease which you are kindly having prepared.

[1] This letter is printed in extracts *op. cit.*, vol. ii, pp. 1183 and 1279.
[2] No. 272.

I return the copy of the Proclamation to Japan by the Heads of Governments of the United States, the United Kingdom, and the Republic of China, which I received from you yesterday.[3] I am willing to sign it on behalf of His Majesty's Government in its present form, and I hope you will issue it as you propose whenever you choose and as soon as possible.

On a minor point, I suggest that the word 'industries' might be added where shown in paragraph 11, otherwise the word 'those' would seem at first sight to apply to Reparations.[4]

> Yours very sincerely,
> WINSTON S. CHURCHILL

[3] See No. 231, note 7.

[4] Mr. Rowan noted on another copy of this letter (on PREM 8/34): 'Shown to Mr. Attlee 11.0 p.m. 26.7—who agreed that it should appear above Mr. Churchill's signature. It has appeared. T.L.R. 26.7': see No. 281. Earlier on 26 July 1945, with reference to a broadcast to Japan by Captain E. M. Zacharias of the U.S. Navy on 21 July (see *F.R.U.S. Berlin*, vol. ii, pp. 1273–4), Mr. Churchill, who resigned his office at 7 p.m. on 26 July, had sent a personal and top secret message to President Truman transmitted to Berlin in Foreign Office telegram No. 221 Onward at 1.5 p.m. that day: 'In view of Zacharias' statement which I read, it would seem important that our document should issue as soon as possible.'

No. 274

Record of Eighth Meeting of Foreign Secretaries held at Cecilienhof, Potsdam, on Wednesday, 25 July 1945 at 12.30 p.m.

F.(*Terminal*)*8th Meeting* [U 6197/3628/70]

Top secret

Present:

M. V. M. MOLOTOV, M. A. Ya. Vyshinski, M. A. A. Gromyko, M. F. T. Gousev, M. K. V. Novikov, M. A. A. Sobolev, M. S. A. Golunski (*Interpreter*).

MR. J. F. BYRNES, Mr. J. C. Dunn, Mr. H. F. Matthews, Mr. W. L. Clayton, Mr. B. V. Cohen, Mr. C. E. Bohlen (*Interpreter*).

SIR A. CADOGAN, Sir W. Strang, Mr. N. Brook, Mr. W. Hayter, Major A. Birse (*Interpreter*).

Contents

Minute	Subject
1.	International Inland Waterways
2.	Transfer of Populations
3.	Preparation of Protocol and Communiqué
4.	Procedure: Date of Next Meeting

1. *International Inland Waterways*
(Previous References: P. (Terminal) 8th Meeting,[1] Minute 4 and 9th Meeting,[2] Minute 4.)

Mr. Byrnes recalled that at the Plenary Meeting that morning[2] Premier Stalin had assented to President Truman's suggestion that the memorandum on this subject by the United States Delegation (P. (Terminal) 33)[3] should be considered by the Foreign Secretaries.

Mr. Byrnes thought that in the first instance the proposals should be considered in detail by a Committee.

It was agreed that a Committe consisting of:
British Delegation: Mr. Ward, Mr. Dean,
United States Delegation: Mr. Riddelberger, Mr. Russel[l],
Soviet Delegation: M. Gerashchenko, M. Lavrishchevo,
should be appointed to consider this proposal and report to the Foreign Secretaries' Meeting.

2. *Transfer of Populations*
(Previous Reference: P. (Terminal) 9th Meeting,[2] Minute 2.)

Mr. Byrnes recalled that at the Plenary Meeting that morning this question had been referred to the Foreign Secretaries for consideration, and he invited the views of his colleagues as to how it should be handled. As he understood it, what was required was a plan for the orderly transfer of the Sudeten Germans from Czechoslovakia into Germany.

Sir Alexander Cadogan said that there was also the question of the transfer of Germans from Western Poland. Though the majority of these might already have left the territory claimed by Poland, this would not dispose of the question entirely if, as was proposed, there was to be a permanent change of domicile. There was also a similar problem on a smaller scale in Hungary.

The United Kingdom Delegation had no detailed plan to cover all these movements; but they suggested that, as the difficulties would arise mainly at the reception end in Germany, the movement might be placed under the control of the Allied Control Council in Germany, who should be instructed to act in consultation with the Governments concerned, namely, the Czechoslovak, Polish and Hungarian Governments. If this could be agreed in principle, the details could be worked out.

Mr. Byrnes said that $2\frac{1}{2}$ million people could not be transferred without causing difficulty and distress; but these difficulties would be much less if the transfer were carried out gradually. He agreed that the Control Council was the right body to control these transfers, and he hoped that it would be possible to agree to instruct the Control Council to provide for the orderly and gradual removal of these populations and to prevent their removal in large numbers all at once.

[1] No. 258. [2] No. 271.
[3] No. 246.

M. Molotov said that the Control Council should certainly receive instructions on this matter. But the authority of the Control Council did not extend outside Germany. It could refuse to admit these people to Germany, but it could not control the action of the other Governments in removing them from their present homes.

Sir Alexander Cadogan suggested that the Conference should ask the Control Council to investigate this problem as it existed, to report on the numbers of people already entering Germany from these areas, and to give an estimate of the time and rate at which they could be absorbed in Germany. At the same time we might tell the three Governments concerned that this investigation was being made and ask them to suspend further transfers until the report had been received, whereupon we would consult with them about future plans. In Hungary he thought that the Control Commission in that country could hold the position until a plan could be made.

Mr. Byrnes suggested that the further step might be taken of authorising the Control Council to make the necessary arrangements in consultation with the Governments concerned. M. Molotov, however, pointed out that the Control Council had not previously been authorised to have dealings with other Governments, and suggested that this point needed further consideration.

It was agreed that a sub-Committee consisting of:

British Delegation: Mr. Harrison,
United States Delegation: Mr. Cannon,
Soviet Delegation: M. Sobolev,

should be appointed to consider and report to the Foreign Secretaries' Meeting what practical arrangements could be made for regulating the transfer of populations in Europe, consequent on the defeat of Germany.

3. *Preparation of Protocol and Communiqué*
(Previous Reference: P. (Terminal) 8th Meeting,[1] Minute 8.)

The Plenary Meeting on the previous day had invited the Foreign Secretaries to appoint a Committee to begin work on the preparation of a communiqué for issue at the end of the Conference.

Sir Alexander Cadogan suggested that the preparation of a draft of the Protocol should also be put in hand. Perhaps this could be done by the same Committee?

Mr. Byrnes, while agreeing that work should start on the drafting of the Protocol, pointed out that this would require a style of drafting somewhat different from that of a statement designed for issue to the Press. He therefore suggested that two drafting Committees should be appointed, one to deal with the Protocol, and the other with the communiqué.

It was agreed that the following Committees should be appointed for these purposes:

Preparation of Protocol:
United States Delegation: Mr. J. Dunn, Mr. F. Matthews, Mr. B. Cohen.

United Kingdom Delegation: Sir E. Bridges, Mr. N. Brook, Mr. W. Hayter, Mr. P. Dean.

Soviet Delegation: M. Gromyko, M. Gribanov, M. Kozyrev.

Preparation of the Communiqué:

United States Delegation: Mr. W. Brown, Mr. Wilder Foot[e].

United Kingdom Delegation: Sir E. Bridges, Mr. N. Brook, Mr. W. Hayter, Mr. P. Dean.

Soviet Delegation: M. Sobolev, M. Golunski.

It was noted that the representatives nominated for these purposes by the United Kingdom Delegation would divide between them, as proved convenient, the duty of attending the meetings of the two Committees.

4. Procedure

It was agreed that the next meeting of the Foreign Secretaries should be held on Friday, 27th July, 1945, at 11 a.m.

Mr. Byrnes expressed the hope that, in the meantime, the Committee[s] which were considering the various subjects still outstanding would make a special effort to reach agreement and produce reports which could be considered by the Foreign Secretaries at their next meeting.

Cabinet Office, Potsdam, 25th July, 1945

No. 275

Letter from Mr. Hayter to M. Gromyko (Berlin)
[*F.O. 934/2/9(28)*]

BRITISH DELEGATION, BERLIN, *25 July 1945*

Dear Monsieur Gromyko,

At our meeting yesterday[1] I suggested, and Your Excellency agreed, that I should send you a letter setting out the points on which we should be grateful for further elucidation of the proposals made by the Soviet Government for altering the system of work of the Allied Control Commissions in Roumania, Bulgaria, Hungary and Finland.

2. Firstly, I should like to place on record my understanding that the proposals in regard to Roumania, Bulgaria and Finland are identical, whereas that in regard to Hungary differs in certain respects, of which the most important is that while in the first three countries directives by the Allied Control Commission are issued after a preliminary discussion with British and American representatives, in Hungary the directives are not issued until they have been agreed to by the British and American representatives.

---

[1] No record of this second meeting of the Sub-Committee on the implementation of the Yalta Declaration on Liberated Europe has been traced: cf. No. 254, minute 1, and *F.R.U.S. Berlin*, vol. ii, p. 380.

3. In this respect the position in Hungary would of course be more satisfactory to us than that proposed in the other three countries. In particular we should wish it to be laid down that our representatives in all the countries concerned must be associated with any decisions of the Control Commission affecting specifically British interests in the countries concerned.

4. There are those further points of difference between Hungary and other countries. Firstly, whereas in the proposal for Roumania which you handed to me[2] the British and American representatives have the right to determine the numbers and composition of their staff, no such provision appears in the Hungarian document.[3] The view of His Majesty's Government, as is well known to the Soviet Government, is that we should have this right in Hungary as in the other three countries.

5. Secondly, paragraph 1(a) of the Hungarian document begins with the words 'during the period before the conclusion of the peace treaty with Hungary'. These words do not appear in the other document. Has this difference any significance?

6. Thirdly, paragraph 4 of the Hungarian document, dealing with exit and entry permits, does not appear in the other document. This is a valuable provision, and we should wish to see it applied to the other countries.

7. In both the documents which you communicated to me it is stated that the British and American representatives are allowed freedom of movement through the country on condition that the Allied Control Commission is warned in advance of the time and route of their journey. It appears from enquiries made from the Soviet authorities in Bulgaria that in exceptional circumstances the Soviet Garrison Commander claims the right to alter the proposed destination or route. The British Government feels that if any such alteration is proposed it should only be for reasons which would be explained to the British representative and regarded by him as satisfactory.

8. There is one further point. Under Article 15 of the Armistice with Bulgaria the British Delegation is entitled to the provision of adequate funds. As recently as July 7th the Soviet authorities in Sofia indicated that they were not prepared to provide further currency unless they were given a detailed account of the uses to which it would be put. No reference is made to this matter in the documents which you have handed to me, and I should be glad to hear from you that no further difficulties on this point are to be expected. Clearly the right of the British representative to determine the numbers and composition of his staff is likely to be meaningless if he is unable to obtain adequate funds for them.

9. You thought it possible that you might not have available here all the information which would enable you to clear up the above point. If this is so, and if the information cannot be obtained before the end of the Conference, perhaps your Embassy in London could supply the answers to

[2] No. 259.   [3] See No. 197.i.

the Foreign Office, to whom I am sending a copy of this letter.

Yours sincerely,

W. HAYTER

No. 276

Letter from M. Novikov to Sir W. Strang (Berlin)[1]

[*F.O. 934/5/42(5)*]

Translation   BERLIN, *25 July 1945*

Dear Mr. Strang,

On instructions from the Peoples' Commissar of Foreign Affairs V. M. Molotov I forward to you herewith an aide mémoire on the activity which is hostile to the Soviet Union in the British, American and French zones of occupation in Austria and Germany as carried out by White emigrés and other persons and organisations hostile to the U.S.S.R.

I shall be grateful to you, Mr. Strang, for an acknowledgement of the receipt of this letter.

Yours sincerely,

K. V. NOVIKOV

ENCLOSURE IN No. 276

Aide Mémoire

Translation

The organisation dealing with problems of the repatriation of Soviet citizens has received information to the effect that White emigrés and other persons and organisations hostile to the U.S.S.R. are widely engaged in the British, American and French zones of occupation in Germany and in the British and American zones in Austria in activities, the object of which is to hinder the return home of Soviet citizens.

In Austrian territory this kind of activity is carried out in the areas occupied by the troops of the Eighth British and Fifth American Armies. It is reported that in the town of Salzburg a committee actually functions under the official title of 'Engineering and Technical Firm of Karyakin' which directs the aforesaid activity and is headed by Colonel Bobrov, a Russian emigré. In the district of Salzburg functions a committee for the non-return of Ukrainians. It is headed by Slipchenko and Mishchenko. Agents of the former Army Corps of Vlasov function

---

[1] This letter from M. Novikov, Secretary of the Soviet Delegation to the Conference at Potsdam, is printed with enclosed aide-mémoire (circulated in the British Delegation as document P. (Terminal) 44 of 27 July 1945) in *Berlinskaya konferentsiya*, pp. 373–5. Cf. *F.R.U.S. Berlin*, vol. ii, pp. 683–4, 1036, for the corresponding communication to the American Delegation. A further letter of 25 July, not here printed, from M. Novikov to Sir W. Strang enclosing an aide-mémoire of even date (circulated as P. (Terminal) 43 of 27 July) concerning the alleged non-application in full of the capitulation of German forces in Norway is printed in *Berlinskaya konferentsiya*, pp. 375–6: cf. *F.R.U.S. Berlin*, vol. ii, p. 1037.

in the region of Klagenfurt under orders of Colonel Rogozhin. General guidance in Austria of activities hostile to the U.S.S.R. is effected by a centre which includes the prominent White emigrés General Kreiter, the engineer Voskresentzev, Ivanov and Lavrov.

Similar activity of White emigrés in Germany in the zone of the First French Army is also reported. In this case this activity is carried out with the active support on the part of the French military authorities of the 'Sécurité Militaire'. The guidance of the activity directed against the U.S.S.R. in the British and American zones of occupation is effected by the so-called 'Ukrainian Central Committee' headed by the White emigré General Skoropadski, Kostyushchenko, Mironenko and Shmega. In accordance with the information received by the Soviet military authorities this committee created, in June of this year, in a number of German towns, including Weissenberg, Kassel and Nuremberg, what were called 'Ukrainian Committees'. Each member of such a committee was supplied with a printed certificate from the 'Central Committee'. Each certificate bears a seal and the signature of the 'President of the Free Ukraine'. Persons carrying these certificates freely move within the Allied zones of occupation in Germany and carry out without interference an activity hostile to the U.S.S.R. in camps for Soviet citizens situated in the British, American and French zones.

The Soviet Government considers it necessary to draw the attention of the British Government and the Government of the United States of America to the aforesaid facts.

25th July, 1945

CALENDAR TO NO. 276

i *26 July 1945 Letter from Mr. Harrison (Berlin) to Mr. Steel (Lübbecke)*. Requests investigation into Soviet complaints made in No. 276. [F.O. 934/5/42(5)].

No. 277

Minute from Sir A. Clark Kerr (Berlin) to Mr. Eden[1]
[F.O. 934/2/19(73)]

[BERLIN,] *26 July 1945*

We thought it best, for purposes of record, to reproduce as far as possible all that Mikolajczyk said, but it may be useful to you if I try to bring out what seemed to me to be the salient points.

---

[1] This covering minute to Nos. 269 and 270 was noted by Mr. D. Allen on 29 July 1945 as seen by Mr. Bevin. On 27 July Mr. Allen had minuted on these three documents: 'The top copy of this interesting record has been sent to Mr. Attlee so that he may if possible read it before he returns here. Copies have also gone to Mr. Warner in the F.O. Sir A. Clark Kerr's recommendation at X [not marked on filed copy] is covered by the paper which we have now prepared suggesting a definite linking of the frontier question with those of supply and reparation [see No. 436, enclosure]. The question of a Trade Agreement and a British newspaper in Warsaw, as well as those of the return of Polish Armed Forces will have to be pursued in London D. A. 27/7.'

It is clear that M. Mikolajczyk's chiefest preoccupation is the independence of Poland which he is still not unhopeful of securing. His hopes are of course mainly based on the result of the elections. You are aware of what he feels about party representation and of his concern that this should be free and fair, so I may perhaps skip that. He does not see much chance of unfettered elections until the Red Army withdraws. This is in progress in Poland proper, but, he argues, the Russians may be counted upon not to budge from the new areas to be absorbed by Poland until these are defined in some manner, provisional or otherwise. He regards it as of first importance that the Poles now living in these areas (many of whom are, as often as not, being treated by the Russians as *Volksdeutsche* and *Reichsdeutsche* and thus being deported in large numbers) should play a full part in these elections. This leads us to his claim that doors must be opened to the west *now* if Poland is not to lose her independence and succumb to Soviet influence. The words he used were these 'It is for you to decide, but for myself as a Pole who has come back to Poland, I say—that Poland will be independent if we have speedy elections; that the elections in their turn are dependent upon the fixing of the frontiers and of the removal of the Red Army from Polish territory.' It seems to me that there is much force in this.

You will see that he claims that the filling of the gap left by the departure of the 8 million inhabitants from Silesia etc. will present no serious problem, inasmuch as 2 of these 8 million are already Poles, 1 million was made up by swallow-immigration of farm labour from Poland, and there are homes to be found for the 4 millions from the Ukraine, and for the surplus population of the overcrowded areas of central Poland. If we tot these figures up we find that they do not fall far short of 8 million. This would seem to demolish to some extent the claim that large regions would remain unpopulated. It will not have escaped you that Mikolajczyk says that the attitude that we and the Americans have assumed about these areas will be used as propaganda by the Communists, who lean towards the Soviet Union rather than towards the west. Mikolajczyk seems now to have completely come over to the Oder Neisse school of thought. His change may be explained, apart from economic considerations, by his anxiety for the independence of Poland and by his fear that a denial of the Polish claims may destroy all chance of an orientation towards the west and you will notice too that he meets your and the Prime Minister's suggestion that a 'belt of Soviet territory' separates Poland from the West by questioning the wisdom of broadening this belt by letting it expand east of the Oder and Neisse.

My own feeling is that, if some arrangement can be made about reparations, food, *etcetera*, it would be prudent in us to be as fluid as possible about the Polish claims. Whatever we do we shall be creating a *Germania irredenta*[2] and the only way to make that secure is to hold Germany down.

[2] An unrecovered Germany.

This is the basis, I gather, of everything. Thus if you take a bite out of the living flesh of Germany, which is what we are doing, it does not much matter if the bite is a bit bigger than we had foreseen. One result will be, it is true a larger piece of *irredenta*, but the work of holding Germany down will not be the harder for that. Another result, however, will be a compact, sturdy, and possibly independent Poland, which is after all what we are aiming at.

You told me to ask Mikolajczyk how best we could help. I did so. In reply he has *inter alia* begged again for an early Trade Agreement. I suggest that we should set this going at once. About the establishment of an airline I spoke to Bierut today. He again welcomed the plan and said that he would take up with the Russians the question of clearance for flights over their zone of Germany.

I suggest too that we should at once pursue the proposal for a British newspaper in Warsaw.

A. C. K.

No. 278

Record by Mr. Winch (Berlin) of a conversation with M. Mikolajczyk

[F.O. 934/2/10(71)]

[BERLIN,] 26 July 1945

I had a short talk yesterday evening with Mr. Mikolajczyk who had come to my hotel in Berlin to dine with the Hulewiczes.[1]

2. Mr. Mikolajczyk is very anxious that some settlement should be reached with regard to the Western Frontier of Poland, as he regards this as an essential prerequesite [*sic*] for the elections. He feels that those members of the Government who wish to postpone the holding of the elections will be on strong ground if they say that elections cannot be held until the area of Poland has been fixed. He also feels that the absence of the Army in Britain will be made a further excuse for the postponement of the elections. He is therefore anxious that the Army and all other Poles in Britain should come to Poland as soon as possible, even if this can only be achieved as a result of British pressure.

3. Two necessary prerequisites for the holding of *fair* elections, Mr. Mikolajczyk thinks, are:–

(i) A clear request by the British and American Government to the Polish Government that a date for the elections, which are to be held in conformity with the Crimea Decisions, should soon be settled, and strong pressure by the two Governments that all parties should be allowed to nominate candidates.

---

[1] Professor Jan Hulewicz, former Deputy Minister of Information in the Polish Government in London, and Mme Hulewicz were then in Berlin on their way to Warsaw.

(ii) The departure of the Red Army from Poland, a possibility which he hoped would be taken up with Marshal Stalin by the British and American representatives in Potsdam.

4. Asked whether he thought that there was a real possibility of the elections being free, Mr. Mikolajczyk said that it was still too early to give a definite reply. If it appeared later that they would not be free, it would be essential for them to be held under international auspices. I suggested that this would mean a foreign observer in every voting booth and an arrangement for the counting of votes by a foreign body. Mr. Mikolajczyk said that he thought a party of 'supervisors' to the number of three or four hundred would be quite sufficient.

5. In conclusion, Mr. Mikolajczyk reiterated that the departure of the Red Army and the N.K.V.D. would be the most important factor in the development of the new Poland. Repeating the view expressed to H.M. Ambassador in Moscow, on the occasion of his visit to Warsaw, Mr. Mikolajczyk said that the Polish people would know how to 'deal with' the Polish security police. By this he means that the members of the security police are at heart decent Poles and could easily be re-educated so soon as they have been deprived of the support of Russian bayonets.[2]

M. B. WINCH

[2] This record was addressed to Mr. D. Allen. It was minuted by him and by Sir A. Cadogan and Mr. Pierson Dixon as follows: 'This is on the same general lines as M. Mikolajczyk's remarks to Mr. Eden and Sir A. Clark Kerr. But three points here are new or at least more explicit than they have hitherto been made: (i) The suggestion that we should ask the Polish Provisional Govt. to name a date for the elections. (ii) The suggestion that we should ask Stalin about the withdrawal of the Red Army from Poland. (iii) The suggestion that international supervision of the elections may be necessary.   Should a suitable opportunity present itself here it might be a good thing to take up (i) and (ii) with M. Bierut and Marshal Stalin respectively. D. Allen 27/7.' 'This might perhaps be sent, with other papers, for Mr. Attlee to read on the way here. A. C. July 27, 1945.' 'The S[ecretary] of S[tate] has had this paper before him. P. D. 29/7.'

No. 279

Record by Mr. Jebb (Berlin) of a conversation with Mr. Dunn
[F.O. 934/5/48(8)]

BERLIN, 26 July 1945

I saw Mr. Dunn last night and the following points arose:

Executive Committee[1]

(1) I outlined the way in which we saw the Committee working and said that Mr. Gerig[2], who had come to see me the day before in London, had quite agreed with this. Mr. Dunn likewise agreed and said that he thought

[1] Of the Preparatory Commission of the United Nations: cf. No. 106.
[2] Alternate American Delegate to the Preparatory Commission of the United Nations.

that the scheme for informal sub-committees was exactly what was required. I urged that more than two Americans should be made available for the international secretariat.

(2) In regard to the officers Mr. Dunn confirmed what Mr. Gerig had said, namely that in the last resort the Americans would prefer to have a Russian Chairman rather than that the chairmanship should rotate. Mr. Stettinius apparently feared that this last proposal, if adopted, might create an awkward precedent for the Security Council and other bodies of the World Organisation. In any case the Americans felt strongly that we should supply the Executive Secretary. In general, they did not mind very much what system was adopted (other than rotation) since as they saw it the Chairman would have no very special authority, the real work being done in the informal sub-committees with the assistance of the Secretariat. Supposing, therefore, that any Vice-Chairmen were needed, they would be quite happy to serve in that capacity, but equally they would not mind if there were no Vice-Chairmen at all.

(3) Mr. Dunn asked me if I had any news regarding the American representative! I said that Mr. Gerig had told me that he believed that Mr. Byrnes would not take any decision on this point until Terminal was over. Mr. Dunn then said that, as he understood it, Mr. Stettinius himself would probably represent the United States if the Senate had ratified the Charter before August 9th. He did not think that Mr. Stettinius would, in that event, stay in London for the whole period of the Executive Committee's existence but would go to the first few meetings and then go back to the United States. If the Senate had not ratified by August 9th then the United States would be represented by a deputy at the opening meeting. Mr. Dunn told me in great confidence that Mr. Stettinius was very keen that he (Mr. Dunn) should be his deputy and that if possible Mr. Pasvolsky[3] and his team of specialists should also come over to his office which would be located in the White House. In any case, communications from the American Delegation to the Executive Committee would go straight to Mr. Stettinius' office and not to the State Department, though Mr. Stettinius would keep in 'close touch' with the latter. Mr. Dunn said that if Mr. Byrnes would like him to be Mr. Stettinius' deputy, he would be very happy to do so and I got the impression that he was genuinely keen on the job.

(4) It was left that when I saw M. Gromyko[4] I should first of all try to find out whether or not the Russians were going to send a special representative or whether they were likely to be represented by their Ambassador in London. If M. Gromyko said that they were definitely adopting the first proposal, then I should be fairly forthcoming as regards a Russian Chairman. If, however, M. Gromyko indicated that M. Gousev was likely to be their representative then I should reserve my attitude while

[3] Special Assistant to Mr. Byrnes.
[4] Cf. No. 280.

indicating that the Americans at any rate would be opposed to a rotating Chairman.

Seat of the Organisation

(5) Mr. Dunn asked me what information I had on this subject and, when I referred to what Mr. Stettinius told Lord Halifax recently,[5] said that he had no knowledge of this. I therefore passed it on to him in great confidence. I also told Mr. Dunn the gist of Sir A. Cadogan's recent conversation with M. Molotov.[6] Mr. Dunn then said that he himself was opposed to locating the seat in the United States. He thought that the main problems with which the Organisation would have to deal, at any rate in the early stages of its existence, would certainly be in Europe or near Europe and that he, for his part, would greatly prefer some place like Copenhagen. I said that we, for our part, had always thought that two major decisions would have to be taken when the matter was seriously discussed. In the first place, was the seat going to be in the territory of any great Power? In the second place, was it going to be in the North American Continent or in Europe, all other areas being in practice out of the question? Mr. Dunn said that he agreed with this and that he imagined that the whole subject would have to be discussed at a fairly early date in the Executive Committee.

GLADWYN JEBB

[5] See No. 204.iii.
[6] See No. 204.

No. 280

Record by Mr. Jebb (Berlin) of a conversation with M. Gromyko
[*F.O.* 934/5/48(9)]

[BERLIN,] *26 July 1945*

I saw M. Gromyko for a few minutes at the Cecilienhof this morning and proceeded to explain to him in the first instance how we proposed that the Executive Committee[1] should work. M. Gromyko did not seem to object to any of this but displayed little interest. He said that what he was interested in was the chairmanship. What was our proposal?

I said that we had no very strong views ourselves and that it would in any case interest us to know whether the Soviet Government was going to appoint a special representative or not. M. Gromyko said that he had no information on this subject, nor could he say whether the Soviet Government could supply any officials for service on the International Secretariat. He repeated that he would like to know what our proposal was in regard to the chairmanship.

[1] See No. 279, note 1.

I then said that so far as I had been able to discover the Americans did not care very greatly for a rotating chairman. M. Gromyko expressed some surprise at this and said that, failing a Russian chairman, it was in his opinion the best solution. At this point we had to break off our conversation and I am going to see him again after tea.

I myself am begining to think that we ought to try to press the Americans to agree to a rotating chairman after all. If they are nervous about its creating a precedent for the World Organisation it should be noted in the first place that it cannot affect the presidency of the Assembly since Article 21 of the Charter lays down that the General Assembly 'shall elect its President for each session'. The relevant Articles regarding the Security Council, the Economic and Social Council and the Trusteeship Council lay down that each of these bodies shall 'adopt its own rules and procedure, including the method of selecting its President'. It is true therefore that if the chairmanship of the Executive Committee rotates it might be argued that the presidency of the three principal organs of the United Nations (other than the General Assembly) should also rotate. But it must be remembered that the presidency of the Council of the League of Nations rotated round the full circle of all the sixteen members whereas the proposal in regard to the Executive Committee is simply that it shall rotate as between the five Great Powers. I do not think that in practice it would be possible to arrive at a system whereby one nation held the presidency of the three major organs of the United Nations in question either in perpetuity or for more than one session. Nor do I think that it would in practice be possible for the Great Powers to make a gesture and agree that the presidency of them should be confided to the representative of a small Power who might be elected on grounds of merit. It is true that different systems might well be adopted for the Security Council and for e.g. the Economic and Social Council. In the former it would be arguable in view of their special position that the chairmanship should rotate among the five Great Powers only; in the latter it would seem preferable that it should rotate among all the eighteen members. Special considerations may also apply perhaps to the Trusteeship Council.

The net result of this seems to be that we should not run any particular risk if we agreed that the chairmanship of the Executive Committee should rotate among the five Great Powers, and incidentally this proposal would have the merit of being one which would be likely to appeal also to the French and the Chinese. I think, therefore, that I might tackle Mr. Dunn again on this subject and see whether I could induce him to send a telegram to the State Department; in the meantime I attach a draft telegram[2] which the Foreign Office, perhaps after consulting the Secretary of State, might send to Washington.

GLADWYN JEBB

[2] Not attached to filed copy: see further Nos. 416 and 422.

Proclamation
by the Heads of Government
United States, United Kingdom and China
[*F 4672/584/61*]

26 July 1945[1]

(1) We, — The President of the United States, the President of the National Government of the Republic of China, and the Prime Minister of Great Britain, representing the hundreds of millions of our countrymen, have conferred and agree that Japan shall be given an opportunity to end this war.

(2) The prodigious land, sea and air forces of the United States, the British Empire and of China, many times reinforced by their armies and air fleets from the west, are poised to strike the final blows upon Japan. This military power is sustained and inspired by the determination of all the Allied nations to prosecute the war against Japan until she ceases to resist.

(3) The result of the futile and senseless German resistance to the might of the aroused free peoples of the world stands forth in awful clarity as an example to the people of Japan. The might that now converges on Japan is immeasurably greater than that which, when applied to the resisting Nazis, necessarily laid waste to the lands, the industry and the method of life of the whole German people. The full application of our military power, backed by our resolve, *will*[2] mean the inevitable and complete destruction of the Japanese armed forces and just as inevitably the utter devastation of the Japanese homeland.

(4) The time has come for Japan to decide whether she will continue to be controlled by those self-willed militaristic advisers whose unintelligent calculations have brought the Empire of Japan to the threshold of annihilation, or whether she will follow the path of reason.

(5) Following are our terms. We will not deviate from them. There are no alternatives. We shall brook no delay.

(6) There must be eliminated for all time the authority and influence of those who have deceived and misled the people of Japan into embarking on world conquest, for we insist that a new order of peace, security, and justice will be impossible until irresponsible militarism is driven from the world.

(7) Until such a new order is established and until there is convincing proof that Japan's war-making power is destroyed, points in Japanese

---

[1] Date of release as notified by the United States Delegation at Potsdam in communicating on 28 July 1945 to the British Delegation this undated and unsigned copy of the proclamation: printed in *B.F.S.P.*, vol. 154, pp. 366–8.

[2] The underlining of this word in the filed copy was apparently inadvertently carried over from a draft: cf. *F.R.U.S. Berlin*, vol. ii, p. 1475, note 3.

territory to be designated by the Allies shall be occupied to secure the achievement of the basic objectives we are here setting forth.

(8) The terms of the Cairo Declaration shall be carried out and Japanese sovereignty shall be limited to the islands of Honshu, Hokkaido, Kyushu, Shikoku and such minor islands as we determine.

(9) The Japanese military forces, after being completely disarmed, shall be permitted to return to their homes with the opportunity to lead peaceful and productive lives.

(10) We do not intend that the Japanese shall be enslaved as a race or destroyed as a nation, but stern justice shall be meted out to all war criminals, including those who have visited cruelties upon our prisoners. The Japanese Government shall remove all obstacles to the revival and strengthening of democratic tendencies among the Japanese people. Freedom of speech, of religion, and of thought, as well as respect for the fundamental human rights shall be established.

(11) Japan shall be permitted to maintain such industries as will sustain her economy and permit the exaction of just reparations in kind, but not those industries which would enable her to re-arm for war. To this end, access to, as distinguished from control of, raw materials shall be permitted. Eventual Japanese participation in world trade relations shall be permitted.

(12) The occupying forces of the Allies shall be withdrawn from Japan as soon as these objectives have been accomplished and there has been established in accordance with the freely expressed will of the Japanese people a peacefully inclined and responsible government.

(13) We call upon the Government of Japan to proclaim now the unconditional surrender of all the Japanese armed forces, and to provide proper and adequate assurances of their good faith in such action. The alternative for Japan is prompt and utter destruction.

No. 282

Second report of the Economic Sub-Committee[1]
P.(Terminal)41 [U 6197/3628/70]

Top secret   *26 July 1945*

Reparations and European oil requirements

The Economic Sub-Committee regrets to have to report that after extensive discussions of the problems of German, Austrian, and Italian reparations, it has failed to come to agreement and consequently must refer these matters back to the Foreign Ministers for decision.

2. The Sub-Committee has recognised the liability of all three nations to exactions on account of reparation.

---

[1] This report, in succession to No. 210, is printed in extracts in *F.R.U.S. Berlin*, vol. ii, pp. 664–5, 866, 1385, and in *Berlinskaya konferentsiya*, pp. 377–8.

3. With respect to Germany, the Sub-Committee is in agreement that substantial reparations should be made. The Sub-Committee has been unable, however, to agree on the method for carrying out a programme of such reparations.

4. The Soviet representatives believe Austria capable of delivering the equivalent of $250,000,000 in kind over six years, and Italy capable of delivering the equivalent of $600,000,000 in kind over a like period, particularly, if in the case of Italy she will no longer have heavy military expenditure. The British and American representatives, on the other hand, point out that both Austria and Italy will require aid from abroad for some time to come, that the United Kingdom, United States and Canada have already supplied more than $500,000,000 of goods to Italy to prevent disease and unrest and that any reparations deliveries from these countries would, in fact, be financed by the nations supplying such goods. They are thus unable to agree to the imposition of any reparation levies on the current production of Austria and Italy. They would be prepared to consider the possibility of certain once-for-all removals of machinery and equipment from direct war industries having no peace-time utility.

5. The Sub-Committee is not yet prepared to make a definite report regarding the proposal of the United States that at least 50,000 barrels a day of oil be shipped from South-Eastern European producing areas to Western Europe or the Mediterranean for the purpose of easing the stringent oil and tanker situation in the supply of the Pacific War. The Soviet representatives indicate that they have not yet been able to obtain full information as to such possibility, although their preliminary data suggest a considerable deficit of petroleum products to meet Soviet needs, and the absence of any substantial surplus in the producing areas. They indicate that they will explore the matter further and report later.

No. 283

Report by the Sub-Committee on Cooperation in solving immediate European economic problems[1]
P.(Terminal)42 [U 6197/3628/70]

Top secret   *26 July 1945*

Cooperation in solving immediate European economic problems

Report of the conclusions reached by the Sub-Committee
created to consider the United States proposal

1. After a discussion of the functions and purposes of the Emergency Economic Committee for Europe and the European Coal Organisation, the

---

[1] Printed under date of 25 July 1945 in *F.R.U.S. Berlin*, vol. ii, p. 1161, and *Berlinskaya konferentsiya*, p. 378.

Soviet representatives agreed to review the documents concerning these organisations in order to decide the Soviet position regarding participation in them. The United Kingdom and United States Governments are already members of these organisations.

2. The United Kingdom and United States representatives informed the Soviet representatives of their desire to reconvene the European Inland Transport Conference and stated that they would welcome assurance that the Soviet Government would participate in the work of the reconvened Conference. The Soviet representative subsequently informed the United Kingdom and United States representatives that the Soviet Government would participate in this Conference.

CALENDAR TO No. 283

i *26 July 1945 F.O. Delegation note on No. 283:* 'A colourless document.' Summarises present position as regards the E.E.C.E., E.C.I.T.O. and E.C.O.: cf. No. 96 [F.O. 934/1/2(28)].

No. 284

Note of a meeting between British and Polish experts in the Conference Room, 20 Ringstrasse, on 26 July 1945 at 3 p.m.
[*F.O. 934/2/10(75)*]

Present:

THE HON. T. BRAND, Mr. Coulson, Mr. Allen, Mr. Weston, Captain Leggett, interpreter.

PROF. GOETEL, President of Mining Academy, Cracow, Dr. Bochenski, member of Mining Academy, Cracow, Dr. Leszczycki, geographer, Cracow University, Dr. Zebrowski, interpreter.

The Polish experts said that they wished to discuss the economic aspects of Poland's claim to a frontier on the Oder and Western Neisse. They then rehearsed all the general economic arguments in support of the Polish proposals on lines already familiar from the various statements of the Polish Delegation.

They read out figures showing Poland's losses and gains in respect of various commodities and natural resources as a result of the proposed frontier changes in the East and in the West. They undertook to furnish all this information in writing.

The following additional points emerged in the course of conversation:

Coal

The new territories contained (*a*) eighteen mines in German Upper Silesia with a production capacity of thirty million tons a year, (*b*) mines in the Walkenburg area near the Czechoslovak frontier with a production capacity of five million tons a year, mainly of coking coal. In these areas steps had been taken by the Poles immediately after the Germans withdrew to start production. Luckily in the Silesian mines 80% of the miners had been Polish and these had remained behind. No figures were available of present production. The Poles estimated it at about 50% of capacity, (say seventeen million tons a year).

In the mines in pre-war Polish territory production had now reached an average of twenty-nine million tons a year (June production was 2,400,000 tons). This was about three quarters of pre-war peak production although under the Germans production had been considerably increased by uneconomic exploitation. As a result of these German methods much replacement of equipment and technical improvements were now urgently needed in all the mines. A second serious difficulty was the lack of transport. In recent months it had been possible to transport away from the pit-head only 34% of the coal actually mined. Despite these difficulties the Poles expected to have a considerable surplus of coal available for export.

Food

50% of Poland's best alluvial soil suitable for wheat production had been lost in the East and this would not be replaced by the proposed compensation in the West. The net result of the present proposals would be that production of rye and potatoes would be increased but that of wheat, millet and maize would decrease. There was therefore a danger that Poland might become a food importing country rather than an exporting country as she had been before the war. In the long run there might be a surplus of rye, potatoes and livestock available for export but in the immediate future Poland would be able to feed her own population only if crops were good and rates of production were raised above those attained under the Germans.

The new territories had been emptied of their population but nevertheless some Spring sowing had been done and it was expected that, with help from the Red Army, enough labour would be available to get all the harvests in. Out of a total of five million hectares of arable land in these territories, two million hectares had been sown with grain this year apart from further areas under potatoes and beet. These territories should produce ample grain to support the local population though there would be a deficiency of fats and meat.

Towards the end of the meeting the Polish experts said that they looked forward in due course to exporting any available surplusses [*sic*] of food to Germany in return for German products which Poland might need.

Transport

Present difficulties were chiefly due to a shortage of rolling stock, only 30% of which remained and that in poor condition and largely needed for the transport of troops and other military purposes. Difficulties had also been caused by Russian attempts to broaden the gauge of the railways west of the Curzon Line. These plans had however been abandoned and all railways in Poland were being restored to the normal European narrow gauge. Control of the railways had also now been restored to Polish hands.

The Poles were placing considerable reliance upon water transport, particularly in moving Silesian coal down the Oder and thence either westwards to Berlin or eastwards by canal to the Vistula. Nearly one million [*sic*] of the Germans' six-hundred-ton barges still remained on the Oder and the Poles were putting these into Commission. They were also beginning the construction of a canal which would eventually link up the Oder in upper Silesia with the Danube across Czechoslovakia.

Forests

Poland had lost in the East 1,384,000 hectares of forest resources which in any case had been seriously depleted by the Germans. It would now be an importing and no longer an exporting country so far as timber was concerned.

Foreign Office, 27th July, 1945

No. 285

*Record by Mr. Hoyer Millar (Berlin) of a conversation with
Mr. Dunn and Mr. Mathews*

[*F.O. 934/5/48(6)*]

BERLIN, *26 July 1945*

I spoke to Mr. Dunn and Mr. Mathews this afternoon about the resolution on the admission of Italy, Spain, etc. to the United Nations which is coming up before the Foreign Secretaries tomorrow.[1] I explained to them why we did not feel able to accept the Russian amendment re-establishing diplomatic relations with Bulgaria, etc. and why we felt that the second alternative amendment, of which we had provisionally informed them yesterday, was unsatisfactory in that it rather skated over the difficulties and suggested that we would in fact be prepared to re-establish diplomatic relations before long with the existing Balkan Governments in their present form. In these circumstances we thought that we ought to stand by our first alternative which implied that we could only re-establish normal diplomatic relations after the conclusion of peace treaties with Bulgaria, etc.

Mr. Dunn and Mr. Mathews said that they quite shared our views and that they felt sure that their Secretary of State would resist any amendment which could be held to mean that the U.S. Government was prepared to establish diplomatic relations with the Balkan Governments in their present form. That being so, they thought that our suggested first alternative

[1] See No. 431, minute 2.

was the best way of meeting the case. I pointed out to them that if we both stood firm on the matter, the Russian Delegation might very well say that in that case they would not agree to any resolution at all—even though this might mean cutting out the anti-Franco part of the resolution. If this happened then we, for our part, should lose that part of the resolution which said that the three Governments would back Italy's candidature for the United Nations. Mr. Dunn said that he quite realised this, but he thought that Mr. Byrnes would prefer to let the whole resolution go rather than budge over the Balkans. Mr. Dunn said that he did not think losing the references to Italy would really matter very much. The fact that we intended to conclude an early peace treaty with Italy would appear in the other resolution about the Council of Foreign Ministers. The peace treaty point was really more important to make public than the United Nations point. It would always be possible for the United States Government in the President's Report to Congress and for H.M.G. in any debate in the House of Commons on Terminal, to make it clear that they for their part would be glad to support Italy's candidature for the United Nations as soon as the peace treaty was signed.

I asked the U.S. Delegation to try to let us know before tomorrow's meeting exactly what lines their Secretary of State decided to take. It is just possible that the Americans may put forward some fresh form of words in the hopes of meeting the Russians to some extent.[2]

F. R. Hoyer Millar

[2] This record was initialed by Sir A. Cadogan on 26 July 1945.

CHAPTER III

Developments during the first part of the Conference at Potsdam
17 — 26 July 1945

No. 286

Mr. Eden (Berlin) to Sir J. Anderson (Received 17 July, 12.47 a.m.)
No. 54 Target Telegraphic [ZM 3861/1/22]

Top secret. Immediate   BERLIN, *17 July 1945, 1.50 a.m.*

Your telegram No. 19 Onward.[1]

Dixon saw Dunn and Matthews today[2] and spoke to them in the sense of your telegram under reference.

2. They admitted inappropriateness of making proposed announcement now though they thought that it might be desirable to include some reference to Italy's eventual admission to the World Security Organisation in any general statement on Italy issued as result of the Terminal Conference. Dunn promised to recommend to Mr. Byrnes that instructions should be sent to Washington to defer making the announcement on July 17.

3. United States Delegation have now telegraphed instructions in this sense to Washington.[3]

Please repeat to Rome, Washington and Caserta.

CALENDARS TO No. 286

i *16 July 1945 Letter from Mr. Dixon (Berlin) to Mr. Hoyer Millar.* Attaches American briefs received from Mr. Dunn and Mr. Matthews on (*a*) Italy (printed *F.R.U.S. Berlin*, vol. i, pp. 681–4); (*b*) future of Allied Commission and Advisory Council for Italy; (*c*) the Italian institutional question; (*d*) creation of democratic organs of local government in Italy. Foreign Office minutes on the briefs [ZM 3867/1/22].

ii *17 July 1945 Mr. Eden (Berlin) Tel. No. 55 Target.* Views expressed by Mr. Dunn and Mr. Matthews to Mr. Dixon on 16 July concerning discussion

---

[1] Repetition to Berlin of No. 149.
[2] This telegram was drafted on 16 July 1945. Cf. No. 178.ii.
[3] See *F.R.U.S. Berlin*, vol. ii, pp. 623–4.

of Italy at the conference: U.S. Govt. favoured conclusion with the Italian Govt. of a *modus operandi* pending a peace treaty. Mr. A. D. M. Ross minuted on this in F.O. on 18 July that 'Mr. Hoyer Millar is proceeding to Terminal to urge the Americans *inter alia* to abandon their idea of a *modus operandi*' [ZM 3863/1/22].

iii   *17 & 20 July 1945   Record of meeting at the Foreign Office on 17 July, and related correspondence.* Work of British Council and Ministry of Information in regard to Italy [LC 3027/82/452].

iv   *21 July 1945   A.F.H.Q. (Caserta) to Sir J. Grigg Tel. No. Mat 830* (transmitted as No. 222 Onward of 26 July to Berlin). Termination of military responsibility for civil supplies in Italy projected for 1 Sept. Italian economy must remain for considerable period dependent on foreign aid [ZM 4069/18/22].

v   *21 & 24 July 1945   Mr. Hopkinson (Rome) Despatches Nos. 315 (E) and P.L. No. 319.* Recently announced Allied industrial plan for Northern Italy has been prepared with view to early withdrawal of A.M.G. and transfer of the territory to Italian Govt. Italian P.M. informed on 18 July of transfer of certain financial responsibilities to Italian Govt. [ZM 4099/2842/22; ZM 4139/7/22].

No. 287

Cabinet Office to Joint Staff Mission (Washington)
No. 893 NOD Telegraphic [R 12178/24/92]

CABINET OFFICE, *17 July 1945, 11.15 a.m. G.M.T.*

Secret. Important

Following from Chiefs of Staff.

Reference Don 859 and 872.[1]

One. We agree Sacmed's interpretation of Clause 3 of Belgrade Agreement.

Two. We also agree Americans draft telegram contained in Don 872, but we feel that Sacmed should be given more specific instruction. We therefore suggest addition of following paragraph to American draft.

---

[1] Joint Staff Mission (Washington) telegram Don 859 of 28 June 1945 to the Cabinet Office had referred to Field-Marshal Alexander's telegram Naf 1023 of 25 June, printed in paraphrase in *F.R.U.S. Berlin*, vol. i, pp. 854–6. Joint Staff Mission telegram Don 872 of 4 July had transmitted the following American draft reply to Naf 1023 concerning the interpretation of paragraph 3 of the Belgrade Agreement (see No. 3, note 8) regarding local Italian and Yugoslav systems of civil administration: 'Position expressed in Naf 1023 of 25th June and your aide memoire to Jugoslavs of 16th June 1945 [*ibid.*, pp. 844–6] is approved. You should continue to press home with the Jugoslavs the position that Allied Military Government will take no action which will prejudice the position of either of the disputing parties and that during Allied Period of Trusteeship, the laws applicable in the territory will be Italian laws purged of all Fascist measures and supplemented by Allied Military Government Proclamations and Orders.'

Three. *Begins:*

We suggest that Sacmed should be advised to compromise as far as possible in administration of area, on following lines:

Yugoslav system of National Committees should be eradicated in whole area, and Italian system reinstalled. In predominantly Yugoslav towns and villages, token Yugoslav administration might be retained and National Committee used in advisory capacity. In mainly Italian towns, particularly Trieste, firmness should be used to sweep away Yugoslav system.[2]

CALENDARS TO NO. 287

i   *17 July 1945   Mr. Broad (Caserta) Tel. No. 1363.* Weekly summary of events in Venezia Giulia. 'Yugoslav-sponsored civil administration has continued its efforts to retain and if possible increase its powers by a policy of passive obstruction to the Allied Military Government' [R 12071/24/92].

ii   *22 July–6 Aug. 1945   Mr. Stevenson (Belgrade) Tels. Nos. 1173 & 1221; Mr. Broad (Caserta) Tel. No. 1448.* Summarizes note No. 1938 of 17 July from Yugoslav Govt.: cf. *F.R.U.S. Berlin,* vol. ii, pp. 1215–8; Yugoslav complaint of A.M.G. civil administration in Venezia Giulia. Full report demanded by F.M. Alexander. Receipt of letter of 25 July on this subject from Marshal Tito and Dr. Subasic to Mr. Churchill (cf. *ibid.,* pp. 1214–5) [R 12365, 12683, 13228/24/92].

[2] Cf. the text of this proposed addition printed *op. cit.,* vol. ii, p. 1213: *v. ibid.,* p. 1219, for a text embodying subsequent American amendments.

No. 288

Sir J. Anderson to Mr. Stevenson (Belgrade)

No. 1037 Telegraphic [R 11700/130/92]

Important   FOREIGN OFFICE, *17 July 1945, 3.5 p.m.*

Repeated to Caserta No. 2234, Washington No. 7550.

Your telegram No. 72 Saving (of July 4th: meeting of Croat Republican Peasant Party).[1]

Please draw Yugoslav Government's attention to the statement that Zara, Fiume and Istria have *returned* to Federal Croatia, and enquire what steps they have taken to correct the erroneous impression given by it and to rebuke the authors of the resolution for using such improper language.[2]

[1] Transmitting a Tanjug press report of a resolution at a meeting of the Zagreb Executive Committee of this party on 1 July 1945. 'It welcomed the return of parts of Dalmatia, Zadar, Rijeka [Fiume] and Istria to Federal Croatia.'

[2] Mr. Stevenson acted on this instruction in a memorandum of 23 July to the Yugoslav Ministry of Foreign Affairs (R 13200/24/92).

i *20 July & 1 Sept. 1945 Mr. Hopkinson (Rome) Tel. No. 203 Saving & Mr. Stevenson (Belgrade) Tel. No. 25 Saving to Rome; 27 July Sir N. Charles (Rome) Tel. No. 214 Saving.* Reports from Italian Foreign Ministry of Yugoslav oppression of Italians in Zara, Lussino and Cherso [R 12610/24/92; R 15544/15199/92].

No. 289

Mr. Hopkinson (Rome) to Mr. Eden (Received 17 July, 10.5 p.m.)
No. 1146 Telegraphic [ZM 3888/3/22]

ROME, *17 July 1945, 7.50 p.m. G.M.T.*

Repeated to (Resmed) Caserta.

My telegram No. 1082.[1]

I shall shortly be reporting fully on situation in Bolzano particularly in relation to the election arrangements. Briefly it can be said that political situation there has deteriorated. South Tyrolese party has come out into the open and has been conducting active and provocative separatist propaganda. There has however been a split amongst the German-speaking population apparently due to fear of extreme left tendencies in Vienna and more moderate and strong Catholic elements are now seeking to establish a new German-speaking party known as Christian Peasant Party. This proposal has so far not materialised owing to intimidation by more extreme separatists.

2. Meanwhile on the strong advice of Provincial Commissioner and the Allied Commission local authorities are continuing to follow a policy of toleration and conciliation though this is becoming more difficult. Italian Government on July 11th announced a decision of the Council of Ministers guaranteeing free use of language in bi-lingual areas not only in private commercial relations, public meetings, religious observances and the press but also in their relations with political administrative and judicial authorities. Teaching and use of the mother tongue in public schools is guaranteed. It is hoped that this will have a calming effect and the prefect is now engaged in working out a special decree for Bolzano which will embody the above principles.

3. Meanwhile there is accumulating evidence to show that French are fomenting Separatist agitation. Immediately after the surrender of the German troops French officers in uniform appeared in Bolzano apparently belonging to some French underground organisation. One of these, a Captain Clairval, who was in close touch with Ammon head of the South Tyrolese Party is reported to have discussed plans for the formation of a greater Bavaria, including Vor-Orlberg [Vorarlberg] Austrian Tyrol and Bolzano Province. Clairval shortly afterwards became involved in an obscure

---

[1] Of 3 July 1945, not printed.

financial transaction with the former Prefect of Bolzano also a South Tyrolese from whom (. . . ? he)[2] obtained 23,000,000 lire for the use of his elements. This was reported to the Allied military authorities and he was arrested. The French authorities at Rome disclaimed all knowledge of his activities.

4. Since French took over their zone in Austria some Separatist notices have been posted by them in Bolzano Province. I am obtaining copies of these from the Province Commissioner. A clandestine radio station is also broadcasting in German to German speaking population in Bolzano apparently from Austria. Station is reported to have broadcast statement that ex-prefect of Bolzano and ex mayor of Bolzano City were to proceed to Paris, London and Washington as leaders of the South Tyrolese movement to discuss the future of Bolzano. This story was repeated by Radio Paris and was subsequently quoted in a Reuter report from London which appeared in the Italian press and has created considerable indignation. It has, as a matter of fact, added to the tenseness in the Province itself and as it is wholly without foundation the Allied Commission at the request of the Italian Government are issuing a *démenti*.

CALENDAR TO No. 289

i *8 & 21 July 1945 Mr. Hopkinson (Rome) Tel. No. 1114, and Despatch No. 311* enclosing letter of 16 July from Signor de Gasperi. Franco-Italian territorial questions in western Piedmont. Italian Govt. will grant a special regime of local autonomy in Val d'Aosta. Mr. Hopkinson anticipates a calming effect also in Bolzano and Udine [ZM 3726, 4161/3/22].

[2] The text is here uncertain.

No. 290

Earl of Halifax (Washington) to Mr. Eden (Received 17 July, 7.23 a.m.)
No. 4975 Telegraphic [UR 2397/1590/851]

Immediate   WASHINGTON, *17 July 1945, 12.50 a.m.*

Following personal for Minister of Food from the Ambassador.

Thank you for your telegram No. 7443[1] of 13[14]th July.

I will telegraph you later about inviting the European Allies to join the Committees of the Food Board. Your people here are waiting daily for a reply from Clinton Anderson[2] but Clayton is at Terminal, new people have come in and, in these circumstances it may take a little time to push the State Department along.

[1] No. 135.
[2] U.S. Secretary of Agriculture.

2. I very fully agree with you that what the French and Belgians want is an assurance that they will have their fair share of available food supplies, but I imagine they must want even more to see the early arrival of some of the things they need most. Pineau is making this very plain over Argentine meat.

3. I have discussed the meat question with your people and, if I understand the problem right, am perturbed that we are apparently prepared to let the French have only our leavings of Argentine meat whether these represent a reasonable share for them or not.

4. As you know I am a layman in these matters but it seems to me that there are only two courses open to you. One is to limit the French and the others to whatever surplus you can spare from Argentine after securing the minimum quantities you require and to enlist for this line the fullest support the Americans may at present be willing to give. The disadvantage of this would seem to be that even if you obtain your minimum quantities you would still have to rely on the United States for large supplies and meanwhile you would probably have had a row with the French and certainly put them in a position to say that you did not intend to give them their fair share when this did not suit your book. I should not feel too happy about the reaction on the American mind when the French made the facts known. As you know this reaction would not be sensibly diminished by anything we might have to say about the relative comfort of the American position.

5. The other course is to give the French and the others a re[a]sonable share of your Argentine supplies even though this might mean you would get somewhat less than you want. It seems to me however that if we could get the Americans to agree now that this is the course you should adopt at this moment when the President's pledge about Argentine supplies[3] still carries weight and in addition secure the most responsible assurance we can that they will do their best to make good what you might lose in the Argentine as a result of treating the French fairly, then I should have thought you would have given yourself the best chance you have of maintaining your ration. As long as we are bound in any case to be dependent on the Americans for so much of our supplies we are somewhat vulnerable in asking them to pool their resources for our benefit if at the same time we are plainly not prepared to pool our supplies for the benefit of others. Americans are more apt to respond in well-doing to a definite lead expressed in action than to any argument as to what constitutes their duty.

6. It is surely in our permanent interest to give the French every help we can. On the other hand I, of course, understand how much you must dislike doing anything which might increase your reliance on American

[3] In response to a message of 18 June 1945 from Mr. Churchill (UR 1920/1916/851) on British difficulties in concluding a long-term meat contract with Argentina in view of possible competition from France and Belgium, President Truman had assured Mr. Churchill in a telegram of 24 June that 'I recognise our obligation to use our influence in keeping other buyers out of Argentine market' (AS 3552/40/2).

assurances of future supplies which you have certainly had no great cause hitherto to trust. But the case for helping the French seems so overwhelming that I would have hoped it might have been within the Prime Minister's power at the present meeting to convince the President in that sense and so resolve this ugly dilemma.

7. I have marked this telegram personal to yourself but if it would help you to have it repeated to Terminal please instruct accordingly.

CALENDAR TO NO. 290

i *18 July 1945* Proposals by E.E.C.E. Sub-Committee on Food and Agriculture (*London*) for modifying methods for coordinating purchasing and allocation by Combined Food Board of foodstuffs in short supply [UR 2377/1600/53].

No. 291

Sir H. Knatchbull-Hugessen (Brussels) to Mr. Eden
(*Received 19 July, 3.10 p.m.*)
No. 240 Saving Telegraphic, by bag [Z 8509/291/4]

Important　　　　　　　　　　　　　　　　　　　BRUSSELS, *17 July 1945*

I am anxious to bring to your urgent attention an appeal which I have received from the Luxembourg Foreign Minister regarding the critical situation created by the impossibility hitherto of restarting the steel industry.

2. M. Bech states that but for two blast furnaces at Differdange, the whole Luxembourg steel industry and in particular the Arbed works have been inoperative for the last nine months. In spite of this Arbed has been paying its employees regularly but its financial reserves are almost exhausted and payments will shortly have to stop which would mean thousands of workers being left idle and unpaid.

3. M. Bech points out that remedy is adequate supply of coke which is the only element lacking to bring blast furnaces again into operation. In view of the fact that Luxembourg has always imported 90% of its solid fuel from Germany and cannot be expected to import metallurgical coke from Belgium, he appeals for arrangements to be made for supplies of German coke to be received as soon as possible.

4. Similar appeal was made to United States Ambassador some two weeks ago and I understand he has telegraphed to Washington.

5. My information bears out the account given by M. Bech. Food position in Luxembourg is reasonably good but position of steel industry is literally disastrous. Supplies of coke from Germany appear to be awaiting a decision as to general policy with regard to German exports.[1]

---

[1] Mr. W. A. Camps of the Relief Department of the Foreign Office noted against this sentence: 'I think not.'

6. Mr. Gridley, chairman of the E.C.O., was informed of the position when in Brussels recently. Representative of the Ministry of Production on my staff learned recently in Luxembourg that case had already been referred to E.C.O. in London by Luxembourg Government.

7. I would emphasise urgent importance of an early decision and would state that I consider M. Bech's appeal entirely deserving of favourable consideration.[2]

CALENDAR TO No. 291

i *26 July 1945 Letter from Sir F. Leith Ross to Sir G. Rendel (respectively Chairman and U.K. rep. on European Committee of U.N.R.R.A.):* encloses Luxembourg aide-mémoire on standstill of Luxembourg iron and steel industry, and criticizes S.H.A.E.F. policy on allocation of coke. Asks if action can be expedited [Z 8822/291/4].

[2] Mr. Coulson in a letter of 21 July 1945 from Berlin informed Mr. Hasler that Mr. Eden had minuted on this telegram: 'These are good people? Can we help? We should do our utmost.' Mr. Coulson added: 'You will know the importance, from the point of view of our own steel industry, of getting Arbed on its feet.' On 27 July Mr. F. L. Simpson of the Western Department of the Foreign Office asked Major R. S. Leage (Civil Affairs, War Office) with reference to this telegram: 'Is there any action the C[ombined] A[dministrative] L[iquidating] A[gency of S.H.A.E.F. Commitments] could take with a view to the inclusion of Arbed's needs in the calculation of August requirements? There does not seem to be any other action which we can take at present on this appeal from the Luxembourg Government since the latter have quite rightly already referred the matter to the E.C.O.'

No. 292

Mr. Labouchere (Stockholm) to Mr. Eden (Received 18 July, 6.10 a.m.)
No. 1121 Telegraphic [F 4320/630/23]

Important. Top secret   STOCKHOLM, *17 July 1945, 9.25 p.m.*

I feel that you should know that the Assistant Head of Political Division of Swedish Ministry of Foreign Affairs informed me to-day that a telegram had been received from Swedish Legation in Washington this morning to the effect that Stalin was bringing Japanese peace proposals to the Potsdam meeting and that his late arrival there was due to last minute discussions with the Japanese.[1]

[1] This telegram was minuted as follows in the Far Eastern Department of the Foreign Office: 'We have heard nothing yet from Terminal. The story of the Konoye Mission to Moscow [see No. 173, note 2] has evidently leaked in Washington; see report from Daily Telegraph of July 18 within. A. J. de la Mare 18/7.' 'I have had this repeated to *Terminal.* J. C. S[terndale] B[ennett] July 19.'

No. 293

Sir J. Anderson to Mr. Hankey (Warsaw)
No. 5 Telegraphic [N 8231/6/55]

Immediate   FOREIGN OFFICE, *17 July 1945, 4.50 p.m.*

Repeated to Moscow No. 3,986, Washington No. 7,557.

My telegram to Moscow No. 3,701[1] (of 1st July) and Moscow telegram No. 2,977[1] (of 7th July) which are being repeated to you.

Before M. Bierut is acknowledged by His Majesty's Government as active [acting] President of the Republic as will be done if His Majesty's Ambassador's letters of credence are addressed to him we should be glad to hear the views of M. Mikolajczyk. Explanations given during Moscow discussions[2] (see paragraph 2 of my telegram to Moscow No. 3,701) suggested that the Praesidium rather than its president would be the repository of the powers of Head of the State. Incidentally Mikolajczyk told us in London that he would not serve under Bierut as President, although you should not of course tax him with this.

2. Addition of Witos (if he has not finally refused, on which I should be glad to be informed)[3] and Grabski to Praesidium would presumably have less practical effect if M. Bierut and not Praesidium is Acting Head of State.

3. Legal Advisor [Adviser] does not consider that we need quarrel on legal grounds with theory expounded in Moscow telegram No. 2,977. But I should like to be sure that M. Mikolajczyk knows of claim now advanced on behalf of M. Bierut and accepts position before His Majesty's Government commit themselves. Please take early opportunity of ascertaining his views.[4]

CALENDARS TO No. 293

i *19–22 July 1945 Mr. Hankey (Warsaw) Tel. No. 21; to and from Mr. Eden (Berlin) Tels. No. 110 Onward and No. 144 Target.* M. Mikolajczyk personally suggests that credentials of Mr. Cavendish Bentinck as H.M. Ambassador to Poland should be addressed to M. Bierut as President of the Praesidium of the National Council. Question of matching the credentials of H.M. and U.S. Ambassadors [N 8876, 9041/6/55; F.O. 934/2/10(25)].

[1] Not printed. These telegrams related to the current location and exercise of the powers of Polish Head of State in relation to the Polish constitution of 1921; cf. below.

[2] Cf. No. 78, note 1.

[3] Mr. Hankey reported in Warsaw telegram No. 22 of 19 July 1945: 'According to Mikolajczyk position as regards Witos is that he is only prepared to accept the post as member of Praesidium if Peasant Party is left entirely free to conduct its activities. At present this is not entirely clear. Discussions are proceeding to clarify the situation and if they do not succeed M. Witos considers M. Mikolajczyk's efforts are bound to fail. In that case he intends to hold himself in reserve.'

[4] Lord Halifax was instructed in Foreign Office telegram No. 7558 of 17 July to Washington to inform the State Department of these instructions.

No. 294

Sir J. Anderson to Mr. Duff Cooper (Paris)
No. 1687 Saving Telegraphic, by bag [R 11918/4/19]

FOREIGN OFFICE, *17 July 1945*

Repeated Saving to Athens No. 118, Washington No. 700, Moscow No. 164, United Kingdom Delegation Berlin No. 57 Onward.

We have been discussing with the United States Government the question of Allied supervision of the forthcoming Greek plebiscite and elections. The agreement signed at Varkiza on February 12th between representatives of the Greek Government and of E.A.M., which put a final end to the Greek civil war, provided for supervision by observers from the great Allied powers. The United States Government have agreed to share the responsibility for supervision with us and have also agreed that the Soviet and French Governments should be asked to participate. The United States Government consider that the approach to the Soviet and French Governments should be made by them and us and not by the Greek Government in view of the efforts which we have made for the restoration of Greece and of the undertakings which we both assumed in the Yalta Declaration on Liberated Territories. A joint approach was therefore made to the Greek Government by British and American representatives in Athens and the Greek Government have expressed their entire agreement with the procedure proposed.

2. The exact wording of the invitation to the French and Soviet Governments is now being worked out between British and American representatives at Terminal. It is proposed that approach to the Russians should be made during Terminal and that concurrent invitation should be made to the French by British and American Ambassadors in Paris. United States Government have suggested that publicity should be given by including an announcement about supervision in the communiqué to be issued at the end of Terminal. Until then matter would be kept secret. We see no objection to this provided that replies from Soviet and French Governments have been received by that date.

3. No action need be taken on this telegram but as soon as agreement has been reached at Terminal I shall be asking you to raise matter with the French Government.

CALENDAR TO No. 294

Tels. No. 46 Onward & No. 101 Target; Mr. Caccia (Athens) Tels. Nos. 1567, 1570, 1571; letters between Mr. Howard and Mr. Hayter (Berlin). Anglo-American discussion of terms and handling of proposed communication concerning Allied supervision of Greek elections and plebiscite (cf. No. 28.iii) [R 12111, 11918, 12240, 12324, 12346, 12355, 12345, 12718/4/19].

No. 295

Sir W. Strang (Lübbecke) to Mr. Eden (Received 21 July, 1.10 p.m.)
No. 8 Saving Telegraphic, by bag [R 12334/1728/92]

LÜBBECKE, *17 July 1945*

Following from King (Frankfurt on Main)

Shortly before dissolution of SHAEF, divisions in charge of repatriation of Yugoslav ex-prisoners of war and civilians expressed concern to political advisers about reports reaching them from Yugoslavia of arrest and ill-treatment of Yugoslavs on their return home. Although no Yugoslav was repatriated against his will, feeling in SHAEF was that most of those who did not object to returning had no knowledge of conditions in Yugoslavia and had been misled by propaganda of Yugoslav repatriation officers appointed by Tito Government.

2. My United States colleague and I replied that in our view repatriation of Yugoslavs willing to go must continue and that there could be no question of warning them about conditions in Yugoslavia. We undertook however to inform our respective Governments of SHAEF's misgivings.[1]

[1] Foreign Office telegram No. 95 Saving of 25 July 1945 to Lübbecke replied: 'I agree with Mr. King's views.'

No. 296

Earl of Halifax (Washington) to Mr. Eden (Received 18 July, 6.50 a.m.)
No. 4985 Telegraphic [N 8805/6453/12]

Important   WASHINGTON, *17 July 1945, 10.22 p.m.*

Repeated to Prague, SHAEF Main (for Kirkpatrick).

My immediately preceeding telegram and your telegram No. 7027.[1]

State Department say that they have set out their views regarding procedure to be followed by military authorities in regard to persons whose surrender is being requested by respective Governments of United Nations for trial as renegades or quislings in a draft directive to the commanders of

[1] These telegrams of 17 and 3 July 1945 respectively are not printed.

the United States Forces of occupation (No. J.F.C. 1349).[2] This document was communicated to Europeam [sic] Advisory Commission on or about May 29th and I presume you have seen a copy. It provides for the apprehension of suspects and for turning them over to their respective governments upon demand, United States commanders are however given discretion to delay action and to report back to Washington if they have reason to believe that any persons whose surrender is requested should not be turned over.

2. You will see however from my immediately following telegram[3] that State Department do not (repeat not) consider it advisable to hand over Yugoslav quislings to present régime at any rate until they (State Department) are satisfied that such persons will receive a reasonably fair trial. State Department's instructions to Caserta referred to in my telegram were also repeated to Murphy thus the United States commanders concerned will have already special guidance as to how they should deal with Yugoslavs claimed by their Governments as quislings.

3. I understand that American directive was based upon and does not substantially differ from a United Kingdom memorandum (EAC(45)14[4] dated February 2[2]nd 1945) which has been laid before the European Advisory Commission. State Department say their own views have not changed and enquire whether His Majesty's Government's position has been modified since the United Kingdom memorandum was issued.

4. While I am not sure effective liaison arrangements exist in these matters since the termination of SHAEF I should have thought arrangement mentioned in paragraph 1 above would be adequate for your purpose if you are simply concerned to establish identical policy. If on the other hand you wish to retain the right to screen individuals, it may not go far enough.

Foreign Office please pass to Prague as my telegram No. 14 and to SHAEF Main.

CALENDARS TO No. 296

i *16 July 1945 Letter from Mr. R. G. D. Laffan (F.O. Research Dept.) to Mr. Howard.* Expresses relief at eventual stopping of transfer of Slovenes to Yugoslav authorities, and concern over the 'wretched condition of the Yugoslav refugees in Italy' [R 11649/1728/92].

ii *22 July 1945 To Lord Halifax (Washington) Tel. No. 7740.* Instructions to discuss with State Dept. question of rendition of captured Yugoslav collaborators, and requirement of a *prima facie* case of treachery. Cases of Ante Pavelić and others [R 12114/329/92]

---

[2] Printed in *F.R.U.S. 1945*, vol. iii, pp. 515–6.

[3] Not printed. This telegram, which was as indicated below, summarized the American instructions to the U.S. representative at Caserta printed in *op. cit.*, vol. v, pp. 1241–2.

[4] Printed with amendments in *F.R.U.S. Berlin*, vol. ii, pp. 422–3, note 6.

No. 297

Letter from Mr. Hasler to Mr. Dixon (Berlin: received 17 July)

[*UR 2023/282/851*]

FOREIGN OFFICE, *17 July 1945*

Dear Bob,

The day before you left I showed you Cabinet Conclusions (45) 13th Meeting of 10th July[1] referring to Eastern European Surpluses.

You will remember that the paper before the Cabinet was put in by the President of the Board of Trade as a result of discussion in the S.L.A. Committee and that it recommended that a warning should be given to the Russians, possibly at Terminal, that the surplus areas in Eastern Europe which were now under Russian control should not only meet their own food requirements but should also make a contribution to the needs of Western Europe.

The Conclusions of the Cabinet were (1) that the Foreign Secretary should suggest to the Prime Minister that an attempt should be made at Terminal to secure agreement to two principles (*a*) that for purposes of supplies as for purposes of reparations, both Germany and Austria should be treated as a single economic unit; (*b*) that, in the absence of special reasons to the contrary, each of the separate Zones of Occupation should draw their supplies from the areas on which they had drawn before the war; (2) invited [*sic*] the President of the Board of Trade to arrange for the British representatives on the Combined Boards to be instructed to see that UNRRA's requirements for Poland and Czechoslovakia were subjected to thorough scrutiny and that supplies provided by UNRRA were regarded as supplementary to those available locally.

Conclusion (2) is being dealt with here and does not concern Terminal.

Conclusion (1) you will see refers in terms only to Germany and Austria. The two points have been covered in the brief which you have on Germany as an economic unit.[2] You will find also that the background on what we know of the food resources of Eastern Europe including the Russian Zone of Germany is in the brief on Eastern European Surpluses.[1]

You will notice that the Conclusions reached by the Cabinet do not cover the main suggestion in the paper before them namely that a general warning should be given to the Russians on their responsibilities for feeding Europe, a question which is a good deal wider than that of feeding the Western Zones of Germany and Austria. I do not know whether we are going too far in thinking that the Cabinet had in mind that, if there was any general discussion about the movement of food supplies from the Russian parts of Germany to the rest, occasion would be taken in the course of this

---

[1] See No. 22.ii.

[2] No. 125.

discussion to draw the general moral that the 'Russian areas' of Europe as a whole ought not to require imports of food.[3]

Yours ever
BILL HASLER

[3] This letter was minuted as follows in the British Delegation at Potsdam: 'This seems to be a point in the first instance for the tripartite economic C[ommi]tee. P. D[ixon]. 17/7.' 'It is difficult to see how this can be worked in at present. But I think it will be possible. Sir D. Waley, Mr. Turner to see. J. C[oulson] 18/7.' 'It has now been raised with a vengeance.' J. C.[oulson] 23/7.'

No. 298

Letter from Mr. Troutbeck to Mr. Harrison (Berlin: received 18 July)
[F.O. 934/1/2(17)]

FOREIGN OFFICE, 17 July 1945

My dear Geoffrey,

There is one point which is worrying us rather in connection with the possible outcome of Terminal. It is this. It seems possible that we may give formal assent to the transfer to Polish administration of at any rate Danzig, East Prussia south and west of Königsberg, Oppeln Silesia and the most eastern portion of Pomerania—see Foreign Office telegram to Washington No: 7412,[1] of which you no doubt have a copy. If this is done, the treatment of Germany as an economic whole may prove a liability rather than an asset to us. It will mean that the Silesian industrial areas and large agricultural territories in the east are withdrawn from Germany, and the whole of Germany will therefore look to the Ruhr and the Saar for its coal, while the prospect of ever getting anything in return in the way of agricultural surpluses will become remote. In other words we shall, as General Weeks has put it, have bought a pup.

I have no doubt that the Delegation has this point well in mind, but we thought it worth while drawing your attention to it.

Yours ever
JACK

CALENDAR TO No. 298

i *17 July 1945 Letter from Mr. Troutbeck to Mr. Pink (21st Army Group)*. H.M.G. did not recognise incorporation of Danzig into Germany and do not yet recognize it as Polish although committed to supporting Polish claim. In practice inhabitants of Danzig should continue to be treated as German citizens for the time being [N 8176/433/55].

[1] See No. 115, note 1.

No. 299

Letter from Sir A. Cadogan (Berlin) to Sir O. Sargent
[N 8979/90/30]

FOREIGN OFFICE [sic], 17 July 1945

My dear Moley,

The Americans, just before embarking, heard about the Russian–Norwegian exchanges on Spitzbergen.[1] I think Lie told us about them somewhere about Nov[ember] last and swore us to secrecy. I think we rather assumed that he w[oul]d tell the Americans too, but they have only just heard of them and are rather exercised.

I promised Jimmy Dunn to give him such inf[ormatio]n as I could. Could you send me a short memo, or papers on the subject, by an early Bag?

As usual, it's difficult to get things moving, and we've done nothing so far except joy-rides to Berlin, inspecting the ruins—particularly of the Chancellery & Hitler's dug-out. Most impressive![2]

Yours
ALEC

[1] Cf. *F.R.U.S. 1945*, vol. v, pp. 91–2.

[2] On 20 July 1945 Sir O. Sargent sent to Sir A. Cadogan a copy of No. 162, and of Oslo telegram No. 92 (see No. 162, note 1) together with Oslo telegram No. 123 of 20 July in reply to Foreign Office telegram No. 110 to Oslo (*v. ibid.*). Sir L. Collier there reported: 'Minister for Foreign Affairs . . . has no objection to the matter being discussed with the Americans at Potsdam . . . hopes, however, that the matter will not be discussed with the Russians in his absence. If they should raise it he would be willing to go to Potsdam at once. They have still said nothing more to the Norwegians.'

No. 300

Minute from Major-General Jacob to Mr. Churchill (Berlin)
E.C.C. (45) 5[1] [UE 3125/3123/53]

Secret   CABINET OFFICE, 17 July 1945

The European Control Committee today[2] considered a telegram (No. 17 Reveal)[3] conveying your wish that they should report on our policy with regard to German research and development establishment. They also had before them your telegram to Field-Marshal Montgomery[4] telling him that no such establishments were to be destroyed.

[1] Reference under which this minute was circulated on 17 July 1945 by the secretariat of the European Control Committee of the Cabinet.

[2] This minute was drafted on 16 July.

[3] Of 13 July, not printed: see No. 134.iii.

[4] Annex to No. 134.iii.

2. No instructions have at any time been issued to S.H.A.E.F. or to Field-Marshal Montgomery requiring the destruction of research and development establishments. General Weeks has confirmed that there is no intention, on the part of the Commander-in-Chief, to destroy any of these establishments. It is possible that any rumours to this effect which may have reached you are founded on one or both of the following two facts:–

(a) There was a proposal at one time to destroy certain vital installations connected with the development of V-2s[5] which were in that part of the Russian zone temporarily occupied by Anglo-American Forces. As far as we know the instruction was not carried out, but certain equipment was removed before the territory was handed over to the Russians;

(b) Certain equipment within the British zone is being dismantled and brought back to England. This might give the impression to someone on the spot that the establishments where this equipment is located were being destroyed, it perhaps not being known to him that the equipment was merely being removed for use elsewhere.

3. The policy for dealing with German research and development establishments which were used for war purposes or for the development of war material has been under discussion at the European Advisory Commission. The U.K. representative on the European Advisory Commission has now been authorised to join in recommending to the four Governments that the Allied representatives in Germany should, when they consider conditions in Germany appropriate, order that all research, experimentation, development or other study relative to war or to the production of war material in public or private establishments, factories, technological institutions, laboratories or elsewhere shall be abolished and forbidden in future. The view of the British Departments who have been studying this question is that, while there would be no objection to our using German establishments for our own purposes for a certain length of time, to perpetuate this practice would be dangerous and inconsistent with the policy recommended by the European Advisory Commission and that in due course all German establishments should be either destroyed or removed bodily to the United Kingdom or elsewhere outside Germany. In the meanwhile we are in no way debarred from making such use of establishments in our own zone as we may desire.

4. Establishments for research and development which are not directly related to war purposes present a more difficult problem which is being studied in London with a view to the formulation of recommendations. These, after they have received the approval of His Majesty's Government could then be discussed with our Allies.

E. I. C. Jacob

---

[5] i.e. Vergeltungswaffe Zwei (Revenge weapon two), a German rocket-bomb.

No. 301

Mr. Roberts (Moscow) to Mr. Eden (Received 30 July)
No. 495 [*C 4279/216/18*]

MOSCOW, 17 July 1945

His Majesty's Chargé d'Affaires at Moscow presents his compliments to His Majesty's Principal Secretary of State for Foreign Affairs, and has the honour to transmit to him the under-mentioned documents.

Reference to previous correspondence:

German Department letter C1962/216/18 of May 23rd.[1]

Description of Enclosure

Name and Date	*Subject*
To: Mr. V. G. Dekanozov, People's Commissariat for Foreign Affairs, dated 17th July, 1945.	

ENCLOSURE IN No. 301

Letter from Mr. Roberts to M. Dekanozov (Moscow)

No. 416/2/45   BRITISH EMBASSY, MOSCOW, *17 July 1945*

(Dear Mr. Dekanozov),

I have been instructed by my government to transmit to the Soviet Government the enclosed four copies[2] of a first list of British properties in the Soviet zone of occupation in Germany. This list is necessarily incomplete and will be supplemented later. As you will see, it does not include the property of subjects of the Dominions, British India, the Colonies or of British Mandated Territories.

2. My government will be grateful if the Soviet Government will take what steps may be possible for the protection of these British properties.[3]

(Yours sincerely),
F. K. ROBERTS

[1] Not printed.

[2] Copy entered separately on C 1962/216/18 is not printed.

[3] H.M. Embassy in Moscow reported in a Chancery letter of 28 July: 'Dekanozov has now replied that the list has been sent to the Soviet military authorities, who have been informed of His Majesty's Government's request that measures shall be taken to safeguard the British property in question.'

No. 302

Memorandum by Mr. Law[1]
C.P.(45)82 [*CAB 66/67*]

Secret   CABINET OFFICE, *17 July 1945*

Non-repatriable Refugees

I desire to draw the attention of the Cabinet to the proposals of the Com-

[1] This memorandum was submitted to the Cabinet by Mr. R. K. Law as Acting Chairman of the Cabinet Committee on the Reception and Accommodation of Refugees.

mittee for the Reception and Accommodation of Refugees as regards the question of non-repatriable refugees.

2. The full scope of this problem cannot be properly assessed for some time to come, and the Committee feel strongly that for the present all refugees displaced as a result of the war must be regarded as eventually repatriable, and that a final decision to regard any as non-repatriable can only ultimately be reached after a careful review of all the relevant circumstances obtaining at the time.

3. The Committee have accordingly considered the existing methods of giving temporary relief to the various categories of refugees, and to the respective functions in this field of U.N.R.R.A. and the Intergovernmental Committee on Refugees, which was set up as a result of the International Conference at Evian in 1938.

4. The Committee are strongly of the opinion that His Majesty's Government in the United Kingdom cannot continue to contribute to the relief of refugees in the proportions which at present govern the finances of the Intergovernmental Committee. Under existing arrangements the operational expenses of the Intergovernmental Committee are divided in equal proportions between the United States and the United Kingdom Governments, a division which, of course, in no way reflects the financial capacity of the two countries. In the case of U.N.R.R.A., on the other hand, the expenses of operation are shared between a number of Governments in proportion to their financial capacity.

5. In the Committee's view, therefore, it should be clearly recognised that the task of giving relief to refugees is in general one for U.N.R.R.A. The Intergovernmental Committee should not undertake this task except as regards certain specific categories of refugees in conditions where it was clear that these did not come within U.N.R.R.A.'s mandate. Nor should it be automatically assumed that because certain categories of refugees did not qualify for relief from U.N.R.R.A., they should be regarded as the responsibility of the Intergovernmental Committee. The manner in which effect would be given to these principles is set out in the Annex to this paper.

6. Ultimately, the time will come when a 'hard core' of refugees will be agreed to be non-repatriable and their future will have to be provided for. The Cabinet Committee on Refugees have expressed no view of this yet, but it may well be found desirable to entrust the task to the Intergovernmental Committee. Before this could be considered, however, they feel that it would be essential to reorganise that body, and, in particular, to adjust the existing financial arrangements so as to provide that the United Kingdom would contribute in proportion to its means instead of, as now, bearing half the burden (the United States bearing the other half) of all operational expenditure.

7. The Committee feel that it would be necessary, in the first place, to communicate the above views to the United States Government (who are directly concerned as regards both U.N.R.R.A. and the Intergovernmental Committee) and to try to get them to agree.

8. I invite my colleagues (*a*) to approve the principles set out in the Annex to this paper, and (*b*) to authorise the Foreign Office to communicate these principles to the United States Government and to try to secure their acceptance of them as suggested in paragraph 7.

R. K. L.

ANNEX TO NO. 302

(*a*) The present relief operations in which the Intergovernmental Committee is engaged with the approval of His Majesty's Government and of the United States Government and of the Executive Committee should be reviewed in order to ascertain whether any of the categories of refugees thus being relieved can be held to come within the mandate of U.N.R.R.A. If so, arrangements should be made to transfer the responsibility for their relief to U.N.R.R.A. as soon as possible.

(*b*) Any proposals which may in future be made to the Intergovernmental Committee to undertake the relief of specific categories of refugees should not be approved until it is quite clear that they are outside the scope of whatever U.N.R.R.A.'s mandate may be at the time. Similarly, in the event of U.N.R.R.A.'s mandate being enlarged, proposals for relief which the Inter-governmental Committee had previously been authorised to accept should be reviewed to ascertain whether they were now properly an U.N.R.R.A. responsibility.

(*c*) When asked to approve any proposals to undertake the relief of specific categories of refugees, the Governments represented on the Executive Committee of the Intergovernmental Committee (in the first place His Majesty's Government) should be furnished with as full particulars as possible of the reasons to support an assumption *prima facie* that the refugees in question would prove to be non-repatriable. It would be clearly understood that, unless these reasons were found to be adequate, His Majesty's Government, for their part, would be unable to approve the assumption of relief activities on behalf of the refugees in question by the Intergovernmental Committee and would press for their inclusion, at any rate for the time being, within the mandate of U.N.R.R.A.

CALENDARS TO NO. 302

i *20 & 31 July 1945 Cabinet Conclusions (C.M. (45) 16) of 20 July, item 2, and minute by Mr. P. Mason (Acting Head of F.O. Refugee Department).* Principles in annex to No. 302 approved and their acceptance by U.S. Govt. should be sought. Comments by Mr. Mason [WR 2232/1/48].

ii *17–28 July 1945 Minutes by Mr. W. A. Camps and others; letter from Mr. Hasler to Mr. Caccia (Athens).* Criticisms of U.N.R.R.A. do not justify a specific complaint [UR 2312/66/850].

iii *20 July 1945 Minute by Mr. F. R. Cowell (F.O. Cultural Relations Dept.)* U.N.R.R.A. assistance for medical and technical institutes [UR 2547/2547/850].

iv *19 & 25 July 1945 Letters from Mr. F. C. Everson (H.M. Embassy, Washington) to Mr. I. L. Henderson; Foreign Office Note No. R.C.(45) 178, for Cabinet Relief Policy Committee* on item 8 of agenda for forthcoming session of U.N.R.R.A. Council (see No. 376, note 2); tactics for proposed U.N.R.R.A. relief to Allied Nationals who are unwilling to be repatriated: supported by H.M.G. and opposed by Soviet Govt. [WR 2245, 2207/1/48].

v *18 July 1945* Note by Countess of Limerick of conversation with Lieut.-General *Sir C. Keightley*, commanding V Corps in Austria and Italy (copy received in F.O. on 10 August; cited N. Tolstoy, *op. cit.*, pp. 338–9). Earlier question of recommending withdrawal of Red Cross personnel in South Austria in respect of repatriation of unwilling displaced persons: explanations by General Keightley in regard to Cossacks (question of their status), and to Yugoslavs, of whom no unwilling persons were now being sent back. Lady Limerick relieved by the information [WR 2396/2155/48].

No. 303

Brief for the United Kingdom Delegation to the Conference at Potsdam
No. 45 [U 5489/5202/70]

Secret   FOREIGN OFFICE, [*17 July 1945*][1]

Posts on Executive Committee and Preparatory Commission[2]

As will be seen from the attached telegram at Flag 'A'[3] the whole question of posts on the Executive Committee of the Preparatory Commission was left open at San Francisco. We suggested that it should be placed on the official agenda for 'Terminal' but the Americans objected to this on the grounds that it was not of sufficient importance to merit consideration by the Big Three. We have therefore suggested, see telegram at Flag 'B',[4] that it should be discussed in the first instance informally by [with] Mr. Dunn and Mr. Sobolev and then referred, if necessary, to the three Foreign Secretaries for decision.

2. When the question was originally discussed in a Big Five meeting at San Francisco it seemed to be a general opinion that the Executive Secretary should be a British national; but as will be seen from the telegram at Flag 'A', Mr. Gromyko eventually objected to this and said that he could only agree if the chairmanship of the Executive Committee was allocated to the Soviet Union. After much argument, however, he made the suggestion that the chairmanship might possibly 'revolve' though it was not clear whether the idea was that it should 'revolve' among five powers or between three or four of them.

3. It is suggested that our general line at 'Terminal' should be that, whatever is decided in regard to posts, the United Kingdom should provide the Executive Secretary, if only for the reason that the committee and commission will meet in London and that it would be in the interests of

---

[1] Date on which this undated memorandum was filed.

[2] Of the United Nations Organisation.

[3] Not printed. For this telegram No. 360 of 29 June 1945 from Mr. Jebb in New York, cf. below.

[4] This short telegram No. 7351 of 11 July to Washington, not printed, was as indicated below.

efficiency for this official to be a British national. If this is accepted then there are, broadly speaking, two possibilities:—

(*a*) the chairmanship and perhaps two vice-chairmanships of the Executive Committee should be divided up among the four remaining powers, the one which is left out being given the chairmanship of the Preparatory Commission, or,

(*b*) the chairmanship of the Executive Committee should 'revolve' among all the five powers and the chairmanship of the Preparatory Commission should be allocated to a small power, e.g. Belgium.

4. There is much to be said for solution 'B' for the following reasons:—

(1) If the chairmanship of the Executive Committee 'revolves', the (British) Executive Secretary will be likely to be more powerful since he would have no immediate chief.

(2) It would avoid having to make a difficult choice as to the actual chairmanship of the Executive Committee since clearly the chairman would have more influence than the two vice-chairmen.

(3) It would in many ways be preferable for the chairmanship of the Preparatory Commission to be allocated to a small power.

5. It is therefore suggested that we should take the initiative in urging solution (*b*). If, however, we cannot get agreement on this then we should take the line that it is for the Americans and Russians in the first instance to settle as between themselves how the posts, other than the Executive Secretary, should be allocated.

No. 304

Sir J. Anderson to Earl of Halifax (Washington)
No. 7570 Telegraphic [F 4310/364/23]

Top secret   FOREIGN OFFICE, *18 July 1945, 2.40 a.m.*

Repeated to United Kingdom Delegation Berlin No. 51 Onward.[1]

Your telegram No. 3754[2] (of May 29th: United States proposals for post-surrender control of Japan).

Sir George Sansom's summary of State Department's document has been examined with him here. It raises a number of issues which will have to be studied in detail and discussed with the Dominions before final conclusions

---

[1] At 2.40 a.m. on 18 July 1945 (received in Berlin at 5.12 a.m. that day): the substance of this telegram was transmitted to the Governments of the Dominions as Dominions Office telegram D. No. 1245 at 8 p.m. on 17 July with a request for any comments, with reference to the relevant Dominions Office telegrams D. Nos. 1243–44 of even date.

[2] This telegram, not printed, had summarized notes by Sir George Sansom, Adviser on Far Eastern affairs to H.M. Ambassador at Washington, on an American draft document, shown to him informally on 28 May 1945 regarding American policy towards Japan: see *F.R.U.S. 1945*, vol. vi, pp. 581–2, 549–54, and Sir L. Woodward, *op. cit.*, vol. v, pp. 519–22.

can be reached. Following comments[3] are entirely tentative and without commitment.

2. The American objectives as described in the preamble of the State Department's document are unexceptionable. The question is whether the methods contemplated for their realisation are those most likely to achieve this aim.

3. It may be assumed that some form of military occupation of Japan will be a necessary sequel of the military operations required for her defeat, if only for the purpose of implementing the purely military requirements of the Allies. But more than one view is possible regarding its scale and duration. Total and protracted military occupation, combined with the assumption of all the functions of government, is likely to be a strain on both manpower and physical resources. Faced with a proud and stubborn race likely to resort freely to assassination, a foreign military government may require the backing of an army much larger in proportion to the population than that required in Germany. This burden may have to be shouldered if it is the only way to render Japan permanently harmless. But is there no other way?

4. Upon defeat, Japan will be deprived of her overseas territories and will be in a position analogous to 1868. She will be militarily impotent and financially weak. A large part of her industrial equipment will have been destroyed and she will be unable to borrow capital. She will be dependent for her very existence on the resumption of international trade and it should be possible for the Allies, especially in the period immediately following her defeat, to decide and control the nature and extent of her exports and imports. The Allies will also be able to defer making new treaties with Japan. Granted agreement between the major Powers including Russia, should it not be possible for them by exercising the positive power of controlling trade and the negative power of withholding treaties, to induce Japan herself to introduce such reforms in her constitution and the working thereof as will justify confidence in her future good behaviour?

5. It is desirable also to consider what place in world economy is to be taken by Japan after defeat; to what extent, if any, Japan's productive capacity is to be used to supply the needs of, for example, South East Asia for essential consumption goods; and what are likely to be the economic and political consequences, and more particularly the reactions on projects for the political re-education of the Japanese people and on the prospects of the liberalisation of Japanese politics, if a large proportion of the urban population of Japan (more than 50% of a total of 76,000,000) is unemployed and inadequately fed.

6. It seems possible that the enforcement of the necessary economic

---

[3] Foreign Office telegram No. 7571 to Washington of 12.55 a.m. on 18 July 1945 (No. 52 Onward to Berlin: not printed) indicated that the present telegram was based on a memorandum by Sir G. Sansom with which the Chiefs of Staff were in general agreement. This memorandum of 20 June suggested alternative means of reaching objectives similar to those advanced in the draft document from the State Department.

controls might be achieved by the military occupation not (repeat not) of the entire country but of certain easily held key points; by the presence of Allied war vessels at ports; and by occasional demonstration flights of massed aircraft.

7. Might it not be preferable also for the Allies, instead of suspending the constitutional powers of the Emperor, to work through those powers or through whatever state administration they may find in being in Japan, using economic sanctions to secure compliance with such requirements as the repeal of obnoxious laws, the dissolution of political societies, the reform of education, freedom of speech and worship etc.?

8. If you see no objection, please make an oral communication on the above lines to the State Department, emphasising that it represents the preliminary departmental reactions of the Foreign Office only, and is entirely without prejudice not only to the views of the Dominions (which must be expressly reserved) but also to the final conclusions of His Majesty's Government in the United Kingdom themselves.[4]

CALENDARS TO NO. 304

[4] Mr. Eden minuted on this telegram to Mr. Dixon in Berlin: 'I don't like this telegram & it should *not* have been sent without my seeing it. It deals with important issues of policy which are essentially for me. Please telegraph at once to W[ashing]ton that no action is to be taken upon it, & if it has been taken it is to be cancelled. Dep[artmen]t must be rebuked for having done this; matter could well have waited to be referred to us here. Incidentally where is State Dep[artmen]t Document? A. E. July 19.' 'This action must be taken this a.m. A. E.': See No. 325. In a minute of 20 July Mr. Foulds explained the background to this telegram (cf. note 3 above), on which Mr. Eden minuted 'I do not want us to recommend to Americans that Emperor should be preserved. They would no doubt like to get such advice & then say they had reluctantly concurred with us. A. E.' (cited Sir L. Woodward, op. cit., vol. v, p. 523). In reply to Mr. Foulds' suggestion that as 'Onward 51 was primarily intended to give the American officials dealing with the Far East in the State Department a very informal indication' of the views of the Far Eastern Department of the Foreign Office 'it does not in any way commit the Secretary of State or H.M.G.', Mr. Eden minuted 'This is rather too subtle for me. F.O. docs. commit me until July 26 anyway.'

No. 305

Major-General Edgcumbe (Budapest) to Sir J. Grigg[1]
No. B.M.M. 585 Telegraphic [R 12267/84/21]

Important. Secret   BUDAPEST, *18 July 1945, 3.37 p.m.*

Repeated to British Military Mission Bulgaria, British Military Mission Roumania.

Reference my B.M.M. 563[2] of 13th July.

First meeting under chairmanship of Marshal Voroshilov held 17th July. Heads of sections attended. Meeting businesslike and cordial and following matters discussed.

1. Deportation of 200,000 (200,000) [*sic*] Swabians with German and Nazi sympathies from Hungary to Germany. This arises from application of Hungarian Government to A.C.C. Marshal has not (repeat not) consulted Soviet Government but personally wishes to help Hungarian Government in every way possible in this matter as he considers these Swabians potential danger to future of Hungary. General Key[3] and I both said this matter must be referred to respective Governments. Minister is sending full report to Foreign Office.

2. Hungarian war criminals. Hungarian Government has applied to A.C.C. for all Hungarian war criminals held in territories under Allied control to be returned for trial and punished by them. Chairman recommends early transfer of most important criminals for trial by Hungarian Government. General Key and I agreed to report this matter to respective Governments. A list of some 557 persons has been prepared by the Hungarian Government and copies are being provided to us together with a list of the most important persons whom Hungarian Government wish to try as soon as possible. Minister is referring this question to the Foreign Office for (? instructions) as to policy.[4] I mentioned to Chairman question of large

---

[1] Received in the Foreign Office at 1 p.m. on 20 July 1945.

[2] This telegram, not printed, had related to the Soviet letter concerning revised arrangements for the A.C.C. in Hungary summarized in No. 197.i.

[3] Chief of the United States military representation on the A.C.C. in Hungary.

[4] In Budapest telegram No. 241 of 18 July 1945 to the Foreign Office Mr. Gascoigne requested telegraphic confirmation 'that it is our policy to hand over Hungarian war criminals situated outside Hungary to Hungarian authorities in Hungary for trial and punishment. I shall transmit names of 40 most important persons involved as soon as this list is available.' Foreign Office telegram No. 262 of 30 July to Budapest replied: 'This is a difficult question on which policy has not yet been decided. If matter is raised again on July 31st you will have to say that you are unable to discuss it since your instructions have not yet arrived.   2. You should if possible endeavour to confirm the use of the term "war criminals" for persons who have been responsible for atrocities committed against members of the United Nations or for other breaches of the rules of war. It seems probably [*sic*] that most of the people on the select list of 40 will be found not to be guilty of war crimes in this sense, but simply of offences against Hungarian law which is a purely domestic matter. Surrender to present Hungarian Government of leaders of Hungary's war effort at the side of Germany is of course quite a different question to which a totally different set of considerations apply.'

number of Hungarian P[risoners of] W[ar] and displaced persons now in Austria which question is linked up somewhat with above and will be discussed at an early date.

3. Reparations. Chairman said agreement had been reached on June 15th without considerable disagreement for (? suitable) reparations by the Hungarian Government. He has asked permission of Soviet Government to hand complete copy of agreement to us and anticipates early approval. He said Czechoslovaks and Yugoslavs now negotiating with Hungarian Government regarding their reparations and understood agreement reached that 70% of one hundred million dollars worth should go to Yugoslavia and 30% to Czechoslavakia but nothing has been published officially. I asked what arrangements there were for coordination of demands of article II [11]⁵ by Soviet High Command and demands of article 12 reparations and chairman said nothing definite yet arranged and that demands for occupying Soviet troops are still being made independently of A.C.C. I referred to compensation to Great Britain under last paragraph article 12 linked with British property under article 13 and asked permission for my staff to deal direct with Hungarian Government over details. Chairman said this point would be discussed fully at the next meeting after my economic section had discussed the matter in detail with Soviet economic division.

4. Procedure and agendas for A.C.C. meetings were discussed and it has been agreed to have meeting of A.C.C. under chairman 10th, 20th and 30th of each month together with conferences of Staffs and heads of sections twice monthly when a proportion of Soviet representatives from the provinces will attend. Points for agendas will be submitted by us and collated by Soviet Staff. This seems satisfactory.

5. Chairman referred to recent occurrence of disagreement of Hungarians P.W. came [sic] from American occupied Austria into Hungary without warning and without any means of checking. He asked us to ensure there was no repetition owing to obvious difficulties which might arise. I am sending full copies of my notes on this meeting by next aircraft.⁶ Minister did not (repeat not) accompany me to this conference as he is not member of A.C.C.

⁵ Of the Armistice agreement signed between the United Nations and Hungary at Moscow on 20 January 1945: printed (Cmd. 7280 of 1947) in B.F.S.P., vol. 145, pp. 788-95.

⁶ Mr. Gascoigne transmitted a copy of these notes (not printed; cf. F.R.U.S. 1945, vol. iv, pp. 837-8) under cover of Budapest despatch No. 192 of 18 July (received in Foreign Office on 31 July). Mr. Gascoigne commented: 'It is too early to say whether the new arrangement, whereby the British and American representations on the Allied Control Commission are in future to be permitted to take a greater share in the tripartite control (my telegram No. 231 [No. 197.i] of the 13 July), will be faithfully adhered to by the Russians, or whether the latter's unilateral policy will continue under a smoke screen of accommodation. In any case in view of the terms of paragraph 1 (a) (iii) of my telegram No. 231 it should certainly be more difficult for the Russians to carry out the control without consulting us and the Americans—although the wording "directives on matters of principle" might lend itself to certain undesirable ambiguity.'

i *18 & 21 July 1945   From & to Mr. Gascoigne (Budapest) Tels. Nos. 240 & 252.*
Instructions for further discussion at A.C.C. of transfer of Swabians from
Hungary: part of larger question of transfers to Germany for decision by the
four occupying Powers; points of subsequent procedure [C 4026/95/18].

ii *18 July 1945   Letters from Mr. Gascoigne (Budapest) to Mr. Howard* enclosing
memorandum from General Edgcumbe. Question of Mr. Gascoigne's
attendance at meetings of A.C.C. [R 12623/84/21].

iii *19 July & 2 Aug. 1945   From and to Major-General Edgcumbe (Budapest) Tel. No.
B.M.M. 591 and War Office Tel. No. 64202.* Guidance regarding compensation
for war-damages and losses to British interests in Hungary [R 13263/183/21].

iv *16–31 July   Situation in Hungary   Mr. Gascoigne (Budapest) Despatches* (a)
No. 178 of 16 July: dependence upon Soviet currency transactions; indications
of Soviet funding of Communist Party in Hungary [R 12694/9311/21].
(b) *No. 180 of 16 July:* Hungarian concern at failure of Soviet authorities to
coordinate demands on Hungarian industrial capacity under the armistice
[R 12847/82/21]. (c) *No. 185 of 17 July:* enclosed report indicates that there
was no effective national resistance movement in Hungary [R 12696/8113/21].
(d) *No. 204 of 19 July:* M. Kovacs, Secretary General of National Peasant
Party, was told in relation to British policy that 'Hungary must first work
her own passage and prove her good faith'; Hungarian minorities
[R 12982/459/21]. (e) *Nos. 208, 213 & 219 of 23, 25 & 31 July:* conversations
with Bishop Grosz and Dr. Zsedenyi, President of Hungarian National
Assembly: situation deteriorating; activities of Hungarian political police
[R 13208, 13209, 13485/26/21].

No. 306

Mr. Le Rougetel (Bucharest) to Mr. Eden (Received 18 July, 5.45 p.m.)
No. 720 Telegraphic [R 12171/28/37]

Immediate   BUCHAREST, *18 July 1945, 3.50 p.m. G.M.T.*

Repeated to Moscow, Washington and Saving to Sofia, Budapest.

My telegrams Nos. 701[1] and 715[2].

There is almost certainly a strong element of window dressing in all this.
The Russians, who have so far defied our criticism are now seeking to
forestall it and to avoid or to defer creating an issue in Roumania where

---

[1] In this telegram of 10 July 1945 Mr. Le Rougetel had reported receipt of a nominal roll
of the Roumanian Executive Committee and of the permanent delegation of the National
Liberation Party, showing majorities still loyal to M. Constantin Bratianu, President of
the National Liberal Party since 1934. M. Tatarescu had sought to sidetrack these organs,
and it would be most unwise to accept from his speech of 1 July an 'impression that a swing
to the Right is now in progress here, and that from now on bourgeois politicians will not
be seriously muzzled provided their hearts are in the right place where Soviet Union is
concerned.'

[2] No. 259.i.

they find that the ground is not yet ripe[3] for communism. If sufficiently pressed they may, therefore, be expected to compromise.

2. For the above reasons I agree with Air Vice Marshal Stevenson that as far as Roumania is concerned the Russians are now leading more from weakness than from strength and do not in the least expect to make the slam which they have bid.

Foreign Office please pass to Washington as my telegram No. 107.

[3] On the filed copy the words 'ground' and 'ripe' were underlined, with a marginal exclamation-mark.

No. 307

Mr. Hopkinson (Rome) to Mr. Eden (Received 18 July, 1.40 p.m.)
No. 1150 Telegraphic [F.O. 934/5/45(1)]

ROME, *18 July 1945, 12.10 p.m. G.M.T.*

Repeated to Resmed, Belgrade and Washington.

Caserta telegram No. 1350[1] to you.

My own feeling is that whatever the difficulties, every conceivable effort should be made to solve the mystery of this crime. Otherwise it seems to me that we should incur a terrible responsibility before history. If scientifically undertaken it ought to be possible to bring the bodies out and in similar cases e.g. Ardeatine Cave[2] identification has proved to be far less difficult than was expected.

2. I also feel strongly that some publicity should be given to this affair. It does not matter whether some of the victims were fascists or not.[3]

Foreign Office please repeat to Belgrade as my telegram No. 55.

[1] In this telegram of 14 July 1945 Mr. Broad had reported 'allegations by Italian Committee of National Liberation in Trieste that between May 2nd and May 5th Yugoslavs threw hundreds of corpses of Fascist policemen and minor officials, collaborators and German soldiers down a disused mine shaft near Basovizza. It is also alleged that many civilians were thrown in alive or compelled to jump in. Carcasses of horses are said to have been thrown in last of all . . . Investigations to date have been unproductive.' In view of technical difficulties and absence of any eye-witness evidence Mr. Broad considered it 'fruitless' to pursue enquiry and asked agreement to the 8th Army's recommendation of closing and sealing the mine-shaft.

[2] In June 1944 there had been discovered in the Ardeatine Caves near Rome the corpses of over 320 Italians, taken hostage and shot in German reprisal for an attack on an S.S. detachment in Rome.

[3] Mr. Eden minuted to Mr. Dixon on this telegram: 'What do you say? If this is a crime of Tito's I would like to unearth it. A. E.' On 20 July Mr. Churchill minuted to Mr. Eden with reference to these telegrams: 'I entirely agree. W. S. C.' Mr. Dixon stated in an explanatory minute of 20 July to Mr. Eden: 'The State Dept. favour continuing the investigation. We might consult the U.S. Delegation, & if they agree, propose to F.M. Alexander that the investigation shd. continue. We shd. then inform London, Washington, Caserta & Rome.' Mr. Eden minuted on this: 'I agree. Please consult F.M. Alexander. A. E. July 21.' Field-Marshal Alexander stated in an undated minute to Mr. Eden: 'I think

i *23 July 1945   Sir D. Osborne (The Vatican) to Mr. Broad (Caserta) Tel. No. 23.* Has received from the Vatican a memo. regarding the alleged fate 'of many Italians and Slavs in concentration camps in Venezia Giulia. Many are reported to have died in the pits and gullies of San Canziano' east of the Morgan Line: Allied protection requested [R 12419/24/92].

that the investigations should be carried on and every effort made to find out the truth. I see no reason why we should consider "whitewashing" the guilty or if it proves a false tale why unfair suspicion should be allowed to remain. H. R. A.' On 23 July Mr. Eden instructed the Foreign Office in Berlin telegram No. 160 Target: 'I consider that full investigation should be carried out. This is also the Prime Minister's view and Field-Marshal Alexander whom I have consulted also agrees.'

No. 308

Earl of Halifax (Washington) to Mr. Eden (Received 19 July, 7.20 a.m.)
No. 5031 Telegraphic [ZM 3892/1/22]

Immediate   WASHINGTON, *18 July 1945, 10.20 p.m.*

Repeated to Rome, Resmed's Office Caserta[1].

My telegram No. 4994[2].

Mr. Reber at State Department spoke this morning as follows to a member of my staff.

2. State Department were somewhat surprised at the tone of the Foreign Office reply to their message announcing the intention of the United States Government to support officially Italy's admission in due course to the World Security Organisation. Since Soviet Ambassador at Rome had made a statement to the press on July 13th[3] in which he said that the U.S.S.R. would be the first to support unconditionally Italy's admission to the World Security Organisation, the State Department assumed that His Majesty's Government had addressed a similar protest to the Soviet Government although no mention of this fact was made in their communication.

[1] Further repeated to the British Delegation at Berlin as Foreign Office telegram No. 76 Onward of 19 July 1945.

[2] This telegram of 17 July, not printed, had reported action on the instructions in No. 149 (cf. note 3, *ibid.*), and receipt by the State Department of the instructions referred to in No. 286, paragraph 3.

[3] On 19 July Mr. Harvey minuted to Mr. Hoyer Millar at Berlin on this telegram: 'This is the first indication that we have had from any source, officially or Press, of the statement said to have been made by the Soviet Ambassador in Rome, nor can such a statement even now be traced. We are telegraphing to Rome for a report.' On 21 July Mr. Hopkinson telegraphed from Rome that he could find no evidence that such a statement was made 'either to a foreign correspondent or to the Italian press.' On 24 July Lord Halifax reported in Washington telegram No. 5132 that according to the State Department the Soviet Ambassador's statement 'was made in a conversation with Signor Parri as reported by an Italian press correspondent quoting "a most reliable source of information" '.

3. Mr. Reber emphasised once more that he felt there was no real difference of view between His Majesty's Government and the United States Government as regards their ultimate objectives in Italy. Nevertheless he could not help thinking that His Majesty's Government had not fully appreciated the difficulty of political conditions in Italy to-day. It was necessary to recognise that the present Italian Government although showing promise of being reasonably effective, was basically a weak one. Without Allied support it could not hope to survive for long. He felt that some support was well worth giving because Parri Government was at least representative of all parties in Italy, and if it failed it would only be succeeded by one whose general complexion would be far less favourable from the Allied point of view.

4. Ways and means of giving support were difficult to find. Italy needed supplies but with the existing world shortages there was an obvious limit to the assistance she should be given in this sphere. Politically Italy was irked by the delay in bringing to an end her anomalous position as a 'co-belligerent'. As it was obvious that final peace terms could not be settled for many months to come it was necessary to find other means of dispelling Italian inferiority complex in this respect. It had seemed to the State Department that sponsorship of Italy's admission to the Security Organisation was just such a step and one moreover which did not conflict with the general lines of agreed Allied policy.

5. As it happened the Americans and British had once more allowed the Soviet Government to take the initiative showing that the Communist party in Italy would not be slow to derive the maximum political credit from the statement of the Soviet Ambassador and any American or British declaration would now come too late to counteract effectively that statement. In other words, while it was agreed that both Governments were anxious to prevent Italy drifting out of the western orbit, we were slow to take such steps as were open to us to achieve this end and too often allowed the initiative to pass out of our hands. Mr. Reber could not help feeling that in part at least these delays and uncertainties must be laid at the door of His Majesty's Government.

6. It was pointed out to Mr. Reber that His Majesty's Government while desiring to see a peaceful and democratic Italy ultimately restored to her position as one of the Western Powers and while as anxious as United States Government to prevent Italy turning exclusively to the east for political and economic inspiration, could not easily forget the part that Italy had played in the war against the British Empire. Moreover, if Italy were allowed to gain the impression that she had already worked her passage home it would render the task of concluding a satisfactory peace treaty extremely difficult, and would inevitably create a state of mind in Italy which would tend to reject out of hand terms of a peace such as we had in mind. It was a question of balancing immediate and possible transitory political advantage against long-term objectives. It was the feeling of His Majesty's Government that by concentrating solely on the former there was a danger of sacrificing the latter.

7. Mr. Reber replied that the United States Government appreciated that Italy had not yet worked her passage home, and he believed there would be no divergence of views between United States Government and His Majesty's Government as to the nature of terms of peace to be imposed on Italy. He nevertheless considered the immediate danger of Italy taking the wrong political turning and so committing herself to a Communistic form of Government was so great as to make it imperative to adopt all means at our disposal to forestall such a development. He added that State Department had revealed these views to United States Delegation at Terminal and expressed the hope that an opportunity would be found there to discuss freely and frankly the whole question of Anglo-American policy towards Italy.[4]

[4] Mr. S. Reber's record of this conversation with Mr. G. H. Middleton is printed in *F.R.U.S. Berlin*, vol. ii, pp. 624–5.

No. 309

Mr. King[1] (Salonica) to Mr. Caccia (Athens)
No. 30 Saving Telegraphic, by bag [*R 12457/4/19*]

SALONICA, *18 July 1945*

Repeated to Foreign Office No. 20 Saving.[2]

1. Situation has been disturbed since my last report of July 6th by reaction to the anti-Greek press and radio campaign of Belgrade and Moscow. The local newspapers of the Left add fuel to this fire by giving lurid details of the monarcho-fascistic terror said to be reigning in Macedonia, and by presenting reports from Belgrade and Moscow of the persecution of the Macedonian Slavs as if they were statements of fact: Those of the Right do likewise with sensational and often entirely false accounts of frontier incidents. The result is chatter of impending war producing in its turn fear and hesitation in returning to normal life.

2. The unguarded state of the frontiers continues to facilitate the escape of criminals from Greek justice and the entry of agents and agitators. Most of the frontier posts themselves are in a state of ruin. A display of force in the frontiers is also essential if the numerous frontier incidents of the last fortnight are to cease.

3. The deployment of the Gendarmerie continues satisfactorily and in Western Macedonia has reached pre-war strength, but this is not sufficient for present commitments. Support from the National Guard is still required to deal with the armed bands reported from all the more remote mountain areas.

[1] Mr. A. H. King was Acting British Consul-General at Salonica.
[2] Received on 24 July 1945 at 2.40 p.m.

4. The National Guard is behaving better, but beatings of village men and women are still all too frequent particularly in the Kilkis district. Several cases have also occurred in which National Guards have seized hidden arms and promptly handed them out again to local royalists. Local British commanders are doing what they can to put a stop to these malpractices.

5. The state of the prisons is a plague spot which is becoming worse. Nearly 5000 people are awaiting trial in inhuman and insanitary conditions. The present prison intake far exceeds the output of the Courts. Judges and prosecutors are insufficient in numbers and ludicrously paid with all the usual evils as a result.

CALENDAR TO No. 309

i *20–26 July 1945 To and from Mr. Caccia (Athens) Tels. No. 1545, Unnumbered and 126; Mr. King (Salonica) to Mr. Caccia No. 31 Saving. Letter from Mr. Howard to Mr. Hayter (Berlin).* Propaganda in regard to situation in Greece. Mr. Howard considers that Mr. Caccia's unnumbered tel. of 22 July 'provides a first hand and authoritative answer to the wild charges which are being made by Tito and company' [R 12288/4/19; R 12811/3549/19; R 12367/11/67; R 12397/3/19; F.O. 934/1/1(23)].

No. 310

Sir W. Strang (Lübbecke) to Mr. Eden (Received 18 July, 12.15 p.m.)
No. 48 Telegraphic [N 8850/1866/15]

LÜBBECKE, *18 July 1945, 10.22 a.m. G.M.T.*

Repeated to Copenhagen.

Following from Steel.

21st Army Group have referred to me a request from the Danish Minister of Foreign Affairs to be allowed to visit Flensborg to discuss questions affecting the Danish minority in South Schleswig. I advise that this request should be refused on the ground that a visit in the present circumstances would be inopportune.

2. It seems to me that if the Danish Government wish to take up questions affecting Danish minority in South Schleswig they should continue to do so through the proper channels, i.e. His Majesty's Legation or General Dewing's Mission at Copenhagen. A visit by Mr. Moller is[1] Flensborg would in the present circumstances almost certainly lead to patriotic demonstrations by the Danish minority coupled with demands for return of South Schleswig to Denmark. This would be embarrassing not only to our Military Authorities but also to the Danish Government, if they are really sincere in their claim that they do not wish to encourage irredentism

---

[1] It was suggested on the filed copy that this word should read 'to'.

746

amongst the Danes in this area. I therefore hope that it will be possible to persuade Mr. Moller that such matters should continue to be dealt with in Copenhagen where the atmosphere should be more favourable to discussion.

Foreign Office please repeat to Copenhagen as my telegram No. 4.

CALENDAR TO NO. 310

i *10 & 18 July 1945 Mr. Randall (Copenhagen) Tels. Nos. 316 & 361.* Danish Government attach importance to requested visits from Danish minority in South Schleswig to Denmark. Mr. Randall considers there would be 'small risk' in granting concessions. M. Möller has emphasised Danish Government have no territorial ambitions in Schleswig. If visits continue to appear obstructed 'we shall I feel sure be in for some rather serious crisis' [N 8402, 8865/1866/15].

No. 311

Czechoslovak Aide-Mémoire (Received 19 July)

[*N 8858/365/12*]

18 July 1945

1. The Government of Czechoslovakia is anxious to start trade negotiations with His Majesty's Government and submits a list of commodities which Czechoslovakia means to procure in the Sterling Area.

We have included in this list the most important raw materials, a few semi-finished articles and finished goods, and we wish to point out that most of the items are of vital importance for the restarting of our industry. We are fully aware that some of the commodities are in short supply and that the delivery would involve certain sacrifices for His Majesty's Government, but we hope that with the help of His Majesty's Government, the restarting of our industry will make it possible to increase our exports to your country in the shortest possible time.

2. We hope that His Majesty's Government will grant to the Government of Czechoslovakia an adequate long term credit to facilitate the purchase of a part of our requirements. These credit negotiations were started with H.M. Treasury some time ago and we hope that they will be concluded without any difficulty.

3. We are desirous of negotiating for additional short and medium term business credits with City Bankers, which should be already based on our exports.

4. We should be most grateful if His Majesty's Government would give us friendly support in the following matters which are probably partly subject to the decision of the Great Powers:–

Transport question:–

(*a*) Repatriation of Czechoslovak railway waggons from Germany.

(*b*) To facilitate goods traffic between Hamburg and Prague and Bremen and Prague.

(c) To facilitate goods traffic between Belgian ports and Prague.

(d) To facilitate air traffic between London and Prague at least three times a week.

Financial questions:–

(a) Release of the blocked accounts of Czechoslovak citizens, banks and firms.

(b) Removal of Czechoslovak firms from the Black List of the Board of Trade, in consideration of the fact that Czechoslovakia is no longer an enemy country within the meaning of the Trading with the Enemy Act, 1939.[1]

We are certain that your kind help will prove to be a first and most important step towards re-establishment of permanent mutual and friendly trade relations between both our nations.

ENCLOSURE IN NO. 311

List of urgent Czechoslovak requirements

List of urgent Czechoslovak requirements to be imported from the Sterling area (including certain commodities from outside Sterling area, but supplied by British-owned Companies; such as e.g. Borax, Quebraccho, etc.)

I. Textile Raw Materials: Wool, Egyptian Cotton, Indian Cotton, Jute, Sisal, Textiles Waste a/ for Wool spinning industry, b/ for paper industry.

II. Oilseeds, Vegetable Oils & Edible Fats: Arachid, Cotton seed and Palm kernels, Oils /Cottonseed Oil, Groundnut Oil etc./Fish Oil.

III. Raw Materials for Leather Industry: Raw Hides and Skins, Mimosa, Quebraccho.

IV. Base Metals and Alloys: Copper, Tin, Lead, Zinc, Magnesium, Ferro Alloys, Pyrites.

V. Chemical Products & various raw materials: Nickel-Sulphate, Pharmaceuticals including Vitamins, Chemical Intermediates, Dye-Stuffs, Crude Borax, Mica, Red Phosphorus, Industrial Diamonds, Shellac, Gums.

VI. Finished and Semi-finished Articles: Clothing (e.g. surplus stocks from Civil Defence Stores etc.), Textile Machinery Spares and Spindles, Machine Sewing Needles, Typewriters, Radio Valves, Sewing Machines spare parts, Electrodes (chiefly carbon), Transmission Belts (leather, cotton, composition belting), Nibs for fountain pens, Celluloid, artificial horn (rods) and other artificial resins.

VII. Spot requirements to be determined in consultation with British Authorities as and when occuring.

CALENDAR TO NO. 311

i *12 July 1945   To Mr. Nichols (Prague) Tel. No. 142.* Welcomes proposed visit by Dr. Ripka, Czechoslovak Minister of Foreign Trade. 'Insofar as circumstances permit we would be glad to resume and expand pre-war trade with Czechoslovakia . . . There will, however, be a difficult intervening period . . . A major question is whether Czechoslovakia will be able to escape being forced into the Russian political and economic orbit' [N 8111/365/12].

[1] Printed in *B.F.S.P.*, vol. 143, pp. 180–90.

No. 312

Sir J. Anderson to Mr. Eden (*Berlin: received 18 July, 11.45 p.m.*)
No. 61 Onward Telegraphic [*UE 3074/32/71*]

FOREIGN OFFICE, *18 July 1945, 5.30 p.m.*

Top secret. Most Immediate

For Prime Minister from Chancellor of the Exchequer.
Your telegram Target 65.[1]

The President's note[2] shows how ill-informed he is about our general financial position. We are in fact in worse financial straits today, especially with the eventual end of lend-lease in sight, than we have ever been before. Our dollar balances are higher than we estimated they would have been if we had failed to obtain the further help we were asking last autumn.[3] They are not higher than what we then indicated and what Mr. Morgenthau then accepted as a reasonable objective, having regard to the size and inevitable growth of our overseas liabilities. Part of the improvement is due to the prolongation of the war in Europe, which has increased our earnings from the personal expenditure of American troops in U.K., but these gains have been greatly exceeded by the increased overseas obligations we have incurred for the same reason, namely the prolongation of Stage I.[4] You will be aware that we aim at keeping our reserves at a certain level in order not to be in a critical and indeed helpless position when Lend-Lease comes to an end.

2. On our general financial position, if the President will agree to satisfactory conditions for the winding up of Lend-Lease and for assistance to follow Lend-Lease on terms we can accept, we can of course ease up on difficult items such as those mentioned in the third paragraph of the President's note. All this was to be the subject of the conversations which I hope the President will agree to our opening in Washington in September.

3. I suggest you reply that all these matters can be taken up in these conversations but meanwhile it is a complete fallacy to suppose that we have surplus dollar resources.

4. You could add that both in the matter of disposals and relief to Europe, in an earnest endeavour to meet the Americans I have already authorised proposals to the State Department which go considerably beyond what I could conceivably have justified on any other ground. In particular we have informed the State Department that we are willing to continue relief during the military period in Italy until UNRRA takes over relief there in the early autumn and to make a further contribution to the general work

---

[1] No. 174.i.
[2] No. 174, annex.
[3] Cf. No. 26, note 7.
[4] i.e. the period prior to the defeat of Germany.

of UNRRA for next year.[5] Both these proposals are at present under discussion with the State Department, though I have not yet any Parliamentary authority for this further relief expenditure.

5. The President's memorandum takes us all greatly by surprise. Brand, who has just arrived from Washington and is with me now, has reached within the last few days a not unsatisfactory understanding about Lend-Lease outside munitions with the FEA administrator, Mr. Crowley.[6]

6. Turning now to the question of munitions, Lyttelton and I have just seen the President's directive of 5th July restricting supplies of munitions to what will be used in the war against Japan and not for any other purpose. This is quoted in ZO 608 from Washington.[7] Our Staff views on this question are contained in the note covering a draft memorandum to the President which was submitted to you by the Chiefs of Staff.[8] They have full supporting information. Lyttelton and I personally agree with these views. The first two paragraphs of the President's memorandum of 17th July do not appear to be nearly so restrictive as his Directive of 5th July and suggest that the door is still open. I hope you may feel it possible to press for agreement on lines suggested in Chiefs of Staff note.

CALENDARS TO NO. 312

i   *18 July 1945   To Mr. Eden (Berlin) Tel. No. 62 Onward.* Message from Sir J. Anderson to Mr. Churchill referring to No. 312. Wonders if President Truman is working on right figures of British gold and dollar reserves, at present at 1.8 billion dollars. British overseas liabilities against them are approximately 13 billion [UE 3074/32/71].

ii *18–19 July 1945   Minutes by Sir R. Campbell, Mr. N. Butler and Mr. E. Hall-Patch:* gravity and questionability of American attitude in regard to termination of lend-lease. [UE 3133, 3074/32/70].

iii *17 July 1945   Lord Halifax (Washington) Tels. Nos. 254 & 255 Empax:* open letter from Mr. J. S. Knight of *Chicago Daily News* to Lord Beaverbrook: growth in America of anti-British feeling and criticism of British war-effort [AN 2230/36/45].

iv *18 July & 1 Aug. 1945   Minutes of 9th and 10th meetings of the British Supply Council (Washington):* status of Stage II programme and military agreements; dependence on favourable decision at Potsdam for lend-lease eligibility of U.K. civil aircraft programme [UR 3704, 3711/73/71].

[5] Cf. *F.R.U.S. 1945*, vol. ii, pp. 993–4.

[6] See No. 26.i.

[7] Of 13 July, not printed: see No. 199, paragraph 3(a) for the second paragraph of President Truman's directive here cited.

[8] No. 26.iv.

No. 313

Letter from Sir J. Anderson to Sir W. Monckton (Berlin)
[*F.O. 934/1/2(22)*]

Personal. Copy   TREASURY CHAMBERS, *18 July 1945*

My dear Monckton,

Many thanks for your letter of the 12th July[1] about the deindustrialisation of Germany. This matter is the key both of your discussions and of the German settlement generally, and it is vital that our policy should be clear and consistent. I have felt, on reading your letter, that we were not at one on the matter, and I am therefore writing at once to give you my personal views. I am circulating your letter and my reply to my colleagues: in a few days we shall have to reconsider the question of industrial disarmament in the light of the Control Commission's comments on the APW proposals,[2] for which the Cabinet asked and which will doubtless be reaching us any day now; and I hope that my colleagues will take that opportunity to express their views on the general questions which we are discussing.

2. The technical aspects of industrial disarmament are complicated, very important, and controversial. They cannot be dismissed as mere detail; they must be discussed at a high level, and during those discussions attention is apt to be focussed first on one and then on another particular industry in which the speakers have reason to be strongly interested. In such discussions there is always the danger—which I think, in fact, we have so far avoided—of losing sight of the fundamental principles involved. I should like to go back to them at this point when you, in Moscow, have got to the stage of discussing industry by industry and we, in London, are considering a plan which has reached some degree of detail.

3. Our basic position is stated in paragraphs 2 and 3 of the draft of a note for the use of the United Kingdom Delegation on the European Advisory Commission, attached to the Minister of State's paper C.P. (45)36,[3] which the Cabinet agreed you should have as interim guidance. After stating our general objective of adopting a drastic policy over a selected field of industry and removing surplus capacity, the note continues:–

'. . . [4] but they (i.e. the United Kingdom Delegation) feel that any policy of excessive deindustrialisation would be likely to defeat our own ends in that it would create conditions of depression and unrest under which there would be little hope of the emergence of a peaceful Germany. The United Kingdom Delegation attach great importance to maintaining a clear distinction between measures imposed for purposes of security, and other measures which may be adopted for reparation or other reasons. The former, in their opinion, should be carried out regardless of their

[1] No. 117.
[2] See No. 154, note 3.
[3] For this paper of 14 June 1945 (UE 2630/86/77: not printed) see below.
[4] Punctuation as in original quotation.

751

effect on Germany's capacity to make reparation for the damage she has done, or of the difficulties they may create for the occupying Powers, since the primary object must be to prevent Germany from ever again becoming a threat to the peace of the world.'

4. I hold entirely to this statement of principle. Our programme of security is of such overriding importance that it must be considered first, and separately; only when our minds are clear on what we want for this end should we go on to consider how the other aspects of our policy towards German industry and economy fit into it. I should sum up our desiderata somewhat as follows:–

(a) Our programme must commend itself to public opinion in this country both now and at all future times when we may have to call for approval of action in support of it. It serves no purpose to impose prohibitions or restrictions which will seem unjust a generation hence; and it may be harmful to rest the programme on once-for-all action which will be condemned in retrospect, so that efforts to reverse it will receive support.

(b) We can rely on a long, but not an indefinite, period of direct control. After that period the number and scope of restrictions which we can enforce will be limited, and they must appear plainly justifiable. Yet it is only after that period that the danger will appear.

(c) Therefore we must chiefly rely on action taken and completed within that period, which carries with it the seeds of permanence and stability.

(d) For all these reasons we should aim at a change in Germany's industrial structure which will leave them, at the end, in a stable and self-supporting position which they have an interest to maintain. If we reduce them to a state of misery and chaos, or even leave them in a position where ordinary peaceful development is unnaturally difficult for them the system will not last.

(e) We should aim at economy of effort. If a given set of measures will in themselves make Germany incapable of waging war, there is no need to add further measures which will increase her poverty and discontent without effectively adding to security.

(f) While the central and essential measures must be taken regardless of cost, the very fact that we give them this priority must make us chary of adding to their number. Subsidiary measures should not be taken if they do not effectively add to security, but on the other hand would add to the cost of the programme to us, in supplies, manpower or money.

(g) Industrial security must not be regarded as a measure by itself, or as a measure sufficient in itself. It can only be an adjunct to military and political security—helpful if our arrangements on that side are well-founded, useless and even harmful, because it is falsely relied on, if it is not constantly backed up by willingness to enforce the scheme by arms, if necessary.

(h) Therefore it should be fitted in to the general scheme of security;

and, in particular, we must not sacrifice to it any hopes of removing the German will to war. It must not simply lead to revolt.

(i) If we succeed in devising a scheme which meets these criteria, it must not be stultified by other aspects of our German policy.

5. The scheme which we have worked out may be criticised in detail, but broadly it satisfies the criteria I have mentioned, and I think we can be content to stand by its broad lines. The Russian scheme, so far as I understand it from your letter and from the minutes of the first four meetings of Committee No. 1,[5] does not commend itself to me. As I understand it, the choice of industries to be eliminated, and the extent of elimination, has been determined, so far as we know it, on a double basis: industrial disarmament is in practice made almost subordinate to reparation. A very wide range of deindustrialisation is justified partly on the Russian desire of reparation (which is legitimate enough) but partly also on grounds of security. I am not in the least convinced by the argument that every kind of heavy industry constitutes war potential to some degree. Certainly it does; so do coal-mining and farming. The fact that a given industry constitutes war potential seems to me an irrelevance, since our own experience shows us that there is hardly a form of economic activity that does not. The question we must ask is different: how few, not how many, industries must we strike out to make Germany powerless to fight? If we have struck them out, the job is done, and the fact that a locomotive factory could be turned into a tank factory is without importance. I remain convinced that the draconian attack on selective industries is the only possible one. I am interested to note traces of this line of thought in the very interesting talk which Turner had with Mr. Sabourov.[6] His general approach to the problem is apparently like our own in this respect: though the mixed motives as regards reparation and the disregard of others of the criteria mentioned above make this scheme less attractive to me than our own.

6. I realise, of course, that once-for-all deliveries will not be confined to plant removed for reasons of disarmament—indeed, that stands in your instructions. But I do not think that it is pedantic to insist on the difference of motive between deliveries that are based on industrial disarmament, and those that are not. First, we must ensure that we are not asking for deliveries of a kind which will militate against our disarmament programme. This is largely a matter of manufactured goods, and I do not think there will be much dispute on that. Second, and more important, different arguments apply to the two classes. We recognise an absolute priority to disarmament. Reparation, outside the field of disarmament, is more open to argument. I would not have you think we are seeking to favour Germany at Russia's expense, or to 'see that Russia obtains a small rather than a large amount of once-for-all deliveries'. The question is not so absolute.

[5] The British notes of these meetings, of 2–7 July, of Committee No. 1 of the Allied Reparations Commission in Moscow are not printed.

[6] No. 117.i.

They should certainly get a large amount, but they are not the sole judges of what is large and what is small. We should not, in my view, be ashamed of expressing our own opinion on that matter. I hope that we shall reach agreement; but it has never been out of my mind that the difference between us may prove fundamental. We should have a clearer view of this after Terminal; until we know better where we stand, I should not wish to give way on the main issue.

7. Our ideas of industrial disarmament do not lead us to far-reaching deindustrialisation, or to any burden which, in the long run, Germany could not easily carry. I should not, therefore, accept arguments of this order as decisive in that field. We must argue it out as a matter of pure reparation. Here, as I see the matter, we have two main desiderata, subject to which reparation should be developed and not cut down, within the agreed limits. First, reparation deliveries must not be at our expense, in the broadest sense. They must not lead to our having to inject supplies into Germany without hope of repayment; they must not involve an intolerable commitment for our Commander in the administration of our zone, though by this I do not mean that important deliveries should be held up for a mere matter of minor convenience. We have already seen, in the context of the first charge,[7] that this will prove difficult to establish.

8. Second, while reparations are an important aim in themselves, and must not take last place, they have not an overriding priority. I suggested, at a recent meeting of the APW Committee on this subject, that the priority for policy decisions should be: security, German standard of living, reparations and German exports. I have already dealt with security. By giving second place to the German standard of living, I do not, of course, mean that we must increase that standard at the expense of reparation. This is sufficiently shown by our adherence to the statement of principles.[8] But a minimum standard is essential, not only as a matter of administration which affects us as a controlling power, but also as a long-range political matter. We come back here, indirectly, to the theme of security. Our aim must be, in the long run, to secure stability in Germany. We cannot afford, politically or materially, to police Germany indefinitely by force of arms. If, by our reparation programme, we drive Germany below the level of tolerable existence—not below her deserts, since this is a criterion which is irrelevant in a matter which is primarily one of our own interests—we shall not achieve this aim, and we shall have agreed to a policy which it would be hard to defend to Parliament or the public.

9. It is here that I fear a deep divergence between ourselves and the Russians. You have said in your letter that they take a short view. They appear to be indifferent, or largely indifferent, to the economic future of Germany. They may be far more ready than we are to continue in occupation for an indefinite period. All this should be clearer after Terminal; mean-

[7] Cf. No. 152, paragraph (4).
[8] Cf. No. 116, annex.

while, we ought not, in the field of reparation, to commit ourselves to a policy which may prove incompatible with our long-term interests; still less should we drift into a position where we can only put on the brake by appearing to disregard the interests of industrial disarmament.

10. Your letter has thrown a good deal of light on your interesting telegram No. 3009,[9] which we had before us at the last meeting of the Reparations Committee. What you say gives a good example of the different way in which we and the Russians may view things. To our mind paragraph 7[8] means what it says: that during the reparation period the standard of life in Germany should be somewhere between those of Belgium and Bulgaria. We cannot regard it as justifying the creation of a sub-Balkan condition of chaos. Some degree of deindustrialisation, not in itself incompatible with the formula, follows inevitably from industrial disarmament as we understand it. Beyond that there will be further deliveries; they will be on such a scale as to achieve, in total, the desired effect. But there is nothing in the formula to take them further, and we think it undesirable to take them further. I agree that, as is stated in the telegram, any suspicion that we simply wanted to be kind to the Germans would create a deplorable effect—as it would on our own public. But this is no reason why we should withhold from the Russians our true motives. If we do not do so, either we sacrifice our policy unargued—which is not to be thought of—or we attempt to cut down the Russian demands on the Germans in each case with no expressed reason, and the implication that we are simply trying to be kind to the Germans.

11. After Terminal, I should hope that your position in this respect will be a good deal easier, since the main issues will have been discussed at the highest level, and you will not be in the invidious position of having to break the ice in discussions on a matter on which the Russians are particularly touchy.

12. At the end of your letter you suggest that, if I or my colleagues dissent from your views, I should send a telegram direct to the Delegation during your absence at Berlin. You will see from this letter that in some important respects I differ from the views which you have expressed. I have not sent a telegram to the Delegation, partly because at this stage I am sending you my personal views before consulting my colleagues, but partly also because you alone know how you have left matters with the Delegation in your absence, and if any redirection of their work is required in the light of what I have said, you alone can judge.

13. One hesitates, at a distance, to make any suggestion on what is primarily a question of tactics; but, if you agree with the general lines of what I have said, I would like you to consider whether it is wise to start off this very delicate and difficult question on the technical level. You yourself have drawn attention to the dangers of the procedure. Experts examine

[9] This telegram of 8 July, not printed, had made the suggestion recorded in No. 116, paragraph 4(*b*).

755

industry after industry, and on each one, taken separately, strong arguments for drastic action appear, till at the end we are found to be practically committed to agreement, on economic security grounds, to a programme which we have rejected as a whole. The essence of industrial disarmament as I see it, is political, and the problem must be taken as a whole. We found, in our domestic examination of the problem, that great confusion arose whenever we adopted a piecemeal approach, and one always accumulated more recommendations for action than seemed reasonable when the problem was examined as one. If it is practicable at this stage, would it not be wise to call a halt to the technical discussions, or at least to conduct them subject to the strictest reserves, until the general policy has been more fully discussed, either at Terminal, if it so happens, or after your return to Moscow between the Heads of the Delegations? Otherwise, as you yourself point out, we may end up by finding that the subject has been decided before it has been considered; and you may yet find yourself burdened by Russian suspicion, due to your experts' attempts to moderate the Russian proposals in individual cases on grounds which only assume their full validity when applied to the complete policy.

14. I must, I think, comment frankly on the last page of your letter. The issue is wider than any distinction between commonsense and logic, or between general principles and the technical approach. What the Russians are proposing is, in short, an extreme version of views expressed earlier in the year in Washington, and described there as the 'Morgenthau Plan'. When these views became known they caused a great shock to the State Department and to the War Department, as well as to any informed American opinion. They were equally condemned over here in every paper.

If we were to be an acquiescing partner to a policy which, as you recognise, would have disastrous consequences when applied, there would be a sharp revulsion of feeling both here and in the United States. We have no wish to let Germany off lightly or to prevent Russia recouping some of her physical losses from German plant and assets, but for the sake of the sanity and peace of Europe we cannot push the policy of destroying Germany's economy to the point of a complete breakdown.

Yours ever,
JOHN ANDERSON

CALENDARS TO No. 313

i *19 July 1945* (a) *Letter from Sir J. Anderson to Sir W. Monckton (Berlin).* Comments on No. 152 in regard to (1) Reparation Plan; hasty concessions should not be made on disarmament; (2) allocation of reparation receipts should be agreed by all reparation-receiving Powers; (3) agrees with formula on procedure for bringing in other Powers; (4) war booty. We should not yield on unaccepted principle of the first charge 'especially in view of the Russian attitude about deindustrialisation.' (b) *22–23 July Letter from Sir D. Waley (Berlin) to Mr. Playfair and ensuing correspondence* concerning (2) above [UE 3241/624/71].

ii *12–21 July 1945   British requirements from Germany. (a) Ministry of Production paper* concerning urgent requirements for immediate action; (*b*) *correspondence of 17–18 July* between Mr. O. S. Franks (Ministry of Supply), Mr. Hall-Patch, Mr. Coulson (Berlin) and Mr. R. C. G. Somervell (Allied Reparations Commission, Moscow) regarding lists of plant and equipment in steel, non-ferrous and chemical industries required from British Zone of Germany, and possibility of obtaining requirements from American Zone; Mr. Hall-Patch requests circulation of the information 'so that nobody gives away light-heartedly anything which may be of interest to us'; (*c*) *record of 19 July by Mr. Hasler* of interdepartmental meeting on German exportable surpluses; (*d*) *War Office Tel. No. 7 Sugra* to British Element of Control Commission transmitting first list of urgent British requirements from Germany to prevent destruction or dissipation; exportable surpluses to be ascertained [UE 3102, 3185/2615/77; UE 3229/2689/71].

iii *11–23 July 1945   Letters from Mr. E. W. Playfair (Treasury) to Mr. Hall-Patch and others; memo. (EIPS/134) and meeting (EIPS/29/135) of Economic and Industrial Planning Staff.* Treatment of Krupps, IG. Farbenindustrie and Hermann Göring Werke in British Zone [UE 3511/86/77].

iv *22 July 1945   Tel. No. 61 Victim to Moscow:* in view of inequality between British and Russian occupation costs urges agreement to principle that cost of imports for occupying forces be included in the first charge [UE 2992/624/77].

v *23 July 1945   U.K. Delegation (Moscow) brief* on disarmament and control of the German engineering industry [UE 3481/624/77].

vi *25 July 1945   Covering memo. by Mr. W. Mabane (Minister of State, F.O.) to report of the German Science and Industry Committee* on industrial disarmament of Germany [UE 3141/18/53].

No. 314

Sir J. Anderson to Mr. Eden (Berlin: received 19 July, 7.30 a.m.)
No. 72 Onward Telegraphic [F.O. 800/417/65]

FOREIGN OFFICE, *19 July 1945, 5.10 a.m.*

Top secret. Most Immediate

Following is repetition of Naf 1042 (FX 24640) dated 18th July, 1945 (T.O.O. 181707Z).
Begins:
For: Combined Chiefs of Staff. British Chiefs of Staff.
Info: Terminal Personal for Field Marshal Alexander.
Signed: Alexander.
Cite: FHGCT.
For your information following is outline of a report made by General McCreery G.O.C. Eighth Army on recent contracts [contacts] with the Russians.

1. Representatives of 8th Army with United States and French colleagues had two meetings with Russian authorities in Vienna on 16th July.

2. Russians claimed that agreements made with EAC have not been ratified by Governments, they therefore had no authority from Moscow to make any decisions for implementing these agreements. Occupation of Styria by Eighth Army and move of advance party of the three Allies into Vienna could not therefore be discussed.

3. Although Marshal Koniev had written to General McCreery agreeing to the meeting and stating that he believed that many questions could be settled at the meeting, Russians also declining to discuss such questions as signal communications, roads, railways and civilian supplies. Reactions of the Allied Party to the un-cooperative attitude of the Russians forced Russian representative to refer the matter to Marshal Koniev who agreed to an immediate discussion of these questions by specialist officers of the Four Powers. Good progress was then made on most of these points.

4. Agreement was reached on road communications and establishment of combined signals and railways boards. Guarantees also given for telephone and telegraph facilities within Vienna and between zones of occupation and Vienna. Boards will not of course function until agreement reached for movement of advance parties into Vienna.

5. Koniev's Chief of Staff stated that Koniev would issue invitations to three Allied commanders for Staff meetings to be followed by a commanders meeting as soon as instructions were received from Moscow.

6. It is apparent that Russia can continue to stall us regarding move into Vienna and Styria unless steps are taken on the highest level to ensure despatch of necessary instructions to Marshal Koniev from Moscow. It is considered that nothing further can be achieved through local contacts. In compliance with instruction based on Fan 582[1] first approach to Russia regarding move into Styria was made on 1st July and it is considered undesirable to risk a third rebuff by local Russian commander.

7. All these Allied parties left Vienna 17th July.[2]

CALENDARS TO NO. 314

i *16–19 July 1945 Correspondence concerning arrangements for entry into British zone of occupation in Austria and western sectors of Vienna: (a) Mr. Mack (Vienna) to Mr. Harvey, General McCreery (8th Army) Tels. Nos. AC/401–3:* 'French continue to be treated as poor relations . . . Russians are still removing material . . . While Russian staff are friendly and anxious to cooperate they are not (r[e]p[ea]t not) kept in the picture by Moscow' *(AC/403). (b) To General McCreery Tel. No. 61150; Mr. Hopkinson (Rome) Tel. No. 1158; to Mr. Eden*

---

[1] This telegram of 29 June 1945 (U 5127/20/70: not printed) from the Combined Chiefs of Staff to Field-Marshal Alexander and Generals Eisenhower, Deane and Gammell conveyed instructions for the withdrawal of British and American forces from the Soviet Zone of Germany and their advance into their zones of occupation in Austria in execution of the understanding reached with Marshal Stalin on 17 June: see No. 35.

[2] A paraphrase of this telegram is printed in *F.R.U.S. Berlin*, vol. ii, pp. 669–70.

(Berlin) Tel. No. 82 Onward. Requests for Austrian situation to be taken up at Potsdam [C 4435, 4295, 4157/317/18; C 4069, 4057/205/3; U 5558/11/70].

ii *20 July 1945 Brief for Mr. Eden (Berlin).* Suggests expedition of outstanding U.S. and Soviet ratifications of E.A.C. agreements for Austria may clear difficulties reported in No. 314 [F.O. 934/4/25(1)].

No. 315

Sir J. Anderson to Mr. Eden (Berlin: received 20 July, 1 a.m.)
No. 86 Onward Telegraphic [U 5558/11/70]

FOREIGN OFFICE, *19 July 1945, 11.30 p.m.*

Top secret. Immediate

[Repeated to Moscow, Washington, Caserta and Rome for Mr. Mack.][1]

For the Secretary of State from Sir Orme Sargent.

My telegram No. 82 Onward[2] (of 19th July: Withdrawal of Russian Forces from British areas in Austria).

It seems not improbable that the reason why the Russians are stalling in this way is to give them time to complete the virtual stripping of Styria before we get there. Head of Economic Division of British Element[3] is now in London and has circumstantial evidence of large-scale removals of machinery and industrial equipment of all kinds from Vienna and Styria. He also has evidence of large-scale requisitioning by the Red Army of food stocks, cattle, farm implements etc. in Styria.

2. This information has been obtained in the course of several visits by British military officers to Vienna and also from reliable Austrian sources in Styria. Sources can therefore not be quoted, but the general picture has been reported in the Press.

3. On the 22nd April H.M. Chargé d'Affaires in Moscow addressed an official letter to Mr. Vyshinski which contained the following passage:

'My Government are sure that the Soviet Government will agree that our common purpose might well be prejudiced by unilateral action on the part of any one of the occupying powers in regard to the removal of industrial plant and equipment, regardless of whether or not this was German-owned, or the elimination without regard to their attitude towards the Nazis of Austrians who might prove useful in re-establishing Austrian administration and economy. My Government propose therefore that the representatives to be sent to Vienna may be empowered to deal with such questions, and that the Soviet Commanders on the spot should meanwhile be instructed to hold their hand. My Government would also urge the importance of taking all possible steps to maintain Austrian agriculture in full production.'

---

[1] Supplied from another copy on F.O. 934/4/25(4).
[2] o. 314.i(*b*).
[3] Of the Allied Commission for Austria, Mr. E. A. Berthoud.

4. If you decide to raise this question of Austria at Terminal you may consider it appropriate to draw attention at the same time to the anxiety we have been caused by reports of this unilateral action on the part of the Soviet authorities of occupation, which seems likely to create formidable difficulties for the Allied Council and in particular to the British Commander-in-Chief.

CALENDARS TO No. 315

i *19–20 July 1945 Correspondence between Mr. Playfair, Mr. Berthoud and Mr. Troutbeck.* 'Russian depredations in Austria' and questions concerning Austrian reparation and restitution [C 4199/317/3].

ii *25 July 1945 Mr. J. W. Nicholls (Graz) Tel. No. 2 Saving.* Report of impressions of Russian behaviour in Styria [C 4730/317/3].

No. 316

Letter from Mr. Howard to Mr. Hayter (Berlin)
[*F.O. 934/2/9(26)*]

Immediate   FOREIGN OFFICE, *19 July 1945*

Dear William,

I enclose copies of the following telegrams: M.1443, M.1444,[1] M.1448 and M.1457[2] from the Military Mission in Bulgaria; BMM/563[3] and BMM/565[4] from the Military Mission in Hungary; Gascoigne's telegram No. 231[4] and Le Rougetel's telegram No. 715[5]. I also enclose a copy of our telegram No. 239[6] to Gascoigne and his reply confirming certain statements in his telegram No. 231.

You will see from these telegrams that the Russians have now made proposals for the reorganisation of the Control Commissions in all three Balkan countries. There are, however, discrepancies between the proposals communicated to our various Heads of Missions. The most important concerns the procedure for the communication of directives to the Governments of the countries concerned. You will see from paragraph 2 of M.1444[1] and from paragraph 2(2) of Le Rougetel's telegram No. 715[5] that in Bulgaria and Roumania we are apparently to be given the right to discuss all matters of importance before directives are issued by the Control Commission, but have no guarantee that the views we express will not be overruled. Gascoigne and the Head of our Military Mission in Hungary are, however, positive

---

[1] See No. 136, note 2.   [2] No. 136.i.
[3] See No. 305, note 2.   [4] No. 197.i.
[5] No. 259.i.   [6] No. 197.ii.

that the communication addressed to the latter provides that directives shall be issued to the Hungarian Government only after *agreement* has been reached with the British and United States Representatives, i.e. that we shall have the right of veto. The second discrepancy is that, while in Roumania and Bulgaria we are to have the right to decide upon the size of the staffs of our Missions, in Hungary this is specifically reserved for the decision of the Chairman of the Control Commission. It appears, however, from paragraph 3 of Gascoigne's telegram No. 231[4] that General Edgcumbe has reached what he considers to be a satisfactory arrangement with Voroshilov.

You will see that the reactions of our Representatives on the spot vary, and that while Gascoigne appears to be fully satisfied, our Representatives in Bulgaria and Roumania—more cynical and disillusioned maybe—are in varying degrees doubtful of the true intentions of the Russians. It certainly seems very probable that the move has been precisely timed to avoid or minimise discussion at Terminal. We think, however, that, while after our past experience some scepticism is certainly justified, there is at the very least nothing to be lost by accepting the Russian offer. The argument in paragraphs 5 and 7 of M.1448[2] does not seem to be valid, since if we express a view in a Control Commission and find it overruled we are not in any way debarred from announcing this fact. In any event, we have never on any previous occasion publicly dissociated ourselves from any action of the Control Commissions, although we have sometimes threatened to do so.

The Delegation will no doubt wish these developments to be discussed with the Americans, but we suggest that as soon as that has been done, the second step is to discuss the matter with the Russians as we had planned in order to discover what their intentions are and to tighten up as far as possible those parts of their proposals which are sufficiently vague to give a loophole for differences of interpretation. The first point to be cleared up with them is whether or not they interpret the communication addressed to our Representatives in Hungary in the same sense as we do, and if they do, to discover why we are asked to accept a materially less advantageous position in Roumania and Bulgaria. The discussions held in Moscow last October do not seem to provide an explanation of this discrepancy, since, although we then agreed to a lower 'percentage' of interest in Roumania, we were given the same 'percentage' for Bulgaria as we were for Hungary.[7] It still seems to us very difficult to believe that the Russians have in fact agreed to genuinely tripartite control of the Hungarian Commission. If it turns out that there is a misunderstanding on this point, then the promise of discussions in the Control Commission before directives are issued clearly fails to meet the requirements set out in the last paragraph of the brief which you took to Terminal,[8] and we would suggest that the Delegation should press, as we proposed, for a much more watertight arrangement for associating our Representatives with decisions affecting British interests.

[7] See No. 185, note 4.   [8] See No. 82, note 4.

On the assumption that it is the Bulgarian and Roumanian proposals which correctly represent the Russian intentions, we should in addition wish to secure further concessions as regards the movement of our Representatives. You will see from telegram from Bulgarian Military Mission of 12th July No. M/1443[1] § 2, that in Bulgaria the Russians have reserved the right to alter the destination or route of projected tours. We could perhaps scarcely object to their retaining some control, but we suggest that, while noting this concession with approval, the Delegation should insist that it is interpreted as putting upon the local Soviet authorities the onus of producing clear and adequate reasons for any alterations. Similarly, even though the Commissioner in Hungary is satisfied with an oral understanding he has reached with Voroshilov about the size of his staff, we think that we should be given just the same right of fixing the number for ourselves as we are now to have in the other two countries. These are small points, but as we all know from our experience of the last nine months such points can give rise to continual argument and irritation unless they are settled by absolutely definite agreement at high level.

We also hope that, while welcoming the conclusion of the long-standing argument about the size of our Mission in Bulgaria, the Delegation will point out that this concession must be accompanied by adequate provision of funds, to which we were entitled under the Armistice. As you know, we are still having difficulty on this point.

These developments will no doubt be regarded by the Americans as a partial success of their policy and make them even more strongly opposed to our proposals for the conclusion of peace treaties. But these developments do not in fact affect the two main questions which are preoccupying us and the Americans respectively, namely, the conclusion of peace treaties and the replacement of the present puppet governments by something more representative; and even if we obtained 100% satisfaction as regards the working of the Control Commissions, we should be no further on in respect of our other requirements. We assume that the Delegation will first wish to discover exactly what concessions we have got or can get from the Russians over the Control Commissions before deciding whether or not to submit our peace proposals. The question really at issue is whether we should make peace treaties with the present Governments of these countries or whether we should refuse to make peace with them until they have Governments with which we are satisfied. If we adopt the first course, our rights in the Control Commissions will cease to have much importance as the Commissions will disappear as soon as peace treaties are signed. If, on the other hand we adopt the second course, the Commissions may continue indefinitely. The Soviet Government will then enjoy the advantages deriving from a military occupation and a political protectorate whereas we and the Americans will continue to be deprived of normal diplomatic relations with these countries. We therefore do not think that these developments need prevent the presentation of our peace proposals in spite of the fact that it looks from your letter to me of 16th July[9] that they will not be supported by the Americans.[10]

Yours ever
(For D. F. Howard)
DUGALD STEWART

CALENDAR TO NO. 316

i   *22 July 1945*   *To Mr. Houstoun-Boswall (Sofia) Tel. No. 717.* Refers to No. 136.i and summarizes No. 316. Even if no improvements can be secured at Terminal, the Soviet proposals are worth a trial [R 11903/23/7].

<hr>

[9] No. 142.i.

[10] With reference to this letter, Mr. Haigh forwarded to Mr. Hayter on 27 July corresponding Russian proposals of 12 July concerning the Control Commission in Finland (cf. No. 136, note 2). Mr. Haigh explained: 'We are anxious that Finland should not be left out of any discussions at Terminal about these proposals, as we are anxious to participate in Finland in any advantages which may be obtained in the Balkans out of discussions with the Russians.'

No. 317

Sir J. Anderson to Mr. Stevenson (Belgrade)

No. 1054 Telegraphic [R 12206/24/92]

Important   FOREIGN OFFICE, *19 July 1945, 5.50 p.m.*

Repeated to Athens No. 1532, Caserta No. 2244, Sofia No. 706, Moscow No. 4019, Washington No. 7618.

My telegram No. 1033[1] (of July 15th: Yugoslav press campaigns on Greek Macedonia, Carinthia and Venezia Giulia.)

Deputy Under-Secretary of State spoke to the Yugoslav Ambassador on July 17th on the lines of my telegram under reference, lamenting, among other things, the fact that Greece and Yugoslavia two of the United Nations who had undergone the same brutal tyranny from the Germans and Italians, should not now be collaborating in the work of rehabilitation. Instead of that the Yugoslav Government were exploiting the Macedonian question in order to carry on violent propaganda against Greece, and were delaying the re-establishment of normal diplomatic relations by the exchange of Ambassadors.

2. M. Leontic dilated on the subject of 20,000 Macedonians who had he said fled from Greece into Yugoslavia, to which Sir O. Sargent replied that if this was the case it was precisely a subject for amicable discussion between

<hr>

[1] No. 157.

763

the two Governments with a view to a return of these victims of the civil war to their homes in Greece. M. Leontic, having declared that the Greek authorities were persecuting the Slav minority in Northern Greece, was reminded that a similar accusation was being made against the Yugoslav authorities in Istria in regard to their treatment of the Italian minority there, but M. Leontic naturally denied this accusation.

3. M. Leontic was also warned of the possible effect on Anglo-Yugoslav relations of the campaign which was being carried on against British military government in Carinthia. M. Leontic alleged that in the local administration in the Slovene districts, our military government had appointed only one Slovene as against eleven Austrians, notwithstanding the fact that the vast majority of the population was Slovene. But for the most part M. Leontic preferred to evade the issue by discussing the injustice of the plebiscite held in Klagenfurt after the last war.[2] Sir O. Sargent denied his facts.

4. M. Leontic protested that Yugoslavia had no territorial ambitions, not even as regards Greek Macedonia. He regretted that Yugoslavia was so misunderstood in this country, where she was looked upon as being entirely Communist. In any case, how could she be Communist and Chauvinist in the same breath? Sir O. Sargent said that he did not see that one necessarily excluded the other. Anyhow the extent to which Yugoslavia was Communist would become more apparent after we had seen in the autumn how the elections were held and what result they produced.

5. M. Leontic undertook to report the conversation to his Government. Sir O. Sargent had previously explained to him that you had been instructed to speak in the same sense to Marshal Tito, and that the Secretary of State would have liked to have spoken to M. Leontic himself if he had had the time before leaving for Berlin.[3]

CALENDAR TO No. 317

i *18 & 20 July 1945* Mr. Stevenson *(Belgrade)* Tel. *No. 1139 & Despatch No. 174.* Representations by Yugoslav Govt. against alleged terrorisation of Slavs in Greek Macedonia [R 12207, 12958/3549/19].

[2] For this plebiscite of 10 October 1920 cf. *D.B.F.P.*, First Series, vol. xii, No. 248 *et passim.*

[3] Copies of this telegram and No. 157 were enclosed in a letter of 19 July from Mr. Howard to Mr. Hayter at Berlin. Mr. Howard wrote: 'Sargent would like you to suggest to the Secretary of State that he should himself speak to Molotov using some of the arguments in our telegram No. 1033 to Belgrade.' Sir A. Cadogan and Mr. Eden minuted as follows: 'Things have already been said, along these lines, at the Conference here. We might take any further opportunity that offers, but I don't think we need seek it out. A. C. July 21, 1945.' 'I should like to know how Mr. Stevenson has fared. I think we should ask him to repeat here his account of interview with Tito. A. E. July 22': see No. 335.

No. 318

Mr. Hankey (Warsaw) to Mr. Eden (Received 19 July, 9.20 p.m.)
No. 24 Telegraphic [N 8959/6/55]

Top Secret   WARSAW, *19 July 1945, 6.47 p.m.*

I had a conversation with M. Grabski yesterday. He is unkempt and rather deaf but being a professor with 40 years experience he has contacts all over Poland, and he seemed to know what was going on.

2. M. Grabski said the present situation was thoroughly unsatisfactory. There were no civic liberties. The press was entirely controlled by security authorities. Many Voivods (provincial Governors) had a Russian adviser behind the scenes and had to accept his advice. The security police (often called Polish N.K.V.D. and undoubtedly under Russian control) was still arresting people though the situation was improving. There was not much freedom of political activity as the difficulties of M. Popiel showed (see my telegram No. 23[i]). All this was done under cover of a state of siege. Now the war was done there was no further excuse for the state of siege and it was highly unpopular. He knew the people were getting tired of Obber [Osobka]-Morawski, the present Polish Prime Minister. At a recent meeting in Warsaw he himself had received five times as many cheers as the Prime Minister and M. Mikolajczyk 25 times as many. More significant still at the march past of P.P.R. some of them even shouted for Mikolajczyk. The P.P.R. were recruited largely from people who could otherwise get no bread.

3. M. Grabski said the essential thing was to ensure free and unfettered elections. But this would only happen if Great Britain and America insisted upon it. In his opinion His Majesty's Government must not allow the Polish armed forces to return unless it was absolutely clear that the constitutional liberties could be restored. This was the only hope.

4. M. Grabski told me that he had a difficult time in Praesidium where he was in a minority of 1 to 5. His deafness must make it even harder.

5. He told me that a proposal is on foot for a general amnesty to get numerous armed bands out of the forests and to encourage the armed forces overseas to return. The Communists were, however, trying to exclude all leaders of the Home Army as well as those in London responsible for their activities. Such a restriction would defeat the purposes of the amnesty.

6. M. Grabski said that when he was in South Poland recently he saw within 50 miles of Krakow at least 15 large convoys of Russian troops moving eastward taking with them considerable numbers of cattle and horses. The Russians insisted that the livestock was German but he could certify from his own knowledge of agriculture that they were types of cattle and horses found not in Germany but in Poland. Incidentally stories of looting by undisciplined Russian soldiery and displaced persons moving east reach me independently from Poznanic [*sic*] as well as from the south. M. Grabski insisted that the withdrawal of Russian troops was imperative.

No. 319

Memorandum by Sir O. Sargent[1]

[*N 8746/211/55*]

FOREIGN OFFICE, *19 July 1945*

Sir A. Clark Kerr's telegrams, Target Nos. 45 to 51 [i].

I have the following comments on certain points in these telegrams, taken *seriatim*.

(*a*) *Target No. 46* [i] *paragraph 2.* I cannot help thinking that it is most important for M. Mikolajczyk at the present time to stay in Poland, consolidate his position there, set the Present [Peasant] Party on its feet and give a lead to the other Ministers imported into the new Polish Government. It is perhaps a little surprising that M. Mikolajczyk is being allowed, apparently, so much latitude to do this; he should surely make the most of the opportunity and attempt to build up so strong a position as soon as possible that if his opponents were tempted to try to clip his wings popular clamour throughout the country would prevent them doing so. The original proposal for a visit from M. Mikolajczyk and M. Gomulka was made in connexion with the transfer to the new Government of the affairs of the old Government. But the Polish Provisional Government have appointed their commission for this purpose and it is becoming pretty clear that negotiations with them will be lengthy and detailed. There is no practical need for M. Mikolajczyk and M. Gomulka to come for this purpose. M. Mikolajczyk could no doubt do good work in persuading Poles here to go back and M. Gomulka might benefit from direct contact with us. But I do not feel quite sure that Sir A. Clark Kerr may not have pressed the proposal for the visit too strongly upon M. Mikolajczyk and I think it would be wise to tell Mr. Hankey to say to M. Mikolajczyk that we should not at all wish to urge him to come in the immediate future, if he feels that his time could better be spent in consolidating his position inside the country.

(*b*) *Target No. 47* [i] *paragraph 5.* It is interesting to learn that M. Mikolajczyk thinks that the bulk of the Red Army will be withdrawn within the next two months and that the NKVD will go with them. It would be

---

[1] This memorandum was addressed to Mr. Eden.

interesting to have more details about this, about the reasons for M. Mikolajczyk's optimism as regards the departure of the NKVD and the specific points which are to be left in Russian occupation. If Sir A. Clark Kerr cannot provide more information, we could ask Mr. Hankey to enquire of M. Mikolajczyk.

(c) *Target No. 47 paragraphs 6 and 7.* These are on the whole encouraging. It will be noted that M. Popiel has apparently been allowed to revive the Christian Labour Party—presumably as a Party—and to issue a manifesto. Or perhaps this has not been done with the sanction of the Polish Government, but they are merely not interfering at present. It would be interesting to know from Sir A. Clark Kerr which of these alternatives is the case.

(d) *Target No. 47 paragraph 8.* It is interesting to notice that the Communist element in Poland is, as in other Soviet controlled countries, thinking that they stand to gain by delaying elections. M. Ripka, who is here on a short visit, tells me the same is true in Czechoslovakia. In that case, he said, the reason was that the Communists hoped that the deplorable impression made by the Russian armies would in time be forgotten. It may also be that the Communists think they stand to gain from the deplorable conditions and distress likely to be prevalent next winter.

We should note that M. Mikolajczyk is anxious to get as many Poles from the West as possible back to Poland before Christmas. It should be observed that M. Mikolajczyk talks of the Government as though he were Leader of the Opposition.

(e) *Target No. 47 paragraph 9.* It is for consideration whether the effect upon the food situation of Europe of the presence of the very large Russian armies in the granary of Europe should not be taken up by ourselves and the Americans at Terminal. I am submitting you a separate minute on this point.[2]

(f) *Target No. 47 paragraph 10.* We are consulting the Treasury and the Board of Trade; it may be that it will be useful at an early stage for the Poles to send people here to discuss trade etc., but we certainly should not open such discussions until at least the basis of our discussions with the Polish Government's Commission regarding Polish Government property etc. are agreed.

(g) *Target No. 48* [i]. It is very satisfactory to learn that the Ministry of Posts and Telegraphs, offered to M. Thugutt, has gone to one of Mikolajczyk's men and that the Communists made no difficulty about honouring their understanding on this matter.

(h) *Target No. 49* [i].

Para. 1. (a) It is strange that neither the Prime Minister nor the Minister for Foreign Affairs know much about the basis of discussions with the Polish Government's Commission here which we have suggested to Warsaw. One would have thought that it was a most important question for the Warsaw Government. Combined with the action of the Soviet

---

[2] No such minute has been traced in Foreign Office archives: see, however, No. 367.

Delegation at Terminal in raising the question of the liquidation of the London Government etc. it looks as if the Warsaw Government with Russian help hope to evade our proposals and this is to some extent borne out by the Warsaw Government's attempt to send here a further party of officials, before replying about the basis of discussions. It is significant that this party contains three persons concerned with the Merchant Marine and the prospective Military Attaché.

(b) Something has gone wrong with the first sentence.[3] Perhaps Sir A. Clark Kerr can elucidate. I propose to instruct Mr. Hankey to press the Polish Government for a clearer and more satisfactory statement on this matter.

(c) We should not let the Polish Prime Minister get away with the suggestion that supplies are being dropped to Polish dissidents by General Anders. Mr. Hankey will be instructed to inform the Prime Minister that this matter has been thoroughly looked into and there is no question of supplies being sent by General Anders or anybody else.

Para. 2. (a) The proposal that the Warsaw Government should send a Mission to discuss the return to Poland of Polish merchant shipping under our control needs further consideration. The Ministry of War Transport say that if the Warsaw Government were reasonable and were ready to join U[nited] M[aritime] A[uthority], they would not necessarily be unwilling to terminate our charters and let the Polish shipping go back. If Warsaw sent a Mission consisting of reasonable people, it might help with the Polish merchant seamen who are at present causing considerable difficulty. The Treasury, however, are naturally anxious, pending discussions with the Warsaw Government regarding their acknowledgement of the financial obligations towards us of the old Polish Government and security for them, not to release any potential assets in our hands. It would in any case be premature to start discussions on the question of shipping before we had started discussions with the main Warsaw Commission on the question of their taking over Polish property in this country.

(b) We have not yet been able to discuss the problem of Polish prisoners of war and displaced persons with the Americans and other British authorities concerned. We have only just succeeded in getting a general picture of SHAEF's treatment of them and the matter is further complicated by the breaking up of SHAEF, although it appears that displaced persons are still being dealt with by a joint American–British organisation. We cannot however agree to the Polish Mission going to Germany until the whole of this problem has been thoroughly examined.

(i) *Target No. 50* [i]. We had understood from various sources that M. Strasburger was being offered the London Embassy. This would be much more satisfactory than M. Kot, who would be little less than disastrous.

---

[3] 'The Polish Government's request for an amnesty for Poles now in Polish military prisons': cf. No. 513.ii.

It is most unfortunate that M. Mikolajczyk continues to place confidence in M. Kot. Mr. Hankey was requested before his departure to drop M. Mikolajczyk a broad hint that we should not want M. Kot, but I suggest that the Secretary of State should instruct Mr. Hankey to inform M. Mikolajczyk privately but definitely.[4]

(*j*) *Target No. 51* [i]. This is more or less in line with what we had understood from the Polish Government's previous statements. It might be worse.

O. G. SARGENT

CALENDARS TO No. 319

i *16 July 1945 Sir A. Clark Kerr (Berlin) Tels. Nos. 45–51 Target.* Reports his conversations with Polish Ministers in Warsaw on 12–14 July: assurances from M. Bierut on 12 July (No. 46 Target) of his desire for good Anglo-Polish relations, and of 'Poland's intention to do all she could to maintain her former contacts with the West' and to ask soon for British economic help; cautious optimism from M. Mikolajczyk on 13 July (No. 47 Target) for Polish recovery from present 'state of chaos': discussion with M. Osobka-Morawski on 13 July (No. 49 Target) on Polish Commission in London, amnesties for Polish prisoners, etc. Assurances from M. Osobka-Morawski (No. 51 Target) concerning political conditions for forthcoming Polish elections [N 8746–52/211/55].

ii *17–18 July 1945 From and to Mr. Hankey (Warsaw) Tels. Nos. 8–9, 13–14, & 10.* Proposed Polish Commission should not proceed to London for discussion on assets until agreement secured on basis for discussion stipulated in No. 41 [N 8689, 8852/1938/55].

iii *11 & 19 July 1945 (a) to Sir A. Clark Kerr (Moscow) Tel. No. 3884. (b) To Mr. Hankey (Warsaw) Tel. No. 14.* In regard to refuting stories about continued British assistance for Polish underground movement, Air Ministry confirm no flights have been made from Italy to Poland under British auspices since 28 December 1944 and that at no time were British aircraft sent to any part of Poland not occupied by Germany [N 8293/6/55].

[4] Sir O. Sargent here added a marginal note: 'M. Mikolajczyk has since told Mr. Hankey that M. Strasburger, who had been summoned to Warsaw, is to be appointed Ambassador to London. This would be in every way an admirable appointment. O.G.S.' Cf. No. 293.ii.

No. 320

Mr. Hankey (Warsaw) to Mr. Eden (Received 19 July, 11.17 p.m.)
No. 25 Telegraphic [N 8878/6/55]

Immediate   WARSAW, *19 July 1945, 9.12 p.m. G.M.T.*

It is officially confirmed that Polish authorities have taken over Stettin.[1]

2. French Ambassador who has just been in East Prussia confirms that

[1] In Warsaw telegram No. 63 of 29 July 1945 Mr. Hankey further conveyed a report confirming 'that the main part of Stettin on West bank of the Oder is now controlled by Polish civil authorities. The naval dockyard forms a Russian enclave.'

German population has already been largely removed and saw further parties along the road with their belongings.

3. No one here has yet mentioned (. . . ? Western)[2] frontier to me (though many have mentioned Lwow) and pending Berlin decisions I have felt it (. . . ? wise)er[2] not to raise subject myself unless instructed to. Meanwhile Polish Government is conducting a press and poster campaign to persuade people of agricultural and . . . al,[2] merits of Pomerania and Silesia and general tendency is to treat the whole question of western frontier as settled. I find it hard therefore not to agree with last sentence of paragraph 3 of Moscow telegram repeated to me as your telegram No. 4.[3]

4. Whatever is decided at Terminal, may I express the hope that largest possible percentage of that part of Eastern Germany which will in any case become Polish (e.g. Danzig Allenstein etc.,) may be transferred definitely as soon as possible.

Please pass to Moscow as my telegram No. 2 and to Terminal.

[2] The text is here uncertain.
[3] Repetition to Warsaw of No. 155.

No. 321

Mr. Roberts (Moscow) to Mr. Eden (Received 19 July, 11.30 a.m.)
No. 3205 Telegraphic [N 8934/158/30]

Secret   MOSCOW, *19 July 1945, 9.3 a.m. G.M.T.*

Norwegian Counsellor told me yesterday[1] in strict confidence that in reply to a request for Soviet concurrence in the establishment of Norwegian wireless station at Kirkeness for communication with Oslo, Peoples Commissariat for Foreign Affairs had stated that the Soviet military authorities had no objection provided that only Norwegian and no British military personnel operated the station.

Please repeat to Oslo.

[1] This telegram was drafted on 18 July 1945.

No. 322

Mr. Duff Cooper (Paris) to Mr. Eden (Received 19 July, 2.45 p.m.)
No. 1005 Telegraphic [U 5818/19/70]

Immediate. Top secret   PARIS, *19 July 1945*[1]

I understand from SHAEF Mission that the Russians have offered to supply the French with 200 Yaks[2] free of charge and are offering also to

[1] The time of despatch is not recorded.
[2] Russian fighter-aircraft designed by M. A. S. Yakovlev.

supply them with equipment. The Air Minister, a Communist, urges acceptance of offer but Air Staff are opposed to doing so on the ground that machines are inferior to British and American ones. The Air Minister on the other hand points out delays and disappointments which have occurred in deliveries from the United Kingdom and I am assured in this respect he has strong case.

Can the Air Ministry do anything to expedite matters in order to prevent French Air Force from falling completely into the hands of the Soviet?

No. 323

Sir J. Anderson to Sir R. Bullard (Tehran)
No. 434 Telegraphic [E 5045/20/34]

FOREIGN OFFICE, *19 July 1945, 6.20 p.m.*

Repeated to Moscow No. 4001, Government of India, M.E. Min's Office No. 99 Saving, Bagdad No. 43 Saving (for P.A.I.C.), Washington No. 673 Saving.

Your telegram No. 691[1] (of 11th July: Soviet interference in Persian affairs).

We have spoken to representatives of the *Observer* and *Economist*. As a result one item has already appeared in the *Observer* and we hope that an article will shortly appear in the *Economist*. At our suggestion, *Daily Mail* are sending a man to Tehran forthwith (see my telegram No. 425).[2] We have also spoken to the new *Times* correspondent for the Middle East, who is expected to arrive in the Middle East next month. We have urged him to visit Tehran as soon as possible.

2. It would be helpful if the United States Ambassador could secure the visit to Tehran of some responsible American journalists.

3. You may also like to consider the possibility of suggesting to the Government of India that they should secure the despatch to Tehran of a representative of some reputable Indian paper.

4. Perhaps you could bring home to the Persian Minister for Foreign Affairs the need for the Persian Government to do something themselves to publicise their own case. We suggest that they should try to use their missions for putting out, especially in this country and in the United States of America, their own version of what is happening in Persia. It should not be beyond the powers of a Persian mission abroad to explain to local journalists that the Persian Government are having considerable administrative difficulties owing to the obstructive tactics of the parliamentary minority which alone of Persian parties appears able to secure the reporting of its views in the Moscow press and wireless.

[1] No. 91.
[2] Not printed.

i *19 July 1945 To Sir R. Bullard (Tehran) Tel. No. 17 Saving:* conversation of 17 July between Sir R. Campbell and M. Taqizadeh, Iranian Ambassador in London. Iranian anxieties in regard to 'violent Russian press campaign' and to tense situation in Iran [E 5303/20/34].

No. 324

Sir J. Anderson to Sir H. Seymour[1] *(Chungking)*
No. 769 Telegraphic [F 4283/186/10]

Secret   FOREIGN OFFICE, *19 July 1945, 3.15 p.m.*

Repeated to Moscow No. 4010.

Chinese Ambassador on 13th July expressed great uneasiness to Secretary of State[2] about Soong's talks with Soviet Government in Moscow.

2. Secretary of State replied in the negative to question whether Soviet Government had asked His Majesty's Government for any concessions in the Far East. The Ambassador said that China might be prepared to give Russia trade facilities at some port such as Port Arthur but could not give her naval bases.[3]

i *21–2 July 1945 Sir H. Seymour (Chungking) Tels. Nos. 719–20.* Principal points to be raised by Dr. Soong on forthcoming visit to London include revival of scheme for a loan based on 1944 credit, and political relations: 'He thinks British and Chinese interests in general coincide and would like to explore ground with a view to closer understanding between the two countries' [F 4457/186/10].

[1] H.M. Ambassador to China.
[2] This conversation had been briefly reported in F.O. despatch No. 456 of 13 July 1945 to Chungking, not printed.
[3] In Chungking telegram No. 718 of 12.36 p.m. G.M.T. on 21 July (received 2.15 p.m. that day) Sir H. Seymour reported: 'In conversation on July 20th Dr. Soong appeared hopeful in regard to the Moscow conversations. He thought that if all went well he might leave for Moscow about July 29th. He said that the Chinese at any rate now knew the Russian desiderata, and observed that he believed that it was possible in dealing with the Russians to take a firm stand on one's own undoubted rights.'

No. 325

Mr. Eden (Berlin) to Sir J. Anderson (Received 19 July, 3.8 p.m.)
No. 95 Target Telegraphic [F.O. 934/3/14(1b)]

Immediate   BERLIN, *19 July 1945, 5.11 p.m.*

Please pass following immediate to Washington from Private Secretary.

Foreign Office telegram No. 7570[1] of 17th July, repeated to Terminal No. 51 Onward.

Secretary of State does not want any action taken on telegram under reference until you hear further from him. If action has been taken please cancel it.

[1] No. 304.

No. 326

Sir J. Anderson to Mr. Roberts (Moscow)
No. 4012 Telegraphic [F 4443/1057/23]

Immediate. Top Secret   FOREIGN OFFICE, *19 July 1945, 2.10 p.m.*

Repeated to Terminal unnumbered (for Foulds from Sterndale Bennett).

. . .[1] at the instance of the Japanese Government Hirota, former Premier and Ambassador at Moscow, has recently held conversations with Malik, the Soviet Ambassador to Japan in an attempt to sound out the views of the Soviet Government on the war in the Far East and also to come to some understanding for future relations between Japan and Russia.

2. These conversations have been in progress spasmodically throughout the month of June and Malik, after consultation with his Government, has made it clear that any proposal for closer relations between the two countries after the expiration of the Neutrality Pact[2] in April next must originate from the Japanese side who must make concrete proposals for the settlement of outstanding questions.

3. As a result of these conversations Hirota on June 29th put specific proposals to Malik. These were (a) an agreement for mutual assistance and non-ag[g]ression, (b) 'neutrality' of Manchuria, (c) cancellation of Japanese fishing rights in Northern waters in exchange for supplies of oil from Russia, (d) discussion of any other question which Russia might wish to raise. The Japanese Ambassador in Moscow was instructed to seek an interview with Molotov before the latter went to Berlin in order to support Hirota's proposals and to expedite a Russian reply. Sato grudgingly agreed to act accordingly while pointing out that the proposals were completely at variance with present world trends and that there was no reason why Russia, who had only recently abrogated the Neutrality Pact, should wish to make a new pact with Japan.

4. . . .[1] the Japanese Government have resolved to send Prince Konoye, former Premier and an elder statesman close to the Throne, on a special mission to Moscow to convey a message from the Emperor to Marshal

[1] A confidential reference is here omitted.

[2] The Treaty of Neutrality between Japan and the U.S.S.R., with Declaration regarding Mongolia and Manchukuo, signed at Moscow on 13 April 1941 for a period of five years, is printed in *B.F.S.P.*, vol. 144, pp. 839–40.

Stalin and President Kalinin. This message is to the effect that so long as Great Britain and America insist on unconditional surrender, Japan has no alternative but to fight to the end; but that the Emperor is grieved at the continued loss of life to both sides in the war in the Far East and that his dearest desire is to see peace restored. Sato is understood to have communicated the substance of this message to the Soviet on July 13th and to have asked for their concurrence in the despatch of the Mission[3] . . .[1]

[3] See No. 173, note 2.

No. 327

Letter from Viscount Cranborne to the South African High Commissioner in London[1]

No. WR 207/1/13 [U5583/50/70]

Top secret   DOMINIONS OFFICE, *19 July 1945*

My dear High Commissioner,

Emrys Evans has shown me your letter of 9th July[2] regarding the future status and disposal of the Italian territories in Africa.

2. His Majesty's Government in the United Kingdom are glad to learn from your letters that the Union Government agree in principle to the cession *pro tempore*[3] of Italian colonies to the Four Powers. As regards the Union Government request that they should be formally consulted by the four Great Powers before any final decision is reached we have been considering how best to meet the Union Government's wishes. On present information, we do not expect that this will come up in any detailed form at the present Berlin meeting. But, should matters progress faster than at present seems likely, we will endeavour to get put on record at Berlin an agreement between the three Powers that the United Kingdom Government would, on behalf of the other Powers, as well as on their own behalf, consult the Union Government regarding the future of Italian territories in Africa.

Yours sincerely,

CRANBORNE

[1] A copy of this letter was received in the Foreign Office on 20 July 1945.
[2] See No. 118, note 9.
[3] For the time being.

No. 328

Minute by Mr. Scott Fox

[U 5801/16/73]

FOREIGN OFFICE, *19 July 1945*

At the discussions which have been taking place for the past three weeks between the Attorney General and the U.S., French and Soviet representatives about the establishment of an Inter-Allied Tribunal for the trial of major German war criminals and organisations, it has become increasingly clear that the other 3 Delegations are proposing to include in these trials a much larger number of defendants than was contemplated when the matter was discussed in the Foreign Office.

So far the question of defendants has only come up incidently [*sic*] in the discussions. The Americans objected to a proposal that the 4 prosecutors should act only by a majority vote. Judge Jackson, the American representative, said that the Americans had in their custody some 350 Germans whom they wished to try before the Inter-Allied Tribunal and that they would be reluctant to agree to any provisions whereby the representatives of the other powers could prevent them bringing these Germans before the Tribunal. Sir T. Barnes[1], in a private conversation after the meeting, tackled Judge Jackson on the 350 figure; he explained that this figure was really that of the list supplied by the U.S. J[udge] A[dvocate] G[eneral] and that not all of these would in fact be tried.

The Attorney General in his anxiety to reconcile the American view that the parties to the agreement should not be bound by the majority rule referred to by Judge Jackson above and the Soviet insistance that the prosecutors of the 4 powers must in all circumstances act as a body if the whole basis of the proposed agreement was not to be undermined, said at yesterday's meeting that his view was that he would prefer to see provision made for the inclusion rather than the exclusion of defendants in any disputed cases.

There is little doubt that the Americans hold more of the major criminals than the other 3 powers but on the bases of the American figure it would be difficult to keep down the number of defendants for the Inter-Allied trials to below the figure of say 500 or 600. (In addition it is proposed that the trial should be open to any member of the German organisations like the S.S. and Gestapo, who might be disposed to appear to contest the announced intention of the court to convict those organisations of criminal conspiracy.) This figure appears to be acceptable to the French and Soviet representatives. For instance, the latter, in agreeing to the first trial taking place at Nuremberg pointed out that agreement was to last for one year and that in view of the number of defendants involved a number of subsequent trials would have to take place, probably in different localities, at the discretion of the Tribunal. And the French representative said that his Govt. had several hundred 'economic' criminals whom they wanted to bring before the Tribunal.

I have discussed the position with Sir Basil Newton.[2] There is no doubt that such a large number of defendants will mean two things. Firstly, that persons will be included against whom it will be difficult to prove a satis-

[1] H.M. Procurator-General and Treasury Solicitor.
[2] Sir Basil Newton was superintending the War Crimes Section of the German Department of the Foreign Office.

factory case—in the eyes of history at least. Secondly, that the trials will be unduly protracted. Sir Basil Newton considers that it would be preferable to confine the Inter-Allied trial to a very small list of defendants about whose guilt there can be no doubt, and about whom the Four Powers are in full agreement. These would be outstanding figures. This list might be on the lines of the 10 or 12 names proposed for the first trial (Göring, Hess, Ribbentrop, Ley, Keital [sic], Kaltenbrunner, Rosenberg, Hans Frank, Frick and Streicher; and possibly Von Schirach and Sauckel[3]). The remaining suggested defendants could be tried subsequently by any of the Four Powers concerned in their *National* courts in the same way as Germans guilty of specific war crimes are tried. This might incidentally suit the Americans who, brought up against the problem of reconciling United States with continental procedure, have been showing a tendency to regret their own suggestion of an Inter-Allied trial, & might welcome the suggestion to try the bulk of the criminals in their hands independently and in their own way.

One difficulty about this suggestion is that the other three Powers are anxious to include all the Germans in question in the Inter-Allied trails [trials] because they consider that, as these persons cannot be accused of specific war crimes, they could only be convicted under the general charge of conspiracy which is to form the basis for the indictment for the trials before the Inter-Allied Tribunal. These Germans would evidently include a large number of representatives of German economic life, about whose guilt of any hitherto accepted crime we are far less confident than the other three powers appear to be and also presumably a number of those in the 'intermediate' category mentioned in paragraph 23 of my minute in U 4958.[4] However, provided the main conspiracy charge, including the economic aspect, is proved at the Inter-Allied trial, it would probably be possible to base the subsequent proceedings at the National courts on the results of that trial in the same way as it is proposed to convict members of the S.S. and Gestapo in the National courts for their membership of the organisations which will have been declared criminal by the Inter-Allied court. None the less it would I think be difficult to persuade our Allies not to include any representative of German economic life in the Inter-Allied trial, not only because they feel very strongly about the guilt of Schacht[5] at least, but also because it would probably prove difficult for the Prosecutors to make out a good case before the Inter-Allied Tribunal as regards the criminal character of German economic activities unless there was an actual representative of these activities before the court. In this connection

[3] Obergruppenführer Baldur von Schirach, formerly leader of the Hitler Youth, had been Gauleiter and Reichsstatthalter of Vienna. Obergruppenführer Fritz Sauckel, Gauleiter and Reichsstatthalter of Thuringia, had been Plenipotentiary-General for the Employment of Labour.

[4] Of 19 June 1945, not printed.

[5] Dr Hjalmar Schacht had been President of the Reichsbank and Minister without Portfolio.

it should be noted that the Soviet representatives have from the first been reluctant to try the S.S. and Gestapo as criminal organisations[6] on the grounds that the function of the Inter-Allied court is to try only the persons of the major criminals.

Another difficulty which would have to be got round is that the Russians have only been persuaded to accept Nuremberg as the place for the first trial on condition that subsequent trials before the Inter-Allied Tribunal should take place elsewhere in accordance with whatever decision is reached by the Tribunal's headquarters which is to be established at Berlin. If there is to be only one trial by the Tribunal they will doubtless press very hard for it to take place at Berlin or elsewhere in the Soviet zone. In the last resort it seems to me that we might suggest a compromise whereby each Prosecutor should bring *independent* prosecutions at subsequent Inter-Allied trials. In that case the court would remain an Inter-Allied body but each Power could name their own defendants and frame their own cases against those defendants on their own responsibility.

I believe that the Attorney General is proposing to the other three representatives a formula to reconcile the United States-Soviet difference referred to above, whereby any German would on the proposition of any one of the four Powers be tried by the Tribunal, unless all the other three Powers were opposed to it. If, therefore, we are not to risk finding ourselves in the position of having encouraged a big extension of the list of defendants, it is important to advise him of the Foreign Office views without delay.[7]

D. Scott Fox

[6] The preceding part of this sentence was sidelined on the original.

[7] This paragraph was sidelined on the original. Sir B. Newton minuted below: 'I agree generally. It seems to me important that at any rate the first big trial should be above reproach. It follows (*a*) that there must be no suggestion of trying individuals for offences (notably economic offences) which were not crimes when they were committed. Condemnation for such offences would shake public confidence in the new International Court now and create a precedent for grave injustices in the future. (*b*) the first trial at least should be limited to a few leaders about whose authority and responsibility there would be no shadow of doubt. Whereas we have in mind a list of about a dozen, we have reason to fear that the United States are working on a list of 300 or more, the French 400 or 500, and the Russians, although they have not yet defined their attitude, have indicated that they expect that large numbers will be tried by the Tribunal. As explained in the last para. of Mr. Scott Fox's minute, we are proposing to allow any of the four Powers to include whoever they want in the list of defendants for the Inter-Allied trials provided they can find one other Power to support them. This seems a risky procedure. Whilst the above is being considered I took the opportunity this morning to mention our misgivings to the Attorney General & also to the Treasury Solicitor, & finally also to Sir John Anderson— see further minute & note attached. B. N. 20th July 1945.'

'At a very brief interview this morning with the Chancellor before he saw the Attorney General I explained that, while it was very important that the present international discussions should succeed, I had certain misgivings that the trials might be unduly enlarged, particularly by the inclusion of economic offences. I left with the Chancellor a copy of the attached note [annex below] in which I have tried to sum up the essence of what I had in mind. I had previously explained these views at greater length to the Attorney General

*Copy of note left with Sir John Anderson before his interview with
the A[ttorney] G[eneral] this morning*

B.N. 20/7/[45]

The first big trial must be above any reproach.
It follows

(*a*) there must be no suggestion of trying individuals for offences (notably
economic offences) which were not crimes when they were committed.
Condemnation for such offences would shake public confidence in the new
International Court now and create a precedent for grave injustices in the future.

(*b*) the first trial at least should be limited to a few leaders about whose
authority and responsibility there would be no shadow of doubt. It is suggested
therefore that at any rate in this trial no one should be included unless there is
unanimity amongst the four Powers, or at least three to one in favour.

CALENDARS TO No. 328

i *24 & 26 July 1945   Notes of meeting between representatives of U.N. War Crimes Commission and of Central Register of War Criminals and Security Suspects (CROWCASS);
Record by Mr. G. W. Shaw (F.O. Research Dept.) of his conversation with Czechoslovak
representative on U.N. War Crimes Commission* [U 6171/29/73; N 9534/6453/12].

himself, and also separately to the Treasury Solicitor, Sir Thomas Barnes.   B. N. 20th July
1945.'
'[To] Mr. Troutbeck, Sir O. Sargent. I hope you will agree with this action which had
to be taken at short notice. The position is explained in detail in the attached typed minute
[No. 328] of the 19th July by Mr. Scott Fox. B. N. 20/7.'
'Sir B. Newton's note is in accordance with the views all along expressed by the German
Department. My only fear is that the pass has already been sold. I understood that we had
agreed to a general charge—including such things as preparing a war of aggression and
entering into a common plan to dominate Europe—which could not possibly be regarded
as having in any hitherto accepted legal sense been crimes when they were committed.
I thought the whole purpose of the proposal was to create a new international law, which
must obviously involve trying people for things which were not crimes at the time, however
morally offensive they may have been. If Sir B. Newton's view is accepted, it seems to
mean going back to the Moscow conception when the whole emphasis was laid on the
atrocity aspect. I should personally welcome this, though I imagine it would mean reversing
the work of many months. It would also mean letting out of the net not only the Schachts
but also the S.S., Gestapo, etc., except in so far as any particular individual in those bodies
could be found guilty of a war crime in the hitherto accepted sense of the term. For many
of them there would be insufficient evidence. The same would apply to the General Staff,
though I am not clear that it was in fact ever the intention to name it as one of the bodies
guilty of criminal conspiracy, despite its having been the master planner.   J. M. Troutbeck
20th July, 1945.' 'O. G. Sargent July 21.'
Sir B. Newton noted in the margin of the third sentence of Mr. Troutbeck's minute
above: 'I hope the charge will have also to include responsibility for actual crimes or
offences ag[ain]st existing treaties. B. N.' Sir B. Newton noted in the margin of the last
sentence of Mr. Troutbeck's minute: 'The inclusion of the General Staff is still undecided,
but the U.K. delegation have suggested Keitel. B. N.'

No. 329

Mr. Roberts (Moscow) to Mr. Eden (Received 20 July, 3.42 p.m.)
No. 3211 Telegraphic [C 4194/24/18]

MOSCOW, *20 July 1945, 1.25 p.m. G.M.T.*

Repeated to Washington.

My telegram 3199[1].

Areas of Soviet military administration in Germany as published in Soviet press of July 11th (see my telegram 3102)[1] were as follows:

(*a*) Micklenburg [*sic*] and Western Pomerania excluding Stettin;

(*b*) Brandenburg including part of Frankfurt district with City of Kottbus;

(*c*) Saxony Province, including Anhalt;

(*d*) Thuringia;

(*e*) Saxony State including Western part of Lizegnitz [Liegnitz] Province in Silesia.

2. This announcement passes over in silence the arrangements for all territory east of the Oder and Western Neisse, and for Stettin it may be possible to find out at Terminal, extent of Soviet supervisory control of these areas.

Please pass to Terminal[2] and Warsaw.

[1] Not printed.

[2] Mr. Allen minuted on 21 July 1945 on the copy of this telegram repeated to Berlin as No. 111 Onward of 20 July: 'This appears to confirm what the Russians have told us about their support of Polish claims. D. A. 21/7.'

No. 330

Mr. Steel (Lübbecke) to Mr. Eden (Received 20 July, 10 p.m.)
No. 60 Telegraphic [F.O. 934/5/40(3)]

Immediate   LÜBBECKE, *20 July 1945, 8.2 p.m. G.M.T.*

Repeated to Copenhagen.

Following from Steel.

My immediately preceding telegram [i].

Military Government have now referred to me a further request by the Danish Government for permission to send a Danish subject to Flensborg to take over the job of general secretary to Danish minority movement in

779

south Schleswig. I consider this request should be refused. There is no reason why Danish minority in south Schleswig should not have an organisation to look after its interests but staff of this organisation must surely be found from amongst members of Danish minority. If we were to agree that a Dane from Denmark could be imported for this job we should be conniving at an almost Hitlerite[1] manoeuvre by the Danish Government to organise minority movement from Copenhagen for their own political ends.[2]

Foreign Office please repeat immediately to Copenhagen, as my telegram No. 6.

CALENDARS TO No. 330

i *20 July 1945 Mr. Steel (Lübbecke) Tel. No. 59.* Reasons for view of 21st Army Group that proposed visit by M. Möller to Flensborg (cf. No. 310) is undesirable. Danish minority in South Schleswig are showing great activity. However, military authorities are prepared to agree to another request by M. Möller to visit his son's grave there. Berlin Tel. No. 158 Target of 22 July informed the Foreign Office: 'Secretary of State considers that we should certainly agree to M. Möller's request' [F.O. 934/5/40(3)].

ii *20–21–July 1945 Mr. Randall (Copenhagen) Tels. Nos. 366, 369, 374.* Possible repercussions of M. Möller's proposed visit to Flensborg, but strong arguments in favour [N 8964, 8971, 8996/1866/15].

[1] Mr. Eden put a question mark in the margin against this word.

[2] Mr. Eden in Berlin minuted to Sir A. Cadogan on this telegram with reference to it and to No. 330.i: 'Doesn't Steel seem rather anti-Dane in these telegrams? A. E.' On 22 July 1945 Mr. D. Allen referred Mr. Eden's minute to Mr. Warner at the Foreign Office for his views. In reply Mr. Warner on 24 July forwarded a copy of No. 374 as helping 'to explain the attitude to this question of the Commander in Chief, Germany. It will also explain why, for the time being at least, we could not allow a Dane to be sent from Denmark to act as General Secretary to the Danish Minority.'

No. 331

Earl of Halifax (Washington) to Mr. Eden (Received 20 July, 3.55 p.m.)

No. 5051 Telegraphic [Z 8584/103/17]

WASHINGTON, *20 July 1945, 10.3 a.m.*

Your telegram No. 6831.[1]

From various discussions which members of my staff have had with different

[1] This telegram of 27 June 1945 (UE 2528/2/53), not printed, had enquired as to American intentions in restricting economic policy towards France, discussed by Lord Halifax and Mr. Grew on 8 June, as reported in Washington telegram No. 4018 (UE 2435/2/53), not printed. Mr. Grew had stated 'that although General de Gaulle had now climbed down as far as the Val d'Aosta question was concerned, the United States authorities considered, until he showed a more amenable attitude in regard to the situation in the Levant, it would be inexpedient to show much cooperation in the economic field. He instanced the fact that no military supplies were now being sent by the Americans to the French and added that this temporary unwillingness to show cooperation should stop short at the point where it gave needless offence to the French.'

members of the State Department, I am inclined to think that the conversation reported in my telegram No. 4018[1] was provoked by the immediate situation in the Levant and does not (repeat not) represent the considered policy of the United States Government.

2. Indeed, the steps which the President has taken over coal, the desire of F[oreign] E[conomic] A[dministration] to permit nothing to stand in the way of the speedy procurement of mining supplies needed if there is to be coal for export from the Ruhr and Saar, and the attitude of the United States officials who have taken part in the food discussions which M. Pineau has been having here, all go to show that the President and his advisers, the State Department, and F.E.A. are at one in admitting that France must be helped and that it is in the long term interest of the United States to see that she is, since they realise she has an essential part to play in the world.

3. At the same time it is noticeable that in most agencies of the Government there is a feeling that the French are rather tiresome, that in helping to liberate France the United States has already done a great deal and that if the French were to get somewhat worse treatment than the Belgians or the Norwegians it would be no more than they deserve.

In short, whilst the policy of the United States Government is that a strong and united France is necessary both to Europe and to the United States, the French themselves have not made a number of important officials in the various agencies concerned too eager to act in accordance with that policy.

CALENDAR TO No. 331

i *21 July 1945* Mr. Shone (Beirut) Tel. No. 694. Discussion with American Minister of possibilities of further American participation in economic activities in the Levant (cf. No. 66, note 1) [E 5352/420/89].

No. 332

Viscount Cranborne to Mr. Mackenzie King (Ottawa)[1]
D. No. 1255 Telegraphic [Z 8637/537/41]

Top secret   DOMINIONS OFFICE, *20 July 1945, 1.35 p.m.*

Soviet Delegation have tabled Spain (and Tangier) for discussion at Potsdam Conference. It is likely that they will raise question of continuance of Franco régime in Spain.

2. Our views on subject remain as set out in my telegram D. No. 446[2] of

---

[1] This telegram was also sent to the Governments of Australia, New Zealand and South Africa.

[2] Not printed. This telegram (Z 1907/118/41) had summarized Foreign Office telegram No. 2282 of 10 March 1945 to Washington, for which see Sir L. Woodward, *op. cit.*, vol. iv, pp. 38–9.

15th March. The United States Government have expressed themselves as in substantial agreement with our policy (see my telegram D. No. 587).[3] While we do not like the present régime in Spain and see no prospect of satisfactory relations with Spain so long as it remains in power, we would not favour its substitution by another form of totalitarian régime, especially if this were the result of another civil war, which would almost inevitably be the case.

3. Incidentally, since the defeat of Germany, Spanish Government have shown themselves quite forthcoming on such questions, as handing-over of German official premises, expulsion of undesirable Germans, blocking of German assets and handing-over of German ships in Spanish ports.

[3] Of 10 April, not printed. This telegram had summarized the American communication of 6 April printed in *F.R.U.S. 1945*, vol. v, pp. 672–3.

No. 333

Viscount Cranborne to Mr. Mackenzie King (Ottawa)[1]
D. No. 1263 Telegraphic [Z 8403/16/28]

Secret   DOMINIONS OFFICE, *20 July 1945, 10.30 p.m.*

My telegram 16th July D. No. 1238[2] paragraph 6. Tangier.

French Provisional Government informed United Kingdom Embassy, Paris,

(a) that they were prepared to abandon idea of pursuing exchanges of view with United States and Soviet Government through diplomatic channel, but

(b) that they hoped in return that we should be ready to open negotiations on Tangier in Paris early in August, to which Soviet Government would be invited.

French further suggested

(c) that negotiations should be preceded at end of July by unofficial and secret talks between United Kingdom United States and French representatives only. They said that this would be acceptable to United States if we agreed.

2. His Majesty's United Kingdom Ambassador Paris has been instructed to explain to French Provisional Government that

(a) we are unable to join in communication to Soviet Government until final decision has been taken as to Soviet request at Berlin meeting;

(b) if procedure described in paragraph 1(c) is adopted, we might prefer a slightly later date.

[1] This telegram was also sent to the Governments of Australia, New Zealand and South Africa.
[2] Not preserved in Dominions Office archives and untraced in Foreign Office archives.

3. Spanish Government have meanwhile represented to His Majesty's Chargé d'Affaires, Madrid, that

(*a*) in their view Soviet Government's claim to participate in Tangier conversations had no juridical basis;

(*b*) if U.S.S.R. took part in Tangier settlement only course open to Spain would be denunciation of Tangier *status quo* and return (as far as Spanish nationals in Tangier were concerned) to capitulation régime;

(*c*) Spain would never (repeat never) consent to Soviet participation.

4. His Majesty's Chargé d'Affaires Madrid has been instructed to reply to effect that

(*a*) since Russia was signatory of Act of Algeciras we cannot agree that claim of U.S.S.R. to participate in Paris talks has no juridical basis; U.S.S.R. is entitled to accede at any time to Tangier Convention under Article 56, and is in same juridical position as United States of America;

(*b*) although it is no doubt open to Spain to refuse to participate in administration of Tangier, in our view it is not possible for her to return to régime of capitulations in view of fact that Spain agreed (Article 13 of Convention) that capitulations should be *abrogated* in zone;

(*c*) Spanish Government, while of course free to take whatever action they wish in face of Soviet demand for participation in Paris talks, would be well advised in their own interests not (repeat not) to take any action that would precipitate a crisis.[3]

CALENDARS TO NO. 333

i   *21–7 July 1945   From and to Mr. Duff Cooper (Paris) Tels. Nos. 1011, 1282, 1027, 1290; to Sir A. Clark Kerr (Moscow) Tel. No. 4163.*   Action on instructions (*a*) cited in para. 2 of No. 333 and (*b*) in pursuance of decision in No. 233, minute 8, that arrangements for Soviet participation in conversations be made. M. Meyrier annoyed at (*a*) but welcomed (*b*), accepting 6 August as date for opening of conversations [Z 8644, 8765/16/28].

ii   *22 July 1945   Mr. Bowker (Madrid) Tel. No. 556.* Action on instructions cited in para. 4 of No. 333. Assurance from Spanish Under-Secretary of State that Spanish Government had no intention of precipitating a crisis. Spanish Government convinced, however, that participation of Russia in conversations would have 'most dangerous consequences' [Z 8660/16/28].

iii   *24 July 1945   Letter from Mr. Hoyer Millar (Berlin) to Mr. P. Garran (F.O. Western Dept.)* Had foreseen difficulty over P. (Terminal) 28: see No. 226, note 15; but this was avoided at meeting recorded in No. 233 [Z 8731/16/28].

---

[3] These instructions had been conveyed to Mr. Bowker in Foreign Office telegram No. 584 of 3.15 p.m. on 19 July 1945 to Madrid. This telegram had added: 'For your own information, under Article 56 there is no provision for renunciation of the Tangier Convention at all but only for its revision by common agreement. If Spain however chose to renounce, the other powers might be quite prepared to accept her renunciation and proceed to amend the Convention without Spain's participation.'

No. 334

Mr. Broad (Caserta) to Mr. Eden (Received 20 July, 11.5 p.m.)
No. 1384 Telegraphic [R 12329/24/92]

CASERTA, *20 July 1945, 9.33 p.m. G.M.T.*

Repeated to Belgrade and Rome.

My telegram No. 1363.[1]

Allied Force Headquarters have telegraphed to Combined Chiefs of Staff pointing out that a special civil police force of high quality is urgently required in Venezia Giulia.

2. They state that in their belief this police force should be equipped, maintained, administered and commanded as a combined United States and United Kingdom commitment exercised through Military Commandant. Allied Force Headquarters have accordingly requested approval to equip and maintain a police force of approximately 3500 as a combined commitment.

CALENDAR TO No. 334

i *21 July 1945* Mr. Hopkinson *(Rome) to* Mr. Broad *(Caserta) Tel. No. 321.* Question of increase in Carabinieri should be deferred until a decision is taken on proposed police mission in Italy [ZM 4037/3/22].

[1] No. 287.i.

No. 335

Mr. Stevenson (Belgrade) to Mr. Eden (Received 20 July, 5 p.m.)
No. 1156 Telegraphic [R 12343/24/92]

BELGRADE, *20 July 1945, 2.50 p.m.*

Repeated to Moscow, Sofia, Resmed (Caserta), Athens, Washington.

Your telegram No. 1033.[1]

I spoke to Marshal Tito this afternoon[2] as directed leaving with him an aid[e]-memoire in the sense of paragraph 2 and paragraph 3 of your telegram under reference.

2. In reply Marshal Tito said that so far as concerned his own utterances, he considered it to be his duty to explain fully and clearly to the Yugoslav people the problems of foreign affairs, which faced the Government. In this connexion he took exception to the phrase 'inflammatory utterances of responsible Yugoslav statesmen', which I had included in my aid[e]-memoire. I said that it was not my intention to accuse him of deliberately trying to rouse Yugoslav people to war, but I could assure him that the impression

[1] No. 157.
[2] This telegram was drafted on 19 July 1945.

caused by his speeches and those of other members of his Government could be accurately described as 'inflammatory'.

3. As regards the attitude of the press, Marshal Tito said the Greek newspapers were largely to blame. Some weeks ago they had started a campaign against Yugoslavia, in the course of which they had put forward claims to Yugoslav territory. He could not prevent the Yugoslav press from replying to these and other attacks, particularly in the Turkish press. He agreed with me fully, however, that the best way of dealing with not only frontier incidents, but general differences of opinion, was by way of direct negotiations between the two Governments. He would be very glad to reach a direct settlement with the Greek Government.

4. Similarly as regards Venezia Giulia and Carinthia, he maintained that the attitude of the Yugoslav press was provoked by the unfriendly tone of certain organs of the British press. In this connexion he mentioned *Nineteenth Century* Magazine and *Time and Tide*. Unfounded accusations had, he said, been made in the British press against the Yugoslav military administration in Istria. For instance a revolt was alleged to have broken out in Fiume and to have been put down with the utmost brutality by Yugoslav troops. This was entirely untrue. Here again, however, he agreed with me that the right way to settle any incidents was by way of direct negotiation between either the military authorities on the spot or the Governments concerned. He had recently received a report of an incident . . .[3] Gorizia in the course of which Slovenes had been killed and wounded by British troops. He intended to take this and other incidents up direct with me.

5. I then spoke to Marshal Tito on lines of paragraph 4 of your telegram under reference, saying that this attempt to appeal to the people of Britain over the head of the Government had made a very unfavourable impression. He replied that he much regretted this as he had had no intention whatever of producing any such impression. He had merely wished to show in a symbolic way that amongst the staunchly democratic peoples of Great Britain and America there were some individuals who were fascist minded. I took note of this rather lame explanation of his words.

6. I gained the impression from Marshal Tito's demeanour during our conversation that our representations would have a salutory effect on him (see also my immediately following telegram).[4] I am not, however, optimistic about any marked improvements in the attitude of the local press.

Pass to Caserta, Athens and Washington as my telegrams Nos. 651, 73 and 211 respectively.

CALENDAR TO No. 335

i   *19 July 1945   Military Attaché (Belgrade) to 8th Army Tels. Nos. 433 & 434.* Transmits reports of torture and shootings by O.Z.N.A. (Committee for the Protection of the People) police formations in June in Celje area [R 12998/6/ 92].

---

[3] The text is here uncertain.   [4] No. 336.

No. 336

Mr. Stevenson (Belgrade) to Mr. Eden (Received 20 July, 4.50 p.m.)
No. 1157 Telegraphic [R 12325/24/92]

BELGRADE, *20 July 1945, 3.18 p.m. G.M.T.*

Repeated to Moscow, Sofia, Resmed (Caserta), Athens, Washington.

My immediately preceding telegram.[1]

I took advantage of this interview to discuss with Marshal Tito the general unfriendly attitude of Administration, and in particular of the Yugoslav General Staff, towards the British in this country. I told him that not only was the General Staff entirely unco-operative, but generally unpleasant. The attitude of minor officials in most branches of the Administration had been recently increasingly hostile. I was informed on good authority that in Yugoslav schools, children were openly told that the British were fascist. There were constantly recurring cases of attempts to (. . . ? persecute)[2] Yugoslavs who were either employed by British officials or who even made their acquaintance. The incidents in themselves were generally of a minor character, but when added up they appeared to amount to a deliberate policy. I was sure that it was not the policy of Marshal Tito himself or of the leaders of the movement, but there seemed to have been issued somewhere a directive which fostered this hostile attitude. I was at a loss to understand the reasons which lay behind this. Could it be that it was the object of certain currents within the National Liberation Movement to disturb relations between Great Britain and Soviet Russia by provoking us into open hostility and then appealing to Moscow for help? This might seem, and probably was, a far-fetched explanation, but it showed how far I was from being able to understand the reasons for the present unfriendly attitude of the Yugoslav authorities.

2. Marshal Tito replied he had in fact noticed in the past an attitude of unfriendliness and even of hostility to Great Britain particularly in the Yugoslav Army. The faults might have been all on the Yugoslav side but in any event such an attitude was, as he had made clear in the past, not only against his orders but against his deepest convictions. His aim was to maintain the most cordial relations with Great Britain, who had helped so considerably in the Yugoslavs' liberation. He would see to it that immediate and stringent orders and directives were issued to all concerned which would, he hoped, better the situation. I thanked him for this and as he had mentioned the possibility of there having been incidents in which British officers and soldiers might have been to blame, I said he could count on me to do all in my power to make local relations as harmonious as possible. I asked he should pay particular attention to improve the attitude of the Yugoslav General Staff. He promised to do so, and in this connexion agreed

---

[1] No. 335.
[2] The text is here uncertain.

without hesitation to allow me to operate two transport aircraft within the country for the purpose of maintaining touch with the Consulates, a matter on which I had failed, despite repeated efforts, to extract any kind of a reply from the General Staff.[3]

Foreign Office pass to Caserta, Athens and Washington as my telegrams Nos. 652, 74 and 212 respectively.

---

[3] Sir A. Cadogan and Mr. Eden minuted on this and the preceding telegram, repeated to Berlin: 'Mr. Stevenson spoke well. A. C. July 23, 1945.' 'Yes. Now let us see if there is any improvement. A. E. July 24.' Mr. Stevenson was informed in Foreign Office telegram No. 1083 of 3 p.m. on 25 July to Belgrade: 'I approve your language.'

No. 337

Sir R. Bullard (Tehran) to Mr. Eden (Received 20 July, 4.20 p.m.)

No. 728 Telegraphic [*E 5278/20/34*]

TEHRAN, *20 July 1945, 1.49 p.m. G.M.T.*

Repeated to Moscow; Saving to M.E. Min[ister]'s Office, Bagdad (for P.A.I.C).

Your telegram No. 417.[1]

General Officer Commanding-in-Chief considers that the interests of security require the exclusion of Soviet Delegation from Abadan and oil fields. In view of the Soviet attitude towards applications by foreigners to go to Azerbaijan and of the much greater importance of oil supplies to us than any military interest in Azerbaijan to the Soviet Government this seems perfectly reasonable. Whether Kermanshah should be included in the ban is being discussed.

(2) Unfortunately welfare facilities for Persian labour in the Anglo-Iranian Oil Company are not so good that they would be convincing to the Soviet delegates who would in any case not be there to praise the A.I.O.C. Facilities for education are excellent but housing is weak and we cannot expect the Soviet delegates to take into consideration that the war has greatly increased the number of workers while reducing supplies of building material and that A.I.O.C. labour is in any case better housed than other Persians living nearby.

(3) Welfare work among Persian labour is one of the questions that I intend to study when I visit Abadan late July.

---

[1] No. 93.i.

No. 338

Major-General Hayes[1] *(Chungking) to Sir J. Grigg*
(Received 20 July, 5.40 p.m.)
No. o/o114 Telegraphic [F 4449/1147/10]

Top secret. Important   CHUNGKING, *20 July 1945, 9 a.m.*[2]

Ref your 58502 (M.O.12) July 9th.[3]

Have discussed question with Ambassador and General Carton de Wiart and we are agreed project suggested is not now practical. Following represents our combined opinions.

1. Project is closely bound up with American attitude still tending to harden towards British military organizations in China. Americans regard China as their theatre and barely tolerate our presence here at all.

2. They are in any case extremely suspicious of our activities and I face continual crises, obstructions, pin pricks and the like. Hitherto these difficulties have been mitigated by a policy of complete frankness with Wedemeyer on the part of General Carton de Wiart and myself. We are both completely committed to keeping him informed of all (repeat all) we do in the military field. On any other basis we would have had to close down completely some months ago.

3. We both have gained the impression that Wedemeyer is personally opposed to any action by the British in China directed to the reoccupation of Hong Kong. Canton is now known to be one of the objectives of forth-coming offensive by American trained (? concentration)[4] of Chinese Combat Command and it may be that Hong Kong is another. On the other hand I have no doubt the China Combat Command even with extensive help from the sea including necessary landing craft and other special equipment will have great difficulty capturing Hong Kong island if Japanese suicide garrison fight to last.

4. In unlikely contingency Japanese garrison choosing to surrender possibility that China Combat Command will be forestalled into Hong Kong by local Chinese communist guerillas cannot be ruled out. Indeed according to latest reports of Japanese belonging to Communist (?word omitted)[4] Japanese themselves may connive at such a course.

5. Only British available close at hand for task in question are small

---

[1] General Officer Commanding British Troops in China and Head of the British Military Mission to China.

[2] Time of origin.

[3] Not printed. This telegram had instructed preparation of a project relative to the possibility at Hong Kong of 'seizure, or anticipated seizure of colony by Chinese forces of any type. In that event Colonial Office consider very necessary to forestall assumption of civil administration by Chinese.'

[4] The text is here uncertain.

elements of British Army aid group. Have had greatest difficulty clearing them with Americans and any attempt on my part to build them up will certainly be viewed by Americans with grave suspicion and will meet every sort of obstacle.

6. In view of para. 2 above any leakage of our plans will prejudice if not destroy British military position in China which is already deplorably weak. B[ritish] A[rmy] A[id] G[roup] is watched and reported on by both local Americans and Chinese. It is still regarded with suspicion by both and my own view is Americans at all events have already concluded it has some future role in connection with Hong Kong.

7. All . . .[4] country is of course controlled by the Chinese and Americans have a hand in it too. Without agreement with both it will probably be impossible for even bare minimum personnel to move into Hong Kong under any circumstances. A few might conceivably get themselves smuggled through but even this is a forlorn hope. A better bet in my opinion would be to despatch an advanced party of civil affairs unit to the colony from outside China by sea or air the necessary (? facilities)[4] for it's arrival being given by a high grade agent, previously planted there for the purpose.

8. To sum up, our military position in China is now so difficult and precarious, that in our opinion, it is essential that any project of this nature, if it is to have any hope of success, must (repeat must) be previously cleared with both Chinese and Americans and at highest level. It would be useless to approach Wedemeyer on subject initially, since he sticks rigidly to his directives and would merely refer the matter to Washington. Neither will it be sufficient to project with Americans alone since Wedemeyer when approached will certainly feel it necessary in his capacity as C[hief] O[f] S[taff] to Generalissimo (?to) (?tell)[4] the latter.

9. The (? bigger)[4] question of allied strategy in Far East is doubtless under consideration now and feel sure it is unnecessary for me to stress the importance from the point of view of our prestige and future relations with China that we should recapture Hong Kong Island and if possible the whole (? colony)[4]. And our (? plans)[4] I suggest should include some measures however slight to save our remaining prisoners from possible massacre at the last moment.[5]

[5] On 25 July 1945 Colonel Stanley wrote to Mr. Eden: 'My dear Anthony, I should very much have liked to have a talk with you tomorrow about a matter connected with Hong Kong. It is of great urgency as it may be that the only way for it to be dealt with is that it should be raised in personal conversations with the Americans, either between you and Byrnes or between the Prime Minister and the President. But unfortunately I cannot get back from Bristol until Friday [27 July] morning and I hear that you are planning, if all goes well, to leave then for Potsdam. I do hope you can spare a few minutes tomorrow to let George Gater [Permanent Under Secretary, Colonial Office] explain the position to you. Orme Sargent is, I think, already aware of it and it has been discussed with your office. Of course you could not give a decision at such short notice, but you might be able to advise me as to the best course to pursue. Yours ever, Oliver Stanley': see further No. 550.

No. 339

Sir J. Anderson to Sir H. Seymour (Chungking)
No. 779 Telegraphic [UR 2209/1999/853]

Immediate   FOREIGN OFFICE, 20 July 1945, 7.10 p.m.

Repeated to Government of India, External Affairs Department New Delhi.

Your telegram No. 667[1] (of 6th July: Cholera experts for China).

You will now have received Government of India's telegram No. 6325[2] of 17th July. We hope their offer will be accepted and that it will be possible to arrange air passages at once. These doctors should be able to reach Chungking sooner than any sent from United States of America.

We attach great importance to participation of British or British Indian personnel in this work, as some offset against UNRRA's tendency to rely solely on American staff in Far East.[3]

CALENDARS TO No. 339

i   *19 & 20 July 1945*   *Letters from Mr. D. Ogilvy (H.M. Embassy, Washington) to Mr. Hasler and Mr. P. J. Stent (F.O. Relief Dept.)* Importance of British appointments to U.N.R.R.A. missions in the Far East, 'our backyard' [UR 2524/12/850].

ii   *26 July 1945*   *British Food Mission (Washington) Tel. No. 5397 Amaze:* no further supplies available for Far Eastern relief requirements: position is serious. Minuting in F.O. [UR 2622/82/851].

[1] Not printed.

[2] This telegram (not printed) had conveyed an offer from the Government of India of doctors and vaccine to assist in an outbreak of cholera in Chungking and neighbourhood.

[3] Sir H. Seymour reported in Chungking telegram No. 311 of 30 July 1945 at 10.44 a.m. to the Government of India with reference to its offer: 'Director of National Health Administration and Chief Medical Officer U.N.R.R.A. express their great appreciation of your generous offer of assistance but consider that as cholera epidemic is now abating quite rapidly they would not be justified in bringing the doctors in question to China. They hope, however, that offer of vaccine may be kept open in case it should be needed later on.'

No. 340

R.A.F. Delegation (Washington) to the Air Ministry[1] (Received 21 July)
No. 1182 Sever Telegraphic [UE 3143/16/53]

Secret   WASHINGTON, 20 July 1945, 8.4 p.m. G.M.T.[2]

The Senate passed the Bretton Woods bill[3] by 61 votes to 16 after a three days debate.

[1] For the Joint American Secretariat (J.A.S.).

[2] Time of origin.

[3] This bill provided for the participation of the United States in the International Monetary Fund and the International Bank for Reconstruction and Development agreed at Bretton Woods (see No. 42, note 10): the U.S. Act approved on 31 July 1945 is printed in *Documents on American Foreign Relations*, vol. vii, pp. 537–45.

2. The bill was passed in the form in which it emerged from the Senate banking and currency committee. Copies of that text with the three amendments incorporated by the Senate committee were airbagged to you on July 9th.

3. The bill now goes back to the House for consideration of these three amendments. The administration anticipates no difficulty in their acceptance by the House and the Bill should be ready for the President's signature in a matter of days.

4. Most of the amendments to the bill were voted on Thursday[4] and defeated by substantial majorities. The most dangerous was sponsored by Senator Ball. It would have required member nations to abolish discriminatory currency practices within three years or be barred from use of the fund. The amendment was clearly aimed at Great Britain. It found support with Senator Vandenberg who up to that moment had voted against every other amendment to the bill. Vandenberg argued that this amendment would not handicap the Bretton Woods proposals but would merely encourage the member nations 'to live up to their end of the bargain'. The amendment was defeated by 46 votes to 29 and undoubtedly gave the administration its biggest worry.

5. Bernstein[5] who had followed the three days debate very closely told us after the vote that what impressed him most was the sympathetic understanding of Britains special problem by many speakers including die-hard Republicans and their recognition of American responsibility for helping in the solution of this problem. Bernstein said that the debate had committed many prominent members of the opposition to utmost co-operation by the United States in over-coming Britains transition period difficulties. He added 'when such measures of co-operation and aid are discussed in congress it will be very difficult for Senator Taft and his like to go back on what they have said in the course of the last three days'.

6. We are air bagging you copies of the Congressional record covering the debate.

CALENDARS TO No. 340

i *21 July 1945 Lord Halifax (Washington) Tel. No. 382 Saving.* Economic weekly summary: 'The fight for Bretton Woods in the United States is won' [UE 3240/42/53].

ii *18–27 July 1945 Correspondence between Sir P. Liesching (Board of Trade) and Sir W. Eady* on U.S. commercial policy [UE 3284/113/53].

---

[4] 19 July 1945.
[5] Mr. E. M. Bernstein was Assistant Director of Monetary Research in the U.S. Treasury Department.

No. 341

Letter from Sir O. Sargent to Sir A. Cadogan (Berlin)[1]
[F.O. 934/5/39(1)]

Immediate & Secret   FOREIGN OFFICE, 20 July 1945

Dear Alec

We have seen President Truman's communication to the Prime Minister about Lend-Lease and our dollar balances,[2] and as you will easily believe, we were disagreeably impressed by it. Its contents, besides being unsatisfactory, are not directly related to the work of Terminal, and to have discharged it at us at the beginning of the proceedings seems to us ominous as well as boorish.

In addition to the two replies which the Chancellor of the Exchequer has already sent to the Prime Minister,[3] the Secretary of State may care to have our comments. It seems to us that from the political point of view there are two possible explanations:–

(1) that this action is proof of the sort of 'America first' attitude recently attributed to Mr. Truman and Mr. Byrnes by visitors from the United States, and, incidentally, also by Dorothy Thompson[4] in a recent article (i.e. international matters will be viewed from the over-narrow point of view of American interest). This particular manifestation may be the result of pressure from American exporters (there has lately been a telegram reporting non-official complaints of an alleged British export campaign in Latin America. This may have been intended as a means of justifying before the event the attitude now taken by the United States Government). In any case, it seems that American foreign policy will be made by two ex-senators with the traditional restricted outlook of Congress; or

(2) that it may be intended as a means of putting us on notice before the Terminal discussions really get under way that, for a timely revival of our strength and, therefore, influence, we are dependent on the United States, and that therefore what they decide in matters of policy 'goes', wherever our views may differ from theirs. In another very secret connexion[5] it has seemed to us that the key to the Americans' attitude might be an intention to use their predominant position in that particular sphere of activity in order to put over their conception of how the world should behave and be arranged.

It is just possible that records being so badly kept in Washington, the present American bigwigs do not realise how far President Roosevelt and

---

[1] This letter was read by Sir A. Cadogan on 21 July and by Mr. Eden on 22 July 1945.
[2] No. 174, annex.
[3] Nos. 312 and 312.i.
[4] Miss Dorothy Thompson was an American journalist and commentator.
[5] The reference may have been to atomic research.

his advisers had committed themselves morally if not documentarily as regards Lend-Lease and other things in Stage II.

Yrs

O. G. SARGENT

No. 342

Record by Mr. Berkeley Gage of a conversation in Washington with Mr. Hickerson on 20 July 1945[1]

[AN 2438/35/45]

I called on Mr. John Hickerson (whom I had previously met in San Francisco) this morning, prior to my return to the North American Department of the Foreign Office.

Mr. Hickerson asked what my impressions had been of opinion towards Britain and the British Commonwealth in the cities which I had just visited (Seattle, St. Paul and Minneapolis, Chicago, Detroit, New York and Washington). I said I had found a variety of contrasting and often conflicting views, mainly from businessmen, pressmen and others whose views might not have been entirely representative, since my contacts had been weak on the labour side. I said I seemed to discern three main trends from the opinions which had been expressed to me, namely, (1) that the future of the world lay between the two 'colossi' America and Russia, because the British Commonwealth had been so weakened economically by the war and was so scattered in its components that it could not compete in importance with the other two and could almost be overlooked in American policy: (2) that the British Commonwealth could not survive without American support but that it was a vital American interest and counter-balance to Russia and should be supported by the United States as such, the B[ritish] C[ommonwealth of] N[ations] playing the role of a junior partner: and (3) that Britain was as full of tricks as a monkey and would again out-smart the United States in the foreign commercial fields and in the political field (by dragging her into something which was not a United States interest) as it always had before thanks to the ineptness of the United States State Department. This latter category seemed to feel that Britain would make full use of 'unfair' commercial practices, such as frozen sterling balances, her allegedly superior position in the field of communications (viz. Reuters agencies and civil aviation bases) and fuel supplies (oil supplies in Persia

---

[1] This record of a conversation with Mr. J. D. Hickerson, Acting Director of the Office of European Affairs in the State Department, was brought back to the Foreign Office (received by 2 August 1945) by Mr. Gage, Assistant Head of North American Department, on his return via Washington from the San Francisco Conference. A copy was also transmitted under cover of Washington despatch No. 995 of 2 August (received, 13 August: see note 2 below) signed for Lord Halifax by Mr. J. Balfour.

and British-controlled territories) and lend-lease materials in order to be first after the war in the export markets. I also found in some circles a fear that Britain would, through her policy in Europe, drag the United States into a war with Russia. Generally speaking there seemed to be an uncertain balance between admiration and suspicion of us, little realisation that Britain's life-blood was the proper balance of her exports and imports, or that a prosperous Britain was an American commercial asset, nor that British policy in Europe was rendered extremely difficult by the absence, anyhow until recently (I was not fully up-to-date) of an American policy which could be co-ordinated with ours. While I had been glad to find generally a wholehearted acceptance of the United Nations Charter, there seemed to be a certain suspicion of Russia (in some cases a rather rabid suspicion) as well as of ourselves.

Mr. Hickerson expressed interest and then, speaking very deliberately, asked me to bear in mind when I returned to England that the State Department held the view that Britain was a major American interest, politically, economically and sentimentally.[2] In other words, the State Department wanted us to be strong and prosperous and would support any practical measures directed to that end. It must be admitted that Britain was not in a strong position at present and needed American help. He hoped something would come out of the impending visit to the United Kingdom of American economic experts. He expected that there would be difficulties both in the United States and in the United Kingdom with private commercial interests (in the United States the question of the reduction of tariffs would have to be handled with particular care) but these difficulties must be got over in the interests of both countries. It was most important that there should be an atmosphere of complete confidence and frankness between the officials of both countries in which all problems could be freely discussed. Let us by all means slam at each other as hard as we felt like, behind locked doors if necessary, but once agreement had been reached let us stand by that agreement and not later accuse each other of letting the other side down. He cited as an example of how not to do things certain Anglo-American discussions which once took place over the question of Spanish wolfram. The United Kingdom officials had, after discussion, given way to the United States point of view, but later there had been recriminations and the Spanish had alleged to United States officials that they had been told by British officials that the United Kingdom had opposed the United States view that all wolfram exports to enemy countries should be prohibited. Another bad example had been the Chicago Aviation Conference where the Americans

<hr>

[2] Covering Washington despatch No. 995 commented on this: 'Whilst this statement may not reflect the unanimous view of the State Department, I consider it deserves attention as coming from an official who is not prone to enthusiasms.' The despatch had observed that 'Mr. Hickerson, who is normally a somewhat taciturn person, evidently expressed himself very freely and frankly on this occasion. His remarks are the more encouraging as he holds a position of considerable responsibility in dealing with Anglo-American relations.'

had thought that Britain had been playing a selfish game and Britain had thought that she had been double-crossed by Mr. Berle. Another cause of suspicion was unauthenticated rumours that one side or the other was not playing the game in commercial matters. Such rumours should always be tracked down to their source and publicity given to the truth where necessary.

As regards relations with Russia, Mr. Hickerson said that he held the view that Russia had every motive to keep the peace and that none of the wild suspicions voiced in certain circles were justified. He himself had been impressed by the conciliatory attitude of the Soviet delegates at San Francisco. He believed that the international era of communism was over but that it was still necessary for Britain and America to stand up for the right of European nations to get the type of government they desired, bearing in mind Russian security requirements in the nations bordering her territories.

In general, Mr. Hickerson made it clear that the State Department advocated the closest possible collaboration with Britain and the British Commonwealth within the United Nations Charter and not in opposition to Russia but as an aid to better relations with her in the case of both Britain and America. He added that he hoped that instructions would shortly be issued to all United States officials in this sense.

I told Mr. Hickerson that what he had told me would be a great encouragement to me in my work in London. I agreed with him that the closest possible collaboration and the utmost frankness between the officials of both countries was most desirable in our mutual interest, and that I would do all I could to encourage this idea. I had had little experience of Anglo-American problems, but my impression had been when I left London in April that we had certain inhibitions with regard to our future economic relations with the United States which could best be resolved by a thorough survey of the whole situation. For this reason I was very glad indeed to hear that American experts were going to London. I also expressed personal agreement with his views on Russia and on the behaviour of the Soviet delegates at San Francisco.

I also spoke to Mr. Tom Wa[i]les and Mr. Ted Achilles of the British Commonwealth Division of the State Department. They were less forthcoming than Mr. Hickerson. When I mentioned the fear I had heard expressed on my tour that Britain might drag the United States into a war with Russia they seemed to think that this fear had some point and that Britain should indeed avoid doing so! I said that there was no more validity in this view than in the other one I had heard even more frequently expressed that war between America and Russia was inevitable.[3]

[3] Mr. N. Butler observed in a minute of 2 August on this record: 'Sir A. Cadogan will have been able to judge at Potsdam whether President Truman and Mr. Byrnes share the feeling toward us of this State Department official.' Sir A. Cadogan minuted: 'Rather difficult to say. The impression I got was that both the Pres. and Mr. Byrnes were rather on the "mediation" tack. The President's slick and snappy manner (whether natural or assumed)

is rather inclined to result in quick decisions about which he does not consult us and in which he appears to ignore our interests. But that may be due to inexperience, and he may improve in that respect. A. C. Aug. 4. 1945' (minute cited in part by Robert M. Hathaway, *Ambiguous Partnership: Britain and America 1944–7*—New York, 1981—p. 179).

No. 343

Minutes of a meeting of the Provisional Sub-Committee on Industry and Materials of the Emergency Economic Committee for Europe held at 4 Carlton Gardens, London S.W.1., on Friday, 20 July 1945

E.E.C. (I. and M.) (45) 3rd Meeting [UR 2309/1600/53]

Confidential

Present:

Mr. Roger Nathan (in the Chair)

Belgium Mr. van der Plancke

Denmark Mr. E. Kristiansen

France Mr. M. Jaoul

Norway Mr. V. Paus, Mr. J. H. Meyer (for part of the time), Mr. S. F. Wennevold (for part of the time)

United Kingdom Miss L. S. Sutherland, Hon. M. R. Bridgeman (for part of the time), Mr. H. Broadley (for part of the time)

United States of America Mr. S. Timberg

Observers:

U.N.R.R.A.: Mr. A. S. J. Baster

Secretary:

Mrs. K. H. Munro

1. The minutes of the second meeting were approved.

2. *Relations with the Food and Agriculture Sub-Committee*

THE CHAIRMAN welcomed Mr. Broadley, the Chairman of the Sub-Committee on Food and Agriculture, and invited him to outline to the meeting such problems as he thought could profitably be tackled jointly by the two Committees.

MR. BROADLEY said that the Sub-Committee on Food and Agriculture, like that on Industry and Materials, was still in its infancy. A beginning had been made by asking countries to supply information from which it would be possible to draw up a statement of what was required to maximise the 1946 harvest. The survey covered needs of fertilisers, agricultural machinery, seeds and other materials. Once this information had been received the Committee would be in a better position to review the problems with which it was faced and it would then be possible to see how far the Industry and Materials Committee could be of assistance.

(a) Fertilizers

He mentioned the Working Committee on Fertilizers which was being set up (as agreed the same morning at the E.E.C.E. meeting)[1] under the chairmanship of Commandant Bernard, to take over the day to day executive work connected with the production and distribution of fertilizers and at the same time to sit as a Committee for the discussion of problems arising from this work. He suggested that the Industry and Materials Sub-Committee should send a representative to the Fertilizers Working Party when it met in this second capacity.

THE COMMITTEE:

    (a) agreed and appointed the Belgian Delegate as its representative on the Fertilizers Working Party.

(b) Agricultural Machinery

MR. BROADLEY, continuing his survey, said that the second problem under consideration was the requirement and supply of tractors. Figures for essential minimum needs had been asked for and he proposed that when these were received they should be discussed at a meeting of the Food and Agriculture Sub-Committee with a member of the Industry and Materials Committee present, or that, if necessary, a joint meeting should be held.

THE COMMITTEE:

    (b) Agreed that the British member should represent it at meetings of the Food and Agriculture Sub-Committee at which tractors and agricultural machinery were under discussion.

(c) Insecticides

MR. BROADLEY suggested that the Industry and Materials Committee might also wish to be associated with any work undertaken on insecticides. The Chairman did not consider it necessary for the Committee to send a representative to discussions on this matter but asked Mr. Broadley to keep the Committee informed of any development in which it might be interested.

(d) Storage and Preservation of Food Stuffs

MR. BASTER suggested that it would be useful to the Committee, for instance when discussing questions of transportation, to have before them an estimate of the 1946 crops.

MR. BROADLEY said that the Food and Agriculture Sub-Committee was collecting information about crops. Figures for 1944/5, including the 1945 harvest, should be available in their preliminary form by the middle of August, and in final form by November. The Food and Agriculture Committee had also asked for estimates of the target figures both for herds and for acreage during 1946. These would of course be tentative, but would provide some guidance, for instance in assessing needs of processing factories. He undertook to have both sets of figures circulated to the Industry and Materials Committee. THE CHAIRMAN suggested that in addition to gifures

---

[1] The reference was to the sixth meeting of the E.E.C.E., on 17 July 1945 (record on UR 1600/1600/53).

[figures] for actual production, it was important to know what provision could be made for the preservation of stocks, particularly since the possibility of providing any surplus for export would depend on such storage facilities.

After some discussion it was agreed that it would be useful to have a survey made of existing facilities for refrigeration, processing, packing, etc., and from this information to estimate what would be needed in the way of further equipment, spare parts and fuel, at any rate in so far as such needs could not be met through normal channels and gave rise to any difficulties.

THE COMMITTEE:

(d) Invited Mr. Broadley to raise this matter at the next meeting of the Sub-Committee on Food and Agriculture and to report back to the Industry and Materials Sub-Committee any proposals for joint action.

(e) Invited Mr. Broadley to attend a future meeting of the Industry and Materials Sub-Committee when the necessary information bearing on the problems so far discussed had been received.

(f) Instructed the Secretary to arrange with the Secretary of the Food and Agriculture Sub-Committee that they should receive copies of each others papers, and to bring to the notice of the Sub-Committee any points of common interest arising from the papers of the Sub-Committee on Food and Agriculture.

3. *Statement on the General Position of Petrol, Oil and Lubricants in Europe*

THE CHAIRMAN welcomed Mr. Bridgeman, from the Ministry of Fuel and Power, and invited him to give the Committee a general survey of the present European position of P[etrol,] O[il and] L[ubricants], which he thought would be one important bottleneck in the restoration of European industry.

MR. BRIDGEMAN said that it was extremely difficult from his point of view to deal with Europe as a whole in view of the different conditions prevailing in countries which were, and which were not, still a military responsibility, in neutral countries, and in those which came into the Russian zone. He asked, therefore, whether the Committee were interested in any particular aspect of the problem.

MISS SUTHERLAND suggested that the Committee's immediate concern was with the countries of North West Europe, and in particular the question of how far European self-help was possible or desirable.

MR. BRIDGEMAN said that in France, Belgium, Holland, Denmark and Norway, requirements of P.O.L. were put in to the Four Party Committees,[2] and that when approved they were passed to the military representative for inclusion along with military requirements in the overall needs of the Area. In the case of areas of British responsibility, the total requirement was then passed through the War Office to the Ministry of Fuel and Power, who made arrangements for supply in consultation with Washington. With the end of

---

[2] These committees had been established in liberated countries with representatives from the government concerned, the relevant S.H.A.E.F. Mission and British and U.S. civil authorities to discuss procedure and priorities for supplies.

military responsibility on the 1st September in France, Belgium, and Holland, and at a somewhat later date in Norway and Denmark, this position would be changed. The actual transition would be gradual and would depend on the rate at which such material as pipelines, tankers and installations generally could be turned over from military to civil control. In the post-military period, requirements would continue to be co-ordinated by the Ministry of Fuel and Power, but if the several countries agreed, would be passed through the British Embassies instead of the military representatives.

In reply to questions, Mr. Bridgeman said that the supply position for P.O.L. was the most difficult in the case of fuel oil. The lubricant position varied from time to time and as between different grades, and though not good was not serious.

THE CHAIRMAN thanked Mr. Bridgeman and in summing up said he felt convinced that for the present there was nothing that this Committee could do to improve the P.O.L. position in Europe.

4. *Textiles*

THE CHAIRMAN said that it had been agreed the same morning at the meeting of the E.E.C.E.[1] that the time limit for the receipt of replies to the Textile Questionnaire should be extended to the 28th July. In the meantime there was nothing further to report, and Item 3 on the Agenda therefore did not arise. It should, however, be possible to go further into the matter at the next meeting.

5. *Iron and Steel*

THE CHAIRMAN referred to the suggestion made at the Second Meeting of the Sub-Committee (Minute 4)[3] that the Iron and Steel industry should be among the topics investigated by the Sub-Committee. He referred to the difficulties European countries were experiencing in obtaining essential requirements, but felt that the industry was so closely related to the supply of coal that proposals for its assistance in Europe might prove rather academic.

MISS SUTHERLAND suggested that the Committee might consider (with the advice of experts) the desirability of setting up a Working Party to prepare an analysis of the types of iron and steel, e.g. sheet and tinplate, where the minimum demands of European countries could not readily be met from overseas sources and to examine the best way of meeting these deficiencies at an early date from European production. The Working Party could draw attention to bottlenecks in production of which it might be possible to deal with over a limited field of iron and steel production though not over the field of the whole industry, e.g. in the case of fuel supplies, it ought be possible to indicate what quantities were necessary to produce the minimum requirements of the deficiency items and thus to provide a report which the E.E.C.E. could pass on to E.C.O., drawing their attention

---

[3] The record of this meeting of 3 July is not printed.

to the urgency of coal supplies for this particular purpose.

MR. TIMBERG suggested that it would also be useful to strengthen the case by examining the end-uses for which these deficiency iron and steel requirements were intended, e.g. sheet for the housing programmes.

THE COMMITTEE:

(*a*) Agreed that the Iron and Steel industry should be discussed further at its next meeting and expert advice taken.

(*b*) Invited the Chairman and the Belgian, British and Norwegian representatives to bring expert advisers to the next meeting.

6. *Date of Next Meeting*

The Committee agreed that the next meeting should take place on Wednesday 1st August, at 4.30. p.m.

Lancaster House, London, S.W.1., 28th July, 1945

CALENDARS TO No. 343

i *17–27 July 1945   Coal supplies for Western Europe:* (*a*) *European Coal Organisation: First Meeting of Production Sub-Committee* (*London: ECO/PSC/2*) [UR 2310/1600/53]; (*b*) *Memo.* (*C.P.*(*45*)*85*) *by Mr. O. Lyttelton and extract from Cabinet Conclusions 16*(*45*): *Letters from Sir G. Laithwaite* (*Cabinet Office*) *to Mr. N. Brook* (*Berlin*). Increased bunkering requirements [F.O. 934/1/2(29)] (*c*) *R.A.F. Delegation* (*Washington*) *to Joint American Secretariat Tel. Dorpoc 643.* U.S.A. will supply 6 million tons of coal, excluding bunker coal, before the end of 1945 [UR 2665, 2483/2109/851]. (*d*) *To Lord Halifax* (*Washington*) *Tel. No. 7866.* Italian membership of E.C.O. considered premature but need for supplies recognized [UR 2335/1600/53].

ii *18 July 1945   Extract from Cabinet Conclusions 15* (*45*). Preference for use of German rather than home-produced timber [UR 3083/64/77].

iii *19–20 July 1945   Lord Halifax* (*Washington*) *Tels. Nos. 5019–20, 5072.* Arrangements for first conference of Food and Agriculture Organisation [UE 3072, 3077, 3128/1/53].

iv *20–23 July 1945   Letter from Mr. J. W. Taylor* (*Commercial Counsellor at Prague*) *to Mr. Hasler; Mr. Nichols* (*Prague*) *Tel. No. 2 Absent.* Unsatisfactory position of U.N.R.R.A. mission in Prague owing to Soviet prohibition on travel [UR 2635, 2519/6/850].

No. 344

Letter from Lieut.-Colonel Mallaby (*Berlin*) *to Lieut.-Colonel Melville*[1]
No. J.S.(*T*)/*3* [*CAB 119/12*]

Top secret   [BERLIN,] *20 July 1945*

I should have written before to tell you what the chances of your being

---

[1] Lieut.-Colonels H. G. C. Mallaby and A. D. Melville were on the Military Staff of the Offices of the Cabinet and Minister of Defence.

sent for were but no doubt you assumed that as you heard nothing you were not required. Although, as you will have seen from the papers and minutes which have come home, we have been fairly busy, I could not have justified a request to General Hollis to send for you. In point of fact, although I have worked pretty hard throughout the day, I have not had to work after dinner. I am afraid you will be disappointed when I tell you that I think it is a very enjoyable Conference. The surroundings are most pleasant, the accommodation comfortable and the weather good. You need not believe all you read in the press about the luxury of our living. As a matter of fact, we are living rather less luxuriously than we did at Cairo or Quebec, but there is certainly no lack of food and drink.

On the whole, the results of Combined Chiefs of Staff meetings have been encouraging and satisfactory, at any rate a great deal better than we expected. You will have seen that there was no difficulty in getting agreement in principle to the Coronet force, though there may, of course, be considerable difficulties when the details are discussed with General MacArthur. We already know, however, that he is not opposed to the proposal and has already begun to think out how he might make it work.

Our chief vexation has been the paper on Basic Objectives which has been handed about between Lord Leathers and Lord Cherwell and the Treasury and has ended up very much as it began. It is being taken by the Combined Chiefs of Staff tomorrow[2] and I doubt whether it will get a very fair passage.

The Directors of Administrative Plans have not been notic[e]ably busy, but as you know, Brigadier Ransome always manages to make it appear that the whole Conference revolves round him. He has, moreover, been most useful in arranging to take people for trips into Berlin and has quickly acquired the skill of a guide. I have not yet had time to go into Berlin, though the whole Conference goes off tomorrow morning to see a British parade in the British Sector.

I think the most likely date of our return is next Wednesday,[3] though some of us might be delayed a little longer. Will you please show this letter to anyone who may be interested.

CALENDAR TO NO. 344

i   *22 July 1945   Lt.-Col. Mallaby (Berlin) to Major M. F. Berry (Cabinet Office).*
Further progress of C.C.S. at Potsdam: all 'should now be ready for the Final Report with the exception of Basic Objectives which is causing the maximum of difficulty and ill-temper' [CAB 119/12].

---

[2] Cf. No. 218, minute 1 and note 4.
[3] 25 July 1945.

No. 345

Minute from Sir O. Sargent to Mr. Eden (Berlin)
[E 5138/8/89]

FOREIGN OFFICE, 20 July 1945

I understand that you have asked for the Department's comments on Paris telegram No. 992[1] about the Levant.

2. If the French are now prepared to withdraw all their troops from the Levant as a unilateral gesture, our troops would of course all be withdrawn too, as we have publicly proclaimed. We ought certainly to take the opportunity to divest ourselves of any further obligations towards the Syrian and Lebanese Governments as suggested by Mr. Duff Cooper in paragraph 3 of this telegram.

3. The French however, would surely be very foolish from their own point of view to make such a unilateral gesture, leaving all other Franco-Syrian problems unregulated. Indeed, it hardly seems likely that they will do this. They had much better agree to a conference, as we have proposed, at which they would agree to troop withdrawals in return for definite assurances (which we would try to help them to obtain) as regards fair treatment of legitimate French interests.

4. If there is a conference, the Syrians and Lebanese must of course be represented at it; but this need not preclude a talk between yourself and M. Bidault in Paris.

5. If you do discuss the Levant with M. Bidault, it will be important to avoid anything which would amount to, or which France or the Levant States or anyone else could represent as, a settlement of the future of the Levant behind the backs of the States themselves. I also submit that we should not commit ourselves to the French as regards the support they may expect from us if and when the Levant question is referred to the World Organisation. It would, I think, be valuable if you could find out what ideas the French have about the position and interests they want to preserve; and if you could advise moderation in any direct discussions with the Levant States or at a conference, or pending discussion of the dispute by the World Organisation, should neither direct Franco-Levantine conversations nor a conference materialize.

O. G. SARGENT

[1] No. 120.

No. 346

Letter from Mr. Hayter (Berlin) to Mr. Howard[1]
[F.O. 934/1/1(12)]

BRITISH DELEGATION, BERLIN, 20 July 1945

Dear Douglas,

Southern Department subjects had a field day today.

[1] The date of receipt in the Foreign Office is uncertain.

The Russians produced their promised paper on the Yalta Declaration (copy enclosed)[2]. As you will see it consists of assertions that everything is lovely in the Bulgarian garden and of wild accusations about Greece. No doubt the Russians thought that attack was the best form of defence. The Secretary of State dealt with the Greek part of this with great thoroughness, and was well supported by Byrnes who said that from the American point of view there was a great difference between Greece, where anyone could go and see for himself what was going on, and Bulgaria and Roumania which were closed to the outside world.

It so happened that the letters about the Greek elections[3] had gone in this morning. After a lot of argument Byrnes produced a suggestion that he should write a paper proposing the observation (at the plenary in the afternoon the Prime Minister made a great point of observation, not supervision)[4] of elections, more privileges for British and Americans on the Control Commissions and improved facilities for press correspondents. We said that we were strongly in favour of these ideas and Molotov said rather grumpily that he would consider the paper when it was produced. Cannon is drafting it tonight and we hope to see it before the morning meeting.

At one point Molotov suggested reminding the Greek Government that it was their duty to observe the Varkiza Agreement. We did not take this up at the time, but I am trying to sell the idea that we should agree to this (which in itself seems harmless enough) on condition that the Russians agree to reminding the Yugoslavs about the Tit[o]-Subasic Agreement.

Roumanian oil and Turkey got squeezed out today. We hope to give Turkey a run tomorrow, but the Americans have suggested that we should keep Roumanian oil back until the Yalta Declaration stuff makes a little more progress. This seems to us sound.

W. G. HAYTER

[2] No. 201.
[3] See No. 200, note 9.
[4] See No. 208, minute 1.

No. 347

Letter from Mr. Lawford to Mr. Dixon (Berlin)
[*F.O. 934/5/55(1)*]

FOREIGN OFFICE, *20 July 1945*

My dear Bob,

You may remember[1] that before he left the Secretary of State asked for a file of 'Examples of Russian bad faith' for Terminal. The attached notes represent what I have been able to collect from the Departments.

[1] An annotation by Mr. J. N. Henderson on the filed copy here referred to the minute in No. 84.iv.

There are of course other Russian shortcomings connected with the E.A.C., the French sector in Berlin, the Soviet attitude towards E.C.O., E.E.C.E., P.E.I.T.O. and U.M.A., and the production and distribution of food in Eastern Europe. On all these subjects I understand that you already have briefs.[2]

Yours ever
NICHOLAS

ENCLOSURE IN NO. 347

Roumania and Bulgaria

In Roumania and Bulgaria we have experienced two striking examples of Russian bad faith in the sense of violation or evasion of written undertakings:–

1. The recent removal of further oil equipment from British-owned Roumanian companies was conducted in violation of a categorical undertaking given in Moscow on the 4th January.

2. By obstruction and procrastination, the Russians have so far permitted the Bulgarians to evade their obligation to deliver reparations to Greece. The Russians are themselves under a definite obligation to keep the Bulgarians up to the mark.

It might also be argued that the Russians have deliberately violated the Yalta declaration upon liberated territories by their actions in Roumania, but there is little doubt that they genuinely interpret that declaration in a sense widely differing from our own and the United States Government's interpretation.

The majority of our complaints in these countries arise not from violation of agreements, but from complete failure to accord us the co-operation to which we are entitled. As the chief participants in the Control Commission, the Russians have assumed the general trusteeship of Allied interests. So far from fulfilling this obligation, they have taken every opportunity of increasing their own interests at the expense of ours. The most important of our complaints under this heading are:–

(1) the restrictions imposed upon our representatives in these countries (brief[3] on this point was taken to Terminal);

(2) continued attacks, both direct and indirect, on British commercial interests, including the exclusion of British commercial representatives;

(3) an extreme disinclination to inform the British representatives of important actions taken in the name of the Control Commission.

Implementation of the Yalta Prisoner of War Agreement

Even after making full allowance for priorities created by the conduct of military operations and for the different standards of comfort etc. prevalent in Russia, the fact remains that the Soviet authorities entirely failed to give effect to several of the most important provisions of the Yalta Agreement. The following are our principal sources of grievance.

I. *Lack of facilities for British contact officers.* Contact teams were allowed to make one short visit to Lublin, Lwow and Volkovysk, but they were not allowed

---

[2] Mr. Dixon minuted on this: '? + Lena Goldfields, & send enclosure to P.M. P.D. 21/7.' Undated brief No. 9 for the U.K. Delegation at Potsdam on Lena and Tetiuhe Bonds (N 12546/137/38) is not printed.

[3] See No. 82, note 4.

to do the job for which they had been sent. In the case of Lwow, the British team was ordered to leave after only a few days' stay and while liberated prisoners were still passing through. When they refused, they received orders to remain in their hotel. The contact team at Volkovysk was not allowed to administer the camp there and was finally ordered to leave while a party of 28 prisoners were still in the camp. At Lublin, it was found impossible to do anything for the benefit of the liberated British and United States prisoners who were found to be living in totally inadequate conditions.

The only place at which British repatriation teams were allowed to remain was Odessa, but even there they were not allowed to function properly. They were not permitted to live in the camp itself, as Soviet repatriation officers are in the United Kingdom, nor to interview British ex-prisoners of war save in the presence of a Soviet officer. Furthermore, every time these British officers wished to enter the camp they were obliged to ask for a Soviet escort. Insistence on these conditions gradually lapsed, but they remained nominally in force throughout.

The Soviet authorites have based their refusal to allow our repatriation officers to proceed to other areas on the argument that Odessa was the only collecting point in existence. Returning prisoners were, however, unanimous in asserting the presence of large numbers of British stragglers in many areas of Poland. One of the most objectionable aspects of this Soviet attitude has been their

II. *Refusal to grant British repatriation officers access to sick British prisoners of war in various hospitals*, where, by all accounts, they were receiving quite inadequate attention.

III. *Maltreatment.* There have been cases of liberated British prisoners of war—known by the Soviet authorities to be such—being forced to work at dismantling factories, etc. There have also been cases of the rape of British women and innumerable instances of the robbery of returning British prisoners of war under threat of arms.

IV. *Slowness of evacuation.* The apparent lack of any organisation responsible for collecting liberated prisoners of war in the forward areas, and the chaotic conditions of rail transport in the rear of the Red Army, have combined to make evacuation a lengthy and hazardous process.

Whenever substantiated, these matters have been brought to the attention of the Soviet authorities. The replies received have been couched in the most general terms, have produced no counter evidence and have merely rejected our complaints out of hand. Thus, for example, the repeated maltreatment of liberated British prisoners was more or less written off as the work of 'marauders and other bandit elements' in the rear of the Red Army. On the other hand, His Majesty's Government are held fully responsible for innumerable instances (all without foundation) in which Soviet citizens liberated by the Allied Armies are said to have been improperly treated by the Polish Armed Forces, or by German civilians.

Despite their extremely bad record in this matter, the Soviet Government have tried, both by public statement and by innumerable notes of protest, to present themselves as the injured party. The truth of the matter is that the best that the best [*sic*] that the Russians have done for our men has been considerably lower, in general, than the worst which we have offered to theirs, and the interpretations given to the Yalta agreement by the British and Soviet authorities respectively simply do not bear comparison.

Persia

There is no Soviet act in Persia which can be quoted as an outstanding case of

Soviet 'bad faith' towards ourselves. Nevertheless, the whole policy of the Soviet authorities in Persia is based on the misuse of the powers granted by the Anglo-Soviet-Persian Treaty of Alliance, which were intended to further the prosecution of the war against Germany, to undermine Persian independence which the Soviet Government are under a joint obligation with us to maintain.

Examples:–

(1) Interference with the movement of Persian troops, gendarmeries and police.

(2) Interference in Persian internal politics.

(3) Misuse of censorship to prevent Persian news from reaching the outside world except through Moscow, combined with the use of the Moscow press and wireless to put out anti-Persian articles.

(4) Continued control of the northern section of the Persian railways, inspite of the fact that aid to Russia through Persia has ceased; and interference at all times with growing supplies by rail.

Agreement of 27th June 1942[4] *as regards payment for aircraft*

Between August, 1941 and July, 1943 His Majesty's Government supplied to the Soviet Union aircraft and aircraft engines to the value of some $33,000,000 which had originally been purchased for dollars in the United States of America.

2. The Soviet Government is obliged under Article 2(d) of the Agreement of the 27th June, 1942 'Concerning the financing of military supplies and other military assistance from the Government of the United Kingdom of Great Britain and Northern Ireland to the Government of the Union of Soviet Socialist Republics' to pay for these aircraft. The relevant clause reads as follows: 'Military supplies, which have originally been bought and paid for by the British Government in United States dollars, shall be paid for by the Soviet Government at the time of delivery in United States dollars at the same prices as the British Government originally paid for them'. The agreement was made retroactive to the period from the 22nd June, 1941 and it was agreed that it should remain in force until six months after the signing of an armistice between the British and Soviet Governments on the one hand and the German Government on the other. These provisions were brought to the notice of the Soviet Government in September 1941 during the Moscow Conference when the original draft text of the 1942 agreement was submitted for consideration. The Soviet Government raised no objections.

3. On the 13th June, 1945, when His Majesty's Ambassador at Moscow pressed Monsieur Mikoyan for payments the latter said the Soviet authorities had not heard about payment until a year or eighteen months after the agreement had been signed. Why had they not been warned at the time of delivery? How could they be expected to pay for something they had not ordered? When the Soviet Government agreed to the insertion of a clause making the Agreement retroactive, they had had in mind only certain deliveries of rubber and tin, not aircraft.

4. These arguments are disingenuous. The necessity of paying in gold or its equivalent for military supplies which His Majesty's Government had purchased for dollars in the U.S.A. and which were to be passed on to Russia in the same form as we had received them was formally brought to the attention of the Soviet Government by Sir Stafford Cripps on the 20th September, 1941, and deliveries

---

[4] Printed in *Vneshnyaya politika Sovetskogo Soyuza v period Otechestvennoy voyny* (Foreign Policy of the Soviet Union in the period of the Patriotic War: Moscow, 1944f.), vol. i, pp. 264–5.

of rubber and tin were specifically excluded from the agreement of the 27th June, 1942 as they had been dealt with under the Agreement of the 16th August, 1941[5] 'Concerning mutual deliveries, credit and methods of payment.' If the Soviet Government persists in its refusal to pay for these aircraft and aeroplane engines, it will have been guilty of a breach of faith by defaulting on an agreement freely entered into by both sides.

CALENDARS TO No. 347

i *17–21 July 1945 Mr. Hankey (Warsaw) Tels. Nos. 7 & 26; to Sir A. Clark Kerr (Moscow) Tel. No. 4050.* Difficulties of British P.O.W.s in Poland: 'it is evident that Russian authorities have in many cases ignored Yalta agreement about freed British subjects.' Instructions to Moscow on 21 July for enlisting Soviet assistance in repatriating some 200 British remaining in Poland [F.O. 916/1200; N 9160/4869/55].

ii *19 July 1945 (a) Letter No. 1 from General Ratov, Soviet representative for repatriation, to General Sir A. Thorne, Allied Commander in Norway; (b) 21 Army Group telegram No. L.M.4/1.27–80 to War Office.* (a) Soviet complaints of treatment of Soviet citizens in Norway and of non-repatriation, with reference to Latvians, Estonians, Lithuanians, Ukrainians and White Russians. (b) Accreditation of General Ratov for Denmark is not authorized [N 8600, 9074/409/38].

iii *20 July 1945 General Gammell (Moscow) to A.F.H.Q. Tel. No. MIL/4196.* Soviet complaints of treatment of Soviet citizens in Italy [N 9223/409/38].

iv *26 July 1945 British Note to M. Koukin (Counsellor in Soviet Embassy, London).* Protest at conduct of certain Soviet repatriation officers in the U.K. concerning their recent claim to authority in respect of two Poles [N 8685/409/38].

[5] Printed in the appendix to Cmd. 7297 of 1948.

No. 348

Sir J. Anderson to Mr. Eden (Berlin: received 21 July, 1.45 p.m.)
No. 112 Onward Telegraphic [U 5558/11/70]

Top secret. Immediate   FOREIGN OFFICE, *21 July 1945*, 7.5 a.m.

Personal for the Secretary of State from Sargent.

My telegram number 86 Onward[1] (of 19th July: Austria).

General McCreery foresees that the Russians will take the same line as they did over Berlin and try to place on us the responsibility for feeding our sector in Vienna. He asks for instructions. The position is that, without American help, we cannot supply food except for a short period, still less fuel. Moreover a serious question of principle is involved, even more serious than in the case of Berlin.

[1] No. 315.

2. War Office have been discussing the question with us, and would like to send Stopford and Berthoud, Head of the Economics Division of the British Element of the Austrian Commission, who is now in London, to Terminal in the hope that, in the light of their explanations and of any advice given by Field Marshal Alexander, you and the Prime Minister will be able to determine upon precise instructions to General McCreery. Whilst we realise the political importance of not abandoning our position in Austria, it is for consideration whether in view of the additional commitment involved we should occupy our zone in Vienna, and indeed Styria, unless the Russians agree that deficiencies in Austria should be met from normal sources. In the case of Vienna's food requirements, these are in the main Lower Austria and/or the countries of the Danube basin which are also under Russian control, whilst coal was mainly drawn from Silesia and Poland.

3. Unless we hear from you to the contrary, Stopford and Berthoud will proceed to Terminal Sunday morning, 22nd July.[2]

CALENDARS TO No 348

i *17–23 July 1945 A.C. Tel. No. 3308 to General Winterton (Military Mission, Vienna); General McCreery (8th Army) Tels. Nos. AC/404 & 407; to and from Mr. Eden (Berlin) Tels. Nos. 135 Onward & 181 Target; minuting in Berlin by Mr. Coulson and Sir A. Cadogan.* Importance of treating Austria as an economic entity. Possibility of Soviet attempt to make British entry into Vienna conditional on immediate provision of supplies. Arrangements with Soviet authorities for take-over of British sector in Vienna and British zone. Instructions pursuant to No. 241, minute 14 [UE 3171/139/71; F.O. 934/4/25 (6–7); U 5658/11/70; C 5051/317/3].

ii *24 July–2 Aug. 1945 Protocol of meeting in Vienna of Chiefs of Staff of Allied Forces in Austria on 24 & 25 July; Telegrams between General Winterton (Vienna) and General McCreery (8th Army) COS 558–9 & A.C./339.* Arrangements for Allied occupation of Vienna, access thereto, and zones in Austria. Discussion with Soviet Deputy Commissioner on 1 August on working of control machinery [C 4714, 4294, 4306, 4490/317/3].

[2] Mr. Coulson minuted on this telegram in Berlin: 'Mr. Harrison & I discussed with Sir A. Cadogan. We agreed: (a) that politically we could not go back on our zones; (b) that there could be no objection to Mr. Stopford and Mr. Berthoud coming here. I have asked Administration to arrange beds & offices for them. J. E. C. 21/7.'

No. 349

Sir J. Anderson to Mr. Eden (Berlin: received 22 July, 1.5 a.m.)
No. 122 Onward Telegraphic [F.O. 934/2/10(33)]

Immediate   FOREIGN OFFICE, *21 July 1945, 5.10 p.m.*[1]

Following for Sir A. Cadogan from Sargent.

We have given cursory consideration here to Polish memorandum[2]

[1] Time of origin.   [2] See No. 115, note 5.

mentioned in your telegram Target 105.[3] It makes the expected claim to the Oder-Western Neisse frontier including Stettin but advances no fresh arguments and calls for no special comment except that it glosses over the problem of how to dispose of the present German population. Annex IV is worth a glance from point of view of Silesian coal.

2. You have I think all the necessary information to enable you to state fully the British case in reply to the Soviet memorandum P (Terminal) 12[4] of the 20th July. I gather from Allen's letter to Warner of the [1]9th July[5] that the Americans have been reluctant to raise the matter as they do not want to get deeply involved in its economic aspects until a clearer picture has emerged as a result of the work of the special Economic Committee. But the political aspect of the question is just as important if not more important than the economic aspect. You will I am sure agree that if the Potsdam Conference broke up without our having clearly stated our views on this subject, our silence would always be quoted against us afterwards, just as our silence about Abyssinia at the Stresa meeting[6] was quoted against us by Mussolini.[7]

[3] Not printed.
[4] No. 202.
[5] No. 189.ii.
[6] The Anglo–Franco–Italian Conference at Stresa in April 1935. For the question of Abyssinia in this connexion see *D.B.F.P.*, Second Series, vol. xiv, No. 230, note 5; cf. *ibid.*, pp. x-xi.
[7] Mr. Eden and Sir A. Cadogan minuted on this telegram: 'A. C. Should we put in something in writing? A. E.' 'Mr. Allen. Are you considering a written statement of our views? It might be useful. A. C. July 23/45.'

No. 350

Letter from Sir O. Sargent to Sir A. Cadogan (Berlin: received 22 July)
[*F.O. 934/2/10(74)*]

FOREIGN OFFICE, *21 July 1945*

Dear Alec

I enclose a copy of Warner's record [iii] of his interview with the Chairman of the Warsaw Government Commission for taking over Polish State property this morning and the translation [iii] of the communication Hankey may expect to receive from the Warsaw Government in reply to the basis of discussions with the Commission, which we suggested in our telegram No: 3843 of the 8th July to Moscow.[1]

You will see that it looks as if discussions will shortly open on a satisfactory basis and as if the Warsaw Government's attitude to the whole matter was not going to be too unreasonable. The last sentence of the penultimate

[1] No. 41.

paragraph of the record also tends to suggest that Warsaw may take a fairly sensible attitude about the Polish armed forces.

This being so, it seems to us most important that we should not allow ourselves to be bullied by Vyshinsky, on the Drafting Committee, into giving away any point beforehand. Harriman is quite right; this is none of the Soviet Government's business.[2]

You will see my record [ii] of a talk with Drohojowski yesterday in which he delivered three messages from Mikolajczyk and copies of Hankey's telegrams Nos: 23 and 24[3] about the treatment which Popiel is receiving and Grabski's difficulties in the praesidium. I hope it may be possible to take the offensive with the Russians on these points and not confine ourselves in the draft resolution to generalities about the elections. Incidentally, you will have noticed that Mikolajczyk is not keen on very early elections.

A further point that occurs to me is that the Prime Minister at the second plenary meeting said our policy was to *persuade* as many as possible of the military and civilian Poles to go back to Poland.[4] Our line in fact is to ensure, so far as possible, that they should have an appropriate chance of opting. It seems to me dangerous to commit ourselves to persuading. The border-line between persuading and compelling may not be very distinct to the Russians and Warsaw communists.

In sum it looks as if we may be able to have a discussion on a reasonable and orderly basis with the Warsaw Government about all these matters and I feel pretty sure that this is what our friends in Poland want; I hope therefore that we shall not prejudice these discussions in advance by making promises to the Russians at Terminal, who are of course campaigning on behalf of the anti-Mikolajczyk communists in the Warsaw Government.[5]

Yrs

O. G. SARGENT

[2] Cf. No. 189.ii.

[3] Nos. 318.i and 318 respectively.

[4] See No. 184, minute 5.

[5] Mr. Allen minuted in Berlin: 'The first part of the attached letter from Sir O. Sargent to Sir A. Cadogan is now out of date, in as much as our draft statement on Poland was finally agreed at the plenary session on the 21st July. The Foreign Office were anxious that we should not prejudice the discussions which may shortly begin with representatives of the Polish Provisional Government in a reasonably promising atmosphere by giving promises to the Russians on questions such as the transfer of Polish State property in the United Kingdom and the assumption of liability for Polish debts. In fact, I think, we have not given anything very serious away on this point in the statement as finally agreed. The field has been left clear for bilateral discussions between H.M.G. and the Polish Provisional Government. More serious are the questions raised in Warsaw telegrams Nos. 23 and 24 [see note 3] which are referred to in Sir O. Sargent's letter . . . Sir O. Sargent suggests that we should take the offensive with the Russians on these points. I am afraid that the time has in fact passed for this and I doubt whether we should in any case get anywhere if we were to raise them with the Soviet representatives here. On the other hand an opportunity for discussing these questions should arise if representatives of the Polish Provisional Government accept our invitation to come here. We should, I think, be in a strong position in pointing out to them that they cannot seriously expect us to agree to their extending their authority right up to the line of the Oder and the Western Neisse

i *19 July 1945 Minutes of First Meeting of Polish Armed Forces (Service Depts.-F.O.) Committee.* Problems arising from British recognition of Polish Provisional Govt.: facilitating repatriation, control over Polish High Command, etc. [N 9135/123/55].

ii *20–22 July 1945 (a) Record by Sir O. Sargent of conversation with M. Drohojowski (b) To Mr. Hankey (Warsaw) Tels. Nos. 27 and 33; Mr. Hankey (Warsaw) Tel. No. 30.* Messages from M. Mikolajczyk: (i) Polish effort to build up Praesidium as a super-government: question of credentials of H.M. and U.S. Ambassadors; (ii) elections should not be held in Poland pending withdrawal of Russian troops; (iii) he would like to visit London. [N 8990, 9009/6/55, N 9863/211/55].

iii *21 July 1945 Record by Mr. Warner of conversation with members of Polish Commission to London.* Unofficial discussion of draft Polish note (annexed) in reply to communication in No. 41. Poles disappointed at Mr. Warner's reaction that note was not straightforward acceptance of proposed basis for discussions with commission [N 9197/6/55].

iv *24 July & 4 Aug. 1945 To Mr. Eden (Berlin) Tel. No. 200 Onward: to Mr. Hankey (Warsaw) Tel. No. 143.* Refutes press allegations against Polish military authorities in London involving Interim Treasury Committee; meeting on 1 August between the I.T.C. and Polish Commission on financial liquidation of former Polish Govt. in London [N 9325/123/55, N 9876/1938/55].

so long as the reports which we are receiving from Warsaw about general conditions in Poland proper are so extremely unsatisfactory. D. Allen 22nd July 1945.' Sir A. Cadogan minuted 'If we allow the Poles to go as far as the Western Neisse, we certainly should at least get some *quid pro quo* of this sort. But I am not sure that we should trade that area for simple assurances by the Poles. A. C. July 23, 1945.' Mr. Eden commented: 'I am strongly against Western Neisse anyway. But I agree that we should take up these points with Poles when they come—Mr. Allen might prepare brief for me—Sir A. Clark Kerr should also see this. I think that it would be good if I had a talk to them myself; even better if P.M. and I could do it together. A. E. July 24.'

No. 351

Sir J. Anderson to Mr. Eden (Berlin: received 22 July, 10 a.m.)
No. 131 Onward Telegraphic [R 12360/81/67]

FOREIGN OFFICE, *21 July 1945, 8.15 p.m.*[1]

From Foreign Office for Secretary of State.

You will doubtless not want to leave unanswered the assertions made in paragraph 2 of the Russian paper P. (Terminal) 11[2] of the 20th July about the Yalta Declaration on Liberated Europe. The briefs taken to Terminal,

---

[1] Time of origin.　　　　[2] No. 201.

and particularly that dealing with Greek internal affairs,[3] will provide most of the answers to this astonishing document, but I thought it might be useful to you to have some further ammunition.

We cannot for the moment accept the contention either that 'due order' exists in Roumania and Bulgaria or that the Governments of these countries are 'trusted by the population.' Our briefs drew attention to the terroristic activities of the Communist-controlled secret police and militia in these countries, particularly in Bulgaria, but we might mention as an example of these activities the fact that, according to reports which we believe to be true, between 40,000 and 50,000 persons were murdered by the militia in the past six months in addition to the 2,000 odd executed after trial as 'war criminals'. The offence of the great majority of these people was, of course, opposition to the present Government and not collaboration with the Germans. A second example of the methods of the militia is the affair of Petkov's secretary,[4] of which Hayter knows the details. The pretence that all is in order within the Bulgarian Government has been finally exposed by the latest crisis resulting from the publication by an Agrarian Minister of the true facts. Hayter took with him a note on this point serving as an addendum to one of our briefs[5] and there have been no further developments.

The statement that the Governments of these countries faithfully carry out the obligations they assumed under the Armistices is, of course, equally unacceptable. The failure of the Bulgarian Government to make reparation deliveries to Greece is the most serious example of this. The Russian claim also offers a good opportunity for pointing out that the Bulgarians, so far from demobilising their army, as they are bound to do by the Armistice Terms, appear to have been permitted even to increase it. I hope the Delegation can also find an opportunity for pointing out that, while these three countries are obliged by the Armistice Terms to suppress fascist organisations and technically, at any rate, have done so, many of the members of these organisations, notably the Iron Guard,[6] have simply transferred their allegiance to the local Communist Party, which has welcomed them with open arms.

As regards Hungary, neither the Soviet memo. nor the American memo.[7] on which it comments devotes much attention to the situation there. While that situation is certainly not satisfactory, and will probably deteriorate in the same way as that of Roumania has, it is at present better in some ways

[3] No. 84.ii.

[4] Cf. *F.R.U.S. 1945*, vol. iv, p. 238f. for the death in May 1945 of Mlle. Mara Racheva, private secretary to M. Petkov and formerly to his predecessor as Secretary-General of the Bulgarian Agrarian Party, Dr. G. M. Dimitrov, while she was under arrest following the escape of Dr. Dimitrov from house arrest to refuge in the U.S. Mission.

[5] Brief No. 8 for the British Delegation at Potsdam on the political situation in Roumania, Bulgaria and Hungary, drafted on 9 July 1945 (R 11694/81/67), is not printed. The addendum to this brief was a note of 12 July by Mr. Howard summarizing the Bulgarian development reported in No. 90.

[6] In Roumania.

[7] See No. 170, note 2, for P. (Terminal) 4.

than that in Roumania or Bulgaria, and we too are not yet in a position to make a fuss about it.

Since the Russians will of course deny our facts, could not a very effective point be made by contrasting the iron censorship imposed in the Soviet-controlled Balkan countries with the complete freedom of speech and of the press, which is permitted in Greece? If the situation in the Russian-controlled countries is as satisfactory as they pretend, why two months after the end of the German war are they still so anxious to prevent newspaper correspondents from entering these countries and objective reports from leaving them? If we have anything to hide in Greece, why do we not even try to do so?[8]

[8] Mr. Eden minuted on this telegram to Mr. Dixon: 'I hope Dept. have records of what I said at F. S. meeting [see No. 200, minute 6]. War Cabinet should surely see too? Please speak to Sir A. C[adogan] about a written note by us on Bulgaria. A. E.'

No. 352

Sir J. Anderson to Mr. Eden (Berlin)[1]
No. 133 Onward Telegraphic [UE 3156/86/77]

Top secret. Immediate   FOREIGN OFFICE, *21 July 1945, 11.50 p.m.*

For Foreign Secretary from Sir O. Sargent.

We have considered with other Departments of His Majesty's Government concerned the definition of Restitution put forward by the United States Delegation;[2] and the amendments thereto proposed by Sir D. Waley.[3] From the political point of view the Department considers it of primary importance that the European Allies should be entitled to restitution of identifiable and recoverable monetary gold, valuables and securities which were their property before occupation and which were looted by the enemy. We very much hope it will prove possible to secure this. The inclusion of identifiable monetary gold in any Restitution policy agreed at Terminal would materially lessen the bitterness with which other European Allies, especially the French, would look upon a policy settled by the Three Great Powers without consultation with them.

[1] Time of receipt at Berlin is uncertain.   [2] See No. 213, note 5.
[3] Cf. No. 175.i, and *F.R.U.S. Berlin*, vol. ii, p. 848.

No. 353

Mr. Randall (Copenhagen) to Mr. Eden (Received 21 July, 8.20 p.m.)
No. 375 Telegraphic [N 9047/1866/15]

COPENHAGEN, *21 July 1945, 6.18 p.m.*

Repeated to Political Adviser to the Commander in Chief Germany.

Your telegram No. 223.[1]

[1] Repetition to Copenhagen of No. 330.

I agree appointment of Danish national would be unnecessary and politically undesirable. I should have no objection to Military Government so replying to Danish Government. You may however prefer that I should inform Danish Government, adding perhaps that it would be better in future if this kind of political request were made through diplomatic channels.

Confidential. I presume I am correct that His Majesty's Government would be opposed to Danish annexation of or mandate over German territory inhabited by Danish minority, and that it is reasonable to assume that the American and Soviet Governments would concur in this view. Danish Minister for Foreign Affairs has more than once, while repeating his well-known views against annexation asked me whether the three principal Allied Governments had considered the question of the Danish-German frontier regions and in particular whether the future of Kiel had yet been taken up.[2]

Foreign Office please repeat to 21st Army Group for Mr. Steel as my No. 9.

[2] On 23 July 1945 Foreign Office telegram No. 234 to Copenhagen replied: 'First paragraph. I agree to the action you propose. Second paragraph. See my telegram No. 37 Saving [No. 374] which should reach you 24th July.'

No. 354

Sir J. Anderson to Sir W. Strang (Lübbecke)
No. 100 Telegraphic [N 8996/1866/15]

Most Immediate   FOREIGN OFFICE, *21 July 1945, 7.45 p.m.*

Repeated to Copenhagen No. 229 Most Immediate.

Copenhagen telegram No: 374[1] (of 21st July: Desire of Danish Minister for Foreign Affairs to visit Danish minority in South Schleswig).

We think it right that Mr. Christmas Moller should be allowed to visit the grave of his son and trust that every courtesy will be afforded him.

2. As for his further request to spend a few hours talking privately to leaders of Danish minority we for our part see no objection to his having such private conversations, but if the Commander-in-Chief agrees to his entering the British zone for this purpose, Mr. Randall should point out to him beforehand that the administration of the British zone is solely a British responsibility under the terms of the four Power Agreement and that we must therefore ask him not to indulge in any activity that could be regarded as political.

3. I agree that Danish request reported in your telegram No: 60[2] (of 20th July) is unreasonable though we should hardly describe it as 'an almost Hitlerite manoeuvre'.

[1] No. 330.ii.   [2] No. 330.

i *22–4 July 1945 Lübbecke Tels. Nos. 62 & 66; Mr. Randall (Copenhagen) Tel. No. 380.* Arrangements for M. Möller's visit to South Schleswig [N 9016, 9021, 9169/1866/15].

No. 355

Sir J. Anderson to Mr. Hopkinson (Rome)
No. 1878 Telegraphic [ZM 4121/1/22]

FOREIGN OFFICE, *21 July 1945, 1.45 a.m.*

Repeated to Washington No. 682 Saving, Resmed's Office Caserta No. 223 Saving, Terminal No. 113 Onward (by bag).

The question of a Peace Treaty with Italy was raised by Count Carandini[1] in the course of two conversations on July 18th. He was told that we favoured an early and comprehensive settlement so that a new chapter in Anglo-Italian relations could begin. Count Carandini agreed, but maintained that if our terms were to be severe it would be preferable to conclude a *modus vivendi*. A heavy blow to the present Italian Government might prove fatal for the future of democracy in Italy.

2. Count Carandini thought that Italian opinion would accept a treaty providing for the retention of Trieste and the Istrian littoral the cession of that part of Cyrenaica called Marmorica up to Tobruk and the retention under Italian trusteeship of the rest of the Italian colonies. He asked whether it would help if the Italian Government were to tell us officially precisely what sacrifices they were prepared to make in order to bring about a 'just' peace settlement. No response was made to this suggestion nor to an offer that the Italian Government should spontaneously hand over the Dodecanese to Greece.

3. The Deputy Under-Secretary of State told Count Carandini that he saw no advantage in a Peace Treaty which merely evaded the difficult problems which would have to be faced sooner or later. It was a pity that it had not been possible to face these problems straight away when fighting had ceased, but Sir O. Sargent was certain that the longer we put off grasping the nettle the more difficult it would be to reach an agreed settlement.

4. Sir O. Sargent urged strongly the importance of elections before the winter (*a*) because it was important that the Italian Government, who would have to grapple with a terribly difficult economic situation during the winter, should be fortified by a popular vote; (*b*) because the Communists might derive an altogether fictitious strength by exploiting economic difficulties which were bound to occur during the winter; and (*c*)—and

[1] Italian Representative in London with the personal rank of Ambassador.

this was Count Carandini's own point—because it was desirable that the elections should be held while the British and American troops were still in the country so as to prevent disorders and victimisation. Count Carandini offered to put these considerations to his Government.

5. In reply to a question Count Carandini declared that he was in favour of the Peace Treaty being signed before the elections and was confident that the present Government had sufficient authority in the country to do so. If it was being negotiated after the elections and during the time when the Constituent Assembly was meeting, it would become the subject of discussion and intrigue in the Assembly which might further complicate and seriously delay the work of that body. (No doubt Count Carandini made a mental reservation as regards the severity of the Treaty.)

CALENDARS TO No. 355

i   *18–20 July 1945   Records by Mr. Harvey & Sir O. Sargent* of conversations summarized above. Mr. Hoyer Millar in Berlin stated in a minute of 20 July to Sir A. Cadogan: 'The general impression which both Mr. Harvey and Sir Orme Sargent got from Count Carandini's conversations was that the Italian Government was starting up their old game of black-mail' in an attempt either to secure agreement to 'a soft peace treaty now' or a *modus vivendi* so as to 'postpone the unpleasant parts of the peace treaty indefinitely' [U 5615/50/70].

ii   *25 July 1945   Letter from Mr. Hoyer Millar (Berlin) to Mr. Harvey.* Use of documents in regard to assertions by Professor L. Rougier (cf. No. 565.i); appointment of Allied Chief Commissioner in Italy (cf. No. 193, minute 6); considerations at the Potsdam Conference regarding an Italian peace treaty, colonies and reparation [F.O. 934/2/6(26)].

iii   *31 July 1945   Minute by Mr. Ross.* On 30 July Count Carandini said that Italian Govt. would like some indication of British intentions regarding peace treaty so as to be able to guide Italian public and warn H.M.G. of provisions whose imposition might spell danger [U 5615/50/70].

No. 356

Mr. Roberts (Moscow) to Mr. Eden (Received 22 July, 2.55 a.m.)
No. 3255 Telegraphic [R 12350/4476/44]

Immediate   MOSCOW, *21 July 1945, 10.45 p.m.*

Repeated to Istanbul (Constantinople) No. 26, Washington No. 532.

All papers 21st July, under heading 'American Observer on Foreign Policy of Soviet Union' devote 75 lines to extracts from 'Christian Science Monitor' article by Stevens[1] commenting on Soviet demand for regulation of certain problems affecting its interests, particularly return of Soviet territories Kars Artvin and Ardahan. Stevens says that in demanding

---

[1] Mr. E. W. Stevens had recently been an American war-correspondent in Moscow.

return of these territories bordering Caucasus U.S.S.R. wishes to recover last hitherto unclaimed portion of Russian territory lost when U.S.S.R. was weak. Territories are historically Armenian and acquired by Turkey 1920 by force. Population is not mainly Armenian because Turks killed all Armenians during last war. This does not strengthen Turkey's right to disputed territory. Soviet demand will receive wide support among all Armenians who usually prefer Russians to Turks.

2. Noting justice of Soviet demands for control over Dardanelles, Stevens earnestly warns against Turkish attempts to create Greco-Turkish anti-Soviet bloc with British support. Soviet Union being a Black Sea power and interested in sea communications is just as interested in Dardanelles as United States in Panama. Perhaps also Axis warships were allowed through Dardanelles contrary to Montreux Agreement against interests of U.S.S.R. and Allies. Stalin will undoubtedly insist on future Dardanelles security requiring more substantial measures than verbal Turkish promise not to violate Montreux again.

3. Stevens says danger in this issue arises less from Soviet demands than sensitive British attitude over Mediterranean power balance. Exploiting this, Turks try to create Turkish-Greek bloc closely linked with Britain to bar Soviet influence from Mediterranean. Such barrier is equivalent to wedge in Great Power unity.[2]

Please pass to Terminal.

CALENDAR TO No. 356

i   *22 July 1945   Mr. Roberts (Moscow) Tel. No. 3257.* Comments on Mr. Stevens' article, which 'contains the most detailed public statement which has yet appeared here about Soviet territorial and other claims against Turkey', and affords opportunity to Russians to suggest difference of view between British and Americans [R 12366/4476/44].

[2] Mr. McDermott minuted and Mr. Howard initialed on this telegram: 'It is not surprising the Russians welcome this. Incidentally there is a good deal of truth in it. Copy [to] M[iddle] E[ast] Min.   G. L. McDermott 22/7.'   'D. H. 23/7.'

No. 357

Field-Marshal Viscount Wavell[1] *(New Delhi) to Mr. Amery*
(Received 21 July, 3.45 p.m.)
No. 1186 S. Telegraphic [F 4791/364/23]

NEW DELHI, *21 July 1945, 6.40 p.m.*

Important. Top secret and personal

Your telegram 16085[2] of July 18th. In year following last war Indian feeling towards Japan was made up of first admiration for Japanese efficiency

[1] Viceroy and Governor-General of India.
[2] It would appear that this untraced telegram referred to the American draft document noted in No. 304, note 2.

and progress and status of Japan as only first class oriental power and second fear of Japanese trade competition.

2. First was weakened by Japanese aggression in China, revived with Japanese success in present war, and will disappear though perhaps not wholly with unconditional surrender of Japan. Second is still strong and India hopes to keep out Japanese good(? s omitted) and capture Japanese markets after this war.

3. Indian politicians and business men would therefore I think support severe policy provided it was carried out with maximum co-operation of Japanese. Any suggestion that Japanese are being humiliated or crushed to greater extent that Germans might revive sentiment in first above.

4. From Indian aspect I therefore consider Foreign Office approach outlined in your 16087[3] greatly preferable to that of State Department.

[3] This untraced telegram had repeated Dominions Office telegram No. 1245 (see No. 304, note 1), as explained in a letter of 28 July 1945 from Mr. D. M. Cleary of the India Office to Mr. Sterndale Bennett (received, 4 August) enclosing a copy of the present telegram from the Viceroy. Mr. Cleary stated: 'The Secretary of State concurs in the Viceroy's conclusions as expressed in paragraph 4 of his telegram.'

No. 358

Letter from Sir W. Monckton (Berlin) to Sir J. Anderson
[F.O. 934/1/2(22)]

Copy   BRITISH DELEGATION, BERLIN, *21 July 1945*

My dear Chancellor of the Exchequer,

Thank you for your letter of the 18th July.[1] I do not think there is any substantial difference between us, but I do not think I stated my difficulty plainly.

As regards industrial disarmament, I have adopted throughout our negotiations the line which you have restated and, where the Russians have sought to justify a very wide range of deindustrialisation on grounds of economic security, we have questioned the validity of their argument on the lines which you suggest.

I agree with the desiderata about reparation to which you refer in paragraphs 7 and 8 in your letter and I fear that, as you say, as regards reparation there is reason to expect a deep divergence between ourselves and the Russians. In so far as the Russians try to go beyond anything justified by paragraph 7 (Standard of living) of the Reparation Principles and to create a sub-Balkan condition of chaos in Germany, I shall contest their view vigorously. My difficulties and doubts arise in so far as the Russians keep strictly *within* the ambit of paragraph 7.

[1] No. 313.

A great deal of deindustrialisation is justified by the elimination or reduction of key industries on the ground of economic security and by the fact that Germany will no longer be producing armaments. Germany will have a smaller territory and a reduced population in the remaining territory. This reduced population has to have a modest standard of living. Taking all this into consideration, my experts have expressed the view that it would be justifiable to reduce German steel production to something like 7 million tons a year, as against the existing level before the collapse of something like 23 million tons. In the same way, taking each of the metallurgical and chemical industries in turn (apart from the key industries which must be dealt with from the point of view of economic security) very considerable reduction can be justified while keeping within a quite reasonable interpretation of paragraph 7. As you say in your letter, there is likely to be a wide divergence between the Russians and ourselves as to the extent to which deindustrialisation should be carried. It may well be that the Moscow Commission will not, by itself, be able to bridge the gap and the matter will have to be referred to the two [*sic*] Governments for settlement. The view which I suggested in my letter was that though we should be on very strong ground if we could successfully argue that the Russian proposals would reduce the German standard of living *below* the kind of level contemplated by paragraph 7, we should be on much more difficult ground if we could not successfully argue this. At the same time I was impressed by the danger that a degree of deindustrialisation which might come well within a reasonable interpretation of paragraph 7 might still create serious trouble for our Army of Occupation. I felt that I must ask you to consider, on the one hand, the political difficulty of resisting Russian proposals which could not successfully be shown to be inconsistent with paragraph 7 and, on the other hand, the danger of carrying deindustrialisation a good deal further than is politically wise.

I am afraid, as I said at the outset, that I may not have succeeded in putting my point clearly. You say that the Russians are proposing an extreme version of the Morgenthau Plan and you write as if I had suggested that we might become an acquiescing partner to such a policy. One of our great troubles has been that the Russians have never put forward their Plan and we do not know how far they intend to go. None of their suggestions goes as far as the Morgenthau Plan, though, of course, the suggestion that steel production might be reduced to 3 million tons a year goes a long way in that direction. But the point which I was trying to make in my letter is that even if the Russian Plan falls far short of the Morgenthau Plan and keeps well within the scope of paragraph 7, it may well be found to involve a greater degree of deindustrialisation than H.M. Government would be prepared to contemplate.

I am not quite sure how far I made this point plain and to what extent, therefore, it was before your mind when you wrote to me. I would infer, however, from your reply that, in your view, H.M. Government should resist a degree of deindustrialisation which will be dangerous from the general standpoint, even if it could not be successfully criticised as going beyond the scope of paragraph 7.

Before I received your letter my own mind had been moving in that direction and I was confirmed in this by talks which I have had with General Weeks and Sir Percy Mills. I enclose a note [ii] of a talk on the 18th July which you may find of interest.

As regards the tactics, we have not failed to conduct the technical discussions subject to the strictest reserves. I fully agree with you that it would be a good thing if we could call them off altogether until the general policy has been more fully discussed, but we could not secure this without the concurrence of the Americans who are anxious to get on with the business, chiefly because many of them are impressed with the danger that the capital plant and equipment will rapidly deteriorate unless it is moved quickly and that the Western European countries, as well as Russia, are in such urgent need of equipment that the greatest possible progress should be made before the winter comes.

I shall, however, as soon as I am back in Moscow concentrate on getting the Russian Plan put forward as soon as possible in a comprehensive form and it may well be that at that stage my right course would be to come back to London and ask you to consult with your colleagues and give me the necessary instructions as to the lines which I am to follow.

I must apologise for the length of this letter, but I wanted to do my best to make it quite clear to you how I feel about these questions which are, I realise, of vital importance to us and indeed to the world.

Yours ever,
WALTER MONCKTON

CALENDARS TO No. 358

i   *17 July 1945   Letter from Mr. Playfair (Treasury) to Mr. E. A. Radice (Assistant Secretary in the Economic Advisory Branch of the F.O.).* Refers to views of Lords Keynes and Cherwell on estimated percentage reduction in German standard of living from applying principle 7 in annex to No. 116. M. Maisky has estimated that the German standard of living would have to be about 25% below the pre-war level. This figure would suit H.M.G., as a controlling Power, better than the 40% previously estimated. Invites comments [UE 3126/139/71].

ii *18 July 1945   Note by Sir W. Monckton of discussion with General Weeks and Sir P. Mills (Berlin).* Both General Weeks and Sir P. Mills criticised principle 7 in annex to No. 116: Russians might claim that it committed us to wholesale deindustrialization of the Ruhr. Sir W. Monckton thought, however, that there was 'room for considerable elasticity' in applying all the principles. A statement is needed of facts and arguments upon which General Weeks and Sir P. Mills could rely in opposing the pastoralization and excessive deindustrialization of Germany. Such a statement would depend on Conference's decision on German-Polish border [F.O. 934/1/2(22)].

No. 359

Letter from Mr. Hoyer Millar (Berlin) to Mr. Harvey (Received 24 July)
[*Z 8823/537/41*]

BRITISH DELEGATION, BERLIN, *21 July 1945*

My dear Oliver,

I understand from a letter[1] which Peter Garran sent me on July 20th that you are seeing Victor Mallet[2] again on Monday[3] to have a final talk with him before he leaves for Madrid. That being so, I had better tell you how matters stand here in respect of Spain at the present moment.

I arrived here on Thursday afternoon just in time to go to a meeting of the Heads of Governments at which the Russians produced a proposal (P (Terminal) 8)[4] that the three Governments should recommend to the United Nations that they should break off relations with the Spanish Government and generally intervene in Spanish internal affairs in order to 'render support to the democratic forces in Spain'.

I think that this Russian recommendation has now got watered down into a suggestion that the Conference should pass a resolution intimating that the three Governments for their part would not be prepared to support an application from the present Spanish Government to join the World Security Organisation. The Russians have not yet admitted that they would, in fact, be satisfied with such a resolution, but a drafting committee has been set up to prepare the draft of such a paper. We had our first meeting of this committee this afternoon; Maisky and Gousev are the Soviet representatives, Mat[t]hews and Cannon represent the United States, and Pat Dean and I attend for our Delegation. At the meeting Maisky was inclined to try and introduce into the resolution the same sort of sentiments as appeared in the original Soviet paper. However, in the end we managed to persuade him to accept a more or less straightforward draft prepared by us with at his request certain additions at the end indicating why we did not care for the Franco régime. I enclose a copy of this draft herein.[5] It is still subject to approval by the Heads of the three Delegations and has to be considered at a further meeting of the drafting committee tomorrow.

The idea is that this resolution, or the substance of it, will eventually be published in the final communiqué issued at the end of the Conference. It will not, I am afraid, please Franco or make Victor Mallet's arrival any easier. However, it is a great deal milder than the original Soviet proposal, which, if pressed, might cause us a good deal of embarrassment.

Tangier. So far, although the Soviet Delegation have put Tangier on the agenda,[6] nothing has been said on the subject.

[1] Not printed (Z 9281/16/28).
[2] Sir V. Mallet was about to proceed as H.M. Ambassador to Madrid.
[3] 23 July 1945.
[4] The memorandum cited in No. 194, minute 7.
[5] No. 225, annex.
[6] Cf. No. 170, minute 2, and No. 171.

Italy. At the moment the situation is rather obscure. You will have seen the original paper (P (Terminal) 5)[7] put forward by the U.S. Delegation, without, as far as I know, previous consultation with our own people. This paper provided for some kind of *modus vivendi* pending the eventual peace settlement and is obviously objectionable. After a certain amount of discussion with the State Department people and preparation of certain counter drafts by ourselves, the Americans produced a revised version of their paper (P (Terminal) 20)[8] which is much simpler and I think more or less acceptable as it stands, though we have suggested a redraft for the last paragraph of which I enclose a copy[9] herein.

Unfortunately, however, progress on this revised American paper has been stymied by the Russians, who want to see some similar resolution adopted in regard to the Balkan ex-enemy satellites together with a recommendation that the Allied Governments will resume diplomatic relations with Bulgaria etc. Neither the Americans nor ourselves can accept this last stipulation and the Russians seem to be taking the attitude that in that case they cannot agree to any action being taken in respect of Italy. Just what will happen I do not yet know, but I should not myself very much mind if no three-Party resolution about Italy were in fact adopted and if, instead, we were to issue a purely Anglo-American statement about our future policy towards Italy. This might serve to discredit the Russians in the eyes of the Italians.

You will have seen our telegrams Target Nos. 93 and 118 about the question of Mr. Douglas and Admiral Stone.[10] I hope this disposes of the problem satisfactorily. At all events, Matthews of the State Department seemed fairly happy on the subject when I spoke to him this afternoon, though he emphasised the great difficulty which the State Department had had in persuading Douglas to go to Italy and the embarrassment which they had been caused by the delay in making his appointment effective.

Yours ever,

DERICK

P.S.   It looks pretty certain as if the Resolution of the Conference recommending the setting up of the Council of Foreign Ministers will have a passage saying that one of the first tasks of this Council shall be to consider the preparation of the peace treaty for Italy. That being so, it is all the more important that E.I.P.S. should lose no time in producing their recommendations about the economic aspects of the treaty. Playfair sent me a letter[11]

---

[7] See No. 208, minute 4.

[8] See No. 214, minute 4 and note 9.

[9] See i below.

[10] These telegrams (not printed) of 19 and 20 July respectively announced the imminent departure of Colonel Douglas for Italy to study economic conditions before becoming Chief Commissioner of the Allied Commission for Italy in succession to Rear Admiral Ellery Stone, and confirmed the arrangements made by Field-Marshal Alexander and Mr. Stimson: cf. *F.R.U.S. Berlin*, vol. ii, pp. 1100–3.

[11] Of 11 July 1945 (U 5552/50/70), not printed.

the other day which I passed on to Sammy Hood, suggesting that the Foreign Office might usefully write to E.I.P.S. impressing on them the urgency of the matter. If such a letter has not already been sent to E.I.P.S. it might be as well to send it now, basing our arguments on the proceedings of the Conference here, all of which point to the Italian peace treaty having to be considered fully in the near future.

F. R. M.

CALENDARS TO NO. 359

i *21 & 22 July 1945* Minutes by Mr. Hoyer Millar on P. (Terminal) 20; attaches redraft of para. 3; however, American proposals for possible dropping of this paper agreed by Sir A. Cadogan and Mr. Eden [F.O. 934/2/6(11)].

ii *22–4 July 1945 Correspondence between Mr. Hoyer Millar (Berlin) and Mr. Harvey; minute by Mr. Hoyer Millar.* Question of the surrender by the Spanish to the French authorities of M. Pierre Laval, Minister for Foreign Affairs in the Vichy régime; M. Maisky raised the subject at the meeting of 21 July of the drafting committee on Spain and the U.N. Mr. Harvey enclosed telegrams (Nos. 7613 and 5090 to and from Washington respectively of 19 and 21 July) concerning proposal that M. Laval be landed from Spanish aircraft in Italian territory under Allied control and there be surrendered to French authorities [Z 8257, 8632, 8735/5491/41; F.O. 934/4/26(10)].

No. 360

Letter from Mr. Stewart to Mr. Hayter (Berlin)
[F.O. 934/4/28(4)]

FOREIGN OFFICE, 21 July 1945

Dear William

You sent us the Secretary of State's copy of Washington telegram No. 4915[1] recording the instructions sent by the State Department to Harriman about Roumanian oil. Against the sentence reporting that Harriman was to threaten that the Americans would cease to supply the Russians with technical data, equipment and petroleum products the Secretary of State minuted: 'Have we no like card to play? If so we should not hesitate to play it as U.S. does here'.

While we are concerting with the Ministry of Fuel and Power a final reply to this question, it may be useful to recall to you:

(1) that we have already considered at length the possibility of threatening to cut off oil deliveries and have concluded that nothing can be done because it is very doubtful whether we shall send further supplies to Russia even if the Russians do meet our requirements in Roumania;

[1] Of 14 July 1945, not printed: see below and *F.R.U.S. Berlin*, vol. i, pp. 423–6.

(2) we have already played one such card. The Russians have been pressing for details of certain patents possessed by Astra Romana[2] in Roumania. The Military Mission have been instructed to reply that there can be no question of meeting this request until the Russians repair the damage they have done to the company.

Yours ever

DUGALD STEWART

CALENDARS TO No. 360

i   *20 July 1945   Letter from Mr. Gallop to Mr. M. R. Bridgeman (Ministry of Fuel and Power).* 'It was finally decided that no general "oil brief" should be prepared' for Potsdam Conference. Mr. Bridgeman should take up the general question of oil supplies for Eastern Europe with Petroleum Attaché at U.S. Embassy and coordinate a simultaneous approach to Moscow [W 8964/12/76]

ii   *20 & 21 July 1945   British Military Mission (Roumania) to War Office Tel. No. R.A.C. 1980/956; Mr. Le Rougetel (Bucharest) Tel. No. 732.* Roumanian decree law of 19 July on transfer of German shares in oil companies and banks to Russian ownership, apparently on instructions from Gen. Susaikov in name of Control Commission. French suggestion for representations to Soviet Government. Minute by Mr. Eden to Sir A. Cadogan: 'Another example we might use here? A. E.': cf. No. 347 [F.O. 934/2/9(16)].

iii   *21 July 1945   British Military Mission (Roumania) to War Office Tel. No. RAC 1993/923.* Transmits note from Gen. Vinogradov on oil-pipes and equipment removed from Roumania [R. 12362/80/37].

iv   *24 July 1945   (a) Mr. Le Rougetel (Bucharest) No. 223,* enclosing Roumanian note of 20 July on position on British oil interests in Roumania; *(b) 3 Aug.: British Military Mission (Roumania) to War Office:* Roumanian note 'is evasive and unsatisfactory in the extreme'; points for reply [R 13202, 14195/10102/37].

[2] Cf. No. 48, note 8.

No. 361

Letter from Mr. Howard to Mr. Hayter (Berlin)

[F.O. 934/2/9(14)]

Secret   FOREIGN OFFICE, *21 July 1945*

Dear William

Sargent has asked me to send you the attached copy of a telegram from the Military Mission in Roumania[1] and to ask for your comments on paragraph 4. I enclose Bucharest telegram No. 723[2] which seems to have some bearing on it.

It is very difficult to guess from here exactly what sort of story the Russians have been telling the Roumanians. Can you throw any light on the matter?

Yours ever,

DOUGLAS

[1] Enclosure 1 below.   [2] Enclosure 2 below: text supplied from R 12209/24/92.

ENCLOSURE 1 IN No. 361

Air Vice-Marshal Stevenson (Bucharest) to Sir J. Grigg
(Received in Foreign Office, 20 July, 9.30 a.m.)
No. RAC 1966/956 Telegraphic

Immediate. Secret   BUCHAREST, *19 July 1945, 5 p.m.*

Copy

Private and Personal for P.U.S. from Commissioner.
(Begins)

You will see from RAC 1964/956 Elfu 142[3] that final text of agreement on Russian-Roumanian Oil Combine is likely to prove disastrous for British (? and other) interests on account of privileges exclusive rights and advantages granted to Combine and also because wording is most ambiguous and could be given wide interpretation by Russians.

2. A revised text drawn up at our suggestion on 15th July was much better and clearer and merely granted Combine 'most favoured nation' treatment. It was fully accepted on 16th July by M. Tatarescu (Minister for Foreign Affairs).

3. However following a private meeting between Tatarescu and Krutikov[4] the satisfactory text was rejected at the last minute and then reverted to present form which grants virtual monopoly to the Combine.

4. Tatarescu excused his sudden *volte face* by telling his colleagues 'Much bigger things are at stake. I have been told what is being discussed at Potsdam and only the Soviet Union can save Roumania from the loss of Northern Transylvania and other territories.' It is understood that this statement was made to Tatarescu by Krutikov.

5. Please pass to Foreign Office.

ENCLOSURE 2 IN No. 361

Mr. Le Rougetel (Bucharest) to Mr. Eden (Received 19 July, 12 noon)
No. 723 Telegraphic

Immediate   BUCHAREST, *19 July 1945, 9.55 a.m. G.M.T.*

Repeated to Washington, Moscow, Belgrade.

My United States Colleague has been informed by a source which he considers reliable that Groza accompanied by Budnaras[5] met Tito at Varsatz during last week-end and discussed Yugoslav demands for cession of Roumanian Banat.

2. Groza returned in a state of depression and Tatarescu is said to have observed that the Soviet Union was the only country which could now guarantee Roumania's territorial integrity. This fits in with reports now circulating here to the effect that Great Britain and the United States are prepared to acquiesce in

---

[3] This telegram of 19 July 1945 is not printed.
[4] First Assistant People's Commissar for Foreign Trade of the Soviet Union.
[5] M. Emil Bodnaras was in charge of the Patriotic Defence organisation of the Roumanian Communist party.

the partition of Transylvania. I have reason to believe that these reports emanate from Soviet sources.[6]

Foreign Office please pass to Washington as my telegram No. 108.

[6] Mr. Hayter replied to Mr. Howard in a letter of 25 July from Berlin: 'To the best of my knowledge and belief Transylvania and Roumanian frontiers generally have never been mentioned here by anyone. Either Tatarescu or Krutikov must be lying.' In regard to enclosure 2 above Mr. Stevenson had reported in Belgrade telegram No. 1189 of 4 p.m. on 24 July: 'I questioned Yugoslav Minister of Foreign Affairs today about alleged meeting between Marshal Tito and M. Groza. 2. Dr. Subasic said that he knew nothing of any such meeting and he very much doubted whether it had taken place. He went on to say, as he had informed me previously . . . Yugoslav claims on Roumanian Banat would be confined to a slight rectification of frontier on economic grounds in connexion with certain irrigation and drainage works. This claim would be put forward at proper time.' On 26 July Mr. Le Rougetel reported in Bucharest telegram No. 744 of 9.45 a.m.: 'My United States colleague now tells me that the King has confirmed the fact that Groza and Tito met as stated in my telegram 723. 2. It seems that His Majesty was rather perturbed by vagueness of Mr. Groza's account of what transpired and his emphasis on its secrecy. He asked the King not to tell any member of his household about this meeting.'

No. 362

Letter from Mr. Stewart to Mr. Hayter (Berlin)
[F.O. 934/2/9(11)]

FOREIGN OFFICE, *21 July 1945*

Dear William

You will remember that before you left we asked the War Office to instruct Oxley to ask the Russians to explain their troops movements in Bulgaria.

I enclose a copy of a telegram reporting the result of these enquiries. Sargent has asked that the attention of the Delegation should be drawn to the marked passage.[1]

Yours ever
DUGALD STEWART

ENCLOSURE IN No. 362

*Major-General Oxley (Sofia) to Sir J. Grigg (Received in
Foreign Office, 20 July, 1 p.m.)*

No. M. 1493 Telegraphic

Immediate. Secret　　　　　　　　　　SOFIA, *19 July 1945, 12.25 p.m.*

Repeated to A.F.H.Q. (for General Morgan).

From General Oxley.

Reference 60413 (CA6) of 17th July[2] not to A.F.H.Q.

I saw General Biryusov this morning[3] and among other things I asked him

[1] The eighth and ninth sentences, beginning 'He paused here', in the main paragraph of the enclosure below.

[2] Untraced in Foreign Office archives.

[3] For this conversation with the Deputy Chairman of the A.C.C. in Bulgaria, cf. *F.R.U.S. Berlin*, vol. ii, p. 1062.

whether there was any foundation in rumour that Russian Army of Occupation in Bulgaria had been largely increased. I pointed out that I had myself noticed troops passing through Sofia and had also seen them on the move while on my last tour. I said that I proposed to come and ask him directly rather than believe rumours often maliciously exaggerated. I therefore asked him whether he would care to reply to two definite questions. Had Russian Army of Occupation been increased and if so what was significance of this? He replied Russian Armies in South East Europe were in process of being regrouped as a result of withdrawals from Hungary, Austria and Yugoslavia. He emphasised that withdrawal north east from southern part of this area necessitated move through Bulgaria. He paused here and I asked him whether they were moves through Bulgaria back to Russia. He paused again and then somewhat astonishingly replied that there were other countries beyond Bulgaria and that he was not aware of plan of the General Staff in this matter. He then proceeded to counter attack and said he was informed that we had largely increased our garrison in Greece. He further stated that Greek Press were putting out highly inflammatory statements one of which was to the effect that they proposed to march through Bulgaria to Moscow. He said he presumed that they could be likened to a flea on the back of an elephant who feels that much stronger. It is gratifying to observe that we are rated as high as an elephant. I endeavoured to allay his fears in this matter and pointed out that there had been no increase of British troops in Greece and he said he accepted this statement. I then explained to him that Greeks were, like the other Mediterranean races, an excitable people and at the present time suffering they had undergone in last four years made them more so than ever and that too much attention should not be paid to the irresponsible part of their Press. If there was anything worrying at any time he had only to ask me and I would make every effort to get him reliable information. Meeting ended in many professions of mutual esteem.

Calendars to No. 362

i   *11 July 1945*   *Letter from Sir O. Sargent to Brig. Hirsch (War Office).* Discusses Russian troop movements in Bulgaria and requests the action indicated in first paragraph of No. 362 [R 11575/247/7].

ii   *26 July 1945*   *Dominions Office Tel. D. No. 1307 to Govts. of Canada, Australia, New Zealand, South Africa.* Alleged Soviet-Roumanian diplomatic and military agreements. Roumanian Armistice Commission state that about 1 million Soviet troops will remain in and be supplied from Roumania for at least a year [R 11977/169/37].

No. 363

Letter from Mr. Houstoun-Boswall (Sofia) to Mr. Hayter (Received 30 July)
No. 10/67/45 [R 12798/1237/7]

Personal   SOFIA, *21 July 1945*

My dear Hayter,

    Athens Chancery letter 84/56/45 of June 29th,[1] copied to us under your

---

[1] Not printed.

number R11365/1237/7, about the possibility that the United States may be ready to receive a representative of the Bulgarian Government at Washington.

It is my belief that this idea is by no means dormant. So I hope that you will not be unduly surprised if some day or other Washington does consent to receive a Bulgarian representative. And my own view is that we would be wise to think along the same lines. If hitherto we have been frightened of offending Greece, there is no longer any reason for that, now that the only obstacle, as far as I can see, to the presence of a Greek liaison officer or representative of some sort in Sofia, is the failure of the Greeks themselves to send one. After all, I am here representing His Majesty's Government (informally and without any juridical basis, if you will—but I *am* here): and I cannot see what advantage it is to us to continue to refuse to receive in London some informal sort of Bulgarian representation. After all, despite all their faults the Bulgarians did turn over and fight on our side—though I know that is not a popular thing to admit: nevertheless they did do so.

I suggest to you too that, although from the strictly 'protocolaire' point of view it may not be correct for British representatives in Ankara, Bucharest and Belgrade to receive their Bulgarian opposite numbers, in adopting such a formal attitude we are really the only people who suffer, because our representatives are thus deprived of contacts which might provide them with useful information on occasions. Moreover, those Bulgarian diplomats, who have an acute and easily understandable inferiority complex, would be peculiarly sensitive to any display of ordinary human decency from the British representatives at their posts. There is little enough that we *can* do to counteract Russian influence, but there is a great deal that we can do to enhance British influence. And one of the best ways to do that is by the exercise of a little ordinary civility, which costs nothing at all. If we treat Bulgarians as pariahs, just because they are Bulgarians, we drive them into the arms of the Russians or anybody else; whereas if, while withholding our approval from the manner in which their totalitarian government behaves—backed as it is by the Militia, which is known to be the tool of the Communist Party, we unbend somewhat to Bulgarians because some Bulgarians seem to be decent men, we can do ourselves a great deal of good.

I do not know how this will strike you, but it has been my experience in life that it is quite futile to be stuffy just for the sake of being stuffy. I personally find it difficult to reconcile our desire to make peace (even at the risk of irritating the United States of America) with this curious 'all Bulgars are cads because they are Bulgars' attitude.

Yours ever
W. E. HOUSTOUN BOSWALL

CALENDAR TO No. 363

i *18 Aug. 1945 Letter from Mr. Howard to Mr. Houstoun-Boswall (Sofia).* In the light of the record of the Bulgarian Govt., argues on balance against accepting an unofficial Bulgarian representative in London [R 12798/1237/7].

No. 364

Mr. Roberts (Moscow) to Mr. Eden (Received 22 July, 3.40 p.m.)
No. 3245 Telegraphic [E 5353/808/89]

MOSCOW, *22 July 1945, 2.7 p.m.*

Repeated to Beirut, M.E. Min[ister].

The new Syrian Minister called today[1] and gave me an account of his first interviews with Kalinin, Dekanozov and Kavtaradze.[2]

2. The Minister had taken the line that Syria was a very small country whose future was dependent upon the great powers. He could only hope that they had no aggressive designs. Dekanozov made the stock reply that the United Nations' Charter was sufficient protection for all the smaller powers. The Minister asked why, in that case, it was necessary for the Big Three to meet in Berlin to which Dekanozov replied that this meeting was mainly to discuss German questions. He and Kavtaradze then said that the Soviet Union had already shown that it was directly interested in Persia, but they disclaimed any special interest in other Middle Eastern countries.

3. The Minister told Kalinin that he was very anxious to see as much as possible of the Soviet Union, and in particular to study the Kolkhoz System,[3] which might provide useful lessons for his Government in dealing with large Government-owned estates in Syria. He was promised full facilities but is not unduly optimistic.

4. The Minister took up with the P[eoples] C[ommissariat for] F[oreign] A[ffairs] on his arrival the recent article on the Arab League (see my telegram No. 3234 [3134][4]). He explained certain inaccuracies to the head of the press department and has been promised an interview with the writer of the article to pursue the matter in more detail.

5. The Minister had hoped that the reception given to the patriarch[5] on his recent visit to Syria would have resulted in the patriarch helping the Minister in Moscow. After some difficulty he had visited the patriarch, but found that it was the latter who wanted help. He asked the Minister not to fail to tell the Soviet Government how useful the visit had been. The Minister contrasted the great fuss made of the patriarch by the Soviet Minister in Syria with his obvious insignificance in Moscow.

6. The Minister said that he intended to return to Damascus in September. He doubted whether he would himself come back to Moscow, as there was very little for a Syrian representative to do here.

Foreign Office please pass to Beirut unnumbered and M.E.Min. as my telegram No. 8.

[1] This telegram was drafted on 21 July 1945.
[2] MM. V. G. Dekanozov and S. I. Kavtaradze were Soviet Deputy People's Commissars for Foreign Affairs.
[3] Soviet system of collective farming.
[4] Moscow telegram No. 3134 of 14 July (E 5151/3/65) is not printed.
[5] Of Moscow and All Russia.

No. 365

Mr. Roberts (Moscow) to Mr. Eden (Received 22 July, 1.45 p.m.)
No. 3246 Telegraphic [E 5353/808/89]

MOSCOW, *22 July 1945*, *11.44 a.m.*

Repeated to Beirut, M.E.Min's Office Cairo, Istanbul (Constantinople).

My immediately preceding telegram.[1]

The Syrian Minister told me that he had also mentioned the question of Alexandretta to the Soviet Government and had said that he hoped for Soviet support in obtaining the return of the Sanjak to Syria. I gathered that there had been no Soviet response.

2. When I expressed surprise that he should have raised this question now in Moscow and asked whether his Government had raised it in other capitals he said that His Majesty's Government and the French Government were of course aware of the Syrian demands so were the Turkish Government. He claimed that the Turks had not yet recognised Syria because the Syrians would not formally recognise that Alexandretta was Turkish. The minister seemed to think that in view of recent Soviet demands upon Turkey and of Turkey's weak post-war position this was an appropriate moment to regain Alexandretta for Syria. After some discussion he said however that this was not a matter of the first urgency and that it was enough for the Syrian Government to put their case without pressing it for the time being.

Foreign Office please pass to Beirut unnumbered and to M.E.Minister and Istanbul as my telegrams Nos. 9 and 25 respectively.

[1] No. 364.

No. 366

Sir J. Anderson to Mr. Randall (Copenhagen)
No. 232 Telegraphic [N 8589/9/15)

Important. Secret   FOREIGN OFFICE, *22 July 1945 7.20 p.m.*

Repeated to Moscow No. 4075, Washington No. 685 Saving, United Kingdom Delegation Berlin No. 141.

Your telegram No. 234 [324][1] (of 11th July: Russians in Bornholm).

It has not (repeat not) been our intention to raise the question of Bornholm with the Russians at the Potsdam meeting. If, however, the Russians should raise the question of the withdrawal of Allied Forces from Denmark, we should doubtless say that we are already withdrawing our forces and propose to continue to do so as and when their tasks are completed and that we assume the Russians will do likewise.

[1] No. 104.

2. If the Danish Government wish to discover when the Russians propose to leave Bornholm, they should surely ask them direct. In order to avoid discrimination, they would no doubt wish at the same time to ask us when we propose to withdraw our troops from Denmark.

3. Our own plans are as described in paragraphs 2, 3 and 4 of my telegram No. 19 Saving (of 30th June).[2]

4. Please speak to the Minister for Foreign Affairs on the lines of paragraphs 1 and 2 above. You may add that, if the Danish Government were to ask us when we propose to withdraw our Forces from Denmark, our reply would be on the lines indicated in paragraph 3 above.

5. It would obviously be most satisfactory that the withdrawal of British and Russian Forces from Danish territory should be decided independently and on purely military grounds. Only if the Russians were to make difficulties about this would it be advisable to consider the purely political suggestion of simultaneous withdrawal. Simultaneous withdrawal would, under present plans, mean that the Russians would stay in Bornholm until mid-October, unless the Danish Government asked us to make the arrangements contemplated in paragraph 3 of my telegram No. 19 Saving. Even then, such arrangements would necessitate the retention of a mission from 21st Army Group until the military tasks enumerated in paragraph 2 of my telegram No. 19 Saving were completed by the Danes themselves. The task of the British Naval personnel could not be delegated to any other organisation; and the need for the R.A.F. staging post would remain. The leave camps scheme might continue for some time to come. The proposal for simultaneous withdrawal might well lead to the Soviet Government claiming analogous facilities in Bornholm.

6. On purely military grounds there seems no reason why the Russians should not withdraw from Bornholm in advance of the final withdrawal of British Forces from the rest of Denmark. But if the Danish Government fail to obtain from Soviet Government a satisfactory undertaking regarding early withdrawal we should then be willing to consider the advisability of trying to hasten their withdrawal by arranging for simultaneous withdrawal of both British and Russian forces.

[2] See No. 104, note 1.

No. 367

Letter from Sir O. Sargent to Sir A. Cadogan (Berlin)

[*F.O. 934/2/10(49)*]

FOREIGN OFFICE, *22 July 1945*

Dear Alec

In Target No. 47[1], paragraph 9, Sir A. Clark Kerr reports M. Mikolajczyk's description of the effect of the presence and behaviour of the Red Army in

[1] No. 319.i.

Poland upon the harvest and food situation. M. Mikolajczyk seems to expect the Red Armies to withdraw in the course of the next two months, but if, in doing so, they devastate the countryside and take away all machinery and four-footed beasts, the position for the future will not be much remedied by their departure.

The story of the devastation of Poland is, of course, only part of the general process going on wherever the Russian armies are encamped, from the Russian zone in Germany down to Bulgaria, no distinction being made between Allied and ex-enemy countries.

The result is that what used to be the granary of Europe is going to be reduced to famine conditions unless UNRRA can intervene in time and with sufficient supplies. Similarly, the removal of machinery, means of transport, etc., is going to delay very seriously the rehabilitation of these countries, and produce widespread unemployment.

I don't know whether it would be possible or wise to place on record at Terminal these all too well known facts. Although such an indictment would not undo what has been done, and might not even bring about much relief for the future, it would at any rate put the Soviet Government on the defensive, and might perhaps strengthen our bargaining position in other directions.

No doubt you have already thought of all this, but if so, just tear this letter up.[2]

Yrs
O. G. SARGENT

[2] Sir A. Cadogan minuted on this to Mr. D. Allen: 'If we haven't said all this, I think we've gone as far as we can in hinting it, and are trying to find the remedy. A. C. July 23/45.'

No. 368

Sir J. Anderson to Mr. Eden (Berlin: received 22 July, 11.45 p.m.)
No. 147 Onward Telegraphic [C 4112/22/18]

Top secret. Immediate   FOREIGN OFFICE, *22 July 1945, 9.36 p.m.*

Following for Secretary of State for Foreign Affairs from Sir Orme Sargent.

We have received a copy of record of Sir W. Monckton's conversation with Maisky on June [July] 20[1] about a special 4-Power regime for the Rhineland and Westphalia.

2. As you know, the French have hitherto done most of the running on this question, and any discussion of it in their absence would inevitably cause much heart burning. If this question is raised officially by the Russians at Terminal would not the best course be to refer it to the new Council of Foreign Secretaries on which the French would be represented and with

[1] See No. 204.ii.

which it should be possible to associate the Belgians and the Dutch?

3. A further reason for not committing ourselves for the present is that no decision on the problem has yet been taken by the Cabinet or by the Chiefs of Staff.

No. 369

Letter from Mr. Duff Cooper (Paris) to Mr. Harvey (Received 27 July)
No. 75/76/45 [Z 8820/13/17]

PARIS, *22 July, 1945*

My dear Oliver

At a tête-à-tête lunch with Duncannon[1] on July 17th, Etienne Burin des Rosiers, the member of General de Gaulle's Cabinet dealing with foreign affairs, expressed concern at the difficulties to be overcome, if an effective Anglo-French alliance was to be concluded; he admitted that he was voicing de Gaulle's views in the matter. He began by saying what we already know and in fact what Monsieur Bidault already said to the Foreign Secretary at the end of February last (Foreign Office telegram No. 358 Saving[2] of the 4th March) that he did not see how an alliance could be concluded without a simultaneous settlement of the German and Levant questions. He amplified this by saying that he thought it would be necessary to include in the treaty a definite statement in regard to our joint attitude towards and treatment of Germany in the future with perhaps a declaration that never again would Germany be allowed to exercise sovereignty over the Rhineland. He did not indicate what kind of settlement of the Levant question should be included in the treaty but said that we would have to state our common interests and aims in the Middle East.

2. Duncannon asked Burin des Rosiers whether it would not be possible to conclude an alliance in more general terms than this; the reply was that it would be useless to do so, unless these outstanding disputes were settled first, otherwise the treaty would be empty and pointless. In view of our reluctance to come to a settlement of these questions Burin des Rosiers said that General de Gaulle was under the impression that we definitely did not want to conclude a treaty. Duncannon said that he thought that this was far from being the case, but that in addition to our possible desire to conclude an alliance in more general terms than the French contemplated, and our differences in the Levant, he had the personal impression that there was perhaps also an even simpler and purely mechanical explanation of the delay, i.e. that there had not been time before San Francisco or between San Francisco, the General Elections in England and the Potsdam Con-

---

[1] Viscount Duncannon was a Second Secretary in H.M. Embassy in Paris.

[2] Not printed: see No. 62, note 5.

ference for the authorities concerned to settle down with a French Delegation to work out a joint draft. Duncannon told Burin des Rosiers that he was in any case making a great mistake if he thought there was any unfriendly reluctance on our part to conclude a treaty. Surely the reverse was the case as our efforts before San Francisco had shown? The two of them seem to have concluded however, that there appeared to be general agreement on both sides regarding the desirability of an alliance, but differences of opinion as to its scope and exact terms. Duncannon ventured the opinion that after the Potsdam Conference a suitable draft could be drawn up to form the basis of discussions; and Burin des Rosiers did not dissent.

3. We have a good opinion of Burin des Rosiers who, while Monsieur Bidault's relations with General de Gaulle were strained and while the former was in San Francisco, seemed to be acting almost as Foreign Secretary! In any case the Quai d'Orsay seem to refer all important questions to him and rely on him to put matters to de Gaulle in the most favourable light. Since, however, during the above conversation, des Rosiers seemed merely to be voicing the opinions of de Gaulle, Duncannon found it difficult to discuss with him the matter of an alliance objectively and comprehensively. Indeed, since the Levant crisis there seems to have been a noticeable change in des Rosiers' attitude. Before the crisis he was always able to discuss Anglo-French relations in an unbiassed way, but although he is still as before very polite he seems recently to have become almost as intransigeant as his Chief in his outlook.

4. From all this it may appear that the alliance will have to be concluded with General de Gaulle's successor. If, however, after the Potsdam Conference we really set our hearts upon an alliance and give sufficient time to work it out, I think that due to the widespread feeling in France in favour of it, it should not be so difficult to get General de Gaulle to agree to a text. If on the other hand we are unable to agree to conclude the treaty on the more comprehensive lines proposed by the General, the French may go forward on their own and begin to create their Western European group with Belgium and Holland. Alphand's recent visit to these two countries and the economic agreements concluded with them,[3] are pointers in this direction.

5. I am sorry to say that the Prime Minister recently expressed to me in conversation his own lack of enthusiasm for an alliance. I did my best to correct his views but am uncertain as to how much effect I produced.

Yours ever

DUFF COOPER

---

[3] An agreement of mutual consultation between France, the Netherlands, Belgium and Luxembourg had been concluded in Paris on 20 March 1945; this agreement (printed in *U.N. Treaty Series*, vol. 2, pp. 299–305) had been initialed there for France and Belgium on 23 February, at the time of the conclusion of a Franco–Belgian agreement on exchange of information on their respective populations and of a Franco–Belgo–Luxembourg commercial agreement: cf. *The Times* of 24 February 1945, p. 3, and of 21 March, p. 3.

No. 370

Letter from M. Paris (London) to Sir R. Campbell (Received 25 July)

No. 454 [E 5445/420/89]

[FRENCH EMBASSY, LONDON,] *23 July 1945*

Cher Sir Ronald,

Un de mes collaborateurs a déjà confirmé officiellement à M. J. T. Henderson, par lettre du 19 juillet[1], les réserves expresses qu'avait inspiré au Ministère des Affaires Etrangères la démarche des autorités britanniques à Washington, en vue d'obtenir une participation américaine à certains organismes au Levant, et en particulier à celui des céréales.

Sur de nouvelles instructions de mon Département, j'ai l'honneur de vous faire savoir que le Gouvernement français attacherait un prix tout particulier à ce que le Gouvernement britannique veuille bien renoncer à son projet d'associer des fonctionnaires américains aux dits organismes. L'organisation du commerce des céréales avait été en effet, établie en vertu d'un accord exclusivement franco-britannique; le Gouvernement britannique ayant décidé unilatéralement d'assurer seul des responsabilités et des attributions qui appartenaient au Gouvernement français, celui-ci estime que c'est seulement entre ses mains que le Gouvernement britannique pourrait s'en décharger.

De plus, cette initiative est en contradiction avec les engagements qui ont été pris en 1941[2] à l'égard du Gouvernement français, aux termes desquels le Gouvernement britannique a reconnu la situation prédominante et privilégiée de la France par rapport aux autres puissances, et affirmé son intention de n'empiéter en aucune manière sur les positions françaises.

Je vous prie d'agréer, Cher Sir Ronald, l'expression de mes bien dévoués sentiments.[3]

J. PARIS

[1] Not printed. In this letter No. 436 (received, 23 July 1945) M. P. Francfort of the French Embassy, in confirmation of a conversation which he had had with Mr. Henderson on 17 July, had conveyed the reserves indicated in regard to the British démarche (cf. No. 66, note 1, and No. 94) 'en vue d'obtenir une participation américaine à l'Office des Céréales Panifiables et d'autres organismes analogues au Levant.'

[2] See No. 64.i.

[3] Mr. J. T. Henderson minuted: 'This letter contains notable inaccuracies. A. We cannot well recall an invitation to the Americans, once issued. B. We are not off-loading our responsibilities onto the Americans, only trying to broaden the international basis of help to the Levant States. C. In the letter from Mr. Oliver Lyttelton [see No. 64.i] what we freely admitted was that "France should have the dominant privileged position in the Levant among all *European* nations." D. We said "we have no desire to encroach in any way upon the position of France", which is not quite "les positions françaises". I explained, incidentally, to M. Francfort, that we got the idea as one way of showing the French that we did not want to supplant them, that we desired, by associating the Americans with us, to disclaim any monopoly of influence, etc. He waved these assertions aside. Perhaps we need not reply. J. Thyne Henderson 27/7.'

No. 371

Mr. Hopkinson (Rome) to Mr. Eden (Received 23 July, 8.50 p.m.)

No. 1174 Telegraphic [ZM 3978/3/22]

Important   ROME, *23 July 1945, 6.20 p.m. G.M.T.*

Repeated to Resmed, Caserta.[1]

My despatch No. 279.[2]

Please see Naf 1043 [i] July 21st which was repeated to British Chiefs of Staff.

2. For reasons given in my despatch under reference I consider course B. in paragraph 4 represents the most practical means of securing a fair decision on the institutional question. Most intelligent observers seem to agree that if a straight plebiscite were held decision would be in favour of the monarchy. On the other hand the difficulty of getting the Italian Government to agree at this stage to substitute this method for that laid down by decree law number 151 would be immense. Moreover while I appreciate the objection indicated by Sacmed to course B. the election to constituent assembly and subsequent debates in the assembly itself would afford an opportunity of putting the case before the public before a final decision is taken in a way which is perhaps more discreetly democratic as we know it than a straight vote by a plebiscite. Furthermore, since members of the Government and the constituent assembly would realise that their decision on this issue has got to be submitted for ratification by the people and that if their recommendations were rejected it would almost certainly lead to a fall of the Government and fresh election, it would tend to cause them to be more moderate in preparation for other parts of the constitution.

3. My own view therefore is that an all out effort should be made to secure the adoption of course B. in the fulfilment of our obligations to restore democratic form of Government under the Moscow declaration on Italy. It will not be easy as Signor Nenni whose Ministry is responsible for the setting up of machinery for Constituent Assembly will be strongly opposed to it. On the other hand he himself in editorial statements in *Avanti* has said that the Constituent Assembly must if necessary, be packed in order to ensure a Republican solution to the institutional question and Allied Governments are thus legitimately entitled to ask for safeguards. Incidentally he also yesterday broke the institutional truce by a violent attack on the monarchy in a speech at a big meeting in Milan. Chief Commissioner is consulting Allied Force Headquarters as to whether protest should be made to the Italian Prime Minister.

---

[1] Also repeated to Washington and by the Foreign Office to Berlin as No. 188 Onward.
[2] Of 5 July 1945, not printed.

i *20–28 July 1945 F.M. Alexander (A.F.H.Q.) to C.C.S. Tels. Nos. Naf 1043 &*
1046; Mr. Balfour (Washington) Tel. No. 5246. Views of F.M. Alexander and
of State Department on Italian institutional question. F.M. Alexander considers
(Naf 1043 of 20 July) that eventual referendum, preferably under Allied
supervision, would be fairest way of settling issue; three possible methods
for obtaining a referendum include course B, that Italian Government be
requested to make provision, in supplementary decree on procedure, for a
referendum on the constituent assembly's decision, under decree law No.
151, on the institutional question [ZM 3560, 3963, 4083/3/22].

ii *28 July 1945 Mr. Broad (Caserta) Tel. No. 1413.* Allied protest at republican
speech by Signor Nenni [ZM 4088/3/22].

No. 372

Mr. Fraser (Wellington) to Viscount Cranborne (Received 23 July, 9.15 p.m.)
No. 195 Telegraphic [U 5517/50/70]

WELLINGTON, *23 July 1945, 11.55 p.m.*

Immediate. Top secret and Personal

From Prime Minister. Begins.

Consideration has been given to the question of the proposed Peace
Treaty with Italy referred to in your telegram D. No. 1225[1] and other
relevant communications. I would like to state at the outset of my remarks
that I do not, and never have, felt particularly happy about the policy
adopted towards Italy. For my part I would have preferred a policy of
delay in concluding any final peace. Nevertheless the force of circumstances
to which your various communications refer is recognised and I realise that
at this stage it is not possible to retract steps already taken.

Our former objection to the conclusion of a separate peace with Italy
arose from a consideration that it might increase tendencies in the United
Nations to regard the war with Japan as a matter of secondary importance.
I think that this objection still holds good and in my view it is unfortunate
that the immediate and paradoxical development should be the declaration
of war on Japan by Italy herself. This in my view should not have been
permitted.

If the United States as the leader of the war against Japan is eager and
determined to bring about the conclusion of the Peace Treaty with Italy
then our former objection is likely to be of little practical avail. Moreover
a new situation has arisen as a result of the territorial trusteeship provisions
in the United Nations Charter in so far as the disposal of Italy's Colonial
territories is concerned.

---

[1] Dominions Office telegrams Nos. 1225–7 of 14 July 1945 had remitted to the governments of the Dominions for their comments additional draft heads for political sections of
an Italian peace treaty in accordance with the decision in No. 118, conclusion 3.

Because of these new factors we recorded our acquiescence in the proposal as set out in New Zealand telegram No. 97[2] of 24th April—the comments now added are of a general and provisional character because of your indication that nothing more is expected at the Berlin meeting than a preliminary discussion.

We are greatly surprised that the standing of those United Nations which are at war with Italy is not more clearly recognised in the relevant paragraph of your memorandum dated 4th June.[3] We see no good reason why a Peace Conference, representative of all the associated Powers, should not in due course be held. It is admitted that preparation of the Peace Settlement and the direction of such a Conference must be assumed by a limited number of States but in addition to the Four Powers and to those you referred to as having 'a primary interest in the Italian settlement' I feel that the views of other Powers which have contributed substantially to Italy's defeat such as New Zealand should also be taken into special consideration.

We also hold the view that the residuary functions and rights which you propose should be entrusted to the Four Powers should belong to the whole of the 'Associated Nations' and that those functions and rights should be exercised on their behalf by a council not composed exclusively of the Four Powers.

We have also given consideration to the possible use of the United Nations Organisation when it comes into existence but so far as the cession of Italy's European territories is concerned we see advantages in any such cessions being made to the associated Nations rather than to the United Nations Organisation.

It seems better that Italy should not be able to place upon the United Nations Organisation the odium of the penalties which she must justly incur.

The position as regards Colonial territories is different and it seems to us that there is a strong case for ceding these territories to the United Nations Organisation. We trust that most or all of these territories will be the subject of trusteeship arrangements. Their cession to the United Nations would solve the question of sovereignty in a more satisfactory manner than was the case of the mandates. Moreover as the United Nations Organisation must in any event approve the terms of trusteeship arrangements in these particular cases it should also decide the allocation of the trusteeships. It may be desirable that Italy herself should hold some of the trusteeships and the cession of these territories would therefore be without special odium for the Organisation.

We do not propose to comment in detail at this state on the proposed transfer of territories in Europe. We note however that certain small rectifications of frontier are proposed in favour of one of the Four Powers, France.

---

[2] Not printed (D.O. 35/1827).
[3] It would appear that the reference was to a memorandum of 14 June (U 4782/50/70): an earlier draft of the memorandum of 5 July noted in No. 31, note 1.

While these rectifications may appear reasonable in themselves, and while it is a matter for congratulation that France appears to have abandoned her pretensions in the region of Aosta, the question does arise whether the Four Powers would not strengthen their position of leadership in these negotiations if they were able to conform absolutely to the terms of the First Article of the Atlantic Charter.

On the question of Italian armaments (your telegram D. No. 1224,[4] paragraph 2 (4)), we assume that these will be controlled by the Associated Powers. While the policy of building up to a certain degree the strength and efficiency of the Italian armed forces may offer certain advantages, we presume that nothing will be done which could be invoked as a precedent for the reconstitution on any considerable scale of the armed forces of Germany.

I would like in conclusion to refer to the political aspects of what appear at this distance to be the policy of the Allies in Italy—the wisdom of which, from the knowledge at my disposal, seems on occasion to be open to doubt. In particular, the power of the Allies appears to have been used to discriminate in favour of elements which must be regarded as reactionary as against more progressive forces such as the Trade Unions. In my opinion, every possible effort should be made to ensure that full liberty is given to democratic liberal forces to frame and operate such a constitution as commends itself to the majority of the people. I fully realise that it is not always possible at this distance to obtain the clearest picture in the light of all the facts and I would be glad to get reassurances on the points referred to in this paragraph. Ends.[5]

CALENDAR TO No. 372

i *20 & 27 July 1945 Mr. Chifley (Canberra) Tels. Nos. 196 & 203, with F.O. minutes.* Australian reactions to proposed peace treaty with Italy. Proposed procedure would offer little chance of effective voice to Dominions in important part of settlement, and appears inconsistent with undertakings. Objections raised by Mr. G. G. Fitzmaurice, Assistant Legal Adviser, on 2 August to proposed cession of Italian colonies to U.N. [U 5517, 5724/50/70].

[4] Not preserved in Dominions Office archives. Untraced in Foreign Office archives.
[5] Mr. Eden minuted on this telegram: 'Mr. Fraser should be reassured. A. E. July 25.'

No. 373

Mr. Hankey (Warsaw) to Mr. Eden (Received 23 July, 11.15 p.m.)
No. 39 Telegraphic [N 9107/6/55]

Important   WARSAW, *23 July 1945, 9.23 p.m.*

I attended meeting of National Home Council on July 21st and July 22nd as well as a public demonstration on the 22nd. The proceedings, which are recorded in my immediately preceding telegrams,[1] did not strike me very favourably. The names of the new members, especially Messrs. Mikolajczyk, Grabski, Witos and Zulawski were greeted with acclamation. But Witos was not there and everyone knew he had still not accepted. Further Mikolajczyk did not take the oath and did not speak for reasons given below. The Polish Prime Minister received his vote of confidence by a perfunctory show of hands before anyone had been allowed to comment on his speech. One should add that comments were mostly of rather a secondary nature. In short National Home Council is not a people's democratic assembly but a voting machine carefully parked on them. I was told the public was also pretty carefully selected. Public demonstration today consisted almost exclusively of PPR (Communists) with a carefully arranged clack of speaking choruses. It seemed to me to have remarkably little spontaneity but Communists certainly know what they want.

2. Reason for Mikolajczyk's abstention is that Monsieur Bi . . .[2] [? Bierut] has refused to accept any of his nominations of Peasant Party men to National Home Council although Mikolajczyk was prepared to accept 38 persons only against PPR strength of 100. Bi . . . 's[2] object is to force Mikolajczyk to fuse his party with stooge Peasant Party formed under Lublin. Mikolajczyk thinks he may have to agree but will do so unwillingly as it means having Communists everywhere inside his organisation.

3. Owing to meeting of National Home Council I have still not been able to get an interview with the President, but unless instructed to the contrary and unless Mikolajczyk asks me not to, in view of subsequent developments, I think it would be useful if I emphasised to him the importance you attach to freedom of political action in the preparation of election for Christian Labour and Peasant Parties, as also for the left wing of the National Democrats (see my telegram No. 23)[3] in accordance with decisions reached in the Crimea and Moscow. At present things are moving in the wrong direction.

[1] Not printed.
[2] Punctuation as in filed copy.
[3] No. 318.i.

No. 374

Sir J. Anderson to Mr. Randall (Copenhagen)
No. 37 Saving Telegraphic, en clair [N 8996/1866/15]

FOREIGN OFFICE, *23 July 1945*

Repeated to Office of Political Adviser to Commander-in-Chief Germany No. 88 Saving.

My telegram No. 100[1] of 21st July to Political Adviser to Commander-in-Chief, Germany (repeated to you as my telegram No. 229).

[1] No. 354.

The following background, for your own information, may help to explain reluctance of Commander-in-Chief, Germany, to permit visit of Mr. Christmas Moeller.

2. The so-called Danish minority in South Schleswig, though of Danish origin, consists of German citizens. Our policy is not to differentiate between German citizens on grounds of race and to break completely with the policy followed after the last war of establishing minority rights. This means that, unless our policy is revised, we cannot admit any Danish right to intervene in the affairs of the Danish minority in South Schleswig.

3. There are however other possible solutions such as:–

(a) the re-incorporation of South Schleswig into Denmark, and

(b) an exchange of populations between the Danish and German minorities on either side of the present frontier.

Responsible Danish spokesmen have made repeated declarations against a revision of the frontier. We have not so far received any proposals from the Danes for an exchange of populations.

4. The problem is being studied here, but it cannot be considered in isolation, since a decision in respect of the Danish minority would have repercussions upon other minorities, e.g. the Slovene population in the British zone of Austria. It may therefore be some time before our minds are clear on the subject. Meanwhile, it is important not to create precedents which would prompt e.g. Marshal Tito to claim the right to visit the Slovene minority in Carinthia, even for such personal conversations as Mr. Christmas Moeller wishes to have with the leaders of the Danish minority in South Schleswig.

5. I am afraid there is little in the above which will help you in calming down the Danish Government. But you will perhaps be able to impress upon them that we cannot be rushed into giving privileged treatment to a section of the German citizens in our zone of occupation on the grounds of their Danish origin, in view of the tremendous political problems which we have to face in our zone and of the precedents which would thereby be created in respect of other minorities who would claim similar privileges. While we cannot admit that the Danish Government have any *locus standi* in pleading for special treatment for any group of German citizens in our zone, we shall nevertheless be glad to examine any proposals which they may care to put forward for dealing with the problem of South Schleswig.

CALENDARS TO No. 374

i   *25 & 30 July 1945   Correspondence between Mr. Haigh and Mr. Randall (Copenhagen)* on Danish minority in South Schleswig [N 9263, 9951/1866/15].

ii *26 & 27 July 1945   From and to Lübbecke Tels. Nos. 73 & 123.* F.O. confirm favourable attitude towards M. Möller's private visit to South Schleswig [N 9288/1866/15].

No. 375

Letter from Mr. Coulson (Berlin) to Mr. Hall-Patch[1]
[F.O. 934/1/2(25)]

Personal   BERLIN, *23 July 1945*

My dear Edward

You will see from the minutes of a recent meeting[2] that we have fought the supply problem of Berlin to the highest level and have so far met with no success. The Poles have been invited to come, and it may be that we can have detailed discussions with them about the supplies which they can provide. I think on the whole, however, this is unlikely.

The same question has, as you know, now arisen over Vienna. Almost by a miracle we found time to interest the Secretary of State in it, and brought him and Mr. Byrnes together for a moment this morning. Mr. Byrnes also showed great interest and said he would get the President to raise it at the Big Three meeting this afternoon.[3] Unfortunately, the existing American instructions though they provide that their Commander should not agree to feed the U.S. sector of Vienna, say that this should not delay his moving in. In the extreme chaos existing here, we could not reconcile these instructions with our own views in time, and the only hope is that something will come out of the President's intervention this afternoon.

These two issues have now become closely bound up with the definition of war booty and therefore the whole reparation plan. The Russians have suggested a very wide definition of booty. This has fired Mr. Byrnes and Mr. Pauley with the idea of confining Russian reparation to what they can get out of their own zone, though they will also get something out of our zones in return for goods, such as coal, and food which they or the Poles could supply. We had a meeting with the Russians and Americans about this this afternoon, of which you will be getting a record in due course.[4] This idea, if it is pursued, will obviously help in our trouble of feeding our zones in Germany and also the liberated areas. It is, however, in a very rudimentary state at the moment.

It is not possible to keep you regularly informed about these things, though I think you will be getting most of the reparation stuff from the Treasury, whom Waley keeps informed. We are normally completely occupied with briefs and meetings, from about 9 a.m. to 2 a.m.

I hope, however, that the above will give you some idea of the composite picture.

J. E. COULSON

---

[1] Date of receipt is uncertain.

[2] See No. 226, minute 7.

[3] *Annotation by Mr. Coulson:* 'Stalin agreed to ask Koniev to make a temporary arrangement': cf. No. 258, minute 6.

[4] *Annotation by Mr. Coulson:* 'Advance copy enclosed': not attached to filed copy. See No. 240.

No. 376

Minute from Mr. Hasler to Sir G. Rendel[1]
[*UR 2596/114/850*]

FOREIGN OFFICE, *23 July 1945*

Our immediate UNRRA problems are centred round the Council meeting.[2] At this meeting we hope that new financing arrangements will be agreed upon which will enable UNRRA to carry on in Europe until the harvest of 1946 and in some countries until the end of 1946. It is obvious however that from now on there will be increasing attention, particularly in the supplying countries, to the problems of changing over from the UNRRA period to the succeeding period when the non-paying countries will purchase their own supplies. This means that we shall have to study carefully the effects in each of the non-paying countries of the UNRRA programmes and the manner in which UNRRA's operations can be adjusted so as to ease the transition by encouraging the local Governments to take over.

2. Our current problems over getting UNRRA in operation have tended to obscure the fact that the problems of disengaging UNRRA are really the most delicate of all. Moreover the success or failure of UNRRA will be judged in history by the unsolved problems it leaves behind. The problem will differ very greatly as between one country and another. The policy appropriate to Czechoslovakia for instance will be quite different from that required for Greece. The problems will be difficult and we shall clearly have to pay great attention to them. Moreover the U.K. will have to play a leading part in this connection since the American tendency will be to cut off suddenly without regard for the consequences. If we are to exercise an influence we shall have to know much more about what is really happening in the non-paying countries.

3. At present we know next to nothing of what UNRRA is achieving in the non-paying countries. It was clear in the discussions we had in the Treasury[3] that there was considerable doubt about the ability of some of them to absorb the quantities of supplies now planned. While in others it looked, from the London end, as if the emphasis was not correctly placed as between one type of supply and another.

4. It has been suggested from Athens that I should pay a short visit to Greece to look at UNRRA problems on the spot. I was not able to go out at the time originally suggested, but it seems to me that it would be most useful if I were to pay this visit shortly after the Council meeting and to concentrate there upon building up a much fuller picture than we now possess of the future of the UNRRA programme there. If this trip does

---

[1] An Acting Under-Secretary of State superintending Refugee and Relief Departments.
[2] The third session of the U.N.R.R.A. Council was to open in London on 7 August 1945.
[3] No record of these discussions has been traced in Foreign Office archives.

materialise it would be useful at the same time if I could spend a short time in Italy, since we shall have just authorised UNRRA to take over responsibility in Italy and will be anxious to do anything we can to help UNRRA do this quickly. Whether it would be possible or desirable to attempt at the same time any similar analysis of the position in Yugoslavia I do not know.

5. It is not necessary at this stage to take any final decision on the question of a visit. I should like to know however whether in general you favour the idea. I have reason to believe that the Treasury would approve and I certainly think that something of the sort will be necessary if we are to have a proper basis upon which to build our UNRRA policy in the period after the council.[4]

W. J. HASLER

[4] Sir G. Rendel minuted: 'Yes. I agree provided the work can be adequately carried on here & you are not away too long. G. W. R. 25.vii.45.'

No. 377

Minute by Mr. Mason on rendition of Allied nationals
[WR 2208/1138/48]

FOREIGN OFFICE, 23 July 1945

I am very sorry that these papers[1] have been held up so long. The various papers on the subject have been quite impossible to get into one file: instead of being all entered WR (as I think they should have been) some have been entered Northern, some Southern and yet again some UE.[2] Even now all the papers are not here, but I cannot hold the matter up any longer and must piece the story together as best I can.

2. I understand that on the 29th March of this year a circular note[3] was sent to all Allied Governments (it is apparently to be found on UE papers) stating that before handing over nationals of Allied countries uncovered by our armed forces we should require the Allied Governments concerned to produce a *prima facie* case that the persons wanted by them had some legitimate charge to answer in their own country, e.g. they were quislings, renegades or even war criminals.

3. In accordance, I presume, with the line taken in their[4] circular note there seems to have been a good deal of correspondence earlier this year between SHAEF and the Chiefs of Staff in Washington and through other channels aimed at getting agreed military directives that no persons of the

[1] See paragraphs 4–9 below.
[2] WR and UE were respectively the prefixes for files of Refugee Department and of Economic Relations Department in the Foreign Office.
[3] Not printed (U 1527/29/73).
[4] It was suggested on the filed copy that this word should read 'this'.

kind mentioned above should in fact be handed over until the stipulation about a *prima facie* case had in effect been carried out. This seems to have led to a good deal of argument, among others, with the French Government. There are intimations, though it is not altogether clear, that the idea was to hold the position on these lines at least so long as the war against Germany actually continued.

4. At the same time, however, discussions appear to have been going forward on other papers which resulted eventually in the drawing up of Directive No. 40 for the Allied Commanders in Chief (No. 40 in the Handbook of Directives Flag A)[5] which was circulated to the European Advisory Commission after, apparently, having been approved by the relevant Cabinet Committee (the A.P.W. Committee). That Directive states categorically that 'you will be furnished by each United Nation Government with a list of their nationals whose apprehension is desired. You will take all possible steps to apprehend the persons named in such lists and you will hand them over to the appropriate authority of the United Nation concerned as arranged with that Government'. This is unequivocal and is in direct conflict with the policy mentioned above (para 2).

5. In accordance with the policy laid down in Directive No. 40 mentioned in the immediately preceeding [*sic*] paragraph it will be seen from SCAF 436 and FACS 248 [i] (at Flag B) that Belgian, Dutch, French and Luxembourg nationals were handed over by SCAEF and this action was endorsed by the Combined Chiefs of Staff—I am not quite clear on what date—without any *prima facie* case being required.

6. The next point in the story is twofold. First, the Yugoslav Government made a formal request for the handing over of a list supplied by them of quislings and traitors. This matter is being dealt with at present on Southern Department papers and I understand that it is proposed to insist on the production of a *prima facie* case before the persons in question are actually handed over to the Yugoslav Government. In the second place a Committee was held on the 20th June, of which there is a record on WR 1875[6] (at Flag C), when it was decided that it would be necessary to persist in requiring a *prima facie* case before any quislings or renegades were handed over and to reach agreement with the United States on this point. A letter was sent on the paper mentioned to Sir Frederick Bovenschen on July 2nd asking for his concurrence.

7. The next point appears to have arisen on papers at present entered Northern when it came to notice that there was a possibility of some Slovak nationals being handed over by American forces to the Czech Government as traitors. The Americans were asked to hold their hands (and they in fact did so) until we could reach a joint policy based on the production of a *prima facie* case, on the lines put forward at the Foreign Office meeting held on the 20th June (WR 1875[6] see above). The Americans retorted (see

[5] No flagged papers are annexed to the filed copy. Cf. No. 296, notes 2–4.
[6] Not printed. This paper, which included no minute of the meeting of 20 June 1945, contains a summary record by Mr. I. L. Henderson of the particulars given below.

N.8805[7] Flag D) that they and we had both presented proposals to the European Advisory Commission providing for the handing over of persons to Allied Governments without any conditions attached—these are in fact the directives mentioned in paragraph 4 above. They were apparently prepared to make an exception about the Yugoslavs (and as noted in paragraph 6 these have been dealt with separately) but they enquired whether our position has changed—if so their own had not—since the Directives to the European Advisory Commission were issued.

8. The situation seems in short to be that we have pursued, possibly unwittingly, two quite separate policies, firstly of pressing, both with Allied Governments and with the Combined Chiefs of Staff, for the retention of persons desired by Allied Governments pending the production of a *prima facie* case, and secondly, in the European Advisory Commission and with the approval of the relevant Cabinet Committee, of directing the Chiefs of Staff to hand over any persons required by Allied Governments without questions asked.

9. Now Sir Frederick Bovenschen in replying on WR 2079 [ii] (Flag E) to the Foreign Office letter in WR 1875,[6] has pointed out these inconsistencies and asks them [*sic*] whether we really intend to go back, as would be implied in the proposals in WR 1875, on the line already taken by the European Advisory Committee. He makes other points too but this, I think, is the main one.

10. I hope that I have traced this story correctly but it is so difficult in the absence of many of the papers and full records, that I shall be more than grateful for any comment that can be made by other Departments who would, perhaps, attach any important papers in their possession.

11. It is naturally most difficult to suggest a constructive way out of this apparent impasse since to pursue further the line originally suggested by us in the Circular Note of March 29th last[3] referred to at the beginning of this memorandum and renewed in WR 1875[6] would presumably make it necessary to go back to the Cabinet Committee and ask them to revise or modify the Directive No. 40[5] referred to in paragraph 4: and we should also have to square that point with the Americans too.

12. All I can suggest, therefore, is that we should take the line both in replying to Sir Frederick Bovenschen and with the Americans that we do not wish to go back broadly speaking on the line in Draft Directive No. 40 but that as regards certain countries, particularly in Eastern and South Eastern Europe we shall find it essential in practice to ask for production of a *prima facie* case before implementing the instructions in Draft Directive No. 40. This would of course entail an emendation in the lines suggested in WR 1875[6] where it was proposed that for the sake of conformity all countries including the Western European Allies should be asked to produce a *prima facie* case. This may be unfortunate but I doubt if it will matter so much in practice since it will be clear from the documents mentioned above (SCAF

[7] No. 296.

436 and FACS 248 [i] Flag B) practically all the Western quislings appear already to have been handed over.

P. Mason

Calendars to No. 377

i *9 July 1945   Combined Chiefs of Staff to F.M. Alexander (A.F.H.Q.) Tels. Nos. Fan 588–9.* Transmits texts of tels. SCAF 436 and FAC 248 on disposal of Allied and neutral nationals captured when serving in enemy forces; application in regard to Czechoslovakia [WR 2079/1138/48].

ii *6 July 1945   Letter from Sir F. Bovenschen (War Office) to Sir O. Sargent.* Difficulties in applying policy, in reversal of previous F.O. view regarding Russians, of requiring *prima facie* case before rendition of alleged Allied traitors [WR 2079/1138/48].

iii *18 July–2 Aug. 1945   A. V. M. Stevenson (Bucharest) Tel. No. RAC 1940/117.* Soviet approval of repatriation of Roumanians from Western Germany and Italy. Minutes on question of repatriation of those of Bessarabian and Bucovinan origin by Mr. Stewart, Mr. Galsworthy, Mr. Brimelow (on the principle of British policy on repatriation) and by Lord Dunboyne of F.O. Refugee Dept. [R 12522/5819/37].

No. 378

Letter from Mr. Howard to Mr. Hayter (Berlin)[1]
[F.O. 934/3/11(15)]

Top secret   FOREIGN OFFICE, *23 July 1945*

Dear William,

Moley[2] has asked me to send you my enclosed minute [i] about a talk I had with Gavrilovic[3] on 20th July.

Moley's comment is that he is 'afraid there is little prospect of our being able to get the Conference to consider the Yugoslav scandal in view of the fact that President Truman, most surprisingly, has said that he sees no need to raise the Yugoslav question at present and is prepared to give Marshal Tito the benefit of the doubt.'

Yours ever,
Douglas

Calendars to No. 378

i *20 July 1945   Record by Mr. Howard of a conversation with Dr. Gavrilovic,* who considered that Tito–Subasic agreement was now 'a complete farce' [F.O. 934/3/11(15)].

---

[1] The date of receipt of this letter, initialed by Mr. Hayter on 28 July 1945, is uncertain.
[2] Sir Orme Sargent.
[3] Dr. S. Gavrilovic was an Under-Secretary in the Yugoslav Ministry for Foreign Affairs.

No. 379

Letter from Mr. Howard to Mr. Hayter (Berlin)
[F.O. 934/2/9(22)]

FOREIGN OFFICE, *23 July 1945*

Dear William,

As you know, the Bugarian Armistice provided that 'on the conclusion of hostilities against Germany the Bulgarian armed forces must be demobilised and put on a peace footing under the supervision of the Allied Control Commission'.[1] Our information is that so far from carrying out this provision of the Armistice, the Russians are themselves supplying equipment to the Bulgarian Army and may even be promoting its expansion. The best estimate of the exact size to which the Russians have agreed seems to be fifteen divisions. Sargent wishes to suggest that the Delegation should raise this matter with the Americans and Russians, pressing the latter to state their intentions and generally to clarify the position. Would you put this suggestion forward?

Yours ever,
DOUGLAS

[1] Clause 1(d) of Armistice terms of 28 October 1944: *B.F.S.P.,* vol. 145, p. 526.

No. 380

Letter from Mr. Hayter (Berlin) to Mr. Howard
[F.O. 934/3/17(6)]

Top secret and Personal   BRITISH DELEGATION, BERLIN, *23 July 1945*

Dear Douglas,

Southern Department questions got quite an airing yesterday.

At the Foreign Secretaries' meeting in the morning we had the Yalta Declaration and Roumanian oil.[1] On the Yalta Declaration Molotov made it quite plain that he would have nothing to do with supervision of elections.

[1] See No. 224, minutes 2 and 4.

The other two questions in the American paper[2] about the Yalta Declaration (facilities for the Control Commissions and freedom of the press) were referred to a Sub-Committee consisting principally of Gromyko, Cannon and myself. This Sub-Committee met after dinner last night. Fired by two glasses of vodka and a glass of Armenian brandy I became very eloquent on the subject of freedom of the press, but I can't say we got very far. We did not discuss Control Commissions because the Russians were not ready with their paper.[3] We are going to meet again tonight.

When the Sub-Committee finally reports I thought of suggesting that we should make some further statement about elections, and we might then get in our word about the elections in Bulgaria, in accordance with your suggestions.[4]

As regards Balkan peace treaties, the present position is that they are to be referred to the proposed Council of Five Foreign Ministers to be taken up next in order after the Italian peace treaty. I think this is the best we shall get.

The discussion on Roumanian oil was inconclusive. Vyshinski made a long, tortuous and untruthful statement which was very badly interpreted. Byrnes backed us up fairly well, and the matter was left for further considera-tion. I think that both the Secretary of State and Cadogan feel that the worst part of our case is the companies claim to keep the oil equipment obtained from Germany during the war. However, Mark Turner has put up a very good case for this, and we hope to have another try tomorrow.

Turkey came up at the Plenary in the afternoon.[5] We had just been having a curiou[s] discussion about Colonial Trusteeship, in the course of which the Russians had not denied a suggestion by the Prime Minister that they were seeking to obtain 'large tracts of the North African shore'. Consequently when we came to Turkey the Prime Minister spoke with considerable fire. Molotov replied with a long statement in the course of which he referred to the Treaty of Unkiar Skelessi and the Russian-Turkish Treaty of 1805. Please tell Geoffrey[6] that I consider that I have been most harshly treated on not being properly briefed on these important topics. Finally, Truman said he would like time to consider the Russian proposals and the question was adjourned until today.

Yours ever,
W. HAYTER

P.S. Turkey came up again at the Plenary this afternoon,[7] and the President suggested that 'the freedom of the Straits should be guaranteed by all of us'. By this he seemed to mean that an international régime should be instituted for all international waterways; he lumped the Kiel Canal,

[2] No. 219.i.
[3] See No. 254, minute 1, and No. 259.
[4] Cf. No. 200.i.
[5] See No. 226, minute 9.
[6] Mr. McDermott.
[7] See No. 241, minute 10.

the Rhine, the Danube and the Dardanelles together. Joe[8] asked for time to think this over; no doubt he will say tomorrow that he quite agrees and that he thinks a similar régime should be applied to the Suez and the Panama Canals.

During the discussion on Turkey yesterday the Prime Minister suggested that the Turks had been intimidated by Russian troop concentrations in Bulgaria. Joe took this up this afternoon and said that the Russians had less troops in Bulgaria than we had in Greece. When the Prime Minister asked him how many troops he thought we had in Greece, Jo[e] said four or five divisions. On being told that we had only two divisions, or about 40,000 men in all, Joe claimed only to have 30,000 men in Bulgaria. Have we any figures about this? One other point about the Turkish debate today was that Joe said that the Turks could not have an Alliance without territorial concessions. He seemed to imply that if they were prepared to forego the Alliance they would not be required to make territorial concessions. The impression certainly was that the claim for Kars and Ardahan would not be strongly pressed.

[8] Marshal Stalin.

No. 381

Letter from Mr. N. Butler to Mr. Balfour (Washington)
[AN 2182/355/45]

FOREIGN OFFICE, *23 July 1945*

Dear Jock,

Before leaving for Potsdam the Secretary of State passed to the Department for comment the Ambassador's letter of July 2nd about Tarawa [i], remarking only that Mr. Grew had sent a very firm reply to Congressman Anderson.

You will appreciate that the Ambassador's appeal that we should get the matter reconsidered and his original proposal adopted presents us with quite a formidable problem. The Colonial Office were opposed on principle to handing over to a foreign government territory which included a large number of British subjects, some 3,000 in this case. This objection was shared by the Prime Minister of New Zealand: he and the then Prime Minister of Australia, whom our own Prime Minister wished to be consulted, were both opposed to the project, and Mr. Churchill accepted their advice.

As you know, in order to get a decision reversed, it is generally necessary, and always helpful, to adduce some fresh consideration. It is possible that both the Australian and New Zealand Governments are feeling less alarmed as to American imperialism in the South East Pacific than they were in January 1944, or again that they are more disposed to assist us in making a gesture in that part of the world to the United States Government. Apart from this, various questions occur to us on which the Embassy can really judge better than we.

The Americans have fought many notable battles since Tarawa, at Iwojima and Okinawa, and you will know from the famous picture of the hoisting of Old Glory on the former[1] that for the time at any rate Iwojima has left Tarawa in the shade. Congressman Anderson is of no particular influence so far as we are aware. Is there evidence of substantial feeling behind the point of view advocated in his speech, and is Grew's firm reply not likely to give a fair quietus to it on at least the negative side? By which I mean that we shall not be seriously criticised for not making the gesture if our decision is that way. We have heard that it is at least possible that the Americans will wish to transfer the graves of their dead back to the United States. This would not necessarily apply in all conditions; on the other hand, if the public feeling is that way, this would diminish the appropriateness of the proposed gesture.

Apart from these practical points, I regret that I have misgivings whether Dr. Evatt would be at all disposed to make it easy for us to make a friendly gesture in his part of the world to the United States. I have a feeling that he would wish to retain a monopoly for himself. I may be doing him injustice, but I would like you to consider a suggestion that I made in Washington, namely, that the Embassy should sound out the Australian and New Zealand Ministers there as to whether (*a*) they think it likely that their Governments would be ready to reconsider their previous objections, and (*b*) whether the Ministers themselves would use their influence in that sense.

Until we have had further advice from you on some or all of the above points, I would hardly feel justified in setting in motion all the wheels that would need to grind through successfully in order to obtain a reversal of the decision taken a year and a half ago. I will tell Lord Halifax of this letter if I have an opportunity when he gets to London, and he may be able to answer some of the points himself offhand.[2]

N. M. BUTLER

CALENDAR TO NO. 381

i   *2 July 1945   Letter from Lord Halifax (Washington) to Mr. Eden.* In view of recent speech in House of Representatives and letter from Congressman Anderson suggesting American negotiation for possession of such islands as Tarawa in Gilbert and Ellice Islands, urges reconsideration of British policy: spontaneous gift of Tarawa to the U.S. would bring great return in goodwill [AN 2182/355/45].

[1] This photograph, taken on 23 February 1945, was first published in the *Los Angeles Times* of 25 February 1945.

[2] Mr. Butler minuted on 7 August 1945: 'Discussed w[ith] Ld. Halifax who agreed that we should await Mr. Balfour's reply. He regards the question as a matter of opinion, and his opinion is that the gesture wd. be a very good investment. N. M. B. 7/8.'

No. 382

Letter from the South African High Commissioner in London to Viscount Cranborne[1]

No. 116/90/20/10 [D.O. 35/1970: WR 222/3/4]

SOUTH AFRICA HOUSE, *23 July 1945*

My dear Secretary of State,

Post-war Treatment of Japan

With reference to your Circular telegrams D. Nos. 1243, 1244 and 1245,[2] my Prime Minister has asked me to convey to you the following message:—

I have grave doubts about the Japanese Policy attributed to the State Department, which appears impracticable, dangerous and likely to prolong the war unnecessarily. The Japanese will fight to the death against such a policy of annihiliation [*sic*]—nor is it in the long range interest of Peace. To eliminate Japan so completely exposes future peace in Asia to grave risks either at the hands of Russia or China. A vacuum is created into which many fresh devils may enter. Rather administer thorough defeat to Japan and impose certain severe conditions which will prevent rapid military recovery but leave her to manage her own affairs and avoid military government by foreigners which will fail and saddle all the odium of failure on the occupying powers. I prefer the older methods of peace-making to these new drastic methods which are too destructive of existing systems for which no alien rule can provide an effective substitute. I am much more in agreement with the Foreign Office criticism of the scheme though even that goes too far in my opinion. The West cannot govern the East on American lines and the scheme will not only fail but cover the Western failure with just odium for far-reaching reactions. I must admit that this criticism applies also to a minor extent to our plans for dealing with Germany which I fear will also break down and bring odium on the occupying powers. These conquered peoples must be allowed to govern themselves and be responsible for their own failures, while the Allies should remain in the background for reasons of security. Nor is it wise to remove all restraints from the future path of new powers like Russia and China whose policies may follow very different lines from what may be envisaged to-day. While thoroughly defeating Germany and Japan and taking security precautions for future, I would not destroy the balance in Europe or Asia to an extent which will open the door to new unforeseen dangers, which may take many unforeseen forms. I fear we are destroying both Germany and Japan with results which no one can foresee and which the Charter could not control. After all the war is not against peoples but against ideologies and gangster Governments which one hopes will be destroyed and finally discredited by defeat. We cannot recreate the

---

[1] Received not later than 24 July 1945.

[2] Not printed. These Dominions Office telegrams had reference to the memorandum of 20 June 1945 by Sir G. Sansom: see No. 304, notes 1–3.

World but only deal with patent evils such as Nazism and Bushido or whatever the Japanese disease is called.

I have sent copies for information to the other Dominion High Commissioners.[3]

Yours sincerely,

G. HEATON NICHOLLS

[3] In a letter of 24 July 1945 Lord Cranborne thanked Mr. Heaton Nicholls for conveying this message from Field-Marshal Smuts: Lord Cranborne would see that it was brought to the notice of Mr. Churchill and Mr. Eden.

No. 383

Mr Roberts (Moscow) to Mr. Eden (Received 3 August)
No. 511 [F 4746/186/10]

MOSCOW, *24 July 1945*

Sir,

I have the honour to report that the Prime Minister and Minister of Foreign Affairs of China, Mr T. V. Soong, arrived in Moscow for conversations with the Soviet Government on June 30th. The way was paved for this visit by General Hurley's conversations with Marshal Stalin in Moscow last April[1] and by subsequent contacts between Chinese and Soviet statesmen in San Francisco under American auspices. Mr Soong left on July 14th, as explained in my telegram No. 3133[2] of that date, with the intention of returning to Moscow and resuming his conversations with Generalissimo Stalin and other Soviet representatives after the Potsdam Conference.

2. Mr Soong was accompanied on his visit by the Deputy Minister of Foreign Affairs, Mr Victor Hoo, who was a student in Leningrad and speaks excellent Russian, by a small staff, and by the Soviet Ambassador to China, Mr Petrov. He was met at the airport by various prominent Soviet officials including Mr Molotov, and the Diplomatic Corps. On arrival he at once made a statement that he believed that sincere and friendly collaboration between China and the Soviet Union would make a tremendous contribution to the establishment of a firm peace. This note was maintained throughout his stay.

3. Mr Soong had the first of several meetings with Generalissimo Stalin the same evening, and conversations with Soviet officials continued for the whole fortnight of his stay. The Soviet press reported a luncheon given by Mr Molotov to Mr Soong on July 2nd and a reception given by Mr Molotov the next day to enable the Diplomatic Corps and other leading Soviet personalities to meet Mr Soong. On July 13th Generalissimo Stalin gave him and his party an official Kremlin banquet, which was described,

[1] Cf. *F.R.U.S. 1945*, vol. vii, pp. 338–40.   [2] No. 133.

according to custom, as having taken place 'in a warm, friendly atmosphere'. At the same time a joint Soviet-Chinese communiqué was published reporting the friendly atmosphere and broad mutual understanding in which 'questions of very great importance' were discussed. I enclose an English translation[3] of this communiqué. During the night of July 13th/14th Generalissimo Stalin and Mr Molotov left for Potsdam and Mr Soong left by air for Chungking on July 14th to report developments to date and prepare for the resumption of conversations after the Potsdam meeting. He was seen off by M. Lozovski, who deals with Far Eastern affairs in the People's Commissariat for Foreign Affairs. It remains to be seen whether on his final departure Generalissimo Stalin will himself come to bid him farewell, as he did in the case of Mr Matsuoka[4] some years ago. The Soviet Ambassador to China also left with Mr Soong, but Mr Hoo remained in Moscow ostensibly to maintain contact with the Soviet Government.

4. It cannot have been wholly an accident that Mr Soong's visit coincided with that of another personality also recognised by the Soviet Government as a Prime Minister, but presumably regarded by Mr Soong as a rebel Chinese subject: Marshal Choibalsan, the Premier of the Mongolian Peoples' Republic. The Marshal, it will be remembered, was one of the leaders of the Mongolian Independence Movement in 1918, and came to study military science in Moscow in 1927, becoming a Marshal in the Mongolian People's Army in that year. After holding various offices in the small *Hural* or Council of State and on the Committee of the 'Mongolian People's Revolutionary Party' he became Prime Minister of his Republic in March 1939 at the age of 44. He has always been at pains to emphasise his country's connexion with the U.S.S.R., and is identified with the policy of material aid to the Soviet Union. Indeed, his official pronouncement after the Japanese attack on Pearl Harbour was devoted to praise of the Red Army 'in the name of the whole Mongolian people'. Marshal Choibalsan arrived on July 4th and was duly accorded the same honours as Mr Soong. He was met at the airport by Mr Molotov and the same Soviet officials as had met the Prime Minister of China. On July 5th he was accorded an interview with Generalissimo Stalin, and the Kremlin reception in his honour took the form of a luncheon on July 7th, six days before the dinner in honour of Mr Soong. The Mongolian Prime Minister left Moscow on July 8th; and as he was not expected to return, he was duly seen off by Mr Molotov. No communiqué was published on the conversations, though the luncheon at the Kremlin of course took place 'in a warm, friendly atmosphere'. So far as is known Mr Soong and Marshal Choibalsan did not meet each other.

5. Mr Soong and his party were carefully nursed by the United States Ambassador, who even postponed his departure to Potsdam on their

[3] Not here printed.
[4] On the departure of M. Y. Matsuoka, Japanese Minister for Foreign Affairs, from Moscow on 13 April 1941 after the conclusion that day of a non-aggression pact between Japan and the Soviet Union.

account. They attended the Independence Day celebrations at the American Embassy on the 4th July, and also lunched with Sir A. Clark Kerr on the 11th July. Before luncheon on that day Mr Soong explained to His Majesty's Ambassador the scope of his negotiations with the Soviet authorities and their progress up to that date, on the understanding that no written report would be made of their conversation, but that Sir A. Clark Kerr would report what he had said orally to Mr Churchill.[5] In these circumstances the Chinese Ambassador and Mr Hoo have continued to maintain the utmost discretion about the Moscow conversations and have revealed none of the anxieties shown by the Chinese Ambassador in London, as reported in your telegram No. 769 to Chungking.[6] The Ambassador has gone so far as to indicate that after the Moscow talks an important pronouncement would probably be made in Chungking which should relieve the tension between the Government and the Chinese Communists and he has recently shortened the odds which he has been laying against an early end to the war in the Far East. This is however as much a tribute to recent Anglo-American naval and air activity against Japan as to his obvious confidence, which is widely shared in Moscow, that the Soviet Union will participate in the Far Eastern war. I have heard from foreign journalists here that the Japanese Embassy have shown the greatest anxiety over the course of the Potsdam talks and that they have sent home most of their women. The Japanese Ambassador certainly showed considerable despondency about his country's prospects in conversation with the International Red Cross delegates, who passed through Moscow to Manchuria and Japan early this month.

6. Before Mr Soong's visit to Moscow the Soviet press had begun to show a slightly increased interest in Chinese internal affairs and in the course of the Pacific War. The references to Chinese internal affairs were on familiar lines critical of the Kuomintang on the grounds that it was neither a truly democratic system of government nor an efficient organiser of the Chinese war effort. A few highly critical articles were also appearing about Manchuria under the Japanese yoke. Little, if anything, has been published here this year about developments in those areas of China under Communist control. The space given to Far Eastern affairs has however been very small in comparison with that given to developments in Europe. During and since Mr Soong's visit, apart from factual reporting of the Pacific war in a sense increasingly careless of Japanese reactions, there has only been one article about the Far East, a *Tass* report from Vladivostok critical of General Ho Ying-chin's attitude towards the war, quoted in my telegram No. 3055.[7] As a large volume of *Tass* material is constantly poured into Moscow from the Far East, it is clear that the Soviet authorities are deliberately playing down the Far East to their own public, partly no doubt because of their continued preoccupation with the settlement of Europe, but more probably

[5] Cf. No. 180.
[6] No. 324.
[7] Of 11 July 1945 (F 4169/325/10), not printed.

because they have not yet finally decided what course should be set and do not wish to commit themselves in advance.

I am sending a copy of this despatch to His Majesty's Ambassador at Chungking.

I have, &c.,
FRANK K. ROBERTS

No. 384

Sir J. Anderson to Earl of Halifax (Washington)
No. 7765 Telegraphic [UR 2391/9/850]

Important. Secret   FOREIGN OFFICE, 24 July 1945, 2.25 a.m.

Following for Marris[1] from Haden [Hasler].

1. You will have seen Jackson's telegram,[2] reporting a conversation with Iliuschenko on the possibility of U.S.S.R. asking for U.N.R.R.A. assistance, and Lehman's reply[3] suggesting discussion with the United States and United Kingdom Governments. We have now told U.N.R.R.A. here that in our view everything should be done to avoid bringing this matter to a head, since if the Russians make a formal request for assistance a situation will be created in which action will have to be taken which will create bad blood one way or the other. We consider that the wisest course would be for U.N.R.R.A. to explore the matter further with the Russians before it reaches a more formal stage and to point out to them that a Russian request for assistance from U.N.R.R.A. would make necessary a thorough scrutiny of Soviet finances. What the Russians would be asking would be, in effect, that the United States and the United Kingdom, having failed to come to terms with the Russians on the financing of supplies outside the Protocol,[4] should now provide these supplies free. All the contributing Governments had in one way or another committed themselves to their Parliaments on the basis that U.N.R.R.A. would provide free relief only to those countries which were unable to pay for supplies. They could not be expected to accept such a major change as the U.S.S.R. becoming a non-paying country without being absolutely sure that U.S.S.R. was not in fact able to pay. This being so, how would the Russians wish to proceed, bearing in mind that they would presumably not wish to make a formal request for assistance unless they were fairly certain of it succeeding?

2. I understand that the State Department have informed Clayton of what has passed and I am bringing Coulson up to date on how matters stand. We shall presumably discuss this with Clayton here. Meanwhile,

---

[1] Mr. A. D. Marris was an Economic Adviser attached to H.M. Embassy in Washington.
[2] The information in this telegram, No. 2012 Enjoy of 12 July 1945 (not printed), is summarized in No. 97.
[3] No. 97.i.
[4] See No. 97, note 2.

you may, if you think fit, inform State Department of substance of my paragraph 1.

3. All of this seems to emphasise the importance of the Resolution 23 Committee[5] making a thorough examination of the Chinese case, since if this is done in an easy-going manner, it will be quoted against us.

CALENDARS TO No. 384

i   *24 July 1945   Letter from Mr. Hasler to Mr. Coulson (Berlin).* Refers to No. 97 and discusses implications of conversation with M. Iliuschenko [F.O. 934/5/53(1)].

ii   *30 July 1945   Mr. Balfour (Washington) Tel. No. 5281.* In discussion on Chinese case U.S. representative on Resolution 23 Committee took line that it should not take into account effect which Soviet application for aid might have on U.N.R.R.A. resources. Committee's subsequent recommendation that China be regarded as non-paying country up to June 1946 indicates that present Committee will not be an effective instrument for limiting U.N.R.R.A's financial commitments [UR 2631/252/852].

[5] This subcommittee to the U.N.R.R.A. Committee on Supplies had been established in November 1943 under Resolution 23 of the First Council Session of U.N.R.R.A. to advise the Director-General on the ability to pay of countries applying for U.N.R.R.A. assistance.

No. 385

Mr. Hankey (Warsaw) to Mr. Eden (Received 24 July, 3.25 p.m.)
No. 42 Telegraphic [N 9228/35/55)

WARSAW, *24 July 1945, 1.48 p.m. G.M.T.*

In spite of I think genuine desire on the part of the Polish President and Government to work closely with the Russians, the latter seem to be making it as hard as possible for the people to like them. Stories of rape and plunder come in from all parts of Poland, from Poles of all classes and from British prisoners-of-war.

2. In order to protect the Polish harvest the Polish Government have now got the Russians to sign agreement not to requisition goods in Poland east of the 1939 frontier, and new territories (. . . ? will be)[1] taking the harvest in somewhat under half the area. The Russian army has however apparently no proper supply system and the trouble will only be cured when it is gone.

Please repeat to Moscow as my telegram No. 6.

[1] The text is here uncertain.

No. 386

Mr. Hankey (Warsaw) to Mr. Eden (Received 24 July, 6.50 p.m.)
No. 44 Telegraphic [N 9170/6/55]

Immediate   WARSAW, *24 July 1945, 4.30 p.m. G.M.T.*

My telegrams Nos 23 and 39.[1]

I learn on good authority that members of Peasant Party (Mikolajczyk's branch) who held provincial meeting in Lublin were all arrested on July 22nd and last night had still not been released.

2. There is practically no freedom of political activity at present in this country. The N.K.V.D. control the police and the police control most overt political activity in such a way that only P.P.R. and stooge groups of other parties allied with them (including stooge group of Peasant Party) can do anything. It is being borne in on me more and more that free and unfettered election procedure will be a complete sham unless free association and opinion is given to other parties in accordance with Moscow decisions (. . . ? including)[2] Peasant Party (Mikolajczyk) and Christian Socialist Party (Popiel) . . .[2] also to left wing National Democrats.

3. I earnestly hope Secretary of State and possibly also Prime Minister will (. . . ? feel)[2] able to speak severely to President Bierut, Polish Prime Minister and if possible to get Americans to do the same.

Please pass to Terminal at once with telegrams under reference[3] and to Moscow as my telegram No. 7.

CALENDARS TO NO. 386

i   *24 July 1945   Letter from Sir O. Sargent to Sir A. Cadogan (Berlin).* Concern for some satisfaction concerning participation of Polish parties in forthcoming elections: suggests ways of securing this at Potsdam; initialed by Sir A. Cadogan on 26 July and minuted by Mr. D. Allen: 'This is now out of date in view of the arrival of the Polish delegation and the P.M.'s and S. of S.'s conversations with them. D. A. 26/7' [F.O. 934/2/10(68)].

ii   *26 July 1945   Mr. Hankey (Warsaw) Tel. No. 1 Saving.* Position of members of Polish Home Army [N 9666/6/55].

---

[1] Nos. 318.i and 373 respectively.

[2] The text is here uncertain.

[3] Mr. D. Allen minuted and Sir A. Cadogan initialed in Berlin upon repetitions to the British Delegation of these telegrams: 'These three telegrams are disturbing . . . and provide ample justification for the fears expressed by M. Mikolajczyk privately here [cf. No. 268.i] . . . The P.M.'s and S. of S.'s conversations with the Polish Delegation [Nos. 267–270] . . . have provided us with the opportunity of taking up with them most of these points in accordance with the sense of the minutes on Sir O. Sargent's letter [i] . . . D. Allen. 25/7.' 'A. C. July 26, 1945.'

No. 387

Mr. Randall (Copenhagen) to Mr. Eden (Received 24 July, 3.20 p.m.)
No. *391 Telegraphic* [U 5697/20/70]

COPENHAGEN, *24 July 1945, 1.41 p.m. G.M.T.*

Repeated to 21st Army Group.

Danish Foreign Minister asked me yesterday whether I could throw any light on the report in some Danish papers that Russians were in favour of a unified Germany while His Majesty's Government and the United States Government advocated a splitting up of Germany. I replied in the negative but confirmed Mr. Christmas Moller's remark that a large body of British liberal and labour opinion was opposed to the dismemberment of Germany. I said that it was conceivable that a strong move for independence or autonomy would develop in certain German regions. Mr. Christmas Moller agreed but said that a forced dismemberment would in his opinion be a disastrous error and would lead to the appearance of another Hitler in ten years. He added that he would hardly have thought that the Western Powers would have wished to see a divided Germany lying between them and a large unified Russia.

This is partly an explanation and proof of the sincerity of Mr. Christmas Moller's opposition to Denmark's acquisition of South Schleswig; he cannot believe in lasting German weakness and fears future German vengeance.

Foreign Office please repeat to 21st Army Group as my telegram No. 13.

No. 388

Mr. Eden (Berlin) to Sir J. Anderson (Received 24 July, 1.45 p.m.)
No. *196 Target Telegraphic* [F.O. 934/4/20(16)]

Top secret. Important   BERLIN, *24 July 1945, 3.35 p.m.*

For Foreign Office from Foreign Secretary.

Your telegram Onward No. 124[1] paragraph 2 (of July 21st: French sector in Berlin).

I had some doubt whether the French sector in Berlin should come entirely out of ours, leaving us and France in an inferior position to the United States of America and the U.S.S.R. As, however, Field Marshal Montgomery is content with this arrangement, and provided the proposal in General Week's [*sic*] report of July 20th to the War Office[2] is acceptable in Whitehall, I agree that the United Kingdom Delegation should be authorised to accept the Soviet formula given in your telegram Onward No. 89.[1]

---

[1] No. 222.i.   [2] Cf. No. 389.

No. 389

Sir J. Anderson to Mr. Eden (Berlin: received 25 July, 6.45 a.m.)
No. 196 Onward Telegraphic [U 5619/20/70]

Top secret. Immediate FOREIGN OFFICE, *24 July 1945, 11.53 p.m.*

For Foreign Secretary from Foreign Office.

Your telegram Target 138.[1] Neither we nor War Office have received clear statement of General Week's proposals but we understand that they consist in giving to the French the two districts of Reinickendorf and Wedding and that this can be effected without inconveniencing our own people in Berlin and without any consequential alteration in the existing Soviet sector. If we are correct in assuming that there are no technical objections to this proposal we recognise there may be administrative advantage in reducing the size of the British sector, though these would be correspondingly offset if feeding of French sector remained a British responsibility. The decision whether or not to accept Soviet formula contained in our telegram Onward 89[1] seems however to turn on political considerations. Can we afford to leave the Russians in possession of eight districts as compared with the United States, British and French sectors of six, four and two districts respectively? Will this mean that Russian views in all matters affecting Berlin will in future prevail against ours because they will always be able to argue that their responsibility is far larger than that of the British?

2. If you consider as a matter of tactics it would be better to concede this point to the Russians, we should be grateful for early intimation to that effect in order that we may conclude without delay the necessary Agreement at the E.A.C.[2]

---

[1] No. 222.i.

[2] This telegram crossed No. 388, as explained in Foreign Office telegram No. 213 Onward of 6.20 p.m. on 25 July to Berlin, which added: 'Unless we receive contrary instructions we shall accept Soviet formula at meeting of E.A.C. tomorrow morning': see further No. 417.

No. 390

Mr. Eden (Berlin) to Sir J. Anderson (Received 24 July, 1.35 a.m.)
No. 194 Target Telegraphic [U 5819/19/70]

Top secret. Immediate BERLIN, *24 July 1945, 3.30 a.m.*

Following from the Foreign Secretary.

Paris Tel No. 1005[1]

I am disturbed at this development and consider that we must press on with our offer to equip the ten additional French squadrons. Please tell

---

[1] No. 322

the Air Ministry the importance I attach to this and concert with them how best to hasten the discussions with the French.

2. I shall be glad to know what truth there is in the allegation of 'delays and disappointments' in deliveries of British aircraft to the French.

3. Please repeat to Paris.

No. 391

Sir J. Anderson to Mr. Eden (Berlin: received 25 July, 12.20 a.m.)
No. 192 Onward Telegraphic [ZM 3978/3/22]

Top secret. Immediate   FOREIGN OFFICE, *24 July 1945, 10.10 p.m.*

Following from Foreign Office for Foreign Secretary.

Please see Onward No. 188 repeating Rome tel. No. 1174[1] of 23rd July: Italian Institutional Question.

We agree with views expressed in this tel. Course B is in fact the solution proposed in our despatch No. 1020 to Washington,[2] of which Mr. Hoyer Millar has a copy. Any representations to the Italian Government would however, in our view have to be made with considerable circumspection and on a strictly joint Anglo-American basis if we are not to defeat our own ends by appearing openly to be intervening in favour of the monarchy.[3]

[1] No. 371.
[2] See No. 12, note 1.
[3] In minuting in Berlin on this telegram and on No. 371, Mr. Hoyer Millar summarized his discussion with the U.S. Delegation, of which a record had been sent to Mr. Harvey (No. 441.i): 'The Foreign Office will therefore be in a position to take whatever action they think necessary on Rome telegram No. 1174 and Naf 1043 [No. 371.i]. F. R. H. M. July 27th, 1945.'

No. 392

Sir J. Anderson to Mr. Eden (Berlin: received 25 July, 12.32 a.m.)
No. 195 Onward Telegraphic [R 12416/4/19]

Immediate. Top secret   FOREIGN OFFICE, *24 July 1945, 6.30 p.m.*[1]

Following for Secretary of State from Sir O. Sargent.

Sofia telegrams Nos. 843 and 844[2] (Onward 185 and 186) and Athens

[1] Time of origin.
[2] In these telegrams of 23 July 1945 (received in Foreign Office and Berlin on 24 July) Mr. Houstoun-Boswall had reported receipt from the Allied Control Commission in Bulgaria of a Bulgarian note of 19 July to the A.C.C. in favour of early Allied establishment of 'regular diplomatic intercourse' with Bulgaria (cf. *F.R.U.S. Berlin*, vol. ii, pp. 711–3). Mr. Houstoun-Boswall commented: 'Acting Commissioner and I are not impressed by this specious document which reiterates all old arguments with which we are familiar here. We feel sure that it has been concocted with the approval, if not at the suggestion, of local

telegrams Nos. 1577[3] (Onward 174), 1583 (Onward 178) and 1584 (Onward 176) [i]. Our first impression is that the Bulgarian note to the A.C.C., the Yugoslav note to the Greek Government and the resignation of M. Sophianopoulos[4] perhaps also Sophianopoulos's demand for a 'representative' government are all part of a concerted plan by the Soviet Government to launch a diplomatic offensive against us in the Balkans.[5]

2. Our considered views on each question will follow as soon as possible.

CALENDAR TO NO. 392

i *23–4 July 1945 Mr. Caccia (Athens) Tels. Nos. 1583–4.* On 22 July M. Sophianopoulos informed Mr. Caccia of his resignation since he believed that 'present service Government must go and be replaced by a political Government covering all parties'. President of the Council, Admiral P. Voulgaris, subsequently informed Mr. Caccia that he had accepted office under protest and would go if H.M.G. thought it in the interests of Greece. The Regent, Archbishop Damaskinos, wished for frank advice from H.M.G. as to change of Govt. in Greece in the interests of Greek relations with other Allied Powers such as U.S.S.R. Requests urgent instructions [R 12416/4/19].

Soviet authorities . . . This communication does however seem to provide an admirable opportunity for a general discussion [annotation by Mr. Eden: 'Where? Berlin? A. E.'] of the very unsatisfactory internal situation of Bulgaria.'

[3] In this telegram of 23 July (received in Foreign Office on 23 July and in Berlin on 24 July) Mr. Caccia had reported receipt from the Director General of the Greek Ministry of Foreign Affairs of a copy of a Yugoslav note of 22 July to the Greek Government complaining of alleged Greek persecution in Macedonia (cf. *F.R.U.S. 1945*, vol. viii, pp. 328–9). 'Director General said that such a document would not be accepted by the Greek Government. They did not admit that there was any Yugoslav minority in Greece nor that the Yugoslav Government had any right to meddle in internal Greek affairs . . . If the history of the pre-war years was to be repeated, such a document could only be a prelude to some act of aggression but in this case Greece relied with complete assurance on the support of His Majesty's Government and on their close association with the Soviet as well as the United States Government.'

[4] Greek Minister for Foreign Affairs.

[5] Mr. Eden minuted on this: 'I agree; against us & against all free Govts. Press should be encouraged to point this out—with moderation. It should also be presumed in press that these matters will be discussed at Berlin. Our plain speaking has had some effect with Russians at conferences.'

No. 393

Sir J. Anderson to Mr. Eden (Berlin: received 25 July, 12.59 a.m.)
No. 194 Onward Telegraphic [U 5751/191/70]

FOREIGN OFFICE, *24 July 1945, 10.45 p.m.*

Top secret. Most Immediate

Private and Personal for Foreign Secretary from Dominions Secretary.

We have just learnt from Target 173[1] that the question of Trust Territories

[1] This telegram of 23 July 1945, not printed, summarized the discussion recorded in No. 226, minute 8.

has been raised by the Russians and is to be discussed by you and the other Foreign Secretaries. You will of course know how extremely delicate this question is, but you may not be aware that at San Fransisco the Soviet Delegation made repeated efforts to cut out from the Trusteeship Chapter all safeguards with regard to existing League of Nations mandates. If they had had their way, there would have been no security for existing mandatories pending the negotiation of new Trusteeship agreements. They also did their utmost to prejudice the opposition [position] of Trustee powers in respect of the negotiation and administration of new Trusteeship Agreements. What was behind their attitude we never found out. But it is rather significant that they should have raised the question again. As you will know, it is one that concerns not only ourselves but also Australia, New Zealand and South Africa, and these countries would certainly regard it as a breach of faith with them if we entered into any arrangements with the United States and Russia without full previous consultation with them. Moreover, this is a matter which, since the signature of the Charter, now concerns all the United Nations and in particular France and Belgium. I would therefore most strongly urge that we should enter into no commitment at Terminal on this question, which has the most serious potentialities for the future of Empire collaboration. Oliver Stanley, whom I have consulted, asks me to say that he is in full agreement with this telegram.

No. 394

Sir J. Anderson to Lord Killearn (Cairo)[1]
No. 1133 Telegraphic [W 9911/24/802]

Secret   FOREIGN OFFICE, 24 July 1945, 7.40 p.m.

Repeated to Washington No. 7758, M.E. Min's Office No. . . . [sic] Resmed's Office Caserta No. 2275.

On June 21st His Majesty's Ambassador at Washington addressed a note to United States Government,[2] in response to latter's request for an assurance on the subject, stating *inter alia* that His Majesty's Government had no intention of opposing United States Government or any other Government in the acquisition of *landing rights* for civil aircraft in any country.

2. We have ascertained that United States Government are interpreting this statement as meaning that His Majesty's Government have abandoned their opposition to grant of unconditional Fifth Freedom rights[2] to United States civil air lines and are interpreting it in this sense to certain foreign Governments on whom they are renewing their pressure to sign civil aviation agreements favourable to themselves.

---

[1] This telegram was also addressed to H.M. representatives at Beirut as No. 544, Bagdad No. 422, Tehran No. 449, Istanbul No. 128, Rome No. 1900, Lisbon No. 530, and Saving to H.M. representatives at Paris No. 1741, Brussels No. 156, The Hague No. 10, Copenhagen No. 38 and Oslo No. 20.
[2] See i below.

3. His Majesty's Government have of course in no way modified their policy of opposition to grant of unrestricted Fifth Freedom rights and you are authorised so to inform Government to which you are accredited if you think there is any danger of their being misled into yielding to United States pressure.

(Cairo only. Please pass copy to M.E.Min.).

CALENDARS TO No. 394

i *6 & 22 July 1945 From and to Earl of Halifax (Washington) Tels. Nos. 4667 & 7727.* Conversation on 2 July with Mr. S. W. Morgan, Chief of Aviation Division of State Dept., on British note of 21 June (see *F.R.U.S. 1945*, vol. viii, pp. 71–3) regarding landing rights for U.S. air companies in Middle East: denial that U.S. sought exclusive rights to airfields: problems arising from Anglo-American divergence at Civil Aviation Conference at Chicago in Nov.-Dec. 1944 over 'fifth freedom' of the air. Instructions thereon [W 9274, 9963/24/802].

ii *16 July–5 Aug. 1945 From and to Sir H. Stonehewer-Bird and Mr. G. H. Thompson (Bagdad) Tels. Nos. 541, 578, 581 & 424, 467, 475.* Urged that Iraqi Govt. should not be rushed into granting unrestricted 'fifth freedom' rights to U.S. airlines: British position explained to U.S. colleague [W 9496, 9714, 10282, 10339, 10464/24/802].

iii *22–30 July 1945 To Mr. Caccia (Athens) Tel. No. 1557; Mr. Shone (Beirut) Tel. No. 717; to Mr. Thompson (Bagdad) Tel. No. 98; to Sir M. Peterson (Istanbul) Tel. No. 205.* Attitudes of Greek, Syrian, Lebanese and Turkish Govts. to granting 'fifth freedom' rights to U.S. airlines, and British reactions. Minute by Mr. Cheetham on likely need for 'some more positive plan for resisting U.S. pressure' [W 9963, 10139, 10187, 10203/24/802].

iv *30 July 1945 Lord Killearn (Cairo) No. 1086* enclosing communication to Egyptian Prime Minister on British policy on international air transport and the 'fifth freedom' [W 10901/24/802].

v *9 Aug. 1945 Letter from Mr. Gallop to Sir D. Gainer (Rio de Janeiro).* Reply to No. 128. Explains British opposition to unrestricted 'fifth freedom' rights; Anglo-American competition in regard to external telecommunication services of Saudi Arabia [W 10012/75/802].

No. 395

Letter from Mr. Cullis[1] to Mr. Mack (Rome)

[C 3946/141/3]

FOREIGN OFFICE, *24 July 1945*

Dear Mack,

I enclose a copy of some notes [i] sent to Harrison by the irrepressible Robert[2], on the situation in the American and French zones. I should not

---

[1] Mr. M. F. Cullis was a member of the German Department of the Foreign Office.

[2] Archduke Robert of Austria, younger brother of the Archduke Otto, sons of the former Emperor Charles.

necessarily place great reliance on these Hapsburg reports, but in the present case our own evidence tends to bear out his statement of the ineptitude with which United States military government has tackled the denazification problem. Altogether, it is a characteristic example of how the Americans dissipate the great potential good will that awaits them.

It is satisfactory to hear that the French in Tyrol-Vorarlberg (the zone, incidentally, where the Archdukes are believed to have maintained the most active contacts) are doing much better.

I forget whether I told you that Otto and one or two of his brothers have—according to Robert, and there is no reason to disbelieve it—travelled *incognito* all over the three Western zones of Austria. Clearly he has the French in his pocket!

Yours ever,
M. F. CULLIS

CALENDAR TO NO. 395

i *10 July 1945 Letter from Archduke Robert of Austria to Mr. Harrison* enclosing a report from the Tyrol [C 3946/141/3].

No. 396

Mr. Shepherd (Helsinki) to Mr. Eden (Received 7 August)
No. 114 [N 9908/356/56]

Confidential HELSINKI, *24 July 1945*

Sir,

I have not so far made any comments on the Foreign Office secret circular despatch of March 30th[1] regarding the effect of our external financial position on our foreign policy. This is partly because (*a*) as pointed out in paragraph 17 of the circular, Finland is one of those Scandinavian countries where the maintenance of flourishing trade relations should present no difficulty, (*b*) partly because the direction of Finnish foreign trade and the general economic situation of the country are still somewhat uncertain, (*c*) but also, and perhaps mainly, because the attitude which we may propose towards Finland must depend to an appreciable extent on our policy with regard to the Scandinavian States in general with special reference to Russia.

2. As regards the first consideration, there seems every reason to hope that economic relations with Finland will not only regain their pre-war characteristic but will develop in a manner favourable to us. We bought before the war 45% of Finland's total exports but Finnish imports from the United Kingdom were only 19%. We are likely to be in the market when

---

[1] Not printed (UE 813/813/53).

865

normal trade conditions return for similar quantities of Finnish forest and agricultural products and while abnormal post-war conditions prevail our demand for anything Finland can supply is likely to be exceptionally high. Finland, like other European countries affected by the war, is in need of raw materials and machinery in order to build up her worn out and war damaged industries; while for the next two years she will be requiring more than normal imports of foodstuffs during the period required to rehabilitate the land which is short of fertiliser and to carry through the necessary re-allocation of arable land to accommodate the refugees from Karelia.[2] Finnish imports from Germany before the war amounted to 17% of the total and it seems likely that this figure will fall to little over zero and will give us the opportunity to replace Germany in the Finnish market. There may be some competition from the United States but the Finnish capacity for earning dollars is small and we should find Finland a valuable unit of the sterling area. The only fly in this ointment is the Soviet Union. There was comparatively little trade with Russia before the war partly owing to difficulties connected with the Soviet organisation, partly owing to a strong disinclination on the part of the Finns to allow business with Russia to assume large proportions. This attitude completely changed as a result of the defeat of Finland and even without a strong Communist party there would be great inducement from a political point of view to the development of trade between Finland and Russia. This inducement will undoubtedly be strengthened by the influence of the Communist party which is indeed likely to do everything it can to diminish Finnish trade with the west in order to strengthen Finnish dependence on Russia and emphasize the necessity for Finland to regard itself as definitely and permanently coming within the Russian sphere. The development of this trade is rather difficult to forecast. During the immediate years ahead Russia will probably require timber products which she would not normally import, especially paper, of which her manufactures, even in peace time, were comparatively small. At the present time, the Finns are giving Russia all they can in addition to reparations deliveries and deliveries under Article 14 of the Armistice, in return for foodstuffs and essential raw materials. There is also a strong possibility that the Finnish Army will in the not very distant future be re-organised and re-armed on the Russian model with Russian weapons. It is certain, therefore, that we shall find Russia a strong trade competitor.

3. The development of Finland as a medium of good trade relations depends, of course, on her weathering the economic storms which still beset her. Reparations and restitution deliveries are burdensome and there is a general decrease in the average production of individuals which I believe is characteristic of post-war periods. The financial situation, though not entirely out of hand, is precarious, and while interim rates of exchange which involve sterling and the dollar have been fixed in Finland itself, the

[2] In the aftermath of the Finnish cession of the Karelian Isthmus to the Soviet Union by the peace of 12 March 1940: *B.F.S.P.*, vol. 144, pp. 383–8.

effective value of the Finnmark is a matter for speculation. It is certainly decreasing fairly quickly. The internal price level is rising rapidly and wages are rising as well, so that the spiral of inflation is proceeding, if not unchecked, with only occasional touches of the brake. In spite of efforts to curtail it, the Black Market still flourishes and is likely to continue to flourish until the volume of consumer goods is sufficient to absorb surplus purchasing power. Labour conditions are also unstable, partly owing to price difficulties, partly owing to political subversion, and partly owing to difficult relations between employers and employees, a branch of the social structure in which Finland appears to have been curiously backward, in spite of her social progressiveness in some other respects.

4. The extent to which official support of resumption of trade relations with Finland will be required depends to a considerable extent on the policy which we propose to adopt with regard not only to Finland, but to Scandinavia as a whole. There is presumably no doubt that we shall do our utmost to retain and improve our interests in the other Scandinavian countries, but Finland is in an intermediate position. She is definitely in the Russian defensive sphere and it is a matter for consideration whether, after a certain point, British interests in Finland would not invoke counter measures by Soviet Russia which might not only nullify our own efforts but might even have the opposite effect. It is possible that Russia may wish to use Finland as an outlet to the west and that efforts on our part to develop Finnish cultural interests in Britain would not be unpalatable to the Russians. It is certain, however, that there would be strong Russian reaction to a situation in which Finnish relations with the west would be strong enough to keep alive anti-Russian feeling to an extent where Finland might become a dangerous or even inconvenient neighbour.

I have, &c.,

F. M. SHEPHERD

CALENDARS TO No. 396

No. 397

Letter from Mr. Roberts (Moscow) to Mr. Harvey (Received 28 July)
No. 405/5/45 [*U 5786/445/70*]

Secret. Personal   MOSCOW, *24 July 1945*

My dear Oliver,

We were very glad to see a copy of your letter U 4283/445/G [i] of the 4th June [July] to Maurice Peterson about the 'Western group'. We had in any case been intending to bring our own views up-to-date in the light of Duff Cooper's despatch No. 290[1] of 11th March and Maurice Peterson's despatch No. 82[2] of the 6th March, both of which reached us recently in the print. There is nothing in your letter of the 4th June [July] from which we should dissent but it may perhaps be useful if we summarise recent developments as seen from Moscow in expansion of the Ambassador's despatch No. 772[3] of November 19th 1944.

I was certainly surprised to find the Soviet Ambassador at Angora giving such a definite endorsement to the idea of a Western grouping[4] as that reported in paragraph 11 of Peterson's despatch No. 82[2] of 6th March. Although Stalin has in the past and more particularly in 1941 given a sort of general blessing to the idea of closer arrangements among the Western

---

[1] With reference to earlier correspondence concerning suggestions for the formation of a Western European system of alliances (cf. Sir L. Woodward, *op. cit.*, vol. v, pp. 190–1) Mr. Duff Cooper had there envisaged (in his paragraph 5) 'the possibility of the formation of a group of Western Democracies under French leadership enjoying the support and patronage of the U.S.S.R. We should also admit the possibility—I do not say the likelihood —of such a group feeling sufficiently strong with Russian support to act independently, and to be unwilling to seek the collaboration of Great Britain who, if she collaborated, must of necessity become the dominating member of the group.' Mr. Duff Cooper represented the urgency of 'securing political agreement with France, framed if possible in the clauses of a treaty of alliance . . . It is to Great Britain that Belgium looks for leadership and security, and I have little doubt that Holland will soon be looking in the same direction . . . We must beware lest reluctance on the part of Great Britain to take a decision, or delay in taking it, drive those who would be our friends into the arms of others and leave us in a position of dangerous isolation.'

[2] Sir M. Peterson had there (R 5551/3168/67) reported a conversation with the Soviet Ambassador at Ankara, M. Vinogradov, mainly on the situation in Eastern Europe: '11. A reference to France afforded me an opportunity of raising point . . . whether Monsieur Vinogradov reflected the view expressed by Marshal Stalin to the Secretary of State in 1941 that we should enter into special arrangements with the countries of Western Europe in order to create a security zone against Germany. Monsieur Vinogradov's reaction to this was that in his understanding Moscow entirely approved such a proposal—it was to be understood that the régime in Spain would have to be modified before that country could join—but felt that the matter was primarily one for the Western nations to settle between themselves.'

[3] Not printed. Sir A. Clark Kerr had there transmitted the memorandum printed as No. 119, annex IJ.

[4] Mr. Falla noted here: 'But M. Vinogradov is, as I remember, relatively light-hearted for a Soviet diplomat. P. S. Falla 2/8.'

European states, the Russians have never committed themselves definitely to support any specific scheme and there has always been an underlying note of suspicion in their reactions whenever the question has been raised in the British press. This note of suspicion has been less marked in the private comments of leading Soviet statesmen than in articles published in the Soviet press. In fact I have not yet seen a single article in the press here encouraging in any way the formation of a Western group to balance the many critical articles.

There is of course one common note underlying all this Soviet suspicious criticism, i.e. fear of the motives of the advocates of a Western *bloc*. You will remember that Walter Lippman[n] came in for severe handling last May when his new book[5] on the military aims of the United States was interpreted here as dividing the world up into groups, the chief of which would be a Western Atlantic maritime system under Anglo-American leadership and an Eastern land-grouping around the Soviet Union. The Russians particularly objected to this because it definitely aligned two of the Big Three in a grouping which might be turned against the Soviet Union and because they feared Lippman's aim was to attract a regenerated Germany within this grouping. Lippman's subsequent explanations, although—surprisingly enough—they were published here, were not regarded as convincing. Soviet criticism started up again later in May in connexion with the San Francisco Conference when 'reactionary' forces in America and in England were accused of advocating a Western grouping against the Soviet Union comprising a restored Germany. Towards the end of May the *Yorkshire Post* was attacked for articles suggesting that Soviet policy had divided Europe into Eastern and Western *blocs*. The *Yorkshire Post* was reminded that it was the Anglo-Soviet treaty knitting Europe together which had saved the continent from Fascist imperialism. The *Economist* campaign for a Western *bloc* drew down further and even stronger criticism in the middle of June to the effect that, despite assurances to the contrary, such a *bloc* must clearly be aimed against someone and was therefore bound to lead to strife between Eastern and Western Europe.

By this time the Russians had it firmly fixed in their minds that the main advocates of a western grouping abroad were elements whom they regarded as hostile to the Soviet Union. This applies even to the relatively innocent *Economist* and with much greater force to the Catholic press in England, to the Polish Emigre Government, to Spanish official spokesmen and above all to such dangerous 'Fascist beasts' as the Turkish journalist Yalçin. All these 'enemies' of the Soviet Union were accused of wishing to divide the world into *blocs* and groups of states; and early in July the Soviet press was attacking not merely the Western *bloc* as such but all other *blocs*, e.g. Northern, Anglo-American, Continental or South-Eastern. The moral drawn was that the guarantee of general peace and security was not to be

[5] *U.S. War Aims* (London, 1944).

found in isolated *blocs* but in the genuine democratisation of European states, whatever that may mean.

The Soviet press can hardly be blamed for showing itself suspicious about a Western grouping when this idea was so warmly advocated by the enemies or at best the critics of the Soviet Union. All the above criticisms also appeared at a time when Soviet relations with her Western Allies and more particularly with us were going through a period of severe strain. This no doubt accounted for the sharpness of Soviet press reactions, but the reactions in themselves were entirely consistent with Soviet policy. As the Ambassador pointed out in the enclosure to his despatch No. 772[3] of November 19th the Russians regard our post-war attitude towards Germany as the touchstone of our good faith as an ally and look to us to collaborate closely with them in enforcing on Germany the maximum possible measure of economic disarmament. They also want to act quickly before our memories of the war and of German barbarism grow dim. All the Soviet criticisms which have appeared about the Western *bloc* arise out of the fear that its advocates intend Germany (or a large part of Germany) to be included within that *bloc*, that she should therefore receive relatively mild treatment and that she will in the end become the centre of an anti-Soviet European system. You will remember that Sir Walter Layton's proposals[6] for the organisation of a United States of Europe without British or Soviet participation, although quite different from the idea of a Western group, came in for equally strong criticism in the Soviet press for the simple reason that it would inevitably have led to the restoration of German predominance in Europe.

This continued Soviet preoccupation with the future of Germany provides I think an adequate explanation for the apparent dualism between the violent public criticism of foreign advocates of the Western *bloc* and the relative encouragement given privately by Soviet official representatives from Stalin downwards to our tentative ideas for closer arrangements in the West. His Majesty's Government, unlike the *Economist* and other press advocates of the Western *bloc*, have made it clear to the Soviet Government that whatever regional defence arrangements in the West they might eventually wish to promote would be subordinated to the world organisation to continued Three-Power collaboration and to the Anglo-Soviet Treaty, which is expressly framed to prevent the revival of the German danger.

Since our exchanges with Molotov last November we have had no further official conversations with Soviet leaders about the Western *bloc*, but Stalin has twice referred to the subject in connexion with the Polish problem. His first reference—a public one—was at the time of the signature of the Polish–Soviet Treaty last April[7]. He then said that if the barrier against

---

[6] Sir W. Layton, Chairman of the News Chronicle Ltd. and of the Star Newspaper Company Ltd., had made these proposals in a pamphlet *How to deal with Germany: a plea for European Peace* (London, October 1944).

[7] This treaty of friendship, mutual assistance and post-war collaboration, signed in Moscow on 21 April 1945, is printed in *B.F.S.P.*, vol. 145, pp. 1166–8: *v. ibid.*, pp. 238–40 for a similar Soviet-Czechoslovak treaty of 12 December 1943.

German aggression which had been set up in the East by the Soviet treaties with the lesser Slav states were completed 'by an alliance of our (i.e. the Slav) countries with our Allies in the West, then it might be boldly said that German aggression would be bridled and that it would not be easy for her to run amok'. This was not an invitation to His Majesty's Government to promote the establishment of a Western group but rather an encouragement to the lesser Slav states and to Poland in particular to enter into direct treaty relations with the United Kingdom and France which would supplement the Soviet Union's treaties with those countries. Stalin returned to this theme in his speech at the Kremlin banquet on June 23rd after the Polish settlement in Moscow. He then said that Germany might rise again and that experience showed that she could easily regain her military strength. In that event Poland and Russia alone would be unable to resist German attack. The Soviet Union would therefore welcome the conclusion of alliances by Poland with Great Britain, France, the United States of America, as well as with the smaller Slav countries. There is therefore, the highest authority for the view that all Soviet thinking about regional groupings is dominated by the problem of Germany which the Soviet authorities do not regard as finally settled.

For the present however the Soviet authorities seem to be less interested in regional groupings than in securing the continuation of Three-Power collaboration to hold down Germany and to maintain world peace within the framework of the United Nations Organisation. As long as they are uncertain about the future relationship between the Three Great Powers they are likely to maintain a rather reserved attitude towards a Western group.

It will not have escaped your attention that the Soviet system in Eastern Europe is not an Eastern group properly so-called.[8] Soviet relations with the lesser Slav states are based upon bi-lateral treaties and not on any multilateral system. Despite the provision in the Soviet-Czech Treaty[7] for Polish accession nothing has yet been done to knit together the Soviet-Czech and Soviet-Polish Treaties. The Soviet Government also appear to have been more lukewarm recently about the idea of a Yugoslav-Bulgarian pact. On this analogy our safest line, if we wish to allay Soviet suspicions, would seem to be to follow the Soviet model and concentrate upon bi-lateral treaties with France and with our other Western neighbours. From the Russian point of view it would clearly be better to restrict these treaties in the first place to members of the United Nations and not to bring in Spain, Portugal, or Italy. If at the same time we concluded bi-lateral treaties with Poland, and with the other lesser Slav allies, as advocated by Stalin himself it would be very difficult even for these suspicious people to raise any objections.

The above is no doubt a counsel of perfection and we are probably not yet prepared to embark upon an elaborate treaty system covering Eastern as well as Western Europe. But if we want to carry the Russians with us and

---

[8] There is here a marginal question-mark.

avoid future trouble we should be well-advised to decide as soon as possible upon our plans for Western Europe and to show that we have a definite policy there. It is clearly dangerous to leave the formulation of these ideas to British and American publicists, most of whom are rather suspect to the Russians. As long as our policy appears unsettled whether in Western Europe, Germany or the Balkans, the Russians will either suspect our intentions, or alternatively be tempted to profit from our uncertainty. There are no signs yet of the Soviet Union encouraging the formation of a Western group under French leadership as suggested in Paris despatch No. 290[1] although there is certainly a growing Russian interest in developments in France and also in Belgium. But it is clearly an essential part of Soviet policy that Western Europe should be strong enough to resist any revival of German aggression and, if nobody else gives the necessary lead, the Russians may feel impelled to do so themselves. But the present rulers of Russia have little confidence in France and would clearly prefer to work with us. While therefore we must certainly admit the possibility of matters developing on the lines foreshadowed in paragraph 5 of Paris despatch No. 290,[1] the Russians would I think expect us to show clearly that we intend, within the framework of the United Nations' Organisation, of continued Big-Three collaboration and of the Anglo-Soviet alliance, to take the lead in establishing a Western barrier against German aggression similar to that set up in the East under Soviet leadership.

Your comments [i] on paragraph 7a and b of Peterson's despatch[9] go beyond the scope of this letter. As regards the Russian Navy we agree that it cannot be a serious menace for many years, but there is an increasing interest here in the Red Fleet and we intend to cover this subject in a separate despatch. As regards the economic brake upon Soviet policy, I think myself that we (or rather the Americans) could make really effective use of the financial lever. This is also the view of most Americans here. The Russians can probably restore their own economic position without Western assistance, although it would mean delays and hardship. But they could not I think also cope singlehanded with the heavy responsibilities they have incurred in their new zones of influence in Eastern and Central Europe and from which they cannot now withdraw without immense loss of prestige. Whether internal conditions in America and England and in particular the fears of unemployment will permit an effective use of the financial lever is another question, which deserves fuller treatment than it can be given at the end of this letter.[10]

[9] No. 165 of 18 May, not printed.

[10] Mr. Falla minuted on 2 August that 'this useful letter' could be read in conjunction with Annex 1 to No. 119, particularly paragraphs 21–2. After summarizing the main points in the present letter Mr. Falla concluded in his last paragraph: 'The moral of all this would seem to be that we should be well advised to go ahead with our proposals for a Western Group while Germany is still prostrate and there can be no question of our attempting to draw her into an anti-Soviet system. The first step in this direction which has been suggested is the conclusion of a Franco–British Treaty or equivalent mutual defence arrangements—

I am sending copies of this letter to Holman at Paris, Balfour at Washington, Helm at Angora and Aveling at Brussels.

Yours ever
FRANK K. ROBERTS

CALENDAR TO No. 397

i *4 July 1945 Letter from Mr. Harvey to Sir M. Peterson (Angora)*. F.O. views on formation of a Western Group based upon France jointly with Great Britain and excluding Italy, Spain and Portugal [U 4283/445/70].

see paragraphs 12–17 of the brief (*flag B* [flags not attached to filed copy: see annex 1 to No. 119]). In the light of developments since the question was last mooted, it may now be possible to consider intimating to the French that we should receive favourably an approach on their part for a Treaty. In the event of such a decision of policy being taken, it would be necessary to tell the Dominion Governments and to keep them informed of the progress of any negotiations—see Z. 1457/13/17 (*flag C*). The question of outstanding Anglo–French commitments which would have to be abrogated if a new Treaty were signed is discussed on U 322/1/G (*flag D*).' Mr. Jebb minuted below: '(I regret that these papers have been held up owning to the absence of Mr. Ward and my having to cope with the Executive Committee of the United Nations). In the meantime, I note that Mr. [Harold] Laski has made a statement in Paris to the effect that we should "form a single state out of the two nations" (Britain and France). I am not sure how far Mr. Laski was speaking with authority, but I have myself urged for some time that any "Western European Grouping" would only make sense if it were founded on something like a customs union. I understand that at the last [Office] meeting on this subject this particular objective was ruled out as too remote a possibility, and it may be so; but in any case I think that we ought to study the effects of such a union in detail. In any case there seems now to be very general agreement that somehow or other we must come together with France to the utmost possible degree, and I certainly should myself support the general line suggested by Mr. Falla in the last paragraph of his minute. Gladwyn Jebb   13th August 1945.'

No. 398

Minutes of a Meeting held at the Foreign Office on 25 July 1945
[*UE 3621/813/53*]

Top secret

Economic Relations with France and Western Europe

Those present were:
Mr. Ronald (*Foreign Office*) in the Chair.
Mr. Fraser (*From His Majesty's Embassy Paris*).
Sir Wilfrid Eady, Mr. Rowe Dutton, *Treasury*.
Sir Percivale Liesching, Mr. Welch, Mr. Hughes, *Board of Trade*.
Mr. Toseland, *Department of Overseas Trade*.
Professor Robbins, *Cabinet Office*.
Mr. Harvey, Mr. Hall-Patch, Mr. Stirling, Professor Webster, Mr. Hasler, Sir Anthony Rumbold, Mr. Simpson, *Foreign Office*.

1. MR. RONALD said that the purpose of the meeting was to discuss

Mr. Duff Cooper's despatch No. 629[1] of the 12th June in which he had suggested that the policy governing our economic relations with France should be founded on the view that Western Europe was an area in which it was vital for the success of our foreign policy that there should be strong economic ties with the United Kingdom and that France was the key to this area.

2. Mr. Ronald said that the proposal that a Western Bloc should be formed on the basis of a close Anglo-French association had been under consideration for many months but that little progress had been made. Papers on the subject had been drafted for submission to the Dominion Prime Ministers' meeting in May 1944 and for the use of the United Kingdom Delegation to the Dumbarton Oaks Conference. Neither of these drafts however had been acceptable to the Prime Minister and they were therefore not used. The subject had been put before the Prime Minister again in November 1944, but his reaction had been to express apprehension in view of the hopeless weakness of the Allied countries. He had said that he feared that it would lead to an impossible commitment by the United Kingdom to defend these countries, that it would involve a large British Army on the continental model which would not be acceptable to Parliament and that in his view our policy should be to maintain the defences of our island and rely upon our strength in the air and on the sea. When the proposal had come before the Prime Minister more recently he had again expressed misgivings about the burdens which a Western Bloc would impose on the United Kingdom, but had said that the matter should be discussed in the Cabinet at the proper time. Meanwhile the French, the Belgians and the Dutch, who had made various approaches to us, had had to be put off with fair words.

3. The Foreign Office saw many advantages in the proposal of a Western Bloc based on an alliance with France. They thought that it would prevent the Western countries from again being eaten up 'one by one', prevent them from turning to the Soviet Union for their salvation, provide depth to the defences of the United Kingdom and prevent a European aggressor from again obtaining the use of the manpower of Western Europe for slave labour. The Chiefs of Staff had also expressed themselves in favour of the project which they thought 'would at any rate be a start in the building up of a strong association of nations in Western Europe which would provide us with the depth which is becoming increasingly necessary to our defence'.[2]

4. It would be useful to know how the Treasury and Board of Trade felt about the economic concomitants of an association of this kind. The proposal would have eventually to be brought before the Cabinet and it was therefore desirable at once to formulate the issues upon which Ministers would have to take decisions.

---

[1] This despatch (on UE 2504/813/53) in reply to Mr. Eden's circular despatch of 30 March (cf. No. 396, note 1) is not printed: see below.

[2] Cf. Annex 1B to No. 119.

5. SIR WILFRID EADY said that in general terms the Treasury regarded a close association with the Western European powers as clearly in the economic interests of our country. The restoration of economic stability in Western Europe was urgently necessary, especially owing to the gravely disturbed conditions both in Germany and in other European countries. European markets were important to British economy. To give a start to this policy the Treasury had concluded Payments Agreements with some of the Western European countries and also the Scandinavian countries.

Development of association, both politically and economically, with Western Europe involved three considerations, that the scheme was within the framework of the San Francisco ideas, that any plan did not involve transferring to the United Kingdom some of the political and financial weaknesses of the other partners, and that both politically and economically the association could not be regarded as designed in opposition to [a][3] policy of economic co-operation with the United States.

The San Francisco difficulty was now out of the way. Whether the association added to our anxieties or not depended upon its terms; the association might in fact strengthen us rather than otherwise. As regards the United States it was important that they should be kept informed of the object of any Western European pact and of its principles. Other things being equal the Treasury would regard it as advantageous to enter into this association.

Sir Wilfrid Eady said that there were also financial reasons why we should hesitate before we entered into bilateral trade negotiations with the United States. We had very important financial negotiations to conduct and wished to avoid these negotiations being subject to pressure for bilateral trade concessions. Therefore if the multilateral approach to the United States broke down he agreed that we would be wise, on commercial policy, to clear our flanks with the Europeans first. The Europeans would still look to us for a lead. Indeed, even if a multilateral approach to trade policy came out of the talks with the United States he felt that the Western Europeans would want to know our standpoint first. Joint talks with the Western Europeans with the Americans sitting at the table would be impracticable.

Sir Wilfrid Eady said that when the Dutch and Belgians had talked normally [informally] to the Treasury about a Customs Union it appeared that they had been thinking of an association of two low tariff systems. At that time they had to be told that the moment for discussing such an idea was inopportune, at any rate if it involved possibilities of extension to the United Kingdom.

As far as the French were concerned he doubted whether long-term commercial policy was so important in their eyes as the immediate problems of supply. They were apt to accuse us of standing in the way of a solution of these problems and if talks on commercial policy were to be successful the French would have to recognise that we were not holding up available

---

[3] All insertions in the present, circulated, text are from an earlier text on this file.

supplies by any deliberate policy. The French rate of exchange was the major difficulty at present in the way of any commercial talks. The French recognised that, but claimed that until the supply of coal to France was much improved they did not dare to shake confidence by touching the exchange rates. Meanwhile we should try to begin by operating on them at the points where we already had contact, as for example on the Control Commission for Germany where the French had appointed one or two excellent men to whom the Americans were beginning to listen.

6. Sir PERCIVALE LIESCHING said that there could be a great improvement in our trading relations with Western Europe, but that progress towards such an improvement was held up by the absence of a Cabinet decision on our commercial policy. In any case, the idea of a Customs Union in Western Europe or between this country and France was much too ambitious to aim at as the first objective of our policy. A Customs Union between two such equal powers as the United Kingdom and France was a very difficult proposition. It would in any case presuppose a strong political tie and, even with such a tie, it would under the current philosophy of full employment imply complete mobility of labour between the two countries and this was difficult to visualise. It would be very difficult to find remedies for the various problems which a Customs Union would bring in its train for the Government of each of the countries concerned.

7. Moreover a Customs Union would involve a common level of tariffs suitable both to the highly developed metropolitan countries and to their colonial dependencies whose economic circumstances were very different. This was a formidable difficulty. We should also have to reckon with the fact that the Dominions might suffer and that there might be a re-orientation on their part towards the United States.

8. The Board of Trade certainly felt that it was necessary to get into closer touch with the Europeans, but we could not consider our relations with Europe in isolation [sic] from our commitments to the United States under Article VII.[4] If the multilateral system foreshadowed in our current Article VII talks proved unobtainable, we could at present always fall back on Dominion preference. But the great advantage of the approach through Article VII was that it would make the United States set an example to the world of an all-round out [cut] in tariffs (to which, incidentally, we could of course ourselves contribute). These talks had now reached the point where it seemed likely that a proposal could be made to the rest of the world. But without Cabinet direction it was impossible for us to open any useful discussion with the Western Europeans. The United States would shortly have to issue an invitation to other countries and it was very desirable that we should, if possible, be associated with them in some way in the issue of this invitation. In fact there was everything to be said for our taking the lead. In any case we ought to be in a position to insist on taking part in any talks which the Americans might have with other countries arising out of

---

[4] Of the Anglo–American Lend Lease Agreement of 23 February 1942: cf. No. 26, note 2.

Article VII. The present position was that, unless the Americans relapsed in the meantime from the multilateral approach, the Cabinet would during the month of August be invited to express tentative reactions as to whether there was a presumption of success in such an approach. If the Cabinet responded favourably, the next step would be for the Americans to issue a statement of principles. Since we would want to be associated with the American initiative, that would be the moment at which we should begin discussions with the French. If, however, the Americans decided on a more cautious bilateral approach, he for his part would be inclined to advise that we should let them know that we thought that conversations should start with the European countries. Anglo-American trade relations could continue to be governed by the 1938 Agreement[5] with certain modifications.

9. SIR WILFRID EADY said that there were also financial reasons why we should be slow in entering into bilateral negotiations with the United States, and he agreed that we ought to clear our flanks with the Europeans first. In the event of a failure of the multilateral project, the Europeans would still look to us for a lead. In fact, this was the case on either assumption. He felt that joint talks with the Western Europeans, with the Americans in the chair, would be impracticable.

10. MR. FRASER said that from the point of view of French psychology it was important that we should talk to them alone and first. SIR P. LIESCHING agreed and thought that the French would anyhow want to talk to us.

11. PROFESSOR ROBBINS said that it seemed to him that the project of a political association of Western European Powers did not stand or fall by what happened on the economic side. In fact the French thought of their problems in terms of a ganging up of Western Europe against America.

12. SIR PERCIVALE LIESCHING said that conversely we did not want to be handcuffed in carrying out and following the course of action which he had outlined on the economic side by what happened on the political side.

13. MR. HARVEY said that the Foreign Office favoured the formation of a Western bloc in order that both we and our Western European Allies should carry more weight in the counsels of the Big Three. So far, however, we had had nothing much to offer to the other Western European countries. The Foreign Office had never thought it would be necessary to have anything so provocative as a Customs Union. What they looked forward to was a regional group on the lines contemplated at San Francisco the other potential partners in such a group being just as anxious as we were to be covered by the formula of the United Nations Charter. Until such a regional group could be formed we should do whatever we could for these countries on the economic side.

14. PROFESSOR WEBSTER pointed out that there was really no analogy between a political or military association and an economic association. It had to be assumed that a political association in Western Europe would

[5] This Anglo–American trade agreement signed in Washington on 17 November 1938 is printed in *B.F.S.P.*, vol. 142, pp. 183–92.

have American help for defence purposes, whereas an economic association would in some measure be directed against the United States. We should, moreover, clearly distinguish in our minds between a military association such as might be favoured by the Military Staff Committee set up under the United Nations Organisation and a political association of a more old-fas[h]ioned kind.

15. MR. FRASER said that the Embassy in Paris were all deeply anxious about the state of affairs in France. The French felt very lonely, they distrusted the Americans and they were not naturally well disposed towards the Russians. They must have somebody to associate with on economic grounds alone. M. Herriot had said that the French might in the long run have no alternative but to succumb to a more powerful Eastern European unit. It was because they held views such as these that the French talked so earnestly of a Customs Union with us. They were already talking seriously with the Dutch and Belgians about a common economic policy.[6] Moreover, they looked to us to interpret them to the Americans and it would be tragic if we lost the opportunity of playing this part. He therefore thought that we should start talking to them on commercial policy as soon as possible, and he would like someone to go to Paris for this purpose.

16. MR. HARVEY said that it was very important that we should appear to have a policy of our own. This was largely a psychological factory [factor] and he thought that we could probably offer the French a good deal to [of] support and encouragement by talking to them on our own, even though we had [no] cards in our hand. SIR PERCIVALE LIESCHING agreed, but pointed out the difficulties of talking to the French on our own in advance of any decision by the Cabinet on our commercial policy and in view of our commitments to the United States. But what Mr. Fraser and Mr. Harvey had said emphasised the disadvantage of acting as an actual co-sponsor with the Americans of any talks on commercial policy. On the contrary, it would be to our advantage to be among the invited Powers, although we must associate ourselves at the outset with any statement of principles which the Americans might make.

17. PROFESSOR ROBBINS thought it important that the French should be weaned from an undue attachment to logic. They tended to think exclusively in terms of alternative extremes.

18. SIR WILFRID EADY said that when the Dutch and Belgians had talked to us about a Customs Union they had really been thinking of an association of two low tariff systems. They had had to be told that the moment for discussing such an association was inopportune. So far as the French were concerned, meanwhile, it was the immediate problems of supply which

---

[6] Mr. Fraser requested Sir A. Rumbold in a letter of 15 August 1945 from Paris (received by 18 August) that: (a) the following words should here be added to the record: 'but they had several times made it clear in conversations with members of the Embassy that they had little hope that any measures they might agree upon would be fruitful unless the United Kingdom would come in and take the lead'; (b) the last sentence of this paragraph be deleted. This letter was circulated on 31 August to those who had attended the meeting.

really haunted them, and they accused us of standing in the way of a solution of these problems. Before we could have successful talks with them on commercial policy they would have to alter their ideas about the role we played in supply matters. Until the problem of the supply of coal was settled, for example, there was nothing substantial which we could do for the French on the commercial side. Meanwhile, in order to soothe their nerves, we should try to operate on them at the points where we had contact with them, as for example on the Control Commission for Germany, where the French had several excellent men, and where consequently the Americans were beginning to listen to them. MR. RONALD thought that we were doing what we could to help the French, both over coal and meat. MR. HASLER thought that we were not doing as much as we could to help them over coal.

19. MR. RONALD, in summing up the discussion, said that, until the time came to talk to the French on the longer-term issue of commercial policy, we must do what we could for them on the shorter-term issues in which they were anyhow more immediately interested. All Departments represented at the meeting seemed to be in favour in the long run of our forming some kind of Western European group based on a close association with France, in order to secure certain political and strategic advantages. The strategic aspect would have an economic counterpart in so far as there would have to be a standardisation of military equipment and a rationalisation of the industries of the various countries producing for war purposes. Besides this immediate economic counterpart, Departments appeared to be anxious that any measures should be taken which were likely to promote a multilateral commercial system, but stopping short of an actual Customs Union of Western European powers.

20. He wondered whether there were any points upon which, in the light of this discussion, Departments should now be working. He did not personally think that there was any work for officials to do, since action now lay with Ministers.

21. MR. HALL-PATCH said there seemed to be general agreement that a closer association of the Western Powers was desirable. The implications of such an association would require careful study before decisions could be expected from Ministers. *Prima facie* such an association had a strong appeal. The U.K., France, Holland and Belgium and their dependent territories alone would form a large potential market and a source of many key raw materials. There was nothing in this conception which was incompatible with the San Francisco decisions, and, if the World Security Organisation broke down, it provided a possible alternative. If any of the British Dominions were to join such a group, it would become a very powerful combination. There was a tendency in the U.S. to consider the U.K. as an exhausted and rather second-rate Power. The U.S.S.R. for their part treated us with scant consideration. If we became the recognised and vigorous leader of a group of western powers with large dependent territories, we would gain that weight in the counsels of the Big Three the need of which had been stressed by Mr. Harvey. The obvious starting point for such a grouping

was a close association with France. We were, at present, waiting upon suggestions from France.

It seemed desirable not to wait for others to make suggestions as to possible methods of collaboration. We should review the situation and decide for ourselves what, from our point of view, would be the most desirable goal at which to aim during the next twenty or twenty-five years. The Departments represented seemed to think that an association of the Western Powers was desirable; the Chiefs of Staff for their own purposes felt the same. The Treasury and the Board of Trade had, however, drawn attention to various difficulties which at present stood in the way. In spite of these difficulties there was need of an agreed long-term policy. With such a policy we should have a definite goal at which to aim whatever the difficulties and fluctuations of the next few years. Meanwhile, the short-term decisions forced upon us in the transition period would not be taken without relation to each other, and they could, as far as possible be fitted into an agreed general framework. Only if there were a definite goal known to all departments would it be possible for them consciously and deliberately to work towards it. For these reasons it seemed therefore desirable that a considered paper on long-term policy should be prepared for submission to Ministers.

22. Sir Wilfrid Eady, commenting on Mr. Ronald's question as to what work there was for Departments to do, said that there were two fields of activity which came to his mind at once. One was the reconciling of the Western European Powers to the machinery of the Combined Boards or the modification of that machinery in such a way as to satisfy them, and the second was the question of Reparations. It also occurred to him that it would be wise to present to the Western Powers our account in respect of their indebtedness to us under Civil Affairs. The account would be a large one and might come to them as a shock. Mr. Hasler said that he thought the amount was already generally known, but if not there was no reason why it should not be communicated to the countries concerned at once.

23. Mr. Harvey, referring to Mr. Hall-Patch's suggestions, said that he thought that a long term directive could be sought from the Cabinet after the elections had taken place. Meanwhile, he would like to observe that it was clearly in the intentions of the Soviet Union to diminish the position of the French and to prevent the formation of a Western bloc.

24. Sir Percivale Liesching said that in considering the merits of a Western bloc we must not only compute the assets. [On the contrary, we must try to draw up a balance sheet. The proposal would entail liabilities as well as assets.] Some of the colonial territories of the countries concerned, which were often pointed out as a source of strength for such a bloc, might in point of fact be difficult to defend and would be liabilities rather than assets.

25. Mr. Hall-Patch said that it was clear that there were any number of studies which could profitably be prepared by departments on the assumption that an association of the Western Powers was desirable. These studies would have to cover all the facets of the problem.

No. 399

Mr. Eden (Berlin) to Sir J. Anderson (Received 25 July, 10.5 p.m.)
No. 220 Target Telegraphic [F.O. 934/4/30(7)]

Top secret   BERLIN, *25 July 1945, 12.5 p.m.*

Your telegram Onward No. 194[1] (of July 24th: trusteeship)
Following private and personal for Dominions Secretary from Foreign Secretary.

I agree with all you say. We had a bit of a dust-up with the Russians but have yielded nothing (repeat nothing). They will no doubt return to the charge on the next international occasion.[2]

---

[1] No. 393.
[2] In Berlin Mr. Ward minuted on this telegram and No. 393: 'The Russians put us on notice that they would revert to their Trusteeship paper (raising the future of the Italian colonies and of the present mandates) before the Council of Foreign Ministers at its first session. We & the U.S. did not demur and must be regarded as accepting to discuss. Molotov did not make it clear whether the Soviets would also raise the question of Korea at the C. of F.M.'s 1st mtg. This was raised here orally by the Soviet Delegation. But Mr. Foulds may care to advise F.E. Dept. to be ready with views on Korea against the end of August, in case F.E. Dept. have not spotted all the relevant passages in the minutes. J. G. W. 29/vii.' Mr. Foulds noted 'I have done this   L. H. F. 29/7.' Cf. No. 454.

No. 400

Mr. Eden (Berlin) to Sir J. Anderson (Received 25 July, 3.10 p.m.)
No. 229 Target Telegraphic [F.O. 934/5/41(4)]

Immediate. Top secret   BERLIN, *25 July 1945, 3.40 p.m.*

Discussion on Turkey came to inconclusive end last night.[1]

2. Yesterday's discussion was principally concerned with the President's proposal that the freedom of the Straits should be approved and guaranteed by an international authority, including the Three Great Powers.

3. Stalin refused to agree that this would be any substitute for Russian bases in the Straits. Eventually, he said that he thought the question was not yet ripe, and that the Soviet Government would resume their interrupted talks with the Turks.

4. The question of Kars and Ardahan was not mentioned yesterday, but Stalin indicated on July 23rd, that, if there were no territorial concessions, Turkey could not expect an Alliance.[2]

5. The Russians may now intensify their pressure on Turkey. We would advise the Turks to keep their heads and to maintain firmly in reply to

---

[1] See No. 258, minute 4.
[2] See No. 241, minute 10.

Russian approaches that this question must be settled on an international basis. At the end of the session the President undertook to try to make the Turkish Government see the advantages of international control. We hope the Turks will realise the very great importance of the President's proposal, under which the United States themselves would join in a guarantee of the freedom of the Straits, and will reflect carefully upon it.

6. Sir M. Peterson should inform the Turkish Government of the course of the discussions as described above, and advise them to act in accordance with paragraph 5.

Please repeat to Angora, Moscow and Washington.

No. 401

Mr. Duff Cooper (Paris) to Mr. Eden (Received 25 July, 5.30 p.m.)
No. 1024 Telegraphic [E 5455/8/89]

Important   PARIS, *25 July 1945, 5.15 p.m.*

Repeated to Beirut, M.E. Min's Office.

I see from Beirut political summary No. 170[1] not only that a team of British officers and . . .[2] non commissioned officers is engaged in training Syrian security services but also that British Council is dealing with the provision of British educational facilities in Syria to fill the gap left by French schools.

2. So long as these activities continue I trust I shall not be instructed to continue to assure the French Government that we have no intention of taking over the position hitherto occupied by the French in the Levant.

CALENDARS TO No. 401

i *31 July 1945 Letter from F.O. Eastern Dept. to H.M. Chancery in Paris.* Notes that with reference to No. 401 Office of Min. Resident in Middle East 'have taken upon themselves to set your minds at rest about our "imperialist" activities in the Levant'. French Embassy in London have not so far accused us of bad faith on these counts [E 5455/8/89].

[1] Not preserved in Foreign Office archives. The relevant extracts from this summary, undated in copies supplied subsequently, read: 'Colonel Abdullah Atfeh has now submitted a report on the proposals for the re-organisation of the Syrian security services which were prepared by the British military authorities. Lieutenant-Colonel Scott and a training team of British officers and N.C.O's have been lent by Ninth Army to the Syrian Government to assist in training the Syrian security services in the use of the new mechanical equipment and arms provided by the British Army.'

'The British Council representative discussed with the Minister of Education on the 2nd of July the question of providing British educational facilities in Syria to fill the gap left by the French schools, which in future will have little or no attendance. Two alternatives were considered namely that the British Council should open a school, or—should this not be possible—that the necessary funds should be collected by local subscription.'

[2] The text is here uncertain.

ii *22, 24, 27 July 1945* To Mr. Eden (Berlin) Tels. Nos. *149 & 175 Onward;*
Sir A. Cadogan (Berlin) Tel. No. *250 Target.* Implications of movement of
additional British troops to Levant: likely effect on French opinion: question
to be settled in London [E 5385–6/8/89; F.O. 934/5/44(4)].

iii *26 July 1945* Letter from Sir W. Croft (Chief Civil Assistant to Minister of State
in Cairo) to Sir R. Campbell. Decision re British assistance to Syrian gendarmerie
apparently taken by General Paget without consultation of political
authorities. Problem of balancing military and political considerations in
the Levant [E 5487/8/89].

iv *25–6 July 1945* Mr. Shone (Beirut) Tels. Nos. *24–6 Saving:* conditions in Syria;
possible withdrawal of British and French forces, and steps to facilitate
Franco-Syrian settlement [E 5631–2/8/89].

v *26 July 1945* (date of M. Massigli's communication to, and discussion with,
Sir R. Campbell) French note on Anglo-French relations in the Levant [E 5540/8/
89].

No. 402

Sir J. Anderson to Mr. Eden (Berlin: received 25 July, 7.30 p.m.)
No. 210 Onward Telegraphic [R 12398/3549/19]

Top secret. Immediate   FOREIGN OFFICE, *25 July 1945, 5.16 p.m.*

From Foreign Office for Secretary of State.

Athens telegram No. 1577[1] (Onward No. 174) (of July 23rd: relations
between Greece and Yugoslavia).

We have just told Tito that if he has complaints to make about the
situation in Greece he should take the matter up through the normal
diplomatic channel instead of running a campaign in the Yugoslav press.[2]
We cannot, therefore, object to the presentation of a note to the Greek
Government, nor do we feel that the terms of the note[1] are so offensive that
the Greek Government should reject it.

2. In advising the Greek Government about their reply we regard it as
essential that they should not suggest that the Yugoslav Government have
any right to intervene as regards the treatment of Greek citizens in Greece,
because these people are of Slav origin. We do not wish to revive the
conception of racial minorities which after the last war gave rise to the
minority treaties, and we must *not* therefore admit that any State has the
right to assume the protection of its racial minorities in any other State (cf.
case of Danish minority in Schleswig dealt with in our telegram to Copenhagen No. 37 Saving).[3] This would equally prevent the Greek Govt. from
intervening on behalf of the 'Greek' minority in Albania.

3. In our view the correct method of dealing with this dispute between

[1] See No. 392, note 3.
[2] See No. 335.
[3] No. 374.

Yugoslavia and Greece is for it to be referred to the World Organisation. Until the World Organisation comes into being and has set up machinery to deal with such questions, recourse could be had to the Moscow declaration of 1943,[4] which provides for joint action by the four signatory Powers to settle disputes threatening world security. Reference could also be made to Article 106 of the United Nations Charter in order that France should be associated with the four Powers who signed the Moscow declaration.

4. We recognise that to invoke this machinery would be a cumbersome method of dealing with a relatively unimportant local problem. We feel, therefore, that the Greek Government should first attempt to settle it direct with the Yugoslav Government. Any such local arrangements, however, should not prejudice the principle referred to in paragraph 2 above.

5. We suggest, therefore, that the Greek Government should accept the Yugoslav note and should reply on following lines. First they should reject claim of Yugoslav Government to intervene on behalf of Greek citizens. Treatment of Greek citizens is a purely internal Greek matter which does not concern any other government. Secondly they should set out their own account of the situation in Greek Macedonia, refuting as fully as possible Yugoslav allegations about persecution of Slav minority. Thirdly they should state that they have nothing to hide and that they would agree to a joint Greek-Yugoslav Commission being established in order to ascertain the facts and to enquire into allegations that Greek citizens had fled into Yugoslavia and to arrange for their return. If necessary it might discuss an exchange of populations so as to eliminate 'minorities' in both countries. Finally they should suggest that if the Yugoslav Government do not wish to seek a settlement of this dispute by friendly negotiation with the Greek Government, matter should be referred to the Great Powers on lines suggested in paragraph 3. In that event Greek Government would naturally expect that any Allied Commission which might be established would examine situation on both sides of the frontier.

6. Since the Greek Government have communicated the contents of the Yugoslav note to the U.S. Government as well as ourselves, you will no doubt wish to discuss matter with U.S. Delegation. We consider it most desirable that we should give joint advice to the Greek Government.

Repeated to Athens No. 1573, Belgrade No. 1092, Caserta No. 2288, Moscow No. 4131 and Washington No. 7818.

CALENDAR TO No. 402

i   *31 July & 6 Aug. 1945   Mr. Caccia (Athens) Tel. No. 1616; to Mr. Balfour (Washington) Tel. No. 8118.* Greek and American reactions to Yugoslav notes to them. Mr. Bevin feels strongly that any Allied commission of investigation as suggested by U.S. Govt. should include France: see *F.R.U.S. 1945*, vol. viii, pp. 328–36 *passim*, *F.R.U.S. Berlin*, vol. ii, p. 1065 f. [R 12926, 13074/3549/19].

---

[4] See No. 85, note 1.

No. 403

Sir J. Anderson to Sir R. Bullard (Tehran)
No. 453 Telegraphic [E 5482/103/34]

Immediate   FOREIGN OFFICE, 25 July 1945, 9.20 p.m.

Repeated to Moscow 4135, Washington 7825, M.E. Min 1300, Bagdad 447, Govt. of India.

It has been agreed at Terminal that British and Soviet forces should be withdrawn from Tehran at once; and that Council of Foreign Ministers at their first meeting in September 1945, should consider the further stages in the withdrawal of Allied forces from Persia.[1]

2. You should at once get in touch with your Soviet colleague and as soon as he receives the necessary instructions you should arrange for simultaneous notification to the Persian Government of the decision to withdraw from Tehran. You should not (repeat not) at present mention proposed discussion by the Foreign Ministers of further withdrawals. You should keep your United States colleague informed.

3. Co-ordination of arrangements for withdrawal of British, Soviet and American forces from Tehran will need to be arranged locally by representatives of the Embassies concerned. I will telegraph again as to this, but meanwhile you should see signal[2] which War Office are addressing to Commander in Chief Middle East regarding withdrawal of British forces.

---

[1] See No. 241, minute 13.
[2] This telegram No. 62632 of 26 July 1945 instructed General Sir B. Paget that, in particular, as regards withdrawal from Tehran 'your estimate of two months is likely to be unacceptable on political grounds and you should plan to effect withdrawal if in any way possible in a very much shorter time . . . Foreign Office advise us that retention survey party which is carrying out work at special request Persian Govt. need not be considered by you and this will be another matter for Ambassador to discuss with Russians.'

No. 404

Earl of Halifax (Washington) to Mr. Eden (Received 26 July, 4.20 a.m.)
No. 5195 Telegraphic [UR 2538/9/850]

Immediate   WASHINGTON, 25 July 1945, 10.52 p.m.

Your telegram No. 7765.[1]
Klentsov[2] called on U.N.R.R.A. yesterday and on behalf of Government of U.S.S.R. made formal application for U.N.R.R.A.'s assistance and stated

---

[1] No. 384.
[2] M. V. Klentsov was Soviet delegate to the third session of the U.N.R.R.A. Council.

that U.S.S.R. needed help in capital approximately 700,000,000 dollars.[3] Klentsov spoke of U.S.S.R. and not (repeat not) of White Russia or Ukraine.

CALENDAR TO No. 404

i   *30 July–2 Aug. 1945   Letters from Mr. D. Ogilvy (Washington) to Mr. Hasler; Mr. Balfour (Washington) Tel. No. 5341.* Reactions to Soviet request for U.N.R.R.A. assistance: State Dept. 'much distressed' [UR 2784, 2819, 2693/9/850].

[3] With reference to this information Mr. Hasler added in a letter of 27 July 1945 to Mr. Coulson in Berlin: 'With an ineptitude which surpasses anything yet shown the UNRRA staff immediately called a Press Conference and announced this to the world. I gather that they did this without any prompting from the Russians, and from a mistaken idea that this would put UNRRA more on the map. It is clear that the Russians are going to press this thing very hard and very quickly. They are evidently determined to get this pound of flesh at the Council meeting and it looks to me very much as if they will oppose any extension of UNRRA's mandate for Italy for example only if they have got it [*sic*]. You may pass this news on to Clayton unless he had got it from his own people.' On 3 August Sir O. Sargent minuted with reference to the present telegram: 'It would be fatal to begin haggling with the Russians over this. It is a blatant try-on which ought to be turned down at once. If they trot out the Chinese precedent I should have thought it would be easy to show that the circumstances in Russia and in China are completely different. O. G. Sargent.'

No. 405

Joint Staff Mission (Washington) to the Cabinet Office
(Received 26 July, 12.15 a.m. G.M.T.)
No. Don 917 Telegraphic [UE 3226/139/71]

Secret. Important   WASHINGTON, *25 July 1945, 9.25 p.m. G.M.T.*[1]

Reference Don 878[2]—Continuation of Combined Supply Machinery for Germany.

We had further discussion on 20 July with representatives of State and War Departments from which it is clear that Americans now have considerable less anxiety that the co-ordinated handling of supply problems in the Western Zones of Germany would prejudice the success of early establishment of quadripartite arrangements. Moreover both Departments are impressed with the advantages of a co-ordinated scheme for handling German imports. We think therefore that the way is clear for early agreement (the importance of which is realised in all quarters) provided we now

[1] Time of origin.   [2] No. 9.

reach an understanding on the machinery required and the financial arrangements involved.

2. Americans are anxious that arrangements covering the period until the effective functioning of quadripartite machinery should be such as to be capable of expansion into quadripartite machinery with the least possible change or dislocation. Therefore in deciding on the interim machinery they feel we should both have clearly in mind the form which we hope later quadripartite organization will take.

3. Proposals set out in paragraphs 4 to 9 below were put forward by American side at meeting on 20 July. Americans have subsequently learned that same issues are under discussion at Terminal. Hence before submitting any formal proposals they desire to exchange views with their representatives there. However we think it important to report to you their views as expressed at the meeting.

4. The following principles have been put forward by the Americans:–
(a) Zonal estimates to be co-ordinated in C[ombined] R[esources and] A[llocations] B[oard] on basis of agreed interim policies covering consumption standards and levels of industrial activity. Agreement on policies should be reached by Zone Commanders who should so far as possible use CRAB as informal instrument for obtaining such agreement. Object is to avoid any appearance of establishing without consultation with Russians policies which might be or appear to be permanent.
(b) Deficiencies in one zone to be met as far as practicable by surpluses from other zones.
(c) Zonal programmes of requirements for imports to be submitted simultaneously to Combined Boards by the Governments of the occupying powers separately from any other programmes.
(d) Instructions to be issued to Combined Boards and any other interested Governmental Agencies in U.S.A., and U.K. to ensure equal priorities for programmes of all zones.
(e) Zone Commanders to have the right to agree as to diversion of supplies from one zone to another in case of emergency.

5. Actual procedure which Americans contemplate can best be described under three heads.
(a) Procedure inside Germany (para 6 below).
(b) Procedure outside Germany (para 7 below).
(c) Financial arrangements (paras 8 and 9 below).

6. For procedure inside Germany CRAB should be used acting as specified in Mel 891[3] of 30 June.

7. Procedure outside Germany would be as follows. Import programmes for three zones after agreement in CRAB would be submitted through Zone Commanders to respective Governments (with copies to other Zone

[3] See No. 9, note 5.

Commanders for transmission to their Governments). Governments would put programmes through their representatives in Washington to Combined Boards (presumably after exclusion of non-R[eserve] C[ommodity] L[ist] items which would be procured independently by respective Governments). These programmes would be considered simultaneously by Combined Boards subject naturally to necessity for action on other programmes if any programme were unduly delayed. Combined Boards would be directed to give equal priority to all zonal programmes in making allocations. After allocations were made arrangements for procurement and shipment would be responsibility of respective Governments acting through their own agencies.

8. As regards finance Americans are strongly of opinion that only practicable arrangement is that each country should bear initial financing of procurement for its own zone. This would apply to the French as well as ourselves and to American supplies from U.K. as well as to British supplies from U.S.A. There are two main reasons for this view. First the financing by the U.S.A. of supplies from the U.S.A. for the British and French zones would inevitably necessitate screening by the War Department in Washington of the programme for the British and French zones. This would stultify or duplicate one of the functions which it is intended CRAB should perform. It would also in American view increase difficulties of development into quadripartite arrangement since it would in effect transfer to Washington the whole function of approval and control of supplies to Germany. Secondly, War Department have no funds beyond a very limited period to finance supplies for British or French zones and after that limited period (which is almost covered by requirements already stated by SHAEF up to November arrivals and in part already approved and allocated by C[ombined] C[ivil] A[ffairs] C[ommittee]) neither War Department nor any other U.S. Department has funds for this interim financing.

9. Any proceeds of current exports from Germany would in the American view be made available as a pool out of which repayment would be made to the three (ultimately the four) Governments in proportion to the interim financing burden assumed by each. Americans agree that the task of repaying out of the pool those who have provided the interim finance of imports should be the joint responsibility of the controlling powers.

10. This telegram has been seen by State Department and War Department.

CALENDARS TO No. 405

i 25 July–1 Aug. 1945   From and to J.S.M. (Washington) Tels. Nos. Don 918 & Nod 911; Mr. Balfour (Washington) Tels. Nos. 5318 & 5329. General acceptance of principles and proposals in paras. 4–9 of No. 405, subject to certain qualifications (recommended by J.S.M. in Don 918 and authorized in Nod 911 of 30 July) is welcomed by State Department [UE 3226, 3320/139/71].

19 July 1945 J.S.M. (Washington) Tel. No. Don 903. Proposal reported in No. 9.i is unworkable and should be rejected: wider implications for initial financing of imports for British zone [UE 3112/139/71].

No. 406

Minutes of a Meeting of the European Advisory Commission held at Lancaster House, London, S.W.1., on Wednesday, 25 July 1945 at 5.30 p.m.

E.A.C. (45) 6th Meeting [U 5785/20/70]

Top secret

Present:

MONSIEUR R. MASSIGLI (*in the Chair*), Monsieur de Leusse, Professor A. Gros.
SIR R. I. CAMPBELL, Viscount Hood.
MR. G. F. SAKSIN, Mr. N. V. Ivanov.
MR. J. G. WINANT, Mr. E. A. Lightner, Jnr., Colonel G. R. Hall.
Secretariat: Lieutenant M. W. Boggs, U.S.N., Mr. T. A. Marchenko, Mr. W. D. McAfee, Mr. B. V. Ivanoff.

Agenda

1. Approval of the text of the Agreement[1] between the Governments of the United Kingdom, the United States of America and the Union of Soviet Socialist Republics and the Provisional Government of the French Republic on certain Additional Requirements to be imposed on Germany.

2. Approval of the Report[2] by the European Advisory Commission to the Governments of the United Kingdom, the United States of America and the Union of Soviet Socialist Republics and the Provisional Government of the French Republic.

THE COMMISSION–

1. Approval of text of the Agreement between the Governments of the United Kingdom, the United States of America and the Union of Soviet Socialist Republics and the Provisional Government of the French Republic on certain Additional

(*a*) approved the text of the Agreement between the Governments of the United Kingdom, the United States of America and the Union of Soviet Socialist Republics and the Provisional Government of the French Republic on certain Additional Requirements to be imposed on Germany (the text of the Agreement, in English, Russian and French, is annexed);

(*b*) decided to submit the Agreement between the Governments of the United Kingdom, the United States of America and the Union of Soviet Socialist Republics and the Provisional Government of the French Republic on certain Additional Requirements to be imposed on Germany to the Governments of the United Kingdom, the United States of America and

---

[1] For this agreement, whereof the annexed text is not here printed, see No. 29, note 5.
[2] Annex below.

889

Requirements to be imposed on Germany.	the Union of Soviet Socialist Republics and the Provisional Government of the French Republic for consideration and approval.
2. *Report by the European Advisory Commission to the Governments of the United Kingdom, the United States of America and the Union of Soviet Socialist Republics and the Provisional Government of the French Republic.*	Approved the text of the Report by the European Advisory Commission and decided to transmit it, signed by the four Representatives on the European Advisory Commission, as a covering document to the text of the Agreement on certain Additional Requirements to be imposed on Germany, to the Governments of the United Kingdom, the United States of America and the Union of Soviet Socialist Republics and the Provisional Government of the French Republic. (The text of the Report, in English, Russian and French, is annexed.)[3]

Representative of the Government of the United Kingdom on the European Advisory Commission:	Representative of the Government of the United States of America on the European Advisory Commission:	Representative of the Government of the Union of Soviet Socialist Republics on the European Advisory Commission:	Representative of the Provisional Government of the French Republic on the European Advisory Commission:
(Signed) R. I. CAMPBELL	*(Signed)* JOHN G. WINANT	*(Signed)* G. F. SAKSIN	*(Signed)* R. MASSIGLI

Lancaster House, London, S.W.1, 25th July, 1945

ANNEX TO No. 406

Report[4] by the European Advisory Commission to the Governments of the United Kingdom, the United States of America and the Union of Soviet Socialist Republics and the Provisional Government of the French Republic

1. Pursuant to the Declaration regarding the Defeat of Germany and the Assumption of Supreme Authority with respect to Germany, signed at Berlin on the 5th June, 1945, wherein it is stated, in Article 13 (*b*), that the Allied Representatives will impose on Germany additional political, administrative, economic, financial, military and other requirements, the European Advisory Commission has, in accordance with its terms of reference, considered certain of the more urgent of those additional requirements. Accordingly, it submits herewith, for consideration and approval by the four Governments, an Agreement regarding certain Additional Requirements to be imposed upon Germany.

2. It will be recalled that the Commission agreed in March 1944, when discussing the terms of surrender of Germany, that certain broad political and economic requirements should be imposed upon Germany at the time of, or shortly after, the surrender, in addition to the mainly military requirements, to be contained in the Instrument or Declaration of Surrender. The most important

[3] The Russian and French texts are not annexed to filed copy.
[4] Printed in *F.R.U.S. Berlin*, vol. ii, pp. 1008–1011.

military requirements were announced in the Declaration of the 5th June, 1945. The Commission believes that the enclosed Agreement on Additional Requirements, representing the agreed views of the four Governments, will furnish guidance to the Allied Representatives regarding additional measures to be imposed on Germany. The Commission accordingly recommends that the Agreement on Additional Requirements, as soon as it is approved by the four Governments, be transmitted to the Allied Representatives in Berlin. The Commission recommends that the four Governments authorise the Allied Representatives to decide whether publication of this document shall be in whole or in part.

3. The Commission has several comments to make with regard to certain specific provisions in the Agreement on Additional Requirements.

(a) The Commission recommends that in exercising control over German research relating to war or the production of war material, as set forth in sub-paragraph 13(b), the Allied Representatives should, when they consider conditions in Germany appropriate, supplement this provision by issuing the following order to the German people:–

All research, experimentation, development or other study relative to war or the production of war material, whether in public or private establishments, factories, technological institutions, laboratories or elsewhere, is hereby abolished and forbidden in future.

(b) The Commission recommends that in giving effect to the provisions of sub-paragraph 15 (b) the Allied Representatives should also require the German authorities to hand over, for delivery to the Allied Government concerned, any drawings, plates and other special technical equipment utilised directly for the production of monetary tokens for issue by Germany in territories formerly occupied by her or elsewhere.

(c) In connection with the provisions of sub-paragraph 16 (b) the Commission recommends that all property, assets, rights, titles and interests in Germany held for or belonging to any country, other than Germany and the countries referred to in sub-paragraph 16 (a), which has at any time since the 1st September, 1939, been at war with any of the United Nations, be taken under the provisional control of the Allied Representatives and preserved, pending subsequent transfer to the countries of ownership under arrangements to be worked out with the appropriate Allied Control Commissions or organs in those countries.

(d) In connection with the execution of the provisions of sub-paragraph 26(a) the Commission recommends to the four Governments approval of the following understanding:

Vessels of the United Nations surrendered to the Allied Representatives in accordance with sub-paragraph 26 (a) will be returned by the Allied Representatives to the respective Allied States which own or owned, or whose nationals own or owned, such vessels. Nothing in this provision shall alter in any manner any existing agreements and procedures among any of the United Nations with respect to the pooling of the vessels surrendered by Germany under the provisions of sub-paragraph 26 (a).

(e) In connection with the execution of the provisions of paragraphs 14, 15, 16 and 19, the Commission invites the attention of the four Governments to the great importance of effecting as full and as prompt restitution as possible of property which has been looted by the Germans from occupied Allied countries. It points out the urgency of providing the Allied Representatives in Germany with guidance concerning the principles and procedures which should govern the restitution of looted Allied property, in accordance with the Declaration made at London on the 5th January, 1943, on Enemy Acts of Dispossession.

4. During the consultations which the European Advisory Commission has carried on, under instructions of the four Governments, with representatives of the European Allied Governments concerning the Declaration of the 5th June, 1945, these Governments have expressed, both in writing and orally, their great interest in the additional requirements which are to be imposed upon Germany. In view of this concern, the Commission recommends that the four Governments instruct it to communicate the Agreement on Additional Requirements, upon its approval by the four Governments, to the interested Allied Governments. In so doing the Commission would point out to the representatives of those Governments that these additional requirements do not purport to be complete and will be supplemented by specific orders and instructions to be issued by the Allied Representatives.

Representative of the Government of the United Kingdom on the European Advisory Commission:	Representative of the Government of the United States of America on the European Advisory Commission:	Representative of the Government of the Union of Soviet Socialist Republics on the European Advisory Commission:	Representative of the Provisional Government of the French Republic on the European Advisory Commission:
(Signed) R. I. CAMPBELL[5]	*(Signed)* JOHN G. WINANT	*(Signed)* G. F. SAKSIN	*(Signed)* R. MASSIGLI

Lancaster House, London, S.W.1, 25th July, 1945

CALENDARS TO NO. 406

i *25 July 1945 E.A.C.: UK Delegation Circular No. 232* circulating record by Sir R. Campbell of informal meeting of the E.A.C. on 23 July: discussion of difficulties in way of signature of Agreement on Additional Requirements and of covering report: British withdrawal of amendment to para. 3 (*d*) of report [U 5746/20/70].

ii *26 July 1945 E.A.C.: UK Delegation Circular No. 233* circulating note on No. 406 recording agreement on title of Agreement and oral statement by Sir R. Campbell of British reservation concerning paragraph 3 (*d*) of report: acceptance of return of vessels on basis of ownership rather than of flag is a departure from well-established principle which should not be regarded as a precedent for the future [U 5749/20/70].

[5] In signing this report Sir R. Campbell, in accordance with instructions from the Overseas Reconstruction Committee (No. 29.ii), placed on record a reservation with regard to paragraph 3 (*d*): see ii below. Notification of approval of the report and agreement was given to the European Advisory Commission by H.M. Government on 2 August, by the Soviet Government on 4 September, by the French Government on 10 September, and by the United States Government on 8 September subject to the omission of article 38 of the agreement, which was accordingly omitted from the final text issued as proclamation No. 2 of the Allied Control Council at Berlin on 20 September 1945: printed in B.R. von Oppen, *op. cit.*, pp. 68–79.

No. 407

Memorandum by Mr. Jebb
[*U 5998/12/70*]

FOREIGN OFFICE, *25 July 1945*

Reflections on San Francisco
(*A paper written before the General Election*)

On arriving back in this country after ten weeks' absence at San Francisco, the British official is struck by the widespread lack of interest in this country in all questions connected with the World Organisation. America is another world. There the question is anxiously debated in all sections of the community. Sometimes rather unrealistically it is true; but generally speaking the approach is one of constructive criticism and tempered enthusiasm. There is no question of the interest which Americans take in the whole affair, and the general impression created is that they are willing and anxious to assume responsibilities and will not fall by the way-side if the United Nations does not work out in quite the way which is now expected.

2. Here, on the other hand, if anybody can be induced to talk about the subject at all, it is in a mood of d'sillusionment, not unmixed with cynicism. No one seems to think that it greatly matters whether there is a World Organisation or not, and most people fall back on the stock argument that, if constituted on the lines now proposed, it will simply be a Great Power Alliance which will last just so long as the interests of the Great Powers do not clash. There is, of course, a great deal of truth in this simple thought, but the approach is negative rather than positive and ignores the hopeful features of the Charter and notably the very fact that a machine will now be constituted whereby the Great Powers can attempt to settle their own difficulties as well as those of other people. There seems to be no popular conception of the immense importance attaching to some positive role by this country and to the enormous dangers of a purely cynical outlook on the problem as a whole. 'Where there is no vision the people perish'.[1]

3. Yet it cannot be denied that in the production of the great plan now brought to fruition at San Francisco, H.M.G. in the U.K. played a very great, perhaps even a preponderating part. The essential features of the original British papers circulated before Dumbarton Oaks have all been incorporated in the final document, with one notable exception on which more will be said later. The very basis of the scheme, namely, continued co-operation between the Great Powers, and notably between the Soviet Union, the United States and the United Kingdom, had its origin in this country and was imparted by devious means to our two great Allies. The Military Staff Committee is a purely British invention, and the Economic

---

[1] Quotation from *The Book of Proverbs*, chapter xxix, verse 18.

and Social Council is modelled on the Bruce report[2] which was in accordance with with [*sic*] British ideas. The Declaration on Colonial Policy was largely based on our initiative. Finally, the famous Yalta Voting Formula[3] was originally produced by the British Delegation at Dumbarton Oaks.

4. If we examine the Charter in detail, moreover, we find that the Purposes and Principles (Articles 1 and 2), the criteria for election to the Security Council (Article 23), the crucial Articles 24 and 25 whereby States pledge themselves to carry out the decisions of the Security Council, Article 37 which entitles the Security Council to frame an indictment against a Great Power if need be, Article 38 dealing with disputes other than those likely to produce a breach of the peace, Article 44 allowing a non-member of the Council to vote on decisions concerning the employment of its forces, almost all of the military paragraphs (Articles 47–50), and Art. 99, which provides for the Secretary General bringing to the attention of the Security Council any matter which in his opinion may endanger the peace, were the result of great and successful efforts made by the United Kingdom Delegation, which, as is known, consisted of representatives of all the major political parties.

5. These points must be noted in any fair attribution of responsibilities. But at the same time it must be recalled that our policy has been, and presumably still is, not to emphasise our achievements in public, but rather to allow the Americans to claim the principal credit for the production of the Charter as a whole. This they have not failed to do in their equivalent of a 'White Paper',[4] presumably with the object of persuading the American people that the new Organisation is, so to speak, their own property, thereby overcoming the forces of isolationism. It is also true, I think, that many Americans really believe that most of the important features in the Charter originated in the United States. I understand that they have practised the same kind of self-deception in regard to R.A.D.A.R.,[5] the secret of which was furnished to them by us at the beginning of the war. But I have no doubt that, although irritating, this general attitude is on balance to our advantage seeing that we want the Americans to regard the World Organisation as their special interest in order that they should play their full part in its operation. Nevertheless there may be a point at which the absence of even the smallest blast on our own trumpet produces an impression among our own people that we have done nothing except plod dutifully in the footsteps of the United States; and it is for consideration whether we should not—perhaps in the Secretary of State's speech during

---

[2] The League of Nations report of the Special Committee on the development of international cooperation in economic and social affairs, under the chairmanship of Mr. S. M. Bruce, Australian High Commissioner in London, issued on 22 August 1939: cf. supplement to *The Monthly Summary of the League of Nations 1939*, vol. xix.

[3] In section I of the Protocol of the Yalta Conference: cf. No. 30, note 2.

[4] Cf. Department of State publication No. 2349, Conference Series 71: *Charter of the United Nations: Report to the President on the Results of the San Francisco Conference by the Chairman of the United States Delegation, the Secretary of State, June 26, 1945.*

[5] Radio Detection and Ranging.

the ratification debate—make some appropriate allusion to our own part in the production of the San Francisco document.

6. However this may be, it is indisputable that our major foreign political objectives have largely been secured by the constitution of the new World Organisation. Thus the United States, we hope, will shortly be committed to intervene if trouble breaks out anywhere in the world. The Soviet Union will shortly be bound by the most solemn obligations, which it must surely hesitate to repudiate. And, finally, the position of the smaller states, their independence and integrity, have all been made vastly more secure than they would have been if no Organisation had been agreed upon—and the position of the smaller states has always been considered to be one of the major interests of Great Britain.

7. In the long run too, the prospects seem to be better, and not worse, than they were in 1919. An Organisation has now been created which will include all the existing major powers. Those powers which recently bid for domination of the world have been, or shortly will be, smashed to pieces, and are not likely to recover for a very long period. It is therefore essential that the major powers should continue their cooperation for a long period to come, and it is not unreasonable to hope that they may do so. There seem, therefore, to be considerable grounds for self-congratulation and indeed for some small measure of enthusiasm. Why, therefore, do we have this mood of apathy and disillusion in Great Britian [sic], and what are the compelling reasons for the cynicism which now prevails?

8. I think that the chief reason is sheer fatigue. It seems quite probable that, by and large, the average citizen of this country has worked harder during the last five years than the citizen of any other country. But this by itself does not altogether explain the phenomenon. There is, for instance, also the thought, whether formulated or unformulated, that whereas in 1919 we were the almost undisputed leaders in urging the establishment of international machinery for the preservation of peace, now that leadership has passed to Russia and America and that all that we can do is to follow in the wake of one or the other as our outlook on, and our station in life, may determine. This, in itself, I suggest, is partly due to the fact that there is an unresolved conflict between Right and Left in the United Kingdom, and perhaps more to the fact that this country alone is obviously less important than its two great Allies until and unless it can either develop a workable Commonwealth system in regard to Foreign affairs, or establish some entity in Western Europe, or both.

9. Frankly, I think that our failure to do either of these things was partly responsible for an impression which a number of my foreign colleagues gained at San Francisco to the effect that we were playing a secondary rather than a primary part. There were other reasons for such an impression which, however mistaken, was fairly widespread. In the first place the demands of the General Election deprived the Delegation of nearly all its leaders before the really crucial debates took place in the Technical Committees. Lord Cranborne, of course, stayed on and played what was

perhaps the outstanding rôle in the discussions on Trusteeship. But in all other matters we had to continue with Lord Halifax as the sole political representative of His Majesty's Government, and he was, of course heavily engaged in all the Five Power discussions, with the result that he could only very occasionally intervene (with great success) in the Committee's debates. Consequently a depleted band of permanent and temporary civil servants had to carry on as best they could; and, apart from anything else, it is no reflection on them to say that Civil Servants, however capable and distinguished, are at a disadvantage when coping in public with eminent foreign and Dominion politicians. The Canadians, also owing to their election, were in a precisely similar position.

10. But more important still was the unfortunate clash which took place with the representatives of Australia and New Zealand. Dr. Evatt from the outset adopted the attitude that H.M.G. had made various concessions to the Dominions' point of view during the Dominion talks which preceded the Conference, and had subsequently declined to carry these out. He ignored the other equally important consideration, universally accepted at the Empire talks, that any views expressed in London might have to be modified at San Francisco, if that were necessary to secure the paramount objective, namely the acceptance of the Charter by the United States and the Soviet Union. Whatever justification Dr. Evatt may have had for asserting that we had changed our attitude—and I should myself have thought that there was very little—the fact remains that Dr. Evatt and Mr Fraser, who was influenced by him, were obviously not prepared to follow the lead of the United Kingdom, and tended to act, not primarily as members of a great Commonwealth of Nations, but rather as small or middle nations. It is only fair to add that Dr. Evatt's views were not shared by Mr Forde, the Deputy Prime Minister of Australia, and leader of the Australian delegation, and that the Canadian delegation, an unusually able one, were generally helpful and cooperative. Field Marshal Smuts for his part was so convinced of the paramount importance of avoiding any breach in the unity of the Big Three that he instructed the South African delegation from the start of the Conference to accord the United Kingdom representatives their constant and whole-hearted support on all occasions. It is clear however that membership by the United Kingdom of the Big Three Club will increase the importance of consulting the Dominions in advance on all important questions of foreign policy, and that even with such consultation, it may not be possible to prevent the expression of dissenting views on some issues by one or other of the Dominions. It is arguable that, if we were ever to come to some working arrangement with France, our hand might be very considerably strengthened and to that extent therefore the solution of the Commonwealth problem may be bound up with any plans which we may have for increased unity in Western Europe.

11. There was also a third element which detracted from the force with which the U.K. Delegation was able to argue its case. That was the undeniable fact that we were on record as disapproving the Russian proposal

that parties to a dispute should vote on the enforcement sections of the Charter. It was quite true that the Americans also had (after some hesitation) rallied to our thesis at Dumbarton Oaks; but this fact was not generally known and was certainly never publicised by the Americans themselves. Consequently, whereas the Russians and to some extent also the Americans could argue with force and conviction that the Yalta Voting Formula was the best possible solution of the problem, we could only say that it was the best solution possible in the circumstances, and this created an impression that we were half-hearted and were being dragged along reluctantly by our two powerful friends. It was suggested that, if we had had our way, we would have sided with the smaller powers against the greater, but that we had sacrificed our principles to expediency. Finally, this attitude of ours in regard to parties to a dispute not voting was confused with a secret willingness to dispense altogether with the famous 'Hidden Veto', which of course was a totally different thing. For the 'Hidden Veto' is nothing else than the principle of unanimity of the Permanent Members of the Security Council (other than parties to a dispute) in all matters relating to the pacific settlement of disputes. If this principle were abandoned, it would mean, for instance, that a dispute between Holland and Belgium could be dealt with quite regardless of the opinion of Great Britain, France and the United States, and a dispute affecting Turkey quite regardless of the feelings of the Soviet Union and the United Kingdom. It was from the first a rather unreal issue, and in any case bore no relation to the simple proposal that parties to a dispute should not vote.

12. On this last issue there is no doubt that there is widespread opinion in this country opposed to the Yalta Voting Formula and that such opinion is largely responsible for the lack of interest to which allusion has been made above. I suggest that the best way to deal with such opinion is not be apologetic in regard to the Yalta Voting Formula, but rather to suggest that the main principle enshrined in it is one which is best adapted to the realities of the world of today. To confuse the ideal with the real is a very dangerous matter in Foreign Affairs; and fundamentally what we have to do is to choose between behaving as a Great Power or joining the ranks of the 'Little 45'.[6] A resolute attitude on this point, and an expressed determination to play our part as a Permanent Member of the Security Council with special responsibilities, might give rise to some criticism, but in the long run would avoid serious misunderstandings and even more extensive criticism in the future.[7]

GLADWYN JEBB

[6] Of the fifty governments represented at the Conference of San Francisco the Little 45 complemented the Big Five (cf. No. 42, note 5) in popular parlance in regard to the United Nations.

[7] In accordance with an authorization by Mr. Ernest Bevin this memorandum was circulated to King and Cabinet.

Mr. Roberts (Moscow) to Mr. Eden (Received 7 August)
No. 519 [N 9839/627/38]

Secret   MOSCOW, *25 July 1945*

Sir,

I have the honour to enclose herein a translation of an Order of the Day[1] which Generalissimo Stalin issued on July 22nd, on the occasion of Red Navy Day. Among other things, it praises the Red Navy's work during the war in protecting the flanks of the Red Army, striking at enemy shipping, and ensuring the uninterrupted use of its own communications. But the most important section of this Order of the Day states that the Soviet people want to see their fleet becoming stronger and more powerful and that they will build for it new ships and new bases. It also maintains that the duty of the fleet is to keep on training and improving seamen, to master the experience acquired in the war, and to increase the skill, discipline, and cohesion of its officers and men.

2. Red Navy Day was celebrated throughout the Soviet Union. The celebration in Moscow consisted of a Water Sports Meeting at which sailors from the various Soviet fleets took part. Special emphasis has however been laid upon the parades of the Baltic Fleet at Kronstadt, of the Black Sea Fleet at Sevastopol and of the Pacific Fleet at Vladivostok. I have not seen any special mention of a parade of the Northern Fleet at Archangel or Murmansk. This therefore suggests a return to old Russian naval traditions. In connexion with the Baltic Fleet parade, Peter the Great's description of the Gulf of Finland as the 'window to Europe' has been quoted. There have also recently been many public references to victories of the Russian Black Sea Fleet against the Turks in the days of Catherine the Great.

3. The contents of Stalin's Order of the Day and its publication on the front pages of the newspapers along with a photograph of Stalin suggest that the Soviet Government are anxious to interest the people in building a bigger fleet than the Soviet Union has hitherto possessed. It is the first Order of the Day which Stalin has issued to the Red Navy on the occasion of Red Navy Day, and it fits in with a number of other signs that the Soviet Government have begun to think in terms of a stronger fleet which will mark the resurgence of Russia as a great naval power. During the 1930's the Soviet Union embarked on what was meant to be a rapid expansion of its navy, particularly its submarine, cruiser, and destroyer fleets, and at the beginning of 1938 the increasing importance of the Red Navy appeared to be symbolised in the establishment of a separate People's Commissariat for the Navy distinct from the People's Commissariat for Defence which had previously dealt with naval matters. On January 15th, 1938, M. Molotov also told the first session of the Supreme Soviet of the U.S.S.R. that 'the

---

[1] Not here printed: see *The Times* of 23 July 1945, p. 3.

mighty Soviet State ought to have a seagoing and ocean-going navy commensurate with its interests and worthy of its great cause', and two days later *Pravda* went even further by asserting that 'for the prestige of a great power it is essential that she should be as strong at sea as on land.' In 1939 the Soviet Government took a further step towards improving the position of the fleet by decreeing that July 23rd was to be known as Red Navy Day, and in 1939 and 1940 they arranged special celebrations and gave Red Navy Day a good deal of publicity in the Soviet press.

4. Between 1941 and 1943 they perhaps not unnaturally ignored Red Navy Day, though the press appears to have given steady and adequate coverage to the navy's wartime achievements, and it was not until 1944 that they reverted to the policy adopted in 1939 and 1940 by again singling out Red Navy Day for special attention. Even so, in 1944 the articles on Red Navy Day confined themselves to describing the importance of the fleet's wartime activities without reference to the need for a big ocean-going navy. But in October, 1944, a leader in *Red Fleet* on the need for Soviet naval officers to know foreign languages again talked of the Soviet Union possessing its own 'powerful ocean-going fleet'. In February, 1945, the Union of Soviet Writers arranged a special discussion on the theme of the Soviet navy in literature, and during the debates it was repeatedly emphasised that the U.S.S.R. was on the eve of building a big seagoing and ocean-going navy and that Soviet writers ought to reflect this navy in Soviet literature. This discussion received little publicity in the Soviet daily press. But it occupied over a page and a half of the four pages of No. 7 of the *Literary Newspaper*.

5. On Red Navy Day this year some of the leaders and articles in the Soviet press have again taken up the theme of a powerful ocean-going fleet. For example, the leading article in *Trud* recalls M. Molotov's speech in 1938 about the need for 'a seagoing and ocean-going navy commensurate with the interests of the mighty Soviet power' and says that these words expressed the hopes of the whole Soviet people. 'Our country', it adds, 'is a great sea power. Fourteen seas and two oceans wash its shores. The sea coasts of the U.S.S.R. are twice as long as its land frontiers. The sea routes of our country are important for our contacts with other lands, for the economic development of the Soviet Union'. An article in the same paper by Admiral Levchenko, a vice-commissar for the navy, was even more pointed. 'A strong and mighty seagoing and ocean-going fleet will be built' it says. 'This is the will of the Communist Party, the Soviet Government, and the whole of our people. It is a matter of honour and glory for industrial workers, engineers and technicians, and the working masses to take an active part in building a big fleet. This will be accomplished by reinforcing the ships and units of the fleet with new personnel, by self-sacrificing labour from shipbuilders and workers in allied trades, by the widespread propagation of naval knowledge, and by close contact between workers and sailors.'

6. Throughout the war the Soviet Government have tried to enhance the prestige of the Red Navy by introducing new titles and uniforms for

its commanding personnel, by publicising its exploits in the press and to a certain extent in the cinema, and by playing up Russia's naval traditions and past naval victories. Whether they now intend to launch an intensive campaign for making the Soviet people 'navy conscious' is still not clear, though it is not without significance that on July 24th the Soviet press published calls to socialist emulation in Soviet shipbuilding yards from workers of the Ordzhonikidze Baltic yard and in the Soviet river fleets from workers in the Dnieper Basin. But the Soviet Government's growing interest in the naval bases and strategic waterways such as Koenigsberg, Kirkenes, Bear Island, Bornholm, the Bosphorus and Dardanelles and Port Arthur, in the disposition of the Italian and German fleets, and in the construction of new ports and the repair of old ones (see War Office Weekly Intelligence Review for April 25th)[2] can almost certainly be taken as a sign of their determination to develop the policy of building an ocean-going fleet worthy of their interests and power.

7. The Soviet Union nevertheless has a long way to go before it can become a great sea power. Apart from a number of modern submarines and smaller craft, the Soviet fleet consists at present mostly of old Russian ships (the only battleship mentioned in connexion with the recent Red Navy Day parades is the aged 'October Revolution') or of equally old second-hand ships acquired from His Majesty's Government and the United States Government as a result of the Italian capitulation. The Soviet fleet is also ill-balanced, particularly as regards cruisers and capital ships, and it is entirely without aircraft carriers. The experience of the Royal Navy, which has worked with the Russians at Murmansk and Archangel, does not suggest that the Russians have great confidence in their own seamanship or that, with the possible exception of their submarine arm, they can yet compare with other first class or even second class navies. Russian ships have shown some reluctance to put to sea and to engage the enemy. They have been unreliable in making their small contribution to the escorting of allied convoys and have shown little initiative or even common sense as regards such important matters as mine-laying. In so far as the Red fleet has distinguished itself in the war against Germany, it has been mainly in connexion with amphibious operations such as the defence of Sevastopol, in fighting in and around the Kerch Straits, and in Baltic operations when Soviet sailors have done most of their fighting on land. It is therefore not unnatural that British naval officers who have worked with the Russian Navy during this war are not impressed by its efficiency or potential fighting qualities.

8. On the other hand Soviet junior officers and ratings in conversation with their British opposite numbers have shown great pride and enthusiasm about the future of the Red Navy and the greatest confidence that the public statements made by Stalin and Molotov will bear fruit in a considerable modernisation and expansion of the Red Navy in the early future. The officer cadre, more particularly in the higher ranks, is very much larger

[2] Not here printed.

than would be needed for a navy of the present size and it would appear that this has been done deliberately to provide for expansion later on. The quality of these officers is of course uncertain and many of them have had very little experience at sea. American naval officers in the Soviet Union, who have had less experience than British officers of day to day cooperation with the Red Navy, are inclined to take a less critical view of its potentialities. They consider that there will be an early and rapid expansion. Their own experience has taught them that naval personnel can be trained relatively quickly and the experience of this war has shown that technical equipment, which can be provided by Russian science and industry, is as important a factor as good seamanship.

9. There is I think little doubt that the Soviet Union will now make great efforts to increase her naval strength. She is once again a first class power with interests throughout the world and it is therefore only natural that she should want to reconstruct and even to expand her navy. She will certainly wish to profit from the German defeat and to become the dominant naval power in the Baltic, thus realising the aims of Peter the Great. This will certainly be coupled with a close interest in Denmark and in freedom of passage through the Baltic into the North Sea. She will equally wish to reassert her naval superiority in the Black Sea and to secure freedom of egress into the Mediterranean through the Dardanelles. This war has shown so clearly the importance of Murmansk and Archangel as the emergency life-line for Russia that Russia will certainly try to ensure liberty of action for her fleet in Northern waters and she may want bases in Bear Island and Northern Norway. It is too early yet to say what are the Russian intentions in the Far East but the interest already shown here in the future of Port Arthur and of Korea suggests a definite intention to increase Soviet naval strength in the Pacific. For some years to come Russia is however likely to be fully occupied in restoring her naval position in the Baltic and the Black Sea where the bulk of the Soviet merchant marine will also presumably be concentrated. The Russians have a long way to go before they are in a position to concentrate any naval strength in the Mediterranean or in waters outside the immediate proximity of the Soviet Union.

10. It may well be doubted whether the Red Navy, even when expanded, will ever become more than 'a loyal helper of the Red Army', as Stalin called the Red Navy in his Order of the Day. But it would be unwise if we were to overlook some of the possible implications of the re-emergence of Russia as a great naval power with a big seagoing and ocean-going fleet and suitably disposed bases. This would be all the more dangerous if the Soviet Government maintain the pressure they are now exerting in the Aegean as well as in the Dardanelles area and if they attempt to spring surprises like the 60,000 ton battleships with fourteen 16-inch guns which Krylov, the famous Russian designer, admitted that they were building in the years before the war in a conversation with an American journalist and a member of the Embassy staff in September, 1944, after a ceremony at

which His Majesty's Ambassador had invested him with honorary membership of the Society of Naval Architects.[3]

I have, &c.,

FRANK K. ROBERTS

[3] Rear-Admiral H. J. Egerton, Senior British Naval Officer, North Russia, had been consulted and had concurred in this despatch.

No. 409

Letter from Mr. Hayter (Berlin) to Mr. Howard [1]

[*F.O. 934/2/9(13)*]

BRITISH DELEGATION, BERLIN, *25 July 1945*

Top secret and Personal

Dear Douglas,

You will have seen how we stand about Turkey from the telegram[2] sent off today. There are only two things to add to this. The first is that the President has not yet despaired and has asked the Foreign Ministers (who have appointed a Sub-Committee) to continue to study his International Waterways proposal, with particular reference to the Dardanelles. The second is that I am reliably informed that after dinner with the Prime Minister Joe said that, if we did not want to give him bases in the Dardanelles, could we let him have one somewhere else, for instance Dedeagach.

Peace Treaties with the Balkans have become curiously entangled, as you will see from the attached document,[3] with a number of utterly irrelevant subjects, such as a moral booster for Italy, a kick in the pants for Franco, and the admission of Switzerland to the World Organisation. It is still uncertain whether anything will come of this business. The Russians pressed us very hard to put something in about the resumption of diplomatic relations with Bulgaria, etc. The Americans were almost ready to agree to a weasel-worded formula saying that the Three Governments would immediately consider the question of resumption of relations, but we pointed out that it was no good trying to use words to paper over cracks, especially as the President had made it plain repeatedly that the United States Government had no intention whatever of recognising the present Bulgarian and Roumanian Governments.

The Sub-Committee on the Yalta Declaration will be meeting again this afternoon and will undoubtedly reach a deadlock. I doubt if this matters

[1] The date of receipt is uncertain.
[2] No. 400.
[3] Not attached to filed copy: cf. No. 260.

very much from our point of view. The Russians had already killed the passage about elections, the declaration about the press would not have been worth the paper it was written on, and we do not want to press for genuinely tripartite Control Commissions because of the dangerous repercussions on the situation in Italy. But it will be a nasty blow to poor little Cannon.

We put in a masterly compromise proposal about Roumanian oil,[4] the joint work of Mark Turner and myself, and what the Russians will say we don't know.

During a discussion about whether the Bulgarian and Roumanian Government were Communist or not[5] the following dialogue took place:

Molotov. 'Tatarescu is not a Communist.'
Secretary of State. 'No, his record is quite a different one.'
Molotov. (trying again) 'The King of Roumania is not a Communist.'
Secretary of State. 'Nor is he a member of the Roumanian Government.'
Molotov. 'No, but he appointed it.'
Secretary of State. 'With some assistance from M. Vyshinsky.'
Vyshinsky. (smirking and not attempting to deny it) 'Anyway, I put a priest in the Government.'

The high point of the Conference to my mind was the occasion when Joe explained the basis of his foreign policy. The Prime Minister had been talking about Bulgaria 'crouching in the Balkans, fawning upon Germany.' Joe in his reply did not attempt to defend Bulgaria, but said 'Feelings of revenge are not a good guide for foreign policy. I do not wish to teach my colleagues a lesson, but policy should be based on the calculation of forces.'[6] One had always known this was so in Joe's case, but it was nice to get it from the horse's mouth.

W. HAYTER

[4] See No. 264.
[5] See No. 254, minute 2.
[6] Cf. No. 208, minute 4.

No. 410

Letter from Mr. Allen (Berlin) to Mr. Warner (Received 26 July)
[*N 9609/6/55*]

BERLIN, *25 July 1945*

Dear Christopher,

We are sending you some telegrams[1] this morning about yesterday's talks with the formidable delegation which the Polish Provisional Government have sent here in response to the Big Three's invitation. It does not at

[1] Berlin telegrams Nos. 225–8 Target of 25 July, not printed, summarized the discussions recorded in No. 254, minute 4 and annex, Nos. 257, 267, 268 and No. 271, minute 3.

present look as though we are likely to get anywhere on the question of the Polish Western Frontier. Last night's talk in the Secretary of State's house which went on until 1.30 a.m. was, however, useful. I have had two brief private words with Mikolajczyk. He seems to be far from cheerful about the present trend of events in Poland. I enclose translations of two notes[i][2] which he handed to me privately. In giving me these he said that he felt that the battle for Poland's independence was now joined. In commenting upon the attitude of Poles abroad he said rather grimly that this was now a fight and where there was fighting people were apt to get hurt or even killed. Patriotic Poles should, however, accept this risk. He said that conditions had deteriorated during the last few days since he had his conversation with Clark Kerr in Warsaw[3] and he was now running into difficulties in organising the Peasant Party.

Yours ever,
Denis Allen

Calendar to No. 410

i *24 July 1945 Translations of two notes by M. Mikolajczyk on Polish affairs:* need for prompt Polish acquisition of frontier on the Neisse and of Stettin, for Soviet withdrawal from Poland, for safeguarding freedom there [N 9253, 9609/6/55].

[2] Mr. Allen minuted on these notes: 'These papers, which M. Mikolajczyk handed to me most confidentially as representing his own views, show that he has his own reasons for supporting M. Bierut's line on the Western frontier question. A copy of each has been submitted to Sir A. Cadogan separately and one has been given to S. of S. D. A. 25/7.'
[3] See No. 319.i.

No. 411

Mr. Eden to Sir N. Charles (Rome)
No. 1917 Telegraphic [C 5051/317/3]

Immediate   FOREIGN OFFICE, *26 July 1945, 2 p.m.*

Following from Harvey for Mack.

Target No. 210[1] from Terminal repeated to A.F.H.Q. as OZ 4576 (of 24th July: Feeding of Vienna).

Record of discussion at Terminal on July 24th [23rd][2] on feeding of Vienna stated that Stalin had said it would be helpful if the British and United States Governments would recognise the authority of Dr. Renner's Government for purposes of organising food supply for all zones of Vienna; and that this proposal was agreed [*sic*][2] to by the Conference.

[1] No. 258.i.
[2] See No. 241, minute 14.

2. Harrison tells us that this does not accurately represent what passed, and he is taking up the question of amending the record.[3] Harrison reports that Prime Minister said: 'As regards recognition of the authority of the Renner Government, we recognise that this is important and we consider that it is one of the first questions to tackle when our people are established in Vienna. As regards the distribution of food in Vienna we agree that it is in principle desirable to work through a single Austrian administration. We wish to disturb local administrative arrangements as little as possible.'

3. It may be useful for you to bear this in mind in case it should be claimed that any decision at Terminal amounts to recognition of the Renner Government.

4. Harrison also reports that he gathers from discussion with American representatives at Terminal that Americans appear ready to recognise Renner Government with less reconstruction than we would like. They agree that it is a matter for local discussion between Allied representatives in Vienna. Americans appear to think that our main objection to the Renner Government is that it is too far to the left. You should take every opportunity of pointing out to your American colleagues that this is not the basis of our complaint against the Renner Government. What we object to is that it is quite unrepresentative of Austria as a whole, being based only on Vienna and two at most out of all the Austrian provinces.

5. If American attitude is maintained we may find it hard to get the sort of Austrian Government we want, but meanwhile we see no reason to modify instructions[1] already issued to General McCreery.

[3] The reference was to No. 258, minutes 6–7: *v. ibid.*, notes 15 and 16.

No. 412

Mr. Eden to Mr. Caccia (Athens)
No. 1579 Telegraphic [R 12416/4/19]

Immediate   FOREIGN OFFICE, *26 July 1945, 3.35 p.m.*

Repeated to Terminal No. 224 Onward (*Important*), Washington No. 7838, Moscow No. 4143, Belgrade No. 1098, Resmed's Office Caserta [No.] 2290.

Following from Sir O. Sargent.

Your telegrams Nos. 1583 and 1584[1] (of July 23rd: political situation in Greece).

We have discussed this with the Secretary of State who agrees that you should at once advise Regent and Admiral Voulgaris on following lines:

(*a*) the present service government should remain in power.

(*b*) we hope that a respectable non-party man will be appointed Minister for Foreign Affairs.

[1] No. 392.i.

(c) the service character of the government should be maintained.

2. We are considering other measures designed to strengthen the Regent's position and to curb demand for a change of government. We will telegraph shortly about this.

No. 413

Sir M. Peterson (Istanbul) to Mr. Eden (Received 26 July, 10 p.m.)
No. 193 Telegraphic [R 12667/44/44]

Top secret   ISTANBUL, *26 July 1945, 7.37 p.m. G.M.T.*

Repeated to Moscow, Washington, Angora.

Your telegram No. 137.[1]

I saw the Turkish Prime Minister this afternoon at his villa near Istanbul, leaving aide-mémoire with him. Counsellor will make similar démarche with Ministry of Foreign Affairs in Angora tomorrow.

Prime Minister studied aide-mémoire attentively and in a state of some perturbation. He finally made the following comments:

(a) In general he hoped the Allies were not going to tend to give way to Russia over everything. If they did they might confirm and make permanent Russian influence over countries in which it was as yet precarious.

(b) He thought that the United States Government and indeed His Majesty's Government might have given Turkey notice that they were going to raise question of internationalisation. He assumed that what was now contemplated was not revision but scrapping of Montreux.

(c) Much must depend on what was meant by internationalisation but in the absence of more precise information M. Sarajoglu was disposed to consider that it would imply a return to the system prevailing between Lausanne and Montreux.[2] This for Turkey would imply demilitarisation and acceptance of an International Commission in Istanbul.

2. To these objections I replied:

(a) that on the evidence available Soviet did not seem to be particularly pleased with the suggestion of internationalisation,

(b) I did not know whether His Majesty's Government had been aware of the Presidents intention to put forward this solution. But whether they were or not they had at least taken prompt steps to let Turkey know that it had been raised,

(c) I could only suggest that we should wait and see what precisely was

---

[1] Repetition of No. 400.

[2] The system of free passage through the demilitarised Straits established under the Lausanne Convention and article 23 of the treaty of peace with Turkey signed at Lausanne on 24 July 1923 (*B.F.S.P.*, vol. 117, pp. 550, 592–600) had been revised at Montreux in 1936: see No. 3, note 9.

meant by the term 'international control' and I stressed the importance for Turkey of having America associated with internationalisation of the Straits.

3. Prime Minister cheered up sufficiently to reflect (your paragraph 4) that Turkey was not in the least interested in concluding a treaty of alliance with Russia. He did not know which side had spoken first of a treaty of alliance but if it had been the Turkish Ambassador in Moscow it must have been in pursuance of general instructions given him to go to the utmost possible lengths to meet the Russians. He agreed there was nothing to do save to await American proposals when he would wish to speak to me again. He returns to Angora Monday[3] night for the re-opening of the assembly.

4. The United States Embassy is badly placed at the moment to handle questions of this importance. The Ambassador is in hospital in Istanbul for another 3 weeks or so and the Embassy at Angora is in charge of a First Secretary who has been expecting to leave for months past.

Please repeat to Terminal.[4]

Foreign Office please repeat to Moscow Washi[n]gton as my telegrams No. 57 and 93 respectively.

CALENDAR TO No. 413

i   *2 Aug. 1945   F.O. brief for Mr. Bevin* on Turco-Soviet relations with particular reference to the question of the Straits [R 13083/4476/44].

[3] 30 July 1945.
[4] Repeated from the Foreign Office as telegram No. 255 Onward of 28 July 1945 to Berlin where it was minuted by Mr. Hayter and initialed by Sir A. Cadogan as follows: 'The Americans are still pursuing the Straits question, rather faintly in the Waterways Sub-Ctee. But I am afraid it is over as far as Terminal is concerned. W. G. Hayter 29/7.' 'A. C. July 29 1945.'

No. 414

Mr. Eden to Sir A. Cadogan (Berlin)
No. 225 Onward Telegraphic [U 5819/19/70]

Top secret   FOREIGN OFFICE, *26 July 1945, 4.50 p.m.*

For Sir A. Cadogan from Sir O. Sargent.

Reference Target No. 194.[1]

Air Ministry are fully aware of the importance attached to our offer to equip ten additional French Squadrons. We are informing the French that the Air Ministry are ready to begin conversations in London any time after August 1st to settle methods of implementing offer.

[1] No. 390.

2. The delays and disappointments in delivery of British aircraft to the French referred to by Mr. Duff Cooper come under three heads:

(i) *Availability*. R.A.F. requirements for their own purposes have not always made it possible for the French to be supplied with the aircraft they have requested.

(ii) *Assignment*. Lease-Lend material of American origin cannot be assigned to the French nor can material of British origin that is of similar type to American or 'dollar purchased' without the concurrence of the Americans and the latter have often been sticky in giving their concurrence.

(iii) *Security*. Secret equipment cannot be transferred to the French under existing directive.

3. Air Ministry do not think there is serious risk of the French Air Force coming under excessive Soviet influence even if they accept the offer referred to by Mr. Duff Cooper.

No. 415

Mr. Roberts (Moscow) to Mr. Eden (Received 26 July, 8.58 p.m.)
No. 3290 Telegraphic [U 5738/42/70]

MOSCOW, *26 July 1945, 6.45 p.m.*

Repeated to Tehran, Istanbul (Constantinople), Paris.

Sir A. Clark-Kerr's letter of 30th March to Sir O. Sargent.[1]

Soviet authorities seem to be making considerable efforts to prepare the ground for forthcoming Trades Union Conference at Paris. They are apparently anxious both to ensure support for their delegation at the Conference from the delegations of other major powers, and also to arrange for the presence of as many delegations from smaller powers as possible who will be amenable to their influence.

2. Soviet Press is beginning to show increased interest in this subject. Article in *Trud* referred to in my telegram No. 3278[1] has been followed up in the Press of 25th July by a report of the visit of Soviet Trade Unionists, headed by Kuznetsov, to the United States as guests of the C[ongress of] I[ndustrial] O[rganizations] with the object of strengthening the unity between Soviet and American Trades Unions; and by an account of the Cleveland Conference of the A[merican] F[ederation of] L[abour] under the heading 'Movement for International Trades Union Unity in A.F.L. Organizations' which describes the meeting as a struggle of the rank and file anxious for international unity against a reactionary leadership.

3. In general, the Soviet Press gives considerable prominence to Trade Union movements everywhere, representing them as spearheads in the struggle not only for improved material conditions for the working class but also for rallying into a unified block (under Communist guidance) all the 'progressive democratic' forces in a country. The pattern seems to be as follows:–

[1] Not printed.

(*a*) In countries under Soviet occupation, stress is laid on the enlistment of all workers into Government-sponsored Trade Unions. Typical article in *Trud* of 24th July entitled 'Trade Unions, strength of Roumanian Democracy' describes the gradual rallying of all Roumanian workers and intellectuals to the new Trade Unions, who are not only restoring the industrial life of the country, but helping to democratise the country, purge Government departments and reorganise the police. These Unions must be represented at the Paris Conference. Reports on Polish affairs regularly bring out the importance of the efforts being made to enlist all workers into the new unitary Trades Unions.

(*b*) In countries less subject to Soviet control, emphasis is laid on the attempts by Communist parties to bring all Trades Unions under a common leadership, which goes hand in hand with their attempts to fuse as far as possible the Communist and Socialist parties. This theme has appeared recently in reports on France, Belgium, United Kingdom, the United States, Mexico and other countries, as well as in Germany, where amalgamation has happily been effected in the Russian zone, and only opposition of the Allies to Trades Union movements prevents it being applied to the rest of Germany.

(*c*) In countries like Persia and Turkey, the Soviet Press is beginning to call attention to the appalling conditions of the working class, for which efficient and powerful Trades Unions are the obvious remedy. That such Trades Unions would be sympathetic to the Soviet Union as the great champion of all free democracy is assumed. The Soviet Union's smaller southern neighbours are apparently expected to admit these Trojan horses without further delay. British Trades Union delegation now in Soviet Union have told me of the effort made in Tehran to enlist their support for demand of obviously unrepresentative but Soviet-sponsored Persian Trades Unions to secure invitation to Paris Conference.

Please repeat to Tehran, Istanbul (Constantinople) and Paris Saving as my telegrams Nos. 100, 29 and 95 respectively.

CALENDAR TO NO. 415

i *26 July 1945 Record by Mr. Ross of a conversation with Baron Malfatti (Labour Attaché, Italian Embassy).* Discussion of visits by Italian trades unionists to the Soviet Union and to Great Britain. Baron Malfatti notices 'a great tendency in Italy to regard Russia as the only progressive country, largely because she was unknown' [ZM 4233/19/22].

No. 416

Sir A. Cadogan (Berlin) to Mr. Eden (Received 26 July, 4.45 p.m.)
No. 244 Target Telegraphic [F.O. 934/5/48(4)]

Top secret. Immediate   BERLIN, *26 July 1945, 6.30 p.m.*

Please pass to Washington from Sir A. Cadogan.

Preliminary discussions at Terminal have disclosed the fact that Mr.

Stettinius is reluctant to agree to a proposal that the chairmanship of the Executive Committee of the Preparatory Commission of the United Nations should rotate among the Five Great Powers on the grounds that this might create an undesirable precedent in connexion with the World Organisation. Mr. Dunn has also stated that in the last resort the Americans would prefer to have a Russian Chairman rather than a rotating one.

2. We, for our part, see no strong objection to either course provided that we ourselves are awarded the Executive Secretaryship; but if, as seems possible, the Russians appoint M. Gousev, we feel that there would be serious inconveniences attaching to the proposal for a Soviet Chairman. In any case, we do not think that the dangers which Mr. Stettinius foresees, if it should be decided to have a rotating Chairman, are very real. The presidency of the three major organs of the United Nations (other than the General Assembly, the Court and the Secretariat) would almost certainly in practice have to rotate anyhow and it is arguable that in the case of the Security Council it would be greatly preferable if it rotated between the permanent members only rather than between all members as in the case of the League of Nations. In the Security Council indeed the five permanent members will play an even more important role than they did in the Council of the League of Nations and the League system in this respect was itself open to criticism in that at criticial moments there was apt to be a weak representative of an unimportant nation in the chair. On the other hand, the presidency of the Economic and Social Council might well rotate among all 18 members.

3. It would be useful therefore if you could at once see Mr. Stettinius and ask him whether on reflection he could not agree to inform the United States Delegation at Terminal that, if this should be necessary in order to gain agreement, he would be prepared to withdraw his objection to a rotating chairman of the Executive Committee.

No. 417

Minutes of a Meeting of the European Advisory Commission held at Lancaster House, London, S.W.1., on Thursday 26 July 1945 at 7 p.m.
E.A.C.(45)7th Meeting [U 5847/20/70]

Top secret

Present:
Monsieur R. Massigli (*in the Chair*), Monsieur de Leusse, Professor A. Gros.
Sir R. I. Campbell, Viscount Hood, Brigadier F. G. French.
Mr. G. F. Saksin, Mr. N. V. Ivanov.
Mr. J. G. Winant, Mr. E. A. Lightner, Jnr., Colonel G. R. Hall.

Secretariat: Lieutenant M. W. Boggs, U.S.N., Mr. T. A. Marchenko, Mr. E. A. Paton-Smith, Mr. B. V. Ivanoff.

Agenda

1. Approval of the text of Agreement[1] between the Governments of the United Kingdom, the United States of America and the Union of Soviet Socialist Republics and the Provisional Government of the French Republic regarding Amendments to the Protocol of the 12th September, 1944, on the Zones of Occupation in Germany and the Administration of 'Greater Berlin.'

2. Approval of the Report[2] by the European Advisory Commission to the Governments of the United Kingdom, the United States of America and the Union of Soviet Socialist Republics and the Provisional Government of the French Republic.

THE COMMISSION–

1. *Approval of text of the Agreement between the Governments of the United Kingdom, the United States of America and the Union of Soviet Socialist Republics and the Provisional Government of the French Republic regarding Amendments to the Protocol of the 12th September, 1944, on the Zones of Occupation in Germany and the Administration of 'Greater Berlin.'*

(a) approved the text of the Agreement between the Governments of the United Kingdom, the United States of America and the Union of Soviet Socialist Republics and the Provisional Government of the French Republic regarding Amendments to the Protocol of the 12th September, 1944, on the Zones of Occupation in Germany and the Administration of 'Greater Berlin,' the boundaries of the zones of occupation in Germany being as marked on the annexed map 'D' in accordance with the texts of the above-mentioned Protocol and of the present Agreement (the text of the present Agreement in English, Russian and French and map 'D'; which supersedes map 'A' annexed to the Protocol of the 12th September, 1944, are annexed);[3]

(b) decided to submit the Agreement between the Governments of the United Kingdom, the United States of America and the Union of Soviet Socialist Republics and the Provisional Government of the French Republic regarding Amendments to the Protocol of the 12th September, 1944, on the Zones of Occupation in Germany and the Administration of 'Greater Berlin,' with the annexed map 'D,' to the Governments of the United Kingdom, the United States of America and the Union of Soviet Socialist Republics and the Provisional Government of the French Republic for consideration and approval.

[1] Printed in Cmnd. 1552 of 1961, pp. 45–8.
[2] This report of 26 July 1945 concerning a French zone of occupation in Germany and sector in Berlin, not here printed, is printed in *F.R.U.S. Berlin*, vol. ii, pp. 1003–4.
[3] *Note in filed copy:* 'Russian and French texts and map not reproduced.'

2. *Report by the European Advisory Commission to the Governments of the United Kingdom, the United States of America and the Union of Soviet Socialist Republics and the Provisional Government of the French Republic.*	Approved the text of the Report[2] by the European Advisory Commission and decided to transmit it, signed by the four Representatives on the European Advisory Commission, as a covering document to the text of the Agreement regarding Amendments to the Protocol of the 12th September, 1944, to the Governments of the United Kingdom, the United States of America and the Union of Soviet Socialist Republics and the Provisional Government of the French Republic. (The text of the Report in English, Russian and French is annexed.)[4]

Representative of the Government of the United Kingdom on the European Advisory Commission:	Representative of the Government of the United States of America on the European Advisory Commission:	Representative of the Government of the Union of Soviet Socialist Republics on the European Advisory Commission:	Representative of the Provisional Government of the French Republic on the European Advisory Commission:
(*Signed*)	(*Signed*)	(*Signed*)	(*Signed*)
R. I. CAMPBELL	JOHN G. WINANT	G. F. SAKSIN	R. MASSIGLI

Lancaster House, London, S.W.1, 26th July, 1945

CALENDARS TO NO. 417

i *17–26 July 1945 Correspondence between Foreign Office and French and U.S. Embassies (London).* Announcement of Agreement in E.A.C. on 26 July on zones of occupation in Germany: cf. *F.R.U.S. Berlin*, vol. ii, p. 1005, note 2 [U 5556, 5748, 6177/20/70].

ii *30–31 July 1945 Letter from Sir A. Cadogan (Berlin) to M. Gousev; minute by Sir R. Campbell* circulating record of informal meeting of E.A.C. on 27 July. Arrangements for announcement and publication of agreements on the occupation and control of Austria [F.O. 934/4/25(12); U 5871/11/70].

[4] Notification of approval of this report and agreement was given to the E.A.C. by H.M. Government on 2 August, by the United States Government on 29 July, by the French Government on 4 August and by the Soviet Government on 13 August.

No. 418

Mr. Eden to Mr. Roberts (*Moscow*)

No. 71 Victim Telegraphic [*UE 2722/624/77*]

FOREIGN OFFICE, *26 July 1945, 8.23 p.m.*

Repeated to Washington No. 86 Victim and Paris No. 99 Victim (Saving).

Your telegram No. 13 Victim,[1] paragraph 4 (of 27th June; supplies from Germany) and my telegram No. 58 Victim[2] (of 18th July; interim deliveries).

[1] Not printed.   [2] No. 152.ii.

For your information United Kingdom element of Control Commission have now been warned by telegram of following urgent United Kingdom requirements from Germany:– Hides, skins, leather, carbon black, synthetic rubber, rubber chemicals, rubber thread, rayon type fabric, paranitrochlorbenzene, polyisobutylene, dimethyl and dibutyl phthalates, silica gel, phthalic anhydride, opium, fuel injection pumps, hosiery needles, paperboard and corrugated fibre board, potash, timber, pig lead, zinc sheets, camphor (technical).

2. Telegram states that as soon as agreement on policy is reached firm requirements for some or all of the above are likely to be put forward and in the meantime it is hoped that arrangements will, as far as possible, be made for location and listing of exportable surpluses of these materials and for prevention of their destruction or dissipation.

3. The above list is not necessarily inclusive and lists of further requirements are promised.

4. You should also know the Working Party on German export surpluses appointed by the Emergency Economic Committee for Europe is about to invite all Members of the E.E.C.E. including Americans and ourselves to submit by 1st August lists of not more than 20 items (counting chemicals and pharmaceuticals as one item) of urgent requirements from Germany and Austria. War material, coal, power and such transportation equipment as comes under the Provisional European Inland Transport Organisation are to be excluded as they are covered by other machinery.

CALENDARS TO No. 418

i *24 July 1945   Allied Commission on Reparations (Moscow). Notes of a meeting* of representatives to discuss system of accounting for reparations deliveries; Soviet representative was generally receptive [UE 3482/624/77].

ii *26 July 1945   Mr. Holman (Paris) Tel. No. 1 Saving Victim.* French criticism of alleged decisions and discussions on reparation at Yalta, Moscow and Potsdam. M. Pleven stated on 24 July that France could not accept without protest any reparation settlement concluded in her absence [UE 3245/624/77].

No. 419

Mr. Roberts (Moscow) to Mr. Eden (Received 26 July, 9.11 p.m.)
No. 3295 Telegraphic [F 4567/630/23]

Secret. Important   MOSCOW, *26 July 1945, 7.18 p.m. G.M.T.*
Repeated to United Kingdom Delegation Berlin, Chungking.

A story is circulating among foreign correspondents and diplomatists here that Admiral Nomura and other Japanese representatives are now in Moscow to ask for Soviet mediation to end the war in the Far East. The United States Embassy think that there is probably some foundation for this story, which was killed by Soviet censorship.

913

2. I also understand from journalists that the Japanese Embassy are very nervous about the Potsdam talks and are preparing for early Soviet entry into far eastern war.

3. There have been a few instances recently of Soviet officers talking openly to casual foreign acquaintances about the movements of their units to the Far East.

Foreign Office please pass to Terminal[1] and Chungking.

[1] With reference to this telegram, repeated to Berlin as No. 235 Onward of 26 July 1945, Foreign Office telegram No. 286 Onward of 30 July to Berlin commented: 'In our view story in paragraph 1 is improbable. If Admiral Nomura had visited or was in Moscow we should almost certainly have heard of it. He gave a press interview in Japan on the 5th July.' In Berlin Mr. Foulds minuted to Mr. Dixon: 'This canard no doubt had its origin in some leakage about the Japanese proposal to send Prince Konoye to Moscow. L. H. Foulds 31/7.' 'P. D. 31/7.'

No. 420

Mr. Roberts (Moscow) to Mr. Eden (Received 7 August)
No. 514 [N 9934/325/38]

MOSCOW, 26 July 1945

His Majesty's Chargé d'Affaires at Moscow presents his compliments to His Majesty's Principal Secretary of State for Foreign Affairs, and has the honour to transmit to him the undermentioned documents.

Reference to previous correspondence:
Foreign Office telegram No. 3998[1] of July 18th.
Description of Enclosure

Name and Date	Subject
To: Mr. V. G. Dekanozov, People's Commissariat for Foreign Affairs, dated 26th July, 1945.	

ENCLOSURE IN NO. 420

Letter from Mr. Roberts (Moscow) to M. Dekanozov
No. 396/4/45

BRITISH EMBASSY, MOSCOW, 26 July 1945

(Dear Mr. Dekanozov),

The Government of India are considering as part of their post-war development plans, the expansion of the existing Indian organisations connected with agricultural research and the introduction of large-scale experiments in cooperative

[1] Not printed.

farming. In view of the wide experience in these fields gained in the Soviet Union, the Government of India feel that in both these matters it would be useful if a small party of scientists and agriculturists could be sent to the Soviet Union to study at first hand the working of collectivised and state farming and to visit leading scientific institutions in this country. The Government of India find that there is very little direct information available in India about developments in the Soviet Union either in respect of systems of farming or in respect of the application of biological science to agriculture and livestock improvements. Although it is realised that Indian conditions are vastly different from those obtaining in the U.S.S.R., the Government of India feel that first-hand study on these lines would prove very useful to them.

2. The Government of India would therefore like to send a small delegation composed of both agricultural scientists and practical farmers to study the advances made in the Soviet Union in agriculture and animal husbandry, and to discuss and consult with leading Soviet scientists in these subjects. It is proposed that the scientists in the delegation would be experts in plant and animal genetics and breeding, plant physiology, entomology and mycology. The total number of delegates would not exceed ten. The duration of the visit would naturally be determined by the nature of the facilities which the Soviet Government felt able to provide and the number of centres which in the opinion of the Soviet authorities would best repay visits by the delegation.

3. If the Soviet Government feel able to grant the necessary facilities for the above visit in the near future, the Government of India would be grateful to receive a rough indication of possible itineraries of such a visit, together with an approximate estimate of the total cost involved. The delegation are of course likely to be especially interested in visiting those parts of the Soviet Union where soil and climatic conditions are similar to those prevailing in the various regions of India.

4. I should be grateful to learn whether this proposal is acceptable to the Soviet Government. You will realise that it is for practical reasons desirable that an agricultural visit of this kind should take place before winter sets in, and I should therefore be greatly obliged for an early reply.

(Yours sincerely),
F. K. ROBERTS

No. 421

Letter from Sir O. Sargent to Sir W. Strang (Lübbecke)
[C 3858/3086/18]

FOREIGN OFFICE, *26 July 1945*

My dear William,

We have all read with much interest your despatch No. 1[1] of the 13[11]th July, enclosing a report on conditions in the British Zone.

There are, as I am sure you will agree, certain aspects of the situation that must cause anxiety.

[1] No. 103.

(1) Observers quoted by you frequently stress the high morale, the will to survive and rebuild, and, in general, the resilience of the German people. The impression created often appears to be the rather erroneous one that the German people, to use a sporting metaphor, have taken a count but are now once more gamely struggling to their feet—in short that they 'can take it'. The real conclusion to be drawn from this state of affairs however appears to me to be that the German people are less war weary and show higher morale because they have not as yet, certainly not in the country districts, nor in the smaller towns, suffered as much in the war years from want of food, clothing and fuel as we and the people in Allied liberated territories. They have in fact been cushioned by the Displaced Persons. Their war effort does not seem to have been as intensified as ours and they have only begun to know what it means to be 'occupied'. Morale, it would seem, is higher in large part because up to the present many of them have suffered less. They are therefore facing the hardships of the coming winter with some considerable initial advantages over the inhabitants of Allied liberated territories. Would you say that this is a correct appreciation and if so how would you propose that the situation ought to be handled?

(2) The displaced persons are evidently regarded by many Germans and military government officers alike as public enemy No. 1 to the re-establishment of law and order. I quite see the reasons why they cannot be allowed to run wild, but their excesses should not call for undue sympathy as the Germans are themselves solely responsible for this problem and have now to reap a whirlwind of their own sowing. The Germans should clearly not be allowed to exploit this problem and to use it as a bridge linking them and our occupation forces. Military Government officers coming, as they inevitably must, into close and daily contact with the suffering and hardship of the population are more liable to become the victims of exaggerated sympathy, and it would be highly undesirable if their opinion were to be allowed to lapse into 'softness' when the forces in general and the people in this country still feel very strongly and differently on this question of German responsibility for the suffering caused by the war. The repatriation of displaced persons, except for a relatively small number, or the rounding up of them into camps should automatically bring this source of mischief to an end.

(3) It is interesting to note the widespread desire among the Germans themselves for a more rigorous policy of de-nazification, and also the view expressed by some members of the Military Government that Nazi experts who have been retained are more a hindrance than a help to the revival of economic and social life. I trust therefore that the purge of Nazis from office and posts of influence will be vigorously pursued. There should be no room for doubt as to our policy in this direction or as to our aim to encourage all genuinely anti-totalitarian movements. Whether 'Antifa'[2] qualifies under this heading I am of course unable to judge.

[2] A German anti-fascist organisation (Kampfbund gegen den Faschismus).

(4) I trust that the hesitancy in dealing with Trade Unions will be dispersed by the results of the Potsdam Conference.

(5) It is somewhat disturbing to find that essential work is often handicapped by shortage of Military Government staff. If there is one thing for which the whole of Europe is crying out, it is coal. Yet at the time of your visit to Essen the Ruhr Coal Control apparently had a 'totally inadequate clerical staff'. Is this situation being remedied? We shall be under fire if coal shortage can be attributed to this kind of reason.

O. SARGENT

No. 422

Letter from Mr. Jebb (Berlin) to Mr. Ronald (Received 28 July)
[*U 5788/5202/70*]

BRITISH DELEGATION, BERLIN, *26 July 1945*

Dear Nigel

I have sent you by this bag the records of my various talks up to date,[1] and as you will no doubt see in the telegram distribution tomorrow Alec[2] decided to send off my draft to Washington without referring it to the Foreign Secretary in London.[3] We are now bending our efforts to try and get the Americans to agree to a 'rotating' Chairman. If they do agree, then I think we shall try to arrange an exchange of letters between Cadogan, Gromyko and Dunn.

What an astonishing turnover![4] We are all agog to know who is going to come out here tomorrow or the next day to represent His Majesty's Government.

Yours ever
G. J.

[1] See Nos. 279–80.
[2] Sir Alexander Cadogan.
[3] See No. 416.
[4] In the result of the British general election, declared on 26 July 1945, the Labour Party secured an overall majority of 146 seats in the House of Commons. At 7 p.m. that day Mr. Churchill resigned his office and at 7.30 p.m. Mr. Attlee was invited to form a Government. Mr. Eden continued to work in the Foreign Office on 26 and 27 July, and surrendered his seals of office to H.M. the King shortly after 10 a.m. on 28 July. Mr. Eden was succeeded by Mr. Bevin, whose appointment had been announced in the evening of 27 July.

CHAPTER IV

Proceedings of the Conference at Potsdam after assumption of office by Mr. Attlee

27 July — 1 August 1945

No. 423

Mr. Eden to Sir A. Cadogan (Berlin: received 27 July, 2.35 a.m.)
No. 236 Onward Telegraphic [F.O. 934/2/8(7)]

Most Immediate   FOREIGN OFFICE, *27 July 1945, 12.30 a.m.*

Following for Cadogan from Bridges.

Please convey following as personal messages from Mr. Attlee to President Truman and to Generalissimo Stalin.

Begins:

On resignation of Mr. Churchill, His Majesty The King has entrusted me with the formation of a Government. You will I am sure realise that owing to the immediate and urgent tasks before me I shall be unable to return to Potsdam in time for the Plenary Meeting fixed for 5 p.m. on Friday 27th July.

I plan to arrive in Potsdam in time for a meeting late on Saturday 28th July and should be much obliged if provisional arrangements could be made accordingly if this would suit your convenience. I greatly regret the inconvenience caused by this postponement.   *Ends.*

No. 424

Mr. Eden to Sir A. Cadogan (Berlin: received 27 July, 2.40 a.m.)
No. 237 Onward Telegraphic [F.O. 934/2/8(7)]

FOREIGN OFFICE, *27 July 1945, 12.35 a.m.*

Most Immediate. Top secret

Following for Cadogan from Mr. Attlee.

You will have seen my messages[1] to President Truman and Generalissimo Stalin.

---

[1] No. 423.

You have my authority to continue to act for the Foreign Secretary until my return to Potsdam. I hope therefore that you will continue to hold meetings of Foreign Secretaries.

No. 425

Mr. Eden to Sir A. Cadogan (Berlin: received 27 July, 2.58 a.m.)
No. 238 Onward Telegraphic [F.O. 934/2/8(13)]

FOREIGN OFFICE, *27 July 1945, 12.25 a.m.*

Immediate. Top secret and Strictly Personal

Following for Cadogan and Brook from Bridges and Dixon.

For your information only. As Mr. Attlee wishes to return to London as soon as possible and does not expect resumed discussions to last more than two or three days it is important that minimum time shall be spent over agreeing the final protocol and communiqué.

2. We therefore hope that you will make all progress possible at present stage in framing these documents. It would also help if you could send material showing progress made and any documents produced since the party left so that we can read them on the journey out.

No. 426

Sir A. Cadogan (Berlin) to Mr. Eden (Received 27 July, 11.40 a.m.)
No. 251 Target Telegraphic [F.O. 934/2/8(23)]

Top secret BERLIN, *27 July 1945, 1.30 p.m.*

Following for Bridges from Brook.

Many thanks for your personal telegram.[1]

We shall certainly do our best to push ahead but fear that the Russians may be a drag on rapid progress. The meeting of Foreign Secretaries arranged for this morning has had to be postponed until this afternoon at the Russians' request. Moreover, the Russians have a good deal of the initiative on the Protocol Committee for we were forced to accept a proposal put forward by them and supported by the Americans that on each of the subjects to be included in the Protocol the first draft should be prepared by the Delegation which had put that subject on the Conference's Agenda. This means that over the greater part of the field the initiative on the Protocol Committee must rest with the Russians and the Americans. It also excluded from formal consideration nearly all the drafts which we had

[1] No. 425.

prepared in readiness for the Committee's first meeting, though I handed these over for what they were worth to the representatives of the two other Delegations. The Protocol Committee is meeting again this evening and I will send you the results of their work together with the minutes of the Foreign Secretaries' meeting by the first opportunity. I hope this will be by bag due at Foreign Office 0100 hours your time tomorrow . Anything which misses this will come by bag due at Foreign Office 0900 hours your time Saturday.[2]

CALENDAR TO No. 426

i *26 July 1945 Minute from Mr. Brook to Mr. Hayter (Berlin).* Note of first meeting that morning of Drafting Committee on the Protocol [CAB 21/864].

[2] 28 July 1945.

No. 427

Minute by Mr. Dent

[UE 3221/624/77]

FOREIGN OFFICE, *27 July 1945*

I understand that Sir J. Anderson called a meeting yesterday to consider whether any definite instructions could be given to the Delegation at Terminal on this new proposal[1]. A meeting was first held in Mr. Hall Patch's room to consider the question from an F.O. point of view.

[1] See No. 252, note 1. On 26 July 1945 Mr. Troutbeck had minuted: 'The idea discussed in R.M. (45) 11 that the Russians should meet nine-tenths of their reparation claims out of their own zone, while Western Germany should meet the reparation claims of all the other claimants needs a good deal of thinking about.

'In the first place it is difficult to believe that such a system would not divide Germany completely into two parts, however much we might try to avoid that result.

'Secondly, Eastern Germany would, under this system, almost certainly be reduced to complete destitution and, unless measures are taken to prevent it, great numbers of the inhabitants would try to escape into the Western zones.

'Thirdly, conditions in the Eastern zone would probably be such that to push the German population from Czechoslovakia into that area would be little less than murder by starvation. They wd. therefore try to get into the western zones.

'Fourthly, the result would be that the Western zone, in addition to having to supply the Russians with additional equipment, would also have to meet all the claims of the minor Allies. The Russians would be able to wash their hands happily of that problem. We should therefore be faced with the alternative of either having to strip the Western zones up to the same kind of degree as the Russians will be stripping the Eastern zone or to rouse the furious indignation of the Allies that we were pampering Germany at their expense.

'Fifthly, it is not quite clear from the paper whether the Poles as well as the Russians are to have their claims met out of Eastern Germany but, on the assumption that the Russians will be taking the whole lot themselves, it looks as though the Poles (and also

The following points arise

(a) this proposal would lend impetus to the various influences tending towards the division of Germany into one or more parts.

(b) It had hitherto been our policy to treat Germany as one economic unit. Should we resist the proposal because in view of (a) above it was prejudicial to our overall economic policy, should we attempt to modify it with the object of making it as little prejudicial to our policy as possible, or should we make it the occasion and the excuse for changing our policy.

(c) From the point of view of simplifying the administration of reparation and avoiding trouble with the Russians the proposal had obvious attractions.

2. It was the general feeling that we should not wish to change our policy of treating Germany as one economic unit, or to use an American proposal as an excuse for doing so. On the contrary in view of (c) above we should endeavour to get the proposal so modified (in particular resist the American idea, not in this paper, that there should be separate import programmes for each zone) that in all respects except Reparation Germany should continue to be treated as one economic unit, and that with respect to reparation the principle of allocation by zones should be understood to have been adopted as a matter of administrative convenience and not by virtue of any agreement that the Controlling Powers were ceasing to treat Germany as a whole.

3. At the interdepartmental meeting there was some support for the views expressed in para. 2 above, and Sir J. Anderson recommended the Delegation to see how far they could get along such lines short of committing H.M.G. In the present political situation he felt it was impossible to give the Delegation positive instructions until the decision had been referred to the new Cabinet[2].

JOHN S. DENT

the Czechs) will also be claiming from our zone. J. M. Troutbeck 26th July, 1945.' Mr. Hall-Patch recorded on this in a minute of 27 July: 'Discussed in Chancellor's Office yesterday evening.'

[2] Mr. Hall-Patch minuted on this: 'Sir D. Waley & Mr. M. Turner were to return to Berlin & see how far they could get on the lines of para. 3 above. I am afraid it will not be very far. E. L. H. P. 27/7.'

No. 428

Mr. Eden to Sir A. Cadogan (Berlin: received 27 July, 3.50 p.m.)
No. 243 Onward Telegraphic [F.O. 934/2/8(10)]

FOREIGN OFFICE, *27 July 1945, 1.45 p.m.*

Most Immediate. Top secret and Strictly Personal

Following for Cadogan from Dixon.
My telegram No. Onward 238.[1]

[1] No. 425.

So far as we can see object of resumed meeting will be to 'harvest' points on which agreement has already been reached.

2. Feeling here is that we ought also to make an attempt to reach agreement on

(1) reparation and residuary supply problems for Germany.

(2) a tripartite warning to the Balkan States to keep quiet. On this latter point Sir O. Sargent is sending you a telegram.[2]

3. Finally we feel that the Delegation ought to be prepared for Russian attempt to re-open questions which they have withdrawn e.g. Syria and the Lebanon.

4. It would therefore be most useful if we could have brief statement by telegram, which could be discussed with Mr. Attlee and the new Foreign Secretary setting forth

(*a*) points on which agreement has been reached.

(*b*) points on which attempt should be made to reach agreement at Terminal and if not how far they could be dealt with at the Foreign Ministers' Conference in September.

(*c*) points on which Russians may be expected to re-open and on which we should stand firm.

5. Above are only our own ideas.

CALENDAR TO NO. 428

i   *27 July 1945   Letter from Mr. Ward (Berlin) to Viscount Hood.* Progress at Potsdam on proposals for Council of Foreign Ministers: positions of France and China [F.O. 934/3/16(8)].

[2] No. 531.

No. 429

Memorandum by Sir A. Cadogan (Berlin)
[*F.O. 934/2/9(23)*]

BERLIN, *27 July 1945*

The Balkans

Balkan questions are at present being dealt with in two documents:

(1) A proposal about the admission of various States to the World Organisation (P. (Terminal) 35[1]—copy attached). The Russians are endeavouring to insert into this document a clause binding us to consider at an early date the resumption of diplomatic relations with the Balkan Satellites of Germany. We are resisting this, for two reasons. Firstly, it is constitutionally impossible for us to resume diplomatic relations with a country with which we are technically at war. Secondly, the Americans

[1] No. 260.

have been taking the line, with which we ourselves are in full agreement, that the Governments in these countries are unrepresentative and owe their position to Russian bayonets; consequently, we do not wish to enhance their position by resuming diplomatic relations with them. This paper will come up in the plenary meeting tomorrow.

(2) A memorandum by the U.S. Government on the Yalta Declaration (P. (Terminal) 21[2]—copy attached). There is also a Soviet memorandum (P. (Terminal) 11[3]—copy attached). The American memorandum has three proposals:

(a) the observation of elections in certain countries. This the Russians have already turned down;

(b) facilities for the Press to report on conditions in Bulgaria, Roumania and Hungary. Here the Russians have refused to agree to the abolition of political censorship or to free entry for press representatives;

(c) improved conditions for our representatives on the Control Commissions. The Russians have recently made proposals which mark a step forward, and we hope to reach agreement on a recommendation welcoming these proposals and accepting them as a basis for further discussion. No text has, however, yet been settled.

The Russians have made a severe attack on our policy in Greece, and have tried to make out that the situation in the ex-Satellite countries is perfect. It seems desirable to refute this contention. There is attached the draft[4] of a possible statement which might be made when the meeting of the Foreign Secretaries or the plenary meeting consider the report of the Sub-Committee dealing with the American memorandum on the Yalta Declaration (the draft is based on the assumption that an agreement about the Control Commissions will by then have been reached). In addition to refuting the Soviet contentions about conditions in the Balkans, the draft also attempts to revive a proposal made recently by the British and American Ambassadors in Belgrade, at the suggestion of the Yugoslav Minister for Foreign Affairs, that a reminder should be addressed to the Yugoslav Government to observe the provisions of the Tito-Subasic Agreement, on the basis of which His Majesty's Government and the American and Soviet Governments recognise the present Government.

There is one other Balkan question, namely the removal by the Red Army of oil equipment belonging to British firms in Roumania. In regard to this we have put in a paper (P. (Terminal) 40[5]—copy attached) suggesting

---

[2] No. 219.i.   [3] No. 201.

[4] Annex below. An earlier draft of this statement had been submitted by Mr. Hayter under cover of a minute of 26 July 1945 wherein he had proposed that the occasion of such a meeting 'might be taken to make a general statement of the views of His Majesty's Government in regard to the Balkan situation. It might be better to do this orally rather than to put in a paper on Bulgaria as suggested by Mr. Eden, which would no doubt lead to another paper from the Russians.' On 27 July a copy of the British draft was given to the American Delegation on a noncommittal basis.

[5] No. 264.

investigation by an impartial committee. The Americans at once agreed with this proposal. The Russian reaction is still awaited.

A. C.

ANNEX TO No. 429

Draft Statement

The agreement in regard to the Control Commissions is welcomed, and it is hoped that as a result of the proposals which the Soviet Government have made the conditions for British representatives on these Commissions will become more satisfactory than they have been in the past, and that they will be able to co-operate usefully with their American and Soviet colleagues.

2. The Soviet refusal to consider the supervision of elections is regretted. We intend to accede to the Greek Government's request to supervise the elections in that country, and we hope that the United States Government will join us. We have every reason to think that the result will faithfully reflect the will of the Greek people.

3. We have far less confidence about the result of the Bulgarian elections, which are apparently to be held next month. In these elections it appears that no organised opposition will be tolerated. This has been categorically confirmed quite recently by the Minister of the Interior. It is clear that elections in such circumstances will be a complete farce. His Majesty's Government will be obliged to inform the Bulgarian Government that they will be unable to recognise as representative any government elected by these means.

4. It is also to be regretted that no agreement could be reached in regard to the press. It must be frankly stated that there has been much uneasiness in many quarters in London about the impossibility of obtaining news about conditions in the ex-satellite countries. A reassuring statement by the Conference would therefore have an excellent effect. But the Soviet representatives on the Sub-Committee were unable to agree to any provision for facilitating the entry of press representatives into the countries concerned, nor could they guarantee the abolition of political censorship. In these circumstances no statement about present conditions in these countries could be issued which the British Government would be able to endorse. It is still to be hoped that the Soviet Delegation will agree that we should state publicly that press correspondents can go freely to these countries and report freely there on all that they see, as they can in Italy or in Greece.

5. It will be remembered that earlier in the Conference the Soviet Delegation put in a paper on the subject of the Yalta Declaration,[3] which referred to conditions in the ex-satellite countries and in Greece. There are certain points in this statement which call for comment.

6. The Soviet memorandum says that the Governments of the satellite states are faithfully carrying out the obligations assumed by them under their respective instruments of surrender. As regards Bulgaria, this statement cannot be accepted. It will be remembered that at the Plenary Meeting on July 20th Marshal Stalin said that Bulgaria was required to pay reparations, and Russia, together with the other Great Powers, would see to this.[6] This assurance is welcomed. But Bulgaria has not yet paid any reparations to Greece, which has so far received from Bulgaria only a few horses and mules, all in very bad condition. On the same occasion

[6] See No. 208, minute 4.

Marshal Stalin said that now that the German war was over the Bulgarian forces would be demobilised to peacetime strength. This statement is also welcomed, since hitherto there has been no sign of disarmament. We cannot therefore say that Bulgaria has fulfilled the armistice so far, though in view of the Marshal's statement we can be sure they will shortly be obliged to do so.

7. Nor do our reports confirm the statement in the Soviet memorandum that in the case of the satellite states 'due order exists and legal power is acting'. On the contrary according to our recent reports the secret police and militia in Bulgaria are carrying on terrorist activities, and according to reports which we believe to be true between 40,000 and 50,000 persons were murdered by the Bulgarian militia in the past six months. These are quite different from the 2,000 executed after trial as war criminals, and the offence of the great majority was opposition to the present Government and not collaboration with the Germans. We cannot of course be sure that these reports are true, since we have hitherto been denied facilities for seeing conditions in the country for ourselves, but we have every reason for believing that they are not far from the mark. If so it is hardly true to say that the position in Bulgaria compares favourably with the situation in Greece. At least it has not happened in Greece that a Prime Minister and a leader of a democratic party have been obliged, in fear of their lives, to take refuge in foreign Legations.[7]

8. As regards Greece, there is nothing to add to Mr. Eden's statement when the Soviet paper was introduced at the meeting of the Foreign Secretaries on July 20th, and the memorandum by Mr. Churchill circulated to the other Delegations on July 22nd.[8] If the Soviet Government do not believe these reports they should send someone to Greece to see for themselves, and meanwhile refrain from broadcasting to the world these unsupported charges. They can be assured of facilities to see everything they want.

9. The Soviet document refers to the Varkiza Agreement. His Majesty's Government could not agree to the recommendation as drafted, but they would not object to a friendly reminder to the Greek Government to observe the terms of the Agreement, provided that a similar communication should be made by the Conference to the Yugoslav Government on the subject of the Tito-Subasic Agreement. Both Agreements form the basis of the Governments in the countries concerned, and both have been endorsed by His Majesty's Government.

10. The Conference might therefore recommend that these two neighbouring United Nations, whose relations have recently been somewhat disturbed, should endeavour to live in peace in the future. A document for insertion in the protocol[9] might accordingly be prepared on the following lines:

'The Conference expressed the hope that friendly relations might be established and developed between the two neighbouring United Nations, Greece and Yugoslavia, and that these countries, after the many trials of war and of Fascist occupation which they had suffered in common, might now enter a period of prosperous and democratic development on the lines respectively of the Varkiza Agreement and the Tito-Subasic Agreement.'

[7] General N. Radescu, after being compelled under communist pressure to resign from being Roumanian Prime Minister in February 1945, had sought refuge in the British Mission in Bucharest. For the case of Dr. Dimitrov in Bulgaria see No. 351, note 4.

[8] See No. 200, minute 6, and No. 228.

[9] Marginal annotation by Sir A. Cadogan: '+ condemnation of way in which Balkan states are attempting to anticipate the peace settlement.'

No. 430

Minute from Mr. Dixon to Mr. Rowan (Berlin)
[*F.O. 934/5/42(2)*]

27 *July 1945*

Your minute of 23rd July[1] about the return of Soviet citizens against their will to the Soviet Union.

The difficulties about the Prime Minister's proposal are the following:

(1) Under the Crimea Agreement (copy attached)[2] His Majesty's Government are fully pledged to the return to the Soviet Union of undoubted Soviet citizens (i.e. all persons who possess Soviet citizenship by reason of their coming from within the 1939 boundaries of the Soviet Union.) On this point, this agreement repeats the pledge given by my Secretary of State to M. Molotov in October, 1944.[3] We cannot therefore make any proposal involving a claim to retain persons who do not wish to go back to the Soviet Union, without committing a clear breach of the Crimea Agreement and the Secretary of State's undertaking.

(2) The question whether Soviet citizens should be sent back against their will has been very carefully considered on several occasions and although unpleasant consequences often occur to the persons concerned, it has always been decided that we have no option but to send these people back, because

(*a*) if we had not been prepared to do so the Soviet Government would have made even greater difficulties about sending back our own liberated British subjects whether they wanted to come or not;

(*b*) the majority (though not quite all) of the Soviet citizens in question do not want to go back because they have[4] collaborated more or less with the Germans and their claims upon our sympathy are therefore small;

(*c*) we have no means of checking the truth of the stories which these people tell as they change their names and identities with great frequency. The only people who can find out whether they are genuine or not are the Soviet Government;

---

[1] No. 248.

[2] Not attached to filed copy: see No. 44, note 2.

[3] At a meeting at 4.30 p.m. on 16 October 1944 at an Anglo–Soviet Conference in Moscow: '*Mr. Eden* raised the question of the repatriation of Russians in England. . . . *Mr. Molotov* wanted to ask a question in principle. Were H.M.G. agreed of the opinion that all Soviet citizens without exception should be returned to Russia as soon as possible. *Mr. Eden* said: "Yes, and they were already provided with tonnage for them." *Mr. Molotov* said he was interested in this question of principle. So far he had had no reply from the British Government. *Mr. Eden* replied that there was no doubt in his mind. There may have been some doubt or misunderstanding about the Soviet citizens in Egypt, but those in England would come back on transports' (British record: PREM 3/434/7).

[4] The following seven words and some other extracts are cited by N. Tolstoy, *op. cit.*, p. 419; further extracts are cited by Ian Colvin in *The Daily Telegraph* of 18 March 1975, p. 3.

(*d*) if these people are not sent back the problem of their disposal would be very formidable since many of them are extremely undesirable characters.

(3) Almost all the British subjects who were liberated by the Soviet advance have now been recovered by us. Those remaining are nearly all either in hiding or living voluntarily for the time being with Polish or Czech families. An offer, therefore, not to demand the return of any British subjects should they not wish to come would be worth very little, and in fact we have never asked for any British subject to be sent back against his will, and so far as we know there have been no examples of this being necessary.

(4) The Soviet Government would never understand our motives in refusing to send back Soviet citizens who did not wish to return, and they would regard us as harbouring traitors.

In practice a few Soviet citizens who have really good reasons for not wishing to return have probably been allowed to escape, but it is very difficult to do this in the United Kingdom since the Soviet Government know all about the Soviet citizens who are there. It may be possible to arrange for the unobtrusive disappearance of a few genuine recalcitrants but in view of our clear commitments, it is impossible in our view to propose to the Soviet Government that only those Soviet citizens who wish to return should be sent back. They would misunderstand and resent any such proposal very much.

Privately, we very much dislike sending some of these people back, particularly as we know that some of them are executed on arrival, but the decision to do so was most carefully considered and we do not see how we can go back on it now without a serious row with the Soviet Government.[5]

[5] This minute was initialed by Sir A. Cadogan. Mr. Rowan minuted at Berlin to Mr. Dixon on 30 July 1945 (cf. N. Tolstoy, *loc. cit.*): 'Many thanks for your minute dated 27 July about the return of Soviet citizens to the Soviet Union. I agree that there is no need to take any further action in this matter. I return your file herewith but have kept the top copy of your minute. T. L. R. 30.7.45.' This minute was initialed that day by Mr. Dixon and on 31 July by Mr. Dean.

No. 431

Record of Ninth Meeting of Foreign Secretaries held at Cecilienhof, Potsdam, on Friday, 27 July 1945 at 4 p.m.

F. (*Terminal*) 9th Meeting [*U 6197/3628/70*]

Top secret

Present:

M. V. M. MOLOTOV, M. A. Ya. Vyshinski, M. I. M. Maisky, M. A. A. Gromyko, M. F. T. Gousev. M. S. A. Golunski, M. K. V. Novikov, M. B. F. Podtzerob, M. V. N. Pavlov (*Interpreter*).

MR. J. F. BYRNES, Mr. W. A. Harriman, Mr. E. W. Pauley, Mr. J. C. Dunn, Mr. H. F. Matthews, Mr. W. L. Clayton, Mr. C. E. Bohlen, Mr. B. V. Cohen, Mr. E. Page (*Interpreter*).

Sir A. Cadogan, Sir A. Clark Kerr, Sir W. Strang, Mr. N. Brook, Mr. W. Hayter, Major L. M. Theakstone (*Interpreter*).

Contents

Minute	Subject
1.	Outstanding Business
2.	Neutral and ex-Enemy States: Admission to United Nations
3.	Reparations: Germany
4.	Reparations: Austria and Italy
5.	Germany: Economic Problems
6.	Europe: Oil Supplies
7.	Europe: Immediate Economic Problems
8.	Roumania: Removal of Allied Industrial Equipment

1. *Outstanding Business*

MR. BYRNES suggested that the meeting should review the items of business at present outstanding. According to his information these were:

(a) *Germany: Economic Principles*
(Previous Reference: P. (Terminal) 7th Meeting,[1] Minute 3: See also P. (Terminal) 15.)[2]

(b) *Reparations from Germany*
(Previous Reference: P. (Terminal) 7th Meeting,[1] Minute 2: See also P. (Terminal) 41.)[3]

(c) *Reparations from Austria and Italy*
(Previous Reference: P. (Terminal) 8th Meeting,[4] Minute 1; See also P. (Terminal) 41.)[3]

(d) *Europe: Oil Supplies*
(Previous Reference: F. (Terminal) 4th Meeting,[5] Minute 5: See also P. (Terminal) 41.)[3]

(e) *Neutral and Ex-enemy States: Admission to United Nations*
(Previous Reference: P. (Terminal) 8th Meeting,[4] Minute 3: See also P. (Terminal) 35.)[6]

(f) *Balkans: Elections and Facilities for Official and Press Representatives.*
(Previous Reference: P. (Terminal) 6th Meeting,[7] Minute 3 and F. (Terminal) 7th Meeting,[8] Minute 1: See also P. (Terminal) 21 and 34.)[9]

(g) *Interim Arrangements for Italy and the Satellite States*
(Previous Reference: P. (Terminal) 5th Meeting,[10] Minute 6: See also P. (Terminal) 20.)[11]

(h) *Roumania: Removal of Industrial Equipment*
(Previous Reference: P. (Terminal) 8th Meeting,[4] Minute 1: See also P. (Terminal) 40.)[12]

---

[1] No. 241.　　　[2] No. 210.　[3] No. 282.　　　[4] No. 258.
[5] No. 214.　　　[6] No. 260.　[7] No. 226.　　　[8] No. 254.
[9] See No. 219.i, and No. 259.　[10] No. 219.　[11] See No. 214, note 9.　[12] No. 264.

(i) *Western Frontier of Poland*
   (Previous Reference: P. (Terminal) 9th Meeting,[13] Minute 3: See also
   P. (Terminal) 12.)[14]

(j) *Europe: Immediate Economic Problems*
   (Previous Reference: P. (Terminal) 7th Meeting,[1] Minute 7: See also
   P. (Terminal) 42.)[15]

(k) *War Crimes*
   This had been on the original Agenda submitted by the British Delegation (P. (Terminal) 1)[16] but it had not so far been discussed.
M. MOLOTOV suggested, and it was agreed, that this was a matter for
discussion by a Plenary Meeting.

(l) *Transfer of Populations*
   (Previous Reference: F. (Terminal) 8th Meeting,[17] Minute 2.)

(m) *International Inland Waterways*
   (Previous Reference: F. (Terminal) 8th Meeting,[17] Minute 2: See also
   P. (Terminal) 33.)[18]

SIR ALEXANDER CADOGAN suggested a further subject:
(n) *Germany: Political Questions*
   (Previous Reference: P. (Terminal) 3rd Meeting,[19] Minute 3: See also
   P. (Terminal) 39.)[20]

There were two minor points which had originally been included in the
Economic Principles but which the Soviet Delegation had regarded as being
more political than economic in character. The British Delegation had now
proposed P. (Terminal) 39[20] that these might be added to the agreed Statement of Political Principles.
M. MOLOTOV recalled that another outstanding question was:

(o) *The German Fleet and Merchant Navy*
   (Previous Reference: P. (Terminal) 9th Meeting,[13] Minute 1: See also
   P. (Terminal) 9.)[21]

2. *Neutral and Ex-Enemy States: Admission to United Nations*
   (Previous Reference: P. (Terminal) 8th Meeting,[4] Minute 3: see also
   P. (Terminal) 35.)[6]
MR. BYRNES recalled that discussion of this matter had been adjourned
without agreement because, although President Truman had acquiesced in
the draft statement (P. (Terminal) 40 [35][6]) as amended in discussion,
subject to further consideration of the drafting, Mr. Churchill had not been
able to accept it.
SIR ALEXANDER CADOGAN agreed that Mr. Churchill had not been able
to accept the draft as it then stood. In particular, he had felt unable to
accept the suggestion of the Soviet Delegation that the following should be
added to the end of paragraph 3:

[13] No. 271.   [14] No. 202.   [15] No. 283.   [16] No. 171.   [17] No. 274.
[18] No. 246.   [19] No. 194.   [20] No. 263.   [21] See No. 189, note 8.

'The Three Governments agree to consider, each separately, in the immediate future, the question of establishing diplomatic relations with Bulgaria, Finland, Hungary and Roumania.'

Mr. Churchill had explained that it was constitutionally impossible for the British Government to enter into full diplomatic relations with Governments with which they were technically still at war. Sir Alexander Cadogan asked, therefore, whether it would be acceptable to the other Delegations that the sentence proposed by the Soviet Delegation should be amended so as to read:

'The conclusion of peace treaties with responsible democratic Governments in these States will enable the three Governments to establish normal diplomatic relations with them and to support their application for admission to the United Nations.'

M. Molotov said that, so far as he was aware, the only actual amendment to the draft statement put forward by Mr. Churchill was in the first sentence of paragraph 3, where he had suggested that instead of 'preparing peace treaties *with* Bulgaria, Finland, &c. . . .'[22] the sentence should read, 'preparing peace treaties *for* Bulgaria, Finland, &c. . . .'[22] The Soviet Delegation had been prepared to accept this amendment.

Sir Alexander Cadogan agreed that Mr. Churchill had not put forward any other amendment to the text. He had, however, as Mr. Byrnes had pointed out, been unable to accept the Soviet amendment; and the British Delegation was now putting forward a new suggestion, in the hope that agreement might be reached.

Mr. Byrnes recalled the history of this proposal. When President Truman had put forward his original proposal that Italy's application for admission to the United Nations should be publicly supported, he had not expected that it would meet with serious objection. A counter-proposal had, however, been put forward, to include in the statement a reference to neutral countries; then amendments were suggested, and accepted by the United States Delegation, to the terms in which the statement referred to the Italian Government; then it appeared that agreement could not be reached unless the statement also included a reference to other ex-enemy satellite States. The proposal had been discussed at numerous meetings, and no agreement had been reached. That being so, Mr. Byrnes thought it might be wise if the United States Delegation withdrew their original proposal. He thought it more important to avoid continuing disagreement on the matters now under discussion than to secure the issue of a public statement indicating merely what attitude the three Governments would take towards Italy at some future date. There were many important matters, such as the German Fleet and Merchant Navy, Reparations, the Western Frontier of Poland, &c., on which it was vital to get agreement in the few days that remained before the Conference came to an end.

M. Molotov pointed out that a good deal of time had been given up to

[22] Punctuation as in original quotation.

discussing this question which, as Mr. Byrnes had pointed out, had been raised originally by the United Stated Delegation. His impression was that, when it was last discussed at the Plenary Meeting, agreement was not far off, provided a suitable draft could be prepared. Mr. Byrnes's proposal to drop the whole matter should, he thought, be submitted to the Plenary Meeting.

It was agreed that the position should be reported to the next Plenary Meeting.

3. *Reparations: Germany*
(Previous Reference: P. (Terminal) 7th Meeting,[1] Minute 2.)

M. MOLOTOV said that the Soviet Delegation were not satisfied with the course of the discussions on Reparations in the Economic Committee. (See P. (Terminal) 41.)[3]

At the Crimea Conference (paragraph 4 of Protocol on Reparations),[23] the Soviet and United States Delegations had agreed that 'the Moscow Reparation[s] Commission should take in its initial studies as a basis for discussion the suggestion of the Soviet Government that the total sum of reparation (from Germany, in capital goods and current deliveries) . . .[22] should be 20 billion dollars and that 50 per cent. of it should go to the U.S.S.R.' The United Kingdom Delegation had been of opinion that, pending consideration by the Moscow Commission, no figure of reparation should be mentioned. He understood, however, from M. Maisky that the United States representative on the Economic Committee (Mr. Pauley) had now withdrawn his support for the total figure on which the Soviet and United States Delegations had agreed at the Crimea Conference. He asked whether this represented the present view of the United States Government.

MR. BYRNES said that President Roosevelt had not agreed at the Crimea Conference that reparations should be exacted from Germany to the extent of 20 billion dollars. What he had done was to accept that figure as a basis for discussion and detailed study by the Moscow Reparations Commission. All that Mr. Pauley had now said on the Economic Committee was that, as a result of the study which had been given to this matter by the Reparations Commission, he had reached the conclusion that, in the circumstances now existing in Germany, he could not regard it as practicable to exact reparations from Germany up to a total amount of 20 billion dollars.

M. MOLOTOV said that the Soviet Government, in framing their proposals for reparations, had proceeded on the assumption that the United States Government had accepted the basis of a total reparation of 20 billion dollars. It was on this basis that they had put forward their detailed proposals at the present Conference regarding the branches of the German economy from which reparations might be drawn and the dates by which they might be exacted. Now, however, he understood that Mr. Pauley had officially withdrawn his agreement to accept the decision of the Crimea Conference. Was this now the official view of the United States Government?

[23] See No. 30, note 2.

MR. BYRNES said that he was anxious to avoid any misunderstanding on this point. Both the United States Government and their representative, Mr. Pauley, had accepted the figure of 20 billion dollars as a basis for discussion. Mr. Pauley had discussed this problem at Moscow for more than a month on that basis; and for a time discussions had proceeded on the same basis in the Economic Committee at the present Conference. It was as a result of these discussions, and in view of his investigations of conditions as they now existed, that Mr. Pauley had formed the view that it would not in fact be practicable to exact this total of reparation from Germany.

Since the Crimea Conference the position had changed. In the first place, much property in Germany had been destroyed by the Russian Armies and by the United States forces in the course of their military operations. Secondly, the figures discussed at the Crimea Conference had been based on the assumption that reparations would be exacted from Germany as a whole. It was a very different situation if large parts of Germany, including the industrial areas in Silesia, were to be turned over to Poland. Thirdly, important differences had arisen over the definition of 'war booty,' and it had become clear that the Russians, in pursuance of their interpretation of 'war booty', had already seized and removed a large proportion of the plant and equipment in Germany from which reparations might have been payable. Thus, in the United States zone in Berlin, almost all the machinery had been stripped from the plant of the International Telegraph and Telephone Company. Four other plants, one a Rayon plant, and another a Zeiss plant, had also been stripped. It was these considerations which had led Mr. Pauley to the conclusion that it would not be practicable to exact reparations from Germany up to a total of 20 billion dollars.

M. MOLOTOV replied that the Soviet Government were willing to reduce their original claim of 10 billion dollars as the Soviet share of reparations from Germany. Would the United States Delegation suggest an alternative basis of discussion? He understood that they were thinking of an arrangement by which each of the occupying Powers would take reparations from its own zone. If agreement were not reached on a plan extending to Germany as a whole, the Soviet Government would certainly take reparations from their zone of occupation.

MR. BYRNES said that the United States Government sought nothing for themselves by way of reparations. They were, however, entitled to reparations and they asserted their claim because they would have to look after the interests of other Allied countries such as Belgium, Holland and eventually, no doubt, Yugoslavia. 500 million dollars had already been given to Italy, and more would have to be given to France. The United States Government were not, however, removing machinery from Germany, as the Soviet Government were doing. The United States Army had been instructed not to remove industrial equipment, and had not removed any save a small quantity of specialised war production plant which was required for experimental and research purposes. What most impressed him in this matter was that, more important than money or machinery, was the need to remove all potential sources of friction between the Allied Governments. He feared that the reparation plans which had been discussed hitherto would prove a continuing source of friction between the three Great Powers; and for this reason he would be glad if some different basis could be found for dealing with reparations.

M. MOLOTOV said that it must not be forgotten that neither the United States nor Great Britain had been occupied by the German Armies. The Soviet Union and Poland, however, had been invaded and had suffered great losses in human life and in property. They therefore had an indisputable right to claim reparations. He admitted that some plant might have been removed by the Soviet authorities, but it was only a fraction of that which had been destroyed in the Soviet Union during the German occupation. Even if the United States Government and Great Britain did not ask for one dollar in reparation, the Soviet Government would maintain their claim, which was morally justified. The Economic Committee had merely agreed that large reparations must be made by Germany, but M. Molotov declared that this was an empty phrase which did not satisfy the Soviet Delegation.

MR. BYRNES said that the task before the Conference was to find a solution which would be acceptable to everybody. Little progress was being made towards this end, and it seemed to him that the question would have to be submitted to the Plenary Meeting. Alternatively, it might be taken up again at the Foreign Secretaries' Meeting when representatives of the new British Government had arrived at the Conference. Was Sir Alexander Cadogan in a position to indicate the view of the British Delegation?

SIR ALEXANDER CADOGAN said that he could not make any substantial contribution to the discussion at this stage. As he saw it, no one wished to deprive the Soviet Government of their just claims, but agreement had not yet been reached on the methods and definitions by which those claims should be satisfied.

It was agreed that the discussion should be resumed at the meeting of Foreign Secretaries on the following day or on the day after. The result of the discussion should then be reported to the Plenary Meeting.

4. *Reparations: Austria and Italy*
(Previous Reference: P. (Terminal) 8th Meeting,[4] Minute 1.)

M. MOLOTOV said that the Soviet Delegation could not regard as satisfactory the course of the discussions in the Economic Committee on the payment of reparations by Austria and Italy (see P. (Terminal) 41).[3] The Soviet Government considered that Italy [Austria][24] was capable of delivering the equivalent of 250 million dollars over a period of six years. They proposed that this should be distributed between Great Britain, the United States, U.S.S.R. and Yugoslavia. The goods in which this reparation was to be

[24] Cf. *Berlinskaya konferentsiya*, p. 213, also *F.R.U.S. Berlin*, vol. ii, p. 432, in accordance with No. 261 above.

made was a matter for further discussion. Would the other Delegations accept these proposals as a basis for consideration?

Mr. Byrnes said that the United States Delegation were satisfied that it would be unreasonable to hope for any reparations from current production in either Austria or Italy. The Governments of the United States, United Kingdom and Canada had already found it necessary to send goods to Italy to the value of 500 million dollars in order to prevent disease and unrest, and the United States Delegation believed that it would be necessary to provide further relief for Italy up to at least the same amount. The United States Government were unwilling to advance money and goods to any country in order to finance their payment of reparations. The only form of reparations which the United States Delegation were prepared to consider, in the case of Austria or Italy, was the removal of plant and equipment which was used directly for war production and had no peacetime use. Even to this the United States Government laid no claim: they were, however, willing that others should take it by way of reparations.

M. Molotov said that United States territory had not been overrun by Austrian troops. Soviet territory had been invaded by Austrian forces, who had done substantial damage. It was wrong that Austria should escape punishment.

Mr. Byrnes said that he appreciated the sacrifices made by the Soviet Union in the loss of human lives; but for that, no material reparation could compensate them. Loss of property was, however, a different matter. He himself saw no great difference between losing a building worth 100 thousand dollars and spending 100 thousand dollars in the prosecution of the war; and the 400 billion dollars spent by the United States Government in their war effort was a loss of property.

M. Molotov said that the war expenditure of the Soviet Government had also been enormous; but they had suffered devastation over and above that expenditure. Was it right that those who had been responsible for this devastation should go unpunished, without being required to pay even the minimum reparation? Roumania was required to pay reparations, under the terms of surrender which had been signed by the United States Government. Was it right that Austria and Italy should be required to pay nothing?

Mr. Byrnes said that the United States Government looked for no reparations from Roumania. If the principle were adopted that any country was entitled to reparation which had suffered damage from occupation by enemy forces, Greece should be given a claim to compensation from Italy.

M. Molotov said that the Soviet proposals provided for the payment of reparations by Italy to Greece, Albania and Yugoslavia, and it would be for the three Great Powers to decide the extent to which claims from these countries should be met.

Mr. Byrnes made the further point that there was now some question of relief being provided to Austria by U.N.R.R.A., and he understood that no country which was paying reparation would be regarded as eligible for relief from U.N.R.R.A. M. Molotov said that he was not aware of any such provision in the Charter of U.N.R.R.A. MR. BYRNES said that this was a matter of fact which could be ascertained, but it seemed to him that if a country could afford to pay reparations it was not entitled to relief.

SIR ALEXANDER CADOGAN said that the British Delegation shared the views which had been expressed by Mr. Byrnes on behalf of the United States Delegation regarding the extent to which reparation could be exacted from Italy and Austria.

> It was agreed that it should be reported to the Plenary Meeting that the Foreign Secretaries had been unable to agree on the question of reparations from Austria and Italy. While the Soviet Delegation adhered to their view that reparations should be exacted from these countries on the scale suggested in their memoranda (P. (Terminal) 36 and 37),[25] the British and United States Delegations were of the opinion that it would be impracticable to exact any reparation levies on the current production of either of these countries, though they would be prepared to consider the possibility of certain 'once-for-all' removals of machinery and equipment which had been used directly for war production and had no peace-time use.

5. *Germany: Economic Problems*
(Previous Reference: P. (Terminal) 7th Meeting,[1] Minute 3.)

M. MOLOTOV recalled that of the statement annexed to P. (Terminal) 15,[2] only paragraph 18 and the additional paragraph put forward by the Soviet Delegation remained to be considered.

MR. BYRNES said that he was satisfied that no decision could be reached on this issue until the question of reparations had been settled.

> It was agreed that consideration of this matter should be deferred.

6. *Europe: Oil Supplies*
(Previous Reference: F. (Terminal) 4th Meeting,[5] Minute 5.)

Mr. Byrnes said that the Economic Committee (see paragraph 5 of P. (Terminal) 41)[3] were not yet prepared to make a definite report on the proposal put forward by the United States Delegation (P. (Terminal) 18).[26] The Soviet representative had required further information. Unless this was now available the matter could not profitably be discussed at the present meeting.

> It was agreed that this matter should be left over until the Economic Committee was in a position to make a further report.

7. *Europe: Immediate Economic Problems*
(Previous Reference: P. (Terminal) 7th Meeting,[1] Minute 7.)

Mr. Byrnes referred to the memorandum from the Economic Committee (P. (Terminal) 42)[15] reporting that the Soviet Government had agreed to participate in the work of the European Inland Transport Conference, but were considering further whether they could participate in the Emergency

[25] Nos. 261–2.
[26] See No. 214, note 10.

935

Economic Committee for Europe and the European Coal Organisation. Should this information be reported to the Plenary Meeting at once, or should it be held over until the Soviet Government had reached a decision on the two outstanding points?

Sir Alexander Cadogan said that the Soviet decision to participate in the European Inland Transport Conference was most gratifying and should be reported to the Plenary Meeting. The report could add that the Soviet Government were considering whether they could participate in the other two organisations.

It was agreed that a report on this matter should be made to the Plenary Meeting on the lines suggested by Sir Alexander Cadogan.

8. *Roumania: Removal of Industrial Equipment*
(Previous Reference: P. (Terminal) 8th Meeting,[4] Minute 1.)

Sir Alexander Cadogan asked whether the Soviet Delegation had been able to consider the proposals put forward in the latest memorandum by the British Delegation (P. (Terminal) 40).[12]

M. Molotov said that a written reply (subsequently circulated as P. (Terminal) 46)[27] to the suggestion made in this memorandum had been addressed that day to Sir Alexander Cadogan.

Cabinet Office, Potsdam, 27th July, 1945

CALENDARS TO No. 431

i *27 July 1945 U.K. Delegation Minute (Berlin) to Mr. Attlee No. P.M./45/ Terminal 1.* Summary of previous consideration at conference of question of admission to the U.N. of Italy, Spain and Balkan States: question of establishing diplomatic relations with the latter [F.O. 934/5/48(11)].

ii *28 July 1945 U.K. Delegation brief (Berlin)* on economic principles to govern the treatment of Germany in initial control period. Soviet Delegation has rejected principles 18–19 in No. 210. Unless it accepts them, the British Delegation should not agree to the remainder [F.O. 934/1/2(39)].

[27] No. 432.

No. 432

Memorandum by the Soviet Delegation (Berlin)[1]
P. (Terminal) 46 [U 6197/3628/70]

Top secret   27 July 1945
Removal of Allied Industrial Equipment especially in Roumania

In its memorandum of the 24th July (P. (Terminal) 40)[2] the British Delegation once more raises the question of the legitimacy of the removal by the Soviet Command from Roumania of oil equipment by way of war booty.

[1] Printed under date of 25 July 1945 in *Berlinskaya konferentsiya*, pp. 379–80.
[2] No. 264.

The Soviet Government has repeatedly explained its point of view on this question and referred to definite facts proving that the oil equipment under discussion, consisting mainly of pipes, is German military equipment and war booty for the Red Army.

It should be recalled that beginning as long ago as the summer of 1940, the British Oil Companies and enterprises in Roumania were seized by the Germans and used by them up to the 23rd August, 1944, for supplying the German Army with oil products. In aide-mémoires from the People's Commissar for Foreign Affairs of the U.S.S.R. dated the 30th November, 1944, and the 4th January, 1945,[3] full details were already quoted to confirm the above statement nor [*sic*] leaving any doubt that the Allied Control Commission in Roumania had in this matter acted in full accord with Article 7 of the Agreement on the Armistice with Roumania and with Article 2 of the Protocol to this Agreement. There is, therefore, at the present time, no need to expound the Soviet point of view on this question.

As to the suggestion contained in the British Memorandum of the 24th July to instruct a committee, consisting of three persons who are citizens of Allied countries, to investigate the problem as to whether these pipes were British or German property, the Soviet Delegation considers the reference of this problem to a joint examination by Soviet representatives and British representatives in respect of oil equipment and pipes removed from the territory of the enterprises with the participation of British capital to be more useful. The Soviet representatives, together with the British representatives, could examine the facts and documents which could be presented to the British party.

CALENDAR TO No. 432

i *27 July 1945 Letter from Mr. Howard to Mr. Hayter (Berlin)* enclosing Bucharest telegrams Nos. 740 & 743 of 25 July: removal of British oil equipment in Roumania: reactions to discussions in No. 224, minute 4, and No. 254, minute 3. Can only suggest that British Delegation should record strong protest against deliberate attack upon British interests, of which removal of oil equipment is only an example. Sir A. Cadogan minuted on this in Berlin: 'I imagine we shall not reopen this argument here, but shall confine ourselves to the discussion of our proposal for arbitration. A. C. July 28/45.' [F.O. 934/4/28 (7)].

[3] Not printed.

No. 433

Memorandum by United Kingdom Delegation (Berlin)

[F.O. 934/5/48(5)]

[BERLIN,] *27 July 1945*

Posts on Executive Committee and Preparatory Commission[1]

His Majesty's Government in the United Kingdom have been carefully

[1] Of the United Nations. The filed copy of this memorandum was inscribed at head by Mr. Jebb on 27 July 1945: 'Handed to Mr. Dunn and M. Gromyko.'

considering this question and have come to the conclusion that the following solution would be the best one:

A. *Executive Committee*

(i) The chairmanship should rotate among the five Permanent Members of the Security Council. This proposal would avoid the perhaps rather invidious choice of one Great Power as a permanent Chairman and might be more likely on the whole to appeal to the Committee itself. Further, if one permanent Chairman were selected, there might have to be a number of Vice-Chairmen whose precise duties might be rather difficult to determine. In any case, it does not appear that a decision to make the chairmanship rotate need necessarily create a precedent, since it is clearly unlikely that the Security Council, the Economic and Social Council and the Trusteeship Council will select the representative of any one Power as a permanent president.

(ii) The post of Executive Secretary should be allotted to the United Kingdom. This is considered very desirable if not essential, owing to the fact that the Committee will meet in London and that it will be necessary for the Executive Secretary to have many dealings with the British Government Departments on administrative matters.

B. *Preparatory Commission*

It is thought that the chairmanship of this body might suitably be allotted to the representative of some 'middle' Power. If it is necessary to have Vice-Chairmen, these might also be drawn from the ranks of the 'middle' or smaller Powers. The Preparatory Commission will in fact have to approve the work of the Executive Committee and no doubt will in practice have to accept it subject perhaps to minor amendments. Consequently, it would seem that a gesture towards the 'middle' and smaller Powers will be desirable if such acceptance is to be secured with the minimum of delay and friction.

CALENDAR TO NO. 433

i *28 July 1945 Letter from Mr. Jebb to M. Gromyko (Berlin).* Hopes for Soviet agreement to recommendations in No. 433, with which U.S. Delegation is now prepared to agree. Encloses memorandum on suggested working of International Secretariat [F.O. 934/5/48(5)].

No. 434

Mr. Eden to Sir A. Cadogan (Berlin: received 27 July, 7.45 p.m.)
No. 247 Onward Telegraphic [F.O. 800/417/65]

Top secret. Most Immediate   FOREIGN OFFICE, *27 July 1945, 5.29 p.m.*

Following for Cadogan from Bridges.

Mr. Attlee plans to leave Northolt at 13.30 hours B[ritish] S[ummer] T[ime] tomorrow, Saturday, 28th July. His party will include the Foreign

Secretary in the new Government whose appointment, it is expected, will be announced late tonight.

2. This is the earliest hour at which the party can hope to get off and the time of departure may have to be an hour later.

3. It is clear, therefore, that the earliest time at which Mr. Attlee and his colleague would be ready for a meeting would be after dinner on Saturday night.

4. We must leave it to you, in the light of your knowledge of the situation at your end, and of the amount of preliminary consultation with Ministers which will be necessary, to decide whether to fix up a meeting at, say, 21.30 hours Saturday 28th Berlin time, or whether it would be better to have the first meeting on the morning of Sunday, 29th July.

5. Mr. Attlee also leaves it to you to make the necessary communication about the time of his arrival to President Truman and Generalissimo Stalin. It is absolutely necessary for Mr. Attlee to attend a meeting at 11.00 hours on Saturday 28th and he has used his utmost endeavours to return to Potsdam at the earliest possible moment.

6. The detailed particulars of those returning with Mr. Attlee will be communicated in a separate telegram.

No. 435

Sir A. Cadogan (Berlin) to Mr. Eden (Received 27 July, 11.5 p.m.)
No. 255 Target Telegraphic [F.O. 934/2/8(13)]

Top secret   BERLIN, *27 July 1945, 9 p.m.*

Following for Bridges from Brook.

1. We have toiled all day and caught nothing.

2. The Russians began by asking that the meeting of Foreign Secretaries should be postponed from 11 a.m. to 4 p.m. When we did meet[1] they proposed for discussion subjects on which it was clear at the outset that no decision could be reached in the absence of British Ministers. Thus we discussed the admission of neutral and ex-enemy States to the United Nations, reparations from Germany, reparations from Austria and Italy; and all we decided was to put it on record that the Foreign Secretaries could not reach agreement and must report the position to the Plenary Meeting.

3. After the meeting at 4 p.m. the Russians reluctantly agreed to have a further meeting of the Committee on the Protocol. Dunn handed in the drafts which the United States Delegation had prepared and we produced our one outstanding draft on the Straits. The Russians then said that they were not ready to produce any of their drafts, nor were they ready to

---

[1] See No. 431.

comment on the others. They asked for time to finish their work and study ours. Dunn and I stressed the need for making progress, and the Russians said they would do their best to let us have their drafts and comments in time for another meeting after the Plenary tomorrow, Saturday.

4. I am sorry that we cannot report better progress. It is pretty clear, however, that the Russians are stalling until British Ministers return. I doubt whether we shall be able to make any further headway tomorrow until the Prime Minister arrives.

No. 436

Letter from Mr. Allen (Berlin) to Mr. Warner (Received 28 July)
[*C 4402/4216/18*]

Confidential   BRITISH DELEGATION, BERLIN, *27 July 1945*

Dear Christopher,

Copies have gone to you of a minute by Clark Kerr of the 26th July addressed to the Foreign Secretary[1] and covering a long record[2] of a conversation with Mikolajczyk. You will have seen that in his covering minute Clark Kerr suggests that we should be wise to be as fluid as possible in our attitude towards the Polish claims to the Oder-Neisse frontier. We had in fact already been reconsidering this whole question in the light of our various conversations with the Polish Delegation. As a result John Coulson and I have now produced a joint paper, of which a copy is enclosed, suggesting a possible basis upon which a compromise agreement might still be reached here. This paper has been approved by Cadogan as the basis for discussion with General Weeks of the Control Commission and with the American Delegation.[3] If they are receptive, we shall submit

[1] No. 277.

[2] Nos. 269–270.

[3] A covering minute of 27 July 1945 by Mr. Coulson in Berlin read as follows: 'The attached memorandum has been prepared in an attempt to find a way round the economic difficulties inherent in a settlement of the Polish western frontier. It has not yet been discussed with the British Element of the Control Commission. But if the latter think the proposals worth pursuing, we intend to sound the Americans out on it. They have taken a strong line against any concessions to the Poles on the frontier question and we could not circulate a paper of this kind, which represents a compromise, without explaining our intentions to them fully in advance and endeavouring to reach agreement with them.' On 28 July copies of Mr. Coulson's minute and of the enclosure below were passed by the Foreign Office to No. 10 Downing Street, whence Mr. P. F. R. Beards, Private Secretary to Mr. Attlee, wrote that evening to Mr. Frank Giles, Private Secretary to Mr. Bevin, 'I am not quite clear whether you wish this document to be sent out to the Prime Minister at Terminal. If so, I think it should go out in tonight's box, which closes here at 11 p.m.' Mr. Beards' letter was opened at 11.10 a.m. on 29 July by Miss B. Evans, a clerical officer in the Foreign Office, and forwarded with enclosure to the British Delegation at Potsdam. There Mr. Coulson noted: '(I think it is too late to submit this) J. E. C. 29/8' [*sic*].

recommendations on these lines to our new masters, whoever they may be, as soon as they arrive here. As regards the other points mentioned in Clark Kerr's minute, we are, as you know, pursuing with the Russians here the question of clearance for flights over the Soviet zone for a British air service to Warsaw. We are not, however, doing anything about the question of an early trade agreement with the Poles or the proposal for a British newspaper in Warsaw. You will, no doubt, be pursuing these at your end as well as the other questions, such as the return of the Polish Armed Forces and merchant marine, about which Mikolajczyk has expressed anxiety.[4]

Yours ever,
DENIS

P.S.   Michael Winch, who is now at last hoping to get off to Warsaw, is taking a copy of this with him.

ENCLOSURE IN No. 436

Polish Western Frontier and Supplies From Transferred German Territory

1. The main outstanding economic point on which a solution is urgently required at this Conference is how to obtain for Germany her normal supplies of coal from Silesia and food from East Prussia and give the Allied Control Council a basis on which to plan German economy. Unless we get this coal, Ruhr coal will have to provide practically all German hard-coal requirements and none will be left for export. Unless we get the food, we shall have to increase imports into Germany at the expense of ourselves and liberated countries. The chief difficulties to overcome are:

(a) the Poles are in actual possession of the territory and the Russians have washed their hands of it;

(b) if we arrange for the Poles to be paid for any supplies sent to Germany, we abandon the position we have hitherto taken that all pre-1937 Germany must be subject to reparation; if on the other hand we ask for these supplies to be handed over free of charge, the territory will be little use to Poland and she will not agree.

2. We have no exact information about production in the disputed territory. As regards coal, the Poles tell us that production must be something like 50% of normal, i.e. at the rate of about seventeen million tons a year. If this is so, even if the Poles made available five millions to the common pool in Germany, they would still have twelve million tons for their own use or for export, in addition to production in old Poland which in June had already reached 2,400,000 tons a month. As regards food, the Poles say that two million hectares have been sown with grain. If they are lucky their supplies will just meet requirements; if they are unlucky, there may be a deficit in the territory. Thus we shall have no certainty that there is really an exportable surplus from this area and we cannot therefore ask for a fixed amount to be handed over. The Poles say that they have no shortage of labour either in the mines or in the fields.

3. The United States Delegation have ventilated the idea that the Russians

---

[4] Mr. Warner wrote in the margin of the last two sentences: 'Noted.'

should get all their once-for-all reparation deliveries out of their own zone. If they want capital equipment from the Western zone, they must pay for it by deliveries of coal and food from the East. The Russians have not, however, accepted this proposal and will not accept it unless much qualified. We cannot rely on getting agreement; in any case barter arrangements on these lines would be cumbersome and would neither fit conveniently into a reparation policy [n]or a system of normal trading. Moreover, they will necessarily take time, whereas the problem of food and fuel is urgent. Meanwhile a temporary settlement of the Polish frontier may be reached and it seems preferable to take the opportunity of this to conclude a definite arrangement which will guarantee, so far as this is possible, that the Allied Control Council will get the supplies they need.

4. The conversations with the Polish delegation have shown that the Poles will be content with nothing less than their full territorial claims and that they have wholehearted Russian support for them. There is considerable substance in the arguments which they adduce to show that the area up to the Oder and the Western Neisse must be treated as a whole and that Poland must have control of the entire Oder-Neisse river system if the possession of Upper Silesia is to be of fullest advantage. M. Mikolajczyk argues strongly that the early settlement of the Western frontier question is an indispensable condition of the development of free political life in Poland: only when the Poles know where they are, he says, in regard to the western territories, will the Polish Provisional Government be able to arrange the orderly return of the Poles abroad, to secure the full withdrawal of the Soviet armies and the cessation of Russian political interference, and to hold free elections. The Poles have clearly done little more than begin the vast task of administering and settling the new territories but all their planning is being based upon the confident assumption that they will be able to absorb them. It is evident that the difficult problem of the transfer of German populations has to some extent solved itself already by the departure of a considerable proportion of the Germans, who are unlikely to be allowed back, and the new settlers will have to be brought in to occupy the country.

5. We are therefore faced with a situation of fact which we shall in practice have no chance of altering. Neither the Russians nor the Poles are at all likely to heed our warnings that it is contrary to Poland's long term interests to push so far west. They will argue with some justice that these lands have for practical purposes already ceased to be German, that Germany will feel a sense of grievance anyway, whether she is deprived of Stettin or only of Danzig and East Prussia, that so long as the Allies are strong and Germany weak she will be unable effectively to exploit her grievance and that to deprive her of her Eastern territories will contribute to her permanent weakening. It is therefore for consideration whether we should gain anything by continuing, now that our warnings and doubts have been placed on record, to withhold our acquiescence in a situation which we shall have to recognise sooner or later. If we maintain our present position we shall stand little chance of striking a bargain with the Russians such as will bring us alleviation of our practical supply difficulties in Germany. Nor will any half-way measure, such as agreeing to the transfer to Polish administration of Upper Silesia only, help us in this respect. Only if we indicate now our readiness to fall in with Polish ideas, shall we be in a position to demand a price for our acquiescence. The longer we wait the less chance we shall stand of getting anything in return. Moreover a long period of delay during which we refuse to recognise the fact of Polish occupation and administration of the areas can only lead to

numerous legal embarrassments and difficulties (compare the position in the Baltic States).

6. A possible basis for a bargain might be found on the following lines. It would be confirmed that, as agreed at the Crimea, the eventual delimitation of the Polish-German frontier should await the final territorial settlement in this part of Europe. Meanwhile, however, it would be understood that in practice the Polish Provisional Government would be permitted to assume full political authority (but not sovereignty) over all the territories east of the line which they claim and be allowed full freedom to administer these territories under Polish law. In return the following conditions must be agreed upon among the three great Powers and accepted by the Poles:–

(i) Until such time as agreement to the contrary has been reached among all the four Powers represented on the Allied Control Council in Germany, all the territory of Germany as it existed on the 31st December 1937 shall continue to be subject to the supreme authority of the Allied Control Council and the Polish authorities administering areas within that territory shall be deemed to be doing so as agents for the Commander-in-Chief of the Soviet zone.

(ii) While it is agreed in principle that all Germans should in due course be transferred from the lands eventually ceded to Poland, none shall be evicted pending such cession without the agreement of the Allied Control Council.

(iii) The Control Council shall be entitled to call upon the Polish Provisional Government to provide up to five million tons of coal yearly, free of cost: this should be used to meet the needs of Greater Berlin, any balance being available to the Control Council for use in Germany as they may direct.

(iv) The Control Council may call upon the Poles to deliver to them all foodstuffs in the former German territory handed over to them which are surplus to that area's requirements, delivery of up to one million dollars being free of charge.

(v) Any balance of coal and foodstuffs handed over beyond the figures mentioned in (iii) and (iv) above to be paid for as soon as possible out of the proceeds of German exports.

7. An arrangement on these lines is not strictly logical. If we maintain that this territory is still under the jurisdiction of the Control Council, then no payment should be made to the Poles and all the proceeds of the territory, if exported outside Germany, should be available to Germany either to pay for imports or for reparation. If, on the other hand, the territory is regarded as Polish, then the Poles should be paid for all exports from it, whether to Germany or to any other country. The arrangement proposed, therefore, is by way of being a compromise. It recognises Poland's *de facto* position and places it upon a basis of inter-governmental agreement, it provides that Poland should, as it were, pay a rent for the territory she is provisionally occupying, and it means in fact that this territory will only to a limited extent be called upon to make reparation payments.[5]

British Delegation, 27th July, 1945

[5] Mr. Warner and Mr. O'Neill minuted in the Foreign Office on this memorandum: '[To] Mr. Troutbeck. I like this paper. One point occurs to me; in regard to (1) [para. 6] on penultimate page. Wd. it be feasible that Poles shd. be regarded as agents of the Allied Control Council instead of as agents of Soviet C-in-C? M. Mikolajczyk has said that in fact everything west of the old German frontier is entirely run by the Russians & it wd. be a help, if feasible, to loosen their hold. C. F. A. Warner 28/7.' '(Mr. Troutbeck is away today.) If we feel obliged to abandon our resistance to the Oder–Neisse line—no discussion of this

943

here is much use at the moment, but I hope we shall not—then I agree that this compromise proposal is about as good as we could get. I don't think it would help to regard the Poles as agents of the Control Council rather than of the Soviet C-in-C. This might give them a right of representation on the Control Council, ['Surely not. C. F. A. W.'] which we don't want. Moreover the whole of our case rests on the argument that the areas in question are part of the Soviet-occupied zone of Germany. We should be flying in the face of our occupation agreement if we proposed that they should be regarded as part of Germany but not part of the Soviet zone. If the Russians ever admit the authority of any agency in Germany over these areas, then surely it would be that of their own C-in-C, not that of the Control Council, which could exercise authority not directly but only through him. Finally, would it make much difference in practice? C. O'Neill 30.7.' Mr. Warner noted marginally against the first clause of the penultimate sentence: 'I am not sure: they have *refused* to admit his responsibility for the Polish admin.n of the Polish occupied area. C. F. A. W. 31/7'; and after the last sentence: 'I think it very likely wd. I cannot assess the importance of the other difficulties you raise: but I think politically it wd. undoubtedly pay us to have the Polish admin.n formally independent of the Soviet authorities & direct under the Allied Control Council. C. F. A. W. 31/7.'

No. 437

Record by Sir A. Cadogan (Berlin) of a conversation with Mr. Byrnes
[F.O. 934/2/8(20)]

[BERLIN], *27 July 1945*

I called on Mr. Byrnes this evening to inform him of Mr. Attlee's plans and I have reported in a telegram[1] to London the result of our discussion on that point.

Mr. Byrnes took the opportunity to indicate to me in outline the way in which he saw the possibility of a solution of the major questions still awaiting solution by the Conference.

On the one hand there was the reparation question, and in this matter he was inclined to favour an arrangement whereby the Russians would take what they required from their Zone of Occupation and should be allowed to have, say, one and a half billion dollars worth of material and equipment from the Western Zones. In exchange for this they would have to promise the supply of an equivalent value in coal and foodstuffs from German territory under their control. Obviously this amount would not be forthcoming at once and delivery would have to be spread over, say, five or six years, subject to an express written agreement on the point.[2]

On the other hand, we should have to agree to the immediate transfer to Polish administration of all the territory up to the Oder, including Stettin and the *Eastern* Neisse. Mr. Byrnes showed me a draft on this point, of which he did not give me a copy, in which it was stated that the final definitive

[1] No. 438.
[2] For a discussion on German reparation and other subjects between Mr. Byrnes and M. Molotov at a meeting at 6 p.m. that day see *F.R.U.S. Berlin*, vol. ii, pp. 449–52, and *Berlinskaya konferentsiya*, pp. 218–222.

allocation of this territory to Poland must await the peace settlement, but that Polish administration could be set up in it forthwith. I asked him whether, in his view, this would enable the Poles to hold elections in this territory as that was the Poles insistent demand. Mr. Byrnes was not very clear on this point, but eventually indicated that he thought this could be arranged.

The two above solutions would, of course, be inter-dependent and the transfer of the administration of the territory indicated to the Polish Government would be dependent on the firm agreement by the Soviet Government to supply over a number of years the requisite quantities of coal and food-stuffs.

A. C.

No. 438

Sir A. Cadogan (Berlin) to Mr. Eden (Received 28 July, 12.20 a.m.)
No. 261 Target Telegraphic [F.O. 800/417/66]

Top secret. Most Immediate   BERLIN, *28 July 1945, 2.1 a.m.*

Following for Bridges from Cadogan.

Your telegram Onward No. 247.[1]

I have informed Mr. Byrnes and M. Molotov of Mr. Attlee's plans.

I myself should have thought that not much time would be gained by meeting tomorrow night[2] and that the time might be more profitably spent in discussion within the Delegation. But Mr. Byrnes told me President was becoming impatient and had hoped it might be possible for him to leave as early as Sunday night.[3] He consulted the President, who said he would be prepared to sit as late as necessary tomorrow night.

I then saw M. Molotov and informed him of what Mr. Byrnes had told me. He too thought it would be desirable, if possible, to meet tomorrow night, and Russians of course do not mind how late they sit. I left it therefore that Mr. Attlee would aim at a meeting tomorrow night, but that it would depend on his departure not being seriously delayed, and on his having time to prepare for the meeting on his arrival here.

[1] No. 434.
[2] This telegram was drafted on 27 July 1945.
[3] 29 July.

No. 439

Sir A. Cadogan (Berlin) to Mr. Eden (Received 28 July, 12.30 a.m.)
No. 259 Target Telegraphic [F.O. 934/2/8(10)]

Most Immediate. Top secret   BERLIN, *28 July 1945, 12.30 a.m.*

Following from Cadogan for Dixon.

Your telegram Onward No. 243.[1]

Our views are as follows.

2. Your paragraph 4(a). Agreement has been reached on the following points:

(a) Council of Foreign Ministers.
(b) Germany, political principles (subject to two minor additions).
(c) Germany, economic principles (with certain major exceptions).
(d) Poland.
(e) Tangier.
(f) Persia.
(g) Western frontiers of U.S.S.R. (Königsberg).
(h) Territorial Trusteeship (Italian Colonies).
(i) Co-operation in solving immediate economic problems in Europe (Soviet membership of European Inland Transport Organisation, European Coal Organisation, European Emergency Economic Committee).

3. The Russians have withdrawn their proposal about Syria and the Lebanon and we do not expect them to revive it.

4. The discussions on Turkey have come to an inconclusive end, (see telegram Target No. 229).[2]

5. Your paragraph 4(b). We think an attempt should be made to reach agreement on the following subjects at Terminal:

(a) Germany, economic principles (points still outstanding).
(b) Reparations.
(c) Polish Western Frontier.
(d) Yugoslavia (reminder to the Yugoslav Government about Tito-Subasic Agreement).
(e) United Nations Organisation (admission of Italy and other States and exclusion of Spain).
(f) Roumania (removal of oil equipment by the Red Army).
(g) Reparations from Austria and Italy.
(h) Transfer of German populations from Poland and Czechoslovakia.
(i) Balkans (elections; facilities for press representatives; position of British and American representatives on Control Commissions).
(j) International Waterways.
(k) European Oil Supplies.

6. Of the above (f) (i) (j) and (k) might if necessary be left to be dealt with at the Foreign Ministers' Conference in September.

7. Your paragraph 4(c). We think we should be able to resist any attempt by the Russians to reopen questions already settled by the Conference. But there are a number of questions on which the Russians wish to see agreement and which are still open. The most important of these are:

Spain (this is covered by the proposed Resolution on the exclusion of Spain from the World Organisation).

[1] No. 428.　[2] No. 400.

German Fleet and Merchant Navy.

8. We have sent home by bag tonight in envelope addressed to you, briefs on the following subjects[3]:

Polish Internal Questions.

Polish Western Frontier.

Admission of certain State[s] to the World Organisation and exclusion of Italy.

Balkan Questions (written before receipt of Onward 242.[4] You will no doubt be briefing the Prime Minister on the lines of the latter but you may wish to show him our brief which indicates the stage reached here on Balkan questions).

[3] Cf. Nos. 277, 436 enclosure, 431.i and 429.
[4] No. 531.

No. 440

Note by Sir A. Cadogan (Berlin)
[F.O. 934/2/8(19)]

[BERLIN,] 28 July 1945[1]

The main outstanding problems of the Conference are:–

(1) Reparations from Germany

(2) Economic Treatment of Germany as a whole

(3) Polish Western Frontier.

These are all tied up together. (There are a number of minor questions that might be settled without great difficulty if we could solve these central problems).

1. Mr. Byrnes has outlined a comprehensive solution as follows:

(1) It is agreed that Russia (including Poland) is entitled to 50% of German reparation. Approximately half the national wealth of Germany is situated in the Russian Zone. The Russians are in process of stripping this Zone. They will strip it much more completely than we shall strip ours. Let us therefore deem that Russia, by this process, is practically satisfying her claim. But Russia has great need of machinery from the Western Zones, particularly the Ruhr. Let us allow her a fixed proportion of the machinery which we decide to remove from the Western Zone, but let us agree to do so only in return for Russia agreeing to furnish coal and food to Berlin and the other parts of Germany normally dependent on such supplies from the Russian (and Polish) administered areas. After the Conference there will have to be a detailed and specific agreement fixing the amount of coal and food and the period over which it is to be supplied.

[1] A copy of this note was evidently given to Mr. Attlee and Mr. Bevin upon their arrival at Potsdam that evening (cf. Sir L. Woodward, *op. cit.*, vol. v, p. 428.)

Our condition will be fulfilled only when this detailed agreement has been concluded by Russia.

(2) Tell Russia that if she agrees to the above we will agree to an area of Germany being here and now handed over to Polish administration. (This may involve the definitive allocation of such an area to Poland later on).

A settlement on these lines was discussed in London with Sir John Anderson who said he would recommend it to his successors, provided that the British Control Commission agree. The British Control Commission agreed, provided that the offer is made in the form outlined above and not in the form of offering to exchange machinery from the Ruhr for supplies from the Russian (and Polish) administered areas, which would be an illogical way of putting the case so long as we are aiming at treating Germany as a single economic unit. The offer involves recognising the transfer to Poland of certain areas of Germany. (I do not at the moment go into the question of what, exactly, these areas would be). In regard to this point, it is true that we have hitherto maintained that all territorial transfers must await the Peace Settlement and if we depart from this principle in one case, we may be embarrassed in maintaining it in others. But the 'Peace Settlement' must be getting nearer anyhow and must we not make up our minds that the time is very near (perhaps the Foreign Ministers meeting in September) when we shall have to grasp this nettle? The Soviet Delegation have said that they can only accept a plan such as that outlined by Mr. Byrnes if they can obtain, as reparation, machinery from the Ruhr. As the Ruhr is in the British Zone, the Americans consider that the ball is in our court. So far as we can ascertain, the American Delegation would be in agreement with us if we made a statement on the lines of the attached draft.

2. As a background to all this, it may be explained that up till recently we and the Americans have been strongly in favour of treating Germany as a single economic unit. The Russians have also accepted this as an abstract principle. General Eisenhower and Field Marshal Montgomery feel that we should make a genuine effort to go on with this principle. Others in the American Delegation have been greatly impressed by seeing how thoroughly the Russians have stripped Berlin and think it unrealistic to suppose that it will be possible, in fact, to treat all four Zones as a single economic unit.

ANNEX TO NO. 440

Draft Statement to be made by the Prime Minister
about reparation

1. The United States Delegation have pointed out that approximately 50% of Germany's natural wealth is in the territory for the occupation of which the Soviet Government is responsible. They therefore suggest that the claims of the Soviet Government and of Poland for reparation should be satisfied by the deliveries and removals which the Soviet Government have effected, or are in a position to effect, from what is within their Zone of Occupation. The Soviet

Delegation stated that they can consider the American Delegation's proposal only if Russia obtains industrial plant and equipment from the Ruhr. H.M. Government consider that for a number of reasons the claims of the Soviet Government and Poland would be fully met by what lies within the Russian Zone. Nevertheless, as part of a settlement covering this and other matters, H.M. Government are ready to agree that Russia should also be entitled to receive from the Western Zones, and particularly from the Ruhr, 10% of such equipment, particularly from the heavy metal industries, as it is decided to remove. H.M. Government know that it is a matter of urgent importance to the Soviet Government to obtain plant and equipment of this kind, particularly from the Ruhr, for the reconstruction of Russian industry on which such grave losses have been inflicted by the enemy.

2. H.M. Government are glad to meet the wishes of the Soviet Government in this way as part of a comprehensive settlement under which the Soviet Government would also agree to meet the wishes of the British and American Governments on another matter. In the past the Greater Berlin Area has obtained very substantial supplies of food, coal and fuel from territory now occupied by Russia, including territory which is being administered by Poland.

There are at present approximately 2 million people in the Zones of the Greater Berlin Area occupied by the American, British and French Governments. These people cannot be left to starve or be deprived of all coal. In the past they have obtained supplies of food and fuel from the Eastern territory of Germany as it existed in 1937. The American and British Governments cannot agree that in future, instead of being supplied from these sources, food should be supplied from Northern America and coal should be supplied from the West to the detriment of the nations of Western Europe where a calamitous shortage of coal at present exists. The principle must therefore be accepted that the Soviet Government will make itself responsible for supplying food, coal and other fuel to the Western Zones and in particular to the whole of the Greater Berlin Area from Eastern Germany, including the territory now administered by Poland. It will be for the Control Council to agree upon the detailed arrangements. What we require is an agreement signed by all four Governments specifying the amounts of named commodities to be delivered over an agreed period of years.

3. The Reparation Plan must provide that payment for necessary imports and for the needs of the occupying forces will form a first charge on all exports from Germany. But H.M. Government will agree, so far as they are concerned, that this 'first charge' should not apply to once-for-all deliveries in which the Soviet Government are primarily interested.

4. The French Government should be represented on the Allied Commission on Reparations at an early date.

5. The Governments entitled to reparation should be invited as soon as possible to submit data to the Allied Commission on Reparations under the procedure which that Commission propose. It should be made clear that the Plan for Reparation and the shares in reparation of all the Governments entitled to reparation which are not represented at the present Conference will be a matter for settlement by common agreement between all the Governments entitled to reparation.

6. The other main outstanding problem before the Conference is that of the Polish Western Frontier. This is a matter which must be finally settled at the Peace Conference. If, however a satisfactory agreement is concluded in regard to the

949

Western Zones and the whole of the area of Greater Berlin obtaining supplies from the Russian Zone of Occupation, H.M. Government would be ready to recognise the arrangement made by the Soviet Government that certain areas of Germany within the agreed Russian Zone of Occupation should be administered by the provisional Government of Poland and would at the Peace Conference give their support to the Polish claim to such territory.

28th July, 1945

CALENDARS TO No. 440

i   *28 & 30 July 1945   Letters from Sir D. Waley (Berlin) to Sir W. Eady (H.M. Treasury) with enclosures, from Mr. Playfair to Mr. Hall-Patch:* report conversations on 27 July on treatment of Germany as an economic unit with (*a*) Generals Weeks and Robertson and Mr. S. P. Chambers, Chief of Finance Division, Control Commission for Germany (British Element), (*b*) Mr. Pauley and others who thought treatment of Germany as economic unit unrealistic but that Generals Eisenhower and Clay agreed with F.M. Montgomery and General Weeks that genuine effort to achieve it should be made [T 236/264: OF 213/3/2e; PREM 8/48; UE 3381/624/77].

ii   *28 July 1945   Letter from Sir D. Waley to M. Maisky (Berlin).* Comments on, and proposes amendment to, American proposal on reparations (cf. Nos. 252 & 427) [T 236/264: OF 213/3/2e].

No. 441

Minute from Mr. Hoyer Millar to Sir A. Cadogan (Berlin)
[*ZM 4085/1/22*]

[BERLIN,] 28 July 1945

During the last day or two I have had two long conversations on the subject of Italy with Mr. Dunn, Mr. Mat[t]hews and Mr. Cannon of the United States Delegation. The first conversation was on the subject of the general policy of our two Governments towards Italy; the second conversation dealt only with the terms of the proposed Italian Peace Treaty.

I attach below records of the two conversations [i]. I have already sent copies of these records to the Foreign Office and I hardly think it is worth your while looking at them in any detail. Shortly, the position is as follows:

The Americans are in entire agreement with us as to the general policy which our two Governments should follow towards Italy—i.e. of trying to build Italy up into a respectable member of European society; of persuading her to look to the West rather than to the East, and of encouraging her to stand more and more on her own feet.

The Americans are also in general agreement with us as to the way in which this policy should be implemented by our two Governments in the near future. They agree that a very early Peace Treaty is desirable; that our two Governments should press the Italians to hold elections before the end of the year; that, from the political point of view, it would be very useful if

Anglo–American troops could remain on in Italy until after the elections; that steps must be taken to help the Italians equip and maintain reasonably strong armed forces and that the possibility of the United States playing their part in this in spite of Lend-Lease difficulties should be explored in Washington; that some kind of Anglo-American military mission will probably be necessary; that both our Governments should step up our propaganda in Italy; that UNRRA should be encouraged to take over supply responsibilities in Italy as soon as practicable; that the other economic functions of the Allied Commission should be transferred to some kind of Anglo-American advisory body consisting of high-powered British and American economic advisers attached to their respective Embassies; that the remaining activities of the Allied Commission should be transferred to the Italians as soon as practicable; that Italy should be given as much help in the economic sphere as possible, especially as regards coal; and that although it is desirable to do away with the Allied Advisory Council, it would be unwise to take any steps in this direction at this moment.

The only points where we and the Americans did not see eye to eye concerned (*a*) the Police Mission. The Americans doubted the necessity for any such Mission and were clearly most disinclined to contemplate an American Mission. It was agreed that consideration of this question could be deferred for some months; (*b*) the Institutional Question. Sir Noel Charles and the Allied Commission for Italy feel strongly that we shall get a much fairer solution of the monarchy question if this is decided by plebiscite rather than by a Constituent Assembly and they have been urging that we and the Americans should take some active steps to induce the Italian Government to declare that the monarchy question should be settled by a plebiscite. We in the Foreign Office have always felt rather nervous about this and have thought that it savoured too much of intervention in Italian internal affairs. The Americans feel even more strongly than we do, and made it clear that they felt that the Italians ought to be left to settle this question themselves. They are not likely to go further than agree that if the Italian Government should spontaneously consult the British and American Ambassadors, the latter could suggest to them the desirability of a Constituent Assembly, referring part or all of its recommendations to a plebiscite for eventual endorsement.

As regards the Peace Treaty, the Americans seemed in general agreement with our proposals concerning the territorial provisions. They seemed quite to agree that all Italian colonies should be removed from her and put under trusteeship and they like our idea of letting Italy administer Tripolitania under the trusteeship system. Their views about Venezia Giulia were not very different from ours though they favour the 'Wilson' line[1] rather than the existing 'Morgan' line as the line of division; and as

[1] As proposed by President Wilson in a memorandum communicated to the Italian Delegation in Paris on 27 October 1919, printed in *D.B.F.P.* First Series, vol. iv, No. 121, enclosure 1. This line and the Morgan Line (see No. 3, note 8) are shown on the British map facing p. 252 in *F.R.U.S. 1945*, vol. ii.

regards Bolzano, they contemplate giving part of it back to Austria, whereas we were more inclined to leave it to Italy.

As regards the military clauses of the Treaty the Americans obviously had not made much progress on this subject in Washington. However, they seemed to think our proposals quite reasonable and the only point to which they appeared to take exception was the idea of permanently demilitarising Sicily and Sardinia.[2]

F. R. HOYER MILLAR

CALENDARS TO NO. 441

i *27–8 July 1945 Letters from Mr. Hoyer Millar (Berlin) to Mr. Harvey* transmitting records of his conversations with U.S. Delegation [ZM 4085/1/22; F.O. 934/2/6(25)].

ii *28 July 1945 Minute by Mr. Hoyer Millar;* developments in regard to P. (Terminal) 20: No. 214, note 9 [F.O. 934/2/6(30)].

[2] Sir A. Cadogan minuted on this: 'We and the Americans seem to be pretty well in line. A. C. July 29, 1945.'

No. 442

Brief by United Kingdom Delegation[1]
[*F.O. 934/1/5(12)*]

[BERLIN,] *28 July 1945*

War Crimes

This matter was placed on the Agenda by the British Delegation in order that any matters still outstanding might if necessary be settled by the Conference. For the last six weeks discussions have been going on in London between British, Soviet, United States and French representatives with a view to the establishment of an International Military Tribunal in Germany to try the principal Nazi leaders and organisations for their part in planning and organising the war and carrying it on in defiance of the rules of war. The present state of the discussions is briefly shown in the annex to this brief.

In the absence of the French, and since the four representatives in London have not agreed that the matter should be discussed in detail at this Conference, it does not seem possible to try and settle the outstanding points here.[2] We could, therefore, simply state that we placed the matter on the Agenda so that any outstanding points could, if necessary be discussed and settled, but that the detailed questions still under discussion in London are hardly

[1] This brief was submitted by Mr. Dean under a covering minute of even date, largely treating the same points, to Sir A. Cadogan.

[2] In his covering minute Mr. Dean added: 'Also we are not fully informed of the latest position since some of the latest conversations in London took place between the heads of delegations only and the head of the British delegation was the Attorney General in the last Government.'

suitable for further discussion here. We therefore wish to withdraw the matter unless any other Delegation wishes to raise any question in connexion with it.

It would be a pity, however, to take this course if it could be avoided, since it might arouse Soviet suspicions that we are not in earnest about these trials (which is the contrary of the fact) and public opinion in them [*sic*] is so great[3] that a statement however general would be very valuable. It is therefore suggested that we should attempt to obtain the agreement of the United States and Soviet Delegations to a statement on the lines of the attached draft proposal[4] for insertion in the Protocol and Communiqué. Such a statement taking note of the recent discussions, reaffirming the intention of the Big Three to prosecute and punish those major war criminals and expressing the hope that the trials will begin as soon as possible might be very useful in speeding up the preliminary arrangements and would also have a good effect on public opinion at home and abroad.

The Americans are likely to agree with the proposed draft paragraph.[5]

ANNEX TO NO. 442

The position about *minor war criminals* is reasonably satisfactory. The intention is that they should be dealt with by the authorities of the state whose nationals they have wronged or at the scene of their crimes and this intention is in fact being carried out.

The question of dealing with *major war criminals* has been under discussion in London between British, United States, Soviet and French representatives. The British representative has been the Attorney General, and he has had a team of officials and others working with him. These discussions have led to substantial agreement being reached on a draft agreement and charter for the establishment of a Four Power Military Tribunal in Germany, but three questions are still unsettled. These are:–

(1) *Article 6 of the Charter*. This contains a definition of the charges to be brought. By definition these acts will amount to criminal violations of international law. We and the Americans have prepared a most careful draft which is sound in law, but the French and Soviet representatives find it difficult to reconcile it with certain theories of Continental law and desire to widen it. It is most important that this Article should be properly drafted both from the point of view of the trials themselves and of the view which posterity will take of it.

(2) *Article 15 (i)(b), and last sub-paragraph*. This raises the difficult question

---

[3] A corresponding passage in the covering minute read 'public opinion is extremely interested in these trials'.

[4] This draft statement, not here printed, was the same as the second paragraph of No. 467. Mr. Bevin minuted on this draft: 'Agreed. E. B.'

[5] Mr. Dean added in a postscript of 28 July 1945 to his covering minute of that date that he had ascertained this. Mr. Dean there further reported that the American experts 'have some doubt whether in practice it will be possible to establish an international Court consisting of representatives of the Four Powers for these trials, but they have not abandoned hope of doing so yet. They are afraid of Soviet procedure and methods which might discredit the trial seriously.'

how the final designation of the defendants is to be made. It is proposed that there shall be four prosecutors who in this respect will act as a committee, and the Americans are anxious that, if they are divided two to two, those in favour of trying any given individual shall have their way. The French support this. We and probably the Russians are opposed to it since it undermines the international basis of the court and, more serious, may place us in the position of having to take part in the trials of persons whom we do not believe to be properly triable as major criminals. In the last resort we may have to accept the Americans' view and if, in consequence, they attempt to bring to trial somebody whom they [?we] consider not to be a war criminal at all, we shall have either to argue them out of it or resort to administrative delay.

(3) *Article 22.* This deals with the venue of the trial. For political reasons we are most anxious that the trial should not be held in the Soviet Zone since it is most important that it should take place in conditions which will be approved by public opinion now and in the future. We and the Americans have suggested Nuremberg and the Russians have provisionally agreed to this for the first trial provided that the headquarters and administrative office of the court is at Berlin. Our intention is, if possible, to try about a dozen of the leading Nazis in the first trial on a charge of criminal conspiracy, and if we accomplish this it will not so much matter if subsequent trials take place in other parts of Germany. It is, however, clearly of the utmost importance that the first trial should include most of the principal Nazis, since we have far less control over the venue of subsequent trials.

Finally, our strongest card in these negotiations is the fact that we and the Americans hold between us almost all the principal Nazi leaders. This has enabled us to lay down procedure in the Charter which is broadly in accordance with Anglo-American procedure and to insist that the first trial should at least take place in the United States Zone.

It is most important to get the trial started soon and we have been aiming for early September. It seems unlikely, however, that we can accomplish this, but it will be most helpful towards attaining an early start if the Conference could express a view in its favour.

CALENDAR TO No. 442

i   *28 July 1945   Letter from Mr. R. A. Clyde (British War Crimes Executive) to Mr. Scott-Fox; letter from Mr. Scott-Fox to Mr. Dean (Berlin).* Outstanding points on draft charter on war crimes. Importance of progressing with negotiations in London. Question of release of captured German documents [U 5745, 5860/29/73].

No. 443

Mr. Eden to Sir A. Cadogan (Berlin: received 28 July, 7.50 a.m.)
No. 256 Onward Telegraphic [F.O. 934/5/48(5)]

Important   FOREIGN OFFICE, *28 July 1945, 2.40 a.m.*[1]

Following received from Washington telegram No. 5237 27th July. Begins:

[1] Time of origin.

Terminal telegram Target No. 244.[2]

I to-day spoke to Stettinius as instructed[3] and he told me that the United States Delegation to Terminal already possessed authority, if it were necessary to gain agreement, to acquiesce in a rotating Chairman of the Executive Committee. He incidentally gave me to understand that excepting in the case of the Secretariat the United States Government were not committed to the idea of permanent Chairmen for the major organs of the United Nations.

2. In response to an enquiry on my part he said that although the point was not yet decided Mr. Hiss[4] will probably be the United States representative on the Executive Committee. He added that he himself proposed to visit London for a few days at the end of August.

3. Please pass to Terminal for Sir A. Cadogan.

[2] No. 416.
[3] For this conversation on 26 July 1945 between Mr. Balfour and Mr. Stettinius cf. *F.R.U.S. Berlin*, vol. ii, pp. 639–40.
[4] Mr. Alger Hiss was Director of the Office of Special Political Affairs in the State Department.

No. 444

Mr. Bevin to Sir A. Cadogan (Berlin: received 28 July, 1.55 p.m.)
No. 258 Onward Telegraphic [F.O. 800/417/65]

Top secret. Most Immediate FOREIGN OFFICE, *28 July 1945, 11.45 a.m.*

Following for Hayter from Dixon.

Foreign Office party leaving for Terminal to-day is as follows: Mr. Bevin, Mr. Ridsdale, Mr. Henderson, Detective Minikin and self. We leave Northolt at 13.45 local time arriving Gatow 18.40 local time.

2. Mr. Bevin proposes living in Mr. Eden's house. Could you please arrange for a desk to be put into the sitting-room of the house. Please tell the Chef to prepare dinner for six people tonight.

3. Mr. Bevin may require typhus innoculation immediately on arrival at Terminal. Please arrange for doctor to be available to provide this at the house.

No. 445

Mr. Morrison[1] to Mr. Bevin (Berlin: received 28 July, 10.5 p.m.)
No. 268 Onward Telegraphic [F.O. 800/417/65]

Top secret. Immediate FOREIGN OFFICE, *28 July 1945, 7.27 p.m.*

For Bridges from Eady.

[1] Mr. Herbert Morrison, newly appointed Lord President of the Council, was in charge of government business and the Foreign Office in the absence of Mr. Attlee and Mr. Bevin at Potsdam.

Chancellor[2] considers new lines of reparations proposal acceptable in principle. He regards it as important that the acceptance should be subject to

(a) a satisfactory agreed reparations programme;
(b) acceptance of the prior charge on exports;
(c) full acceptance of Germany as one economic unit for purposes of Control Commission.

CALENDARS TO No. 445

i *28 July 1945 Memorandum from Sir W. Eady to Dr. Dalton.* Background to new proposals on reparations, on which the Americans are impatient to get an agreement. Advises acceptance: 'I agree. H. D. 28/7' [T 236/264: OF 213/3/2e].

ii *28 July 1945 Lord Halifax (Washington) No. 973.* Consideration is being given by State Department to British views on possibility of White Russia and the Ukraine entering separate reparation claims and seeking separate representation on an Inter-Allied Reparation Commission [UE 3475/624/77].

[2] Dr. Hugh Dalton had succeeded Sir John Anderson as Chancellor of the Exchequer.

No. 446

Record of a Meeting between Mr. Attlee, Mr. Bevin and Generalissimo Stalin at Potsdam on 28 July 1945 at 10 p.m.[1]

[*F.O. 800/417/64*]

Present:

PRIME MINISTER, Foreign Secretary, Major Birse (*Interpreter*).

GENERALISSIMO STALIN, M. Molotov, M. Pavlov (*Interpreter*).

After introducing the Foreign Secretary the PRIME MINISTER said he had returned to resume the work at the Conference.

The GENERALISSIMO remarked that the Prime Minister had had a great victory. It appeared to have been unexpected and how was it to be explained?

The PRIME MINISTER agreed that it had been unexpected, but there had been a wave of opinion in favour of Labour.

The GENERALISSIMO thought that the British people had decided that the war was over, that Japan was far away and that the Americans could finish it off. They were turning their minds to peace problems.

[1] Before this meeting Mr. Attlee and Mr. Bevin accompanied by Sir A. Cadogan had that evening had a meeting with President Truman and Mr. Byrnes accompanied by Admiral Leahy at the President's residence at 2 Kaiserstrasse, Babelsberg. No official British or American record of this meeting has been traced. Mr. Byrnes recalled: 'Soon after their arrival, Mr. Attlee and Mr. Bevin called on the President and the four of us discussed the work of the conference. The President mentioned the Soviet demand for East Prussia and indicated on a map the changes in the boundary lines of Germany, Poland and the Soviet Union that thus would be effected. Mr. Bevin immediately and forcefully presented his strong opposition to those boundaries' (James F. Byrnes, *Speaking Frankly*—New York & London, 1947—p. 79). Cf. also Fleet Admiral William D. Leahy, *I Was There* (London, 1950), p. 490.

The PRIME MINISTER denied it. He wished to put the point that the people wanted to finish the war in the Far East because peace and liberty were indivisible. We would not let down the Americans. It was true that minds were turning towards a period of reconstruction.

The GENERALISSIMO thought the leaders in Britain had agreed it was necessary to finish the war with Japan, but the people felt the chief war was over.

The PRIME MINISTER pointed out that Britain looked upon it as her duty to fight in the Far East and her contribution in land forces had been the greatest. We had a million men in Burma. We had had great casualties.

The FOREIGN SECRETARY observed that Britain had become a debtor to India to the extent of one thousand million pounds.

Turning again to the Election results, M. MOLOTOV thought that some big event must have occurred to create such surprising results.

The PRIME MINISTER replied that Labour enthusiasts were sometimes led away by great meetings in which the electors would cheer and applaud a Labour candidate, but they forgot the silent voters. The reverse had happened in this case.

With regard to Mr. Churchill, the Prime Minister said the nation distinguished between Mr. Churchill the leader of the nation in war and Mr. Churchill the Conservative Party leader. The people wanted a parliament based on a definite programme. Many people looked upon the Conservatives as a reactionary party which would not carry out a policy answering to peace requirements.

The Prime Minister emphasised the point that in this Election the middle classes and technical classes had voted Labour.

The FOREIGN SECRETARY spoke of the great support given by the Trade Unions.

The GENERALISSIMO turned to the question of Japan. He thought Japan had refused the ultimatum made by President Truman, Mr. Churchill and Generalissimo Chiang Kai-Shek. Japan had now made a second approach to Russia for mediation. (This was later discussed at the Plenary Session).[2]

The Generalissimo asked how long the Conference would last. The President was in a hurry.

It was agreed that the Conference might end in two or three days.

[2] See No. 447, minute 3.

No. 447

Record of Tenth Plenary Meeting held at Cecilienhof, Potsdam, on Saturday, 28 July 1945 at 10.30 p.m.

P. (Terminal) 10th Meeting [U 6197/3628/70]

Top secret

Present:

PREMIER STALIN, M. V. M. Molotov, M. A. Ya. Vyshinski, M. F. T. Gousev,

M. A. A. Gromyko, M. K. V. Novikov, M. A. A. Sobolev, M. B. F. Podtzerob, M. S. A. Golunski (*Inrerpreter*).

PRESIDENT TRUMAN, Mr. J. F. Byrnes, Mr. Joseph E. Davies, Fleet-Admiral W. D. Leahy, Mr. W. A. Harriman, Mr. E. W. Pauley, Mr. J. C. Dunn, Mr. H. F. Matthews, Mr. W. L. Clayton, Mr. C. E. Bohlen (*Interpreter*).

MR. ATTLEE, Mr. Bevin, Sir A. Cadogan, Sir A. Clark Kerr, Sir W. Strang, Sir E. Bridges, Sir D. Waley, Mr. N. Brook, Mr. P. J. Dixon, Mr. W. Hayter, Major A. Birse (*Interpreter*).

Contents

Minute	Subject

1. *Foreign Secretaries' Report*

M. MOLOTOV submitted a Report on the proceedings at the meetings of the Foreign Secretaries held on the 25th and 27th July. These proceedings are recorded in the Minutes of those Meetings—F. (Terminal) 8th[1] and 9th[2] Meetings.

The Conference took note of M. Molotov's report. In particular, they expressed their satisfaction at the decision of the Soviet Government to participate in the work of the European Inland Transport Conference; and took note that the Soviet Government were reviewing the question of their participation in the Emergency Economic Committee for Europe and the European Coal Organisation (P. (Terminal) 42[3] and F. (Terminal) 9th[2] Meeting, Minute 7).

2. *Subjects for Discussion*

M. MOLOTOV said that, as a result of the Foreign Secretaries' Meeting on the previous day, there were two subjects for discussion:

(*a*) *Neutral and Ex-enemy States: Admission to the United Nations; and*

(*b*) *Reparations from Austria and Italy.*

Other subjects which might be discussed at the present meeting were the *Western Frontier of Poland* and *The German Fleet and Merchant Navy*.

PRESIDENT TRUMAN said that he was prepared to discuss any subject which his colleagues wished to raise.

MR. ATTLEE said that he also was ready to discuss any subject. He would like to take this opportunity of expressing his regret that the domestic affairs of the United Kingdom should have delayed the progress of the Conference. The British Delegation were now willing to meet as often and as long as was necessary to complete the business of the Conference.

[1] No. 274.   [2] No. 431.   [3] No. 283.

3. Japan: Request for Mediation

PREMIER STALIN said that the Soviet Government had received from the Japanese Government a proposal that they should act as mediators between the Japanese Government and the British and United States Governments. Although he had not been informed beforehand of the call to surrender published by the British and American Governments, he nevertheless considered it his duty to inform them, in strict confidence, of this development.

Premier Stalin explained that he had received a letter from the Japanese Ambassador in Moscow, the effect of which was as follows: When last the Japanese Ambassador had expressed a desire to state the policy of his Government in regard to Japanese-Soviet relations and the war, the Soviet Government had replied that they were unable to answer, since the message from the Japanese Emperor had not contained a sufficiently definite proposal.[4] In order to be more precise, therefore, the Japanese Ambassador had been instructed to explain that the proposed mission of Prince Konoye was to ask the Soviet Government to mediate between the Japanese Government and the British and American Governments with a view to bringing to an end the present war, and to negotiate on questions relating to Soviet-Japanese relations. He further desired to state that the mission had received the special authority of the Emperor and that his only object was to achieve the Emperor's desire to avoid further bloodshed on both sides. He expressed the hope that the Soviet Government would consider the proposal and agree to receive the mission;[5] as was well known, Prince Konoye, an ex-Prime Minister, was trusted by the Emperor and was prominent in Japanese political circles.

Premier Stalin added that this communication contained nothing that was not already known: it was simply a further attempt to obtain the collaboration of the Soviet Government in the furtherance of Japanese policy. The Soviet Government had, therefore, returned an unhesitating negative.[6]

---

[4] A translation of a Soviet note of 18 July 1945 in this sense to the Japanese Ambassador in Moscow is printed in *F.R.U.S. Berlin*, vol. ii, p. 1251.

[5] A Foreign Office telegram of 29 July to Moscow, repeated unnumbered to the British Delegation in Berlin (received on 30 July), communicated similar secret information on this Japanese approach to the Soviet Government. This information, which included a reference to Japanese inability to accept unconditional surrender (cf. *F.R.U.S. Berlin*, vol. ii, p. 1258), generally corresponded to Marshal Stalin's above statement based upon M. Sato's communication of 25 July (*ibid.*, vol. ii, pp. 1262–3). According to the Soviet and American records of this meeting of the conference on 28 July (*The Tehran, Yalta and Potsdam Conferences: Documents*, p. 263, and *F.R.U.S. Berlin*, vol. ii, p. 460 respectively) an English translation of M. Sato's communication to the Soviet Government was read out in the course of Marshal Stalin's statement. For translations of relevant documents from the archives of the Japanese Foreign Ministry see further *F.R.U.S. Berlin*, vol. ii, pp. 1250–1, 1257–9, 1263–4.

[6] The corresponding Soviet and American records here read: 'We intend to reply to them in the same spirit as the last time' (*Conferences: Soviet Documents* p. 263); 'the answer

Mr. Truman and Mr. Attlee expressed their gratitude to Premier Stalin for the information which he had given them.[7]

4. *Neutral and Ex-enemy States: Admission to United Nations*
(Previous References: P. (Terminal) 8th Meeting,[8] Minute 3, F. (Terminal) 9th Meeting,[2] Minute 2.)

M. Molotov[9] said that this subject had been discussed at the Plenary meeting on the 24th July, but the Foreign Secretaries had had different impressions of the conclusions then reached. The Soviet Delegation had understood that the matter had been settled after acceptance of the amendment proposed by Mr. Churchill for the substitution in paragraph 3 of P. (Terminal) 35[10] of 'peace treaties *for*' instead of 'peace treaties *with*.' Sir Alexander Cadogan had, however, put forward another amendment; and the Foreign Secretaries' Meeting, after discussion, had decided that they must bring the matter up again at a Plenary Meeting.

Premier Stalin said that the amendment suggested by Sir Alexander Cadogan referred to 'responsible democratic Governments.' As he had emphasised in earlier discussions, such a reference to 'responsible' Governments would give offence to the existing Governments of these satellite States, as it would imply they were irresponsible. If, on the other hand the word 'recognised' was used, the statement would not give offence, and it would mean that each of the three Powers could recognise these Governments when they were ready to do so. He was under the impression that this view had already been accepted by the Plenary Meeting.

Mr. Byrnes recalled the previous discussions of this matter. The President had agreed in principle to the text as amended by the Soviet Delegation, and had suggested that it should be referred to a drafting Committee. In making this suggestion the President had had only one alteration in mind, viz., the substitution of 'examine' for 'consider' in the additional sentence of paragraph 3. There was, therefore, no disagreement in substance between the Soviet Delegation and the United States Delegation. Mr. Churchill had, however, doubted the wisdom of making any such declaration about the diplomatic recognition of the satellite States, and had been unable to accept the addition proposed on this point by the Soviet Delegation.

Mr. Byrnes said that the original proposal of the United States Delegation had been limited to a statement about the admission of Italy to association with the United Nations. It had then been proposed that the statement should include an indication that Spain would not be regarded as eligible

would be in the negative' (*F.R.U.S. Berlin*, vol. ii, p. 460); 'Our answer of course will be negative' (*ibid.*, p. 467). For the Soviet reply on 8 August, cf. *ibid.*, p. 1298, note 3.

[7] The question of terms for the surrender of Japan was raised informally by Mr. James Forrestal in an officially unrecorded conversation, also covering other subjects, with Mr. Ernest Bevin on 29 July: cf. *F.R.U.S. Berlin*, vol. ii, p. 477.

[8] No. 258.

[9] This statement is ascribed to Marshal Stalin in the Soviet record, *Conferences: Soviet Documents*, p. 264, also in *F.R.U.S. Berlin*, vol. ii, p. 467; cf., however, *ibid.*, p. 461.

[10] No. 260.

for such admission so long as she remained under the control of the present political régime. The British Delegation had then proposed that the statement should cover other neutral countries. Then the Soviet Delegation had put forward the paragraph about the other satellite States. Then it had been proposed to modify the language in the paragraph dealing with those States so as to conform with that dealing with Italy. It now appeared that concessions made to meet the views of the Soviet Delegation were not acceptable to the British Delegation, and amendments proposed to meet the British point of view were not acceptable to the Soviet Delegation. If, therefore, the Soviet Delegation and the British Delegation could now reach agreement, the United States Delegation would be content to go forward with this declaration: but, if this could not be achieved, then the United States Delegation would withdraw their original modest request for a statement indicating the views of the three Great Powers on the admission of Italy to association with the United Nations.

At Mr. Attlee's request SIR ALEXANDER CADOGAN explained the position of the British Delegation. As he understood it, the text of the statement (P. (Terminal) 35)[10] had been agreed except for two amendments:

(*a*) That already mentioned by Premier Stalin, substituting 'recognised Governments' for 'responsible Governments.' This amendment was acceptable to the British Delegation.

(*b*) The additional sentence proposed by the Soviet Delegation at the end of paragraph 3:

'The three Governments agree to consider, each separately, in the immediate future, the question of establishing diplomatic relations with Bulgaria, Finland, Hungary and Roumania.'

Mr. Churchill had explained that it would be misleading to make a public statement to this effect, as it was not constitutionally possible for us to resume normal diplomatic relations with States with which we were still technically at war. He had therefore suggested a compromise in the following sense: 'The conclusion of peace treaties with recognised democratic Governments in these States will enable the three Governments to establish normal diplomatic relations . . . ,'[11] but this had not been acceptable to the Soviet Delegation.

PREMIER STALIN said that he could see no reason for any difference in the relations between Italy and the Allies on the one hand, and between the other satellite States and the Allies on the other hand, because in none of these countries, except Finland, was there an elected Government. Yet Italy had been granted full diplomatic recognition by the Soviet and United States Governments and, in Mr. Churchill's phrase, 90 per cent. recognition by the United Kingdom Government. He could not see any ground for the discrimination on which the British Delegation were insisting.

MR. BEVIN said that one point of difference was that we had known a great deal about the Italian Government before we recognised it and we

[11] Punctuation as in original quotation.

knew nothing about the Governments in the other countries. PREMIER STALIN said that the United Kingdom Government could find out more about these Governments before deciding to recognise them.

MR. BEVIN then asked why we should be committed to considering recognition before we had had an opportunity of finding out about these Governments.

PREMIER STALIN replied that Russia had known very little about the Italian Government when she had recognised it. The first step towards easing Italy's position had been the resumption of diplomatic relations. Now it was proposed to take the second step by referring publicly to the question of her admission to association with the United Nations. What he was proposing for the other satellite States was that the first step, of offering to consider the resumption of diplomatic relations, should be taken now. If it was proposed to take the second step in respect of Italy, it was not unreasonable to ask that the first step should be taken in respect of the other satellite States.

MR. ATTLEE repeated that we could not resume full diplomatic relations with a State with which we were technically at war. The paragraph proposed by the Russians would give the impression that we were going to do so; but this was impossible. The amendment proposed by the British Delegation stated only what was possible, viz., that, after the conclusion of peace treaties with these States, we would consider the resumption of diplomatic relations with them.

PREMIER STALIN suggested that the paragraph might read, 'The three Governments agreed to consider, each separately, the question of establishing *complete or partial diplomatic relations . . .* '[11]

MR. ATTLEE did not think this could be accepted.

PREMIER STALIN then suggested that the United States proposal to substitute 'examine' for 'consider' should be adopted.

MR. ATTLEE said that a change of word would not change the sense of the paragraph.

MR. BEVIN added that we must be absolutely straight with the British people and we did not want to cover up with words the real effect of what had been decided. If we were going to recognise the satellite States, then we would be ready to say so, but this was not possible at the present time. He would prefer to accept the offer, made earlier in the meeting by Mr. Byrnes, that the whole project for a declaration about the admission of neutral and ex-enemy States to the United Nations should be withdrawn.

PREMIER STALIN said that in the circumstances this seemed to be the best course.

> The Conference agreed not to proceed further with the proposal for a statement on the admission of neutral and ex-enemy States to association with the United Nations.

5. *Reparations: Austria and Italy*
   (Previous Reference: F. (Terminal) 9th Meeting,[2] Minute 4.)
   M. MOLOTOV reported that the Foreign Secretaries had considered this

matter but had failed to reach agreement; they had therefore decided that it must be submitted to the Plenary Meeting.

PREMIER STALIN said that the Soviet Government was prepared to agree that reparations should not be exacted from Austria. Austria had not fought as a separate State, and had been forced into the war by Germany; and she had had no armed forces separate from the German armed forces.

It would be impossible, however, to convince the Soviet people that reparations should not be exacted from Italy, which not only was a separate State but had sent armies as far into the Soviet Union as the Volga and had devastated the country.

PRESIDENT TRUMAN said that the Governments of the United States and the United Kingdom had sent to Italy, in order to prevent disease and unrest, goods to the value of 500 million dollars; and the United States Delegation believed that it would be necessary to provide further relief for Italy up to at least the same amount. The United States Government were unwilling to contribute money to any country in order to finance their payment of reparations. If there were war plants in Italy which were needed by the Soviet Government to re-establish their industry, the United States Government saw no objection to their being taken as reparations. It must be clearly understood, however, that the first charge on Italian exports must be the repayment of the advances already made to Italy.

PREMIER STALIN said that he understood the point of view of the United States Delegation. The Soviet people had, however, a moral right to reparations in view of the fact that for $3\frac{1}{2}$ years their territory had been occupied and devastated on an enormous scale. President Truman had referred to the possibility of obtaining military equipment and this would certainly be useful. The Soviet Government had no intention of asking for too much, but they would like to know at what figure the total value of such equipment should be put. Under their Armistice terms Finland, Hungary and Roumania had each agreed to pay reparations to the value of 300 million dollars. The question was how much would be the total value of reparations from Italy on the basis specified by President Truman.

PRESIDENT TRUMAN said that he was unable to give an immediate answer to that question: it was a matter which would have to be investigated.

MR. ATTLEE agreed with the view expressed by President Truman. The British Government had every sympathy with the sufferings of the Russian people. But the United Kingdom had also suffered under the attacks of Italy, and the British people would not tolerate a situation in which Italy was required to pay reparations and could do so only because of the advances made by Great Britain and the United States. In his view, apart from the 'once for all' removal of military plant referred to by the President, Italy could not pay reparations: in fact she could only live at all through the assistance given to her by Great Britain and the United States.

MR. BEVIN asked whether the military plant and machinery referred to by Premier Stalin was that used directly for war production, with no peacetime use. PREMIER STALIN replied that he had referred to the machinery of military factories. Although such machinery might have been exclusively military in the past, it could now be turned over to peace-time production. The Soviet Government were arranging such a turnover in their war factories. He was not, however, asking for a precise enumeration at the present Conference of the categories of plant which might be removed. All he suggested was that the Conference should decide in principle that machinery and plant of this kind might be removed from Italy in payment of reparations and that the total amount of such reparations should be reviewed in the light of this decision.

PRESIDENT TRUMAN though there was little difference between the three Delegations. His only object was to have it plainly understood that the advances made by the United States to Italy must not be used to enable her to pay reparations.

PREMIER STALIN agreed that such advances should not be touched.

MR. BEVIN said that, as he saw it, the matter resolved itself into a question of priorities. In the first priority would be payments for the advances made by Great Britain and the United States, and reparations would be in the second priority. The next step would be to investigate how much was left over for reparations after allowance had been made for the first priority.

> The Conference (a) took note that the Soviet Government agreed that no reparations should be exacted from Austria; and (b) agreed to resume consideration of the question of reparations from Italy at a later meeting.

6. *Procedure: Time of Next Meeting*

MR. ATTLEE said that the Conference had now reached a stage at which it seemed that progress was more likely to be made at Plenary Meetings; and he suggested that there would be no advantage in holding a Meeting of Foreign Secretaries on the following morning. For his part, he would be ready to agree that Plenary Meetings should be held more frequently in order that the business of the Conference might be cleared up as rapidly as possible.

> It was agreed that on the following day there should be no Meeting of Foreign Secretaries and that a Plenary Meeting should be held at 4 p.m.

Cabinet Office, Potsdam, 28th July, 1945

CALENDARS TO NO. 447

i *27 & 30 July 1945 Letters from Mr. Coulson and Mr. Brand (Berlin) to Mr. Ronald.* Implementation of proposals on cooperation in solving immediate European economic problems. Questions of Soviet and Polish participation in E.E.C.E. and E.C.O. [F.O. 934/5/38(1); UR 2704/1600/53].

ii *29 July 1945 Minute from Sir D. Waley to Sir A. Cadogan (Berlin); F.O. Delegation minute to Mr. Bevin (Berlin).* Agreement that Austria should not pay reparations is satisfactory but unless Russian removals of Austrian plant and equipment cease it 'will have been an empty victory' [UE 3373/720/77].

No. 448

Letter from Mr. Oldham[1] to Mr. Bevin (Berlin)
[F 4673/584/61]

OFFICES OF THE CABINET, GREAT GEORGE STREET, 28 July 1945

My dear Secretary of State—

I have just received the following telegram from my Minister for External Affairs, Dr. Evatt, who has asked that it be immediately conveyed to you.

Begins.

Personal from Dr. Evatt.

I am delighted at your appointment and hope it will be followed by complete re-examination by yourself of some of the Potsdam negotiations, which take no account of the right of this country and the promises as to peace and armistice terms made on several occasions, including War Cabinet meeting at which you were present. Please see telegrams [i][2] referring to them. The last straw is the publication of the ultimatum to Japan[3] without any reference to Australia, who for more than two years bore the brunt of the Pacific struggle from the British point of view. The first we heard of this was in the newspapers. The Foreign Office talks about Dominion rights but in practice does its best to evade them.

Best wishes.

Ends.[4]

Yours faithfully
JOHN OLDHAM

CALENDAR TO NO. 448

i 27 July 1945 Mr. Chifley (Canberra) to Dominions Office Tel. No. 205. In view of previous undertakings asks that political and diplomatic decisions affecting initial post-hostilities and peace arrangements in Europe at Potsdam, in particular proposals for Council of Foreign Ministers, should be regarded as tentative in light of Dominion interests [D.O. 35/1950: WR 222/48/5].

---

[1] Mr. J. E. Oldham was senior liaison officer between the Australian Government and the Foreign Office.

[2] See also No. 372.i.

[3] No. 281.

[4] Mr. Bevin replied in a personal message to Dr. Evatt sent from Potsdam in a letter of 29 July 1945 from Mr. Dixon to Mr. Oldham: 'Many thanks for your telegram. I will go into the matter which you raise at the earliest possible moment.' With reference to this correspondence Sir E. Machtig remitted to Sir O. Sargent on 30 July a copy of his letter of even date to Sir E. Bridges at Potsdam concerning a public protest by Dr. Evatt on 29 July in general accordance with No. 448, cited in part by P. Hasluck, The Government and the People 1942–1945, p. 593: cf. also The Times of 30 July 1945, p. 4. Sir E. Machtig informed Sir E. Bridges that 'we in London had no idea that the Potsdam statement was coming out until it actually appeared. . . . On the substance, we at the Dominions Office feel bound to say that Dr. Evatt has a case when he contends that the Australian Government had a right to be consulted before any modification of "unconditional surrender" for Japan was decided upon, having regard to the assurances which had been given to

him by Mr. Churchill. . . . Even if circumstances had not permitted of full consultation with Australia, we think at the very least that we ought to have been in a position to let them have in advance a warning that a statement on these lines was to be issued. . . . We fully recognise the difficulties under which the Potsdam Conference has been working.' On 4 August a similar representation was received from the New Zealand Government in their telegram No. 213 of that date (F 4885/364/23), not printed: cf. P. Hasluck, *loc. cit.*

No. 449

Mr. Bevin (Berlin) to Mr. Morrison (Received 29 July, 9.45 a.m.)
No. 267 Target Telegraphic [E 5697/8/89]

Top secret. Immediate   BERLIN, *29 July 1945, 11.37 a.m.*

Private Office from Rowan.
Please despatch[1] following:
Begins:
Personal from Prime Minister to Gen. Paget.
I am informed that you are proposing to send an additional brigade into the Levant States. Increases in the number of troops in the Levant States may cuase [cause] trouble in other directions and can only be justified by Military necessity. I rely on you not to increase the garrison beyond the minimum required to maintain order.
Ends.

[1] It was noted on the filed copy that this message had been passed that day to General Headquarters, Middle East.

No. 450

Note of First Staff Conference with Prime Minister and Foreign
Secretary, held at 23 Ringstrasse on Sunday,
29 July 1945 at 10.30 a.m.
[F.O. 934/2/8(15)]

Top secret

THE RT. HON. C. R. ATTLEE, M.P., PRIME MINISTER, The Rt. Hon. Ernest Bevin, M.P., Secretary of State for Foreign Affairs, Sir A. Cadogan, Sir E. Bridges, Sir D. Waley, Mr. P. J. Dixon, Sir A. Clark Kerr, Sir W. Strang, Mr. N. Brook, Mr. T. L. Rowan, and officials of the Foreign Office.

Contents

Minute No.	Subject
1.	Neutral and Ex-Enemy States: Admission to the United Nations
2.	Western Frontier of Poland
3.	German Fleet and Merchant Navy
4.	Greece and Yugoslavia

5. Roumania: Removal of Industrial Equipment
6. Reparations: Austria and Italy
7. International Inland Waterways
8. European Oil Supplies
9. Consultation with French Government

1. *Neutral and Ex-Enemy States: Admission to the United Nations*

SIR ALEXANDER CADOGAN said that Mr. Byrnes had told him that morning that the United States Delegation were anxious to revive this proposal, and intended to put forward for discussion at the next Plenary Meeting the following revised formula:

'The Three Governments agree to examine, each separately, in the near future in the light of the conditions then prevailing, the establishment of diplomatic relations with Finland, Roumania, Bulgaria and Hungary, to the extent possible prior to the ratification of peace treaties'.

He thought that, if this formula proved acceptable to the Soviet Delegation, we could agree to it.

THE PRIME MINISTER said that he assumed that the object of the Soviet Delegation, in pressing for some such declaration in respect of the ex-enemy satellite States in the Balkans, was to gain credit for the existing regimes in those States. What would be the effect of such a declaration on the genuinely democratic parties in those countries?

SIR ALEXANDER CADOGAN said that they might at first be discouraged by such a declaration. On the other hand, the new formula would not require us to recognise the existing Governments: we need not take any action under it until we were satisfied that responsible democratic Governments had been established.

In further discussion the suggestion was made that this proposal might be linked up with the request which we had made for better facilities for the Press and for the free expression of political opinion in those countries. Might it not be made clear to the Soviet Delegation that, if these facilities were made available, we should be the more likely to feel able to consider favourably the resumption of diplomatic relations. It could also be made clear that we should feel free to announce publicly, if the question were raised, that we had agreed to this declaration in the expectation that these facilities would be granted, and that we did not intend to resume diplomatic relations with these countries until we had more information about conditions there and were satisfied that there was due freedom for the Press and for the expression of opinion. If the Soviet Delegation could give us any assurance on that point, it would help us to accept the new formula now suggested.

It was agreed that the United States Delegation should be informed that, if they put forward the new formula now proposed, the United Kingdom Delegation would take the line indicated above.

2. *Western Frontier of Poland*

THE FOREIGN SECRETARY said that he had been considering whether the Soviet Government's proposals regarding the Western Frontier of Poland might afford an opportunity to reach a simultaneous settlement of a wide complex of problems which had been raised in discussions at the Conference. It would be worth trying to get a provisional settlement of Poland's Western Frontier which would enable practical arrangements to be made for the administration of this territory but would be subject to review at the Peace Conference in the light of experience in the meantime. Such a provisional settlement should enable us to secure agreement for the withdrawal of Soviet troops from these territories and for the holding of elections for a constituent assembly. We might at the same time get the Soviet Government to agree that, from her enlarged territory, Poland should provide a stated quantity of supplies over the next three years or so, to assist in the provision of essential supplies for Germany and Western Europe.

As part of the same understanding we might promise that we would seek to secure the holding of early elections in Greece, and for the early election of a constituent assembly in Italy. This might enable us to press for the holding of similar elections in the satellite countries of Eastern Europe, without appearing to single out those countries as requiring special treatment.

The Foreign Secretary said that, if such a general agreement could be reached, he would be prepared to make some concession on reparations— e.g. to offer the Russians more than 10 per cent., possibly up to 20 per cent.— of 'once for all' deliveries from the Ruhr.

Discussion then turned on the precise line which might be agreed for the Western frontier of Poland.

THE FOREIGN SECRETARY said that he would have preferred a line running to the East of the Oder and along the Eastern Neisse.

SIR ALEXANDER CADOGAN said that the United States Delegation were thinking in terms of a line along the Oder, leaving Stettin to the Poles, and thence proceeding along the *Eastern* Neisse. They would resist Poland's claim to the territory west of the Eastern Neisse; but, if the line of the Eastern Neisse were accepted, they would favour some settlement which would make it possible for immediate elections to be held in the territory provisionally ceded to Poland under the settlement.

SIR ARCHIBALD CLARK-KERR said that the Soviet Delegation and the Polish Provisional Government would press very strongly for the line of the *Western* Neisse. He himself believed that they would in practice be allowed by the Soviet Government to occupy the whole of this area; and there was much to be said for accepting the full claim, as part of a general settlement, rather than be forced subsequently to accept a *fait accompli* secured by unilateral action on the part of the Soviet Government.

THE PRIME MINISTER pointed out that there was a difference between our accepting a *fait accompli* and becoming accessories *before* the fact. It was pointed out that, even from that point of view, there would be advantages for us in having made the concession as part of a general settlement.

Points in further discussion were:

(a) It might be possible to avoid taking definite decision at this stage between the line of the Eastern Neisse and the Western Neisse. The pre-war population in the area between these two rivers had been about 3 million. There was no reliable evidence to show what number of Germans remained in this area. It would be helpful if, before a final decision had to be taken, a report could be made by experts (after examination on the spot into the existing conditions in the area) on the comparative merits of the two alternative lines.

A variant of this suggestion would be to suggest that a provisional decision should be taken now in favour of the line of the Western Neisse, on the understanding that this would be subject to review in the light of such a report by experts.

Sir Archibald Clark-Kerr thought that M. Mikolajczyk might be willing to accept the latter alternative.

(b) Was it necessary that the French Government should be a party to any decision on this question?

It was explained that the Control Council for Germany was responsible for the administration of the whole area within the 1937 frontiers of Germany. The French were members of the Control Council; and it followed that, strictly speaking, they should be made parties to any decision involving the removal of any of this area from the jurisdiction of the Council.

(c) The suggestion of holding an enquiry by experts had the further advantage that it would give time in which public opinion in the United Kingdom could become accustomed to the idea of Poland's acquiring so large a stretch of territory in the west. The original proposal to postpone further discussion of this question until the Peace Conference was open to the objection that the Poles would consolidate their position in the meantime, with the support of the Soviet Government, and we should be faced at the Peace Conference with a *fait accompli*. There would be advantages if, before we were faced with that situation, we had at least secured facilities to go and see for ourselves what was happening in these areas.

(d) As one of the major problems involved was the transfer of the German population of these areas into Germany, it would not be enough for us merely to obtain up-to-date information about conditions in these areas themselves. If, as we were told, large numbers of the German residents had already fled, we should also need to know where they had gone and what had happened to them. This would involve obtaining better information about conditions in the Soviet zone of occupied Germany.

Sir William Strang confirmed that, according to his information, most of the German refugees who had moved into Germany from neighbouring countries had gone into the Soviet zone. Some were prisoners of war, some had died and some had been deported eastwards and into the Baltic States; but of those who had fled into Germany most were in the Soviet zone. Some further information on this point should be forthcoming as a result of the proposal (which was likely to be brought forward to the Plenary Meeting by the Committee on Transfer of Populations) that the Control Council for Germany should be authorised to report on the problems arising out of this transfer of population into Germany from neighbouring countries.

THE PRIME MINISTER said that he would like to have fuller information about the present conditions generally in Germany; and SIR ALEXANDER CADOGAN undertook to submit a recent report which had been forwarded to the Foreign Office by Sir William Strang.

The Conference went on to consider the general approach to the complex of problems connected with the question of Poland's Western Frontier.

THE FOREIGN SECRETARY said that, while he would prefer for the moment to leave himself a choice between the line of the Eastern Neisse and that of the Western Neisse, he would like to consider what the Soviet Delegation might be prepared to concede in return for a settlement of Poland's full claim. He thought we might aim at getting, in return, a favourable settlement of the reparations issue and an agreement on supplies of food and fuel from the eastern areas (including the territories claimed by Poland) for Western Germany.

He was anxious to promote the rapid reconstruction of Poland's economic life. He thought it important that Poland should re-open trade with the Scandinavian countries, for this would afford a counter-pressure to Russian influence on Poland. Equally, he would like to see an early resumption of normal trading in South-East Europe. It was in our interest to promote the early resumption of the two main trade cycles in Europe which centred, respectively, on the Baltic and on Genoa.

As regards the method of approach, the Foreign Secretary said that before putting any concrete proposals at a Plenary Meeting, he would like to have a private conversation between the Prime Minister and himself on the one hand and, on the other, Premier Stalin and M. Molotov. In such a conversation he would present the main issues which had been covered in discussion that morning as inter-connected problems. It would be un-profitable to seek decisions on each of these problems separately until some understanding had been reached about the general attitude of the two Delegations. If the Russians believed that we were prepared to make a general settlement over the whole of this field, they might be more accommodating on some of the points to which we attached special importance. Would there be any objection, from the point of view of the United States Delegation, to our making such a separate approach to Premier Stalin?

SIR ALEXANDER CADOGAN said that no objection could be raised by the United States Delegation. It would, however, be as well to let President Truman know beforehand that we intended to make such an approach, and he would himself think it preferable to discuss the whole position with the President before approaching Premier Stalin.

THE PRIME MINISTER said that he and the Foreign Secretary would see President Truman and Mr. Byrnes during the course of the day and explain to them what they had in mind; and subject to that interview, would make a separate approach to Premier Stalin on the general lines indicated by the Foreign Secretary in the course of the discussion.

3. German Fleet and Merchant Navy

THE FOREIGN SECRETARY asked whether difficulty would arise later if a decision was taken at this Conference about the disposal of the German Fleet, without providing for the French to have some share of it.

It was pointed out that the distribution which had been suggested by the Admiralty, and approved by a Cabinet decision of the late Government, had made provision for a share to be given to the French.

As regards the German merchant fleet, Premier Stalin had already agreed that this should be treated as reparations; and the best way of meeting the French position on this aspect of the matter was to secure agreement to their being admitted to the Reparation Commission.

4. Greece and Yugoslavia

MR. DIXON recalled that the British Delegation had raised at the Conference (P. (Terminal) 3rd Meeting,[1] Minute 9) the question of implementing the Tito–Subasic Agreement in Yugoslavia; and the Soviet Delegation had raised (P. (Terminal) 3rd Meeting, Minute 1) the question of frontier disturbances by Greece. Neither Delegation was likely to be satisfied with the progress so far made on these questions.

It had now been proposed by the Foreign Office that the Conference might agree upon the terms of a statement covering in a single declaration certain aspects of the present situation in both Greece and Yugoslavia. This might contain a reminder to Yugoslavia about the need for implementing the Tito–Subasic Agreement, and a reminder to Greece about the need for compliance with the Varkiza Agreement.

It was agreed that the Foreign Office should prepare the draft of a Memorandum on this subject for submission to the Conference.

5. Roumania: Removal of Industrial Equipment

SIR ALEXANDER CADOGAN recalled that the United Kingdom Delegation had proposed (P. (Terminal) 40)[2] that these issues should be the subject of investigation by an independent Committee of three Allied Nationals drawn from States not interested in the dispute. To this proposal the Soviet Delegation had now replied (P. (Terminal) 46)[3] that it would be preferable to refer the matter for joint examination by representatives of the Soviet and United Kingdom Governments. This counterproposal had none of the advantages of an independent enquiry, and the effect of accepting it would be merely to transfer the dispute to a lower level.

It was agreed that it would be preferable to suggest that the dispute about the removal of the Allied industrial equipment from Roumania should be remitted for consideration by the Council of Foreign Ministers at their first meeting in September.

[1] No. 194.   [2] No. 264.   [3] No. 432.

6. *Reparations: Austria and Italy*

It was recalled that at the Plenary Meeting the previous day (P. (Terminal) 10th Meeting,[4] Minute 5), the Soviet Delegation had agreed that it would be impracticable to exact reparations from Austria.

As regards Italy, though some progress had been made, final agreement had not been reached. It was possible, however, that the Soviet Delegation might accept the proposal put forward by the Foreign Secretary at the Plenary Meeting the previous day if a suitable formula could be devised.

> It was agreed that Sir David Waley should prepare a draft formula, for inclusion in the Protocol, dealing with reparations from Austria and Italy on the lines of the discussion at the Plenary Meeting on 28th July. (P. (Terminal) 10th Meeting,[4] Minute 5).

7. *International Inland Waterways*

MR. WARD recalled that in their Memorandum P. (Terminal) 33[5] the U.S. Delegation had recommended the appointment of interim navigational agencies for the Danube and the Rhine. In the Committee to which this Memorandum had been referred, the U.S. representatives were seeking to extend the same system of international control to the Kiel Canal and the Black Sea Straits. The Russian representatives were maintaining that they had no authority to discuss these further questions.

THE PRIME MINISTER said that, while he favoured the principle of international control for the main inland waterways, he thought this was a matter for ultimate decision by the World Organisation; and he suggested that the preparatory work should be remitted to the Council of Foreign Ministers. He thought it unlikely that the present Conference could reach any conclusions about the control of the Black Sea Straits; and the control of the Kiel Canal was for the present a matter for the Control Council for Germany.

> It was agreed that the matters raised in the Memorandum by the U.S. Delegation (P. (Terminal) 33)[5] might be disposed of by reference to the Council of Foreign Ministers.

8. *European Oil Supplies*

> It was agreed that this question[6] should also be remitted to the Council of Foreign Ministers.

9. *Consultation with French Government*

SIR WILLIAM STRANG recalled that the Conference had decided (F. (Terminal) 6th Meeting,[7] Minute 4) that the telegrams inviting the Governments of France and China to join the new Council of Foreign Ministers should be despatched 48 hours before the issue of the communiqué at the end of the Conference.

---

[4] No. 447.   [5] No. 246.

[6] The rest of this sentence is deleted on another copy (PREM 4/79/1) and the following substituted in manuscript: 'was suitable for remission to the Council of Foreign Ministers, but that as the U.S. Delegation had raised it, they should be left to press it at the present conference.'

[7] No. 233.

It was also desirable that the French Government should be notified in advance of the decisions of the Conference regarding the political principles to govern the treatment of Germany in the intial control period.

It was agreed that it was desirable that communications on both these points should be despatched to the French Government during the course of the day; and the Foreign Office were invited to ascertain whether the other two Delegations would proceed accordingly.

Cabinet Office, Potsdam, 29th July, 1945

CALENDARS TO NO. 450

i *29 July 1945 Record by Mr. Hoyer Millar of conversation with Mr. Dunn:* admissions to United Nations. British position agreed in minute 1 above was explained [F.O. 934/5/48(12)].

ii *29 July 1945 Letter from Mr. Ward (Berlin) to Viscount Hood:* disposal of German fleet and merchant navy; encloses brief of 28 July covering draft of No. 466 [U 5378, 5978/5397/70].

iii *28 July 1945 Minute from Sir W. Strang to Sir A. Cadogan (Berlin)* suggesting procedure acceptable to U.S. Delegation for communications to French Govt. as discussed in minute 9 above. Soviet Delegation are being consulted [F.O. 934/4/20(22)].

No. 451

Letter from Mr. Hayter (Berlin) to Mr. Howard[1]

[*F.O. 934/2/9(24)*]

Top secret & Personal   BRITISH DELEGATION, BERLIN, *29 July 1945*

Dear Douglas,

It is perhaps worth making one point in connection with Istanbul telegram No. 193[2] of July 26th. In paragraph 1 (*b*) the Turkish Prime Minister is reported as complaining that we gave Turkey no notice about internationalisation. In point of fact this proposal was produced by the President in the middle of a session without any warning to the British Delegation, so that we were in no position to give the Turks advance notice.

I am afraid this Conference is going to be another Yalta as far as Southern Department subjects are concerned. Everyone here is panting to get away, and it seems unlikely that my stirring speech about the Balkans, of which I sent you a copy,[3] will ever be delivered. At a Delegation meeting this morning it was suggested that we might try to get a declaration by the Conference asking the Balkan countries to stop squabbling.[4] I enclose a first

---

[1] The date of receipt is uncertain.
[2] No. 413.
[3] Untraced in Foreign Office archives.
[4] See No. 450, minute 4, and No. 429, annex.

draft of this which has not been cleared with anyone yet. I am far from certain that anything on these lines will ever see the light of day.

It seems very unlikely that we shall get anything now about the Yalta Declaration. Even the proposed statement about the mess the Russians have made in the position of the Control Commissions seems to have got stuck in the Russian Delegation. We are in the difficult position that the Russians are asking us to confirm that their proposals shall be the basis for the future work of the Commissions, while we ourselves are so answering for the meaning of the proposals that we cannot commit ourselves to describing them as satisfactory. But we do not wish to press too hard for their improvement for fear that they would be quoted against us at present in Italy.

I held out as long as I could against the inclusion of any reference for the resumption of diplomatic relations with the Balkan satellites in the proposed declaration about the admission of various states into the World Organisation. However under strong American pressure we have agreed to say that each Government will consider separately how far it is able to go in the direction of the resumption of diplomatic relations before the conclusion of peace treaties. This has not yet come up in the Plenary or been cleared with the Russians. But when it does we shall make it plain that we have no intention of resuming diplomatic relations with Bulgaria or Roumania until conditions improve there, and that if pressed we shall not hesitate to say so. This proposal is of course merely papering over the cracks.

As regards Roumanian oil equipment you probably know by now that the Russians have put in a counter paper[5] which turns down our proposed neutral commission. While we were thinking what to do next the Americans have produced a paper[6] on the general question of the treatment of Allied property in ex-axis countries. Apparently some of their Delegation visited the I.T. & T.[7] factory in the American zone of Berlin and found it stripped down to the concrete; this brought home to them vividly the state of affairs likely to be encou[n]tered when American owners were able to visit their property again in Europe. We think we should be able to support all the American paper and hope that they will press its acceptance strongly on the Russians. We have not yet had time to examine it very closely. I rather doubt whether anything will come of it during this meeting; probably it will be referred along with all our other topics, to the Council of Foreign Ministers in September.

I hope to be back about Wednesday or Thursday[8], though this may be

---

[5] No. 432.

[6] Cf. the American memorandum—P (Terminal) 49 of 29 July 1945: not here printed—printed under date of 25 July in *F.R.U.S. Berlin*, vol. ii, pp. 744–5. Cf. also the American memorandum on 'Removals from Germany of properties of United Nations or neutral nationals'—P (Terminal) 48 of 29 July: not here printed—printed under date of 25 July, *ibid.*, p. 870.

[7] International Telegraph and Telephone Company: cf. *op. cit.*, pp. 902–3.

[8] 1 or 2 August.

optimistic. I should like to go on leave almost immediately, not spending more than a day at the office if possible. Would this fit in with your plans, and have you any more news about your future movements?

Yours ever,

W. G. HAYTER

CALENDAR TO No. 451

i 27 July–1 Aug. 1945 Correspondence on removal from Germany of United Nations or neutral property: Mr. E. W. Playfair to Mr. H. S. Gregory (Trading with the Enemy Dept.); Mr. Dent to Mr. Playfair commenting on P. (Terminal) 48: cf. note 6 above [UE 3328/2615/77].

No. 452

Minute from Sir A. Clark Kerr to Mr. Bevin (Berlin)
[F.O. 934/2/10(80)]

[BERLIN,] 29 July 1945

I have just seen Mikolajczyk. He tells me that a fresh agreement has been reached with the Russians to stop the stripping of factories in the new areas of Poland. Under this agreement the Poles are to get 120,000 railway trucks, of which 10,000 are damaged. He hints that this accommodating attitude on the part of the Russians springs from the anxieties we have shown about the probable failure of new areas of Poland to provide any contribution towards the common pot. He thinks that there may be good prospect of Poland's being able to bear a share now that she is to get some means of transport.

2. He says that the attitude of Stalin towards the Poles has been markedly friendlier. Stalin listened to grievances he put forward and showed readiness to redress them. Stalin admitted that the Red Army had been a little grasping.

3. Stalin remarked to Mikolajczyk on the morrow of the elections that the result showed that the British people were more preoccupied with internal post-war problems than with the war with Japan and with the holding down of Germany.

4. The Communists in the Polish Government see in the result of the el[e]ctions a good hope that the policy of His Majesty's Government concerning Poland will change and that we will show more sympathy for the Bierut faction and relax our pressure for early elections.

Mikolajczyk thinks that it is very important that their minds should be disabused.

5. Stanczyk arrives this afternoon and will probably attend the Meeting.[1]

[1] See No. 453.

6. Mikolajczyk says that much of his influence in Poland has dwelt in the belief on the part of the Communists that he had Mr. Churchill behind him. He is anxious that his colleagues should get the impression that this support will be sustained and he says that it would help him if the Foreign Secretary gave him a warm welcome and suggested a private talk.[2]

A.C.K.

CALENDAR TO No. 452

i   *28 July 1945 Mr. Hankey (Warsaw) Tel. No. 66.* Reactions in Poland to result of British general election [N 9400/211/55].

[2] Mr. Dixon noted that day that this paper had been seen by Mr. Bevin.

No. 453

Record of a meeting at the Prime Minister's residence
Potsdam, on 29 July 1945 at 3 p.m.
[*F.O. 934/2/10(81)*]

Present:
THE PRIME MINISTER, The Foreign Secretary, Sir A. Cadogan, Mr. Peck, Mr. Allen, Captain Leggett (*interpreter*).
M. BIERUT, Professor Grabski, M. Mikolajczyk, M. Stanczyk, M. Minc, M. Modzelewski, M. Zebrowski (*interpreter*).

M. BIERUT set forth the general arguments of the Polish delegation in support of their claim to a frontier on the Oder and the Western Neisse on lines similar to those which he had previously followed in conversation with Mr. Churchill and Mr. Eden.[1]

He said that the decision of the Great Powers that Poland should be shifted to the west was a just one provided the frontiers were determined in such a way that Poland should not be wronged and that she should have full opportunity for healthy development as a homogeneous State. Poland had no imperialistic designs but must have a certain minimum of territory in which to live and develop. The present claims were supported by all Polish parties. When they were considered in relation to the density of population in pre-war Poland and to the needs of her present population they would be found to be modest. The pre-war density of population in the territories now claimed was slightly less than the average for the whole of pre-war Poland.

M. MIKOLAJCZYK said that he wished to address himself to three questions.

First, he recalled the Crimea Agreement to the effect that the final delimitation of Poland's frontiers in the west should await the peace settle-

[1] See Nos. 257, 267–8.

ment. But these lands now contained only one and a half million Germans and economic life was at a standstill; there were four million Poles from east of the Curzon Line for whom homes had to be found; and from the general international point of view agriculture and industry in the new territories must be brought into full production as soon as possible if Poland were to make her proper contribution to the needs of Europe. These tasks could only be undertaken by the Poles themselves. In fulfilling them, however, the Poles did not wish to be accused of establishing a *fait accompli* without the approval of the Great Powers. They therefore urged that at the present Conference a formula would be found whereby Polish administration of the new territories could be legalised and Poland thereby enabled to make her contribution to the rehabilitation of Europe.

Second, he explained that the territories claimed had been important to Germany (*a*) as an armaments base, and (*b*) as a profitable source of profit from transit trade. The areas had, however, in no sense been essential to Germany's internal economic life. Poland, however, needed the territories (*a*) as an integral part of their own balanced internal economy and (*b*) so that they could control transit trade with Czechoslovakia, Roumania and Hungary. They planned to link the Oder with the Danube by a canal across Czechoslovakia. The Oder system was also linked by canal and waterway with the Vistula and thence with Soviet Russia so that possession of the Oder would play an important part in the development of economic relations between Poland and the Soviet Union. The Germans could sabotage the Oder system either by controlling Stettin (just as they had bottled up the Vistula trade by their control of Danzig after the last war) or by controlling the whole system of tributary rivers, canals and dams centred in the Western Neisse basin. It was essential that both of these means of damaging Poland's economy should be denied to the Germans.

Third, it had been asked why Poland needed territory that had been inhabited by nine million people in order to settle four million Poles from the East. There were three replies to this question:

(*a*) according to Polish computations the population of the areas claimed before the war had not exceeded seven million and at present it was one and a half million. Before the war the eastern territories had absorbed the overflow of population from the crowded parts of central Poland (where the population density was 140 per square kilometre as against an average of 83 per square kilometre for the whole of Poland). (THE PRIME MINISTER here interjected that the density of population was a relative question depending upon the degree of industrialisation and the whole economic organisation of any given territory. If therefore the Poles proposed to develop industry in the new territories they could not argue that the same area of territory was still required as had previously been needed to house a primarily agricultural population.)

(*b*) Of the pre-war population of the new territories two million had really been of Polish race and these, even though now deported to other parts of Germany, would have to return to their homes.

(*c*) Before the war the German population had already tended to move out of these areas whereas seasonal migrants from Poland had been moving into them.

M. MIKOLAJCZYK urged that these factors which showed the dynamic character of the Polish population problem should be taken into account in assessing their territorial claims.

MR. BEVIN asked what steps His Majesty's Government, who were asked to approve the Polish claims, could take to ascertain the facts of the case. Could they send representatives, possibly with representatives of other interested countries, such as the United States, to investigate the situation on the spot.

M. BIERUT said that British representatives could certainly go there and see for themselves. Mr. Clayton of the American delegation, who was interested in industrial and economic developments in Poland, hoped to go there tomorrow.

MR. BEVIN said the the present British Government reaffirmed the policy of making no final territorial arrangements until the peace settlement. They stood for an independent Poland. But what they were now asked amounted in fact for all practical purposes to settling Poland's territorial status now. His Majesty's Government could not mislead the British public in such matters by pretending that what would in reality become a final settlement was a purely provisional one. In the Labour Party they were accustomed to call a spade a spade.

M. BIERUT complained that at the Crimea Poland's eastern frontier had been settled without waiting for the peace conference. This had created urgent problems for the Poles for which they must find a solution at once; not only had four million Poles been turned out of their homes in the east, but there were millions of deported Poles in Germany and western Europe for whom new homes must be found on Polish territory.

MR. ATTLEE suggested that British public opinion, which had felt strongly about the Germans' removal of thousands of Poles from their homes, would ask, if told that only one and a half million people remained in the disputed territories, where the others now were.

M. BIERUT said that the answer was that they had left during the course of military operations.

MR. BEVIN said that the general view taken of a possible settlement in Great Britain was on the basis of the Eastern Neisse rather than the Western Neisse. How many Poles could be settled in the territory to the east of the Oder and the Eastern Neisse and how quickly could the four million from eastern Poland be moved? How many Poles would have to be settled in the new territories in the next six months?

M. BIERUT said that these questions were difficult to answer in terms of figures. The Polish Government's studies had always been based on the Western Neisse. The question was whether Poland was to be weak or to enjoy adequate conditions for development as a properly balanced industrial and agricultural State. The problem was one affecting all the countries of

Europe. If the disputed territories remained empty they would become a desert, the mines would be flooded and industry ruined. The Polish authorities had therefore already sent their own experts to take charge of these industries and twenty-five thousand miners had been sent to the Walkenburg coalfield.

M. MIKOLAJCZYK stated that the Poles in the eastern territories were obliged to decide before 1st November whether they wished to move and that they would have to leave before 1st January. Therefore the Polish Government must begin its arrangements for their reception immediately. The Poles did not wish to be blamed for having failed in their responsibilities not only towards their own people but also towards Europe as a whole.

M. MINC said that in the east the Poles had lost the two large cities of Vilna and Lwow and that their large urban populations must be housed. There were not enough large towns east of the Eastern Neisse and they therefore needed Stettin and Breslau. It must be remembered that Warsaw had been completely destroyed, Danzig almost completely and 46% of Poznan.

MR. BEVIN asked the Poles to consider whether they could not accommodate their surplus population in the territories east of the Oder and the Eastern Neisse while their further claims were investigated.

Mr. Bevin then said that he wished to ask three further questions:
first, assuming that the frontier question had been provisionally settled, how soon thereafter would elections be held, and would all parties be allowed to compete in them?

M. BIERUT replied that free elections under the liberal rules laid down by the 1921 Constitution would be held as soon as the frontiers had been defined and the deported populations had been brought back and settled within those frontiers. This should mean that within a few months after the definition of the frontiers conditions requisite for the holding of elections should have been created. Any and every group of Poles that had a programme and candidates to put forward would be allowed to participate. The very liberal and progressive nature of the 1921 Constitution was in itself the best possible guarantee that the elections would be the most democratic that could be contrived anywhere.

MR. BEVIN said that his next question related to the withdrawal of Soviet troops.

M. BIERUT replied that they were already withdrawing. He expected that the process would be completed within a certain time, but suggested that more precise information could be obtained from the Soviet Government.

MR. BEVIN asked in the third place whether, once the frontier had been settled, the Poles would assist the Allies in supplying the rest of Europe and in particular Germany.

M. MIKOLAJCZYK replied that from the next harvest the Poles would certainly have no surplus of agricultural products available for export.

But if only in their own interests they would be anxious to do all they could to help as soon as possible over coal and industrial products.[2]

CALENDARS TO No. 453

i   *29 July 1945   U.K. Delegation notes for conversation with Polish Delegation* [F.O. 934/2/10(81)].

ii *29 July 1945   Minute by Mr. D. Allen* attaching papers from Polish Delegation (indicating views of Prof. S. Grabski on a balanced economy for Poland; Polish assumption that Polish administration is already established up to line of Oder and Western Neisse) [C 4404/4216/18].

---

[2] After this meeting, at 4.30 that afternoon, Mr. Attlee and Mr. Bevin accompanied by Sir A. Cadogan held a meeting with President Truman and Mr. Byrnes (cf. No. 450, minute 2). No official British or American record of this meeting has been traced. Mr. Truman recalled (Harry S. Truman, *Year of Decisions 1945*—London, 1955—p. 331) that at this meeting the British representatives were informed of a conversation which Mr. Truman and Mr. Byrnes, accompanied by Admiral Leahy and Mr. Bohlen, had held at noon that day with M. Molotov accompanied by M. Golunsky: see *F.R.U.S. Berlin*, vol. ii, pp. 471–6, and *Berlinskaya konferentsiya*, pp. 234–43. Reference to this conversation was made in the following letter of 29 July 1945 from Sir D. Waley in Berlin to Sir W. Eady in the Treasury (T 236/264): 'My dear Wilfrid, There is not much news to-day. German reparation was not discussed by the Big Three last night. It was touched on at a meeting by the Prime Minister and the Foreign Secretary and the President and Mr. Byrnes this afternoon, but Cadogan tells me that the discussion was in very general terms. It appears, however, that though Pauley told me that the next move should lie with us, Mr. Byrnes had a talk with Molotov without prior consultation with us. I am not clear what he said. Molotov merely replied that he would consult Stalin, who is unwell to-day. Everyone still seems to hope that the Conference will end on Tuesday. It is an odd world. Yours ever, Sigi [P.S.] Cadogan and I have arranged to see Clayton and Pauley as soon as they, on their side, have found out what has passed.'

No. 454

Minute by Mr. Foulds (Berlin)
[F.O. 934/4/30(8)]

[BERLIN,] *29 July 1945*

It will be recalled that at the Sixth Plenary Meeting on the 22nd July M. Molotov stated, with reference to the Soviet Memorandum on trustee territories (P (Terminal 13)[1] that the Soviet Delegation desired, in addition to raising the question of the former Italian colonies and of mandated territories to discuss Korea.[2] It was eventually agreed that the Foreign Ministers would discuss the Russian demands on the 23rd July, but in fact M. Molotov on that day spoke only about Italian colonies, making no further mention of Korea.

---

[1] No. 203.
[2] Cf. No. 226, minute 8.

980

In conversation yesterday with Mr. Eugene Dooman of the State Department, who was formerly Counsellor of the American Embassy at Tokyo, I speculated as to whether M. Molotov's purpose in alluding to Korea in the same breath as the Italian colonies had not been to convey a hint that Russia would expect her Allies to acquiesce in her assuming trusteeship for Korea in return for her refraining from demanding the trusteeship for some Italian colony.

Mr. Dooman said that if that were the idea the Russians would get a surprise. American public opinion would be far more sensitive to Russian encroachment in the Far East than in Europe, and Korea in American eyes was becoming a test case for the efficacy of the World Organisation.

L. H. FOULDS[3]

[3] This minute was initialed that day by Sir A. Cadogan.

No. 455

Report from Marshal Zhukov to Marshal Stalin (Berlin)

P. (*Terminal*) 47 [U 6197/3628/70]

Top secret   29 July 1945[1]

Removal by the Allies of equipment and other property from the factories in the Soviet Zone of occupation

(Handed in by the Soviet Delegation)

Hereby I report that the Americans and British, when withdrawing from the Soviet zone of occupation, *i.e.*, from the territory of Saxony, Thuringen, and province of Saxony and province of Me[c]klenburg, removed the following equipment, property and technical experts:—

Morsleben, near the town of Helmstadt [Helmstedt], Province of Saxony, from the aviation equipment plant of the Company 'Ascania Werke' in the salt mines were removed to Braunschweig:–

200 universal metal-cutting machine-tools.

All technical documentation.

All optical instruments from the laboratory.

Town of Hadmetsleben [*Hamersleben*], near town of Oschetsleben [Oschersleben] (Saxony).

The 'Junkers' underground plant in the salt mines:–

All the optical instruments were damaged, the microscope and microphotocamera's lenses were removed.

Unseburg, near town of Stassfuhrt [Stassfurt]

From the underground plant of B.M.V. [B.M.W.] Company in the salt mines were removed:–

(*a*) All technical documentation for new motors and the turbine 0018.

[1] Date of circulation to the British Delegation of the present translation of this report, printed under date of 28 July 1945 in *Berlinskaya konferentsiya*, pp. 392–9.

(*b*) Chief designer of the new reactive turbine 0018 and a group of technical experts, with their families, were taken away.

Town of Schenebeck [Schönebeck]

From the Junkers' plant producing HE-162 aircraft were removed:–

(*a*) 50 turbines of the firm B.M.W. were dismantled from the finished HE-162 aircraft.

(*b*) Chief engineer of the plant and a group of technical experts with their families.

Beendorf, near town of Helmstadt

From the Siemen's plant situated in the salt mines, the pit 'Maria', for the production of the aviation equipment and autopilots for the V-1 and V-2 aircraft were removed:–

All technical documentation; all optical instruments and the laboratory.

Chief engineer of the plant and a group of technical experts with their families.

Tartun [Tarthun], near the town of Schenebeck

From the underground Junkers' aviation plant were removed:–

Technical documentation and draughts.

Chief engineer and a group of designers and technologists with their families.

Town of Stassfuhrt

From the Berlepsch salt mine were removed:–

10 precise geodesic instruments and devices.

From the pits 'Ludwig-1' and 'Ludwig-2' of the 'Ludwig' mine from the underground Commissary stores of the German War Office were removed:–

More than 100 railway cars of ammunition and fabrics, including the the fabrics produced by the Russian Morozov Factory.

Town of Kleimwansleben [Kleinwanzleben], westward of the city of Magdeburg.

From the Institute of beet-sugar production (a research Institute of world-wide importance) were removed in April:–

All the main laboratory equipment and the scientific and research works.

Two doctors of Biological Sciences with their families.

Town of Merseburg

From the 'Leyna [Leuna]' plant producing Synthetic gasoline, carbon and ammoniac were removed:–

A suitcase full of platinum (that was in the store in the plant).

28 engineers.

The Americans gave permission to Krupp to remove the plant. The Commander of the Soviet 129 Rifle Corps stopped the removal of the equipment, but all the principal technical staff has been taken away.

Town of Helle [Halle]

Twenty-four scientists, including the outstanding physiologist, the Nobel prizewinner Professor Doctor Emil Abderhalden, were taken away from the

Institute of Physics and Chemistry.

The laboratory of the Institute was removed.

From the Siebbel plant were removed:

The draught-designs of new speed aircraft.

Chief designer of the plant.

Town of Schkopau

1,400 tons of finished rubber products and 40 klg. of platinum were removed from the Buhna plant.

Simultaneously 26 leading chemical engineers, including inventors, research-workers with their families and personal belongings were taken away. Many engineers raised a protest against this, but they were made to leave by force.

Village of Berka (Saxony)

Up to 100 tons of gold were removed from the store of medical supplies.

Town of Niedersachswerfen (Saxony)

A plant producing V-1 and V-2 weapons was partially removed.

Town of Ilfelde [*Ilfeld*] (Saxony)

The equipment of plant producing Faust-cartridges was partially removed.

Town of Langensaltz [*Langensalza*] (Saxony)

The workers of Krupps and Junkers plants were taken away.

The machine-tools of the aviation school-factory producing aircraft JU–88 were partially removed.

City of Ienna [*Jena*]

From the Zeiss plant were removed:–

The central optical Control Laboratory.

The reproduction laboratory.

The physics laboratory.

The electro-technical laboratory.

The range-finder laboratory.

The crystallographic laboratory.

The metallographic laboratory.

The microscopic laboratory.

The medical laboratory.

The geodesic laboratory.

20 million R.M. worth of finished optical-mechanical devices.

All the original draughts of all kinds of optical-mechanical production.

77 leading experts, including the Chief Engineer of the plant, 3 professors and 35 Doctors of Technical sciences.

From the 'Schott' optical plant were removed:–

The optical control laboratory.

The physics laboratory.

The range-finder laboratory.

The crystallographic laboratory.

The microscopic laboratory.

The geodesic laboratory.

3 million R.M. worth of the finished production.

All kinds of draughts for all kinds of optical production.

50 key-experts, including the Chief Engineer of the plant, Doctor of Technical Sciences Berger.

Town of Weida

From the Berlin Physical and Technical Institute were removed:–

All the supplies of radium and pollonium [polonium].

2 complexes of quarz clocks.

A series of etaloons [*sic*] and measuring instruments (magnitons [*sic*], vacuum pumps, electromagnets, &c.).

Modern technical literature.

The draughts of apparatus of new constructions.

The records of physical observations.

13 experts of the high frequency laboratory, including Doctor Schaibe, the head of the laboratory and Doctor Meller, President of the Institute.

Town of Eisenach

From the Bavarian motor-building plant were removed:–

302,000 R.M. worth of equipment.

Engineers and designers of the plant.

Town of Gera

From the Siemens-Hallske electro-technical enterprise were removed:–

The most valuable equipment and finished production, for example, the newest signal-speaking system for railroads.

All technical key-personnel, including Keyser, the manager, and Patz, the Chief Engineer.

From 'Califon-Fabric' were removed:–

All chemical experts and the manager of the factory.

City of Jegeln [Egeln]

From the aircraft factory 'Junkers' was removed, the Chief Engineer with drawings.

City of Bad-Blannenburg [Blankenburg]

A part of the laboratory of the firm 'Telefunken' was removed.

Twenty experts in military wireless technique were removed.

City of Leipzig

From the factory of the firm 'Leis Schoper' were removed:–

Drawings of non-contact contained fuzes.

Three experts.

Drawings and two experts were removed from the factory where gyroscopic compasses for U-boats of the firm 'Schitzsche' were manufactured.

City of Zwickau

From the 'Horch' factory of the 'Autounion' concern were removed:

Electrical torpedo drawings.

The Chief Designer of torpedoes.

City of Verdau [Werdau]
(*a*) Three experts and drawings were removed from the 'Schwarzkopf' factory, where principal engines and governing instruments for torpedoes were manufactured.
(*b*) Three experts and drawings were removed from the 'Siemens' naval instruments factory.

City of Bitterfeld
From the 'I.G. Farben Industrie' were removed:–
25 experts.
Recipes, reports on research work, drawings, patents for production of chlorine, calcium, chloride, hydrogen, chloride-benzole chlorineiron, &c.

City of Berngurg [Bernberg]
From the 'Deutsche Solne [Solway] Werke' were removed:
10 experts.
Recipes.
Reports on research work.
Drawings.
Patents on production of calcinated soda; sodium hydroxide, bicarbonate, calcium, chloride, and cement.

City of Playen [Plauen]
From the works of the firm 'Horn' were removed:–
All technical documentation.
Specimens and manufactured goods of automatic control of the plane and flying bombs.
Chief Constructor—Doctor Edhard Horn—and his two assistants.
Many documents, drawings, were blown up and burned.

City of Ka[h]la (Thuringen)
From the works of the firm 'Gustloff Werke Reimag' were removed:
Original drawings of Me.-262, the reaction engines and turbines.
All copies documents and experimental specimens are burned.

Village of Molsdorg [Morsdorf] (Thuringen)
Research laboratory of the firm 'Siemens S[c]hukert' for the application of high frequency currents and ultra-violet rays for glueing of wood, its drying, increasing of vitamins in food-stuffs, catalytic agent for chemical process, change of atom structure of some solutions, &c.
All reports on finished works and researches as well as research personnel of four men and staff technical personnel with most valuable apparatus were removed.

City of Suhl
From the artillery-rifle works of 'Gustlaw', where there has been a central engineering bureau for rifle and small calibre artillery production and the largest laboratory were removed:
All designers to the last.
All engineers which worked directly in shops.

Technical experts with drawings and technical data.

Village of Merkers (near city of Gotha)

Some time ago, from Berlin to the mines of Kaiserode and Grossgerzen were removed:–

Gold and other valuables of German State Bank, paintings and other objects of art of State museums of Berlin, acts and apparatuses of Königsberg canals.

According to the Manager of the Kaiserode joint stock company and the chief mining engineer, from this mine were removed all these valuables, including:–

Gold of the German bank—over 100 tons.

Paper currency, approximately 4 railroad cars' load.

All paintings and other valuables from Berlin museums.

Acts and instruments of the Königsberg canal board.

Village of Wertenrode [*Wernröde*] (Harz)

It is reported that in the potassium mine in Wertenrode were hidden 250 extremely valuable paintings, 4 sculptures, 48 gaubelins [gobelins] and 3 boxes containing the so-called Royal treasures from the Prussian Royal Palace (crowns, swords, sceptres, &c.).

Enquiries made of local inhabitants revealed that cultural valuables hidden in Wertenrode were removed by the Americans round about the 8th April, 1945.

According to incomplete information received from a Commission investigating synthetic oil plants in the area of Magdeburg, Chemnitz, Leuna ('Treglitz', 'Schwartzfaide' and 'Ruland' factories), managers, chemical experts, mechanics and technical documents were removed.

In all, up to 80 per cent. of all military doctors, all gold, silver, deposited in banks were removed from the province of Thüringen.

In addition, the British city of Beuzenburg [*Boitzenburg*]

Partly removed the equipment from the Dornier aircraft factory.

Removed ready-made output from the motor-boat and self-propelled barges.

Experts with families—6 persons.

Part of turbine drawings.

City of Haltberstadt [*Halberstadt*] (*province of Saxony*)

From the works 'Malakhite' for production of engines 'B.M.W.' were removed:–

Model of reaction turbine 004.

Its drawings.

Experts, engineers and technologists—6 persons.

City of Wernigorode [*Wernigerode*]

From the works of 'Rautenbach' for aircraft engine castings were removed:–

X-ray apparatus for inspection of castings—7.

Precision machine tools (including 1 S.I.P.)—2.
All drawings of production objects.
Equipment of metallography and mechanic laboratories.
From the branch works of the firm 'Junkers' were removed:–
All drawings for turbine 004 and motor.

Village of Königshütte (near Elbingerode)
A number of parts and equipment of Kiev Movie studio were removed:–
Movie apparatus—3.
Parts of movie projectors.

City of Ostervik [Osterwieck]
From the clothing factory of brothers 'Asmole-Galle,' all the equipment of the factory was removed.

City of Salbelel [Salzwedel]
200,000 tons of gasoline and workshop equipment were removed from the airfield.

City of Oschersleben
Removed: a part of the equipment, drawings of all sorts of production, leading and technical personnel of the 'Junkers' aircraft factory that produced turbine fighter planes.

The investigation into the removal of equipment and valuables is continuing.

No. 456

Minute from Mr. Dixon to Mr. Coulson (Berlin)
[UE 3464/2615/77]

Top secret   [BERLIN,] *29 July 1945*

The Secretary of State has called for a report on the experimental German stations in our zone. These stations, I understand, contain the 'wind tunnels' used in connection with jet propelled aircraft. Mr. Bevin is also interested in the experimental rocket stations, of which I believe there is one at Brunswick.

The Secretary of State wishes to be sure that there is no danger of our handing over any of this equipment to the Russians as part of reparation. He considers that the equipment should be very valuable to us and has in mind that we should either remove it to the United Kingdom or continue to use if for experimental purposes *in situ*.[1]

P.D.

[1] Mr. Coulson minuted in reply: 'We regard the equipment of these experimental stations as "booty". Before we got into Germany an Anglo–American organisation was set up, called the Combined Intelligence Objectives Sub-Committee, whose job it was to decide on the intelligence information of this kind which we wanted to get out of Germany, and arrangements were made for parties of men to go as early as possible to all the likely spots. A great deal of experimental material has been taken in this way, even out of what is now

the Russian Zone; as witnessed by Marshal Zhukov's report [No. 455] which Marshal Stalin circulated yesterday. There is no question of our allowing any of this "booty" to be handed over as reparation. J. E. Coulson July 29th, 1945.' Mr. Bevin minuted: 'Noted E. B.'

No. 457

Mr. Morrison to Mr. Bevin (Berlin: received 29 July, 8.59 p.m.)
No. 278 Onward Telegraphic [PREM 3/139/9]

FOREIGN OFFICE, 29 July 1945, 5.40 p.m.[1]

Immediate. Top secret

Following for Rowan from Colville (Nocop).[2]

Mr. Churchill is drafting a statement on the use and development of T[ube] A[lloys] as intended before the change of government. Throughout the last four years aided by Sir John Anderson and Lord Cherwell he has as Minister of Defence conducted the handling of this matter in its non-technical aspect. He thinks it of great importance that the early beginnings before America came into the war should have due prominence, as this establishes our case for the very large British share conceded by President Roosevelt to Mr. Churchill in the project.[3] He will be glad if the Prime Minister chooses to issue this from 10, Downing Street, explaining that it is a statement Mr. Churchill had intended to make public, when the time comes, simultaneously with those of President Truman and Mr. Stimson to the text of which he had agreed.[4]

CALENDAR TO NO. 457

i *23–4 July 1945 Letter from Mr. D. Rickett (Cabinet Office) to Mr. Rowan (Berlin); Minute from Lord Cherwell to Mr. Churchill:* Anglo-American coordination of draft statements on atomic development [PREM 3/139/9].

[1] Time of origin.
[2] A designation of restricted circulation.
[3] Cf. M. Gowing, *op. cit.*, pp. 164, 340–1.
[4] See No. 110, note 3, and No. 110.ii.

No. 458

Letter from President Truman to Mr. Attlee (Berlin)[1]
[UE 3550/32/71]

THE WHITE HOUSE, WASHINGTON, AT BABELSBERG (BERLIN), 29 July 1945

Copy

My dear Mr. Prime Minister:

In accordance with my letter of July 25,[2] I enclose a copy of a memoran-

[1] This letter is printed with enclosure in *F.R.U.S. Berlin*, vol. ii, pp. 1184–5.
[2] No. 272.

dum directive on the issuance of Lend-Lease munitions, which I have today
sent to the Joint Chiefs of Staff. This directive eliminates the delivery of
Lend-Lease material for the occupation of Axis countries. In other respects I
believe it adequately covers your expressed desires.

I have noted the suggestion in the letter of July 24,[3] that postwar economic
arrangements be discussed in Washington, say in September. Mr. W. L.
Clayton, Assistant Secretary of State, will be in London shortly for the
U.N.R.R.A. Council meeting, and I have instructed him to engage in
informal conversations with your people about these matters. When he has
reported to me in Washington, we shall be able to decide upon arrangements
for further discussions with your representatives.

Very sincerely yours,
HARRY TRUMAN

ENCLOSURE IN No. 458

Copy of Memorandum Directive to the Joint Chiefs of Staff

Top secret

Referring to my memorandum of 5 July, 1945,[4] quoted herewith following:
'Approval of the issue to Allied Governments of Lend-Lease munitions of war
and military and naval equipment will be limited to that which is to be used in
the war against Japan, and it will not be used for any other purpose.'
It may be given the following interpretation:

1. Issue of Lend-Lease munitions of war and military and naval equipment to
all Allied Governments, including Latin American countries is authorized when
in the opinion of the Joint Chiefs of Staff it is to be used in direct support of
redeployment of American troops, or Allied troops in connection with their
redeployment in support of the war against Japan.

2. Supply of Allied service units that are directly serving United States forces
in any area with subsistence, supply, and equipment (except arms and
ammunition) is authorized.

3. Until the receipt of further instructions issue of Lend-Lease munitions of
war and military and naval equipment to the U.S.S.R. is authorized in accordance
with my directive of 11 May, 1945,[5] when in the opinion of the Joint Chiefs of
Staff it can be considered as for use in the war against Japan.

4. Until the receipt of further instructions issue of Lend-Lease munitions of
war and military and naval equipment to the British Empire is authorized for
the direct support of redeployment of American troops, and of British troops in
connection with their re-deployment in support of the war against Japan, taking
into account commitments for approved combined operations against Japan. In
accordance with my memorandum of 17 July, 1945, to the Prime Minister,[6]
and subject to the elimination of the requirements for occupational forces in Axis
countries, such issue should be generally in accord with schedules of requirements

---

[3] Annex I to No. 251.
[4] See No. 26, note 4.
[5] Cf. *F.R.U.S. 1945*, vol. v, pp. 999–1001.
[6] Annex to No. 174.

and other terms arrived at by British and American supply representatives in October-November 1944, subject to changing strategic demands as well as to usual supply, procurement, and allocation considerations and procedures.

5. Replacement and maintenance on a military Lend-Lease basis of French units which have already been equipped by the U.S. under the North African Rearmament Program, Metropolitan Rearmament Program, and Air Forces Program is authorized for subsistence until August 31, 1945, and for other items of equipment and supply until September 30, 1945.

6. Supply of maintenance items for U.S. equipment now in the possession of Allied armies may be issued for purposes other than those specifically approved in this memorandum against payment under such terms and conditions as may be determined by the State Department and Foreign Economic Administration in accordance with established procedure.

H. S. T.

July 29, 1945

CALENDAR TO No. 458

i *29 July 1945* *Minute from Mr. Rowan to Mr. Attlee (Berlin)*. Attaches No. 458 and draft, prepared by Sir R. Sinclair, for reply at No. 503. Sir R. Sinclair is confident that this is as good as we can hope to get. Mr. Churchill would have been in agreement [PREM 4/17/15].

No. 459

Memorandum by Mr. Jebb (Berlin)

[U 6311/2600/70]

[BERLIN,] *29 July 1945*

The attached exchange of minutes between Mr. Eden and Mr. Attlee[1] raises issues of the greatest importance and affects our entire foreign policy. One thing is clear, namely that we should be well advised to press for a reference of the whole problem of 'bases' to the World Organisation (Military Staff Committee) as soon as it is constituted, and in the meantime to try to arrange for it to be discussed with the Russians on a technical level. I lately endeavoured in London to induce the Chiefs of Staff to agree to some fairly early meeting between the representatives of the General Staffs of the five prospective Permanent Members of the Security Council in order

(*a*) to discuss the method of work of the Military Staff Committee, and

(*b*) to exchange views in a preliminary way regarding the 'special agreement' which the Five Powers themselves will probably jointly make with the Security Council.

[1] See Nos. 179 and 238, also No. 237 cited below.

It seemed to me that on this 'special agreement' almost everything would depend; and it is clear that it cannot be negotiated until there is at any rate broad agreement on such major problems as the control of the Straits, the Suez Canal and (I should personally have thought) the entrances to the Baltic.

2. The Prime Minister suggests:

(*a*) that apart from any other considerations, we are not in a position to resist a Russian claim physically to dominate the Straits and an attempt to place herself in a strategic position to enforce her right to have 'free access to the oceans'; and

(*b*) that if these objectives on the part of the Russians were obtained they would have 'only a relative importance in the light of modern war conditions now that air power transcends all frontiers and menaces all home-lands'.

He also suggests that, in view of our economic position, we may not ourselves be able to continue to be solely responsible for the defence of the Suez Canal area and Singapore.

3. No-one can predict the future development of the technique of warfare, but it is at least arguable that there is an antidote to every conceivable offensive weapon. It is also arguable that air power itself is now largely out of date. General Eisenhower is reported to have said that it might pay the United States to scrap all their existing aeroplanes and concentrate entirely on research, rockets being presumably the weapon of the future. But even rockets may perhaps be countered by blowing them up in the air by specially directed anti-aircraft fire, and if that situation were arrived at then land and sea bases might play a very much more important part than now seems likely. I only make these observations to draw attention to the fact that present manoeuverings for position on the part of Russia, and indeed on the part of other Powers, may be of very real importance. At any rate the Russians themselves seem to think that they are, and in these matters they are certainly not unintelligent.

4. A further most important consideration is what is meant by 'power politics'. I should like myself to think that this term refers to a *misuse* of power in the conduct of foreign policy. If this is so, the term could apply, for instance, to Hitler's attempt to dominate Europe. But until such a time as the Great Nations are prepared voluntarily to renounce their sovereignty, or at any rate some essential part of it, until such a time in fact as a World State has been created, international politics can only be an expression of power. Marshal Stalin said this in so many words during the present talks in Potsdam;[2] and however much we may deplore it it is impossible to contest the truth of his observation.

5. In any case the World Organisation, as expressed in the Charter signed at San Francisco, is undoubtedly based on the physical power of the major states. This means that it will only work if they co-operate among themselves,

[2] Cf. No. 208, minute 4.

and this in its turn means it will only work if they come to some broad agreement regarding mutual respect for their various interests. The effort to achieve such a harmonising of interests is now proceeding and will continue whatever policy we adopt. In the course of it bargaining will be necessary. If such bargaining is to take place, it can only be on a basis of power. A state which has no power cannot make any bargain. A state with insufficient power can only make a bad bargain. But each state concerned must at least say what it wants, and this entails making it clear that in the last resort there are certain interests which it cannot abandon except under compulsion. And compulsion may mean war.

6. It may well be, of course, that in these circumstances we shall find it advisable and necessary to abandon many positions in order to defer to Russian views; but there is presumably a point beyond which we could not go. This point it is very necessary to determine. To yield to *any* Russian demand would clearly mean that we were not prepared to play the part of a Great Power which has been allotted to us in the present World Organisation. If we took this line we should be powerless to uphold the rights of the smaller states who look to us for assistance, and our own future would be decided not by us but by other people. Supposing, therefore, that the general thesis that we must stand up for what we consider our rights is accepted, what is the nature of the bargain which we might conceivably hope to drive with the Russians in Eastern Europe and in the Middle East?

7. I suggest that this problem can be analysed as follows:

(*a*) The Russians, who are certainly pursuing entirely national ends, have as their immediate objectives the physical control of the Straits and the political control of Turkey and Greece. By 'political control' is meant the formation of a government in those countries broadly equivalent to the governments now constituted in Roumania, Bulgaria and Yugoslavia. The achievement of either objective would be almost certain to involve the achievement of the other. It is true that the Russians may at the moment be pursuing these objectives by a kind of 'defensive offensive'. In other words, it may be our own attempt to keep our end up in the other Balkan countries mentioned which has led to the recent Russian attack on our Greek policy, and even to a worsening of their relations with the Turks. It is arguable that, if we by one means or another made it clear that we did not propose to interfere in Roumania, Bulgaria and Yugoslavia, we might induce the Russians for the time being to revert to their previous attitude in regard to e.g. Greece. At Yalta, for example, Marshal Stalin went out of his way to express approval of our Greek policy and it is notable that the attack on it in Potsdam only took place the day after we had presented our paper on Yugoslavia[3]. The objectives, however, remain. Whether the Russians pursue them actively depends entirely on their estimate of the opposition which such action would be likely to arouse. And this in its turn very largely depends on whether

[3] See Nos. 194, minute 9, and 200, minute 6.

they think that it would be likely to involve a real break with England and America.

(*b*) Do we then for our part consider that the attainment by the Russians of the immediate objectives referred to above is something which we could in the last resort agree to, or are we prepared to risk a show-down in order to prevent it? It seems to me that this question depends very largely on whether in such a show-down we should be sure of American support. If we are sure of it we ought, presumably, to oppose the Russian demands for the reason that the creation of a sort of Russian Scapa Flow in the Sea of Marmora, and the establishment of an E.A.M. Government in Greece and of some kind of similar régime in Turkey would undoubtedly have an unfavourable effect on our whole position in the Middle East and indeed in the world. If, however, we are not sure of it then there is a great deal to be said for our at least leaving open the way for retreat and fighting, as it were, a rearguard action, which might conceivably result in the Russians achieving their objectives to only a limited extent.

(*c*) As the Prime Minister points out, one of the weak points in our case is the fact that, whereas at present we oppose the establishment of Russian bases in the Straits, we continue to have bases of our own in the area of the Suez Canal. This attitude is clearly illogical; and if we intend to maintain our present position in the Suez Canal we can in the long run only resist a similar Russian claim in the Straits on the grounds that neither we nor the Americans wish them to have such bases, and are, if necessary, prepared to oppose any such claim on their part by force.

(*d*) If we are not prepared to take this line—and indeed it could only be taken in complete harmony with America—then we must either let the Russians have their bases in the Straits with the probable effect on the political situation in Turkey and in Greece indicated above, or we must, so to speak, regularise the position, either by agreeing to have no bases in the Suez Canal ourselves provided the Russians leave the control of the Straits to Turkey, or alternatively by suggesting that the Russians should assist us in the control of the Suez Canal provided that they allow us to take part in the control of the Straits.

(*e*) It should be noted that any self-denying ordinance on our part might be combined with the retention of British forces in Cyprus, Palestine[4] and Aden, which are, after all, British possessions, though it might also have to be combined with our agreeing to having no base in Iraq, provided that the Russians cleared out of Northern Persia and genuinely respected Persian independence.

8. No attempt is made in this paper to suggest what line we ought to pursue, the object simply being to analyse the position. What is, however, abundantly clear is that, whether the question of bases by itself, or the allied question of Russian policy in Turkey and in Greece as well, is referred to the

---

[4] This word is queried on the original by Sir A. Cadogan to whom this memorandum was addressed.

World Organisation, or alternatively whether it is discussed in accordance with Article 106 of the Charter by the Big Five in advance of the constitution of the United Nations, the same issues will arise and the same bargaining will be necessary. If it is clearly recognised that the whole functioning of the World Organisation and the whole preservation of peace during the coming years depends in the first instance on a harmonising of the interests of the Three Great Powers then the first essential is for each of these three to know what it wants and what concessions it is in the last resort prepared to make. At the moment only the Russians seem to have a clearly defined national policy. The absence of such a policy in England and America, more than any other single factor, is likely to give rise to misunderstandings and difficulties which, if they are allowed to continue, may darken the prospects of the World Organisation we are seeking to create.

Conclusion

The Chiefs of Staff should be asked, as a matter of urgency,

(*a*) to re-examine the question of the possible establishment of Russian bases in the Straits (and the consequential establishment of pro-Russian Governments in Greece and Turkey) in the light of the Terminal discussions and of the considerations advanced in paragraph 7 of this paper;

(*b*) To state what exactly would be likely to be the military effect of the establishment of Russian bases in the entrances to the Baltic (1) with and (2) without the establishment there of corresponding British bases;

(*c*) to produce in rough outline the kind of 'special agreement' which we, together with our four principal Allies, might be prepared to make with with [*sic*] Security Council;

(*d*) to indicate in detail the way in which, as they see it, the Military Staff Committee ought to function.[6]

GLADWYN JEBB

[5] Sir A. Cadogan minuted on this: 'This must be dealt with in the F.O. Sir O. Sargent shd. first see this paper. A. C. July 30, 1945.'

No. 460

Minute from Mr. Brook to Mr. Hayter (Berlin)
[*F.O. 934/2/8(14)*]

OFFICES OF THE WAR CABINET, GREAT GEORGE STREET [*sic*], *29 July 1945*

I agreed with Mr. Walter Brown[1] this evening our amendments to the U.S. draft of a skeleton communique. He accepted all our suggestions. The enclosed copy incorporates them.

[1] Special Assistant to Mr. Byrnes.

Mr. Brown gave me a draft paragraph[2] on 'military talks' which has been drafted by Admiral Leahy. I have not included this in the roneo-d version. I am showing it in the first instance to General Ismay.

NORMAN BROOK

ENCLOSURE IN NO. 460

Top secret

Terminal

First Draft of Communique

Report on the Tripartite Conference of Berlin

I

On July 17, 1945, the President of the United States, Harry S. Truman, the Chairman of the Council of Peoples Commissars of the Union of Soviet Socialist Republics, Generalissimo J. V. Stalin, and the Prime Minister of Great Britain, Winston S. Churchill, together with Mr. Clement R. Attlee, met in the Tripartite Conference of Berlin accompanied by the foreign secretaries of the three governments, the Chiefs of Staff, and other advisers.

There were nine meetings ending July 25. The Conference was then interrupted for two days, while the results of the British general election were being declared.

On July 28 Mr. Attlee returned to the Conference as Prime Minister, accompanied by the new Foreign Minister of Great Britain, Mr. Ernest Bevin. There were . . .[3] additional meetings. The Conference ended on . . .[3]

Important decisions and agreements were reached and they are announced in this report. Views were exchanged on a number of other questions that deeply concern the three Governments and consideration of these matters will be continued by the Council of Foreign Ministers which was agreed upon here.

This Conference strengthened the ties among the three governments and extended the scope of their collaboration and understanding.

President Truman, Generalissimo Stalin and Prime Minister Attlee leave this Conference with renewed confidence that their governments and peoples, together with the other United Nations, will succeed in creating a just and enduring peace.

II

Establishment of a Council of Foreign Ministers

The Conference reached an agreement for the establishment of a Council of Foreign Ministers to continue the necessary preparatory work for the peace settlement and to take up other matters which from time to time may be referred to the Council by agreement.

Text of the agreement is as follows:

'(1) There should be established a Council composed of the Foreign Minister[s] of the United Kingdom, the Union of Soviet Socialist Republics, China, France, and the United States.

'(2)(i) The Council shall normally meet at London, which shall be the permanent seat of the joint Secretariat which the Council will form. Each of the Foreign Ministers will be accompanied by a high-ranking Deputy, duly authorised to carry on the work of the Council in the absence of his Foreign Minister, and by a small staff of technical advisers.

---

[2] Untraced.   [3] Punctuation as in original.

'(ii) The first meeting of the Council shall be held in London not later than September 1st, 1945. Meetings may be held by common agreement in other capitals as may be agreed from time to time.

'(3)(i) As its immediate important task, the Council shall be authorised to draw up, with a view to their submission to the United Nations, treaties of peace with Italy, Roumania, Bulgaria, Hungary and Finland, and to propose settlements of territorial questions outstanding on the termination of the war in Europe. The Council shall be utilised for the preparation of a peace settlement for Germany to be accepted by the Government of Germany when a government adequate for the purpose is established.

'(ii) For the discharge of each of these tasks the Council will be composed of the Members representing those States which were signatory to the terms of surrender imposed upon the enemy State concerned. For the purposes of the peace settlement for Italy, France shall be regarded as a signatory to the terms of surrender for Italy. Other Members will be invited to participate when matters directly concerning them are under discussion.

'(iii) Other matters may from time to time be referred to the Council by agreement between the Member Governments.

'(4)(i) Whenever the Council is considering a question of direct interest to a State not represented thereon, such State should be invited to send representatives to participate in the discussion and study of that question.

'(ii) The Council may adapt its procedure to the particular problem under consideration. In some cases it may hold its own preliminary discussions prior to the participation of other interested States. In other cases, the Council may convoke a formal conference of the State chiefly interested in seeking a solution of the particular problem.'

The Three Governments have each addressed an identical invitation to the Governments of China and France to adopt this text and to join in establishing the Council.

The establishment of the Council of Foreign Ministers for the specific purposes named in the text will be without prejudice to the agreement of the Crimea Conference that there should be periodic consultation among the Foreign Secretaries of the United States, the Union of Soviet Socialist Republics and the United Kingdom.

The Conference also considered the position of the European Advisory Commission in the light of the agreement to establish the Council of Foreign Ministers. It was noted with satisfaction that the Commission had ably discharged its principal tasks by the recommendations that it had furnished for the terms of Germany's surrender, for the zones of occupation in Germany and Austria, and for the inter-Allied control machinery in those countries. It was felt that further work of a detailed character for the co-ordination of Allied policy for the control of Germany and Austria would in future fall within the competence of the Allied Control Commission at Berlin and the Allied Commission at Vienna. Accordingly, the Conference agreed to recommend to the Member Governments of the European Advisory Commission that the Commission be now dissolved.

III

Germany

The Allied armies are in occupation of the whole of Germany and the German people have begun to atone for the terrible crimes committed in their name by those leaders whom, in the hour of their success, they loudly applauded and blindly obeyed.

Agreement has been reached at this Conference on the political [and economic][4] principles to govern the treatment of Germany during the initial control period. The text of this agreement is appended[5] to this report.

The purpose of this agreement is to carry out the Crimea declaration on Germany. [The German people will be compelled to compensate to the greatest possible extent for the loss and suffering that their country caused to the United Nations and for which they cannot escape responsibility.][4] German militarism and Nazism will be extirpated and the Allies will take in agreement together, now and in the future, the other measures necessary to assure that Germany never again will threaten her neighbo[u]rs or the peace of the world.

It is not the intention of the Allies to destroy or enslave the German people. It is the intention of the Allies that the German people be given the opportunity to prepare for the eventual reconstruction of their life on a democratic and peaceful basis. If their own efforts are steadily directed to this end, it will be possible for them in due course to take their place among the free and peaceful peoples of the world.

IV

Reparations from Germany
(Text to be agreed upon)

V

Austria

During the course of the Conference, final approval was given to the Agreement on Zones of Occupation in Austria and the Administration of the City of Vienna, and the Agreement on Control Machinery in Austria, recommended by the European Advisory Commission. The two Agreements, having likewise been approved by the Provisional Government of the French Republic, come into force at once.

VI

Poland

The following statement was approved:

'We have taken note with pleasure of the agreement reached among representative Poles from Poland and abroad which has made possible the formation, in accordance with the decisions reached at the Crimea Conference, of a Polish Provisional Government of National Unity recognised by the Three Powers. The establishment by the British and United States Governments of diplomatic relations with the Polish Provisional Government has resulted in the withdrawal of their recognition from the former Polish Government in London, which no longer exists.

'The British and United States Governments have taken measures to protect the interest of the Polish Provisional Government as the recognised government of the Polish State in the property belonging to the Polish State located on their territory and under their control, whatever the form of this property may be.

---

[4] Square brackets in the original.
[5] Not appended to filed copy: see No. 603, section II.

They have further taken measures to prevent alienation to third parties of such property. All proper facilities will be given to the Polish Provisional Government for the exercise of the ordinary legal remedies for the recovery of any property of the Polish State which may have been wrongfully alienated.

'The three powers are anxious to assist the Polish Provisional Government in facilitating the return to Poland as soon as practicable of all Poles abroad who wish to go, including members of the Polish Armed Forces and the Merchant Marine. They expect that those Poles who return home shall be accorded personal rights and rights of property on the same basis as all Polish citizens.

'The three powers note that the Polish Provisional Government in conformity with the Crimea decision has agreed to the holding of free and unfettered elections as soon as possible on the basis of universal suffrage and secret ballot in which all democratic and anti-Nazi parties shall have the right to take part and to put forward candidates, and that representatives of the Allied press shall enjoy full freedom to report to the world upon the developments in Poland before and during the elections.'

VII
Removals of Populations
(Text to be agreed upon)

VIII
Other Agreements on Liberated Europe
(Text to be agreed upon)

IX
International Waterways
(Text to be agreed upon)

X
Withdrawal of troops from Iran
(Text to be agreed upon)

XI
Other Agreements
(Text to be agreed upon)

XII
Military Talks
(Text to be agreed upon)

XIII
Lists of Delegations
(Text to be agreed upon)

No. 461

Minute from Mr. Rowan to Sir E. Bridges[1] *(Berlin)*
[*PREM 3/430/14*]

Private   BERLIN, *30 July 1945*

You may wish to see the attached copy of a note dictated by the Prime

[1] This minute was addressed to '*Sir Edward Bridges* (For Yourself Alone)'.

Minister about the question of Mr. Churchill and Mr. Eden returning to this Conference. I send you this for your private information only and shall be glad if I may have the enclosure back.

T. L. R.

ENCLOSURE IN No. 461

On the evening of Thursday, the 26th, I had a talk with Mr. Eden on the question of participation in the Potsdam talks by a representative of the Conservative Party. He told me that Mr. Churchill did not want to go, and discussed the question as to whether it would be advisable for him to attend. He said that he was, of course, quite willing to help in every way, but he was most clearly not at all keen. I told him that I should be consulting with my colleagues on the general principle involved. He told me that if no invitation was sent I could be quite sure that neither the Prime Minister, himself, nor his Party generally would feel in the least disturbed by it.

July 30, 1945

No. 462

Note of Second Staff Conference with Prime Minister and Foreign Secretary, held at 23 Ringstrasse on Monday, 30 July 1945 at 10 a.m.

[*F.O. 934/2/8(16)*]

Top secret

Present:
THE RT. HON. C. R. ATTLEE, M.P., PRIME MINISTER, The Rt. Hon. Ernest Bevin, M.P., Secretary of State for Foreign Affairs, Sir A. Cadogan, Sir E. Bridges, Sir D. Waley, Mr. P. J. Dixon, Sir A. Clark Kerr, Sir W. Strang, Mr. N. Brook, Mr. T. L. Rowan, and Officials of the Foreign Office.

Contents

Minute No.	Subject
1.	Future meetings of the conference
2.	Reparations
3.	German fleet and merchant navy
4.	Neutral and ex-enemy states: admission to the United Nations
5.	Consultation with the French Government
6.	War crimes
7.	Yalta declaration on liberated Europe

1. *Future meetings of the Conference*

SIR ALEXANDER CADOGAN said that the U.S. Delegation had heard that Premier Stalin, who was indisposed, would be unable to attend any meeting that day. Mr. Byrnes had suggested that, in these circumstances, a meeting of Foreign Secretaries might be held during the afternoon, possibly at 4 p.m.

It was agreed that we should support this suggestion.

999

2. *Reparations*

It was suggested that, at the meeting of Foreign Secretaries that afternoon, we might seek to make further progress towards an agreement on reparations.

SIR DAVID WALEY said that, with this in view, he had prepared short statements [i] on some of the main issues on which it seemed possible that a settlement might now be reached. He suggested that these statements might be handed in at the meeting in support of oral explanations of the views of the British Delegation.

(i) *The 'First Charge'*

Sir David Waley suggested that we should seek to have included in the Statement of Economic Principles a declaration that 'payment for approved imports into Germany shall be a first charge against the proceeds of exports out of current production and out of stocks of goods'. He submitted a short statement on this point, and confirmed that this would meet the views of the Control Council for Germany.

This statement was approved, subject to amendment of the final sentence so as to read—'Meanwhile each Zone Commander remains responsible to his own Government for administering his own Zone'.

(ii) *The Soviet Share of Reparation*

Sir David Waley submitted a short statement on the attitude of the U.K. Government towards the Russian claim to receive plant and equipment from the western zones of occupation, particularly the Ruhr. He explained that this statement was based on the longer memorandum[1] prepared by the U.S. Delegation.

THE PRIME MINISTER asked whether the proposed deliveries to the Russians from the western zones should not be expressed as in exchange for deliveries of food and other supplies from the Russian zone.

SIR DAVID WALEY explained that the British representatives on the Control Council were anxious that this agreement should not be so expressed as to appear to contemplate a direct exchange—so much machinery being exchanged against so much food. They feared that, if the matter were so expressed, there would be endless wrangles over each particular consignment either way. The point of principle was, however, covered by the opening words of the statement, which made it clear that the offer was made 'as part of a settlement covering this and other matters'.

THE FOREIGN SECRETARY suggested that it should be made clear in the statement that the agreed Reparation Plan would have to provide on the one hand for eliminating the German war potential and, on the other hand, for leaving to Germany sufficient industrial equipment to enable her to maintain an approved standard of living. It was agreed that the statement should be amended so as to make this clear.

---

[1] Cf. i below.

(iii) *Reparations from Italy*

SIR DAVID WALEY explained that it would be preferable to deal with reparations from Italy on the basis of a general principle, rather than seek to determine a total amount of reparation payable. The Soviet Government would find it difficult to agree to a lower figure than that fixed for the satellite States in eastern Europe; and it was clear that it would be impossible to exact reparations of that order from Italy.

(iv) *Reparations from Austria*

SIR DAVID WALEY recalled that Premier Stalin had now agreed (P. (Terminal) 10th Meeting,[2] Minute 5) that no reparations should be exacted from Austria. It would be desirable that the Conference should further agree that the removal of plant and equipment and other goods from Austria, as war booty or otherwise, should in future be a matter to be settled by the Control Council.

It was agreed that this further suggestion might be raised at the meeting of Foreign Secretaries, but that it should not be pressed if it seemed likely to endanger the main decision, already reached, that no reparations should be exacted from Austria.

(v) *Supplies for Zones of Occupation in Germany*

The following points were raised on a draft statement about the sources of supply for the several zones of occupation in Germany, including the area of Greater Berlin.

(*a*) It was agreed that this document should begin by stating the general principle that each zone, including the Greater Berlin area, should draw its supplies so far as practicable from the areas of Germany on which it had drawn before the war.

(*b*) The statement should then continue to make the special point regarding food supplies in the interim period until the 1946 harvest became available. While it was recognised that during this period the Russian zone would have little or no surplus which could be made available for other zones, it should be agreed that the Russian zone should supply during this period enough food to ensure that this zone and the whole of the Greater Berlin area would be self-supporting and would maintain a nutritional standard up to the minimum level established for Germany as a whole.

(*c*) It was proposed that the part of Germany now administered by Poland should supply 5 million tons of hard coal a year to the western zones and the Greater Berlin area for a period of 3 years.

It was agreed that it was of secondary importance whether this should be made as a free supply. If payment were demanded, we could agree that it might be made by way of exports to this area from Germany.

(*d*) It was pointed out that we should require from the eastern areas of pre-war Germany, not only food and coal, but also timber and potash.

[2] No. 447.

It was agreed that this point should be covered in one or other of the statements which were to be handed in at the meeting of Foreign Secretaries that afternoon.

It was agreed that Sir David Waley should revise the draft statements in the light of the discussion; that the revised statements should be shown to the U.S. Delegation before the meeting of Foreign Secretaries that afternoon; and that they should be handed in at the meeting in support of oral explanations of the views of the British Delegation on these questions.

3. *German fleet and merchant navy*

THE FOREIGN SECRETARY said that he had approved the draft of a memorandum on this subject, which he proposed to submit to the meeting of Foreign Secretaries that afternoon.

4. *Neutral and ex-enemy states: admission to the United Nations*

THE PRIME MINISTER said that the U.S. Delegation would probably put forward, at the meeting of Foreign Secretaries that afternoon, the amendment to the proposed declaration on this subject which had been discussed at the First Staff Conference the previous day.[3] If so, the Foreign Secretary would indicate that the United Kingdom Government were prepared to accept this formula.

5. *Consultation with the French Government*

As there had been no Plenary Meeting or meeting of Foreign Secretaries on the previous day, it had not been possible to arrange for the despatch of the telegrams inviting the Governments of France and China to join the Council of Foreign Ministers, and informing the French Government of the decisions of the Conference regarding the political principles to govern the treatment of Germany in the initial control period.

It was agreed that this question should be raised at the meeting of Foreign Secretaries that afternoon, so that these telegrams could be despatched later in the day.

6. *War crimes*

THE FOREIGN SECRETARY suggested, that, until other arrangements could be made, the Lord Chancellor might be invited to carry out the duties in connection with the work of the War Crimes Commission which had hitherto been undertaken by the Attorney-General.

THE PRIME MINISTER undertook to telegraph to the Lord Chancellor in this sense during the course of the day.

THE FOREIGN SECRETARY said that he had prepared the draft of a paragraph on War Crimes for insertion in the Protocol of the present Conference.

It was agreed that the meeting of Foreign Secretaries that afternoon should be invited to agree in principle that a paragraph on these lines be included in the Protocol.

[3] See No. 450, minute 1.

7. *Yalta Declaration on Liberated Europe*

The Meeting of Foreign Secretaries had appointed a Committee to consider two aspects of this question—the powers of Allied representatives on Control Commissions, and the freedom of the Press. The Committee had not been able to reach agreement on these points; and it was possible that the United States Delegation (at whose instance these questions had been raised at the Conference) would ask that the position should be discussed at the meeting of Foreign Secretaries that afternoon.

It was agreed that, if these questions were raised, the British Delegation might take this opportunity of submitting their proposals for a declaration on the Tito-Subasic Agreement and the Varkiza Agreement.[4]

Cabinet Office, Potsdam, 30th July, 1945

CALENDARS TO No. 462

i *30 July 1945 Minute from Sir D. Waley to Sir E. Bridges (Berlin).* Attaches draft statements on the first charge, Soviet share of reparations, supplies for Berlin area and West Germany from the East, Italian and Austrian reparation. Lists objections to attached American proposals itemizing goods for Soviet share of reparation [F.O. 934/1/4(33)].

ii *30 July 1945 Brief by Mr. Hoyer Millar* on Admission to the United Nations. Suggests and explains policy laid down in minute 4 above. Attaches redrafts of annex to No. 260 [F.O. 934/5/48(13)].

iii *30 July 1945 Mr. Bevin (Berlin) Tel. No. 283 Target.* Request by Mr. Attlee to Viscount Jowitt, Lord Chancellor, to take up discussions in War Crimes Commission: hopes for early agreement [U 5838/29/73].

[4] Cf. No. 429, annex, and Nos. 465, 479.

No. 463

Record of a Meeting held at the Prime Minister's Residence,
Potsdam, at 11.30 a.m. on 30 July 1945
[F.O. 934/2/10(87)]

Present:

THE PRIME MINISTER, The Foreign Secretary, Sir A. Cadogan, Sir A. Clark Kerr, Mr. Peck, Mr. Allen, Captain Leggett (*interpreter*).

M. BIERUT, Professor Grabski, M. Mikolajczyk, M. Stanczyk, M. Modzelewski, Professor Goetel, M. Zebrowski (*interpreter*).

Elections

MR. ATTLEE said that he would like some information about the position of the political parties in Poland under the 1921 Constitution, to which, he understood, the present Polish Government had returned.

M. BIERUT replied that under the 1921 Constitution all democratic parties representing the workers, the peasants and democratic bourgeois elements, had the right to exist and to carry on their activities. In reply to a further question by Mr. Attlee he said that the term 'democratic party' covered all parties which did not support Nazi ideas and tendencies.

Mr. Attlee said that the 1921 Constitution had been drawn up before the days of the Nazi Movement and asked on what basis these parties were now excluded.

M. Bierut said in 1921 there had been no parties which did not acknowledge the Constitution and therefore in theory at least, none had been excluded though in practice the Communist Party had been prevented from working and its members had been arrested and its organisation disbanded in accordance with the provisions of the old penal code relating to subversive activities and in contravention of the Constitution. The Constitution had subsequently been changed by the Sanacja Regime after the coup d'état of 1926[1] when the Fascist ideas had been introduced which were given expression in the 1935 Constitution.

Mr. Attlee commented that the treatment of the Communist Party after 1921 proved that the existence of a written Constitution was not in itself an adequate guarantee of free political institutions. Everything depended upon how the Constitution was applied. What was the position now in this respect? The present Government intended to return to the 1921 Constitution but how far did they propose to modify it by administrative action?

M. Bierut said that the present Polish Government, being provisional, would not interfere with electoral procedure. Any changes that might be required would be left to the Constituent Assembly which would be elected on a basis of universal suffrage in accordance with the 1921 rules. In the elections for this Constituent Assembly all parties would be allowed to put forward candidates except those, if any, which produced Nazi or Fascist programmes.

Mr. Attlee asked who would decide this point. Here was an example of the manner in which the Government could interfere by administrative action.

M. Bierut replied that at present the National Council, as the highest constitutional body in Poland, would decide such problems. In reply to a further question he confirmed that theoretically the National Council would have power to exclude from the elections parties of which it did not approve. At present however the four parties in the Government coalition were collaborating harmoniously in the National Council.[2] There was no permanent opposition since all parties understood the enormous problems with which the Government were faced and were unwilling to cause them embarrassment.

---

[1] The Sanacja Regime of 'moral renovation' was a term applied after the Polish *coup d'état* of 12 May 1926 whereby Marshal Pilsudski became Minister for War in the new government of M. Bartel.

[2] Another copy of this record (N 9608/6/55) carries a marginal query by Sir O. Sargent against this sentence.

Mr. Attlee asked by what method the Constituent Assembly would be elected, whether on a basis of single member constituencies, electoral lists or proportional representation.

M. Bierut said that he could not answer in detail since the electoral law had not yet been voted by the National Council but there were five general principles that would certainly be followed: the voting should be universal, secret, equal, direct and proportional. In reply to a further question he explained that a special electoral law was required because the 1921 Constitution had merely contained a general provision guaranteeing the full right of citizens to representation. Before 1926 it had always been the practice of the Sejm to pass a general electoral law before the elections. The present electoral law would follow similar lines. The procedure would probably be that in every electoral district the parties, either individually or in blocs, would present their electoral lists. The number of representatives of each party elected would be as nearly as possible proportionate to the number of votes cast. Any surplus votes would be transferred to a national list from which further representatives would be chosen on the basis of the proportion of votes cast for each party.

Mr. Attlee asked whether any party would be excluded from these elections.

M. Bierut replied that the four parties in the Government coalition represented the whole of the democratic movement in Poland. Parties opposing the present system could only work underground. Two broad categories would be excluded from the elections:

(a) Supporters of Marshal Pilsudski's Sanacja who had been associated with the production of the 1935 Constitution, and

(b) Extreme nationalist organisations such as the National Radical Wing (O.N.R.) of the National Democrat Party or the illegal armed underground movement known as the National Armed Forces (N.S.Z.).

Mr. Bevin asked whether the Polish representatives could not make some rather more precise statement than they had hitherto given on the length of time likely to elapse between any settlement of the frontier question and the holding of elections.

M. Bierut replied that the date of the elections was related to the problem of repatriation of the several million Poles still abroad. These Poles had the right to vote in the elections and how soon they could be brought home would depend very largely upon the assistance which the Allied Powers were able to give by organising their repatriation, providing transport, etc. The election would be held as soon as possible after their repatriation but the precise date must be settled by the National Council. When asked to suggest a possible outside date he said that it would probably take two months to prepare the electoral lists after the return of the emigrants, so that assuming that repatriation could be completed in three months it should be possible to hold the elections in five or six months after an agreement on frontiers had been reached. The Polish Provisional Government had concluded an agreement with the Soviet Government to repatriate all

Poles from the Soviet Union before the 1st January. It might be done more quickly than this but would inevitably take some time. As regards the Poles in Western Europe, the Polish Provisional Government recognised that their repatriation could not be compulsory though they wished as many as possible to return and expected at least half a million to do so. As a result of the war there were Poles scattered all over the world and the Government hoped that most if not all of these could be brought back before the elections were held.

MR. BEVIN asked whether the Polish Provisional Government could not give an assurance that the elections would be held by, say, February at the latest. Some such declaration of the Government's intentions would have a considerable effect upon British public opinion and would help to establish the necessary basis of confidence. Could the Polish Delegates not give some general assurance that they would make every effort to deal with the problems of repatriation and the organisation of the elections so as to ensure that the nation's will could be expressed not later than the end of February?

M. BIERUT said that the date of the elections could only be settled by the competent Polish authorities. All Polish political parties were interested in the early holding of elections and the Polish people, having suffered dictatorship, would cling enthusiastically to the democratic prerogatives which had now been restored to them and would if necessary fight for their rights. The Polish Provisional Government could not accept commitments on such a matter, particularly when it might be felt that they were being forced upon the Polish nation from outside. The Polish nation was conscious of having reached political maturity and would not accept any foreign guarantee of its political rights. He appealed to the British people to trust the Polish people in this matter. The present Government had nothing to fear from elections, which could only strengthen their position. They had every intention of holding them but a definite commitment given to a foreign power on such a subject would not be understood. The Polish Provisional Government had accepted the Provisions of the Crimea Declaration relating to democratic elections and had repeatedly reaffirmed that they stood by these principles.

Polish Forces under British Command

MR. ATTLEE said that the Polish troops serving with the British forces had brought great honour to Poland and popularity for themselves. The British people would wish to know what was to happen to them and what provision would be made for finding them homes and land, particularly those who came from the Eastern territories now transferred to the Soviet Union.

M. BIERUT replied that both the men and their officers would be welcomed back to Poland. The Polish Provisional Government considered, now that the Government had been recognised by the Great Powers, that these Polish forces should be placed under the authority of the Polish High Command in Poland as soon as possible. They wished no distinction to be made between those who had served Poland at home and those who had fought abroad. Land would be provided in the new territories West of the 1939 German frontier and measures would be taken to ensure that they enjoyed the full protection of the State.

M. MODZELEWSKI said that a study of the Polish press would show that the whole Polish nation was proud of the Polish troops who had fought at Tobruk and Monte Cassino and that they would be given all assistance on their return. The Polish Provisional Government were however concerned about reports which had reached them from Italy to the effect that Generals of the Polish 2nd Corps were arresting and deporting men under their command who had declared their wish to return to Poland. A note [i] would be addressed to His Majesty's Government on this subject.

M. BIERUT then confirmed, in reply to a further question by MR. BEVIN, that all Polish troops and workers abroad would be allowed to return to Poland with their families and that they would be given protection and facilities for finding work and land on equal terms with all other Polish citizens. In fact soldiers deserved and would receive even better treatment than civilians. Those who had fought in the West would receive in the new Western territories the same treatment as those who had fought on the Eastern front or in Poland.

Press

MR. BEVIN said that if some settlement were reached at the present Conference it would help His Majesty's Government if they could receive an assurance that the press would be free in Poland and that foreign correspondents would be allowed to send uncensored news out of any territories that might be allotted provisionally to Poland.

M. BIERUT repeated the assurance he had given to Mr. Eden[3] that some British correspondents had already visited Poland and that British correspondents in Poland would in general be granted the same treatment as Polish correspondents in British territory.

In reply to a further question, M. Bierut confirmed that freedom of religion already existed in Poland and would be maintained. Visitors would be able to satisfy themselves on this point.

R.A.F. Air Service to Warsaw

MR. BEVIN asked whether M. Bierut had yet spoken to the Soviet Delegation about our desire to establish an official courier service to Warsaw via Berlin.

M. BIERUT replied that he had not yet done so. He was, however, conscious of the need for such a service and would try to settle the matter with the Russians here.

He went on to state that it was not only a question of Soviet permission for an R.A.F. service. The Poles were interested in securing from Great Britain aircraft which would enable them to operate a service of their own. They looked forward to concluding a convention with the British authorities

[3] See No. 267.

which would grant the Poles a share on a basis of reciprocity in the air traffic between Poland and Great Britain.

MR. BEVIN stated that any such arrangements would take time and what we were at present interested in was a purely interim arrangement to enable us to communicate with our Embassy in Poland. The early establishment of such communication between London and Warsaw was in the interests of the Poles as well as of ourselves.

Foreign Office, 30th July, 1945

CALENDARS TO No. 463

i *30–1 July 1945 Letter from Mr. D. Allen (Berlin) to Mr. Warner; To Mr. Bevin (Berlin) Tel. No. 318 Onward;* Polish note complaining of alleged pressure on Polish forces in Italy not to return to Poland; proposed interim reply pending result of British investigations [N 9715/123/55].

ii *26 July 1945 Mr. Hankey (Warsaw) No. 12.* Report by Mr. L. H. Massey (Third Secretary) on Polish press and information about Great Britain [N 12407/45/55].

No. 464

Minute from Mr. Harrison to Mr. Bevin (Berlin)
[F.O. 934/4/20(24)]

[BERLIN,] *30 July 1945*

The question of the dismemberment of Germany was discussed at the Crimea Conference and as a result a Committee was set up, consisting of Mr. Eden (Chairman), Mr. Winant and Mr. Gousev to study 'the procedure for the dismemberment of Germany'.

The terms of reference of the Committee, as finally agreed, will be found at Flag A.[1] The important point is contained in M. Gousev's statement that: 'The Soviet Government understand the decision of the Crimea Conference regarding the dismemberment of Germany not as an obligatory claim for the dismemberment of Germany but as a possibility for exerting pressure on Germany with the object of rendering her harmless in the event of other means proving inadequate'.

The Committee met twice informally. At the second meeting it was agreed that, as soon as any of the three representatives had proposals or suggestions to put forward, these would be communicated to his colleagues. None of the representatives has so far submitted proposals. The Foreign Office did, however, do a certain amount of work on the subject and circulated on March 19th to the Armistice and Post-War Committee definite proposals for dividing Germany into three, four or five States. The

---

[1] Not attached to filed copy. Cf. No. 74.ii, and for the following.

Foreign Office paper was referred to the Economic and Industrial Production Sub-Committee. There the matter rests.

The general trend of this Conference suggests that, whatever the *de facto* result of dividing Germany into zones of occupation may be, the idea of planned and deliberate dismemberment is dead. It should be noted that in his proclamation to the Soviet people on May 9th Marshal Stalin included the following passage: 'Germany is utterly defeated. The German troops are surrendering. The Soviet Union is celebrating victory, although it does not intend either to dismember or destroy Germany.'

The question arises what should be done about the London Dismemberment Committee. Mr. Bevin presumably inherits Mr. Eden's position and responsibilities as Chairman. There are two possible courses. Either the whole thing can be allowed tacidly [tacitly] to drop; or some formal action should be taken here in Berlin to establish whether the Committee set up at Yalta is still expected to produce a report.

The first course, which might give rise to misunderstanding later on, is not altogether satisfactory, and Mr. Eden had it in mind to try to 'clarify the position a little here'.

I assume we do not desire to precipitate a further discussion at this Conference regarding the dismemberment of Germany. A possible line might be for Mr. Bevin to say that he had learned of the responsibility he has inherited as Chairman of the London Dismemberment Committee, set up at Yalta; that the Committee has hitherto made no progress; and that he is anxious to know whether, in the light of Marshal Stalin's proclamation of May 9th when he said the Soviet did not intend 'either to dismember or destroy Germany' and of the experience gained during the past three months in occupying Germany, his Soviet and United States colleagues consider that the Committee still has a useful function to perform.

G. W. HARRISON

No. 465

Memorandum by the United Kingdom Delegation (Berlin)[1]
P. (Terminal) 51 [U 6197/3628/70]

Top secret   *30 July 1945*

South-East Europe

The United Kingdom Delegation suggest that it might be desirable for the Conference to issue at its conclusion a statement on the following lines:–

The three Heads of Government noted with regret that charges of aggressive action were being made by Governments in South-East Europe against their neighbours, and that fears were entertained of attempts to

---

[1] Printed in *F.R.U.S. Berlin*, vol. ii, pp. 1074–5: cf. Sir L. Woodward, *op. cit.*, vol. v, pp. 488–9.

anticipate the peace settlement by violent and unilateral action. The three Heads of Government would be strongly opposed to any such attempts, which would be contrary to the principles for which the war has been fought and which are embodied in the Charter of the United Nations. They are confident that the Governments of the countries concerned, which have so recently suffered in common the trials of war and of Fascist occupation, will find peaceful means of solving their differences, and that their people will now be enabled to enter a period of prosperous and democratic development, on the lines laid down in such documents as the Varkiza Agreement and the Tito-Subasić Agreement.

No. 466

Memorandum by the United Kingdom Delegation (Berlin)[1]
P. (Terminal) 52 [U 6197/3628/70]

Top secret   30 July 1945

Disposal of the German Fleet and Merchant Ships

When this question was discussed at the Third Plenary Meeting on the 19th July, on the basis of the Soviet Delegation's Memorandum of that date,[2] certain conclusions were reached and it was agreed to leave the matter until the last stage of the Conference.

2. The British Delegation have given further consideration to the questions raised in the Soviet Memorandum, in the light of the discussion on the 19th July, and submit the following suggestions as a basis for the decisions of the Conference on the subject. These suggestions relate to the numbered paragraphs of the Soviet Memorandum:–

(1) (a) It was agreed on the 19th July that the German surface ships should be shared equally between the Three Powers. The British Delegation suggest that consideration should now be given to allotting a share to France[3] which is an equal party to the terms of surrender for Germany and is a full member of the Control Council for Germany. The allocation of specific vessels is, it is suggested, a matter upon which an expert commission should submit recommendations to the Three Governments, after it had drawn up a list of all available surface ships, including those under con-

[1] Printed in *F.R.U.S. Berlin*, vol. ii, pp. 977–9.
[2] See No. 194, minute 6.
[3] The preceding part of this sentence reflected a manuscript insertion by Lord Hood in the draft of this memorandum on U 5825/5397/70. In submitting the amended draft to Mr. Bevin, Lord Hood stated in a covering minute of 28 July 1945: 'The French claim to a share of the German warships was not mentioned at the Plenary discussion and the British Delegation consider it impractical to raise it now. It seems to be deliberate Russian policy to ignore the French. Conversely it seems to be in our interests to ensure that France plays her full part as fourth partner in German affairs. The Foreign Office would therefore suggest that we should try to obtain some German warships for the French.'

truction or already launched, and those under repair which can be quickly ompleted. Any ships requiring more [*sic*] than three months for completion hould be removed from Germany by the country to whom they are allocated. Remaining ships under construction will be destroyed.

(*b*) At the same time it was agreed in principle that the German U-boats hould be dealt with separately, the greater part being destroyed. A token number would be retained for equal division among the Three Powers for purposes of research. The question of a French share of the retained U-boats hould also be considered. Here, again, it is suggested that the expert commission should be instructed to make concrete proposals after full investigation of the numbers of U-boats—seaworthy, damaged and under construction or repair—which are in the hands of the Allied authorities. Each of the Three Powers would be responsible for arranging the destruction of U-boats in its control, apart from the token number which it may be agreed to retain.

In deciding the allocation of German warships, the British Delegation consider that account should be taken of the Roumanian and Bulgarian warships available to the Soviet Union.

(2) The Soviet request for a proportional share of the German Navy's reserve of armaments, ammunition and supplies was not discussed at the Plenary Meeting on the 19th July. The Soviet request is acceptable in principle to the British Delegation, who must point out, however, that these stores have been dispersed by the Germans and that the first step must be the preparation of an inventory which should be one of the tasks assigned to the proposed expert commission.

(3) It was agreed in principle that there should be a division of the surrendered German merchant shipping, but no final conclusion was reached as to the proportions to be allotted to the different Allied States. Mr. Churchill expressed the view that account should be taken of merchant shipping which had passed under the control of the Soviet Government as the result of the armistices with Finland and Roumania. President Truman emphasised the need for German shipping in the war against Japan and for bringing supplies for the rehabilitation of Europe.

The meeting agreed in principle that without prejudice to the preparation of a scheme for the division of surrendered German merchant ships, all such ships should be available for use in support of the Allied war effort against Japan.

The British Delegation maintain their point of view that in the division of the surrendered German merchant shipping account should be taken of the shipping taken as reparation by the Soviet Union from the Satellite States. Account should also be taken of the need for providing ships for local German purposes, in accordance with any recommendations which may be made by the Allied Control Council for Germany. Subject to these conditions, the British Delegation renew the suggestion made by Mr. Churchill on the

19th July that a fourth part be made available for division between the other Allied States whose merchant marines have suffered substantial losses at the hands of Germany. The share of the Soviet Union would in that case be one quarter of the total available.

The shares of the various Allied States would be counted as reparation receipts.

(4) The British Delegation cannot agree to the timetable proposed by the Soviet Delegation, since, as pointed out above, there is much essential preliminary investigation and listing to be done before the transfer of ships can begin. The British Delegation suggest that the following timetable should be approved in principle by the Conference:–

(*a*) *Warships.*—Transfers will be carried out as soon as possible after Governments have approved the recommendations of the proposed expert commission.

(*b*) *Merchant Ships.*—Proposals for the allocation of specific German merchant ships, in accordance with such decision on allocation as may be agreed by the Conference, should be agreed as soon as possible between the three Governments, in the light of recommendations made by the experts, and particular ships would then be earmarked. The transfer of these ships would take place as soon as they became available after the end of the Japanese war.

(5) The Plenary Meeting on the 19th July agreed in principle upon the formation of a Three Power Naval Commission with reciprocal rights for each party to make the investigations required for their work in any territory under the control of the other parties. As mentioned above, the British Delegation propose that there shall be established an expert commission to deal with German warships. Its composition and duties are suggested in paragraphs (1) and (2) above.

As regards merchant ships, the British Delegation suggest that detailed recommendations to give effect to the proposals in paragraphs (3) and (4) (*b*) should be worked out between suitable expert representatives nominated by the three Governments to deal with merchant ships, in consultation with representatives of other interested Governments.

3. There is the possibility that any public announcement that German warships are to be divided amongst the Allies may result in the German crews scuttling ships which might be ordered to sail to Allied ports. It is therefore desirable that no announcement of the division of the German Navy be made, at any rate until the expert commission has completed its investigations, which should include the detailed arrangements for carrying out the transfer of ships. A similar delay is necessary before making any definite announcement about the division of the surrendered German merchant ships.

No. 467

Memorandum by the United Kingdom Delegation (Berlin)[1]

P. (*Terminal*) 53 [U 6197/3628/70]

Top secret

30 July 1945

War Crimes

The British Delegation placed this matter on the Agenda of the Conference. They consider it most desirable, in view of the great public interest throughout the world in the major war criminals being brought to just and speedy punishment, that an agreement should be reached between the Three Governments to insert a paragraph on the lines suggested below in the Protocol and Communiqué.

'The Three Governments have taken note of the discussions which have been proceeding in recent weeks in London between British, United States, Soviet and French representatives with a view to reaching agreement on the methods of trial of those major war criminals whose crimes under the Moscow Declaration of October 1943, have no particular geographical localisation. The Three Governments reaffirm their intention to bring these criminals to swift and sure justice. They hope that the negotiations in London will result in speedy agreement being reached for this purpose, and they regard it as a matter of great importance that the trial of these major criminals should begin at the earliest possible date.'

[1] This memorandum, dated 13 July 1945, perhaps in error, and communicated unnumbered to the American and Soviet delegations on 30 July, is printed *op. cit.*, vol. ii, p. 986. Cf. Sir L. Woodward, *op. cit.*, vol. v, p. 465.

No. 468

Memorandum by the Soviet Delegation (Berlin)[1]

P. (*Terminal*) 62 [U 6197/3628/70]

Top secret

30 July 1945

Proposals on Reparations from Germany

1. The exactions of once for all removals from the national wealth of Germany in the way of reparations (plants, factories, capital equipments, materials, &c.) will be effected by each Government in its zone of occupation during the period of two years after the capitulation.

2. The removals should have as their purpose to contribute to the speediest economic restoration of the countries which have suffered from the German occupation, taking also into account the necessity to reduce by all means the German war potential.

3. In view of the tremendous losses sustained by the Soviet heavy industries

[1] Printed in *Berlinskaya konferentsiya*, pp. 412–3.

and the very limited number of similar German plants in the Soviet zone of occupation; in view also of the general deficiency of resources in this zone, the U.S.S.R. in addition to the removals effected in its own zone must receive on the reparation account from the Western zones, more particularly from the Ruhr district, 5.5–6 million tons of capital equipment in good state and complete form according to a specially compiled list. This equipment will have to contribute to the restoration of those branches of the Soviet industry, in the first place, of iron and steel, chemical and engineering industries, which were destroyed by the enemy. Those removals should start immediately and end not later than the 10th May, 1947. A special body should be created for this purpose by the Allied Commission on Reparations.

4. U.S.S.R. shall also receive shares to the amount of 500 million dollars of those industrial and transport enterprises remaining in the Western zones which are most important from the angle of the greatest possible limitation of the German war potential.

5. The exaction of the annual deliveries in kind from current production shall be effected not by zones, but from Germany as a whole, and the Allied Commission on Reparations shall work out a general plan of the exaction as well as distribution of these deliveries among the Nations entitled to it. The total amount of such deliveries is fixed at 8 billion dollars for the period of ten years. The share of the U.S.S.R. in the annual deliveries from current production shall be 50 per cent. of the total sum.

6. The list of commodities from current production to be delivered on the reparation account may include:–

Coal, brickets, metal, metal manufactures, cement, building materials, metal scrap, timber, potassium, paper, sugar, chemical and ceramic products, machines, river ships, medical instruments, agricultural produce, domestic animals, &c.

The basis of calculations is world prices of 1938 in dollars plus 10 per cent.

7. The Allied Commission on Reparations shall work out a plan concerning distribution of the German foreign investments, and German claims among the Nations entitled to receive reparations.

8. In regard to that part of the reparations which shall be covered by the once for all removals, U.S.S.R. undertakes to settle the reparation claims of Poland from its own share. United States and United Kingdom will do likewise in respect of France, Yugoslavia, Czechoslovakia, Belgium, Holland and Norway.

No. 469

Record of Tenth Meeting of Foreign Secretaries held at Cecilienhof, Potsdam, on Monday, 30 July 1945 at 5 p.m.

F. (Terminal) 10th Meeting [U 6197/3628/70]

Top secret

Present:

M. V. M. MOLOTOV, M. A. Ya. Vyshinski, M. A. A. Gromyko, M. F. T. Gousev,

M. I. M. Maisky, M. S. A. Golunski, M. K. V. Novikov, M. A. A. Sobolev, M. B. F. Podtzerob, M. V. N. Pavlov (*Interpreter*).

Mr. J. F. Byrnes, Mr. W. A. Harriman, Mr. E. W. Pauley, Mr. J. C. Dunn, Mr. H. F. Matthews, Mr. W. L. Clayton, Mr. C. E. Bohlen, Mr. B. V. Cohen, Mr. E. Page (*Interpreter*).

Mr. E. Bevin, Sir A. Cadogan, Sir A. Clark Kerr, Sir E. Bridges, Mr. N. Brook, Sir D. Waley, Mr. P. J. Dixon, Mr. W. Hayter, Major L. M. Theakstone (*Interpreter*).

Contents

1. *Chairmanship*

Mr. Byrnes said that it had been the procedure hitherto for each of the Foreign Secretatires [*sic*] to take the Chair in turn at these meetings; and he suggested that on this occasion Mr. Bevin should preside. M. Molotov agreed.

Mr. Bevin thanked his colleagues for extending this invitation to him. Before proceeding with the business of the meeting he asked that M. Molotov should convey to Premier Stalin on their behalf an expression of the regret with which they had heard of his illness and their hope that he would make a speedy and complete recovery.

2. *Subjects for Discussion*

Mr. Bevin proposed that the following questions should be considered:
    (*a*) *Council of Foreign Ministers:* invitations to the Governments of France and China.

(*b*) *Germany: Political Principles.* Notification to the French Government.

(*c*) *Reparations:* Germany, Austria and Italy.

(*d*) *German Fleet and Merchant Navy.*

(*e*) *Germany: Political Principles* to govern the treatment of Germany in the initial control period (certain additional points).

(*f*) *Yugoslavia* (Tito–Subasic Agreement).

(*g*) *War Crimes.*

MR. BYRNES submitted a memorandum on:

(*h*) *German External Assets.*

He also suggested that the meeting might call for:

(*i*) *Progress Reports* on the work of the various Committees which had not yet reported.

M. MOLOTOV asked that the following three subjects should be placed on the agenda:

(*j*) *German troops in Norway.* (P. (Terminal) 43).[1]

(*k*) *Activities of Russian Fascists in Austria and Germany.* (P. (Terminal) 44).[2]

(*l*) *The Ruhr*, on which the Soviet Delegation suggested that there might be an exchange of views.

3. *Council of Foreign Ministers: Communications to Governments of France and China*

(Previous Reference: F. (Terminal) 6th Meeting,[3] Minute 4.)

(*a*) *Invitations to Join the Council*

At the meeting on 23rd July the Foreign Secretaries had approved the terms of telegrams to be despatched by each of the Governments of the three Powers, separately, to the Governments of China and France informing them of the proposed establishment of the new Council of Foreign Ministers and inviting them to join it. They had further agreed that these telegrams should be despatched 48 hours before the release of the final communiqué to be issued at the end of the Conference.

MR. BEVIN suggested that the time had now come when these communications should be sent, and proposed that the telegrams should be despatched that day.

(*b*) *European Advisory Commission*

SIR ALEXANDER CADOGAN explained that the Committee which had prepared these telegrams had agreed that, in the telegram to the French Government, a paragraph should be added about the position of the European Advisory Commission. This paragraph pointed out that further detailed work for the co-ordination of Allied policy for the control of Germany and Austria should in future fall within the competence of the Allied Control Commission in Berlin and the Allied Commission in Vienna; and continued that the Conference had therefore agreed to recommend to the French Government that the European Advisory Commission might now be

---

[1] See No. 276, note 1.   [2] See No. 276, enclosure.   [3] No. 233.

dissolved. Although this additional paragraph had been agreed by the Committee, it had not hitherto been formally approved by the meeting of Foreign Ministers.

Sir Alexander Cadogan proposed that it should now be approved, subject to one verbal amendment. He thought it would be preferable that, in order to avoid giving offence to the French Government, the recommendation in the final sentence should be expressed as coming from the Governments of the three Great Powers rather than, in terms, from the present Conference.

It was agreed (*a*) that each of the three Governments should despatch that day communications in the agreed terms to the Governments of France and China; and (*b*) that the communication to the French Government should include an additional paragraph about the dissolution of the European Advisory Commission in the terms proposed by the Committee, subject to the amendment suggested by Sir Alexander Cadogan.[4]

4. *Reparations: Germany*

(Previous Reference: P. (Terminal) 10th Meeting,[5] Minute 5.)

MR. BYRNES said that he had communicated to the other two Delegations a paper on this subject (which was read out and subsequently circulated as P. (Terminal) 63),[6] as follows:

'Reparations claims of Russia and Poland to be satisfied from the Russian zone plus:

(*a*) 25 per cent. of such industrial capital equipment as we determine is not necessary for a peace economy and should be removed from the Ruhr on condition that there would be exchanged an equivalent value in food, coal, potash, zinc, timber, clay products and oil products, to be made available to us by the Soviets.

(*b*) An additional 15 per cent. of such industrial capital equipment as is determined unnecessary for a peace economy should be transferred

---

[4] Berlin telegrams Nos. 290–2 Target of 31 July 1945 (not printed), for repetition to Paris, Chungking, Washington and Moscow, conveyed instructions for these British communications to the governments of France and China. The British communication to the French Government was made jointly with the Soviet and American communications (cf. *F.R.U.S. Berlin*, vol. ii, pp. 1543–4) on 31 July. The British communication to the Chinese Government was made on 1 August. That day Sir H. Seymour reported in Chungking telegram No. 768 that owing to a discrepancy in texts as received by his United States colleague and himself, an addition had been made to the British note to match the American one: after the second sentence of the approved text in section IB of No. 603 had been inserted: 'In order that Council may represent those nations having broadest interests in peace settlements in Asia and Europe, it is proposed that Council be composed of Foreign Ministers of those states which are to have permanent seats on Security Council of United Nations in accordance with decision of San Francisco Conference' (cf. *op. cit.*, vol. ii, p. 616).

[5] No. 447.

[6] This paper of 30 July, as cited below, circulated on 31 July, is printed in *F.R.U.S. Berlin*, vol. ii, p. 921.

from the Ruhr to the Soviet Government without payment or exchange of any kind in return.'

Mr. Byrnes said that the agreement which the United States Delegation had just proposed was conditional upon agreement on two other proposals, which would have to be considered with it.

The first of these was the United States proposal (P. (Terminal) 35)[7] about *Admission to the United Nations* (previous reference: P. (Terminal) 10th Meeting,[5] Minute 4). This had been discussed on many occasions at the Conference and had finally been withdrawn. In the hope of reaching agreement, he submitted an amended version of this paper (subsequently circulated as P. (Terminal) 58).[8] Two changes had been made:

(*a*) The insertion of the following at the end of paragraph 3: 'The three Governments agree to examine, each separately, in the near future, in the light of the conditions then prevailing, the establishment of diplomatic relations with Bulgaria, Finland, Hungary and Roumania, to the extent possible prior to the ratification of Peace Treaties with those countries.'

(*b*) The further addition to paragraph 3 of the words 'The three Governments express the desire that, in view of the changed conditions resulting from the end of the war in Europe, representatives of the Allied press shall enjoy full freedom to report to the world on developments in Roumania, Bulgaria, Hungary and Finland.'

Mr. Byrnes pointed out that the first of these amendments was designed to meet the Soviet point of view and also the objections raised by the British and United States Delegations to the amendment previously suggested by the Soviet Delegation.[9] The second amendment was, it would be noted, substantially in the same language as that already approved for the proposed statement on Poland (P. (Terminal) 23).[10]

The second matter on which agreement should in his view be reached concurrently with agreement on reparations and admission to the United Nations, concerned the *Western Frontier of Poland* (previous reference: P. (Terminal) 9th Meeting,[11] Minute 3). The United States Delegation were prepared to make a proposal which would permit administration by the Polish Provisional Government of the area claimed by them, pending a final arrangement of the actual frontier at the Peace Conference.

In submitting this proposal Mr. Byrnes pointed out that it involved a sacrifice of the views already expressed by the United States Delegation on several points. International agreement was, however, full of compromise; and he was willing to make this agreement, if it were possible to agree on all three proposals at once. If this were not possible, it would be necessary for the Foreign Secretaries to report to the Plenary Meeting, and it would then

[7] No. 260.
[8] This paper of 30 July (not here printed) is printed *op. cit.*, vol. ii, pp. 629–30.
[9] See No. 258, minute 3, No. 431, minute 2, and No. 447, minute 4.
[10] See No. 219, note 6.
[11] No. 271.

be for the three Heads of Government to decide whether to continue discussions on these matters or to leave them for settlement at some future Conference. He personally thought that these matters ought to be settled now, because on their determination depended the settlement of several other problems, such as the economic principles governing the treatment of Germany.

MR. BEVIN said that the British Delegation had considered the question of *Reparations* in its broadest aspects and submitted the following paper, which was read out (and subsequently circulated in P. (Terminal) 65)[12]:

The Soviet Union Share of Reparation

'As part of a settlement covering this and other matters, His Majesty's Government are ready to agree that Russia, in addition to obtaining reparation removals and deliveries from the Russian Zone of Occupation, shall also be entitled to receive from the Western Zones, and particularly from the Ruhr, 10 per cent. of such equipment, particularly from the heavy metal industries, as it is decided to remove under an agreed Reparation Plan, which will have to provide on the one hand for eliminating German war potential to an adequate degree and which will have, on the other hand, to leave to Germany a sufficient industrial equipment to enable her to maintain approved living standards. It is the policy of His Majesty's Government that, in order to eliminate German war potential, there must be very considerable removals from these heavy metal industries, but they cannot express an opinion about the precise amount until a comprehensive Plan has been worked out.

'The Reparation Plan will have to be such as to enable the Powers (other than the Soviet Union and Poland) entitled to reparation to obtain from the Russian Zone adequate amounts of annual deliveries of timber and potash. It will be for the Allied Commission on Reparations to work out the details.'

M. MOLOTOV, in discussing the respects in which this proposal differed from that of the United States Delegation, said that according to the British proposal Russia would only get 10 per cent. of equipment from the United States and British zones, whereas under the United States proposal she would get 25 per cent. of equipment with payment and 15 per cent. without payment.

MR. BEVIN explained that the British Delegation had chosen a slightly different basis for calculation from that of the United States Delegation, and that the question really was whether the Russians preferred 10 per cent. from both the Western zones, or a higher percentage from the Ruhr only. Mr. Bevin added that the British Delegation had taken into account the economic

---

[12] Not printed. This document of 31 July, circulated only to the British Delegation, comprised the three British papers printed below under the headings *The First Charge, The Soviet Union Share of Reparation* and *Source of Supply for the Zones of Occupation, including the Greater Berlin Area*, in that order. Cf. No. 462, minute 2, also Sir L. Woodward, *op. cit.*, vol. v, pp. 451–2.

principles which they had in mind for the treatment of Germany. They, therefore, preferred to treat the supply of goods rather separately from reparations. He was concerned lest the supply of goods between zones might lead to disputes; for instance, he foresaw some difficulty in exchanging potatoes for machinery, since the basis of exchange might be hard to determine. He therefore hoped that the meeting would reach agreement about the source of supplies for all the zones of Germany, and would keep the question of reparations rather separate. The question of source of supplies had been dealt with in a second paper which he handed round. These two problems hung together and the main difference between the United States Delegation's proposal and his own approach to the problem was one of method. The following paper was then handed round and read out (and subsequently circulated in P. (Terminal) 65)[12]:

Source of Supply for the Zones of Occupation, including the Greater Berlin Area
'(a) As a general principle in the absence of special reasons for the contrary, each of the Zones of Occupation, including the Greater Berlin Area, will draw its supplies so far as practicable from the areas of Germany on which it had drawn before the war.

'(b) *Food.*—During the period until the 1946 harvest is available for consumption, it is recognised that the Zone of Occupation for which the Soviet Government are responsible may have little or no surplus foodstuffs to supply to the Western Zones. But during this period the Zone of Occupation for which the Soviet Government are responsible should supply enough food to ensure that this Zone and the whole of the Greater Berlin Area will be self-supporting and will maintain a nutritional standard up to the minimum level established by the Control Council for Germany as a whole without foodstuffs having to be imported from the Western Zones.

'From the 1946 harvest onwards, the Zone of Occupation for which the Soviet Government are responsible should provide for supplies to the Greater Berlin Area and also to the Western Zone to approximately such extent as was customary in the past. This follows as a result of the general principle of treating Germany as a single economic unit.

'(c) *Coal.*—That part of German territory within the 1937 frontiers which is administered at present by Poland should supply 5 million tons of hard coal a year to the Western Zones and to the Greater Berlin Area for a period of 3 years.

'(d) Alternatively, an agreement covering specific quantities of food and coal and other fuel should be worked out by the Control Council, and when such an agreement has been concluded, this agreement and the agreement that the Soviet Government should obtain industrial plant from the Western Zones and, particular[ly,] from the Ruhr, will come into operation simultaneously.'

Mr. Bevin said that he regarded the proposal which he had just read out as a fair approach to the reparations issue. There was, however, another factor which concerned the Economic Principles for governing Germany and which, with the two papers just read out, made the British Delegation's case complete. He accordingly read out the following document (subsequently circulated in P. (Terminal) 65)[12]:

The First Charge
'The following should be included in the Economic Principles:
"Payment for approved imports into Germany shall be a first charge against the proceeds of exports out of current production and out of stocks of goods."
'This corresponds with what M. Molotov said at the meeting of Foreign Secretaries on the 23rd July. "Approved imports" means imports approved by the Control Council. If the Control Council does not approve imports which any one of the four Governments regards as essential a new situation arises and will have to be dealt with by the four Governments. Meanwhile, each Zone Commander remains responsible to his own Government for administering his own Zone.'

M. Molotov said that he thought that both Mr. Byrnes' and Mr. Bevin's proposals contained a number of elements which could be included in an acceptable agreement, but that they required amendment and additions.

As regards Mr. Bevin's proposals, M. Molotov said he had only just heard them for the first time; it would not therefore be possible to reach a decision on them that afternoon, since time was required to study them. On the other hand, Mr. Byrnes' proposals dealt with these issues in a simpler form. He would like to restate the essence of the Soviet Delegation's point of view.

The Soviet Government were anxious to receive a considerable proportion of German equipment, in order to rehabilitate the Soviet factories which had been destroyed. From their point of view, Mr. Byrnes' proposals were nearer the Soviet Governments' wishes. The question of greatest importance to the Soviet Delegation, however, remained obscure in both proposals; both spoke of percentages, whether 25 per cent. or 10 per cent., but those were percentages of an unknown figure. Could it be said that the 25 per cent. quoted by Mr. Byrnes would be the equivalent of 800 million dollars or 2 million tons of equipment? If this were established, the whole question could be settled, so far as the Soviet Delegation were concerned. The Soviet Delegation were, of course, principally concerned to know how much equipment they would receive; and they preferred to speak of reparations not from the Ruhr only, but from the Western zones.

Mr. Byrnes repeated that he had realised the desire of the Soviet Delegation to have an estimate in dollars of the amounts available. But that was impossible, since no information was available about the amount of equipment which could be taken for payment of reparations. This amount depended in turn upon how much equipment was required to maintain the essential economy of Germany. The same thing applied to an estimate in tons. Further, there was the question what value should be given to each piece of equipment. Should it be the cost price or the value of the article to-day? The experts among the representatives of the United States on the Reparations Commission at Moscow did not themselves agree on an estimate of the amount of equipment available, either in dollars or in tons. It was for that reason that his Soviet friends must accept the United States Delegation's statement in good faith that the economy of Germany would be carried out in accordance with the uniform principles laid down by all the four Powers. When the United States Delegation spoke of a percentage and said they would agree to hand over to Russia a certain percentage of equipment, they had said all that it was possible to say if quarrels and misunderstandings at a later date were to be avoided. The three Governments were going to trust one another on matters of much greater importance than this, and the Soviet Delegation could therefore rest assured that, when the United States Delegation proposed to hand over a certain percentage of a certain commodity, this promise would be carried out in good faith.

Mr. Byrnes, in conclusion, said that he was not wedded to any particular plan. He had thought, however, that the United States proposal put the matter as simply as it could be expressed. Moreover, the United States plan was specific and calculated to avoid misunderstandings in the future.

M. Molotov asked whether Mr. Bevin meant 10 per cent. of all equipment in the Western zones, or 10 per cent. of the equipment in those zones which it was decided could be removed from Germany.

Mr. Bevin said that the British offer of 10 per cent. meant 10 per cent. of the equipment which it was calculated could be removed from the western zones. In arriving at this figure, regard must, of course, be had to the position of the other Allies.

Mr. Byrnes said that under the United States plan, the Soviet Government would be free to exercise its discretion as to removals of equipment from the Russian zone, without interference from the United States, Great Britain or the French. The United States plan had taken the form of a percentage of machinery and equipment to be taken from the Ruhr, because it was the machinery and equipment in this area in which the Soviet Government were specially interested. After the Soviet Government had drawn their percentage of reparations from the Ruhr, there would have to be an adjustment between the United States and the British Governments, and the former would compensate the latter with machinery drawn from the American zone in respect of any excess of machinery drawn from the British zone. A separate agreement on this point would be made between the United Kingdom and the United States Governments and this fact could be mentioned in the final Protocol. Arrangements would also have to be made to meet the claims of France, Holland and Belgium and other Allies. But by presenting the Russian share as a percentage of equipment to be drawn from the Ruhr only, confusion was avoided with other competing claims.

M. Molotov said that Mr. Byrnes' proposal was in the main acceptable, but it failed to define the minimum amount, and also the type, of equipment which would be made available from the West as reparations for the Soviet Union.

Mr. Bevin said that it was impossible to give a minimum figure because we did not know how much equipment was available. There was no use therefore in promising specific amounts at this stage. He did not suppose that Great Britain would obtain much in the way of reparations, but he felt that due regard must be taken of the claims of France and of other countries.

M. Molotov asked who would decide how much equipment was to be made available from the western zones.

Mr. Byrnes and Mr. Bevin suggested that it should be the Control Council, subject to appeal in the event of disagreement to the Zone Commander, who was responsible for the economy of his zone.

M. Molotov thought that the decision how much equipment could be made available for reparations should be decided by the Control Council or by the Reparations Commission, so that it would be possible for the Soviet Government to take part in the decision as one of the four Governments concerned.

Mr. Bevin thought the matter should be dealt with by an advisory body, perhaps the Reparations Commission when the French had been included in membership, but working in close association with the Control Commission. As already stated, there should be a right of veto by the Zone Commander.

Mr. Byrnes said that, provided this right of veto was maintained, he would agree with this proposal.

M. Molotov said that this should be put on record.

M. Molotov then reverted to his argument that the Soviet Delegation could not accept a decision which did not contain minimum figures. He had suggested a financial definition. If this was not acceptable, the minimum amount might be expressed in tons. If no agreement could be reached on this point, the matter should be submitted to the Big Three.

Mr. Byrnes said that the United States Delegation could not agree to a minimum stated in tons. Value was not dependent on weight. The most desirable and necessary plant might weigh much less than other less valuable machinery.

Mr. Bevin said that he would find it difficult, under Mr. Byrnes's plan, to explain to the British public why the greater part of the Soviet demands had been met from the British zone.

M. Molotov suggested that the United States plan might be made to apply not to the British zone alone, but to both the British and American zones.

Mr. Byrnes said that he would have no objection to this, but if the plan covered both zones, the percentages allocated to the Soviet Delegation should be halved.

M. Molotov said that the Soviet Union was the Allied country with the greatest interest in reparations. They were most anxious to secure the share of 50 per cent. agreed at the Crimea Conference. According to Mr. Byrnes' plan, they would receive too little. He suggested that they should receive 25 per cent. of reparations from the West by way of exchange, and another 25 per cent. without payment.

MR. BEVIN said that if the United States proposal could be expressed as the removal of 12½ per cent. from the British and American zones on the basis of exchanges, and 7½ per cent. without payment, this would save him much political difficulty.

M. MOLOTOV then suggested, as reparations from both zones, 20 per cent. on the basis of exchange and 20 per cent. without payment, from both zones but mainly from the Ruhr.

MR. BYRNES said that Mr. Bevin's suggestion would give the Soviet Union the same amount of machinery that he had contemplated when he put forward his plan. He reminded M. Molotov that he had coupled the United States proposal about reparations, which went far beyond anything previously discussed, with the concession suggested by the United States Delegation on the question of Poland's Western Frontier. He also coupled it with the proposal about admission to the United Nations, which involved a concession by the British Delegation. He earnestly hoped, therefore, that the Soviet Delegation would make the concession which he suggested about percentages.

M. MOLOTOV said that the proposed decision on the Western Frontier of Poland would be a concession, not to Russia, but to Poland.

MR. BYRNES said that at the recent meeting at which the Polish representatives had put their case on this matter,[13] none of them had made as eloquent a plea for it as had M. Molotov.

M. MOLOTOV replied that, since a large part of Poland had been incorporated in Russia, the Soviet Government had adopted a specific attitude about Poland's Western Frontier and felt bound to support the Polish Provisional Government in their claim.

MR. BEVIN pointed out that the British Delegation had not agreed to the United States Government's proposal about Poland's Western Frontier. Nor had they agreed to the United States proposal as regards reparations. He wished to make that point clear, and added that he thought that the percentages suggested by the United States Government, namely, 12½ per cent. and 7½ per cent., were very favourable to Russia.

M. MOLOTOV repeated that the offer was too little and would leave the Soviet Union without the equipment which she required. The Germans had advanced as far as Stalingrad and had removed all the equipment from the Donetz Basin. As a result, the Soviet Union could not even meet one-fifth of the demand for agricultural machinery and had nothing with which to restore her railways and bridges. He therefore suggested 25 per cent. from

---

[13] See annex to No. 254.

the Ruhr on the basis of exchanges and 15 per cent. from each of the Western zones.

MR. BYRNES said that 15 per cent. from both zones was the equivalent of 30 per cent. from the Ruhr alone. M. Molotov's latest proposal, therefore, totalled 45 per cent. Mr. Byrnes asked M. Molotov whether he was in a position to reach agreement that afternoon on the three proposals which he had linked together.

M. MOLOTOV said that he thought this question should be referred to the Big Three.

Discussion then reverted to the proposal which Mr. Bevin had submitted on '*The First Charge.*'

M. Molotov said that he would like to make the following addition at the end of Mr. Bevin's formula:

'As regards the rest, priority should be given to reparations, as compared with the satisfaction of other economic needs.'

M. MOLOTOV then quoted two examples to show how this formula would work. (The instances given by M. Molotov were those which he had already quoted at the meeting of Foreign Secretaries (F. (Terminal) 6th Meeting,[3] Minute 3).

MR. BYRNES said that from the start of the Conference it had been clear that it was going to be difficult to get agreement on German reparations. It was partly for this reason that he had put forward the proposal which had been discussed that afternoon. If the Soviet Government accepted his proposals there would be no need for them to enter into the difficult questions of German imports and exports, because they would get from the Western Zones whatever percentage of reparation deliveries had been agreed, and any difficulties that might arise over imports and exports would have to be settled by the British and Americans. This was the great advantage of his proposal from the Soviet point of view and one of the reasons why he had put it forward.

M. MOLOTOV said that he thought agreement could be reached provided a definite figure could be settled for the total of reparations due to the Soviet Union.

MR. BEVIN suggested that the British proposals on this matter be adopted, on the understanding that, so far as reparations were concerned, the percentage agreed to be due to the Soviet Union would be delivered in any case and would not be affected by that part of his proposal which related to the normal flow of goods in and out of Germany.

M. MOLOTOV said that this suggestion overlooked the fact that the Soviet Union would have to obtain the greater part of their reparations deliveries from their own zone, and that there was no certainty that these would in fact be delivered. It seemed to him that agreement had been reached on all points except one—the question of the total figure to be fixed for reparations due to the Soviet Union.

MR. BYRNES reminded the meeting that his three points in his proposal had to be taken as a whole. If agreement could not be reached on one of them without its being submitted to the Plenary Meeting, then all three must be so submitted.

This course was agreed to.

5. *Reparations: Austria and Italy*
(Previous Reference: P. (Terminal) 10th Meeting,[5] Minute 5.)

It was recalled that at the last Plenary Meeting Premier Stalin had agreed that reparations should not be exacted from Austria. M. MOLOTOV asked whether further consideration might now be given to the question of reparations from Italy.

MR. BYRNES said that this question had already been discussed at length without agreement being reached and he himself saw no agreement in prospect. If, however, his colleagues so desired, the Plenary Meeting might be asked to resume their discussion of this problem. If such a request were to be made it should, he thought, be made by M. Molotov.

> It was noted that M. Molotov would raise this question at a Plenary Meeting.

6. *German Fleet and Merchant Navy*
(Previous Reference: P. (Terminal) 9th Meeting,[11] Minute 1.)

MR. BEVIN said that the British Delegation had prepared a memorandum setting out their detailed proposals on this question (P. (Terminal) 52).[14] He suggested that a technical committee should be appointed to consider it.

M. MOLOTOV submitted a memorandum by the Soviet Delegation on the same question (subsequently circulated as P. (Terminal) 55).[15]

> It was agreed to appoint a Committee consisting of:
> *United States Delegation:* Admiral Cook, Mr. Russel[l];
> *United Kingdom Delegation:* Admiral MacCarthy, Mr. Ward, Mr. Weston;
> *Soviet Delegation:* Admiral Kuznetzov, M. Sobolev;
> to examine the questions raised in P. (Terminal) 52 and 55 and to report to an early meeting of Foreign Secretaries.

7. *German External Assets*

MR. BYRNES said that he was submitting that day a memorandum on Germany's External Assets (since circulated as P. (Terminal) 56).[16]

> It was agreed that the Economic Committee should be invited to consider and report to the meeting of Foreign Secretaries on the issues raised in this memorandum.

8. *Germany: Political Principles*
(Previous Reference: P. (Terminal) 3rd Meeting,[17] Minute 3.)
(a) *Notification to French Government*

MR. BEVIN suggested, and it was agreed, that the French Government, as

[14] No. 466.   [15] No. 470.

[16] Not here printed. This document comprised the American memorandum of 30 July and the annex headed 'Text of proposed declaration by the Big Three and France' listed as Attachment 2 in the texts of these papers printed in *F.R.U.S. Berlin*, vol. ii, pp. 961–2.

[17] No. 194.

one of the occupying Powers, ought to be informed in advance of the decisions reached by the Conference regarding the political principles which should govern the treatment of Germany in the initial control period.

(b) *Additional Principles*

Mr. Bevin said that the United Kingdom Delegation had submitted a memorandum (P. (Terminal) 39)[18] on the 24th July suggesting that two further paragraphs should be added to the Statement of Political Principles to govern the treatment of Germany in the initial control period. These were as follows:

(a) 'So far as practicable, there shall be uniformity of treatment of the German population throughout Germany.'

(b) 'Subject to normal regulations, there shall be free circulation of nationals of the Powers represented on the Control Council in all zones by land and air.'

The first of these additional paragraphs was accepted.

As regards the second, M. Molotov said that such a provision should not be included in the Statement without an examination of certain technical details which could not be carried out by the Conference; and he suggested that this paragraph should be referred for technical examination by the Control Council for Germany.

Mr. Byrnes said that it appeared to him that the paragraph sought merely to establish a general principle, for the guidance of the Control Council, who would be left to work out its practical application. The position of the Control Council would be fully protected by the phrase 'Subject to normal regulations'. He thought that the Statement of Political Principles would be improved by the addition of this paragraph, and he hoped that M. Molotov would see his way to accept it.

M. Molotov said that he could not accept the principle of this new paragraph until its detailed implications had been examined.

At Mr. Bevin's suggestion, it was then agreed that the second additional paragraph proposed by the British Delegation should be referred for examination by the Control Council for Germany, who should be asked to submit their recommendations about it to the first meeting of the Council of Foreign Ministers in September, 1945.

M. Molotov then suggested that a third addition should be made to the Statement of Political Principles by adding at the end of paragraph 8 (iv)[19] the following:

'Assistance will, however, be rendered to the establishment of a central German administration composed of secretaries for respective branches of administration—in the first instance of central administrative institutions for foreign trade, industry, finance, transport and communications. The central German administration shall act under the direction of the Control

[18] No. 263.   [19] See No. 190.

Council, and it will be their task to co-ordinate the activities of the Provincial Governments in order to ensure the fulfilment of the decisions of the Control Council and the exercise of functions connected with the solving of problems of an all-German character.'

M. Molotov said that it was necessary that a central administration should be established in Germany to function within defined limits. The Statement of Economic Principles implied this, but did not state it specifically. It was desirable that it should be so stated.

Mr. Bevin said that, in his view, the draft proposed by the Soviet Delegation described the constitution and functions of the central administration in too much detail. Would it not be wiser to ask the Control Council to advise on the steps to be taken to establish a central German administration, its constitution and its functions? If the published Statement of Principles included such a paragraph, it would certainly be asked later whether the Control Council had been consulted, having regard to its responsibilities in this matter.

Mr. Byrnes said that the Conference had given directions to the Control Council on various matters concerning them without first asking their advice; and if the Conference throught it necessary to have a central German administration for certain economic purposes, he himself saw no reason why they should not give a general directive to that effect to the Control Council. If, however, the British Delegation felt doubtful about the wisdom of outlining the constitution and functions of the administrative body to be set up, without first consulting the Control Council, it might be enough to include in the Statement the first sentence and the first half of the second sentence (stopping at the words 'Control Council') in the additional paragraph proposed by M. Molotov. That would establish the necessary central administration, but would leave it to the Control Council to define its functions.

It was agreed:

(1) That the first additional paragraph (*a*) proposed by the British Delegation in P. (Terminal) 39[18] should be included after paragraph 1 in the Statement of Political Principles.

(2) That the three Governments should each instruct its Ambassador in Paris to communicate to the French Government the text of the Statement of Political Principles before this was announced in the communiqué to be issued at the end of the Conference.

(3) That the Control Council for Germany should be invited to consider the detailed implications of adopting the second additional paragraph (*b*) proposed by the British Delegation in P. (Terminal) 39,[18] and to report their views to the first meeting of the Council of Foreign Ministers in September 1945.

(4) That a decision on the third addition proposed by the Soviet Delegation should be deferred until the following day in order that the British Delegation might have a further opportunity of considering it.

9. *Yugoslavia*

(Previous Reference: P. (Terminal) 3rd Meeting,[17] Minute 9.)

MR. BEVIN said that in the memorandum which he had submitted on South-East Europe (P. (Terminal) 51)[20] he had suggested that the Conference might issue a statement noting with regret that Governments in South-East Europe were making charges of aggressive action against their neighbours, and that fears were entertained of attempts to anticipate the peace settlement by violent and unilateral action. The draft statement went on to say that any such attempts would be contrary to the principles for which the war had been fought and which were embodied in the Charter of the United Nations; and it expressed the hope that the Governments of these countries would find peaceful means of solving their differences, and that their peoples would be enabled to enter a period of prosperous and democratic development on the lines laid down in such documents as the Varkiza Agreement and the Tito–Subasić Agreement.

M. MOLOTOV said that the Soviet Government had also circulated at that meeting a memorandum on conditions in the Trieste–Istria district (since circulated as P. (Terminal) 61).[21] He would like his colleagues to consider that memorandum; and he would also like further time to consider the memorandum by the British Delegation, which had not yet been translated into Russian.

It was agreed that discussion of P. (Terminal) 51 and 61 should be deferred.

10. *War Crimes*

MR. BEVIN submitted a memorandum by the United Kingdom Delegation (P. (Terminal) 53)[22] suggesting the inclusion in the Protocol and Communiqué of a paragraph on War Crimes.

M. MOLOTOV also submitted a memorandum on this subject by the Soviet Delegation (P. (Terminal) 57).[23] This contained a list of the first ten war criminals, who were already in Allied hands and, in the view of the Soviet Delegation, should immediately be brought to trial. M. Molotov said that people in many countries expected the Berlin Conference to promise early action in this matter.

MR. BYRNES said that the United States representative on the War Crimes Commission, Mr. Justice Jackson, had discussed this matter with him recently. He understood that the Commission had not yet reached agreement about the tribunal before whom these war criminals should be tried, but hoped to agree very soon on a definition of 'war crime,' and had virtually reached agreement on the means of securing the surrender of the persons

---

[20] No. 465.

[21] No. 475.

[22] No. 467.

[23] See No. 471. It would appear that M. Molotov here submitted this memorandum in the somewhat variant text printed in *F.R.U.S. Berlin*, vol. ii, p. 985: cf. *ibid.*, p. 984, note 1, p. 985, note 1, and *Berlinskaya konferentsiya*, p. 416, note.

charged. He would prefer to ascertain the views of the Commission before settling the terms of the declaration to be made by the Conference in this matter.

M. Molotov said that the Soviet Delegation already had positive information from their representative about the stage which had been reached in the work of the Commission. Agreement had now been reached on all save one or two minor points. There had been some divergence of view about the place at which the trials should take place. Berlin, Nuremberg and other places had been suggested: but the Soviet Government were prepared to agree to any of these.

Mr. Bevin and Mr. Byrnes said that they were glad to hear that Nuremberg was acceptable to the Soviet Government, as they would both prefer that the trials should be held there.

Mr. Bevin asked whether, in the light of the discussion which had just taken place, the meeting would not be satisfied with the draft statement put forward by the British Delegation in P. (Terminal) 53.[22]

M. Molotov thought it would be preferable to place on record the names of certain people to be tried forthwith.

Mr. Byrnes did not think it would be wise to mention the names of selected individuals at this stage. The representatives of the three Governments on the War Crimes Commission would have their own views, based on their expert and detailed consideration of all the charges, as to which cases should be tried first; and it was for the Commission to decide how best to proceed. Moreover, there was room for much difference of opinion about priorities. Thus, there were even differences between two lists which had been shown to him by M. Molotov.[23] Moreover, every country in Europe had its favourite Nazi war criminal; and if any of these were omitted from the list, there would be endless difficulties in explaining why we had discriminated between certain war criminals and others.

M. Molotov said that, in his view, the statement contained in P. (Terminal) 53[22] did not go far enough. Public opinion expected the Conference to move forward in this matter, and would not be satisfied in 1945 with reminders of what had been said in 1943.

It was agreed that discussion of this matter should be deferred.

11. *Fascist Activities in Germany and Austria*

(Previous Reference: P. (Terminal) 9th Meeting,[11] Minute 4.)

M. Molotov referred to the memorandum by the Soviet Delegation (P. (Terminal) 44)[2] recording the information which had reached the Soviet Government on hostile activities in Germany and Austria by Russian Fascists formerly in the service of the Germans. The object of the Soviet Delegation in submitting this memorandum was to obtain from the British and United States Delegations an assurance that enquiries would be made and measures taken to put an end to the activities referred to, to disband the organisations and to make it impossible for them to reappear. He enquired whether the British and United States Delegations were in a position to give such assurances.

Mr. Byrnes said that on receiving the memorandum the United States Delegation had immediately asked for reports from their Commanders-in-Chief. These had not yet been received, but it was hoped that they would arrive by the following day. As soon as they arrived he would communicate with M. Molotov.

Mr. Bevin said that similar action had been taken by his predecessor and he hoped to receive reports shortly. If they did not reach him before the end of the Conference he would communicate with the Soviet Government through the diplomatic channel.

M. Molotov hoped that the assurances mentioned would be received before the end of the Conference. Mr. Bevin said that if the facts, as reported by the Commanders-in-Chief concerned, justified action, he would take it; he must, however, have the facts first.

12. *German Troops in Norway*
(Previous Reference: P. (Terminal) 9th Meeting,[11] Minutes 3 and 4 (c).)

M. Molotov referred to the memorandum on this subject by the Soviet Delegation (P. (Terminal) 43).[1]

Mr. Bevin said that he was now in a position to send a full reply to the Soviet Delegation. The draft would be submitted to the Prime Minister that evening, and the reply sent to M. Molotov without delay.

13. *Future Business*

M. Molotov gave notice of the following questions raised in memoranda submitted by the Soviet Delegation:

(a) *Administration of the Ruhr Industrial Area.* (Subsequently circulated as P. (Terminal) 59.)[24]

(b) *Repatriation of Soviet Citizens from the Baltic, Western Ukraine and Byelo-Russia.* (Subsequently circulated as P. (Terminal) 60.)[25]

14. *Agenda for Eleventh Plenary Meeting*

M. Molotov said that Premier Stalin hoped to be able to attend a Plenary Meeting the following afternoon.

Mr. Bevin suggested that the agenda for this meeting should be arranged by consultations between the three Delegations.

It was agreed that the next Plenary Meeting should take place at 4 p.m. on Tuesday, the 31st July, 1945, the Agenda being arranged by consultation between the three Delegations beforehand.

Cabinet Office, Potsdam, 30th July, 1945

[24] No. 472.   [25] No. 473.

No. 470

Memorandum by the Soviet Delegation (Berlin)[1]

P. (Terminal) 55 [U 6197/3628/70]

Top secret
30 July 1945

German Navy and Merchant Marine

1. One third of the total strength of the German surface navy, including ships which at the beginning of Germany's surrender were under construction or in repair, shall be transferred to the Soviet Union.

2. A larger part of the German submarine fleet shall be sunk. A part of the submarine fleet, viz., submarines presenting the greatest interest from the technical standpoint shall be preserved and divided between the U.S.S.R., Great Britain and the United States of America.

3. One third of all stock of armaments, ammunition and supplies of the German navy shall, according to the classes of vessels, be transferred to the Soviet Union.

4. One third of the German merchant marine shall be transferred to the Soviet Union.

5. The transfer of vessels and ships of the German navy and merchant marine shall begin on the 1st August and their receipt shall be completed by the 1st November, 1945.

6. A Maritime Technical Commission will be set up to hand and take over vessels of the German navy and merchant marine located in the ports and bases in Allied countries and [as] well as in Germany and other countries.

[1] Printed in *Berlinskaya konferentsiya*, p. 421.

No. 471

Memorandum by the Soviet Delegation (Berlin)[1]

P. (Terminal) 57 [U 6197/3628/70]

Top secret
30 July 1945

War Criminals

The following paragraph is suggested for insertion in the Protocol and the Communiqué of the Conference:–

1. The Conference recognised it as necessary that an International Tribunal should be set up in the near future to try the principal war criminals whose crimes, as is stated in the Moscow Declaration of the 1st November, 1943, have no geographic location.

2. The Conference decided that in the first place the following chiefs of the Hitler clique should be tried by the International Tribunal: Göring, Hess, Ribbentrop, Ley, Keitel, Doenitz, Kaltenbrunner, Frick, Streicher, Krupp.

[1] Printed *op.cit.*, p. 416.

3. The leaders of the three Allied Governments declared that, in accordance with the Moscow Declaration of the 1st November, 1943, they will take all measures in their power to secure the surrender for trial of war criminals who have taken shelter in neutral countries. Should any of these countries refuse to surrender the war criminals who have taken shelter in its territory the three Allied Governments will consult each other as to the steps which it will be necessary to take to ensure the implementation of their firm decision.

No. 472

Memorandum by the Soviet Delegation (Berlin)[1]
P. (*Terminal*) 59 [U 6197/3628/70]

Top secret   30 July 1945

The Ruhr Industrial District

Considering the Ruhr Industrial District as a part of Germany and having in view the necessity of completely curtailing Germany's war potential, the Conference has deemed it expedient:–

(1) To determine that the Ruhr Industrial District shall be, in respect of administration, under the joint control of the United States, United Kingdom, U.S.S.R., and France.

(2) The administration of the Ruhr Industrial District shall be exercised by an Allied Council composed of representatives of the United Kingdom, United States, U.S.S.R., and France.

(3) The Industry of the Ruhr District will be utilised for reparation purposes in conformity with the common reparation plan.

(4) To establish immediately, in order to secure prompt accomplishment of this decision, a provisional Allied Council composed of representatives of the United States, United Kingdom, U.S.S.R., and France, which in a month's time will carry out the necessary preparatory work and will assume the provisional administration of the Ruhr District.

[1] Printed *op. cit.*, p. 414.

No. 473

Memorandum by the Soviet Delegation (Berlin)[1]
P. (*Terminal*) 60 [U 6197/3628/70]

Top secret   30 July 1945

Soviet citizens from Baltic, Western Ukraine and Byelorussia

According to the information of the Soviet Repatriation Authorities, General Torn [Thorne], Commander of British troops in Norway, having

[1] Printed *op. cit.*, p. 428.

quoted the British Government's order, refused to deliver to these authorities citizens of the Soviet Baltic Republics, who are at the present time in Norway, as well as Soviet citizens who had emigrated from the Western Ukraine and Western Byelorussia, several thousand persons altogether.

A similar situation exists in Great Britain, from which country 287 Soviet citizens—emigrants from the Soviet Baltic Republics and from the Western Ukraine and Western Byelorussia—were not permitted to leave for their native country by the British Authorities.

Drawing the attention of the Government of Great Britain to these facts, the Soviet Government expects that the British Military Authorities will immediately issue instructions authorising the delivery to the Soviet Repatriation Military Authorities of all Soviet citizens who have emigrated from the Baltic Republics, the Western Ukraine and Western Byelorussia.

CALENDAR TO No. 473

i *31 July 1945 Letter from Mr. Dean (Berlin) to Mr. Warner; U.K. Del. Brief on Soviet citizens from Baltic Republics, Western Ukraine and Byelorussia.* Divergence between British and Soviet definitions of Soviet citizens. A reply to No. 473 'will be sent in the ordinary way through diplomatic channels' [F.O. 934/5/42 (11)].

No. 474

Letter from Mr. Bevin to M. Molotov (Berlin)[1]
[F.O. 934/5/51(4)]

BRITISH DELEGATION, BERLIN, *30 July 1945*

Dear M. Molotov,

At the Plenary Meeting on July 25th last Generalissimo Stalin said that the Soviet Government had received information to the effect that German troops in Norway were not being properly disarmed. Mr. Churchill undertook to have enquiries made and to submit a report on the facts.[2]

M. Novikov subsequently communicated to Sir W. Strang an aide-mémoire[3] setting out the information in the hands of the Soviet Government.

I have now received the following report from the competent authorities in London, and I am happy to be able to tell you that the allegations contained in the Soviet aide-mémoire of July 25th are without foundation.

The true situation is as follows:

At the conclusion of hostilities with Germany there were in all 365,000 Germans in Norway. These were all collected into reservations, up to ten

---

[1] A copy of this letter, circulated to the British Delegation as P. (Terminal) 64 of 31 July 1945, was sent by Mr. Bevin to Mr. Byrnes on 31 July: printed in *F.R.U.S. Berlin*, vol. ii, pp. 1038–40.

[2] See No. 271, minutes 3–4.

[3] See No. 276, note 1.

miles square in area, in which they were confined to within one kilometre of the camps. A small number of Germans connected with communications, supply and technical services are 'exempt' from confinement in these reservations and work in depots and similar installations.

After collection into the reservations, the Germans in Norway were all disarmed except for the officers and two per cent of the other ranks. These were allowed to retain pistols and rifles respectively, with a very small quantity of ammunition, to maintain order and discipline amongst themselves. There are in all about 7,300 Germans thus allowed to bear arms. No German is allowed to bear arms outside his reservation, depot or similar installation.

The Soviet aide-mémoire of July 25th referred to reports that German troops stationed in the area between the towns of Mo and Trondjem, numbering about 260,000 men and those in the region of Tromso numbering about 140,000 men were in possession of their arms and war equipment. The true facts are as follows:

In the Mo-Trondjem area there are 49,688 Germans, of whom 1,400 have been allowed to retain arms and 7,500 are 'exempt' from confinement in reservations, In the Bodo-Tromso area, out of a total of 120,000 men, 2,750 are armed and 13,300 exempt from confinement. It will be seen therefore that the reports referred to in the Soviet aide-mémoire are incorrect and devoid of foundation.

I should like to take this opportunity of raising a point connected with the evacuation of the German troops from Norway. 108,000 of the Germans in Norway originated from the Russian Zone of Occupation in Germany. The British military authorities are at present responsible for the disposal of 54,000 of these Germans, the United States military authorities having offered to take responsibility for the remaining 54,000. It would much facilitate the work of evacuation if the Soviet authorities would accept direct from Norway those 54,000 Germans originating from the Russian Zone in Germany who are now the responsibility of the British military authorities. If the Soviet Government agree in principle to this proposal, I would suggest that arrangements for transporting these Germans direct from Norway to the Russian Zone in Germany might be worked out by the appropriate British, Soviet and possibly Swedish authorities.

E. BEVIN

No. 475

Memorandum by the Soviet Delegation (Berlin)[1]
P. (Terminal) 61 [U 6197/3628/70]

Top secret   *30 July 1945*

Conditions in Trieste-Istria District

The Soviet Government have taken knowledge of the message of Mr. I. Subasić, Minister of Foreign Affairs of Yugoslavia, and Marshal I. Brose

[1] Printed in *Berlinskaya konferentsiya*, pp. 426–7.

[Broz]-Tito, Prime Minister of Yugoslavia, to the Heads of the Three Governments concerning conditions in Trieste–Istria District. It is said in that message that Italian Fascist laws, which had been in action until the 8th September, 1943, were restored on the territory of Trieste-Istria in consequence of Allied military authorities' activity. Former Italian institutions are being restored; persons who had occupied executive posts in the period of German occupation are permitted to participate in the civil administration. At the same time, obstacles are being made to the activities of democratic institutions of the local Yugoslavian administration which had been created during the period of struggle against occupants, in a number of cases these institutions are ignored by the representatives of the Allied military authorities.

The Government of Yugoslavia request that the laws which had been in action until the 8th September, 1943, on Trieste–Istria territory be revoked, that the possibility of normal activities should be given to the democratic institutions of the local administration represented by the people's committees having the support and confidence of the population, and that in such cases, when those institutions do not correspond to the proper requirements, their replacement should be effected by the way of free democratic elections.

The Soviet Government consider desirable that the proposals of the Government of Yugoslavia, expressed in the message of Mr. I. Subasić, Minister of Foreign Affairs, and Marshal I. Brose[Broz]-Tito, Prime Minister of Yugoslavia, should be met by the Conference of the Heads of the three Governments.

No. 476

Minute from Sir E. Bridges to Mr. Bevin (Berlin)
[CAB 21/864]

[BERLIN,] *30 July 1945*

A meeting was held this morning of the Committee which is drafting the Protocol of the Conference. At this meeting the Soviet representative, Mr. Gromyko, wished to insert a paragraph dealing with a complaint made by the Russians about a British camp in Italy at Cesenatico in which there were some Ukrainians who had fought against us. Mr. Churchill had given an explanation which Premier Stalin accepted.[1] I, therefore, took the line that it was entirely inappropriate to include in the Conference a reference to a matter which (a) was a relatively minor point; (b) had been disposed of, and (c) only affected two of the Powers at the Conference. I offered to arrange an agreed exchange of documents between ourselves and the Russians if this was thought necessary, but Mr. Gromyko said that the

---

[1] See No. 258, minute 5.

question whether this matter should be mentioned in the Protocol would have to be referred to the Foreign Secretaries.

Later in the meeting the Russians also proposed to insert a paragraph in the Protocol to the effect that there had been an exchange of views at the Conference about Syria and the Lebanon. This is inoffensive in itself, but the U.S. representative, Mr. Dunn, took the point that it was undesirable to have any more points than could be avoided mentioned in the Protocol and not in the Communique. He also agreed with the view I expressed, namely, that there was no point in including in the Protocol anything except agreed decisions, and he would therefore prefer to have this matter left out.

The Russians are, of course, in these two instances, seeking to include in the Protocol matters in which they are interested or have raised points against us. If they take this line there is no reason why we should not propose for inclusion in the Protocol such matters as (i) *Roumania and Bulgaria:* the unsatisfactory position of the British element of the Control Commission, or (ii) the removal of British oil equipment from Roumania, on neither of which we have received any satisfaction. But I am sure the right line is to eliminate from the Protocol all matters except those on which there are agreed decisions on substance.[2]

E. E. B.

[2] Mr. Bevin minuted on this: 'I agree. Limit it to decisions. E. B.'

No. 477

Minute by Mr. T. Brand (Berlin)
[*F.O. 934/1/2(37)*]

[BERLIN,] *30 July 1945*
German coal production: P. (Terminal) 54[1]

It is unlikely that this question will be raised at the Conference, unless the Russians bring it up on the President's memorandum informing the Soviet Government of the instructions which have been given to the Western Zone Commanders to take all possible measures to increase coal production and make the maximum quantities available for export.

2. The position is as follows. The Potter-Hyndley Report estimated that North-West Europe, Italy, Greece and French North Africa would need imports of at least 30,000,000 tons of coal by the end of April 1946, if a disastrous coal famine is to be avoided. Somewhere between 6 and 9 million tons of this can be provided from overseas, leaving a deficit of 21 to 24

[1] P. (Terminal) 54 of 30 July 1945 comprised a memorandum of 27 July from President Truman for Marshal Stalin with annexed directive to General Eisenhower on coal, printed in *F.R.U.S. Berlin*, vol. ii, pp. 1028–30.

million tons to be provided from Germany of [? or] Poland. The figure of requirements of 30,000,000 tons mentioned above assumes consumption of only one third to one half of 1938 standards.

3. The British and American Governments have already issued their instructions to the Zone Commanders and it is believed that the French will do so in the near future if they have not already done so. The target figure for export stated in the instructions is 25,000,000 tons. Difficulties in production and transport make it improbable that this target will be reached. The first estimate from the Allied Control Commission was that only 8,000,000 tons would be available for export up to 30th April 1946, but General Weeks stated recently that he hoped to improve on these figures and get up to 12 to 16 million tons.

4. The Russians may raise the following points:–

(i) That export of coal must not be prejudicial to the restoration of German economy. Our answer to this would be that the instructions allow the Zone Commander to retain whatever coal he considers necessary for the general security of his troops and the zone, but that, as far as the restoration of economic life is concerned, the choice is deliberate. If it is a question of whether liberated areas or Germany should suffer, let it be Germany.

(ii) That current deliveries of coal should be in accordance with reparation percentages rather than the urgent needs of the various European countries. In this case our reply would be:–

(a) That, during this winter, the proceeds of exports of coal will be needed to pay for imports; there will therefore be no reparation receipts from export of coal during the period covered by the instructions.

(b) That the need for coal in liberated areas is so great that the allocation of the German exportable surplus must be in accordance with need, adjustments for reparation account being made later.

5. We should also resist any suggestion that the Ruhr should bear the whole burden of hard coal supplies for Germany. Supplies for Greater Berlin and the Eastern Zone should come from Silesia. We should also press the Russians to take all measures to increase brown coal production in their area.

6. If the Russians complain that the Americans, the French and ourselves have taken unilateral action, our reply would be that the need for increased production of coal was so great that immediate action was necessary, and that Field Marshal Montgomery has been instructed to discuss this policy at the Allied Control Council. We might at the same time take this opportunity of repeating our invitation to the Soviet Government to join the European Coal Organisation. The present position is that they are considering the documents setting up the European Coal Organisation and will let us know their views later. We are anxious that Russia should join this Organisation, because a concerted plan cannot be worked out without including the large Polish exportable surplus. It is probable that

an invitation will be sent in the near future to the Polish Government to join the European Coal Organisation, but Poland may not be willing to come in unless the Russians are in also.

T. H. B.

CALENDAR TO No. 477

i *27 July 1945   Letter from Mr. Hasler to Mr. Brand (Berlin).* Refers to Nos. 191.iv, 233.ii, and 271.ii: preparation of instructions to F.M. Montgomery on coal: position regarding British coal exports [UR 2483/2109/851].

No. 478

Mr. Morrison to Mr. Bevin (Berlin: received 31 July, 12.44 a.m.)
No. 294 Onward Telegraphic [N 9539/6/55]

FOREIGN OFFICE, *30 July 1945, 10.30 p.m.*

Top secret. Most Immediate

Following from Sir Orme Sargent to Sir A. Cadogan.

It appears from what M. Mikolajczyk said to Mr Eden and Sir A. Clark Kerr on the 25th July[1] as if the tussle between him and the Communists in Poland has already reached a crucial stage. It looks to us as if our friends will have lost the game if we can do nothing at Potsdam to secure proper opportunities for M. Mikolajczyk and M. Popiel to organise their parties, to secure that M. Mikolajczyk's candidates are accepted by the National Council and to prevent the Praesidium from being made into a super Government.

2. It seems from what M. Mikolajczyk told Mr Eden that M. Bierut's promises and talk about 23 political parties and freedom of expression at elections are worth nothing. What seems to be required is

(i) that we should get at Potsdam, if there is still time, formal assurances of a satisfactory nature from the Poles in full conference (and also undertakings from the Russians about the withdrawal of the Red Army and NKVD from Poland) and

(ii) that we should have some sanction which we and the Americans could apply if these assurances were not fulfilled.

3. We are not clear here how it is proposed to leave the question of Polish Western frontier at the termination of the conference. But it occurs to us that it might be possible, if we are prepared to do anything for the Poles on this matter, to use it as such a sanction, by withholding fulfilment of anything we may be prepared to do pending the carrying out to our satisfaction of assurances of the kind referred to in the preceding paragraph.

---

[1] See Nos. 269–270.

Alternatively, or perhaps in addition, would it be possible to link with the carrying out of such assurances our attitude on the questions of the Polish Armed Forces, merchant marine, return of refugees to Poland, etc., reparations—indeed everything that sooner or later we have to discuss with the Warsaw Government.

4. We are too much out of the picture here to know whether these suggestions are at all practicable and indeed whether the Poles are still at Potsdam. But I think it just worth while sending you this telegram as we have seen that the Prime Minister and Foreign Secretary saw the Poles yesterday afternoon[2] and that on the question of political freedom in Poland Bierut seems[3] only to have repeated the same sort of stuff as he had said to Mr Churchill and Mr Eden.[4]

(Repeated to Warsaw No. 103, Moscow No. 4221, Washington No. 7973.)

[2] Cf. No. 453.

[3] The ensuing passage is cited by Sir L. Woodward *op. cit.*, vol. v, p. 433.

[4] This telegram was minuted in Berlin by Mr. D. Allen and Sir A. Cadogan as follows: 'We had in fact already been thinking on these lines and the S. of S. is pressing the Poles for assurances in return for our agreement to the Western frontier, which should cover point (1) in para. 2. We have not however yet asked the Russians for assurances about the withdrawal of the Red Army. M. Mikolajczyk attaches importance to this and I should have thought we might well have raised the matter at the plenary session today. D. Allen. 31/7.' 'This was done, and we got the best we could out of the Russians—which is not *entirely* satisfactory. A. C. July 31, 1945.'

No. 479

Brief by United Kingdom Delegation
[*F.O. 934/3/17(6)*]

[BERLIN,] *30 July 1945*

Yalta Declaration

The Soviet Government have made proposals for the improvement of the position of the British and United States representatives. These proposals required clarification, for which we have asked.[1] But subject to this we hope that conditions for British representatives on these Commissions will become more satisfactory than they have been in the past, and that they will be able to co-operate usefully with their American and Soviet colleagues.

2. The Soviet refusal to consider the supervision of *elections*[2] is regretted. We intend to accede to the Greek Government's request to supervise the elections in that country, and we hope that the United States Government will join us. We have every reason to think that the result will faithfully reflect the will of the Greek people.

3. We have far less confidence about the result of the Bulgarian elections,

[1] In regard to Allied Control Commissions in former Satellite States: see No. 275.
[2] See No. 206.

which are apparently to be held next month. In these elections it appears that no organised opposition will be tolerated. This has been categorically confirmed quite recently by the Minister of the Interior. It is clear that elections in such circumstances will be a complete farce. His Majesty's Government will be obliged to inform the Bulgarian Government that they will be unable to recognise as representative any government elected by these means.

4. It is also regretted that no agreement could be reached in regard to the *press*. It must be frankly stated that there has been much uneasiness in many quarters in London about the impossibility of obtaining news about conditions in the ex-satellite countries. A reassuring statement by the Conference would therefore have an excellent effect. But the Soviet representatives on the Sub-Committee were unable to agree to any provision for facilitating the entry of press representatives into the countries concerned, nor could they guarantee the abolition of political censorship. In these circumstances no statement about present conditions in these countries could be issued which the British Government would be able to endorse. It is still to be hoped that the Soviet Delegation will agree that we should state publicly that press correspondents can go freely to these countries and report freely there on all that they see, as they can in Italy or in Greece.

5. It will be remembered that earlier in the Conference the Soviet Delegation put in a paper on the subject of the Yalta Declaration,[3] which referred to conditions in the ex-satellite countries and in Greece. There are certain points in this statement which call for comment.

6. The Soviet memorandum says that the Governments of the satellite states are faithfully carrying out the obligations assumed by them under their respective instruments of surrender. As regards Bulgaria, this statement cannot be accepted. It will be remembered that at the Plenary Meeting on July 20th Marshal Stalin said that Bulgaria was required to pay reparations, and Russia, together with the other Great Powers, would see to this.[4] This assurance is welcomed. But Bulgaria has not yet paid any reparations to Greece, which has so far received from Bulgaria only a few horses and mules, all in very bad condition. On the same occasion Marshal Stalin said that now that the German war was over the Bulgarian forces would be demobilised to peacetime strength. This statement is also welcomed, since hitherto there has been no sign of disarmament. We cannot therefore say that Bulgaria has fulfilled the armistice so far, though in view of the Marshal's statements we can be sure they will shortly be obliged to do so.

7. Nor do our reports confirm the statement in the Soviet memorandum that in the case of the satellite states 'due order exists and legal power is acting'. On the contrary according to our recent reports the secret police and militia in Bulgaria are carrying on terrorist activities, and according to reports which we believe to be true between 40,000 and 50,000 persons were murdered by the Bulgarian militia in the past six months. These are

[3] No. 201.　　　　　　　　　[4] See No. 208, minute 4.

quite different from the 2,000 executed after trial as war criminals, and the offence of the great majority was opposition to the present Government and not collaboration with the Germans. We cannot of course be sure that these reports are true, since we have hitherto been denied facilities for seeing conditions in the country for ourselves, but we have every reason for believing that they are not far from the mark. If so it is hardly true to say that the position in Bulgaria compares favourably with the situation in Greece. At least it has not happened in Greece that a Prime Minister and a leader of a democratic party have been obliged, in fear of their lives, to take refuge in foreign Legations.

8. As regards Greece, there is nothing to add to Mr. Eden's statement when the Soviet paper was introduced at the meeting of the Foreign Secretaries on July 20th,[5] and the memorandum by Mr. Churchill circulated to the other Delegations on July 22nd.[6] If the Soviet Government do not believe these reports they should send someone to Greece to see for themselves, and meanwhile refrain from broadcasting to the world these unsupported charges. They can be assured of facilities to see everything they want.

9. The Soviet document refers to the Varkiza Agreement. His Majesty's Government could not agree to the recommendation as drafted, but they would not object to a friendly reminder to the Greek Government to observe the terms of the Agreement, provided that a similar communication should be made by the Conference to the Yugoslav Government on the subject of the Tito-Subasic Agreement. Both Agreements form the basis of the Governments in the countries concerned, and both have been endorsed by His Majesty's Government.

10. The Conference might therefore recommend that these two neighbouring United Nations, whose relations have recently been somewhat disturbed, should endeavour to live in peace in the future. A document[7] for insertion in the protocol has accordingly been circulated.

British Delegation

[5] See No. 200, minute 6.
[6] No. 228.
[7] No. 465.

No. 480

Minute from Mr. Bevin to Mr. Attlee (Berlin)
No. P.M./45/Terminal/2 [E 5474/15/31]

[BERLIN,] *30 July 1945*

I have seen the memorandum on Palestine which President Truman sent to Mr. Churchill on July 24th. (Flag A.)[1]

[1] Annex below: printed in *F.R.U.S. Berlin*, vol. ii, p. 1402. *V. ibid.*, p. 1406, for Mr. Attlee's interim reply of 31 July 1945 to Mr. Truman in the sense proposed below.

2. I suggest that you should reply to the President that the new Government will give early and careful consideration to the President's memorandum. The President will certainly understand that no statement on policy could be given to him until we have had time to consider the matter.

3.[2] I consider the Palestine question urgent and when I return to London I propose to examine the whole question, bearing in mind the repercussions on the whole Middle East and the U.S.A.

4. I should add that the Colonial Office have been consulted by the Foreign Office about the President's memorandum and agree that the reply to the President should be on the lines proposed above.

E. Bevin

Annex to No. 480

Memorandum from President Truman to Mr. Churchill (Berlin)

Copy   THE WHITE HOUSE, WASHINGTON [BABELSBERG], *24 July 1945*
Subject: Palestine.

There is great interest in America in the Palestine problem. The drastic restrictions imposed on Jewish Immigration by the British White Paper of May, 1939,[3] continue to provoke passionate protest from Americans most interested in Palestine and in the Jewish problem. They fervently urge the lifting of these restrictions which deny to Jews, who have been so cruelly uprooted by ruthless Nazi persecutions, entrance into the land which represents for so many of them their only hope of survival.

Knowing your deep and sympathetic interest in Jewish settlement in Palestine, I venture to express to you the hope that the British government may find it possible without delay to take steps to lift the restrictions of the White Paper on Jewish immigration into Palestine.

While I realise the difficulties of reaching a definite and satisfactory settlement of the Palestine problem, and that we cannot expect to discuss these difficulties at any length at our present meeting, I have some doubt whether these difficulties will be lessened by prolonged delay. I hope, therefore, that you can arrange at your early convenience to let me have your ideas on the settlement of the Palestine problem, so that we can at a later but not too distant date discuss the problem in concrete terms.[4]

Harry Truman

[2] This paragraph and other related extracts are cited by N. Bethell, *The Palestine Triangle*, p. 202.

[3] Cmd. 6019.

[4] This memorandum was minuted in the Eastern and Refugee Departments of the Foreign Office: 'The President's démarche is no doubt intended largely "for the record"; and the nature of our reply will at least be indicated in some public statement after his return to the United States. The Zionists have been deplorably successful in selling the idea that, even after the Allied victory, emigration to Palestine represents for many Jews "their only hope of survival". One advantage of temporising would be, I hope, the dissipation of this idea. H. Beeley 27/7.' 'The C[olonial] O[ffice] will prepare the first draft of a note for the

i   *14, 19 July & 1 Aug. 1945   Tel. No. 3906 to Sir A. Clark Kerr (Moscow); Mr. Le Rougetel (Bucharest) Tel. No. 721; Mr. Roberts (Moscow) Tel. No. 3373.* Reported possibility of relaxation of Soviet attitude on emigration to Palestine discounted [WR 2011, 2184, 2290/2011/48].

ii *19, 31 July & 3 Aug. 1945   Sir E. Grigg (Cairo) Tel. No. 700; Lord Killearn (Cairo) Tel. No. 73 to Khartoum; Tel. No. 1179 to Lord Killearn (Cairo).* Considerations regarding proposed visit to Palestine by Soviet Military Mission in Middle East and request to visit the Sudan in connection with repatriation of Soviet citizens [WR 2290/2011/48; N 9575/409/38].

iii *23, 24 & 27 July 1945   Minute by Mr. Mason; letter from Mr. Mason to Mr. Hayter (Berlin); letter from Col. Hammer (War Office) to Mr. Mason.* Attitude in regard to allowing Jewish missions to visit Germany; transmission to Potsdam of message from World Jewish Congress; record of meeting on 25 July between Lord Dunglass and Jewish representatives on situation of Jews in Germany [WR 2267/4/48; F.O. 934/5/49(1)].

iv *30 July 1945   Mr. Gascoigne (Budapest) No. 215.* Little Jewish anxiety to emigrate to Palestine, but reports some anti-semitism in Hungary [WR 2403/4/48].

v   *27 July–2 Aug. 1945   (a) Letter from Sir G. Gater to Sir R. Campbell re No. 480* enclosing brief note on formulation of a new policy for Palestine *(b) Memo. of 30 July from Sir O. Sargent to Mr. Bevin (Berlin)* submitting F.O. appreciation of international repercussions of various policies considered for Palestine. Suggests consultation with Arabs regarding continuation of Jewish immigration on temporary basis; if Arabs refuse, matter could be referred to the 'Big Five' *(c) Draft brief for Mr. Bevin* on Palestine [E 5539, 5601/15/31].

vi *2 Aug. 1945   Record by Sir R. Campbell of conversation with Mr. Gallman (U.S. Embassy in London):* Zionist pressure on U.S. Govt.; need for balancing of Jewish and Arab interests in regard to Palestine [E 5646/15/31].

guidance of the British Delegation. I agree that we must be extremely careful what we reply to President Truman, as he will have to say something in public (or to the Zionist leaders) when he gets back to America. C. W. Baxter 27/7.' 'From Refugee Dept's standpoint (as from that of others) it is important not to give the impression that Palestine, rather than the countries of which they are nationals, is the proper home of all Jews. P. Mason 27.7.'

No. 481

Letter from Mr. Colville (Chequers) to Mr. Rowan (Berlin)
[PREM 3/430/14]

CHEQUERS, *30 July 1945*

My Dear Rowan

Mr. Churchill asks me to say that he would think it a great courtesy if the Prime Minister would let him know the results of the Conference since, having taken part in so much of it, he would naturally be interested to know how things finally develop. In particular Mr. Churchill is anxious to hear whether Marshal Stalin cross-examined the President about T[ube] A[lloys] which had, of course, been mentioned to the Marshal before Mr. Churchill left and, if so, he would be interested to know what Stalin's reactions were.[1]

Yours ever
JOCK COLVILLE

[1] Mr. Rowan minuted on this letter on 31 July 1945 to Mr. Attlee: 'If you agree with the first suggestion in the attached letter, which seems reasonable, I will discuss with Sir E. Bridges the best method of conveying the results of the Conference to Mr. Churchill. The second matter you could no doubt conveniently raise with the President when you hand him the document on T.A. T. L. R. 31.7.45.' Mr. Attlee minuted: 'Yes C. R. A.'

No. 482

Mr. Bevin (Berlin) to Mr. Morrison (Received 31 July, 12.24 a.m.)
No. 287 Target Telegraphic [F.O. 800/417/66]

Top secret. Most Immediate   BERLIN, *31 July 1945, 2.20 a.m.*

For Private Office from Rowan.

Following for Lord President of the Council from Prime Minister:
Begins:

It will not be possible to conclude the work of the conference by Tuesday[1] evening and I have therefore decided to stay here another day, returning to London on Thursday morning. I am sorry not to be back for the first day of the new Parliament,[2] but it is clear that my duty is to remain here as most important issues are at stake.

Ends.

2. For Private Office only.

Please transfer appointments made for Wednesday to Thursday at same time.

[1] 31 July 1945.   [2] On 1 August.

No. 483

Note by the British Secretariat (Berlin)
P. (Terminal) 66 [U 6197/3628/70]

Top secret   *31 July 1945*

Reparations: Italy and Austria

(Circulated to the United Kingdom Delegation only)

The two papers annexed were handed round by the Secretary of State for Foreign Affairs at the meeting of Foreign Secretaries on the 30th July

(F. (Terminal) 10th Meeting),[1] and are now circulated for information.

Italian Reparations[2]

Italy shall be liable to make reparation to those of the United Nations against which she went to war. It is recognised, however, that such reparation must not be at the expense of those States which are furnishing or may continue to furnish Italy with minimum essential supplies or at the expense of the maintenance of Italy's economic stability.

It is recommended that the Council of Foreign Ministers should deal with the problem on this basis when considering the Italian peace treaty.

Austrian Reparations

Reparations will not be exacted from Austria. Removal of plant and equipment and other goods from Austria as war booty or otherwise will, in future, be a matter to be settled by the Control Council.

CALENDAR TO NO. 483

i *4 Aug. 1945 Letter from Mr. Playfair (Treasury) to Mr. B. Trench (E.I.P.S.):* treatment of Italian reparation at Potsdam [UE 3477/1817/77].

---

[1] No. 469.

[2] This paper is printed in *F.R.U.S. Berlin*, vol. ii, p. 1096. The paper below on Austrian reparations is printed *ibid.*, p. 666.

No. 484

Minute from Mr. Allen to Sir A. Cadogan (Berlin)
[F.O. 934/2/10(90)]

[BERLIN,] *31 July 1945*

Late last night the Foreign Secretary instructed me to prepare a paper on the lines of the attached document[1] with a view to crystallising the present situation on the Polish question.

I understand that the Secretary of State proposes to hand this document to the Polish delegation when he meets them this morning at 11.0. Spare copies of the document have been prepared for this purpose.

I also gathered that the Secretary of State had in mind to circulate this paper, or something like it, to the Conference before this afternoon's meeting, as embodying the views of the U.K. delegation. I am less happy about this. If we were to raise the questions of free elections, facilities for the press, etc., in the Conference at this stage the Russians might well accuse us of reopening a question which had already been settled in the statement on Poland agreed after considerable negotiation in the early stages of the

---

[1] Annex I below, initialed as having been seen by Sir A. Cadogan.

Conference (P (Terminal) 23, copy attached).[2] This contains in fact as much as we are likely to be able to get agreed by the Conference on these subjects. To reopen the matter now might well cause serious delay and would involve the risk of reopening also the difficult question of Polish Government assets and liabilities.

I therefore submit that we should concentrate on obtaining privately from the Polish delegation the best assurances we can on the various questions with which we are concerned, with a view to using them as supporting material when the time comes to defend the Terminal Communiqué in Parliament. As regards a document to be circulated to this afternoon's meeting of the Conference I attach a draft (A)[3], the contents of which are restricted solely to the frontier question and the safeguards which we can properly ask for in direct relation to this question.

If agreement on the lines of this draft formula could be reached by the Conference it might be embodied in the Communiqué with an introductory passage on the lines of draft B,[4] also submitted herewith. The draft formula would also have to be submitted to and endorsed by the Polish Delegation.[5]

D. ALLEN

ANNEX I TO No. 484

Before they express a final opinion in regard to the claim of the Polish Provisional Government to a frontier on the Western Neisse and the Oder including Stettin the British Delegation desire to receive satisfactory assurances from the Polish Delegation on the following points:–

1. What measures do the Polish Provisional Government propose to take to carry out the decision of the Crimea Conference, which has been accepted by the Polish Provisional Government, in regard to the holding of free and unfettered elections as soon as possible on a basis of universal suffrage and secret ballot, in which all democratic and anti-Nazi parties shall have the right to take part and to put forward candidates?

2. Will there be freedom of the press in Poland and will foreign correspondents be permitted to enter and to move freely in whatever territories may be transferred to Polish administration and to send out uncensored news concerning developments in Poland before and during the elections?

3. Will there be freedom of religion throughout all territories under Polish administration?

4.[6] Will Poles who return to the new Western territories transferred to Polish administration be given the same opportunities for finding homes and work as Poles in pre-war Polish territory?

---

[2] See No. 219, note 6.
[3] Annex II below, initialed by Mr. Allen.
[4] Annex III below.
[5] Mr. Allen subsequently noted on this minute: 'This was seen by Sir A. Cadogan, Sir A. Clark Kerr and S. of S. before today's meetings with the Poles and this afternoon's Plenary Session, at which agreement was reached. D. A. 31/7.' Cf. Nos. 487, 490 and 495, minute 3.
[6] Marginal annotation on another copy: 'This para. was revised before the paper was handed to the Poles. D. A. 31/7'. Cf. No. 487, note 1.

1047

5. Will the Polish Provisional Government do all in their power to facilitate the early establishment of a British military air service between London and Warsaw via Berlin to enable His Majesty's Government to maintain regular official communication with H.M. Embassy at Warsaw?

The attitude of the British Delegation towards the proposal of the Polish Provisional Government that the present Conference should endorse the transfer to Polish administration of all German territory up to the line of the Oder and the Western Neisse will be influenced by the nature of the replies received to the above questions.

31st July, 1945

ANNEX II TO NO. 484

Western Frontier of Poland: Draft Memorandum
by U.K. Delegation

The U.K. Delegation, having taken account of the views expressed on this subject by the Soviet Delegation (P (Terminal) 12)[7] and the U.S. Delegation (P (Terminal)[?70]),[8] are prepared, subject to a satisfactory agreement being reached on the questions of reparation from and supplies to Germany, to agree to a formula on the lines of the following draft which they submit for the approval of the Conference:

'It is understood that the final delimitation of the frontier between Poland and Germany shall, as agreed in the Crimea, await the Peace Conference. Having regard, however, to the depopulation of Eastern Germany caused by the operations of the war and to the necessity for resuming full production in these regions in the interests of the restoration of the economic life of Europe, it is agreed that, pending a final decision concerning the question of sovereignty over these regions, the following territories shall be administered by the authorities of the Polish Provisional Government:– the free city of Danzig; the parts of East Prussia south of a provisional boundary line running from the Gulf of Danzig south of Koenigsberg and north of Braunsberg and Goldap to the junction of the frontiers of Lithuania, Poland and East Prussia; and all the lands to the east of a line running north from the Czechoslovak frontier along the Lausitzer Neisse and the left bank of the Oder to the Sea west of Swinde-munde [*sic*], leaving Stettin to the east. In all these territories Poles shall enjoy in all respects,[9] including participation in free elections, the same rights as Poles in the pre-war territories of Poland west of the Curzon Line.

This provisional arrangement shall be subject to review in the light of developments in the territories in question pending the Peace Conference. For this purpose the Governments of the U.K., U.S.A. and U.S.S.R. shall be accorded such facilities as they may desire for their representatives to visit the territories and study conditions on the spot.'[10]

---

[7] No. 202.   [8] No. 494.

[9] This clause was as amended in Mr. Allen's hand from the previous text: 'All these territories shall be administered under Polish law and Poles shall enjoy there, in all matters'.

[10] This paragraph was as amended in Mr. Allen's hand from the previous text: 'This provisional arrangement shall, in so far as concerns the territories lying between the rivers Oder and Lausitzer Neisse north of the Czechoslovak frontier and the Oppeln district of Silesia, be subject to review in the light of developments in this area pending

ANNEX III TO No. 484

At the instance of the Soviet Delegation the Conference considered the question of the western frontier of Poland. It was agreed to invite a delegation from the Polish Provisional Government of National Unity to submit to the Conference that Government's views upon the extent of the accessions of territory to be received by Poland in the north and west in accordance with the Declaration on Poland agreed by the Crimea Conference. The Polish delegation submitted to the Conference arguments in support of their claim to a frontier running from the Czechoslovak frontier along the Lausitzer Neisse River and the left bank of the River Oder, and thence west of Stettin to the sea west of Swinemunde. Having heard the arguments of the Polish delegation, the Conference reached the following agreement, which was endorsed by the Polish delegation.

the Peace Conference and for this purpose the Governments of the U.K., U.S.A. and U.S.S.R. shall be accorded such special facilities as they may desire for their representatives to visit the area and study conditions on the spot.' Immediately following in the previous text was a concluding paragraph: 'The arrangement shall also be without prejudice of the supreme authority of the Allied Control Council in Germany, which shall continue to extend, until agreement to the contrary is reached among all four controlling Powers, over all the territories of Germany as it existed on 31st December 1937.' This paragraph was deleted by Mr. Allen, who noted in the margin: 'Sir A. Clark Kerr is strongly in favour of leaving this out, as giving the Russians an excuse for continued interference. Mr. Harrison and I think we *can* now drop it. D. A. 31/7.'

No. 485

Letter from Sir D. Waley (Berlin) to Sir W. Eady
[T 236/265: OF 213/3/2f]

BRITISH DELEGATION, BERLIN, *31 July 1945*[1]

My dear Wilfrid,
For the sake of the record I will try to give a picture of how things are moving. Yesterday morning we had a meeting with the Prime Minister and Foreign Secretary which went over our statements about the first charge, the Soviet share of reparations and supplies for the Western Zones and the Greater Berlin Area and also Italian and Austrian Reparations.[2] The papers were approved in the form in which I sent to you yesterday. I suggested that we should show them to the Americans and we went round to see Pauley at 12 noon. He had to leave to see Byrnes at 12.15. We showed him our texts and he promised to show them to Byrnes. He then showed us his own paper,[3] of which I also sent you a copy, and said that he had told the President and Byrnes that this was his own view and not agreed or discussed with us.

---

[1] This letter, drafted early that day, was sent on 1 August 1945 as an enclosure in No. 508, *q.v.*
[2] See No. 462, minute 2.
[3] Cf. No. 462.i.

The next thing was that Byrnes lunched with Molotov.[4] He gave Molotov the American proposal that Russia should obtain 25% of what is decided available for removal from the Ruhr as a swap against deliveries from the Russian Zone and Silesia and 15% as free reparations. You will note that the 25% and the 15% apply to what is decided to be removable after leaving Germany with what is required for her peacetime needs and does *not* relate to the whole of the industrial plant and equipment in the Ruhr. We and the Americans agree that, broadly speaking, one half of the plant and equipment in the British and American Zones as a whole is to be found in the Ruhr. Thus, the American proposal could also be expressed as $12\frac{1}{2}\%$ of the equipment in the Western Zones as a swap and $7\frac{1}{2}\%$ as free reparations. The Americans thought that, in fact, the Russians wanted to take their removals from the Ruhr. They were quite ready to adjust matters by satisfying other claimants from other parts of the Western Zones and they thought that the higher percentage figures would make a better impression on the Russians.

Byrnes came to see the Secretary of State at 3.30. They began by talking about the Western frontier of Poland and I was not present for this part of the discussion. I understand that whereas the Secretary of State is only willing to agree to the Polish claim for territory on condition that there is freedom of the Press, free elections and free access to foreign newspapers, etc., Byrnes also sold the pass on this subject by agreeing to the cession of territory without clearly making these conditions. However, this is only gossip so far as I am concerned.

Byrnes then went with the Foreign Secretary to see the Prime Minister and the Secretary of State was present for part of the talk, though he had to leave before the end. The Prime Minister was very kind and let me do a good deal of the talking. I did my best to convince Byrnes that his system of swaps is utterly inconsistent with the idea of treating Germany as a single economic unit. I said that the peasant in Brandenberg who sells his potatoes to Berlin has to be paid by receiving boots and shoes from Berlin and cannot be paid by Russia receiving steel plant. I pointed out that if a line is drawn across the middle of Europe, so that there is a frontier with Russia on one side and the Western Powers on the other side, this has an importance far transcending reparations. Mr. Byrnes said that we could try to obtain

[4] Cf. *F.R.U.S. Berlin*, vol. ii, pp. 480–3, for an American record of a meeting between Mr. Byrnes and M. Molotov, at 4.30 p.m., on 30 July 1945. Cf. also *Berlinskaya konferentsiya*, pp. 243–6, for this meeting in Russian record which began (translation): 'Byrnes said that he had come to have a talk with Molotov before the meeting. He wanted to reach an understanding with Molotov on a number of questions before he, Byrnes, met the English. The first question was about Poland. The President had now changed his initial position and was putting forward a new proposal to fix the Western frontier of Poland along the Western and Eastern [*sic*] Neisse. This new proposal had not yet been agreed with the English. Molotov asked whether Byrnes thought that the English would agree to this proposal. Byrnes replied that he thought that they would.'

what we both want as regards supplies to the Western Zones and the whole of the Berlin Area by making two parallel and interdependent agreements instead of by his system of swaps. He said 'God be with you and I am on your side'. I replied that God and Mr. Byrnes was a powerful combination and went on trying to convince him of the objection to swaps. The discussion had to be terminated as the meeting of Foreign Ministers took place at 5 p.m.[5]

At the meeting of Foreign Ministers, the Russians handed round their paper asking for specific quantities of plant from the Western Zones, but this was never discussed. Mr. Byrnes then put forward the proposal which he had already put to Molotov at lunch and the Secretary of State put forward our proposals which he explained clearly and forcibly. Molotov said that he preferred the American proposal to ours, but that the removals should be from the Western Zones as a whole and not solely from the Ruhr. The Secretary of State said that since half the plant was in the Ruhr, the American proposal could then be expressed as $12\frac{1}{2}\%$ from the Western Zones as a swap and $7\frac{1}{2}\%$ from the Western Zones as free reparations. Mr. Byrnes said that if, in fact, the removals for Russia came mainly or wholly from the Ruhr, he would adjust matters by arranging for removals for other claimants to reparation to come from outside the Ruhr. The Secretary of State took note of this point and said it should be placed on formal records.

Molotov then said that he could not accept the American plan unless a definite amount were stated. The least he could accept would be plant to the value of $800 million, or, if it were preferred, 2 million tons. He said that this meant 2 million tons weight and not 2 million tons capacity, but he may have misunderstood his own brief on this point. The Americans and the Secretary of State firmly refused to promise specific values, so that it was decided that the matter must come before the Big Three at the meeting fixed for 4 p.m. this afternoon.

We are to have a meeting with the Prime Minister and Foreign Secretary at 10 a.m. this morning. Some of us feel that the system of swaps is so utterly wrong that we should refuse to be a party to it. I think the Secretary of State feels that the difference between two parallel agreements and a system of swaps is not so fundamental.

I should have made it clear earlier that the proposal which Mr. Pauley showed us at noon was not produced or referred to at the meeting and presumably was not shown to Molotov or made use of in talking to him. The Americans were just as firm as we were in refusing to discuss specific figures.

Yours ever,[6]

---

[5] See No. 469.
[6] Filed copy unsigned: cf. note 1 above.

No. 486

Note of Third Staff Conference with Prime Minister and Foreign Secretary, held at 23 Ringstrasse on Tuesday, 31 July 1945 at 10 a.m.
[F.O. 934/2/8(18)]

Top secret

Present:

THE RT. HON. C. R. ATTLEE, M.P., PRIME MINISTER, The Rt. Hon. Ernest Bevin, M.P., Secretary of State for Foreign Affairs, Sir A. Cadogan, Sir E. Bridges, Sir D. Waley, Mr. P. J. Dixon, Sir A. Clark Kerr, Mr. N. Brook, Mr. T. L. Rowan, Mr. W. Hayter, and Officials of the Foreign Office.

Contents

Minute No.	Subject
1.	Reparations
2.	Western Frontier of Poland
3.	Administration of the Ruhr
4.	Germany: Political Principles
5.	German Fleet and Merchant Navy
6.	Transfers of Population
7.	Yugoslavia
8.	War Crimes
9.	German External Assets
10.	Subjects still outstanding
11.	Agenda for Plenary Meeting

1. *Reparations*

THE FOREIGN SECRETARY summarised the discussion which had taken place on this subject at the meeting of Foreign Secretaries the previous evening.[1] Mr. Byrnes had made his offer conditional upon simultaneous settlement of the Polish Western Frontier and the proposed declaration on the admission of certain States to the United Nations. M. Molotov had not been ready to accept the American offer on reparations as it stood, and Mr. Byrnes had not been ready to accept anything but a simultaneous settlement of all three issues. As a result the discussion had been exploratory and non-committal. The Foreign Secretary said, however, that the impression which he had taken away from the meeting was that the Russians would be ready, before the end of the Conference, to accept the best offer they could get on reparation deliveries from the Western Zones: they would press for an absolute figure, instead of a percentage: and, if this was refused (as it must be refused), they would probably try to get agreement on deliveries to Russia from the two Western zones of 10% against exchanges and 10% without exchanges.

[1] See No. 469, minute 4.

As regards 'the first charge', the U.S. Delegation now appeared to attach less importance to this point as they were prepared to guarantee that the Russians should receive the agreed percentage of deliveries of plant from the western zones. It had, however, appeared that the Russians were not so much concerned about the effect of the 'first charge' formula on deliveries from the west—they evidently expected to receive them in any event to the extent of any agreement reached—but were apprehensive about its effect on reparation deliveries from their own zone. They evidently realised that they had removed so much capital equipment from that zone that little would be forthcoming from current production; and it was their general principle that any deficit on production programmes should fall on internal consumption.

SIR DAVID WALEY said that the most disturbing feature of the new American solution of the reparation problem was its implication that the U.S. Government had abandoned hope of successful co-operation with the Russians in administering Germany as a single economic unit. The arguments used by members of the U.S. Delegation in support of their latest plan seemed to be based on a defeatist view that the Russian zone would be administered as a separate unit, with lower standards of living and few facilities for interchange of goods with other parts of Germany. To the extent that acceptance of the American reparations plan involved encouraging this attitude towards Germany's economic problems, there might be something to be said, even at this late stage, for making one last attempt to get the reparation problem handled on some different basis.

THE FOREIGN SECRETARY said that he saw no practical advantage in further discussions with the U.S. Delegation about the philosophic basis of their reparations plan. What they clearly wanted was to make the best bargain they could and terminate this part of the discussions as quickly as possible. In these circumstances he thought it would be best to try to settle the reparations problem on the general lines of the American plan, but to pursue the question of treating Germany as an economic unit in separate discussions on the exchange of supplies between the various areas of Germany. The Russians were clearly willing to consider proposals for treating Germany as an economic whole, as was shown by their latest proposals for including in the Statement of Political Principles a passage about the need for some central German administration.[2]

SIR DAVID WALEY agreed. His advice would be to accept the methods suggested in the latest American proposal on reparations, and to pursue our objective of getting Germany treated as a whole, for economic purposes, through the U.S. representatives on the Control Council who, unlike those who were advising President Truman on the reparations problem, strongly favoured co-operation between the three zones in economic matters. Even though the latest reparations plan was based on the opposite philosophy, there was a good prospect of our being able to secure a satisfactory economic

[2] See No. 469, minute 8(*b*).

treatment of Germany, especially in the matter of exchanges of goods, through the medium of the Control Council. There should be no inconsistency between treating Germany as a unit for certain economic purposes and at the same time pursuing the policy, favoured by the Coalition Government, of relying on provincial Governments in political matters and discouraging the growth of a central political government in Germany.

After further discussion the following conclusions were reached:

(1) At the Plenary Meeting that afternoon the British Delegation should maintain the attitude which the Foreign Secretary had taken up in the discussion at the Foreign Secretaries' meeting the previous evening, but should be prepared, if necessary in order to reach agreement, to accept a basis of deliveries of equipment to Russia from the two western zones up to a total of 10% against exchanges and 10% without exchanges.

(2) The general plan for this removal of equipment from the western zones should be prepared by the Control Council, subject to veto by the Zone Commander, in accordance with a formula agreed between the British and U.S. Delegations. This formula should be communicated to the Russian Delegation in advance of the meeting.

(3) It should be placed on record that nothing in this reparations plan was inconsistent with the agreed Statement of Economic Principles to govern the treatment of Germany during the initial control period. A formula on this point should also be prepared for delivery to the two other Delegations at the meeting.

(4) In announcing our acceptance of this plan, care would have to be taken to avoid the impression that the Conference had settled the whole of the reparations problem without reference to the French and other Governments interested. This point should be kept in mind in the preparation of the communique to be issued at the end of the Conference.

2. Western Frontier of Poland

THE FOREIGN SECRETARY said that, although the U.S. Delegation had indicated their readiness to concede the full Polish claim, the British Delegation had not yet assented to this and he hoped that it might still be possible to secure from the representatives of the Polish Provisional Government some further assurances in return for our agreement to the decision which the Russian and U.S. Delegations were already prepared to accept. In particular, he would like to have some assurances about elections in Poland which were more definite than the general statement included in paragraph 4 of P. (Terminal) 23.[3]

It would be inexpedient to suggest at this stage any amendment of the agreed declaration contained in P. (Terminal) 23. It was true that this had been agreed at a time when the question of Poland's Western Frontier had not been opened at the Conference; but, if we were now to suggest amendment of the final paragraph of the agreed statement, we should thereby

[3] See No. 219, note 6.

enable the Russians to re-open the other matters mentioned in the statement and should risk a revival of the lengthy arguments which had already been put forward about the assets and liabilities of the former Polish Government in London.

These considerations need not, however, prevent the Foreign Secretary from pressing the representatives of the Polish Provisional Government, in consultations outside the Conference, to give further assurances—particularly on the matters dealt with in paragraph 4 of P. (Terminal) 23. It could be made clear to them that satisfactory assurances on these points would make it easier for the British Delegation to agree at the Conference to acceptance of Poland's territorial claims.

The Foreign Secretary said that he was seeing M. Mikolajczyk later in the morning and would take this line in discussion with him.

3. *Administration of the Ruhr*

The Soviet Delegation had submitted a memorandum (P. (Terminal) 59)[4] proposing that the industrial district of the Ruhr should be brought under the joint administrative control of the United States, the United Kingdom, the U.S.S.R. and France.

THE FOREIGN SECRETARY said that, when this question had been mentioned at the meeting of Foreign Secretaries the previous evening,[5] he had declined to comment, on the ground that such a proposal could not be discussed without consultation with the French Government.

> It was agreed that, if this matter were raised again, the British Delegation should take the line that this was not a question which could be discussed at the present Conference, in the absence of representatives of the French Government. At some later stage there might be advantages in referring the long-term question of international control over the Ruhr for consideration by the Council of Foreign Ministers.

4. *Germany: Political Principles*

At the meeting of Foreign Secretaries the previous evening, the Soviet Delegation had proposed that there should be added to the Statement on Political Principles a paragraph foreshadowing the establishment of a central German administration.[2]

THE FOREIGN SECRETARY said that he had asked for time to consider this proposal. He was now prepared to accept the suggestion in principle, and a revised version of the Soviet draft had been prepared.[6] He hoped that it would be possible to get this revised version agreed with the Soviet and U.S. Delegations before the Plenary Meeting that afternoon.

5. *German Fleet and Merchant Navy*

THE FOREIGN SECRETARY said that the Committee which had been appointed to consider this question should be able to submit their report in time for consideration at the Plenary Meeting that afternoon.

[4] No. 472.　　[5] See No. 469, minute 13.　　[6] See No. 495, minute 7.

As regards the Merchant Navy, the former Prime Minister had indicated that ships sunk while assigned to the Allied shipping pool would be replaced. He thought that we need not make any difficulty over this, especially as the Russians had made the concession that any merchant ships earmarked for them might continue to be used under Allied control until the end of the Japanese war.

6. *Transfers of Population*

THE FOREIGN SECRETARY said that a draft statement on this question had been prepared, and an attempt would be made to get it agreed with the Russian Delegation during the course of the morning. It could then be brought up for ratification at the Plenary Meeting in the afternoon.

It was indicated that, if agreement was reached, the French Government should be informed in advance of any public announcement, as this was a matter which affected the Control Council for Germany.

7. *Yugoslavia*

THE FOREIGN SECRETARY said that he proposed to invite the Plenary Meeting that afternoon to consider the memorandum on this subject by the British Delegation (P. (Terminal) 51)[7].

The Soviet Delegation would probably take the opportunity of asking that the meeting should also discusss their memorandum (P. (Terminal) 61)[8] on conditions in the Trieste-Istria district. We had not, however, been able to obtain any information from our representatives in this area about the allegations contained in the Soviet memorandum; and he proposed to take the line that this complaint could not be dealt with at the Conference but would be answered in due course by correspondence through the diplomatic channel.

8. *War Crimes*

Memoranda had been circulated on this subject—P. (Terminal) 53[9] by the British Delegation and P. (Terminal) 57[10] by the Soviet Delegation. The main point at issue was whether any public statement should include a list of names of the principal war criminals who should be put on trial in the near future.

THE FOREIGN SECRETARY summarised the arguments, put forward at the meeting of Foreign Secretaries the previous evening, against giving such a list of names.[11] It was likely that we should have the support of the U.S. Delegation in resisting the inclusion of such a list.

It was also undesirable that the statement should include, as proposed by the Soviet Delegation, any reference to the surrender of war criminals by neutral countries.

It was agreed that at the Plenary Meeting that afternoon the British Delegation should press for the publication of a statement on the general lines proposed in P. (Terminal) 53.[9]

[7] No. 465.   [8] No. 475.   [9] No. 467.
[10] No. 471.   [11] See No. 469, minute

9. *German External Assets*

Sɪʀ Dᴀᴠɪᴅ Wᴀʟᴇʏ said that a Committee was meeting later in the morning to consider a memorandum on this subject which had been circulated by the U.S. Delegation (P. (Terminal) 56)[12].

At this meeting he proposed to point out that in a matter of this kind, where the title to property was a matter to be established in the courts, there was some disadvantage in making a public declaration implying the unilateral assumption of jurisdiction over such property. If, however, it appeared that the U.S. Delegation strongly favoured the making of such a declaration, he thought we need not maintain our objection to it.

It was agreed that the attitude of the British Delegation on this question should be on the lines indicated by Sir David Waley.

10. *Subjects still outstanding*

Tʜᴇ Fᴏʀᴇɪɢɴ Sᴇᴄʀᴇᴛᴀʀʏ referred to the following questions which were still outstanding:

(*a*) *Removal of Equipment by Allied Forces from Soviet Zone in Germany*
(P. (Terminal) 47)[13].

It was agreed that, if the Soviet Delegation reverted to this question before the end of the Conference, we should take the line that it was a matter which could best be dealt with by correspondence through the diplomatic channel.

(*b*) *International Inland Waterways*
(P. (Terminal) 33)[14]

No progress had been made by the Committee to which this question had been referred.

It was agreed that we need take no action to expedite the submission of a report by this Committee.

(*c*) *German Coal Production*
(P. (Terminal) 54)[15]

The U.S. Delegation had not yet asked for this memorandum to be placed on the Agenda. On this matter we should leave the initiative with the Americans.

(*d*) *German Troops in Norway*
(P. (Terminal) 43)[16]

A reply[17] to the allegations made by the Soviet Delegation had now been sent by the Foreign Secretary, after consultation with the Prime Minister.

(*e*) *Soviet Citizens from Baltic, Western Ukraine and ByeloRussia*
(P. (Terminal) 60)[18]

It was agreed that this allegation by the Soviet Delegation could best be handled through the diplomatic channel.

---

[12] See No. 469, note 16. [13] No. 455. [14] No. 246. [15] See No. 477, note 1.
[16] See No. 276, note 1. [17] No. 474. [18] No. 473.

11. *Agenda for 11th Plenary Meeting*

It was agreed that the following Agenda should be suggested for the Plenary Meeting that afternoon:

(*a*) Reparations
(*b*) Western Frontier of Poland
(*c*) Admission to United Nations
(*d*) Germany: Economic Principles
(*e*) German Political Principles: Soviet addition
(*f*) Transfer of German populations from Poland and Czechoslovakia
(*g*) German Fleet (if Sub-Committee's report is ready)
(*h*) Yugoslavia
(*i*) War Crimes.

It was further agreed that this proposed Agenda should be communicated to the Soviet and U.S. Delegations in advance of the Meeting.

No. 487

Note of a Conversation between Mr. Bevin and M. Mikolajczyk at the Foreign Secretary's House, Potsdam, on 31 July 1945 at 11 a.m.

[N 9659/6/55]

Top secret

MONSIEUR MIKOLAJCZYK explained his fears about the present situation in Poland on the lines of his remarks at an earlier conversation as recorded in the attached minute by Sir A. Clark Kerr (Annex I). Monsieur Mikolajczyk emphasised in particular that the real fight for Polish independence was now taking place in Poland itself. There was on all sides a strong desire that Poland should be really free and the present Four Party Government was still distrusted on this account. The agreement reached in Moscow was not called in question but most people doubted whether the changes that had been made in the Polish Provisional Government would be far-reaching enough to ensure genuine independence for Poland.

Before free elections could be held two conditions must be fulfilled. First the Red Army must go. One hundred thousand Russian troops had already left and their behaviour as they withdrew was distressing for the Poles and increased their doubts about the possibility of co-operation with the Russians. Many Red Army forces still remained, however, including two hundred and sixty thousand cossacks who had to be drafted to the Lublin area to keep order.

Second, encouragement must be given to Poles abroad, including those remaining east of the Curzon Line to return. So far only three hundred thousand Poles had returned from the east. These were mostly townsfolk; the peasants had so far preferred to stay where they were. A factor strengthening their feeling of uncertainty was the conditions of life in the western territories where, so long as the Red Army remained, Poles were apt to find themselves obliged to do forced labour for the Russians.

Monsieur Mikolajczyk said that he had done his best to persuade Monsieur Bierut that His Majesty's Government had not only the right but even the duty under the Crimea Declaration, to intervene in Polish internal affairs so long as their intervention served the cause of Polish independence. He added that he thought it important that if any statement were made in Parliament on the Polish situation emphasis should be laid on Monsieur Bierut's assurance that the elections would be held on the basis of the electoral procedure laid down under the 1921 Constitution. It was important that he should be pinned down to this.

MR. BEVIN said that he understood Monsieur Mikolajczyk's difficulties and wished Monsieur Mikolajczyk to understand his. The view of the Labour Party had always been that Poland should not receive more than the territory east of a line following the Eastern Neisse and the Oder and running to the east of Stettin. If the Prime Minister and he were to agree here to more than this they must have in return some satisfactory assurances from the Poles about internal conditions in Poland. He handed Monsieur Mikolajczyk a paper, of which a copy is attached at Annex II,[1] and asked him to urge the Polish Delegation to return helpful replies on these five points.

In connexion with Point I, he explained that what he required was some definite statement about the date on which elections would be carried out.

It was agreed that the Foreign Secretary should receive the whole Polish Delegation again at 2.30 p.m. on the same day.

Foreign Office, 31st July, 1945

ANNEX I TO No. 487

Foreign Secretary[2]

What Mikolajczyk was trying to tell you in the scurry of his visit this morning[3] was this:

The chiefest of his preoccupations is to secure the independence of Poland, which he feels is still in doubt, but which he thinks to be still within reach, if something like the following conditions is fulfilled.

First, the Red Army will have to go. This is already in progress and is, I understand, to be completed within the next two months, excepting at certain specific points designed to safeguard the Russian lines of communications.

Second, the N.K.V.D. must go. This, he hopes, will happen concurrently with the withdrawal of the Red Army. You will remember that he said that the Polish

[1] Not printed. This paper, which was identical with annex I to No. 484 except for paragraph 4 (cf. No. 484, note 6), is printed by Sir L. Woodward, *op. cit.*, vol. v, pp. 434–5.

[2] The present text, supplied from F.O. 934/2/10(89), was ticked by Mr. Bevin.

[3] For the timing of this otherwise unrecorded conversation between Mr. Bevin and M. Mikolajczyk on the morning of 30 July 1945, cf. Sir L. Woodward, *op. cit.*, vol. v, p. 431, note 1.

people, when the time came, would know how to deal with the Polish version of the N.K.V.D. which the Russians have set up in Poland.

Third, 'free and unfettered elections', which can only be achieved by unrestricted expression of opinion by all political parties,—i.e. political manifestos and party newspapers—and supervision of the elections by the Allies, (I fear that this last is more than we can hope to get, because Molotov will resist it hotly on the ground that it is wounding to Polish pride).

Fourth, he then moved on to the question of the Western Frontiers and said that the area between the two rivers Neisse was essential to his purpose, for the reason that:

(1) he must have land to offer to the four million Poles now east of the Curzon Line in order to tempt them to come home to Poland. An agreement for their repatriation had been reached with the Russians and Poles wishing to return had to opt by the 1st January, after which date they would become irrevocably Soviet citizens. Time was running out and the people concerned were still in doubt whether it would be worth while to move into Poland. Mikolajczyk was ready to see the Eastern Provinces go hang, but the Poles now living there were precious to Poland and he must get them home.

(2) He then spoke of the importance of the system of the control of the waters of the Oder which would remain in German hands unless the region between the two Neisses were given to Poland. This would mean that the Germans would be able, at their will, to make the Oder unnavigable, and thus to destroy much of the economic value of the Oder basin.

(3) He suggested that as time went on these regions would be in a position to contribute to the supplying of Germany with food and coal. Meanwhile the stripping of factories must stop.

He put special stress upon the importance of our meeting Polish territorial claims for the additional reason that his Communist colleagues would use our hesitation as an instrument of propaganda to show that all good things in Poland came from Russia while we and the Americans were unsympathetic and niggardly. This would help the group that leaned towards the Sovi[e]t Union—i.e. Bierut and his associates,—to swing back into the arms of Russia a Poland which he (Mikolajczyk) was bent upon turning towards the West. But, whatever we did, in the end the Russians would see to it that the Poles got the Western Neisse and the credit would go to them.

In another minute[4] I ventured to remind you of the importance of maintaining the impression that Mikolajczyk has your full support. Such strength as he has, and it is still by no means negligible, dwells in the belief on the part of his Communist colleagues, that His Majesty's Government are wholly behind him. Since his return to Poland he has drawn upon this deeply and not without success, and any special fuss you could make of him would therefore be of value to him.

After you left this afternoon he told me that what Bierut had said about the use of the 1921 Constitu[t]ion and the complete freedom of elections[5] was largely nonsense and was a deliberate effort to pull the wool over your eyes. He hoped therefore that you and the Prime Minister would take another opportunity to put to Bierut some of the searching questions he had to answer this morning. He said that on the way home Bierut had complained bitterly about our intolerable interference in the internal affairs of Poland and had rejected the argument that

[4] No. 452.   [5] See No. 463.

the interest of His Majesty's Government was justified by the pledges undertaken as a result of the Crimean Conference.

I hope that you may find time to see Mikolajczyk again, for he gathers prestige from every moment he spends in your presence.

Finally, there remains the question of getting the Poles in the West back to Poland. I suggest that the next time you see the Polish Government it would be well to make it clear to them that a prerequisite of this would be the creation of a feeling of confidence in the new regime either by some form of a persuasive public declaration, or by sending to London a small but convincing mission to explain in person to the waverers the importance and the advantages of an early return.

A. C. K.
30th July, 1945

No. 488

Mr. Bevin (Berlin) to Mr. Morrison (Received 31 July, 9.15 a.m.)
No. 293 Target Telegraphic [F.O. 934/4/20(22)]

Top secret. Most Immediate　　　　　　　　BERLIN, *31 July 1945, 11.5 a.m.*

Please pass following Most Immediate to His Majesty's Ambassador, Paris. Begins:

You should concert with your United States and Soviet colleagues in making the following most urgent communication to the Provisional French Government.

'The Governments of the United States of America, the United Kingdom and U.S.S.R. have agreed upon the following political principles which they consider should govern the treatment of Germany in the initial Control period. It is their intention to communicate the text of these principles to the Commanders-in-Chief of their respective forces of occupation in Germany after the conclusion of the present Conference, and to instruct them to be guided by these principles in their action in their respective zones of occupation, and to concert with their colleagues on the Control Council in working out the application of these principles in such a way as to ensure appropriate uniformity of action in the zones of occupation.

'It is the earnest wish of the three Governments that the Provisional Government of the French Republic will be able to associate itself with these principles, and to send similar instructions, after the conclusion of the Conference, to the Commander-in-Chief of the French forces of occupation.

'The three Governments would be grateful if the French Provisional Government would treat the present communication as strictly secret until such time as an official statement is issued by the Conference.'

2. Text of principles is contained in my immediately following telegram.[1]

---

[1] Not printed. This telegram conveyed the text of the political principles as agreed in No. 469, minute 8(*b*).

3. You should know that paragraph 2 was inserted at Foreign Secretaries meeting on July 30th. I understand that text telegraphed to your United States colleague earlier that day may be incomplete in that respect.

4. You should further know that Soviet Delegation have proposed an amendment to paragraph 9(iv), the text of which has not yet been finally agreed. You have discretion to concert with your United States and Soviet colleagues whether to communicate the document as it stands to the French Provisional Government with the reservation that paragraph 9(iv) is incomplete or whether to wait until you receive the final agreed text, probably in the course of July 31st. We are, of course, particularly anxious that the French Government should receive communication as long as possible before the conclusion of the Conference, which may be not more than forty-eight hours distant.

Ends.[2]

[2] In a letter of even date at Berlin Mr. Harrison informed M. Golunski of the instructions conveyed in this telegram and of the British amendment advanced in No. 495, minute 7. This letter is printed in Russian translation in *Berlinskaya konferentsiya*, pp. 435–6.

No. 489

Record of conversation at a luncheon party given by M. Molotov at Potsdam on 31 July 1945

[*F.O. 800/417/64*]

Present:

THE SECRETARY OF STATE, Sir Alexander Cadogan, Sir Archibald Clark Kerr, Major Theakstone (*Interpreter*).

M. MOLOTOV, M. Vyshinski, M. Maiski, M. Gousev, M. Novikov, M. Pavlov (*Interpreter*).

British General Elections

These were discussed at length, most of those present joining in the conversation. The Secretary of State announced the appointment of Mr. Shinwell to the Ministry of Fuel and Power and Sir Stafford Cripps to the Board of Trade. He explained that apart from being an excellent diplomat and lawyer, Sir Stafford was a most efficient business-man, having successfully managed an explosives works during the last war. The Secretary of State confirmed that the result of the General Election had been quite unexpected. He had thought that Mr. Churchill's popularity would have assured him of a majority of 50 votes. Here M. Molotov recalled Mr. Attlee's last remark to him before returning to England to hear the results of the Election. Mr. Attlee had at that time evidently held the same opinion. The Secretary of State pointed out Mr. Churchill's mistake in trusting in Lord Beaverbrook's knowledge of British public opinion. Mr.

Maiski said he had followed the election speeches and found the Tories' anti-socialist propaganda puzzling. M. Molotov added that this kind of propaganda was out of date by about 40 years. All agreed that Mr. Churchill was a war leader whose services the nation would never forget. The Secretary of State said that Mr. Churchill's place would be among the elder statesmen of the country.

Nationalisation

In reply to an enquiry from M. Molotov on the Labour Government's immediate programme, the Secretary of State said that they were considering the nationalisation of the coal industry, the national transport and the Bank of England. Private banks were to come under Government control.[1]

Britain's Foreign Policy

Talking of Mr. Eden and of his great ability as a Foreign Secretary, M. Molotov received from the Secretary of State an assurance that the continuity of the British foreign policy would be preserved. The Secretary of State explained that his party drew its inspiration from the foreign policy of Arthur Henderson[2] which, he thought, had met with Russian approval. M. Molotov agreed that Mr. Henderson was held in high esteem in the Soviet Union.

War Criminals

Sir Archibald Clark Kerr wanted to know why the Russians had omitted from their list the name of Rosenberg while including that of Krupp. M. Molotov said that they were not certain whether Rosenberg had been captured, while Krupp was on their list as a representative of the German war industry. Some amusing exchanges were made on the subject whether the criminals should be shot before or after making a statement before the Tribunal. The Secretary of State wondered why medical officers had removed from the captured Nazis the poison phials which many of them were carrying in their mouths. M. Molotov emphatically declared that the criminals' statement must be heard before they are shot.

The Gestapo

M. Molotov suddenly faced the Secretary of State with a question how soon the Labour Government proposed to establish their Gestapo. He was surprised to hear in reply that the British Government were going to consult Russia but was relieved when he heard that the reason was that most of the Gestapo documents were in Russian hands. M. Molotov thought that a fair share of these documents had fallen into British and American hands as well.

---

[1] The preceding part of this record, typed as a draft, was, on the subsequent instruction of Mr. Dixon, omitted from the circulated text (on N 10154/165/38), otherwise unamended apart from presentation of abbreviations.

[2] Secretary of State for Foreign Affairs from 1929 to 1931.

The End of the Conference

M. Molotov wanted to know how soon this Conference would end. The Secretary of State replied that it would end as soon as M. Molotov had agreed to all his proposals. M. Molotov thought that the Conference would come to an equally speedy end if the S/S agreed with his proposals. Both sides were agreed that it was no use to prepare a formula which each side interpreted in its own way. It was thought to be far better to proceed slowly and work out precise statements which admitted of no alternative explanation. The S/S said that he would have to report to the House of Commons the results of this Conference and once these had been ratified, Russia could find no better guarantee in the world for the fulfilment of all that was undertaken.

Public Opinion in U.K. and U.S.S.R.

The S/S referred to England as a great, powerful and free country with an enlightened public opinion. While agreeing with him and insisting that the U.S.S.R. was an equally powerful country, rich in natural resources, M. Molotov urged upon the S/S not to think that there was no influential public opinion in Russia.

Looking to the Future

The S/S said that England wanted peace and would direct its foreign policy towards this aim. M. Molotov was anxious that Russia too should enjoy lasting peace. When asked by the S/S how he defined the term 'lasting', M. Molotov replied that he meant a peaceful life for two generations. The S/S did not think this to be sufficient. M. Molotov said that if peace lasted for two generations, i.e. until the end of the present century, people would get out of the habit of settling their disputes by war and external peace would follow. M. Molotov expressed satisfaction with the newly created United Nations Organisation but thought that it was not strong enough. The S/S replied that the strength of the United Nations lay in the goodwill of the three great democracies. The S/S said that it was wrong to follow blindly the ideas of the old teachers. Karl Marx was a brilliant economist but the world had progressed since his day. The same applied to the great British economists of whom both the S/S, Sir Alexander Cadogan, M. Molotov and M. Vyshinski mentioned quite a few. M. Molotov agreed that Marx' theories had to be further developed before they could be applied to present-day problems.

Repin's Painting of the Zaporozhtzi

When on his way to the drawing-room after lunch, the S/S paused in front of a large reproduction of Repin's famous painting[3] and heard M. Molotov's explanation of the scene depicted. Pointing to the scribe, the S/S said that he was the only respectable person among the crowd of wild

[3] The original of the painting 'The Cossacks of Zaporozh'e' write a letter to the Turkish Sultan' by the Russian artist I. E. Repin (1844–1930) hangs in the Russian Museum in Leningrad.

Cossacks. This led to a conversation on diplomats and such views were expressed as, for instance, that diplomacy would run much more smoothly if Foreign Offices exchanged diplomats so that if, say, the British Foreign Office wished to despatch a note to the U.S.S.R., it would entrust its composition to a Soviet diplomat who worked in Downing Street. M. Vyshinski claimed that Sir Archibald Clark Kerr was one of the best diplomats since he was excellent at composing notes of which he (M. Vyshinski) received over ten a day.

The English Language

The S/S asked M. Molotov whether he was content to regard the English language as the language of diplomacy. M. Molotov said that the English and Americans were lucky in that they could easily understand each other. He said that the importance of English was recognised in his country and that its study was quite the fashion there.[4]

[4] Mr. Bevin wrote on this text: 'Noted. E. B.'

No. 490

Record of a Meeting at the Foreign Secretary's House,
Potsdam, on 31 July 1945 at 2.45 p.m.
[*F.O. 934/2/10(91)*])

Present:
SECRETARY OF STATE, Sir A. Cadogan, Sir A. Clark Kerr, Mr. Allen, Captain Leggett (*interpreter*).

M. BIERUT, M. Grabski, M. Gomulka, M. Mikolajczyk, M. Stanczyk, M. Minc, M. Modzelewski, M. Zebrowski (*interpreter*).

MR. BEVIN stated that the proposal of the Polish Delegation that the present Conference should endorse their claim to a frontier on the Oder and the Western Neisse raised for the British Delegation new problems upon which they had no opportunity of consulting the recently formed British Government. For this reason it was necessary for them, when the matter came up before the Heads of Governments, to satisfy themselves that the action they were taking could be justified to British public opinion and that they had taken all precautions to make sure of the conditions that would prevail in the new Poland that they were helping to create. He had therefore submitted to M. Mikolajczyk that morning certain questions (annexed)[1] not with any idea of interfering with Polish sovereignty but in order to ascertain how, if His Majesty's Government were to support the Polish claims, the Polish Provisional Government proposed to carry out

[1] For this document, not annexed to filed copy, see No. 487, note 1.

the Crimea decisions. Whatever majority His Majesty's Government enjoyed, they were responsible to British public opinion and he therefore must be in a position to give Parliament a satisfactory indication of the attitude of the Polish Provisional Government on the points which he had raised. He therefore hoped that the Polish Delegation would be able to give short and direct answers to the questions he had put to them through M. Mikolajczyk.

M. BIERUT said that the questions were the same as had been discussed at earlier meetings with the British Delegation when he had given broad and exhaustive answers. In reply to a comment by MR. BEVIN that his answers had been evasive and indefinite, M. BIERUT said that he would reply in writing if desired, but that all members of the Polish Delegation agreed with the positive answers which he had already given. He had already emphasised that the answers given expressed the spontaneous will of the Polish nation and Government. The Government's policy was to hold elections in the shortest possible time. Their attitude on this question could not, however, be considered as a concession to meeting another Government's point of view.

MR. BEVIN asked M. Bierut to be frank. He himself was not in the habit of evading the issue. The position was that if the Polish Delegation wanted the British Delegation's vote in support of their proposals they must give a definite answer to our questions as to what will happen to the people who will live in the territories transferred to Polish administration. That question would be asked by British public opinion and His Majesty's Government were not asking for something but were giving something away and they were entitled to have an answer. He asked whether in reply to point 1 the Polish Delegation could not give an assurance that, subject to the withdrawal of the Soviet troops and to the speeding up of the repatriation of Poles abroad, the Polish Provisional Government would make every effort to hold free elections early in 1946. M. BIERUT said that British public opinion could be assured that elections under the Crimea Declaration would be held once a provisional settlement of the frontier question had been reached and as soon as repatriation had been completed. The Polish Provisional Government would try to make a declaration on these lines.

MR. BEVIN said that he had not consulted the United States or Soviet Delegations about this matter because he regarded Poland as a sovereign State. He wished, however, on his return to be able to make a statement to Parliament on the following lines: 'I have met the Polish Delegation. They have given me an assurance that they will hold elections under the 1921 constitution and will, if this lies within their power, aim at carrying through these elections in the early part of 1946. Meanwhile the Polish Provisional Goverment will, in conjunction with their Allies, do all they can to secure the fullest repatriation of Poles from abroad. The precise date of the election will however be affected by the date of withdrawal of Soviet troops from territory under Polish administration.' Would some such statement express the intentions of the Polish Provisional Government?

M. Bierut repeated that the whole Polish Delegation, which represented the three most important parties in the Government coalition and spoke for the Polish Government and nation, were agreed in their intention to see elections held in the shortest possible time.

Mr. Bevin said that he must be in a position to give some definite indication of the date. Otherwise His Majesty's Government and the British Parliament would feel that the matter was being put off indefinitely. M. Bierut must help him to help Poland.

M. Bierut said that in any case the elections would take place early in 1946 and possibly earlier and it was agreed that a statement might be made to the effect that the elections would be held as early as possible but not later than early in 1946.

In regard to point 2 M. Bierut first complained that it would be difficult for him to give an assurance that might enable foreign countries to send unlimited numbers of press correspondents to Poland. Mr. Bevin assured him, however, that he was merely asking for the normal facilities and M. Bierut finally agreed that this question might be answered in the affirmative.

Point 3 was also answered in the affirmative, M. Bierut indicating that freedom of religion already existed in Poland.

On point 4 M. Bierut pointed out that a declaration on the lines desired had already been made by the Polish Prime Minister in a recent statement before the National Council. He undertook, however, to see that a further statement was made on this question so that the intentions of the Polish Provisional Government might be placed beyond doubt.

Mr. Bevin said that he would like to ask, purely as a suggestion and not in any sense as a condition, whether the Polish Provisional Government, when a provisional frontier settlement had been reached, would not send representatives to make personal contact with Poles abroad and seek to remove their fears about conditions in Poland. M. Bierut agreed to this suggestion.

On point 5 M. Bierut said that he had spoken to the Soviet Delegation about the proposed British air service to Warsaw, but that they had stated that the matter must be taken up with them by the British Delegation.

Mr. Bevin stated in conclusion that, on the strength of the assurances that he had received from the Polish Delegation and in the belief that the Polish Provisional Government would give effect to them and in the spirit of friendship which he hoped would animate future relations between Poland and Great Britain, he was ready, if the Soviet and the United States Delegations also agreed, to support the Polish Provisional Government's claim to a provisional frontier on the Oder and the Western Neisse. He proposed, however, in informing the Conference of his agreement to convey to them the substance of the assurances which he had received from the Polish Delegation. M. BIERUT agreed to this.[2]

British Delegation, Potsdam, 31st July, 1945

[2] This record was minuted in the Foreign Office (N 9922/6/55): 'Not bad. But they have not done anything specific to meet the attempts to side-track and restrict M. Mikolajczyk, &c. Copy to Warsaw, *urgent*, Moscow, W'ton. C. F. A. Warner 1/8.' 'Am I right in thinking that, as a result of being bounced by the Americans, we have agreed to the Oder–Neisse frontier without receiving any assurances from the Polish Govt. regarding either free elections or what is more important freedom of speech & meetings for the parties not represented in the Govt.? O. G. Sargent Aug. 1.' 'Now see record attached. C. F. A. Warner 1/8.' 'Nothing said about freedom of speech & meetings—unless that is supposed to be covered by the reference to the 1921 Constitution. Let us speak about this with Mr. Allen. O. G. Sargent Aug. 2.'

No. 491

Note by Sir D. Waley (Berlin)
P. (*Terminal*) 67 [*U 6197/3628/70*]

Top secret   *31 July 1945*

German Reparation
(Circulated to the United Kingdom Delegation only)

The Americans intend to submit the attached document to the Plenary Conference this afternoon. Down to the end of (1) (*b*) it is the same as the document produced yesterday (P. (Terminal) 63),[1] except that in accordance with the Foreign Secretary's request 12½ per cent. and 7½ per cent. from the United States and United Kingdom zones has been substituted for 25 per cent. and 15 per cent. from the Ruhr. I made it clear that this change is essential, but I understand that the Americans may nevertheless propose to the Russians 25 per cent. and 15 per cent. from the Ruhr as an alternative.

The next sentence about delivering capital equipment within two years and products within five years is new. This was agreed verbally between Mr. Byrnes and M. Molotov.

The rest of paragraph (1) is the document agreed with the Americans at the meeting yesterday. I have given a copy to M. Maisky.

Paragraph (2) is new. There is no objection to it.

Our acceptance of the American proposal should be 'subject to the understanding that this proposal involves no departure from paragraph 13 of the Economic Principles (P. (Terminal) 15)[2] which provides that during the period of occupation Germany shall be treated as a single economic unit. To this end common policies shall be established in regard to (*inter alia*) . . .[3] (*d*) import and export programmes for Germany as a whole.'

S. D. W.

[1] See No. 469, note 6.
[2] No. 210.
[3] Punctuation as in original quotation.

(1) Reparations claims of U.S.S.R. and Poland shall be met by removals from the zone of Germany occupied by the U.S.S.R., plus:–

(*a*) 12½ per cent. of such industrial capital equipment as is unnecessary for a peace economy, and should be removed from the zones of Germany occupied by the United States and United Kingdom in exchange for an equivalent value of food, coal, potash, zinc, timber, clay products, petroleum and petroleum products, and such other commodities as may be agreed upon.

(*b*) 7½ per cent. of such industrial capital equipment as is unnecessary for a peace economy, and should be removed from the United States and United Kingdom zones, to be transferred to the Soviet Government without payment or exchange of any kind in return.

Removals of industrial capital equipment should be completed within two years of the date hereof in exchange for products to be delivered by the U.S.S.R. in agreed instalments within five years of the date hereof. The determination of the amount and character of the industrial capital equipment unnecessary for a peace economy and therefore available for reparation shall be made by the Allied Commission on Reparations, with France added, working in consultation with the Control Council subject to the final approval of the zone commander in the zone from which the equipment is to be removed.

(2) Reparations claims of other countries entitled to reparations should be met from the Western zones of occupation.

---

[4] With regard to this document, cf. *F.R.U.S. Berlin*, vol. ii, p. 512, note 2, also p. 945.

No. 492

Minute from Mr. Coulson to Sir A. Cadogan (Berlin)
[*F.O. 934/1/4(34)*]

[BERLIN,] *31 July 1945*

Mr. Brand, Mr. Turner and myself are seriously worried about the effect of the American proposals about reparation. The Americans have pushed us into a very awkward situation and it is difficult to see how to retrieve ourselves. But we have prepared the enclosed memorandum in the hope that something may be saved from the wreckage. It is, we hope, in a form in which, if you agree, it can be pushed up before this afternoon's meeting. It explains the dangers in more detail than has hitherto been done.[1]

J. E. Coulson

---

[1] Mr. Coulson subsequently noted on this minute: 'Seen by Sir A. Cadogan & S. of S., but there was no opportunity of compromise on this item. J. C. 31/7.' See No. 495, minute 2.

Reparation and German Economic Unity

It is understood that the line we intend to take is to accept the American plan, but

(*a*) insist that the percentage of capital equipment given to the Russians from the western zone should not exceed 10% against exchange of goods and 10% without payment.

(*b*) make clear that the plan is to be worked without prejudice to the economic unity of Germany.

2. There has never been a very full discussion of the manner in which the American plan conflicts with the idea of German economic unity and it is doubtful whether its implications have been fully realised, in particular the fact that Russia will receive no current deliveries from the western zones and that there will thus be no normal interchange of goods between the east and west of Germany.

3. The chief objections on this account are as follows:

(*a*) there will be no exports from the Soviet zone because the Soviet Government will take all available goods as reparation. If therefore the eastern zone requires imports this must be arranged in one of two ways either

(i) the western zones will export in order to pay for the imports. We could not agree to this because we should thus reduce for Russia's benefit the amount of current reparation deliveries available to other countries. It would therefore be necessary to fall back on

(ii) the Soviet Government arranging for themselves any imports they needed for their own zone. They would naturally get these by exclusive arrangements with countries in their sphere of influence, thus leading to a closed eastern European economic system.

(*b*)if all current deliveries for countries other than Russia are to come from the western zones, exports to pay for imports will also come from the western zones. This means that the foreign trade of the western zones will be taken outside the German economy looked at as a whole. In turn this implies separate financial arrangements in regard to foreign trade, which may have even further implications. For instance, why should the Powers controlling the western zones agree to pay into the central pool the proceeds of import duties when no similar receipt is obtained from the Russian zone? Thus the whole financial structure of Germany will be imperilled, & in a short time we should find separate financial systems and two mark rates in the different halves of Germany.

(*c*) the western Powers will be left with highly industrialised zones which will have to look to the west and overseas to sell their manufactured products in order to exist. We would therefore be deliberately creating trade competition for ourselves and the Americans unless we produced a further reduction of the standard of living in our own zone.

(*d*) under the American system imports and exports could not be agreed by the Allied Control Council for the whole of Germany, because the Russians would be taking the maximum possible out of their own zone by way of current deliveries. This would inevitably cause a disparity between the standards of living in the east and west. The result would either be an impassable barrier between them or an undesirable movement of population from the east to the west.

(*e*) it is inconceivable that a Germany which is not treated as an economic unit could very long be treated as a political unit.

4. Thus, however much we may safeguard the principle of economic unity on paper, the American plan, if followed as the Americans appear to understand it, will from the outset make it impossible to administer Germany as a unit. This is all the more unfortunate in that the Americans are producing this long-term result merely to get over the short-term difficulty of dividing up reparation removals of German capital equipment and of securing some supplies over a limited period. For this short-term purpose they will in effect be preventing all normal interchange of goods between the east and west of Germany.

5. These are very serious consequences indeed. It thus seems that we should clutch at every possible straw which will help us to avoid the worst features of the American plan.

6. It is doubtful whether the Russians have fully realised that, under the American plan, they will get no current reparation deliveries whatever from any of western zones. It is suggested that, in this afternoon's discussion,this should be made very clear to them. If they show signs of asking for current deliveries from the west, this would give us an opportunity of suggesting that current reparation receipts from all zones should be dealt with on a uniform basis and that the Russians should be entitled to their normal share of 50%. In this case they should get their 10% of capital equipment without payment. As regards the other 10% they could, if they wished, take this in return for an equivalent deduction from their claims to continuing deliveries. As part of their bargain the Soviet Government must undertake to provide supplies for Western Germany and Greater Berlin according to our previous proposals.

Foreign Office, 31st July, 1945

No. 493

Note by Sir D. Waley (Berlin) on P. (Terminal) 56[1]
P. (Terminal) 68 [U 6197/3628/70]

Top Secret   *31 July 1945*

German External Assets
(Circulated to the United Kingdom Delegation only)

We reached agreement at the Economic Sub-Committee with the Americans to drop their proposal and to substitute a recommendation that appropriate steps should be taken by the Control Council to exercise control and the power of dispossession over German external assets not already under control of the United Nations which have taken part in the war against Germany.

M. Maisky said that the Soviet Delegation would not be ready to deal with this matter at the Plenary Conference to-day.

S. D. W.

[1] See No. 469, note 16.

No. 494

Draft proposed by the United States Delegation (Berlin)[1]
P. (Terminal) 70 [U 6197/3628/70]

Top secret   *31 July 1945*

Western frontier of Poland

In conformity with the agreement on Poland reached at the Crimean Conference the three Heads of Government have sought the opinion of the Polish Provisional Government of National Unity in regard to the accession of territory in the north and west which Poland should receive. The President of Poland and members of the Polish Provisional Government of National Unity have been received at the Conference and have fully presented their views. The three Heads of Government reaffirm their opinion that the final delimitation of the western frontier of Poland should await the peace settlement.

The three Heads of Government agree that, pending the final determination of Poland's western frontier, the former German territories east of a line running from the Baltic Sea through Swinemünde, and thence along the Oder River to the confluence of the western Neisse River and along the western Neisse to the Czechoslovak frontier, including that portion of East Prussia not placed under the administration of the Union of Soviet Socialist Republics in accordance with the understanding reached at this conference and including the area of the former free city of Danzig, shall be under the administration of the Polish State and for such purposes should not be considered as part of the Soviet zone of occupation in Germany.

[1] Printed in *F.R.U.S. Berlin*, vol. ii, pp. 1150–1.

No. 495

Record of Eleventh Plenary Meeting held at Cecilienhof,
Potsdam, on Tuesday, 31 July 1945 at 4 p.m.
P. (Terminal) 11th Meeting [U 6197/3628/70]

Top secret

Present:

PREMIER STALIN, M. V. M. Molotov, M. A. Ya. Vyshinski, M. I. M. Maisky, M. F. T. Gousev, M. A. A. Gromyko, M. K. V. Novikov, M. A. A. Sobolev, M. B. F. Podtzerob, M. S. A. Golunski (*Interpreter*).

PRESIDENT TRUMAN, Mr. J. F. Byrnes, Mr. Joseph E. Davies, Fleet-Admiral W. D. Leahy, Mr. W. A. Harriman, Mr. E. W. Pauley, Mr. J. C. Dunn, Mr. H. F. Matthews, Mr. B. V. Cohen, Mr. C. E. Bohlen (*Interpreter*).

Mr. Attlee, Mr. Bevin, Sir A. Cadogan, Sir A. Clark Kerr, Sir W. Strang, Sir E. Bridges, Mr. N. Brook, Sir D. Waley, Mr. P. J. Dixon, Mr. W. Hayter, Major A. Birse (*Interpreter*).

Contents

1. *Foreign Secretaries' Report*

Mr. Bevin said he had submitted a written report (P. (Terminal) 69)[1] of the meeting of Foreign Secretaries held on the previous day. He suggested that, if other Delegations had no comments on this, it might be accepted without being read.

It was agreed to note with approval the report contained in P (Terminal) 69.[1]

2. *Reparations: Germany*

(Previous Reference: F. (Terminal) 10th Meeting,[2] Minute 4.)

Mr. Byrnes briefly summarised the attitude of the United States Delegation towards this matter. Three questions had caused special difficulty at the Conference, viz., the Polish Western Frontier, the admission to the United Nations of neutral and ex-enemy States, and Reparations from Germany. The United States Delegation were prepared to make concessions to the Soviet point of view on the first and second of these, in return for some concession on German reparations. On this their proposals were as follows:

'(1) Reparations claims of U.S.S.R. and Poland shall be met by removals from the zone of Germany occupied by the U.S.S.R., plus

(a) 12½ per cent. of such industrial capital equipment as is unnecessary for a peace economy, and should be removed from the zones of Germany occupied by the United States and United Kingdom in exchange for an equivalent value of food, coal, potash, zinc, timber, clay products, petroleum and petroleum products, and such other commodities as may be agreed upon.

---

[1] This report, summarizing No. 469 is not here printed: see *F.R.U.S. Berlin*, vol. ii, pp. 500–3.

[2] No. 469.

(*b*) 7½ per cent. of such industrial capital equipment as is unnecessary for a peace economy, and should be removed from the United States and United Kingdom zones, to be transferred to the Soviet Government without payment or exchange of any kind in return.

Removals of industrial capital equipment shall be completed within two years of the date hereof in exchange for products to be delivered by the U.S.S.R. in agreed instalments within five years of the date hereof. The determination of the amount and character of the industrial capital equipment unnecessary for a peace economy and therefore available for reparation shall be made by the Control Council, under policies laid down by the Reparations Commission subject to the final approval of the zone commander in the zone from which the equipment is to be removed.

(2) Reparations claims of other countries entitled to reparations shall be met from the Western zones of occupation.'

PREMIER STALIN said that, while he understood the reasons which had led Mr. Byrnes to link these three questions, he himself was not prepared to consider any one of them as contingent on another. They were separate and unconnected subjects, each of which should be considered on its merits. The first question was German Reparations: but before he dealt with that he must refer to a related matter. He had already circulated a Report (P. (Terminal) 47)[3] on the equipment and other property removed by the Allies from the Soviet Zone of Germany; and he had also received a later report (subsequently circulated as P. (Terminal) 72)[4] on further substantial removals of railway rolling-stock.

PRESIDENT TRUMAN remarked that rolling-stock ought to be controlled by a single transportation organisation operating over Germany as a whole. He had asked the Commander-in-Chief of the United States Zone for a report on the earlier memorandum submitted by Premier Stalin: meanwhile, he could give an assurance that no removals, either of equipment or of people, from the Russian zone had been effected by the United States forces on instructions from the United States Government.

PREMIER STALIN said that he accepted this statement. He had referred to the matter only to show that it was not only the Russians who removed property from Germany.

On the question of reparations from Germany the Soviet Delegation put forward the following proposals:[5]

'(1) Reparations will be exacted by each Government in its own zone of occupation. They will be of two kinds: once-for-all deliveries withdrawn from the national property of Germany (equipment, materials) which will be withdrawn during the two years following the capitulation, and yearly deliveries of goods from current production which will be exacted during the ten years following the capitulation.

---

[3] No. 455. [4] No. 497.
[5] The Russian text of these proposals is printed in *Berlinskaya konferentsiya*, pp. 431–2.

(2) The object of reparations is to further the rapid restoration of the economy of the countries which have suffered from German occupation, due regard being paid to the need for an all-round reduction of Germany's war potential.

(3) Over and above the reparations exacted from its own zone, the U.S.S.R. will in addition receive from the Western zones:

(a) 15 per cent. of such basic industrial equipment as is serviceable and complete, in the first instance metallurgical, chemical and machine building equipment, which by the decision of the Control Council for Germany and on the report of the Reparations Commission is due to be removed from the Western zones on account of reparations; this equipment will be handed over to the Soviet Union in exchange for food-stuffs, coal, potash, timber, clay products and oil products of equivalent value in the course of five years.

(b) 10 per cent. of the basic industrial equipment which is being withdrawn from the western zones on account of reparations without payment or exchange of any kind.

The determination of the quantity of the equipment and materials due for removal from the western zones on account of reparations must be carried out within not more than three months.

(4) Apart from this, the U.S.S.R. will receive on account of reparations:

(a) 500 million dollars' worth of shares in industrial and transport undertakings in the western zones;

(b) 30 per cent. of German foreign investments;

(c) 30 per cent. of German gold which is now at the disposal of the Allies.

(5) The U.S.S.R. will undertake to settle from its own share of reparations the reparations demands of Poland. The United States and Great Britain will act in the same way with regard to France, Yugoslavia, Czechoslovakia, Belgium, Holland and Norway.'

Premier Stalin thought that in the proposals now before them there was a basis for agreement. There was agreement on the following principles: that reparations should be exacted by each Government in its own zone; that reparation deliveries for the Soviet Union should be supplied from the western zones as a whole and not from the Ruhr only; that some of these deliveries should be in exchange for goods from the Russian zone; and finally that the Control Council, under the general direction of the Reparation Commission, should determine what was available for reparations. The main differences between his proposals and those of the United States Delegation were that he wished a time-limit to be fixed for the determination of the total amount due to the Soviet Union under the proposed agreement, and that he had asked for higher percentage deliveries from the western zones.

In discussion the following points were made:

(i) *The Time-Limit.* (Paragraph 3 of Soviet proposals.)

PRESIDENT TRUMAN said that he was prepared to accept the principle of a time-limit for the determination of the total amount of reparation deliveries due to the Soviet Union.

MR. BEVIN thought that three months would be too short a period; he would, however, accept six months.

PREMIER STALIN agreed to a time-limit of six months for this purpose.

(ii) *Equipment available for Reparations.* (Paragraph 3 (*a*).)

MR. BEVIN pointed out that Premier Stalin's proposals, while they envisaged that the amount of equipment available for reparations would be determined by the Control Council, did not provide any criterion by which the Control Council should judge what could be made available. He suggested that the criterion which he had originally put forward[6] should be expressed in the proposed agreement—*i.e.*, that the equipment taken as available for reparations should be that which was not required for a peace economy. As he understood it, the Control Council would first determine what industrial equipment should be left to Germany as necessary for a peace economy, and the balance should then be regarded as available for reparations. MR. BYRNES recalled that this point had been covered in the United States proposals; and PREMIER STALIN agreed to accept the wording of the United States proposals on this point.

MR. BEVIN also pointed out that France was closely concerned with the general question of removal of equipment from the Western Zones. If, as proposed, the Reparations Commission was to work out the general principles governing the amount of equipment available for removal, it was more than ever important that France should be represented on the Reparations Commission. PREMIER STALIN said that he would raise no objection to this; and it was agreed that France should be represented on the Commission.

(iii) *Additional Soviet requirements.* (Paragraph 4.)

MR. BYRNES explained that the German assets frozen in the United States had already been the subject of legislation under which a procedure had been laid down for dealing with claims against them. It would not be possible for the United States Delegation to give away such assets. A[s] regards assets in neutral countries, he understood that in South America, for example, the Governments would apply all frozen German assets towards the cost of compensation for the losses (of shipping, &c.), which they had suffered at German hands.

As regards the gold, according to his information, most of that now in the hands of the United States was identifiable as having been looted by the Germans; and the United States Government proposed that all such gold should be restored to its rightful owners.

---

[6] See No. 469, minute 4.

PREMIER STALIN said that he would be prepared to restrict this claim to 30 per cent. of all *German* gold in Allied hands. He was also prepared to accept a suggestion by Mr. Bevin that the foreign assets claimed by the Soviet Union should be limited to those in neutral countries.

MR. BYRNES said that on consideration the United States Delegation were not prepared to accept any of the additional claims put forward by the Soviet Delegation (in paragraph 4 above).

PREMIER STALIN said that if the United States Delegation would not accept paragraph 4 of his proposals, it might be necessary to increase the percentages in paragraph 3 (*a*) and (*b*) above.

In further discussion, PRESIDENT TRUMAN said that, if the Soviet Delegation would withdraw paragraph 4 of their proposals, he would agree to the figures of 15 per cent. and 10 per cent. for Russian receipts from the Western Zones, as proposed in paragraph 3.

MR. BEVIN said it would be difficult for us to meet the claims of other Allies such as France, Belgium, and Holland, out of the balance remaining if these percentages were assigned to Russia. He suggested that a compromise might be reached on 12½ per cent. against exchanges and 10 per cent. without exchanges.

PREMIER STALIN said that the United States Delegation were prepared to accept the Russian proposals. Why did the British Delegation hesitate?

MR. BEVIN replied that most of the equipment would be taken from the British zone. Great Britain wanted little for herself in reparations, but it was largely from her zone that the claims of the other Allies would have to be satisfied.

PREMIER STALIN said that France did not deserve to obtain much by way of reparation. It should be remembered that she had signed an armistice with Germany and had broken the common Allied front. He estimated that 150 enemy divisions on the eastern front had been provided or supplied from France. These considerations should be set against any claim which France might make to reparations.

MR. BYRNES suggested that the wording in paragraph 2 of the United States proposals (P. (Terminal) 67)[7] would avoid the difficulty of enumerating the Allies whose claims would have to be considered.

MR. BEVIN suggested that, if the Russian demand for 15 per cent. and 10 per cent. was agreed, these deliveries plus what was taken from the Russian zone would give Russia more than 50 per cent. of all the reparations exacted from Germany.

PREMIER STALIN thought that these proposals would give Russia less than 50 per cent. of the total. He pointed out that 15 per cent. would be exchanged for other goods and only the 10 per cent. would be direct reparations.

MR. BEVIN then suggested that a better settlement would be 17½ per cent.

[7] No. 491, annex.

against exchanges and $7\frac{1}{2}$ per cent. in direct reparations.

PREMIER STALIN said that he could not accept this suggestion. His proposal for 15 per cent. and 10 per cent. was a fair claim and should be accepted.

MR. BEVIN then indicated that he would accept the percentages claimed by Premier Stalin.

It was agreed that a drafting Committee consisting of:
United States Delegation: Mr. Clayton, Mr. Pauley;
British Delegation: Sir David Waley, Mr. Turner;
Soviet Delegation: M. Vyshinski, M. Gromyko;
should prepare a note of the agreement on reparations from Germany which had been reached in the course of the discussion recorded above.

3. *Western Frontier of Poland*
(Previous Reference: P. (Terminal) 8th Meeting,[8] Minute 2.)

MR. BYRNES said that, as part of their attempt to secure agreement on Reparations and on the proposed statement on the admission of neutral and ex-enemy States to the United Nations, the United States Delegation had put forward a proposal which would permit the Polish Provisional Government to take over, on a provisional basis pending final determination of their western frontier in the peace settlement, the administration of the territory in the eastern part of pre-war Germany to which they were laying claim. The proposals of the United States Delegation were set out in a Memorandum (subsequently circulated as P. (Terminal) 70)[9] which had already been handed to the British and Soviet Delegations.

MR. BEVIN said that he would like to know more precisely what was involved in this proposal for provisional administration of this territory by the Polish Provisional Government. Thus, was it proposed that the administration of this territory, which was within the Soviet zone of occupation, should be handed over entirely to the Polish Provisional Government? Would all Soviet troops be withdrawn from this area? What assurances could be given that the Polish Provisional Government would be enabled to bring into force at an early date the conditions envisaged in paragraph 4 of the agreed statement on the Polish question (P. (Terminal) 23)?[10]

Mr. Bevin said that he had received representatives of the Polish Provisional Government that morning and had discussed some of these questions with them. All these points were of great importance from his point of view, as he would have to defend in the British Parliament any change of responsibility for this territory, and Parliament would be greatly influenced by the account which he was able to give of what changes were actually going to take place in this territory as a result of the decision now proposed by the United States Delegation. The Polish representatives had assured him that it was their firm intention to hold free and unfettered elections on the basis of universal suffrage and secret ballot, under the 1921

[8] No. 258.   [9] No. 494.   [10] See No. 219, note 6.

1078

Constitution, and that it was their aim to do so not later than the early part of 1946, provided that conditions were established which made it possible to hold such elections. They had assured him that they intended to give full facilities to the press. They would also ensure freedom of religion throughout their country. A further point in which the British Government were deeply concerned was the repatriation of Poles from abroad, not only civilians but also members of the Polish forces; and he had asked the Polish representatives for an undertaking that Poles returning to Poland would receive exactly the same treatment as Poles already resident in Poland.

Mr. Bevin said that he observed from the memorandum by the United States Delegation that it was proposed that the area under discussion should not be considered part of the Soviet zone of occupation. He understood that, although this area would come under Polish administration, it would remain under the jurisdiction of the Control Council for Germany. If it were proposed to exclude the area from this jurisdiction, it would presumably be necessary to obtain the agreement of the French, who were members of the Control Council.

PREMIER STALIN said the area was now in the Russian zone of occupation, with which the French were not concerned.

MR. BEVIN asked whether, in Premier Stalin's view, each occupying Power was free to transfer to other countries portions of its occupation zone.

PREMIER STALIN said that this was a special case, because Poland had no western border. The three Great Powers had undertaken at the Crimea Conference to take steps to determine the uncertainty about Poland's Western Frontier. No final boundary would, however, be settled in advance of the peace treaty.

MR. BYRNES said that everyone was agreed that no boundaries should be finally determined in advance of the peace settlement. This was recognised in the first paragraph of the United States Memorandum; but the present position was that Poland was already administering a large part of the disputed area. All that was now proposed was that the three Great Powers should agree that, as an interim measure, Poland should continue this administration. It was not intended that there should be a Polish representative on the Control Council. PREMIER STALIN agreed.

MR. BEVIN asked whether all Soviet troops would be withdrawn from this area.

PREMIER STALIN said that all Russian troops would have been withdrawn from the area if it had not been on the lines of communication to the Russian armies of occupation under Marshals Zhukov and Koniev. But no more Russian troops would be left in the area than were needed to protect these lines of communication. Already four-fifths of the Russian troops had been withdrawn from the area, and further withdrawals were contemplated. The area was already entirely under Polish administration.

MR. BEVIN referred to one point which particularly concerned the Russians and the British, viz., the early establishment of a British military air service between London, Berlin and Warsaw, so as to enable His Majesty's Government to maintain regular contact with their Embassy in Poland. He would be grateful if the Russians would agree to this air service as soon as possible.

PREMIER STALIN pointed out that British aircraft already flew over the Russian zone on the way to Berlin. If the British came to an agreement with the Polish Government on this matter, the Soviet Government would be ready to give any facilities necessary on their part, but they would wish to obtain reciprocal facilities for a Russian service from Moscow to London *via* France. It was for decision between the British and the Polish Governments whether the aircraft between Berlin and Warsaw were flown by British or Polish pilots; but between Warsaw and Moscow Russian pilots would have to be used. He imagined that on a service from Moscow to London French and British pilots would be used on the stage from Paris to London. If agreement could be reached on these lines, then a through service between London, Paris and Warsaw could be established.

MR. BEVIN said that this wider question needed detailed discussion, but he would be glad if he could have Premier Stalin's immediate support for the limited project of an air service as far as Warsaw.

PREMIER STALIN undertook to do all that he could to help in establishing this service.

It was agreed:

(1) That the proposals in the United States Memorandum on Poland's Western Frontier (P. (Terminal) 70)[9] should be endorsed by the Conference.

(2) That President Truman should convey the decision of the Conference on this question to the representatives of the Polish Provisional Government who were now in Potsdam.

(3) That each of the three Governments should at once inform the French Government of this decision.

4. *Neutral and Ex-enemy States: Admission to United Nations*
(Previous References: P. (Terminal) 10th Meeting,[11] Minute 4, and F. (Terminal) 10th Meeting,[2] Minute 4.)

MR. BYRNES said that when this question had last been considered by the Plenary Meeting on the 28th July it had been found impossible to reach agreement on the draft then under discussion, and the United States Delegation had agreed to withdraw the proposal which they had originally put forward for a statement on the admission of neutral and ex-enemy States to association with the United Nations. On reflection, however, the United States Delegation had decided to put forward a further draft on this question (P. (Terminal) 58)[12] as part of their attempt to secure agreement on the

[11] No. 447.
[12] See No. 469, note 8. With reference to this draft a brief of 31 July 1945 by the British Delegation in Berlin stated that the Delegation could 'accept the paper as it stands. Presumably, however, in doing so the Delegation will wish to make it clear that acceptance of the sentence about establishing diplomatic relations with Bulgaria, etc., does not imply any departure from our previously expressed view—i.e. that we are not prepared to

three problems of reparations, Poland's Western Frontier, and the attitude of the Great Powers towards the admission of certain States to association with the United Nations. The further draft which they had now circulated differed in two respects from that (P. (Terminal) 35)[13] which was under discussion at the meeting on 28th July:

(a) At the end of paragraph 3, the following sentence had been inserted:
'The three Governments agree to examine, each separately, in the near future, in the light of the conditions then prevailing, the establishment of diplomatic relations with Bulgaria, Finland, Hungary, and Roumania, to the extent possible prior to the ratification of peace treaties with those countries.'

(b) Immediately after paragraph 3 a new paragraph had been added in the following terms:
'The three Governments express the desire that, in view of the changed conditions resulting from the termination of the war in Europe, representatives of the Allied Press shall enjoy full freedom to report to the world on developments in Bulgaria, Finland, Hungary, and Roumania.'

The first of these amendments was designed to meet the views of the Soviet Delegation, and also the objections raised by the British and United States Delegations to the amendment previously suggested by the Soviet Delegation. The second amendment used language substantially the same as that already approved in the proposed statement on Poland (P. (Terminal) 23).[10]

PREMIER STALIN said that the Soviet Delegation could accept the first of these amendments if the phrase 'conclusion of peace treaties' was substituted for 'ratification of peace treaties.'

PRESIDENT TRUMAN and MR. ATTLEE accepted this amendment.

As regards the second amendment, PREMIER STALIN suggested that for the words 'The three Governments express the desire that . . .'[14] representatives of the Allied Press shall enjoy full freedom to report . . .'[14] there should be substituted 'The three Governments have no doubt that . . .'[14] representatives of the Allied Press will enjoy full freedom to report . . .'[14]

PRESIDENT TRUMAN and MR. ATTLEE indicated that they could accept this amendment.

It was agreed that the three Governments should make a declaration on the admission of neutral and ex-enemy States to association with the United Nations in the terms of the revised draft (P. (Terminal) 58)[12] circulated by the United States Delegation on the 30th July, subject to the two amendments noted above.

re-establish relations until we are better satisfied as to the conditions within the satellite countries and as to the nature of their Governments' (F.O. 934/5/48(12)).
[13] No. 260.
[14] Punctuation as in original quotation.

5. *Germany: Economic Problems*

(Previous Reference: F. (Terminal) 9th Meeting,[15] Minute 5.)

PRESIDENT TRUMAN recalled that the Foreign Secretaries, at their meeting on the 27th July, had agreed to postpone further consideration of the draft Statement of Economic Principles to govern the treatment of Germany in the initial control period (P. (Terminal) 15)[16] until the question of reparations had been settled. It was now possible to review the Statement of Economic Principles in the light of the decision reached (see Minute 2 above) on the reparations problem.

In discussion, the following points were raised:

(a) *Paragraph 13*

MR. BYRNES suggested, and it was agreed, that the word 'banking' should be inserted, after 'currency,' in sub-paragraph (e) of this paragraph; and that a new sub-paragraph should be added as follows:

'(g) Transportation and communications.'

(b) *Paragraph 14*

MR. BYRNES suggested that the following should be substituted for the second sentence in this sub-paragraph:

'Except where determined by the occupying Power concerned to be required for payment for necessary imports, no grant of credit to Germany or Germans shall be permitted.'

Mr. Byrnes explained that in consequence of the agreement now reached on the reparations problem, discretion might be given to occupying Powers, if they thought fit, to give credit to Germans for the purposes indicated in the amendment. In reply to a question by Premier Stalin, he said that this discretionary power, if approved, would be exercisable in all zones of occupation.

MR. BEVIN said that he felt some doubt about the wisdom of this amendment. He himself would prefer to omit entirely the second sentence in paragraph 14 (d) of the Statement.

MR. BYRNES said that he had no objection to this course; and it was agreed that this sentence should be deleted.

(c) *Paragraph 18*

It was decided that, as a result of the agreement now reached on the reparations problem, this paragraph could be omitted from the Statement.

(d) *Paragraph 19*

PREMIER STALIN recalled that the Soviet Delegation had suggested[17] the addition of a new paragraph in the following terms:

'After payment of reparations, enough resources must be left to enable the German people to subsist without external assistance. In working out the economic balance of Germany, the necessary means must be provided to pay for imports in so far as they are approved by the Control Council.

[15] No. 431.   [16] No. 210.   [17] See No. 233, minute 3(b).

The exports to pay for such imports will have priority over reparations and internal consumption.'

Mr. Byrnes said that, as it had now been agreed in the reparations settlement that the Russians should receive a specific percentage of the plant and equipment scheduled for delivery as reparations from the western zones, it was no longer necessary to include this paragraph dealing with exports and imports.

Mr. Bevin said that he was still concerned to secure that payment for improved [approved] imports into Germany should be a first charge against the proceeds of exports. It would be most unfortunate if the decision reached on the reparations problem had the effect of dividing Germany into several separate zones for all economic purposes; and, in view of that decision, he was the more anxious to secure agreement that Germany should be treated as an economic unit for purposes of the normal exchange of goods. He thought that the Conference should consider this point further before deciding not to add to the Statement of Economic Principles the additional paragraph 19 put forward by the Soviet Delegation.

Premier Stalin thought that Mr. Bevin's point would be met by the establishment of a central German administration for economic purposes; and he recalled that the Soviet Delegation had put forward, at the meeting of Foreign Secretaries on the previous day, a proposal to add a paragraph on this point to the Statement of Political Principles (F. (Terminal) 10th Meeting,[2] Minute 8).

Mr. Bevin agreed. This proposal was to be considered later in the meeting, and he suggested that a final decision on the proposed addition of a new paragraph 19 to the Statement of Economic Principles should be held over until the Conference had discussed the proposal for the establishment of a central German administration of economic questions. In the light of the decision taken on that point, the Economic Committee might consider whether something on the lines of the proposed paragraph 19 would still be required.

It was agreed:

(1) That the Economic Committee should consider and report forthwith on the question of including a paragraph on the lines of the new paragraph 19 proposed by the Soviet Delegation; and

(2) That the Statement of Economic Principles annexed to P. (Terminal) 15[16] should be approved, subject to the amendments agreed upon at the meetings of Foreign Secretaries on the 22nd and 23rd July (F. (Terminal) 5th Meeting,[18] Minute 3 and 6th Meeting,[19] Minute 3) and to the further amendments approved in the discussion recorded above and to the report of the Economic Committee.

[18] No. 224.   [19] No. 233.

6. *Germany: Administration of the Ruhr*

(Previous Reference: F. (Terminal) 10th Meeting,[2] Minute 13.)

In connection with the discussion recorded in the preceding Minute, M. MOLOTOV suggested that the meeting should consider the memorandum submitted by the Soviet Delegation (P. (Terminal) 59)[20] proposing the establishment of an Allied Council to administer the industrial district of the Ruhr.

MR. BEVIN said that, as he had pointed out when M. Molotov gave notice of this memorandum at the meeting of Foreign Secretaries the previous day, these proposals were of very close concern to France, and it was quite impossible for him to discuss them in the absence of representatives of the French Government. He was not clear why this question had been raised at the present Conference.

PREMIER STALIN said that the Soviet Delegation had brought this up because at earlier conferences the suggestion had been put forward that the Ruhr should be separated from Germany and placed under some form of international control. On earlier occasions this suggestion had met with some approval. It flowed from the idea, which had previously been favoured by the Heads of the three Governments, that Germany might be dismembered after the war. More recently, however, the views of the three Governments on the dismemberment of Germany had been modified; and at the present time the general feeling seemed to be in favour of treating Germany as a unit for economic purposes. For this reason he was anxious to know whether the British and United States Governments were now of opinion that the Ruhr should be treated as a part of Germany. If Mr. Bevin felt unable to discuss the further proposals for Allied control which were outlined in the remainder of the memorandum by the Soviet Delegation, could not the Conference at least consider whether they accepted the opening words of the memorandum which expressed the view that the industrial district of the Ruhr should be treated as part of Germany. If this were the view of the three Governments, he would be glad if a statement to that effect could be included among the decisions of the present Conference.

PRESIDENT TRUMAN pointed out that the Ruhr fell within the jurisdiction of the Control Council for Germany, and said that in his view it should be regarded as part of Germany.

MR. BEVIN said that he would not wish to express any firm opinion on this question without further examination of the records of earlier discussions and of the relevant facts bearing on the question. He was content that for the present the Ruhr should remain within the jurisdiction of the Control Council for Germany; but he would prefer to have an opportunity for consultation with his colleagues in the British Government before committing himself to any view about the long-term arrangements for control over the industrial district of the Ruhr. Meanwhile, he was willing to agree that this

[20] No. 472.

long-term problem should be referred for consideration by the Council of Foreign Ministers.

It was agreed that the issues raised in the memorandum by the Soviet Delegation (P. (Terminal) 59)[20] should be referred for consideration by the Council of Foreign Ministers.

7. *Germany: Political Principles*
(Previous Reference: F. (Terminal) 10th Meeting,[2] Minute 8.)

At the meeting of Foreign Secretaries on the previous day, the Soviet Delegation had suggested an addition to paragraph 8 [9] (iv) of the Statement of Political Principles regarding the need for the establishment of a central German administration for specified economic purposes. Discussion of this suggestion had been deferred so that the British Delegation might have a further opportunity of considering it in detail.

MR. BEVIN said that he agreed in principle with this proposal by the Soviet Delegation, but wished to suggest some verbal amendments to their draft. He proposed that the existing paragraph 8 [9] (iv) should read as follows:

'For the time being, no central German Government shall be established. Notwithstanding this, however, certain essential central German administrative departments, headed by State Secretaries, shall be established, particularly in the fields of finance, transport, communications, foreign trade and industry. Such departments will act under the direction of the Control Council.'

It was agreed that the sub-paragraph set out above should be incorporated in the Statement of Political Principles to govern the treatment of Germany during the initial control period.[21]

8. *Transfer of Populations*
(Previous Reference: F. (Terminal) 8th Meeting,[22] Minute 2.)

MR. BYRNES said that a Sub-Committee appointed to study this question had prepared a Report circulated as (P. (Terminal) 74)[23] and that there was agreement on all but the last paragraph, which read as follows:

'The Czechoslovak Government, the Polish Provisional Government and the Control Council in Hungary are at the same time being informed of the above and are being requested, meanwhile, to suspend further expulsions pending an examination by the Governments concerned of the report from their representatives on the Control Council.'

He urged the meeting to agree to the inclusion of the whole of this final paragraph in order to prevent any further expulsions of Germans from

---

[21] This amendment was telegraphed that day to Mr. Duff Cooper at Paris (cf. No. 488). At 5 p.m. on 1 August he accordingly communicated to M. Bidault a note comprising the text as in No. 603, section IIA (cf. also *F.R.U.S. Berlin*, vol. ii, pp. 1544–5).

[22] No. 274.

[23] Not printed. The text of this report, headed 'Transfer of German Population' and dated 1 August, was identical with section XII of No. 603: cf. iv below.

Czechoslovakia and Poland since these were greatly adding to the work of the occupation authorities in Germany.

M. MOLOTOV said that the purpose of the document was to ensure that the transfers of population took place in an orderly manner. He thought that it was hardly possible for the Conference to reach decisions on this matter without consulting the Governments of Hungary, Poland and Czechoslovakia.

PREMIER STALIN said that any decisions which the Conference might reach on this matter could not be carried out. It was not the fact that the Polish, Czechoslovak and Hungarian Governments were driving the Germans out. The Germans had created such a condition of affairs for themselves in these countries that they preferred to flee, and it was impossible for them to remain in these countries, even if the Conference were to obtain from the Polish and Czechoslovak Governments formal consent that they might do so. To attempt to obtain such consent would be, in Premier Stalin's view, a mere shot in the dark, for it would not take account of the existing situation.

MR. BYRNES said that the last paragraph was designed as an inducement to Governments to refrain from expelling Germans pending the report of their representatives on the Control Council. If these Governments were not expelling Germans then, of course, the action suggested would not be effective. If, however, the Governments concerned had acquiesced in the expulsion of Germans, agreement between the Big Three might make them willing to co-operate in the transfer of populations, and to regulate the movement in an orderly manner.

Mr. Byrnes added that there was a difference in the statements of fact. According to information at his disposal there had been cases where Germans had been forced to leave and this had increased the burden of the occupying Powers to an intolerable extent. The United States Delegation merely suggested inviting these Governments to co-operate in so far as they could help to improve the situation.

PREMIER STALIN replied that the Polish and Czechoslovak Governments would tell Mr. Byrnes that no orders had been given to expel the Germans. The Germans had fled of their own accord. If the United States Delegation insisted, he would agree to their suggestion, though he did not expect any considerable results.

PRESIDENT TRUMAN said that he would appreciate it very much if Premier Stalin would agree. This might make it possible to organise such transfers of population as were still to be made.

MR. ATTLEE agreed with President Truman and said he thought it important to bring to the notice of the Polish and Czechoslovak Governments that the activities of their peoples were laying an intolerable burden on the occupying Powers.

PREMIER STALIN said that he would not object to the issue of this statement.

MR. BEVIN suggested that, since the French Government were represented on the Control Council for Germany, they should be informed of the decisions of the Conference on the question of transfers of German populations from Czechoslovakia, Poland and Hungary. This was agreed.

9. *German Navy and Merchant Marine*
(Previous Reference: F. (Terminal) 10th Meeting[2] Minute 6, and P. (Terminal) 9th Meeting,[24] Minute 1.)

PREMIER STALIN said that he would like a definite decision on this question. The views of the Soviet Delegation had been clearly expressed, and it had been agreed in principle that one-third of the Navy should be handed over to the Soviet Government; that the majority of the submarines should be sunk; and that the merchant marine should be left at the disposal of the Allies until the end of the Far-Eastern War.

PRESIDENT TRUMAN said that he was informed by his naval representative that the question was not yet ready for discussion.

PREMIER STALIN asked whether it could be definitely agreed that the question should be considered on the following day. Or was it possible to refer it to the Foreign Ministers?

PRESIDENT TRUMAN said that he was prepared to discuss it on the following day.

MR. BYRNES said that the Committee which had been set up to study this question were meeting later that evening and hoped to reach agreement. He thought it would save time to await their Report.

It was agreed to discuss this matter at the next Plenary Meeting.

10. *Yalta Declaration on Liberated Europe*
(Previous Reference: P. (Terminal) 6th Meeting,[25] Minute 3.)

MR. BYRNES recalled that the United States Delegation had circulated a paper on this subject (P. (Terminal) 21)[26] on which the Conference had not reached agreement. He thought, however, that there had been substantial agreement on the first two paragraphs and he therefore asked that consideration should now be given to the third paragraph which read out as follows:

'3. The three Governments agree that the Control Commissions in Rumania, Bulgaria and Hungary, in acknowledgement of the changed conditions since the cessation of hostilities in Europe, will henceforth operate on a tripartite basis under revised procedures providing for tripartite participation, taking into account the interests and responsibilities of the three Governments which together presented the terms of armistice to the respective countries.'

M. MOLOTOV[27] said that this question had not been placed on the agenda but that nevertheless it was quite possible that when the Soviet Delegation had looked at it they might not object. The Soviet Delegation had also

[24] No. 271.
[25] No. 226.
[26] No. 219.i.
[27] This statement is ascribed to Marshal Stalin in the Soviet record, *Conferences: Soviet Documents*, pp. 289–90.

circulated a paper (P. (Terminal) 11),[28] which had been directed chiefly towards Greece. Moreover he had circulated the previous day a paper on Yugoslavia and the conditions in the Trieste–Istria District (P. (Terminal) 61).[29]

MR. BEVIN suggested that the wisest course might perhaps be to decide not to proceed further with any of these three papers.

It was decided not to proceed further with discussion of P. (Terminal) 11,[28] 21[26] and 61.[29]

11. *War Criminals*
(Previous Reference: F. (Terminal) 10th Meeting,[2] Minute 10.)

The meeting considered the following redraft (subsequently circulated as P. (Terminal) 71) of a paragraph on war crimes for insertion in the Protocol and Communique, which had been put forward by the British Delegation:

'The Three Governments have taken note of the discussions which have been proceeding in recent weeks in London between British, United States, Soviet and French representatives with a view to reaching agreement on the methods of trial of those major war criminals whose crimes under the Moscow Declaration of the 1st November, 1943, have no particular geographical localisation. They trust that the negotiations in London will result in complete and speedy agreement being reached, and they regard it as a matter of great importance that the trial of these major criminals should begin at the earliest possible date.

'The Three Governments reaffirm their intention to bring these criminals to swift and sure justice. They declare that should any of these war criminals have taken shelter in neutral countries, they will consult together as to any steps which it may be necessary to take to ensure the implementation of this firm intention.'

M. MOLOTOV said that the Soviet Delegation agreed to accept this British draft as a basis for discussion. They had, however, one small amendment to make, namely, the insertion of the words 'such as Göring, Hess, Ribbentrop, Ley, Keitel and Doenitz' after the words 'major criminals' in the last sentence of paragraph 1.

MR. ATTLEE said that the difficulty which the British Delegation saw was that, if certain names were now included in the statement to be issued, it might be found that there was a discrepancy between their list and the list to be drawn up by the War Crimes Commission now sitting in London.

PREMIER STALIN said that the Soviet Delegation's amendment did not necessarily imply that the individuals named should be tried; but only gave certain names as examples. People in all countries were waiting for these criminals to be named and, if the Conference did not mention them, a shadow would be cast on their prestige.

MR. BYRNES said that every country had its own favourite Nazi criminals,

[28] No. 201. It would appear, however, from the Soviet and American records of this meeting that this reference should be to No. 515.
[29] No. 475.

1088

and if the Conference failed to name these it would be difficult to explain why we had shown discrimination.

PREMIER STALIN interjected to say that that was the reason for the insertion of the words 'such as' in his amendment.

MR. ATTLEE said that he did not think that the insertion of a list of names strengthened the argument. The world knew quite well who the major war criminals were.

PREMIER STALIN said that if the Conference was silent, some circles might think that the Three Powers had the intention of saving some of the criminals.

MR. BYRNES said that Mr. Justice Jackson, the United States representative on the War Crimes Commission, with whom he had discussed the matter the previous evening by telephone, hoped that the War Crimes Commission would agree on an international tribunal either that afternoon or the following day. Mr. Justice Jackson would telephone the result of this meeting in London at 1 p.m. the following day. It would be a help if M. Stalin could urge the Soviet representative on the London Commission to reach agreement. If agreement were reached in London the Conference could include it in their own statement, which would thereby be made very effective.

PREMIER STALIN repeated that, if the Conference did not name some of the most hated major War Criminals, the declaration on the matter in the Protocol would not have its full worth. He had also consulted his Russian legal representatives on the War Crimes Commission, and they thought that it would be wise to put some names in.

PRESIDENT TRUMAN suggested that, as a report was expected from London to-morrow morning, it might be better to resume discussion of this matter at their next meeting. This was agreed.

12. *International Inland Waterways*
(Previous Reference: F. (Terminal) 8[th Meeting],[22] Minute 1).

PRESIDENT TRUMAN said that he was much concerned that this matter, which he had raised in the United States Delegation's paper of the 23rd July (P. (Terminal) 33),[30] and had mentioned on that and the following day, should be fully discussed. His paper offered a suggestion for the proper control of the inland waterways of Central Europe, which he was convinced had been the hotbed of war for the last 200 years. If these lines of communication could be internationalised and properly controlled, they would be a great factor in preventing wars in the future. He quite realised that it might not be possible to agree at the present time on the details of such a scheme, but he thought that the matter should certainly be fully considered before the final peace treaties were made.

M. MOLOTOV[31] pointed out that discussion on the question of the Black

[30] No. 246.
[31] This observation is ascribed to Marshal Stalin in the Soviet record, *Conferences: Soviet Documents*, p. 292.

Sea Straits, on which the President's suggestion had originally been raised, had been postponed. To study the question of Inland Waterways the Conference would need a considerable number of experts who knew the full details of the Central European waterways. He therefore doubted whether it would be possible to discuss the matter fully before the end of the Conference.

PRESIDENT TRUMAN agreed and suggested that the matter should be raised at the Foreign Secretaries meeting in September 1945, by which time the various Delegations would have had the opportunity to marshal their facts and consider the views of their experts.

The Conference agreed to this suggestion.

13. *Procedure: Arrangements for further Meetings*

The Conference agreed to meet again at 3 p.m. the following day and, if necessary in order to allow time for winding up the results of the Conference, also at 9 or 10 p.m.

It was agreed that the Foreign Secretaries should meet the following morning at 11 a.m.

Cabinet Office, Potsdam, 31st July, 1945

CALENDARS TO No. 495

i *31 July 1945 Economic assets of Germany east of the Oder-Neisse line.* Paper by E.I.P.S., with covering letters from E.I.P.S. to F.O. and from F.O. to U.K. Delegation in Berlin [UE 3382/3260/77].

ii *31 July 1945 U.K. Delegation (Berlin) Brief on Economic Principles for Germany.* Importance of securing agreement to British formula on the first charge, for inclusion in appendix to No. 210 as proposed in No. 469, minute 4; objections to Soviet alternative draft [F.O. 934/1/2(14)].

iii *1 Aug. 1945 Letter from Mr. Harrison (Berlin) to Mr. Troutbeck:* formula for communicating instructions to Commanders-in-Chief on political principles for Germany [C 4413/24/18].

iv *27–31 July 1945 Sub-Committee on transfer of German populations:* minutes with draft reports on 'very sticky' discussions on 25–30 July. Third revised draft agreed as final report on 30 July [F.O. 934/5/43(2–4, 7)].

v *31 July–1 Aug. 1945 Correspondence between Mr. Bevin and M. Molotov (Berlin):* early return to the British flag of British-owned river craft on Roumanian stretch of Danube [W 10421, 10598/142/803].

No. 496

Letter from Mr. Dixon to Mr. Peck (Berlin)
[UE 3629/2615/77]

BRITISH DELEGATION, BERLIN, *31 July 1945*

I return herewith your copy of Mr. Eden's minute P.M./45/323 of July

12th which you sent me with your letter of July 29th.[1]

Our view is that we should not pursue this particular question. We have decided that the line to take on Marshal Zhukov's recent report[2] about British (and United States) depredations is that we should not quarrel about our respective booty. But in case there *is* any discussion of that report, we have prepared a note of points to make, including the stripping of Austria.

P. DIXON

CALENDAR TO No. 496

i *30 July 1945 U.K. Delegation Note (Berlin).* Comments upon No. 455. 'Almost all the towns' mentioned there 'are in areas which were held by American troops before they were handed over to the Russians.' Suggests points for reply if necessary [PREM 8/48].

---

[1] In this letter, not printed, Mr. Peck had enclosed to Mr. Dixon a copy of Mr. Eden's minute at No. 36.i and had explained that Mr. Attlee would like Mr. Bevin to examine it 'in the light of the latest charges made against us of British depredations.'

[2] No. 455.

No. 497

Report from Marshal Zhukov to Marshal Stalin (Berlin)[1]
P. *(Terminal) 72 [U 6197/3628/70]*

Top secret   *31 July 1945*

The removal by the Allies of railway rolling stock from the Soviet zone of occupation (Circulated by the Soviet Delegation)

I report that during the withdrawal of their troops from our zone, which was temporarily occupied by them, the Americans and British had removed, without our consent, the following quantities of rolling stock:–

Americans

1. Directorate of Erfurt:–

Goods wagons, loaded	9,722
Passenger coaches	278
Engines, all types	87

2. Department of Magdeburg:

Goods wagons, loaded	655
Goods wagons, empty	939
Passenger coaches	322

---

[1] Printed in *Berlinskaya konferentsiya*, pp. 432–3.

1. Directorate of Schwerin:

Goods wagons, loaded	..	..	..	..	36
Goods wagons, empty	..	..	..	..	1,200
Engines, all types	..	..	..	..	15

Total Rolling Stock Removed

	By the Americans	By the British	Total
Goods wagons, loaded ..	10,377	36	10,413
Goods wagons, empty ..	939	1,200	2,139
Passenger coaches ..	600	..	600
Engines, all types ..	87	15	102

I request that you should raise with the Allies the question of returning to our Occupation Zone of [*sic*] the aforesaid rolling stock, since we have in our zone an extremely small quantity of rolling stock.

No. 498

Note by Sir D. Waley (Berlin)
P. (Terminal) 73 [U 6197/3628/70]

Top secret   *31 July 1945*

German Reparations
(Circulated to the United Kingdom Delegation only)

The attached Note shows the progress made by the Drafting Committee. I think we should withdraw our Reserve if the Russians withdraw their Reserve on Article 3 and give an oral assurance in lieu of Article 7.

S. D. W.

ANNEX TO No. 498

German Reparation[1]
(*Agreed with Reserves noted by Drafting Committee.*)

1. Reparation claims of U.S.S.R. shall be met by removals from the Zone of Germany occupied by the U.S.S.R.

2. The U.S.S.R. undertakes to settle the reparation claims of Poland from its own share of reparations.

3. The reparations claims of the United States, the United Kingdom and other countries entitled to reparations shall be met from the Western Zones [2]and from German external assets.[2]

---

[1] Printed in *F.R.U.S. Berlin*, vol. ii, pp. 930–1.
[2] *Note in filed copy:* 'Reserved by Soviet Delegate.'

4. In addition to the reparations to be taken by the U.S.S.R. from its own zone of occupation, the U.S.S.R. shall receive additionally from the Western Zones:–

(a) 15 per cent. of such usable and complete industrial capital equipment, in the first place from the metallurgical, chemical and machine manufacturing industries as is unnecessary for the German peace economy and should be removed from the Western Zones of Germany, in exchange for an equivalent value of food, coal, potash, zinc, timber, clay products, petroleum or petroleum products, and such other commodities as may be agreed upon.

(b) 10 per cent. of such industrial capital equipment as is unnecessary for a peace economy and should be removed from the Western Zones, to be transferred to the Soviet Government on reparations account without payment or exchange of any kind in return.

Removals of equipment as provided in (a) and (b) above shall be made simultaneously.

5. The amount of equipment to be removed from the Western Zones on account of reparations must be determined within six months from now at the latest.

6. Removals of industrial capital equipment shall begin as soon as possible and shall be completed within two years from the date of the determination specified in paragraph 5. [3]Until the determination of the general volume of equipment to be removed, deliveries will be carried out as advance deliveries in regard to such equipment as the Allied Commission on Reparations and the Control Council shall decide to be available. The delivery of products covered by 4 (a) above shall be made by the U.S.S.R. in agreed instalments within five years of the date hereof. The determination of the amount and character of the industrial capital equipment unnecessary for the German peace economy and therefore available for reparation shall be made by the Control Council under policies fixed by the Allied Commission on Reparations, with the participation of France, subject to the final approval of the Zone Commander in the Zone from which the equipment is to be removed.

7.[4] The Soviet Government will make no claim to securities of Corporations in Western Zones, to German external assets, nor to German gold.

---

[3] *Note in filed copy:* 'Reserved by the United Kingdom Delegation.'
[4] *Note in filed copy:* 'Reserved by Soviet Government. United States and United Kingdom Delegations would accept an oral assurance instead of this clause.'

No. 499

Mr. Morrison to Mr. Bevin (Berlin: received 1 August, 12.15 a.m.)
No. 314 Onward Telegraphic [E 5697/8/89]

FOREIGN OFFICE, *31 July 1945, 10.5 p.m.*

Top secret. Most Immediate

Following is text of C.I.C. 781/34740, T.O.O. 311630Z.[1]
Begins
Top Secret and personal for Prime Minister from General Paget.

[1] *i.e.* time of origin, 31 July 4.30 p.m. G.M.T.

Reference Target 267² of 29th July.

I shall not increase garrison in Levant beyond minimum necessary to ensure order and to safeguard French lives and property.

Ends

² No. 449.

No. 500

Mr. Bevin (Berlin) to Mr. Morrison (Received 31 July, 11.10 p.m.)
No. 305 Target Telegraphic [F.O. 934/2/10(91)]

Immediate. Top secret   BERLIN, *31 July 1945, 11.40 p.m.*¹

During the past few days a series of conversations with the Polish Delegation have been held at which it has been pointed out to them that, if His Majesty's Government are to be expected to support the Polish claims to administer all territory east of the Oder and the Western Neisse, His Majesty's Government are entitled to ask in return for satisfactory assurances regarding the conditions that will obtain in the new Poland that will thus be created. At a final meeting on 31st July,² the Secretary of State succeeded in extracting from M. Bierut assurances on the following points: the holding of elections at latest early next year, freedom of the press, freedom of religion, non-discrimination against Poles returning from abroad and the early establishment of a British military air service between London and Warsaw.

2. The United States Delegation had stated at the Foreign Ministers' Committee on 30th July,³ without giving us prior notice of their intentions, that they supported the Soviet Delegation's proposal that the frontier claims of the Polish Provisional Government should be accepted as a provisional arrangement pending the final delimitation of the frontier at the Peace Conference. In the circumstances, the British Delegation at the Plenary Session on 31st July informed the Conference⁴ of the assurances received from the Polish Delegation and stated that on the strength of these assurances and in the belief that the Polish Provisional Government would carry them out, His Majesty's Government were prepared to fall in with the Soviet and American views in regard to the frontier. This statement followed a discussion of the question of reparations from Germany at which agreement was reached covering the question of supplies for Germany from Russian sources.

3. The Secretary of State asked at the Plenary Session when the Red Army would be withdrawn from territory under Polish administration. Marshal Stalin said that Soviet troops would be withdrawn except those

¹ Time of origin.
² See No. 490.
³ See No. 469, minute 4.
⁴ See No. 495, minute 3.

required for guarding 2 lines of communication. He added that four fifths of the Soviet Army had already been withdrawn by agreement with the Polish Government. Secretary of State also drew attention to the fact that, since France was a member of the Allied Control Council in Germany, there was a certain irregularity about making here, in the absence of French participation, any agreement involving the withdrawal of part of 1937 Germany from the supreme authority of the Control Council. On his suggestion, it was agreed that the French Provisional Government should be informed in advance of any public announcement of the terms of the agreement reached.

4. The text of the agreement is contained in my immediately following telegram (Target No. 306).[5] This should be repeated to Paris and His Majesty's Chargé d'Affaires should communicate it in confidence to the French Provisional Government as the fourth Power represented upon the Allied Control Council in Germany. He should, if possible, concert his action with his United States and Soviet colleagues, who will no doubt be receiving similar instructions, but if they do not, he should not delay his own action later than 1st August.

[5] Not printed. This telegram of 1.15 a.m. on 1 August 1945 to the Foreign Office (received at 11.30 p.m. on 31 July) transmitted the text of No. 494, communicated by Mr. Duff Cooper to M. Bidault on 1 August at 5 p.m.

No. 501

Mr. Morrison to Mr. Bevin (Berlin: received 1 August, 1.35 a.m.)
No. 316 Onward Telegraphic [F 4646/47/23]

Top secret   FOREIGN OFFICE, *31 July 1945, 11.28 p.m.*

For Sir A. Cadogan from Sir O. Sargent.

Onward No. 259[1] (of the 28th July: Command boundaries in Indo-China).

We have now received the views of the Chiefs of Staff. In their discussion with the U.S. Chiefs of Staff they originally recommended that approach to Chiang Kai-shek should be by the President and Prime Minister, but at the

[1] This telegram, not printed, referred to a letter of 25 July 1945 (not printed) from General Hollis to Sir A. Cadogan asking whether the Foreign Office in conjunction with the State Department would initiate an approach to Generalissimo Chiang Kai-shek concerning command boundaries in Indo-China: cf. No. 249, enclosure, para. 14, and No. 255, note 5. The Foreign Office telegram had given a preliminary reaction 'that this is scarcely an appropriate matter for action by the Foreign Office and State Department through the normal diplomatic channel and we feel that the approach has in any case little chance of success unless it is in the form of a direct request from the President and the Prime Minister jointly or in parallel telegrams from Potsdam. We are, however, consulting the Chiefs of Staff.'

instigation of the U.S. Chiefs of Staff it was agreed in the Final Report to recommend that the approach should be by the two Governments.

2. If the Prime Minister agrees to propose a direct approach from the President and himself (which the Foreign Office consider to be the only course which has any hope of success) we would suggest that it would be better to avoid all reference to past history since this might only result in raising question of Siam as well as Indo-China. We suggest that message should simply say that the Prime Minister and the President, on the advice of the Combined Chiefs of Staff, had reached the conclusion that it was desirable to make the proposed division of Indo-China *for operational purposes*, thus leaving in the China theatre that part of Indo-China which covers the flank of projected Chinese operations in China and at the same time enabling SACSEA to develop operations in the southern half of Indo-China.

3. Chiefs of Staff are entirely agreeable to our sending advice in above sense. They feel that further reference to the U.S. Chiefs of Staff, who have now returned to America, on method of approaching Generalissimo would ead to undesirable delay.

No. 502

Letter from Mr. Attlee to President Truman (Berlin)
[*PREM 3/139/9*]

Most secret   BERLIN, *31 July 1945*

Dear Mr. President,

T.A.

Mr. Churchill has informed me of the general position and has sent me the attached draft of a statement[1] which we propose to issue when you and Mr. Stimson make your statements. I shall appreciate any comments you may have and gladly consider any amendments you may wish to suggest.

---

[1] Not printed. This statement, subject to some small subsequent amendments, proposed by Sir J. Anderson and accepted by Mr. Churchill, was the same as that issued on 6 August and printed in *The Times* of 7 August 1945, p. 4. Mr. Churchill had sent this draft to Mr. Attlee under cover of the following letter of 29 July: 'Dear Attlee, I have prepared this statement, based on data supplied by Anderson and Cherwell, which requires your immediate consideration in view of what is in prospect. The Americans showed us their two proposed statements, and we should, in fairness and courtesy, show them ours. They accepted from us several amendments drafted in our joint interests on their papers, and of course their views should also be considered. It is however our right and need to establish the historical facts leading to the present position, which redound to the credit and efficiency of our war-time administration. I have drafted the statement in the first person as I should have made it myself, but it would be quite easy to put it into the third person as an announcement by you. Yours sincerely W. S. C.'

2. You will see that the statement which was prepared by Mr. Churchill is in the first person, and as at present advised, I propose to issue it in this form with a short covering statement on the lines of the second enclosure[2] to this letter.

3. I should greatly appreciate an opportunity of a short talk with you on this matter before the Conference ends; and in due course advance information of the time and date at which your statements will be issued.

Yours sincerely,
C. R. ATTLEE

ENCLOSURE IN No. 502

You will all have seen the important statements which have been made by President Truman and by Mr. Stimson, the United States Secretary for War, about the atomic bomb. The problems of the release of energy by atomic fission have been solved and an atomic bomb has been dropped on Japan by the United States Air Force.

President Truman and Mr. Stimson have described in their statements the nature and vast implications of this new discovery. You will, however, expect to hear some account of the part which this country has played in the remarkable scientific advances which have now come to fruition. Before the change of Government Mr. Churchill had prepared the statement which follows and I am now issuing it in the form in which he wrote it.

[2] Enclosure below.

No. 503

Letter from Mr. Attlee to President Truman (Berlin)[1]
[UE 3550/32/71]

BERLIN, 31 July 1945

My dear Mr. President,

Thank you for your letter of July 29[2] on the subject of Munitions Supplies on Lend Lease in Stage II. While I will not disguise my disappointment that it has not been found possible to accept in its entirety our understanding as set out in the memorandum which was attached to Mr. Churchill's letter of July 24,[3] I sincerely appreciate your desire, as stated in your letter of July 25,[4] to get a construction of the new Lend Lease Renewal Act so as to cause the least difficulty and embarrassment to us in the prosecution of the war against Japan.

[1] Printed in *F.R.U.S. Berlin*, vol. ii, pp. 1186–7.
[2] No. 458.
[3] Annex I to No. 251.
[4] No. 272.

In accepting your decision I earnestly trust you will agree:

(*a*) That detailed instructions applying this decision to the British and defining the portion of our Stage II requirements as now revised which under this decision can qualify for Lend Lease can be agreed as soon as possible with our representatives in Washington and

(*b*) That meantime the shipment of supplies destined for the Far Eastern operational theatre or for bases or lines of communication serving that theatre may go forward without delay. There are, I am told, supplies of that category which are currently available in Washington and are urgently required by us in connection with forthcoming operations.

With reference to the application of this decision to the British referred to in (*a*) above, I enclose a draft which, from the informal discussions which have taken place here, would seem to provide a basis for agreement in Washington consistently with your letter; and I would venture to express the hope that those who are charged with the day to day executive action under this arrangement may be given to understand your desire to place a liberal construction upon the document as finally agreed.

In particular I trust that your decision which eliminates our requirements for occupational forces will not be taken to imply that the efficient maintenance of these forces is of small importance, and that they can be stripped of equipment. The effective control of Germany and Austria is a vital matter for us, and its importance is specifically recognised in paragraph 4 of the C.C.S. final report[5] which you and my predecessor recently approved.

I have noted what you say about post-war economic arrangements and I shall look forward to hearing from you after Mr. Clayton has reported to you in Washington.

May I conclude by assuring you of my personal appreciation of the most helpful attitude you have adopted in dealing with this matter which is of such great importance to us.

Yours very sincerely,

[C. R. ATTLEE]

ENCLOSURE IN NO. 503

1. Requirements accepted under the terms of the President's letter of 29th July are to include the following:

(i) Items included in the schedules of British requirements which are to be shipped directly to the Far East or to units outside that area but designated for that area.

(ii) Items required for bases which serve the Far Eastern operational theatre even although the bases themselves are outside of the area.

(iii) Items required for the lines of communication to the Far Eastern Operational theatre provided they are to be used in connection with the prosecution of the war against Japan.

(iv) Items required for essential military purposes in other areas and needed

---

[5] See No. 255, note 5.

solely to replace similar items which, owing to the time factor, have had to be transferred to the Far Eastern operational theatre.

(v) Such proportion of the components required for the manufacture of military stores outside the United States as may be held to be required for the prosecution of the war against Japan.

Note. The first four classifications cover main items and spares, and all five classifications shall qualify for Lend-Lease irrespective of whether the items are made solely in the United States or not.

2. The requirements as defined above shall be accepted for procurement to the extent that production facilities exist and as far as possible they shall be produced in addition to the United States own needs.

3. Assignments shall be made to the British (within the total quantity accepted for procurement) where the items are in easy supply. Where, however, the items are in short supply the share of available supplies allocated to the British must continue to be conditioned by the consideration of operational priorities.

CALENDARS TO NO. 503

i   *31 July 1945 Mr. Balfour (Washington) Tel. No. 567 Remac.* Anglo-American disposal of surplus stores and fixed assets [UE 3307/146/71].

ii   *1 Aug. 1945 R.A.F. Delegation (Washington) to Air Ministry Tels. Nos. 109–110 Uslon.* Communication from Mr. R. P. Patterson, U.S. Under-Secretary of War: American supply of war material under Lend Lease. No indication that No. 503 has been taken into account [UE 3412/32/71].

No. 504

Letter from Mr. Hayter (Berlin) to Mr. Howard[1]
[F.O. 934/2/9(27)]

BRITISH DELEGATION, BERLIN, *31 July 1945*

Top secret and Personal

Dear Douglas,

The remaining Southern Department questions sunk without trace today.

When we put in our proposed statement about South-Eastern Europe[2] yesterday, of which I sent you a copy, Molotov countered with a paper about Venezia Giulia[3] (copy enclosed). When the question came up at the Plenary today[4] the Russians circulated a further extremely offensive statement about Greece[5] (copy enclosed). This was passed round at the meeting, and the decision was taken on the spot to withdraw our paper on condition

---

[1] The date of receipt is uncertain.
[2] No. 465.
[3] No. 475.
[4] See No. 495, minute 10.
[5] See No. 495, note 28.

that the Russians withdrew both of theirs, which they were not unnaturally quite ready to do.

The President circulated at the Plenary a paper on Control Commissions in Roumania, Bulgaria and Hungary[4] (copy enclosed). The Russians said they had not had time to consider it. We could accept it as it stands, subject possible to the addition of an extra paragraph extending it to Finland, but I expect that the Russians will probably try to extend it to Italy. This would upset Derick,[6] particuarly the bit about 'prior joint consideration of directives' and I am doubtful whether it will go through.

The paper on Admission to the United Nations was accepted this afternoon.[7] This contains the paragraph about peace treaties with satellites and the establishment of diplomatic relations with them. It also contains a paragraph saying that the Three Governments have no doubt that representatives of the Allied press will enjoy full freedom to report to the world upon developments in Roumania, Bulgaria, Yugoslavia and Finland. This, for what it is worth, is about the only Southern Department point that has gone through at this Conference.

The Americans have also circulated a paper entitled 'The Use of Allied Property for Satellite Reparations or War Trophies'[8] which, with a few amendments, would take care of our complaints about Roumanian oil equipment. It will come up tomorrow, the last day of the Conference, and has about as much chance as a snowball in hell.

Yours ever,
W. HAYTER

[6] Mr. Hoyer Millar.
[7] See No. 495, minute 4.
[8] See No. 451, note 6.

No. 505

Mr. Bevin (Berlin) to Mr. Morrison (Received 1 August, 9.35 a.m.)
No. 311 Target Telegraphic [R 13007/4/19]

Top secret. Immediate   BERLIN, *1 August 1945, 11.30 a.m.*

Private Office from Peck.

Please send following from Prime Minister to Regent of Greece.

Begins:[1]

Your Beatitude must be aware that it is the desire of H.M.G. to assist the Greek people both in restoring their country and in choosing their future régime and Government in conditions of freedom and tranquillity. We hope to see the Varkiza Agreement fully carried out, and we are concerned at reports of right wing excesses in contravention of this Agreement. We attach importance to the execution by Admiral Voulgaris's Government of the measures they have adopted to prevent all violations of the Agreement

[1] The following message (for which cf. No. 557) is printed by Sir L. Woodward, *op. cit.*, vol. v, p. 491.

by extremists either of the right wing or of the left. It is our earnest hope that law and order may be established throughout Greece on a fair and impartial basis, in order that the Greek people may be enabled to express their will as soon as possible.

Ends

No. 506

Brief for Mr. Attlee
[*F.O. 934/1/5(15)*]

[BERLIN,] *1 August 1945*

War Crimes[1]

Please see Onward telegram No. 317 attached.[2]

The difficulties to which the Lord Chancellor refers arise from the fact that Justice Jackson, who is the U.S. Chief Representative and Chief Prosecutor, is very afraid of Soviet methods being adopted at the trials, thus bringing them into discredit. Further, the Americans hold most of the major criminals—(and we hold the rest)—and they are very anxious to be free to try before the International Military Tribunal any person whom they consider to be a major criminal, even though the other prosecutors hold the contrary view.

These facts have led the Americans to drive a very hard bargain in the way of establishing the Court and procedure in accordance with Anglo-Saxon ideas. This is all to the good, but the Soviet representatives, who have throughout been helpful, clearly distrust the Americans. The American threat to withdraw altogether and proceed with trials on their own is backed up by the fact that they hold most of the major criminals and is linked with their desire to have freedom to try anybody they wish.

It would be most helpful if the Prime Minister could have a word with President Truman and say that H.M. Government attach the greatest importance to these trials being conducted on a quadrupartite [*sic*] basis if this is at all possible and that we should not break up into a series of national trials—even by mutual agreement—unless this really proves necessary. The Russians cannot afford to keep out of the trials except on a major point of difference and as we have now agreed that the first and most important trial shall be held at Nuremberg, i.e. in the U.S. Zone, we shall be able to control the procedure and keep it respectable and orderly. There is no real reason why there should be a break at present and if we and the Americans are determined to make the trials a success on a Four-Power basis, there is no reason why we should not succeed.

The major criminals have sinned against all the world and should be tried if possible internationally. A national trial, however well run, would not satisfy public opinion nearly so well either now or in the future.

[1] This brief was initialed at head by Sir A. Cadogan.
[2] Annex below: text supplied from U 5838/29/73.

Mr. Morrison to Mr. Bevin (Berlin: received 31 July, 11.55 p.m.)
No. 317 Onward Telegraphic

Top secret.   Immediate   FOREIGN OFFICE, *31 July 1945, 10.30 p.m.*

Following from Lord Chancellor to Prime Minister.
Trial of Major War Criminals
Your telegram of 30th July (Target No. 283).[3]

Have discussed matters today with Maxwell Fyfe. The differences outstanding could easily be surmounted given goodwill. Insistence on these difficulties by Americans makes me fear that they will be used as an excuse for breaking away from the idea of a joint trial to trials by individual nations. I have invited the representatives to meet me in the immediate future. But if you could do anything at your end to promote goodwill it would greatly assist me.

[3] No. 462.iii.

No. 507

Report of the Special Committee (Berlin)[1]
P. (*Terminal*) 75 [*U 6197/3628/70*]

Top secret   *1 August 1945*

The German Navy and Merchant Marine

Enclosure: (a) Decisions of the Tripartite Conference on Distribution of the German Navy.
(b) Decisions of the Tripartite Conference on Distribution of the German Merchant Marine.

1. The Committee met at 1030, 31st July, 1945, in consideration of above subject. The Committee's recommendations, Enclosure (A) and Enclosure (B), are based upon tentative decisions reached during plenary sessions of the Tripartite Conference beginning 17th July, 1945. These enclosures are drafted in the form of decisions in order to facilitate final action in the plenary session of the Tripartite Conference. [?For] Those parts of the enclosures in which agreed recommendations could not be made the divergent views are set forth in each of the specific paragraphs involved.

2. The Committee feel bound to draw the attention of the Conference to the possibility that any public announcement that German warships are to be divided amongst the Allies may result in the German crews scuttling ships which might be ordered to sail to Allied ports. It is therefore desirable that no announcement of the division of the German Navy be made, at any rate until the expert commission has completed its investigations, which should include the detailed arrangements for carrying out the transfer of ships. A similar delay is necessary before making any definite announcement about the division of the surrendered German merchant ships. The Committee

[1] This report by the committee appointed in No. 469, minute 6, is printed in *F.R.U.S. Berlin*, vol. ii, pp. 980-3, and *Berlinskaya konferentsiya*, pp. 440-4.

accordingly recommend that the Conference might confine publicity to the following announcement:

'The Conference agreed in principle upon arrangements for the use and disposal of the surrendered German Fleet and merchant ships. It was decided that the Three Governments would appoint experts to work out together detailed plans to give effect to the agreed principles. A further joint statement will be published simultaneously by the Three Governments in due course.'

N. G. KUZNETSOV,
Admiral of the Fleet,
U.S.S.R. Navy

C. M. COOKE, JR.,
Vice-Admiral,
United States Navy

E. D. B. McCARTHY,
Rear-Admiral,
Royal Navy

ENCLOSURE A IN No. 507
Decisions of the Tripartite Conference on Distribution of the German Navy

1. The Tripartite Conference agree upon the following principles for the distribution of the German Navy:

(*a*) The total strength of the German surface navy, excluding ships sunk and those taken over from Allied Nations, but including ships under construction or repair, shall be divided equally among the U.S.S.R, United Kingdom, and United States.

(1) (The British representatives expressed the view that a portion of the German Navy should be allotted to France and that, therefore, full agreement with the above principle must be subject to final decision of the Plenary Conference.)

(*b*) Ships under construction or repair mean those ships whose construction or repair may be completed within three to six months, according to the type of ship. Whether such ships under construction or repair shall be completed or repaired shall be determined by the technical commission appointed by the Three Powers and referred to below, subject to the principle that their completion or repair must be achieved within the time limits above provided, without any increase of skilled employment in the German shipyards and without permitting the reopening of any German shipbuilding or connected industries. Completion date means the date when a ship is able to go out on its first trip, or, under peace-time standards, would refer to the customary date of delivery by shipyard to the Government.

(*c*) The larger part of the German submarine fleet shall be sunk. The Committee are not able to make a recommendation as regards the number of submarines to be preserved for experimental and technical purposes.

(1) It is the opinion of the British and American members that not more than 30 submarines shall be preserved and divided equally between the U.S.S.R., United Kingdom, and United States for experimental and technical purposes. Paragraph 1 (*a*) (1) also applies to submarines.

(2) It is the view of the Russian members that this number is too small for

their requirements and that U.S.S.R. should receive about 30 submarines for its own experimental and technical purposes.

(*d*) All stocks of armaments, ammunition and supplies of the German Navy appertaining to the vessels transferred pursuant to sub-paragraphs (*a*) and (*c*) hereof shall be handed over to the respective Powers receiving such ships.

(*e*) The Three Governments agree to constitute a tripartite naval commission comprising two representatives for each Government, accompanied by the requisite staff, to submit agreed recommendations to the Three Governments for the allocation of specific German warships and to handle other detailed matters arising out of the agreement between the Three Governments regarding the German fleet. The Commission will hold its first meeting not later than the 15th August, 1945, in Berlin, which shall be its headquarters. Each delegation on the Commission will have the right on the basis of reciprocity to inspect German warships wherever they may be located.

(*f*) The Three Governments agree that transfers, including those of ships under construction and repair, shall be completed as soon as possible, but not later than the 15th February, 1946. The Commission will submit fortnightly reports, including proposals for the progressive allocation of the vessels when agreed by the Commission.

Enclosure B in No. 507

Decisions of the Tripartite Conference on Distribution of the German Merchant Marine.

1. The Tripartite Conference agree upon the following principles for the distribution of the German Merchant Marine:–

(*a*) (1) It is proposed by the Soviet and American representatives: The German Merchant Marine, surrendered to the Three Powers and wherever located, shall be divided equally among the U.S.S.R., the United Kingdom, and the United States. The actual transfers of the ships to the respective countries shall take place as soon as practicable after the end of the war against Japan. This distribution shall not preclude any of the Parties from making further allocation of part of its share to other Allied Nations.

(2) The British representatives considered it essential to allot a share of not less than one quarter to the lesser maritime Allied States whose merchant marines have lost so heavily in support of the common cause against Germany. Accordingly, the British Delegation proposed the following alternative draft of sub-paragraph (*a*) (1):–

'One quarter of the German merchant marine surrendered to the Three Powers and wherever located shall be allotted to the Soviet Union and the remainder shall be divided between the United Kingdom and the United States who will provide an appropriate share to the Allied States whose merchant marines have suffered substantial losses in support of the common cause against Germany. The actual transfers of the ships to the respective countries shall take place as soon as practicable after the end of the war against Japan.'

(*b*) The allocation, manning, and operation of these ships during the Japanese War period shall fall under the cognisance and authority of the Combined Shipping Adjustment Board and the United Maritime Authority.

(*c*) While actual transfer of the ships shall be delayed until after the end of the war with Japan, a Tripartite Shipping Commission shall inventory and value all available ships and recommend a specific distribution in accordance with sub-paragraph (*a*) (as approved).

(*d*) The British and American representatives propose the following sub-paragraph:–

'German inland and coastal ships determined to be necessary to the maintenance of the basic German peace economy by the Allied Control Council of Germany shall not be included in the shipping pool thus divided among the Three Powers.'

The Soviet representatives do not agree to this inclusion.

(*e*) The Three Governments agree to constitute a tripartite merchant marine commission comprising two representatives for each Government, accompanied by the requisite staff, to submit agreed recommendations to the Three Governments for the allocation of specific German merchant ships and to handle other detailed matters arising out of the agreement between the Three Governments regarding the German merchant ships. The Commission will hold its first meeting not later than the 1st September, 1945, in Berlin, which shall be its headquarters. Each delegation on the Commission will have the right on the basis of reciprocity to inspect the German merchant ships wherever they may be located.

(*f*) (The British representatives suggested the need to add the following provision:

'The shares of the various Allied States will be counted as reparation receipts.'

The Soviet Delegation considered that this was unnecessary in view of the new policy agreed by the Conference on reparations.

The American representatives took no position in this matter.)

No. 508

Letter from Sir D. Waley (Berlin) to Sir W. Eady
[*T 236/265: OF 213/3/2f*]

BERLIN, *1 August 1945*

My dear Wilfrid,

I dictated the enclosed letter[1] early yesterday, but I did not get back to my desk again until after midnight so it was never sent off. The enclosed draft,[2] though not finally settled, shows what has been decided about German Reparation. The more we thought about that particular view in the American Plan which consists in swapping potatoes from Brandenberg as against steel plant in the Ruhr, the less we liked it. But Ministers decided that we should have to accept it, since the Americans had sold the idea to Molotov and could not be persuaded to alter it. Though it is based on a philosophy quite inconsistent with treating Germany as an economic unit, I do not think that it is really a deciding factor as to whether Germany will

[1] No. 485.
[2] Annex to No. 498.

be so treated or not. That will depend how the Control Council works in practice.

It is a good thing that we have secured a decision that the plan for removing industrial equipment should be drawn up by the Allied Reparation Commission and the Control Council jointly. It is also a good thing that France is to become a member of the Allied Commission on Reparations and also that it has been decided that Austria is not to pay reparations.

Forgive a short letter as I am just off to a series of meetings which will no doubt, as usual, last until midnight.

Yours ever,

p.p. S. D. WALEY[3]

CALENDAR TO No. 508

i *30 July & 1 Aug. 1945 Correspondence between Sir W. Eady and Sir D. Waley (Berlin).* American attitude and intentions on feeding of Berlin [T 236/264–5].

[3] Signature inserted on original over unidentified initials.

No. 509

Record of Eleventh Meeting of Foreign Secretaries held at Cecilienhof, Potsdam, on Wednesday, 1 August 1945 at 11 a.m.

F. (*Terminal*) *11th Meeting* [*U 6197/3628/70*]

Top secret

Present:

M. V. M. MOLOTOV, M. A. Ya. Vyshinski, M. A. A. Gromyko, M. F. T. Gousev, M. K. V. Novikov, M. A. A. Sobolev, M. B. F. Podtzerob, Admiral N. G. Kuznetzov, M. V. N. Pavlov (*Interpreter*).

MR. J. F. BYRNES, Mr. W. A. Harriman, Mr. J. C. Dunn, Mr. H. F. Matthews, Mr. B. V. Cohen, Mr. E. Page (*Interpreter*).

MR. BEVIN, Sir A. Cadogan, Sir W. Strang, Sir E. Bridges, Mr. N. Brook, Mr. P. J. Dixon, Mr. W. Hayter, Major L. M. Theakstone (*Interpreter*).

Contents

8. Fascist Activities in Germany and Austria
9. Repatriation of Soviet Citizens
10. Preparation of Protocol
11. Yalta Declaration on Liberated Europe: Procedure of Control Commissions in Bulgaria, Hungary and Roumania
12. Facilities for Radio Correspondents
13. Council of Foreign Ministers
14. German Fleet and Merchant Navy
15. Agenda for the Plenary Meeting.

1. *Reparations: Germany*
(Previous Reference: P. (Terminal) 11th Meeting,[1] Minute 2.)

Mr. Byrnes asked whether a report had been submitted by the Committee appointed at the Plenary Meeting on the previous day to prepare a note of the agreement reached on Reparations.

M. Vyshinski said that the Committee were not yet ready to report.

It was agreed that this report should be made to the Plenary Meeting that afternoon.

2. *Germany: Economic Problems*
(Previous Reference: P. (Terminal) 11th Meeting,[1] Minute 5.)

Mr. Byrnes asked whether the Economic Committee had yet reported on the questions outstanding on the draft Statement of Economic Principles.

M. Molotov said that this report was not yet ready.

It was agreed that this report should be submitted to the Plenary Meeting that afternoon.

3. *War Crimes*
(Previous Reference: P. (Terminal) 11th Meeting,[1] Minute 11.)

Mr. Byrnes said that the only question outstanding on this subject was whether the redraft (P. (Terminal) 71)[2] put forward by the United Kingdom Delegation should be modified by adding the names of some of the war criminals who would shortly be put on trial.

Mr. Bevin said that the British Delegation were not in favour of including in this statement the names of specific war criminals. The most effective way of meeting this point would be for the three Powers to ensure that all possible measures were taken to get the trials started at the earliest moment.

Mr. Byrnes said that the determination of those war criminals who were to be tried had been left to the selected prosecutors, and he felt that this responsibility should not be taken away from them. He therefore urged that names should not be included in the statement.

M. Molotov said that this point must be decided by the Plenary Meeting.

4. *Allied Property in Satellite Countries: Seizure as Reparations or War Trophies*

Mr. Byrnes suggested that the meeting should discuss the memorandum

[1] No. 495.
[2] See No. 495, minute 11.

1107

(P. (Terminal) 49)[3] which the United States Delegation had submitted on this subject on the 25th July. The United States Delegation were not asking for discussion of the Memorandum (P. (Terminal) 48)[3] which they had submitted on the same day on Removals from Germany of Properties of United Nations or Neutral Nationals.

M. MOLOTOV agreed that this was an important matter, but suggested that it should first be considered by a Committee.

It was agreed that a Committee should be set up as follows:

United States Delegation: Mr. Russell, Mr. Cannon.

Soviet Delegation: M. Gousev, M. Arkadyev.

British Delegation: Mr. Turner, Mr. Coulson.

to examine and report on the United States Memorandum (P. (Terminal) 49).[3]

5. *German External Assets*
(Previous Reference: F. (Terminal) 10th Meeting,[4] Minute 7.)

MR. BYRNES said that the Memorandum on this subject by the United States Delegation (P. (Terminal) 56)[5] was still before the Economic Committee. Discussion of this question must, therefore, be deferred.

6. *European Oil Supplies*
(Previous Reference: F. (Terminal) 9th Meeting,[6] Minute 6.)

MR. BYRNES said that the Memorandum (P. (Terminal) 18)[7] submitted by the United States Delegation on this matter was also before the Economic Committee, who were still awaiting the views of the Soviet representative. Consideration of this matter must, therefore, be deferred.

7. *Roumania: Removal of Allied Industrial Equipment*
(Previous Reference: F. (Terminal) 9th Meeting,[6] Minute 8.)

MR. BEVIN said that proposals for dealing with this question had been put forward by the British Delegation (P. (Terminal) 40)[8] and by the Soviet Delegation (P. (Terminal) 46).[9] The difference between the two proposals was that, while the British had wished to refer the matter to arbitration by a Committee of three Allied Nationals drawn from States not interested in the dispute, the Russians had now proposed a joint investigation by Russian and British representatives. He preferred the British proposal for an independent investigation. He feared that reference to an Anglo-Russian Commission of investigation would only result in transferring the dispute to a lower level.

M. MOLOTOV said that discussions on this question had hitherto been conducted through diplomatic channels. He now proposed the appointment of Russian and British representatives to investigate on the spot in Roumania the relevant documents and facts. So far these had not been examined. He hoped that a settlement might be reached after this examina-

[3] See No. 451, note 6.   [4] No. 469.   [5] See No. 469, note 16.
[6] No. 431.   [7] See No. 214, note 10.   [8] No. 264.   [9] No. 432.

tion, but, if not, other methods of resolving the difficulty could then be considered.

MR. BYRNES said that when this question had first been raised by the British Delegation, he had drawn attention to the fact that it also affected the property of United States companies in Roumania.[10] It would therefore be necessary for a United States representative to participate in the investigation on the spot.

M. MOLOTOV suggested that there should be two separate Commissions of investigation—one consisting of Russian and United States representatives to examine the claims concerning United States property, and the other consisting of Russian and British representatives to examine the claims concerning British property.

MR. BYRNES agreed. For many weeks United States oil experts had been waiting in Roumania, but so far they had not reached any agreement with the Russian experts. He thought that a date should be fixed for the first meeting of these Commissions, and suggested that they should begin their work not later than the 10th August.

In reply to questions by Mr. Bevin and Mr. Byrnes, M. MOLOTOV stated that these Commissions would not be limited to the examination of documents only, but would also be given all facilities for examining the property and other relevant facts on the spot.

> It was agreed that the three Governments should take immediate steps to appoint representatives to act on Commissions of investigation to examine documents and facts relating to the claims put forward by the British and United States Governments as regards the removal of Allied industrial equipment in Roumania. The Commissions should begin their work not later than the 10th August, and would be provided with all the facilities for carrying out a full examination on the spot.

8. *Fascist Activities in Germany and Austria*
(Previous Reference: F. (Terminal) 10th Meeting,[4] Minute 11.)

M. MOLOTOV asked whether the British and United States Delegations were yet in a position to reply to the points raised in the Memorandum (P. (Terminal) 44)[11] which the Soviet Delegation had submitted on this question. If not, would it be possible to place it on record that the British and United States Delegations would institute an urgent investigation into this matter and would take measures to prevent the continuance of the activities of which complaint was made?

MR. BEVIN said that it had been agreed at the Crimea Conference that the British and United States Governments would take steps to prevent any action which was hostile to the Soviet Union in the British and American zones of Germany and Austria. If the Soviet Government had reason to believe that such activities were being carried on, and brought this to the notice of the British or United States Government, as they had done in this

---

[10] See No. 224, minute 4. [11] See No. 276, note 1.

case, then it was the duty of those Governments to act in accordance with their undertakings at the Crimea Conference. In the present case enquiries had been instituted, and if the complaints proved to be well founded appropriate action would be taken. He hoped that M. Molotov would be satisfied with this assurance.

M. MOLOTOV said that he accepted Mr. Bevin's statement of the position.

9. *Repatriation of Soviet Citizens*
(a) *Soviet Citizens from the Baltic, Western Ukraine and Byelo-russia*
(Previous Reference: F. (Terminal) 10th Meeting,[4] Minute 13.)

M. MOLOTOV drew attention to the memorandum on this subject (P. (Terminal) 60)[12] which had been circulated by the Soviet Delegation.

MR. BEVIN said that this was a matter which could appropriately be handled through the diplomatic channels. He had asked the authorities in London to make immediate enquiries, and he would send a reply to the Soviet Government as soon as he got back to London.[13]

M. MOLOTOV said that he was satisfied with Mr. Bevin's statement.

(b) *Interpretation of the Yalta Agreement: Access to Camps*

M. MOLOTOV said that he was about to circulate another paper indicating that the Yalta Agreement on the repatriation of Soviet citizens was not being fully observed.[14] Many Soviet citizens had not yet returned home, in spite of the fact that the war had ended some months ago. The Soviet Government wished to be assured that their representatives for repatriation would be admitted to all camps in which Soviet citizens were held by the British or United States authorities.

MR. BYRNES said that the United States military authorities had been doing everything in their power to help Soviet citizens to return home. They had no interest in retaining them, as they already had enough people to feed in their zone. M. Molotov could therefore rest assured that the United States authorities would do everything possible to facilitate the return of Soviet citizens to Russia.

[12] No. 473.
[13] Mr. Bevin replied to No. 473 in a note of 25 August 1945 (on N 9621/409/38) from the Foreign Office to M. Gousev. Mr. Bevin there stated: 'As you are aware, His Majesty's Government have not yet recognized the incorporation of these territories into the Union of Soviet Socialist Republics, and their policy with regard to displaced persons from these territories is to permit the repatriation of all those who are willing to return home via the U.S.S.R., but not to force any of them to return to their homes if they express reluctance to do so. I regret therefore that I am unable to comply with Monsieur Molotov's request that all the persons displaced from these territories should be handed over to the Soviet repatriation authorities. No obstacles will be placed in the way of displaced persons from these territories who wish to be repatriated, and instructions are already in force that they shall be handed over to the Soviet authorities; but those who are reluctant to return home will not be compelled to do so and will not be handed over to the Soviet authorities.'
[14] This paper has been traced in Foreign Office archives only in a Russian text dated July 1945 as in the translation printed in *F.R.U.S. Berlin*, vol. ii, pp. 1165–6. A Russian text is printed under date of 1 August in *Berlinskaya konferentsiya*, p. 445.

Mr. Byrnes and Mr. Bevin undertook to give careful consideration to the memorandum which M. Molotov was proposing to circulate on this subject.

10. *Preparation of Protocol*
(Previous Reference: F. (Terminal) 8th Meeting,[15] Minute 3.)
Mr. Byrnes said that the Committee which had been appointed to prepare a draft Protocol of the Conference had found themselves unable to agree on a number of points. These, he thought, would have to be resolved by the Foreign Secretaries.

(a) *Trusteeship Territories*
Mr. Byrnes said that, although the memorandum submitted by the Soviet Delegation on this subject[16] had dealt with the general question of trusteeship, discussion at the Conference had been limited to the question of the disposal of the Italian colonies. It had been pointed out that the question whether any of the former Italian colonies should be restored to Italy was bound to arise in the course of the work which the new Council of Foreign Ministers would have to do in preparation for the peace treaties. It had, therefore, been noted that the question of Italian territories would be considered by the Council of Foreign Ministers at their meeting in September. A draft paragraph to this effect had been prepared by the British and United States Delegations for inclusion in the Protocol [i]. The Soviet representative on the Committee was, however, unable to accept this draft. He had understood it to be the intention of the Conference that the Council of Foreign Ministers should consider, not only the disposition of the Italian colonies, but also the general issues regarding territorial trusteeship which had been raised in the memorandum by the Soviet Delegation.

M. Molotov said that he did not wish to press the point which had been put forward by the Soviet representative on the Committee. He would be prepared to accept the draft paragraph which had been agreed between the British and United States Delegations, provided that the opening words were amended so as to read: 'The Conference considered a proposal by the Soviet Government on the question of trusteeship territories . . .'[17]

(b) *Black Sea Straits*
M. Molotov said that he was prepared to accept the wording for this paragraph which had been proposed by the British and United States Delegations.

(c) *Western Frontier of U.S.S.R.*
Mr. Byrnes said that on the draft of this paragraph there were several points of difference; but all of these were related to the desire of the British and United States Delegations to make it clear that there would be no actual

[15] No. 274.
[16] No. 203.
[17] Punctuation as in original quotation.

transfer of territory in advance of the peace settlement. It was most important that there should be no ambiguity on this point; and the United States Delegation had been disturbed by the Soviet objections to the inclusion of the word 'provisionally' in the first paragraph, and the words 'subject to expert examination of the actual frontier' in the second paragraph.

M. MOLOTOV said that on the substance of this question there was no misunderstanding between the three Delegations. The Soviet Delegation fully accepted the position that there could be no actual transfer of territory in advance of the peace settlement and, further, that the actual frontier could not be delimited in detail without expert examination on the spot.

After discussion, it was agreed that the outstanding points of difference on this draft could be removed by the following changes—(i) For the title substitute 'City of Koenigsberg and the adjacent area'; (ii) In the first paragraph, omit the word 'provisionally'; and (iii) For the last paragraph substitute: 'The President of the United States and the British Prime Minister have declared that they will support the proposal of the Conference at the forthcoming peace settlement.'

(d) Austria

M. MOLOTOV said he would be prepared to accept the first two sentences of the draft prepared by the British and United States Delegations, if those Delegations would agree to delete the third sentence of the draft. This reference to interim arrangements for feeding the civil population of Vienna was not an essential part of the paragraph and was not, in his view, suitable for inclusion in the Protocol.

It was agreed to omit the third sentence of this draft.

MR. BYRNES suggested that it should be an instruction to the Committee that the Protocol should not cover all the matters discussed at the Conference, but should include only matters of some importance on which decisions had been taken. M. MOLOTOV agreed.

It was agreed that the Drafting Committee should continue their work on the basis indicated above.

11. *Yalta Declaration on Liberated Europe: Procedure of Control Commissions in Bulgaria, Hungary and Roumania*
(Previous Reference: F. (Terminal 7th Meeting,[18] Minute 1.)

MR. BYRNES recalled that at their meeting on the 22nd July, the Foreign Secretaries had appointed a Committee to consider, *inter alia*, modifications of the procedure of the Control Commissions in Roumania, Bulgaria and Hungary. The Committee had not been able to reach agreement on all the matters referred to them, but he asked that the Foreign Secretaries should now consider the following draft of a statement on the procedure of these Control Commissions:

'1. The Three Governments have taken note that the Soviet Representatives on the Allied Control Commissions in Roumania, Bulgaria and

[18] No. 254.

Hungary, have communicated to their United Kingdom and United States colleagues proposals for improving the work of the Control Commissions now that hostilities in Europe have ceased.

'2. These proposals include provisions for regular and frequent meetings of the three representatives, improved facilities for British and American representatives, and prior joint consideration of directives.

'3. The Three Governments agree that the revision of the procedures of the Allied Control Commissions in these countries will now be undertaken, using as a basis of discussion the above-mentioned proposals, and taking into account the interests and responsibilities of the three Governments which together presented the terms of armistice to the respective countries.'

M. Molotov said that the second paragraph of this draft did not accurately reflect the position, and suggested that it should be omitted.

Mr. Byrnes said that the United States members of the Allied Control Commissions in Roumania, Bulgaria and Hungary had met with many difficulties. There had not been regular meetings of the Commissions, nor did the United States representatives receive advance notice of the issue of directives. He therefore urged that paragraph 2 of the draft should be retained, as it contained precisely the assurances which were required.

M. Molotov said that, if Mr. Byrnes was not prepared to omit paragraph 2, it would be necessary to amend it so as to correspond more exactly with the precise proposals which the Soviet authorities had put forward, e.g., for the procedure of the Allied Control Commission for Hungary (see P. (Terminal) 81).[19] Thus, the draft statement referred to 'regular and frequent meetings.' The actual proposal made in respect of the Commission for Hungary was that 'meetings should be called once every ten days, and in case of necessity even more often.'

After some further discussion, Mr. Bevin suggested that the statement should incorporate the detailed proposals for the procedure of the Control Commission for Hungary, provided that these would also apply to the Commissions for Bulgaria and Roumania.

M. Molotov agreed that the proposals put forward by the Soviet authorities in respect of Hungary should also apply to Bulgaria and Roumania.

It was agreed that a drafting Committee, consisting of:

United States Delegation: Mr. Russell, Mr. Cannon;
Soviet Delegation: M. Lavrishtchev, M. Novikov;
British Delegation: Mr. Hoyer Millar;

should prepare a revised draft statement on the Allied Control Commission procedure in Roumania, Bulgaria and Hungary, which should include paragraphs 1 and 3 of the United States Memorandum quoted

---

[19] Not printed. Under the heading 'Hungary: system of work for the Allied Control Commission' this document of 1 August 1945 comprised the 'Text of a letter transmitted on 12th July to the Representatives of the United States and United Kingdom Governments on the Allied Control Commission in Hungary' as cited in No. 518, minute 7.

above, and should incorporate the substance of paragraphs 3–5 of the Soviet proposals for Control Commission procedure in Hungary (P. (Terminal) 81).[19]

12. *Facilities for Radio Correspondents*
(Previous Reference: P. (Terminal) 5th Meeting,[20] Minute 4; P. (Terminal) 11th Meeting,[1] Minute 4.)

MR. BYRNES said that the statements which the Conference had agreed to issue on Poland and on the admission of neutral and ex-enemy States to the United Nations, declared that 'representatives of the Allied Press shall enjoy full freedom to report to the world upon developments . . .'[17] He suggested that in both these statements the words 'and radio' should be added, after 'Allied Press,' so as to make it quite clear that the facilities to be granted to Press correspondents would also be extended to radio reporters.

M. MOLOTOV said that, in some countries, radio undertakings were owned by Governments, while the Press was privately controlled. The same rules could not, therefore, be applied to both in every case. He suggested that the agreement about the Press should remain as it now stood. As regards the radio, there would be neither permission nor prohibition: each case would be decided on its merits. The decision would vary in different countries. For instance, the Russians would not permit a Hearst radio correspondent to speak on the Moscow radio. The question of freedom for radio reporting raised many difficulties, and he did not think it could be dealt with in general words in these two statements.

MR. BYRNES said that he would raise this question at the Plenary Meeting that afternoon.

13. *Council of Foreign Ministers*
(Previous Reference: P. (Terminal) 5th Meeting,[20] Minute 2.)

MR. BYRNES said that he had just been informed that the Chinese Government had accepted the invitation to join the Council of Foreign Ministers.

14. *German Fleet and Merchant Navy*
(Previous Reference: P. (Terminal) 11th Meeting,[1] Minute 9.)

The meeting considered the report (P. (Terminal) 75)[21] of the Committee appointed to prepare detailed recommendations on this question.

MR. BYRNES said that the first question on which agreement had not been reached in the Committee was the distribution of *warships*.

M. MOLOTOV recalled that it had already been decided at a Plenary Meeting (P. (Terminal) 3rd Meeting,[22] Minute 6) that the German warships should be divided into three parts.

MR. BEVIN said that, as regards the warships, he was prepared to agree to a division into thirds.

[20] No. 219.   [21] No. 507.   [22] No. 194.

On *submarines*, Mr. Bevin said that the question was how many should be destroyed. Mr. Churchill had said that only a token number should be retained. The British and United States Delegations suggested that only 30 submarines should be preserved. This was a matter on which the British people felt very strongly, since no less than 30,000 British seamen had lost their lives during the war by U-boat warfare alone while carrying supplies by sea to Russia and elsewhere. On this point the British and United States Delegations were not prepared to make any concession. No German submarines should be retained except for experimental purposes, and in his opinion 30 was adequate for those purposes.

M. Molotov said he was prepared to agree.

On the question of the German *merchant marine*, Mr. Bevin said that the British Delegation were anxious to ensure that Germany should retain a reasonable amount of shipping for the purpose of carrying on the minimum essential economic life of the country. He proposed that the Control Council should decide what shipping was required for this purpose, in terms of tonnage and types. The balance remaining should then be divided into thirds, on the understanding that the Soviet Government would allot a fair proportion to Poland out of the Soviet third, while Great Britain and the United States would allot from their share a proportion for France and other Allied countries.

M. Molotov pointed out that the proposals contained in P. (Terminal) 75[21] did not mention specific countries. He was unwilling to assume this special responsibility for Poland.

Mr. Bevin said that he wished to limit the liability of the British and United States Governments to allot from their shares to other Allied countries. He thought that their liability should be specifically limited to meeting the claims of France, Greece, Norway, Holland and Belgium. If the Soviet Government would look after Poland, the British and United States would look after the claims of these other Allies.

M. Molotov said that he understood that the Three Powers had already covered this point in their agreement on reparations.

Mr. Bevin replied that he wished to make it quite clear that in his view what was now under discussion was the distribution of booty, not of reparations.

He pointed out that, of the total shipping losses suffered by the Allies during the war, Great Britain had suffered 48 per cent., the United States 15 per cent., Norway $10\frac{1}{2}$ per cent., France 7 per cent., Poland [Holland] $5\frac{1}{2}$ per cent., and the U.S.S.R. 1 per cent.

M. Molotov thought there must be some misunderstanding about this. He could not accept this last figure. What was the corresponding figure for Poland?

Mr. Bevin said that Poland's losses were about the same as those of Holland. He wished to present to the Conference a fair interpretation of Mr. Churchill's undertaking at the previous meeting at which this matter had been discussed (P. (Terminal) 3rd Meeting,[22] Minute 6) and he was therefore willing to accept the division into thirds if he received a definite undertaking that Poland should have her proper proportion of this booty from the share allotted to the U.S.S.R. Great Britain would then undertake, with the assistance of the United States, to deal with claims from Norway, France, Holland, Belgium and Greece.

M. MOLOTOV said that as Yugoslavia was an Ally, she would be offended if she were left out. Great Britain and the United States should make an allotment to her also.

MR. BEVIN replied that he must leave the Soviet Union to make any allotment which was necessary to Yugoslavia. After our tremendous losses, he did not think that we could meet any further claims from our own share.

MR. BYRNES said that he was doubtful whether it was wise to enumerate the Allied countries who should be recognised as claimants to a share. He thought that to do so would be to invite other countries to file claims; for example, certain South American countries had lost some shipping.

M. MOLOTOV said that he wondered whether this proposal would leave the Soviet Union with any ships, since they were to be used first in the war against Japan.

MR. BYRNES replied that, although nobody could say definitely what would be left after the Japanese war, he knew from information which was also supplied to the Soviet and British Governments, that we were not losing very many ships at present in the Japanese war and he thought the prospect was less gloomy than M. Molotov suggested. If the Soviet Union had only to undertake to allot a share to Poland they would have quite a satisfactory proportion left for themselves.

MR. BEVIN said that, if the Soviet Government would agree that Poland should get the same percentage of the allotment made to the U.S.S.R. as Great Britain would give to the other Allies, then he would undertake to be responsible for Yugoslav claims, since he wished to get the matter settled.

M. MOLOTOV said that he must reserve the position of the Soviet Government on this point.

It was agreed:

(1) that the German Navy should be divided equally between the Three Powers;

(2) that thirty submarines should be retained for distribution among the Three Powers, and the remainder destroyed;

(3) that the draft announcement in P. (Terminal) 75[21] should be approved;

(4) that the outstanding point about the allotment of the merchant marine to the other Allies should be submitted to the Plenary Meeting that afternoon.

15. *Agenda for the Plenary Meeting*

It was agreed that in addition to those subjects, which at the present meeting had been remitted for decision by the Heads of Governments, the two following points should be submitted:

(1) *External Assets of Germany.*—Report from the Economic Sub-Committee on P. (Terminal) 56.[5]
(2) *The Additional Article 19 of the Economic Principles*[23] upon which the Economic Sub-Committee had failed to reach agreement.

Cabinet Office, Potsdam, 1st August, 1945

CALENDAR TO No. 509

i   *30 July 1945   Third revise of draft protocol* discussed in minute 10 above
(cf. *F.R.U.S. Berlin*, vol. ii, pp. 1594–1600) [CAB 21/864].

[23] See No. 495, minute 5.

No. 510

Letter[1] from Mr. Harrison (Berlin) to Mr. Troutbeck (Received 2 August)
[C 4415/95/18]

BRITISH DELEGATION, BERLIN, *1 August 1945*

My dear Jack,

Transfers of German Populations

You will have seen from the records of the Conference that a Sub-Committee was set up on July 25th consisting of Sobolev, Cannon and myself 'to consider and report to the Foreign Secretaries' meeting what practical arrangements could be made for regulating transfer of populations in Europe, consequent on the defeat of Germany'.[2]

The Sub-Committee met three times, taking as a basis of discussion a draft which I circulated.

I attach a copy of the document[3] as it finally emerged. The negotiations were not easy—no negotiations with the Russians ever are—but I hope the result will not be too unsatisfactory. William Strang and General Weeks are content.

We had a great struggle, which had to be taken up to the Plenary Meeting, about including the last three and a half lines. Sobolev took the view that the Polish and Czechoslovak wish to expel their German populations was the fulfilment of an historic mission which the Soviet Government were unwilling to try to impede. The view of the Soviet Government was that it was the function of the Allied Control Council in Germany to facilitate the reception of the transfer[r]ed populations as rapidly as possible. Cannon and I naturally strongly opposed this view. We made it clear that we did

---

[1] Reproduced by Alfred de Zayas, *Nemesis at Potsdam: the Anglo-Americans and the expulsion of the Germans: background, execution, consequences* (Revised ed., London, 1979), pp. 232–4.
[2] See No. 274, minute 2.
[3] For this document—P. (Terminal) 74, not printed–see No. 495, note 23.

not like the idea of mass transfers anyway. As, however, we could not prevent them, we wished to ensure that they were carried out in as orderly and humane a manner as possible and in a way which would not throw an intolerable burden on the occupying authorities in Germany. Uncle Joe finally agreed to join in requesting the Polish and Czech Governments and the Control Council for Hungary to suspend expulsions until the report of the Allied Control Council in Germany was available. This may prevent mass expulsions for the time being, but I have no doubt that hundreds of Germans will continue to move westwards daily. Fortunately, the Russians and the Americans will bear the first brunt of the influx.

We did our best to get some reference to the absorptive capacity of Germany, but here the Russians dug their toes in, on the grounds that they at all events have no doubt whatsoever about Germany's capacity to absorb millions of transferees. The position is to some extent safeguarded by the phrase in paragraph 2 'having regard to the present situation in Germany'.

I think one thing was established at this Conference, namely that the problem is now not going to be anything like on the scale we had originally foreseen. The Poles claim that there are only one to one and a half million Germans of whom they wish to dispose left in the area they are taking over up to the Oder-Neisse line. Benes has two and a half millions and there are a quarter of a million Schwaben. This makes a grand total of under four millions. Goodness knows this will be a big enough problem, and of course the millions of Germans who lived east of the Oder must have got somewhere. But people who have been in Germany have got the impression, rightly or wrongly, that there are fewer Germans in the Reich than had been supposed. Everyone agrees that one of the very first things to be done, as soon as possible, is to take a census, however rough and ready it may be.

You will have seen from telegrams[4] which I sent off this morning to Paris, Prague and Warsaw that H.M. Representatives in those countries are being instructed to concert in communicating to the French, Polish and Czechoslovak Governments the text of the Agreement.[3] The French are being invited to send appropriate instructions, after the conclusion of the Conference, to the Commander-in-Chief of the French forces of occupation in Germany.

It will in addition be necessary for us to communicate the text of the Agreement officially to Field-Marshal Montgomery and request him to concert with his colleagues on the Control Council in implementing it. I presume the War Office should do this as soon as possible. Will you bring this to their attention?

The War Office should also be moved to inform our Representative on the Allied Control Commission in Hungary of the Berlin Agreement unless

---

[4] Nos. 313 and 314 Target of 1 August 1945, not printed. At 5 p.m. that day Mr. Duff Cooper communicated a note to M. Bidault as there instructed. Cf. *F.R.U.S. Berlin*, vol. ii, pp. 1945–6.

this could be done through Joe Gascoigne (your letter C 4026/95/18 of July 22nd).[5]

Yours ever
GEOFFREY HARRISON

CALENDAR TO No. 510

i   *2 Aug. 1945   Mr. Hankey (Warsaw) Tel. No. 87; Mr. Murray (Prague) Tel. No. 310.* Reactions of Polish and Czechoslovak Foreign Ministers respectively to British communication of agreement on transfer of German populations [C 4422, 4445/95/18].

[5] Not printed.

No. 511

Letter from President Truman to Mr. Attlee (Berlin)
[*PREM 8/109*]

THE WHITE HOUSE, WASHINGTON, AT BABELSBERG (BERLIN), *1 August 1945*

Dear Mr. Prime Minister:

I have your letter[1] with regard to the new weapon to be used on Japan. It seems to me to be all right, although I have not compared it carefully with our proposed statement. I think you are very generous to release Mr. Churchill's statement *in toto*. I take it that is what we agreed on.

I shall be most happy to see you during the day, at the Conference, or at any other time that is suitable to you.

It certainly has been a very great pleasure to be associated with you in this Conference, and I am exceedingly happy that our two countries are so thoroughly in agreement on policies for world peace.[2]

Sincerely yours,
HARRY S TRUMAN

[1] No. 502.
[2] Mr. Rowan remitted this letter to Mr. Attlee under cover of the following minute of even date: 'Attached is a reply from the President about T.A., together with a reply to him for your consideration. The President's first paragraph is not absolutely clear, but at this afternoon's meeting you will no doubt clear up with him the following points:—
(*a*) Whether Stalin has cross examined the President at all (see flag 'A' [cf. No. 481]).
(*b*) Whether you may assume that our statement is approved, or whether the President will send you a further communication. (*c*) Try to ascertain when roughly the President thinks the statement will be issued. T. L. R.' The following was noted by Mr. Rowan in the margin against (*a*) 'No', (*b*) 'O.K.' (*c*) 'Next few days.'

No. 512

Letter from Mr. Attlee to President Truman (Berlin)[1]
[PREM 8/109]

BERLIN, *1 August 1945*

Dear Mr. President,

Thank you so much for your letter of to-day[2] about the new weapon to be used on Japan. If it is quite convenient to you, I will come to see you for a few minutes after the Plenary Session this afternoon.

I am deeply touched by the very kind words you use about me and I, too, have been greatly encouraged by the unity which exists between our two countries on policies for world peace. I shall work with all my strength to maintain this unity unimpaired during the difficult years which lie before us.

May I also thank you warmly for the great personal consideration and kindness which you have shown to me and which has been such a help, specially during these last few days.

Yrs sincerely
C. R. A.

---

[1] Printed in *F.R.U.S. Berlin*, vol. ii, p. 1375.
[2] No. 511.

No. 513

Mr. Morrison to Mr. Bevin (Berlin: received 1 August, 4.10 p.m.)
No. 327 Onward Telegraphic [N 8946/6/55]

Immediate　　　　　　　FOREIGN OFFICE, *1 August 1945, 12.30 a.m.*[1]

Addressed to United Kingdom Delegation Berlin telegram Onward No. 327, 1st August. Repeated to Warsaw, Washington and Moscow.

Following for Sir Alexander Cadogan from Sir O. Sargent.

You may care to consider in consultation with United States Delegation, if not too late, whether further approach could not usefully be made to Stalin by President Truman and Prime Minister about releasing the 16 Polish political leaders.[2]

2. We suggest it might be pointed out that we are about to open discussions with Polish Government on matters relating to late London Government's affairs which we hope will result in creating an atmosphere more favourable to the return to Poland under orderly conditions of as many

---

[1] Time of origin.
[2] See Sir L. Woodward, *op. cit.*, vol. iii, pp. 540–8.

Poles as possible. This would be greatly helped if there were an increase of confidence amongst Poles abroad in regard to the conditions they may expect to find when they return and nothing which Soviet Government could do would be better calculated to restore their confidence than the release of these democratic leaders. It might be worth pointing out that there has been an amnesty for Polish prisoners in British territory (see my telegram No. 118 to Warsaw [ii]) and that we feel entitled to request the assistance of the Soviet Government to this extent in creating a favourable atmosphere for the solution of these difficult problems.[3]

CALENDARS TO NO. 513

i   *17 July 1945   Letter from Mr. Colville to Mr. V. G. Lawford* enclosing telegram from former Polish President Raczkiewicz asking Mr. Churchill to secure at Potsdam release of sixteen Polish prisoners in Moscow [N 8870/6/55].

ii   *1 Aug. 1945   To Mr. Hankey (Warsaw) Tel. No. 118.* Refers to Nos. 319.i & 513 : instructions to inform Polish Govt. of amnesty for Poles in Polish military prisons in British territory, and to press Polish Govt. to consider further measures to increase confidence of Poles returning home [N 8946/6/55].

[3] Mr. D. Allen and Sir. A Cadogan minuted on this telegram: 'This is rather late in the day but perhaps there would be an opportunity for a word on the subject to the Russians tonight. We should be fully justified in putting it to them that we have made large concessions to their point of view over Poland at this conference and in asking them to make their contribution in the form of a last minute good will gesture on this question of an amnesty for the 16. The arguments in para. 2 of this telegram are all apposite. D. Allen. 1/8.' 'The P.M. said that he wd. try to find an opportunity of a word with Marshal Stalin. I reminded him of it at the end of last night's meeting, but I don't know whether he actually did it. I asked the President whether he wd. do likewise. He said he had already raised the matter with Stalin during the Conference, but had got nothing out of him. If he got an opportunity, he might raise it again. But I do not know whether he was able to do so. A. C. Aug 2, 1945.' 'At Sir A. Cadogan's suggestion I had a word with Mr. Harriman and Mr. Dunn just before the last Plenary meeting and found that although they were strongly opposed to our raising this question in open session they were all in favour of its being mentioned privately to Marshal Stalin, though non-committal about giving us any support themselves. I gathered from Major Birse, who was interpreting, that Mr. Attlee did speak to Marshal Stalin on the question when saying goodbye after the final session. Marshal Stalin was apparently receptive though non-commital and M. Molotov, who was standing near interposed to say that most of the Poles (i.e. those who had received short sentences) would in any case be released in the very near future. So far as I could gather no very definite promise was obtained in regard to the release of the remainder. D. Allen. 3rd August, 1945.'

No. 514

Record by Sir A. Clark Kerr (Berlin) of a conversation with M. Bierut
[N 9861/211/55]

[BERLIN,] *1 August, 1945*

I passed on to Monsieur Bierut this morning your message of goodwill and explained to him that you[1] counted confidently upon the faithful fulfilment of the assurances he gave you yesterday.

He beamed with joy and used that very word to express his gratification. He made me a speech about the gratitude the Poles felt for all we had done for the cause of Poland. We could be assured that the new Government would make every effort to maintain the closest and friendliest relations with us, diplomatic, cultural and economic. He said that he knew that some mistrust was felt for his Government, but he hoped that this would pass. This gave me an opportunity to read him a little sermon upon how this could be best achieved.

He then said that Mr. Truman had told him of the decisions, taken yesterday, about the Western frontiers and he asked me to convey to you an expression of the warm thanks of the Polish Government for this 'happy solution' of Poland's difficulties.

Monsieur Stanczyk was present. He asked me to tell you and the Prime Minister that he hoped to be in London shortly in order to continue the talk he had had with you here.

A. C. K.

---

[1] This record was addressed to Mr. Bevin, who initialed it 'E. B.'.

No. 515

Memorandum by the Soviet Delegation (Berlin)[1]

P. (Terminal) 76 [U 6197/3628/70]

Top secret   *1 August 1945*

Composition of the Greek Government

In view of the fact that at the present time in Greece order has been disturbed, law is not being observed, and, moreover, the Varkiza agreement between the Greek Government and democratic elements is obviously not being carried out, it should be recommended to the British Government to cause the Regent of Greece to modify the composition of the Greek Government in the spirit of the agreement concluded in Varkiza on the 12th February, 1945, between representatives of the then existing Greek Government and representatives of Greek democracy.

---

[1] Printed under date of 31 July 1945 in *Berlinskaya konferentsiya*, p. 438, and in the present translation by Sir L. Woodward, *op. cit.*, vol. v, p. 489.

No. 516

Note by Sir D. Waley (Berlin)
P. (Terminal) 77 [U 6197/3628/70]

Top secret   *1 August 1945*

German Reparation: Report [1] of Drafting Committee

(Circulated to the United Kingdom Delegation only)

Owing to a difference of view regarding the inclusion of German external assets in paragraph 3, full agreement was not reached on paragraphs 1 to 6 of the attached draft.[2] The United States and United Kingdom representatives considered that, in return for the percentages of capital equipment to be received by the U.S.S.R. under the terms of paragraph 4, the Soviet Government had agreed to refrain from exercising a claim to German external assets, gold captured in Germany or securities of German corporations in the Western zones. The Soviet representative was of the view that this decision had not yet been taken, and that the matter should be referred to the Heads of Government.

The United States and United Kingdom representatives did not accept paragraph 7, which was proposed by the U.S.S.R. representative.

S. D. W.

[1] A text of this report is printed in *F.R.U.S. Berlin*, vol. ii, pp. 929–30.
[2] *Note in filed copy:* 'See P. (Terminal) 73', No. 498.

No. 517

Note by Sir D. Waley (Berlin)
P. (Terminal) 78 [U 6197/3628/70]

Top secret   *1 August 1945*

Germany: Economic Questions
Third Report of Economic Committee

(Circulated to the United Kingdom Delegation only)

Paragraph 1 of the annexed Report[1] relates to the 'first charge.' I suggest that we should say that we regard it as essential to lay down the principle that 'payment for approved imports into Germany shall be a first charge against the proceeds of exports out of current production and out of stocks of goods.' (This was the text that we handed round on the 30th July.)[2] We should add, since agreement has not been reached on an article in the Economic Principles, the matter will have to be dealt with in the arrange-

[1] Annex I below, printed in parts in *F.R.U.S. Berlin*, vol. ii, pp. 828, 964, 1387, and in *Berlinskaya konferentsiya*, pp. 448–9.
[2] See No. 469, minute 4.

ments which will be made for deliveries out of current production to the countries entitled to reparation.

The Americans are likely to propose the text shown in the paper headed 'United States Draft.'[3] The Soviet Delegation object to paragraph (c) on the ground that one should not contemplate failure to agree. I think they are right. We must not pre-judge what will happen if there is failure to agree or restrict our Commander-in-Chief's freedom of action, but we should not have a text contemplating failure to agree.

German External Assets

2. The British and American representatives agree to recognise that 'appropriate steps should be taken by the Control Council to exercise control and the power of disposition over German-owned external assets not already under the control of the United Nations which have taken part in the war against Germany.' This, in fact, has already been recommended by the European Advisory Commission on the 26th July.[4] The Soviet objection will presumably be withdrawn if the text about German reparations is settled. If the Russians have renounced their claim to any share of German external assets, they have no interest in the matter.

S. D. W.

ANNEX I TO NO. 517

Third Report of the Economic Sub-Committee to the Foreign Ministers

1. The Economic Sub-Committee considered the questions of a statement regarding German external assets and a proposed Article 19 of the Economic Principles relating to payment for imports into Germany.

2. With respect to the question of German external assets no decision was reached. The Soviet representatives, after a general explanation of the problem had been made, requested fuller information and reserved their position pending the furnishing of such information.

3. The Sub-Committee also failed to reach agreement in the matter of a proposed Article 19 of the Economic Principles.

The Soviet representatives reported that they were not yet in a position further to discuss the matter of oil supplies from the East.

ANNEX II TO NO. 517

United States Draft

Article 19

(a) Payment of reparations should leave sufficient resources to enable the German people to subsist without external assistance.

(b) Payment for imports into Germany approved by the Control Council shall be a first charge against the proceeds of exports out of current production and out of stocks of goods.

---

[3] Annex II below, printed in parts in *F.R.U.S. Berlin*, vol. ii, pp. 812, 827, and in *Berlinskaya konferentsiya*, p. 450.

[4] In paragraph 3 (c) of annex to No. 406.

(*c*) If the Control Council fails to agree, each zone commander may still import into his own zone such supplies as his Government considers essential, for the payment of which he may assess a first charge on exports of current production and stocks from his own zone.

(*d*) The above clause will not apply to the equipment and products referred to in paragraphs 4 (*a*) and 4 (*b*) of the Reparations Agreement.

No. 518

Record of Twelfth Plenary Meeting held at Cecilienhof, Potsdam, on Wednesday, 1 August 1945 at 3 p.m.

P. (Terminal) 12th Meeting [U 6197/3628/70]

Top secret

Present:

PREMIER STALIN, M. V. M. Molotov, M. A. Ya. Vyshinski, M. I. M. Maisky, M. F. T. Gousev, M. A. A. Gromyko, M. K. V. Novikov, M. B. F. Podtzerob, Admiral N. G. Kuznetsov, M. S. A. Golunski (*Interpreter*).

PRESIDENT TRUMAN, Mr. J. F. Byrnes, Mr. Joseph E. Davies, Fleet-Admiral W. D. Leahy, Mr. W. A. Harriman, Mr. E. W. Pauley, Mr. J. C. Dunn, Mr. H. F. Matthews, Mr. W. L. Clayton, Mr. C. E. Bohlen (*Interpreter*).

MR. ATTLEE, Mr. Bevin, Sir A. Cadogan, Sir A. Clark Kerr, Sir W. Strang, Sir E. Bridges, Mr. N. Brook, Sir D. Waley, Mr. T. L. Rowan, Mr. P. J. Dixon, Mr. W. Hayter, Major A. Birse (*Interpreter*).

Contents

1. *Foreign Secretaries' Report*

MR. BYRNES said that at the meeting of Foreign Secretaries that morning reference had been made to the following subjects:

(a) *European Oil Supplies*
(Previous Reference: F (Terminal) 11th Meeting,[1] Minute 6.)

The memorandum (P. (Terminal) 18)[2] which the United States Delegation had submitted had been referred to the Economic Committee, who had not been able to submit any final report on this matter. Further discussion of this question must, therefore, be deferred.

(b) *Roumania: Removal of Allied Industrial Equipment*
(Previous Reference: F (Terminal) 11th Meeting[1] Minute 7.)

The British Delegation had now agreed to accept the proposal, put forward by the Soviet Delegation in P. (Terminal) 46,[3] that a Commission composed of representatives of the British and Soviet Governments should conduct an investigation in Roumania with a view to establishing the facts of this matter so far as concerned British companies. A similar Commission, composed of representatives of the United States and Soviet Governments, was to make investigations as regards American companies. It had been agreed that both these Commissions should begin work in Roumania within the next ten days.

The Conference took note, with approval, of the arrangements made for dealing with this matter.

(c) *Fascist Activities in Germany and Austria*
(Previous Reference: F (Terminal) 10th Meeting,[4] Minute 11 and 11th Meeting,[1] Minute 8.)

A further discussion had taken place on this matter, which had previously been raised at the meeting of Foreign Secretaries on the 30th July. Mr. Bevin had recalled that at the Crimea Conference the British and United States Governments had agreed that they would not allow, in ex-enemy territory under their control, any propaganda or other activities hostile to the Soviet Union. The British Government would continue to act in the spirit of that agreement; and if it were found, as a result of the enquiries which had already been set on foot, that the complaints made in the memorandum by the Soviet Delegation (P. (Terminal) 44)[5] were well founded, appropriate action would be taken. M. Molotov had expressed himself as satisfied with this assurance.

(d) *Repatriation of Soviet Citizens*
(Previous Reference: F. (Terminal) 11th Meeting,[1] Minute 9.)

M. Molotov had drawn attention to memoranda submitted by the Soviet Delegation about the repatriation of Soviet citizens from various parts of Europe. He had said that the Soviet Government attached particular importance to the points raised in these memoranda, and hoped they

[1] No. 509.
[2] See No. 214, note 10.
[3] No. 432.
[4] No. 469.
[5] See No. 276, enclosure and note 1.

would receive full consideration by the Governments of the United Kingdom and the United States.

Mr. Byrnes and Mr. Bevin had undertaken to consider these memoranda and to send a reply to the Soviet Government through the diplomatic channel.

(e) Preparation of Protocol
(Previous Reference: F. (Terminal) 11th Meeting,[1] Minute 10.)

In the preparation of the draft Protocol a number of points had arisen on which the representatives of the three Delegations had been unable to reach agreement on the drafting; these outstanding differences had been considered and resolved by the meeting of Foreign Secretaries that morning.

The substance of Mr. Byrnes's report on other matters discussed by the Foreign Secretaries at their meeting that morning is recorded in Minutes 2, 5, 6, 7, 9, 10 and 11 below.

> The Conference took note with approval of Mr. Byrnes's report of the progress made by the meeting of Foreign Secretaries on these matters.

2. *Reparations: Germany*
(Previous Reference: F (Terminal) 11th Meeting,[1] Minute 1.)

At the Plenary meeting the previous day a Committee had been appointed to prepare, for insertion in the Protocol, a statement of the terms of the agreement reached on reparations from Germany.[6]

Mr. Byrnes now reported that the Committee had prepared such a draft[7] but had been unable to reach complete agreement on the reference to be made to German external assets. He recalled that in their proposals (P. (Terminal) 79)[8] put forward the previous day the Soviet Delegation had asked for:

(a) 500 million dollars' worth of shares in industrial and transport undertakings in the western zone;

(b) 30 per cent. of German foreign investments; and

(c) 30 per cent. of the German gold now at the disposal of the Allies.

The United States Delegation had been unable to accept these proposals and his understanding was that Premier Stalin had withdrawn them, in return for the agreement of the United States Delegation to the higher percentages of deliveries of capital equipment from the western zones. The Soviet representative on the drafting Committee, however, was not prepared to agree to this interpretation of the decision, and this point had therefore to be referred back to the Plenary Meeting.

Premier Stalin agreed that at the meeting on the previous day he had withdrawn the proposals of the Soviet Government referred to by Mr. Byrnes; but what he had intended to withdraw was claims related to the

---

[6] See No. 495, minute 2.

[7] *Note in filed copy:* 'P. (Terminal) 73 [No. 498]: see also P. (Terminal) 77', No. 516.

[8] Not printed. This document of 1 August 1945, entitled 'Reparations: Germany. Soviet Proposals', comprised the text of these proposals (beginning '1. Reparations will be exacted') as cited in No. 495, minute 2.

western zones. The Soviet Government were ready to renounce all claim to shares in undertakings in the western zones, gold found by the Allies in the western zones, and a corresponding share of German external assets. This might be expressed by saying that all assets in countries west of the demarcation line between the Russian zone and the western zone of occupation should be at the disposal of Great Britain and the United States, while all assets to the east of that line should be at the disposal of the Soviet Union. Thus, assets in e.g. France, Belgium and Holland and the Western Hemisphere would be at the disposal of Great Britain and the United States; those in Finland, Bulgaria and Roumania, for example, would be at the disposal of the Soviet Union.

MR. BEVIN asked whether Premier Stalin's suggestion might be expressed by saying that all German external assets located in the areas occupied by the Russian Armies would be at the disposal of the Soviet Union, while all such assets located elsewhere would be at the disposal of Great Britain and the United States. PREMIER STALIN agreed. This would mean that German assets in, e.g., Yugoslavia and Czechoslovakia would be at the disposal of Great Britain and the United States, while those in Austria would be divided.

This proposal of the Soviet Delegation was accepted by President Truman and Mr. Attlee.

MR. ATTLEE added that he had one further suggestion to make. It had been agreed at the previous meeting that France should be invited to become a member of the Allied Commission on Reparations. Should not telegrams be sent at once from each of the three Governments inviting the French Government to join the Commission? These should be despatched without delay in order to reach the French Government before the agreement was publicly announced in the communiqué issued at the end of the Conference.

PREMIER STALIN asked whether Poland should not also become a member of the Commission. Poland had suffered greatly and had a stronger claim to reparations than France. On what criterion was France to be included before Poland?

PRESIDENT TRUMAN said that he hoped Premier Stalin would not think it necessary to reopen the decision which they had reached the previous day that France should become a member of this Commission. All that was now under discussion was whether an invitation to France to join the Commission should be sent before the conclusions of the Conference were promulgated.

PREMIER STALIN said that he would not press his point.

It was agreed:

(1) That the three Governments should at once despatch separate telegrams inviting the French Government to become a member of the Allied Commission on Reparations.[9]

[9] Foreign Office telegram No. 8 Victim to Paris of 1 August at 5.20 p.m. instructed Mr. Duff Cooper to make an immediate communication in this sense to the French Provisional Government in concert with his American and Soviet colleagues: cf. *F.R.U.S. Berlin*, vol. ii, pp. 1546–7.

(2) That the Committee which had prepared the draft statement on reparations should now revise it in the light of the agreements recorded above.

3. *Supplies for the Berlin Area*

Arising out of the discussion recorded in the preceding Minute, MR. ATTLEE said that he had a practical suggestion to make following the agreement on reparations from Germany. In Paragraph 6 of the draft agreement (P. (Terminal) 73)[10] prepared by the Committee there was a reference to the arrangement whereby the Soviet Union was to receive from the western zones deliveries of capital equipment in advance of the determination of the general volume of equipment to be removed. His suggestion was that there should similarly be advance deliveries, to the British and United States Sectors of Berlin, of the supplies which were to be provided by the Soviet Union in exchange for capital equipment under paragraph 4 (*a*) of the Reparations Agreement. He recalled that, under the emergency agreement for supplying Berlin,[11] which was valid for 30 days from the 15th July, the Commanders-in-Chief in the British and United States zones were providing 40,000 tons of food a month and 2,400 tons of coal a day for the British and American sectors. He suggested that the Soviet Union should now agree in principle to furnish such supplies from the date of the expiry of the emergency agreement as advance deliveries on account of reparations, and that the Control Council should be instructed to draw up immediately a programme of food, coal and fuel to be imported during the next six months into the Greater Berlin area, sufficient to raise the standard of the whole population of that area to an agreed level.

MARSHAL STALIN said that, while he saw no objection to some arrangement being reached on the lines suggested and quite understood the reasons for its being put forward, he was not prepared to decide this matter now. He could not enter into any commitment until he knew what quantities of supplies were involved, and what arrangements could be made by the Control Council. He had little doubt that he would be able to agree in principle to some arrangement on the general lines suggested by Mr. Attlee; but he must first have the matter studied by the Control Council and consider the details in the light of their report. He was not ready to take a decision at the present meeting.

It was agreed that a final decision on this matter could not be taken by the Conference.

4. *Reparations: Austria*

(Previous Reference: P. (Terminal) 10th Meeting,[12] Minute 5.)

MR. ATTLEE recalled that it had been agreed that no reparations should be exacted from Austria. He suggested that this agreement should be included in the Protocol.

[10] No. 498. [11] See No. 70. [12] No. 447.

Premier Stalin and President Truman agreed.

5. *Germany: Economic Problems*
(Previous Reference: F. (Terminal) 11th Meeting,[1] Minute 2.)
Mr. Byrnes referred to the third Report of the Economic Committee
(P. (Terminal) 78)[13] on the inclusion in the Statement of Economic
Principles of provisions relating to (*a*) German external assets, and (*b*)
payment for imports into Germany.

(*a*) *German external assets*
The United States and British representatives wished to include the
following statement:
'Appropriate steps should be taken by the Control Council to exercise
control and the power of disposition over German-owned external assets
not already under the control of United Nations which have taken part
in the war against Germany.'
The Soviet representative on the Committee had been unable to accept
this paragraph; but in view of the agreement since reached on Reparations
(see Minute 2 above) the Soviet Delegation might now be able to agree to
the inclusion of these words in the Statement of Economic Principles.
Premier Stalin agreed.

(*b*) *Payment for Imports into Germany*
The Committee had failed to reach agreement on a formula, for inclusion
in the Statement of Economic Principles, on the claim of the British Delegation that payment for approved imports into Germany should be a first
charge against the proceeds of exports from current production or from
stocks of goods.
Alternative drafts were submitted by the British and United States
Delegations. After discussion, it was decided to include in the Statement a
final paragraph in the following terms:
'Payment of reparations should leave enough resources to enable the
German people to subsist without external assistance. In working out the
economic balance of Germany the necessary means must be provided to
pay for imports approved by the Control Council in Germany. The
proceeds of exports from current production and stocks shall be available
in the first place for payment for such imports.[14]
'The above clause will not apply to the equipment and products referred
to in paragraph 4 (*a*) and 4 (*b*) of the Reparations Agreement.'
It was agreed that, subject to the addition of the two paragraphs set
out above, the Statement of Economic Principles to govern the treatment of Germany in the initial control period should be included in the
Protocol and Communiqué of the Conference.

[13] No. 517.
[14] This paragraph is cited by Sir L. Woodward, *op. cit.*, vol. v, p. 456.

6. *War Crimes*
(Previous Reference: P. (Terminal) 11th Meeting,[15] Minute 11, and F. (Terminal) 11th Meeting,[1] Minute 3.)

MR. BYRNES said that this matter had been discussed that morning by the Foreign Secretaries, and the only question outstanding was whether the proposed Statement should name particular war criminals who would be put on trial in the near future. Subject to this one point, the draft put forward by the British Delegation (P. (Terminal) 71)[16] had been approved.

PREMIER STALIN thought that a list of names was necessary, in order to satisfy public opinion in the Allied countries. A list would have the further advantage of making it clear that it was intended to try some German industrialists. It would also remove any uncertainty about Rudolph Hess.

MR. BEVIN said that he could give a clear undertaking that Hess would be handed over for trial without delay. PREMIER STALIN said that he did not doubt this; but would it not be well to remove any doubts there might be in the minds of the general public in Allied countries?

PRESIDENT TRUMAN said that Mr. Justice Jackson, the United States representative on the prosecuting Commission for war crimes trials, had told him that it would handicap the work of the Commission if a list of names were published by the three Governments before the trials took place. It was hoped that the first trials would start within thirty days.

After some further discussion, PREMIER STALIN said that he would be ready to accept the British draft statement if a further sentence were added to the effect that the first list of war criminals to be tried would be published within thirty days.

It was agreed:

(1) That the first list of war criminals to be tried should be published before the 1st September, 1945.

(2) That a public declaration should be made on war crimes, in the terms of the draft put forward by the British Delegation (P. (Terminal) 71)[16] with the addition of a sentence to the effect of (1) above.

(3) That the French Provisional Government should be associated with this declaration.[17]

7. *Yalta Declaration on Liberated Europe: Procedure of Control Commissions in Bulgaria, Hungary and Roumania*
(Previous Reference: (F. (Terminal) 11th Meeting,[1] Minute 11.)

MR. BYRNES said that a report had been received from the Committee appointed by the Foreign Secretaries that morning to prepare a revised draft of a statement on the procedure of the Control Commissions in Bulgaria, Hungary and Roumania.

---

[15] No. 495.

[16] See No. 495, minute 11.

[17] Mr. Duff Cooper was that day instructed accordingly and on 2 August communicated to the French Provisional Government a note in this sense. Cf. *F.R.U.S. Berlin*, vol. ii, p. 1547.

The draft submitted by the Committee was as follows:

'The Three Governments took note that the Soviet Representatives on the Allied Control Commissions in Roumania, Bulgaria and Hungary have communicated to their United Kingdom and United States colleagues proposals for improving the work of the Control Commissions, now that hostilities in Europe have ceased.

The Three Governments agreed that the revision of the procedures of the Allied Control Commissions in these countries would now be undertaken, taking into account the interests and responsibilities of the Three Governments which together presented the terms of armistice to the respective countries, and accepting as a basis, in respect of all three countries, the Soviet Government's proposals for Hungary as annexed hereto.

Text of a letter transmitted on 12th July to the Representatives of the United States and United Kingdom Governments on the Allied Control Commission in Hungary

In view of the changed situation in connection with the termination of the war against Germany, the Soviet Government finds it necessary to establish the following order of work for the Allied Control Commission in Hungary.

1. During the period up to the conclusion of peace with Hungary the President (or Vice-President) of the A.C.C. will regularly call conferences with the British and American representatives for the purpose of discussing the most important questions relating to the work of the A.C.C. The conferences will be called once in ten days or more frequently in case of need.

Directives of the A.C.C. on questions of principle will be issued to the Hungarian authorities by the President of the Allied Control Commission after agreement on these directives with the English and American representatives.

2. The British and American representatives in the A.C.C. will take part in general conferences of heads of divisions and delegates of the A.C.C., convoked by the President of the A.C.C., which meetings will be regular in nature. The British and American representatives will also participate personally or through their representatives in appropriate instances in mixed commissions created by the President of the A.C.C. for questions connected with the execution by the A.C.C. of its functions.

3. Free movement by the American and British representatives in the country will be permitted provided that the A.C.C. is previously informed of the time and route of the journeys.

4. All questions connected with permission for the entrance and exit of members of the staff of the British and American representatives in Hungary will be decided on the spot by the President of the A.C.C. within a time limit of not more than one week.

5. The bringing in and sending out by plane of mail, cargoes and diplomatic couriers will be carried out by the British and American representatives on the A.C.C. under arrangements and within time limits

established by the A.C.C., or in special cases by previous co-ordination with the President of the A.C.C.

I consider it necessary to add to the above that in all other points the existing Statutes regarding the A.C.C. in Hungary, which was confirmed on the 20th January, 1945, shall remain in force in the future.'

PRESIDENT TRUMAN and MR. ATTLEE said that this draft was acceptable to the United States and British Delegation[s].

> It was agreed that the draft set out above should be adopted for inclusion in the Protocol of the Conference.

8. *Poland*
(Previous Reference: P. (Terminal) 11th Meeting,[15] Minute 3.)

PRESIDENT TRUMAN said that representatives of the Polish Provisional Government had called upon him that morning; and he had communicated to them the decision of the Conference on the question of Poland's Western Frontier. He had handed them a written statement of the decision in the terms agreed by the Conference. The Polish Delegation had asked him to convey their thanks to all three Governments.

MR. BEVIN mentioned that he had now made the necessary arrangements with the Polish Provisional Government for reciprocal facilities for an air service between London and Warsaw.

9. *Facilities for Radio Correspondents*
(Previous Reference: F. (Terminal) 11th Meeting,[1] Minute 12.)

MR. BYRNES explained that at the meeting of Foreign Secretaries that morning he had suggested that in the proposed statements on Poland and on the admission of neutral and ex-enemy States to the United Nations the references to facilities for correspondents of the Press should be amended so as to extend to radio correspondents.

PRESIDENT TRUMAN said that the position of radio correspondents was different in the United States from some other countries. Broadcasting companies in the United States were on the same footing as the Press, and they expected to receive the same facilities. American radio representatives worked like Press reporters: they would have nothing to do with the broadcasting system in the country to which they were accredited.

PREMIER STALIN said that, in his view, this was not a matter which could be regulated by a general formula applying to all countries. It was essentially a matter for bilateral arrangements between particular countries, on a reciprocal basis. He could not agree to any mention of radio correspondents in the two statements mentioned by Mr. Byrnes.

MR. ATTLEE agreed with the views expressed by Premier Stalin.

> It was agreed that, in the statements on Poland and the admission of certain States to the United Nations, no reference should be made to facilities for radio correspondents.

10. *German Fleet and Merchant Navy*
(Previous Reference: F. (Terminal) 11th Meeting,[1] Minute 14.)

The only outstanding question on this matter was whether the share of the

German merchant marine which was to go to Poland would be drawn from that portion which had been allocated to the Soviet Union.

PREMIER STALIN said that he withdrew the objection which the Soviet Delegation had made to this proposal at the meeting of Foreign Secretaries that morning.

The Conference:

(1) Endorsed the conclusions reached at the meeting of Foreign Secretaries regarding the German Fleet and Merchant Navy.

(2) Agreed that the point raised by the British Delegation regarding Poland's share of the German Merchant Marine should be met by including in the Protocol a paragraph to the following effect:

> 'The United Kingdom and the United States will provide out of their shares of the surrendered German merchant ships appropriate amounts for other Allied States whose merchant marines have suffered heavy losses in the common cause against German, except that the Soviet Union shall provide out of its share for Poland.'

11. *Allied Property in Satellite Countries: Seizure as Reparations or War Trophies* (Previous Reference: F. (Terminal) 11th Meeting,[1] Minute 4.)

MR. BYRNES said that the United States Delegation were anxious that a decision should be reached on this matter before the end of the Conference.

PREMIER STALIN said that there had been little time to consider the proposals of the United States Delegation; and no report had yet been received from the committee which had been appointed that morning to examine them. The Soviet Delegation would, however, do their best to consider these proposals before the final Plenary Meeting that evening; and he was willing that the matter should be brought forward for discussion at the meeting.

MR. ATTLEE agreed. He thought that the proposals put forward by the United States Delegation in the memorandum (P. (Terminal) 49)[18] would need some further consideration: as they stood, they might prove inequitable. Thus, the memorandum contemplated that, if the Occupying Power would not or could not return Allied property which it had removed from a satellite State, compensation should be payable by the satellite State. He would have thought it more equitable that in such circumstances the compensation should be payable by the Power which had removed the property. Alternatively, if compensation were paid by the satellite State, the amount of that compensation might be counted against reparations. Further, paragraph 3 of the memorandum contemplated that satellite States should be required to provide foreign exchange in order to facilitate reparation payments out of current production. He saw no sufficient reason to discriminate in this matter between reparation deliveries from current production and other exports.

PREMIER STALIN said that, on Mr. Attlee's first point, he saw no reason why compensation should not be payable by the satellite States in respect of

[18] See No. 451, note 6.

any Allied property which had been removed and could not be returned. It must not be forgotten that the satellite States had waged war against the United Nations; and it was not, therefore, unreasonable that they should be required to provide compensation for loss suffered in their territories by Allied nationals as a result of the war.

It was agreed that this matter should be further considered at the Plenary Meeting that evening.

12. *International Inland Waterways*
(Previous Reference: P. (Terminal) 11th Meeting,[15] Minute 12.)

PRESIDENT TRUMAN recalled that at the Plenary Meeting on the 31st July it had been agreed that the proposals put forward on this subject by the United States Delegation (P. (Terminal) 33)[19] should be referred to the Council of Foreign Ministers. He understood that no reference to this decision had yet been included in the drafts which were being prepared for the Protocol and the Communiqué. He hoped the Conference would agree that this matter might be mentioned in both the Protocol and the Communiqué.

PREMIER STALIN said that in his view it would be enough if the decision reached at the Plenary Meeting on the 31st July were recorded in the Protocol. He saw no occasion to mention this matter in the Communiqué. The Conference had not discussed it at any length; it had been raised incidentally in connexion with the proposal for revision of the Montreux Convention; and it was not contemplated that the Communiqué should include any reference to discussions about the Black Sea Straits.

PRESIDENT TRUMAN said that he would prefer the Communiqué to include a reference to all matters on which the Conference had reached a decision. He was anxious to be in a position to say, when he returned to the United States, that he had not entered into any secret agreements at the Conference; and that all the effective decisions of the Conference were recorded in the Communiqué.

PREMIER STALIN referred to the procedure followed at earlier conferences of the three Heads of Government. Under this procedure all decisions reached had been recorded in a Protocol which was agreed at the end of the Conference; but the Communiqué had contained only those decisions on matters of political principle which were of general interest and could with advantage be made public. Decisions which were purely formal in character —as was the decision to refer to the Council of Foreign Ministers the United States proposals on inland waterways—should not in his opinion be included in the public announcement. It did not, however, follow that these decisions, and other decisions which were included in the Protocol but not in the Communiqué, were 'secret arrangements' in the sense in which President Truman had used that term. Though he did not himself think it worth while to include a reference to this particular decision in the Communiqué,

[19] No. 246.

he saw no reason why any of the three Governments should not feel free to disclose the fact if they thought it worth while to do so, that this question was to be referred to the Council of Foreign Ministers.

PRESIDENT TRUMAN said that he would not press his point if, as he understood, he would be free to say, in discussions about international waterways in the United States Senate, that the Berlin Conference had decided to refer this matter to the Council of Foreign Ministers.

It was agreed that the decision reached by the Conference on the United States proposals regarding inland waterways should be included in the Protocol of the Conference, but not in the Communiqué.

Cabinet Office, Potsdam, 2nd August, 1945

CALENDAR TO No. 518

i *1 Aug. 1945 Minute from Sir A. Cadogan to Mr. Bevin enclosing note.* Suggestion for advance supplies for Berlin as proposed in minute 3 above. British agreement to advance deliveries to Russians from the Ruhr should be conditional on obtaining satisfaction here [F.O. 934/1/4(38)].

No. 519

Letter from Sir E. Bridges (Berlin) to Sir E. Machtig
[D.O. 35/1950: WR 222/48/20]

CABINET OFFICE, BRITISH DELEGATION, THREE
POWER CONFERENCE, *1 August 1945*

Dear Machtig,

I have now had a chance of discussing with the Foreign Office the draft telegram which you gave me on Saturday morning[1] about telegrams Nos. 203 and 205 from the Commonwealth Government.

[1] This draft telegram from Sir E. Machtig to Sir E. Bridges, handed to the latter on 28 July 1945, had summarized Australian telegrams Nos. 203 and 205 (respectively Nos. 372.i and 448.i) and proposed that they be brought to the notice of Mr. Attlee and Mr. Bevin. Sir E. Machtig commented: 'While it is obviously going to be quite impossible to meet Dr. Evatt wholly, it might perhaps be practicable so to frame communique to be issued at end of Potsdam Conference so as to take some account of Australian contentions. It may too be possible to draw some distinction between procedure in relation to Europe, where Australian claim for consultation is obviously lesser, and procedure in relation to Japan. But whether or not it proves practicable to meet them to any extent, it is, I think, of first class importance that before final Potsdam communique is issued we should reply to Australian telegrams and give them advance information of what is to be published.' This draft telegram was passed to Mr. Dixon by Sir E. Bridges under cover of an explanatory minute of 29 July. Mr. Dixon replied in minutes of 29 and 30 July: 'I think that it would help if, besides the action suggested by Sir E. Machtig, a personal message was sent from the Prime Minister or the Foreign Secretary to the Commonwealth Prime Minister explaining what we are doing, in particular in regard to peace settlements. A similar message would no doubt also have to be sent to the other Dominion Prime Ministers. P. D. 29th

I thank you also for your letter of the 30th July.[2] It will, I think, be best if I send you rather a full answer.

At the Commonwealth Meeting in April this year, Mr. Churchill said that he had always thought there would be a Peace Conference or perhaps an Armistice Conference. He continued that unlike the World Organisation it will be confined to peoples like the Dominions who had played an important part in the war.

We must, I think, recognise that things are working out differently from what was thought likely by Mr. Churchill so short a time ago as April. The whole conception on which we are now working is that it is no use bringing forward the matters which will have to be settled at a Peace Conference unless and until the issues in question have been worked out beforehand in a smaller body; and the body which it is contemplated shall do this work is the Council of Foreign Ministers.

In so far as Dr. Evatt is thinking in terms of the Pacific or Far Eastern settlement, Australia has no reason for anxiety, since Australia would surely be regarded as one of the States which is 'directly interested' in the Far Eastern settlement. But so far as concerns the European settlement, one must admit that the position is different, and I do not see how a representative of the Autralian Government could be invited to attend meetings of the Council of the Foreign Ministers when the peace treaties with the Axis-satellites are under consideration, without opening the door to admission of a host of the lesser European allies. And it is precisely this which on grounds of businesslike procedure it is essential to avoid.

Dr. Evatt will, therefore, presumably ask how Australia's position in regard to the European peace treaties will be safeguarded. Here I think it is necessary to go into details as to the various stages concerned.

The first stage is when it is decided that the time has come to draw up a peace treaty with a particular country, as, for example, the decision which has been made to draw up a peace treaty with Italy. We take it that Australia does not object to this course so far as Italy is concerned, and I should imagine that there would be no difficulty in letting the Dominion Governments know as and when it is proposed to draw up peace treaties for other countries.

The next stage is the actual drafting of the peace terms. The Dominions will, as heretofore, have been fully consulted on the draft terms and given an opportunity to make their comments.

July, 1945.' 'I have spoken to the Foreign Secretary, who agrees with the action proposed. Mr. Bevin is particularly anxious that the interests of the Commonwealth, Canadian & S. African Govts. shall be safeguarded in connexion with the peace treaty with Italy. He sees no objection to our reaching agreement here between the 3 Powers, without consultation with the Domns. Govts., on the desirability of concluding an early peace treaty with Italy, & I have told him that it is the intention to consult the Domns. about our draft text of the Treaty. But in Mr. Bevin's view, the Domns. Govts. shd. be brought into the actual treaty-making as fully as possible. I think that the S. of S. wd. like to see the draft of any reply you send to Sir E. Machtig . . . . P. D. 30/7.'

2 See No. 448, note 4.

The third stage is when we come to discuss these terms at the Council of Foreign Ministers. As already stated, we don't see how as a general rule the Dominion representative could attend at the Council for the discussion of European peace treaties, although it might be possible to bring them into an occasional meeting on Italy (e.g. their losses in fighting Italy surely give them a 'direct' interest apart from their interest in the Italian colonies). If discussions in the Council of Foreign Ministers reveal marked differences of opinions which would lead to substantial modification of the draft terms as communicated to the Dominions, we would, as always, do our best to let them know what is going on and so far as possible give them an opportunity of expressing their views. (There may be a question whether our machinery is wholly satisfactory for this purpose. See later.)

The fourth state is the actual conclusion of the treaty, and I assume that there would be no difficulty in the Dominion Governments being signatories.

To sum up, the real point as so often seems to be is how to make the machinery of consultation effective. Speaking for myself, I feel some doubts whether in the organisation of these Conferences we have paid quite sufficient attention to means for keeping the Dominions in close touch. It is precisely at those moments when there is something important that the Dominions ought to be told that everybody concerned is overwhelmed with business. I am sure we ought to consider whether, if the Dominions Secretary is not to attend such Conferences, there should not be provision for representation of the Dominions Office in the secretariat, so as to ensure that there is someone who is keeping an eye open for points which the Dominions ought to be told quickly.

One might, I suppose, go a stage further and consider whether there are any members of the staffs of the Dominion High Commissioners who could be worked into the secretariat. But I suppose the trouble here is that if we had one such person, one would have to have four and that would be impracticable.

There is one last point which I ought to mention, namely, the suggestion you made to me orally on Saturday that [? in] paragraph 4 (ii) of the draft dealing with the Establishment of a Council of Foreign Ministers there should be substituted for 'the States chiefly interested' the expression 'the States concerned.' This suggestion has been fully considered here, but we felt that it was too late to propose this alteration. I may say that we and the Americans had considerable difficulty in getting even the present wording accepted by the Russians, who have shown themselves at this Conference to have an even more ruthless 'Great Power' complex than in the past.

May I add that we recognise very fully your anxieties in this matter. We therefore suggested that a personal telegram should be sent by the Prime Minister to the Dominion Prime Ministers shortly before the end of the Conference summarising the main conclusions and outlining the main points likely to feature in the Communique. The Prime Minister has agreed to this course, and the telegram will be reaching you later to-day.

I hope it will include some words of a general re-assurance that the position of the Dominions has been borne in mind.

Yours sincerely,
E. E. BRIDGES

CALENDAR TO NO. 519

i *31 July–1 Aug. 1945 Minutes by Mr. Hoyer Millar, Mr. Ward and Sir A. Cadogan* (*Berlin*) on draft of the above: consultation with Dominions on peace-making, especially in regard to Italian peace treaty, in light of establishment of Council of Foreign Ministers [CAB 21/880].

No. 520

Mr. Bevin (Berlin) to Mr. Morrison (Received 1 August, 3.40 p.m.)
No. 318 Target Telegraphic [F.O. 934/2/8(22)]

Top secret. Most Immediate   BERLIN, *1 August 1945, 5.20 p.m.*

Following for Machtig from Bridges.

This telegram contains text of the personal telegram from the Prime Minister to Dominion Prime Ministers. Please arrange for very early despatch. For your information it is contemplated that the report of the Conference will be released for publication at about 2100 hours BST, Thursday, 2nd August.

Begins[1]

As the Berlin Conference draws to its close I am sending you this personal message from myself, to supplement the Final Report, which will be telegraphed to you as soon as it is settled.

As you will have seen from the regular official telegrams reporting the progress of the Conference, its scope has been wider and the problems more intricate than at any preceding one. As at the Crimea, the procedure followed was that the Foreign Secretaries met in the mornings to thrash out the questions raised by each Delegation, referring some for examination by Committees and submitting others to the Plenary Meeting in the afternoons. I had the advantage of attending the Plenary Meetings from the beginning, and have thus been able to maintain the continuity of the British side in spite of the change of Government. The atmosphere has been one of goodwill and cordiality, combined with the utmost freedom and frankness of discussion. It has been evident that all three Delegations have felt deeply their responsibility for the future of the world; and in our approach to all major questions we have throughout had it in mind that the unity and continued co-operation of the three Governments is the first and greatest essential for the preservation of world peace.

---

[1] This message is substantially cited by Sir L. Woodward, *op. cit.*, vol. v, pp. 498–9.

The most important items in the Report will be:–

(a) Poland: Western Frontier and Political Settlement
(b) Germany: Political and Economic Principles, including Reparations
(c) Italy and South East Europe
(d) The Council of Foreign Ministers.

Some remarks on each of these points follow:–

(a) Poland

The conclusion on the Polish boundary was only reached after long and searching discussions with the Polish representatives. In this matter, as in some others, we found decisions already being shaped for us by events. We made it our prime concern to see that the new Poland would be independent, democratic and in free communication with the world at large. We have obtained assurances from the Polish representatives of their firm intention to put into full effect the political settlement in Poland which the Conference had already agreed.

(b) Treatment of Germany

The political principles and some of the economic principles were settled, without much difficulty. The rest of the latter turned mainly on the decision about German reparations, which proved one of the most difficult questions to settle provoking long and arduous discussion. Our object throughout was to avoid any plan which would stultify the principle of the economic unity of Germany or produce a situation in which Germany could pay reparations only at the indirect expense of the United States and ourselves. The plan finally agreed on is in substance the American plan.

(c) Italy and South East Europe

We were under pressure from the American side to take some further step towards admitting Italy to the United Nations and from the Soviet side to recognise the Governments of the Satellite States. The statement on 'Admission to the United Nations' secures both of these without prejudicing any points which we regard as essential. We found greater willingness than hitherto to admit the Press to South East Europe, though whether we shall see free elections is more open to doubt. The statement has the advantage of administering a public rebuke to Franco.

(d) The Council of Foreign Ministers

In the new Council of Foreign Ministers we hope we have a machine for continuing co-operation between the Great Powers. While the immediate task is to formulate Peace Treaties and prepare for the eventual peace settlement in Europe, we hope to use the Council as an instrument for the settlement of other outstanding questions: some of which as you will have seen, have already been referred to it.

In general I feel that we have made considerable progress towards a better understanding between the three Governments and that the decisions reached will provide a firm basis for a further advance. You will, I know, give the documents we have produced your most earnest consideration; and your comments would be most welcome. Moreover, if you wish the

Foreign Secretary will be ready to discuss each item with the High Commissioners in London. *Ends.*

No. 521

Mr. Chifley (Canberra) to Viscount Addison[1] *(Received 1 August, 6.40 p.m.)*
No. 209 Telegraphic [*D.O. 35/1950:WR 222/48/17*]

Most Immediate. Top secret   CANBERRA, *1 August 1945, 11.59 p.m.*

Addressed Secretary of State for Dominion Affairs No. 209 repeated External Wellington No. 133 Top Secret.

Our telegram No. 205[2] 27th July. Council of Foreign Ministers.

More recent information on Potsdam meeting indicates that Council Foreign Ministers will be in effect semi-permanent body whose conclusions or recommendations are intended broadly to settle in advance all basic issues affecting general peace settlement. Non-participation in its discussions would therefore exclude us in effect from decisive processes of peace-making, situation quite at variance with our definite understandings with you.

2. Suggestion still to be elaborated that lesser states will take part on invitation in Council's discussions does not measure up to our conception of effective participation as principal in Council's work. Such *ad hoc* arrangement would neither recognise our right to participate as principal in all decisive stages of peace deliberations nor assure us opportunity of stating our views at time and in manner most appropriate for our purposes.

3. We have never questioned leading role of Three Great Powers in such matters as will come before Council. However, inclusion among Council's members of France and most significantly China (in respect European affairs) justifies inclusion of Australia as member. Measured in terms of relative war effort and overall contribution to victory, Australia can fairly stand alongside either these Powers, and in terms European war commitments and post-war interests in Europe has more than equal right to effective participation than China.

4. These general considerations have been strongly reinforced by our examination on information available of specific matters which have been under discussion at Berlin Conference. We make particular mention of

(*a*) Italy. On this we hold emphatically that no preparations for peace treaty should be proceeded with without our full participation at all stages, mere communication of views by telegram is quite inadequate.

(*b*) Former Enemy Territories. You will recollect that in April last,

---

[1] Secretary of State for Dominion Affairs in succession to Viscount Cranborne.
[2] No. 448.i.

Australian Government expressed views regarding disposition of Italian Colonies and general question including future of former Japanese possessions is of closest concern to us. Particularly in view of leading part taken by Australia in trusteeship discussions at London and San Francisco.

(c) Polish Provisional Government. Our concern here is also direct as we refer to our earlier representation of Polish interests in Soviet Union.[3]

(d) Turko-Soviet relations. Australia took prominent part in Montreaux [sic] Conference and is closely interested in future of Straits area by reason of its political and strategic importance to Near East and Mediterranean.

(e) German Merchant Marine. In our telegram No. 161[4] 21st June we reserved full right to lodging claim for reparations from Germany. We consider we are entitled to independent share of allocation of German Merchant Marine and armed vessels. Our losses in this respect have been relatively heavy.

(f) Allied Policy in Germany. We have deep interest in revival of genuine democracy in Germany and in promoting of conditions which will safeguard against any resurgence of German Fascism. Number of specially qualified Australians have been nominated for service with British Control Commissions in Germany and Austria and we consider that further essential step would be attachment of Australian Military Mission to Control Council for Germany.

5. For above reasons we hold strongly that Council's present membership would not be regarded as rigid and that, in view its decisive peace-making and other functions, inclusion Australia by appropriate arrangement as principal to its discussions is essential as minimum recognition our part in war.

6. In regard to future of Japan, we have given preliminary consideration to your telegrams D. No. 1243, No. 1244 and No. 1245[5] and will shortly be communicating fully.

Our general attitude is as follows

(1) Full Australian participation as principal in decisions on policy and in control arrangements.

(2) Stern policy.

(3) Emperor as Head of State and Commander-in-Chief of Armed Forces to be given no immunity for Japan's acts of aggression and war crimes which in evidence before us are shown to have been of most barbarious character.

(4) Full occupation until such time as democratic and genuinely popular regime is fully established.

[3] After the severance of diplomatic relations between the Polish and Soviet Governments on 26 April 1943 Polish interests in the Soviet Union had been represented by the Australian Legation in Moscow.
[4] Untraced.
[5] See No. 304, note 1.

(5) Economic disarmament covering all industries, not merely those of war character. We fear combination or [? of] monopoly interest and imperial prestige as basis for resurgence of aggressive Fascism.

(6) Complete surrender of Merchant Navy to Allied Nations.[6]

[6] Lord Hood minuted on this telegram in the Foreign Office: 'This telegram shows some misunderstanding of the role of the new Council of Foreign Ministers, and particularly in regard to the extent of Chinese participation in respect of European affairs. In regard to the preparation of Peace Treaties with Italy and the European Satellites, we shall no doubt have to try to arrange for the participation of Dominion representatives at some stage in the Council's deliberations. In spite of what the Government of Australia say their interest in these treaties is, however, not very direct. If, however, the Council in due course goes on to prepare a Peace Treaty with Japan, the claim of the Australian and New Zealand Governments to participate at all stages will become very much stronger. I expect the Dominions Office will want to send some reply to this, but we might wait to see how the other Dominions Governments react to the establishment of the new Council. Hood 2nd August, 1945.'

No. 522

Letter from Mr. Attlee (Berlin) to Mr. Churchill
[*PREM 8/109*]

Most secret   [BERLIN,] *1 August 1945*

The Conference[1] is ending to-night in a good atmosphere. I would like to let you know the broad results before the communique is issued.

We have, of course, been building on the foundation laid by you, and there has been no change of policy.

It was clear, when the Conference was suspended that the vital points were Reparations and the Polish Western Frontier. On the former the Russians were very insistent on their pound of flesh. We were firm on the need for supplies of food etc. from the Eastern zone for the rest of Germany and on not allowing reparations to have precedence of maintaining a reasonable economy in Germany. On Poland the Russians insisted on the Western Neisse and eventually the Americans accepted this. We were, of course, powerless to prevent the course of events in the Russian zone. We have tied the Poles down as closely as we can with specific pledges on elections, press facilities and repatriation of fighting Poles. We therefore agreed on the Western Neisse as the western boundary of Polish administration pending the Peace Conference decisions. Other questions proved soluble when these major matters were disposed of.

Uncle Joe was not in a good mood at the start caused I think by an indisposition which kept him in bed for two days. Thereafter he was in good form. The President was very co-operative. My having been present from the start was a great advantage, but Bevin picked up all the points extremely

[1] The opening and concluding formulations of this letter are missing from the filed copy.

quickly and showed his quality as an experienced negotiator in playing his hand. I think that the results achieved are not unsatisfactory having regard to the way the course of the war had dealt the cards. I hope you have been able to get some rest. If you would care to come and see me to hear more details I should be delighted.

I was most grateful to you for sending me the statement on T.A. and I have sent it to the President with certain minor changes which I am sure you will agree do not affect its general sense. The President has just told me that they have no comments and I enclose herewith a copy of my covering statement and of your draft[2] in the form in which I sent it to the President. The President told me that Uncle Joe had not cross-examined him at all on this matter.

P.S. We have reached a satisfactory agreement on the German Fleet, especially on U-Boats. Of these all are to be sunk except 30 which are to be divided equally between the Three Powers for experimental and technical purposes.

[2] See No. 502, enclosure and note 1.

No. 523

Mr. Bevin (Berlin) to Mr. Morrison (Received 1 August, 5.30 p.m.)
No. 321 Target Telegraphic [F.O. 800/417/66]

Top secret. Immediate   BERLIN, *1 August 1945, 7.30 p.m.*

For Rawlins[1] from Miss Bright.

Provisional air programme for tomorrow (Thursday) as far as we can give you at present is as follows. Will send further detail as soon as arrangements firm.

Flight A, E.T.D.[2] 0830 Local Time, Prime Minister and party; E.T.D. 0930, schedule Dakota with Mr. Weston and part of Communications Staff;

Flight B, E.T.D. 1245, Foreign Secretary and party including Sir A. Cadogan;

Flight E, E.T.D. 1430, Admiral Macarthy and party;

Flight F, E.T.D. 1500, General Ismay and party;

Flight C, E.T.D. 1515, secretaries and photographers;

Flight D, E.T.D. 1600, Cabinet and Communications Staff; E.T.D. 1730, second schedule Dakota, Marines.

Sir Edward Bridges will travel either in Flight A or Flight F.

[1] Major F. W. Rawlins was Chief Clerk in the Cabinet Office.
[2] Estimated time of departure.

No. 524

Memorandum by Mr. Foulds (Berlin)

[F 4715/47/23]

Top secret   FOREIGN OFFICE [*sic*], *1 August 1945*

Command in French Indo-China.

On 24th July President Truman and Mr. Churchill approved a recommendation by the Combined Chiefs of Staff that that portion of French Indo-China lying south of 16° North latitude should be included in the South-East Asia Command, leaving the rest of French Indo-China in the China Theatre.[1] This recommendation was in the nature of a compromise, the British Chiefs of Staff having previously proposed that the whole of French Indo-China should be transferred from the China to the South-East Asia Theatre.

2. The President and Mr. Churchill agreed that the British and United States Governments should now approach Generalissimo Chiang Kai Shek to secure his concurrence in the division of the territory between the two Theatres.

3. In the past Chiang Kai Shek has shown himself very sensitive to encroachments on the China Theatre, although he has an informal oral understanding with Admiral Mountbatten by virtue of which both of them are at liberty to carry on operations and pre-operational activities in French Indo-China. The Foreign Office consider that the present proposal will not appeal to the Generalissimo and that the only course which has any hope of securing his concurrence in it is for the Prime Minister and the President to approach him direct.

4. Should the Prime Minister agree, it is suggested that he might like to propose to President Truman that each of them should send a message to the Generalissimo in the sense of the enclosed draft.[2] If this course is acceptable to the President, the message from the Prime Minister to the Generalissimo could be telegraphed to His Majesty's Ambassador at Chungking with instructions to arrange with his American colleague for its delivery at the same time that the latter delivers the corresponding message from the President.

5. The Foreign Office believe that there would be advantage in despatching both messages from Potsdam.

L. H. F.

[1] See No. 255, note 5.

[2] Not printed. This draft was the same as the message in No. 525.

No. 525

Mr. Bevin (Berlin) to Mr. Morrison (Received 1 August, 6.15 p.m.)
No. 324 Target Telegraphic [F.O. 934/3/12(19a)]

Top secret. Immediate   BERLIN, *1 August 1945, 8.16 p.m.*

Please pass Immediate to Chungking.

Begins. My immediately preceding telegram.[1]

Following is text of personal message from Prime Minister to Generalissimo.

Begins. At the Potsdam Conference the President of the United States and I, in consultation with the Combined Chiefs of Staff, have had under consideration future military operations in South-East Asia.

2. On the advice of the Combined Chiefs of Staff we have reached the conclusion that *for operational purposes* it is desirable to include that portion of French Indo-China lying south of 16° north latitude (repeat 16° north latitude) in the South-East Asia Command. This arrangement would leave in the China Theatre that part of Indo-China which covers the flank of projected Chinese operations in China and would at the same time enable Admiral Mountbatten to develop operations in the southern half of Indo-China.

3. I greatly hope that the above conclusions will recommend themselves to Your Excellency and that, for the purpose of facilitating operations against the common enemy, Your Excellency will feel able to concur in the proposed arrangements.

4. I understand that the President of the United States is addressing a communication to Your Excellency in a similar sense.   *Ends.*[2]

[1] Not printed. This telegram of 8 p.m. to the Foreign Office (received at 6.05 p.m.) on 1 August 1945 referred to No. 501 and requested transmission to Chungking of a notification that Mr. Attlee and President Truman 'have agreed to propose to Generalissimo Chiang Kai shek that the southern half of French Indo-China should be included in South-East Asia Command.' Sir H. Seymour was instructed to concert with his American colleague the delivery of the message in the present telegram.

[2] Sir H. Seymour replied in Chungking telegram No. 786 of 1.44 p.m. (received 4.10 p.m.) on 4 August: 'Generalissimo is now at his country house and United States Ambassador and I arranged to present messages separately. President's message was delivered on August 2nd and Prime Minister's on August 3rd. 2. Generalissimo asked on each occasion whether new arrangement affected Siam and we both pointed out that messages referred solely to Indo-China. 3. Generalissimo said he would give reply shortly.'

No. 526

Record of Thirteenth Plenary Meeting held at Cecilienhof,
Potsdam, on Wednesday, 1 August 1945
at 10.30 p.m.
P. (Terminal) 13th Meeting [U 6197/3628/70]

Top secret

Present:

PREMIER STALIN, M. V. M. Molotov, M. A. Ya. Vyshinski, M. I. M. Maisky,

M. F. T. Gousev, M. A. A. Gromyko, M. K. V. Novikov, M. B. F. Podtzerob, M. S. A. Golunski (*Interpreter*).

PRESIDENT TRUMAN, Mr. J. F. Byrnes, Mr. Joseph E. Davies, Fleet-Admiral W. D. Leahy, Mr. W. A. Harriman, Mr. E. W. Pauley, Mr. J. C. Dunn, Mr. H. F. Matthews, Mr. W. L. Clayton, Mr. C. E. Bohlen (*Interpreter*).

MR. ATTLEE, Mr. Bevin, Sir A. Cadogan, Sir A. Clark Kerr, Sir W. Strang, Sir E. Bridges, Mr. N. Brook, Sir D. Waley, Mr. T. L. Rowan, Mr. P. J. Dixon, Mr. W. Hayter, Major A. Birse (*Interpreter*).

Contents

1. *Reparations: Germany*
(Previous Reference: P. (Terminal) 12th Meeting,[1] Minute 1.)

MR. BYRNES said that the Economic Committee had considered how the draft statement on reparations should be amended to meet the point about foreign assets which had been raised by Premier Stalin at the Plenary Meeting that morning. Representatives of the three Delegations had agreed that this point could be met by inserting words in the first and third paragraphs of the draft statement which would make it clear that reparation claims would be met by removals from the respective zones 'and from appropriate German external assets.'

It was agreed that these words should be added to paragraphs 1 and 3 of the draft statement on reparations.

MR. BYRNES said that he wished to propose a further amendment in paragraphs 8 and 9 of the draft statement. It was stated in paragraph 8 that the Soviet Government 'renounced all claims to shares of German enterprises' located in the western zones of occupation in Germany. Paragraph 9 recorded a corresponding waiver of claims, by the British and United States Governments, to shares of German enterprises located in the eastern zone of occupation. The suggestion which he wished to make was that it should be made clear that both these paragraphs referred only to claims 'in respect of reparations.' Otherwise it might be thought that the three Governments waived all claims of any description to shares in German enterprises.

It was agreed that the draft statement on reparations should be amended by inserting the words 'in respect of reparations' after the word 'claims' in paragraphs 8 and 9.

[1] No. 518.

2. *Allied Property in Satellite Countries: Seizure as Reparations or War Trophies*
(Previous Reference: P. (Terminal) 12th Meeting,[1] Minute 11.)

M. MOLOTOV[2] said that the Soviet Delegation had now been able to examine the proposals on this subject which had been submitted by the United States Delegation (P. (Terminal) 49).[3] They were prepared to accept these proposals in principle; but there would not now be time to settle the precise wording before the end of the Conference, and they suggested that a detailed agreement should be negotiated through the diplomatic channel.

> It was agreed that the Conference should accept, in principle, the proposals put forward by the United States Delegation (P. (Terminal) 49), but should leave the drafting of a detailed agreement on this matter to be worked out through the diplomatic channel.

3. *Protocol*
The following points were raised in discussion of the draft Protocol:

(*a*) *Allied Property in Satellite Countries: Seizure as Reparations or War Trophies*
It was agreed that a paragraph should be added noting the decision recorded in the preceding Minute.

(*b*) *Western Frontier of Poland*
This paragraph, in describing the line of the proposed frontier, stated that it would run 'through Swinemünde.' It was agreed that, to avoid ambiguity, this phrase should be amended so as to read: 'immediately west of Swinemünde.'

(*c*) *City of Koenigsberg and the Adjacent Area*
This paragraph stated that the Conference agreed in principle to the proposal of the Soviet Government 'subject to expert examination of the actual frontier.'

PREMIER STALIN suggested that for this phrase there should be substituted: 'The exact line on the ground should be established by experts from the U.S.S.R. and Poland.'

MR. BEVIN said that the British and United States Governments had agreed to support, in principle, the proposal which the Soviet Government would put forward at the peace settlement; but he would find it very difficult to agree that these Governments should be committed to support a frontier line which had been defined by the Soviet Government and the Polish Provisional Government alone.

PREMIER STALIN said there must be some misunderstanding about his suggestion. The Conference had agreed broadly where the frontier should run: it remained to define the actual line of the frontier on the ground. This was a matter of adjustment, by a kilometre this way or that, in order to avoid local inconvenience. Detailed adjustments of this kind were surely matters which could be left to the two interested parties.

[2] This statement is ascribed to Marshal Stalin in the Russian record, *Conferences: Soviet Documents*, p. 308.
[3] See No. 451, note 6.

Mr. Attlee said that the final determination of the frontier must await the peace settlement; and it would be for the Peace Conference to decide what expert examination was required to determine the line of the frontier in detail. It was not for the Conference to pre-judge the decision by what experts that determination should be carried out.

Premier Stalin said that, in view of the discussion, he would withdraw his suggestion.

> It was agreed that no change should be made in the wording of this paragraph of the Protocol.

(d) Admission to the United Nations

The first sentence of the proposed statement on this subject read as follows: 'The three Governments consider it desirable that the present anomalous position of Italy, Bulgaria, Finland, Hungary and Roumania should be terminated by the conclusion of Peace Treaties, so that as soon as possible thereafter relations between them and the ex-enemy States can, where necessary, be re-established on a normal footing.'

M. Molotov pointed out that, since this part of the statement was drafted, the Conference had agreed[4] to include, in paragraph 3, an undertaking that the three Governments would examine, in the near future, in the light of conditions then prevailing, the establishment of diplomatic relations with those States 'to the extent possible prior to the conclusion of Peace Treaties with those countries.' He suggested that there was an inconsistency between these two sentences; and therefore proposed that the word 'thereafter' should be deleted from the first sentence.

Mr. Attlee maintained that there was no inconsistency between these two passages in the statement. The first sentence referred to the re-establishment of normal relations; the other passage referred only to the establishment of something less than full diplomatic relations prior to the conclusion of Peace Treaties.

Premier Stalin said that, in his view, the first sentence of the statement, as it now stood, stultified the promise held out in the later passage. He would not be satisfied with the substitution, suggested by Mr. Bevin, of the phrase 'full diplomatic relations' in the first sentence of the statement in place of the present reference to 'normal' relations. He could not understand why the British Government were so reluctant to contemplate the restoration of diplomatic relations with these countries. If his point could not be met he feared that it would not be possible to publish an agreed statement on this question.

After some further discussion Mr. Bevin suggested that the point might be met by omitting the second part of the first sentence of the proposed statement. The whole of the first paragraph would then read as follows: 'The three Governments consider it desirable that the present anomalous position of Italy, Bulgaria, Finland, Hungary and Roumania should be

[4] Cf. No. 495, minute 4.

terminated by the conclusion of Peace Treaties. They trust that the other interested Allied Governments will share this view.'

PREMIER STALIN said that he would be satisfied with this amendment; and it was agreed that the first paragraph of this statement should read as set out immediately above.

(e) Industrial District of the Ruhr

MR. BYRNES pointed out that the Russian text of the Protocol included a paragraph on the Ruhr. There was no corresponding paragraph in the English text. It was agreed that the Protocol should not contain any reference to the discussion about the Ruhr.

The Conference:

(1) Approved the draft Protocol,[5] subject to amendment on the points noted at (a) to (e) above; and

(2) Agreed that the final comparison of the English and Russian texts of the Protocol should be carried out on their behalf by:

United States Delegation: Mr. J. Dunn.

British Delegation: Sir Edward Bridges.

Russian Delegation: M. Vyshinski.

4. Communiqué
(a) Text

The Conference considered the draft of a Communiqué setting out those of the decisions of the Conference which could appropriately be made public.

Agreement was reached on a number of drafting amendments.

It was further agreed that the Communiqué should not include any reference to the following subjects, on which decisions had been recorded in the Protocol: Reparations from Austria; Oil equipment in Roumania; Iran; Tangier; Black Sea Straits; International Inland Waterways; European Inland Transport Conference; Directives to Military Commanders on Allied Control Council for Germany; Seizure of Allied Property in Satellite Countries as Reparations or War Trophies.

It was also agreed that the Communiqué should not include details of the agreement reached on the disposal of the German Fleet and Merchant Navy, or details of the proposed modification of the procedure of the Allied Control Commission in Hungary.

(b) Signature

M. MOLOTOV said that he presumed that the Communiqué would be signed by the three Heads of Government. In what order was it proposed that the signatures should apprear? In the Communiqués issued at earlier Conferences, Mr. Churchill's name or President Roosevelt's name had been placed first; and it had been understood, betwen Mr. Churchill and President Roosevelt, that on the next occasion for the issue of a Communiqué by the three Heads of Government Premier Stalin's name would appear first.

[5] Cf. No. 602, note 2.

It was agreed that the Communiqué in respect of the present Conference should be signed by the three Heads of Government in the following order: Premier Stalin, President Truman, Mr. Attlee.

(c) *Time of Release*

It was agreed that the Communiqué[6] should be released at 9.30 p.m. G.M.T. on Thursday, 2nd August, 1945.

This meant that it would appear in the morning newspapers on the 3rd August; but could be released on the radio at any time after 9.30 p.m. on the 2nd August.

5. *Messages to Mr. Churchill and Mr. Eden*

MR. ATTLEE proposed, and it was agreed, that on the conclusion of the Conference messages should be sent to Mr. Churchill and Mr. Eden in the following terms:

To Mr. Churchill

'President Truman, Generalissimo Stalin and Prime Minister Attlee, assembled at the final session of the Berlin Conference, desire to send a message of greetings to Mr. Winston Churchill. They wish to thank him for all his work in the first part of the Berlin Conference which helped greatly to lay the foundations of its successful conclusion.

They remember with gratitude the untiring efforts and the unconquerable spirit with which at earlier conferences and throughout the war he served our common cause of victory and enduring peace. The whole world knows the greatness of his work, and it will never be forgotten.'

To Mr. Eden

'President Truman, Generalissimo Stalin and Prime Minister Attlee, assembled at the final session of the Berlin Conference, send to Mr. Eden their greetings and thanks for his help in the first part of the Conference. They recall the lasting value of his work at earlier conferences and international meetings, which had contributed so much to victory, unity and peace.'

Cabinet Office, Potsdam, 2nd August, 1945

[6] No. 603.i.

No. 527

Letter from Mr. Attlee (Berlin) to Mr. Eden
[PREM 3/430/14]

Top secret   BERLIN, *1 August 1945*

My dear Eden,

The Conference ended tonight in a good atmosphere. I would like to let you know the broad results before the communique is issued.

We have, of course, been building on the work you did and there has been no change of policy. It was clear that without agreement on Poland

and reparations we should get nowhere. We had wanted to stand on the Eastern Neisse but the Americans rather suddenly gave way. We therefore agreed to the Western Neisse after having had long meetings with the Poles from whom we extracted very specific pledges on elections, Press facilities and the repatriation of the Polish Forces. There was a long wrangle on reparations at which we had to concede a higher percentage of reparation deliveries than we should have liked. We received satisfaction on the supply of food etc. to Western Germany and on giving precedence to the maintenance of German economy at a reasonable level. Other matters proved less difficult and on the whole I am not dissatisfied with the result. Uncle Joe was very glum at our first meeting, the result of indisposition which hung us up for two days. The President was very co-operative, but tended to a certain lack of interest at the later stages. Bevin picked up all the points very quickly and showed his skill as a negotiator.

If you would care to come and see me to hear more details, I should be delighted.[1]

Yours ever
C. R. A.

[1] Mr. Eden replied in a letter of 2 August 1945 from Binderton House, Chichester: 'My dear Clem, Thank you for your letter & for telling me the broad results in this way. It will be interesting to read the full communiqué to-morrow. I agree with you in a strong preference for curtailing these excessive Polish demands to the West. I cannot believe that it is to Poland's own interest to obtain territories to the Western Neisse. Thank you also for your action in proposing thanks in a message to me from the Berlin Conference. As I mentioned in the House I am grateful that you should have thought of this. I hope to spend all next week here but if after that either you or Ernest Bevin want to see me on any point I am, of course, available. I hope, though, that you will both get a few days off. It must have been hard going to conclude the conference and form a govt. in the same week. Yours ever Anthony' (Bodleian Library, Oxford: MS. Attlee dep. 18, fols. 102–3).

CHAPTER V

Developments during the second part of the Conference at Potsdam

27 July — 2 August 1945

No. 528

Mr. Eden to Mr. Hankey (Warsaw)

No. 78 Telegraphic [N 9153/123/55]

Important   FOREIGN OFFICE, *27 July 1945, 10.45 p.m.*

Repeated to Washington (by bag) No. 697 Saving, Terminal (by bag) No. 251, and later to Sir W. Strang, Caserta, M.E. Minister.

Please deliver following official communication to Polish Provisional Government. You should discuss it with M. Mikolajczyk beforehand if possible and if he has important comments or suggestions to make, telegraph them to me before delivering note.[1]

2. (Begins).

His Majesty's Government in the United Kingdom desire to convey to the Polish Provisional Government of National Unity their views regarding the Polish Armed Forces under British Command.

2. These military naval and air forces have borne a brave part as our allies against the enemy in Germany, Italy and elsewhere. They have fought, suffered and died with great gallantry under British command. So long as they remain under British command, His Majesty's Government are

---

[1] With reference to this paragraph, Sir O. Sargent telegraphed Sir A. Cadogan at Berlin in Foreign Office telegram No. 266 Onward of 28 July 1945 at 7.40 p.m.: 'You may have an opportunity at Terminal of discussing our communication with M. Mikolajczyk . . . Unless he advises strongly to the contrary I think it would be best, however, that it should be presented by Mr. Hankey in Warsaw. It would be difficult for you to discuss it at Terminal without full knowledge of the complicated considerations that affect our attitude. Moreover, we do not want the Russians to be brought in and desire to proceed if possible step by step.' Berlin telegram No. 302 Target of 31 July by bag (received, 1 August at 2 p.m.) replied that the communication had been shown to M. Mikolajczyk, 'who has however offered no comment. There seems therefore no reason why Mr. Hankey should not deliver note if he has not already done so, unless he prefers to await early return of M. Mikolajczyk to Warsaw.'

responsible for their welfare and also for ensuring their maintenance as disciplined formations.

3. His Majesty's Government desire that all Polish nationals in the Armed forces who wish to return to Poland should do so as soon as the necessary arrangements can be made. His Majesty's Government moreover consider it their duty to ensure so far as possible that these officers and men should have a proper opportunity of making an unbiassed and unhurried decision, with a full understanding of the facts, and free from fear or compulsion, that orderly arrangements should be made for the return to Poland of those who wish to do so, and that none should be compelled to go against their will. His Majesty's Government are sure that the Polish Provisional Government will agree with these views and will be glad to receive their confirmation.

4. It then remains to consider how the desired results can be achieved.

5. The members of the Polish armed forces under British command are naturally at the present time in a state of some uncertainty and mental stress as a result of the withdrawal of recognition by His Majesty's Government from the ex-President and the Government to whom they have owed allegiance. It is not to be expected therefore that all of them will be ready to make their final decision at once.

6. In the view of His Majesty's Government, the first necessity is that the members of the Polish Armed Forces under British command should be informed of the conditions which the Polish Provisional Government are prepared to offer those who desire to return to Poland. In particular His Majesty's Government would be glad to receive the assurance of the Polish Provisional Government that these men will be guaranteed personal rights and rights of property on the same basis as all Polish citizens and will not be victimised for their former allegiance. His Majesty's Government would therefore be glad as a first step to receive from the Polish Provisional Government a full statement on this subject for their own information and consideration and for subsequent publication among the Polish officers and men under British command here and overseas.

7. Since it is essential that discipline should continue to be preserved in the Polish forces, orderly arrangements will have to be made for ascertaining the wishes of members of those Forces and for transferring to Poland from time to time those who wish to go.

CALENDARS TO No. 528

having any authority over Polish Armed Forces under British command; suggests that such forces be released from oath of allegiance [N 9662/123/55].

iv   *1 Aug. 1945*   *Minutes of 4th Meeting of Interim Treasury Committee for Polish Questions.* Statements by Polish delegation on devastation of Poland's economy [N 9876/1938/55].

v   *15 Aug. 1945*   *Letter from Mr. Warner to Mr. S. Hoare (Home Office).* F.O. had resisted a qualification proposed by Home Office to statement in communication to Polish Provisional Govt. in No. 528 that no Poles should be compelled to return against their will. F.O., however, do not consider that this communication should prevent forcible repatriation in individual cases on special grounds [N 9153/123/55].

No. 529

*Minute of discussion at Allied Control Commission
(Soviet) H.Q. Bucharest on 27 July 1945*
[*R 14495/217/37*]

Present:

U.S.S.R.: COL. GEN. SUSAIKOV (Deputy Chairman of the A.C.C.), Mr. A. P. Pavlov (Soviet Political Representative), Officers in Attendance.

U.S.A.: BRIG. GEN. SCHUYLER, Lt. Col. Tucker, Officers in Attendance.

Britain: A.V.M. STEVENSON, Col. Forster, Officers in Attendance.

(1) THE BRITISH COMMISSIONER stated that, as the war is now over, he considered that the Soviet Control officers in the oilfields, refineries and offices of the British oil companies should be withdrawn. These companies had worked and would continue to work loyally in accordance with demands, without the control officers.

(2) COL. GEN. SUSAIKOV and MR. PAVLOV enquired what the objection was to the continued presence of these control officers. The British Commissioner asked Col. Forster to reply.

(3) COL. FORSTER said that, apart from the fact that the European war is over, there is now another consideration of the greatest importance. The Soviet Union had recently entered the Rumanian oil industry as a competitor of the British companies and it was unreasonable that these companies should have to continue to give Soviet officers free access to all their most valuable information such as geological and production records, refinery processes etc.

(4) COL. GEN. SUSAIKOV asked by whom information of this type was being demanded from the companies.

(5) COL. FORSTER stated that A.C.C. officers were responsible.

(6) COL. GEN. SUSAIKOV and MR. PAVLOV retorted blandly that the A.C.C. had nothing to do with the new Soviet oil company.

(7) COL. FORSTER replied that there was always the possibility of A.C.C. officers (who had had access to British company files) being transferred to

the new Soviet company. He furthermore submitted that the only right the A.C.C. had in (British) oil companies was to see that the proper quantities and qualities of oil were delivered under the Armistice. Nothing in the Armistice Convention gave the right to the use of their technical records.

(8) COL. GEN. SUSAIKOV and MR. PAVLOV angrily commented that Soviet officers were being accused of espionage and that the honour of Red Army officers could not be impugned in this manner. Addressing A.V.M. Stevenson, Col. Gen. Susaikov then stated that the present occassion [sic] was a meeting with the *Commissioner*.

(9) THE BRITISH COMMISSIONER and COL. FORSTER both apologised but insisted that there was no question of accusations of espionage or of the honour of the Red Army. The British Commissioner added that things were now getting back to a normal commercial basis and commercial rights and interests should be respected.

(10) The meeting then passed to the next point on the Agenda.[1]

Notes

(a) At the close of the meeting Col. Gen. Susaikov said to Col. Forster that if people could not quarrel occassionally [sic] when trying to do business, there would never be any business done. Col. Forster concurred.

(b) There is not the slightest doubt that for at least eight months past the Russian A.C.C. officers have made it their business to gain every possible scrap of information from the oil companies, very much of which is of such a purely local nature that it could never be of service for the development of the oil industry in the Soviet Union. On at least one recent occassion they demanded the details of a patented refinery process which they stated was for the ex-German and now Soviet-controlled Petrol Block refinery.

They have also recently developed a regular practice of switching crude oil away from British companies to other refineries, so that the British companies are compelled to pay the others heavy refining charges, although their own plants are working far below full capacity.

[1] Cf. No. 539.i.

No. 530

Mr. Caccia (Athens) to Mr. Eden (Received 27 July, 3.40 p.m.)
No. 1596 Telegraphic [R 12679/4/19]

Immediate　　　　　　　　　　　　ATHENS, *27 July 1945, 2.30 p.m. G.M.T.*

Following for Sir O. Sargent.

Your telegram No. 1579.[1]

The Regent summoned me to see him this morning, and asked me faithfully to report the following.

[1] No. 412.

2. (*a*) A large section of Greek opinion has, in typical fashion, interpreted British (. . .? election)[2] in purely Greek terms. A victory for Churchill would have been taken to mean continued support for the Regent and the present Government. A victory for the Labour Party should herald a change of British policy towards Greece. Although no one could yet decide what that change would be, it was certain that those Republican leaders who with the Communist party had been demanding a political Government rather than a (. . .? service)[2] Government would now become still more vocal.

(*b*) He himself knew that the Greek interpretation of British events was warped. At the same time it would become increasingly difficult for him to resist (. . .? any)[2] opposition if there was no outward sign that British foreign policy towards Greece remained constant.

(*c*) For our own personal information we should know President of the Council had yesterday evening pressed him to accept his resignation. The Regent had refused to consent but it showed that Admiral Voulgaris was entirely sincere in his assertion that he had no desire to continue as President of the Council if that were against the interests of Greece. Consequently the greater became the criticism of present Government at home and abroad, the more difficult it would be for the Regent to persuade Admiral Voulgaris to continue.

(*d*) He, the Regent, had no confidence that an all Party Government was a practical possibility. If necessary this could be put to the test and his guess would be that after usual party negotiations it would be found that such a Government could not at present be formed in Greece. However if for the sake of Greece's good name abroad such an attempt should be made he was always ready to try his best and he knew Admiral Voulgaris would not constitute any obstacle. Further, if the attempt failed Admiral Voulgaris could be 'rebaptised'.

(*e*) Even if an all Party Government could be formed, the basic problem concerning (. . .? restoration of)[2] law and order would remain precisely the same. Improvement depended principally upon clothing, equipping and despatching of sufficient police and gendarmerie to establish law and order. In his view it was not a question of adding anything to the statute book or seeking for men of better faith than were now in the Government.

3. In view of the above considerations he had a single request. Appearances in politics were often as important as realities. He therefore begged that if His Majesty's Government wished him to continue in the course prescribed in your telegram they should choose some means of making their policy clear at the earliest possible moment. For Greece this was a vital and urgent necessity and he earnestly requested that what he said might be taken into immediate consideration. He realised he was asking a great deal; but it was his plain duty to Greece to do so and he could not do otherwise.

[2] The text is here uncertain.

4. I subsequently saw Admiral Voulgaris who confirmed once again that he had no personal wish to continue as President of the Council and that advice of His Majesty's Government should be given solely with a view to the interests of Greece without taking into account any personal considerations.

5. Both he and the Regent greatly hoped His Majesty's Government and United States Government would be of one mind on this and other questions affecting Greece. It was also to Greece's interest that Russia should not boycott her indefinitely.

CALENDAR TO No. 530

i *28 July 1945   Mr. Caccia (Athens) Tel. No. 1599.* Uncertain attitude of Greek republican leaders to suggestion from Communist Party for an all-party government [R 12732/4/19].

No. 531

Mr. Eden to Sir A. Cadogan (Berlin: received 27 July, 6.30 p.m.)
No. 242 Onward Telegraphic [R 12717/11875/19]

Top secret. Important   FOREIGN OFFICE, *27 July 1945, 4.22 p.m.*

Onward telegram No. 195.[1]
Following for Sir A. Cadogan from Foreign Office.
Our views on the questions referred to in that telegram have been sent separately.[2]

2. It is our impression that a concerted campaign which is now being launched against the Greeks by all her neighbours—and even Roumania—and that it is [*sic*] assuming dangerous proportions.

3. Hitherto, there have been only isolated and spasmodic attacks on the Greek Government by the press and radio, principally in Moscow and Belgrade, and occasional sharp criticism in political speeches by Tito. We are now faced with this concerted onslaught which it is difficult to believe is not the result of guidance from Moscow (cf. Belgrade telegram No. 1145 and Moscow telegram No. 3270[3]). It is bad enough of course that Greece's allies should attack her in this way; but it is much worse that the defeated Roumanians and Bulgarians (to say nothing of the Albanians) should be encouraged to indulge in slanderous attacks on Greece.

---

[1] No. 392.
[2] See No. 402, and i below.
[3] These telegrams of 19 and 24 July 1945 respectively (R 12230, 12464/2808/92: not printed) concerned a report of an unconfirmed eye-witness account of a meeting between Marshal Tito and high Russian officials including M. Vyshinski near Novi Sad on 13–14 July.

4. The action we have taken so far to stop this state of affairs is as follows. We instructed H.M. Ambassador in Moscow to draw the attention of the Soviet Government to the anti-Greek press and radio reports emanating from Moscow and to express the hope that steps would be taken to put an end to this development.[4] This, as was to be expected, achieved little or no result. H.M. Ambassador in Belgrade was also recently instructed to inform Tito of H.M.G.'s displeasure at his recent utterances about Greece and to suggest that any Yugoslav grievances should be dealt with through the diplomatic channel and not by public speeches.[5] The Greek Government have also been advised to remain calm and not to indulge in press counter attacks against the Yugoslavs. If, as seems likely, orders have now been given by Moscow for a continuance of this campaign, our representations will bear no result and we may have to consider what, if any, further steps we can take.

5. You will see from Onward telegram No. 210[6] that we are suggesting that the Greek reply to the recent Yugoslav note about Yugoslavs in Greek Macedonia should be

(a) that a Greek–Yugoslav commission should investigate the situation on both sides of the frontier, or

(b) that an appeal should be made to the five Great Powers or the World Organisation, as soon as the latter functions.

But this reply is not going to restore calm if Tito, counting on Russian support, is out for mischief. Given Balkan mentality and the unsettled conditions and the nervous tension in Yugoslavia and Greece, there may be incidents which, though of minor importance in themselves, may rapidly assume larger proportions.

6. In this connexion we would draw your attention to Caserta telegram No. 1346[7] reporting that Field Marshal Alexander had made recommendations to the Combined Chiefs of Staff in connexion with the line to be adopted by the British forces in Greece in the event of Greek frontier incidents. The Field Marshal's recommendations have been considered by the Chiefs of Staff, whose reactions are unfavourable for the following reasons:

(i) Allied resources in Mediterranean are insufficient to support such a policy.

(ii) Absence of American troops in Greece makes it impossible to entertain idea of unilateral British action in Balkans. Undesirable to commit British troops to another task of unpredictable dimensions.

(iii) British forces are scheduled to leave at end of 1945.

The Chiefs of Staff suggest that Sacmed be instructed that British troops in Greece continue their role of maintaining internal order but will *not* be specifically disposed to assist in safeguarding Greek frontiers, nor will they

---

[4] See No. 47, note 1. [5] See Nos. 157 and 335.
[6] No. 402. [7] No. 121.

become involved in frontier incidents unless directly attacked. Foreign Office have been asked for their comments before Chiefs of Staff submit their conclusions to the Prime Minister.

7. We appreciate the military objections of entering into a commitment which might be of long duration, but we fail to see how, if a frontier incident occurs, which it is beyond the power of the slender Greek forces to put down, the British forces can stand aside. It seems to us, looking at the problem from the political aspect, that so long as our forces are there they ought to assist the Greeks not only to maintain internal order but to protect their frontiers. The military situation on the frontier is from the Greek point of view disturbing to a degree. Their own forces are negligible whereas on the other side of the frontier it is calculated that there are some 30,000 Albanians, 30,000 Yugoslav and 24,000 Bulgarian troops excluding the main Yugoslav and Bulgarian divisions in those countries. There is, moreover, the uncomfortable feeling that Russia lurks in the background especially as contrary to Stalin's assertion at Terminal that there are only 30,000 Russian troops in Bulgaria,[8] War Office estimate them at least as 100,000 and General Oxley, who has just arrived from Sofia, puts the present figure at 200,000 or more (see also in this connexion General Oxley's telegram M. 1493[9] of July 19th).

8. On the other hand, Stalin is now aware that we only have 40,000 troops in Greece and no armoured divisions. This information will probably be passed on to Tito who, with or without Russian encouragement, may feel tempted to take action.

9. It looks as though the Soviet Government are preparing to challenge our policy of building up a strong independent Greece and Turkey friendly to Great Britain, and at the same time to strengthen the position of their own client, Bulgaria. So long as Yugoslavia, Greece and Turkey are on good relations with one another Bulgaria is bound to be completely isolated in the Balkans. Since it is the present policy of the Soviet Government to build up Bulgaria as their outpost in the Balkans, with a window on the Eastern Mediterranean, it is only natural that they should endeavour to embroil Greece and Yugoslavia with one another in Europe in the hope that this will force Yugoslavia to co-operate with Bulgaria, if possible to the extent of political union.

10. If this Russian challenge to our position in Greece and Turkey is successfully countered in its early stages it is probable that the Soviet Government will not persevere in their present policy. But if any part of Greek territory is occupied without any military action on our part it will need very little to launch Yugoslavia and Bulgaria on a large-scale invasion for the purpose of obtaining their objectives—Slavonika [Salonika] in the case of Yugoslavia and Thrace in the case of Bulgaria. If this should happen the stage would be set to enable the Soviet Government to overthrow the

[8] See No. 241, minute 10.
[9] Enclosure in No. 362.

Greek Government and revive E.A.M. and also to reduce Turkey by a war of nerves to a state where she would be prepared to give the Soviet Government the bases on the Straits which she has demanded, and generally to force her into the Russian orbit.

11. It looks therefore that if we are to maintain our policy of building up a strong and independent Greece and Turkey as our bastions in S.E. Europe we must show ourselves capable of preventing from the outset all encroachments on Greek territory, even in the form of incursions from Yugoslavia or Bulgaria, lest they develop into actual military invasions by the armies of these two countries.

12. You will see from paragraph 4 of Caserta telegram No. 1346[7] that Field Marshal Alexander suggests that a warning should be given by the principal Allied Powers to Yugoslavia, Bulgaria, Albania and Greece condemning the means by which they are apparently trying to anticipate the Peace Settlement. We should be glad of your views as to the possibility or desirability of raising this matter at Terminal, and of issuing a joint warning to the countries concerned. This will at any rate force the Soviet Government into the open.

13. This telegram has not been seen by Mr. Eden.

CALENDAR TO No. 531

i *27 July 1945 To Sir A. Cadogan (Berlin) Tel. No. 253 Onward.* Further comments on No. 392: sees no reason to take any notice of Bulgarian note [R 12421/21/7].

No. 532

Mr. Eden to Sir A. Cadogan (Berlin: received 27 July, 10.40 p.m.)
No. 248 Onward Telegraphic [R 12707/4/19]

Top secret. Immediate   FOREIGN OFFICE, *27 July 1945, 6.45 p.m.*

Repeated to Athens No. 1593, Washington No. 7881, Moscow No. 4168, Belgrade No. 1109, Caserta No. 2300.

From Sir O. Sargent to Sir A. Cadogan.

My telegram No. 1579[1] to Athens (of July 26th: political situation in Greece) (Onward 224).

If there is to be no change of government we must produce convincing arguments for rejecting the demands for a representative government. This should not be too difficult, since we can point out that:

(*a*) a change of government now would interrupt the measures being taken to restore Greek economy and finances just at the moment when these measures are producing results;

[1] No. 412.

(*b*) the last all-party government under Papandreou failed dismally, and after the civil war and the passions which it has aroused there is even less chance to-day of the party leaders working amicably together:

(*c*) there is no reason to suppose that an all-party government could organise and hold elections and a plebiscite on a fairer or more impartial basis than the present Service Government. On the contrary, party rivalries would be brought into the government, which is not the case at present, and the chances of holding fair elections would be very remote.[2]

2. I am impressed, however, by the danger that if the campaign for a representative government is allowed to continue unchecked the Communist and Republican Parties may succeed in making it impossible for elections to be held this year or may boycott the elections if they take place. The forthcoming announcement of Allied supervision will do something to prevent this, but I have been considering whether there are any other steps open to us. One possible measure would be to set up a commission, on which all the principal parties would be represented, with the task of advising the Greek Government on the preparations for the plebiscite and elections. This could be regarded as a development of the provision in the electoral law already passed by the Greek Government, whereby local commissions formed of representatives of the three principal parties will scrutinize the work of revising the electoral rolls.

3. Another possibility would be to revive the idea of establishing a consultative assembly which would include the leaders of all the political parties. The Regent and Admiral Voulgaris suggested this some months ago, but we took the line that it would give more trouble than it was worth since it would certainly come into conflict with the Government. I am still rather doubtful whether this proposal is worth pursuing but, like the suggestion in the preceding paragraph, it would give the politicians something to do and might ease the pressure for a change of government.

4. We should welcome Mr. Caccia's opinion on paragraphs 3 and 4 [*sic*] above, and you may also wish to discuss the question with the American Delegation before we say anything to the Greek Government.[3]

CALENDAR TO No. 532

i   *28 July 1945   Mr. Caccia (Athens) Tel. No. 1601:* views on No. 532: is strongly opposed to suggested establishment of consultative assembly but less so to the alternative of an advisory commission [R 12736/4/19].

[2] This phrase is cited by Sir L. Woodward, *op. cit.*, vol. v, p. 490.

[3] Sir A. Cadogan replied to Sir O. Sargent in Berlin telegram No. 278 Target of 29 July 1945 at 9.30 p.m.: 'I doubt if we can have any useful Anglo-American discussions on Greece here in the time that is left to us, particularly as the U.S. Delegation's Greek expert has already gone home. Perhaps you would therefore pursue this question direct with the State Department.' On 1 August Mr. Balfour reported in Washington telegram No. 5344 (received 2 August) discussion on paragraphs 2 to 4 of No. 532 with the State Department 'whose preliminary (repeat preliminary) reaction is to favour the proposed inter-party commission . . . We have not (repeat not) discussed first paragraph of your telegram under reference formally with State Department but from informal conversations with members

of Near Eastern Division we gather that, like yourselves, State Department do not at present consider anything would be gained by substituting an all-party for the present Service Government.'

No. 533

Sir W. Strang (Lübbecke) to Mr. Eden (Received 27 July, 2.50 p.m.)

No. 74 Telegraphic [N 9373/2977/59]

Important   LÜBBECKE, *27 July 1945, 1.6 p.m. G.M.T.*

I am informed by CDPX[1] at Frankfurt that the French Government have agreed with the Soviet Government to hand over as Soviet citizens all former citizens of the Baltic States.

2. CDPX, after consulting United States Political Adviser propose:

(*a*) To move out of France into Germany all Baltic nationals under their control.

(*b*) Not to hand over any more to the French, and

(*c*) To convey a discreet warning to all those already handed over. May I have your views?[2]

CALENDARS TO No. 533

i   *28 July 1945   Mr. Stevenson (Belgrade) Tel. No. 1222.* French rendition of seven Yugoslavs regarded as war criminals reinforces need for decision on British policy [R 12734/329/92].

ii   *26 & 31 July 1945   Letter from Mr. Hoyer Millar (Berlin) to Mr. Harvey; Mr. Norton (Berne) Tel. No. 1267.* Judged inopportune to raise at Potsdam question of Soviet-Swiss relations. Arrival in Switzerland of Soviet delegation on repatriation; Swiss reluctance to allow forcible repatriation [F.O. 934/5/50(1); Z 9002/1535/43].

[1] The Combined Displaced Persons Executive had been established on the termination of S.H.A.E.F. for the general coordination of arrangements concerning displaced persons and prisoners of war: cf. M. J. Proudfoot, *European Refugees 1939–1952* (London, 1957), p. 168, note 1.

[2] Foreign Office telegram No. 140 of 2 August 1945 to Sir W. Strang stated in reply: 'We have no knowledge of any such Soviet–French agreement; but should not be surprised if the report were true. We agree with (*a*) and (*b*) of your second paragraph, but not with (*c*). Such a warning would be likely to lead to a clamour from Baltics in French hands to be taken under our protection, which would place us in an awkward position *vis-à-vis* both the French and the Russians.'

No. 534

Minute by Lord Dunboyne[1]

[WR 2155/2155/48]

FOREIGN OFFICE, 27 July 1945

I have spoken with Major Maby CA/DP, W.O.[2] about this [i]. He confirms that H.M.G.'s policy is being adhered to and that no-one is being forcibly repatriated from British occupied zones. Soviet citizens are of course covered separately by the Yalta Agreement but they form the only exception to the rule.[3]

DUNBOYNE

CALENDARS TO NO. 534

i *13 July & 3 Aug. 1945 Correspondence between Miss S. J. Warner (British Red Cross) and Mr. Mason.* Red Cross concern at reports from southern Austria of forced repatriation of Russian and Yugoslav refugees. British Red Cross would deprecate identification with what appears a rather anti-humanitarian policy. Mr. Mason replies that so far as is known at departmental level of War Office forcible repatriation of such refugees is not taking place and would be contrary to directives issued, except in the case of such Soviet nationals as are clearly covered by the terms of the Yalta agreement [WR 2155/2155/48].

ii *23 & 28 July 1945 British Embassy (Belgrade) tel. No. 465 to War Office. W.O. tel. No. 63266:* 'Our policy is that no Yugoslav should be repatriated unless he expresses free wish to return' [R 12839/1728/92].

iii *28 July 1945 Letter from Mr. Warner to Colonel Hammer (War Office).* Legal Adviser has stated that in fulfilment of the Yalta Agreement British authorities, while not going unnecessarily out of their way to assist Soviet authorities, should, failing enforcement of discipline by Soviet authorities, exercise the necessary measures of constraint as part of the process of repatriation. In the U.K. British guards are instructed not to use firearms in any circumstances, though some physical force has been used now and then. Every effort should be made to avoid use of force by British military authorities, as in regard to 55 Soviet citizens in Rome transit camp: if Soviet authorities agree to provide an armed guard and to use the force necessary, this would establish precedent for treatment of much larger group of Cossacks in Austria [N 9357/409/38].

---

[1] A member of the Refugee Department of the Foreign Office.
[2] Displaced Persons Branch of the Civil Affairs Directorate of the War Office.
[3] This minute was initialed on 31 July 1945 by Mr. I. L. Henderson.

No. 535

Mr. Eden to Earl of Halifax (Washington)
No. 7873 Telegraphic [C 49/47/18]

Immediate   FOREIGN OFFICE, *27 July 1945, 9.20 p.m.*

Repeated Immediate to Minister Resident Cairo No. 1315, Resmed Caserta No. 2299, High Commissioner Rome No. 1925, and to Moscow No. 4162, Malta.

P.W.E. Political Warfare Directive (European Theatres) for week beginning 28th July, 1945.

Information and Publicity to Germany and Austria.

1. The following points from the first Standing Directive of the Information Services Control Branch Political Division of the British Element of the Control Commission, set the main objectives for all media in the immediate future.

'The best allies of Nazism in Germany are idleness, boredom and fear of the future.'

'Everything possible will be done, and as soon as possible, to counteract these states of mind.'

'The first phase of austerity, aloofness and rigid restraints is now over. The phase of increasing freedom and hope for the Germans is being entered.'

'A sense of direction, purpose and responsibility among the Germans must be stimulated. This will require the adoption of measures which will lead towards greater freedom of self-expression and frankness of discussion among the Germans.'

2. Make it clear whenever possible that the cerellary [corollary] of the policy of making Germans help themselves and each other is that free discussion and criticism by Germans should have as first targets their own countrymen in positions of responsibility, and as first objectives greater effort and achievement in reconstruction.

3. Use frankly the unavoidably depressing facts about German food, communications, employment and health as problems bequeathed by Hitler's war; but lay emphasis on the power of ordinary people to organise themselves for self-help and for the execution of the instructions of Allied government and local administrations.

4. The encouraging and constructive approach to the German audience must not exclude the occasional reminder of their complicity in the aggressions and crimes of the last 12 years. New evidence on this theme is to be selected with great care and is sometimes best released first through a German spokesman or newspaper. The long-term objective is to stimulate German inquiry into and revelation of the crimes of the past.

5. Emphasise that political reliability alone is not a sufficient title to responsible work. Technical efficiency and ability to command obedience from Germans and to cooperate with Allied officials are also essential.

6. Maintain the food production campaign by constant plugging. Germans still expect plugging. Encourage improvisation in the harvesting

and lifting of crops. Emphasise the importance of reporting to local authorities spare parts, batteries etc. in local garages and workshops; also vehicles capable of repair or adaptation.

7. Use figures of removals and arrests of local Nazi office-holders regularly to show the purge going steadily on. At the same time illustrate the magnitude of the problem by citing the high percentage of officials removed in specific localities. So far as possible make practice in this respect appear uniform throughout the Allied zones.

8. Speculation about the outcome for Germany of the Potsdam conference is still to be avoided pending the issue of provisional or final communiques. Do not encourage Germans to expect decisions which will immediately improve their lot.

9. Avoid all statements on the return of approved anti-Nazi prisoners to Germany from United States of America and United Kingdom.

10. Use available material to explain to Germans how the present system of military government works, emphasising particularly local examples.

11. The following points in Directive of July 20th[1] should be followed further: No. 2 (discouragement of return to the Ruhr); No. 8 (concentration of political activity on local problems); No. 12 (evidence from Austria of return to normal).

CALENDAR TO NO. 535

i 27 July 1945 Minutes of a British meeting in Hamburg on broadcasts to German schools from Radio Hamburg [C 5029/28/18].

[1] No. 43.iii.

No. 536

Mr. Eden to Earl of Halifax (Washington)
No. 7859 Telegraphic [E 5376/14/89]

FOREIGN OFFICE, 27 July 1945, 1.55 a.m.

Repeated to Beirut No. 564, M.E. Min's Office No. 1314, Paris No. 1770 Saving.

Your telegram No. 5109[1] (of July 21st: discussions regarding the Levant).

Please inform States Department of this tentative suggestion. Appointment of a neutral commission with wide terms of reference would have two main advantages:

(*a*) if Levant problem eventually comes before World Organisation,

[1] Not printed. This Washington telegram of 10.8 p.m. (received, 22 July at 5.55 a.m.) had asked whether the tentative suggestion in paragraph 6 of No. 148 should be passed to the State Department.

that body would have an impartial report as a basis for its discussions; (*b*) meanwhile, the very fact that commission was in the Levant studying the situation would tend to keep Syrians and Lebanese on their best behaviour, in order to give no ground whatever for the charge that they are incapable of maintaining order or that they are displaying unjustifiably anti-French attitude.

No. 537

Sir V. Mallet (Madrid) to Mr. Eden (Received 28 July, 1.25 p.m.)
No. 571 Telegraphic [Z 8861/829/41]

Important   MADRID, *27 July 1945, 10 p.m.*

Repeated Saving to Gibraltar, Lisbon, Tangier.

I presented my letters[1] to General Franco today. He was obviously all out to make a favourable impression and although I told him several blunt home truths he remained quite complacent and smilingly insisted that relations would improve.

2. During the three quarter of an hour's talk through interpreter, I told him the British people desired friendly relations with the Spanish people but my visit to England had convinced me of the universal feeling of distrust towards the existing régime in Spain. The régime was associated in British minds with friendship towards Fascists and Nazis and both deeds and speeches during the war would not be forgotten. Reminding him of Mr. Churchill's letter,[2] I told him that the British would not forget that he had openly expressed the hope of German victory. General Franco who instantly interrupted with long dissertations attempted to convince me that pro-Germanism of the Spanish Government had been grossly exaggerated. He insisted that it had never been his intention even in 1940 to join with our enemies. When I referred to the Blue Division, he attempted to minimise it as a 'mere drop of water'.

3. General Franco dilated upon his programme of social reform and education which he considered closer to the ideals of the British Labour party than those of the Conservatives. He made no direct allusion to the British election. When he asserted that Spain did not wish to live in isolation from her neighbours and friends, I replied that she was already very isolated and that I could foresee that under the new British Government she might become even more isolated than ever.[3]

4. Full report by bag.

[1] Of credence as H.M. Ambassador to Spain.
[2] See No. 194, note 12.
[3] Mr. Garran observed in a minute of 30 July 1945 on this paper: 'Sir V. Mallet is opening strongly, but General Franco's complacency has survived this first attack as it survived so many from Lord Templewood.' This minute was initialed that day by Mr. O. C. Harvey.

i *26 July 1945 Sir V. Mallet (Madrid) No. 412.* Conversation on 26 July with new Spanish Foreign Minister, who said that his appointment signified General Franco's intention to work for more cordial relations with western Allied Powers [Z 9172/537/41].

ii *24 July 1945 Mr. Bowker (Madrid) No. 403,* enclosing copy of letter of 21 July to Governor of Gibraltar: question of conversion of part of Spanish neutral ground into recreational area for Spanish and British nationals in interests of Anglo-Spanish relations [Z 8894/8894/41].

No. 538

Letter from Mr. Ward (Berlin) to Mr. Gallop (Received 28 July)

[W 10195/142/803]

Most Immediate   BRITISH DELEGATION, BERLIN, 27 July 1945

Dear Rodney,

You will no doubt have been as much surprised as we were to find the question of 'Inland Waterways' suddenly injected into this Conference.

The first sign of what was coming was the proposal of the American Joint Chiefs of Staff to the Combined Chiefs of Staff here which we reported in our telegram No. Target 170.[1] The Combined Chiefs of Staff approved this proposal for a 'Danube Navigation Agency' and sent the Foreign Office and State Department Delegations here a letter of the 24th July (first enclosure).[2] I also enclose (second enclosure) a copy of paper C.O.S. (Terminal) 10[3], comprising the memorandum by the First Sea Lord which persuaded our Chiefs of Staff to endorse the American proposal.

Meanwhile, while the Combined Chiefs of Staff were still considering the matter, the President suddenly weighed in at the 7th plenary meeting on the 23rd July (see Delegation's Minutes,[4] Item 10) with a paper numbered P (Terminal) 33[5], which you will have seen (third enclosure). Although the paper only proposed the setting-up of 'Interim Navigation Agencies for the Danube and Rhine', the President in his remarks went on to say that the same principles should be applied to the Kiel Canal and to the Black Sea Straits, which was the subject under discussion. The discussion in the plenary meeting on the 23rd July was adjourned and the further discussion at the 8th plenary meeting on the 24th (see Item 4 of the British Delegation's Minutes)[6] on the matter was again adjourned. At the Foreign Secretaries' meeting on the 25th, after the Prime Minister and

[1] No. 232.ii.
[2] Not printed: see *F.R.U.S. Berlin*, vol. ii, pp. 652–3.
[3] No. 251.ii(a).
[4] No. 241.
[5] No. 246.
[6] No. 258.

Mr. Eden had left, the American Secretary of State suddenly trotted out his Inland Waterways proposal again and on his suggestion it was agreed to refer the matter to a sub-committee,[7] to which the unfortunate Dean and myself were nominated.

We went to see Riddleberger, who is handling the matter on the American Delegation, the next day, when he produced the document, attached as the fourth enclosure,[8] which reproduces the American proposal and takes in the President's suggestion that analogous régimes of 'free and unrestricted navigation' should also be established for the Kiel Canal and the Straits. We questioned the wisdom of linking inland waterways with such a contentious and political question as the Straits, and made various other drafting criticisms of the American document. He made it plain, however, that he was bound by the line which the President had taken and that his document had already been approved.

Consequently, we thought it best to go along with the Americans, but we produced our own alternative text, which is attached as the fifth enclosure.[9] This text was agreed with Strang and Weston of the Ministry of War Transport (the Admiralty Delegation had already departed) and was approved by Cadogan. The main differences between our text and the American document are that we place the references to the Kiel Canal and the Straits in separate paragraphs, which can easily be dropped out of the document or transferred to separate papers, and that we pay regard to the special conditions surrounding the Kiel Canal and the Straits. We also think it advisable in the second paragraph not to specify the actual parties who will become members of the Rhine and Danube Agencies and to leave a loophole by which other countries who have a direct interest in the navigation on these rivers but are not riparian States (e.g. Belgium), can participate if the Member States agree.

The Sub-Committee met for the first time this evening, and the Russians were represented by a certain Gerashenko (Director of a Division in the Russian Foreign Office) and two more obscure individuals whose names are irrelevant. They were presented with the alternative American and British drafts, which were laboriously explained to them. They promised to study them, but said that they awaited instructions from Moscow, in particular as to the attitude of the Soviet military authorities, and it was agreed that we should meet again on the 29th. The one positive statement which the Russians made was that they did not regard the Sub-Committee as having any authority to consider the question of the Kiel Canal and the Straits, although they were perfectly prepared to discuss arrangements for the Rhine and the Danube.[10] (As usual at these Conferences, there are no agreed minutes or conclusions, and consequently there is generally a wrangle as to what exactly was decided.)

[7] See No. 274, minute 1.
[8] This document, not here printed, is printed *op. cit.*, vol. ii, pp. 656–7 and 1435.
[9] This document, not here printed, is printed *ibid.*, vol. ii, pp. 657–8 and 1436.
[10] Marginal comment against this sentence: 'Good'.

On returning from the meeting, we saw your telegram Onward No. 228, repeating your No. 7846[11] to Washington, from which we gather that you are alarmed at the implications of the American proposal. We do not think you will get any coherent explanation from the State Department about the President's initiative, which we happen to know was taken suddenly and presumably as a result of the recommendation of the United States Joint Chiefs of Staff. From his remarks at the 7th plenary meeting, the President seems to have had a somewhat naïve hope that he could wangle a settlement of the Straits question under cover of the general question of international arrangements for 'Inland Waterways'.

We have assumed that as we ourselves raised the matter of the Danube with the Russians in September last,[12] we should certainly want to support the American initiative, whatever doubt we may feel about the possibility of dealing with the highly political Straits question in this way. Having regard to the fact that the President had raised the matter of the Rhine and the Danube directly in this way, we did not find anything in the brief which you sent out to us by bag[13] which is inconsistent with the proposals made in our draft paper. In any case, even if you do not think that this is the moment to push the question of the Danube and the Rhine, it would have created the most unfavourable impression on the Americans if we had failed to back their proposal.

The idea of some sort of international régime for the Kiel Canal, initially based upon the Four-Power Control Council for Germany, was blessed in the departmental brief which was entitled 'Security Arrangements for the Baltic Sea Gateways and the Kiel Canal',[14] which we brought out with us and which had the approval of the Chiefs of Staff.

In these circumstances, I hope you will agree that we are bound to support the American initiative in linking the question of Interim Agencies for the Danube and the Rhine with the Straits and the Kiel Canal, and that if the Russians maintain their refusal to bring in the two latter questions, we should continue to support the Americans in trying to get some Three-Power understanding about the two rivers. So far as we can see our proposals cannot possibly do any harm and they may do some good by establishing the broad principle of Three-Power co-operation in these matters. If the Conference took a favourable decision on our or the American paper the next step would probably be a reference to the Council of Foreign Ministers in London, who in their turn would have to propose the establishment of the necessary technical bodies to work out the detailed arrangements.

We should be very grateful for your comments on this letter as soon as possible. Meanwhile, we shall go ahead on the lines indicated above.

[11] No. 246.i.

[12] For British proposals to the Soviet Government in September 1944 for the establishment of a provisional international administration for the Danube, cf. No. 251.ii(*b*), also *F.R.U.S. 1944*, vol. ii, p. 738.

[13] No. 251.ii(*b*).

[14] See No. 109, annex II.

Forgive this rather incoherent letter, dictated at speed late at night!

Yours ever

JACK WARD

CALENDARS TO No. 538

i   *28 July–2 Aug. 1945   From & to Lord Halifax (Washington) Tels Nos. 5261, 8022 & 710 Saving.* Refers to No. 246.i: views of State Dept. on formation of interim navigation agencies for Danube and Rhine and on forum for discussion: British criticism; Lancaster House Conference [W 10201/142/803].

ii *27 July 1945   Memo by 21st Army Group:* proposals for Rhine navigation agency [F.O. 934/5/38(12)].

iii *Correspondence respecting resources of the Continental Shelf and fisheries: (a) 8, 10 & 20 July 1945   Lord Halifax (Washington) Tel. No. 4743; Letter from Mr. Wright (Washington) to Mr. R. Dunbar (Head of F.O. Treaty Dept.); Govt. of Newfoundland Tel. No. 43 Saving to Viscount Cranborne.* American reactions to British comments on proposed U.S. announcement on above (cf. *F.R.U.S. 1945*, vol. ii, pp. 1516–19, 1522–3); views of Government of Newfoundland [T 10553, 11210, 12043/366/380], (b) *19 July 1945   To Mr. E. H. G. Shepherd (H.M. Minister, Reykjavik) No. 59.* Bad effect upon Anglo-Icelandic relations of severe Icelandic fines on British fishing trawlers [N 8359/5669/27].

No. 539

Air Vice-Marshal Stevenson (Bucharest) to Mr. Lawson[1]
No. RAC 2065/195 Telegraphic [R 12729/10/37]

Most Immediate. Top secret   BUCHAREST, *28 July 1945, 1 a.m.*

Repeated A.F.H.Q.

From Air Vice Marshal Stevenson.

My RAC 2053/195 [i] to-day's date. Thus from foregoing I respectfully submit to His Majesty's Government that unless in Potsdam we are able to get Russia to accept fully tripartite agreement on all directives prior to issue to Roumanian Government, the administration by A.C.C. in this country will be no better than that of last ten months. Under this administration British interests and opportunities for expanding our trade have undergone progressive deterioration due to Russian policy of a deliberate attempt to remove the last vestige of British influence here.[2]

---

[1] This telegram to Mr. J. J. Lawson, Secretary of State for War in succession to Sir J. Grigg, was received in the Foreign Office on 28 July 1945 at 7.30 p.m.

[2] Mr. Stewart minuted and Mr. Howard initialed on this paper as follows: 'These telegrams [Nos. 539, 539.i and 259.i(b)] show that, as was to be expected, A.V.M. Stevenson's effort to raise the question of the "new deal" in the Control Commission has secured no results. Gen. Schuyler has (see R 12686) reserved his position. A.V.M. Stevenson has, I think rightly, not taken the same line. RAC 2057 (R 12728/G) confirms our expectation

i *28 July 1945 A.V.M. Stevenson (B.M.M. Roumania) to War Office Tels. Nos.
RAC 2053–2064/195.* Reports meeting on 27 July of Allied Control Commission
under new charter, including discussion of Russian seizures in Roumania,
duration of Soviet occupation, Roumanian trade agreements, removal of
controls on British firms [R 12710, 12757/217/37; R 12814, 12758/27/37;
R 12728/12728/37; R 12759/169/37; R 12889/422/37; R 12890/335/37;
R 12883/219/37; R 12773/1685/37; W.O. 32/15327].

that in its present form the "new deal" is in practice only a paper concession and in the
telegram in this paper A.V.M. Stevenson asks for action at Terminal. In fact we have
already made to the Delegation all the points he raises, but Sir O. Sargent wishes these
tels. to be passed on. Letter [not printed] attached. All the tels. are being given Cabinet
Dist[ribution]. D. L. Stewart 29/7.' 'D. H. 30/7.'

No. 540

Mr. Hankey (Warsaw) to Mr. Bevin (Received 28 July, 9.55 p.m.)
No. 57 Telegraphic [F.O. 916/1200:KW2/117/784]

WARSAW, *28 July 1945*, *5.57 p.m. G.M.T.*

Your telegram No. 4050 to Moscow.[1]

The Soviet Ambassador whose help I had enlisted now informs me that
the Soviet Military Command in Poland is in process of dissolution, that
troops are leaving the country and that in two or three weeks there will be
no military organisation left. (I feel sure however some troops will remain
on the lines of communication.) The organisation for repatriating (. . .?
prisoners of)[2] war has already ceased work.

2. I have asked the Provisional Polish Government for assistance in
tracing and collecting stragglers. Many have Polish wives.

3. Arrangements made by the Polish Red Cross here are [? in] general
extremely primitive and unsatisfactory, we are searching for premises in
which to organise collecting centre ourselves in face of great difficulties.
The cost will be charged in Extraordinaries.[3] I cannot see any alternative.

i *2 Aug. 1945 Mr. Roberts (Moscow) Tel. No. 3384.* Suggests dealing with
Polish Govt. direct regarding British P.O.W.s in Poland and protesting to
Soviet Govt. because three British P.O.W.s were set to work [F.O. 916/1200:
KW 2/117/794].

---

[1] No. 347.i.
[2] The text is here uncertain.
[3] Exceptional expenditures.

No. 541

Sir M. Peterson (Istanbul) to Mr. Bevin (Received 28 July, 3 p.m.)
No. 199 Telegraphic [E 5543/808/89]

ISTANBUL, *28 July 1945, 1.12 p.m. G.M.T.*

Repeated to Beirut No. 38, Moscow and M.E. Min's Office No. 87.

Your telegram No. 547 (*sic* ?125) repeating Moscow telegram No. 3246.[1]

I hope we shall intervene firmly at Damascus to put an end to this kind of mischief making which is particularly inappropriate on the part of the Syrians who owe everything (and possibly a great deal too much) to us.

Foreign Office please repeat to Moscow as my telegram No. 58.[2]

[1] No. 365.
[2] With reference to this telegram Mr. Roberts observed in Moscow telegram No. 3376 of 1 August 1945 at 9.15 a.m.: 'Since this information was given to me by Syrian Minister in the course of a frank private conversation, I think it would be preferable to take the matter up with him here in the first place rather than through his Government in Damascus. Otherwise he may well be less frank in future about his conversations with the Soviet Government. In any case my impression is that he did not intend formally to invoke Soviet intervention and that he only mentioned the matter in the course of general conversation, without realising that Soviet Government might not distinguish between a passing remark and a formal démarche.'

No. 542

Sir R. Bullard (Tehran) to Mr. Bevin (Received 28 July, 7.15 p.m.)
No. 766 Telegraphic [E 5531/103/34]

Immediate   TEHRAN, *28 July 1945, 5.38 p.m. G.M.T.*

Repeated to Moscow, Washington, M.E. Min[ister], Bagdad.

Your telegram No. 453[1].

Your telegram under reference reached me two days ago but the Soviet Ambassador has received no instructions. News that Tehran was to be evacuated which I conveyed to the Ambassador was obviously unwelcome to him and I do not think immediate evacuation is so pleasing to the Soviet Government that they will hasten to instruct their representative here. I suggest we should hint to the Russians that unless their instructions reach their representative in Tehran soon we shall inform the Persians whose note[2] has not yet received definite reply that evacuation of Tehran is to be proceeded with forthwith.

[1] No. 403.
[2] For the Iranian note of 19 May 1945 to the British Government requesting the withdrawal of Allied troops from Iran see Sir L. Woodward, *op. cit.*, vol. iv, p. 473.

2. Every day's delay adds to the risk that the Russians may succeed in pushing into the post of Prime Minister a man who would rig the election for them and in general do their bidding.

Foreign Office please pass to Bagdad as my telegram No. 44 and to Washington as my telegram No. 34.

No. 543

Letter from Mr. Cheetham to Mr. Ward (Berlin)
[*W 10195/142/803*]

Most Immediate   FOREIGN OFFICE, *28 July 1945*

Dear Ward,

In the absence of Rodney Gallop I am answering your letter of 27th July about Inland Waterways.[1] I have discussed it with Howard and Troutbeck and it has been shown to Sargent.

2. We have no objection to your supporting the United States intiative, in linking the river questions with those of the Straits and the Kiel Canal although, of course, we should never ourselves have suggested linking the problems of inland waterways proper with others of such a highly delicate and contentious nature. The question of the Straits is anyhow being pursued quite separately with the Turks and whatever discussions take place at Berlin they are not likely to affect the latter negotiations.

Yours ever,
N. J. A. CHEETHAM

[1] No. 538.

No. 544

Letter from Mr. Harvey to Mr. Hopkinson (Rome)
[*ZM 3943/1/22*]

Confidential   FOREIGN OFFICE, *28 July 1945*

My dear Henry,

Your despatch No. 285[1] (25/10/45) of 10th July about the State Department's ideas on the establishment of a quasi federal state in Italy.

We do not think that it is any business of ours to press the Italian Government on this question, although some measure of decentralisation might remedy an evil of the Fascist system. In any case, the Italian Government have themselves put regional autonomy in their public programme. We

[1] Not printed.

are proposing at the Potsdam Conference that there should be a tripartite declaration on Italy in general terms,[2] and if this goes through we hope to secure the insertion of an appreciative reference to the Italian Government programme, in which the intention to hold elections and to introduce some measure of local autonomy would be mentioned as steps taken in accordance with the declaration on Italy by the Moscow Conference of Foreign Secretaries (1943). We are not prepared to go further in the direction of 'lecturing' the Italian Government which we think might cause some resentment from Signor Parri who seems fully conscious of what the real needs of Italy are.

On the other hand, we shall try to ensure that the Ministry for Information devote special attention in their plans of [for] Italy to the idea of local government and local initiative, which is such an important factor in our own political life.

Yours ever

O. HARVEY

CALENDAR TO No. 544

i *31 July 1945 Cabinet Office to J.S.M. (Washington) Tel. No. Nod 914.* Publicity for British relief to Italy 'to counteract false impression that U.S. has supplied practically all relief supplies to Italy' [ZM 4217/18/22].

[2] Cf. annex 3 to No. 212.

No. 545

Mr. Balfour (Washington) to Mr. Bevin (Received 29 July, 12.55 a.m.)
No. 5238 Telegraphic [W 10207/24/802]

WASHINGTON, 28 July 1945, 10.20 p.m.

Repeated to M[iddle] E[ast] Min[ister]'s Office.

Your telegram No. 7,727.[1]
Aide-mémoire based on your telegram No. 6,234[2] was left by Mr. Makins with Taft this morning. Point in paragraph 4 of your telegram under reference was not raised and is left over for Civil Air Attaché to pursue with Civil Aviation Division of State Department.

2. Taft said that he was glad to have this communication and would have an opportunity of discussing it with Air Co-ordinating Committee

[1] No. 394.i.
[2] Of 12 June 1945, not printed. The British aide-mémoire of 26 July handed to Mr. C. P. Taft, Director of the Office of Transportation and Communications in the State Department, on 27 July is printed in *F.R.U.S. 1945*, vol. viii, pp. 73–5.

which consists of Under Secretaries concerned at War, Navy, Commercial and State Departments before he leaves for London on July 29th.

3. Taft made two other preliminary comments. He said that State Department had been encouraged by reports which they had had from their Civil Air Attachés in London and Cairo of recent conversations with our representatives, and which he regarded as having improved the atmosphere. Secondly he mentioned the address which had been given in London by Mr. Wright Chairman of C[ivil] A[eronautics] A[dministration] as Mr. Wright's . . .[3] lecture which apparently gave a qualified endorsement of United Kingdom position on Fifth Freedom. Taft made it clear that while United States Government were extremely anxious to reach a settlement with His Majesty's Government their position at the present time remained unchanged from that which they had taken up at the Chicago Conference.

4. I recommend that opportunity should be taken for a full discussion with Taft while he is in London.

[3] The text is here uncertain.

No. 546

Mr. Balfour (Washington) to Mr. Bevin (Received 29 July, 8.30 a.m.)
No. 5255 Telegraphic [E 5538/14/89]

Immediate   WASHINGTON, *28 July 1945, 10.34 p.m.*

Repeated to Beirut, M[iddle] E[ast] Min[ister]'s office, Paris Saving.

Your telegram No: 7,859.[1]

Since this is an important step, may I request confirmation that considerations expressed in Beirut telegram No: 710[2] of July 26th have been taken into account and that not withstanding them you wish me to approach State Department?

Foreign Office please pass to Paris as my telegram No: 130 Saving.

CALENDAR TO No. 546

i *4 Aug. 1945 To Mr. Balfour (Washington) Tel. No. 8089.* Proposal for fact-finding commission for the Levant is rejected; but instructions to inform State Dept. of proposal for commission of disinterested Powers [E 5538/14/89].

[1] No. 536.
[2] Mr. Shone had there commented with reference to paragraph 6 of No. 148: 'As regards proposal for neutral fact-finding commission I welcomed this when first mooted . . . But now that so much time has elapsed since the French took military measures in Syria it seems to me that such a commission might have great difficulty in getting the necessary evidence. Moreover it might have the effect of stirring up the mud not only of Franco-Syrian but also of Franco-British disputes which we hope may be gradually settling.'

No. 547

Mr. Balfour (Washington) to Mr. Bevin (Received 29 July, 4.37 a.m.)
No. 5271 Telegraphic [U 5794/12/70]

WASHINGTON, *28 July 1945*[1]

Senate ratified United Nations Charter this afternoon by 89 votes to two, Senators Langer and Shipstead voting against.

CALENDAR TO No. 547

i   *1 Aug. 1945   Minute by Mr. G. G. Fitzmaurice, Assistant Legal Adviser to the F.O.* Winding up of old Permanent Court of International Justice [U 6627/ 1372/98].

[1] The time of despatch is not recorded.

No. 548

Memorandum by Mr. Playfair
No. EIPS/134 [UE 3376/86/77]

Secret   LONDON, *28 July 1945*

The Treatment of I.G. Farbenindustrie, Krupp's
and the Hermann Göringwerke

(Note by the Acting Chairman)

Following the informal meeting of E.I.P.S. on Tuesday, 24th July [i], a meeting took place on the next day between Sir Wilfred Eady, Sir Percy Mills, Mr. Hall-Patch, Mr. Franks, Mr. Ritchie and myself to discuss further procedure.

Sir Percy Mills informed us that our understanding of the facts was not quite correct. The Americans had merely informed General Weeks and Sir Percy Mills of the action which they were taking and had not requested them even informally to take similar action in the British Zone. The idea of taking similar action had emanated entirely from the British side.

The following conclusions were reached:–

(*a*) It was highly desirable that the Control Commission, British Element, should have something to show for the occupation of the British Zone. Hitherto they had been largely concerned with the immediate day to day problems of saving something from the wreck of the German economy.

(*b*) The big chemical, steel and heavy engineering complexes, particularly I.G. Farbenindustrie and Hermann Göringwerke, formed the most important part of Germany's industrial war potential. Special measures must be taken to control these concerns and their more important works. Control should not be carried out as a part-time job by teams which were also concerned with the control of the smaller fry.

(*c*) Sir Percy Mills said that the proposal with regard to Krupp's was to make the gesture of blotting out the Essen works, recognising however that this would be a political and psychological act and would not, of itself, deal a vital physical blow at Germany's industrial war potential. There was general sympathy for the proposal, but it was agreed that action must await approval by Ministers of the industrial disarmament proposals.

(*d*) Given the need to take special measures to control I.G. Farben-industrie and the Hermann Göringwerke and to appoint special teams for these tasks, it was agreed that they would be likely to do a more effective job and that there would be more flexibility if they were appointed as controllers supervising a German management than if they were made the actual management of the firm and thus had to concern themselves with all the detail of everything that went on.

(*e*) Sir Percy Mills stated that Mr. C. S. Robinson[1] was coming to London that day and was going to look for a really good man to head the control team for the I.G. Farbenindustrie factories in the British Zone. Sir Percy Mills thought he should recruit a man of similar calibre to control the Hermann Göringwerke factories in the British Zone. It was agreed that Sir Percy Mills should have every support in these endeavours.

(*f*) It was agreed that there was no need to refer this matter to Ministers for decision, but when the Economic Division had made further progress they should make a report to Ministers.

(*g*) Sir Percy Mills confirmed that there was no intention of allowing I.G. Farbenindustrie factories in the British Zone to become subject to American control. The controllers of these factories would be British officers and while they would collaborate informally with the Americans there could be no question of the British officers abandoning their responsibility to the British Element.

In view of the above there is no need to proceed further with the draft paper which was discussed at the informal E.I.P.S. meeting on Tuesday, 24th July.

E. W. PLAYFAIR

Economic & Industrial Planning Staff, Lansdowne House. 28th July, 1945

CALENDARS TO No. 548

i *24 July 1945 Record (EIPS/29/136) of informal meeting of E.I.P.S.* on British treatment of I.G. Farbenindustrie etc. [UE 3376/86/77].

ii *28 & 30 July 1945 Correspondence between Mr. Playfair and Mr. Dent.* Submission to E.E.C.E. of list of supplies from enemy countries in relation to decisions at Potsdam on interim deliveries [UE 3311/2615/77].

---

[1] Deputy Chief of the Economic Division of the Allied Control Commission for Germany (British Element).

No. 549

Sir M. Peterson (Istanbul) to Mr. Bevin (Received 11 August)
No. 268 [R 13467/4476/44]

Top secret   ISTANBUL, *28 July 1945*

Sir,

The first news of the Potsdam discussions in so far as they affect Turkey contained in Sir John Anderson's telegram No. 137[1] of July 25th, combined with the change of government in Great Britain, make it perhaps expedient for me to attempt to review Turkey's position in the world to-day.

2. It is no exaggeration to say that in every sphere of Turkey's activities— internal as well as external and over the whole range of commerce and industry—the dominating factor at the moment is the uneasy state of Russo-Turkish relations.

3. It is not easy to say precisely how this has come about and why these relations should have deteriorated to so marked an extent since the time when, a little more than twenty years ago, a real sympathy existed between the Russia of Lenin and the Turkey of Mustafa Kemal. Russian dissatisfaction with Turkey's attitude during the war may[2] have played a part, stimulated as it has been by incidents which it is difficult to assess to-day such as the Turkish reinforcement of their eastern frontier at the moment when the Russians had their backs to the wall at Stalingrad. However this may be, most Turks have come to believe that the primary source of Soviet discontent lies in the Treaty of Alliance between Great Britain and Turkey (French participation has slipped into the background) concluded in October 1939[3] immediately after the mission of Monsieur Saracoglu (the present Prime Minister) to Moscow which resulted in the failure of Soviet efforts to draw Turkey into a Russo-Turkish alliance and equally in the failure of Monsieur Saracoglu's own proposals for a triple alliance between Great Britain, Russia and Turkey.

4. The Anglo-Turkish Alliance seems to represent for Russia a derogation from the principle which she purports to assert that countries adjoining the Soviet Union must refrain from allying themselves with any third power: while there may also be in the Soviet conscience an uneasy feeling that such service as Turkey rendered to the Allies during the war and which consisted in the interposition of a buffer state between the Axis in the Balkans and the area of the Middle East is to-day capable of being transformed into a similar check on Soviet ambitions.

5. The particular demands which the Soviet Union has seen fit to make

---

[1] Repetition of No. 400.

[2] On the filed copy this word was endorsed in the margin with a query and an exclamation-mark.

[3] The Treaty of Mutual Assistance between the United Kingdom, France and Turkey, signed at Angora on 19 October 1939, is printed (Cmd. 6165 of 1940) in *B.F.S.P.*, vol. 151, pp. 213-7.

upon Turkey in connection with the proposed renewal of the Russo-Turkish Treaty of Amity denounced by the Soviet Government in March of this year fall under three heads. While it is true that in the Turco-Russian conversations, which began in Moscow on June 7th last and which have been continued intermittently both at Moscow and Angora since that date, no demands have been presented in writing, the Turks believe with every apparent justification that Russia has unmistakeably intimated her desire for these concessions. Firstly, Russian bases in the Straits (by which term is of course meant the entire waterway connecting the Black Sea with the Aegean). Secondly, a revision of Turkey's eastern frontier as laid down by the Russo-Turkish Treaty of 1921. And thirdly, Russia is understood to insist upon a revision of the Montreux Convention of 1936 governing the passage of vessels of all kinds along this waterway, in respect of which Russia is no longer content to enjoy no greater privileges than 'the Emperor of Japan'.

6. The attitude of Turkey towards these demands is, firstly, that nothing will induce her to concede to Russia military bases in the Straits. The Turkish Prime Minister has repeatedly told me that Turkey would fight rather than make these concessions which she would regard as tantamount to the surrender of her independence. Monseiur Saracoglu indeed went so far as to say in conversation on July 26th that Turkey would fight even if Great Britain and America were to support Russian demands for such bases. I do not think that he is bluffing or that such words may be classed as mere histrionics.

7. To the demand for frontier revision Turkey's reply is that it is put forward on false premises. The Treaty of 1921 was concluded at a time when the Soviet Union indeed was weak, but Turkey herself was certainly no stronger. The Treaty was freely negotiated and contained a signal concession to the Soviet Union in the return of Batum. The districts of Kars and Ardahan were Turkish territory up to 1878 and between that time and 1921 they have not been genuinely Russian territory. The Russian attempt to base these territorial demands on the alleged needs of the Armenian people are not taken seriously in Turkey and may indeed be no more than the Russian method of replying to the alleged Pan-Turanian activities of the Turkish Government—activities which as appears from my despatch No. 118[4] of 5th April have been grossly exaggerated in Moscow.

8. Towards the Russian insistence on the revision of the Montreux Convention Turkey has maintained a conciliatory attitude which it may be possible to sustain even if the demand for revision is converted into one for the establishment of a totally different régime.

9. A subsidiary cause of the tension existing between Russia and Turkey lies in the situation in the Balkans where the Turks believe—and so far as I can see with every reason—that Russia is seeking to establish a Slav *bloc* to include Roumania as well as Yugoslavia and Bulgaria and to be directed

---

[4] Not printed.

towards the attainment of access to the sea at the expense of Greece and possibly of Turkey.

10. In the face of what the Turks regard as this Russian menace a remarkable unanimity has been achieved in Turkey and the defects both of the present Turkish internal régime and of the existing administration headed by Monsieur Saracoglu tend to be lost sight of by all save a small group of malcontents amongst whom the better elements are unwilling to push the President too hard so long as the Russian danger persists while the less patriotic elements are more than suspect of being in Russian pay.

11. Indeed were it not for the Russian danger following upon the strain which the five and a half years of war in Europe have imposed upon Turkey, criticism of the country's internal régime would inevitably be much more vocal than it is at present. The Turkish system of government is on the face of it more a facade of democracy than a genuinely democratic organisation. Not only is there a single party, the People's Party, which itself throws off a small 'official' opposition group, but the head of that party is no other than the President of the Republic himself. This latter point is regarded by genuinely patriotic reformers such as Monsieur Rauf Orbay (who broke with Atatürk himself on the same issue) as being the negation of democratic government notwithstanding the analogy to the contrary which exists in the constitution of the United States.

12. So long as President Ismet Inönü shows no signs of stepping down from his dual position it seems unlikely that any genuine opposition party can be formed (since no prominent Turk is anxious to place himself in direct opposition to the President) and tentative efforts in this direction, such as have been widely canvassed in Turkey during the summer and have in fact led to the Party's recent decision not to present official candidates for six vacant constituencies, are likely to be of no more than propaganda value.

13. A step of greater importance recently taken has perhaps been the permitted publication of the debates in the Grand National Assembly and of the periodic press conferences held by the Prime Minister.

14. Finally in the domain of commerce and industry Russian influence is detrimentally evidenced[5] through the strain imposed on Turkey's resources by the continued maintenance of the Turkish army on a footing of mobilisation. The recent release of one class from the colours has had the effect only of reducing the percentage allotted in the budget estimates to military expenditure from fifty-four percent to forty-six percent. Moreover, apart from direct expenditure on the Army and to a less extent the Air Force, Turkish economy suffers acutely from the shortage of manpower resulting from continued mobilisation.

15. It would not perhaps be justifiable to ascribe to expenditure on defence the whole responsibility for the unsatisfactory foundations upon

---

[5] On the filed copy the two preceding words were annotated in the margin: 'Horrible.'

which Turkey's commercial system is at present based.[6] But it may well be the need of meeting military expenditure out of proportion to the country's resources which has led the Turks to base their system of taxation principally upon what may be described as 'indirect taxation deducted at source' with the consequent enormous and continuing rise in prices. The development of government monopolies—exercised principally but not wholly by the banks—for the distribution of practically all the chief articles of importation into Turkey has yielded considerable sums for the revenue (the Minister of Monopolies boasted in a recent Assembly debate that the Sugar Monopoly had yielded no less than Turkish Liras sixty millions in the space of a year) but it is also responsible for the prevalence of a very high level of internal prices which tends to create discontent and impair the stability of the Turkish state. The system by which the banks, and in particular the Sümer Bank, obtain direct and immediate control of many primary articles of importation such as wool and, after exacting for themselves as agents of the government a profit which in some cases reaches two hundred percent, subsequently turn the distribution over to the birliks, or government-controlled unions, means that by the time the article has reached the consumer its price has attained an almost prohibitive level. The effect on the private trader, more particularly if he be a foreigner or a member of the non-Moslem minorities, is such as to constitute a virtual stranglehold on Turkey's foreign trade.

16. To sum up. So long as His Majesty's Government continue to support Turkey, the latter country will continue to represent a valuable bulwark against Soviet penetration to the south and into the Mediterranean area. But until Turkey is relieved of the menace constituted by the present attitude of the Soviet Union towards her, Turkey cannot play the rôle which she otherwise would in the comity of nations and in particular cannot hope to achieve an industrial expansion which she has made one of her principal aims and which, even if realised only in part, would be of benefit throughout the Middle East Area. On the reverse side of the picture the continued malaise in Russo-Turkish relations must constitute a source of anxiety to those nations which are concerned to see the San Francisco Charter become an effective instrument of peace and security.

17. I am sending a copy of this despatch to His Majesty's Representatives at Washington and Moscow.

I have, &c.,

MAURICE PETERSON

[6] Marginal annotation in filed copy against this sentence: 'No indeed'.

No. 550

Letter from Sir G. Gater to Sir A. Cadogan (Berlin)
No. 54144/38/45 [F.O. 934/3/12(18)]

Top secret   COLONIAL OFFICE, *28 July 1945*

My dear Cadogan,

Before the Election results Colonel Stanley had been impressed with the urgent need to clarify our position in respect of the administration of Hong Kong on the liberation of the Colony. In view of the information we now have as to operational plans in China he had come to the conclusion that there was no time to be lost in approaching Chiang Kai Shek with a view to reaching an understanding with him in the event of the liberation of Hong Kong by Chinese forces, on the lines of the agreement which we already have with the Americans regarding British territories in American operational spheres.[1]

Owing to the fact that the Generalissimo's Chief of Staff is an American General, who is reported to be personally opposed to any action by the British in China directed to the reoccupation of Hong Kong, we feel that, before approaching Chiang Kai Shek, we should do anything we can to make sure of American support for our proposal, and in view of the high political issues involved we feel that our preliminary approach to the Americans should be on the highest possible level. I enclose a note on the facts of our position in respect of Hong Kong.

In view both of the urgency of action and the desirability of taking it up with the Americans at a very high level, it seemed to Colonel Stanley that the opportunity of Terminal should not be lost for this purpose, and if this is to be done I must in the circumstances put it at once to you for your consideration and in the hope that you may feel it possible to take action before Terminal disperses. We shall in any case have to go to the Chinese but it will be an immense help if we can clear it first with the Americans.

I have consulted Sargent as to this course which I am taking in writing to you and I have his concurrence in doing so. I shall, of course, report immediately to our new Secretary of State as soon as he takes office.[2]

Yours v. sincerely
G. H. GATER

---

[1] See enclosure below.

[2] In a Foreign Office letter of 10 August 1945 Mr. Sterndale Bennett informed Mr. G. E. J. Gent of the Colonial Office, with reference to the present letter, 'that the proposal to speak to the President about the administration of Hong Kong in the event of its recapture by the Chinese was duly referred to our Secretary of State but it did not prove possible to take the necessary action with the Americans at Potsdam. Mr. Bevin has now directed that the matter shall be taken up through the usual channels with the United States Government before approaching Chiang Kai-shek.'

Note

Top Secret

Arrangements for the Administration of Hong Kong in the event of its liberation by regular Chinese forces

1. At present Hong Kong is in the operational sphere of Generalissimo Chiang Kai Shek whose Chief of Staff is the American General Wedemeyer. We therefore have to be prepared for the contingency of the Colony being liberated by Chinese Forces operating (virtually) under American direction. According to information provided by the U.S. Chiefs of Staff to the British Chiefs of Staff at Terminal, an offensive is contemplated by American-trained Chinese forces in the direction of Canton and Hong Kong in the fairly near future.

2. Even assuming that the Chinese are prepared in such circumstances to hand back Hong Kong to His Majesty's Government it would nevertheless be embarrassing to have to receive it from them. The question whether it is practicable for Hong Kong to be recaptured by British (including Dominion) forces, or with the participation in some degree of British forces, is one for the appreciation of the Chiefs of Staff. If neither course is practicable we shall have to accept the position.

3. In that case it is, at all events, important that we should be able to assume the administration of this British Colony as soon as the military situation allows, and obtain an agreement that from the outset of any initial period of military administration our Civil Affairs policies should be accepted, and that the Civil Affairs administration should be conducted by British personnel.

4. At present we have no understanding with the Chinese Government (as we have with the U.S. Government)[3] in respect of their acceptance of British Civil Affairs policies in any British territory included in their operational sphere. A most embarrassing situation may therefore arise in the event of Hong Kong being liberated by Chinese forces unless there is clear agreement with Chiang Kai Shek in advance as to our role in the administration of Hong Kong.

5. General Wedemeyer's position as Chief of Staff to the Generalissimo is such that any agreement of this nature, and the measures necessary to implement it, would in practice require his support and co-operation. Both the British G.O.C. in China and General Carton de Wiart have formed the impression that General Wedemeyer is personally opposed to any action by the British in China directed to the reoccupation of Hong Kong, and that he would in any case feel obliged to refer any matter of this kind to Washington.

6. In these circumstances it seems very desirable that, before approaching Chiang Kai Shek, we should make sure of American support for our proposal. If these negotiations, first with the Americans and then with the Chinese, are conducted through the usual channels there is a danger that they may drag on for several months, whereas as indicated in paragraph 1, time may be very short.

[3] *Note in filed copy:* 'See Annex.'

The Charter of the Combined Civil Affairs Committee at Washington (under the co-Chairmanship of British and American representatives) was approved by the Combined Chiefs of Staff in September, 1943. Paragraph six of this Charter reads as follows:

> 'Six. When an enemy occupied territory of the United States, the United Kingdom or one of the Dominions is to be recovered as a result of an operation, combined or otherwise, the military directive to be given to the force commanders concerned will include policies to be followed in the handling of civil affairs as formulated by the government which exercised authority over the territory before enemy occupation. If paramount military requirements, as determined by the Force Commander, necessitate the departure from those policies, he will take action and report through the Chiefs of Staff to the Combined Chiefs of Staff.'

2. There is thus clear agreement with the Americans that in British territories in the Far East which are in an American command, the policies to be followed on the liberation of those territories shall be laid down by H.M.G. and accepted by the American Force Commander.

3. This agreement relates to policies only. We have assumed, however, that it carries the implication that British Civil Affairs personnel should be used to carry out British policies, and this is tacitly agreed by the Americans. We have support for this assumption in the procedure that has been followed in Borneo. In that connection we informed the Americans, through the Civil Affairs Committee (London), that we had collected in London a nucleus Civil Affairs Unit for Borneo comprising experienced administrative and technical officers who were in the service of the local Governments prior to enemy occupation and that these British staffs would be at the disposal of the American Force Commander. Following on this, General MacArthur stated in September, 1944, that the presence in Australia of British Officers, who would later participate in Civil Affairs activities in Borneo, would be welcome. In January, 1945, we were informed by telegram that the complete Borneo Unit was required to assemble in Australia without avoidable delay, and they have now taken post in the field.

CALENDAR TO No. 550

i *28-9 July 1945* (a) *Letter from Mr. Sterndale Bennett to Mr. Foulds (Berlin)* transmitting copy of the above. (b) *Revised F.O. Brief* on arrangements for the administration of Hong Kong in the event of its liberation by regular Chinese forces [F 4855/1147/10].

No. 551

Mr. Morrison to Lord Killearn (Cairo)[1]
No. 59 Intel Telegraphic [W 589/118/50]

Top secret. Immediate   FOREIGN OFFICE, 29 July 1945, 5.30 a.m.

Berlin Conference

Following is position in regard to some of subjects discussed.

(a) Conference approved 'Political Principles to Govern Treatment of Germany in Initial Control Period'[2] of which main points are:

(i) Demilitarisation of Germany and elimination or control of industrial war potential.

(ii) Realisation of defeat and Nazi war guilt to be brought home to German people.

(iii) Destruction of Nazism in all its forms; purging of Nazis from official and industrial life.

(iv) Preparation for eventual reconstruction of German political life on a democratic basis and for eventual peaceful co-operation in international life by Germany.

(v) Right of assembly and of public discussion for democratic political parties to be allowed and encouraged throughout Germany.

(vi) Decentralisation of political structure; introduction of representative and elective principles in local self-government.

(vii) No central German government to be established for the time being.

(viii) Reorganisation of judicial system: abolition of racial and other discriminatory laws.

(ix) Control of education.

(x) Freedom of speech, press and religion and freedom to form trade unions to be permitted subject to maintenance of military security.

(b) Peace Conference. Experience of Versailles Conference after last war gives warning against embarking on a general conference until ground has been fully prepared. It has therefore been decided to establish Council of Foreign Ministers of United Kingdom, United States, U.S.S.R., France and China to prepare peace treaties with Italy and Axis satellites, and to propose settlement of outstanding territorial questions, China to take an active part only in discussions on matters affecting Asiatic interests or matters of world-wide concern.

---

[1] This circular telegram was also addressed to H.M. representatives at Addis Ababa, Algiers, Athens, Bagdad, Beirut, Belgrade, Berne, Budapest, Buenos Aires, Caserta, Chungking, Copenhagen, Havana, Helsingfors, Istanbul, Mexico City, Moscow, Oslo, Prague, Rome, S.A.C.S.E.A. (Mr. Dening), Sofia, Stockholm, Tangier, Warsaw, Washington, and *en clair* by bag to Bucharest, Brussels, Lisbon, Madrid, Paris, Jedda, Rabat, Reykjavik.

[2] See No. 495, minute 7.

(*c*) Poland's western frontiers. Russians are supporting extreme Polish claim for Oder–Western Neisse frontier, including Stettin. Russians have already handed this area over to Polish administration. We and Americans maintain question should be settled at Peace Conference; area in question should meanwhile be regarded as part of Germany for purposes of reparations and supply. Mr. Churchill thought Polish claims went altogether too far. At Stalin's suggestion representatives of Polish Provisional Government were invited to Potsdam to state their case. Poles headed by M. Bierut have refused to modify their claims.

(*d*) Stalin has proposed that, pending final settlement at Peace Conference, U.S.S.R. should include in her western frontiers north-eastern corner of East Prussia, including Konigsberg, in view of Soviet need for an ice-free port in the Baltic. President and Mr. Churchill agreed that Soviet claim would be supported at peace settlement.

(*e*) Turco-Soviet relations. Stalin has insisted that Russia should have bases in the Straits and has indicated that without territorial concessions, namely Kars and Ardahan, Turkey could not expect an alliance with Russia. He said he thought that Soviet government would resume talks direct with Turks. President proposed that freedom of Straits should be approved and guaranteed by an international authority including the three Great Powers. No agreement has been reached.
Americans have undertaken to try to make Turks see advantages of international control and we are doing the same.

(*f*) Tangier. We have agreed to participation of Soviet Government in talks in Paris with French and United States governments but refused to discuss question of future régime for Tangier and question of Spain's position there before Paris meeting.

(*g*) Spain. Soviet Delegation suggested that relations with Franco should be broken off and democratic forces in Spain supported in order to enable democratic régime to be established by Spanish people. President and Mr. Churchill said that, while we had no love for Franco, we were opposed in principle to interfering in Spain's internal affairs which were for Spain herself to settle.

(*h*) Levant States. Russians proposed Four-Power Conference. Mr. Churchill explained our position, outlined past history of question and deprecated Conference suggested. He said while we would like to see some special privileges conceded to the French, French government would have to secure them in negotiation from Levant States governments. The immediate problem was to ensure tranquil[l]ity in an area where the primary responsibilities rested on His Majesty's Government. In view of Mr. Churchill's statements Soviet proposal was withdrawn.

No. 552

Mr. Morrison to Sir N. Charles (Rome)
No. 1929 Telegraphic [N 9356/409/38]

FOREIGN OFFICE, 29 July 1945, 6.50 p.m.

Following for Mr. Mack.

My immediately following telegram[1] contains a memorandum on 'obstacles to the return of Soviet citizens from Austria and Germany' which on the 25th July the Soviet Delegation at Terminal asked permission to circulate for consideration by the Foreign Secretaries.

2. The complaint that anti-Soviet propaganda is being carried on by White Russians and other persons inimical to the Soviet Government in camps where Soviet citizens are awaiting repatriation is one that has been frequently repeated by the Soviet Government. In some cases it has been found that, owing to the difficulty of finding suitable interpreters, White Russians or other persons who are not entirely in sympathy with the Soviet régime have been allowed to mingle with the Soviet citizens who are awaiting repatriation, but in many other cases investigations have proved that the complaints have had little or no foundation.

3. The complaint in M. Novikov's aide mémoire is more detailed than some and should enable the competent military authorities to check the facts and supply material for an answer.

4. Please institute enquiries so far as the Soviet complaint refers to the British zone in Austria. Sir W. Strang has been asked to take similar action as regards the British zone in Germany.[2]

CALENDARS TO No. 552

i 27 & 31 July 1945 Letters from Mr. Pink (Lübbecke) to Mr. Brimelow. Transmission to Soviet authorities of Gen. Galloway's reply to complaints about British treatment of Russian POWs and displaced persons: 21 Army Group 'have made enormous efforts to do well by these Russians' [N 9697/409/38].

ii 30 July 1945 To Mr. Bevin (Berlin) Tels. Nos. 287 & 298 Onward. Messages (a) from Mr. Steel to Sir W. Strang requesting guidance for meeting with Russians on displaced persons when it is proposed to resist Soviet request for more liaison officers in British zone, and urge speedier Russian reception of those repatriated; (b) from Sir O. Sargent to Sir A. Cadogan agreeing with (a) [N 9652/409/38].

iii 1 Aug. 1945 Mr. Roberts (Moscow) No. 532. Transmits correspondence with Commissariat for Foreign Affairs concerning complaints about Soviet treatment of liberated British POWs, having regard to Yalta agreement on repatriation; Soviet explanations considered wholly unsatisfactory [F.O. 916/1201: KW2/117/806].

---

[1] Not printed: see enclosure in No. 276.
[2] See No. 276.i.

No. 553

Mr. Morrison to Mr. Balfour (Washington)
No. 7943 Telegraphic [F 4605/364/23]

Top secret   FOREIGN OFFICE, *29 July 1945, 7.15 p.m.*

Target No. 95.[1]

Following for Balfour from Campbell.

Suspension of action on Foreign Office telegram No. 7570 to Washington[2] was due to doubts about possible American reaction to paragraph 7. It was felt that recommendation from us that Imperial powers should be maintained might conceivably tempt Americans to say later, if they found it convenient, that they had reluctantly concurred in *our* view. This is a position which we should like to avoid.

2. Paragraph 7 should accordingly be amended as follows:

'Might it not be preferable also for the Allies, instead of assuming all the functions of government in Japan, to work through a Japanese administration, using economic sanctions to secure compliance with such requirements as the repeal of obnoxious laws, the dissolution of political societies, and the reform of education, freedom of speech and worship, etc.?'

3. Our telegram No. 7570 has it is true been overtaken in some respects by the proclamation to Japan issued from Potsdam, but there appears to be no conflict with that proclamation.

4. In discussion with State Department on treatment of Japan after surrender, therefore, you should still be guided by our telegram No. 7570 as amended above, but you should make it clear that the views are the purely departmental views of the Foreign Office and are entirely without prejudice to ministerial conclusions which await the observations of the Dominions.

[1] No. 325.   [2] No. 304.

No. 554

Minute from Sir R. Campbell to Sir O. Sargent
[UE 3595/1094/53]

FOREIGN OFFICE, *29 July 1945*

American Economic Policy and Economic Policy of H.M.'s new Government

A propos of something I said to you at luncheon yesterday about statements made in the last few months, and attitudes adopted, by certain present Ministers, please see article in the left-hand column of the first page of today's *Observer*.[1] I think the matter is there put very clearly and succinctly; and I believe Mr. Hall Patch would agree that this is so: also Mr. Opie.[2]

There is a chance of the U.S. coming away from their old economic heresies, which hit us so hard, & towards what was our traditional economic philosophy.[3] Were we to play in with this new American tendency we stand to secure large reductions of American import tariffs[4] & thus benefit our exports, in certain directions at any rate. The Administration are keen on the new trend. But at the very same moment there is a risk of our going the other way and welshing on the principles of 'Article 7'.[5] Further, & specifically there is the possibility that our policies will involve a certain amount of State trading which will hamper the application of Article 7 principles.

A serious conflict of attitude in the economic field therefore may be in store for us. This will not only detrimentally affect our economic collaboration and the degree and conditions of American help in the economic field, but it will also affect our general collaboration & the whole view the Americans take of us as partners in world affairs—'Discrimination', 'exclusiveness', 'monopoly', 'imperialist economy'—all these words will be trotted out against us and gain spontaneous and often unthinking response from the U.S. public. Is this point worthy of mention in your 'Stocktaking after VE Day'?[6] It is important in estimating the prospects of Anglo-American co-operation (paras 12 & 13).

It is to be remembered that the Americans are ready to accept the necessity for us to maintain controls &c on a temporary basis that is, during the 'transitional period' for which they are ready to admit a duration of three or possibly as much as five years after the end of hostilities. And during this period they would be ready to continue to help us notwithstanding our maintenance of a policy contrary to their aims and beliefs.

But this tolerance is dependent upon the assurance that, after the transitional period—or even progressively during it—we abandon a restrictive system and promote & then fully adopt the system of an expanding economy and multilateralism.

R. I. CAMPBELL

[1] This article, entitled 'Early restart of Anglo–U.S. trade talks', by the correspondent of *The Observer* in Washington referred to the forthcoming visit to London of Mr. W. L. Clayton in the context of Anglo-American trade relations, and asked: 'Will Britain, under a Labour Government, want to return to the free convertibility of her currency? Will she be willing to return to multilateral trading and give up the preference system?'

[2] Economic Adviser to H.M. Embassy, Washington.

[3] Marginal note by Sir R. Campbell: 'Abandoned in the 1930s under pressure of the exorbitant American Tariff policy: and of course remaining in limbo during the war period.'

[4] Marginal note by Sir R. Campbell: 'The Administration has just secured new powers to effect further reductions, in the renewed Trade Agreements Act.'

[5] Of the Lend Lease Mutual Aid Agreement: see No. 26, note 2.

[6] No. 102.

[P.S.] You will no doubt wish to verify the foregoing from Mr. Hall Patch and Mr. Butler.[7]

[7] On 13 August 1945 Mr. Hall Patch recorded on this paper: 'This was discussed at a meeting in Sir O. Sargent's room at which Sir R. Campbell, Mr. N. Butler & myself were present. My minute of Aug. 3rd is the result': see Volume III.

No. 555

Minutes of First Meeting of the Control Council (Germany) held in Berlin on 30 July 1945 at 1.15 p.m.
CONL/M(45)1 [C 4505/3943/18]

Secret

Member. Present
GENERAL OF THE ARMY EISENHOWER (*Chairman*), MARSHAL ZHUKOV, FIELD MARSHAL MONTGOMERY, LIEUT. GEN. KOENIG[1].

Others Present
America Lieut. Gen. Clay, Ambassador Murphy, Maj. Gen. Parks.

Britain Sir William Strang, Lieut. Gen. Robertson, Lieut. Gen. Weeks, Maj. Gen. Whitely, Brig. Hill.

France Lieut. Gen. Koeltz, Ambassador St. Hardouin.

Soviet Union Army General Sokolovski, Col. Gen. Serov, Col. Gen. Kourosov, Mr. Vishinski, Mr. Sobolev, Mr. Sabourov, Lieut. Gen. Vassiliev.

Secretariat: Brig. Grazebrook, Col. Rootham, Col. Hammond, Col. Vialet, Col. Dupont, Maj. Prechepenko.

1. General Eisenhower, by general agreement, took the chair for this meeting.

2. *Activation of Control Machinery*
General Eisenhower stated that the United States staff had prepared a paper on the activation of the Control Machinery (CONL/P(45)1).[2] He suggested that the Commanders-in-Chief designate their Deputies to consider certain suggested amendments and submit an agreed version of this paper to the Control Council by the 4th of August, for confirmation by the Council at its next meeting on 10 August 1945.

The Council approved the above suggestion.

3. *Order on procedure for meetings*
(a) *Date of meetings.* General Eisenhower proposed that in the future the

[1] The above list and minute 5 below are printed in *F.R.U.S. 1945*, vol. iii, pp. 366-7: cf. also *ibid.*, pp. 820-3.
[2] Not attached to filed copy. An amended text of this American paper, beginning '1 Organisation Meeting of the Control Council' and ending 'the report will indicate the points of agreement and of disagreement' was included in CONL/P(45)7 of 31 July 1945: *loc. cit.*, pp. 825-9.

Control Council should meet on the 10th, 20th, and 30th day of each calendar month. Marshal Zhukov added that in addition the Council should meet at such other times as were necessary. Field Marshal Montgomery suggested that in the month of February, the 3rd statutory meeting should be on the last day of the month.

The Council approved the above proposals and further agreed that Council meetings would be held hereafter at 1400 hours, Berlin time.

(b) *Chairmanship.* The Council agreed

(i) that the chairmanship would rotate by calendar months in alphabetical order of countries as follows: America, Britain, France, and Soviet Russia.

(ii) that General Eisenhower should be Chairman for August.

(c) *Secretaryship.* The Council agreed that the country providing the Chairman should also provide the Chief Secretary for the calendar month.

4. *Progress report of preparation of Control Council building*

The Council took note of a report on the progress made in the preparation of the Control Council building. In this regard, it was noted that the building will be ready for use by the Council at its next meeting on 10 August 1945.

5. *French sector of Berlin*

Field Marshal Montgomery stated that he had been authorized by his government to offer the two districts of Reinic[k]endorf and Wedding, including the Hermann Goering Barracks, to the French as their sector in Berlin. General Koenig stated that he had been authorized by the French government to accept this offer. General Eisenhower agreed with these views and stated that he would make available all possible facilities for the French occupation of their sector. Marshal Zhukov stated that since this decision did not affect the Russian sector, he had no observations to offer. The Council agreed that certain details regarding the French sector should be worked out by the Deputies to the British, French, and American Commanders, respectively. General Koenig requested that facilities should be given to the French to enable them to effect rapid occupation of their sector in Berlin. The other three members of the Council agreed that their Deputies would assist General Koenig's Deputy in every way possible to effect this.

6. *British—USSR boundary adjustment*

Field Marshal Montgomery requested the Council to ratify the agreement which had already been made between himself and Marshal Zhukov on certain adjustments of the present boundaries of the Soviet/British Zone, as enumerated in CONL/P(45)5.[3]

The Council ratified the agreement.

7. *British proposals on airfield requirements in Berlin*

Field-Marshal Montgomery brought to the notice of the Council the necessity for each of the controlling powers to have adequate airfield facilities at Berlin. After some discussion, it was agreed:

[3] Not attached to filed copy: cf. *op. cit.*, p. 822.

(*a*) That the British would submit to the Council a definite proposal in writing on this subject.

(*b*) That the British should continue to use Gatow Airfield after the conclusion of the Potsdam Conference, until the airfield question is settled.

(*c*) That fueling, servicing, and other similar air facilities would be available to the French at Tempelhof until the airfield questions is [*sic*] settled.

Field-Marshal Montgomery stressed that in his opinion each country should have its own airfield at Berlin. Marshal Zhukov reserved his opinion on this point.

8. *Co-ordinating Committee*

After some discussion, the Council agreed:

(*a*) That the Coordinating Committee could not be established until the Council had ratified the document on the activation of the Control Machinery (reference CONL/P(45)1).[2]

(*b*) That until that time, the four Deputies shall meet as required to perform any task required of them by the Council.

(*c*) That their Deputies would meet here at 1000 hours tomorrow, 31 July 1945, to consider the US proposals for activation of Control Machinery.

(*d*) That the recommendations of the Deputies on this subject would be available to the members of the Council by 4 August 1945, if possible.

The Deputies were designated as follows: US—Lt. General Clay, UK—Lt. General Robertson, France—Lt. General Koeltz; and Soviet Union—Army General Sokolovsky.

9. *Records of meetings*

On the suggestion of General Eisenhower, the Council agreed that the Allied Secretariat shall furnish an agreed record of conclusions within 24 hours of each meeting to the members of the Council or their Deputies for confirmation and signature.

10. *Press communique*

Field-Marshal Montgomery proposed that a press communique of the first meeting of the Control Council should be issued. The Council agreed that the four Political Advisers should draft and issue to their respective press agencies an identical communique.

11. *Supplies for Berlin*

Marshal Zhukov raised the question of British and US coal and food for Berlin, and stated that the quantities promised had not yet reached the city. Field Marshal Montgomery said that his information was that the material had been placed in trains and had reached the boundaries of the Russian Zone. Certain delays had subsequently arisen.

The Council agreed that a report on this subject should be submitted to it by the Deputies, who might call upon the Kommandatura for detailed information.

12. *Date of next meeting*

The next meeting of the Control Council will take place at the Allied Building, located at 32 Elsholz Strasse in the United States sector, at 1400 hours, Berlin time, on 10 August 1945.

Meeting adjourned at 1445 hours, Berlin time.

CALENDARS TO No. 555

i *30 July 1945 Letter from Sir W. Strang (Berlin) to Mr. Harvey.* Describes and encloses communiqué of above meeting: 'the atmosphere was excellent. Zhukov readily agreed to let us go on using the Gatow air field' pending settlement of general question of use of airfields [C 4380/3943/18].

ii *31 July 1945 Minutes of meeting of Deputies to members of Control Council (Berlin):* procedure, activation of control machinery, coal and food for Berlin [C 4719/3943/18].

iii *1 Aug. 1945 Minutes of ninth meeting of Conference of the Chief of Staff (British Zone) at Lübbecke* [C 4636/3943/18].

No. 556

Lieut.-General Sir R. McCreery (Cassacco) to Mr. Lawson
(Received 31 July, 12.5 a.m.)
No. M/336 Telegraphic [C 5052/317/3]

MAIN BRITISH TROOPS, AUSTRIA, *30 July 1945, 4.15 p.m.*[1]

Top secret. Immediate

Following from Mack personal for Harvey F.O.

Your tel 1917 to Rome.[2]

First. I discussed this question with Erhardt[3] at Verona (repeat Verona) on 29th July and emphasized the points in your para 4 which I had made to him some time ago. He is in favour of the British plan and told me privately that as a result of our earlier conversation he had advised General Clark to this effect.

Second. I gather from him that what is worrying the Americans is that they have a suspicion that H.M. Government would refuse to accept Renner. I told him that this was not (repeat not) so. Although there might be Austrian leaders with cleaner hands as regards Austria's relations with Germany H.M. Govt. had no (repeat no) personal objection to Renner of which I was aware. It was in my view not (repeat not) unlikely meeting in Vienna which I have (?considered advisable) of representatives of the provinces including Vienna would invite Renner to remain as Head of the

---

[1] Time of origin.

[2] No. 411.

[3] Mr. J. G. Erhardt was Political Adviser for Austrian Affairs to General Mark Clark, Commanding General of American forces in Austria and U.S. Military Commissioner for Austria.

new Provisional Austrian Govt. If so he would have the wider endorsement which he at present lacks and the only endorsement which was possible in the absence of free election. The essentials were that the new Government should accept Allied policy and should be acceptable all provinces. Erhardt agreed.

Third. Erhardt asked who would select the representatives of Vienna at proposed meeting. I expressed the view that Renner should be invited to do so in consultation with his colleagues. Erhardt agreed.

Fourth. If you approve my language I think British and U.S.A. policy will be in line in Vienna. The French have already told us they agree our plan.

Fifth. Erhardt also told me that State Department's policy is to place the responsibility for the administration of Austria on Austrian shoulders as soon as possible. This too is in accord British policy.

Sixth. As regards your 1 and 2. It is possible that we shall find that food distribution in Vienna is in hands the municipality and not (repeat not) the Renner Govt.

Seventh. Erhardt is anxious he should not (repeat not) be quoted to any U.S.A. official.[4]

CALENDAR TO No. 556

i *30 July 1945   Letter from Mr. Mack (H.Q., 8th Army) to Mr. Troutbeck* enclosing correspondence with Mr. Nicholls at Graz: British entry there; communist representation in Styrian Provisional Govt. [C 4578/205/3].

[4] Mr. Troutbeck minuted to Mr. Harvey on 31 July 1945 on this telegram: 'We discussed this telegram in the department and some doubt was expressed about the wisdom of para. 3, viz. leaving it to Dr. Renner and his colleagues to select the representatives of Vienna at the proposing [*sic*] meeting of provincial representatives. Mr. Cullis prepared a draft on this point. I am inclined myself to leave it. It is true that Dr. Renner claims to represent the whole of Austria, and that the Viennese representatives should not, if his claim were admitted, come within his purview any more than say Styrian representatives. But we do not admit his claim. On the other hand to reject his right to speak even for Vienna would mean that the Russians would challenge the right of the govts. who have set up in Carinthia & Styria to speak for those provinces. So all the delegates from every province wd. have to be selected by the Allied Council. But surely it is much better that Austrians shd. do the selecting. I think Mr. Mack was therefore right.   If this is agreed, we might send him a short telegram expressing approval.' Mr. Harvey agreed with Mr. Troutbeck and replied to Mr. Mack in War Office telegram No. 64402 of 3.50 p.m. on 2 August: 'We fully approve line you took.'

No. 557

Mr. Morrison to Mr. Bevin (Berlin: received 31 July, 11.55 p.m.)
No. 289 Onward Telegraphic [R 12845/4/19]

Top secret. Immediate   FOREIGN OFFICE, *30 July 1945, 7.45 p.m.*
Following from Sir O. Sargent for Sir A. Cadogan.

Your telegram Target No. 278[1] (of July 29th: Political situation in Greece).

We feel that it would be better not to take up with the State Department the points referred to in Onward 248[2] until we can give them an indication of our policy in general towards Greece and in particular with regard to a change of Government.

You will have seen from Athens telegrams Nos. 1596[3], 1599[4] (Onward 271) and 1601[5] (Onward 273) that in the absence of any such clear indication of British policy the Regent himself is finding it increasingly difficult to deal with the pressure for a change of government. Our view remains that a change of government at this moment would be entirely unjustified. The arguments for this were set out in paragraph 1 of Onward 248[2] and are strengthened by Athens telegrams under reference. These re-emphasise our conclusion that complete establishment of law and order throughout Greece and preparations for a plebiscite and elections depend on physical facts such as speed with which gendarmerie can take over from National Guard and not on composition of the Greek Government. Moreover, it is clear from these telegrams that even if we wished to establish an all-party government, it is very doubtful whether we could do so, since the Popular Party, which represents about half Greece, would refuse to co-operate with Republicans and Communists.

2. The question is therefore whether we should advise the Greek Government to give way to the campaign now being waged by press and radio in Russian and Russian-dominated Balkan States. I am sure that we should not do so, particularly since the clamour for a change of government in Greece itself appears to come only from a few self-seeking politicians and not from the mass of the people (Athens telegram No. 1584).[6]

3. If agitation for a change of government is allowed to continue it may seriously prejudice internal stability in Greece and preparation for plebiscite and elections. I consider it important therefore that we should make our views known without delay. This is certainly a matter which we should if possible discuss with the Americans, but if this is not possible I think we shall have to go ahead without them.

4. Simplest method of stating H.M.G.'s policy would be in answer to a question in Parliament, but I consider that it might be dangerous to delay announcement until Parliament meets. I suggest therefore that the Prime Minister might send a message to the Regent. Message need not state explicitly that we are against change of government but it should be clear that this is our view. Message might emphasise our continued interest in Greek affairs and our desire to assist the Greek people both in restoring their

[1] See No. 532, note 3.
[2] No. 532.
[3] No. 530. *Note in filed copy:* 'Not repeated to Terminal.'
[4] No. 530.i.
[5] No. 532.i.
[6] No. 392.i.

country and in choosing their future regime and government in conditions of freedom and tranquil[l]ity. Reference might be made to our desire to see Varkiza agreement fully executed and our concern at reports of Right-Wing excesses in contravention of this agreement. Message could stress the importance we attach to the Voulgaris Government's carrying through without fear or favour measures they have adopted to prevent all violations of the agreement by extremists either of the Right-Wing or the Left. Law and order must be established throughout Greece on a fair and impartial basis in order that the Greek people may be enabled to express their will as soon as possible.

Repeated to Athens No. 1615, Moscow No. 4218, Washington No. 7966, Belgrade No. 1132, Caserta No. 2323.

CALENDAR TO No. 557

i *31 July 1945 Mr. Caccia (Athens) Tel. No. 1614.* Refers to No. 532 and discusses proposed advisory commission in relation to holding Greek elections in 1945 and to attitude of Regent to changes in government [R 12875/4/19].

No. 558

Mr. Morrison to Mr. Bevin (Berlin: received 30 July, 10.52 p.m.)
No. 291 Onward Telegraphic [*R 13221/11875/19*]

Immediate. Top secret   FOREIGN OFFICE, *30 July 1945, 8.45 p.m.*

Ismay from Hollis.

The Chiefs of Staff this morning considered Onward No. 242[1] from Foreign Office to Sir Alexander Cadogan on the Greek situation. Chiefs of Staff were particularly worried about paragraph 7 of the Foreign Office telegram which states 'we fail to see how, if a frontier incident occurs, which it is beyond the power of the slender Greek forces to put down, the British forces can stand aside.

It seems to us, looking at the problem from the political aspect, that so long as our forces are there they ought to assist the Greeks not only to maintain internal order but to protect their frontiers'.

2. You will remember that on 26th July the Chiefs of Staff prepared a draft reply to Naf. 1037,[2] which you sent to the Foreign Office for comment before submitting it to the Prime Minister, together with a recommendation that the Foreign Office should be invited to consider what action could be

---

[1] No. 531.
[2] The substance of this draft reply, not printed, to telegram NAF 1037 (see No. 121, note 3) was in accordance with the views of the Chiefs of Staff as summarized in No. 531, paragraph 6. The covering letter of 26 July 1945 from General Sir H. Ismay to Sir O. Sargent, not printed, was as indicated below.

taken regarding a diplomatic warning to Balkan countries. In case you have not a copy of the draft reply to Naf 1037, I am repeating it in my immediately following telegram.[3]

3. In reply to your letter to the Foreign Office of 26th July informing them of the Chiefs of Staff views, Sir Orme Sargent stated that he was unable for the moment to give you the Foreign Office views on this subject, but sent a copy of Onward 242 giving his personal and the provisional views of the Foreign Office on this matter. Thus the Chiefs of Staff reply to Naf 1037 has not yet been sent.

4. The Chiefs of Staff instructed me to inform you that they entirely adhered to the views expressed in their draft reply to Naf 1037 and to say that if this frontier threat could not be resolved by diplomatic action on the highest level and involved participation by British troops in military action of unforeseeable dimensions, the effect on any acceleration of our demobilisation plans will be extremely grave.[4]

5. It appears from Target 278[5] that Anglo-American discussions on Greece are unlikely to take place at Terminal. Nevertheless, the Chiefs of Staff thought that you should be aware of their views in case this question arose.[6]

6. A copy of this telegram is, of course, being sent to the Foreign Office.

CALENDARS TO No. 558

i *30–31 July & 2 Aug. 1945* (a) *Extracts from 186–7th meetings of Chiefs of Staff.* Discussions leading to despatch of No. 558 and its amendment (note 4 above) [R 13042/11875/19]; (b) *requested report J.P. (45) 184 Final of 2 Aug. by Joint Planning Staff on situation in Greece.* Serious implications of an involvement of British forces in defence of Greek frontiers [R 13223/11875/19].

ii *1 Aug 1945* Extract from 188th meeting of Chiefs of Staff. Letter from Gen. Ismay to Sir A. Cadogan (Berlin) enclosing copy of minute to Mr. Attlee covering report J.I.C. (45) 237 (O) (Final) of 31 July on developments in S.E. Europe: possibility of Yugoslav and Bulgarian offensive intentions against Greece [R 13104, 13222/11875/19].

[3] Not printed.
[4] At the request of the Chiefs of Staff, conveyed in Foreign Office telegram No. 310 Onward of 4.18 p.m. on 31 July 1945 to Berlin (received 6.20 p.m.), the last clause, beginning 'the effect on', was deleted and the following substituted: 'we do not possess the military force to implement such a policy and there would have to be a drastic recasting of our mobilization plans.'
[5] See No. 532, note 3.
[6] General Sir H. Ismay in Berlin enclosed a copy of the present telegram in a letter of 31 July to Sir A. Cadogan. General Ismay observed: 'You have probably already seen the attached telegram, a copy of which has been sent to the Foreign Secretary, but I felt it right to draw your particular attention to paragraph 3, from [which] you you [sic] will see that the reply, which the Chiefs of Staff propose to send to Naf 1037 of 12th July, is held up pending Foreign Office concurrence. It seems very important that Field Marshal Alexander should not be left without instructions for much longer.'

No. 559

Cabinet Office to Joint Staff Mission (Washington)
No. COS (W) 39 Telegraphic [U 6005/3276/70]

CABINET OFFICE, *30 July 1945, 7.50 p.m. G.M.T.*

Top secret. Important

Following from Chiefs of Staff.
Ref. COS(W) 23, and Fan 601.[1]

1. Request you put the following views to the U.S. Chiefs of Staff regarding Combined Command in Mediterranean.

2. Conditions in Europe particularly in the South East where several frontiers are in dispute, are such that it would be of advantage to retain, for some considerable time yet, an authority in the Mediterranean with power to concert naval, military, air and political activities. We consider, therefore, that Sacmed and the present system of command should be retained for the present and the situation reviewed in three months time.

3. Sacmed should retain his present area of responsibility less Turkey and the Dodecanese. Responsibility for these territories has been delegated by Sacmed to the Middle East Command for some considerable time and we suggest that they should now be officially transferred to the Middle East.

4. Remarks in paragraph 5 to 8 below deal with combined command *after* it has been decided that the appointment of Sacmed should be abolished and AFHQ dissolved.

5. A small Anglo-American Army Headquarters, the commander of which should be responsible to the Combined Chiefs of Staff will be required to replace AFHQ until

(*a*) The Allied Commission, which should be subordinate to the Anglo-American Army H.Q. is dissolved.

(*b*) Allied Military Government in Bolzano, the area about Tarvisio, Venezia Giulia, Pantellaria, Lampedusa and Linosa has ceased.

(*c*) Allied Administrative commitments such as responsibilities for repair and docking of ships, civil affairs, communications, labour, fuel, local resources and financial matters, have ceased.

6. The Allied Commander should co-operate with the Commanders-in-Chief of the other two Services on Inter-Service matters.

7. The Anglo-American Army Headquarters should be responsible for all Italy, including the occupied part of Venezia Giulia, Sardinia, Sicily, Pantellaria, Lampedusa and Linosa.

---

[1] In pursuance of decisions reached in No. 123.i, telegram COS (W) 23 of 11 July 1945, not printed, from the British Chiefs of Staff to the British Joint Staff Mission in Washington had conveyed instructions for the presentation of memorandum C.C.S. 866/2 of 12 July: printed in *F.R.U.S. Berlin*, vol. i, p. 711. The amendment therein to the draft message to Field Marshal Sir H. Alexander, printed *ibid.*, was incorporated in the final message transmitted in telegram FAN 601 (not printed) of 20 July from the Combined Chiefs of Staff to Allied Forces Headquarters.

8. We propose that Greece and the Aegean Islands, including Crete, would be transferred to the Middle East Command.

9. We suggest that the British Chiefs of Staff should act as the executive agents of the Combined Chiefs of Staff to the Allied Army Commander mentioned in paragraph 5.

10. Field Marshal Alexander has recommended that we should now set up within the general framework of AFHQ a British Army theatre command and staff on the lines of M[editerranean] T[heatre of] O[perations] U[nited] S[tates] A[rmy] through which Sacmed should exercise command in his capacity as commander of the British land forces and which should be responsible for the maintenance of the British forces in Austria. We propose to approve this and you may inform the U.S. Chiefs of Staff of our intention.

11. You should obtain the concurrence of the Combined Chiefs of Staff to the draft directive to Sacmed, contained in our immediately following telegram [i].

CALENDAR TO No. 559

i *30 July 1945 Cabinet Office Tel. No. COS (W) 40 to J.S.M. (Washington).* Draft directive from Combined Chiefs of Staff to F.M. Alexander [U 6045/3276/70].

No. 560

Mr. Morrison to Mr. Roberts (Moscow)
No. 4219 Telegraphic [E 5531/103/34]

Immediate   FOREIGN OFFICE, *30 July 1945, 8.55 p.m.*

Repeated to Tehran No. 470 Important, Bagdad No. 457, M.E. Min. No. 1334, Washington No. 7968, Government of India.

Tehran telegram No. 766[1] (July 28th: Allied withdrawal from Tehran).

Please inform Soviet Government that in view of decision reached at Terminal, we assume they are instructing their Ambassador at Tehran to make appropriate communication to Persian Government. You should add that Sir R. Bullard has instructions to keep in touch with his Soviet colleague with a view to making simultaneous notification to Persian Government; but that he will in any case inform Persian Government shortly of the decision to withdraw Allied forces from Tehran. (See my telegram No. 471 to Tehran.)[2]

---

[1] No. 542.
[2] This telegram of even date (despatched at 9.20 p.m.) referred to the present telegram to Moscow and instructed Sir R. Bullard: 'You should inform Persian Government not later than August 2nd, whether or not your Soviet colleague has received instructions by then.'

No. 561

Letter from Sir L. Collier (Oslo) to Mr. Warner (Received 8 August)
No. 22/5/45 [N 10006/158/30]

OSLO, *30 July 1945*

Dear Warner,

I reported, in paragraph 8 of my letter of 21st June,[1] about inter-allied relations in Norway, that the Russians seemed to be searching for an excuse to take action of their own against the Germans in the north of the country; and you will now presumably have heard from Potsdam of the extraordinary declaration made by the Russians there, alleging that a quarter of a million Germans were armed and unguarded in north Norway.[2] Thorne has disposed of that particular story; but he doubts if we have heard the last of these Russian moves, as he believes that the Russians were much disappointed at finding us in occupation of the Tromsö region after the German collapse, and had planned to occupy it themselves.

Our local Intelligence people in the north maintain, indeed, that the Russians had worked out a plan for the occupation of all north Norway on the German collapse: I have seen no evidence of this, and it is, as you know, contrary to the information we had before I left London, to the effect that the Russians were not making any preparations for an advance from the Kirkenes area, but on the contary were withdrawing some of their troops to Murmansk. They may, however, have changed their minds when they realised that German resistance was collapsing in Norway as well as in Germany itself; and there are certainly plenty of signs that they are now taking a considerable interest in this part of the world.

One of these signs has been the publication in the press of to-day, of an interview with General Ratov (See Stockholm despatch No. 2 of June 6th)[3] on the lines of the notorious Golikov interview mentioned in my letter of July 16th,[4] complaining of the refusal of the Allied Command in Norway to include in the repatriation of Russian ex-prisoners six thousand men who, from the context, are evidently people claiming to be Poles.

Yours ever
LAURENCE COLLIER

CALENDARS TO NO. 561

i *17, 30 July & 6 Aug. 1945 Correspondence between Sir L. Collier (Oslo) and Mr. Warner.* Some deterioration in relations between Norwegian civilians and

---

[1] Not printed.
[2] See No. 276, note 1, and No. 474.
[3] The reference is uncertain.
[4] Not printed. An interview by a Tass correspondent with Colonel-General F. I. Golikov on the repatriation of Soviet prisoners of war had been published in *Pravda* on 30 April 1945. In this connection Genera. Golikov had alleged shortcomings on the part of British and American authorities.

British airborne forces. Progress in evacuating German troops from Norway, and proposed reduction of British forces [N 9177, 9490/158/30].

ii *24 July 1945 Sir L. Collier (Oslo) No. 33.* Conversation on 23 July with M. Lie on Scandinavian cooperation [N 9493/15/63].

No. 562

Letter from Mr. Nichols (Prague) to Mr. Warner (Received 2 August)
No. 3/31/45 [N 9894/207/12]

PRAGUE, *30 July 1945*

My dear Christopher,

In my letter of July 23rd[1] reporting on Beneš's interview with Reuter's correspondent I commented on the fact that Beneš had publicly stated that it was his intention to keep between 300,000 and 500,000 Germans in this country and not 800,000, the figure previously mentioned. I taxed the President with this the other day, when my wife and I lunched alone with the Beneš's, and he confirmed what I had supposed, namely that this was a tactical move. He has not really changed his opinion, which is that 800,000 is probably the right number to keep.

2. It may be worth adding that there have been many rumours, gathering in intensity in the last few days, that Beneš intended to resign and had in fact already threatened resignation. I did not believe these for a moment, but thought it would be interesting to ask the President if he knew of them and, if so, what was their origin. He said he knew all about them, that they were completely untrue and that he could only suppose that they had been put about by the extremists on the Right in order to make trouble for the parties of the Left. The Right parties knew perfectly well that he was not prepared to go so far as were the Left parties and that he was having a tussle with the Left parties on certain of the measures they were proposing, e.g. nationalisation, etc., etc. He assumed that the extremists on the Right held that if they set these rumours afloat they might be believed by the population, who would then draw the conclusion that matters must be very bad indeed if he, the President, were ready to resign, and the Left might thereby be discredited.

3. I should perhaps add in fairness that Beneš did not seem too certain himself that this explanation was the right one, but it was the only one which suggested itself to him. Anyway, there is no truth in the resignation rumour.[2]

---

[1] No. 59.iv.

[2] With reference to this rumour Mr. Nichols further reported in his letter No. 3/32/45 of 4 August 1945 to Mr. Warner (received 8 August): 'It is perhaps worth noting that in the course of the usual week-end speechifying two spokesmen of the political parties took the trouble to refer to and refute these rumours. 2. The National Socialist Deputy Prime Minister, M. J. David, spoke at Melnik of "rumours being spread by irresponsible re-

I still myself think that Beneš will so manage to steer matters in this country as to ensure that the extremists do not have matters all their own way and that in a few years time this country will be no more Left—let alone Communist-minded than, say, New Zealand or Norway. However, it is always foolish to prophesy.

Yours ever
PHILIP NICHOLS

CALENDARS TO NO. 562

i   *23 July 1945*   Mr. *Nichols* (*Prague*) *Tel. No. 57 Saving:* discusses Czechoslovak policy on transfer of German populations [N 9235/207/12].

ii   *30 July 1945*   Mr. *Nichols* (*Prague*) *No. 71.* Reports recent visit to Slovakia [N 9885/48/12].

actionary elements alleging some disagreement between the parties and the President" and emphatically denied that there was any basis of truth in them; and at Pilsen on the same day (Sunday, the 29th July) the General Secretary of the Communist Party delivered a vigorous attack on "all stupid gossip about dissensions in the Government and between the Communists and the President". He, too, attributed the rumours to reactionary circles who were continuing the work of Dr. Goebbels, and appealed to all Communists to act as "vigilant guardians of unity".'

No. 563

Memorandum by Field-Marshal Sir B. Montgomery (Berlin)[1]

[C 4522/267/18]

[BERLIN,] *30 July 1945*

Six Points about Germany

1. Critical period coming this winter. If we weather that storm we will never look back.
    We must win the 'battle of the winter'.
2. Minimum requirements in troops. Three Corps; eleven Divisions.
    Tug-of-war with release scheme.
3. *Economic*
    Imports paid for by exports.
    No question of reparations yet.
4. To save time we must be able to deal direct with Whitehall ministries.

---

[1] On 31 July 1945 Mr. Pierson Dixon minuted in Berlin to Mr. Harrison and Sir W. Strang on this manuscript memorandum: 'This memo was handed to the S. of S. last night by F.M. Montgomery. The S. of S. proposes to examine his proposals on return to London. Meanwhile you may care to make some comments.' Mr. Bevin minuted below: 'Would like to refer to this in my speech on F[oreign] A[ffairs]. E. B.' Mr. Bevin made a speech on foreign affairs in the House of Commons on 20 August: *Parl. Debs., 5th ser., H. of C.,* vol. 413, cols. 283–300.

A Department, with our own P.U.S., under the S of S for War: but not under the War Office.

Approval for this machinery.

5. Need for Whitehall to realise the problem in Germany.

6. Need for a sympathetic Press.
   A good example: fraternisation.[2]

B. L. M.

CALENDARS TO NO. 563

i   *30 July 1945   Minute from Sir W. Strang to Sir A. Cadogan (Berlin)* Attaches No. 43.ii and third revise of F.M. Montgomery's Personal Message No. 3 to population of British Zone of Germany: cf. *The Times*, 7 August 1945, p. 4 [C 5131/24/18].

ii   *31 July 1945   Minutes of first meeting of Interdepartmental Finance Working Party of A.C.A.O. on Germany and Austria* (F.W.P.—45—M.1): questions concerning payment for imports by exports from British Zone [UE 2728/2689/71].

iii   *1 Aug. 1945   Letter from Major-General C. S. Sugden (Director of Military Operations, War Office) to Viscount Hood*: opposition of F.M. Montgomery to participation in occupation of British Zone by contingents from smaller Allied Powers [U 5902/20/70].

[2] No comments on this memorandum by Mr. Harrison or Sir W. Strang have been traced. In the Foreign Office, however, Mr. Troutbeck minuted on it: 'As to the first point, it is realised on all sides that next winter will be a critical period from the point of view of food, fuel and housing. It is very natural that Field Marshal Montgomery should make it his aim to get through this period without serious outbreaks of disease, starvation or disorder. It has however to be remembered that the coming winter will be an equally critical period for our liberated Allies who will have no Field Marshals to fight their battles for them, and that the supply position will be such that we may have to choose between feeding the Allies and feeding the Germans.

'*Point 2*. The Foreign Office should, I think, certainly support the Field Marshal in maintaining a sufficient number of troops to carry out the purposes of the occupation.

'*Point 3*. The Berlin Protocol provides that the "proceeds of exports from current production and stocks shall be available in the first place for payment for such (approved) imports". These imports have to be approved by the Control Council, and there may well be argument as to how much is necessary. For example the living standards for the German people agreed at Potsdam may prove insufficient to produce the coal for which the whole of Europe is crying out. This whole question is, I understand, under urgent consideration now.

'*Point 4*. I understand that the Whitehall Organisation for dealing with the current work of the Control Commission is now under consideration, but the idea of a special P.U.S. for the Commission has been dropped.

'*Point 5*. This matter was raised at a recent Cabinet meeting where it was agreed that every encouragement should be given to Ministers to visit Germany.

'*Point 6*. The News Department will no doubt continue to give the press all the guidance it can but, as the Control Commission is the primary responsibility of the War Office, the matter lies rather in the hands of the War Office Public Relations Officers. But the Field Marshal cannot expect to escape press criticism and, if he starts shooting Russian displaced persons on sight, as he is proposing to do, he will no doubt get it. J. M. Troutbeck 9th August 1945.' This minute was countersigned by Mr. O. C. Harvey on 11 August.

No. 564

Mr. Morrison to Mr. Nichols (Prague)
No. 1 Arfar Saving Telegraphic [N 10093/10093/12]

FOREIGN OFFICE, *31 July 1945*

The name 'Safehaven' has been given to negotiations and operations having as their objectives:

(*a*) the uncovering of enemy assets of every description held outside Germany, particularly, in neutral countries; and

(*b*) the denial to the enemy, through such measures as freezing, of the use of these assets.

2. Negotiations in Portugal, Spain, Sweden and Switzerland have resulted in comprehensive measures being instituted in those countries for the attainment of these objectives. In view of the length of time that the enemy had to perfect his arrangements and of his known mastery of the art of concealment, it is necessary that these measures should be reinforced by similar legislation in ex-occupied countries whose economy may have been utilised by the enemy in furtherance of his policy to spread and conceal his assets abroad.

3. We are already receiving from Germany a great deal of valuable detailed information, which I am anxious to supplement or corroborate by as much information as can be obtained from countries which were occupied by the enemy. The wide-spread nature of organisations like the Bata concern lends itself to operations of the kind which we are anxious to uncover and I consider it essential that the Czechoslovak Government should take steps to conduct a thorough investigation into the real ownership of ostensible Czechoslovak assets abroad.

4. I shall be glad if you will consider what procedure might be adopted in order to collect, collate and make available to me any information of use in connection with 'Safehaven' operations, and if you will invoke the cooperation of the Czecho-Slovak government in the institution of a thorough and efficient investigation into the real ownership of nominally Czechoslovak assets in foreign countries, so that we can request the foreign governments concerned to freeze any assets suspected of having an enemy taint. You will appreciate that the sooner this task is undertaken the better for our ultimate objective.

5. Side-by-side with this investigation I should like to see a similar enquiry conducted into enemy assets within the country, with the object of ensuring that any enemy property is effectively blocked.

CALENDAR TO No. 564

i *18–24 July 1945 From & to Lord Halifax (Washington) Tels. Nos. 5014–15, 7783*
Transmits American proposals for interim offices for German affairs with authority over Germans living abroad; objections to inclusion of Eire [C 4019/32/18; C 4050, 4085/4050/18].

No. 565

Mr. Morrison to Mr. Steel (Lübbecke)
No. 134 Telegraphic [Z 8932/5491/41]

Most Immediate   FOREIGN OFFICE, *31 July 1945, 12.20 p.m.*

Repeated to Resmed's Office Caserta No. 2328 (Most Immediate), Lisbon No. 557 (Immediate), Paris No. 1803 Saving, Madrid No. 622, San Sebastian No. 4.

Laval is reported to have left Barcelona airport this morning at 7.15 a.m. in the aircraft in which he arrived,[1] with German crew. Destination of aircraft is unknown, but it is believed that German pilots wanted to return to Germany.

2. If aircraft lands in British zone of occupation, Laval and any other Frenchmen who may be with him should be handed over as soon as possible to suitable French authorities.

3. Please consult with Commander-in-Chief and make suitable arrangements accordingly.[2]

CALENDAR TO No. 565

i *31 July 1945 Memorandum by Mr. Hoyer Millar.* Allegations by Professor L. Rougier of an agreement between Marshal Pétain and Mr. Churchill in autumn 1940 are untrue (cf. Cmd. 6662 of 1945) [Z 9192/255/17].

---

[1] Cf. No. 359.ii.

[2] The British Chiefs of Staff informed the British Joint Staff Mission in Washington in telegram COS(W) 44 of even date at 6.55 p.m. (repeated to A.F.H.Q., U.S. Forces, European Theatre Main and Rear, 21 Army Group): 'Owing to delay caused by undecipherable telegram, Foreign Office were not aware that Spanish Government had yet made plans for releasing Laval. 2 . . . Destination unknown but he had instructions to return whence he came. 3. Spaniards have consistently refused to organise handing over Laval to the French in conformity with clause in their Treaty with French that there will be no extradition of political prisoners. Spaniards are only concerned to get him out of their country. 4. Under these circumstances if he lands in territory under Allied command, we propose that he should be detained and handed over to the nearest and most appropriate French authorities as quickly as possible. German aircraft crew should be treated as prisoners of war and the aircraft confiscated.'

No. 566

Mr. Roberts (Moscow) to Mr. Bevin (Received 31 July, 3.40 p.m.)
No. 3360 Telegraphic [R 12927/127/92]

Important   MOSCOW, *31 July 1945, 1.44 p.m. G.M.T.*

Repeated to Belgrade.

My immediately preceding telegram [i].

Visits of this kind by Moscow correspondents are of course from our point of view wholly unsatisfactory substitute for that greater freedom for journalists in south east Europe for which British and American delegations have I understand been pressing at Terminal. As has been pointed out by this Embassy on various occasions Moscow correspondents of foreign newspapers and agencies are not allowed by the Soviet censors to report anything critical of Soviet policy and unless they are prepared to prejudice their chances of obtaining re-entry visa their reports even from abroad must not be on lines objectionable to Soviet Government. Their despatches therefore can in fact amount to little more than plain statements of Soviet case.

2. In the case of Finland His Majesty's Ambassador recommended, it is true, that it would be better for first visit to be paid by British journalists from Moscow and not from those resident in Sweden. But this was because of the risk that British journalists in Sweden might to some extent have been infected with anti-Soviet prejudices and because it seemed desirable that Finns should not be led up garden path about British policy. Position in south east Europe is wholly different and if as we should we can get British journalists into this area they ought surely to be people who can afford in cases where they think this right to face the displeasure of the Soviet authorities.

3. If as I understand to be the case there are some British correspondents already in Belgrade they might well object to the arrival in their parish of other journalists working for the same papers. If there are not, this must I assume, be because necessary permission has not been forthcoming from the Yugoslav Government and it would be all the more undesirable that Yugoslav Goverment should handpick journalists who are not entirely free agents owing to their Moscow commitments.

4. The most satisfactory procedure in all such cases would seem to be for foreign governments to invite British newspapers to send correspondents direct from Britain and for the newspapers rather than for the foreign Government to make their own nominations. Although I do not suggest that any steps should be taken which might interfere with the present visit to Yugoslavia, it might be possible to say to Yugoslav Government either in London or Belgrade that selection of Moscow corespondents strikes us as odd and that we should have expected Yugoslav Government to follow procedure mentioned above.

Foreign Office please pass to Belgrade as my telegram No. 76.

Mr. Brimelow, Mr. Ridsdale and Mr. Warner. Information from correspondent of *The Times* in Moscow that M. Alexandrov, a director of propaganda, recently stated that Soviet Govt. intended to use Soviet agencies rather than foreign correspondents to disseminate information on U.S.S.R. Soviet policy thought likely to be effective until newspapers refuse to accept censored reports [N 10667/592/38].

No. 567

Sir N. Charles (Rome) to Mr. Bevin (Received 31 July, 8.25 p.m.)
No. 1206 Telegraphic [ZM 4135/3/22]

Important   ROME, *31 July 1945, 5.46 p.m. G.M.T.*

Repeated to Resmed's Office (Caserta) Saving.

My telegram No. 981.[1]

A[dvisory] C[ouncil for] I[taly] has been informed by Allied Commission that S.A.C.M.E.D. proposes to hand back to jurisdiction of Italian Government provinces of Apuania and Lucca and (. . .? territory)[2] of Emilia on August 3rd and commune of Ancona on August 4th.

2. S.A.C.M.E.D. considers transfer desirable in order to show continued confidence in the Italian Government and to release personnel for work in Venezia Giulia.

3. Although state of law and order in Emilia is still far from satisfactory and trouble must be expected after transfer takes place this will at least give us opportunity of seeing how far Italian Government is capable of coping with the situation before the rest of the north is handed back.

CALENDARS TO No. 567

i *1 Aug. 1945   Memorandum by Mr. J. M. Addis (F.O. Southern Dept.)* on civil administration in Venezia Giulia. Refers to Nos. 469, minute 9, and 475: proposed negative reply to Yugoslav request for use there of Yugoslav committee-system [R 13089/6/92].

ii *2 Aug. 1945   F.M. Alexander (A.F.H.Q.) Tel. No.Naf 1051 to Combined & British Chiefs of Staff.* Submits proposals for interim policy towards Italian armed forces in light of internal situation in Italy and intended return to Italian civil administration of all Italy less Venezia Giulia [ZM 4209/1/22].

[1] This telegram of 13 June 1945 is not printed.
[2] The text is here uncertain.

No. 568

Mr. Morrison to Mr. Balfour (Washington)
No. 7991 Telegraphic [R 12718/4/19]

Important   FOREIGN OFFICE, *31 July 1945, 5.50 p.m.*

Repeated to Athens No. 1618, Moscow No. 4239, Terminal No. 307 Onward by bag, Paris No. 1806 Saving.

Athens telegram No. 1570[1] and Target No. 136[2] (of July, 21st: Allied supervision of Greek plebiscite and elections).

British Delegation at Terminal now state that there is little possibility of further progress being made with this subject at Potsdam. Soviet Government will clearly not agree to participate in supervision. We have not yet received French Government's reply, but should be grateful if you would consult State Department about timing and wording of announcement.

2. If announcement refers only to elections and does not mention plebiscite point is sure to be noticed in Greece and will be interpreted to mean that we and United States Government are in favour of holding elections first and of deferring plebiscite indefinitely. We still feel that for the present we should take no decision on this point and we are therefore anxious that the announcement should give no indication of any preference one way or the other. Mr. Caccia has suggested that we might use some general phrase such as 'supervision of consultation of the popular will'. Something on these lines might do, but this phrase seems to us too artificial in English. A better alternative might be to quote from the Varkiza Agreement, which refers both to plebiscite and elections, and afterwards to refer to Allied supervision without specifying whether it will be exercised over one or both.

3. We feel that announcement should be made as soon as possible after French Government's reply has been received[3] and would therefore welcome early views of State Department.[4]

---

[1] No. 294.i.

[2] This telegram, not printed, had reported receipt of No. 206 and submission of No. 201.

[3] Mr. Duff Cooper reported in Paris telegram No. 1041 of 31 July 1945 at 6.10 p.m.: 'Minister for Foreign Affairs has replied that the French Provisional Government gladly agrees to participate in Four Power supervision of Greek elections. They also agree that a communiqué on the subject should be published at the end of the Potsdam Conference if replies of the Four Powers arrive in time and the Greek Government has been officially informed.'

[4] Mr. Balfour replied to this telegram in Washington telegram No. 5335 of 1 August at 11.01 p.m. (received 2 August): 'State Department have not yet received any report from United States Delegation about discussions at Terminal regarding Greek elections. Official in charge of Greek desk agrees that announcement regarding Allied supervision should be issued as soon as possible and is working on a draft text of which they will communicate to us in due course.'

No. 569

Mr. Houstoun-Boswall (Sofia) to Mr. Bevin (Received 31 July, 9.20 p.m.)
No. 863 Telegraphic [R 12876/21/7]

Important. Secret   SOFIA, *31 July 1945, 6.45 p.m.*

Repeated to Moscow, Washington.

Your telegram No. 734.[1]

Deputy Commissioner and I do not think our object would be best served by raising this matter with Allied Control Commission because General Biryusov would almost certainly reply:

a. that it did not lie within the competence of A.C.C.,

b. that Petkov's letter had been addressed to Bulgarian Prime Minister and dealt with a purely Bulgarian domestic matter (M. Georghiev has in fact already condemned the letter in his opening speech of (. . .? July 29th)[2]),

c. that if he (Biryusov) were to be approached in the sense of Petkov's suggestion the matter would have to be referred to the (. . .? three)[2] Allied governments concerned for decision.

2. United States political representative shares this view. But before deciding whether or not you would still wish action to be taken with A.C.C. it would be well to recall that in paragraph 1 of his note of July 11th (see military mission's telegram M/1444 to War Office)[3] General Biryusov undertook to hold meetings 'not less than once every ten days'. No meeting has yet taken place possibly because Russian proposals are under discussion at Terminal (your telegram No. 717).[4] Nevertheless, should divergences between the three (. . .? governments)[2] about Bulgarian elections be made public, it is just possible that General Biryusov might maintain that (although in the note no right is given to British and United States (. . .?

---

[1] This telegram of 29 July 1945 had reference to M. Petkov's letter of 26 July reported in No. 90.i (printed in *F.R.U.S. Berlin*, vol. ii, pp. 724–5). In view of possible forcible reaction by Bulgarian communists Mr. Houstoun-Boswall was warned against any direct encouragement of M. Petkov since 'we cannot protect him from what may be the consequences.' In discussions at Potsdam on the political situation in Soviet-controlled Balkan countries 'the Russians have refused to admit that the Governments in power are anything but perfect. We do not however, consider that we should lose this further opportunity of recording our objections to the Bulgarian Government and to the method for holding the forthcoming elections.' The recent Russian proposals for Allied Control Commissions (see No. 136, note 2) provided for Allied consultation in such cases as M. Petkov's appeal. 'We therefore consider that after consultation with his United States colleague the Deputy Commissioner should ask for a meeting of the Commission to discuss the matter and should take full advantage of it to express our concern at the situation disclosed by these developments. Do you consider that we should be well advised to take the line that while ready to supervise free and unfettered elections, we should not care to do so if the elections were held under the undemocratic restrictions laid down in the Electoral Law?'

[2] The text is here uncertain.

[3] See No. 136, note 2.

[4] No. 316.i.

representatives)² to ask for a meeting) he would, had he been approached, have been happy at least to discuss the matter. Were he to take this line I for my part think we could ourselves contend (if it suited us) that we had not raised the matter with A.C.C. because subject did not seem to be within its competence.

3. It seems to us that if His Majesty's Government and United States Government wish to influence the projected Bulgarian elections the best way would be by public Anglo-American declaration at an early date— (in default of any agreement with Russians on the subject) in a sense similar to that suggested in my telegram No. 709,⁵ saying that our two governments would refuse to recognise any Bulgarian Government formed as a result of elections held under present electoral law.

4. At the same time we ought to be clear as to where such a declaration might lead us. As matters at present stand, Bulgarian elections will be the first to be held in liberated Europe (i.e. under Yalta declaration) and are therefore in the nature of a 'test case' both for ourselves and Russians. For clearly there is a vast unanimity [sic] between Anglo-Saxon and militarists conception of democracy.⁶ In other words, whatever course the Bulgarian elections may take is liable to be followed by elections in Roumania, Yugoslavia, Hungary, etc. U.S.S.R. may consider it worth making some concession to western opinion in all these instances, in which case the Anglo-American declaration in question might induce her to issue the necessary moderating instructions to the Bulgarian Government. In the contrary event however (i.e. if she felt the principle at stake in all these countries was too great to admit of any concession) U.S.S.R. might ignore our declaration and back the present Bulgarian Government up to the hilt, in which case we might find ourselves in the position of having to deal with a Bulgarian Government which we had declared beforehand that we could not recognise.

5. We ought in fact to guard against a position in which (to use a chess simile) we used our queen to operate solely against a pawn (the Bulgarian Government) instead of against the more valuable pieces, the Soviet Government. The crux of the matter in fact resides in problem of what are our essential interests in Bulgaria as compared with (. . .? those of)² Soviet Government (of [?cf] my despatch No. 87)⁷ and until that question is settled it is difficult to see where we really are in this country and what our objects in it should be.

6. I have consulted my United States colleague who I understand is telegraphing in a somewhat similar sense to Washington.⁸ But I would add I still adhere to my view that effective inter-Allied supervision of elections is

⁵ Of 12 June, not printed.
⁶ This sentence was queried on the filed copy.
⁷ Of 5 April (R 7279/23/7), not printed.
⁸ Cf. F.R.U.S. Berlin, vol. ii, pp. 728–32.

in any case not (repeat not) practicable unless it is done with adequate forces as e.g. in the case of the Saar.[9]

7. Present Bulgarian Government place great hopes on change of Government in England, as is clear from telegrams of congratulation sent to Mr. Attlee by Bulgarian Prime Minister and National Committee of Patriotic Front and from extravagant statements made by Social Democrat (Left-Wing) Minister of Commerce in his election speech of July 29th. Therefore failure to express our disapproval might be interpreted by them to mean that His Majesty's Government condone police . . .[2] system which has been instituted here.

Foreign Office please pass to Washington as my telegram No. 96.

[9] An international force, comprising British, Italian, Netherland and Swedish contingents, had been sent to maintain order in the Saar Territory for the holding of a plebiscite in January 1935 on its future determination: cf. *D.B.F.P.* Second Series, vol. xii, chap. II.

No. 570

Mr. Balfour (Washington) to Mr. Bevin (Received 31 July, 11.20 a.m.)
No. 5298 Telegraphic [Z 8973/50/36]

Secret   WASHINGTON, *31 July 1945, 3.38 a.m. G.M.T.*

State Department inform me that the United States Delegation at Terminal will raise the question of whether the time has not come to say something to the Portuguese Government concerning Portuguese participation in operations to expel the Japanese from Portuguese Timor, a matter which has laid dormant since the staff conversations in Lisbon last year.[1]

2. I understand the State Department think that we cannot continue indefinitely to leave the Portuguese Government in the dark. Much of course depends on available shipping and plans for training the Portuguese Expeditionary Force. In this connexion I should be glad to know whether a decision has yet been taken as regards Ceylon (telegram No. Z 4155 of July 3rd refers)[2] which I could pass on to the State Department.[3]

CALENDARS TO No. 570

i *23 July 1945 Letter from Mr. Ashley Clarke (Lisbon) to Mr. Hoyer Millar.* Prospect of Anglo-Portuguese conversations concerning Beira as an outlet for Rhodesian products [Z 8778/5044/36].

[1] Cf. No. 183, minute 3, also *F.R.U.S. Berlin*, vol. ii, pp. 1351–2.

[2] This telegram, not printed, from the British Chiefs of Staff to Lieutenant-General H. E. Wetherall, Commander-in-Chief Ceylon, had proposed basing Portuguese training forces in Ceylon.

[3] Foreign Office telegram No. 8046 of 3 August 1945 to Washington replied that H.M. Embassy at Lisbon had been instructed on 27 July 'to concert with United States Embassy communication to Portuguese Government giving views of Combined Chiefs of Staff [cf. No. 249, appendix E]. 2. No decision has yet been taken regarding Ceylon.'

ii *1 Aug. 1945   Letter from Major-General Hollis to Mr. Garran.* Chiefs of Staff consider it impossible to accept Portuguese sloops in an Australian port or in Ceylon (cf. No. 249.i) [Z 9059/50/36].

iii *31 July–4 Aug. 1945   Question of a transfer to U.S. Navy of British facilities in Azores. Letter from Mr. Garran to Mr. J. Ordway (U.S. Embassy in London); to and from Mr. Ashley Clarke (Lisbon) Tels. Nos. 555 & 793; minutes by Mr. Garran and Mr. Hoyer Millar.* Transfer of wireless station on Terceira, agreed by F.O., has not been authorized by Portuguese Govt. *Minute by Mr. Bevin:* 'It seems that there is good ground for Portuguese suspicions. A watchful eye must be kept. I cannot help feeling that while we have kept the agreement for us to enter the Azores in the letter we seem to have departed from the spirit of [it] in order to satisfy the U.S.A. I am very anxious that agreements shall be faithfully kept. E. B.' [Z 8656, 8798, 9055, 9386/28/36].

No. 571

Minute by Mr. N. M. Butler
[W 10686/12/76]

FOREIGN OFFICE, *31 July 1945*

When in Washington in the first week of July, I got to lunch with me Mr. Loy Henderson, recently United States Minister in Bagdad, and now Head of the Near Eastern Office of the State Department. In the course of conversation, he volunteered that he hoped that we would not imagine that the United States Government were wishing to make Saudi-Arabia into a sphere of influence. I replied to the effect that, while this might not be the desire of the State Department, we thought it possible that the Navy or War Departments might have other ideas, particularly in connexion with their supplies of oil fuel. Mr. Henderson replied that this was not really so; he continued that the Standard Oil Company of California (or he may have said the Oil Combine), which held the concessions in Saudi-Arabia, had become rather staggered at the magnitude of the proposition which they had to handle, so much so that they would be quite relieved to bring in other oil interests to share with them. Mr. Henderson continued that this was ruled out by the Red Line Agreement reached at San Remo,[1] and that he inclined to think that this Agreement, which might have served a useful purpose in its day, was now out of date and even prejudicial. He threw this out as a personal opinion. I asked whether the Standard Oil Company of California had in mind the possibility of including merely the American East Coast companies, or perhaps British companies also. My

---

[1] A Group Agreement of 31 July 1928 between private European and American oil companies in respect of operations in the Middle East: cf. D. J. Payton-Smith, *Oil: A Study of war-time policy and administration* (H.M.S.O., 1971), pp. 32–7. A map attached to the agreement featured a red line delineating areas of operation.

impression from Mr. Henderson's reply was that he was not in a position to answer this question, but that the possibility of including some or all of the participants in the Iraq Petroleum Company would not be excluded.

Next day, I met Mr. Wilkinson[2] accidentally in the Embassy, and mentioned to him what Mr. Henderson had said to me. He commented that he inclined to agree that the Red Line Agreement had served its term, and that it might usefully have been revised a year ago: he seemed to think that this would be more difficult now. This was an off-hand and private opinion, and I doubt whether Mr. Wilkinson would wish it to be quoted.

N. M. BUTLER

[2] Mr. Harold Wilkinson was British Petroleum Representative in the United States.

No. 572

Letter from Mr. A. R. Fraser (Paris) to Mr. Welch (Received 3 August)[1]
No. C.D. 69/45 [UE 3568/813/53]

Copy   PARIS, *31 July 1945*

Dear Welch,

With reference to previous correspondence and to last week's inter-departmental meeting on economic relations between the Western European Powers,[2] I write to let you know that M. de Louvencourt, who used to be in the Ministry of National Economy, told Godfrey[3] a couple of days ago that he had been transferred to the Ministry of Foreign Affairs to work in a special section which has been set up in connection with the Committee now established as a result of the Franco-Belgo-Dutch-Luxembourg agreements of earlier this year[4] to discuss economic policy. Apparently this special section is to be under M. de la Baume, who was head of the Economic Section of the Foreign Office before the war and afterwards Ambassador to Switzerland. He is now to be French delegate to the Committee. The Committee will meet about once a month and will set up a number of sub-Committees, one of which to deal with coal will be established in London. M. de Louvencourt is to be a sort of Economic Secretary-General.

In his conversation with Godfrey, M. de Louvencourt, who sought the interview but explained that he did so on his own initiative, stressed the feeling of his friends and colleagues (as others have done and I have more than once reported accordingly) that the discussions cannot get very far

[1] Mr. A. R. Fraser was Commercial Minister in H.M. Embassy in Paris. Mr. A. E. Welch was an Assistant Secretary in the Commercial Relations and Treaties Department of the Board of Trade. The date of receipt was that in the Foreign Office of the unsigned copy sent to Mr. O. C. Harvey.

[2] See No. 398.

[3] Mr. W. Godfrey was Commercial First Secretary in H.M. Embassy in Paris.

[4] Cf. No. 369, note 3.

without the co-operation of the United Kingdom, which they are very anxious to secure. Indeed, he feels that there is some danger that the Committee will get on the wrong lines or follow one not in accordance with our views: this is very accommodating of them. His purpose in meeting Godfrey was, therefore, to ask if he could call on us from time to time and tell us informally what the Committee is doing and, if possible, get from us in return some indication of our attitude towards proposals under discussion and our ideas of the way discussions ought to go.

I am arranging to see M. de Louvencourt as soon as possible and, unless I hear from you to the contrary, I shall encourage him to come as often and as informally as he likes and to talk as much as he wishes. Godfrey made it quite plain to him that at present we could say nothing positive and might not even be able to say anything negative. He understands this; but is, nevertheless, anxious to keep in contact and to let us know how things are getting on.

Permit me to attach an extract from yesterday's Press Summary (a document issued daily in the Embassy). One often sees articles like this in the press.

I have sent a copy of this to Oliver Harvey.

Yours sincerely,

ENCLOSURE IN NO. 572

Extract from Daily Paris Press Comment—29th July, 1945

International Affairs

Attention is still focussed on Britain. In *France-Soir* Vianney[5] contributes a leader on the desirability for Franco-British union based on a common foreign policy and for a common economic plan. He comments:

'La France et l'Angleterre ont devant elles un destin: créer un monde nouveau. Autour d'elles, les nations de l'Ouest européen, autour de leurs Empires l'Afrique entière et la Méditerranée, formeraient un tout harmonieux, tandis que l'Allemagne de l'ouest serait vite absorbée et attirée dans une telle synthèse.

'Ce monde nouveau possédant une puissance économique considérable, condition de toute politique libre et de toute prospérité, serait la base nécessaire du foyer de la civilisation occidentale qu'une nation isolée en Europe ne peut plus désormais supporter. Ce monde serait aussi l'intermédiaire naturel entre la Russie et l'Amérique qu'il saurait dans une audacieuse politique intéresser à lui par des liens commerciaux et culturels profonds, sachant qu'il n'est pire attitude entre les peuples que l'isolationnisme et la fermeture des frontières.'

CALENDAR TO NO. 572

i   *1 Aug. 1945   Mr. Duff Cooper (Paris) Tel. No. 390 Saving.* Summarizes 'an important article', published on 30 July, by M. Beuve-Méry, director of *Le Monde:* considers that Great Britain and France can form nucleus of a group of Western Powers; regrets that time has already been lost [Z 9091/13/17].

[5] M. Philippe Viannay was a journalist contributing to *France-Soir*.

No. 573

Mr. Hankey (Warsaw) to Mr. Bevin (Received 1 August, 4.10 p.m.)
No. 77 Telegraphic [N 9614/35/55]

WARSAW, *1 August 1945, 2.16 p.m. G.M.T.*

My telegram No. 57[1] paragraph 1.

Authorative source in Polish administration confirms that Polish Government will resume full responsibilities for their railways and for Soviet lines of communication on August 15th. A Polish delegation will go to Moscow to negotiate an agreement covering conditions in which Soviet Army may use Polish railways. At present main lines have one broad[2] one European gauge track—all will revert to European gauge. Soviet control officers will be removed from railway administration but he thought they would all come back in some liaison mission. He was gloomy.

2. I took the line with him as with others that one of Poland's main contributions to European security must be provision of lines of communication for Soviet army occupying Germany.[3]

Please repeat to Moscow and to Sir W. Strang.

[1] No. 540.
[2] i.e. Russian gauge of 5 feet.
[3] Mr. C. F. A. Warner commented in a minute of 5 August 1945 on this telegram: 'Para. 2: Mr. Hankey was no doubt "technically" correct. But he need not ever say anything to suggest that we enjoy or approve any of the various Russian means of keeping a hold on Poland, I think.'

No. 574

Mr. Broad (Caserta) to Mr. Bevin (Received 1 August, 8.55 p.m.)
No. 1429 Telegraphic [Z 9022/5491/41]

Immediate   CASERTA, *1 August 1945, 7.29 p.m. G.M.T.*

Repeated to Madrid, San Sebastian, Paris, Washington.

My telegram No. 1422.[1]

Laval did not as anticipated land in Italy. According to Allied Force Headquarters, he arrived at Linz in Austria yesterday and was there arrested and handed to French authorities.

Foreign Office pass to San Sebastian[2] and Saving to Paris as my telegram No. 10.[3]

[1] Not printed.
[2] Summer residence of H.M. Ambassador to Spain.
[3] Mr. Duff Cooper reported in Paris telegram No. 1050 of 4.37 p.m. (received 4.50 p.m.) on 2 August 1945: 'Laval and his wife arrived in Paris on August 1st. He was taken at once to Fresnes Prison.'

No. 575

Mr. Caccia (Athens) to Mr. Bevin (Received 1 August, 9.40 p.m.)
No. 1624 Telegraphic [R 13013/4/19]

Important ATHENS, *1 August 1945, 7.46 p.m. G.M.T.*

Repeated to Washington, Moscow [No.] 57, Belgrade [No.] 42, Resmed's Office (Caserta) No. 745.

Your telegram No. 289 Onward.[1]

You will have seen from my telegram No. 1608[2] that in his statement on July 29th General Plastiras suggested the Regency should be set aside. This suggestion has been marked by Communist press and I have reason to think the Regent expects an attack on himself to develop on the grounds that he is principally responsible for having brought the present Government to power and consequently for everything now wrong in Greece.

2. I trust it is unnecessary for me to emphasise that in the period before plebiscite and election it is essential for the stability of this country that the Regent should remain. May I therefore suggest that any message such as proposed in paragraph 4 of your telegram shou[l]d not only be addressed to the Regent but should contain some expression of confidence in the principles which have guided His Beatitude in the exercise of his office.[3]

3. Above also confirms what you say about danger of delay.

4. Foreign Office please pass to Terminal,[4] Moscow and Belgrade.

[1] No. 557.
[2] This telegram of 30 July 1945, not printed, had reported a press statement on the Greek political position by General N. Plastiras, former Greek Prime Minister.
[3] By Foreign Office telegram No. 1638 of 9.25 p.m. on 2 August to Athens the beginning of the message in No. 505 was amended, before its delivery, to read 'On assuming office as Prime Minister I should like to assure Your Beatitude of the continued interest of His Majesty's Government in the welfare of Greece. As your Beatitude is aware, it is the desire of His Majesty's Government to assist . . . ' etc.
[4] Not transmitted to the British Delegation in Berlin owing to lateness of reception.

No. 576

Major-General Hollis to Lieut.-General Sir J. Gammell (Moscow)
No. 4750 Telegraphic [F 4891/1057/23]

Top secret CABINET OFFICE, *1 August 1945, 9.10 p.m. G.M.T.*

Personal for General Gammell from General Hollis.

Reference your telegram MIL 4050.[1]

The Chiefs of Staff have considered your request in the light of your

[1] This telegram is untraced.

minute to General Ismay asking that your duties should be defined in the light of the decisions reached at Terminal.

2. In the event of a declaration of war by the Soviet Union on Japan:–

(i) You should call on General Antonov on behalf of the Chiefs of Staff and convey to him their satisfaction that the Soviet Union is once again the ally of Great Britain in the war against Japan;

(ii) You should say on behalf of the Chiefs of Staff that His Majesty's Government are prepared to furnish to the Soviet General Staff any operational intelligence regarding the enemy in areas under the British Chiefs of Staff should the Soviet General Staff ask for it;

(iii) Should General Antonov ask for technical information regarding our own equipment, it should be referred to the Chiefs of Staff for decision;

(iv) Should he ask for any information regarding our own intentions, distribution or Order of Battle, you should say that this would also have to be referred to London for a decision.

3. You should not volunteer information contained in (iii) and (iv) above, but leave it to the Russians to initiate requests under these headings.

No. 577

Brigadier Blunt[1] *(Sofia) to Mr. Lawson (Received 3 August, 1 p.m.)*[2]
No. M. 1569 Telegraphic [R 13088/23/7]

BRITISH MILITARY MISSION, BULGARIA, *1 August 1945, 10.35 p.m.*

Immediate. Secret

My M.1444[3] July 12th.

In conversation with C.O.S. and Chief Administrative Officer of Allied Control Commission today I informally asked why General Biryusov had called no meeting of Allied Control Commission although three weeks had elapsed since he stated these would be held every ten days.

2. Reply was that General Oxley had asked for a meeting of Allied Control Commission before leaving Sofia. Although full meeting [?had] not been held he had visited General Biryusov with whom he discussed various matters. Accordingly nothing further had up to present appeared necessary.

3. I said I would like to be quite clear as to whether General Biryusov intended calling meetings every two [?ten] days as stated. Reply was that meetings at regular 10 days interval or even more frequently were envisaged and might either be called by General Biryusov or asked for by British and American representative according to whether any of the three had anything he wanted to discuss.

4. The Russians said that it was intended to hold in immediate future a conference of heads of sections and delegates of Allied Control Commission

[1] Acting Commissioner of British Military Mission in Bulgaria.
[2] Time of receipt in Foreign Office.
[3] See No. 136, note 2.

throughout country. To this meeting representatives of America and Great Britain would be invited. Reports from provinces would be read. Then if necessary full meeting of Allied Control Commission would be called to discuss points which had emerged. Russians suggested general conferences of heads of sections might be held monthly.

5. Impression gained was that Russians considered regular meetings of Allied Control Commission unnecessary and proposed only holding them should there be 'something to discuss'.

No. 578

Mr. Morrison to Sir V. Mallet (San Sebastian)
No. 7 Telegraphic [Z 9145/16/28]

Immediate. Secret   FOREIGN OFFICE, 1 August 1945, 10.20 p.m.

Following from Harvey.

Instructions for the British Delegation to the Tangier talks due to open in Paris on the 6th August have not yet been finally approved. It is to be expected, however, that Delegation will be authorised to aim at securing agreement on the following procedure:

(1) An approach to the Spanish Government, preferably by His Majesty's Government and the French Government alone, calling on them to withdraw at a very early date from their present position in the zone.

(2) Establishment of interim regime of purely temporary character.

(3) Fixing of as early a date as possible for the calling of a full-scale conference of all the Tangier Powers, plus United States of America and U.S.S.R. to negotiate a new Tangier Statute.

2. Whether the Spanish Government will be or can be associated in the interim regime will depend upon the attitude of the representatives of the various Powers at Paris. In any event, it would appear almost certain from the attitude adopted by the Soviet Delegation at Potsdam that Soviet Government will demand that present Spanish Government should not (repeat not) be invited to participate either in the interim regime or at the full-scale conference and it is not impossible that the French Government may support them in this.

3. It would help us in deciding upon the attitude to be adopted by His Majesty's Government in the face of such a situation if you could give me your considered opinion of the probable reaction of General Franco if he were to be excluded in this way from the Interim Regime and the negotiation of a new Tangier regime.

4. Do you consider, in view of the serious blow which this would be to his prestige, that it would still be possible to induce him to withdraw the Spanish troops and administration from the Tangier zone without incident,

or do you consider that he would be likely to dig in his toes and refuse to withdraw, thus making necessary a show of force if not an actual minor military operation to eject Spaniards from the zone? Spanish national pride might be expected to react sharply against the humiliation of exclusion and this might serve temporarily to rally the Spaniards round Franco. At the same time it would presumably bring home to the Spanish people the extent to which they have become isolated as a result of the policy followed by Franco during the war. It would, of course, have to be made plain that exclusion of Spain was only temporary during continuance of Franco regime and that in meantime Spanish interests would be regarded as in trust.

5. If, on the other hand, Franco were to resist and refuse to withdraw, the consequences of a recourse to force might be serious, perhaps involving a rupture of relations with Spain with all its attendant complications, apart from the probability that food supplies for Tangier coming from Spain would be cut off. We could not embark on such a course without first weighing very seriously all the issues involved.

6. Peake, who saw Spanish High Commissioner at Tetuan last week, told us that latter took the line that if arrangements for the future of Tangier were made without due participation by Spain he himself would prefer to wash his hands of it and withdraw from his post. This seems to indicate that General Varela at any rate is not disposed to be bellicose.

7. I should be grateful for your urgent observations by telegram.

CALENDARS TO No. 578

i *31 July–1 Aug. 1945 Correspondence concerning forthcoming four-power conversations on Tangier. Undated memo.* on future of Tangier covering draft instructions for British Delegation. *Minutes by Mr. Hoyer Millar and Sir A. Cadogan (Berlin), and letter from Mr. Hoyer Millar (Berlin) to Mr. Garran.* [Z 9119/16/28].

ii *3 Aug. 1945 Sir V. Mallet (San Sebastian) Tel. No. 12.* Considers General Franco unlikely to resist by force if excluded from interim régime for Tangier; but favourable tendencies in Spain could be reversed [Z 9144/16/28].

No. 579

Letter from Sir M. Peterson (Istanbul) to Sir O. Sargent (Received 10 August)
No. 171/143/45G [R 13427/4476/44]

Secret & Personal   ISTANBUL, *1 August 1945*

My dear Moley,

Many thanks for your Secret & Personal letter of 21st July (R 12179/4476/G).[1]

I agree that Archie's letter[2] (of which I have now had the text) served as a

---
[1] See No. 81, note 3.
[2] No. 19, enclosure.

caveat. But matters have gone somewhat further since then and I must admit I am not satisfied, from the news I have so far received from Potsdam, that any one has up till now grasped the nettle firmly and told the Russians that this bullying of Turkey simply will not do.

2. In a despatch[3] which I sent off by yesterday's bag I tried to summarise the position in this country at the moment and show how it is affected at every turn and in every sphere by the Russian menace. This is bad for trade—which is surely a question of the first importance for us—[4] and also bad for the further development of San Francisco. Also it brings in the Anglo-Turk alliance.

3. As regards the second point I feel that something would have been gained—possibly a great deal—if the Russians had been induced to put it on record that their demands were not demands but merely suggestions advanced in the course of conversation. As things stand at present the Russians are getting it both ways. If they chose (to put it at its worst) to attack Turkey they could say that they had put forward demands and they had not been met.[4]

4. As regards the danger spot at the moment what I meant in my letter of July 10th[5] was of course that the eastern frontier seems to me to be the place where any trouble is likely to begin, precisely because it would be much more 'dangerous' for the Russians to advance on the Straits, which would involve other interests notably our own, would entail their making use of Bulgaria or Roumania or both and would be carried out as it were in the full light of day with Istanbul as it is stuffed with foreign press correspondents. On the other hand the eastern districts of Turkey are rigidly a military zone: nobody visits them (although my Press Attaché has managed to bring off a little tour there from which I expect him back very shortly): and any coup the Russians might attempt there would be shrouded in obscurity and might even, for some time at least, be represented as a mere border disturbance.[4]

5. Our interest in the Straits themselves is quite clear enough not to require further definition by me. But as regards the rest of it—what I call the 'bullying' of Turkey—I see no sign that we have so far been anything like sufficiently definite. I suggest we use two arguments—firstly, that the withdrawal of Turkey from the German sphere of influence into which Turkey had fallen back even since the last war has been *our* work and represents a diplomatic feat of some magnitude and importance. Having got hold of Turkey we have not the least intention of letting her go. We might further argue that the present Russian method of treating Turkey is so reminiscent of Hitler's methods in Europe[4] as to be repugnant to us and indeed in our view to run contrary to, and endanger, the new Security Organization.

[3] No. 549.
[4] The preceding passage was queried in the margin by Mr. G. McDermott: cf. note 6 below.
[5] No. 81.

6. A final point. The Turkish Prime Minister and Chief of the General Staff have up till now, with my full encouragement, resisted what is undoubtedly strong pressure, coming particularly from the General Staff other than Orbay himself, to carry out extensive measures of mobilization. I do not know how long we can go on resisting this pressure, if things do not improve. And indeed I must add I do not feel satisfied that I personally will be justified in using such influence as I have against mobilization.[6]

Yours ever
MAURICE PETERSON

CALENDAR TO No. 579

i *30 July 1945 Letter from Turkish Ambassador to Sir O. Sargent* (without enclosure). Refers to No. 95.ii and requests supply of war materials through a credit [R 12929/43/44].

[6] Mr. McDermott minuted on this letter: 'For general comments on our policy towards Turkey please see R 13646/G [of 16 August: not here printed].

'Paragraph 2 within. Sir M. Peterson is mistaken in thinking that trade, in the sense of trade with Turkey, is a question of the first importance for us. On the contrary the Foreign Office are in the position of having constantly to badger the Treasury, Board of Trade, etc. in order to make them take any real interest in this question. Turkey has few products of interest to us and their prices are still preposterously high.

'Paragraph 3. The Russians have done very much what Sir M. Peterson suggests, i.e. they have claimed that their demands were not demands but suggestions put forward in reply to the requests by the Turkish Government.

'Paragraph 4 seems to me, frankly, rather far-fetched.

'Paragraph 5, first part. The Russians would reply that the withdrawal of Turkey from the German sphere of influence was in the first place reluctant, secondly due to the Allied war effort as a whole, and thirdly incomplete at heart. As regards the last sentence, this accusation has been rather freely thrown about since Hitler's disappearance and moreover I think it is rather exaggerated.

'Now see R 13646/G. G. McDermott. 16th August, 1945.'

This minute was countersigned that day by Mr. D. Howard and Sir O. Sargent.

No. 580

Mr. Roberts (Moscow) to Mr. Bevin (Received 11 August)
No. 530 [N 10185/627/38]

MOSCOW, *1 August 1945*

Sir,

Nearly three months have passed since the end of the war in Europe and the Soviet people have now had time to readjust themselves to the new situation. In his despatch No. 468[1] of July 10th Sir A. Clerk-Kerr [*sic*] referred to certain signs of a relaxation in internal tension within the Soviet Union

[1] No. 78.

and I now have the honour to report upon internal developments during the past months of readjustment from war to peace, with however, the Far Eastern War ever present in the background. When a Soviet journalist was recently asked by a member of the Embassy staff 'how things were going' he replied with a wry smile: 'Peace has come, but it has not yet turned into anything tangible'. This point of view is perhaps extreme. But it indicates a feeling that up to the present peace has brought the Russian people even less than they were inclined to expect in the way of tangible advantages at home.

2. From the moment Germany surrendered the Soviet government made it clear that they were determined not to let the Soviet people relax their efforts. Marshal Stalin's May Day Order had already called on the working masses to 'heal the wounds of the war quickly' and to 'increase the power of the Soviet state', and the authorities promptly seized on this injunction and worked it up into a real campaign. Letters appeared in the press from groups of workers in all parts of the Soviet Union, promising Stalin that they would work hard and untiringly to increase the country's military and economic might and to heal the wounds caused by the war. The newspapers repeatedly stressed the enormity of the tasks ahead and insisted that 'self-denial, organisation, and discipline' were as necessary in the work of peaceful reconstruction as in war. As the 1945 budget and budget discussions had already foreshadowed, great emphasis was laid on the urgency and importance of restoring the economy of the liberated areas particularly agriculture, the coal industry of the Donbass, and the metallurgy of the south. 'The rebuilding of our devastated economy', *Pravda* wrote on May 24th, 'is the concern of the whole country. If carried out at a good pace, it will contribute to a further development of all branches of heavy and light industry, to an increase in the output of the means of production, consumers goods, and foodstuffs'. More recently still, workers in one industry after another have been issuing calls to socialist emulation in overfulfilling their plan of output for 1945. This new socialist emulation campaign began early in July with a call to Soviet metal workers from the Stalin metallurgical combines in Magnitogorsk and Kuznetsk, and it has since been developed on an intensive scale by similar calls from workers in the engineering, building, aircraft, tank, machine-tool, oil, electrical, ship-building, armament, and textile industries, in light industry, the food industry, and also in agriculture, where preparations are now in full swing for gathering a victory harvest. On July 11th, in commenting on socialist emulation in the machine building industry *Pravda* wrote: 'We shall enrich our country by new achievements in production and make her illustrious by heroic labour directed towards strengthening the military economic might of our Soviet socialist state'.

3. Besides insisting on a sustained labour effort, the Soviet government have continued to remind their people that the Soviet Union has played the leading part in the European war and is now looked to by the whole of progressive humanity as the most advanced state in the world. This was

illustrated during the Victory Parade in Red Square on June 24th when Marshal Zhukov told the assembled troops that everyone now recognised that it was the Soviet Union which had taken the main and decisive part in Germany's historic defeat and that the Red Army had freed the peoples of Europe and would go down in history as an army of liberation. It was also illustrated during the much-publicised celebrations in honour of the 220th anniversary of the Academy of Sciences when large numbers of foreign scholars were brought to Moscow and Leningrad to pay tribute to the achievements of science and learning under the Soviet system and returned home full of admiration and praise which could be quoted to the Soviet people as evidence of their country's prestige abroad. This continued insistence on the great international authority of the Soviet Union has been accompanied by an equally vigorous campaign re-emphasising that the real organisers and architects of victory were the Communist Party and its leader, who had transformed the Soviet Union into a mighty, invincible socialist state, and who enjoyed the tremendous advantage of being guided by Marxist-Leninist theory which enabled them to understand the laws of social development and anticipate the future trend of events. 'In the glorious day of our victorious triumph', *Pravda* wrote on May 16th, 'the hearts of the Soviet people are filled with deep gratitude to the great party of Bolsheviks, to the leadership of which our country owes its historic victories in the bitter struggle against German imperialism. . . .[2] Our people have conquered because they have been and are being guided by the most progressive and scientific theory, the theory of Marxism-Leninism'. On June 27th and 28th the Praesidium of the Supreme Soviet paid tribute to Marshal Stalin's contribution to victory by awarding him a second 'Order of Victory', the title of 'Hero of the Soviet Union' with the 'Order of Lenin' and the 'Gold Star' medal, and the newly instituted military title of 'Generalissimo of the Soviet Union'. These awards filled leader writers in the press with lyrical ecstasy, and one of them even called the Generalissimo 'the greatest thinker of all time'. Another referred to Marxism-Leninism as 'the science of sciences' and to 'Comrade' Stalin as 'its crowning glory'.

4. This insistence on a sustained labour effort and the glorification of the Soviet Union, of the Communist Party, and of Generalissimo Stalin have been accompanied by tributes to the country's ordinary men and women. At a banquet in the Kremlin on May 24th in honour of the commanders of the Red Army Stalin proposed a special toast to the Soviet people, first of all to the Russian people with their clear mind, steadfast character, and patience, whose faith in the Soviet government had been 'of decisive force in ensuring victory over fascism, the enemy of mankind'. A fortnight later, the Praesidium of the Supreme Soviet instituted a medal 'For Gallant Labour in the Great Patriotic War, 1941–1945' as a decoration for workers on the Soviet home front. On June 27th at the Kremlin banquet which followed the Victory Parade Stalin proposed the health of the ordinary people, the 'little

[2] Punctuation as in original quotation.

cogs' in the great state machine without whom marshals and commanders of fronts and armies 'are not worth a damn'. 'Their name is legion', he said. 'Nobody writes about them and they are of low rank and have no titles. But they are the people who sustain us as the base holds up the summit'.

5. These well-timed and well-turned tributes from the 'father and teacher' in the Kremlin must have given satisfaction and pleasure to ordinary people throughout the Soviet Union. But the Soviet government have not relied on words alone to keep the 'little cogs' turning as busily and smoothly as during the war. They have also introduced a number of concrete measures which show that they are alive to the need for trying to make the hard lives of ordinary men and women a little more tolerable. A great and victorious people is clearly entitled to expect certain practical rewards of victory, but the expectations of this patient and long-suffering people *are very modest* and its leaders are careful to avoid anything which might encourage the Soviet people to think that they could now relax their efforts.

6. Up to the present the most important step in the direction of more normal conditions has been the law demobilising the thirteen older groups on active service in the Red Army, which the Supreme Soviet passed on June 23rd. (See His Majesty's Ambassador's despatch No. 447[3] of July 3rd). This law lays down that all demobilised servicemen are to receive gratuities based on rank and length of service, free travel home with food, an outfit of clothes and shoes, work within a month in urban districts at least as good as before enlistment together with accommodation and fuel, and in rural districts every possible help in getting work and starting a home. In the liberated areas demobilised servicemen with houses to build or repair are also to be allowed to cut timber free of charge and borrow between 5 and 10 thousand roubles for 5 to 10 years from the All-Union Bank for Financing Municipal and House Building. This demobilisation law which probably covers men between 40 and 52 years of age is already being put into effect and the government seem determined to make a success of it. For example, on July 5th, the newspapers printed an announcement saying that the Public Prosecutor's Office would supervise the way in which the military and local authorities were carrying the law out and that any officials guilty of infringing its provisions would immediately be prosecuted. The following day the press published an account of an interview with the head of the All-Union Bank for Financing Municipal and House Building, who described the terms and conditions of the building loans provided for by the new law. He said that the bank would grant these loans under a decision of the executive committees of local soviets and might make them directly through the ex-serviceman's place of work. When ex-servicemen received the loans, they would have to give the necessary guarantees and apply either for a grant of land for a house or for permission to repair an existing house, and the loans would be issued in instalments against a certificate saying that the previous instalment had been used. The interest on the

[3] Not printed.

loans would be 2% a year. The newspapers also published reports from various parts of the country describing the preparations for demobilising troops, providing them with adequate transport, food, and work, and seeing that they received a proper welcome on arriving home. When the first trainloads of ex-servicemen began to reach Moscow and Leningrad the press carried photographs which showed huge and enthusiastic crowds and local officials greeting them with flowers and political speeches. On July 7th *Red Star* reported that demobilised men would receive not only coupons for two hot meals a day on their way home but food rations for ten days if they came from the field army and for five days if they came from military districts. Men from the field army were also being given extra food weighing from ten to twelve kilograms and consisting of flour, sugar, tinned meat, biscuits, and other foodstuffs. On July 20th the same paper had a report of an interview with the vice-chairman of the All-Union Committee on Architectural Affairs, who stated that ex-servicemen would need architectural help as well as materials when building new houses and that the Committee had worked out a number of new model plans for 2 and 3 roomed houses with a separate kitchen which it proposed to issue on a large scale. He also said that ex-servicemen ought to build single storey brick and wooden houses as far as possible and two storey houses where conditions and resources permitted.

7. Another measure which illustrates the tendency to return to more normal conditions was the Amnesty decree issued on July 7th by the Praesidium of the Supreme Soviet of the U.S.S.R. and summarised in Sir A. Clark-Kerr's despatch No. 469[3] of July 10th.

8. Three further peace-time measures have been of more general application. Firstly, at the beginning of July a decision of the Praesidium of the Supreme Soviet restored normal and supplementary holidays abolished during the war to all industrial and white collar workers in the Soviet Union except in certain unspecified branches of industry where the Council of People's Commissars of the U.S.S.R. has been authorised to postpone holidays until the end of 1945 on condition that the workers receive monetary compensation. The day after this decision was announced *Izvestiya* published a report of an interview with the chairman of the All-Union Central Council of Trade Unions, who said that the trade unions were expanding the system of sanatoria and rest-homes for workers and that in 1945 they would accommodate 750,000 people compared with 270,000 in 1944. He also explained that certificates for holidays in these trade union sanatoria and rest-homes would be issued by local and factory trade union committees, in the first instance to war-wounded, young people, expectant mothers, and workers in heavy or dangerous jobs, and that sanatoria and rest-homes still used as hospitals would be adapted for holidays as soon as they were vacated. But the figures which he quoted make it obvious that the vast majority of workers will have to take their holidays at home or with friends, at any rate in 1945. Secondly, it was announced on June 25th that the Council of People's Commissars of the U.S.S.R. had directed all-union industrial

commissariats to arrange for the plants and undertakings under their control to re-establish or introduce special departments producing consumers goods from industrial by-products. To encourage the process the plants concerned are to be allowed to retain the extra profits and distribute 25% of the goods produced through their own trading systems, where they will be available to the workers themselves. In view of the great demand for articles in common use the importance of this measure is obvious, especially as it fits in with a number of press reports which show that the authorities are trying to increase the output of consumers goods in general. But the shortage of these goods is so acute and widespread that it will be some time before the demand even begins to be met, and up to the present the general public has felt no appreciable relief, though prices are continuing to fall in the open markets and commercial shops. Thirdly, the authorities have recently given back the wireless sets which they called in when the Soviet Union was attacked. This return of sets appears to have been carried out efficiently, at any rate in Moscow, and some of the delighted owners are now trying to make up for lost time by turning their sets full on and leaving them near open windows, particularly early in the morning and late at night.

9. The problem of housing which is one of the most acute in the Soviet Union has not yet been the subject of any new general government measure apart from the provisions of the demobilisation law. But reports in the press clearly indicate that the authorities are trying to infuse new life into existing measures. Up to the present the main emphasis has been on the need for increasing the output of building materials, particularly by using local resources, and on improving the facilities for private house building. On May 22nd *Izvestiya* published a long account of an interview with N. S. Krushchev, chairman of the Council of People's Commissars of the Ukrainian S.S.R. and secretary of the Central Committee of the Ukrainian Communist Party, who described the principles which were being followed in carrying out a recent decree of the Ukrainian government on building houses and farm property for Ukrainian collective farmers. Krushchev said that in the past the main drawback had been that collective farmers who wished to build houses had received very little help from the collective farm administration and had found it difficult to draw on qualified workers such as carpenters, roofers, stove-builders etc. But the Ukrainian government had now made the collective farm as a whole responsible for building houses and farm property and had recommended them to set up permanent building brigades which would do the skilled work themselves and use supplementary labour from the collective farm for the unskilled work. Members of building brigades and collective farmers who helped them would have their working days paid for at the same rate as working days spent on normal collective farm work, and the total of working days needed to build a house would become a charge on the owner, who would have to pay it off over a period of years. General meetings of collective farmers would lay down the number of houses to be built during the year and would also decide who was to have them on the basis of priority for the best

collective farm workers, servicemen, and widows and orphans of servicemen. But the individual farmer would choose the type and size of the house which he preferred. Krushchev also said that the saw mills of the People's Commissariat for Timber and of other government departments would saw the timber needed for collective farm building. But executive committees of rayon[4] soviets would have to organise small enterprises for the local production of other building materials for distribution through consumers' co-operatives. In conclusion Krushchev emphasised that the new arrangements would lead to more and better houses and enable collective farm villages to be developed in future according to a properly conceived plan. On May 25th *Pravda* also reported that in 1945 the Agricultural Bank of the U.S.S.R. had allocated 350 million roubles for credits for the rural population compared with 265 million roubles in 1944. These credits were intended to take the form of long-term loans for building private houses and buying cattle and would be extended not only to collective farmers but to specialists, office workers, and other workers, who lived in rural districts. The government also seem to be trying hard to develop private house building in urban districts. For example, on May 17th the newspapers announced that 325 million roubles had been allocated to provide building loans to manual workers and office workers and that enterprises and institutions were helping their employees to get the necessary building materials and technical advice. The press has recently taken local and factory trade union committees severely to task for not giving private house building as much attention and encouragement as the government consider desirable; and has been calling for an increase in the local production of building materials and for an extension of the practice under which factories set up special building brigades to assist individual builders. Priority however is still given to industrial construction, and private house building in particular still suffers from too acute a shortage of skilled labour and materials and from other drawbacks to develop on anything like an extensive scale.

10. In general, in spite of the measures so far adopted ordinary Soviet citizens may well be pardoned for thinking that peace has not yet brought them very much in the way of tangible advantages. What they probably feel the greatest need of is more consumers goods, better living accommodation, and easier working conditions. Consumers goods and better living accommodation would inevitably be slow in coming even if the government had given them first priority. Easier working conditions could be more quickly achieved if the government really wanted them, and when the Supreme Soviet met in June rumours began to circulate that it would restore the 7 hour working day and possibly the 6 day week and lower the age of compulsory national service for women from 45 to at least 36. But all these rumours proved to be ill-founded, and the only measure which the Supreme Soviet passed was the law demobilising the thirteen older age groups. It is

[4] A district of Soviet administration.

now becoming clear from the press that certain Soviet factories have already begun to relieve some of the strain on their workers by stopping or reducing overtime, and the practice is bound to extend as the return of demobilised soldiers produces a new supply of labour which has to be absorbed. In any case, the Soviet people are notoriously patient, long-suffering, inured to hardships and privation, and as long as the government can hold out prospects of gradual improvement they should have little real difficulty in achieving the sustained labour effort at which they are obviously aiming in order to restore and expand the basic industries and to increase still further the economic and military might of the Soviet Union. Its citizens will have to wait some years yet before they can enjoy the fruits of their labours and of their Government's long-term planning. But they are buoyed-up by pride in their recent victory, by confidence in the wisdom of their leaders, by the conviction that one day things will be better, if not for them, then at least for their children, by the knowledge that they will be spared the scourge of unemployment, which threatens the western world and, last but not least, by the ignorance in which they are kept by their Government of the wider life and better material conditions enjoyed outside the Soviet Union.

I have, &c.,

FRANK K. ROBERTS

CALENDAR TO NO. 580

i   *1 Aug. 1945   Letter from Mr. Roberts (Moscow) to Mr. Warner.* Comments on report by Mr. G. F. Kennan, U.S. Chargé d'Affaires in Moscow, on a visit to Siberia and on conditions in U.S.S.R.: implications for Soviet-American relations. Discusses advisability of economic assistance to U.S.S.R. and Eastern bloc. *Minutes by Mr. Brimelow and Mr. Warner.* Advice against use of economic weapons for political advantage. Little prospect of British economic assistance to U.S.S.R. [N 10346/928/38].

No. 581

Mr. Randall (Copenhagen) to Mr. Bevin (Received 14 August)

No. 81 [UE 3616/535/53]

COPENHAGEN, *1 August 1945*

His Majesty's Minister at Copenhagen presents his compliments to His Majesty's Principal Secretary of State for Foreign Affairs and has the honour to transmit to him the under-mentioned documents.

1229

Description of Enclosure

<table>
<tr><td align="center">*Name and Date*</td><td align="center">*Subject*</td></tr>
<tr><td>Note No. 63 of 24th July, 1945
To Monsieur Christmas Møller,
Royal Danish Ministry for Foreign
  Affairs.</td><td>Supplies for neutral European
countries.</td></tr>
<tr><td>Note No. 87.x.35 of 27th July, 1945
From Monsieur Svenningsen,
Royal Danish Ministry for Foreign
  Affairs.</td><td>Acknowledgement of above.</td></tr>
</table>

ENCLOSURE I IN No. 581

Mr. Randall to M. Møller (Copenhagen)

No. 63

BRITISH LEGATION, COPENHAGEN, *24 July 1945*

Monsieur le Ministre,

I have the honour to inform Your Excellency that His Majesty's Government and the United States Government have been influenced in their attitude with regard to supplies for Neutral European countries during 1945 by the desirability of ensuring that the economic activities of these countries, both during the period of continued hostilities in Europe and in the post-hostilities period, did not conflict with the interests of the Allies.

2. The principal objectives to be aimed at have been:

(*a*) to secure the maximum assistance from the neutral countries at reasonable prices of goods and services required both for immediate wartime needs during the continuance of the war against Japan and for the general rehabilitation of Europe;

(*b*) to ensure that neutral purchases of short supply materials from sources outside the control of the Allies are adjusted to the purchasing arrangements of the Allied supply authorities. This involves agreement with the neutrals not only to restrict their purchases to quantities representing their fair share in relation with the needs of the Allies, but also where required to co-ordinate their actual purchasing operations with those of the Allied supply authorities so as to prevent price competition.

In return for agreements along these lines and in order to maintain in the neutral countries a level of economic capacity sufficient to enable them to play their part in producing the required goods for export, it is necessary to make certain limited allocations to the neutrals of goods from sources under Allied control.

3. During the period of continued hostilities in Europe, it was also necessary to secure certain economic warfare objectives and it seemed desirable to maintain in force the existing agreements made between the British and American Governments and the neutral Governments concerned. These called for certain modifications in the light of changing conditions but in general they involved the maintenance of blockade controls and the limitations on neutral imports from all sources, of a wide range of commodities. It was the policy to include in such agreements provisions for assistance by the neutrals in securing supplies required

by the Allies and provision for co-ordinating neutral purchases of certain commodities with arrangements made for Allied purchase of these commodities.

4. Now that hostilities in Europe have terminated, it will be our object to extend these agreements in a modified form. While many wartime controls will necessarily become inapplicable, it will still remain essential to preserve in respect of certain materials in short supply, an orderly system of allocation and of acquisition. It will therefore be our aim to reach agreements with the European neutrals which, while removing many of the limitations on their trade which have been necessitated by wartime conditions, will secure the objectives outlined in paragraph 2 above.

5. His Majesty's Government and the United States Government wish to bring the above general conclusion which they have reached in this matter to Your Excellency's attention. They will supply you with full particulars of any communications with the neutrals which may in any way affect Danish interests.

I avail myself, Monsieur le Ministre, of this opportunity to renew to you the assurance of my highest consideration.

Enclosure 2 in No. 581

M. Svenningsen to Mr. Randall (Copenhagen)
Journal Nr. 87.x.35

UDENRIGSMINSTERIET, COPENHAGEN, *27 July 1945*

Sir,

I have the honour to acknowledge with thanks the receipt of your note of the 24th inst.[1] concerning the attitude of His Britannic Majesty's Government and of the Government of the United States of America with regard to supplies for neutral European countries, the contents of which I have noted with great interest.

I avail myself of this opportunity to renew to you, sir, the assurance of my highest consideration.

For the Minister,

NILS SVENNINGSEN

Calendars to No. 581

i *27 July 1945 Mr. Duff Cooper (Paris) Tel. No. 38 Grub Saving to Ministry of Food. Letter from Ministry of Fuel and Power to Foreign Office.* Position of France in relation to machinery of Combined Food Board and of Anglo-American Allocation Board for petroleum products [Z 9124/103/17; W 10388/12/76].

ii *1 Aug. 1945 Draft minutes: E.E.C.(45)7th Meeting of E.E.C.E.* Allocation and purchasing of foodstuffs in short supply, etc. [UR 2824/1600/53].

---

[1] Enclosure 1 above.

No. 582

Mr. Balfour (Washington) to Mr. Bevin (Received 2 August, 5.15 p.m.)[1]
No. 572 Remac Telegraphic [*UE 3366/32/71*]

Immediate　　　　　　　　　　　WASHINGTON, *2 August 1945, 4 a.m.*

Harmer from Lee.[2]

Please refer to my telegram No. 571[i] concerning Ministry of Food demand for flour from United States of America, discussion with Food Mission has convinced me that supply case for this demand should be re-examined critically and I suggest full scrutiny by Exchange Requirements Committee. We appear to have been urging need for flour for months even though United Kingdom stocks have remained at above 500,000 tons (six weeks consumption taking into account stocks in bakeries etc.). In addition to very high wheat stocks of nearly 1–1/2 [*sic*] million tons. Flour stocks are now falling, but effect of our having consistently put forward what they regard as unconvincing case from supply standpoint is still likely to affect United States and Canadian attitude. *Prima facie* there seems everything to be said for pressing Ministry of Food to make necessary quantities of wheat available from our present Canadian programme and so avoiding any additional financial burden on Canada. I am convinced that we shall get nowhere with F[oreign] E[conomic] A[dministration] except for possible small increase in allocation for armed forces.

CALENDAR TO No. 582

i　*2 Aug. 1945　Mr. Balfour (Washington) Tel. No. 571 Remac.* British proposal for Canadian provision on Mutual Aid of additional wheat for milling in U.S. Questions of terms of supply and of substantial British stocks [UE 3363/32/71].

[1] Received via Air Ministry.
[2] Mr. F. E. Harmer was an Assistant Secretary in the Treasury. Mr. F. G. Lee was deputy to Mr. R. H. Brand as Treasury Representative for Finance and Supply in Washington.

No. 583

Record by Mr. Mason of a conversation with Mr. Earl Harrison
[*WR 2307/1/48*]

FOREIGN OFFICE, *2 August 1945*

Problem of Non-Repatriable Refugees

Mr. Earl Harrison, United States Representative on the Intergovernmental Committee on Refugees, came to see me this afternoon when we had an hour's conversation on general questions dealing with the problem of non-repatriable refugees and the respective relief functions of UNRRA and the Intergovernmental Committee.

2. Mr. Harrison said that, since he was last in this country in April, Congress had been persuaded to vote an appropriation of $4\frac{1}{2}$ million dollars for the calendar year 1945 towards the operational expenditure of the Intergovernmental Committee. This sum was designed to be equal to the sum of £1,000,000 approved in principle by the United Kingdom with a small margin over in case either the United Kingdom increased its own contribution or operational expenditure was found to be higher than it had been anticipated.

3. I then gave Mr. Harrison a very frank, off-the-record survey of the discussions which had taken place here during the last three or four months in regard to the problem of non-repatriable refugees and the respective relief functions of UNRRA and the Intergovernmental Committee. I said that the Cabinet had now reached decisions on this point which were, in the first place, to be communicated to the United States Government with the aim of reaching an agreed policy. A note setting forth the Cabinet's views had been approved and was about to be sent to the Embassy and I read it textually for Mr. Harrison's personal and confidential information since the questions at issue will have to be decided by him on his return to Washington. The note (and its annex) is of course that approved on WR 2232/G.[1]

4. Mr. Harrison listened carefully and at the end expressed his warm approval of the general line of policy set forth therein, with special reference to the principles set forth in the annex (which is the same document as the annex to CP(45)82 endorsed in Cabinet Conclusions 16(45) paragraph 2 of 20th July—WR 2232/G).[1]

5. Mr. Harrison asked for my views as to how such a policy would work out in relation to three separate points. First, he had just come back from Germany where he had been much impressed (he is a shrewd and level-headed observer) with the good case that many victims of persecution could make out for not wishing to be repatriated. How would that square with the policy of regarding all refugees and displaced persons, for the present, as repatriable? He mentioned particularly Poles and Polish Jews. I said that, as I saw it, there was no question[2] of our requiring persons who did not want to go home, to be repatriated at present, or indeed to take a decision for or against at present (those who volunteered or pressed to go home should, of course, be enabled to do so as soon as possible). Their situation would remain, as at present, with the important consideration that, as they were to be regarded for the moment as ultimately repatriable, they would qualify to benefit from UNRRA's relief and rehabilitation services.

6. Second, Mr. Harrison asked whether there was anything in the present

---

[1] See Nos. 302 and 302.i.
[2] Sir G. Rendel here noted: '(Except Russians under the Yalta Agreement. G. W. R.)'

policy which would prevent the Intergovernmental Committee having representatives in Germany pending ultimate decisions as to non-repatriability. I said, No. I added, again off-the-record, that the Intergovernmental Committee had approached the European Advisory Commission with a view to being allowed to send observers to Germany to assess the scale of the problem with which the Intergovernmental Committee might ultimately have to deal, and that His Majesty's Government, for their part, had felt able to endorse this.

7. Third, Mr. Harrison asked about the situation which might arise, for example in France, where there were categories of displaced persons who fell within UNRRA's mandate but where UNRRA was not allowed to operate. I said that this was covered by the formula in the annex to our note. If the Intergovernmental Committee were asked to undertake the relief of such persons, it would clearly be for consideration whether UNRRA and the Government of the country where the refugees had found asylum ought not to be pressed to arrange for UNRRA to take over these refugees. If, for one reason or another, this proved impossible, then the way would be clear for consideration of such persons coming under the Intergovernmental Committee's relief work, though it must be remembered that it did not automatically follow that persons whom UNRRA were unable to relieve should be considered the responsibility of the Intergovernmental Committee.

8. I said that the essential thing was to emphasise that UNRRA was *the* great relief agency and to ensure, not only that it was accepted as such, but that, where its relief services did not at present operate, and there was relief to be done, its activities should be extended to the fullest practicable degree. I said that it was likely that, during the forthcoming UNRRA Council Session, the United Kingdom delegates would say something with a view to impressing upon UNRRA the need for taking a wide and not a narrow view of its functions in this matter.

9. Mr. Harrison once again said that he felt sure that his Government would be in full general accord with the policy which I had described to him. We agreed that it was not possible to form any useful estimate of when final decisions on non-repatriability were likely to be reached.

10. Finally, as regards the question of reconstituting the Intergovernmental Committee, particularly its financial structure, Mr. Harrison said that his Government most fully shared our views. He agreed with me in thinking that the sooner such re-organisation could be attempted the better, so that the Committee would be well prepared in advance for such responsibilities in relation to non-repatriable persons as might ultimately fall upon it, and he endorsed my tentative suggestion that the matter was one which might well be considered at the meeting of the Plenary Committee of the Intergovernmental Committee next November, notice of the two Governments' intentions in this matter being given to the Executive Committee suitably far in advance.

P. Mason

i 28 July 1945 f.   Activities of U.N.R.R.A. in Europe and Middle East. (a) Second Report of Drafting Committee to U.N.R.R.A. Committee on Supplies (Washington) on efficient use of shipping; (b) Draft minutes of nineteenth meeting of U.N.R.R.A. Committee of Council for Europe (London), especially regarding Poland, displaced persons, allocation of relief supplies; (c) Report CCE (45) 99 of Committee of Council for Europe on operations there in July 1945 [UR 3016/206/850; UR 3150, 3171/160/850].

ii 2 Aug. 1945   U.N.R.R.A. activities in Far East. Records of (a) Interdepartmental meeting—U.C.(45)7—on 31 July on British line at meeting of U.N.R.R.A. Committee on Far East; (b) Conversation between Sir P. Butler, U.K. representative on above committee, and U.S. representative, with annexed documents [UR 2880, 2754/12/850].

No. 584

Sir N. Bland[1] (London) to Mr. Bevin (Received 2 August, 7.10 p.m.)
No. 36 Saving Telegraphic [UE 3364/86/77]

LONDON, *2 August 1945*

Netherland Minister for Foreign Affairs in conversation this morning referred to growing exasperation, particularly in the frontier provinces of Holland, at the delay in restoring to rightful owners property looted by the Germans. Blame for this was attributed by the sufferers to our military authorities and our popularity was declining in consequence.

CALENDAR TO No. 584

i 2 Aug. 1945   Sir N. Charles (Rome) to F.O. Western Dept. Transmits copy of letter to Signor Prunas seeking Italian assistance for Swiss enquiry into works of art entering Switzerland since 1939 [UE 3560/123/77].

[1] H.M. Ambassador accredited to the Netherland Government in London.

No. 585

Mr. Shone (Beirut) to Mr. Bevin (Received 2 August, 11.55 a.m.)
No. 741 Telegraphic [E 5656/420/89]

BEIRUT, *2 August 1945, 9.50 a.m. G.M.T.*

Repeated Saving to Washington, Paris, M.E. Min[ister]'s Office.

My telegram No. 694.[1]

United States Minister showed member of my staff in confidence telegram

[1] Not printed.

from the State Department to Paris instructing United States Minister there to inform M. Bidault (in reply apparently to some complaint of the latter)[2] that although the Americans had been unable to provide officers for Mira, this did not in any way mean that they shared M. Bidault's apprehensions as to the British motives, nor did they see how, had they been able to supply these officers such action could be considered as 'helping the British to kick the French out of the Levant'.

(This phrase had apparently been used by M. Bidault in the telegram under reference).[2]

Foreign Office please repeat to Washington and Paris as my telegrams saving 24 and 56 respectively.

CALENDAR TO NO. 585

i *2 Aug. 1945 Mr. Shone (Beirut) Tel. No. 744.* Information from U.S. Minister about Syrian intention to request despatch of American military mission [E 5655/420/89].

[2] See *F.R.U.S. Berlin*, vol. ii, p. 1399.

No. 586

Mr. Duff Cooper (Paris) to Mr. Bevin (Received 3 August, 4.27 p.m.)
No. 391 Saving Telegraphic [Z 9107/14/17]

PARIS, *2 August 1945*

Repeated to Consular Posts in France, No. 37 Saving Circular.

My telegram No. 370 Saving.[1]

On July 28th, 29th and 30th the Consultative Assembly discussed the Government proposals for a referendum and a draft law governing the powers of the Constituent Assembly. General de Gaulle was present throughout the debate and more than 260 of the 295 delegates attended on the final day. After hearing 29 orators and a speech from General de Gaulle the Assembly voted against the Government proposals which it refused even to examine and voted unanimously in favour of the necessity for Ministers to be responsible before the elected representatives of the people. (It will be recalled that in the Government's plan during the life of the Constituent Assembly Ministers are responsible only to the head of the Government.) A large majority agreed that the Constituent Assembly must ensure greater ministerial stability than hitherto in France, and a final vote produced another large majority in favour of a 'sovereign Constituent Assembly in which overseas possessions would be justly represented'.

[1] Not printed. This telegram of 18 July 1945 (received 19 July) had reported the terms proposed by the French Government for a referendum to be held in October concerning the constitution of a Constituent Assembly: cf. below.

2. The outcome of this long and confused debate is that the Government, which in this instance more than ever before means General de Gaulle, finds itself in opposition to the Assembly, and under normal conditions it would be forced to resign. The main point on which there is unanimous agreement among the parties, and which General de Gaulle refuses to admit, is the responsibility of the Government to the elected Constituent Assembly. This is the key to the whole problem. On the second major point, the referendum, there is a division of opinion.

3. The sequence of events has been as follows. First, the Government submitted its proposals to the Assembly. Before, however, the Assembly could discuss them, General de Gaulle made known in a speech at Brest, reported in my telegram No. 380 Saving,[2] his own personal predilection for a Constituent Assembly with limited powers. Then the Assembly Commission for the Reform of the State considered the Government's proposals and rejected them unconditionally and without even attempting to amend them. The Commission pronounced itself in favour of a sovereign Constituent and Legislative Assembly with full powers and, moreover, acknowledged on the instigation of M. Pierre Cot[3] that no existing organisation, be it Provisional Government or Consultative Assembly, had the right to regulate the attributions of an elected Assembly. The Commission, therefore, rejected by a majority not only the Government's proposals but also any form of referendum which might be substituted in a spirit of compromise for those questions proposed by the Government. The referendum was attacked on the grounds that it calls upon the people to vote for or against an opinion known to be held by the head of the Government; therefore it amounts to a plebiscite or vote of confidence in the Head of the State.

4. Full opportunity was given for the expression of all shades of opinion before the Consultative Assembly. It soon became evident that there was little support except from the extreme Right for the election of a Chamber and a Senate which might revise the Constitution sitting together in a National Assembly. Several elderly Senators spoke at length in favour of this scheme, and they were listened to with patient good humour and sympathetically applauded by their colleagues as men who had served their country long and well and whose political career was now over. The debate then revolved round the two major questions mentioned above. Firstly, the responsibility of the Government to the elected Assembly and secondly, the referendum.

5. Over the first question the Assembly was unanimous and de Gaulle adamant. The General in his speech repeated his fears concerning an all-powerful Assembly and his belief that it would abuse its unlimited power to overturn the Government too frequently. But he went further. He said that if he found himself divided from his followers on such a fundamental question he could no longer continue at the head of the Government. This was a

[2] Not printed.
[3] A Radical Socialist member of the Consultative Assembly.

weapon which he was bound to bring out sooner or later. General de Gaulle knows too well that no political party would relish taking the responsibility of precipitating the resignation of the only man in France capable of leading the country at the moment. On the other hand the parties may suspect that General de Gaulle would never in fact resign, and that his threat is partly a bluff which they may find the courage to call. Thus the General stood firm on the question of limiting the powers of the Assembly.

6. In an attempt to compromise the Socialists produced at the end of the debate a counter-proposal presented by Vincent Auriol,[4] by which the questions in the referendum were re-drafted in a clearer form. The Socialist proposal, which seems a reasonable compromise, provided, moreover, that the Constituent Assembly could only bring about the downfall of the Government by a vote of censure, which must have an agreed majority. This would ensure the greater stability of a Ministry and was an attempt to meet the Government halfway. General de Gaulle welcomed it and said the Government would certainly consider it. But the Commission had already rejected the limitation of the Constituent Assembly's powers, and the point was one on which neither the Right nor the Communists were prepared to compromise. Moreover, General de Gaulle's acceptance of the Socialists' proposal as a basis of discussion actually increased the Assembly's opposition to it, in view of his obstinate determination to limit the powers of the Constituent Assembly. The Communists were determined not to let the Socialists swing the House over to the Government's side when there was so manifestly an anti-Government majority. By appealing to 'all good Republicans' to rally in defence of their liberties the Communists, ably led by Jacques Duclos, succeeded in mobilising the support of the Radicals and the Right against the Socialists' proposal, which was turned down by 107 votes to 98. This narrow majority suggests that it would not be difficult to reach a compromise along the lines proposed by the Socialists and that this may be the final solution.

7. Several attempts were made to redraft the proposal for a referendum so that it might be less open to the charge of being a plebiscite for the Head of the Government. But the Commission had already rejected any referendum and the Assembly confirmed this decision.

8. The Government must now decide whether to revise their proposals in the light of the debate or to keep to their original plan. General de Gaulle is reported to have seen the Socialist leaders after the debate, and it seems probable that he is prepared to revise the Government plan by including in it some of the points contained in the Socialists' counter project.

9. General de Gaulle was respectfully but consistently opposed throughout the debate, but none of his numerous interventions suggested that he was prepared to concede any of the demands of the Assembly. Thus the referendum as it now stands becomes more than ever a plebiscite as the Assembly had feared. General de Gaulle himself admitted during the

---

[4] President of the Commission on Foreign Affairs in the Consultative Assembly.

debate that whatever the limitations placed upon the Assembly it could always in fact get rid of a Government if it wanted. In view of this admission it is difficult to see why the General refuses to allow it full powers, and one is almost forced to agree with the opinion so widely held that he is determined to maintain his personal position and to make it unassailable.

10. The situation is a deadlock between General de Gaulle and the Assembly. As the latter is due to terminate its session in next few days, there is unlikely to be any further debate on the Constitution in the meantime. If he submits his proposals in their present form independently to the country in the elections in October it will be a great strain on his personal prestige, and will oblige the Left parties at any rate to campaign against him.

11. This is the most important debate the Consultative Assembly has ever held. The Assembly rose to the occasion and one delegate told a member of my staff that for the first time he really felt himself to be a member of a parliament interpreting the views of the people. The delegates seemed sincerely determined to protect their liberties against what they believed to be the encroachment of authoritarianism.

Full text of debate by bag.[5]

---

[5] Mr. Hoyer Millar minuted that this telegram 'goes to show what a dictator de Gaulle really is & how much disregard he has for popular opinion. He is surely quite unfitted to fill any post in a properly responsible Govt. F. R. Hoyer Millar 8.8.' Mr. Harvey minuted below: 'I think so. Anyway the Govt. has now decided the issue by revising the terms of the referendum. O. C. H. 8/viii.'

CHAPTER VI

The conclusion of the Conference at Potsdam
2 August 1945

No. 587

Mr. Bevin (Berlin) to Mr. Morrison (Received 2 August, 12.40 a.m.)
No. 332 Target Telegraphic [U 5882/29/73]

Secret. Immediate   BERLIN, *2 August 1945, 2.40 a.m.*

For Private Office from Rowan.
Following from Prime Minister to Lord Chancellor.
Begins:
Trial of Major War Criminals.
Your Onward No. 317.[1] I have spoken to the President today[2] about this and I am sure that we have his entire goodwill. He agreed that it was most important that these trials should be conducted on a quadrupartite [*sic*] basis and should be started soon. I am sure that he will speak to his people in this sense. I hope that speedy results will thus follow.[3] (Ends).

---

[1] Annex to No. 506.
[2] This telegram was drafted on 1 August 1945.
[3] This telegram was minuted in the Foreign Office by Mr. Beaumont and Mr. Scott Fox: 'This may cramp Justice Jackson's style a bit which may make things easier. R. A. Beaumont 2/viii.' 'Speedy results did follow. D. S. F. 3/8.'

No. 588

Minute from Mr. Scott Fox to Mr. Bevin
[U 6172/29/73]

FOREIGN OFFICE, *2 August 1945*

The discussions between the British, United States, Soviet and French representatives for the establishment of an International (Four Power) Military Tribunal for the trial of the principal German war criminals and Nazi organisations were satisfactorily concluded this morning. A copy of the

Agreement in final form is attached.[1] I have not yet received a copy of the Charter in final form but apart from some amendment of Article 6 it will be practically identical to the copy attached.[1]

It is hoped that the Agreement will now be signed on Monday, August 6th, and an urgent decision is required as to who should sign on behalf of H.M.G. If the Secretary of State would prefer that the Lord Chancellor, who conducted the negotiations in their closing stages, should sign, I have reason to believe that Lord Jowitt would be very ready to do so. If the Secretary of State signs himself I will inform Judge Jackson, the American representative, so that he can, in accordance with his own suggestion, ask Mr. Winant to sign for the United States Government. In the cases of Russia and France their representatives at the discussions, General Nikitchentko and Monsieur Falco have full powers to sign, but if the Secretary of State and Mr. Winant sign, the French and Soviet Ambassadors should sign for their Governments.[2]

R. D. J. SCOTT FOX

CALENDARS TO NO. 588

i   *26 July–2 Aug. 1945   Berlin Tel. No. 247 Target; Foreign Office minutes; letter from Mr. Troutbeck to Sir L. Collier (Oslo).* Question of release of captured German documents to Allied authorities in connection with the prosecution of war criminals [F.O. 800/417/66; C 3910, 4365, 4378, 4638/20/18].

[1] Not attached to filed copy: cf. annex to No. 442, and No. 442.i. The Agreement for the prosecution and punishment of the major war criminals of the European Axis, signed in London on 8 August 1945 on behalf of the governments of the United Kingdom, the United States, France and the Soviet Union, and the Charter of the International Military Tribunal are printed in Cmd. 6668 of 1945.

[2] This paper was minuted in the Foreign Office as follows by Mr. F. F. Garner of War Crimes Section, Mr. Pierson Dixon, Mr. Scott Fox and Sir B. Newton: 'Foreign Secretary has agreed with Mr. Winant that he, the Foreign Secretary, will sign on behalf of H.M.G. & Mr. Winant on behalf of the U.S. Govt. In addition, the Agreement will be signed by the Judges, & there will thus be a dual signature—political & judicial—in the case of each nation. The S. of S. wishes signatures to be completed by next week. F. F. G. 3/8.'

'We shd. now find out whether the Russians & the French agree. P. D. 3/8.'

'On reflection Mr. Winant decided that he would prefer not to sign the Agreement. He was afraid that if he did so it might involve getting Congressional approval and that further delay might be caused by the reference back to Moscow necessary in order to get the requisite authority for the Soviet Ambassador.

'When the matter came up at a meeting on Saturday, the representatives of the three other Delegations were evidently in favour of signature by the Lord Chancellor, Judge Jackson, General Nikitchentko and Monsieur Falco only.

'I explained matters to the Secretary of State who agreed that in view of Mr. Winant's objections it would be preferable if he did not sign.

'The Lord Chancellor has been informed that his will be the only signature on behalf of H.M.G. I am arranging to get him the necessary Full Powers.

'Signature is to take place tomorrow at Church House at 11 a.m. It is intended to give the Agreement to the Press on Thursday morning. D. Scott Fox 7th August, 1945.'

'I had some fear, as I mentioned to Mr. Dixon, that signature by the Ambassadors would involve delay. B. N. 8/8.'

No. 589

Mr. Bevin (Berlin) to Mr. Morrison (Received 3 August, 4 p.m.)
No. 337 Target Telegraphic [U 5921/5202/70]

BERLIN, *2 August 1945, 10.25 a.m.*[1]

Following from Cadogan for Jebb:–
M. Gromyko tells me his Government agree to British Secretary.[2]
Also that chairmanship of Executive Committe should rotate among the Big Five, that Chairman of Preparatory Commission should be chosen from Middle Power and Vice-Chairman from Small Powers.[3]

[1] Time of origin.
[2] Of the Executive Committee to the Preparatory Commission of the United Nations.
[3] Mr. Jebb minuted on this telegram on 3 August 1945: 'Excellent.'

No. 590

Mr. Hankey (Warsaw) to Mr. Bevin (Received 2 August, 1.30 p.m.)
No. 78 Telegraphic [N 9668/9668/55]

WARSAW, *2 August 1945, 11.23 a.m. G.M.T.*

I called July 31st on M. Jedrychowski, Minister of Overseas Trade and Shipping, and asked him what his ideas were about resumption of commercial relations with Great Britain.

2. He said that Provisional Polish Government were most anxious to renew commercial relations with Great Britain and America. They did not want their trade to be restricted in any one direction. Principal difficulty was that Poland could not at present export anything useful to Great Britain. There would be no meat fats, cereals or timber available for export for about two years. Only coal was available in any quantity. Poland however needed much from the United Kingdom, especially machinery of all sorts. It seemed to him therefore that Poland would have to buy on credit for two years.

3. I thought it well to explain our economic situation in very general terms and to disabuse him of any idea that immediate extensive credits

were likely to be easily forthcoming. He said Poland's overseas trade position in two years would be strong and credits were a safe investment.

4. I asked him how exchange rate difficulty was got over in his agreements with Sweden and any other non-rouble countries. He said he favoured compensation agreement covering specified lists of commodities. Sweden paid kroner for coal and these were used to pay for ball bearings and other Swedish products. Trade need not be solely between Governments and within specified quotas for governmental and other institutions in Poland could deal with private British firms if desired (much general information about governmental control of trade and industry here is on its way I hope by safe hands). He promised to give me information on current negotiations with Swedes, Danes, Russians and Roumanians but was cagey about giving the texts.

5. Poles are working hard to open Danzig and part of the port will be open on August 5th. Swedish vessels are already unloading but into lighters. Meanwhile reliable informant who was there on July 29th says that Russians are dismantling two-thirds of the port and he saw them himself taking away crane newly installed by the Poles.

6. I see no reason why some British business men (e.g. Leggett of Prudential) should not come and look round though most of their former assets seem to be under Government control and I am informed that insurance business in particular is all under control of a state insurance office. General attitude of present Polish Government is that they are willing and anxious to exchange goods with West but will never again allow foreign capitalism to control their industries.

7. Please show to our future Commercial Secretary.

No. 591

Mr. Bevin to Mr. Balfour (Washington)
No. 8039 Telegraphic [N 9388/123/55]

Important   FOREIGN OFFICE, 2 *August 1945*, 6.55 *p.m.*

Repeated to Warsaw No. 123, Moscow No. 4287, Office of the Political Adviser to the Commander-in-Chief Germany No. 104 Saving, Paris No. 1822 Saving, Resmed's Office Caserta No. 2353, M.E. Min's Office No. 1343.

The transfer of Allied recognition to the new Polish Provisional Government makes it essential that we should decide at once, if possible in agreement with the United States Government, what arrangements are to be made for the present maintenance and future repatriation of Polish displaced persons in Germany. The need is all the more urgent in view of the Polish Provisional Government's suggestion made at Terminal[1] that

---

[1] See Nos. 267 and 267.i.

they should send a mission to discuss with the Allied Control Commission the repatriation of these Poles, and of the fact that the Polish Provisional Government are likely to do their utmost for manpower reasons to get these Poles back to Poland quickly. The subject has just been exhaustively discussed at an interdepartmental meeting here which was addressed by Colonel Ross, who is advising 21st Army Group on Polish affairs.

2. We have so far been at pains to ensure that no Poles, whether displaced persons or members of the Polish Armed Forces or refugees in British territory, should be asked straight away to make a final decision whether or not to return to Poland since it is to be hoped that by waiting the number of those opting to return will tend to increase. We understand, however, that general instructions were issued by SHAEF for the registration of Poles for repatriation, although no repatriation of Poles in Germany has in fact taken place except from the United States zone. We understand that in the United States zone Poles have been asked to decide there and then whether they wish to return to Poland or not. Although as a result between 10 and 15 thousand Poles have been repatriated, sometimes in Russian repatriation convoys in which there were places to fill, it appears that some of the repatriated have already made their way back from Poland.

3. We have of course no wish to obstruct the speedy repatriation of any Poles who have already decided that they wish to return to Poland and since we desire as many as possible eventually to do so, we are ready to give Polish Provisional Government all proper opportunities for appealing to Polish displaced persons to return home and for making their case known to them. But we are advised that there would be grave risk of complete breakdown of discipline if representatives of Polish Government were immediately to replace present Polish Liaison Officers, and freely to organise measures for persuading Poles to return and give their final decision at once. We consider that we have a certain obligation to ensure so far as possible, in the interest both of individual Poles themselves and of Polish Government, that former are not forced to make an immediate final decision in absence of proper means of forming a judgement. M. Mikolajczyk and his friends here lay emphasis on this point. Polish Prisoners of War and displaced persons have been cut off in Germany from all knowledge of outside world for long time and many of them have natural bias against new government. Besides, the fact that in the matter of repatriation Eastwards the Russian Displaced Persons have at present an absolute priority makes it impossible to organise any large scale repatriation of Poles in the immediate future. Also, Poles will be the more encouraged to volunteer for repatriation if the arrangements made for repatriation are orderly and humane and especially if some assurance can be secured from the Polish Provisional Government as to the conditions in Poland to which they will be returning. The fact that a number of those repatriated have already returned to Germany from Poland will already tend to increase the doubts of those in Germany who have not yet decided to return.

4. On all above grounds it seems to His Majesty's Government very

important that orderly and fair arrangements should be agreed with Warsaw authorities for enabling these Poles to make their decision at their leisure, without undue pressure, and with knowledge of relevant factors and for ensuring that the repatriation of those who choose to go is carried out in good conditions. Authority of our military commanders over what is done in their occupation zones and probable anxiety of Polish Provisional Government to secure early return of maximum number of their nationals ought together to make it possible for such arrangements to be made. In this connexion it seems important from political standpoint, both for future Poland and for His Majesty's Government and United States Government, that displaced persons and Prisoners of War who return should carry with them favourable recollections of their treatment by British and United States authorities.

5. We understand that responsibility in respect of displaced persons in the British, American and French zones has now passed from SHAEF to the respective Zone Commanders whose policy is formulated through the Combined Displaced Persons Executive which is intended to last only until some other co-ordinating machinery can be established. It is essential therefore to secure United States agreement to a policy in respect of Polish Displaced Persons which would be implemented through CDPX and its successor by the Allied Commanders in each zone.

6. Please inform the United States Government of the above and endeavour to secure their agreement to the following proposals:—

(a) That no scheme should at present be instituted for the registration for repatriation of Polish Displaced Persons in Germany until first a statement has been obtained from the Polish Provisional Government as to the conditions under which these Poles would return to Poland, and secondly the repatriation of Soviet nationals, which at present has first priority, has been completed and arrangements have been made with representatives of the Polish Provisional Government for the orderly repatriation of Poles. Arrangements should however be made at once by CDPX for Poles who wish to volunteer to return to Poland without being asked to do so to register their wish with their camp commandants or other suitable authorities.

(b) That the Polish Provisional Government should be approached (if possible on similar lines by the United States Government as well as His Majesty's Government) with a request that they should appoint representatives to discuss with the British and American representatives the best manner of handling the problem in an orderly way. For our part we propose that these discussions should not take place in Warsaw or in Berlin but either in London or in British zone (or if it appears suitable to handle matter on Joint British and American basis, in American zone). We should also aim at bringing Warsaw representatives and Polish Liaison Staff at present with Polish displaced persons, into contact. If the transfer of responsibility for these displaced persons from the existing Polish Liaison Officers to representatives of the Polish Provisional Government is to be achieved in a peaceable and orderly fashion it is very desirable that this contact between the two should be effected under British (and American) auspices.

(c) That we should do our best to resist all attempts to discuss the repatriation of these Poles in the Allied Control Commission where it would be the subject of Soviet intervention. (*Inter alia*,[2] we should at once be faced with the Soviet demand that all displaced persons such as Poles refusing to return home should be excluded from the benefits of UNRRA). We should therefore insist upon negotiating the question direct with the Polish Provisional Government, who would of course themselves be responsible for making any necessary arrangements with the Soviet authorities for repatriation across the Soviet zone.

7. Please ask the State Department to let you have their views urgently as we should like to take the initiative by making a communication to the Polish Provisional Government as soon as possible.

8. When we have American views, we can consider best method of carrying French with us as participants in C.D.P.X.[3]

[2] Among other things.

[3] The filed copy of this telegram was initialed at head by Mr. Bevin and minuted by him at foot: 'I agree negotiation in detail should proceed. But regard should be had to the undertaking given by Polish Govnt. at Terminal. The undertaking should be met including discussion with Clark Kerr.' Mr. C. A. E. Shuckburgh, First Secretary designate to Prague, noted on this in a minute of 3 August: 'It seems to me that we are in line with the Sec. of State's views here, and that no action is required.' On this Mr. Warner minuted and Sir O. Sargent countersigned as follows: 'Yes, I think so. I take it the S/S wants us to bear in mind the possibility of using our agreement to various measures of "handing over" to the Warsaw Poles as a sanction for their fulfilment of their "Terminal" undertakings. C. F. A. Warner 5/8.' 'O. G. Sargent. Aug. 6.'

No. 592

Letter from Sir R. Leeper (Oxford)[1] *to Sir O. Sargent (Received 3 August)*
[*R 13082/4/19*]

119, WOODSTOCK ROAD, OXFORD, *2 August 1945*

My dear Moley

I enclose a short paper on Greece in the hope that you may think it useful to the Sec. of State in examining the situation. I leave that to you, as you may have covered all this ground already. I am available at any time if wanted.

Yours ever

R. A. LEEPER

[1] Sir Reginald Leeper, H.M. Ambassador to Greece, was then on leave in England.

Note by Sir R. Leeper on the present situation in Greece

The present Greek Govt. contains no politicians & is therefore known in Greece as a service Govt. This was found to be necessary as a result of the acute divisions between the political parties which made a Govt. representing all political parties impossible.

It was entirely due to H.M.G. that a Govt. representing all parties, including the Communists, entered Athens when the Germans left in Oct. 1944. H.M.G. did everything in their power to keep that Govt. together so that it might disband the private armies, form a National Army & prepare the elections. Owing to the refusal of the Communists to disband ELAS, the private army under their control, the all-party Govt. came to an end & was followed by civil war.

After the civil war a new beginning had to be made. The Archbishop, as Regent, took over the functions of the King & entrusted Plastiras with the formation of a Govt. The Regent's intention was that this Govt. should be non-party, but Plastiras introduced too many of his political friends both into the Govt. & into the army & the Regent removed him. He then made certain that the new Govt. under Voulgaris was purely service i.e. above & outside party conflicts. The only politician left in it was Sophianopoulos because he had already left Greece to represent his country at San Francisco. He has now resigned & has begun a campaign in favour of what he calls a 'representative' Govt. i.e. a Govt. of the parties of the Left including the Communists. Such a change at this moment would cause acute division in the country, would almost certainly lead to renewed disturbances, would cause havoc to the financial & economic reforms undertaken by Varvaressos & would probably mean no elections this year. For these reasons the Regent has rejected the proposal.

The Regent, however, now finds himself in a very difficult position. Sophianopoulos by his proposal has started all the former political intrigues which under the service Govt. were in abeyance until the elections. He has chosen the moment when the Greek population is in a highly nervous state owing to the anti-Greek propaganda of Russia's Balkan satellites—Yugoslavia, Bulgaria & Roumania. The Yugoslav & Bulgarian armies greatly outnumber Greece's one division & are strengthened by large Russian forces greatly in excess of the 40,000 British troops in Greece which are steadily diminishing as a result of demobilisation without replacements. Hence it is impossible for the Regent to carry on with the present Govt. & to calm the fears of the people without a public declaration of support from the new British Govt. Without such a declaration political agitation, fanned by the Communists, may get out of hand, the propaganda from the Balkan neighbours will be intensified & the Greek population will become panicky. Such a situation will be highly embarrassing to H.M.G. with British troops in the country. On the other hand the withdrawal of British troops would almost certainly lead to the provocation of frontier incidents by the Yugoslavs & Bulgarians which might quickly be followed by the occupation of Macedonia & Western Thrace. The loss of these territories would destroy the Greek State economically with consequent disorder & the eventual absorption of the rest of Greece into a Balkan Soviet Federation dominated by Russia who would then be free to deal with Turkey.

The position in Greece may slip very quickly, unless H.M.G. take immediate action. Only those who have lived through recent months in Greece can fully appreciate the nervous tension & the danger of a rapid change for the worse. I suggest that there are two ways of handling this situation:– (*a*) an immediate declaration by H.M.G. of support to the Regent & the Greek Govt. on the same lines as given by the former British Govt.[2] (*b*) an invitation to the Regent to visit London & confer with H.M.G.

I foresee that an immediate declaration may be embarrassing to H.M.G. before they have had time to examine the situation as a new Govt. I therefore strongly recommend the second course which would hold the situation in Greece, give H.M.G. time to examine the situation, enable the Regent to meet British Ministers, to appreciate the situation here & to agree on a policy likely to steady the position in Greece until the elections. The Regent is the only outstanding figure in Greece. He is a man of warm sympathies, an admirer of British ideas of liberty & a strong champion of liberal & progressive views. His contacts in London ought to have a beneficial effect in enlightening British opinion about Greece & in influencing him in the course to pursue in his own country in close accord & understanding with us.

CALENDAR TO No. 592

i   *18 Aug. 1945   Letter from Mr. Howard to Mr. Stevenson (Belgrade)* concerning the inconclusive discussions on Yugoslavia at Potsdam [R 13857/6/92].

[2] Cf. Sir L. Woodward, *op. cit.*, vol. iii, pp. 385f.

No. 593

Sir H. Seymour (Chungking) to Mr. Bevin (Received 2 August, 11.40 a.m.)
No. 769 Telegraphic [U 5917/5559/70]

Immediate   CHUNGKING, *2 August 1945, 9.58 a.m. G.M.T.*

My telegram No. 768.[1]

Following is text of reply addressed by Chinese Minister for Foreign Affairs to you personally.

(Begins).

I am directed by the President of the National Government of China to acknowledge receipt of your message informing him of the proposal of the Governments of the United Kingdom, United States and U.S.S.R. to establish a Council of Foreign Ministers in order to provide appropriate machinery for dealing with peace negotiations and territorial settlements arising from this war in an expeditious manner. The Chinese Government concurs in the proposal and takes great pleasure in accepting the invitation to become a member of the Council of Foreign Ministers and to take part

[1] See No. 469, note 4.

in its work and it fully shares your conviction that China's association with her British, American, Soviet and French Allies in this new body will offer an essential and fruitful introduction to our future association as permanent members of Security Council. (Ends).

2. Last sentence is in direct reply to a phrase in introductory sentence of American note[1] not reproduced in our own.

3. Russian note was delivered yesterday.

No. 594

Letter from Mr. Foulds (Berlin) to Mr. Sterndale Bennett (Received 3 August)
[F 4785/584/61]

Secret   BRITISH DELEGATION, BERLIN, *2 August 1945*

Dear Sterndale Bennett,

Will you please refer to the second paragraph of your letter No. 12[1] of 30th July enquiring whether the question of consulting the Dominions Governments about the proclamation to Japan was ever considered at Potsdam.

I am afraid that the answer is in the negative. As first drafted by the Americans the proclamation was designed to be issued by President Truman and Mr. Churchill only, and we were given to understand that the Americans wished to act quickly. In forwarding our suggested amendments to Mr. Churchill, Mr. Eden said that he presumed Chiang Kai Shek would be consulted. Mr. Churchill replied that he did not think that this was necessary but that he would ascertain President Truman's views.[2] President Truman told Mr. Churchill that night that he thought it would take too long to consult the Chinese and that he was anxious to issue the proclamation as soon as possible. We were taken completely by surprise when we heard on the following day that the Americans had asked Chiang Kai Shek to join in.[3] We have had no explanation of the reason for this sudden *volte face*.

I think the best we can say to Dr. Evatt is that owing to the American insistence on rapid action there was no time to consult the Dominions; that we thought the proclamation was going to be issued in the names of President Truman and Mr. Churchill only, and that we did not know until after the event that the Americans had invited Chiang Kai Shek to participate.

Yours sincerely,
L. H. FOULDS

[1] Not printed. In the light of No. 448, Mr. Sterndale Bennett had there enquired as indicated below.
[2] See No. 221 and note 4 *ibid.*
[3] Cf. No. 231, note 7.

No. 595

Minute from Sir A. Cadogan to Mr. Foulds (Berlin)
[*F 5737/1057/23*]

[BERLIN,] *2 August 1945*

The P.M. last night gave me the annexed paper which had been handed to him by the President.

I am not aware that Marshal Stalin has approached us with any request for a similar letter. Unless he has done so, I presume there is nothing for us to do on this.[1]

A. C.

ANNEX 1 TO No. 595

July 31, 1945

Memorandum for Generalissimo Stalin:[2]

In response to your suggestion[3] that I write you a letter as to the Far Eastern situation, I am attaching a form of letter which I propose to send you at your convenience after you notify me you have reached an agreement with the Government of China. If this is satisfactory to you, you can let me know immediately when you have reached such agreement and I will wire you the letter, to be used as you see fit. I will also send you by fastest courier the official letter signed by me. If you decide to use it it will be all right. However, if you decide to issue a statement basing your action on other grounds or for any other reason prefer not to use this letter it will be satisfactory to me. I leave it to your good judgment.

HARRY S. TRUMAN

ANNEX 2 TO No. 595

July 31, 1945

Dear Generalissamo [*sic*] Stalin:

Paragraph 5 of the Declaration signed at Moscow, October 30, 1943 by the United States, the Soviet Union, the United Kingdom and China, provides:

'5. That for the purpose of maintaining international peace and security pending the reestablishment of law and order and the inauguration of a system of general security, they will consult with one another and as occasion requires with other members of the United Nations with a view to joint action on behalf of the community of nations.'

Article 106 of the proposed Charter of the United Nations provides:

'Pending the coming into force of such special agreements referred to in Article 43 as in the opinion of the Security Council enable it to begin the exercise of

---

[1] Mr. Foulds minuted on this: 'We have not been approached so far as I know. L. H. F. 2/8.'

[2] This memorandum and the unsigned attachment below are printed in *F.R.U.S. Berlin*, vol. ii, pp. 1333–4, and in *Stalin Correspondence*, vol. ii, pp. 258–9.

[3] Conveyed by M. Molotov in his conversation with President Truman and Mr. Byrnes at noon on 29 July 1945 (cf. No. 453, note 2).

its responsibilities under Article 42, the parties to the Four-Nation Declaration, signed at Moscow, October 30, 1943, and France, shall, in accordance with the provisions of paragraph 5 of that Declaration, consult with one another and as occasion requires with other Members of the United Nations with a view to such joint action on behalf of the Organization as may be necessary for the purpose of maintaining international peace and security.'

Article 103 of the Charter provides:

'In the event of a conflict between the obligations of the Members of the United Nations under the present Charter and their obligations under any other international agreement, their obligations under the present Charter shall prevail.'

Though the Charter has not been formally ratified, at San Francisco it was agreed to by the Representatives of the Union of Soviet Socialist Republics and the Soviet government will be one of the permanent members of the Security Council.

It seems to me that under the terms of the Moscow Declaration and the provisions of the Charter, above referred to, it would be proper for the Soviet Union to indicate its willingness to consult and cooperate with other great powers now at war with Japan with a view to joint action on behalf of the community of nations to maintain peace and security.

Sincerely yours,

No. 596

Minute from Mr. de la Mare to Mr. Sterndale Bennett
[F 4839/584/61]

FOREIGN OFFICE, 2 August 1945

In the political warfare directive for the coming week, which was agreed at a meeting last night, we are telling our operators to repeat the Potsdam Declaration to Japan[1] daily at dictation speed. This is in accordance with our discussion the other day and I think it is the right line to adopt for the time being. We have reason to believe that the full text of the Declaration may not have been revealed to the Japanese people by their own authorities.

On the other hand we must, I think, consider how long we should continue to repeat the Declaration. In it we gave categorical terms on a take it or leave it basis and stated that we would brook no delay. On July 28th Suzuki made his public statement to the effect that the Japanese Government would ignore the Declaration.[2] This may not necessarily be the last word of the Japanese Government on this matter but the fact remains that they have put themselves on record with what amounts to a categorical rejection of the Declaration. If, in spite of this fact, we continue to repeat the Declaration too long, the Japanese will certainly come to the conclusion that

---

[1] No. 281.
[2] For this statement by Admiral Baron K. Suzuki, Japanese Prime Minister, cf. F.R.U.S. Berlin, vol. ii, p. 1293 and footnotes.

we are most anxious that they should accept it and this will encourage them to hold out a little longer in the hope that we will sooner or later offer them further modifications. We already have evidence that this line of thought is taking shape in Japan. On July 30th the Chief Editor of Radio Tokyo in a broadcast remarked on the 'softening attitude of the Allies shown at Potsdam' and contrasted this with the 'stiffening attitude of Japan'.

I do not think that any damage will be done by repeating the Declaration for a week or so and I think we can await the return of our Delegation before taking any action. It may be that Mr. Foulds has already discussed this point with the Americans. But if nothing has been done I would suggest that we should consult with the State Department so as to get concerted action. Our own current directive is seen before despatch by representatives of O.W.I. and I believe of the American Embassy also but I think that we should seek the views of the State Department as to how long they consider political warfare organisations should continue to repeat the Declaration if no further reply is forthcoming from the Japanese. This is a matter which should be discussed between the State Department and ourselves rather than between O.W.I. and P.W.E.[3]

A. J. DE LA MARE

[3] Mr. de la Mare added: 'After consultation with Mr. Foulds I have asked Mr. Pilcher, P.I.D., to issue a directive to posts abroad authorising them to drop the repetition of the Potsdam Declaration on August 8th. He will inform O.W.I. of this action A. J. d. l. M. 4/8.'

No. 597

Letter from Mr. Balfour (Washington) to Mr. Sterndale Bennett
(Received 10 August)
[F 5032/364/23]

WASHINGTON, 2 August 1945

My dear Benito

On receipt of the instructions contained in your telegram No. 7943[1] I made arrangements to see Grew and to hand to him the two documents, copies of which are enclosed.[2] You will observe that I, as it were, handed back to him a copy of a summary of the original American paper: it seemed desirable to do this so that there would be no misunderstanding in the minds of the Americans regarding the document on which the work done at the Foreign Office had been based.

Grew expressed interest and appreciation and will pass our paper along to his experts for examination. He did not make any remarks of special interest except to point out that the Potsdam surrender formula represented a

[1] No. 553.
[2] Not here printed: see F.R.U.S. 1945, vol. vi, pp. 581–4.

modification in American ideas somewhat in the direction of our paper, particularly in the respect that it mentions explicitly the establishment of a responsible Japanese government.

Yours ever,

JOCK BALFOUR

No. 598

Sir N. Bland (London) to Mr. Bevin (Received 3 August)
No. 235 [F 4761/4564/61]

Important. Secret   LONDON, *2 August 1945*

Sir,

On Friday, 20th July, at the urgent request of the Netherland Minister for Foreign Affairs, I despatched a telegram (Onward No. 104)[1] to Mr. Eden at Potsdam asking that Dr. van Kleffens, accompanied by the Netherland Prime Minister, Dr. Schermerhorn, and his predecessor, Professor Gerbrandy, might be permitted to visit Potsdam before the dispersal of the 'Big Three' to discuss certain matters of great importance to the Netherland East Indies. On the following Friday evening 20th July, I received a reply (Target No. 235)[1] expressing regret that it was impossible to invite the Netherlands Government to participate in the Three-Power Conference. I venture to observe that Dr. van Kleffens had not asked for participation in the Conference and I cannot find anything in my telegram to suggest that he had.

2. On receipt of Mr. Eden's reply, I at once wrote privately to Dr. van Kleffens to inform him that it was unfavourable and that I should be ready at any time to explain to him by word of mouth the reasons for Mr. Eden's decision.

3. Dr. van Kleffens is still suffering from the effects of a severe dental operation, but he asked me to call this morning, and, when I had conveyed to him the gist of Mr. Eden's message, he embarked on a long harangue about the appalling difficulties which the Dutch were experiencing in obtaining the necessary shipping for transporting essential troops and civil affairs personnel to the Far East. Their modest requirements had been put to the Combined Chiefs of Staff in Washington by the Netherland Liaison Officer in that city, to Mr. Churchill by Professor Gerbrandy and to Sir Alan Brooke by the Netherland Ambassador in London. All these representations had been met with expressions of sympathy, qualified by remarks about shortage of shipping, but so far no visible results whatever had been achieved. The Dutch requirements are set out in a document given me by Dr. van Kleffens, from which I have the honour to enclose a

---

[1] No. 251.i.

copy of the relevant extract [i]. I imagine that this document constitutes the reply to the request referred to in paragraph 3 of Mr. Sterndale Bennett's letter to me of 3rd July [i].

4. Dr. van Kleffens said that it was vital to the peaceful recuperation of the Netherland East Indies that there should be immediately available troops and civilians, who understood the Indies, to take over and maintain order in the islands directly the Japanese were evicted. It was only Dutch ships for which he was asking, ships which had already borne their full share in furthering the interests of the Allies as a whole. Now that the Dutch wanted them for their own purposes—and not theirs alone, but in the interests of many millions of natives who for years had been suffering under the oppression of the Japanese—it seemed that they were still going to be denied the use of them. His Excellency added that he and his Government had come to the end of their tether and that if they could not obtain satisfaction through the exhaustive methods of approach which they had hitherto employed, they would be compelled to take the matter into their own hands.

5. I ventured to suggest to Dr. van Kleffens that it might be useful if he discussed the matter with you, Sir, personally, but he appeared to feel that the Netherland Government had already done all that could be expected of them, and said that he intended to make no more representations to anyone.

6. While I have no doubt that Dr. van Kleffens' attitude is coloured by his conviction that the so-called smaller Powers are unjustifiably excluded from consultations on matters in which they are directly interested (to which I have called attention on previous occasions), nevertheless, I feel that in the present case there is even more substance than usual in his claims. It is only common-sense that the inhabitants of the Netherland East Indies must not be left to their own devices on liberation, nor is there any workable alternative to the Dutch for putting matters right there. And if the Dutch are precluded from getting the right people out there by the strangle-hold on their own shipping, I can only prophesy a reign of chaos in the islands which it will take years to put right. It cannot be in the immediate, or ultimate, interest either of the Dutch, or of ourselves, or of the Americans that this risk should be run, and I cannot urge sufficiently strongly that it should not be, but that steps should be taken to avoid it by granting the Dutch what they need, before they place us in the embarrassing situation, in which we should surely find ourselves, if Dr. van Kleffens' threat to withdraw the ships which he requires from the Allied pool were put into action.

> I have, &c.,
> NEVILE BLAND

CALENDAR TO No. 598

i *3 July 1945 Letter from Mr. Sterndale Bennett to Sir N. Bland (London); Undated extract from a Netherland memorandum.* Netherland participation in the war in the Far East, and military requirements. Earlier staff conversations in Washington [F 3448/52/61; F 4761/4564/61].

No. 599

Letter from Mr. Dening (Kandy) to Mr. Sterndale Bennett
(Received 8 August)
No. 1691 [F 5022/47/23]

HEADQUARTERS, SUPREME ALLIED COMMANDER, SOUTH EAST ASIA, *2 August 1945*

Top secret

Dear Sterndale-Bennett,

With reference to my Top Secret telegram No. 326 [i] you will probably have seen Kanmo 146 [i] of 31st July. The whole of this arose out of the fact that the Supreme Commander directed the staff here to examine urgently the possibility of a walk-in were the Japanese to surrender at short notice.

2. The announcement by the Big Three[1] came as somewhat of a shock, which was by no means a bad thing, for I have been uneasy for quite a time at our total lack of preparedness should the Japanese decide to call it a day.

3. All this turned our minds to the implications of a Japanese surrender, and it is clear to me that they are still very confused. The J[oint] P[lanning] S[taff] have turned out two papers, one dealing with the Zipper-Mailfist area and the other with the S.E.A.C. area. While they are still in draft, and show to my mind a mistaken conception of the task in prospect, they have nevertheless set the machinery in motion, and out of it all should emerge a plan which will show what we can do and how we can do it. It should also show our deficiencies, which are many.

4. One of the most intricate parts of modern amphibious warfare is the loading of the convoys which are to take the fighting forces and their supplies to the battle. But obviously the supplies required for a battle would differ in many respects from those required to make an unopposed landing for the purpose of assuming control from an enemy who has surrendered. In battle, for example, airfield construction is of paramount importance to enable land based aircraft to operate as soon as possible from captured territory, and this means airfield construction units and vast quantities of stores. In the case of surrender all this would fade into insignificance. You can readily appreciate that a different set of circumstances would require a good deal of detailed planning, which takes time.

5. The earlier assumption of control in territories for which we might have expected to fight raises a problem of civil supply which, I must confess, frankly appals me. It is true that shipping space is likely to become available

[1] No. 281.

which would otherwise be required for vast quantities of bombs, shells, ammunition and other warlike stores. But it is not easy to see where the supplies would come from in time. At present only Malaya is catered for at all, and that hardly on the scale likely to be required. I dare say that a certain amount of Japanese shipping would become available to move, for example, Siamese rice to Malaya, but shipping will not help unless there are supplies to ship. The whole problem seems to me to require very urgent consideration in London.

6. If we are prevented by Japanese surrender from fighting battles for the recovery of the S.E.A.C. area, then I am sure you will agree that it is of paramount political importance that we should make the best possible showing in our re-occupation of territories which the Japanese have overrun. Here we have a military machine which is capable of making a good showing within the limitations of its resources provided it is given reasonable time for planning. No other machine could in fact do the task better.

7. But the military machine is only equipped to undertake the limited task of re-occupation and prevention of disease and unrest. It is reasonable to suppose that civil government will expect to assume control much earlier than would be the case if territories had first to be conquered. But civil government cannot assume effective control without the requisite finance and supplies. It emerged from a recent conference between the Governor of Burma and the Supreme Commander that the former, while he has succeeded in obtaining a substantial financial grant, has not succeeded in obtaining anything but a low priority for essential supplies which he must have in order to resume civil government in Burma. This is only a foretaste of what is to come unless H.M.G. is prepared to step up the priorities for British territories in the Far East. I know that the whole world is crying out for goods, but this part of the world has been neglected too long, and unless we are prepared to make a real effort I am afraid that the adverse effect upon our position may well prove to be beyond redemption.

8. Nor are our responsibilities towards British territories only. By the creation of the South East Asia Command, which is predominantly British, we assumed responsibility for the areas contained within its boundaries. That is all to the good provided we discharge that responsibility. If we do, then we stand a fair chance of restoring British prestige in a part of the world where it had sunk to a very low ebb. If we do not, then I should expect that, as the years roll on, the peoples of the Far East will tend to look less and less to Britain and more and more to any Power which is in a position to afford them strategic, political and economic security. This will affect our relations with other European Powers with possessions in the Far East; it will loosen our ties with Australia and New Zealand and affect our relations with China and the United States.

9. To sum up, what is urgently needed now is detailed planning and the allocation of priorities for civil supplies. Given these, there is every hope that we can still make a good job of it.

10. Since writing the above I have learned that we may well be denuded

of most of our shipping resources for the assault on Japan. I need hardly emphasize the adverse effect upon our political position in South East Asia should such a step prove necessary, but I suppose that the decision has already been made by now. What I would urge is that, if an assault on Japan should prove unnecessary, we should exert every effort to ensure that shipping and supplies are made available to South East Asia in order to ensure that re-occupation takes place under the most favourable circumstances. A token representation in the occupation of Japan is politically far less important to us than showing the flag in South East Asia.

Yours ever,
M. E. Dening

Calendar to No. 599

i *31 July 1945 Kandy Tels. No. Kanmo 146 and No. 326.* Contingency of occupying Singapore at short notice as a result of Japanese surrender: 'Politically it is vitally important that our return to territories occupied for so long by Japanese should take place in a manner most calculated to impress the inhabitants with security we are capable of providing' [F 4676/299/61; W.O. 203/5520].

No. 600

Memorandum by Sir D. Waley (Berlin)
[UE 3514/624/77]

2 August 1945

This note is designed as a continuation of the Treasury note of the 16th July[1] and attempts to give an account of the Potsdam negotiations.

The Americans were impressed by the evidence that the Russians have taken from Berlin everything on which they could lay their hands from factory plant to furniture. They assume that they had done the same throughout their Zone of Occupation and felt that it would be certain that they could not or would not account properly for what they have taken. Thus the original plan of giving Russia a share of approximately 50% in all reparation deliveries would have meant that the Russians would already have taken practically everything from their Zone and would then proceed to claim half of what is in ours. The Americans therefore proposed that the Russian share of reparations should be satisfied by the deliveries which they have taken or are in a position to take from the Russian Zone which contains from 40% to 50% of the national wealth of Germany within her

<hr>

[1] No. 165.

1937 frontiers.[2] A further reason for this proposal was that the Russians have, in effect, handed over a considerable part of Germany to Poland with all the natural wealth which it contains.

The Russians said that they would only accept this plan if they obtained adequate deliveries of equipment from the Ruhr,[3] which is the form of reparation which they particularly want. The Americans felt that they should get something in return for giving the Russians a share of equipment from the Western Zones. They had been much incensed when the Russians ceased to supply food and coal for the Zones in Berlin which were handed over to American and British Forces, with the result that we had to agree to import food. They therefore felt that we should stipulate that the Russian Zone and the territory handed over to Poland should continue, so far as possible, to supply food and coal for the rest of Germany, including the whole of Berlin.[3]

Up to this point we were in complete agreement with the Americans and we obtained authority in London to concur in their plan.[4] We felt, however, very strong objection to the method by which the Americans proposed to achieve their objective. Their proposal was that industrial equipment from the Ruhr and the rest of the Western Zones should be handed over to Russia and that in return for a part of this, Russia should hand over specified quantities of food, coal and other goods to the U.S.A. and to the U.K. The industrial equipment is to be delivered over two years while the food, coal and other goods are to be delivered over five years.

The American plan is based on the belief that it will not be possible to administer Germany as a single economic whole with a common programme of exports and imports, a single Central Bank and the normal interchange of goods between one part of the country and another. Some of them, particularly Mr. Harriman and Mr. Pauley, hold the view that the Russian Zone will inevitably be treated as a separate economic unit and that, however undesirable it may be to draw a line across the middle of Germany, this is bound to happen and it is unrealistic to make a bargain except on a basis which assumes that it will happen. On the other hand, we believe that General Eisenhower, General Clay and Mr. Murphy intend to make a genuine effort to administer Germany as a single economic unit and think it wrong that at this stage we should assume that that effort will fail.[5]

We constantly tried to persuade the Americans to alter their plan, but we failed to do so and eventually Mr. Byrnes settled the matter as between the Americans and the Russians before his visit to the Foreign Secretary and Prime Minister, which was arranged in order that this and other outstanding questions should be discussed.[6] We were thus faced with the alternative of

[2] See Nos. 240, 252 and 440.
[3] See No. 266.
[4] See No. 252, note 1, Nos. 427, 445 and 445.i.
[5] Cf. No. 440.i.
[6] Cf. No. 485.

refusing to accept something which had been agreed as between the Americans and the Russians (which would probably have meant no reparation agreement at all) or of accepting the American proposal to which, in this particular respect, we saw strong objections. The Conference was expected to end within the next 24 hours and the decision taken by the Prime Minister and the Foreign Secretary was that we should accept the American plan.[7] It was felt that the detailed arrangements to carry out the plan will be made by the Control Council and that if the Control Council succeeds in its desire to run Germany as a single economic unit, the detailed arrangements will be fitted into that picture.

The American proposal as finally put[8] was

(a) $12\frac{1}{2}$% of such part of the capital equipment in the Western Zones as may be decided to be removable in exchange for an equivalent value of food, coal, etc. and

(b) 10% [? $7\frac{1}{2}$%] of such 'surplus' equipment as reparations.

The Russians asked that (a) should be 15% instead of $12\frac{1}{2}$% and (b) 10% and claimed

(a) shares of industrial enterprises in the Western Zones to the total amount of $500 million

(b) 30% of all German foreign assets

(c) 30% of German gold.

The Americans at once agreed to put up the figure in (a) from $12\frac{1}{2}$% to 15%[9]. British Ministers also agreed provided that other Russian claims were dropped. The Russians dropped their claims, but reopened the matter in a quite shameless way at the last moment and were finally allowed German foreign assets in Bulgaria, Finland, Hungary, Roumania and Eastern Austria.

It is a little difficult the day after negotiations of this kind end to assess how good or bad a deal has been made. The Russians have certainly done very well in obtaining everything in their own Zone and 25% of the surplus industrial equipment in the Western Zones. The Americans guess that this means that they will receive mainly from the Ruhr industrial equipment worth (at 1938 replacement cost plus 15%) some £100 million. It is not at all clear what commodities the Americans expect us to receive in return.

We certainly should desire to remove a great deal of industrial equipment from the Ruhr. We only want a limited amount ourselves and the Western

[7] See No. 486, minute 1.

[8] See No. 495, minute 2.

[9] In the filed copy, after 'the figure in (a)', Sir D. Waley noted 'and (b)', and deleted '$12\frac{1}{2}$% to 15%'. Those percentages were accurate in respect of (a); in respect of agreement that the percentage at (b) be raised from $7\frac{1}{2}$% to 10% see No. 495, minute 2.

European Allies are only entitled to a comparatively small share and though the Russians may have made much too favourable a bargain in obtaining 25%, it is unlikely to do us or any of our Allies any real harm. If the Russians had not been willing to remove some of this industrial equipment, it might have had to be simply destroyed. It is a pity that we renounced any reparation claims to German-owned assets in Bulgaria, Roumania and Finland and a very great pity that we have similarly renounced German-owned assets in Eastern Austria. But we should not really have been able to get much advantage out of a theoretical claim to German-owned assets in countries such as Bulgaria.

The Chancellor of the Exchequer regarded it as important that our acceptance of the American plan should be subject to two [*sic*] points:– (Onward No. 268)[10]

(*a*) An agreed satisfactory reparations programme. This is fully provided for in all the documents, but some at any rate of the Americans, particularly Mr. Pauley, think that it is inevitable that Russia will do what she likes in her own Zone and has no business to interfere with what we do in ours. This may lead to trouble hereafter.

(*b*) Acceptance of the prior charge on exports.
We secured this at the last moment—see paragraph 19 of the Economic Principles. The Americans, who had so passionately advocated this principle swung round to the opposite extreme. They thought that, in fact, exports and imports would have to be arranged on a zonal basis and that the formula would tie their hands. However, they dropped their objections at the last moment.

(*c*) Full acceptance of Germany as one economic unit for the purposes of the Control Commission.
Here again the documents entirely endorse this view, but we know that Mr. Pauley believes it to be quite unrealistic.
It should be added that we succeeded in securing

(1) French membership of the Allied Commission on Reparations[11] and

(2) the decision not to extract reparations from Austria.[12]
I attach copy of a memorandum by Mr. Brand on Food and Coal for Greater Berlin.[13]

S. D. W.

[10] No. 445.

[11] See No. 518, minute 2.

[12] See No. 447, minute 5.

[13] Not attached to filed copy.

i *2 Aug. 1945   Memoranda by Sir D. Waley (Berlin)* on future work of the Allied Commission on Reparation and its future meeting place, citing one of Mr. Byrnes' letters of 1 Aug. to M. Molotov and Soviet reply (cf. *F.R.U.S. Berlin*, vol. ii, pp. 936–7; cf. also *ibid.*, pp. 933–4) [UE 3514/624/77].

ii *31 July 1945   Record by Mr. Lincoln of conversation with the Netherland Counsellor:* allocation of reparations to smaller powers [UE 3380/624/77].

No. 601

Minute from Mr. Coulson to Sir A. Clark Kerr (Berlin)
[*UE 2592/14/77*][1]

2 August 1945

The Protocol records, I think, that the Three Governments were in principle agreed on the question of not using Allied property in satellite countries as reparation or war trophies, but that the wording of an agreement had not been settled and the matter would be pursued through the diplomatic channel.[2]

What actually happened was that a Sub-Committee was set up on the last day to deal with this[3] but did not have a chance of meeting until 7.0. We took the American paper (circulated as P (Terminal) 49)[4] and found that the Russians did not of course accept a good deal of it. We attempted to reach agreement on the lines of the draft report, of which I attach a copy [i], and it seemed as if M. Gusev might accept this, but at the last moment he ran off to consult his lawyers and never reappeared. The above is in case the matter is raised through the diplomatic channel and you require to take action in Moscow. Presumably the Americans will take the initiative.

J. E. Coulson

Calendar to No. 601

i *1 Aug. 1945   F.O. delegation minute to Mr. Bevin attaching report from Sub-Committee on Use of Allied Property for Satellite Reparation or War Trophies* [UE 2592/14/77 of 1946].

[1] Of 1946.
[2] See No. 603, section XX.
[3] See No. 509, minute 4.
[4] See No. 451, note 6.

No. 602

Memorandum of agreement of the protocol of the proceedings of the Berlin Conference

[F.O. 93/1/238]

BERLIN, *August 1 [2]*[1] *1945*

There is attached[2] hereto the agreed protocol of the Berlin Conference.

I. STALIN[3]
HARRY S. TRUMAN
C. R. ATTLEE

---

[1] In the original '1' was struck through in pencil and '2' inserted above.

[2] There was no attachment when the present document was signed by the three Heads of Government, as explained by Mr. W. Armstrong of the Cabinet Office in a letter of 5 November 1945 to Lord Hood:

'As you may be aware, there was no "original" document signed by the three Heads of State. As at Yalta, they had before them final drafts in English and Russian, prepared simultaneously but not compared word for word, and they agreed amendments to the drafts across the table, signed blank sheets of paper and left it to the officials to settle the final form of the agreed amendments and compare the Russian and English texts.

'This process was carried out on the afternoon of 2nd August at two meetings of officials. The first was attended by Mr. Brook, Lt.-Colonel Norman and Major Theakstone, for the United Kingdom Delegation (all members of the Foreign Office having left with the Secretary of State), by Mr. Dunn, Mr. Bohlen and others, for the United States Delegation, and M. Gromyko and Mr. Golunski, for the Soviet Delegation. The meeting was unsatisfactory because Mr. Gromyko had not had full instructions from M. Vyshinski, and it was agreed that there should be a later meeting at a time when M. Vyshinski could attend.

'Mr. Brook had to leave before this later meeting, which was attended, for the United Kingdom Delegation, by Lt.-Colonel Norman and Major Theakstone.'

This later meeting was recorded by Colonel Norman in a note of 7 August to Mr. Brook:

'1. On the afternoon of August 2nd, after you had left, we went through the final text of the Protocol to check it with the Russian version. Those present included:

For U.S.S.R.: M. Vyshinski, M. Gromyko, M. Golunski, plus three others.

For U.S.A.: Mr. James Dunn, Mr. Bohlen, Mr. Wilderfoot.

'2. After three hours prolonged discussion we agreed certain amendments which I have already passed on to you. At the end of the meeting Mr. Vyshinski wanted to have another Protocol agreeing to the amendments to this Protocol, but we finally persuaded him to be content with Mr. Dunn's and my initials on his Russian text where any changes had been made. M. Vyshinski reciprocated to some extent by putting his initials on some of the alterations in my text, which I attach for record purposes, in case any trouble arises in future on the final wording of the Protocol. M. R. Norman. 7th August, 1945.'

This undated text of the Protocol as amended with initials (on F.O. 93/1/238), but unsigned, is otherwise the same, subject to minor verbal variation (cf. amendments in square brackets), as the final fair copy dated 2 August 1945 at No. 603.

Mr. Armstrong concluded his letter of 5 November to Lord Hood: 'I am afraid this procedure can hardly be described as satisfactory, but nothing better was possible in the circumstances.'

[3] In literal transliteration. In the Confidential Print of the Protocol the signature supplied read, in accordance with general usage, J. V. Stalin: see No. 603.

No. 603

Protocol of the proceedings of the Berlin Conference[1]
[U 6197/3628/70]

Top secret   BERLIN, 2 August 1945

The Berlin Conference of the Three Heads of Government of the U.S.S.R., United States and United Kingdom which took place from the 17th July to the 2nd August, 1945, came to the following conclusions:–

I.—*Establishment of a Council of Foreign Ministers*

A. The Conference reached the following agreement for the establishment of a Council of Foreign Ministers to do the necessary preparatory work for the peace settlements:–

'(1) There shall be established a Council composed of the Foreign Ministers of the United Kingdom, the Union of Soviet Socialist Republics, China, France and the United States.

(2) (i) The Council shall normally meet in London, which shall be the permanent seat of the joint Secretariat which the Council will form. Each of the Foreign Ministers will be accompanied by a high-ranking Deputy, duly authorised to carry on the work of the Council in the absence of his Foreign Minister, and by a small staff of technical advisers.

(ii) The first meeting of the Council shall be held in London not later than the 1st September, 1945. Meetings may be held by common agreement in other capitals as may be agreed from time to time.

(3) (i) As its immediate important task, the Council shall be authorised to draw up, with a view to their submission to the United Nations, treaties of peace with Italy, Roumania, Bulgaria, Hungary and Finland, and to propose settlements of territorial questions outstanding on the termination of the war in Europe. The Council shall be utilised for the preparation of a peace settlement for Germany to be accepted by the Government of Germany when a Government adequate for the purpose is established.

(ii) For the discharge of each of these tasks the Council will be composed of the Members representing those States which were signatory to the terms of surrender imposed upon the enemy State concerned. For the purposes of the peace settlement for Italy, France shall be regarded as a signatory to the terms of surrender for Italy. Other Members will be invited to participate when matters directly concerning them are under discussion.

(iii) Other matters may from time to time be referred to the Council by agreement between the Member Governments.

[1] *Note in filed copy:* 'Text compared and agreed with the United States and Soviet Delegations' (cf. No. 602, note 2). This text was published in 1947 as Cmd. 7087. American and Russian texts are printed respectively in *F.R.U.S. Berlin*, vol. ii, pp. 1478–98, and in *Berlinskaya konferentsiya*, pp. 459–480.

(4) (i) Whenever the Council is considering a question of direct interest to a State not represented thereon, such State should be invited to send representatives to participate in the discussion and study of that question.

(ii) The Council may adapt its procedure to the particular problem under consideration. In some cases it may hold its own preliminary discussions prior to the participation of other interested States. In other cases, the Council may convoke a formal conference of the State chiefly interested in seeking a solution of the particular problem.'

B. It was agreed that the three Governments should each address an identical invitation to the Governments of China and France to adopt this text and to join in establishing the Council. The text of the approved invitation was as follows:–

Council of Foreign Ministers

Draft for identical invitation to be sent separately by each of the Three Governments to the Governments of China and France

'The Governments of the United Kingdom, the United States and the U.S.S.R. consider it necessary to begin without delay the essential preparatory work upon the peace settlements in Europe. To this end they are agreed that there should be established a Council of the Foreign Ministers of the Five Great Powers to prepare treaties of peace with the European enemy States, for submission to the United Nations. The Council would also be empowered to propose settlements of outstanding territorial questions in Europe and to consider such other matters as member Governments might agree to refer to it.

'The text adopted by the Three Governments is as follows:–

(Here insert final agreed text of the Proposal.)[2]

'In agreement with the Governments of the *United States and U.S.S.R., His Majesty's Government in the United Kingdom and U.S.S.R., the United States Government, the United Kingdom and the Soviet Government* extend a cordial invitation to the Government of *China (France)* to adopt the text quoted above and to join in setting up the Council. *His Majesty's Government, the United States Government, the Soviet Government* attach much importance to the participation of the *Chinese Government (French Government)* in the proposed arrangements, and they hope to receive an early and favourable reply to this invitation.'

C. The establishment of the Council of Foreign Ministers for the specific purposes named in the text will be without prejudice to the agreement of the Crimea Conference that there should be periodical consultation between the Foreign Secretaries of the United States, the Union of Soviet Socialist Republics and the United Kingdom.

D. The Conference also considered the position of the European Advisory Commission in the light of the Agreement to establish the Council of Foreign Ministers. It was noted with satisfaction that the Commission had ably

---

[2] i.e. section A (1)—(4) above.

discharged its principal tasks by the recommendations that it had furnished for the terms of surrender for Germany, for the zones of occupation in Germany and Austria and for the inter-Allied control machinery in those countries. It was felt that further work of a detailed character for the co-ordination of Allied policy for the control of Germany and Austria would in future fall within the competence of the Control Council in Berlin and the Allied Commission at Vienna. Accordingly it was agreed to recommend that the European Advisory Commission be dissolved.

II.—*The Principles to Govern the Treatment of Germany in the Initial Control Period*
A. *Political Principles*

1. In accordance with the Agreement on Control Machinery in Germany, supreme authority in Germany is exercised, on instructions from their respective Governments, by the Commanders-in-Chief of the armed forces of the United States of America, the United Kingdom, the Union of Soviet Socialist Republics and the French Republic, each in his own zone of occupation, and also jointly, in matters affecting Germany as a whole, in their capacity as members of the Control Council.

2. So far as is practicable, there shall be uniformity of treatment of the German population throughout Germany.

3. The purposes of the occupation of Germany by which the Control Council shall be guided are:—

(i) The complete disarmament and demilitarisation of Germany and the elimination or control of all German industry that could be used for military production. To these ends:—

(*a*) All German land, naval and air forces, the S.S., S.A., S.D. and Gestapo, with all their organisations, staffs and institutions, including the General Staff, the Officers' Corps, Reserve Corps, military schools, war veterans' organisations and all other military and semi-military organisations, together with all clubs and associations which serve to keep alive the military tradition in Germany, shall be completely and finally abolished in such manner as permanently to prevent the revival or reorganisation of German militarism and Nazism;

(*b*) All arms, ammunition and implements of war and all specialised facilities for their production shall be held at the disposal of the Allies or destroyed. The maintenance and production of all aircraft and all arms, ammunition and implements of war shall be prevented.

(ii) To convince the German people that they have suffered a total military defeat and that they cannot escape responsibility for what they have brought upon themselves, since their own ruthless warfare and the fanatical Nazi resistance have destroyed German economy and made chaos and suffering inevitable.

(iii) To destroy the National Socialist Party and its affiliated and super-vised organisations, to dissolve all Nazi institutions, to ensure that they are not revived in any form, and to prevent all Nazi and militarist activity or propaganda.

(iv) To prepare for the eventual reconstruction of German political life on a democratic basis and for eventual peaceful co-operation in international life by Germany.

4. All Nazi laws which provided the basis of the Hitler régime or established discrimination on grounds of race, creed, or political opinion shall be abolished. No such discriminations, whether legal, administrative or otherwise, shall be tolerated.

5. War criminals and those who have participated in planning or carrying out Nazi enterprises involving or resulting in atrocities or war crimes shall be arrested and brought to judgment. Nazi leaders, influential Nazi supporters and high officials of Nazi organisations and institutions and any other persons dangerous to the occupation or its objectives shall be arrested and interned.

6. All members of the Nazi party who have been more than nominal participants in its activities and all other persons hostile to Allied purposes shall be removed from public and semi-public office, and from positions of responsibility in important private undertakings. Such persons shall be replaced by persons who, by their political and moral qualities, are deemed capable of assisting in developing genuine democratic institutions in Germany.

7. German education shall be so controlled as completely to eliminate Nazi and militarist doctrines and to make possible the successful development of democratic ideas.

8. The judicial system will be reorganised in accordance with the principles of democracy, of justice under law, and of equal rights for all citizens without distinction of race, nationality or religion.

9. The administration in Germany should be directed towards the decentralisation of the political structure and the development of local responsibility. To this end:–

(i) Local self-government shall be restored throughout Germany on democratic principles and in particular through elective councils as rapidly as is consistent with military security and the purposes of military occupation;

(ii) all democratic political parties with rights of assembly and of public discussion shall be allowed and encouraged throughout Germany;

(iii) representative and elective principles shall be introduced into regional, provincial and state (*Land*) administration as rapidly as may be justified by the successful application of these principles in local self-government;

(iv) for the time being, no central German Government shall be established. Notwithstanding this, however, certain essential central German administrative departments, headed by State Secretaries, shall be established, particularly in the fields of finance, transport, communications, foreign trade and industry. Such departments will act under the direction of the Control Council.

10. Subject to the necessity for maintaining military security, freedom of speech, press and religion shall be permitted, and religious institutions shall

be respected. Subject likewise to the maintenance of military security, the formation of free trade unions shall be permitted.

B. *Economic Principles*

11. In order to eliminate Germany's war potential, the production of arms, ammunition and implements of war as well as all types of aircraft and sea-going ships shall be prohibited and prevented. Production of metals, chemicals[,] machinery and other items that are directly necessary to a war economy, shall be rigidly controlled and restricted to Germany's approved post-war peacetime needs to meet the objectives stated in paragraph 15. Productive capacity not needed for permitted production shall be removed in accordance with the reparations plan recommended by the Allied Commission on reparations and approved by the Governments concerned or, if not removed, shall be destroyed.

12. At the earliest practicable date, the German economy shall be decentralised for the purpose of eliminating the present excessive concentration of economic power as exemplified in particular by cartels, syndicates, trusts and other monopolistic arrangements.

13. In organising the German economy, primary emphasis shall be given to the development of agriculture and peaceful domestic industries.

14. During the period of occupation Germany shall be treated as a single economic unit. To this end common policies shall be established in regard to:–

(*a*) mining and industrial production and its allocation;
(*b*) agriculture, forestry and fishing;
(*c*) wages, prices and rationing;
(*d*) import and export programmes for Germany as a whole;
(*e*) currency and banking, central taxation and customs;
(*f*) reparation and removal of industrial war potential;
(*g*) transportation and communications.

In applying these policies account shall be taken, where appropriate, of varying local conditions.

15. Allied controls shall be imposed upon the German economy but only to the extent necessary:–

(*a*) to carry out programmes of industrial disarmament and demilitarisation, of reparations, and of approved exports and imports;
(*b*) to assure the production and maintenance of goods and services required to meet the needs of the occupying forces and displaced persons in Germany and essential to maintain in Germany average living standards not exceeding the average of the standards of living of European countries. (European countries means all European countries excluding the United Kingdom and the Union of Soviet Socialist Republics);
(*c*) to ensure in the manner determined by the Control Council the equitable distribution of essential commodities between the several zones so as to produce a balanced economy throughout Germany and reduce the need for imports;

(*d*) to control German industry and all economic and financial international transactions, including exports and imports, with the aim of preventing Germany from developing a war potential and of achieving the other objectives named herein;

(*e*) to control all German public or private scientific bodies, research and experimental institutions, laboratories, &c., connected with economic activities.

16. In the imposition and maintenance of economic controls established by the Control Council, German administrative machinery shall be created and the German authorities shall be required to the fullest extent practicable to proclaim and assume administration of such controls. Thus it should be brought home to the German people that the responsibility for the administration of such controls and any breakdown in these controls will rest with themselves. Any German controls which may run counter to the objectives of occupation will be prohibited.

17. Measures shall be promptly taken:–

(*a*) to effect essential repair of transport;

(*b*) to enlarge coal production;

(*c*) to maximise agricultural output;

(*d*) to effect emergency repair of housing and essential utilities.

18. Appropriate steps shall be taken by the Control Council to exercise control and the power of disposition over German-owned external assets not already under the control of United Nations which have taken part in the war against Germany.

19. Payment of reparations should leave enough resources to enable the German people to subsist without external assistance. In working out the economic balance of Germany the necessary means must be provided to pay for imports approved by the Control Council in Germany. The proceeds of exports from current production and stocks shall be available in the first place for payment for such imports.

The above clause will not apply to the equipment and products referred to in paragraph 4 (*a*) and 4 (*b*) of the Reparations Agreement.

III.—*Reparations from Germany*

1. Reparation claims of the U.S.S.R. shall be met by removals from the zone of Germany occupied by the U.S.S.R., and from appropriate German external assets.

2. The U.S.S.R. undertakes to settle the reparation claims of Poland from its own share of reparations.

3. The reparations claims of the United States, the United Kingdom and other countries entitled to reparations shall be met from the Western Zones and from appropriate German external assets.

4. In addition to the reparations to be taken by the U.S.S.R. from its own zone of occupation, the U.S.S.R. shall receive additionally from the Western Zones:

(*a*) 15 per cent. of such usable and complete industrial capital equipment, in the first place from the metallurgical, chemical and machine manufacturing industries, as is unnecessary for the German peace economy and should be removed from the Western Zones of Germany, in exchange for an equivalent value of food, coal, potash, zinc, timber, clay products, petroleum products, and such other commodities as may be agreed upon.

(b) 10 per cent. of such industrial capital equipment as is unnecessary for the German peace economy and should be removed from the Western Zones, to be transferred to the Soviet Government on reparations account without payment or exchange of any kind in return.

Removals of equipment as provided in (a) and (b) above shall be made simultaneously.

5. The amount of equipment to be removed from the Western Zones on account of reparations must be determined within six months from now at the latest.

6. Removals of industrial capital equipment shall begin as soon as possible and shall be completed within two years from the determination specified in paragraph 5. The delivery of products covered by 4(a) above shall begin as soon as possible and shall be made by the U.S.S.R. in agreed instalments within five years of the date hereof. The determination of the amount and character of the industrial capital equipment unnecessary for the German peace economy and therefore available for reparations shall be made by the Control Council under policies fixed by the Allied Commission on Reparations, with the participation of France, subject to the final approval of the Zone Commander in the Zone from which the equipment is to be removed.

7. Prior to the fixing of the total amount of equipment subject to removal, advance deliveries shall be made in respect of such equipment as will be determined to be eligible for delivery in accordance with the procedure set forth in the last sentence of paragraph 6.

8. The Soviet Government renounces all claims in respect of reparations to shares of German enterprises which are located in the Western Zones of occupation in Germany as well as to German foreign assets in all countries except those specified in paragraph 9 below.

9. The Governments of the United Kingdom and United States renounce all claims in respect of reparations to shares of German enterprises which are located in the Eastern Zone of occupation in Germany, as well as to German foreign assets in Bulgaria, Finland, Hungary, Roumania and Eastern Austria.

10. The Soviet Government makes no claims to gold captured by the Allied troops in Germany.

IV.—*Disposal of the German Navy and Merchant Marine*

A.

The following principles for the distribution of the German Navy were agreed:–

(1) The total strength of the German surface navy, excluding ships sunk and those taken over from Allied Nations, but including ships under

construction or repair, shall be divided equally among the U.S.S.R., United Kingdom and United States.

(2) Ships under construction or repair means those ships whose construction or repair may be completed within three to six months, according to the type of ship. Whether such ships under construction or repair shall be completed or repaired shall be determined by the technical commission appointed by the Three Powers and referred to below, subject to the principle that their completion or repair must be achieved within the time limits above provided, without any increase of skilled employment in the German shipyards and without permitting the reopening of any German ship building or connected industries. Completion date means the date when a ship is able to go out on its first trip, or, under peace-time standards, would refer to the customary date of delivery by shipyard to the Government.

(3) The larger part of the German submarine fleet shall be sunk. Not more than thirty submarines shall be preserved and divided equally between the U.S.S.R., United Kingdom and United States for experimental and technical purposes.

(4) All stocks of armament, ammunition and supplies of the German Navy appertaining to the vessels transferred pursuant to paragraphs (1) and (3) hereof shall be handed over to the respective Powers receiving such ships.

(5) The Three Governments agree to constitute a tripartite naval commission comprising two representatives for each Government, accompanied by the requisite staff, to submit agreed recommendations to the Three Governments for the allocation of specific German warships and to handle other detailed matters arising out of the agreement between the Three Governments regarding the German fleet. The Commission will hold its first meeting not later than the 15th August, 1945, in Berlin, which shall be its headquarters. Each Delegation on the Commission will have the right, on the basis of reciprocity, to inspect German warships wherever they may be located.

(6) The Three Governments agree that transfers, including those of ships under construction and repair, shall be completed as soon as possible, but not later than the 15th February, 1946. The Commission will submit fortnightly reports, including proposals for the progressive allocation of the vessels when agreed by the Commission.

B.

The following principles for the distribution of the German Merchant Marine were agreed:–

(1) The German Merchant Marine, surrendered to the Three Powers and wherever located, shall be divided equally among the U.S.S.R., the United Kingdom and the United States. The actual transfers of the ships to the respective countries shall take place as soon as practicable after the end of the war against Japan. The United Kingdom and the United

States will provide out of their shares of the surrendered German merchant ships appropriate amounts for other Allied States whose merchant marines have suffered heavy losses in the common cause against Germany, except that the Soviet Union shall provide out of its share for Poland.

(2) The allocation, manning and operation of these ships during the Japanese War period shall fall under the cognisance and authority of the Combined Shipping Adjustment Board and the United Maritime Authority.

(3) While actual transfer of the ships shall be delayed until after the end of the war with Japan, a Tripartite Shipping Commission shall inventory and value all available ships and recommend a specific distribution in accordance with paragraph (1).

(4) German inland and coastal ships determined to be necessary to the maintenance of the basic German peace economy by the Allied Control Council of Germany shall not be included in the shipping pool thus divided among the Three Powers.

(5) The Three Governments agree to constitute a tripartite merchant marine commission comprising two representatives for each Government, accompanied by the requisite staff, to submit agreed recommendations to the Three Governments for the allocation of specific German merchant ships and to handle other detailed matters arising out of the agreement between the Three Governments regarding the German merchant ships. The Commission will hold its first meeting not later than the 1st September, 1945, in Berlin, which shall be its headquarters. Each delegation on the Commission will have the right, on the basis of reciprocity, to inspect the German merchant ships wherever they may be located.

V.—*City of Königsberg and the Adjacent Area*

The Conference examined a proposal by the Soviet Government to the effect that, pending the final determination of territorial questions at the peace settlement, the section of the western frontier of the Union of Soviet Socialist Republics which is adjacent to the Baltic Sea should pass from a point on the eastern shore of the Bay of Danzig to the east, north of Braunsberg–Goldap, to the meeting point of the frontiers of Lithuania, the Polish Republic and East Prussia.

The Conference has agreed in principle to the proposal of the Soviet Government concerning the ultimate transfer to the Soviet Union of the City of Königsberg and the area adjacent to it as described above subject to expert examination of the actual frontier.

The President of the United States and the British Prime Minister have declared that they will support the proposal of the Conference at the forthcoming peace settlement.

VI.—*War Criminals*

The Three Governments have taken note of the discussions which have been proceeding in recent weeks in London between British, United States,

Soviet and French representatives with a view to reaching agreement on the methods of trial of those major war criminals whose crimes under the Moscow Declaration of October 1943 have no particular geographical localisation. The Three Governments reaffirm their intention to bring these criminals to swift and sure justice. They hope that the negotiations in London will result in speedy agreement being reached for this purpose, and they regard it as a matter of great importance that the trial of these major criminals should begin at the earliest possible date. The first list of defendants will be published before the 1st September.

VII.—*Austria*

The Conference examined a proposal by the Soviet Government on the extension of the authority of the Austrian Provisional Government to all of Austria.

The three Governments agreed that they were prepared to examine this question after the entry of the British and American forces into the city of Vienna.

It was agreed that reparations should not be exacted from Austria.

VIII.—*Poland*

A. *Declaration*

We have taken note with pleasure of the agreement reached among representative Poles from Poland and abroad which has made possible the formation, in accordance with the decisions reached at the Crimea Conference, of a Polish Provisional Government of National Unity recognised by the Three Powers. The establishment by the British and United States Governments of diplomatic relations with the Polish Provisional Government of National Unity has resulted in the withdrawal of their recognition from the former Polish Government in London, which no longer exists.

The British and United States Governments have taken measures to protect the interests of the Polish Provisional Government of National Unity, as the recognised Government of the Polish State, in the property belonging to the Polish State located in their territories and under their control, whatever the form of this property may be. They have further taken measures to prevent alienation to third parties of such property. All proper facilities will be given to the Polish Provisional Government of National Unity for the exercise of the ordinary legal remedies for the recovery of any property belonging to the Polish State which may have been wrongfully alienated.

The Three Powers are anxious to assist the Polish Provisional Government of National Unity in facilitating the return to Poland as soon as practicable of all Poles abroad who wish to go, including members of the Polish armed forces and the merchant marine. They expect that those Poles who return home shall be accorded personal and property rights on the same basis as all Polish citizens.

The Three Powers note that the Polish Provisional Government of National Unity in accordance with the decisions of the Crimea Conference has agreed to the holding of free and unfettered elections as soon as possible on the basis of universal suffrage and secret ballot in which all democratic and anti-Nazi parties shall have the right to take part and to put forward candidates; and that representatives of the Allied Press shall enjoy full freedom to report to the world upon developments in Poland before and during the elections.

B. *Western Frontier of Poland*

In conformity with the agreement on Poland reached at the Crimea Conference the three Heads of Government have sought the opinion of the Polish Provisional Government of National Unity in regard to the accession of territory in the north and west which Poland should receive. The President of the National Council of Poland and members of the Polish Provisional Government of National Unity have been received at the Conference and have fully presented their views. The three Heads of Government reaffirm their opinion that the final delimitation of the western frontier of Poland should await the peace settlement.

The three Heads of Government agree that, pending the final determination of Poland's western frontier, the former German territories east of a line running from the Baltic Sea immediately west of Swinemünde, and thence along the Oder River to the confluence of the western Neisse River and along the western Neisse to the Czechoslovak frontier, including that portion of East Prussia not placed under the administration of the Union of Soviet Socialist Republics in accordance with the understanding reached at this conference and including the area of the former free city of Danzig, shall be under the administration of the Polish State and for such purposes should not be considered as part of the Soviet zone of occupation in Germany.

IX.—*Conclusion of Peace Treaties and Admission to the United Nations Organisation*

The three Governments consider it desirable that the present anomalous position of Italy, Bulgaria, Finland, Hungary and Roumania should be terminated by the conclusion of Peace Treaties. They trust that the other interested Allied Governments will share these views.

For their part the Three Governments have included the preparation of a Peace Treaty for Italy as the first among the immediate important tasks to be undertaken by the new Council of Foreign Ministers. Italy was the first of the Axis Powers to break with Germany, to whose defeat she has made a material contribution, and has now joined with the Allies in the struggle against Japan. Italy has freed herself from the Fascist régime and is making good progress towards re-establishment of a democratic government and institutions. The conclusion of such a Peace Treaty with a recognised and democratic Italian Government will make it possible for the Three Governments to fulfil their desire to support an application from Italy for membership of the United Nations.

The Three Governments have also charged the Council of Foreign Ministers with the task of preparing Peace Treaties for Bulgaria, Finland, Hungary and Roumania. The conclusion of Peace Treaties with recognised democratic Governments in these States will also enable the Three Governments to support applications from them for membership of the United Nations. The Three Governments agree to examine, each separately in the near future, in the light of the conditions then prevailing, the establishment of diplomatic relations with Finland, Roumania, Bulgaria and Hungary, to the extent possible prior to the conclusion of Peace Treaties with those countries.

The Three Governments have no doubt that in view of the changed conditions resulting from the termination of the war in Europe, representatives of the Allied press will enjoy full freedom to report to the world upon developments in Roumania, Bulgaria, Hungary and Finland.

As regards the admission of other States into the United Nations Organisation, Article 4 of the Charter of the United Nations declares that:–

1. Membership in the United Nations is open to all other peace-loving States who accept the obligations contained in the present Charter and, in the judgment of the organisation, are able and willing to carry out these obligations;

2. The admission of any such State to membership in the United Nations will be effected by a decision of the General Assembly upon the recommendation of the Security Council.

The Three Governments, so far as they are concerned, will support applications for membership from those States which have remained neutral during the war and which fulfil the qualifications set out above.

The Three Governments feel bound, however, to make it clear that they for their part would not favour any application for membership put forward by the present Spanish Government, which, having been founded with the support of the Axis Powers, does not, in view of its origins, its nature, its record and its close association with the aggressor States, possess the qualifications necessary to justify such membership.

X.—*Territorial Trusteeship*

The Conference examined a proposal by the Soviet Government on the question of trusteeship territories as defined in the decision of the Crimea Conference and in the Charter of the United Nations Organisation.

After an exchange of views on this question it was decided that the disposition of any former Italian Colonial territories was one to be decided in connection with the preparation of a peace treaty for Italy and that the question of Italian Colonial territory would be considered by the September Council of Minister[s] for Foreign Affairs.

XI.—*Revised Allied Control Commission Procedure in Roumania, Bulgaria and Hungary*

The Three Governments took note that the Soviet Representatives on the Allied Control Commissions in Roumania, Bulgaria and Hungary have communicated to their United Kingdom and United States colleagues proposals for improving the work of the Control Commissions, now that hostilities in Europe have ceased.

The Three Governments agreed that the revision of the procedures of the Allied Control Commissions in these countries would now be undertaken, taking into account the interests and responsibilities of the Three Governments which together presented the terms of armistice to the respective countries, and accepting as a basis, in respect of all three countries, the Soviet Government's proposals for Hungary as annexed hereto. (Annex I.)[3]

XII.—*Orderly Transfer of German Populations*

The Three Governments, having considered the question in all its aspects, recognise that the transfer to Germany of German populations or elements thereof, remaining in Poland, Czechoslovakia and Hungary, will have to be undertaken. They agree that any transfers that take place should be effected in an orderly and humane manner.

Since the influx of a large number of Germans into Germany would increase the burden already resting on the occupying authorities, they consider that the Control Council in Germany should, in the first instance, examine the problem, with special regard to the question of the equitable distribution of these Germans among the several zones of occupation. They are accordingly instructing their respective representatives on the Control Council to report to their Governments as soon as possible the extent to which such persons have already entered Germany from Poland, Czechoslovakia and Hungary, and to submit an estimate of the time and rate at which further transfers could be carried out having regard to the present situation in Germany.

The Czechoslovak Government, the Polish Provisional Government and the Control Council in Hungary are at the same time being informed of the above and are being requested meanwhile to suspend further expulsions pending an examination by the Governments concerned of the report from their representatives on the Control Council.

XIII.—*Oil Equipment in Roumania*

The Conference agreed to set up two bilateral commissions of experts, one to be composed of United Kingdom and Soviet members, and one to be composed of United States and Soviet members, to investigate the facts and examine the documents, as a basis for the settlement of questions arising from the removal of oil equipment in Roumania. It was further agreed that these experts shall begin their work within ten days, on the spot.

XIV.—*Iran*

It was agreed that Allied troops should be withdrawn immediately from Tehran, and that further stages of the withdrawal of troops from Iran should be considered at the meeting of the Council of Foreign Ministers to be held in London in September 1945.

---

[3] Not here printed. This annex, headed 'Text of a letter transmitted on 12th July to the Representatives of the United States and United Kingdom Governments on the Allied Control Commission in Hungary', comprised the text under that heading in No. 518, minute 7.

XV.—*The International Zone of Tangier*

A proposal by the Soviet Government was examined and the following decisions were reached.

Having examined the question of the Zone of Tangier, the three Governments have agreed that this Zone, which includes the city of Tangier and the area adjacent to it, in view of its special strategic importance shall remain international.

The question of Tangier will be discussed in the near future at a Meeting in Paris of representatives of the Governments of the Union of Soviet Socialist Republics, the United States, the United Kingdom and France.

XVI.—*The Black Sea Straits*

The three Governments recognised that the Convention concluded at Montreux should be revised as failing to meet present-day conditions.

It was agreed that, as the next step, the matter should be the subject of direct conversations between each of the three Governments and the Turkish Government.

XVII.—*International Inland Waterways*

The Conference considered a proposal of the United States Delegation on this subject and agreed to refer it for consideration to the forthcoming meeting of the Council of Foreign Ministers in London.

XVIII.—*European Inland Transport Conference*

The British and United States Delegations to the Conference informed the Soviet Delegation of the desire of the British and United States Governments to reconvene the European Inland Transport Conference, and stated that they would welcome an assurance that the Soviet Government would participate in the work of the reconvened conference. The Soviet Government agreed that it would participate in this conference.

XIX.—*Directives to Military Commanders on Allied Control Council for Germany*

The three Governments agreed that each would send a directive to its representative on the Control Council for Germany informing him of all decisions of the Conference affecting matters within the scope of his duties.

XX.—*Use of Allied Property for Satellite Reparations or 'War Trophies'*

The proposal (Annex II)[4] presented by the United States Delegation was accepted in principle by the Conference, but the drafting of an agreement on the matter was left to be worked out through diplomatic channels.

---

[4] Not here printed. This annex was the same as the American proposal circulated as P. (Terminal) 49: see No. 451, note 6.

XXI. *Military Talks*

During the Conference there were meetings between the Chiefs of Staff of the three Governments on military matters of common interest.[5]

J. V. STALIN
HARRY S. TRUMAN
C. R. ATTLEE

Berlin, 2nd August, 1945

CALENDARS TO No. 603

i *2 Aug. 1945 Report on the Tripartite Conference of Berlin* with covering signed sheet: communiqué published in *The Times* of 3 Aug. 1945, p. 8 (cf. *F.R.U.S. Berlin*, vol. ii, pp. 1499–1514; *Berlinskaya konferentsiya*, pp. 481–500) [F.O. 93/1/238].

ii *3 Aug. 1945 Minute by Sir E. Bridges to General Ismay; communiqué on the Combined Chiefs of Staff meetings at Berlin Conference*, published in *The Times* of 4 Aug. 1945, p. 4 [CAB 21/864].

[5] This text of the protocol, circulated to the Cabinet on 4 August 1945 was discussed at a Cabinet meeting held at 5 p.m. on 7 August: ' 3. The Cabinet had before them a Note by the Secretary (C.P. (45) 95) covering the agreed English text of the Protocol of the proceedings of the Berlin Conference.

'*The Secretary of State for Foreign Affairs* summarised the main conclusions reached by the Conference, and explained the attitude which the United States and Soviet Delegations had taken up towards some of the principal problems which had been discussed.

In discussion the following points were raised:–

(a) As regards the *transfer of populations* there was some ground for thinking that the Czechoslovak Government had behaved with great inhumanity. It was pointed out on the other hand that, according to the Russians, this was not the result of a settled Government policy but of the bitterness of feeling among the Czechoslovak people. Given the history of the last seven years, it was very difficult to keep such feeling within bounds.

(b) We should be at great pains to ensure that *reparation shipping* was not brought here to the detriment of our ship building industry and of our mercantile marine. *The Prime Minister* said that this point had been fully considered at an earlier stage and steps would be taken to safeguard it.

(c) *The Lord Chancellor* said that he was uneasy about the arrangements for the trial of *war criminals*. The procedure proposed was liable to involve great delay. It was most important that we should dispose of these trials as expeditiously as possible. *The Prime Minister* agreed. We must impress on those concerned the importance of avoiding long drawn-out trials.

(d) *The Minister of Fuel and Power* said that he understood that, in connection with the discussions on the Reparations Commission at Moscow, a proposal had been made that over a period of eight years 50 million tons of German coal should be made available for export. He was disturbed at the implications of this proposal; and would take an early opportunity of bringing the matter to the notice of the Cabinet.

The Prime Minister said that he had been present throughout the discussions at the Berlin Conference. Very little had been brought to a conclusion before he and the Foreign Secretary had returned to Berlin after Mr. Churchill's resignation. The Foreign Secretary's success in picking up the threads, and handling so skilfully the discussion of this wide range of complicated problems was a remarkable achievement, for which the Cabinet owed him a great debt of gratitude. He thought that on the whole we could be very well satisfied with the results that had been secured.

The Lord President of the Council said that he would like to express to the Prime Minister and the Foreign Secretary the gratitude and admiration of the Cabinet for the skill with which they had handled the discussions at the Berlin Conference and for the results which they had secured.

The Cabinet:—

Warmly endorsed the views expressed by the Lord President of the Council' (CAB 128/1).

No. 604

Letter from Mr. Attlee to Mr. Churchill
[PREM 3/430/14]

Confidential   *2 August 1945*[1]

My dear Churchill,

I have just got back to England after a good flight, and I am sending at once an advance copy of the communique[2] which will be released to the Press to-night at 10.30 p.m. I have not yet available a copy of the Protocol,[3] but I will send you this as soon as possible.

These two documents will give you the main decisions, but I feel that you would also wish to see the Minutes and papers of the later proceedings. If so, I shall be very pleased to send them to you as soon as they are in print.[4] I think this would be more convenient to you than to have them in typed form.

Yrs. ever
C. R. A.

CALENDAR TO No. 604

i *3 & 5 Aug. 1945 Correspondence between Mr. Churchill and Mr. Attlee.* Mr. Churchill replies on 3 Aug. to Nos. 522 and 604. 'I am sorry about the Western Neisse, and I fear the Russians have laid an undue toll even on the Germany which is not in their zone. This was certainly not the fault of the British Delegation. I should be very glad to have the Minutes and papers on the later proceedings at Potsdam when they are in print.' Thanks for the message in No. 526, minute 5, and suggests verbal amendments to the two draft statements on the atomic bomb (cf. No. 502, note 1): accepted by Mr. Attlee in his reply of 5 Aug; his confidence in C.I.G.S. [PREM 8/109].

[1] The filed copy carries above the dateline the annotation 'Terminal'.
[2] No. 603.i.
[3] No. 603.
[4] i.e. in Confidential Print.

A3